THE USBORNE SCHOOL
ILLUSTRATED
DICTIONARY
AND
THESAURUS

Jane Bingham and Fiona Chandler

Assistant editor: Rachel Wardley

Designed by Susie McCaffrey and Matthew Hart

Assistant designer: Sue Grobecker

Illustrated by Sean Wilkinson, Gerald Wood,
Nicholas Hewetson, Ian Jackson, Peter Dennis, Michelle Ross,
David Cuzik, Ann Johns and Gary Bines

Photography by Mark Mason Studio

Cover design by Russell Punter

Additional illustrations by Joyce Bee, Chris Shields, Kuo Kang Chen, Dan Courtney, Andrew Beckett, Hans Jenssen, Nick Gibbard, Mauruce Pledger,David Wright, Chris Lyon, Isabel Bowring, Peter Geissler, Aziz Khan, Steven Kirk, Jason Lewis, Peter Goodwin, Louise Nixon, Malcolm McGregor, Nicholas Shea, Radhi Parekh, Miranda Gray, Annabel Spencley, Chris Lyon, Norman Young, Treve Tamblin, Sue Stitt, Denise Finney, Tricia Newell, Andy Burton, Robert Walster, David Astin, John Francis, John Gosler, David Hurrell, Elaine Keenan, Andy Martin and Ed Roberts

Definitions by John McIlwain, Sheila Dignen, Jessica Feinstein and Andrew Delahunty

Managing editor (dictionary): Christopher Rawson

Additional editing (thesaurus): Jessica Feinstein

Advisors: Colin Hope, Susan Hitch, George Phillipson, Richard Hatton, John Rostron, Margaret Rostron, Anne Rooney, Bill Chambers, Anne Millard, Michael Reiss, Shelley Harris

The publishers are grateful to the following: AppleCentre, Oxford (60); Benetton Formula Ltd. (196); Boss Trucks Ltd. (102); Cellmark Diagnostics (323); Central Broadcasting Ltd. (438); Penny Dwyer (390); Corporation of Trinity House (144); Flight International (14-15); Ford Motor Company Ltd. (46); GKN Westland Helcopters Ltd. (409); Korg (UK) Ltd. (400); Martin Lunn (427); Douglas MacKenzie, Visitor Services Manager, HMS Victory, Portsmouth (222-223); Massey Ferguson (259); Anne Millard (298, 299, 301, 384-385, 412-413); Minolta Cameras (179); Mitsui Machinery Sales (UK) Ltd. (158); Basil Mustafa (310); New Holland Ford Sales Promotion and Product Support Department (117); Renault UK Ltd. (192); Rolls Royce plc (135); Shell UK Exploration and Production (167); Stephen Bateman (164); Thames Barrier Visitor's centre (28); Thames Valley Police Fingerprint Department (323); Vickers PLC, Defence Systems (21); Yamaha-Kemble Music (UK) Ltd. (200). The picture on page 203 is based on the drawing "Study for the Head of Leda" by Leonardo da Vinci, The Royal Collection, Windsor.

boomerang

THE USBORNE SCHOOL
ILLUSTRATED
DICTIONARY

Rajah
Brooke's
birdwing
butterfly

robotic
arm

grand piano

Contents

Your dictionary 2
Parts of speech 3
Writing English 4
The story of English 6
English today 8
Dictionary 9

kumquat

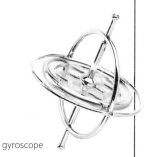
gyroscope

snowflake

hurdling

The Thesaurus section starts
on page 289

harvest mouse

samurai

YOUR DICTIONARY: *A USER'S GUIDE*

This dictionary contains over ten thousand entries and over a thousand pictures, many of them surrounded by picture labels. Here is the entry for "satellite" with its labelled picture.

Finding a word

Entries are listed in alphabetical order. Make a guess at the first few letters of your word, for example, for "satellite", find "sat", then try different ways of spelling the next part.

If you can't find a word

• You may have chosen the wrong first letters. Try some alternative spellings and look out for **spelling guides** at the bottom of the page.

• You may be able to find a related word. For example, you would find the word "slothful" under "sloth".

• The word you want may be a **picture label**. Look for it in the **Index of picture labels** at the back of the dictionary.

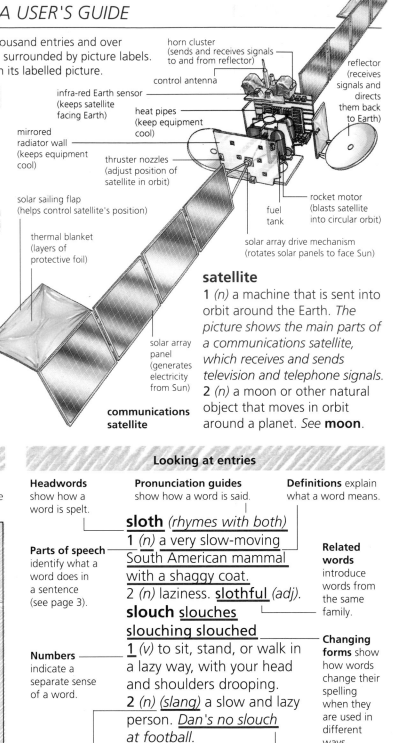

horn cluster (sends and receives signals to and from reflector)

control antenna

reflector (receives signals and directs them back to Earth)

infra-red Earth sensor (keeps satellite facing Earth)

heat pipes (keep equipment cool)

mirrored radiator wall (keeps equipment cool)

thruster nozzles (adjust position of satellite in orbit)

rocket motor (blasts satellite into circular orbit)

fuel tank

solar sailing flap (helps control satellite's position)

solar array drive mechanism (rotates solar panels to face Sun)

thermal blanket (layers of protective foil)

solar array panel (generates electricity from Sun)

communications satellite

satellite

1 *(n)* a machine that is sent into orbit around the Earth. *The picture shows the main parts of a communications satellite, which receives and sends television and telephone signals.*
2 *(n)* a moon or other natural object that moves in orbit around a planet. *See* **moon**.

Looking at pages

Guide words help you to find the right page.

Guide letters help you to find the right letter section.

Spelling guides help you to find tricky words by suggesting other spellings.

Looking at entries

Headwords show how a word is spelt.

Pronunciation guides show how a word is said.

Definitions explain what a word means.

sloth *(rhymes with both)*
1 *(n)* a very slow-moving South American mammal with a shaggy coat.
2 *(n)* laziness. **slothful** *(adj)*.
slouch slouches slouching slouched
1 *(v)* to sit, stand, or walk in a lazy way, with your head and shoulders drooping.
2 *(n)* *(slang)* a slow and lazy person. *Dan's no slouch at football.*

Parts of speech identify what a word does in a sentence (see page 3).

Numbers indicate a separate sense of a word.

Related words introduce words from the same family.

Changing forms show how words change their spelling when they are used in different ways.

Example sentences show how a word is used.

Usage guides show that a word is old-fashioned, poetic, informal or slang. Informal words are used in everyday speech, but not in formal or official writing. Slang is usually only spoken.

Weights, measures, numbers, days, months, countries and nationalities are listed on page 284.

PARTS OF SPEECH: *THE PARTS THAT WORDS PLAY*

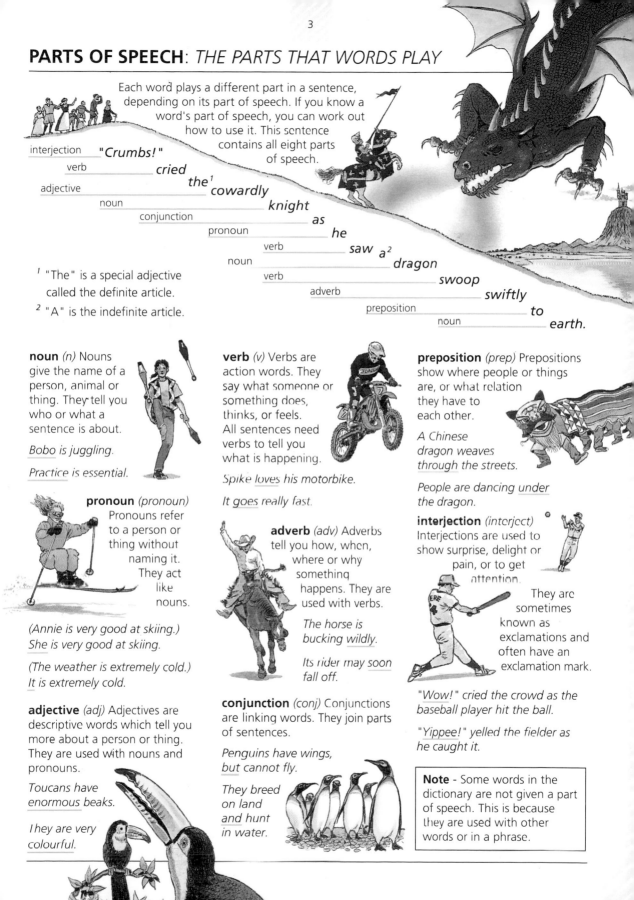

Each word plays a different part in a sentence, depending on its part of speech. If you know a word's part of speech, you can work out how to use it. This sentence contains all eight parts of speech.

interjection **"Crumbs!"**

verb *cried*

adjective *the[1] cowardly*

noun *knight*

conjunction *as*

pronoun *he*

verb *saw a[2]*

noun *dragon*

verb *swoop*

adverb *swiftly*

preposition *to*

noun *earth.*

[1] "The" is a special adjective called the definite article.

[2] "A" is the indefinite article.

---

noun *(n)* Nouns give the name of a person, animal or thing. They tell you who or what a sentence is about.

Bobo is juggling.

Practice is essential.

pronoun *(pronoun)* Pronouns refer to a person or thing without naming it. They act like nouns.

(Annie is very good at skiing.)
She is very good at skiing.

(The weather is extremely cold.)
It is extremely cold.

adjective *(adj)* Adjectives are descriptive words which tell you more about a person or thing. They are used with nouns and pronouns.

Toucans have enormous beaks.

They are very colourful.

---

verb *(v)* Verbs are action words. They say what someone or something does, thinks, or feels. All sentences need verbs to tell you what is happening.

Spike loves his motorbike.

It goes really fast.

adverb *(adv)* Adverbs tell you how, when, where or why something happens. They are used with verbs.

The horse is bucking wildly.

Its rider may soon fall off.

conjunction *(conj)* Conjunctions are linking words. They join parts of sentences.

Penguins have wings, but cannot fly.

They breed on land and hunt in water.

---

preposition *(prep)* Prepositions show where people or things are, or what relation they have to each other.

A Chinese dragon weaves through the streets.

People are dancing under the dragon.

interjection *(interject)* Interjections are used to show surprise, delight or pain, or to get attention. They are sometimes known as exclamations and often have an exclamation mark.

"Wow!" cried the crowd as the baseball player hit the ball.

"Yippee!" yelled the fielder as he caught it.

Note - Some words in the dictionary are not given a part of speech. This is because they are used with other words or in a phrase.

WRITING ENGLISH: *SOME HINTS AND GUIDELINES*

These two pages give some help with spelling and punctuation. You should find them useful to refer to when you are writing.

Spelling English

It is sometimes hard to spell English correctly because it is a mixture of so many languages (see pages 6-7). Here are some patterns to follow and spellings to remember, but watch out for exceptions and use a dictionary to check your spelling.

Making plurals

Most nouns simply gain an **s** to become plural.

dinosaur

dinosaur - dinosaurs	zoo - zoos
book - books	day - days
garden - gardens	house -houses
apple - apples	bicycle - bicycles

dinosaurs

Some words, however, change differently. Here are some word groups for you to remember.

fox

If a word ends in **ch**, **sh**, **s**, **ss**, **x** or **z**, add **es**.

arch - arches	atlas - atlases
match - matches	dress - dresses
dish - dishes	fox - foxes
bus - buses	waltz - waltzes

foxes

If a word ends in **y** and the letter before the y is not a, e, i, o or u, replace the y with **ies**.

berry - berries	country - countries
baby - babies	city - cities
party -parties	puppy - puppies
pony - ponies	library - libraries

berry

berries

Many words ending in **f** drop their final f and gain **ves**.

leaf - leaves	wife - wives
half - halves	thief - thieves
loaf - loaves	dwarf - dwarves
shelf - shelves	wolf - wolves

leaf

leaves

Many words ending in **o** gain **es**.

buffalo - buffaloes	potato - potatoes
cargo - cargoes	echo - echoes
tomato - tomatoes	hero - heroes

buffalo

buffaloes

Odd plurals

Some words change their spelling dramatically when they become plural. These plurals need to be learnt.

woman - women	man - men	foot - feet
child - children	mouse - mice	tooth - teeth

Letter pairs

qu
q is always followed by **u**.

queen	request
quit	squad

gh
When **g** and **h** are written together, **g** always comes before **h**.

sleigh
right
ghost
although

i and e

It is very easy to get these two letters the wrong way round, but this rule should help you.

"i before e, except after c, when the sound is ee."

i before **e**	**e** before **i**
shield	ceiling
believe	receive
thief	conceited
field	receipt

Note - there are some exceptions to this rule, such as *seize, weir, weird*.

Doubling up

Watch out for the double letters in these words.

accommodate	disappoint
accurate	embarrass
address	necessary
beginning	occasion
communicate	parallel

One word or two?

Here are some common words and phrases that are often spelt wrongly.

two words	**one word**
thank you	cannot
no one	someone
all right	altogether

Double or single l ?

It is sometimes hard to know whether words have a single or a double l. The following words have only one l.

already	careful
always	until
awful	welcome

Remember - when full is added to a word, it drops its final l.

Whenever I see a spider, I am full of fear.

Whenever I see a spider, I am fearful.

Tricky endings

-le or -el

Most words end in **-le**.

battle	bubble
trouble	table
able	Bible

but watch out for:-
travel barrel label quarrel

-ic or -ick

Words with two or more sounds (syllables) end in **-ic**. Words with one sound end in **-ick**.

comic	stick
fantastic	lick
artistic	trick

Learning spellings

Follow the four steps below when you are learning to spell a word.
1 LOOK at the word carefully and memorize the order of letters.
2 COVER the word.
3 WRITE it down from memory.
4 CHECK that it is right.

Punctuation

Without punctuation to break thèm up, your sentences would be impossible to read. These guidelines will help you to use some tricky punctuation marks.

Apostrophes

Apostrophes show the owner of something *(The hat that belongs to Ben = Ben's hat)* or mark missing letters *(I am hungry = I'm hungry).*

Apostrophe s

If the owner is singular, add an **apostrophe s**
Ben's hat
Charles's hat

If the owner is plural and ends in s, add an **apostrophe only**
The boys' hats

If the owner is plural, but does not end in s, add an **apostrophe s**
The children's hats

Never use an apostrophe s to make a plural.

Missing letters

Usually, an apostrophe shows that one letter has been dropped, but sometimes more than one letter is missing:
I'd = I would or I had
shan't = shall not
won't = will not

it's and its

it's is only used to show that a letter has been missed out from **it is**.

I'm glad it's a sunny day.

The kangaroo carries its baby in its pouch.

Colons and semi-colons

You can manage without colons and semi-colons in your writing, but they can be very useful. Here are some ways to use them.

Colons can be used to introduce a statement or a list.

At last Harry revealed the secret of his success: three raw carrots every day.

For this trick you need: a pack of cards, a silk scarf and a wand.

Semi-colons are useful for breaking up lists when the items in the list are long and complicated.

We visited the zoo and saw: two giraffes; an elephant with a baby; some performing seals; and a very mischievous monkey.

Inverted commas

You use inverted commas, or speech marks, to show that someone is speaking. Always start someone's spoken words with a capital letter and use a comma to separate speech from the rest of the sentence.

"The view is amazing," said the astronaut.

The astronaut said, "The view is amazing."

"The view," said the astronaut, "is amazing."

THE STORY OF ENGLISH: *A HISTORY OF OUR LANGUAGE*

People first spoke English fifteen hundred years ago. Since then, our language has changed enormously, both in the way it is spoken and written, and in its range of words. These two pages show how English grew and changed as the British were invaded, visited and influenced by people from other countries.

Old English: 5th-11th century

Three main groups of people created Old English: the Anglo-Saxon tribes who settled in England, Christian missionaries from Rome, and Viking and Danish invaders and settlers.

Anglo-Saxons

5th-6th century: Tribes of Angles, Saxons and Jutes from mainland Europe and Scandinavia invaded the British Isles and created a new kingdom of England. People in England spoke Anglo-Saxon, the earliest form of English.

Anglo-Saxon helmet

```
— ANGLO-SAXON WORDS —
fire      day       book
man       what      and
house     earth     you
```

Missionaries from Rome

5th-7th century: Christian missionaries travelled to Britain and founded monasteries. The monks held services in Latin and copied Latin manuscripts.

6th-century monk

```
— LATIN WORDS —
verse     altar
angel     candle
demon     school
pope      hymn
```

Vikings and Danes

8th-11th century: Vikings and Danes from Scandinavia attacked Britain. During the 10th and 11th centuries the Danes ruled over north-east England.

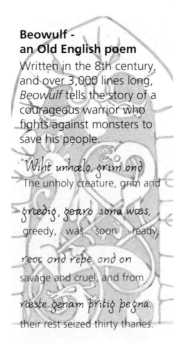

Viking invaders

```
— SCANDINAVIAN WORDS —
leg       knife     skin
want      sky       egg
dirt      get       bull
```

Beowulf - an Old English poem

Written in the 8th century, and over 3,000 lines long, *Beowulf* tells the story of a courageous warrior who fights against monsters to save his people.

"Wiht unhælo, grim ond
The unholy creature, grim and

grædig, gearo sona wæs,
greedy, was soon ready,

reoc ond repe, ond on
savage and cruel, and from

ræste genam þritig þegna.
their rest seized thirty thanes.

Middle English: Late 11th-15th century

In this period, the Normans added French words to the language, some spellings changed and borrowing from Latin continued.

Normans

1066-1300: In 1066, William of Normandy conquered England. French was spoken by the upper classes and used in parliament and the law courts.

William the Conqueror

```
— FRENCH WORDS —
court     crime     feast
royal     fashion   music
attorney  beauty    story
```

Spelling changes

12th-15th century: Old English letters were abandoned. French scribes introduced "qu", "gh", "ch" and "ng" spellings.

The Canterbury Tales - a Middle English poem

Geoffrey Chaucer began writing the *Canterbury Tales* around 1387. The poem presents 23 tales, told by pilgrims.

"Thanne longen folk to goon
Then people long to go

on pilgrimages...And specially
on pilgrimages. . . . And specially

from every shires ende of
from the end of every county of

Engelond to Caunterbury
England to Canterbury

they wende."
they travel.

The birth of modern English: Late 15th-18th century

In this period, English gradually became recognizable as the language that we use today.

Caxton and the rise of printing

1476: William Caxton began printing books in English. This led to a great increase in reading and writing.

15th-century printing press

William Shakespeare

Shakespeare

1590-1612: William Shakespeare used the English language in new and exciting ways in his plays and poetry.

PHRASES FROM SHAKESPEARE

good riddance
a blinking idiot
high time
foul play
a laughing stock
an eyesore

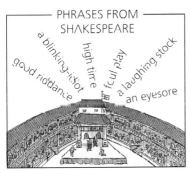

The King James Bible

1611: An English version of the Bible was printed. This version, which was authorized by King James I, was used throughout the country.

PHRASES FROM THE KING JAMES BIBLE

in the twinkling of an eye
the skin of my teeth
a wolf in sheep's clothing
the salt of the earth
the apple of my eye
an eye for an eye

The Renaissance

1475-1650: People became interested in Ancient Greek and Roman writings, and developed new ideas in science and the arts. To express these ideas, they borrowed words from Greek, Latin, French and Italian.

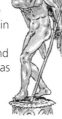

17th-century astronomical sphere

RENAISSANCE WORDS

SCIENTIFIC WORDS
temperature (Latin)
skeleton (Greek)
pneumonia (Greek)
gravity (Latin)
muscle (Latin)
virus (Latin)

MUSICAL WORDS
violin (Italian)
madrigal (Italian)
soprano (Italian)
opera (Italian)
ballet (French)
fugue (French)

ARCHITECTURAL WORDS
cupola (Italian)
balcony (Italian)
grotto (Italian)
dome (French)
portico (Italian)
stucco (Italian)

Dr Johnson's dictionary

1755: Dr Samuel Johnson published his *Dictionary of the English Language*. By this time, English spelling was almost standardized.

Dr Johnson

Traders and explorers

16th-18th century: explorers discovered new countries and merchants traded with them, bringing back new words.

TRADING WORDS

coffee (Turkish)
banana (Spanish)
yam (Portuguese)
apricot (Portuguese)
maize (Spanish)
potato (Spanish)

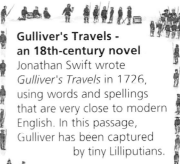

Gulliver's Travels - an 18th-century novel

Jonathan Swift wrote *Gulliver's Travels* in 1726, using words and spellings that are very close to modern English. In this passage, Gulliver has been captured by tiny Lilliputians.

"I attempted to rise, but was not able to stir...I could only look upwards; the Sun began to grow hot, and the Light offended mine eyes."

Modern English: 19th century onwards

No major changes took place in the language after 1800, but English spread around the world and gained thousands of new words.

ENGLISH TODAY: *ITS RANGE AND VARIETY*

English is now a world language, spoken by over 350 million people, with at least 400 million more using it as a second language. Here are some words used by English speakers in different parts of the world.

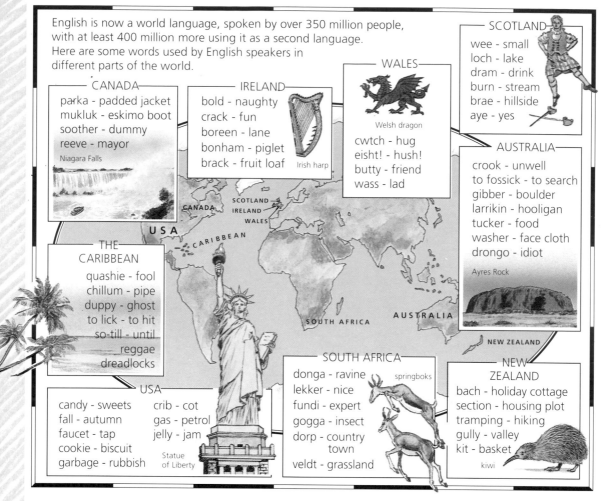

SCOTLAND
wee - small
loch - lake
dram - drink
burn - stream
brae - hillside
aye - yes

CANADA
parka - padded jacket
mukluk - eskimo boot
soother - dummy
reeve - mayor
Niagara Falls

IRELAND
bold - naughty
crack - fun
boreen - lane
bonham - piglet
brack - fruit loaf
Irish harp

WALES
Welsh dragon
cwtch - hug
eisht! - hush!
butty - friend
wass - lad

AUSTRALIA
crook - unwell
to fossick - to search
gibber - boulder
larrikin - hooligan
tucker - food
washer - face cloth
drongo - idiot
Ayres Rock

THE CARIBBEAN
quashie - fool
chillum - pipe
duppy - ghost
to lick - to hit
so-till - until
reggae
dreadlocks

USA
candy - sweets
fall - autumn
faucet - tap
cookie - biscuit
garbage - rubbish
crib - cot
gas - petrol
jelly - jam
Statue of Liberty

SOUTH AFRICA
donga - ravine
lekker - nice
fundi - expert
gogga - insect
dorp - country town
veldt - grassland
springboks

NEW ZEALAND
bach - holiday cottage
section - housing plot
tramping - hiking
gully - valley
kit - basket
kiwi

CANADA *SCOTLAND* *IRELAND* *WALES* *USA* *CARIBBEAN* *SOUTH AFRICA* *AUSTRALIA* *NEW ZEALAND*

New words

English speakers today continue to borrow words from other languages as well as creating new words. "Karaoke" is a recent borrowing from Japanese, while the words listed here are all new arrivals in our language.

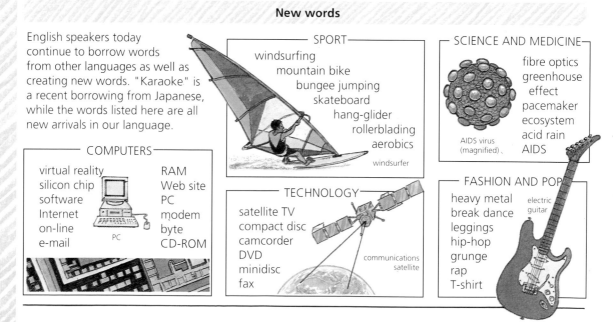

SPORT
windsurfing
mountain bike
bungee jumping
skateboard
hang-glider
rollerblading
aerobics
windsurfer

SCIENCE AND MEDICINE
fibre optics
greenhouse effect
pacemaker
ecosystem
acid rain
AIDS
AIDS virus (magnified)

COMPUTERS
virtual reality
silicon chip
software
Internet
on-line
e-mail
RAM
Web site
PC
modem
byte
CD-ROM
PC

TECHNOLOGY
satellite TV
compact disc
camcorder
DVD
minidisc
fax
communications satellite

FASHION AND POP
heavy metal
break dance
leggings
hip-hop
grunge
rap
T-shirt
electric guitar

Aa

aardvark *(n)* an African mammal with a long, sticky tongue, that it uses to search for insects.

aardvark

abacus abacuses *or* abaci *(n)* a frame with sliding beads on wires, used for counting.

abandon abandoning abandoned
1 *(v)* to leave forever. *Abandon ship!*
2 *(v)* to give up. *As night fell, we abandoned hope of being rescued.*

abattoir *(ab-er-twar) (n)* a place where animals are killed for their meat.

abbey *(n)* a group of buildings where monks or nuns live and work.

abbreviation *(n)* a short way of writing a word. *CD is an abbreviation of compact disc.* abbreviated *(adj)*.

abdicate abdicating abdicated *(v)* to give up being king or queen. abdication *(n)*.

abdomen
1 *(n)* the part of your body between your chest and hips.
2 *(n)* the back section of an insect's body. *See* **beetle**.

abduct abducting abducted *(v)* to kidnap someone. abduction *(n)*.

abhor abhorring abhorred *(v)* to hate someone or something. abhorrent *(adj)*.

abide abiding abode *or* abided
1 *(v) (old-fashioned)* to stay or live somewhere.
2 *(v)* If you **cannot abide** something, you cannot put up with it.

ability abilities
1 *(n)* the power to do something. *I know I have the ability to do better.*
2 *(n)* skill. *Pablo has great ability in art.*

abject *(adj)* miserable and without dignity. *The refugees lived in abject poverty. Sabrina offered an abject apology.*

ablaze *(adj)* on fire.

able abler ablest
1 *(adj)* If you are **able** to do something, you can do it.
2 *(adj)* skilful, or clever. *Our team has many able players.* ably *(adv)*.

able-bodied *(adj)* Someone who is able-bodied has no injuries or disabilities.

abnormal *(adj)* unusual, or not normal. abnormality *(n)*.

aboard *(prep)* on or into a train, ship, or aircraft. aboard *(adv)*.

abode *(n) (old-fashioned)* a home.

abolish abolishes abolishing abolished *(v)* to put an end to something officially. *We voted to abolish school uniform.* abolition *(n)*.

abominable *(adj)* horrible, or disgusting. *An abominable mess.* abominably *(adv)*.

Aborigine *(ab-or-ij-in-ee) (n)* one of the native people of Australia who lived there before Europeans arrived. *This picture shows Aborigines performing a traditional dance.* Aboriginal *(adj)*.

Aborigines

abort aborting aborted
1 *(v)* to remove a fetus from its mother's womb so that the pregnancy ends. abortion *(n)*
2 *(v)* to stop something from happening.

abound abounding abounded *(v)* to have a large amount of something. *The forest abounds with wildlife.*

about
1 *(prep)* on a particular subject. *Tell me about your holiday.*
2 *(adv)* almost, or more or less. *My dad's about 40.*

above
1 *(prep)* higher up, or over. *Above the clouds.*
2 *(prep)* more than. *Above average.*

above board *(adj)* If something that you do is **above board**, it is completely honest and legal.

abrasive
1 *(adj)* rough and grinding, like sandpaper. *An abrasive surface.*
2 *(adj)* rude. *Spike has an abrasive manner.*

abreast *(adv)* side by side. *We walked three abreast.*

abridged *(adj)* shortened. *An abridged novel.* abridge *(v)*.

abroad *(adv)* in or to another country. *We are going abroad this summer.*

abrupt
1 *(adj)* sudden and unexpected. *The car came to an abrupt halt.* abruptly *(adv)*.
2 *(adj)* rude and short-tempered. *An abrupt reply.* abruptly *(adv)*.

abscess *(ab-sess)* abscesses *(n)* a painful swelling, full of a yellow substance called pus.

abscond absconding absconded *(v)* to go away suddenly and secretly, usually after doing something wrong.

abseil *(ab-sail)* abseiling abseiled *(v)* to lower yourself down a steep cliff or mountain face by holding onto a rope. abseiler *(n)*.

absent *(adj)* not present. absence *(n)*, absentee *(n)*, absenteeism *(n)*.

absent-minded *(adj)* If you are absent-minded, you are forgetful and do not think about what you are doing. absent-mindedly *(adv)*.

absolute
1 *(adj)* complete, or total. *Ben looks an absolute idiot in that hat.* absolutely *(adv)*.
2 *(adj)* without any limit. *The dictator had absolute power.*

absolve absolving absolved *(v)* to pardon someone or free them from blame. absolution *(n)*.

absorb absorbing absorbed
1 *(v)* to soak up liquid. *The sponge absorbed the juice.* absorbent *(adj)*.
2 *(v)* to take in information. *The students absorbed all the facts.*
3 *(v)* If something absorbs you, it takes up all your attention.

abstain abstaining abstained *(v)* to stop yourself from doing something. *The prisoners abstained from eating until their demands were met.* abstention *(n)*.

abstract *(adj)* based on ideas rather than things. *Abstract artists paint shapes rather than people or objects.*

absurd absurder absurdest *(adj)* silly, or ridiculous. absurdity *(n)*, absurdly *(adv)*.

abundant *(adj)* If there is an abundant supply of something, there is plenty of it. abundance *(n)*, abundantly *(adv)*.

abuse abusing abused
1 *(ab-yuce) (n)* rude or unkind words. abuse *(ab-yooze) (v)*, abusive *(adj)*.
2 *(ab-yooze) (v)* to treat a person or creature cruelly. abuse *(ab-yuce) (n)*.
3 *(ab-yuce) (n)* wrong or harmful use of something. *Alcohol abuse.* abuse *(ab-yooze) (v)*.

abysmal *(ab-iz-mal) (adj)* very bad, or terrible. **abysmally** *(adv)*.

abyss *(ab-iss)* **abysses** *(n)* a very deep hole that seems to have no bottom.

academic
1 *(adj)* to do with study and learning. *Anna loves sport, but hates academic work.* **academically** *(adv)*.
2 *(n)* someone who teaches in a university or college, or someone who does research.

accelerate accelerating accelerated *(v)* to get faster and faster. **acceleration** *(n)*.

accent
1 *(n)* the way you pronounce words. *Helmut speaks with a German accent.*
2 *(n)* a mark put over a letter in some languages to show how it is pronounced, for example, café.

accentuate accentuating accentuated *(v)* to emphasize or draw attention to something.

accept accepting accepted
1 *(v)* to take something that you are offered. **acceptance** *(n)*.
2 *(v)* to agree to something. *Keri won't accept our plan.* **acceptance** *(n)*, **acceptable** *(adj)*.

access accesses accessing accessed
1 *(n)* an entrance or approach to a place. **accessible** *(adj)*.
2 *(n)* the right to see someone. *Lucy lives with her mother, but her father has access at weekends.*
3 *(v)* to open up a document, program or Web site on a computer.

accessory accessories
1 *(n)* an extra part for something. *Car accessories.*
2 *(n)* something, like a belt or a scarf, that goes with your clothes.
3 *(n)* An **accessory** to a crime is someone who helps another person to commit a crime.

accident *(n)* something that takes place unexpectedly, and which often involves people being hurt. **accidental** *(adj)*, **accidentally** *(adv)*.

acclimatize *or* **acclimatise** acclimatizing acclimatized *(v)* to get used to a different climate or to new surroundings. **acclimatization** *(n)*.

accommodation *(n)* a place where people live. **accommodate** *(v)*.

accompany accompanies accompanying accompanied
1 *(v)* to go somewhere with someone.
2 *(v)* to support a musician or singer by playing a musical instrument. **accompaniment** *(n)*, **accompanist** *(n)*.

accomplice *(ak-um-pliss) (n)* someone who helps another person to commit a crime.

accomplish accomplishes accomplishing accomplished *(v)* to do something successfully. **accomplishment** *(n)*.

accomplished *(adj)* skilful.

accord
1 *(n)* peaceful agreement.
2 If you do something **of your own accord**, you do it without being asked.

accordion *(n)* a musical instrument that you squeeze to make sound, and play by pressing keys and buttons. *See* **instrument**.

according to
1 *(prep)* as someone has said or written. *According to Amy, all boys are stupid!*
2 *(prep)* in a way that is suitable. *You'll be paid according to the amount of work that you do.* **accordingly** *(adv)*.

accost accosting accosted *(v)* to approach someone and talk to them, usually in an insulting way.

account accounting accounted
1 *(n)* a description of something that has happened.
2 *(n)* a sum of money in a bank or building society that you can add to or take from, when needed.
3 **accounts** *(plural n)* records of money earned and spent.
4 *(v)* If you **account for** something, you explain it. **accountable** *(adj)*.

accountant *(n)* an expert in finance and keeping accounts.

accumulate accumulating accumulated *(v)* to collect things or let them pile up. **accumulation** *(n)*.

accurate *(adj)* exactly correct. **accuracy** *(n)*, **accurately** *(adv)*.

accuse accusing accused *(v)* to say that someone has done something wrong. **accusation** *(n)*, **accuser** *(n)*.

accustomed
1 *(adj)* usual. *My accustomed seat.*
2 *(adj)* When you are **accustomed to** something, you are used to it.

ace
1 *(n)* a playing card with only one symbol on it.
2 *(n)* a serve in tennis that is impossible to return.

ache *(rhymes with take) (n)* a dull pain that goes on and on. **ache** *(v)*.

achieve *(ach-eev)* achieving achieved *(v)* to do something successfully, especially after a lot of effort. **achievement** *(n)*.

acid
1 *(n)* a substance that turns blue litmus paper red. Strong acids can burn your skin. **acidic** *(adj)*.
2 *(adj)* sour, or bitter. **acidic** *(adj)*.

acid rain *(n)* rain that is polluted by acid in the atmosphere and damages the environment. *The diagram below shows how fumes containing acids from factories, car exhausts, etc. travel until they meet damp air, then fall as acid rain.*

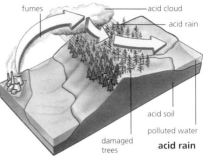

fumes · acid cloud · acid rain · acid soil · polluted water · damaged trees · **acid rain**

acknowledge acknowledging acknowledged
1 *(v)* to admit to something. *I acknowledged my mistake.*
2 *(v)* to show that you have seen and recognized somebody. *Toby walked past without acknowledging me.*
3 *(v)* to let the sender know that you have received a letter or parcel. **acknowledgement** *(n)*.

acne *(ak-nee) (n)* lots of red pimples on the skin, especially on the face.

acorn *(n)* the seed of an oak tree.

acoustic *(a-koo-stik)*
1 *(adj)* to do with sound or hearing.
2 **acoustics** *(plural n)* If a place has good **acoustics**, you can hear sounds and music very clearly inside it.

acoustic guitar *(n)* a guitar which does not need an amplifier.

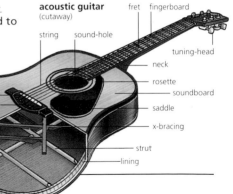

acoustic guitar (cutaway)

fret · fingerboard · tuning-head · neck · rosette · soundboard · saddle · x-bracing · strut · lining · string · sound-hole · bridge · bridge pins

acquaintance *(n)* someone you have met, but you do not know very well.

acquire acquiring acquired
1 *(v)* to obtain or get something.
2 *(n)* If something is an acquired taste, you grow to like it slowly. *Coffee is an acquired taste.*

acquit acquitting acquitted
(v) to find someone not guilty of a crime. acquittal *(n)*.

acrobatics *(plural n)* difficult and exciting gymnastic acts, often performed in the air or on a high wire. *The picture shows a "human column", an example of acrobatics.* acrobat *(n)*, acrobatic *(adj)*.   **acrobatics**

acronym *(n)* a word made from the first or first few letters of the words of a phrase. *Radar is an acronym for radio detecting and ranging.*

across
1 *(prep)* from one side to the other. *We ran across the field.*
2 *(prep)* on the other side. *Emma lives across the street from me.*

acrylic *(ak-rill-ik) (n)* a chemical substance used to make fibres and paints.

act acting acted
1 *(v)* to do something. *We must act now to save the rainforests.* act *(n)*.
2 *(v)* to perform in a play, film, etc.
3 *(v)* to have an effect. *This drug acts very quickly.*
4 *(n)* a short performance. *A comedy act.*
5 *(n)* one of the parts of a play.
6 *(n)* a law made by parliament.

action
1 *(n)* something that you do to achieve a result. *Kamran's rapid action prevented a serious accident.*
2 When you **take action**, you do something for a purpose.

active
1 *(adj)* energetic and busy.
2 *(adj)* An **active** verb is one where the verb's subject does the action, rather than having something done to it. *In the sentence, "I kicked the ball", the verb is active, but in "The ball was kicked", the verb is passive.*

activity activities
1 *(n)* action, or movement. *The playground was full of activity.*
2 *(n)* something that you do for pleasure. *Leisure activities.*

actor *(n)* someone who performs in the theatre, films, television, etc.

actual *(adj)* real, or true. actually *(adv)*.

acupuncture *(ak-yoo-punk-cher) (n)* a way of treating illness by pricking parts of the body with small needles.

acute acuter acutest
1 *(adj)* sharp, or severe. *Acute pain.*
2 *(adj)* able to detect things easily. *Dogs have an acute sense of smell.* acuteness *(n)*, acutely *(adv)*.
3 *(adj)* An **acute** angle is an angle of less than 90°.

AD the initials of the Latin phrase *Anno Domini*, which means "In the year of the Lord". AD is used to show that a date comes after the birth of Christ. *Columbus discovered America in AD1492.*

adapt adapting adapted
1 *(v)* to make something suitable for a different purpose. *We have adapted our garage into a games room.*
2 *(v)* to change because you are in a new situation. *It can be hard to adapt to life in a foreign country.* adaptable *(adj)*.

adapter or **adaptor** *(n)* a type of electrical plug that you use to connect two or more plugs to one socket.

add adding added
1 *(v)* to put one thing with another. *Add the eggs to the flour.*
2 *(v)* to put numbers together to make a total. addition *(n)*.

adder *(n)* a small, poisonous snake, sometimes called a viper. *The common adder is found in Britain.*

common adder (male)

addict *(n)* someone who cannot give up doing or using something. *A drug addict.* addiction *(n)*, addicted *(adj)*.

addictive *(adj)* If something, like a drug, is **addictive**, people find it very hard to give it up. *Tobacco is addictive.*

additive *(n)* something added to a substance to change it in some way. *Jon tries not to eat food with additives.*

address addresses addressing addressed
1 *(n)* the details of the place where someone lives. *What's your address?*
2 *(v)* to write an address on a letter, card, or package.
3 *(n)* the series of letters (and sometimes numbers) that you type into a computer to enable a browser to find a particular Web site or page. *What's the address for that Web site?*

adenoids *(ad-in-oyds) (plural n)* spongy lumps of flesh at the back of your nose.

adequate *(adj)* just enough, or good enough. adequately *(adv)*.

adhesive *(n)* a substance, such as glue, that makes things stick together. adhesive *(adj)*.

adjacent *(adj)* close or next to something or someone. *Our families live in adjacent streets.*

adjective *(n)* a word that describes someone or something. *In the phrase, "A tall, handsome stranger", "tall" and "handsome" are adjectives.* adjectival *(adj)*. See page 3.

adjudicate adjudicating adjudicated *(v)* to judge something, like a competition. adjudication *(n)*, adjudicator *(n)*.

adjust adjusting adjusted
1 *(v)* to move or change something slightly. adjustment *(n)*, adjustable *(adj)*.
2 *(v)* to get used to something new and different. adjustment *(n)*.

ad lib ad libbing ad libbed *(v)* to speak in public without preparing first. ad lib *(adv)*.

administer administering administered
1 *(v)* to govern or control something. *Nat administers the team funds.* administration *(n)*.
2 *(v)* to give something to someone. *The nurse administered the medicine.*

administrate administrating administrated *(v)* to manage and control an organization. administration *(n)*, administrator *(n)*.

admiral *(n)* an officer who holds a very high rank in the British navy. *The picture shows a statue of Admiral Nelson.*

Admiral Nelson

admire admiring admired
1 *(v)* to like and respect someone. admiration *(n)*.
2 *(v)* to look at something and enjoy it.

admit admitting admitted
1 (v) to confess to something, or agree that something is true, often reluctantly. **admission** (n).
2 (v) to allow someone or something to enter. **admission** (n), **admittance** (n).

admonish admonishes admonishing admonished (v) to tell someone off, or to warn someone. **admonishment** (n).

adolescent (n) a young person who is more grown-up than a child, but is not yet an adult. **adolescence** (n), **adolescent** (adj).

adopt adopting adopted
1 (v) When a couple **adopts** a child, they take it into their family and become its legal parents. **adoption** (n).
2 (v) to accept an idea or a way of doing things. The government is adopting a tough approach to crime.

adorable (adj) very sweet and lovable.

adore adoring adored (v) to love someone or something very much. **adoration** (n).

adorned (adj) decorated. **adorn** (v).

adrenaline (n) a chemical produced by your body when you are excited, frightened, or angry.

adult (n) a fully-grown person or animal. **adulthood** (n), **adult** (adj).

adulterate adulterating adulterated (v) to spoil something by adding something less good to it.

adultery (n) If someone commits adultery, they are unfaithful to their husband or wife by having sexual intercourse with somebody else. **adulterer** (n), **adulterous** (adj).

advance advancing advanced
1 (v) to move forward, or to make progress. **advancement** (n).
2 (adj) happening before something else. Advance warning.
3 (v) to lend money. **advance** (n).
4 (n) a movement forward by a group of soldiers.

advanced
1 (adj) If something has reached an advanced stage, it is nearly finished.
2 (adj) Advanced work is not elementary or easy. Advanced level science.

advantage
1 (n) something that helps you or is useful to you. **advantageous** (adj).
2 (n) the first point in a tennis game after the score of deuce.

3 If you **take advantage of** a person or situation, you use them for your own benefit.

advent
1 (n) the beginning of something important. The advent of the computer age.
2 Advent (n) the weeks leading up to Christmas in the Christian church's year.

adventure (n) an exciting or dangerous experience. **adventurous** (adj).

adverb (n) a word usually used to describe a verb. Adverbs tell how, when, where, how often, or how much something happens. "Slowly", "late", and "soon" are all adverbs. **adverbial** (adj). See page 3.

adversary adversaries (n) someone who fights or argues against you.

adverse (adj) unfavourable, or difficult. Adverse weather conditions. **adversely** (adj).

advertise advertising advertised (v) to give information about something that you want to sell. **advertisement** (n), **advertiser** (n).

advice (n) suggestions about what someone should do. Shahid gave me good advice on how to mend my bike.

advisable (adj) If something is advisable, it is sensible and worth doing. **advisably** (n).

advise advising advised (v) to give someone information or suggestions, so that they can decide what to do. Tom advised me to stay at home until the rush hour was over. **adviser** (n), **advisory** (adj).

advocate advocating advocated
1 (ad-voh-kate) (v) to support an idea or plan. I would never advocate violence.
2 (ad-voh-kut) (n) a lawyer who defends someone during their trial.

aerial (air-ee-ul)
1 (n) a piece of wire that receives television or radio signals.
2 (adj) happening in the air. Aerial refuelling.

aerobatics (plural n) skilful or dangerous movements made by aircraft in the sky. The picture shows a plane performing the positive flick roll, an example of aerobatics. **aerobatic** (adj).

aerobics (plural n) energetic exercises performed to music. The sequence of aerobics shown here strengthens the waist and back muscles. **aerobic** (adj).

aerodynamic (adj) designed to move through the air very easily and quickly. The streamlined shape of this Suzuki Nuda motorcycle makes it very aerodynamic.

aerodynamic motorbike

streamlined windscreen

fairing (streamlined bodywork)

angled headlights

aeronautics (singular n) the science and practice of designing and building aircraft. **aeronautical** (adj).

aeroplane (n) a machine with wings and an engine, that flies through the air. See **aircraft**.

aerosol (n) a can containing liquid which is forced out in a fine spray. When you press the button on an aerosol, propellant gas pushes liquid up a tube and out through a nozzle.

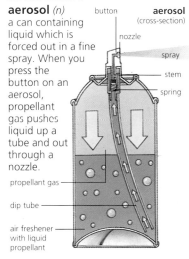

button

aerosol (cross-section)

nozzle

spray

stem

spring

propellant gas

dip tube

air freshener with liquid propellant

aestivate (ee-stiv-ate) aestivating aestivated (v) When animals or insects **aestivate**, they spend the summer in a deep sleep. Their heartbeat, temperature, and breathing rate become very low, so that they can survive heat and drought. **aestivation** (n).

affair
1 (n) a special event. The wedding was a grand affair.
2 affairs (plural n) business connected with private or public life. Personal affairs. Business affairs.

aerobatics

affect affecting affected *(v)* to influence or change someone or something. *Lance's accident affected him badly.*

affected *(adj)* false and unnatural. *Gloria has an affected voice.*

affection *(n)* a great liking for someone or something.

affectionate *(adj)* very loving. affectionately *(adv)*.

affinity affinities *(n)* If you have an affinity with someone or something, you like them and feel close to them.

affliction *(n)* illness, or suffering. afflict *(v)*.

affluent *(adj)* If you are affluent, you have plenty of money. affluence *(n)*.

afford affording afforded
1 *(v)* If you can afford something, you have enough money to buy it.
2 *(v)* to have enough time or ability to do something. *I'm so far ahead, I can afford to relax.*

afloat *(adj)* floating on water.

afraid
1 *(adj)* frightened, or worried.
2 *(adj)* sorry. *I'm afraid I can't come to your party.*

afresh *(adv)* When you start afresh, you begin something again.

aft *(adv)* towards the back of a ship or an aeroplane.

after
1 *(prep)* later than. *After lunch.*
2 *(prep)* following. *The puppy ran after her.*
3 *(prep)* trying to catch someone or something. *The police are after him.*

afternoon *(n)* the time of day between midday and about five o'clock in the evening.

afterwards *(adv)* later.

again *(adv)* one more time. *Say it again, Sam.*

against
1 *(prep)* next to and touching. *Put your ear against the wall.*
2 *(prep)* competing with. *It's the Chicago Bears against the Miami Dolphins tonight.*
3 *(prep)* opposed to. *I'm against killing whales.*

agate *(n)* a hard, semi-precious stone with bands of colour. *The picture shows a piece of agate that has been cut in half and polished.*

agate
(cross-section)

age ageing *or* aging aged
1 *(n)* the number of years that someone has lived or that something has existed.
2 *(n)* a period of time in history. *The Stone Age.*
3 *(v)* to become or seem older.

aged
1 *(rhymes with caged) (adj)* being a particular number of years old. *Anyone aged 12 can join our club.*
2 *(ay-jid) (adj)* Someone who is aged is very old.

ageism *or* **agism** *(n)* prejudice or discrimination because of age. ageist *(adj)*.

agenda *(aj-en-der) (n)* a list of things that need to be done or discussed.

agent
1 *(n)* someone who arranges things for other people. *Travel agent.* agency *(n)*.
2 *(n)* a spy. *Secret agent.*

aggravate aggravating aggravated
1 *(v)* to make a difficult situation even worse.
2 *(v) (informal)* to annoy someone. aggravation *(n)*, aggravating *(adj)*.

aggregate *(ag-rig-ut) (n)* a total created by adding together lots of smaller amounts. *The aggregate of our scores was 25.*

aggression *(n)* fierce or threatening behaviour. aggressive *(adj)*, aggressively *(adv)*.

aggro *(n) (slang)* a short word for aggression.

aghast *(ur-gast) (adj)* shocked, or dismayed.

agile
1 *(adj)* If you are agile, you can move fast and easily. agility *(n)*
2 *(adj)* Someone with an agile mind can think quickly and cleverly. agility *(n)*.

agism *see* **ageism**.

agitate agitating agitated
1 *(v)* to make someone nervous and worried. agitation *(n)*, agitated *(adj)*.
2 *(v)* to stir up a liquid.

agnostic *(n)* someone who believes that you cannot know that God exists. agnostic *(adj)*.

ago *(adv)* before now, or in the past. *Three days ago.*

agony agonies *(n)* great pain or suffering. *David was screaming in agony.* agonizing *(adj)*.

agree agreeing agreed
1 *(v)* to say yes to something. *I agreed to his plan.* agreement *(n)*.

2 *(v)* to share the same opinions. *Dan and I always agree on politics.*
3 *(v)* If something agrees with you, it suits you, or is good for you.

agreement
1 *(n)* the same way of thinking. *Bik and I are in agreement over that book.*
2 *(n)* an arrangement. *We've made an agreement to share the cost of the party.*

agriculture *(n)* farming. *This picture of agriculture in the Middle Ages shows labourers using scythes to mow a field.* agricultural *(adj)*. Also see **farm**.

medieval farming

aground *(adv)* If a boat runs aground, it gets stuck on the bottom in shallow water.

ahead
1 *(adv)* in front. *Go on ahead.*
2 *(adv)* in the future. *You must think ahead.*

aid aiding aided
1 *(v)* to help someone. aid *(n)*.
2 *(n)* money or equipment for people in need. *Foreign aid.*

AIDS *(n)* an incurable illness in which the body's ability to protect itself against disease is destroyed. AIDS stands for acquired immune deficiency syndrome.

AIDS virus
(magnified)

aileron *(ay-ler-on) (n)* a hinged piece on an aircraft wing, used to control balance. See **aircraft**.

ailment *(n)* an illness, though not usually a serious one.

aim aiming aimed
1 *(v)* to hit, throw, or shoot something in a particular direction. aim *(n)*.
2 *(v)* to intend to achieve something. *I aim to become a chef.* aim *(n)*

air airing aired
1 *(n)* the invisible mixture of gases around you that you need to breathe.
2 *(v)* to let air into a room.
3 *(n)* an appearance, or manner. *Wanda has an air of mystery.*

air conditioning *(n)* a system for keeping the air in a building cool and clean when it is hot outside.

aircraft *(n)* a vehicle that can fly. *The picture shows a Boeing 747-400 aircraft, known as a jumbo jet, because of its enormous size. It can carry up to 500 passengers and cruises at around 600 miles (965km) per hour.*

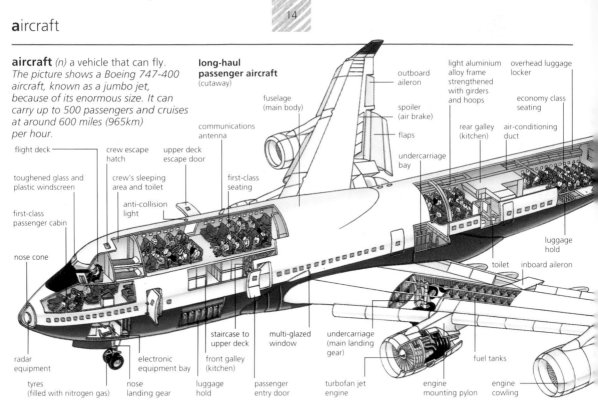

long-haul passenger aircraft (cutaway)

outboard aileron · light aluminium alloy frame strengthened with girders and hoops · overhead luggage locker · fuselage (main body) · spoiler (air brake) · economy class seating · communications antenna · flaps · rear galley (kitchen) · air-conditioning duct · flight deck · crew escape hatch · upper deck escape door · undercarriage bay · toughened glass and plastic windscreen · crew's sleeping area and toilet · first-class seating · anti-collision light · first-class passenger cabin · luggage hold · nose cone · toilet · inboard aileron · radar equipment · electronic equipment bay · staircase to upper deck · multi-glazed window · undercarriage (main landing gear) · fuel tanks · tyres (filled with nitrogen gas) · nose landing gear · luggage hold · front galley (kitchen) · passenger entry door · turbofan jet engine · engine mounting pylon · engine cowling

aircraft-carrier *(n)* a warship with a large, flat deck where aircraft take off and land.

air force *(n)* part of a country's fighting force that can attack or defend from the air.

airline *(n)* a company that owns and flies aircraft, carrying passengers and goods by air.

airmail *(n)* a postal service by which letters, packages, etc. are carried abroad by aircraft.

airport *(n)* a place where aircraft take off and land and where people get on and off them.

airship *(n)* a large air balloon with engines and a passenger compartment hanging underneath it. *The airship below is a Zeppelin, built in Germany in 1910.*

airship (cutaway)

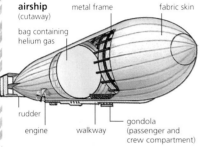

metal frame · fabric skin · bag containing helium gas · rudder · engine · walkway · gondola (passenger and crew compartment)

airtight *(adj)* If a container is airtight, it is so well sealed that no air can get in or out.

airy airier airiest
1 *(adj)* An **airy** room is not stuffy.
2 *(adj)* lighthearted, or casual. *Camilla gave an airy wave.* **airily** *(adv).*

aisle *(rhymes with pile)* *(n)* the passage that runs between the rows of seats in a church, cinema, aircraft, etc.

ajar *(adj)* If a door is **ajar**, it is partly open. **ajar** *(adv).*

alarm alarming alarmed
1 *(n)* a device, containing a bell, buzzer, or siren, that wakes someone or warns them of danger.
2 *(n)* a sudden fear that something bad will happen. *Don't worry, there's no cause for alarm.*
3 *(v)* to make someone afraid that something bad might happen. *I don't want to alarm you, but I can smell smoke.* **alarming** *(adj),* **alarmingly** *(adv).*

alas *(interject)* unfortunately, or sadly. *I'd love to come but, alas, I can't.*

albino *(al-bee-no)* *(n)* a person or animal born without any natural colouring in their skin, hair, or eyes.

album
1 *(n)* a book in which you keep photographs, stamps, etc.
2 *(n)* a collection of pieces of music recorded on a CD, tape, or record.

alcohol *(n)* a colourless liquid found in drinks such as wine, whisky, and beer, which can make people drunk.

alcoholic
1 *(adj)* containing alcohol.
2 *(n)* **Alcoholics** cannot stop themselves from drinking alcohol. **alcoholism** *(n).*

alcove *(n)* a part of a room that is set back from the main area.

alert alerting alerted
1 *(adj)* If you are **alert**, you pay attention to what is happening and are ready for action.
2 *(v)* to warn someone that there might be danger. *Alert the fire brigade!*
3 *(n)* a warning of danger. *A nuclear alert.*

algae *(al-jee)* *(plural n)* small plants that grow without roots or stems in water or on damp surfaces.

algebra *(al-jer-bra)* *(n)* a type of mathematics in which signs and letters are used to represent numbers, for example, $2x + y = 7$.

alias *(ay-lee-uss)* aliases *(n)* a false name, especially one used by a criminal.

alibi *(al-ee-bye)* *(n)* a claim that a person accused of a crime was somewhere else when the crime was committed.

alien *(ay-lee-un)*
1 *(n)* a creature from another planet.
2 *(adj)* different and strange. *Poppy found her new school very alien.*
3 *(n)* a foreigner.

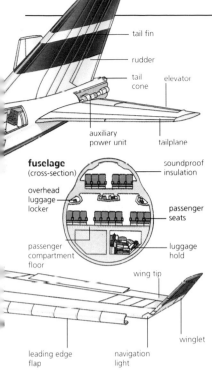

tail fin
rudder
tail cone
elevator

auxiliary power unit
tailplane

fuselage
(cross-section)
soundproof insulation

overhead luggage locker
passenger seats

passenger compartment floor
luggage hold

wing tip
winglet

leading edge flap
navigation light

alike
1 *(adj)* looking or acting the same.
2 *(adv)* in a similar way. *All the children were treated alike.*

alive
1 *(adj)* living.
2 *(adj)* full of life.

alkali *(al-ka-lye) (n)* a substance which turns red litmus paper blue. Strong alkalis can burn your skin. *Toothpaste is an alkali.* **alkaline** *(adj).*

Allah *(n)* the Muslim name for God.

allegiance *(a-lee-jenss) (n)* loyal support for someone or something.

allergic *(adj)* If you are **allergic** to something, it makes you ill. *Ned is allergic to cats.* **allergy** *(n).*

alliance *(n)* a friendly agreement to work together.

alligator *(n)* a large reptile like a crocodile, with strong jaws and very sharp teeth. Alligators live in parts of North and South America and China.

alligator

alliteration *(n)* repeated use of the same sound at the beginning of a group of words, for example, "The gruesome ghost gave a ghastly groan." **alliterative** *(adj).*

allocate allocating allocated *(v)* to decide that something should be used for a particular purpose. *We allocated half the money to charity.* **allocation** *(n).*

allotment *(n)* a small piece of land that people can rent and use to grow vegetables, fruit, or flowers.

allow allowing allowed *(v)* to let someone have or do something.

allowance *(n)* money given to someone regularly.

alloy *(n)* a mixture of two or more metals.

all right
1 *(adj)* good enough, or acceptable.
2 *(adj)* not hurt, or not ill. *Helena fell off her horse, but she's all right now.*
3 *(interject)* You say **all right** when you agree to do something.

ally *(al-eye)* allies *(n)* a person or a country that gives support to another.

almighty
1 *(adj)* very big. *An almighty crash.*
2 *(adj)* possessing total power.

almost *(adv)* very nearly.

alone *(adj)* by yourself. **alone** *(adv).*

along
1 *(prep)* from one end to the other. *We drove along the street.*
2 **all along** *(adv)* all the time. *I knew all along that Hal was lying.*

aloud *(adv)* in a voice that other people can hear. *Reading aloud.*

alphabet *(n)* all the letters of a language arranged in order. *The first six letters of the Greek alphabet are shown below.* **alphabetical** *(adj).*

Greek alphabet

alpha   beta   gamma   delta   epsilon   zeta

already *(adv)* before now. *I've seen that film already.*

also *(adv)* as well.

altar *(n)* a large table in a church or a temple, used for religious ceremonies.

alter altering altered *(v)* to change something. *We've altered our plans.* **alteration** *(n).*

alternate *(ol-ter-nat) (adj)* If something happens on **alternate** days, it happens every second day. **alternate** *(ol-ter-nate) (v).*

alternative
1 *(n)* something you can choose to have or do instead of something else. **alternative** *(adj)*, **alternatively** *(adv).*
2 *(adj)* different from what is usual. *Alternative medicine.*

although
1 *(conj)* in spite of something. *Although it was wet, we had fun.*
2 *(conj)* but. *Natalie is only nine, although she seems much older.*

altitude *(n)* the height of something above the ground. *This plane can fly at very high altitudes.*

alto
1 *(n)* a singing voice that is quite high for a man and quite low for a woman.
2 *(n)* a singer with an alto voice.

altogether
1 *(adv)* in total. *Pippa has seven hats altogether.*
2 *(adv)* completely, or entirely. *What I told you wasn't altogether true.*
3 *(adv)* on the whole. *Altogether, it was a very good party.*

aluminium *(n)* a light, silver-coloured metal.

always *(adv)* If something is **always** happening, it happens all the time or very many times.

Alzheimer's disease *(alts-hi-merz-diz-eez) (n)* a disease that affects a person's brain, making it gradually harder for them to think clearly or remember things. Alzheimer's disease usually only affects people in old age.

a.m. the initials of the Latin phrase *ante meridiem*, which means "before midday". *I get up at 7 a.m.*

amateur *(n)* someone who takes part in a sport or other activity for pleasure rather than for money.

amaze amazing amazed *(v)* to make someone feel very surprised. **amazement** *(n)*, **amazing** *(adj)*, **amazingly** *(adv).*

amber
1 *(n)* an orangey-yellow colour. **amber** *(adj).*
2 *(n)* a yellowish substance, formed from fossilized tree sap, and used for making ornaments and jewellery. *This piece of amber contains an insect that was trapped in the sap before it hardened and fossilized.*

amber

ambidextrous *(adj)* If you are **ambidextrous**, you can use both hands equally well, especially for writing.

ambiguous *(am-big-yoo-uss) (adj)* If something is **ambiguous**, it can be understood in more than one way. *Conrad gave an ambiguous answer.* **ambiguity** *(am-big-you-it-ee) (n).*

ambition

1 (n) something that you really want to do. *My ambition is to be a film star.*
2 (n) a strong wish to be successful. *Jo is driven by ambition.* **ambitious** (adj).

ambivalent (adj) If you feel ambivalent about something , you have two different opinions about it at the same time. **ambivalence** (n).

amble ambling ambled (v) to walk slowly because you are not in a hurry.

ambulance (n) a vehicle that takes people to hospital when they are ill.

ambush ambushes ambushing ambushed (v) to hide and then attack someone. **ambush** (n).

amenity amenities (n) something that is available for everyone to use and enjoy, such as a sports centre.

ammonia (n) a gas or solution with a strong smell. Some cleaning liquids contain ammonia.

ammunition

1 (n) things that can be fired from weapons, such as bullets or arrows.
2 (n) information that you can use against somebody else.

amnesty amnesties

1 (n) an official promise by a government to release prisoners or pardon crimes.
2 (n) a chance to hand in something you should not possess, without being punished.

amoeba (am-ee-ber) amoebas or amoebae (n) a microscopic creature made of only one cell. *The diagram shows the parts of an amoeba.*

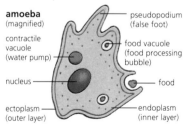

amoeba
(magnified)

pseudopodium
(false foot)

contractile
vacuole
(water pump)

food vacuole
(food processing
bubble)

nucleus

food

ectoplasm
(outer layer)

endoplasm
(inner layer)

among or amongst

1 (prep) surrounded by other people or things.
2 (prep) If you share something among several people, you divide it between them.

amount amounting amounted

1 (n) The amount of something is how much of it there is.
2 (v) If something amounts to a total, it adds up to it.

amp (n) a unit which measures the strength of an electrical current. Amp is short for ampere.

amphibian

1 (n) an animal that lives on land, but breeds in water. *Frogs, toads, and newts are amphibians.* **amphibious** (adj).
2 (n) a vehicle that can travel on land and in water. **amphibious** (adj).

amphitheatre (n) a large, open-air building, built in Roman times, with rows of seats in a high circle around an arena. Amphitheatres were used for public entertainments, such as gladiator and animal fights. *The picture shows a famous amphitheatre.*

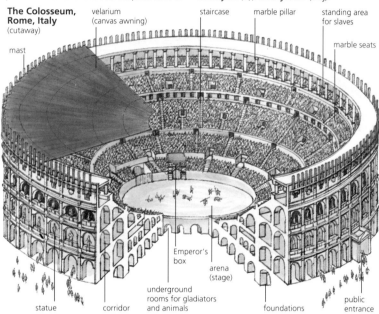

The Colosseum, Rome, Italy (cutaway)

velarium
(canvas awning)

mast

staircase

marble pillar

standing area
for slaves

marble seats

Emperor's
box

arena
(stage)

underground
rooms for gladiators
and animals

statue

corridor

foundations

public
entrance

ample ampler amplest

1 (adj) more than enough. *There was ample food for everyone.* **amply** (adv).
2 (adj) large. *Moira has an ample figure.*

amplifier (n) a piece of equipment that makes sound louder. **amplification** (n), **amplify** (v).

amputate amputating amputated

(v) to cut off someone's arm or leg because it is damaged or diseased. **amputation** (n).

amuse amusing amused

1 (v) to make someone laugh or smile. **amusing** (adj).
2 (v) to keep someone happy and stop them from being bored. *Dad's new camera kept him amused for hours.* **amusement** (n).

anaemic (a-nee-mik) (adj) If you are anaemic, you become easily tired and weak because your blood does not contain enough iron. **anaemia** (n).

anaesthetic (an-iss-thet-ik) (n) a drug or gas given to someone before an operation to prevent them from feeling pain.
anaesthetist (an-ees-the-tist) (n).

anagram (n) a word or phrase made by changing the order of letters in another word or phrase. *Stop is an anagram of post.*

analyse analysing analysed

(v) to examine something carefully in order to understand it. *Let's analyse the problem before we do anything.*
analysis (n), **analytical** (adj).

anarchy (n) a situation with no order and no one in control. **anarchist** (n).

anatomy

1 (n) The anatomy of a person or an animal is the structure of their body.
2 (singular n) the study of how the bodies of people and animals fit together. **anatomical** (adj).

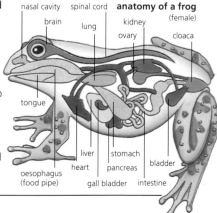

nasal cavity

spinal cord

anatomy of a frog
(female)

brain

lung

kidney

ovary

cloaca

tongue

liver

stomach

bladder

oesophagus
(food pipe)

heart

pancreas

gall bladder

intestine

ancestor *(n)* Your ancestors are members of your family who lived a long time ago. **ancestry** *(n)*, **ancestral** *(adj)*.

anchor *(n)* a heavy metal hook which is lowered from a ship or boat to stop it drifting. **anchorage** *(n)*, **anchor** *(v)*. See **ship**.

anchovy **anchovies** *(n)* a small, edible fish. Anchovies have a salty taste.

ancient *(ayn-shent)*
1 *(adj)* very old.
2 *(adj)* belonging to a time long ago. *Ancient Rome.*

android *(n)* a robot that acts and looks like a human being.

anecdote *(n)* a short, funny story about something that has happened. **anecdotal** *(adj)*.

anemometer *(n)* a scientific instrument used to measure the wind's speed.

anemone *(n)* a small flower, shaped like a cup.

angel
1 *(n)* a messenger of God. **angelic** *(adj)*.
2 *(n)* a very kind, gentle person. **angelic** *(adj)*.

anger *(n)* the feeling of being very annoyed.

angle
1 *(n)* the space between two lines at the point where they touch. *Angles are measured in degrees, for example, 90°.*
2 *(n)* a way of looking at something. *Leroy approached the problem from a different angle.*
3 If something is at an angle, it is sloping and not straight.

angling *(n)*
the sport of fishing with a fishing rod rather than a net. *The picture shows equipment used for freshwater angling.* **angler** *(n)*, **angle** *(v)*.

line

rod ring

carbon fibre rod

float ring

grayling float

split shot

drag nut setting

reel fitting

cork handle

bale arm

reel handle

spool

float
fishing rod

fixed spool reel

bait on hook

angora
1 *(n)* a long-haired variety of rabbit, goat, or cat.
2 *(n)* fluffy wool made from the hair of angora rabbits, mixed with sheep's wool.

angora rabbits

angry **angrier angriest** *(adj)* If you are **angry**, you feel that you want to argue or fight with someone. **angrily** *(adv)*.

anguish *(ang-wish)* *(n)* a strong feeling of misery or distress. **anguished** *(adj)*.

angular *(adj)* Something that is **angular** has a lot of straight lines and sharp corners. *Foxy had a thin, angular face.*

animal *(n)* any living creature that can breathe and move about.

animated
1 *(adj)* lively. *An animated conversation.* **animation** *(n)*, **animatedly** *(adv)*.
2 *(n)* An **animated film** is made by filming a series of drawings very quickly, one after the other, so that the characters in the drawings seem to move. *Artists provide millions of drawings, like the ones below, to make an animated film.* **animation** *(n)*, **animate** *(v)*.

animation sequence

animosity **animosities** *(n)* a strong dislike for someone.

aniseed *(n)* a strong-smelling seed used in sweets and drinks.

ankle *(n)* the joint that connects your foot to your leg.

annex **annexes annexing annexed** *(v)* When one country **annexes** another, it takes control of it by force.

annexe *(n)* an extra building joined on to or placed near a main building.

annihilate *(an-eye-ill-ate)* **annihilating annihilated** *(v)* to destroy something completely. **annihilation** *(n)*.

anniversary **anniversaries** *(n)* a date which people remember because something important happened on that date in the past.

annotate **annotating annotated** *(v)* to write notes explaining a piece of writing. **annotated** *(adj)*.

announce **announcing announced** *(v)* to say something officially or publicly. **announcement** *(n)*.

announcer *(n)* someone who introduces programmes on television or radio.

annoy **annoying annoyed** *(v)* to make someone feel angry. *Dudley really annoys me when he puts on that stupid voice.* **annoyance** *(n)*, **annoying** *(adj)*, **annoyingly** *(adv)*.

annual
1 *(adj)* happening once every year or over a period of one year. *The annual writing competition. An annual subscription.* **annually** *(adv)*.
2 *(n)* a book published once a year.
3 *(n)* a plant that only lives for one year. *Sunflowers are annuals.*

anon
1 *(adj)* **Anon** is short for anonymous.
2 **See you anon** means see you soon.

anonymous *(adj)* written, done, or given by a person whose name is not known. *An anonymous letter.* **anonymity** *(n)*, **anonymously** *(adv)*.

anorak *(n)* a waterproof jacket with a hood.

anorexia *(n)* If someone suffers from **anorexia**, they think that they are too fat and so they eat very little and become dangerously thin. Anorexia is short for anorexia nervosa. **anorexic** *(n)*, **anorexic** *(adj)*.

another
1 *(adj)* one more of the same kind. *Have another sweet.*
2 *(pronoun)* a different one. *I didn't like the red dress, so I chose another.*

answer **answering answered**
1 *(v)* to say or write something as a reply to a question. **answer** *(n)*.
2 *(n)* the solution to a problem. *Is there an answer to world poverty?*
3 *(v)* If you **answer back**, you make a rude or cheeky reply.
4 If someone has **a lot to answer for**, they have caused a lot of trouble.

answerable *(adj)* responsible. *Each leader is answerable for the safety of her group.*

answering machine *(n)* a machine connected to or built into a telephone, which records messages from people who telephone while you are out.

ant *(n)* a small insect with no wings that lives in a group called a colony. See **desert**, **insect**.

antagonize or **antagonise** **antagonizing antagonized** *(v)* If you **antagonize** someone, you make them feel very angry with you. **antagonism** *(n)*, **antagonist** *(n)*.

Antarctic *(n)* the area around the South Pole. **Antarctic** *(adj)*. See **polar**.

anteater (n)
a South American mammal with a very long tongue that it uses to search for ants and other small insects.

giant anteater

antelope (n) a large animal like a deer, that runs very fast. Antelopes are found in Africa and parts of Asia.

antenna antennas or antennae
1 (n) a feeler on the head on an insect. See **beetle**.
2 (n) a piece of wire that receives radio and television signals.

anthem (n) a religious or national song, usually sung by a choir.

anthology anthologies (n)
a collection of poems or stories by different writers which are all printed in the same book.

anthropology (singular n) the study of the beliefs and ways of life of different people around the world. **anthropologist** (n).

antibiotic (n) a drug, such as penicillin, that kills bacteria and is used to cure infections.

antibody antibodies (n) Your blood makes **antibodies** to fight against infection.

anticipate anticipating anticipated (v) to expect something to happen and be prepared for it. *The police anticipate trouble after the match.* **anticipation** (n).

anticlimax anticlimaxes (n)
If something is an **anticlimax**, it is not as exciting as you had expected.

anticlockwise (adv) in the opposite direction from that of the hands of a clock. **anticlockwise** (adj).

anticyclone (n) an area of high pressure in the atmosphere that causes settled weather. *In summer, an anticyclone brings clear skies and warm weather.*

antidote (n) something that stops a poison from working.

antiperspirant (n) a substance which you put on your skin to stop you sweating too much.

antique (an-teek)
1 (n) a very old object that is valuable because it is rare or beautiful.
2 (adj) very old.

antiseptic (n) a substance that kills germs and prevents infection.

antisocial
1 (adj) When someone behaves in an **antisocial** way, they do something that upsets or harms other people.
2 (adj) If somebody is **antisocial**, they do not enjoy being with other people.

antler (n) one of the two large, branching, bony structures on a stag's head. Stags grow and shed new antlers each year. *The diagram shows a new antler.*

velvet (skin)
antler bone
tine (branch)
pedicel (antler base)
skull bone

stag's antler
(cross-section)

anxiety (ang-zye-it-ee) anxieties (n) a feeling of worry or fear.

anxious (ank-shuss)
1 (adj) worried. *Mum gets anxious when I'm late.* **anxiously** (adv).
2 (adj) very keen to do something. *Sid is anxious to do well in his exams.*

anybody (pronoun) any person.

anyhow
1 (adv) in any case. *I didn't want to come anyhow.*
2 (adv) carelessly. *Her clothes were thrown down just anyhow!*

anyone (pronoun) any person.

anything (pronoun) any thing. *I'm not fussy, I'll eat anything.*

anyway (adv) in any case. *I never liked him anyway.*

anywhere (adv) in or to any place. *I'd follow Jo anywhere.*

apart (adv) If two people or things are **apart**, they are separated from each other.

apartheid (a-part-ate) (n) a political system in which people of different races are kept apart from each other.

apartment (n) a set of rooms for living in, usually on one floor of a building.

apathetic (adj) If you are **apathetic**, you do not care about anything or want to do anything. **apathy** (n).

ape aping aped
1 (n) a large animal like a monkey, but with no tail. Gorillas, gibbons, and chimpanzees are kinds of apes. *The picture shows a type of ape, called a chimpanzee, poking a stick into a termite mound to find food.*
2 (v) to copy the way another person behaves or speaks.

ape

aperture (n) a hole behind a camera lens that can be adjusted to control the amount of light that shines on to the film.

apex apexes (n) the highest point of something. *The apex of a triangle.*

apologize or **apologise** apologizing apologized (v) to say that you are sorry about something. **apology** (n), **apologetic** (adj).

apostle (n) one of the twelve men chosen by Christ to spread his teaching. *This picture of the apostle Matthew is taken from the 7th-century Lindisfarne Gospels.*

apostle

apostrophe (a-poss-truh-fee) (n) a punctuation mark (') used to show ownership, for example, "Jane's bag", or to show that letters have been missed out, for example, "can't".

appalling (adj) horrifying and shocking. **appallingly** (adv).

apparatus
1 (n) equipment used for performing sports, especially gymnastics.
2 (n) equipment or machines used to do a job or laboratory experiment.

laboratory apparatus

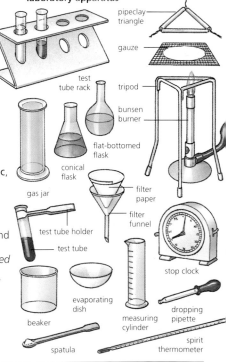

pipeclay triangle
gauze
tripod
bunsen burner
flat-bottomed flask
conical flask
gas jar
test tube rack
filter paper
filter funnel
stop clock
test tube holder
test tube
evaporating dish
beaker
measuring cylinder
dropping pipette
spirit thermometer
spatula

apparent
1 *(adj)* obvious or clear. *Bill's guilt was apparent to us all.*
2 *(adj)* seeming real or true. *Claudia's apparent confidence is really a sham.* apparently *(adv).*

appeal appealing appealed
1 *(v)* to ask for something urgently.
2 *(v)* to ask for a decision made by a court to be changed.
3 *(v)* If something **appeals** to you, you like it or find it interesting.

appear appearing appeared
1 *(v)* to come into sight. appearance *(n).*
2 *(v)* to seem. *Paul appears to be happy.* appearance *(n).*

appendicitis *(n)* If someone has **appendicitis**, their appendix is infected and very painful.

appendix appendices *or* appendixes
1 *(n)* a small, closed tube leading from your bowel. *See* **digestion**.
2 *(n)* extra information at the end of a book.

appetite
1 *(n)* desire for food.
2 *(n)* great enjoyment of something. *Sadjit has a real appetite for work.*

appetizing *or* appetising *(adj)*
Food that is **appetizing** looks and smells good to eat.

applaud applauding applauded
(v) to show that you like something, usually by clapping your hands. applause *(n).*

apple *(n)* a round, usually crispy, fruit. *See* **fruit**.

appliance *(n)* a machine designed to do a particular job. *Our kitchen is full of modern appliances.*

applicant *(n)* someone who has written formally, asking for something, like a job or a place on a course.

application
1 *(n)* a written request for something, like a job. *A job application.*
2 *(n)* a way of using something. *Our computer system has many different applications.*

apply applies applying applied
1 *(v)* to ask for something in writing.
2 *(v)* to be relevant. *These rules don't apply to us.*
3 *(v)* If you **apply yourself** to something, you work hard at it.

appoint appointing appointed
1 *(v)* to chose someone for a job.
2 *(v)* to arrange something officially. *We've already appointed a date for the match.*

appointment
1 *(n)* an arrangement to meet someone at a certain time.
2 *(n)* a job.

appreciable *(adj)* important enough to be noticed. *The company has lost an appreciable amount of money.*

appreciate appreciating appreciated
1 *(v)* to enjoy or value somebody or something. appreciation *(n),* appreciative *(adj),* appreciatively *(adv).*
2 *(v)* to understand something. *I appreciate your point of view.*
3 *(v)* to increase in value. appreciation *(n).*

apprehensive *(adj)* worried and slightly afraid. *Dolores was apprehensive about making her speech.* apprehension *(n),* apprehensively *(adv).*

apprentice *(n)* someone who learns a trade or craft by working with a craftsman and attending college. apprenticeship *(n).*

approach approaches approaching approached
1 *(v)* to move nearer. approach *(n).*
2 *(v)* If you **approach** somebody, you go up to them and talk to them.
3 *(v)* When you **approach** a problem, you think of ways of tackling it. approach *(n).*

approachable *(adj)* If someone is **approachable**, they are friendly and easy to talk to.

appropriate appropriating appropriated
1 *(ap-ro-pree-at) (adj)* suitable or right. appropriately *(adv).*
2 *(ap-ro-pree-ate) (v)* to take something that is not yours.

approve approving approved
1 *(v)* If you **approve of** someone or something, you think that they are acceptable or good. approval *(n).*
2 *(v)* to accept a plan or an idea. approval *(n).*

approximate *(adj)* more or less accurate or correct. *An approximate price.* approximation *(n),* approximately *(adv).*

apricot *(n)* a small, soft fruit with an orange skin. *See* **fruit**.

apron
1 *(n)* a piece of clothing that you wear to protect your clothes when you are cooking, painting, etc.
2 *(n)* the part of a stage in front of the curtain.

apt
1 *(adj)* very suitable. *An apt reply.*
2 *(adj)* quick to learn things.
3 *(adj)* If you are **apt to** do something, you are likely to do it.

aptitude *(n)* a natural ability to do something well.

aqualung *(n)* breathing apparatus for diving. An aqualung consists of an air cylinder with a tube leading to a mouthpiece. *See* **scuba diving**.

aquarium aquariums *or* aquaria *(n)* a glass tank in which you can keep fish. *The picture shows an aquarium for tropical freshwater fish.*

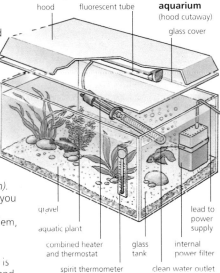

aquarium
(hood cutaway)

hood
fluorescent tube
glass cover
gravel
aquatic plant
combined heater and thermostat
glass tank
spirit thermometer
lead to power supply
internal power filter
clean water outlet

aquatic
1 *(adj)* living or growing in water. *Aquatic plants.*
2 *(adj)* performed in or on water. *Aquatic sports.*

aqueduct *(n)* a large bridge built to carry water across a valley. *The Roman aqueduct shown below was built in France in AD14.*

aqueduct

Arabic
1 *(n)* a language spoken by many people in the Middle East and North Africa.
2 *(n)* **Arabic numerals** are the sort of figures, such as 1, 2, 3, that we use today. *Arabic numerals are easier to use than Roman numerals.*

arable *(adj)* Arable land is used for growing crops.

arbitrate arbitrating arbitrated *(v)* to help two sides to reach an agreement. **arbitration** *(n)*.

arc
1 *(n)* a curved line.
2 *(n)* An **arc** is part of the circumference of a circle. *See* **circle**.

arcade
1 *(n)* a row of arches in a building.
2 **amusement arcade** *(n)* a covered area with machines, such as video games, that you pay to play on.
3 **shopping arcade** *(n)* a covered passageway with shops or stalls.

arch arches arching arched
1 *(n)* a curved structure. Arches often help to support a building or bridge. *The picture shows four different types of arch.*
2 *(v)* to curve. *The cat arched its back and spat.* **arched** *(adj)*.
3 *(adj)* chief. *Joe is my arch-enemy.*

arches

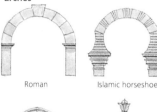

Roman   Islamic horseshoe

Gothic pointed   Gothic ogee

archaeology *or* **archeology** *(ar-kee-ol-oh-jee) (n)* If you study **archaeology**, you learn about the past by digging up old buildings and objects and examining them carefully. **archaeologist** *(n)*, **archaeological** *(adj)*.

archaic *(ar-kay-ik) (adj)* very old-fashioned and not used any more.

archbishop *(n)* one of the most important leaders in the Christian church.

archeology *see* **archaeology**.

archery *(n)* the sport of shooting at targets, using a bow and arrow. **archer** *(n)*.

archipelago *(ar-kee-pel-ag-o) (n)* a group of small islands.

architect *(ar-ki-tekt) (n)* someone who designs buildings and checks that they are built correctly.

architecture
1 *(n)* the activity of designing buildings.
2 *(n)* the style in which buildings are designed. *The selection of buildings below shows how different styles of architecture have been used for places of worship throughout the world and for a range of modern buildings.* **architectural** *(adj)*. *Also see* **building**.

pyramid
(The Great Pyramids, Giza, Egypt)

Greek temple
(The Parthenon, Athens, Greece)

Byzantine cathedral
(St Basil's, Moscow, Russia)

pagoda
(Soochow Lake, China)

Gothic cathedral
(Salisbury, England)

mosque
(The Blue Mosque, Istanbul, Turkey)

Shinto shrine
(Izumo, Japan)

Hindu temple
(Khajuraho, India)

communications tower
(CN Tower, Toronto, Canada)

skyscraper
(Hong Kong and Shanghai Bank, Hong Kong)

external maintenance crane

helipad

internal staircase

terrace

steel support mast

steel hanger

hanging glass curtain wall

10-storey atrium

steel suspension truss

aluminium cladding panel

glass typhoon screen

opera house
(Sydney, Australia)

museum entrance
(Louvre Museum, Paris, France)

arctic
1 **The Arctic** (n) the frozen area around the North Pole. **Arctic** (adj). *See* **polar**.
2 (adj) extremely cold and wintry. *Arctic weather conditions.*

ardent (adj) If you are **ardent** about something, you feel very strongly about it. **ardently** (adv).

arduous (ard-yoo-uss) (adj) very difficult and demanding a lot of effort.

area
1 (n) the size of a surface. To work out the area of a surface, you multiply its length by its width.
2 (n) part of a place. *A poor area of the country.*

arena (n) a large area, used for sports or entertainment. *See* **amphitheatre**, **track and field**.

argue arguing argued
1 (v) to disagree with someone angrily. **argument** (n), **argumentative** (adj).
2 (v) to give your opinion about something. *Sean argued that whaling was cruel.* **argument** (n).

arid (adj) Land that is **arid** is extremely dry because very little rain has fallen on it.

arise arising arose arisen
1 (v) If something, like a problem, **arises**, it comes into being.
2 (v) (old-fashioned) to stand up. *Arise, Sir Francis!*

aristocrat (n) a member of the highest social rank, or nobility. **aristocracy** (n), **aristocratic** (adj).

arithmetic (n) calculations with numbers. Addition, subtraction, multiplication, and division are all types of arithmetic.

arm arming armed
1 (n) the part of your body between your shoulder and your hand.
2 (v) If a country **arms** itself, it gets ready for war.
3 **arms** (plural n) weapons.

armadillo (n) a mammal covered by hard, bony plates. *The nine-banded armadillo, shown below, is found in North and South America.*

nine-banded armadillo

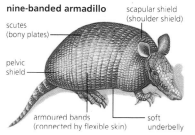

scapular shield (shoulder shield)
scutes (bony plates)
pelvic shield
armoured bands (connected by flexible skin)
soft underbelly

armaments (plural n) weapons and other equipment used for fighting wars.

armchair (n) a comfortable chair with supports for your arms.

armistice (n) an agreement to stop fighting a war.

armour
1 (n) metal covering worn by soldiers to protect them in battle. *See* **knight**.
2 (n) protective scales, spines, or shell that cover some animals, such as an armadillo. *See* **armadillo**.

armoured vehicle (n) a tank or other military vehicle with a strong metal covering. *This armoured vehicle is used for carrying troops.*

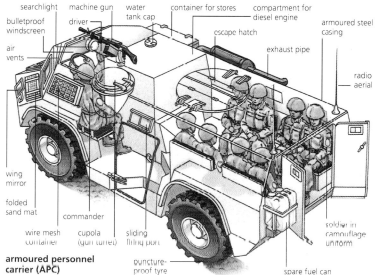

searchlight machine gun water tank cap container for stores compartment for diesel engine
bulletproof windscreen driver escape hatch armoured steel casing
air vents exhaust pipe
radio aerial
wing mirror
folded sand mat
commander
wire mesh container cupola (gun turret) sliding firing port
soldier in camouflage uniform
armoured personnel carrier (APC)
puncture-proof tyre
spare fuel can

armpit (n) the area under your arm where it joins your shoulder.

army armies (n) a large group of people trained to fight on land.

aroma (n) a pleasant smell. **aromatic** (adj).

around
1 (prep) surrounding, or in a circle. *He tied a rope around the tree.*
2 (adv) in many different parts of a place. *We travelled around Spain.*
3 (adv) more or less. *There were around 30 of us.*

arouse arousing aroused
1 (v) to wake someone.
2 (v) to stir up a feeling. *Tarquin's strange behaviour aroused my curiosity.* **arousal** (n).

arrange arranging arranged
1 (v) to make plans for something to happen. **arrangement** (n).
2 (v) to place things so that they look attractive. **arrangement** (n).

3 (v) to change a piece of music slightly, so that it can be played on different instruments. **arrangement** (n).
4 (n) If someone has an **arranged marriage**, their parents have chosen a husband or wife for them.

arrest arresting arrested
1 (v) to take someone prisoner. **arrest** (n).
2 (v) to stop something from developing or happening any more.

arrive arriving arrived
1 (v) to reach a place. *We arrived home early.* **arrival** (n).
2 (v) to come. *At last, the great day arrived.*

arrogant (adj) conceited and proud. **arrogance** (n), **arrogantly** (adv).

arrow
1 (n) a pointed stick, shot from a bow.
2 (n) a sign showing a direction.

arson (n) If someone commits **arson**, they deliberately and wrongly set fire to something.

art
1 (n) the skill of creating something beautiful by drawing, painting, or making things with your hands.
2 (n) something that requires a lot of skill. *The art of Chinese cookery.*
3 **the arts** (plural n) forms of entertainment, such as music, theatre, and film.

artery arteries (n) one of the tubes that carry blood from your heart to all the other parts of your body. **arterial** (adj). *See* **circulation**.

arthritis (n) a disease which makes people's joints swollen and painful.

article
1 *(n)* an object or a thing.
2 *(n)* a piece of writing published in a newspaper or magazine.
3 *(n)* a word, such as "a", "the", or "some", that goes in front of a noun.

articulate *(adj)* If you are **articulate**, you can express yourself clearly in words. **articulately** *(adv)*.

articulated truck *(n)* a truck with a cab and a trailer linked by a flexible joint so that the truck can turn round corners easily. *See* **truck**.

artificial *(adj)* false, not real, or not natural. *Artificial flowers.* **artificially** *(adv)*.

artificial intelligence *(n)* the use of computers to do things that previously needed human intelligence, such as understanding language.

artillery
1 *(n)* large, powerful guns.
2 *(n)* the part of an army that uses large guns.

artist *(n)* someone very skilled at painting, drawing, or making things. *This picture shows a range of tools and materials used by artists.* **artistic** *(adj)*, **artistically** *(adv)*.

aside
1 *(adv)* to one side, or out of the way. *Sarah pushed her brothers aside.*
2 *(n)* a remark made quietly so that not everyone can hear it.

ask asking asked
1 *(v)* to make a request or put a question to someone.
2 *(v)* to invite someone to do something. *I've asked Tim to lunch.*

askew *(ass-kyoo) (adj)* crooked.

asleep *(adj)* sleeping. *The baby soon fell asleep.*

aspect *(n)* one feature or characteristic of something. *Robbie enjoys most aspects of school life.*

asphyxiate *(ass-fix-ee-ate)* asphyxiating asphyxiated *(v)* to suffocate. **asphyxiation** *(n)*.

aspiration *(n)* a strong desire to do something great or important. *In order to succeed, you need to have aspirations.* **aspire** *(v)*.

aspirin *(n)* a drug that relieves pain and reduces fever.

ass asses
1 *(n)* a donkey.
2 *(n) (informal)* a stupid person.

assassinate assassinating assassinated *(v)* to murder an important person, such as a president. **assassin** *(n)*, **assassination** *(n)*.

assault assaulting assaulted *(v)* to attack someone or something violently. **assault** *(n)*.

assemble assembling assembled
1 *(v)* to gather together in one place. *All the school assembled in the hall.*

2 *(v)* to put all the parts of something together. *Follow the instructions to assemble this model.*

assembly
1 *(n)* a meeting of lots of people.
2 **assembly line** *(n)* a series of machines and workers in a factory that each do a job in turn.

assent assenting assented *(v)* to agree to something. **assent** *(n)*.

assert asserting asserted *(v)* If you **assert yourself**, you behave in a strong, confident way so that people take notice of you.

assertive *(adj)* able to stand up for yourself and tell other people what you think or want. **assertiveness** *(n)*, **assertively** *(adv)*.

assess assesses assessing assessed *(v)* to judge how good or bad something is. **assessment** *(n)*, **assessor** *(n)*.

asset *(n)* something or someone who is helpful or useful. *Imran is a great asset to our team.*

assignment *(n)* a special job that is given to somebody. **assign** *(v)*.

assistance *(n)* If someone gives you **assistance**, they do something to help you or to make things easier for you. **assist** *(v)*.

assistant *(n)* a person who helps someone else to do a task or job.

association
1 *(n)* an organization, club, or society.
2 *(n)* a connection that you make in your mind between different things. *Our holiday house has many happy associations for me.* **associate** *(v)*.

assonance *(n)* repeated use of the same vowel sound in words that are close together, for example, "How now brown cow?".

assortment *(n)* a mixture of different things. **assorted** *(adj)*.

assume assuming assumed
1 *(v)* to suppose that something is true, without checking it. *I assume that you're right.* **assumption** *(n)*.
2 *(v)* If you **assume** responsibility for something, you agree to look after it.
3 An **assumed name** is a false name.

assurance
1 *(n)* a firm promise.
2 *(n)* confidence in yourself and in what you can do. *Self-assurance.*

assure assuring assured
1 *(v)* to promise something, or say something positively. *Annie assured me of her support.*
2 *(v)* If you **assure yourself** about something, you make certain about it.

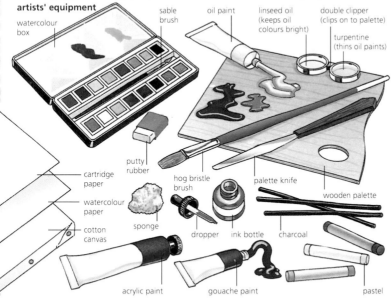

artists' equipment
watercolour box
sable brush
oil paint
linseed oil (keeps oil colours bright)
double clipper (clips on to palette)
turpentine (thins oil paints)
cartridge paper
putty rubber
hog bristle brush
palette knife
wooden palette
watercolour paper
cotton canvas
sponge
dropper
ink bottle
charcoal
acrylic paint
gouache paint
pastel

ascend *(ass-end)* ascending ascended *(v)* to move upwards. **ascent** *(n)*.

ash ashes
1 *(n)* the powder that remains after something has been burnt.
2 *(n)* a tree with long, thin leaves.

ashamed *(adj)* If you are **ashamed**, you feel embarrassed and guilty.

asterisk *(n)* a mark (*) used in printing and writing.

asteroid *(n)* a very small planet that travels round the Sun.

asthma *(ass mer)* *(n)* If you have asthma, you sometimes wheeze and find it hard to breathe. **asthmatic** *(n)*, **asthmatic** *(adj)*.

astonish astonishes astonishing astonished *(v)* to make someone feel very surprised. **astonishment** *(n)*, **astonishing** *(adj)*, **astonishingly** *(adv)*.

astray
1 *(adv)* If something has gone **astray**, it has been lost.
2 If someone **leads you astray**, they encourage you to do something wrong.

astride *(prep)* If you sit **astride** something, like a horse or a bicycle, you sit with a leg on either side of it.

astrology *(n)* the study of stars and planets and the way they are supposed to affect people's lives. **astrologer** *(n)*, **astrological** *(adj)*.

astronaut *(n)* someone who travels in space. *The picture shows an astronaut operating a manned manoeuvring unit (MMU), which is used for moving around outside the spaceship.*

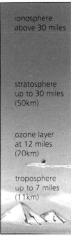

astronomical sphere

astronomical
1 *(adj)* to do with astronomy. *The astronomical instrument shown here dates from the 16th century and was used to work out the positions of the stars.*
2 *(adj)* very large. *An astronomical amount of money.* **astronomically** *(adv)*.

astronomy *(n)* the study of stars, planets, and space. **astronomer** *(n)*.

astute *(ass-tyoot)* *(adj)* If someone is astute, they understand situations and people clearly and quickly.

asunder *(adv)* *(old-fashioned)* in or into pieces. *The veil was torn asunder.*

asylum *(ass-eye-lum)*
1 *(n)* protection given by a country to someone escaping from danger in their own country.
2 *(n)* *(old-fashioned)* a hospital for people who are mentally ill.

asymmetrical *(adj)* A shape that is asymmetrical cannot be divided into two equal halves.

ATB *(n)* The initials ATB stand for all-terrain bicycle. ATBs have wide, tough tyres and many gears so they can be used on a range of surfaces.

atheist *(ay-thee-ist)* *(n)* someone who does not believe that there is a God. **atheism** *(n)*.

athlete
1 *(n)* someone who takes part in sports such as running, jumping, and throwing.
2 *(n)* someone who is very good at sports. **athletic** *(adj)*.

athletics *(n)* competitive sports that involve running, jumping, or throwing. **athletic** *(adj)*. See **track and field**.

atlas *(n)* a book of maps.

atmosphere *(at-muss-fear)*
1 *(n)* the mixture of gases that surround a planet. *The layers of the Earth's atmosphere are shown in this diagram.*
2 *(n)* the air in a particular place. *The atmosphere in some of our cities is very polluted.* **atmospheric** *(adj)*.
3 *(n)* a mood or feeling created by a place or a work of art. *I didn't like the atmosphere in Uncle Merlin's house.* **atmospheric** *(adj)*.

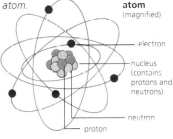

ionosphere	above 30 miles
stratosphere	up to 30 miles (50km)
ozone layer	at 12 miles (20km)
troposphere	up to 7 miles (11km)

layers of the atmosphere

atom *(n)* the smallest part of a substance. Everything is made up of atoms. *The diagram shows the main parts of an atom.*

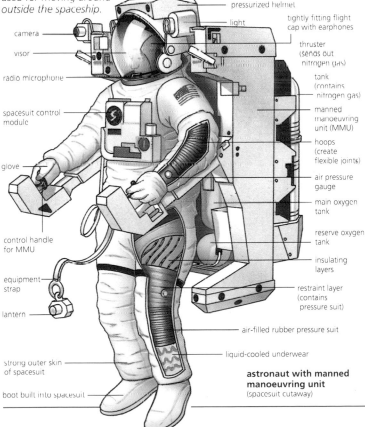

camera
visor
radio microphone
spacesuit control module
glove
control handle for MMU
equipment strap
lantern
strong outer skin of spacesuit
boot built into spacesuit

pressurized helmet
light
tightly fitting flight cap with earphones
thruster (sends out nitrogen gas)
tank (contains nitrogen gas)
manned manoeuvring unit (MMU)
hoops (create flexible joints)
air pressure gauge
main oxygen tank
reserve oxygen tank
insulating layers
restraint layer (contains pressure suit)
air-filled rubber pressure suit
liquid-cooled underwear

astronaut with manned manoeuvring unit
(spacesuit cutaway)

atom (magnified)
electron
nucleus (contains protons and neutrons)
neutron
proton

atomic
1 *(adj)* to do with atoms. *Atomic structure.*
2 *(adj)* using the power created when atoms are split. *Atomic energy.*

atone atoning atoned *(v)* If you atone for something, you make up for it. *Kate atoned for her lateness by working extra hard.*

atrocious *(at-roh-shuss)* *(adj)* disgusting, or terrible.

atrocity atrocities *(n)* a very wicked or cruel act, often involving killing.

attach attaches attaching attached
1 (v) to join or fix one thing to another. **attachment** (n).
2 If you are **attached to** someone, you are very fond of them. **attachment** (n).

attack attacking attacked
1 (v) to try to hurt someone or something. **attack** (n), **attacker** (n).
2 (v) to criticize someone strongly. **attack** (n).
3 (v) to try to defeat an enemy or capture a place where the enemy is. *The troops attacked the castle.* **attack** (n).
4 (n) a sudden period of illness. *A bad attack of flu.*

attainment (n) an achievement. **attain** (v), **attainable** (adj).

attempt attempting attempted (v) to try to do something. **attempt** (n).

attend attending attended
1 (v) to be present in a place or at an event. *Thousands of people attended the concert.* **attendance** (n).
2 (v) If you **attend to** something, you deal with it.

attendant (n) someone who looks after an important person or place. *A museum attendant.*

attention
1 (n) concentration and careful thought. *Attention to detail.*
2 If you **pay attention**, you concentrate on something.
3 When soldiers **stand to attention**, they stand up straight, with their feet together and their arms by their sides.

attic (n) a room in the roof of a building.

attitude
1 (n) your opinions and feelings about someone or something. *Aidan has a positive attitude towards his work.*
2 (n) the position in which you are standing or sitting.

attract attracting attracted
1 (v) If something **attracts** you, you are interested in it. **attraction** (n).
2 (v) If a person **attracts** you, you like them. **attraction** (n).
3 (v) If something **attracts** objects or people to itself, it pulls them towards itself. *Magnets attract iron and steel.* **attraction** (n).

attractive
1 (adj) pleasant, or pretty to look at. **attractiveness** (n), **attractively** (adv).
2 (adj) interesting, or exciting. *An attractive plan.* **attractiveness** (n).

auburn (or-burn) (n) a reddish-brown colour. **auburn** (adj).

auction (n) a sale where goods are sold to the person who offers the most money for them. **auctioneer** (n).

audience
1 (n) the people who watch or listen to a performance, speech, or show.
2 (n) a formal meeting with an important or powerful person.

audio-visual (adj) Audio-visual equipment uses sound and pictures, often to teach people something.

audition (n) a short performance by an actor, singer, etc. to see whether they are suitable for a part in a play, concert, etc.

aunt (n) the sister of your father or mother, or the wife of your uncle.

au pair (oh-pair) (n) a young person from another country who lives with a family and helps them, in order to learn a language.

aural (or-al) (adj) to do with listening. *My piano exam includes an aural test.*

author (n) the writer of a book, play, or poem. **authorship** (n).

authority authorities
1 (n) the right to do something or to tell other people what to do. *The detectives have the authority to search our house.*
2 (n) a group of people with power in a certain area. *A local authority.*
3 (n) someone who knows a lot about a particular subject. *Sam is an authority on computers.*

authorize or **authorise** authorizing authorized (v) to give permission for something to happen. **authorization** (n).

autistic (adj) Someone who is **autistic** has a mental illness which prevents them from communicating normally or from forming proper relationships with other people.

autobiography autobiographies (n) a book that tells the story of the writer's life. **autobiographical** (adj).

autograph (n) a famous person's signature.

automatic
1 (adj) An **automatic** machine can perform some actions without anyone operating it. **automatically** (adv).
2 (adj) An **automatic** action happens without your thinking about it. **automatically** (adv).

automation (n) the use of machines rather than people to do jobs, especially in factories. **automate** (v).

automobile (US) a type of passenger motor vehicle (car, UK).

autumn (n) the season between summer and winter, when it gets colder and the leaves fall from the trees. **autumnal** (adj).

available
1 (adj) ready to be used or bought. **availability** (n).
2 (adj) not busy, and so free to talk to people. **availability** (n).

avalanche (av-er-larnsh) (n) a large mass of snow and ice that suddenly moves down the side of a mountain.

avenue (n) a wide road in a town or city, often with trees on either side.

average
1 (n) In maths, you find an **average** by adding a group of figures together and then dividing the total by the number of figures you have added. *The average of 2, 4, and 6 is 4.*
2 (n) usual, or ordinary.

aviary aviaries (n) a large cage for birds.

aviation (n) the science of building and flying aircraft. *The great age of aviation began in 1903, when Orville Wright first left the ground in the Flyer, shown below.* **aviator** (n).

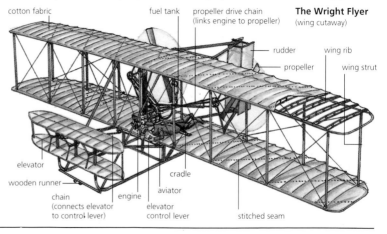

The Wright Flyer (wing cutaway)

cotton fabric · fuel tank · propeller drive chain (links engine to propeller) · rudder · wing rib · propeller · wing strut · elevator · wooden runner · chain (connects elevator to control lever) · engine · aviator · cradle · elevator control lever · stitched seam

avoid avoiding avoided
1 (v) to keep away from a person or place. **avoidance** (n).
2 (v) to try to prevent something from happening. We must avoid making that mistake again **avoidance** (n), **avoidable** (adj).

await awaiting awaited (v) to wait for or expect someone or something.

awake awaking awoke awoken
1 (adj) not asleep. I'm wide awake.
2 (v) to wake up. **awakening** (n).

award awarding awarded (v) to give something to someone officially, often as a prize. **award** (n).

aware (adj) If you are **aware** of something, you know that it exists. **awareness** (n).

away
1 (adv) moving from a place, person, or thing. Rosie ran away from me.
2 (adv) distant from a place. We live three miles away.
3 (adv) not at home, or not present.
4 (adv) in a safe place. Put your money away.
5 (adj) An **away** match is a sports match that you play at your opponent's ground.

awe (n) a feeling of admiration and respect, mixed with a little fear. **awesome** (adj).

awful
1 (adj) terrible, or horrible.
2 (adj) (informal) very great. I spent an awful lot of money. **awfully** (adv).

awkward
1 (adj) causing difficulties. An awkward catch. **awkwardness** (n), **awkwardly** (adv).
2 (adj) not able to relax and talk to people easily. **awkwardness** (n), **awkwardly** (adv).

axe axing axed
1 (n) a tool with a sharp blade on the end of a long handle, used for chopping wood.
2 (v) to bring something to an end, usually in order to save money. 200 jobs will be axed.

axis axes
1 (n) an imaginary line through the middle of an object, around which that object spins. The earth's axis.
2 (n) a line at the side or the bottom of a graph.

axle (n) a rod in the centre of a wheel, around which the wheel turns.

Aztec (n) a member of the Mexican Indian people, who had a great civilization before the conquest of Mexico in the 16th century. **Aztec** (adj).

Bb

babble babbling babbled
1 (v) to talk in an excited way, without making any sense.
2 (v) to make sounds like a baby.

baboon (n) a large monkey that lives in Africa. Baboons have long, dog-like snouts and large teeth.

olive baboons

baby babies (n) a newly born or very young child or animal. **babyish** (adj).

baby-sitter (n) someone who is paid to stay in the house and look after children while their parents are out.

bachelor (n) a man who has never been married.

back backing backed
1 (n) the rear part of your body between your neck and your bottom.
2 (n) the opposite end or side from the front. **back** (adj).
3 (adv) to where someone or something was before. Ed came back.
4 (v) to support someone.
5 **back down** (v) to admit that you were wrong.
6 **back out** (v) to decide not to do something that you had agreed to do.

backfire backfiring backfired
1 (v) If a car **backfires**, there is a small explosion inside its exhaust pipe.
2 (v) If an action **backfires**, it does not work out as you planned it.

background
1 (n) the part of a picture that is behind the main subject.
2 (n) the facts or events that surround something and help to explain why it happened.

backhand (n) a stroke in tennis that you play with the back of your hand facing outwards and your arm across your body. The sequence below shows how to play a backhand.

backhand drive

backpack
1 (n) a large bag that you carry on your back when you are walking or climbing.
2 If you **go backpacking**, you go on a long walk or hike.

backstroke (n) a style of swimming in which you swim lying on your back.

backwards
1 (adv) in the direction that your back is facing. Joe stepped backwards.
2 (adv) in the opposite to the usual way. Say the alphabet backwards.

bacon (n) smoked or salted meat from the back or sides of a pig.

bacteria (plural n) microscopic living things which exist all around you and inside you. Many bacteria are useful, but some cause disease. The diagram shows a simplified bacteria cell, magnified millions of times.

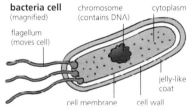

bacteria cell (magnified) — chromosome (contains DNA) — cytoplasm — flagellum (moves cell) — jelly-like coat — cell membrane — cell wall

bad worse worst
1 (adj) not good.
2 (adj) serious. A bad mistake.
3 (adj) not fit to eat. The fish has gone bad.

badge (n) a small sign with a picture or message on it that you pin to your clothes.

badger badgering badgered
1 (n) a mammal with a grey body and a black and white head, that lives in a sett under the ground and comes out at night to feed.
2 (v) to keep asking someone to do something. Fran kept badgering me to let her come with us.

badger's sett (cutaway) — sow (female badger) — sett entrance — tunnel — chamber — cubs on bedding of dry grass and leaves

badly
1 (adv) not well, or not skilfully.
2 (adv) urgently. I want it badly.

badminton

(n) a game like tennis, in which players use rackets to hit a shuttlecock over a high net.

badminton racket and shuttlecocks

frame

string

shaft

plastic shuttlecock

feather shuttlecock

baffle baffling baffled *(v)* to puzzle or confuse someone. **baffling** *(adj)*.

bag *(n)* a container used for carrying things.

baggage *(n)* suitcases and bags.

baggy baggier baggiest *(adj)* hanging in loose folds. *Baggy shorts.*

bagpipes *(plural n)* a musical instrument. To play the bagpipes, you blow air through the blowstick into a bag, and squeeze it out through the drones and the chanter.

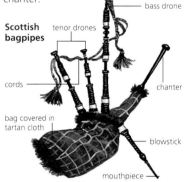

Scottish bagpipes

bass drone

tenor drones

cords

chanter

bag covered in tartan cloth

blowstick

mouthpiece

bail

1 *(n)* a sum of money paid to a court to allow someone accused of a crime to be set free until their trial.

2 *(n)* one of the two small pieces of wood that are placed across the top of cricket stumps. See **cricket**.

bailiff *(n)* a law officer who makes sure that a court's decision is carried out, especially by taking someone's property when they owe money.

bail out see **bale out**.

bait *(n)* a small amount of food used to attract a fish or an animal, so that you can catch them. See **angling**.

baize *(n)* a felt-like material, used for covering card-tables, snooker tables, etc.

bake baking baked

1 *(v)* to cook food in an oven, especially bread or cakes. **baker** *(n)*, **bakery** *(n)*.

2 *(v)* to heat something in order to make it hard. *Bake the clay in a kiln before glazing it.*

balaclava *(n)* a woolly hat that covers your head and neck, like a helmet.

balance balancing balanced

1 *(n)* an instrument used for weighing things.

2 *(v)* When two things **balance** in a pair of scales, they weigh the same and do not tip the scales either way.

3 *(n)* Your **balance** is your ability to keep steady and not fall over.

4 *(v)* If you **balance** something, you keep it steady and do not let it fall.

5 *(n)* When you subtract an amount from another amount, what you have left is the **balance**.

balcony

1 *(n)* a platform with railings on the outside of a building, usually on an upper level.

2 *(n)* the upstairs seating in a theatre.

bald *(borld)* balder baldest

1 *(adj)* Someone who is **bald** has very little or no hair on their head. **baldness** *(n)*, **balding** *(adj)*.

2 *(adj)* A **bald** fact or statement is stated simply, without any attempt to make it more pleasant. **baldly** *(adv)*.

bale out baling out baled out

1 *(v)* to jump out of an aircraft, using a parachute.

2 *(v)* If you **bale someone out**, you help them out of a difficult situation.

ball

1 *(n)* a round object, used in games.

2 *(n)* something made into a round shape. *A ball of wool.*

3 *(n)* a very formal party where people dance.

4 *(informal)* If you **have a ball**, you really enjoy yourself.

ballad *(n)* a song or a poem that tells a story.

ballast

1 *(n)* heavy material, such as water or sand, that is carried by a ship to make it more stable.

2 **ballast tank** *(n)* a large tank in a submarine that is filled with water to make the submarine sink, and with air to make it come to the surface.

ball bearings *(n)* small, metal balls used to help parts of machinery move more smoothly against each other.

ballerina *(n)* a leading woman ballet dancer.

ballet *(bal-ay)*

1 *(n)* a style of dance with set movements.

2 *(n)* a performance using dance and music, often to tell a story. *The picture shows three ballet movements.*

grand jeté

arabesque

pirouette

ballet movements

ballistics *(singular n)* the science and study of missiles that are fired from guns. **ballistic** *(adj)*.

balloon

1 *(n)* a small bag made of thin rubber that is blown up and used as a decoration.

2 See **hot-air balloon**.

ballot

1 *(n)* a secret way of voting for something.

2 **ballot box** *(n)* a box with a slit in the top into which votes are put.

3 **ballot paper** *(n)* a special piece of paper used for marking a vote.

ballpoint *(n)* a pen with a tiny ball at its tip that lets ink flow as you write.

balsa *(n)* a very light wood, used for making models.

bamboo *(n)* a tropical plant with a hard, hollow stem, often used for making furniture.

ban banning banned *(v)*

to forbid something. *Ball games are banned in this park.* **ban** *(n)*.

banana *(n)* a tropical fruit that is long, curved, and yellow.

banana tree

unripe bananas

flower

band banding banded

1 *(n)* a narrow ring of rubber, paper, or other material, that is put around something to hold it together.

2 *(n)* a group of people who play music together.

3 *(n)* a group of people who do something together. *A band of robbers.*

4 *(v)* When people **band together**, they join together in a group in order to do something.

bandage (n) a long piece of cloth that is wrapped around an injured part of the body in order to protect it. **bandage** (v).

bandit (n) an armed robber, usually one of a gang, who attacks travellers.

bang banging banged
1 (n) a sudden loud noise.
2 (v) to knock hard against something **bang** (n).

banger
1 (n) a firework that makes a loud noise.
2 (n) (informal) an old, battered car.
3 (n) (slang) a sausage.

bangle (n) a band of metal, plastic, etc. worn around the wrist.

bangs (plural n) (US) the hair that hangs over your forehead (fringe, UK).

banish banishes banishing banished (v) to send someone away from a place and order them not to return. **banishment** (n).

banister or **bannister** (n) a rail that runs along the side of a flight of stairs.

banjo (n) a musical instrument like a small, round guitar with a long neck.

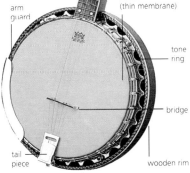

banjo

arm guard

tail piece

bank banking banked
1 (n) a place where people keep their money. Banks also lend money and offer other financial services.
2 (n) the land along the sides of a river or a canal.
3 (n) a place where something is stored and collected. A bottle bank.
4 **bank holiday** (n) a public holiday in Britain when the banks are closed.

tuning peg

headstock

fifth tuning-peg

string

fingerboard

neck

velum (thin membrane)

tone ring

bridge

wooden rim

5 (v) If you **bank on** something, you rely on it.

banknote (n) a piece of paper money.

bankrupt (adj) If a person or company is bankrupt, they cannot pay their debts. **bankruptcy** (n), **bankrupt** (v).

banner (n) a long piece of material with writing on it, often carried in sports crowds and processions.

bannister see **banister**.

banns (plural n) an announcement of a wedding made in a church.

banquet (n) a formal meal for a large number of people, usually on a special occasion.

banter bantering bantered (v) to tease someone in a good-natured way. **banter** (n).

bap (n) a soft bread roll.

baptize or **baptise** baptizing baptized (v) to pour water on someone's head, or to immerse someone in water, as a sign that they have become a Christian. **baptism** (n).

bar
1 (n) a long stick of metal. An iron bar.
2 (n) a long, flat block of something hard. A chocolate bar.
3 (n) a place where drinks, especially alcoholic drinks, are sold.
4 (n) one of the groups of notes into which a piece of music is divided.

barbarian (n) a member of a wild and uncivilized tribe that lived in the past.

barbaric (adj) very cruel. The animals were kept in barbaric conditions.

barbecue
1 (n) a charcoal grill used for cooking meat and other food out of doors.
2 (n) an outdoor meal or party in which food is cooked using a barbecue.

barbed wire (n) wire with small spikes along it, used for fences.

barber (n) someone who cuts men's and boys' hair.

bar code (n) a band of thick and thin lines printed on goods sold in shops which gives information about the goods.

bare baring bared; barer barest
1 (adj) wearing no clothes.
2 (adj) empty. The cupboard was bare.
3 (v) to uncover or reveal something. The dog bared its teeth. Verity bared her secret thoughts.

4 (adj) plain and simple. Just give me the bare facts.

bareback (adv) If you ride a horse bareback, you do not use a saddle.

barefaced (adj) open and undisguised. Barefaced cheek.

barely (adv) only just. Tarquin was so scared, he could barely speak.

bargain bargaining bargained
1 (n) something that you buy for less than the usual price.
2 (v) When you **bargain** with someone, you agree to do something if they will do something else in exchange. **bargain** (n).

barge barging barged
1 (n) a long, flat-bottomed boat, used on canals.
2 (v) If you **barge** into someone, you knock against them roughly or push them out of the way.

baritone
1 (n) the second lowest singing voice for a man. **baritone** (adj).
2 (n) a singer with a baritone voice.

bark barking barked
1 (v) When a dog **barks**, it makes a loud sound in its throat. **bark** (n).
2 (n) the hard covering on the outside of a tree.
3 (v) to shout at someone gruffly. "Attention!" barked the sergeant.

barley (n) a common cereal plant. See **grain**.

bar mitzvah (n) a celebration that takes place on a Jewish boy's 13th birthday, after which he can take part in his religion as an adult.

barn (n) a farm building where crops or animals are kept. See **thresh**.

barnacle (n) a small shellfish that sticks itself firmly to the sides of boats, rocks, and other shellfish. See **scallop**.

barometer (n) an instrument that measures changes in air pressure and shows how the weather is going to change. In the simple barometer shown here, liquid rises in the spout for stormy weather and falls for fine weather.

19th-century barometer

baron (n) a nobleman. In Britain, a baron is a male peer of the lowest rank. **baronial** (adj).

baroness baronesses (n) a noblewoman. In Britain, a baroness is a female peer of the lowest rank or the wife of a baron.

barracks barracks (n) the buildings where soldiers live.

barrage

1 (n) a dam built across a river to control the level of the water.
2 (n) a large amount of something that all comes at the same time. *A barrage of complaints.*

barrel

1 (n) a container for liquids, such as water or beer, which has curved sides and a flat top and bottom.
2 (n) the long part of a gun that looks like a tube. See **blunderbuss**.
3 (n) the part of a dart that you hold. *See* **dart**.
4 If someone has you **over a barrel**, they have made you powerless.

barren

1 (adj) If land is **barren**, farmers cannot grow crops on it.
2 (adj) (old-fashioned) A woman who is **barren** is not able to have children.

barricade barricading barricaded

1 (n) a wall built in a hurry to stop people from getting past.
2 (v) If people **barricade** themselves into a place, they build walls to stop other people reaching them.

barrier

1 (n) a bar, fence, or wall that prevents people, traffic, water, etc. from going past it. *The Thames Barrier is made up of a series of linked gates across the River Thames which can be opened to let water through or closed to prevent flooding. The picture below shows a gate in the closed position.*
2 (n) something that prevents you from communicating properly with someone else. *A language barrier.*

barring

(prep) except for. *We'll be there, barring accidents.*

barrister (n) a lawyer who works in the higher law courts in Britain.

barrow

1 (n) a small cart used for carrying things.
2 (n) a mound of earth made to cover a grave in prehistoric times.

bartender (n) someone who serves behind the bar in a public house.

barter bartering bartered (v)

to trade by exchanging food and other goods, rather than by using money. **barter** (n).

base basing based; baser basest

1 (n) the lowest part of something, or the part that it stands on.
2 (v) to use something as the starting point for something else. *I based my story on a real event.* **basis** (n).
3 (n) the place from which a business, army, etc. is controlled. **base** (v).
4 (n) In baseball or rounders, a **base** is one of the four points to which you have to run in order to score a run or rounder. See **baseball**.
5 (n) In chemistry, a **base** is a substance that will neutralize an acid. Bases react with acids to form salts.
6 (n) In maths, a **base** is the starting point for a counting system. For example, ten is the base of the decimal system.
7 (adj) selfish, or mean. *A base trick.*

baseball field

baseball bat

webbed catching pocket
rubber grip
leather ball with cork centre
flexible leather
hand-stitching
fingers laced together

fielder's glove and baseball

baseball (n) an American game, played with a bat and ball and two teams of nine players. *The picture shows the batting area of a baseball field, beyond which is the centrefield, a large fielding area. Some baseball equipment is also shown.*

basement (n) an area or room in a building below ground level.

bash bashes bashing bashed

1 (v) (informal) to hit something hard.
2 (informal) If you **have a bash** at something, you try it.

bashful (adj) shy. **bashfully** (adv).

basic basics

1 (adj) simple and straightforward.
2 basics (plural n) the most important things to know about a subject.

basin

1 (n) a large bowl used for washing, usually fixed to a wall.
2 (n) a deep bowl, often used for mixing food.
3 (n) an area of land around a river from which water drains into the river.

basis (n) the idea or reason behind something. *The basis of a plan.*

bask basking basked

1 (v) to lie or sit in the sunshine and enjoy it.
2 (v) If you **bask in** someone's praise, admiration, etc., you enjoy it.

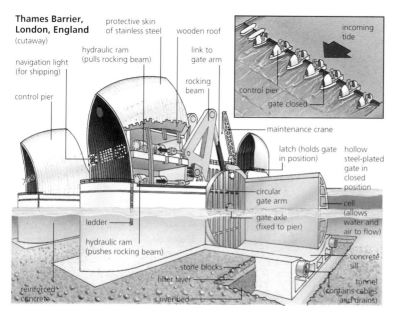

Thames Barrier, London, England (cutaway)

navigation light (for shipping)
control pier
protective skin of stainless steel
hydraulic ram (pulls rocking beam)
wooden roof
link to gate arm
rocking beam
control pier
gate closed
incoming tide
maintenance crane
latch (holds gate in position)
hollow steel-plated gate in closed position
circular gate arm
cell (allows water and air to flow)
gate axle (fixed to pier)
ladder
hydraulic ram (pushes rocking beam)
concrete sill
stone blocks
filter layer
reinforced concrete
river bed
tunnel (contains cables and drains)

basket *(n)* a container, usually with handles, made of cane, wire, etc.

basketball *(n)* a game played by two teams who try to score points by throwing a ball into a high net at the end of a court. *The picture sequence shows a goal being shot in basketball.*

basketball

bass *(rhymes with lace)* **basses**
1 *(n)* the lowest singing voice for a man.
2 *(n)* a stringed instrument that makes a low sound.

bat batting batted
1 *(n)* a small, flying mammal that comes out at night to feed. Bats find their way around by making high-pitched squeaks which send back echoes that are picked up by their sensitive ears.
2 *(n)* a piece of wood used for hitting the ball in games such as cricket, baseball, and table tennis. *See* **baseball**, **cricket**.
3 *(v)* to take a turn at hitting the ball and scoring runs in games such as cricket and baseball. *It's Barry's turn to bat.* **batsman** *(n)*.

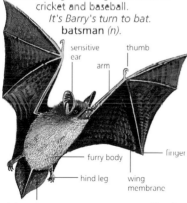

sensitive ear
thumb
arm
furry body
finger
hind leg
wing membrane
tail membrane
serotine bat

batch batches *(n)* a group of things that arrive together or are made together. *A batch of cakes.*

bath
1 *(n)* a large, open container for water in which you sit and wash your whole body.
2 **baths** *(plural n)* a public swimming pool.

bathe bathes bathing bathed
1 *(v)* to go swimming in the sea or in a stream. **bather** *(n)*.
2 *(v)* If you **bathe** part of your body that is sore, you wash it gently in water or antiseptic.

bathroom *(n)* a room that contains a bath or a shower, and often a basin and toilet.

batik *(bat-eek)* *(n)* an Eastern method of printing designs on cloth. Parts of the cloth are covered with wax so that when it is put into the dye these parts are not coloured.

baton
1 *(n)* a short, thin stick used by a conductor to beat time for an orchestra.
2 *(n)* a short stick passed from one runner to another in a relay race.

batsman batsmen *(n)* the person who is batting in cricket.

battalion *(n)* a large number of soldiers.

batten *(n)* a light strip of wood, used to support or strengthen something.

batter battering battered
1 *(v)* to hit someone or something many times. **battering** *(n)*
2 *(v)* If someone **batters down** a door, they break through it by hitting it many times.
3 *(n)* a mixture of milk, eggs, and flour that can be cooked to make pancakes or used to coat food which you fry.

battering ram *(n)* a heavy, wooden beam, sometimes protected by a hut on wheels, that is rammed against an enemy's walls or gates. *Battering rams were used in ancient times and in the Middle Ages.*

medieval battering ram

battery batteries
1 *(n)* a group of machines or heavy guns that are all used together.
2 *(n)* a container that stores chemicals which produce electrical power. *Also see* **car**.

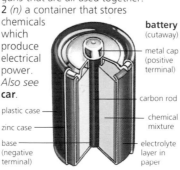

battery (cutaway)
metal cap (positive terminal)
carbon rod
chemical mixture
electrolyte layer in paper
plastic case
zinc case
base (negative terminal)

battery farming *(n)* a system for breeding and rearing poultry or cattle or for producing eggs, in which a large number of animals are kept in small cages or pens.

battle
1 *(n)* a fight between two armies.
2 *(n)* a struggle with someone.

battleship *(n)* a warship armed with powerful guns.

bawl bawling bawled
1 *(v)* to cry loudly like a baby.
2 *(v)* to shout loudly in a harsh voice. *"Get off my roses!" bawled Mr Jones.*

bay
1 *(n)* a part of the coast that curves inwards.
2 If you keep something or someone **at bay**, you fight them off. *Anna managed to keep her fears at bay.*
3 **bay window** *(n)* a window that sticks out from the wall of a house. *See* **building**

bayonet *(n)* a long knife that can be fitted to the end of a rifle.

bazaar
1 *(n)* a street market, especially one held in Middle Eastern countries.
2 *(n)* a sale held to raise money for charity.

BC the initials of the phrase "before Christ". BC is used to show that a date comes before the birth of Jesus Christ. *Julius Caesar died in 44BC.*

beach beaches *(n)* a strip of sand or pebbles where land meets water.

beacon *(n)* a light or fire used as a signal or warning.

bead
1 *(n)* a small piece of glass, wood, or plastic with a hole through the middle that can be threaded on to a string.
2 *(n)* a drop of liquid.

beak *(n)* the hard, horny part of a bird's mouth.

beaker
1 *(n)* a tall drinking cup.
2 *(n)* a plastic or glass jar used in chemistry. *See* **apparatus**.

beam beaming beamed
1 *(n)* a thick ray of light from a torch, car headlight, etc. **beam** *(v)*.
2 *(n)* a long, thick piece of wood, concrete, or metal, used to support the roof or floors of a building.
3 *(v)* to smile widely. **beam** *(n)*.

bean
1 *(n)* Beans are large seeds that you can eat or that can be used to make a drink. *Baked beans. Coffee beans.*
2 *(informal)* If you are **full of beans**, you are very lively.

bear bearing bore borne
1 (v) to support or carry something. *Is the ice thick enough to bear my weight?*
2 (v) When a tree or plant **bears** fruit, flowers, or leaves, it produces them.
3 (v) If you cannot **bear** something, you cannot put up with it, either because it upsets you or because you do not like it at all. *My mum can't bear rap music.* **bearable** (adj).
4 (n) a large, heavy mammal with thick fur. *The picture shows a young male grizzly bear catching a salmon.*

grizzly bear

beard (n) the hair on a man's face.
beast
1 (n) (old-fashioned) a wild animal.
2 (n) (informal) a horrible or unkind person. **beastliness** (n), **beastly** (adj).
beat beating beat beaten
1 (v) to hit someone or something many times. **beating** (n).
2 (v) to defeat someone in a game or contest. *Cuthbert beat me at chess.*
3 (n) the regular rhythm of a piece of music or of your heart.
4 (v) If you **beat** a mixture, you stir it up quickly with a whisk or fork.
beautiful (adj) very pleasant to look at or listen to. **beauty** (n), **beautify** (v), **beautifully** (adv).
beaver beavering beavered
1 (n) an animal like a large rat with a wide, flat tail, that lives both on land and in water. Beavers build dams across streams to create safe areas for their lodges.
2 (v) If you **beaver away** at something, you work very hard at it.

beaver's dam and lodge

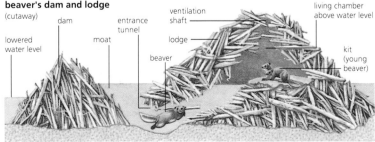

because (conj) for the reason that. *I came because I wanted to see you.*
beckon beckoning beckoned
(v) to make a sign to someone, asking them to come. *Jack beckoned us to follow him.*
become becoming became
(v) to start to be. *When did you become suspicious?*
bed
1 (n) a piece of furniture that you sleep on.
2 (n) a place in a garden where flowers are planted.
3 (n) the bottom of an ocean or river.
bedclothes (n) sheets, duvets, blankets, etc.
bedridden (adj) If you are **bedridden**, you are so ill that you cannot get out of bed.
bedroom (n) a room used for sleeping.
bedsitter (n) a rented room that someone lives and sleeps in.
bee (n) a flying insect with yellow and black stripes that makes honey. *A bee lets other bees know where food is by performing a "dance", in which it waggles its abdomen a certain number of times.*
Also see **hive, honeycomb, insect.**

bee dance

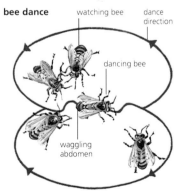

beech beeches (n) a tree with a smooth, grey bark and leaves that spread outwards.

beef (n) the meat from a cow, a bull, or an ox.
beefy beefier beefiest (adj) (informal) big and muscular.
beehive (n) a box for keeping bees so that their honey can be collected. *See* **hive.**
beer (n) an alcoholic drink made from malt, barley, and hops.
beetle (n) a flying insect with hard wing covers. *The goliath beetle weighs as much as a sparrow.*

claw
antenna
compound eye
head
thorax
abdomen
elytron (wing cover)
goliath beetle

beetroot (n) a purplish-red root vegetable. *See* **vegetable.**
before
1 (prep) sooner or earlier than. *The time before last.*
2 (adv) earlier. *I've been here before.*
beg begging begged
1 (v) to ask someone in the street for help, especially for money or food. **beggar** (n).
2 (v) to plead with someone to do something. *Emily begged Tom to go to her party.*
begin beginning began begun (v) to start. **beginner** (n), **beginning** (n).
behalf If you do something on **behalf** of someone else, you do it for them, or in their place. *On behalf of my family, I'd like to thank you all.*
behave behaving behaved
1 (v) to do and say things in a particular way. *Matthew behaved very strangely.* **behaviour** (n).
2 (v) to act properly, and avoid being noisy or causing trouble. *I wish you would behave yourself!*
behind
1 (prep) on the other side, or towards the back of something. *Look behind the curtain!*
2 (prep) further back, or in a lower position. *Joshua finished the race behind me.*
3 (adv) not making good progress. *I'm behind with my work.*

beige *(bayjh)* *(n)* a pale brown colour. **beige** *(adj)*.

belch belches belching belched
1 *(v)* to let out gases from your stomach through your mouth with a loud noise. **belch** *(n)*.
2 *(v)* to send out fire and smoke.

believe believing believed
1 *(v)* to feel sure that something is true. **belief** *(n)*, **believer** *(n)*.
2 *(v)* to support someone or something. *I believe in rights for children.* **believer** *(n)*.

bell
1 *(n)* an instrument which makes a ringing sound. Bells are often cone-shaped and have a clapper hanging down inside them.
2 *(informal)* If something **rings a bell**, you think you have heard it somewhere before.
3 *(n)* a bell-shaped object, especially on a musical instrument. *See* **brass**.

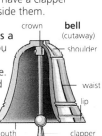

crown
bell *(cutaway)*
shoulder
waist
lip
mouth
clapper

bellow bellowing bellowed
1 *(v)* to shout or roar. **bellow** *(n)*.
2 **bellows** *(plural n)* an instrument used for pumping air into something like an organ or a fire.

belly bellies
1 *(n)* the stomach, or the part of a human's or animal's body that contains their stomach and bowels.
2 **belly flop** *(n)* a dive into water in which you hit the water hard with the front of your body.

belong belonging belonged
1 *(v)* If something **belongs** to you, you own it. **belongings** *(plural n)*
2 *(v)* If you **belong** to a group, you are a member of it.
3 *(v)* If something **belongs** somewhere, that is its proper place.

below
1 *(prep)* lower than. *The temperature is below freezing point.*
2 *(prep)* at or to a lower place. *We hid below the stairs.*

belt belting belted
1 *(n)* a strip of leather or other material that you wear around your waist.
2 *(n)* a moving band of rubber, used for transporting objects or for driving machinery. *Conveyor belt.*
3 *(v)* *(informal)* to hit someone hard.
4 *(v)* *(informal)* to travel very fast.
5 *(n)* an area, or a strip. *Commuter belt. A belt of rain.*

bench benches
1 *(n)* a long, narrow seat for several people, usually made of wood.
2 *(n)* a work table in a workshop or laboratory.
3 *(n)* The **bench** is the word used for a group of judges or magistrates in Britain.

bend bending bent
1 *(v)* If you **bend, bend down**, or **bend over**, you lean forward from your waist.
2 *(v)* If something **bends**, it changes direction by turning to one side. *The road bends to the left.* **bend** *(n)*.
3 *(v)* to change the shape of something so that it is no longer straight.

beneath
1 *(prep)* underneath. *We hid beneath the bedclothes.*
2 *(prep)* lower than, or not worthy. *It's beneath my dignity to talk to her.*

beneficial *(adj)* Something that is **beneficial** is good for you.

benefit benefiting benefited
1 *(v)* If you **benefit** from something, you gain an advantage from it or are helped by it. *We really benefited from our holiday.* **benefit** *(n)*.
2 *(n)* money paid by the government to people who need it, such as people who are poor, ill, disabled, or unemployed.

Bengali *(ben-gor-lee)* *(n)* a language spoken in Bangladesh and the Indian state of West Bengal.

benign *(adj)* harmless. *The tests showed that the lump was benign.*

bent
1 *(adj)* crooked, or curved.
2 *(adj)* *(slang)* dishonest.

bequeath bequeathing bequeathed *(v)* to leave something to somebody in a will. **bequest** *(n)*.

bereaved *(adj)* A person is **bereaved** if a friend or relative of theirs has died. **bereavement** *(n)*.

berry berries *(n)* a small, often brightly coloured fruit, found on bushes or trees.

berth berthing berthed
1 *(n)* a bed in a ship, train, or caravan.
2 *(n)* a place in a harbour where a boat is tied up.
3 *(v)* When a boat **berths**, it comes into harbour and is tied up.

beside
1 *(prep)* next to.
2 If you are **beside yourself**, you are overcome with emotion. *Augustus is beside himself with rage.*

besides
1 *(prep)* as well as, or apart from. *Who went to the match besides Jim?*
2 *(adv)* also, or in addition to this. *I hate boats and, besides, I can't swim.*

besiege besieging besieged *(v)* to surround a place in order to make it surrender. *Enemy troops are besieging the castle!*

best
1 *(adj)* better than everything else.
2 When you **do your best**, you try as hard as you can to do something.
3 **best man** *(n)* the friend of the bridegroom who helps him at his wedding.

bet betting bet
1 *(v)* to risk a sum of money on the result of something, such as a horse race. If you guess the result correctly, you win some money, if not, you lose money. **betting** *(n)*.
2 *(v)* If you **bet** someone that they cannot do something, you dare them to do it. *I bet you can't climb that tree!*
3 *(v)* *(informal)* If you **bet** that someone does something, you predict that they will do it. *I bet Mona trips over that cat.*

betray betraying betrayed
1 *(v)* If you **betray** someone, you deliberately let them down or do something to hurt them. **betrayal** *(n)*.
2 *(v)* If you **betray** your feelings, you are not able to keep them hidden.

better
1 *(adj)* more suitable, or higher in quality.
2 *(adj)* no longer ill or hurting.
3 **better off** *(adj)* richer.

between
1 *(prep)* If something is **between** two things, it has them on either side of it. *Dan stood between two trees.*
2 *(prep)* from one to the other. *We threw the ball between us.*
3 *(prep)* somewhere within two limits. *Nadya left between three and four o'clock.*

beverage *(n)* a drink.

beware If a person or sign tells you to **beware of** something, they warn you to look out for something dangerous or harmful.

bewilder bewildering bewildered *(v)* to confuse or muddle someone. **bewilderment** *(n)*, **bewildered** *(adj)*.

beyond
1 *(prep)* on the far side of something. *We couldn't see beyond the bushes.*
2 *(prep)* If something is **beyond you**, you cannot understand it.

biased *(by-ursd) (adj)* prejudiced, or favouring one person or point of view more than another. *Tim thinks that the referee is biased against our team.* bias *(n).*

Bible *(n)* the holy book of the Christian religion.

bibliography bibliographies *(n)* a list of books on a subject. bibliographical *(adj).*

bicycle *(n)* a two-wheeled vehicle which you ride by steering with handlebars, and pedalling. *The mountain bike shown below is a type of bicycle that has been specially developed for off-road cycling.*

bid bidding bid
1 *(v)* to offer to buy something at an auction for a certain amount of money. bid *(n)*, bidder *(n)*.
2 *(v) (old-fashioned)* to order someone to do something. *Bid the prince to come here!*
3 *(n)* an attempt to do or win something. *Elvis made a bid for fame.*

bidet *(bee-day) (n)* a low bowl in some bathrooms, in which you sit and wash yourself.

biennial
1 *(adj)* happening every two years or over a period of two years.
2 *(n)* a plant that lives for two years.

big bigger biggest *(adj)* large, or important.

bigot *(n)* someone who has a strong and unreasonable dislike of certain other people, especially people of a different race, nationality, or religion. bigotry *(n)*, bigoted *(adj).*

bike biking biked
1 *(n)* a bicycle, or a motorcycle.
2 *(v)* to ride a bicycle or motorcycle. biker *(n).*

bikini *(n)* a two-piece swimming costume worn by women and girls.

bile *(n)* a greenish-coloured liquid that is made by the liver and which helps to digest food.

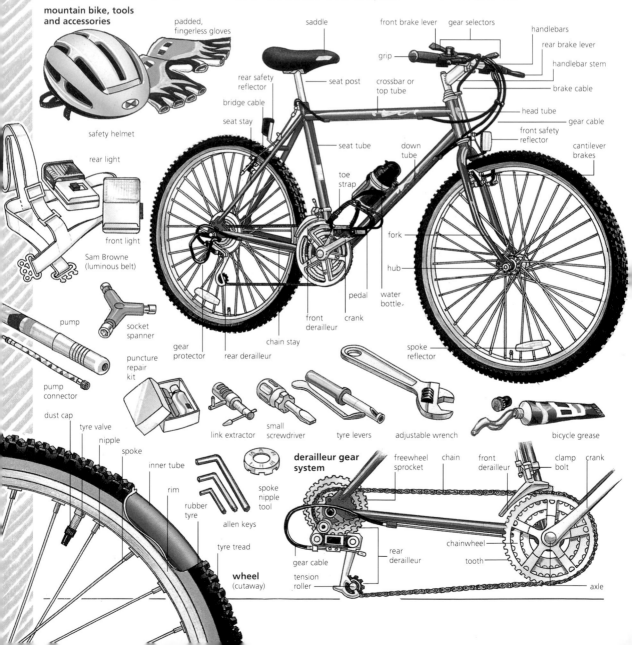

mountain bike, tools and accessories

bilingual *(adj)* If someone is **bilingual**, they can speak two languages very well.

bill
1 *(n)* a piece of paper telling you how much money you owe for something that you have bought.
2 *(n)* a written plan for a new law, to be discussed in parliament.
3 *(n)* the beak of a bird, especially a duck's beak.
4 *(n)* *(US)* a banknote.

billabong *(n)* *(Australian)* a pond that used to be part of a river.

billiards *(singular n)* a game, similar to snooker, in which you use a stick, called a cue, to hit balls around a table and into pockets.

billow billowing billowed
1 *(v)* When a curtain, sail, sheet, etc. **billows**, it is pushed outwards by the wind.
2 *(v)* If smoke or fog **billows**, it rises up in large clouds.
3 *(n)* an ocean wave.

binary
1 *(adj)* made up of two parts or units.
2 *(adj)* **Binary** arithmetic uses only two digits, 1 and 0.

bind binding bound
1 *(v)* to tie something up.
2 *(v)* to wrap a piece of material tightly around something.
3 *(v)* to fasten the pages of a book together and put a cover on them.

binder *(n)* a hard folder with metal rings inside it, used for holding papers.

bingo *(n)* a game in which you cross out numbers on a card as they are called out.

binoculars *(plural n)* an instrument that you look through with both eyes to make distant things seem nearer.

biodegradable *(adj)* Something that is **biodegradable** can be destroyed naturally by bacteria.
Biodegradable packaging helps to reduce waste and pollution.

biography biographies *(n)* a book that tells someone's life story. **biographer** *(n)*, **biographical** *(adj)*.

biology *(n)* the scientific study of living things. **biologist** *(n)*, **biological** *(adj)*, **biologically** *(adv)*.

biplane *(n)* an aeroplane with two sets of wings, one above the other.

bird *(n)* a two-legged creature with wings, feathers, and a beak. All birds lay eggs, and most birds can fly.
Birds can be grouped according to their characteristics and behaviour into 23 orders, or types, and an example of each order is shown below. The picture of an orange chat on the right shows the main parts of a bird's body.

orange chat

ear coverts — crown
nape
secondary feathers
throat
wing
breast
belly
claw
primary feathers
toe
flank
scaly leg
under-tail coverts
tail   thigh

birds

whooping crane
short-eared owl
greater roadrunner
Indian hornbill
waxwing
turtle dove
white-cheeked turaco
sooty-capped puffbird
red and green macaw
king penguin
red-and-yellow barbet
sparkling violet-eared hummingbird
swift
red-throated bee-eater
white-backed mousebird
red-bellied trogon
hoopoe
Canada goose
ostrich
painted buttonquail
red grouse
spotted tinamou
mallee fowl

Some words that begin with a "bi" sound are spelt "by".

birth
1 (n) the event of being born.
2 (n) the beginning of something.
The birth of talking films.
3 When a woman **gives birth**, she has a baby.

birth control (n) the methods used to prevent women from becoming pregnant.

birthday (n) a yearly celebration of the day that someone was born.

biscuit
1 (n) a small, flat cake, which has been baked until it is hard.
2 (n) (US) a round, flat bun, often eaten with butter (scone, UK).

bisect bisecting bisected (v) to divide a line, angle, or shape into two equal parts.

bishop
1 (n) a senior priest in the Christian church who is in charge of priests and churches in a large area called a diocese.
2 (n) a chesspiece that can move diagonally across the board. *The picture shows a bishop from a 12th-century Viking chess set. Also see* **chess**.

bishop chesspiece

bison bison (n) an American buffalo.

bit
1 (n) a small piece or amount of something.
2 (n) the smallest unit of information in a computer's memory.
3 (n) the metal bar that goes in a horse's mouth and is attached to the reins. *See* **tack**.
4 (n) the end part of a drill. *See* **drill**.

bitch bitches bitching bitched
1 (n) a female dog.
2 (v) If you **bitch about** someone, you say unkind or untrue things about them.

bite biting bit bitten
1 (v) to close your teeth around something. *Lindsay bit into the apple and found a maggot!* bite (n).
2 (v) If an insect or snake **bites** you, it pricks your skin and injects poison into your body. bite (n).

bitter bitterest
1 (adj) tasting sharp and slightly sour, often in an unpleasant way.
2 (adj) If you feel **bitter**, you are upset and angry about something.
3 (adj) If the weather is **bitter**, it is very cold indeed.
4 (n) a British beer with a slightly bitter taste.

black
1 (n) the colour of coal, or of the sky at night. black (adj).
2 (adj) Black people are people with naturally dark skin. black (n).

blackberry blackberries (n) a small, black fruit that grows on brambles. *See* **bramble**, **fruit**.

blackboard (n) a dark surface that teachers write on with chalk.

black hole (n) the area in space around a collapsed star that sucks in everything around it, even light.

blackmail (n) the crime of threatening to reveal a secret about someone unless they pay a sum of money. blackmail (v).

blackout (n) If someone has a **blackout**, they become unconscious for a short time. black out (v).

blacksmith (n) someone who makes and fits horseshoes and mends things made of iron.

bladder (n) the organ in your body where waste liquid is stored before it leaves your body. *See* **organ**.

blade
1 (n) a sharp edge on a knife, sword, dagger, etc.
2 (n) the long, thin part of an oar or propeller.
3 (n) a single piece of grass.

blame blaming blamed (v) If you **blame** someone for something, you say that it is their fault. blame (n).

bland blander blandest (adj) mild and rather dull. *Bland food.*

blank blanker blankest
1 (adj) If something is **blank,** it has nothing on it. *A blank cassette.*
2 (n) a cartridge for a gun that makes a noise but does not fire a bullet.
3 **blank verse** (n) a type of poetry that does not rhyme and usually has ten syllables in each line.

blanket
1 (n) a thick cover for a bed.
2 (n) a thick covering of something, such as snow or flowers.

blare blaring blared (v) to make a very loud and unpleasant noise. *His radio has been blaring out all day.*

blaspheme blaspheming blasphemed (v) to say offensive things about God or a religion. blasphemy (n), blasphemous (adj).

blast blasting blasted
1 (n) a loud noise or explosion.
2 (n) a sudden rush of air.
3 (v) to fire a gun.
4 (v) When a rocket or a spaceship **blasts off**, it leaves the ground.

blatant (adj) obvious and shameless *Horace grinned as he told a blatant lie.* blatantly (adv).

blaze blazing blazed
1 (v) to burn fiercely.
2 (n) a large fire.

blazer (n) a smart jacket, often worn as part of a school uniform.

bleach bleaches bleaching bleached
1 (n) a chemical substance used to kill germs or to make cloth white.
2 (v) to make something white or very light. *The sun had bleached Jan's hair.*

bleak bleaker bleakest
1 (adj) A **bleak** place is cold, empty, and depressing.
2 (adj) without hope. *The future looks really bleak.*

bleat (n) the cry made by a sheep or goat. bleat (v).

bleed bleeding bled (v) to lose blood. bleeding (adj).

bleep bleeping bleeped (v) to make a short, high sound. bleep (n).

blend blending blended (v) to mix two or more things together. blend (n).

blender (n) an electrical machine that chops and mixes food.

bless blesses blessing blessed
1 (v) to ask God to look after someone or something. blessing (n).
2 You say **bless you** when a person sneezes, or as a way of thanking someone.

blind
1 (adj) Someone who is **blind** cannot see. blindness (n).
2 (adj) A **blind** bend or corner is so sharp that drivers cannot see round it.
3 (n) a covering for a window that can be pulled over it.
4 (n) A driver's **blind spot** is the area slightly behind him that he cannot see in his rear-view mirror or in his wing mirror.

blink blinking blinked (v) to move your eyelids up and down very quickly. *You blink all the time without realizing it.* blink (n).

blinkers (plural n) leather flaps worn by racehorses on each side of their head so that they can only see straight ahead.

bliss (n) great happiness. *It was bliss to be home again.* blissful (adj), blissfully (adv).

blister (n) a sore bubble of skin, filled with liquid, that is caused by something burning your skin or rubbing against it.

Some words that begin with a "bi" sound are spelt "by".

blitz
1 (n) a sudden attack in which bombs are dropped from the air.
2 (n) If you have a **blitz** on something, you tackle it energetically.

blizzard (n) a heavy snowstorm.

bloated (adj) fat and swollen, often as a result of eating too much.

block blocking blocked
1 (n) a large lump of something hard. A block of wood.
2 (v) to stop something from getting past or from happening. **block** (n).
3 (n) A **block** of flats is a tall building where a lot of people live.
4 **block capitals** (n) capital letters.

blond blonder blondest (adj) Blond men and boys have pale yellow hair.

blonde (n) a woman or girl with pale yellow hair. **blonde** (adj).

blood
1 (n) the red liquid that is pumped around your body by your heart. Blood is made up of red cells, white cells, and platelets, all floating in plasma. **bloody** (adj).
2 **blood donor** (n) a person who lets some blood be taken out of their body to be stored and given to someone else.
3 **blood vessel** (n) one of the narrow tubes in your body through which your blood flows.

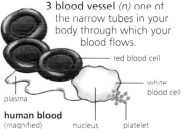

red blood cell

white blood cell

plasma

nucleus   platelet

human blood (magnified)

bloodshed (n) all the killing that happens in a battle or war. We must try to prevent further bloodshed.

bloodthirsty (adj) Someone who is bloodthirsty really enjoys violence and killing. **bloodthirstiness** (n), **bloodthirstily** (adv).

bloom blooming bloomed
1 (n) a flower on a plant.
2 (v) When a plant **blooms**, its flowers come out.
3 (adj) If someone is **blooming**, they look very healthy.

blossom blossoming blossomed
1 (n) the small flowers that appear on trees in the spring.
2 (v) to grow or improve. Francesca has blossomed into a first-rate dancer.

blot blotting blotted
1 (n) a stain caused by spilled ink or paint.
2 (v) to dry ink on a page using a piece of soft paper.

blotch blotches (n) an area of reddened skin, or a stain. **blotchy** (adj).

blouse (n) a piece of clothing, like a loose shirt, worn by women and girls.

blow blowing blew blown
1 (v) to make air come out of your mouth.
2 (v) to move in the wind. The leaves were blowing around.
3 (n) a punch or hit on the body.
4 (n) a disappointment.
5 **blow up** (v) to destroy something with an explosion.

blubber blubbering blubbered
1 (n) the fat under the skin of a whale or seal.
2 (v) to cry noisily.

blue bluer bluest
1 (n) the colour of the sky on a sunny day. **blue** (adj).
2 (adj) sad and depressed.
3 **out of the blue** suddenly.

blueprint (n) a detailed plan for a project or an idea.

blues (singular n) a type of slow, sad, jazz music, first sung by black Americans.

bluff bluffing bluffed
1 (v) to pretend to be in a stronger position than you really are, or to know more about something than you really do. Nat says he's going to win, but I think he's bluffing. **bluff** (n).
2 If you **call someone's bluff**, you challenge them to do what they say they can do, because you think that they are bluffing.

blunder blundering blundered
1 (n) a stupid mistake. **blunder** (v).
2 (v) to move in an awkward and clumsy way, usually because you cannot see where you are going

blunderbuss blunderbusses (n) an old-fashioned gun with a wide-mouthed barrel that fires several lead balls at once. When the trigger of a blunderbuss is released, the flint strikes against the frizzen, making the gunpowder explode and shoot the lead balls out of the barrel.

blunt blunter bluntest
1 (adj) not sharp.
2 (adj) direct and straightforward in what you say. **bluntly** (adv).

blur blurring blurred
1 (v) to make something smeared and unclear.
2 (n) a shape that is unclear because it has no outline or is moving too fast. **blurred** (adj).

blurb (n) writing on or about a product which aims to get people interested in it.

blurt blurting blurted (v) If you **blurt** something out, you say it suddenly, without thinking.

blush blushes blushing blushed (v) When you **blush**, your face turns red because you are embarrassed or ashamed. **blush** (n).

bluster blustering blustered
1 (v) to blow in gusts. The wind blustered round the chimney pots. **blustery** (adj).
2 (v) to act or speak in an aggressive and over-confident way.

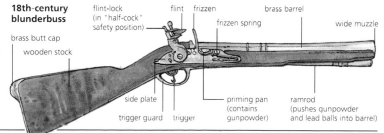

boar
1 (n) a male pig.
2 (n) a type of wild pig.

wild boar

board boarding boarded
1 (n) a flat piece of wood or stiff card. A chess board.
2 (v) to get on to a train, an aeroplane, or a ship.
3 (n) The **board** of a company is the group of people who manage it.

boarder (n) a student who lives at school during the term.

boarding school (n) a school which students live in during the term

boast boasting boasted
1 (v) to talk proudly about what you can do or what you own, in order to impress people. **boastful** (adj), **boastfully** (adv).
2 (v) If a place **boasts** something good, it possesses it. Paris boasts many fine restaurants.

18th-century blunderbuss

flint-lock (in "half-cock" safety position)   flint   frizzen   brass barrel

frizzen spring   wide muzzle

brass butt cap

wooden stock

side plate   priming pan (contains gunpowder)   ramrod (pushes gunpowder and lead balls into barrel)

trigger guard   trigger

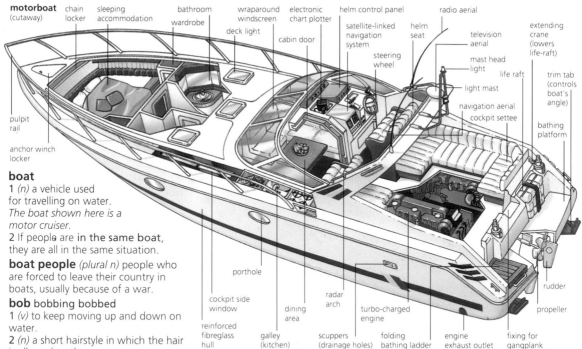

motorboat (cutaway)

chain locker · sleeping accommodation · bathroom · wardrobe · deck light · wraparound windscreen · electronic chart plotter · satellite-linked navigation system · cabin door · helm control panel · steering wheel · helm seat · radio aerial · television aerial · mast head light · extending crane (lowers life-raft) · life raft · light mast · trim tab (controls boat's angle) · navigation aerial · cockpit settee · bathing platform

pulpit rail · anchor winch locker · porthole · cockpit side window · dining area · radar arch · turbo-charged engine · rudder · propeller

reinforced fibreglass hull · galley (kitchen) · scuppers (drainage holes) · folding bathing ladder · engine exhaust outlet · fixing for gangplank

boat

1 (n) a vehicle used for travelling on water. *The boat shown here is a motor cruiser.*
2 If people are **in the same boat**, they are all in the same situation.

boat people (plural n) people who are forced to leave their country in boats, usually because of a war.

bob bobbing bobbed

1 (v) to keep moving up and down on water.
2 (n) a short hairstyle in which the hair is all one length.

bobby pin (n) (US) a piece of bent wire with sides that press together to hold your hair in place (hairgrip, UK).

bobsleigh (bob-slay) (n) a sledge with mechanical steering and brakes, used for racing down a steep, ice-covered run.

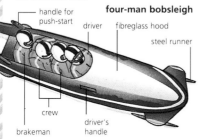

four-man bobsleigh

handle for push-start · driver · fibreglass hood · steel runner · crew · driver's handle · brakeman

body bodies

1 (n) all the parts that a person or an animal is made of. *The human body.*
2 (n) the main part of something, especially a car or an aircraft.
3 (n) a dead person. *The detectives have found another body.*

bodyguard (n) someone who protects an important person from attacks.

bodywork (n) the outer covering of a car or other motor vehicle.

bog (n) an area of wet, spongy land. **boggy** (adj).

bogus (adj) false. *Bill gave a bogus name to the police.*

boil boiling boiled

1 (v) to heat a liquid until it starts to bubble and give off vapour. **boiling** (adj).
2 (v) to cook something in boiling water.
3 (n) an infected lump under the skin.

boiler (n) a tank that heats water for a house or other building.

boiling point (n) the temperature at which a liquid that has been heated turns to gas.

boisterous (adj) If you are boisterous, you behave in a rough and noisy way. **boisterousness** (n), **boisterously** (adv).

bold bolder boldest

1 (adj) Someone who is **bold** is very confident and shows no fear of danger. **boldness** (n), **boldly** (adv).
2 (adj) Bold colours stand out clearly.

bollard (n) a short post placed in a road to stop traffic from going in a particular direction.

bolster bolstering bolstered

1 (v) to support someone or something.
2 (n) (old-fashioned) a long pillow.

bolt bolting bolted

1 (n) a metal bar that slides into place and locks something. **bolt** (v).
2 (n) a strong metal pin, used with a metal nut to hold things together.
3 (v) to run away suddenly.

bomb bombing bombed

1 (n) a container filled with explosives, used in war or to blow up buildings, vehicles, etc.
2 (v) to attack a place with bombs.

bombard bombarding bombarded

1 (v) to attack a place with heavy gunfire. **bombardment** (n).
2 (v) If you **bombard** someone with questions, you ask them lots of questions in a short time.

bombshell

1 (n) a bomb.
2 (n) something which makes you shocked and surprised.

bond bonding bonded

1 (n) a close friendship or connection with someone. *A special bond developed between the boys.*
2 (v) When two things **bond**, they stick together. **bond** (n).
3 **bonds** (plural n) ropes, chains, etc. used to tie someone up.

bone (n) one of the hard, white parts that make up the skeleton of a person or an animal.

human thigh bone (cutaway)

head · soft, spongy bone · bone marrow · hard, compact bone · periosteum (tough outer layer) · shaft

bonfire *(n)* a large, outdoor fire, often used to burn garden rubbish.

bonnet
1 *(n)* the cover for a car's engine. See **car**
2 *(n)* a baby's or woman's hat, tied with strings under the chin.

bonsai *(bonz-eye)*
bonsai *(n)* a miniature tree or shrub, grown in a pot for decoration.

bonsai
(needle juniper)

bonus bonuses
1 *(n)* an extra reward that you get for doing something well. **bonus** *(adj)*.
2 *(n)* a good thing that is more than you expected. *It's a bonus to have a cinema so close to our new house.*

booby trap *(n)* a hidden trap or trick which is set off when someone or something touches it.

book booking booked
1 *(n)* a set of pages that are bound together in a cover.
2 *(v)* to arrange for something to be kept for you to have or use later. *We've booked a holiday in Crete.*

hardback book
(cutaway)

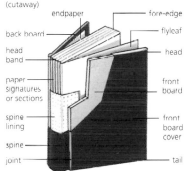

endpaper
back board
head band
paper signatures or sections
spine lining
spine
joint
fore-edge
flyleaf
head
front board
front board cover
tail

book-keeper *(n)* someone who keeps financial records for a business. **bookkeeping** *(n)*.

booklet *(n)* a book with a paper cover and a small number of pages.

bookmaker *(n)* someone who takes money for bets and pays out money to people who win. **bookmaking** *(n)*.

bookworm *(n)* someone who loves reading books.

boom booming boomed
1 *(n)* a very loud, deep sound, like an explosion. **boom** *(v)*.
2 *(v)* to speak in a loud, deep voice. *"Sit down!" the guard boomed at us.*
3 *(n)* a rapid increase in something. *A spending boom.*
4 *(n)* a long pole, used to control the angle of a sail. See **dinghy**, **sail**.

boomerang *(n)* a curved stick that is thrown through the air and returns to the thrower if it misses its target. *Boomerangs were used by Aboriginal hunters in Australia.*

Aboriginal boomerang

boon *(n)* something that makes life easier. *Our dishwasher is a real boon.*

boost boosting boosted
1 *(v)* to increase the power or amount of something. **boost** *(n)*.
2 *(n)* If something gives you a **boost**, it cheers you up.

booster
1 *(n)* a rocket that gives extra power to a spacecraft. See **space shuttle**.
2 *(n)* an injection of a drug, given to increase the effect of an earlier injection.

boot booting booted
1 *(n)* a heavy shoe that covers your ankle and sometimes part of your leg.
2 *(n)* the place, usually at the back of a car, where luggage can be carried. See **car**.
3 *(v)* When you **boot up** a computer, you turn it on and get it ready to work.
4 *(v)* *(informal)* to kick something hard.

booty *(singular n)* valuable objects that are taken away by pirates or an army after a battle.

booze *(n)* *(informal)* alcoholic drink. **boozer** *(n)*, **boozy** *(adj)*.

border bordering bordered
1 *(n)* the dividing line between one country or region and another.
2 *(v)* If one country **borders** another, their boundaries meet.
3 *(n)* a decorative strip around the edge of something.
4 *(n)* a long flowerbed.

bore boring bored
1 *(v)* If something or someone **bores** you, you find them very dull and uninteresting. **bore** *(n)*, **boredom** *(n)*.
2 *(v)* to make a hole in something with a drill. *This machine can bore into solid rock.*
3 *(n)* the hole inside a gun barrel.

borough *(buh-ruh)* *(n)* a town, or an area of a town, that has its own local government.

borrow borrowing borrowed *(v)* to use someone else's belongings for a short time, with their permission.

borstal *(n)* *(old-fashioned)* a prison school for young people aged between 16 and 21. In Britain, borstals are now called detention centres or youth custody centres.

bosom
1 *(n)* a woman's breasts.
2 *(n)* *(old-fashioned)* a man's or a woman's chest.

boss bosses bossing bossed
1 *(n)* someone in charge of a company or someone who people work for.
2 **boss about** *(v)* to keep telling somebody what to do.

bossy bossier bossiest *(adj)* A **bossy** person likes telling other people what to do. **bossiness** *(n)*.

botany *(singular n)* the study of plants. *The picture shows a watercolour painting of a Christmas rose, from an 18th-century book on botany.* **botanist** *(n)*, **botanical** *(adj)*.

botanical drawing

bother bothering bothered
1 *(v)* If something **bothers** you, it makes you feel uncomfortable.
2 *(v)* to interrupt someone who is busy. *Bobo keeps bothering me.*
3 *(v)* to make an effort to do something. *At least Kitty bothered to come to the meeting.*

bottle bottling bottled
1 *(n)* a glass or plastic container for liquids.
2 *(v)* to put things into bottles.
3 *(v)* If you **bottle up** your feelings, you keep them to yourself.
4 *(n)* *(slang)* courage, or spirit.

bottleneck *(n)* a narrow part of a road that causes traffic jams.

bottom
1 *(n)* the lowest part of something. *The bottom of the sea.* **bottom** *(adj)*.
2 *(n)* the part of your body that you sit on.

bough *(rhymes with now)* *(n)* a thick branch on a tree.

boulder *(n)* a large rock.

bounce bouncing bounced
1 *(v)* to spring back after hitting something. **bounce** *(n)*, **bouncy** *(adj)*.
2 *(n)* If someone has lots of **bounce**, they are very cheerful. **bouncy** *(adj)*.

bound bounding bounded
1 *(v)* to move forward quickly with leaps and jumps. **bound** *(n)*.
2 *(v)* If something is **bound to** happen, it will definitely take place.
3 If a place is **out of bounds**, you are not allowed to go there.

boundary boundaries *(n)* the line that separates one area from another.

bouquet (boh-*kay* or boo-*kay*) (n) a bunch of flowers given to someone as a present.

bow bowing bowed
1 (rhymes with cow) (v) to bend low as a sign of respect or to accept applause. **bow** (n).
2 (rhymes with low) (n) a knot with loops.
3 **bow** or **bows** (rhymes with cow) (n) the front of a ship.
4 (rhymes with low) (n) a long flat piece of wood with strings stretched along it, used for playing stringed instruments. See **strings**.
5 (rhymes with low) (n) a curved piece of wood with a stretched string attached to it, used for shooting arrows. *This archer from the Bayeux tapestry draws his bow, ready to shoot, and holds some spare arrows in his hand.*

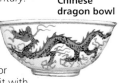

medieval archer

bowels (plural n) the part of your body that carries solids away from your stomach.

bowl bowling bowled
1 (n) a deep dish. *This porcelain dragon bowl was made in China in the 16th century.*

Chinese dragon bowl

2 (v) When you **bowl** in a game like cricket or baseball, you throw a ball for someone to hit with a bat. **bowl** (n), **bowler** (n).

bowls (n) a game played with heavy, wooden balls called bowls.

box boxes boxing boxed
1 (n) a container, especially one with four flat sides.
2 (v) to fight with your fists as a sport. **boxer** (n), **boxing** (n).
3 **box in** (v) If you **box someone in**, you surround them so that they cannot escape.

box office (n) the place in a theatre or cinema where you buy tickets.

boy (n) a male child. **boyish** (adj).

boycott boycotting boycotted (v) to refuse to take part in something or buy something as a way of making a protest. **boycott** (n).

boyfriend (n) the man or boy with whom a woman or girl is having a romantic relationship.

bra (n) a piece of underwear that supports a woman's breasts. Bra is short for brassière.

brace bracing braced
1 (n) an object that supports another object or holds it in place. **brace** (v).
2 (n) a wire device worn inside your mouth to straighten your teeth.
3 **braces** (plural n) two elastic straps worn over the shoulders to hold up a pair of trousers.
4 (v) If you **brace** yourself, you prepare yourself for a shock or for the force of something hitting you.

bracelet (n) a band worn around the wrist as a piece of jewellery.

bracket
1 (n) a support, made of metal or wood, used to hold up a shelf or cupboard.
2 (plural n) **Brackets** are the pair of curved lines that are used to separate some words from the main writing. **bracket** (v).
3 (n) a grouping. *This game is intended for your age bracket and is in my price bracket.*

brag bragging bragged (v) to talk in a boastful way about how good you are at something.

braid (n) (US) a piece of hair that has been divided into three and twisted together (plait, UK).

Braille (brayl) (n) a system of printing for blind people. Braille uses raised dots that are read by feeling with the fingertips. *This picture shows what the word "Braille" looks like when it is printed in Braille.*

B R A I L L E

brain
1 (n) the organ inside your head that controls your body and allows you to think and have feelings.
2 (n) your mind or intelligence.

brainstorm brainstorming brainstormed
1 (v) If people **brainstorm**, they get together to share ideas on a topic or to solve a problem.
2 (n) a sudden idea.

brainwash brainwashes brainwashing brainwashed (v) to make someone accept and believe something by saying it to them over and over again. **brainwashing** (n).

brainwave (n) a sudden good idea.

brainy brainier brainiest (adj) (informal) clever, or intelligent.

brake braking braked
1 (n) You use **brakes** to slow down or stop a vehicle. The brakes press against a wheel and stop it turning.
2 (v) to slow down or stop by using brakes.

bramble (n) a thorny bush that blackberries grow on.

bramble

blossom

branch branches branching branched
1 (n) a part of a tree that grows out of its trunk like an arm.
2 (v) When a road, river, etc. **branches**, it splits into two parts that go in different directions. **branch** (n).
3 (n) A **branch** of a company or organization is one of its shops, offices, etc. in a particular area.

thorn

blackberry

brand branding branded
1 (n) a particular make of a product. *A brand of toothpaste.*
2 (v) If someone **brands** an animal, they burn a mark on to its skin to show that the animal belongs to them. **brand** (n).

brandy (n) a strong alcoholic drink made from wine.

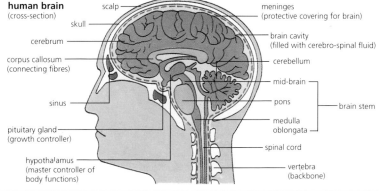

human brain
(cross-section)

scalp
skull
cerebrum
corpus callosum
(connecting fibres)

sinus

pituitary gland
(growth controller)

hypothalamus
(master controller of
body functions)

meninges
(protective covering for brain)
brain cavity
(filled with cerebro-spinal fluid)
cerebellum
mid-brain
pons
medulla
oblongata
spinal cord
vertebra
(backbone)

brain stem

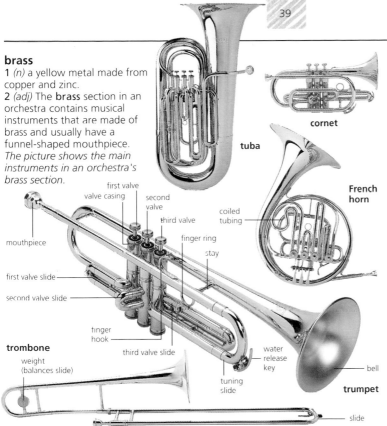

brass
1 *(n)* a yellow metal made from copper and zinc.
2 *(adj)* The **brass** section in an orchestra contains musical instruments that are made of brass and usually have a funnel-shaped mouthpiece. *The picture shows the main instruments in an orchestra's brass section.*

cornet

tuba

French horn

first valve
valve casing
second valve
third valve
coiled tubing
finger ring
stay
mouthpiece
first valve slide
second valve slide
finger hook
third valve slide
water release key
bell

trombone
weight (balances slide)
tuning slide

trumpet
slide

brassière see **bra**.

brass rubbing *(n)* a copy of a picture carved on a brass plate. Brass rubbings are made by rubbing with a wax crayon on a piece of paper placed over the plate. *This brass rubbing is taken from the tomb of a 15th-century knight.*

bravado *(n)* If you are full of **bravado**, you pretend to be braver and more confident than you really are.

brave braving braved; braver bravest
1 *(adj)* If you are **brave**, you show courage and are willing to do difficult things. **bravery** *(n)*, **bravely** *(adv)*.
2 *(v)* If you **brave** something difficult, you face it deliberately.
3 *(n)* a Native American warrior.

brawl *(n)* a rough fight. **brawl** *(v)*.

bray braying brayed
1 *(v)* When a donkey **brays**, it makes a loud, harsh noise in its throat. **bray** *(n)*.
2 *(v)* When a person **brays**, they make a harsh noise like a donkey.

brass rubbing

brazen
1 *(adj)* shameless. **brazenly** *(adv)*.
2 *(adj)* made of brass.

brazier *(bray-zee-er) (n)* a container for burning coals, used to keep people warm out of doors.

bread
1 *(n)* a baked food made from flour, water, and often yeast.
2 *(n) (slang)* money.

breadline If people are **on the breadline**, they have only just enough money to live.

breadth
1 *(n)* the distance from one side of something to the other.
2 *(n)* a wide range. *Jack has a breadth of experience in caring for animals.*

breadwinner *(n)* someone who earns money for a family.

break breaking broke broken
1 *(v)* to damage something so that it is in pieces or it no longer works. **breakage** *(n)*, **breakable** *(adj)*.
2 *(n)* a rest from working or studying.
3 *(v)* If someone **breaks** the rules or the law, they do something that is not allowed.
4 **break in** *(v)* to get into a building by force.
5 **break out** *(v)* to begin suddenly. *Fighting broke out on the streets.*

break dance *(n)* a very energetic and acrobatic form of dance.

breakdown
1 *(n)* If you have a **breakdown** while you are travelling, your car stops moving because its engine has stopped working.
2 *(n)* If someone has a **breakdown**, they are so worried or depressed about something that they become ill.

breaker *(n)* a big sea wave.

breakfast *(n)* the first meal of the day.

breakthrough *(n)* an important step towards achieving something.

breakwater
1 *(n)* a wall built in the sea to protect a harbour from the force of the waves.
2 *(n)* a barrier built on a beach to reduce the force of the waves.

breast
1 *(n)* A woman's **breasts** are the two round fleshy parts on her chest that can produce milk to feed a baby.
2 *(n) (old-fashioned)* a man's or a woman's chest.

breaststroke *(n)* a style of swimming on your front in which you move your arms forwards and out from your chest and kick your legs like a frog.

breath
1 *(n)* the air that you take into your lungs and breathe out again.
2 If you are **out of breath**, you have difficulty breathing.
3 When you say something **under your breath**, you say it very quietly.

breathalyze *or* **breathalyse** breathalyzing breathalyzed *(v)* When drivers are **breathalyzed**, they have to blow into a special bag, called a breathalyzer, which shows whether they have drunk too much alcohol to drive safely.

breathe breathing breathed *(v)* to take air in and out of your lungs.

breather *(n) (informal)* a short rest.

breathtaking *(adj)* very beautiful or impressive. *The view from the cliff was breathtaking.* **breathtakingly** *(adv)*.

breed breeding bred
1 *(v)* to keep animals or plants so that you can produce more of them and control their quality. **breeder** *(n)*.
2 *(v)* When animals **breed**, they mate and produce babies.
3 *(n)* a particular type of animal. *A popular breed of dog.*

breeze *(n)* a gentle wind. **breezy** *(adj)*.

brew brewing brewed
1 *(v)* to make beer.
2 *(v)* to make tea or coffee.
3 *(v)* If something is **brewing**, it is about to start. *There's trouble brewing at home.*

brewery breweries *(n)* a place where beer is made.

bribe bribing bribed
1 *(n)* money or a gift that you offer to someone to persuade them to do something for you, especially something wrong.
2 *(v)* to offer someone a bribe. bribery *(n)*.

bric-a-brac *(n)* various objects, such as ornaments, that are not worth very much.

brick *(n)* a block of hard, baked clay, used for building.

bride *(n)* a woman who is about to be married or has just been married.

bridegroom *(n)* a man who is about to be married or has just been married.

bridesmaid *(n)* a girl or a woman who helps a bride on her wedding day.

bridge bridging bridged
1 *(n)* a structure built over a river, railway, etc. so that people or vehicles can get to the other side.
2 *(n)* a card game for four players.
3 *(v)* If something **bridges a gap**, it provides a connection between two different things.
4 *(n)* an upright piece of wood on a guitar, violin, etc. over which the strings are stretched.
See **guitar**, **strings**.

bridges

suspension bridge

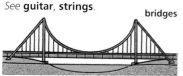

cantilever bridge

beam bridge

arch bridge

bridle *(n)* the straps that fit around a horse's head and mouth, and are used to control it. See **tack**.

bridle path *(n)* a track or path for horse riders or walkers.

brief briefing briefed; briefer briefest
1 *(adj)* lasting only a short time. *A brief visit.* **briefly** *(adv)*.
2 *(adj)* using only a few words. *Be as brief as you can.* **briefly** *(adv)*.
3 *(v)* to give someone information so they can carry out a task. **brief** *(n)*.
4 briefs *(plural n)* underpants.

briefcase *(n)* a bag with a handle, used for carrying papers.

brigade
1 *(n)* a unit of an army.
2 *(n)* an organized group of workers. *The fire brigade.*

bright brighter brightest
1 *(adj)* A **bright** light or colour is strong and can be seen clearly. **brightness** *(n)*, **brightly** *(adv)*.
2 *(adj)* cheerful. **brightly** *(adv)*.
3 *(adj)* *(informal)* clever.

brilliant
1 *(adj)* shining very brightly. *A brilliant diamond.* **brilliance** *(n)*.
2 *(adj)* very clever. **brilliance** *(n)*, **brilliantly** *(adv)*.
3 *(adj)* very good. *It was a brilliant party.* **brilliantly** *(adv)*.

brim *(n)* the wide part that sticks out around the bottom of a hat.

brine *(n)* salty water.

bring bringing brought
1 *(v)* to take something or someone with you. *Bring a friend.*
2 *(v)* to make something happen or appear. *Hooligans bring trouble.*
3 *(v)* If a company **brings out** a product, it starts selling it.
4 **bring up** *(v)* to look after and guide a child as it grows up.
5 **bring in** *(v)* If you **bring something in**, you introduce it. *The government is bringing in new employment laws.*

brink
1 *(n)* the edge of something, like a cliff or a river bank.
2 If you are **on the brink** of something, you are just about to do it. *Jake is on the brink of leaving.*

brisk brisker briskest *(adj)* quick and energetic. *A brisk walk.* **briskly** *(adv)*.

bristle
1 *(n)* one of the long, wiry hairs used to make brushes. **bristly** *(adj)*.
2 bristles *(plural n)* the short, stiff hairs that start to grow on a man's chin if he does not shave. **bristly** *(adj)*.

brittle *(adj)* easily snapped or broken. *Dried flowers can be very brittle.*

broach broaches broaching broached *(v)* When you **broach** a subject with someone, you start to talk or ask about it.

broad broader broadest
1 *(adj)* wide. **broaden** *(v)*.
2 *(adj)* covering the most important points, but not the details. *Give me a broad outline of the story.* **broadly** *(adv)*.

broadcast broadcasting broadcasted
1 *(v)* to send out a programme on television or radio. **broadcaster** *(n)*, **broadcasting** *(n)*.
2 *(n)* a television or radio programme.

broccoli *(n)* a green vegetable with rounded heads on stalks. See **vegetable**.

brochure *(broh-shur)* *(n)* a booklet, usually with pictures, that gives information about a product or service. *A holiday brochure.*

brogue *(brohg)*
1 *(n)* a strong accent, especially an Irish one.
2 brogues *(plural n)* strong walking shoes.

broiler *(n)* *(US)* the part of a cooker that heats food from above (grill, *UK*).

broke *(adj)* *(informal)* If you are **broke**, you have no money.

broken home *(n)* A **broken home** is one where the family is no longer together because the parents have divorced.

bronchitis *(bron-ky-tiss)* *(n)* an illness of the throat and lungs that makes you cough a lot.

bronze
1 *(n)* a hard, reddish-brown metal that is a mixture of copper and tin.
2 *(n)* a reddish-brown colour. bronze *(adj)*.

brooch *(rhymes with coach)* brooches
(n) a piece of jewellery that can be pinned to your clothes. *The Tara brooch, shown here, was made in 10th-century Ireland.*

Tara brooch

brood brooding brooded
1 *(n)* a family of young birds.
2 *(v)* to keep worrying or thinking about something. *Don't brood about your problems.*

brook *(n)* a small stream.

broom *(n)* a large brush with a long handle, used for sweeping floors.

brother *(n)* a boy or man with the same parents as you **brotherly** *(adj)*.

brow
1 *(n)* forehead. *A wrinkled brow.*
2 *(n)* the top of a hill.

brown *(n)* the colour of wood, leather, and coffee. **brown** *(adj)*.

brownie *(n)* a type of chocolate cake with nuts in it.

browse browsing browsed *(v)* to look casually at something. *Max browsed through the newspaper.*

browser *(n)* a computer program that allows you to use the World Wide Web by looking at Web pages and moving between them.

bruise *(brewz) (n)* a dark mark that you get on your skin when you fall or are hit by something. **bruise** *(v)*.

brunette *(n)* a woman or girl with dark brown hair. **brunette** *(adj)*.

brush brushes brushing brushed
1 *(n)* an object with bristles and a handle, used for sweeping, painting, or smoothing hair.
2 *(v)* to use a brush. *Brush your hair before you go out.*
3 *(v)* to touch something lightly.

brutal *(adj)* cruel and violent. **brutally** *(adv)*

brute
1 *(n)* a rough and violent person.
2 *(n)* If you do something by **brute force**, you use a lot of strength instead of skill or intelligence.

BSE *(n)* a slow-developing fatal disease that affects cattle, damaging their brain and making them lose control of their limbs. BSE is also known as mad cow disease. The initials BSE stand for bovine spongiform encephalopathy.

bubble bubbling bubbled
1 *(n)* one of the tiny balls of gas in fizzy drinks, boiling water, etc.
2 *(v)* to make bubbles. *The water bubbled in the saucepan.*

bubbly
1 *(adj)* If a liquid is bubbly, it is full of balls of gas.
2 *(adj)* If a person is bubbly, they are very lively and talkative.

buccaneer *(n)* (old-fashioned) a pirate.

buccaneer

buck bucking bucked
1 *(n)* a male rabbit, kangaroo, etc.
2 *(v)* If a horse **bucks**, it jumps in the air with all four feet off the ground.
3 If you **pass the buck**, you pass the responsibility for something on to someone else.
4 *(n) (slang)* a dollar.
5 **buck up** *(v) (informal)* to hurry up.

bucket *(n)* a plastic or metal container with a handle, used for carrying liquids.

buckle buckling buckled
1 *(n)* a metal fastening on shoes, belts, or straps. *The elaborate buckle shown here was made by Anglo-Saxon craftsmen in the 7th century AD.*
buckle *(v).*
2 *(v)* to crumple. *Hugh's legs buckled under him and he fell.*

buckle

bud *(n)* a small shoot on a plant that grows into a leaf or flower. *See* **plant**.

Buddha
1 *(n)* the name given to Siddhartha Gautama, the teacher who founded the religion of Buddhism.
2 *(n)* a statue or picture of Buddha.

Buddha

Buddhism *(n)* a religion based on the teachings of Buddha and practised mainly in eastern and central Asia. Buddhists believe that you should not become too attached to material things and that you live many lives in different bodies. **Buddhist** *(n)*, **Buddhist** *(adj).*

budge budging budged *(v)* If you cannot **budge** something, you are not able to move it.

budgerigar *(n)* a brightly coloured Australian bird, often kept as a pet.

budget budgeting budgeted
1 *(n)* a plan for how money will be earned and spent. **budgetary** *(adj).*
2 *(v)* If you **budget** for something, you plan how to spend your money so that you can afford it.

buff
1 *(n)* a pale, yellow-brown colour. buff *(adj).*
2 *(n) (informal)* someone who knows a lot about a particular subject. *Barry is a great film buff.*

buffalo buffaloes *(n)* a type of ox with heavy horns.

buffer *(n)* something that softens a blow, especially the springs fixed to the front and back of a railway carriage. *See* **steam locomotive**.

buffet buffeting buffeted
1 *(buff-et) (v)* to strike and shake something or someone. *The wind buffeted the trees.*
2 *(boo-fay) (n)* a meal in which many cold dishes are laid on a table and people serve themselves.
3 *(boo-fay) (n)* a snack bar, usually at a railway station.

bug bugging bugged
1 *(n)* an insect.
2 *(n) (informal)* a minor illness caused by germs. *A stomach bug.*
3 *(n) (informal)* an error in a computer program or system that prevents it from working properly.
4 *(adj) (informal)* If a room is **bugged**, someone has hidden microphones there so that they can listen to what people are saying. **bug** *(n).*
5 *(v) (informal)* If someone or something **bugs** you, they annoy you.

buggy buggies
1 *(n)* a chair on wheels, in which you push young children.
2 *(n) (old-fashioned)* a light, two-wheeled carriage, pulled by a horse. *This buggy dates from the 1800s and has seats for three passengers.*

hooded buggy

folding hood

hood window

suspended body

rest for reins

lamp

open seat

shafts for horse

step

step

rubber tyre

bugle *(n)* a musical instrument like a small trumpet, often used in the army to send signals to the troops. *The picture shows a 19th-century British army bugle.*

bugle

build building built
1 *(v)* to make something by putting different parts together.
2 *(n)* the size and shape of a person's body. *Nick has quite a large build.*
3 **build up** *(v)* to increase or make stronger. *The traffic has built up. You must build yourself up for the race.*

building (n) a structure with walls and a roof. *This cutaway picture of a modern house shows the different parts of a building.*

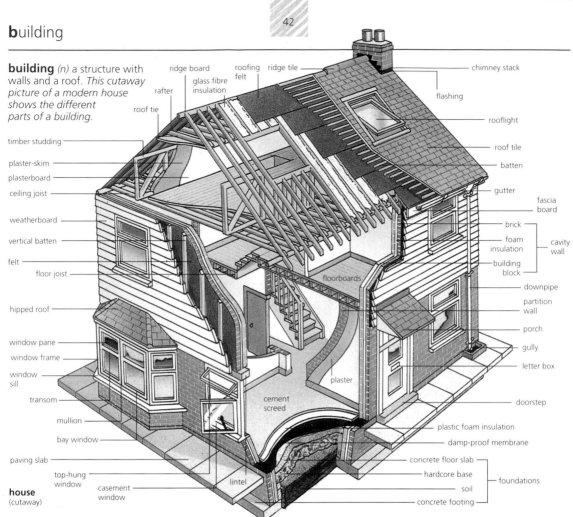

ridge board
roofing felt
ridge tile
chimney stack
glass fibre insulation
rafter
flashing
roof tie
rooflight
timber studding
roof tile
plaster-skim
batten
plasterboard
gutter
ceiling joist
fascia board
weatherboard
brick
vertical batten
foam insulation
cavity wall
felt
building block
floor joist
floorboards
downpipe
partition wall
hipped roof
porch
window pane
gully
window frame
letter box
window sill
transom
plaster
doorstep
mullion
cement screed
bay window
plastic foam insulation
paving slab
damp-proof membrane
top-hung window
concrete floor slab
casement window
lintel
hardcore base
foundations
soil
house (cutaway)
concrete footing

building society building societies (n) an organization with which you can save money and which lends money to people to buy houses.

bulb

1 (n) the onion-shaped root of some plants.

2 (n) the glass part of an electric light or torch that lights up when you switch it on. *When you switch on a light, an electric current travels along the connecting wires inside the bulb and makes the filament glow white hot.*

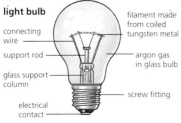

light bulb

connecting wire
filament made from coiled tungsten metal
support rod
argon gas in glass bulb
glass support column
screw fitting
electrical contact

bulge bulging bulged (v) to swell out like a lump. *Sergei's bag bulged with presents.* **bulge** (n).

bulk

1 (n) The **bulk** of something is the main part of it.

2 When you buy **in bulk**, you buy in large quantities.

bulky bulkier bulkiest

1 (adj) large and difficult to handle.

2 (adj) very filling. *Bulky food.*

bull

1 (n) the male of the cattle family.

2 (n) a male elephant, seal, or whale.

bulldozer (n) a powerful tractor with a wide blade at the front, used for moving earth and rocks.

bulldozer

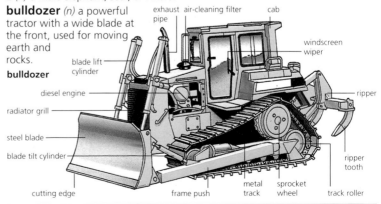

exhaust pipe
air-cleaning filter
cab
windscreen wiper
blade lift cylinder
diesel engine
ripper
radiator grill
steel blade
blade tilt cylinder
ripper tooth
cutting edge
frame push
metal track
sprocket wheel
track roller

bullet (n) a small, pointed metal object fired from a gun.

bulletin (n) a short news report on television or radio.

bulletproof (adj) Something that is bulletproof is made to protect people from bullets. *Bulletproof glass.*

bullfight (n) a public entertainment in which men fight against bulls.

bullion (n) bars of gold or silver.

bullock (n) a castrated bull.

bully bullies bullying bullied (v) to frighten or hurt people who are weaker than you. **bully** (n).

bump bumping bumped
1 (v) to knock into something by accident. **bump** (n).
2 (n) the sound of one thing hitting something else. *I fell out of bed with a bump.*
3 (n) a round lump or swelling.
4 (v) (informal) If you **bump into** someone, you meet them by chance.
5 (slang) If someone has been **bumped off**, they have been killed.

bumph (n) (slang) a lot of printed papers.

bumptious (adj) loud and conceited.

bumpy bumpier bumpiest (adj) very uneven. *A bumpy road.*

bun
1 (n) a small, round cake or bread roll.
2 (n) hair fastened in a round shape at the back of the head.

bunch bunches (n) a group of things or people. **bunch** (v).

bundle bundling bundled
1 (v) to tie or wrap things together loosely. **bundle** (n).
2 (v) to handle someone quickly and carelessly. *We bundled Uncle Hector out of the car.*

bung bunging bunged
1 (n) a piece of cork, rubber, or wood used to close up the opening in a bottle or other container.
2 (v) (slang) to throw something roughly and carelessly. *Bung your bag on the floor.*

bungalow (n) a house with one storey.

bungee jumping (n) a dangerous sport in which someone jumps from a high place and is stopped from hitting the ground by a long piece of elastic attached to their legs.

bungle bungling bungled (v) to do something badly or clumsily.

bunk
1 (n) a narrow bed.
2 **bunk beds** (plural n) two beds stacked one above the other.
3 **bunk off** (v) (slang) to miss something, like a lesson, on purpose.

bunker
1 (n) a place for storing coal.
2 (n) an underground shelter from bomb attacks and gunfire.
3 (n) a large, sand-filled hollow on a golf course.

bunting (n) small flags joined by a string and used for decoration.

buoy (boy) (n) a floating marker in the sea or in a river.

buoyant
1 (adj) able to keep afloat. **buoyancy** (n).
2 (adj) cheerful. **buoyantly** (adv).

burden burdening burdened
1 (n) a heavy load that someone has to carry.
2 (v) to weigh someone down with heavy things. *We burdened Dad with all our bags and cases.*
3 (v) to tell someone about your problems.

bureau (byoor-oh) bureaux
1 (n) a writing desk with drawers.
2 (n) an office that provides information or some other service.

burger (n) a round, flat piece of cooked meat, usually served in a bread roll.

burglar (n) someone who breaks into a house and steals things. **burglary** (n), **burgle** (v).

burn burning burnt or burned
1 (v) to hurt or damage someone or something with heat or fire.
2 (n) a sore area on the skin or a mark on something, caused by heat.

burp burping burped (v) to make a noise in your throat because gases have been forced up from your stomach, usually after eating or drinking. **burp** (n).

burrow burrowing burrowed
1 (n) a tunnel or hole in the ground where a rabbit or other animal lives.
2 (v) to move along under the ground by digging.

bursar (n) the person in a college or school whose job is to look after the money and the buildings.

burst bursting burst
1 (v) to explode or break apart suddenly. *The balloon burst.*
2 (n) a short, concentrated outbreak of something, such as speed, gunfire, or applause.
3 (v) to start doing something suddenly. *Kit burst into tears.*

bury buries burying buried
1 (v) to put a dead body into a grave. **burial** (n).
2 (v) to hide something in the ground or under a pile of things.

bus buses (n) a large vehicle, used for carrying passengers.

bush bushes
1 (n) a large plant with many branches.
2 **The bush** (n) the wild areas of Australia and Africa. **bushman** (n).

bushy bushier bushiest (adj) growing thickly. *Bushy eyebrows.*

business businesses
1 (n) the type of work that someone does. *Hank's in the music business.*
2 (n) the buying and selling of goods and services. *Our company does a lot of business with Japan.*
3 (n) a company or shop that makes or sells things or provides a service.
4 If something is **none of your business**, it is nothing to do with you.

businesslike (adj) efficient and practical.

busker (n) someone who sings or plays music in the street, in order to earn money. **busking** (n).

bust busting busted or bust
1 (n) a woman's breasts. **busty** (adj).
2 (n) a statue of a person's head and shoulders. *This marble bust is of the Ancient Greek scientist, Galen.*
3 (v) (informal) to break something. **bust** (adj).

marble bust

bustle bustling bustled (v) to rush around being busy. **bustle** (n).

busy busier busiest
1 (adj) If you are **busy**, you have a lot of things to do. **busily** (adv).
2 (adj) A **busy** place has a lot of people in it and is full of activity.

butcher (n) someone who sells meat.

butler (n) the chief male servant in a house.

butt butting butted
1 (n) a large barrel for water.
2 (v) to hit with the head or horns.
3 (n) the handle of a gun.

butter (n) a yellow fat made from cream, used in cooking and for spreading on bread. *This picture shows a 19th-century dairymaid using a plunger churn to turn cream into butter.*

buttercup (n) a small, yellow wild flower. *See* **plant**.

butter-making

butterfly

butterfly
butterflies (n) a thin-bodied insect with large, brightly coloured wings. *Also see* **caterpillar**.

clouded yellow

purple tip

Rajah Brooke's birdwing

Danaid egg fly

Adonis blue

peacock

forewing — head — antenna — hindwing — tongue — leg — **high brown fritillary** — thorax

buttocks (plural n) the two fleshy parts of your bottom.

button
1 (n) a round piece of plastic, metal, etc. that is sewn on to clothing and used as a fastener. **button** (v).
2 (n) a small knob on a machine that you press to switch it on or off.

buy buying bought (v) to get something by paying money for it.

buzz buzzes buzzing buzzed (v) to make a noise like a bee or a wasp. **buzz** (n).

bypass bypasses bypassing bypassed
1 (n) a main road that goes around a town rather than through it.
2 (v) to avoid something by going around it. **bypass** (adj).

byte (n) a unit of information that is contained in a computer's memory.

Byzantine
1 (adj) to do with Byzantium, the ancient eastern Roman empire.
2 (adj) in the style of art or architecture used in the Byzantine empire. Byzantine buildings have large domes and rounded arches, and are highly decorated, often with mosaics.

C c

cabbage (n) a large, leafy vegetable. See **vegetable**.

cabin
1 (n) the driver's section of a vehicle.
2 (n) a room for passengers on a ship or plane.
3 (n) a small, wooden house.

cabinet
1 (n) a cupboard with shelves or drawers.
2 (n) a group of top members of a government who advise the leader.

cable
1 (n) a thick wire or rope.
2 (n) a tight bundle of wires used for carrying electricity, television signals, etc.
3 **cable car** (n) a vehicle pulled along by a moving cable, used for carrying people up mountains.
4 **cable television** (n) a television service received by cable with a wide choice of channels.

cactus cacti or **cactuses** (n) a spiky plant that grows in hot, dry countries.

cadet (n) a young person who is training to become a member of the army, navy, air force, or police force.

prickly pear cactus

barrel cactus

cacti

café (kaf-ay) (n) a small restaurant that serves snacks and hot drinks.

cafeteria (n) a self-service restaurant.

caffeine (kaf-een) (n) a chemical found in tea and coffee which makes your brain and body more active.

caftan (n) a long, loose piece of clothing with long sleeves, worn by men in Arab countries.

cage (n) a container in which animals or birds are kept, made of wires or bars. **cage** (v), **caged** (adj).

cajole cajoling cajoled (v) to persuade someone to do something by flattering them.

cake caking caked
1 (n) a sweet food made by baking flour, butter, eggs, and sugar together.
2 (v) If you are **caked** in something, you are covered in it.

calamity calamities (n) a terrible disaster. **calamitous** (adj).

calcium (n) a soft, white element found in teeth and bones.

calculate calculating calculated (v) to work something out, especially a sum. *Andy calculated that it would take two hours to get there by car.* **calculation** (n).

calculating (adj) A calculating person makes clever plans so that things work out the way they want.

calculator (n) a small electronic machine, used for working out sums. *This picture shows the face, the circuit board, and the case of a pocket calculator.*

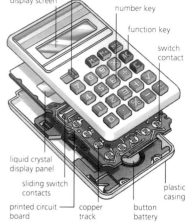

power switch — **calculator** — display screen — number key — function key — switch contact — liquid crystal display panel — sliding switch contacts — printed circuit board — copper track — button battery — plastic casing

calendar (n) a chart showing all the days in a year.

calf calves
1 (n) a young cow, seal, elephant, giraffe, or whale.
2 (n) the fleshy part at the back of your leg, below your knee.

call calling called
1 (v) to shout something out, especially someone's name.
2 (v) to give someone or something a name.
3 (v) to telephone someone. **call** (n).
4 (v) If you **call on** someone, you visit them. **caller** (n).
5 **call off** (v) If you **call something off**, you cancel it.
6 **call collect** (v) (US) to reverse telephone charges from someone who is making the call to the person who is receiving it.

calligraphy (n) the art of beautiful handwriting. *The picture shows a dip-pen and the word "calligraphy", written in the Foundational style.*

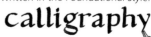

calligraphy

callous *(adj)* hard-hearted and cruel. **callousness** *(n)*, **callously** *(adv)*.

calm calming calmed; calmer calmest
1 *(adj)* peaceful and untroubled. **calmness** *(n)*, **calmly** *(adv)*.
2 *(v)* to soothe an animal or a person.
3 *(n)* peacefulness.

calorie *(n)* a measurement of the amount of energy that a food gives you.

calypso *(n)* a West Indian song with a strong rhythm.

camcorder *(n)* a video camera with a sound recorder, that you can carry around with you. *When light from the camcorder lens reaches the image-sensing chip, an electrical signal is created. This signal travels through electrical circuits to the record-playback head which records magnetic patterns on to the video tape, which also records the sound.*

camcorder
(cutaway)

magnetic video and audio tape — eyepiece
viewfinder (contains playback screen)
videotape cassette
take-up spool
guide roller
pinch rollers (control speed of tape)
microphone
image-sensing microchip
automatic focus zoom lens
record-playback head
tape magnetized with picture and sound signals

camel *(n)* a mammal with one or two humps on its back that is used for carrying people and goods across the desert. *The two types of camel are shown here.*

camels

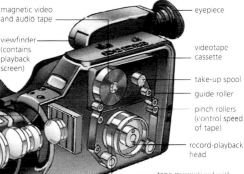

bactrian camel   dromedary

cameo *(kam-ee-oh)*
1 *(n)* a piece of coloured stone with a figure carved out of it.
2 *(adj)* A **cameo** role is a small character part taken in a play or a film, usually by a famous actor.

cameo

camera *(n)* a machine for taking photographs or making films.
See **photography**.

cameraman *(n)* someone whose job is to use a camera to make films and television programmes.

camouflage *(kam-er-flarj)* camouflaging camouflaged
1 *(n)* colouring or covering that makes animals, people, and objects look like their surroundings. *The praying mantis uses camouflage to hide from other creatures.*
2 *(v)* to disguise something so that it blends in with its surroundings.

praying mantis   leaf

camp camping camped
1 *(v)* to have a holiday in a tent. **camping** *(n)*.
2 *(n)* a group of tents together.

campaign *(n)* a series of actions organized over a period of time in order to achieve or win something. *An election campaign.*

camper
1 *(n)* someone who has a holiday in a tent.
2 *(n)* a large vehicle in which you can sleep and cook meals.

can could
1 *(v)* to be able to. *Natalie can speak fluent French.*
2 *(v)* *(informal)* to be allowed to do something. *You can stay out until dark.*
3 *(n)* a metal container. **canned** *(adj)*.

canal *(n)* a man-made waterway used by barges and narrow boats.

cancel cancelling cancelled
1 *(v)* If someone **cancels** something that has been arranged, they say that it is not going to happen. **cancellation** *(n)*.
2 **cancel out** *(v)* If two things **cancel** each other out, they stop the effect of one another. *If you eat all day, it will cancel out the benefit of all the exercise you've taken.*

cancer *(n)* a serious disease in which some cells in the body produce harmful growths. **cancerous** *(adj)*.

candid *(adj)* honest and open in what you are saying. **candidly** *(adv)*.

candidate *(n)* someone taking an examination, applying for a job, or standing in an election. **candidacy** *(n)*.

candle *(n)* a stick of wax with a string or wick running through it, which you burn to give light. **candlelight** *(n)*.

candy candies *(n)* *(US)* a small piece of food, made with sugar or chocolate (sweet, *UK*).

cane caning caned
1 *(n)* the hollow stem of a plant like bamboo, used to make furniture.
2 *(n)* a stick, especially a walking stick or a stick used for beating someone.
3 *(v)* to beat someone with a cane as a punishment.

canine
1 *(adj)* to do with dogs.
2 *(n)* the pointed tooth on each side of your upper and lower jaw.
See **teeth**.

cannabis *(n)* a drug that people smoke to give them a feeling of pleasure. Cannabis is illegal in Britain and in many other countries.

cannibal *(n)* someone who eats human flesh. **cannibalism** *(n)*.

cannon *(n)* a heavy gun which fires large metal balls. *The picture shows an 18th-century cannon.*

cannon
(cutaway)
trunnion (supports barrel)   shot   pricker
cascabel
gun barrel   rammer   wad
muzzle
carriage
wheel   powder charge
towing eye
cannonballs   worm or reamer   sponge

canoe *(n)* a narrow boat that you move through the water by paddling.

canopy canopies
1 *(n)* a piece of cloth used as a cover over a doorway, bed, etc.
2 *(n)* a shelter over something. *Tree tops formed a canopy over the forest floor.*
3 *(n)* a cover over a cockpit.
See **glider**, **helicopter**.

canteen *(n)* an area in an office, school, etc. where you can eat meals.

Some words that begin with a "c" sound are spelt with a "k".

canter cantering cantered (v)
When a horse **canters**, it runs at a
speed between a trot and a gallop.
canter (n).

canvas canvases
1 (n) a type of coarse, strong cloth
used for tents, sails, and clothing.
2 (n) a surface for painting, made
from canvas cloth stretched over a
wooden frame. *Artists paint on
canvases.*

canvass canvasses canvassing
canvassed (v) to ask people for their
opinions or votes. **canvasser** (n).

canyon (n) a deep, narrow river
valley.

cap capping capped
1 (n) a soft, flat hat with a peak at the
front.
2 (n) the top of a bottle, jar, or pen.
3 (v) If you **cap** someone's story, you
tell an even better one.
4 (n) a small amount of explosive on a
piece of paper that makes a bang
when fired in a toy gun.

capable
1 (adj) If you are **capable** of doing
something, you are able to do it.
*Ingrid is capable of winning the
competition.* **capability** (n).
2 (adj) able to do something well and
skilfully. *Danny is a capable tennis
player.* **capably** (adv).

capacity capacities
1 (n) the amount a container can hold.
2 (n) an ability to do something.
*Cosmo has the capacity to absorb
facts very fast.*

cape
1 (n) a sleeveless coat that you wear
over your shoulders.
2 (n) a part of the
coastline that sticks
out into the sea. *The
picture shows Cape
Cod, on the east coast
of North America.*

cape

capillary capillaries
1 (n) a small tube in your body which
carries blood between arteries and
veins.
2 **capillary tube** (n) a very thin tube,
made out of glass. *See* **thermometer**.

capital
1 (n) the main city of a country, where
the government is based.
2 (n) a large letter. *You begin a
sentence with a capital.*
3 (singular n) an amount of money
used to start a business.
4 **capital punishment** (n) punishment
by death.

capitalism (n) a way of organizing a
country so that all the land, houses,
factories, etc. belong to private
individuals rather than the state.
capitalist (n), **capitalist** (adj).

cappuccino (kap-er-cheen-oh) (n)
coffee made with frothy milk.

capricious (adj) Someone who is
capricious is unpredictable and tends
to change their mind without any
obvious reason.

capsize capsizing capsized (v) If a
boat or ship **capsizes**, it turns over in
the water.

capsule
1 (n) a small container of medicine
that you can swallow.
2 (n) the part of a rocket or spacecraft
in which the crew travel.

captain
1 (n) the person in charge of a ship or
an aircraft.
2 (n) the leader of a sports team.
3 (n) an army officer.

caption (n) a short title or
description printed below a cartoon,
drawing, or photograph.

captivate captivating captivated
(v) to delight someone. *Clara
captivated us with her singing.*

captive (n) a person or animal who
has been taken prisoner. **captivity** (n),
captive (adj).

capture capturing captured (v)
to take a person or a place by force.

car (n) a type of passenger motor
vehicle. *The picture shows a cutaway
view of a Ford Mondeo saloon car.*

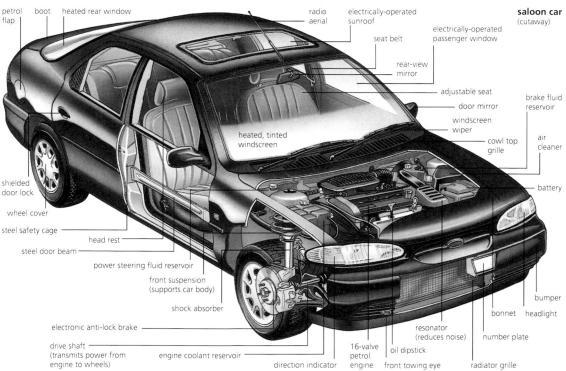

petrol flap | boot | heated rear window | radio aerial | electrically-operated sunroof | **saloon car** (cutaway)

seat belt · electrically-operated passenger window · rear-view mirror · adjustable seat · brake fluid reservoir · door mirror · windscreen wiper · cowl top grille · air cleaner · battery · bumper · headlight · bonnet · number plate · radiator grille · front towing eye · oil dipstick · 16-valve petrol engine · direction indicator · resonator (reduces noise) · engine coolant reservoir · electronic anti-lock brake · drive shaft (transmits power from engine to wheels) · shock absorber · front suspension (supports car body) · power steering fluid reservoir · steel door beam · head rest · steel safety cage · wheel cover · shielded door lock · heated, tinted windscreen

caramel
1 (n) burnt sugar.
2 (n) a sweet made from burnt sugar, butter, and milk.
3 (n) a light brown colour. caramel (adj).

carat (n) a unit for measuring the weight of precious metals.

caravan
1 (n) a small home on wheels which can be towed by a car and is used by people on holiday.
2 (n) a group of people and camels that travel together across a desert.

caravan

carbohydrate (n) one of the substances in foods such as bread and potatoes, that give you energy.

carbon
1 (n) an element found in coal and diamonds and in all plants and animals.
2 carbon dioxide (n) a gas that is breathed out by people and animals, and is used to make drinks fizzy.
3 carbon monoxide (n) a poisonous gas produced by vehicle engines.
4 carbon fibre (n) a light, strong material, made from threads of carbon, and used for fishing rods, racing car bodies, etc.

carburettor (n) the part of a car's engine where air and petrol mix.

carcass carcasses (n) the body of a dead animal.

card
1 (n) stiff paper.
2 (n) a folded piece of card sent on birthdays and special occasions.
3 (n) one of a set of rectangular pieces of card, used in games such as whist and bridge. *The cards shown here were made in France in the 18th century.*

playing cards

cardboard (n) very thick card, used for making boxes.

---

cardiac (adj) to do with the heart.

cardigan (n) a knitted jacket which fastens down the front.

care caring cared
1 (v) If you **care** about someone or something, you are very concerned about what happens to them. caring (adj).
2 If you take care of someone, you look after them.
3 If you do something **with care**, you pay attention to what you are doing.

career (n) the series of jobs that a person has in their life, usually in the same profession. *A career in teaching.*

carefree (adj) Someone who is carefree has no worries.

careful (adj) Someone who is careful takes trouble over what they are doing and does not take risks. carefully (adv).

careless (adj) Someone who is careless does not take much trouble or care over things. carelessness (n), carelessly (adv).

caress caresses caressing caressed (v) to touch gently. caress (n).

caretaker (n) someone whose job is to look after a school or some other public building.

cargo cargoes (n) goods that are carried by ship or aircraft.

caricature (n) an exaggerated picture of someone.

carnival (n) a public celebration. People wear colourful costumes, walk in processions, and dance in the streets at carnival time.

carnivore (n) an animal that eats meat. carnivorous (adj).

carob
1 (n) an evergreen tree whose beans are used to make a food rather like chocolate.
2 (n) a chocolate-like food.

carol (n) a religious song that people sing at Christmas. carol (v).

carpenter (n) someone who makes or repairs the wooden parts of buildings. carpentry (n).

carpet
1 (n) a thick floor covering. carpet (v).
2 (n) a thick layer of something. *A carpet of flowers.* carpet (v).

carriage
1 (n) one of the parts of a train in which passengers travel.
2 (n) a vehicle with wheels that is pulled by horses.
3 (n) Your **carriage** is the way that you stand, sit, and walk.

---

carriageway (n) Motorways and major roads are divided into two carriageways, for traffic travelling in opposite directions.

carrot
1 (n) an orange root vegetable. *See* **vegetable**.
2 (n) If someone offers you a **carrot**, they promise you something nice in order to persuade you to do something.

carry carries carrying carried
1 (v) to hold on to something and take it somewhere. *Please carry this tray.*
2 (v) If a sound **carries**, it can be heard some distance away.
3 (v) If you **carry out** a plan or idea, you put it into practice.

cartilage (n) a strong, stretchy substance found around your joints.

cartography (n) the art of drawing maps. cartographer (n).

carton (n) a cardboard or plastic box, usually containing food or drink.

cartoon
1 (n) a short, animated film.
2 (n) a funny drawing or series of drawings. cartoonist (n).

cartridge
1 (n) a tube of ink used in a fountain pen.
2 (n) a container that holds a bullet or pellets and the explosive that fires them.

cartwheel (n) a circular, sideways handstand.

carve carving carved
1 (v) to cut slices from a piece of meat.
2 (v) to cut a shape out of a piece of wood, stone, etc. carver (n), carving (n).

case
1 (n) a container for carrying clothes when you travel.
2 (n) an example of something. *This is a case of deliberate disobedience!*
3 (n) a trial in a court of law.
4 (n) a crime that the police are investigating.
5 (n) The **case** of a noun or pronoun is the form that it takes, depending on its relationship with other words in the sentence. *"I" is the nominative case, "me" is the accusative case, and "my" is the possessive case.*

cash cashes cashing cashed
1 (n) money in the form of notes and coins.
2 (v) If someone **cashes** a cheque, they get money in exchange for it.
3 (v) If you **cash in** on something, you take advantage of it.

---

cash-and-carry cash-and-carries
(n) a warehouse where you can buy things in large quantities at low prices.

cashier (n) someone who takes or pays out money in a shop or bank.

cashpoint (n) a machine from which people can take out money from their bank accounts, by using a plastic card.

casino (n) a place where people play gambling games such as roulette.

casket
1 (n) (poetic) a jewellery box.
2 (n) (US) a box which contains the body or the ashes of a dead person (coffin, UK).

casserole
1 (n) a stew that is cooked slowly in the oven.
2 (n) a dish with a lid that is used for cooking casseroles.

cassette (n) a flat, plastic box that contains recording tape, used to record and play sound and pictures. A video cassette. See **tape**.

cast casting cast
1 (n) the actors in a play or film.
2 (n) a hard plaster covering that supports a broken arm or leg.
3 (v) When fishermen **cast** their fishing lines or nets, they throw them into the water.

castaway (n) someone left on a deserted island after a shipwreck.

caster sugar or **castor sugar** (n) finely ground white sugar.

castle
1 (n) a large, strong building, often surrounded by a wall and a moat. In the Middle Ages, noble families stayed in castles and soldiers defended them from attack. The picture shows a cutaway view of a medieval castle's keep or tower and a ground plan of the castle. Also see **portcullis**.
2 (n) a chesspiece, also known as a rook, that moves in straight lines across a chessboard. See **chess**.

castle keep (cutaway)

man-at-arms

lord's bedchamber

four-poster bed

parapet

solar (private room for lord's family)

turret

arrow loop (slit for shooting arrows through)

crenellation

crenel   merlon

stables

garderobe (toilet)

forge

toilet chute

blacksmith

knife grinder

storeroom

inner bailey

entrance

great hall

kitchen

spiral staircase

chapel

oven   baker

guard room

main entrance

falcon

well

travelling pedlars

dungeon   minstrel   dovecote

falconers

castle (ground plan)

moat   inner bailey

tower

inner bailey wall

keep

outer bailey

outer bailey wall

drawbridge   gatehouse

barbican (watch tower)

castor sugar *see* **caster sugar**.

castrate castrating castrated *(v)* to remove the sex organs of a male animal so that it cannot breed.

casual
1 *(adj)* not planned. *A casual meeting.* casually *(adv)*.
2 *(adj)* not formal. *Casual dress.* casually *(adv)*.

casualty casualties
1 *(n)* someone who is injured or killed in an accident, disaster, or war.
2 *(n)* the department in a hospital that handles accidents and emergencies.

cat
1 *(n)* any member of the cat family, including lions, tigers, and cheetahs.
2 *(n)* a small, furry mammal, often kept as a pet. *The picture shows a range of domestic cats.*

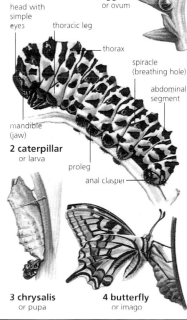

cats
silver classic tabby
chinchilla
red Devon rex
brown Abyssinian
seal-point Siamese

catalogue
1 *(n)* a book listing things you can buy from a company or works of art on show in an exhibition. catalogue *(v)*.
2 *(n)* a list of all the books in a library.

catalyst
1 *(n)* a substance that causes or speeds up a chemical reaction, without changing itself.
2 *(n)* a person or thing that causes something to happen.

catamaran *(n)* a boat with two hulls joined together.

catapult
1 *(n)* a simple, Y-shaped weapon, with elastic stretched over it, used for shooting small stones.
2 *(n)* a large weapon used in the past for firing rocks over castle walls.

cataract
1 *(n)* a waterfall.
2 *(n)* an eye disease in which the lens becomes cloudy and vision becomes blurred.

catarrh *(kat-arh) (n)* the thick liquid that blocks up your nose and throat when you have a cold.

catastrophe *(kat-ass-trof-ee) (n)* a sudden disaster.
catastrophic *(kat-ass-trof-ik) (adj)*.

catch catches catching caught
1 *(v)* to grab hold of something moving through the air. catch *(n)*.
2 *(v)* to get someone whom you are chasing. *The police caught the thieves.*
3 *(v)* If you **catch** a bus or train, you get on it.
4 *(v)* If you **catch** someone doing something wrong, you see them doing it.
5 *(n)* a fastening on a door, box, etc.
6 *(v)* If something **catches on**, it becomes very popular.

categorical *(adj)* clear and plain. *Henry's reply was a categorical "No".*
categorically *(adv)*.

category categories *(n)* a class or group of things that have something in common.

cater catering catered
1 *(v)* to provide food for a lot of people. caterer *(n)*, catering *(n)*.
2 *(v)* to provide people with the things that they need. *This restaurant caters for vegetarians.*

caterpillar *(n)* a worm-like larva that changes into a butterfly or moth. *The pictures show the main parts of a swallowtail caterpillar and the life cycle of a swallowtail butterfly.*

1 egg
or ovum

head with simple eyes
thoracic leg
thorax
spiracle (breathing hole)
abdominal segment
mandible (jaw)
2 caterpillar
or larva
proleg
anal clasper

3 chrysalis
or pupa

4 butterfly
or imago

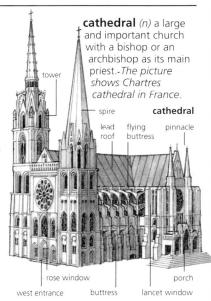

tower
spire
lead roof
flying buttress
pinnacle
rose window
west entrance
buttress
lancet window
porch

cathedral *(n)* a large and important church with a bishop or an archbishop as its main priest.*The picture shows Chartres cathedral in France.*

cathedral

cathode-ray tube *(n)* a glass tube with no air inside it through which rays travel to produce an image on a screen. *See* **television**.

Catholic *(n)* a member of the Roman Catholic Church. **Catholic** *(adj)*.

cattle *(plural n)* cows and bulls.

cauldron *(n)* a large, rounded cooking pot.

cauliflower *(n)* a vegetable with a large, rounded, white centre, surrounded by leaves. *See* **vegetable**.

cause causing caused
1 *(v)* to make something happen.
2 *(n)* the reason that something happens.
3 *(n)* an aim or principle for which people fight.

cautious *(adj)* If you are **cautious**, you try hard to avoid mistakes or danger. caution *(n)*, cautiously *(adv)*.

cavalry
1 *(plural n)* soldiers who fight on horseback.
2 *(plural n)* soldiers who fight in armoured vehicles.

cave *(n)* a large hole underground or in the side of a hill or cliff.

caveman cavemen *(n)* someone who lived in caves in prehistoric times.

cave painting *(n)* a picture painted by a caveman on a cave wall in prehistoric times. *This cave painting of a bison was discovered in northern Spain.*

cave painting

cavern (n) a large cave.
cavernous (adj).

caving If you go caving, you explore caves. **caver** (n).

cavity cavities (n) a hole or hollow space in something solid, such as a tooth.

CB (n) a radio system which people use to talk to each other over short distances. The initials stand for citizens' band.

CD short for **compact disc**.

CD-ROM (n) a disc used with a computer monitor or television screen which produces text and pictures. The initials stand for compact disc read only memory.

cease ceasing ceased (v) to stop.

cease-fire (n) a period during a war when both sides agree to stop fighting.

ceaseless (adj) without stopping. **ceaselessly** (adv).

cedar (n) a large, evergreen tree with needle-like leaves.

ceiling
1 (n) the upper surface inside a room.
2 (n) the upper limit that something can reach. A price ceiling.

celebrate celebrating celebrated (v) to do something enjoyable on a special occasion, such as having a party. **celebration** (n), **celebratory** (adj).

celebrated (adj) famous.

celebrity celebrities (n) a famous person, especially an entertainer or a film star.

celery (n) a vegetable with white or green crisp stalks, often eaten raw in salads. See **vegetable**.

celestial (adj) to do with heaven. **celestially** (adv).

cell
1 (n) a room in a prison or a police station where someone is locked up.
2 (n) a basic, microscopic part of an animal or a plant.

plant cell
(magnified)

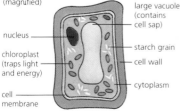

large vacuole (contains cell sap)

nucleus

starch grain

chloroplast (traps light and energy)

cell wall

cytoplasm

cell membrane

cellar (n) a room below ground level in a house, often used for storage.

cellular (adj) made out of, or to do with cells. Cellular tissue.

cellulose (n) the substance from which the cell walls of plants are made.

Celsius (adj) measured on a temperature scale on which water boils at 100° and freezes at 0°. Celsius is also called centigrade.

cement
1 (n) a grey powder, used in building, that becomes hard when you mix it with water and let it dry.
2 (n) a substance that joins two things together. See **tooth**.

cemetery cemeteries (n) a place where people are buried.

censor censoring censored
1 (v) to remove parts of a book, film, play, etc. that are thought to be harmful to the public. **censorship** (n).
2 (n) someone whose job is to censor books, films, plays, etc.

census (n) an official count of all the people living in a country.

cent (n) a unit of money in the USA, Canada, Australia, and New Zealand. One hundred cents make one dollar.

centaur (n) a creature found in Greek and Roman myths which had the body and legs of a horse but the chest, arms, and head of a man.

centenary centenaries (n) the hundredth anniversary of something.

centigrade see **Celsius**.

centipede (n) a small creature with a very long body and lots of legs. The tropical giant centipede shown here measures 20cm.

centipede

central
1 (adj) in the middle. **centrally** (adv).
2 (adj) most important. The central problem.
3 central heating (n) a system for heating a building in which water or air is heated in one place and then carried in pipes all over the building.

centre centring centred
1 (n) the middle of something.
2 (n) a place where people go to do a particular activity. A sports centre.
3 (v) to concentrate on something. The campaign centres on the problems of the elderly.
4 centre of gravity (n) the point on an object at which it can balance.

centrifugal (adj) pulling away from the centre. You can feel the centrifugal effect when you swing an object in a circle.

centripetal (adj) pulling towards the centre. When you swing an object round in a circle, you pull it inwards and exert a centripetal force.

centurion (n)
an officer in the Roman army who was in command of 100 soldiers.

centurion

plumed helmet

woollen cloak

chain mail corselet

decorated belt

dagger

sword

double pleated kilt

twisted vine rod

bronze greave (shin plate)

century centuries (n) a period of 100 years.

ceramics
1 (singular n) the craft of making objects out of clay.
2 (plural n) objects made of clay. **ceramic** (adj).

cereal
1 (n) a grain crop grown for food, such as wheat, oats, or maize.
2 (n) a breakfast food usually made from grain and eaten with milk.

ceremony ceremonies (n) formal actions, words, and often music, performed to mark an important occasion. A wedding ceremony. **ceremonial** (adj), **ceremonially** (adv).

certain
1 (adj) If you are certain about something, you are sure about it. Alex was certain he had posted the letter. **certainty** (n), **certainly** (adv).
2 (adj) particular. The shop is closed at certain times.

certificate (n) a piece of paper given to someone to prove that they have done something. An examination certificate.

CFC short for **chlorofluorocarbon**.

chain
1 (n) a line of metal rings, called links, joined together.
2 (n) a series of connected things. A chain of events.
3 chain store (n) one of a group of shops in different towns that are owned by the same company and sell similar goods.

chair chairing chaired
1 (n) a piece of furniture that you sit on, with four legs and a back.
2 (n) the person in charge of a meeting, also called the chairman, chairwoman, or chairperson.
3 (v) to take charge of a meeting.

chair lift (n) a line of chairs attached to a moving cable, used for carrying people up mountains.

chalet (shall-ay) (n) a small, wooden house with a sloping roof.

chalk
1 (n) a soft, white rock.
2 (n) a stick of soft, white rock, used for writing on blackboards. **chalk** (v).

challenge challenging challenged
1 (n) something difficult that you try to do. **challenging** (adj).
2 (v) If you **challenge** someone, you invite them to fight or to try to do something. **challenge** (n).
3 (v) If you **challenge** something, you question whether it is right or not.

chamber
1 (n) a large room.
2 (n) a hollow place in something.
3 **chamber music** (n) classical music for a small number of instruments.

chameleon (kam-ee-lee-un) (n) a lizard that can change colour to match its surroundings.

chameleon

champagne (n) an expensive, sparkling white wine, usually drunk on special occasions.

champion championing championed
1 (n) the winner of a competition or a tournament. **championship** (n).
2 (v) If someone **champions** a cause, they support it. **champion** (n).

chance
1 (n) the possibility of something happening. We have a chance of winning the cup.
2 (n) an opportunity to do something. Warren has the chance to learn to ski.
3 If you **take a chance**, you try something even though it is risky.
4 If something happens **by chance**, it happens accidentally.

chancellor
1 (n) a name for the leader of an organisation or a country. For example, the Chancellor of Germany is its elected leader.
2 **Chancellor of the Exchequer** (n) the minister in charge of finance and taxes in the British Government.

change changing changed
1 (v) to become different or to make something different. **change** (n).
2 (n) If you pay more money than something costs, the money you get back is called **change**.
3 (n) coins rather than banknotes.

channel
1 (n) a narrow stretch of sea between two areas of land.
2 (n) a television or radio station.

chant chanting chanted (v) to say or sing a phrase over and over again. **chant** (n).

Chanukah see **Hanukkah**.

chaos (kay-oss) (n) total confusion. **chaotic** (adj), **chaotically** (adv).

chapel
1 (n) a small church.
2 (n) a side section of a large church.
3 (n) a place in a school, prison, etc. where Christian services are held.

chapter (n) one of the parts into which a book is divided.

character
1 (n) Your **character** is what sort of person you are.
2 (n) one of the people in a story, book, film, or play.
3 (n) a letter, figure, or other mark used in printing.

characteristic
1 (n) a typical quality or feature. Stubborness is a characteristic of our family. **characteristically** (adv).
2 (adj) typical. Sophie worked with characteristic efficiency. **characteristically** (adv).

charcoal (n) a form of carbon made from burnt wood. Charcoal is used for drawing and as a fuel for barbecues.

charge charging charged
1 (v) to ask someone to pay a particular price for something. **charge** (n).
2 (v) to rush at someone in order to attack them. **charge** (n).
3 (v) When you **charge** a battery, you pass an electric current through it so that it stores electricity.
4 If someone is **in charge** of something, they have to deal with it or take control of it.

chariot (n) a small, horse-drawn vehicle, used in ancient times in battles or for racing. The picture shows a Roman chariot.

Roman chariot

charity charities
1 (singular n) money or other help that is given to people in need.
2 (n) an organization which raises money to help people in need.

charm charming charmed
1 (n) If someone has **charm**, they behave in a pleasing and attractive way. **charmer** (n), **charming** (adj).
2 (v) to please someone and make them like you.
3 (n) a small object that some people believe will bring them good luck. This ancient Egyptian charm represents a sacred eye.

Egyptian charm

chart charting charted
1 (n) a drawing showing information in the form of a table or picture.
2 (n) a map of the stars or the sea.
3 (v) to show information in the form of a chart.

chase chasing chased (v) to run after someone in order to catch them or make them go away. **chase** (n).

chasm (kaz-um) (n) a deep crack in the surface of the earth.

chassis (sha-see) chassis (n) the frame onto which the body of a vehicle is built.

chat chatting chatted
1 (v) to talk to someone in a friendly and informal way. **chat** (n).
2 (v) to communicate with other people through a Web site on the Internet by typing messages on a computer. **chat** (n).
3 **chat room** (n) a Web site on the Internet where people can communicate by typing messages to each other.
4 **chat up** (v) If you **chat** someone **up**, you talk in a friendly way to them because you find them attractive.

château (shat-oh) châteaux (n) a castle or large country house in France. The picture shows the Azay-le-Rideau château in the Loire valley in France.

château

chatter chattering chattered
1 (v) to talk about unimportant things. **chatter** (n).
2 (v) When your teeth **chatter**, they knock together because you are cold.

chauffeur (show-fur) (n) someone whose job is to drive a car for somebody else. **chauffeur** (v).

chauvinist *(show-vin-ist)*
1 *(n)* a man who believes that women are inferior to men.
chauvinism *(n)*, chauvinistic *(adj)*.
2 *(n)* someone who believes that no other country is as good or as important as their own.
chauvinism *(n)*, chauvinistic *(adj)*.

cheap cheaper cheapest
1 *(adj)* not costing very much.
cheapness *(n)*, cheaply *(adv)*.
2 *(adj)* unkind and mean. *That was a cheap trick you played on me!*

cheat cheating cheated *(v)* to act dishonestly in order to win a game or get what you want. cheat *(n)*.

check checking checked
1 *(v)* to look at something in order to make sure that it is all right. check *(n)*.
2 *(v)* to stop something from moving or growing. *We must check inflation.*
3 *(n)* a pattern of different coloured squares. checked *(adj)*.
4 *(n)* (US) a printed piece of paper on which someone writes to tell their bank to pay money from their account (cheque, UK).

checkers *(plural n)* (US) a game played with black and white counters on a squared board (draughts, UK).

check out *(n)* the place in a supermarket where you pay for your goods.

checkup *(n)* a medical examination to make sure that there is nothing wrong with you.

cheek
1 *(n)* the side of your face below your eyes.
2 *(n)* rude and disrespectful behaviour or speech. cheeky *(adj)*, cheekily *(adv)*.

cheer cheering cheered
1 *(v)* to shout encouragement or approval. cheer *(n)*.
2 *(v)* If you cheer up, you begin to feel better.

cheerful *(adj)* happy and lively.
cheerfulness *(n)*, cheerfully *(adv)*.

cheese *(n)* a food made from the solid parts of milk after it has turned sour.

cheetah *(n)* a wild cat with a spotted coat that is found in Africa. Cheetahs can run faster than any other land animal.

cheetah

chef *(sheff)* *(n)* the chief cook in a restaurant.

chemical
1 *(n)* a substance used in chemistry. *Dangerous chemicals.*
2 *(adj)* to do with, or made by chemistry. *A chemical reaction. Chemical fertilizers.* chemically *(adv)*.

chemist
1 *(n)* a trained person who prepares and sells drugs and medicines.
2 *(n)* a shop where you can buy drugs and medicines.

chemistry *(n)* the scientific study of substances and the ways in which they react with each other.

cheque *(n)* a printed piece of paper on which someone writes to tell their bank to pay money from their account.

cherish cherishes cherishing cherished *(v)* to care for someone or something in a kind and loving way.

cherry cherries *(n)* a small red or black fruit with a stone at its centre. *See* **fruit**.

chess *(n)* a game for two people with sixteen pieces each, played on a black and white board.

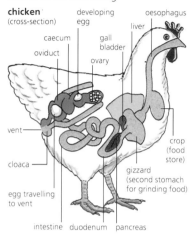

rook or castle
knight
king   bishop
queen
chessboard and pieces
pawn   chequered board

chest
1 *(n)* the front part of your body between your neck and waist.
2 *(n)* a large, strong box.

chestnut
1 *(n)* a large, reddish-brown nut that grows in a prickly case.
2 *(n)* a tree which produces chestnuts.
3 *(n)* a reddish-brown colour. chestnut *(adj)*.

chest of drawers chests of drawers *(n)* a piece of furniture with drawers, used for storing clothes.

chew chewing chewed *(v)* to crush food in your teeth.

chewing gum *(n)* a kind of sweet that you chew for a long time, but do not swallow.

chick *(n)* a very young bird, especially a very young hen.

chicken
1 *(n)* a hen, usually a young one.
2 *(n)* the meat from a young hen. *Roast chicken.*
3 *(n)* (slang) someone who is too scared to do something.

chicken (cross-section)
developing egg
oesophagus
liver
caecum
gall bladder
oviduct
ovary
vent
crop (food store)
cloaca
gizzard (second stomach for grinding food)
egg travelling to vent
intestine duodenum pancreas

chickenpox *(n)* a common disease that gives you red, itchy spots on your skin.

chief
1 *(n)* the leader of a group of people.
2 *(adj)* main, or most important. chiefly *(adv)*.

child children
1 *(n)* a young person who is not yet grown up.
2 *(n)* a son or daughter.

childhood *(n)* the time when you are a child. *Marcus had a happy childhood.*

childish *(adj)* immature and stupid. *Childish behaviour.* childishness *(n)*, childishly *(adv)*.

child minder *(n)* someone who looks after children while their parents are at work.

chill chilling chilled
1 *(v)* to make something cold.
2 *(n)* a feeling of slight coldness. *There is a chill in the air.* chilly *(adj)*.
3 *(n)* a cold. *Don't catch a chill.*
4 *(n)* a feeling of fear. chilling *(adj)*.

chime chiming chimed *(v)* When a bell or clock chimes, it makes a ringing sound. chime *(n)*.

chimney *(n)* a vertical pipe through which smoke escapes from a fire. *See* **building**.

chimpanzee *(n)* a large ape with dark fur, that comes from Africa. Chimpanzees can be very intelligent. *See* **ape**.

chin (n) the part of your face below your mouth.

china
1 (n) very thin, delicate pottery.
2 (n) cups, plates, and dishes made out of china. See **bowl**.

chink
1 (n) a narrow opening.
2 (n) a gentle, jingling sound.

chip chipping chipped
1 (v) to break a small piece off something by accident. **chip** (n).
2 (n) a long, thin piece of potato, cooked in oil.
3 If you have a **chip on your shoulder**, you feel angry because you think you have been treated unfairly.
4 (n) (US) a very thin, flat piece of potato cooked in oil (crisp, UK).
5 (n) a minute piece of silicon, with electronic circuits printed on it, used in computers and electronic equipment. *The magnified silicon chip shown here is small enough to fit on your fingernail.*

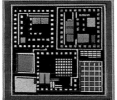
silicon chip
(magnified)

chiropractor (ky-ro-prak-tor) (n) someone who treats back pain and other illnesses by adjusting the spine.

chivalry (shiv-ul-ree)
1 (n) very polite and helpful behaviour, especially by a man towards a woman. **chivalrous** (adj).
2 (n) a way of behaving that a medieval knight was meant to practise.

chlorine (klor-een) (n) a strong-smelling gas which is added to water to kill harmful germs. **chlorinate** (v).

chlorofluorocarbon
(klor-oh-flor-oh-kar bon) (n) a gas containing chlorine and fluorine, that damages the earth's ozone layer.

chlorophyll (klor-oh-fill) (n) the green substance in plants that allows them to use the Sun's energy.

chocolate (n) a sweet food made from beans that grow on the tropical cacao tree. *The picture shows a cacao pod and some dried and roasted beans that can be ground up to make chocolate.* **chocolaty** (adj).

cacao pod and beans   raw beans in pulp
roasted beans

choice
1 (n) the thing or person that you have selected. *Jake was a good choice as team captain.*
2 (n) all the things that you can choose from. *This menu offers a very wide choice.*
3 (adj) of very good quality. *Choice fruit and vegetables.*

choir (kwire) (n) a group of people who sing together.

choke choking choked
1 (v) to struggle to breathe because something is blocking your breathing passages.
2 (v) to kill someone by squeezing their neck until they stop breathing.
3 (v) to block something. *Leaves had choked the stream.*
4 (n) the control in a car that reduces the flow of air to the engine so that the car starts more easily.

cholera (kol-er-ah) (n) a dangerous disease which causes severe sickness and diarrhoea.

cholesterol (kol-est-er-ol) (n) a substance found in foods such as butter and cheese, that is used to carry fats around your body.

choose choosing chose chosen
1 (v) to pick out one person or thing from several.
2 (v) If you **choose** to do something, you decide to do it.

chop chopping chopped
1 (v) to cut something with a knife or an axe. **chop** (n).
2 (n) a small piece of lamb or pork on a bone.
3 (v) If you **chop and change**, you keep changing your mind.

choppy choppier choppiest (adj)
When the sea is **choppy**, it is quite rough.

chopsticks (plural n) narrow sticks for eating food, used by people in Far Eastern countries.

choral (kor-al) (adj) sung by a choir. *Choral music.*

chord (kord)
1 (n) a combination of musical notes played at the same time. *See* **notation**.
2 (n) a straight line that joins two points on a curve. See **circle**.

chore (chaw) (n) a job that has to be done many times, such as washing dishes or cleaning.

choreographer (koh-ree-og-raf-er) (n) someone who arranges dance steps and movements for a ballet or show. **choreography** (n).

chorus (kor-uss) choruses chorusing chorused
1 (n) the part of a song that is repeated after each verse.
2 (n) a large group of people who sing or speak together.
3 (v) to say something all together.

Christ (n) the name given to Jesus, the man whom Christians believe is the son of God and the saviour. *This mosaic of Christ was made in the 12th century.*

Christ

christening (n) a Christian ceremony in which a person is accepted into the Christian church and is given a name. **christen** (v).

Christianity (n) the religion based on the life and teachings of Jesus Christ. Christians believe that Jesus is the son of God, and that they will live with God after they die if they believe in him and follow his teachings. **Christian** (n), **Christian** (adj).

Christmas Christmases (n) the Christian festival which celebrates the birth of Jesus Christ.

chromatography (n) the process of separating parts of a mixture by letting it travel through a material that absorbs each part at a different rate. *You can use chromatography to separate the different coloured chemicals in ink.*

chromosome (n) the part of a cell that carries the genes that give living things their special characteristics. You inherit your chromosomes from your parents.

chronic
1 (adj) (informal) very bad. **chronically** (adv).
2 (adj) If something is **chronic**, it does not get better for a long time. *Chronic bronchitis.* **chronically** (adv)

chronicle chronicling chronicled (v) to record historical events in a careful, detailed way. **chronicle** (n).

chronological (adj) arranged in the order in which events happened. **chronology** (n), **chronologically** (adv).

chrysalis (kriss-er-liss) chrysalises (n) a moth or butterfly at the stage of development between a caterpillar and an adult. A chrysalis is covered by a hard outer shell. See **caterpillar**.

chubby chubbier chubbiest (adj) slightly fat or plump.

chuck chucking chucked (v)
(informal) to throw something
carelessly.

chuckle chuckling chuckled (v)
to laugh quietly. **chuckle** (n).

chug chugging chugged (v)
to make a heavy, regular, thumping
sound while moving along. *The truck
chugged slowly up the hill.*

chunk (n) a thick piece of something.

church churches
1 (n) a building used by Christians for
worship.
2 (n) a group of Christians.

churn churning churned
1 (n) a large metal container for milk.
2 (n) a machine in which milk is made
into butter. *See* **butter**.
3 (v) to move around roughly.
The tractor churned through the mud.

chutney (n) a mixture of vegetables,
fruit, and spices, eaten with meat or
cheese.

cider (sy-der) (n) a fizzy alcoholic
drink made from apples.

cigar (n) a thick, brown roll of
tobacco which people smoke.

cigarette (n) a thin roll of tobacco,
covered with white paper, which
people smoke.

cinder (n) a small piece of wood or
coal that has been partly burned.

cinema (n) a large building where
people go to watch films.

circa (prep) the Latin word for about.
You can also write circa as "c."
*Geoffrey Chaucer was born circa
1340.*

circle circling circled
1 (n) a flat, perfectly round shape.
*The diagrams below show parts of a
circle and other geometric terms
connected with circles.* **circular** (adj).
2 (v) to draw or make a circle around
something. *Circle the correct answer.
The plane circled the airport before
coming in to land.*
3 (n) a group of people who all know
each other. *Dominic has a wide circle
of friends.*
4 (n) a curved, upper area of seating
in a theatre.

parts of a circle

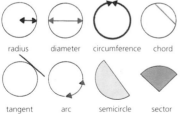

radius   diameter   circumference   chord

tangent   arc   semicircle   sector

circuit (sir-kit)
1 (n) a circular route. *A race circuit.*
2 (n) the complete path that an
electrical current can flow around.
3 **circuit diagram** (n) a diagram that
shows an electrical circuit, using
symbols recognized throughout the
world. *The picture shows some
symbols used in circuit diagrams.*

circuit symbols

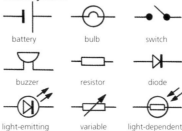

battery   bulb   switch

buzzer   resistor   diode

light-emitting   variable   light-dependent
diode   resistor   resistor

circulation
1 (n) the number of copies of a
newspaper, magazine, etc. that are
bought each day, week, etc.
2 (n) the movement of blood in blood
vessels around the body. *Blood travels
from the heart in arteries, and returns
to the heart in veins. It then travels to
the lungs to collect oxygen, before
returning to the
heart to be
pumped
round again.*

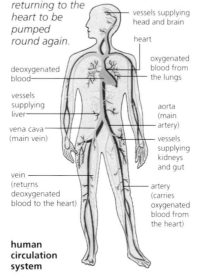

vessels supplying
head and brain

heart

oxygenated
blood from
the lungs

deoxygenated
blood

vessels
supplying
liver

aorta
(main
artery)

vena cava
(main vein)

vessels
supplying
kidneys
and gut

vein
(returns
deoxygenated
blood to the heart)

artery
(carries
oxygenated
blood from
the heart)

**human
circulation
system**

circumcision (n) the removal of the
foreskin at the end of a boy's or a
man's penis, usually for religious
reasons. **circumcise** (v).

circumference
1 (n) the outer edge of a circle.
See **circle**.
2 (n) the distance around the edge of
a circle.

circumspect (adj) cautious, or
careful. **circumspectly** (adv).

circumstance (n)
The **circumstances** of an event are
the things which affect the way that it
happens. *Laura took her exam under
very difficult circumstances.*

circus circuses (n) a travelling show
in which clowns, acrobats, and
animals perform.

cistern (n) a container for storing
water, especially one in the roof of a
house or attached to a toilet.

citizen
1 (n) a member of a particular country
who has the right to live there. *A
British citizen.*
2 (n) a person who lives in a particular
town or city. *A citizen of New York.*

citrus fruit (n) a sharp-tasting, juicy
fruit such as an orange, a lemon, or a
grapefruit.

city cities (n) a very large or
important town.

civic (adj) to do with a city or the
people who live in it. *Civic centre.*

civil
1 (adj) to do with the government or
people of a country, rather than its
army or religion. *The civil service.*
2 (adj) polite. *Please try to be civil to
your great aunt!* **civility** (n).
3 **civil rights** (plural n) the claims that
all members of a society have to equal
treatment and freedom.
4 **civil servant** (n) someone who
works in a government department,
such as a tax office.
5 **civil war** (n) a war between
different groups of people within the
same country.

civilian (n) someone who is not a
member of the armed forces.

civilization
1 (n) a highly developed and
organized society, especially one in
the past. *The ancient civilizations of
Greece and Rome.*
2 (n) an advanced stage of human
development, organization, and
culture.

civilize *or* **civilise** civilizing
civilized
1 (v) to improve a society, so that it is
better organized and its people have a
higher standard of living.
civilized (adj).
2 (v) to improve someone's manners
and education. **civilized** (adj).

CJD (n) a slow-developing, fatal
disease that affects humans,
damaging their brains. One type of
CJD is linked to the cattle disease BSE.
The initials CJD stand for Creutzfeldt-
Jakob disease.

---

*Some words that begin with a "c" sound are spelt with a "k".
Some words that begin with a "ci" sound are "sci", "psy", "si", or "scy".*

claim claiming claimed
1 *(v)* to say that something belongs to you, or that you have a right to have it. *My dad claims unemployment benefit.* claim *(n).*
2 *(v)* to say that something is true. *Ned claims he can beat me.* claim *(n).*

clam *(n)* a large shellfish with two tightly-closed shells.

clamber clambering clambered
(v) to climb up or over something with difficulty.

clammy clammier clammiest
(adj) unpleasantly damp.
Clammy hands.

clamour clamouring clamoured
(v) to demand something noisily.
The children all clamoured for food.
clamour *(n).*

clamp clamping clamped
1 *(n)* a tool for holding things firmly in place.
2 *(v)* to fasten something with a clamp.
3 *(v)* When you **clamp down** on something, you control it more firmly. *The police have clamped down on illegal parking.*

clan *(n)* a large group of related families, especially in Scotland.

clap clapping clapped
1 *(v)* to hit your hands together in order to show that you have enjoyed something. clap *(n).*
2 *(n)* a loud bang of thunder.

clarify clarifies clarifying clarified
(v) to make something clear.
clarification *(n).*

clarity *(n)* clearness. *Ellie writes with great clarity.*

clash clashes clashing clashed
1 *(v)* to fight or argue violently.
clash *(n).*
2 *(v)* If colours **clash**, they look unpleasant together.
3 *(v)* to make a loud, crashing noise.

clasp clasping clasped
1 *(v)* to hold on to something firmly and tightly. *Dawn clasped Gary's hand as they approached the cave.*
2 *(n)* a small fastener, for example on a purse.

class classes
1 *(n)* a group of people or things that are similar.
2 *(n)* a group of people who are taught together.
3 *(n)* a group of people in society.
The middle class.
4 *(n) (informal)* attractiveness and stylishness. *That bike has class!*
classy *(adj).*

classic
1 *(adj)* of very good quality and likely to remain popular for a long time.
A classic film.
2 *(adj)* typical. *A classic example of sixties style.*
3 **classics** *(plural n)* the languages and literature of ancient Greece and Rome.

classical
1 *(adj)* in the style of ancient Greece or Rome. *Classical architecture.*
2 *(adj)* traditional or accepted.
3 **classical music** *(n)* serious music that does not become out of date.

classify classifies classifying classified *(v)* to put things into groups according to their characteristics.
classification *(n).*

clatter clattering clattered *(v)*
When things **clatter**, they bang together noisily. clatter *(n).*

clause
1 *(n)* a group of words which contain a verb and form one part of a sentence. *The sentence "She ran away when she saw the alien" is made up of two clauses: "She ran away" and "when she saw the alien".*
2 *(n)* one section of a formal legal document.

claustrophobia
(klos-trof-oh-bee-yuh) (n) the fear of being in small, enclosed places.
claustrophobic *(adj).*

claw clawing clawed
1 *(n)* a hard, curved nail on the foot of an animal or a bird.
2 *(v)* If a person, animal, or bird **claws** something or someone they scratch at them with their nails or claws.

clay *(n)* a kind of earth that is baked to make bricks or pottery.

clean cleaning cleaned; cleaner cleanest
1 *(adj)* not dirty, or not messy.
cleanly *(adv).*
2 *(v)* to remove the dirt from something. cleaner *(n).*

cleanse cleansing cleansed *(v)* to make something clean or pure.

clear clearing cleared; clearer clearest
1 *(adj)* easy to see through.
clearly *(adv).*
2 *(adj)* easy to understand.
clearly *(adv).*
3 *(v)* to remove things that are covering or blocking a place. *Clear the table.* clear *(adj).*
4 *(v)* to jump over something without touching it. *The horse cleared all the jumps.* clearance *(n).*

5 *(v)* to declare that someone is not guilty of a crime.

clearing *(n)* an area of a forest or a wood that has been cleared of trees.

clef *(n)* a symbol written at the beginning of a line of music, to show the pitch of the notes. *Bass clef. Treble clef. See* **notation**.

cleft *(n)* a split, or a division.

clench clenches clenching clenched *(v)* to hold or squeeze something tightly.

clergy *(plural n)* priests in the Christian church.

clerical
1 *(adj)* **Clerical** work is general office work, for example, filing.
2 *(adj)* to do with the clergy.

clerk *(rhymes with dark) (n)* someone who keeps records in an office, a bank, or a law court.

clever cleverer cleverest
1 *(adj)* able to understand things or to do things quickly and easily.
cleverness *(n),* cleverly *(adv).*
2 *(adj)* intelligently and carefully thought out. *A clever plan.*
cleverly *(adv).*

cliché *(klee-shay) (n)* a phrase that is used so often that it no longer has very much meaning. *"Over the moon" is a cliché.*

click clicking clicked
1 *(v)* to make a short, sharp sound.
click *(n).*
2 *(v) (informal)* If an idea **clicks**, it suddenly becomes clear to you.

client *(n)* someone who uses the services of a professional person, such as a lawyer or an accountant.

cliff *(n)* a high, steep rock face on a coast.

cliffhanger *(n)* a story, film, etc. that is exciting because you do not know what is going to happen next.

climate
1 *(n)* the usual weather in a place.
A warm climate. climatic *(adj).*
2 *(n)* the general situation or mood at a particular time. *A positive economic climate.*

climax climaxes *(n)* the most exciting part of a story or an event, which usually happens near the end.

climb climbing climbed
1 *(v)* to move upwards. climber *(n).*
2 *(n)* an upwards movement or slope.
3 *(v)* to get on or off something using your hands to support and help you.

cling clinging clung *(v)* to hold on to something very tightly.

clinic (n) a room or building where people can go for specialist medical treatment or advice. *A health clinic.*

clip clipping clipped
1 (v) to trim something. *Clip the hedge.*
2 (v) to attach things together with a small fastener.
3 (n) a small metal or plastic fastener.
4 (n) a short piece of a film shown by itself.
5 (v) (old-fashioned) to hit someone. *Sid clipped me round the ear.* clip (n).

clipboard (n) a board with a clip at the top, for holding papers.

clique (rhymes with beak) (n) a small group of people who are very friendly with each other and do not easily accept others into their group. cliquey (adj).

cloak
1 (n) a loose coat with no sleeves, that you wrap around your shoulders and do up at the neck.
2 **cloakroom** (n) a room where you can hang coats, or a room with toilets and basins.

clobber clobbering clobbered
1 (v) (slang) to hit someone.
2 (n) (slang) possessions.

clock (n) an instrument that tells the time. *The picture shows the main working parts of a spring-driven clock. When you wind the clock, you tighten the mainspring which unwinds very slowly. Energy from the mainspring is transferred to the hour and minute hands by a series of wheels. The escape wheel keeps the clock ticking regularly.*

spring-driven clock
balance   hairspring
escape wheel
platform
contrate wheel
minute hand
minute hand square
intermediate wheel
great wheel
centre post
mainspring
barrel
hour hand
hour wheel

clockwise (adv) in the direction that the hands of a clock move. *We ran clockwise round the track.* clockwise (adj).

clockwork
1 (n) a mechanism that makes things like clocks and toys work when they are wound up with a key. clockwork (adj).
2 If things go **like clockwork**, there are no problems.

clod (n) a lump of earth or clay.

clog clogging clogged
1 (v) to block something. *Some leaves had clogged the drain.*
2 (n) a heavy, wooden shoe, often worn in the Netherlands.

Dutch clogs

clone cloning cloned (v) to grow a plant or animal from the cells of a parent plant or animal so that it is identical to the parent. clone (n).

close closing closed; closer closest
1 (rhymes with nose) (v) to shut something.
2 (rhymes with nose) (v) to end something. *The enquiry is closed.* close (n).
3 (rhymes with dose) (adv) near. *Stay close to me!* close (adj).
4 (rhymes with dose) (adj) careful. *Keep a close watch on the children.* closely (adv).
5 (rhymes with dose) (adj) When the weather is **close**, it is very hot and humid.

closed-circuit television (n) a television system that shows things happening nearby. It is often used to watch shoppers or people in banks.

closet (n) (US) a piece of furniture or a small room, used for storing things, especially clothes (wardrobe, UK).

close-up (n) a very detailed view of something, especially a photograph taken from close to a person or thing. close-up (adj).

clot clotting clotted
1 (v) When a liquid, such as blood, **clots**, it becomes thicker and forms lumps. clot (n).
2 (n) (informal) a stupid person.

cloth
1 (n) material made from wool, cotton, etc.
2 (n) a small piece of material used for cleaning.

clothes (plural n) things that you wear, for example, shirts and trousers. clothe (v).

cloud clouding clouded
1 (n) a white or grey mass of water drops or ice crystals suspended in the air. *The picture shows different types of clouds and their approximate levels in the sky.* cloudy (adj).
2 (n) a mass of smoke or dust. cloudy (adj).
3 (v) If something **clouds over**, it becomes less easy to see through.

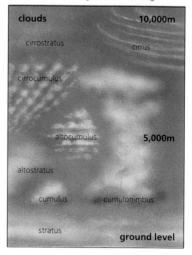

clouds   10,000m
cirrostratus
cirrus
cirrocumulus
altocumulus   5,000m
altostratus
cumulus
cumulonimbus
stratus
ground level

clover (n) a small plant with pink or white flowers, and leaves divided into three parts. *Four-leaved clovers are rare and are believed to be lucky.*

clown clowning clowned
1 (n) an entertainer who wears funny clothes, has a painted face, and tries to make people laugh.
2 (n) someone who does silly or foolish things.
3 (v) to do silly things in order to make people laugh. *Antonio is always clowning around.*

club
1 (n) a group of people who meet regularly to enjoy a common interest.
2 (n) a stick with a metal or wooden head used in the game of golf. See **golf**.
3 (n) a thick, heavy stick used as a weapon. club (v).
4 **clubs** (plural n) one of the four suits in a pack of cards, with a black three-leafed symbol.

clue (n) something that helps you to find an answer to a question or a mystery.

clump clumping clumped
1 (n) a group of trees or other plants growing together.
2 (v) to walk slowly, with clumsy, noisy footsteps. *Edwin clumped up the stairs and woke everyone up.*

clumsy clumsier clumsiest *(adj)* careless and awkward in the way that you move or behave. **clumsiness** *(n)*, **clumsily** *(adv)*.

cluster clustering clustered *(v)* to stand or grow close together. *The flowers clustered around the tree.* cluster *(n)*.

clutch clutches clutching clutched
1 *(v)* to hold on to something tightly.
2 *(n)* the pedal of a car or motorcycle that you press to change gear.
3 *(n)* a number of eggs laid by a hen.

clutter cluttering cluttered *(v)* to fill up a place and make it messy. clutter *(n)*.

co. *short for* **company**.

coach coaches coaching coached
1 *(n)* a bus used for long journeys.
2 *(n)* a large carriage pulled by horses
See **stagecoach**.
3 *(v)* to train someone in a subject or sport. **coach** *(n)*.

coal
1 *(n)* a black rock formed from the remains of ancient plants. Coal is mined from under the ground and burned as a fuel.
2 coals *(plural n)* small pieces of burning coal.

coalfield *(n)* an area where there is coal under the ground and where coal is mined.

coalition *(ko-al-ish-un) (n)* When two or more groups form a **coalition**, they join together for a common purpose.

coarse coarser coarsest
1 *(adj)* If something is **coarse**, it has a rough texture or surface. **coarseness** *(n)*, **coarsely** *(adv)*.
2 *(adj)* If a person is **coarse**, they are rude and have bad manners. **coarseness** *(n)*, **coarsely** *(adv)*.

coast coasting coasted
1 *(n)* the land that is next to the sea. **coastal** *(adj)*.
2 *(v)* to move along in a car or other vehicle without using any power.
3 *(v)* to make progress without much effort. *Lot coasted through his exams.*

coastguard *(n)* someone who watches the sea for ships in danger and who looks out for smugglers.

coat coating coated
1 *(n)* a piece of clothing that you wear over other clothes to keep you warm.
2 *(n)* an animal's fur or wool.
3 *(v)* to cover a surface with a thin layer of something. **coat** *(n)*.

coating *(n)* a covering of something. *The cake had a coating of chocolate*

coat of arms coats of arms *(n)* a design in the shape of a shield that is used as the special sign of a family, a city, or an organization.

crest
mantling
crown
helmet
supporter
arms
Royal coat of arms
DIEU ET · MON DROIT
motto

coax *(kokes)* coaxes coaxing coaxed *(v)* to persuade someone gently and patiently to do something.

cobbles *(plural n)* small, round stones, used in the past for making road surfaces. **cobbled** *(adj)*.

cobra *(n)* a snake with a poisonous bite. Cobras can spread the skin of their neck so that it looks like a hood.

cobweb *(n)* a very fine net of sticky threads, made by a spider to catch flies and other insects.

cocaine *(n)* a powerful drug used by doctors to prevent pain. Cocaine is strongly addictive and is used illegally by some people.

cock
1 *(n)* a fully-grown male chicken.
2 *(n)* a male bird.

cockpit *(n)* the area in the front of a plane where the pilot sits.

cockroach cockroaches *(n)* a large insect which lives in warm, dark places, especially where food is stored. *See* **insect**.

cocktail *(n)* a drink made by mixing several different kinds of drink together. Cocktails are usually alcoholic.

cocoa
1 *(n)* a brown powder made from the roasted beans of the cacao tree, and used to make chocolate.
2 *(n)* a hot, milky drink made with cocoa powder.

coconut *(n)* a very large nut with a hard, hairy shell and sweet, white flesh.

cocoon *(n)* a covering made from threads or mucus, produced by some animals to protect themselves or their eggs.

lynx spider (female)
cocoon (contains eggs)

cod cod *(n)* a fish that is found in Northern Europe and which has white flesh that you can eat.

code
1 *(n)* a system of words, letters, or numbers, used instead of ordinary words to send secret messages. **coded** *(adj)*.
2 *(n)* a set of numbers or letters used to give information briefly.
3 *(n)* a set of rules. *A safety code.*

coeducation *(n)* the system of teaching boys and girls together in the same school. **coeducational** *(adj)*.

coerce *(ko-erss)* coercing coerced *(v)* to force someone to do something. **coercion** *(n)*.

coffee
1 *(n)* a hot drink made from the roasted and ground beans of the coffee shrub.
2 *(n)* a brown powder made from coffee beans and used to make the drink of coffee.

coffin *(n)* a box which contains the body or ashes of a dead person.

cog
1 *(n)* one of the teeth on the edge of a wheel that turns machinery.
2 cog wheel *(n)* a wheel with teeth that turns machinery. *See* **gear**.

coherent *(ko-hear-unt) (adj)* clear and logical. *A coherent argument.*

coil coiling coiled
1 *(v)* to wind something round and round into a series of loops. *The sailor coiled the rope neatly.* coil *(n)*.
2 *(v)* to form loops. *The snake coiled around Perdita's leg.*

coin coining coined
1 *(n)* a piece of money in the form of a metal disc. coinage *(n)*.
2 *(v)* to invent a new word or a new meaning of a word. coinage *(n)*.

Ancient Chinese coins

coincide *(ko-in-side)* coinciding coincided *(v)* If two things **coincide**, they happen at the same time.

coincidence *(ko-in-sid-enss) (n)* a chance happening or meeting. **coincidental** *(adj)*, **coincidentally** *(adv)*.

colander *(n)* a bowl with holes in it, used for draining liquid off food, such as vegetables.

cold colder coldest
1 *(adj)* having a low temperature. cold *(n)*, coldness *(n)*.
2 *(adj)* unfriendly. coldness *(n)*, coldly *(adv)*.
3 *(n)* a common, mild illness that causes sneezing, a sore throat, and sometimes a slight fever.

Some words that begin with a "c" sound are spelt with a "k".

cold-blooded

1 *(adj)* Cold-blooded animals have body temperatures that change according to the temperature of their surroundings. *Reptiles and fish are cold-blooded.*
2 *(adj)* A cold-blooded act is done deliberately and cruelly.

collaborate collaborating

collaborated *(v)* to work with someone and help them to do something. **collaboration** *(n)*, **collaborator** *(n)*.

collage

(kol-arj) *(n)* a picture made by sticking different things on to a surface, for example sticking pieces of cloth on to paper.

collapse collapsing collapsed

1 *(v)* to fall down suddenly from weakness or illness. **collapse** *(n)*.
2 *(v)* to fail suddenly and completely. *The company collapsed after only six months.* **collapse** *(n)*.

collar collaring collared

1 *(n)* the part of a shirt, blouse, coat, etc. which fits round your neck and is usually folded down.
2 *(n)* a thin band of leather worn round the neck of a dog or a cat.
3 *(v)* *(informal)* to catch someone, because you want to talk to them.

colleague

(n) someone who works with you.

collect collecting collected

1 *(v)* to gather things together.
2 *(v)* to fetch someone or something from another place.

collection

1 *(n)* a group of things gathered over a long time. *A shell collection.*
2 *(n)* If you hold a **collection** for something, you take money for it.

college

(n) a place where students can continue to study after they have left school.

collide colliding collided

(v) to crash into something violently, often at high speed. **collision** *(n)*.

colliery collieries

(n) a coal mine.

colloquial

(kol-oh-kwee-al) *(adj)* Colloquial language is used in everyday conversation, but not usually in written English.

colon

1 *(n)* the punctuation mark (:) used to introduce a list of things.
2 *(n)* the part of your large intestine where remaining food is broken down by bacteria, and water removed from it.

colonel

(n) an army officer in command of a regiment of soldiers.

colony colonies

1 *(n)* a country that has been settled in by people from another country and is controlled by that country. **colonial** *(adj)*.
2 *(n)* a large group of insects that live together. *A colony of ants.*

colossal

(adj) extremely large.

colour colouring coloured

1 *(n)* When you say what **colour** something is, you say whether it is red, yellow, black, etc. **colourful** *(adj)*, **colourless** *(adj)*.
2 *(v)* to make something red, yellow, black, etc.
3 *(v)* to influence your opinion about something. *Mum's hatred of noise colours her view of parties.*
4 *(adj)* If you are colour blind, you are unable to see the difference between certain colours. *You may not be able to see the number in this pattern if you are colour blind.*

colour blindness test

colt

(n) a young male horse.

column

1 *(n)* a tall, upright pillar that helps to support a building or a statue. *The picture below shows three styles of Roman column.*
2 *(n)* a row of figures or words running down a page.
3 *(n)* a piece of writing by the same person, or on the same subject, that appears regularly in a newspaper or magazine. **columnist** *(n)*.

Roman columns

Doric   Ionic   Corinthian

coma

(n) a state of deep unconsciousness from which it is very hard to wake up.

comb combing combed

1 *(n)* a flat piece of metal or plastic with a row of teeth used for making you hair smooth and tidy.
2 *(v)* to use a comb to make your hair smooth and tidy.
3 *(v)* to search a place thoroughly.

combat combating combated

1 *(v)* to fight against something. *Regular brushing helps combat tooth decay.*
2 *(n)* fighting between people or armies. **combatant** *(n)*.

combine combining combined

(v) to join or mix two or more things together. **combination** *(n)*.

combustion

(n) the process of catching fire and burning. **combust** *(v)*.

come coming came come

1 *(v)* to move towards a place. *Louise came into the garden.*
2 *(v)* to arrive. *Barney was waiting for his friends to come.*
3 *(v)* If you **come from** a particular place, you were born in that place.
4 *(v)* If something **comes about**, it happens.
5 *(v)* If you **come across** something, you find it by chance.
6 *(v)* If you **come round**, you become conscious again.

comedian

(n) an entertainer who tells jokes and funny stories to make people laugh.

comedy comedies

1 *(n)* a funny play or film.
2 *(n)* anything that makes people laugh. *Merlin's first attempt at skating was a comedy.*

comet

(n) an object that travels around the Sun and leaves a trail of light behind it.

comfort comforting comforted

1 *(v)* to make someone feel less worried or upset. *We comforted the lost child.* **comforting** *(adj)*, **comfortingly** *(adv)*.
2 *(n)* the feeling of being relaxed and free from pain or worries.
3 *(n)* a luxury that makes your life more pleasant and enjoyable. *Home comforts.*

comfortable

1 *(adj)* If you are **comfortable**, you feel relaxed in your body or your mind. **comfortably** *(adv)*.
2 *(adj)* If something is **comfortable**, it allows you to relax and feel pleasure. *A comfortable chair.*

comic

1 *(n)* a magazine containing stories told with pictures.
2 *(n)* someone who tells jokes and funny stories.
3 *(adj)* funny or amusing. **comical** *(adj)*.

comma

(n) the punctuation mark (,) used for separating different parts of a sentence or different words in a list.

command commanding commanded

1 *(v)* to order someone to do something. **command** *(n)*.

2 *(v)* to have control over a group of people in the armed forces.
commander *(n)*.
3 *(n)* Your **command** of something is your knowledge of it and your skill in using it. *Alexia has a good command of Russian.*

commemorate commemorating commemorated *(v)* When you commemorate an event or the life of an important person, you do something special to remember them. **commemoration** *(n)*, **commemorative** *(adj)*.

commence commencing commenced *(v)* to begin something. **commencement** *(n)*.

commend commending commended *(v)* to say that someone has done something very well. *The mayor commended our courage.* **commendation** *(n)*, **commendable** *(adj)*.

comment commenting commented *(v)* If you **comment** on something, you give an explanation or an opinion about it. **comment** *(n)*

commentary commentaries
1 *(n)* a description and comments about an event. *Political commentary.* **commentator** *(n)*, **commentate** *(v)*.
2 *(n)* a description of an event as it is happening, often broadcast on television or radio. *A race commentary.* **commentator** *(n)*, **commentate** *(v)*.

commerce *(n)* the buying and selling of goods in order to make money.

commercial
1 *(adj)* to do with buying and selling goods. *Commercial activities.*
2 *(adj)* having profit as a main aim. *A commercial scheme.*
3 *(n)* a television or radio advertisement.

commercialized or **commercialised** *(adj)* If something is **commercialized**, it has been changed, usually for the worse, in order to make a profit. **commercialization** *(n)*.

commiserate commiserating commiserated *(v)* to share someone else's sadness or disappointment. *We commiserated with Aled over his bad luck.* **commiserations** *(plural n)*.

commit committing committed
1 *(v)* to do something wrong or illegal. *To commit murder.*
2 *(v)* If you **commit** yourself to something, you promise that you will do it or support it. **commitment** *(n)*, **committed** *(adj)*

committee *(n)* a group of people chosen to discuss things and make decisions for a larger group.

commodity commodities *(n)* a product that is bought and sold.

common commoner commonest
1 *(adj)* existing in large numbers.
2 *(adj)* happening often. *A common problem.*
3 *(adj)* ordinary and not special in any way.
4 *(adj)* shared by two or more people or things. *This feature is common to both cars.*
5 common sense *(n)* the ability to think and behave sensibly.
6 The Commons *(plural n)* the House of Commons, the lower house of the British Parliament, whose members are elected.

commonplace *(adj)* If something is commonplace, it happens frequently. *Traffic jams in city centres are commonplace events.*

Commonwealth
1 The Commonwealth *(n)* an association of countries all over the world that used to be ruled by Britain.
2 *(n)* a country made up of several self-governing states that are controlled by a central government. *The Commonwealth of Australia.*

commotion *(n)* a lot of noisy, excited activity.

communal *(adj)* shared by several people. *A communal bathroom.* **communally** *(adv)*.

commune *(n)* a group of people who live together and share things with each other.

communicate communicating communicated *(v)* to share information, ideas, or feelings with another person by talking, writing, etc. **communication** *(n)*, **communicative** *(adj)*.

Communion *(n)* a Christian service in which people eat bread and drink wine in memory of the death and resurrection of Jesus Christ.

communiqué *(kom-yoon-ee-kay) (n)* an official report or statement.

communism *(n)* a way of organizing a country so that all the land, houses, factories, etc. belong to the state and the profits are shared among everyone. **communist** *(n)*, **communist** *(adj)*.

community communities *(n)* a group of people who live in the same area or who have something in common with each other.

commuter *(n)* someone who travels to work each day, usually by car or train. **commute** *(v)*.

compact
1 *(kom-pakt) (adj)* cleverly designed to take up very little space.
2 *(kom-pakt) (n)* a small, flat case containing face powder and a mirror.

compact disc *(n)* a disc with music or information stored on it. *The picture inset below shows the thin metal layer inside the plastic disc, with its pattern of pits and flats, which is read by a laser beam as the disc rotates.*

compact disc

compact disc
(magnified view from below)

flat
pit
laser beam
aluminium layer

companion *(n)* someone whom you spend time with, either through friendship or by chance.

company companies
1 *(n)* a group of people who work together to produce or sell goods or services.
2 *(n)* a group of actors or dancers who work together.
3 *(n)* one or more guests. *We have company this weekend.*

comparative
1 *(adj)* judged against other similar things. *This year's play was a comparative success.* **comparatively** *(adv)*.
2 *(adj)* **Comparative** adjectives and adverbs are used when you compare two things or actions. *"Older" is the comparative of "old"; "more quickly" is the comparative of quickly.* **comparative** *(n)*.

compare comparing compared
1 *(v)* to judge one thing against another and notice similarities and differences. **comparison** *(n)*.
2 *(v)* to be as good as something or somebody else. *Our team compares with any in the area.*

compartment
1 *(n)* one of the small areas into which a railway carriage is divided.
2 *(n)* a separate part of a container, used for keeping certain things. *My purse has a special compartment for stamps.*

compass compasses
1 (n) an instrument for finding directions, with a magnetic needle that always points north. *You can use a compass like the one shown below to follow a route on a map.*
2 **compasses** (plural n) an instrument used for drawing circles, which has two legs connected by a flexible joint. See **geometry**.

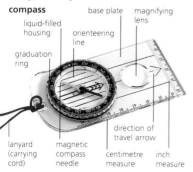

compass

base plate
magnifying lens
liquid-filled housing
orienteering line
graduation ring
direction of travel arrow
lanyard (carrying cord)
magnetic compass needle
centimetre measure
inch measure

compassion (n) a feeling of sympathy for people who are suffering. **compassionate** (adj), **compassionately** (adv).

compatible (adj) If people or objects are **compatible**, they can live together or be used together without difficulty. **compatibility** (n).

compel compelling compelled (v) to make someone do something by giving them orders or by using force.

compensate compensating compensated (v) to make up for something. *Nothing can compensate for my suffering.* **compensation** (n).

competent (adj) If you are **competent** at something, you have the skill or ability to do it well. **competence** (n), **competently** (adv).

competition
1 (n) an event in which two or more people try to do something as well as they can, to see who is the best. **competitor** (n), **compete** (v).
2 (n) a situation in which two or more people are trying to get the same thing. *There was a lot of competition for places at the school.* **compete** (v).

competitive
1 (adj) A **competitive** sport or game is one where the players try to win.
2 (adj) very eager to win.
3 (adj) If a shop offers **competitive** prices, its prices are at least as low as in most other shops.

compile compiling compiled (v) to write a book or a report by bringing together many different pieces of information. **compilation** (n).

complain complaining complained (v) to say that you are unhappy about something.

complaint
1 (n) a statement saying that you are unhappy about something.
2 (n) an illness. *A heart complaint.*

complete completing completed
1 (adj) If something is **complete**, it has all the parts that are needed or wanted. *A complete pack of cards.*
2 (v) to finish something. **completion** (n).
3 (adj) in every way. *The news was a complete surprise.* **completely** (adv).

complex complexes
1 (adj) very complicated. **complexity** (n).
2 (n) a set of strong feelings that you cannot control or forget about, and that causes problems for you. *Nathan has a complex about being short.*
3 (n) a group of buildings that are close together and are used for a particular purpose. *A leisure complex.*

complexion (n) the colour and look of the skin on your face.

complicated (adj) Something that is **complicated** contains lots of different parts or ideas and so is difficult to use or understand. **complication** (n), **complicate** (v).

compliment complimenting complimented (v) When you **compliment** someone, you tell them that you admire them or think that they have done something well. **compliment** (n).

complimentary
1 (adj) If someone is **complimentary** about a person or thing, they praise it. *Jason was complimentary about my new dress.*
2 (adj) free, or without cost. *Complimentary tickets.*

component (n) a part of a machine or system.

compose composing composed
1 (v) to write a piece of music, a poem, etc. **composer** (n).
2 (v) If something is **composed of** certain things, it is made from those things.

compost (n) a mixture of rotted plants that is added to soil to make it richer.

comprehension
1 (n) understanding. **comprehend** (v).
2 (n) a test in which you read or listen to a text and then answer questions about it, to show how well you have understood it.

comprehensive
1 (n) In Britain, a **comprehensive** is a secondary school where pupils of all abilities are taught together.
2 (adj) including everything that is necessary. *A comprehensive list.* **comprehensively** (adv).

compress compresses compressing compressed (v) to press or squeeze something so that it will fit into a small space. **compression** (n).

compromise compromising compromised
1 (v) to agree to accept something that is not exactly what you wanted. **compromise** (n).
2 (n) an agreement that is half way between two opposite views.

compulsory (adj) If something is **compulsory**, there is a law or rule that says you must do it.

computer (n) a machine that can store large amounts of information and do very quick and complicated calculations. **computing** (n).

computer

monitor screen
visual display unit (VDU)
central processing unit (CPU)
memory expansion card
connector
hard disk
floppy drive
power supply case
floppy disk
mouse button
mouse
number keys
letter keys

computer-aided design *(n)* plans and drawings made by giving instructions to a computer and displayed on a computer screen.

comrade
1 *(n)* *(old-fashioned)* a good friend. **comradeship** *(n)*.
2 *(n)* a companion in battle.
3 *(n)* a member of the same trade union or left-wing political group.

concave *(adj)* curved inwards, like the inside surface of a dish. See **lens**.

conceal concealing concealed *(v)* to hide something. **concealment** *(n)*.

concede conceding conceded *(v)* to admit something unwillingly. *Eventually, Natalie conceded that she was wrong.*

conceited *(adj)* If you are **conceited**, you are too proud of yourself and of what you can do. **conceit** *(n)*.

conceive conceiving conceived
1 *(v)* to form an idea in your mind. *Caspar conceived a cunning plan.*
2 *(v)* to become pregnant.

concentrate concentrating concentrated
1 *(v)* to focus your thoughts and attention on something. **concentration** *(n)*.
2 *(v)* to make a liquid thicker and stronger by removing water from it. **concentrate** *(n)*, **concentration** *(n)*, **concentrated** *(adj)*.

concentric *(adj)* Concentric circles all have their centre at the same point.

concept *(n)* a general idea or understanding of something. *Leo has a very vague concept of history.* **conceptual** *(adj)*.

conception
1 *(n)* a general idea that you have formed in your mind. *Do you have any conception of what it's like to be homeless?*
2 *(n)* the act of becoming pregnant.

concern concerning concerned
1 *(v)* to involve you, or to be of interest to you. *These plans concern you.* **concern** *(n)*.
2 *(v)* to be about a particular subject. *This project concerns local history.* **concerning** *(prep)*.

concerned *(adj)* If you are **concerned** about something, you are anxious and worried about it. **concern** *(n)*.

concert *(n)* a performance given by musicians or singers.

concerto concertos or concerti *(n)* a piece of music for one or more solo instruments playing with an orchestra.

concession
1 *(n)* an agreement to allow something that would not normally be permitted. *As a special concession, you can stay up late.*
2 *(n)* a reduction in price for particular types of people. *The theatre offers concessions to students.*

concise *(adj)* saying a lot in a few words. **concisely** *(adv)*.

conclude concluding concluded
1 *(v)* to decide that something is true because of the facts that you have. *I concluded that Bill must have stolen the jewels.* **conclusion** *(n)*.
2 *(v)* to finish or end something. **conclusion** *(n)*.

concoct concocting concocted
1 *(v)* to create something by mixing several different things together. **concoction** *(n)*.
2 *(v)* If you **concoct** an excuse, you invent it.

concrete
1 *(n)* a building material made from a mixture of sand, small stones, cement, and water. **concrete** *(v)*.
2 *(adj)* real, or definite. *The detectives need some concrete evidence.*

concussion *(n)* unconsciousness, dizziness, or sickness caused by a heavy blow to your head. **concussed** *(adj)*

condemn condemning condemned
1 *(v)* to say very strongly that you do not approve of something. *Mahatma Gandhi condemned all violence.* **condemnation** *(n)*.
2 *(v)* to force someone to suffer something unpleasant. *The murderer was condemned to death.*

condense condensing condensed
1 *(v)* When a gas **condenses**, it turns into a liquid, usually as a result of cooling. **condensation** *(n)*.
2 *(v)* to make a piece of writing shorter by taking out unnecessary parts.

condescending *(adj)* If you are **condescending**, you behave as though you are better or more important than other people. **condescension** *(n)*, **condescend** *(v)*.

condition conditioning conditioned
1 *(n)* the general state of a person, an animal, or a thing. *My dog is in good condition. The hostages suffered terrible living conditions.*
2 *(n)* a medical problem that continues over a long period of time. *A heart condition.*

3 *(n)* something that is needed before another thing can happen or be allowed. *One condition of having a bike is that you always lock it up.*
4 *(v)* to train someone to believe certain things or to behave in certain ways. **conditioning** *(n)*.

conditional *(adj)* depending on something else. *I have a conditional place on the course.* **conditionally** *(adv)*.

conditioner *(n)* a thick liquid that you rub into your hair after washing it, to make it strong and shiny.

condolence *(n)* an expression of sympathy for a person who is upset because a friend or relative has just died.

condom *(n)* a thin rubber covering that a man wears on his penis as a contraceptive.

condominium *(n)* *(US)* a block of flats or a housing estate in which each flat or house is owned by the person who lives in it, but the gardens, swimming pool, etc. are shared by all the occupants.

conduct conducting conducted
1 *(kon-dukt)* *(v)* to organize something and carry it out. *The police conducted the murder enquiry.*
2 *(kon-dukt)* *(v)* to stand in front of a group of musicians and direct their playing.
3 *(kon-dukt)* *(v)* If something **conducts** heat, electricity, or sound, it allows them to pass through it. *Copper conducts electricity.* **conduction** *(n)*.
4 *(kon-dukt)* *(n)* behaviour.

conductor
1 *(n)* someone who stands in front of a group of musicians and directs their playing.
2 *(n)* someone who collects bus fares.
3 *(n)* a substance that allows heat, electricity, or sound to travel through it. *Metal is a good conductor of heat.*

cone
1 *(n)* an object or shape with a round base and a point at the top. **conical** *(adj)*. See **shape**.
2 *(n)* the hard, woody fruit of a pine or fir tree.

confectionery *(n)* sweets and chocolates. **confectioner** *(n)*.

conference *(n)* a formal meeting for discussing ideas and opinions.

confess confesses confessing confessed *(v)* to admit that you have done something wrong. **confession** *(n)*.

confetti *(plural n)* small pieces of coloured paper that are thrown over the bride and groom after a wedding.

confide confiding confided *(v)* If you **confide in** someone, you tell them a secret because you can trust them not to tell anyone else.

confident
1 *(adj)* having a strong belief in your own abilities. *Ella is a confident swimmer.* confidence *(n)*, confidently *(adv)*.
2 *(adj)* certain that things will happen in the way you want. *I am confident that it will be sunny tomorrow.* confidence *(n)*, confidently *(adv)*.

confidential *(adj)* secret. confidentially *(adv)*.

confirm confirming confirmed
1 *(v)* to say that something is definitely true or will definitely happen. confirmation *(n)*.
2 *(v)* When someone is **confirmed**, they are accepted as a full member of the Christian church, in a special ceremony. confirmation *(n)*.

confiscate confiscating confiscated *(v)* to take something away from someone as a punishment or because that thing is not allowed. confiscation *(n)*.

conflict conflicting conflicted
1 *(kon-flikt)* *(n)* a serious disagreement.
2 *(kon-flikt)* *(n)* a war, or a period of fighting.
3 *(kon-flikt)* *(v)* When ideas or statements **conflict**, they are different. *Tom's ideas always conflict with mine.*

conform conforming conformed
1 *(v)* If you **conform**, you behave in the same way as everyone else, or in a way that is expected of you. conformist *(n)*, conformity *(n)*.
2 *(v)* If something **conforms** to a rule or law, it does what the rule or law requires. *All these toys conform to strict safety regulations.*

confront confronting confronted
1 *(v)* to meet or face someone in a threatening or accusing way. confrontation *(n)*.
2 *(v)* If a problem **confronts** you, you have to deal with it.

confuse confusing confused
1 *(v)* If someone or something **confuses** you, you do not understand them or know what to do. confusion *(n)*, confusing *(adj)*.
2 *(v)* to mistake one thing for another. *I confused Alex with his twin brother.* confusion *(n)*, confused *(adj)*.

congeal congealing congealed *(v)* When a liquid **congeals**, it becomes thick or solid.

congested *(adj)* blocked-up and not allowing movement. *Congested roads. Congested sinuses.* congestion *(n)*.

congratulate congratulating congratulated *(v)* to tell someone that you are pleased because something good has happened to them or they have done something well. congratulations *(plural n)*.

congregation *(n)* a group of people gathered together for worship.

Congress *(n)* the law-making body of the USA. **Congressional** *(adj)*.

conifer *(n)* an evergreen tree that produces cones. **coniferous** *(adj)*.

conjunction *(n)* a word that connects two parts of a sentence or phrase. *"And", "but", and "if" are all conjunctions. See page 3.*

conjurer or **conjuror** *(n)* someone who performs magic tricks to entertain people. conjuring *(n)*.

conker *(n)* a hard and shiny brown nut from the horse chestnut tree.

connect connecting connected *(v)* to join together two or more things, ideas, or places.

connection
1 *(n)* a link between objects or ideas.
2 *(n)* a train or bus arranged so that people getting off other trains or buses can use it to continue their journey.

connoisseur *(kon-er-ser)* *(n)* someone who knows a lot about a subject, and appreciates things that are of good quality.

conquer conquering conquered *(v)* to defeat an enemy and take control of them by force. conqueror *(n)*.

conscience *(kon-shenss)* *(n)* your knowledge of what is right and wrong, that makes you feel guilty when you have done something wrong.

conscientious
1 *(adj)* If you are **conscientious**, you make sure that you do things well and thoroughly. conscientiously *(adv)*.
2 **conscientious objector** *(n)* someone who refuses to fight in a war because they believe that it is wrong to fight and kill.

conscious
1 *(adj)* awake and able to see, hear, think, etc. consciousness *(n)*.
2 *(adj)* aware of something. *I slowly became conscious that everyone was looking at me.* consciousness *(n)*.
3 *(adj)* deliberate. *I've made a conscious effort to improve.* consciously *(adv)*.

consecutive *(adj)* happening or following one after the other. *Marcia was away for four consecutive days.* consecutively *(adv)*.

consent consenting consented *(v)* If you **consent** to something, you agree to it. consent *(n)*.

consequence *(n)* the result of an action. consequent *(adj)*, consequently *(adv)*.

conservation *(n)* the protection of nature, wildlife, and other valuable things, such as buildings and paintings. conservationist *(n)*.

conservative
1 *(adj)* moderate, cautious, and not extreme. *Marcus has a very conservative dress sense.* conservatively *(adv)*.
2 **Conservative Party** *(n)* one of the main political parties in Britain, promoting private enterprise and competition.

conservatory conservatories *(n)* a glass room attached to a house and used for growing plants.

consider considering considered
1 *(v)* to think about something carefully before deciding what to do.
2 *(v)* to believe that something is true. *Danny considers school to be a waste of time!*
3 *(v)* to take something into account. *We must consider Celia's feelings.*

considerable *(adj)* fairly large. *A considerable amount of money.* considerably *(adv)*.

considerate *(adj)* If you are **considerate**, you think about other people's needs and feelings. considerately *(adv)*.

consideration
1 *(n)* careful thought that you give to something before making a decision.
2 *(n)* a fact that needs to be taken into account before a decision can be made.
3 If you **show consideration**, you care about other people's needs and feelings. considerate *(adj)*.

considering *(conj)* taking into account certain things. *You got here very quickly, considering the weather.* considering *(prep)*.

consignment *(n)* a number of things that are delivered together.

consist consisting consisted *(v)* If something **consists** of different things, it is made up of those things.

consistent (adj) If you are consistent, you always behave in the same way or support the same ideas or principles. **consistency** (n), **consistently** (adv).

console consoling consoled
1 (kon-sole) (v) to cheer up or comfort someone. **consolation** (kon-soh-lay-shun) (n).
2 (kon-sole) (n) the control panel on a machine. A computer game console.

consonant (n) any of the letters in the alphabet except the five vowels.

conspicuous (adj) Something that is conspicuous stands out and can be seen easily. **conspicuously** (adv).

conspiracy conspiracies (n) a secret, illegal plan made by two or more people. **conspirator** (n), **conspire** (v), **conspiratorial** (adj).

constable (n) a British police officer of the lowest rank.

constant
1 (adj) happening all the time and never stopping. The traffic creates a constant noise. **constantly** (adv).
2 (adj) staying at the same rate or level all the time. A constant speed.
3 (adj) If someone is constant, they continue to support a person or an idea without ever changing their mind. **constancy** (n).

constellation (n) a group of stars that form a shape or pattern.

constipated (adj) If you are constipated, you find it hard to pass solids from your body frequently or easily. **constipation** (n).

constituency constituencies (n) an area of a country represented by a Member of Parliament.

constitution
1 (n) the system of laws in a country that states the rights of the people and the powers of the government. **constitutional** (adj).
2 (n) your general health and strength.

constraint (n) something that limits what you are able or allowed to do. **constrain** (v).

construct constructing constructed (v) to build or make something. **construction** (n).

constructive (adj) helpful and useful. Constructive criticism. **constructively** (adv).

consult consulting consulted
1 (v) to go to a person for advice. If you feel ill, you should consult a doctor. **consultation** (n).
2 (v) If you consult a book or a map, you use it to find information.

consultant
1 (n) a senior doctor with specialist knowledge in one area of medicine.
2 (n) a person with a lot of knowledge and experience of something, who gives professional advice to others.

consume consuming consumed
1 (v) to eat or drink something.
2 (v) to use something up. **consumption** (n).
3 (v) If a fire consumes something, it destroys it.

consumer (n) someone who buys goods, eats food, or uses services.

contact contacting contacted
1 When things are in contact, they touch each other.
2 If you are in contact with someone, you write or talk to them.
3 (v) to get in touch with someone.

contact lens contact lenses (n) a small plastic lens that fits closely over your eyeball to improve your eyesight.

contagious (adj) A contagious disease can be caught by touching someone or something already infected with it.

contain containing contained
1 (v) When an object contains something, it holds that thing inside itself or that thing forms a part of it. The chest contained the treasure. This book contains many stories. **container** (n)
2 (v) to keep an emotion under control. I tried to contain my laughter.

contaminated (adj) If something is contaminated, it has been made dirty or impure. Contaminated drinking water. **contamination** (n).

contemplate contemplating contemplated
1 (v) to think seriously about something. Matthew contemplated leaving college. **contemplation** (n).
2 (v) to look at something thoughtfully. Augusta contemplated the view. **contemplation** (n).

contemporary contemporaries
1 (adj) up-to-date, or modern.
2 (adj) If an event is contemporary with another event, they both happened at the same time. A contemporary account of the war.
3 (n) Your contemporaries are people of about the same age as you.

contempt (n) total lack of respect. **contemptuous** (adj).

contend contending contended
1 (v) to compete. The two teams contended for the cup. **contender** (n).

2 (v) to try to deal with a difficulty. Lucy has had a lot to contend with since her parents split up.

content contenting contented
1 (adj) happy and satisfied. **contented** (adj), **contentedly** (adv).
2 (v) If you content yourself with something, you are satisfied with it.

contents (plural n) the things that are inside something or form part of something.

contest contesting contested
1 (kon-test) (n) a competition.
2 (kon-test) (v) to compete or fight for something. **contestant** (n).
3 (kon-test) (v) to claim that something is wrong. Tarquin contested the judges' decision.

context
1 (n) The context of a word or phrase is the writing around it which helps you to understand its meaning.
2 If you put an event or an action in context, you take into account all the things that affect it.

continent
1 (n) one of the seven large land masses of the Earth. **continental** (adj).
2 the Continent (n) the mainland of Europe. **continental** (adj).

continents

continual (adj) happening again and again. **continually** (adv).

continue continuing continued (v) to go on doing something. **continuation** (n)

continuous (adj) When something is continuous, it does not stop. A continuous line. **continuously** (adv).

contort contorting contorted (v) to twist something out of its usual shape. **contortion** (n), **contorted** (adj).

contour
1 (n) an outline.
2 (n) a line joining points of equal height on a map.

contraceptive (n) a device or drug that prevents a woman from becoming pregnant. **contraception** (n).

contract contracting contracted
1 (*kon-trakt*) (*v*) to become smaller.
2 (*kon-trakt*) (*n*) a legal agreement between people or companies, stating the terms on which one will work for the other or sell to the other.

contradict contradicting contradicted (*v*) to say the opposite of what someone else has said. **contradiction** (*n*).

contraption (*n*) a strange and complicated-looking machine.

contrary
1 (*kon-trurry*) (*adj*) opposite.
2 (*kon-trair-ee*) (*adj*) deliberately awkward and difficult.

contrast contrasting contrasted
1 (*kon-trast*) (*v*) to be very different from something else. *Claude's views contrast strongly with mine.*
contrast (*kon-trast*) (*n*).
2 (*kon-trast*) (*v*) to identify the difference between things.

contribute contributing contributed
1 (*v*) to give help or money to a person or an organization. **contribution** (*n*), **contributor** (*n*).
2 (*v*) to write for a magazine or newspaper. **contribution** (*n*), **contributor** (*n*).

control controlling controlled
1 (*v*) to make something or someone do what you want. **control** (*n*).
2 (*plural n*) The **controls** of a machine are the levers and switches which make it work.

controversial (*adj*) If something is controversial, it causes a lot of argument. **controversy** (*n*).

convalescence (*n*) a time during which someone recovers from an illness. **convalesce** (*v*), **convalescent** (*adj*).

convection (*n*) the movement of heat through liquids and gases. *The diagram shows how convection currents are created when a liquid is heated.*

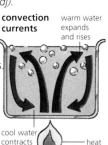
convection currents
warm water expands and rises
cool water contracts and falls — heat

convenience
1 (*n*) something which is useful and easy to use. *This house has been fitted with modern conveniences.*
2 **convenience foods** (*plural n*) foods that are quick and easy to prepare, such as frozen meals.

3 **public conveniences** (*plural n*) public toilets.

convenient (*adj*) If something is convenient, it is useful or easy to use. **conveniently** (*adv*).

convent
1 (*n*) a building where nuns live and work.
2 (*n*) a school for girls, run by nuns.

conventional (*adj*) A conventional person does things in a traditional or accepted way. **conventionally** (*adv*).

conversation (*n*) If you hold a conversation with someone, you talk with them for a while. **converse** (*v*).

convert converting converted (*v*) to make something into something else. *We've converted our loft into a bedroom.* **conversion** (*n*).

convex (*adj*) curving outwards, like the side of a ball. *See* **lens**.

conveyor belt (*n*) a moving belt that carries objects in a factory.

convict convicting convicted
1 (*kon-vikt*) (*v*) to prove that someone is guilty of a crime.
2 (*kon-vikt*) (*n*) someone who is in prison because they have committed a crime.

conviction
1 (*n*) a strong belief in something.
2 (*n*) If you have a **conviction** for a crime, you have been found guilty of committing it.

convince convincing convinced (*v*) If you convince somebody, you make them believe you. **convincing** (*adj*), **convincingly** (*adv*).

convoy (*n*) a group of trucks or other vehicles travelling together.

cook cooking cooked
1 (*v*) to prepare and heat food for a meal. **cooking** (*n*).
2 (*n*) someone whose job is to prepare food.

cookie
1 (*n*) (US) a small, flat cake, which has been baked until it is hard (biscuit, UK).
2 (*n*) a piece of information left on your computer after you have been using a Web page. Cookies are usually used to store information about the choices you have made on a Web page.

cool cooling cooled; cooler coolest
1 (*adj*) rather cold. **coolness** (*n*).
2 (*v*) to lower the temperature of something.
3 (*adj*) unfriendly and distant. **coolly** (*adv*).
4 (*adj*) (*informal*) fashionable.

co-operate co-operating co-operated (*v*) to work together. **co-operation** (*n*).

co-operative (*adj*) If you are co-operative, you work well with other people. **co-operativeness** (*n*).

co-ordinate co-ordinating co-ordinated
1 (*v*) to organize activities or people so that they all work together. **co-ordination** (*n*), **co-ordinator** (*n*).
2 (*n*) a number used to show the position of a point on a line or map.

co-ordinated
1 (*adj*) If you are **well co-ordinated**, you have good control over how you move your arms and legs.
2 (*adj*) Co-ordinated clothes go well together.

cope coping coped (*v*) to deal with something successfully.

copper
1 (*n*) a reddish-brown metal. *See* **mineral**.
2 (*n*) a reddish-brown colour. **copper** (*adj*), **coppery** (*adj*).

copy copies copying copied
1 (*v*) to do the same as someone else.
2 (*n*) A **copy** is made to look or sound exactly the same as something else.
3 (*v*) to make a copy of something.

copyright (*n*) If someone owns the copyright on a book, song, etc. people must ask for their permission before they copy or perform them.

coral (*singular n*) sea creatures, closely related to sea anemones, whose skeletons remain after they die. Coral can be hard or soft. *The picture shows two kinds of soft coral.*

coral   sea fan
brain coral

cord (*n*) a length of string or rope.

cordial
1 (*n*) a sweet, fruit drink. *Lime cordial.*
2 (*adj*) friendly. **cordially** (*adv*).

cordon (*n*) a line of people or objects used to control crowds. *A police cordon blocked the street.*

core (*n*) the centre of something, such as the Earth or an apple.

cork (*n*) soft bark used as a stopper in bottles or to make mats, tiles, etc.

corkscrew
1 (*n*) a tool used for pulling corks out of bottles.
2 (*adj*) spiralling, or turning in circles. *Corkscrew curls.*

Some words that begin with a "c" sound are spelt with a "k".

corn
1 *(n)* the grain of crops such as wheat or barley.
2 *(n)* a small patch of hard skin on your foot.
3 *(n)* (US) See **corn on the cob**, **sweetcorn**.

corner cornering cornered
1 *(n)* the place where two sides of something meet. *A square has four corners.*
2 *(v)* to get a person or animal into a situation where they are trapped.

cornet
1 *(n)* a brass musical instrument like a trumpet. *See* **brass**.
2 *(n)* a cone-shaped wafer with a scoop of ice-cream on top.

corn on the cob *(n)* a stalk of juicy, yellow seeds eaten as a vegetable. *See* **vegetable**.

coronary coronaries
1 *(adj)* to do with the heart.
2 *(n)* a heart attack.

coronation *(n)* the ceremony when a king or queen is crowned.

coroner *(n)* If someone dies suddenly or in an unnatural way, a coroner investigates their death.

corporal *(n)* a soldier of fairly low rank.

corporal punishment *(n)* physical punishment, such as beating.

corporation *(n)* a group of people who work together to run a company or town council.

corpse *(n)* a dead body.

corpuscle *(kor-puss-ul) (n)* a red or white blood cell. *See* **blood**.

correct correcting corrected
1 *(adj)* true, or right. **correctly** *(adv)*.
2 *(v)* to make something right. **correction** *(n)*.

correspond corresponding corresponded
1 *(v)* If two things correspond, they match in some way. **correspondence** *(n)*.
2 *(v)* When you correspond with someone, you write letters to each other. **correspondence** *(n)*.

correspondent
1 *(n)* someone who writes letters.
2 *(n)* someone who reports for television, radio, or newspapers about a special subject or place.

corridor *(n)* a long passage in a building or train.

corrode corroding corroded *(v)* to eat away at something. *Water corrodes metal and makes it rust.* **corrosion** *(n)*, **corrosive** *(adj)*.

corrugated *(adj)* ridged, or rippled. *Corrugated iron.*

corrupt corrupting corrupted
1 *(v)* to make someone bad or dishonest. **corrupt** *(adj)*,
2 *(adj)* If computer data is corrupt, it contains errors which make it useless. **corrupt** *(v)*.

cosmetic
1 cosmetics *(plural n)* beauty products such as lipstick or mascara.
2 *(adj)* changing the way that a person or a thing looks. *Cosmetic surgery.*

cosmic *(adj)* to do with the universe. *Cosmic laws.* **cosmically** *(adv)*.

cosmopolitan *(adj)* If you are cosmopolitan, you feel at home in more than one country.

cosmos *(n)* the universe.

cost costing cost
1 *(v)* to have a certain price. *How much does this cost?* cost *(n)*
2 *(v)* to make someone give up or lose something. *The battle cost many lives.* cost *(n)*.

co-star *(n)* an actor who appears in a film with another actor of equal importance. **co-star** *(v)*.

costly costlier costliest *(adj)* expensive. *Costly gifts.*

costume
1 *(n)* clothes worn by actors.
2 *(n)* clothes worn by people at a particular time in history. *The picture shows a selection of European costume from the last five centuries.*

European costume

1450s 1550s 1630s 1750s 1850s

cosy cosier cosiest *(adj)* comfortable, or snug. *The house was small but cosy.* **cosiness** *(n)*, **cosily** *(adv)*.

cot *(n)* a small bed for a baby, with high sides.

cottage *(n)* a small house, usually in the country. *See* **thatch**.

cottage cheese *(n)* cheese made from curdled skimmed milk.

cotton
1 *(n)* soft, thin material made from the cotton plant and used to make clothes. cotton *(adj)*.
2 *(n)* thread used for sewing.

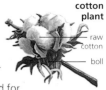
cotton plant
raw cotton
boll

cotton wool *(n)* soft, raw cotton which you use to put cream on your skin.

couch couches
1 *(n)* a long, soft seat with arms and a back, and room for two or more people.
2 couch potato *(n)* (slang) someone who spends most of their time watching television rather than being active.

cough *(koff)* coughing coughed
1 *(v)* to make a sudden, harsh noise as you force air out of your lungs. cough *(n)*.
2 *(n)* an illness that makes you cough.

council *(n)* a group of people chosen to look after the interests of a town, county, or organization.

council tax *(n)* a British tax that pays for local services.

counsel counselling counselled *(v)* to listen to people's problems and give advice. **counselling** *(n)*, **counsellor** *(n)*.

count counting counted
1 *(v)* to say numbers in order.
2 *(v)* to work out how many there are of something. *I counted the planes as they took off.*
3 *(v)* If you can count on something or someone, you can rely on them.

Some words that begin with a "c" sound are spelt with a "k".

counter
1 (n) a small, flat, round playing piece used in some board games.
2 (n) a long, flat surface.
A shop counter.

counteract counteracting counteracted (v) to act against something so that it is less effective. *You should take some exercise to counteract the effects of overeating.*

counterfeit (n) a fake that has been made to look like the real thing.

countless (adj) so many that you cannot count them.

country countries
1 (n) a part of the world with its own borders and government.
2 (n) undeveloped land away from towns or cities. **country** (adj).

countryside (n) undeveloped land away from towns or cities.

county counties (n) an area in some countries, such as Britain, with its own local government.

couple
1 (n) two of something.
2 (n) two people. *A married couple.*

coupon
1 (n) a small piece of paper which gives you a discount on something.
2 (n) a small form which you fill in to get information about something.

courage (n) bravery, or fearlessness. **courageous** (adj), **courageously** (adv).

courgette (kor-jhet) (n) a green, fleshy vegetable like a small marrow. *See* **vegetable**.

courier (koo-ree-er)
1 (n) someone who carries messages or parcels for somebody else.
2 (n) someone who looks after a group of people on holiday.

course
1 (n) a series of lessons.
2 (n) a part of a meal.
3 (n) a piece of ground where a sport is played. *A golf course.*

court
1 (n) a place where legal cases are heard.
2 (n) a place where games such as tennis or squash are played.
3 (n) a place where a king or queen meets visitors and advisors.

courteous (kur-tee-us) (adj) polite and respectful. **courtesy** (n), **courteously** (adv).

courtship
1 (n) attempts by an animal to attract a mate.
2 (n) (old-fashioned) attempts by a man to persuade a woman to become his wife.

cousin (n) Your cousin is the child of your uncle or aunt.

cover covering covered
1 (v) to put something over something else. *Cover the table with a cloth.* **cover** (n).
2 (v) to teach or study something thoroughly. *Have you covered that topic?* **coverage** (n).
3 (v) to travel a certain distance. *We covered twenty miles before nightfall.*
4 (v) to include or provide for. *Does your insurance cover storm damage?*

cow
1 (n) an adult female farm animal that produces milk. *See* **cud**.
2 (n) an adult female seal or whale.

coward (n) someone who is easily scared and keeps away from frightening situations. **cowardice** (n), **cowardly** (adj).

cowboy (n) a man who rears cattle, especially in the USA. *See* **rodeo**.

cox coxes (n) someone who steers a rowing boat and gives orders to its crew. **cox** (v).

crab (n) a creature with a hard shell, eight legs, and two pincers.

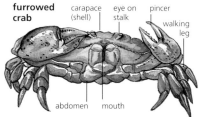

furrowed crab | carapace (shell) | eye on stalk | pincer | walking leg | abdomen | mouth

crack cracking cracked
1 (v) to break or split, often with a loud, sharp noise. **crack** (n).
2 (n) (slang) a form of the drug cocaine.

3 (v) to find the answer to something. *At last, we cracked the problem.*
4 (informal) When you **have a crack at something,** you try to do it.

cracker
1 (n) a thin, plain biscuit, usually eaten with cheese.
2 (n) a paper-covered tube that contains presents, and bangs when you pull it apart.

crackle crackling crackled (v) to make a noise like lots of small bangs. *The dry leaves crackled.*

cradle cradling cradled
1 (n) a wooden bed for a young baby.
2 (v) to hold something or someone in your arms very gently. *Rachel cradled the kitten in her arms.*
3 (n) a protective frame. *A window-cleaning cradle.*

craft
1 (n) work or a hobby where you make things with your hands. *Woodwork, pottery, and needlework are all crafts.*
2 (n) a vehicle, such as a boat or plane.

craftsman craftsmen (n) someone skilled at making things with their hands. **craftsmanship** (n).

crafty craftier craftiest (adj) A **crafty** person is clever at tricking other people. **craftily** (adv).

crag (n) a steep, sharp rock. **craggy** (adj).

cram cramming crammed (v) to fit things into a small space. *I crammed all my clothes into a backpack.*

cramp cramping cramped.
1 (n) pain caused by a muscle tightening suddenly.
2 (v) (informal) If someone or something **cramps your style,** they do not allow you to express yourself freely.

cramped (adj) If a place is **cramped,** there is not enough room in it for everyone or everything.

crane craning craned
1 (n) a machine used for lifting heavy objects.
2 (n) a large wading bird.
3 (v) to stretch your neck so you can see better.

trolley-jib tower crane

trolley travel gear
trolley
hoisting rope
trolley cable
operator's cab
hoisting block
main jib
slewing gear (turns cab and jibs)
hook
hoist cable
load
latticed metal structure
tower mast
counter-jib
concrete counterweight
hoisting gear

crank cranking cranked
1 (n) a bent rod used for winding or lifting something. *See* **bicycle**.
2 (v) to start something, such as a car, by turning a crank.
3 (n) (informal) someone with strange ideas. *A health food crank.*

crash crashes crashing crashed
1 (v) to make a loud noise like thunder.
2 (n) an accident in which a vehicle hits something at high speed. crash (v).
3 (v) When a computer system or program **crashes**, it fails completely.

crate (n) a large, usually wooden box. *A crate of oranges.*

crater
1 (n) a large hole in the ground, caused by something, like a bomb or a meteorite, falling on it.
2 (n) the mouth of a volcano. *See* **volcano**.

crave craving craved (v) to long for something desperately. craving (n).

crawl crawling crawled
1 (v) to move on your hands and knees.
2 (n) a style of swimming on your front in which you use your arms in turn while kicking your legs.

crayon crayoning crayoned
1 (n) a coloured pencil or wax stick used for drawing and colouring.
2 (v) to draw or colour with a crayon.

craze (n) a fashion that does not last very long.

crazy crazier craziest
1 (adj) mad, or foolish. craziness (n), crazily (adv).
2 (adj) (informal) very enthusiastic. *Josh is crazy about football.* craziness (n), crazily (adv).

creak creaking creaked (v) to make a squeaky, grating noise. creak (n), creaky (adj), creakily (adv).

cream
1 (n) a thick liquid taken from the top of the milk. You eat cream with food. creamy (adj).
2 (n) a thick, smooth substance like cream that you put on your skin. *Hand cream.*
3 (n) a yellowy-white colour, or the colour of cream. cream (adj).

crease creasing creased (v) to make lines or folds in something, especially material or paper. crease (n).

create creating created (v) to make or design something. creator (n).

creation (n) something that has been made.

creative (adj) If you are creative, you use your imagination and are good at thinking of new ideas. creativity (n), creatively (adv).

creature (n) an animal, bird, or insect.

crèche (rhymes with fresh) (n) a place where babies and young children can be looked after safely while their parents are busy.

credible (adj) If something or someone is credible, you can believe in them or trust them. credibility (n).

credit
1 If you buy something on credit, you pay for it later.
2 If you or your bank account are in credit, you have money.
3 (n) praise or acknowledgement. *No one gave me credit for my hard work.*
4 (plural n) The credits at the end of a film or television programme tell you who acted in it and made it.

creek
1 (n) a narrow inlet where the sea flows inland for a long way.
2 (n) a small stream.

creep creeping crept
1 (v) to move very slowly and quietly.
2 (v) to crawl along the ground.
3 (n) (slang) an unpleasant person.
4 (informal) If something or someone gives you the creeps, they are unpleasant and frightening. creepy (adj).

cremate cremating cremated (v) to burn a dead body. cremation (n), crematorium (n).

crescent
1 (n) a curved shape.
2 (n) a row of houses, built in a curve.

cress (n) a green plant with tiny leaves which you can eat in sandwiches and salads.

crest
1 (n) a comb or tuft of feathers on a bird's head. crested (adj).
2 (n) the top of something, such as a wave or a hill.
3 (n) a design that represents a noble family, a town, or an organization. *We have a dragon as our school crest.*
4 (n) part of a coat of arms. *See* **coat of arms**.

crevice (n) a crack or split in a rock.

crew (n) a team of people who work together, especially on a ship.

crib cribbing cribbed
1 (n) a small baby's bed.
2 (v) (informal) to copy someone else's work and pretend it is your own.

cricket
1 (n) a game played by two teams of eleven players, with two bats, a ball, and two sets of stumps. cricketer (n).
2 (n) a jumping insect similar to a grasshopper.

cricket equipment

wooden bail

cane handle with rubber grip

wooden stump

protective leg pad

cricket bat

willow blade

plastic box (protects genitals)

padded glove

leather cricket ball with cork centre

crime (n) something that is against the law.

criminal
1 (n) someone who commits a crime. criminally (adv).
2 (adj) to do with crime. *A criminal investigation.*

crimson (n) a deep red colour. crimson (adj).

cripple crippling crippled
1 (n) someone who is lame or disabled. crippled (adj).
2 (v) to stop someone or something from moving or working properly. *The company was crippled by strikes.*

crisis crises
1 (n) a time of danger and difficulty.
2 (n) a turning point or decision point.

crisp crisper crispest
1 (n) a very thin slice of fried potato with salt or other flavours added.
2 (adj) hard and easily broken. *A crisp piece of toast.* crispy (adj).
3 (adj) fresh, dry, and cool. *A crisp winter morning.* crisply (adv).

critical
1 (adj) If you are critical of someone or something, you find faults in them. critically (adv).
2 (adj) important, or serious. *A critical operation.* critically (adv).

criticize or **criticise** criticizing criticized
1 (v) to tell someone what they have done wrong. criticism (n).
2 (v) to point out the good and bad parts in a book, film, etc. critic (n), criticism (n).

croak croaking croaked
1 (v) When a frog **croaks**, it makes a deep, hoarse sound. **croak** (n).
2 (v) If you **croak**, you speak with a deep, hoarse voice. **croaky** (adj).

crochet (crow-shay) crocheting crocheted (v) to make a kind of lace from cotton thread or wool, using a hooked needle. **crochet** (n).

crockery (n) pottery or china that you use at home, such as plates, cups, and saucers.

crocodile
1 (n) a large, scaly reptile with short legs and strong jaws.
2 (n) a neat line of children going for a walk.

crocodile

crook
1 (n) a dishonest person, or a criminal.
2 (n) a long stick with a hook at one end, used by shepherds.
3 (adj) (Australian) (slang) sick, or ill.

crooked
1 (adj) bent. *A crooked path.*
2 (adj) (informal) dishonest.
A crooked deal.

crop cropping cropped
1 (n) a plant grown in large amounts, usually for food. *Potatoes and wheat are crops.*
2 (v) If an animal **crops** grass, it eats it.
3 (v) If something **crops up**, it happens unexpectedly.
4 (n) the pouch in a bird's gullet where food is stored and softened before being digested. *See* **chicken**.

cross crosses crossing crossed
1 (v) to go from one side to the other. *Columbus crossed the ocean.*
2 (adj) angry, or not pleased.
3 (n) The shape x is a **cross**. So is +.
4 (n) a wooden structure in the shape of a cross, on which criminals used to be crucified.
5 (v) If someone **crosses** you, they block your plans.

cross-country (adj)
A **cross-country** race is run through the countryside.

cross-examine cross-examining cross-examined (v) to question somebody very closely.
cross-examination (n).

crossroads (plural n) a place where one road crosses another.

cross-section
1 (n) a diagram which shows the inside of something, by cutting through it.
2 (n) A **cross-section** of the public is a selection of different types of people.

crossword (n) a puzzle in which you answer clues in order to fill blank spaces with words.

crouch crouches crouching crouched (v) When you **crouch**, you bend your legs and lower your body.

crow crowing crowed
1 (n) a large, black bird.
2 (v) When a cockerel **crows**, it makes a loud, crying noise.
3 (v) to boast about something.

crowd crowding crowded
1 (n) a lot of people packed together. **crowded** (adj).
2 (v) If you **crowd** someone, you do not allow them enough room.

crown
1 (n) a headdress worn by a king or queen, made from precious metal and jewels.
2 (n) the top of something. *At last, we reached the crown of the hill.*

crucial (adj) extremely important, or vital. **crucially** (adv).

crucify crucifies crucifying crucified (v) to put someone to death by fastening them to a cross and leaving them to die. **crucifixion** (n).

crude cruder crudest
1 (adj) rough and poorly made. **crudely** (adv).
2 (adj) A **crude** joke is rude and not very funny. **crudity** (n), **crudely** (adv).

cruel crueller cruellest (adj) A **cruel** person deliberately causes pain to others or is happy to see them suffer. **cruelty** (n), **cruelly** (adv).

cruise cruising cruised
1 (n) If you go on a **cruise**, you take a holiday on a ship which calls at several places.
2 (v) to travel smoothly and easily. *We cruised down the river.*

cruiser
1 (n) a motorboat with a cabin. *See* **boat**.
2 (n) a large warship.

crumb (n) a tiny piece of bread or cake.

crumble crumbling crumbled (v) to break into small pieces. **crumbly** (adj).

crumple crumpling crumpled
1 (v) If you **crumple up** a piece of paper, you screw it into a ball.
2 (v) to collapse. **crumpled** (adj).

crunch crunches crunching crunched (v) If you **crunch** something, you crush it noisily. *Ali crunched her carrot.* **crunchy** (adj).

crush crushes crushing crushed
1 (v) to squash something under a heavy weight.
2 (n) (slang) If you have a **crush** on someone, you like them very much, but usually only for a short time.

crust
1 (n) the crisp, outer case of bread or pastry. **crusty** (adj).
2 (n) The Earth's **crust** is its thin, outer layer of land and sea. *See* **Earth**.

crutch crutches (n) one of two, long sticks with padded tops, used to help support someone with injured legs.

cry cries crying cried
1 (v) to weep tears. **cry** (n).
2 (v) to shout out. **cry** (n).

crystal (n) a hard, glassy piece of rock with many sides. Crystals are formed when minerals boil, then cool and solidify. **crystallize** (v), **crystalline** (adj). *See* **quartz**.

cub (n) a young lion, wolf, bear, etc.

cube cubing cubed
1 (n) a three-dimensional shape with six square faces. *A dice is a cube.* **cubic** (adj). *See* **shape**.
2 (v) to multiply a number by itself twice. *3 cubed is 3 x 3 x 3.*

cubicle (n) a small, private area in a changing room or public toilet.

cucumber (n) a long, green vegetable with a watery centre. *See* **vegetable**.

cud (n) undigested food that cows bring up from the first part of their stomachs to chew again. *Grass is formed into cud balls in the rumen, returned to the mouth for chewing and passed into the reticulum where any stones are trapped. The pulp can then be digested.*

digestive system of a cow

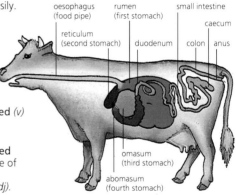

oesophagus (food pipe)
rumen (first stomach)
small intestine
caecum
reticulum (second stomach)
duodenum
colon
anus
omasum (third stomach)
abomasum (fourth stomach)

cuddle cuddling cuddled *(v)* to hold someone closely in your arms.

cue *(kyoo)*
1 *(n)* a long stick used to hit the ball in games like snooker and pool.
2 *(n)* the signal to say some lines or take an action in a play.

cuff
1 *(n)* the end part of a shirt or blouse that goes round your wrist.
2 If you speak **off the cuff**, you give a speech or an answer without preparing it first.

cul-de-sac *(n)* a road that is closed at one end.

culprit *(n)* someone who has done something wrong.

cult
1 *(n)* a religion with a small following.
2 *(n)* a strong, almost religious devotion to a person, an idea, or a way of life. *The hippie cult.*
3 *(n)* A **cult hero** is someone who is very popular and has many followers.

cultivate cultivating cultivated *(v)* If you **cultivate** land, you grow crops on it. **cultivation** *(n)*.

culture
1 *(n)* the arts, such as music, literature, painting, etc. **cultural** *(adj)*.
2 *(n)* The **culture** of a group of people is their way of life, ideas, and traditions.

cultured *(adj)* well-educated.

cunning *(adj)* A **cunning** person is clever at tricking people. **cunning** *(n)*, **cunningly** *(adv)*.

cupboard *(n)* a piece of furniture or a built-in space, used for storing things.

curator *(n)* the person in charge of a museum or art gallery.

curb curbing curbed *(v)* to control and hold back something. *I curbed my desire for another cake.*

curdle curdling curdled *(v)* When milk **curdles**, it goes sour and breaks up into curds and whey.

curds *(n)* the solid part of sour milk, often used to make cheese.

cure curing cured
1 *(v)* to make someone better when they have been ill.
2 *(n)* a drug or course of treatment that makes someone better.

curfew *(n)* a law which prevents people from travelling around freely, especially after dark.

curious
1 *(adj)* eager to find out. **curiosity** *(n)*, **curiously** *(adv)*.

2 *(adj)* strange. *A curious creature.* **curiosity** *(n)*, **curiously** *(adv)*.

curl curling curled
1 *(n)* a curved lock of hair. **curly** *(adj)*.
2 *(v)* to bend into a spiral shape.

currant *(n)* a dried grape.

currency *(n)* the money used in a country.

current
1 *(adj)* happening now. **currently** *(adv)*.
2 *(n)* the movement of water in a river or an ocean, or of electricity through a wire.

current affairs *(plural n)* important events that are happening now and are often discussed on television or in newspapers.

curriculum curricula *(n)* a programme of study for a school or college.

curry curries *(n)* a hot, spicy meal of meat or vegetables, served with rice.

curse cursing cursed
1 *(n)* an evil spell intended to harm someone.
2 *(v)* to swear.

cursor *(n)* a small indicator which shows your position on a computer screen.

curtains *(plural n)* pieces of material that are pulled across a window or a stage to cover it.

curtsy or **curtsey** curtsies curtsying curtsied *(v)* to bend slightly at the knee, with one leg crossed behind the other. Women and girls curtsy to show respect or to accept applause. **curtsy** *(n)*.

curve curving curved
1 *(v)* to bend or turn gently. *The path curved towards the cottage.*
2 *(n)* a bend in something. **curved** *(adj)*, **curvy** *(adj)*.

cushion cushioning cushioned
1 *(n)* a type of pillow used to make chairs or sofas more comfortable.
2 *(v)* to soften the effect of something. *The mattress cushioned her fall.*

custard *(n)* a sweet, yellow sauce made from milk, eggs, and sugar, or from milk, sugar, and custard powder.

custody
1 *(n)* If someone has **custody** of a child, they have the legal right to look after that child. **custodial** *(adj)*.
2 If someone is **taken into custody**, they are arrested by the police. **custodial** *(adj)*.

custom
1 *(n)* a tradition. **customary** *(adj)*.

2 *(n)* something that you do regularly. *A family custom.* **customary** *(adj)*.
3 **customs** *(n)* a checkpoint at country borders, ports, or airports where officials make sure that you are not carrying anything illegal.

customer *(n)* A shop's **customers** are the people who buy things from it.

customize or **customise** customizing customized *(v)* to change something to suit your needs and to make it look unusual. *Garth customized his car.*

cut cutting cut
1 *(v)* to use a sharp instrument, such as scissors or a knife, to divide, shorten, or shape something.
2 *(n)* a skin wound.
3 *(v)* to reduce something. *The shop is cutting its prices.* **cut** *(n)*
4 *(v)* If you are **cut off** from other people, you cannot contact them.
5 *(v)* If you **cut down** on something, like eating sweets, you do it less often.
6 *(v)* If a person or an organization **cuts back**, they reduce the amount of money that they spend. **cutback** *(n)*.

cute cuter cutest *(adj)* charming and attractive.

cutlery *(singular n)* knives, forks, and spoons.

cutting
1 *(n)* something cut off or cut out of something else. *A plant cutting. A newspaper cutting.*
2 *(adj)* If you make a **cutting** remark, you say something hurtful.

cycle *(sy-kul)* cycling cycled
1 *(n)* a series of events which are repeated over and over again. *The cycle of the seasons.*
2 *(n)* a bicycle. See **bicycle**.
3 *(v)* to ride a bicycle. **cyclist** *(n)*.

cyclone *(sy-klone)* *(n)* a very strong wind that blows in a spiral.

cygnet *(sig-net)* *(n)* a young swan. See **swan**.

cylinder *(sill-in-der)*
1 *(n)* a shape with circular ends and straight sides. *Most drink cans are cylinders.* **cylindrical** *(adj)*. See **shape**.
2 *(n)* a tube-shaped container in an engine. See **engine**.

cynical *(sin-ik-al)* *(adj)* Someone who is **cynical** always expects the worst to happen, and thinks that anything people do is for selfish reasons. **cynic** *(n)*, **cynicism** *(n)*, **cynically** *(adv)*.

cytoplasm *(n)* the contents of a cell, apart from its nucleus. See **cell**.

czar or **tsar** *(zar)* *(n)* a Russian king. *The last czar was murdered in 1917.*

Some words that begin with a "cy" sound are spelt "ci", "psy", "si", or "scy".

Dd

dab dabbing dabbed *(v)* to touch a surface gently with something soft. *Henrietta dabbed some ointment on the wound.* **dab** *(n)*.

dabble dabbling dabbled
1 *(v)* to dip something into water and splash it about. *Harvey dabbled his fingers in the stream.*
2 *(v)* If you **dabble** in something, you do it, but not very seriously or very well. **dabbler** *(n)*.

dad or **daddy** *(n)* an informal name for your father.

daffodil *(n)* a spring plant with yellow, bell-like flowers.

daft dafter daftest *(adj)* *(informal)* silly or foolish. *A daft idea.*

dagger
1 *(n)* a short, pointed knife, used as a weapon. *The dagger shown below was made by the ancient Sumerians around 4,000BC.*
2 If you **look daggers** at someone, you look at them in an angry way.

dagger and sheath

daily *(adj)* produced or happening every day. *A daily newspaper.*

dainty daintier daintiest *(adj)* small and delicate. **daintiness** *(n)*, **daintily** *(adj)*.

dairy dairies *(n)* a place where milk is bottled and milk products, such as cheese and yogurt, are made.

dais *(day-us)* *(n)* a raised platform at the end of a hall.

daisy daisies *(n)* a wild flower with white petals and a yellow centre.

dam *(n)* a strong barrier built across a river to hold back water. *See* **beaver**.

damage damaging damaged
1 *(v)* to harm something.
2 *(n)* the harm that something does. *Flood damage.* **damaging** *(adj)*.
3 **damages** *(plural n)* money given to someone by a law court to try to make up for an injury or loss that they have suffered.

damn *(dam)* damning damned
1 *(v)* to say that something or someone is very bad. *The critics damned the play.* **damning** *(adj)*.
2 *(v)* to curse someone or something. **damn!** *(interject)*.

damp damper dampest *(adj)* slightly wet, or moist. **dampness** *(n)*.

damsel *(n)* *(old-fashioned)* a young woman.

dance dancing danced
1 *(v)* to move in time to music. **dancer** *(n)*, **dancing** *(n)*.
2 *(n)* a ball, or a disco.
3 *(n)* the movements that go with a particular kind of music. *Country dance.*

dandruff *(n)* small, white flakes of dead skin found in some people's hair.

danger
1 *(n)* a situation that is not safe. *The children are in danger.*
2 *(n)* something or someone that is not safe. *George's bus is a danger on the road.* **dangerous** *(adj)*, **dangerously** *(adv)*.
3 **danger!** *(interject)* a warning word.

dangle dangling dangled *(v)* to swing or hang down. *Maurice dangled from the drainpipe.*

dank danker dankest *(adj)* unpleasantly wet or damp. *The cellar was cold and dank.*

dappled *(adj)* marked with spots, or with patches of light and dark. *A dappled pony.*

dare daring dared
1 *(v)* to challenge someone to do something. **dare** *(n)*.
2 *(v)* to be brave enough to do something. *Do you dare to dive into the river?* **daring** *(adj)*, **daringly** *(adv)*.

daredevil *(n)* someone who takes risks and does dangerous things.

dark darker darkest
1 *(adj)* without light. *A dark room.*
2 *(adj)* containing more black than white. *Dark blue.*
3 *(adj)* sunset. *I'm not allowed out after dark.*

darkroom *(n)* a room with special equipment and chemicals, where you can develop photographs.

darn darning darned *(v)* to mend a hole in a piece of clothing by sewing across it. **darning** *(n)*.

dart darting darted
1 *(n)* a pointed object that you throw in the game of darts.
2 *(v)* to move forward suddenly. *Stefan darted out into the traffic.*
3 **darts** *(singular n)* a game in which players score points by throwing darts at a board with numbers on it.

dart

flight   shaft   barrel   point

dash dashes dashing dashed
1 *(n)* a small line (–) used as a punctuation mark or in Morse code.
2 *(v)* to move quickly. *I dashed to the shop before it shut.*

data *(n)* information, or facts. *The scientists examined all the data.*

database *(n)* a store of information held on a computer.

date dating dated
1 *(n)* a particular day, month, or year.
2 *(n)* an appointment to meet someone, especially a girlfriend or boyfriend.
3 *(v)* to go out with your boyfriend or girlfriend regularly.
4 *(v)* If something **dates** from a certain time, it was made then.
5 *(n)* a sticky brown fruit with a long thin stone inside it.
6 If something is **dated** or **out of date**, it is no longer fashionable.
7 If something is **up to date**, it is modern.

daughter *(n)* Someone's **daughter** is their female child.

daunt daunting daunted *(v)* If something **daunts** you, it frightens and discourages you. *We were a little daunted by the long climb ahead.*

dawdle dawdling dawdled
1 *(v)* to walk slowly. *The boys dawdled to school.* **dawdler** *(n)*.
2 *(v)* to do something slowly. *Jemima dawdled over her breakfast.*

dawn dawning dawned
1 *(n)* sunrise, or the beginning of the day. **dawn** *(v)*.
2 *(n)* the start of something new. *The dawn of a new age.* **dawn** *(v)*.
3 *(v)* If something **dawns** on you, you begin to understand it.

day
1 *(n)* a 24-hour period, from midnight to midnight.
2 *(n)* the light part of the day.

daydream daydreaming daydreamed
1 *(n)* a dream that you have while you are awake.
2 *(v)* to let your mind wander. **daydreamer** *(n)*.

daze *(n)* If you are **in a daze**, you are stunned and unable to think clearly. **dazed** *(adj)*.

dazzle dazzling dazzled
1 *(v)* to blind someone for a short time with a bright light. **dazzling** *(adj)*.
2 *(v)* to amaze someone. *Tanya dazzled the audience with her playing.* **dazzling** *(adj)*.

dead *(adj)* no longer alive.

dead end
1 *(n)* a street that is closed to traffic at one end.
2 dead-end *(adj)* leading nowhere. *Pete had a dead-end job.*

deadline *(n)* a time by which a piece of work or a job must be finished.

deadlock *(n)* a situation where nothing can be agreed.

deadly deadlier deadliest *(adj)* capable of killing, or likely to kill.

deaf deafer deafest
1 *(adj)* If someone is **deaf**, they cannot hear anything, or they can hear very little. **deafness** *(n)*.
2 *(adj)* If you are **deaf to** something, you choose not to hear it.

deafening *(adj)* very loud. *A deafening crash.* **deafeningly** *(adv)*.

deal dealing dealt
1 *(v)* to do business. *Hugo deals in antiques.* **dealer** *(n)*.
2 *(n)* a business agreement.
3 *(v)* When you **deal with** something, you sort it out.
4 *(v)* to give out cards to people playing a game. **dealer** *(n)*.
5 *(v)* to cover a subject or an area. *Does that book deal with dogs?*

dear dearer dearest
1 *(adj)* highly valued or much loved. *A dear friend.* **dearly** *(adv)*.
2 *(adj)* You use the word **Dear** when you write to someone. *Dear Sir.*
3 *(n)* a kind or sweet person.
4 *(adj)* expensive.

death *(n)* the end of life.

deathly *(adj)* very pale, or very quiet. *His face went deathly white. There was a deathly hush.*

deathtrap *(n)* a place or a vehicle that is very dangerous.

debate debating debated
1 *(n)* a discussion between sides with different views, usually held in public.
2 *(v)* to consider or discuss something. *The family debated where to go on holiday.* **debatable** *(adj)*.

debit debiting debited
1 *(n)* money that you owe. *My account shows a small debit.*
2 *(v)* If a bank account is **debited** with a sum of money, that money is taken out of the account.

debris *(deb-ree) (n)* the scattered remains of something.

debt *(rhymes with pet)*
1 *(n)* an amount of money that you owe.
2 If you are **in debt** to someone, you owe them money or a favour. **debtor** *(n)*.

debug debugging debugged
1 *(v)* to remove the faults in a computer program.
2 *(v)* to remove secret listening devices from a place.

debut *(day-byoo) (n)* a first public appearance. *An acting debut.*

decade *(n)* a period of ten years.

decaffeinated *(adj)* If a drink, like coffee or tea, is **decaffeinated**, it has had most of its caffeine removed.

decapitate decapitating decapitated *(v)* to remove the head of a person or creature.

decathlon *(n)* a competition made up of ten athletic events.

decay decaying decayed *(v)* to rot or break up. **decay** *(n)*.

deceased *(adj)* dead.

deceive deceiving deceived *(v)* If someone **deceives** you, they trick you into believing something that is not true. **deceit** *(n)*, **deceitful** *(adj)*, **deceitfully** *(adv)*.

decent
1 *(adj)* good, or satisfactory. *Decent quality.* **decently** *(adv)*.
2 *(adj)* respectable and proper. *Decent behaviour.* **decency** *(n)*, **decently** *(adv)*.

deception *(n)* a trick that makes people believe something that is not true. **deceptive** *(adj)*, **deceptively** *(adv)*.

decibel *(n)* a unit for measuring the volume of sound.

decide deciding decided
1 *(v)* to make up your mind about something.
2 *(v)* to settle something. *The vote was decided by a show of hands.*

deciduous *(adj)* Trees that are **deciduous** shed their leaves every year.

decimal
1 *(adj)* A **decimal** system uses units of tens, hundreds, thousands, etc. *Decimal currency.*
2 decimal point *(n)* a dot separating whole numbers from tenths, hundredths, thousandths, etc. *The numbers 2.5, 3.75, and 4.624 all use decimal points.*
3 *(n)* a fraction, or a whole number and a fraction, written with a decimal point. *0.5, 6.37, and 82.54 are all decimals.*

decipher deciphering deciphered *(v)* to work out something that is written in code or is hard to understand. *I can't decipher Jim's handwriting.* **decipherable** *(adj)*.

decision *(n)* If you make a **decision**, you make up your mind about something.

decisive *(adj)* If you are **decisive**, you make choices quickly and easily. **decisively** *(adv)*.

deck
1 *(n)* the floor of a boat or ship. *See* **ship**.
2 *(n)* *(US)* a platform with railings on the outside of a building, usually high up (balcony, *UK*).

declare declaring declared
1 *(v)* to say something firmly. *Justin declared that he would never eat meat again.* **declaration** *(n)*.
2 *(v)* to announce something formally. *The government declared that the war was over.* **declaration** *(n)*.
3 *(v)* When you **declare** in a cricket match, you end your team's innings.

decline declining declined
1 *(v)* to turn something down, or to refuse something. *I'm afraid we must decline your invitation.*
2 *(v)* to get worse, or to get smaller. *Ludwig's health began to decline. The population of our village is declining.* **decline** *(n)*.

decode decoding decoded *(v)* to turn something that is written in code into ordinary language.

decompose decomposing decomposed *(v)* to rot, or to decay. **decomposition** *(n)*.

decongestant *(n)* a drug that unblocks your nose, chest, etc. when you have a cold. **decongestion** *(n)*.

decontaminate decontaminating decontaminated *(v)* to remove radioactive or other harmful substances from something or some place. **decontamination** *(n)*.

decorate decorating decorated
1 *(v)* If you **decorate** something, you add things to it to make it prettier. **decoration** *(n)*, **decorative** *(adj)*.
2 *(v)* If you **decorate** a room or house, you paint it or put up wallpaper. **decoration** *(n)*, **decorator** *(n)*.

decrease decreasing decreased
1 *(v)* to become less, smaller, or fewer. *I have noticed a marked decrease in enthusiasm for this project.* **decreasing** *(adj)*, **decreasingly** *(adv)*.
2 *(n)* a loss, or the amount by which something lessens.

decree decreeing decreed *(v)* to give an order that must be obeyed. *The teacher decreed that there should be no more cheating.* **decree** *(n)*.

decrepit *(adj)* old and feeble.

dedicate dedicating dedicated
1 (v) If you **dedicate** yourself to something, you give lots of time and energy to it. **dedication** (n).
2 (v) If you **dedicate** a book to someone, you put their name at the front of it to thank them or to show that you like and admire them. **dedication** (n).

deduce deducing deduced (v) to work out something from clues, or from what you know already.

deduct deducting deducted (v) to take away or subtract something, especially money. **deductible** (adj).

deduction
1 (n) something that is worked out from clues.
2 (n) an amount that is taken away or subtracted from a larger amount.

deed
1 (n) something that is done. A good deed.
2 (n) a legal document saying who owns a house or a piece of land.

deep deeper deepest
1 (adj) going a long way down. A deep well. **deepen** (v).
2 (adj) very intense and strong. Deep sorrow. **deepen** (v), **deeply** (adv).

deep-sea (adj) living or happening in the deeper part of an ocean. Some deep-sea creatures, like this viper fish, make their own light from luminous cells.

deer deer (n) a fast-running wild animal with four legs. Male deer grow bony, branching antlers. See **antler**.

deface defacing defaced (v) to spoil the way something looks.

defeat defeating defeated
1 (v) to beat someone in a war or competition.
2 (n) If you suffer a **defeat**, you are beaten.

defect defecting defected
1 (dee-fect) (n) a fault or weakness in something or someone. **defective** (adj).
2 (dif-ect) (v) to leave your country or political party and join another one.

defend defending defended
1 (v) to protect something or someone from harm. **defence** (n).
2 (v) to support something or some idea by arguing. The strikers defended their action. **defence** (n).

3 (v) to try to stop goals being scored in football, hockey, netball, etc. **defence** (n), **defender** (n).

defendant (n) the person in a court case who has been accused of a crime.

defensive
1 (adj) to do with defending yourself or others. The players took defensive action.
2 (adj) If you are **defensive**, you feel and act as if someone is attacking or criticizing you. **defensiveness** (n), **defensively** (adv).

defer deferring deferred (v) to put something off until later. The outing will be deferred until next term.

defiant (adj) If you are **defiant**, you stand up to someone or to some organization and refuse to obey them. **defiance** (n), **defiantly** (adv).

deficient (adj) lacking something. My diet is deficient in vitamins. **deficiency** (n).

deficit (def-er-sit) (n) If an account shows a **deficit**, more money has been spent than has come in.

define defining defined (v) to explain or describe something exactly.

viper fish

definite
1 (adj) certain. Do we have a definite date for the trip? **definitely** (adv).
2 (adj) clear. These drawings have a very definite outline.
3 definite article (n) the grammatical term for "the".

definition (n) an explanation of what a word or an idea means. This dictionary has 20,000 definitions.

deflate deflating deflated
1 (v) to let the air out of something like a tyre or balloon. **deflation** (n).
2 (v) to make someone feel less confident and important. The teacher's comments deflated Don.

deflect deflecting deflected (v) to make something go in a different direction. The ball was deflected off the post into the goal. **deflection** (n).

deforestation (n) the cutting down of forests.

deformed (adj) If someone or something is **deformed**, they are a strange shape. **deformity** (n).

defraud defrauding defrauded (v) to cheat someone out of money, property, etc.

defrost defrosting defrosted
1 (v) to allow frozen food to thaw out completely.
2 (v) to remove ice from a refrigerator or freezer.

deft defter deftest (adj) skilful, quick, and neat. Deft footwork. **deftness** (n), **deftly** (adv).

defuse defusing defused
1 (v) When someone **defuses** a bomb, they make it safe so it cannot explode.
2 (v) If a situation is **defused**, it is made calmer.

defy defies defying defied
1 (v) If you **defy** a person or a rule, you stand up to them and refuse to obey them.
2 (v) to challenge someone, or to dare them to do something. I defy you to eat all that cake!

degenerate degenerating degenerated (v) to become worse. The lesson degenerated into a riot.

degrading (adj) If a situation or an activity is **degrading**, it makes you feel worthless or disgraced. **degradation** (n), **degrade** (v).

degree
1 (n) a unit for measuring temperature or angles. The symbol for a degree is °. The temperature today reached 20° Celsius. A 90° angle.
2 (n) a qualification given by a university or other institute of higher education.

dehydrated
1 (adj) If you are **dehydrated**, you do not have enough water in your body. **dehydration** (n), **dehydrate** (v).
2 (adj) Dehydrated food has had the water removed from it. **dehydration** (n), **dehydrate** (v).

deign (rhymes with pain) deigning deigned (v) If you **deign** to do something, you lower yourself to do it. The princess deigned to let the peasant kiss her hand.

deity (day-it-ee) deities (n) a god or goddess.

dejected (adj) sad and depressed. **dejection** (n), **dejectedly** (adv).

delay delaying delayed
1 (v) to be late. Don't delay or we'll miss the bus! **delay** (n).
2 (v) to make someone late. The accident delayed me.
3 (v) to put something off until later. Sara delayed doing her homework until the last minute.

delegate delegating delegated
1 (*del-er-gate*) (v) to give someone responsibility for doing a part of your job.
2 (*del-er-gurt*) (n) someone who represents other people at a meeting.

delete deleting deleted (v)
to remove something from a piece of writing or computer text.
deletion (n).

deliberate deliberating deliberated
1 (*der-lib-er-ut*) (adj) planned, or intended. deliberately (adv).
2 (*der-lib-er-ate*) (v) to consider something carefully. deliberation (n).

delicate
1 (adj) finely made, or sensitive. A delicate instrument. delicately (adv).
2 (adj) If a person is delicate, they are not very strong and easily become ill.

delicatessen (n) a shop that sells unusual or foreign foods.

delicious (adj) very pleasing to taste or smell. deliciously (adv).

delight delighting delighted
1 (n) great pleasure. delightful (adj).
2 (v) If something delights you, it pleases you very much.
delighted (adj).

delinquent (n) a young person who is often in trouble with the police.
delinquency (n), delinquent (adj).

delirious (adj) If you are delirious, you cannot think straight because you have a fever or you are extremely happy. deliriously (adv).

deliver delivering delivered
1 (v) to take something to someone. delivery (n).
2 (v) When someone delivers a baby, they help it to be born. delivery (n).
3 (v) (old-fashioned) to rescue someone from something. Deliver us from evil. deliverance (n).

delta
1 (n) the fourth letter of the Greek alphabet. See **alphabet**.
2 (n) an area of land shaped like a triangle, where a river deposits its sediment as it enters the sea.
See **river**.

deluge deluging deluged
1 (n) heavy rain, or a flood.
2 (v) If a river or a storm deluges a place, it floods it.
3 (v) If people deluge you with letters, presents, etc., they send you lots of them. deluge (n).

demand demanding demanded
1 (v) to claim something, or to ask for something firmly. We demand justice!

2 (n) If there is a demand for something, many people want it.

demanding
1 (adj) If somebody is demanding, they are always wanting things and are hard to please.
2 (adj) A demanding job requires a lot of effort.

demeanour (n) the way that you behave.

demo (n) (informal) a meeting or march to protest about something. Demo is short for demonstration.

democracy democracies
1 (n) a way of governing a country, in which the people choose their leaders in elections.
2 (n) a country that has an elected government.

democrat
1 (n) someone who agrees with the system of democracy.
2 Democrat (n) a supporter of the Democratic Party in the USA.

democratic
1 (adj) A democratic system is one where all people have equal rights. democratically (adv).
2 Democratic Party (n) the name of one of the main political parties in the USA.

demolish demolishes demolishing demolished
1 (v) to knock down something and break it up. The builders demolished the old school. demolition (n).
2 (v) (informal) to eat something quickly. Will demolished his lunch in five minutes.

demon (n) a devil, or an evil spirit demonic (adj).

demonstrate demonstrating demonstrated
1 (v) to show other people how to do something or how to use something. Alice demonstrated how to use the computer. demonstration (n).
2 (v) to join together with other people to protest against something. demonstration (n), demonstrator (n).
3 (v) to show something clearly. Alex demonstrated how angry he felt by shouting loudly. demonstrative (adj).

demoralized or **demoralised**
(adj) If you are demoralized, you feel depressed and hopeless.

den
1 (n) the home of a wild animal, such as a lion.
2 (n) a private place where you can work or play.

denim (n) strong, cotton material used for making jeans. denim (adj).

denominator (n) In fractions, the denominator is the number under the line which shows how many equal parts the whole number can be divided into. In the fraction 7/8, 8 is the denominator.

denounce denouncing denounced
(v) to say in public that someone has done something wrong

dense denser densest
1 (adj) thick, or crowded. Dense fog. denseness (n), densely (adv).
2 (adj) (informal) slow to understand. denseness (n), densely (adv)

density (n) The density of an object is how heavy or light it is for its size. Density is measured by dividing an object's mass by its volume.

dent denting dented (v) to damage something by making a hollow in it. dent (n).

dental (adj) to do with your teeth. Dental hygiene.

dentist (n) someone who is trained to check and treat teeth.

denture
1 (n) a plate that fits into your mouth, with a false tooth or false teeth attached to it.
2 dentures (plural n) a set of false teeth.

deny denies denying denied
1 (v) to say that something is not true. Laura denied that she had taken the buns. denial (n).
2 (v) to stop someone having something or going somewhere. The guards denied us entry to the hall.

deodorant (n) a substance used to hide the smell of sweat and to make your body smell fresher.

depart departing departed (v) to leave, especially to go on a journey. departure (n).

department (n) a part of a shop, hospital, university, etc. departmental (adj).

depend depending depended
1 (v) If something depends on something else, it is related to it or influenced by it in some way. The result depends on the skill of our team. dependent (adj).
2 (v) to rely on someone or something. We're depending on your help. dependence (n), dependable (adj), dependent (adj).

dependant (n) someone who is looked after and supported by somebody else.

depict depicting depicted (v)
to show something in a picture, or by
using words. *Paolo's painting depicts
a group of purple aliens.*

deplorable (adj) shockingly bad.
Louis has deplorable taste in clothes.
deplore (v), deplorably (adv).

deport deporting deported (v)
to send someone back to their own
country. *The terrorists were deported
to face trial at home.* deportation (n).

deportment (n) the way that you
stand.

depose deposing deposed (v) If a
king or queen is deposed, they have
their power taken from them.
deposition (n).

deposit depositing deposited
1 (n) a sum of money given as the first
part of a payment, or as a promise to
pay for something. deposit (v).
2 (n) a natural layer of rock, sand, or
mineral found in the ground.
deposit (v).
3 (v) to place, or to lay down. *Dad
deposited the shopping on the table.*

depot (dep-oh) (n) a warehouse, or
a bus garage.

depreciate depreciating
depreciated (v) to lose value.
depreciation (n).

depressed (adj) sad and gloomy.
depress (v), depressing (adj).

depression
1 (n) sadness and gloominess.
2 (n) an area of air at low pressure
which may bring rain.
3 (n) a time when businesses do badly
and many people are poor.
4 (n) a shallow dip in the ground.

deprive depriving deprived (v)
to prevent someone from having
something, or to take something away
from someone. deprivation (n),
deprived (adj).

depth
1 (n) deepness, or a measurement of
deepness.
2 If you study something in depth,
you study it thoroughly.
3 If you are out of your depth, you
cannot understand what is going on.

deputy deputies (n) someone who
helps somebody else in their job and
takes their place when they are ill or
absent. deputize (v).

deranged (adj) insane.

derelict (adj) neglected and in ruins.

derive deriving derived
1 (v) to take or receive
something. *Eva derives a lot
of pleasure from her work.*

2 (v) If a word is **derived** from
another word, it has developed from
it. *The word dictionary is derived from
the Latin word "dictio", meaning word
or phrase.* derivation (n).

derv (n) a fuel used in diesel engines.
Derv stands for diesel-engined road
vehicle.

descant (n) a tune that is played or
sung above the main tune.

descend descending descended
1 (v) to climb down, or go down to a
lower level. descent (n).
2 (v) If you are **descended** from
someone, you belong to a later
generation of their family.
descendant (n)

describe describing described (v)
to create a picture of something in
words. description (n),
descriptive (adj).

desert deserting deserted
1 (dez-ut) (n) a sandy or stony area
where hardly any plants grow because
there is so little rain. *The map shows
the main deserts of the world and is
surrounded by examples of
desert wildlife.* desert (adj).
2 (der-zert) (v) to abandon
someone, or to run away
from the army.
deserter (n).

**deserts and
desert wildlife**

deserve deserving deserved (v)
to earn something because of the way
that you behave. *Uma deserves a
reward for her hard work.*

design designing designed
1 (v) to draw something that could be
built or made. designer (n).
2 (n) the shape or style of something.

desire (n) a strong wish or need for
something or someone. desire (v),
desirable (adj).

desk (n) a table, often with drawers,
used for working at or writing on.

desktop publishing (n) the use of
a computer to arrange words and
pictures on a page, so that the pages
are ready to be printed as part of a
book, magazine, etc.

desolate
1 (adj) deserted, or uninhabited.
A desolate village. desolation (n).
2 (adj) sad and lonely. *After my friend
left, I felt really desolate.*
desolation (n), desolately (adv).

Sturt's desert pea
(Australia)

fennec fox
(North Africa and Middle East)

honey-pot ant
(Australia)

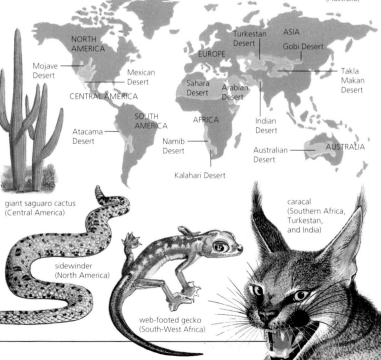

desert

NORTH
AMERICA

Mojave
Desert

Mexican
Desert

CENTRAL AMERICA

SOUTH
AMERICA

Atacama
Desert

Namib
Desert

Kalahari Desert

EUROPE

Turkestan
Desert

ASIA

Gobi Desert

Sahara
Desert

Arabian
Desert

AFRICA

Indian
Desert

Australian
Desert

AUSTRALIA

Takla
Makan
Desert

giant saguaro cactus
(Central America)

caracal
(Southern Africa,
Turkestan,
and India)

sidewinder
(North America)

web-footed gecko
(South-West Africa)

despair despairing despaired *(v)*
to lose hope completely.
*Harry despaired of getting home on
time.* despair *(n)*, despairing *(adj)*.

despatch *see* **dispatch**.

desperate
1 *(adj)* If you are **desperate**, you will
do anything to change your situation.
desperation *(n)*, desperately *(adv)*.
2 *(adj)* dangerous, or difficult.
A desperate shortage of medicine.
desperately *(adv)*.

despise despising despised *(v)*
If you **despise** someone, you dislike
them and have no respect for them.

despite *(prep)* in spite of. *Rollo won
the race, despite falling off his bike.*

dessert *(duh-zert)* *(n)* the sweet
course of a meal.

destination *(n)* the place that
someone or something is travelling to.

destiny destinies *(n)* Your **destiny** is
your fate or the future events in your
life. *Cinderella's destiny was to marry
a handsome prince.*

destitute *(adj)* A **destitute** person
has no money to live on.

destroy destroying destroyed *(v)*
to ruin something or someone
completely. destruction *(n)*.

destructive *(adj)* causing lots of
damage and unhappiness.
destructively *(adv)*.

detach detaches detaching
detached *(v)* to separate one part of
something from the rest of it.
detachable *(adj)*.

detached
1 *(adj)* A **detached** house stands by
itself.
2 *(adj)* If you are **detached**, you are
able to stand back from a situation
and not get too involved in it.
detachment *(n)*.

detail
1 *(n)* a small part of something larger.
2 *(n)* delicate work. *Iona's paintings
are full of detail.* detailed *(adj)*.
3 *(plural n)* If you ask for **details**
about something, you want
information about it.

detain detaining detained *(v)*
to keep somebody back when they
want to go. *The police detained two
men for questioning.*

detect detecting detected *(v)*
to notice, or to discover something.
*I detected a strange smell in the
house.* detection *(n)*.

detective *(n)* someone who
investigates crimes, usually for the
police.

detention
1 *(n)* a punishment in which a pupil
has to stay in school when other
pupils are free.
2 *(n)* If someone is held **in detention**,
they are kept prisoner.
3 **detention centre** *(n)* a type of
prison for young offenders.

deter deterring deterred *(v)*
to prevent or discourage someone
from doing something.

detergent *(n)* liquid or powder used
for cleaning things.

deteriorate deteriorating
deteriorated *(v)* to get worse.
deterioration *(n)*.

determined *(adj)* If you are
determined to do something, you
have made a firm decision to do it.
determination *(n)*.

deterrent *(n)* something that stops
you doing something because you are
afraid of the consequences.
*Burglar alarms are effective deterrents
against crime.*

detest detesting detested *(v)* If you
detest something or somebody, you
dislike them very much.
detestable *(adj)*.

detonate detonating detonated
(v) to set off an explosion.
detonator *(n)*, detonation *(n)*.

detour *(n)* a longer, alternative route
to somewhere, usually taken to avoid
an obstacle.

detract detracting detracted *(v)*
to make something less enjoyable or
valuable. *The rain detracted from the
pleasure of our walk.*

detrimental *(adj)* harmful. *Smoking
is detrimental to your health.*

deuce *(jooss)* *(n)* In tennis, the score
of **deuce** means that both players
have 40 points.

devalue devaluing devalued
1 *(v)* to reduce the value of a currency
in relation to another currency or to
gold. devaluation *(n)*.
2 *(v)* to make something worth less
than it was. *Why do you always
devalue my efforts?*

devastated
1 *(adj)* very badly damaged or
destroyed. *The area was devastated by
the floods.* devastation *(n)*,
devastate *(v)*.
2 *(adj)* shocked and distressed. *I was
devastated by the dreadful news.*
devastating *(adj)*.

develop developing developed
1 *(v)* to grow. *The boys' friendship
developed slowly.* development *(n)*.

2 *(v)* to build on something, or make
something grow. *The farmer is
developing the field as a camp site.*
developer *(n)*, development *(n)*.
3 *(v)* When a film is **developed**, it is
treated with chemicals to bring out
the pictures which have been taken.

deviate deviating deviated *(v)*
to do something different from what
is normal or acceptable. *The cyclist
deviated from his usual route.*
deviation *(n)*, deviant *(adj)*.

device
1 *(n)* a piece of equipment which does
a particular job. *This is a useful device
for taking the tops off bottles.*
2 If you are **left to your own
devices**, you can do what you want.

devil
1 *(n)* In Christianity and Judaism,
the **Devil** is the spirit of evil.
2 *(n)* If you call someone a **devil**, you
mean that they are naughty or
wicked.

devious
1 *(adj)* A **devious** person keeps their
thoughts and actions secret, and
cannot be trusted. deviousness *(n)*,
deviously *(adv)*.
2 *(adj)* complicated and indirect.
We took a devious route back home.

devise devising devised *(v)* to think
something up, or invent something.
Let's devise a way to escape.

devoid *(adj)* without something, or
empty of something. *The house was
devoid of furniture.*

devolution *(n)* the handing over of
some power from a central
government to a local government.

devoted *(adj)* loyal and loving.
devotion *(n)*, devotedly *(adv)*.

devour devouring devoured *(v)*
to eat something quickly and greedily.

devout *(adj)* deeply religious.
devoutness *(n)*, devoutly *(adv)*.

dew *(n)* small drops of moisture
which form overnight on cool surfaces
outside. dewy *(adj)*.

dexterity *(n)* skill, especially in using
your hands. *Simon showed great
dexterity in modelling the clay.*
dexterous *(adj)*.

diabetes *(dye-a-bee-tees)* *(n)*
a disease in which you have too much
sugar in your blood.
diabetic *(dye-a-bet-ik)* *(adj)*.

diabolical
1 *(adj)* extremely wicked. *A diabolical
villain.* diabolically *(adv)*.
2 *(adj)* *(informal)* awful, or terrible.
A diabolical essay. diabolically *(adv)*.

diagnose diagnosing diagnosed
(v) to work out what disease a patient has or what the cause of a problem is. **diagnosis** (n).

diagonal (adj) A **diagonal** line is a straight line joining opposite corners of a square or rectangle. **diagonally** (adv).

diagram (n) a drawing or plan that explains something simply. **diagrammatic** (adj).

dial dialling dialled
1 (n) the face on a clock, watch, or measuring instrument.
2 (v) to enter a telephone number by pressing buttons on a telephone.
3 **dialling tone** (n) the sound you should hear when you first pick up the telephone.

dialect (n) a way of speaking that belongs to a particular place.

dialogue (n) conversation, especially in a play, film, or book.

diameter (dye-am-it-er) (n) a straight line through the centre of a circle, from one side to another. See **circle**.

diamond
1 (n) a very hard, clear, precious stone. See **mineral**.
2 (n) a shape with four equal sides, like a square standing on one of its corners.
3 **diamonds** (plural n) one of the four suits in a pack of cards.

diaphragm (dye-a-fram)
1 (n) the wall of muscle between your chest and your stomach. See **respiration**.
2 (n) the thin disc in a telephone or microphone that vibrates to change voice signals into electrical signals. See **microphone**.
3 (n) the part of a camera made from thin leaves of metal which open and close to control the amount of light reaching the film.

diarrhoea (dye-er-ree-a) (n) a stomach illness which causes normally solid waste to become runny.

diary diaries (n) a book in which people write down things that happen each day, either to use as a record or to plan ahead.

dice dicing diced
1 (plural n) six-sided cubes with a different number of spots on each face, used in games. The singular of dice is die, although most people say dice.
2 (v) to cut something, like vegetables, into cubes. Dice the carrots. **diced** (adj).

dictate dictating dictated
1 (v) to talk aloud so that someone can write down what you say. **dictation** (n).
2 (v) to control something. Mum dictates our bedtimes.

dictator (n) someone who has complete personal control of a country. **dictatorship** (n).

dictionary dictionaries (n) a book like this one that explains what words mean and shows you how to spell them.

didgeridoo or **didjeridu**
(dij-er-ree-doo) (n) a long, decorated tube, made from a hollowed-out branch or tree trunk, which is played as a musical instrument by Aborigines.

didgeridoo

die dying died
1 (v) to stop living, or come to an end.
2 (v) If you are **dying** to do something, you really want to do it.
3 (n) the singular form of the word dice.

diesel (dee-zull)
1 **diesel engine** (n) a type of engine used in trains and motor vehicles. In a diesel engine, the fuel is ignited by heat from compressed air, rather than by a sparking plug.
2 (n) a fuel used in diesel engines that is heavier than petrol.

diet dieting dieted
1 (n) Your **diet** is what you eat. **dietary** (adj).
2 (v) When you **diet**, you choose what you eat in order to lose weight.
3 (n) a controlled eating plan.

difference
1 (n) the way in which things are not like each other. What's the difference between margarine and butter? **differ** (v), **different** (adj), **differently** (adv).
2 (n) The **difference** between two numbers is the amount by which one is less or more than the other. The difference between 5 and 2 is 3.

difficult
1 (adj) not easy. A difficult exam.
2 (adj) A **difficult** person is not easy to get on with.

difficulty difficulties (n) a problem.

dig digging dug
1 (v) to use a spade to move earth.
2 (n) a push, or a poke.
3 (n) an unkind remark.
4 (n) an archaeological excavation.

digestion (n) the process of breaking down food in the stomach, so that it can be absorbed into the blood. This diagram shows the main organs used in human digestion. **digest** (v), **digestive** (adj).

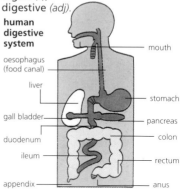

human digestive system

- mouth
- oesophagus (food canal)
- liver
- gall bladder
- duodenum
- ileum
- appendix
- stomach
- pancreas
- colon
- rectum
- anus

digger (n) a large machine, used for moving earth.

digit (dij-it)
1 (n) a finger.
2 (n) a single figure. 625 is a three digit number.

digital
1 (adj) **digital** information is represented as a series of ones and zeros. **digitize** (v), **digitally** (adv).
2 (adj) **digital** equipment works by using information stored as a series of ones and zeros. A digital camera.
3 (adj) A **digital** display shows time, speed, etc. in numbers.

dignified (adj) calm, serious, and in control. **dignity** (n).

dilapidated (adj) shabby and falling to pieces. **dilapidation** (n).

dilemma (n) If you are **in a dilemma**, you have to choose between alternatives.

diligent (adj) hard-working. **diligence** (n), **diligently** (adv).

dilute diluting diluted (v) When you **dilute** a liquid, you make it weaker by adding water. **dilution** (n).

dimension (n) The **dimensions** of an object are its measurements or its size. Objects have three dimensions: length, width, and height.

diminish diminishes diminishing diminished (v) If something **diminishes**, it becomes smaller or weaker. A diminishing flame.

dimple (n) a small dent in a person's cheek or chin. **dimpled** (adj).

dine dining dined (v) to have a meal in a formal way. Lord and Lady Fortescue dined at eight. **diner** (n).

dice

Some words that begin with a "di" sound are spelt "dy".

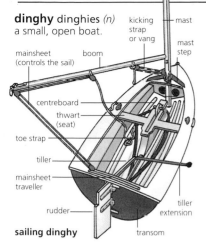

dinghy dinghies (n)
a small, open boat.

kicking strap or vang — mast

mast step

mainsheet (controls the sail)　boom

centreboard

thwart (seat)

toe strap

tiller

mainsheet traveller

rudder

tiller extension

transom

sailing dinghy

dingy (din-jee) dingier dingiest
(adj) dull and shabby. A dingy room.

dinner
1 (n) the main meal of the day, eaten at midday or in the evening.
2 (n) a formal banquet.

dinosaur (n) the general name for the large, land-living reptiles that existed in prehistoric times.
The picture shows a range of dinosaurs and the periods when they existed.

dinosaurs

■ Triassic 248-213 million years ago

■ Jurassic 213-144 million years ago

■ Cretaceous 144-65 million years ago

dip dipping dipped
1 (v) to push something briefly into a liquid. Dip your brush in the water.
2 (v) to slope downwards. dip (n).
3 (v) If you dip a vehicle's headlights, you lower their beams.
4 (n) If you take a dip, you have a short swim.
5 (n) a savoury sauce into which you dip raw vegetables, crisps, etc.

diploma (n) a certificate showing that you have gained a qualification in a particular subject.

diplomat (n) a person who represents their country's government in a foreign country. diplomacy (n).

diplomatic
1 (adj) If you are diplomatic, you are tactful and good at dealing with people. diplomacy (n).
2 (adj) to do with being a diplomat. The diplomatic service.

dire direr direst (adj) disastrous. Dire consequences.

direct directing directed
1 (adj) in a straight line, or by the shortest route. directly (adv).
2 (v) to supervise people, especially in a play or film.

3 (v) to tell someone the way to go. Please direct me to the hotel.
4 (adj) If someone is direct, they have a very straightforward manner. directly (adv).

direction
1 (n) the way that someone or something is moving or pointing. We travelled in a westerly direction.
2 directions (plural n) instructions. Follow the directions carefully.

director
1 (n) one of the senior people in charge of a company.
2 (n) the person in charge of making a film or television programme.

directory directories (n) a book which gives addresses, phone numbers, etc. in alphabetical order.

dirty dirtier dirtiest
1 (adj) not clean. dirt (n).
2 (adj) unfair. A dirty trick.
3 (n) Dirty jokes are rude jokes which may offend some people.

disabled (adj) People who are disabled are restricted in what they can do, usually because of an illness or injury. disability (n).

■ staurikosaurus

■ plateosaurus

■ velociraptor

■ kentrosaurus

■ triceratops

■ parasaurolophus

■ brachiosaurus

■ deinonychus

■ stegosaurus

■ pachycephalosaurus

■ tyrannosaurus rex

■ spinosaurus

disadvantage *(n)* something which causes a problem or makes life more difficult. **disadvantaged** *(adj)*.

disagree disagreeing disagreed *(v)* If you **disagree** with someone, you do not think the same way as they do. **disagreement** *(n)*.

disappear disappearing disappeared *(v)* to go out of sight. **disappearance** *(n)*.

disappoint disappointing disappointed *(v)* to let someone down by failing to do what they expected. **disappointment** *(n)*, **disappointed** *(adj)*.

disapprove disapproving disapproved *(v)* If you **disapprove** of something, you do not think it is a good thing. **disapproval** *(n)*.

disarm disarming disarmed
1 *(v)* to take weapons from somebody.
2 *(v)* If a country **disarms**, it gives up its weapons. **disarmament** *(n)*.
3 *(v)* If someone **disarms** you, they stop you feeling angry.

disaster
1 *(n)* a very serious accident, earthquake, etc. in which many die.
2 *(n)* If something is a **disaster**, it goes completely wrong. **disastrous** *(adj)*, **disastrously** *(adv)*.

disbelief *(n)* refusal to believe something. *My story was greeted with total disbelief.* **disbelieve** *(v)*.

disc or **disk**
1 *(n)* a flat, circular shape.
2 *(n)* a piece of plastic, used for recording music or information. *Compact disc.*

discard discarding discarded *(v)* to throw something away.

discharge discharging discharged
1 *(diss-charge)* *(v)* to tell someone officially that they can go.
2 *(diss-charge)* *(v)* to release a substance into the open. *The factory discharged chemicals into the river.* **discharge** *(diss-charge)* *(n)*.

disciple *(n)* someone who follows the teachings of a leader or a set of ideas.

discipline *(n)* control over the way that you or other people behave. **discipline** *(v)*, **disciplinary** *(adj)*.

disc jockey *(n)* someone who introduces and plays pop music on the radio, at a disco, etc.

disco
1 *(n)* an event at which music is played for dancing.
2 *(n)* a set of sound and lighting equipment used at a disco.

disconnect disconnecting disconnected
1 *(v)* to separate things that are joined together. **disconnection** *(n)*.
2 *(v)* If something, like an electricity supply or a telephone line, is **disconnected**, it is cut off.

discontented *(adj)* not satisfied. **discontent** *(n)*, **discontentedly** *(adv)*.

discontinue discontinuing discontinued *(v)* to stop doing something that you have been doing regularly.

discord
1 *(n)* disagreement between two or more people.
2 *(n)* a mixture of musical notes which sounds unpleasant. **discordant** *(adj)*.

discount *(n)* a price cut.

discourage discouraging discouraged *(v)* If you **discourage** someone from doing something, you persuade them not to do it. **discouragement** *(n)*.

discouraged *(adj)* If you are **discouraged**, you lose your enthusiasm or confidence.

discover discovering discovered
1 *(v)* to find something. *We discovered the treasure.* **discovery** *(n)*.
2 *(v)* to find out about something. *I soon discovered that Abigail was lying.* **discovery** *(n)*.

discreet *(adj)* If you are **discreet**, you know the right thing to say, and can be trusted to keep a secret. **discretion** *(n)*, **discreetly** *(adv)*.

discriminate discriminating discriminated.
1 *(v)* If you **discriminate** against someone, you are prejudiced against them and treat them unfairly. **discrimination** *(n)*.
2 *(adj)* A **discriminating** person knows the difference between things of good and bad quality. **discrimination** *(n)*.

discus *(disk-uss)* discuses or disci *(n)* a large, weighted disc that is thrown in athletics events. *This statue shows an ancient Greek athlete throwing the discus. Also see* **track and field**.

discuss *(disk-uss)* discusses discussing discussed *(v)* to talk over something. *Can we meet to discuss the new plans?* **discussion** *(n)*.

discus thrower

disease
1 *(n)* an illness. *Measles is an infectious disease.*
2 *(n)* sickness. *Disease spread throughout the city.* **diseased** *(adj)*.

disgrace disgracing disgraced
1 *(v)* If you **disgrace yourself**, you do something which other people disapprove of and which makes you feel ashamed.
2 *(n)* If something is a **disgrace**, it is very bad indeed. **disgraceful** *(adj)*.

disguise disguising disguised
1 *(v)* to hide something. *Sebastian tried to disguise his boredom.*
2 *(n)* If you put on a **disguise**, you dress up to look like someone else.

disgusting *(adj)* very unpleasant and offensive to others. **disgust** *(n)*, **disgustingly** *(adv)*.

dish dishes dishing dished
1 *(n)* a bowl used for cooking or for serving food.
2 *(n)* one course of a meal. *A chicken dish.*
3 **dish out** *(v)* If you **dish something out**, you give portions of it to several people.

dishevelled *(adj)* very untidy.

dishonest *(adj)* not truthful. **dishonesty** *(n)*, **dishonestly** *(adv)*.

disillusion disillusioning disillusioned *(v)* If you **disillusion** someone, you destroy their ideas about something.

disinfectant *(n)* a household chemical used to kill germs. **disinfect** *(v)*.

disintegrate disintegrating disintegrated
1 *(v)* to break into small pieces. *The chair disintegrated when Horatio sat on it.* **disintegration** *(n)*.
2 *(v)* to break up. *Emily is sad because her parents' marriage is disintegrating.*

disjointed *(adj)* unconnected, or not flowing smoothly.

disk
1 *(n)* a piece of plastic, used for recording computer data. *Floppy disk.*
2 See **disc**.

dislike disliking disliked *(v)* If you **dislike** something or someone, you do not like them. **dislike** *(n)*.

dislocate dislocating dislocated *(v)* If you **dislocate** a bone, it comes out of its usual place. **dislocation** *(n)*.

dismal
1 *(adj)* gloomy and sad.
2 *(adj)* dreadful. *A dismal failure.*

dismantle dismantling dismantled *(v)* to take something to pieces.

Some words that begin with a "dis" sound are spelt "dys".

dismayed *(adj)* If you are **dismayed**, you are upset and worried by something. **dismay** *(n)*.

dismiss dismisses dismissing dismissed *(v)*
1 *(v)* to allow people to leave. *Our teacher dismissed us early.*
2 *(v)* to sack someone from their job. **dismissal** *(n)*.
3 *(v)* to put something out of your mind. *I've dismissed the idea of having a party.*

disobedient *(adj)* If you are **disobedient**, you do not do as you are told. **disobedience** *(n)*, **disobediently** *(adv)*.

disorderly
1 *(adj)* untidy and disorganized. *A disorderly desk.*
2 *(adj)* A **disorderly** person is uncontrolled and possibly violent

disorganized or **disorganised** *(adj)* muddled and not in order. **disorganization** *(n)*.

disown disowning disowned *(v)* If you **disown** someone, you act as though you do not know them.

dispatch or **despatch** dispatches dispatching dispatched
1 *(v)* to send something or somebody off. *We dispatched Uncle Albert to catch his train.*
2 *(n)* a message, or a report.

dispensary dispensaries *(n)* a place where medicines are prepared and given out. **dispense** *(v)*.

disperse dispersing dispersed *(v)* to scatter. *The crowd dispersed.* **dispersal** *(n)*.

displace displacing displaced
1 *(v)* to take the place of something or somebody else. *When you sit in the bath, you displace some water.* **displacement** *(n)*.
2 *(v)* to move someone or something from their usual place.

display displaying displayed
1 *(v)* to show something. *Jo displayed no emotion as she read my note.*
2 *(n)* a public show or exhibition.
3 *(n)* special behaviour by an animal to attract a mate. *This picture shows part of the courtship display of a bird of paradise.*
4 *(n)* a screen or panel on electronic equipment, showing information.

courtship display

disposable *(adj)* suitable for throwing away after use. *Disposable packaging.* **dispose** *(v)*.

disprove disproving disproved *(v)* If you **disprove** something, you show that it cannot be true.

dispute disputing disputed
1 *(n)* a disagreement.
2 *(v)* If you **dispute** what someone says, you say that you think they are wrong.

disqualify disqualifies disqualifying disqualified *(v)* to prevent someone from taking part in an activity, often because they have broken a rule. **disqualification** *(n)*.

disregard disregarding disregarded *(v)* to take no notice of someone or something. **disregard** *(n)*.

disreputable *(adj)* If someone or something is **disreputable**, they are known for being bad in some way. **disrepute** *(n)*.

disrespect *(n)* lack of respect, or rudeness. **disrespectful** *(adj)*, **disrespectfully** *(adv)*.

disrupt disrupting disrupted *(v)* to disturb or break up something which is happening. *Josh disrupted the meeting by shouting loudly.* **disruption** *(n)*, **disruptive** *(adj)*.

dissatisfied *(adj)* unhappy, or discontented. **dissatisfaction** *(n)*.

dissect dissecting dissected *(v)* to cut something up and examine it. **dissection** *(n)*.

dissident *(n)* someone who disagrees with the laws of a country or other organization. *A political dissident.* **dissidence** *(n)*.

dissolve dissolving dissolved
1 *(v)* to mix with liquid. *Does this tablet dissolve in water?*
2 *(v)* If parliament is **dissolved**, it is officially ended and an election takes place. **dissolution** *(n)*.

distance
1 *(n)* the amount of space between two places.
2 If you see something **in the distance**, it is a long way off. **distant** *(adj)*.

distil distilling distilled *(v)* to purify a liquid, by heating it until it turns into a gas and then letting it cool to form a liquid again. **distillation** *(n)*.

distinct
1 *(adj)* very clear. *Pascale has a distinct French accent.* **distinctly** *(adv)*.
2 *(adj)* clearly different. *The original recording is quite distinct from the cheap copies.* **distinctive** *(adj)*.

distinction
1 *(n)* a clear difference.
2 *(n)* the highest grade in some examinations.

distinguish distinguishes distinguishing distinguished *(v)* to tell the difference between things. *Can you distinguish between a frog and a toad?* **distinguishable** *(adj)*.

distinguished *(adj)* A **distinguished** person is famous for the important things they have done.

distort distorting distorted
1 *(v)* to twist something out of shape. **distortion** *(n)*, **distorted** *(adj)*.
2 *(v)* to try to twist the truth.

distract distracting distracted *(v)* If something or someone **distracts** you, they put you off what you are doing. **distraction** *(n)*.

distress
1 *(n)* a feeling of great pain or sadness. **distressed** *(adj)*, **distressing** *(adj)*.
2 **distress signal** *(n)* a radio message, flare, etc. from a ship or aircraft to show that it is in trouble.

distribute distributing distributed
1 *(v)* to give things out. *Nazim distributed the sweets among his friends.* **distribution** *(n)*.
2 *(v)* to deliver products to various places. **distribution** *(n)*.

distributor
1 *(n)* a person or company that delivers products to various places.
2 *(n)* the part of a car engine which revolves, sending electricity from the ignition system to fire each cylinder in turn.

district *(n)* an area or region.

distrust distrusting distrusted *(v)* If you **distrust** someone, you think that they cannot be trusted. **distrust** *(n)*, **distrustful** *(adj)*, **distrustfully** *(adv)*.

disturb disturbing disturbed
1 *(v)* to interrupt somebody when they are doing something.
2 *(v)* to worry someone.

disturbed *(adj)* If someone is **disturbed**, they are unstable and have difficulty in controlling their behaviour.

ditch ditches ditching ditched
1 *(n)* a long, narrow channel that drains water away.
2 *(v)* If a pilot **ditches** his plane, he makes an emergency landing in water.
3 *(v)* (slang) If one person **ditches** another, they leave them suddenly. *Jodie ditched her boyfriend last week.*

ditto *(adj)* Ditto marks are used in lists to show that what is written above is repeated on the line below.

dive diving dived
1 *(v)* to plunge headfirst into water with your arms stretched out in front of you. **dive** *(n)*.
2 *(v)* to drop down suddenly. *The kite dived to the ground.* **dive** *(n)*.

diver *(n)* someone who uses breathing apparatus to work or explore underwater.
See **scuba diving**.

diverse *(adj)* varied, or assorted. *Hal has a diverse collection of friends.*

diversion
1 *(n)* When a road is closed, a **diversion** takes you on a different route.
2 *(n)* something that takes your mind off other things.

divert diverting diverted
1 *(v)* If someone **diverts** the traffic, they make it take a different route.
2 *(v)* When you **divert** someone's attention from something, you stop them from thinking about it.

divide dividing divided
1 *(v)* to split into parts.
2 *(v)* In maths, if you **divide** one number by a second number, you work out how many times the second number will go into the first.
12 divided by 4 is 3 or 12 ÷ 4 = 3.
3 *(v)* to share something out.
Let's divide the food between us.

divine divining divined
1 *(adj)* to do with God, or like a god.
2 *(v)* to discover something by instinct, magic, or guesswork. **divination** *(n)*.
3 *(adj)* *(informal)* wonderful.

division
1 *(n)* the act of dividing one number by another.
2 *(n)* one of the parts into which something large has been divided. *Football League Division One.*

divorce *(n)* the ending of a marriage by a court of law. **divorce** *(v)*, **divorced** *(adj)*.

Diwali *(n)* a festival of light, celebrated by Hindus and Sikhs in the autumn. *At Diwali, Hindus decorate their doorsteps with rangoli patterns like the one shown here.*

rangoli pattern

D.I.Y. *(n)* home improvements, repairs, and decorations that you do yourself. DIY stands for do-it-yourself.

dizzy dizzier dizziest *(adj)* If you feel **dizzy**, you feel giddy and confused.

DJ *short for* **disc jockey**.

DNA *(n)* the molecule that carries information which gives living things their special characteristics.
The letters stand for deoxyribonucleic acid. *The diagram shows the linked strands of DNA which separate, as a cell divides, to produce two identical new cells.*

DNA

do does doing did done
1 *(v)* to perform an action. *Dad was doing the washing.*
2 *(v)* to deal with something. *Have you done your hair today?*
3 *(v)* to be acceptable. *This bread will do until tomorrow.*
4 *(v)* to get on. *Philippa is doing well at college.*

dock docking docked
1 *(n)* a place where ships load and unload their cargo. **dock** *(v)*.
2 *(n)* In a court of law, the **dock** is where the accused person stands.

doctor *(n)* someone trained to treat sick people.

document documenting documented
1 *(n)* a piece of paper containing important or useful information.
2 *(n)* a file on a computer.
3 *(v)* to write down the facts about something.

documentary documentaries *(n)* a film or television programme made about real situations and people.

dodge dodging dodged *(v)* to avoid something or somebody by moving quickly. *Kirsty dodged the ball.*

doe *(n)* the female of animals such as rabbits, deer, or kangaroos.

dog dogging dogged
1 *(n)* a four-legged mammal that is often kept as a pet.
2 *(v)* to follow someone closely.

dole doling doled
1 *(n)* *(informal)* money paid by the government to people who are unemployed.
2 *(v)* If you **dole out** something, like food or money, you give it out.

dollar *(n)* the main unit of money in the USA, Canada, Australia, and New Zealand.

dolphin *(n)* an intelligent water mammal with a long snout.

bottlenose dolphin
rostrum (beak) forehead
dorsal fin
gape (lower jaw)
flipper
tail fluke

dome *(n)* a rounded roof.

domestic
1 *(adj)* to do with the home. *Domestic chores.*
2 *(adj)* **Domestic** animals are kept by people in their homes as pets. **domesticated** *(adj)*.
3 *(adj)* to do with your own country. *A domestic flight.*

dominate dominating dominated
1 *(v)* to control very powerfully. **domination** *(n)*, **dominant** *(adj)*.
2 *(v)* to be the main feature of a situation. *The castle dominates the view.* **dominant** *(adj)*.

donate donating donated *(v)* to give something as a present. *We donated our profits to charity.* **donation** *(n)*.

dalmatian

golden labrador
withers
buttocks flank
stop
flews
tail
muzzle
shoulder
brisket
loins
elbow
hock sheath
pastern
stifle dew claw

collie

greyhound

chihuahua

west highland white terrier

donkey *(n)* a long-eared mammal, related to the horse.

donor
1 *(n)* someone who gives something, usually to an organization or a charity.
2 *(n)* someone who gives part of their body, usually after they are dead, to help sick people. *A kidney donor.*

doodle doodling doodled *(v)* to draw absent-mindedly while concentrating on something else.

doom *(n)* If you meet your **doom**, you suffer a terrible fate, usually ending in death. **doomed** *(adj)*.

door
1 *(n)* a barrier that opens and closes at the entrance of a building, room, etc.
2 *(n)* a house, or a building. *My friend lives three doors away.*

dormant
1 *(adj)* Animals become **dormant** when they hibernate. They show no signs of action as if they were asleep.
2 *(adj)* A **dormant** volcano is not active at present, but could still erupt.
3 *(adj)* When plants or seeds are **dormant**, they are alive, but not growing.

dormitory dormitories *(n)* a bedroom for several people, usually in a boarding school or youth hostel.

dose
1 *(n)* a measured amount of medicine.
2 *(n)* a brief experience of something unpleasant. *A dose of flu.*

dot dotting dotted
1 *(n)* a small, round point.
2 *(v)* If you **dot** things around, you scatter them in various places.

dot-com company *(n)* a company that does most of its business through a Web site on the Internet. Many dot-com companies offer services or items for sale through their Web site.

double doubling doubled
1 *(v)* If you **double** something, you make it twice as big. **double** *(adj)*.
2 *(n)* If you have a **double**, there is someone who looks just like you.
3 *(n)* When you play **doubles** in tennis, badminton, etc. there are two players on each side.

doubt *(dowt)* doubting doubted
1 *(v)* If you **doubt** something, you are uncertain about it. **doubtful** *(adj)*.
2 *(n)* uncertainty.

dough *(doh)* *(n)* a thick, sticky mixture of flour, water, etc., used to make bread.

doughnut *(doh-nut)* *(n)* a small cake that is made from dough, deep-fried and covered with sugar.

dove *(n)* a bird that makes a gentle, cooing sound. *The dove is often used as a symbol of peace.*

down
1 *(prep)* from a higher to a lower place. *Emma ran down the hill.* **downward** *(adj)*, **down** *(adv)*.
2 *(n)* the soft feathers of a bird. **downy** *(adj)*.
3 *(adj)* If you feel **down**, you feel sad or depressed.

download downloading downloaded *(v)* to copy information or pictures onto your computer from another computer over the Internet. **downloadable** *(adj)*.

dowry dowries *(n)* the money or property that women in some cultures bring with them when they marry.

doze dozing dozed *(v)* to sleep lightly for a short time. *Uncle Arthur has dozed off again.* **doze** *(n)*.

dozen *(n)* a group of twelve.

Dr short for **doctor**.

drab *(adj)* very dull and dreary. *Gertrude wore a drab, grey dress.* **drabness** *(n)*.

draft drafting drafted
1 *(v)* When you **draft** something, like a letter, you make a first rough copy of it. **draft** *(n)*.
2 *(v)* If someone is **drafted**, they are made to join the armed forces. **draft** *(n)*.

drag dragging dragged
1 *(v)* to pull something heavy along the ground.
2 *(v)* If something **drags**, it seems to go slowly. *The lesson really dragged.*
3 *(n)* *(informal)* If something is a **drag**, it is boring.

dragon *(n)* a fire-breathing monster that appears in stories and legends. *In China, people create colourful dragons which dance in their New Year processions.*

Chinese dragon

drain draining drained
1 *(v)* to remove the liquid from something.
2 *(n)* a pipe or channel that takes away water or sewage. **drainage** *(n)*.

drained *(adj)* If you feel **drained**, you have no energy left.

drama
1 *(n)* a play.
2 *(n)* If you study **drama**, you learn about acting and the theatre.
3 *(n)* something which affects people seriously.

dramatic
1 *(adj)* to do with acting and the theatre.
2 *(adj)* very noticeable. *A dramatic change.* **dramatically** *(adv)*.
3 *(adj)* If someone is being **dramatic**, they are making too much fuss about something.

dramatize or **dramatise** dramatizing dramatized
1 *(v)* to adapt a story into a play or film. **dramatization** *(n)*.
2 *(v)* If you **dramatize** an event, you make it seem very exciting.

drapes *(plural n)* *(US)* pieces of material that are pulled across a window or a stage to cover it (curtains, *UK*).

drastic *(adj)* If you do something **drastic**, you take action suddenly and violently. **drastically** *(adv)*.

draught *(draft)* *(n)* a flow of cold air. **draughty** *(adj)*.

draughts *(drafts)* *(plural n)* a game played by two people with black and white counters on a squared board.

draw drawing drew drawn
1 *(v)* to make a picture with a pencil, pen, etc. **drawing** *(n)*.
2 *(v)* to pull something. *The carriage was drawn by horses. The band drew enormous crowds.*
3 *(n)* If a competition ends in a **draw**, both sides are level.
4 *(n)* a competition where something is picked out. *A lucky draw.*

drawback *(n)* a problem, or a disadvantage.

drawer *(n)* a sliding box in a piece of furniture, used for storing things.

drawing pin *(n)* a small pin with a flat, round head, used for fastening paper on noticeboards, walls, etc.

drawing room *(old-fashioned)* *(n)* a formal room where guests are entertained.

dread dreading dreaded *(v)* If you **dread** something, you are very afraid of it. **dread** *(n)*, **dreaded** *(adj)*.

dreadful
1 *(adj)* very unpleasant. *A dreadful accident.* **dreadfully** *(adv)*.
2 *(adj)* very bad. *A dreadful film.*

dreadlocks *(plural n)* a West Indian hairstyle, where the hair is grown long and twisted into strands.

dream dreaming dreamed
or **dreamt**
1 (v) to imagine events while you are asleep. **dream** (n).
2 (v) If you **dream** of doing something, you really want to do it. **dream** (n).

dream time
(n) Aborigines believe that life began in the **dream time**, when the world was created by animal, plant, and human ancestors. *This painting shows the Rainbow Serpent giving birth to the Aboriginal people in the dream time.*

Aboriginal bark painting

dreamy dreamier dreamiest (adj) If you are dreamy, you are always day-dreaming and imagining things. **dreamily** (adv).

dreary drearier dreariest (adj) dull and miserable. **drearily** (adv).

dredge dredging dredged (v) to scrape sand, mud, etc. from the bed of a river or harbour. **dredger** (n).

drench drenches drenching drenched (v) to make something completely wet.

dress dresses dressing dressed
1 (v) to put clothes on.
2 (n) a piece of clothing, worn by women and girls, that covers their body from shoulders to legs.
3 (n) a general name for clothes. *Formal dress.*
4 (v) If you **dress a wound**, you clean it, put ointment on it, and cover it.

dresser
1 (n) a tall piece of kitchen furniture with shelves and cupboards.
2 (n) (US) a piece of furniture with drawers, used for storing clothes (chest of drawers, UK).

dressing
1 (n) a covering for a wound.
2 (n) a type of sauce for salads.

dressing gown (n) a loose robe, worn over your nightclothes.

dressing table (n) an item of bedroom furniture, often with a mirror and drawers.

dress rehearsal (n) the last rehearsal of a play, in full costume.

dribble dribbling dribbled
1 (v) to let saliva trickle from your mouth.
2 (v) When you **dribble** in football, hockey, etc. you run with the ball, touching it often and keeping it close to you.

drift drifting drifted
1 (v) When something **drifts**, it moves wherever the water or wind takes it.
2 (n) a pile of sand or snow, created by the wind.
3 (v) to move or act without any sense of purpose. *Ollie spent the whole day just drifting about.* **drifter** (n).

drill drilling drilled
1 (n) a tool, used for making holes.
2 (v) to use a drill.
3 (n) a way of doing something which is governed by strict rules. *Fire drill.*

electric drill (cutaway)

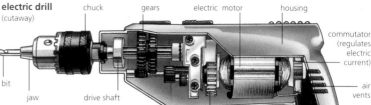

bit
jaw
chuck
drive shaft
gears
electric motor
cooling fan
on/off switch
handle
housing
commutator (regulates electric current)
air vents
switch lock

drink drinking drank drunk
1 (n) a liquid that you swallow.
2 (v) to swallow liquid.
3 (n) an alcoholic liquid. **drinker** (n).

drip dripping dripped
1 (v) When a liquid **drips**, it falls down slowly, drop by drop. **drip** (n).
2 (n) (informal) a silly and rather boring person.

dripping (n) fat obtained from meat while it is cooking, which can often be used again.

drive driving drove driven
1 (v) to control a vehicle. **driver** (n), **driving** (n).
2 (v) to force someone into a desperate state. *Losing his passport drove Matt to despair.*
3 (n) a private road leading to a house.
4 (n) energy. *Jenny will succeed, because she has a lot of drive.*

drivel (n) If someone talks **drivel**, what they say is rubbish.

drizzle (n) light rain. **drizzle** (v).

drone droning droned
1 (v) to make a steady, dull sound.
2 (v) to talk in a dull and monotonous way. *Hector droned on about cricket.*
3 (n) a male bee which does not make honey and has no sting.
See **honeycomb**.
4 (n) a pipe attached to a bagpipe.
See **bagpipes**.

drool drooling drooled
1 (v) to let saliva trickle from your mouth.
2 (v) If you **drool over** something, you really like and want it.

droop drooping drooped
1 (v) to hang down, or to sag.
2 (v) When people **droop**, they run out of energy.

drop dropping dropped
1 (v) to let something fall. *Nancy dropped her bag on the sofa.*
2 (v) to go downwards. *The acrobat dropped to the floor.* **drop** (n).
3 (n) a small quantity of liquid. *A drop of water.*
4 (v) If you **drop out**, you stop doing something. **dropout** (n).
5 (v) When players are **dropped**, they are left out of a team.

drought
(rhymes with shout)
(n) a long spell of very dry weather.

drown drowning drowned
1 (v) When someone **drowns**, they die because their lungs fill with water.
2 (v) to make a louder noise than something else. *The noise of the drill drowned my singing.*

drowsy drowsier drowsiest (adj) sleepy. *This medicine may make you feel drowsy.* **drowsiness** (n), **drowse** (v), **drowsily** (adv).

drug
1 (n) a chemical substance used to treat illness.
2 (n) a substance that people take because of its effect on them. Drugs are dangerous and usually cause addiction.
3 (v) to make someone unconscious by giving them a drug. **drugged** (adj).
4 **drug addict** (n) someone who cannot give up using drugs.

drugstore (n) (US) a shop where medicines and various other items are sold.

drum drumming drummed
1 *(n)* a musical instrument, with a hollow body covered with a stretched skin, that makes a loud noise when you hit it.
2 *(v)* to beat a drum or other surface with drumsticks or your fingers. *Joe drummed his fingers on the table.* **drummer** *(n)*.

drum kit — tom-tom holder
snare drum — tom-tom
crash cymbal
cymbal stand — ride cymbal
hi-hat
snare drum stand
bass drum
hi-hat pedal — bass drum pedal — floor tom

drumstick
1 *(n)* a stick used to hit a drum.
2 *(n)* the cooked leg of a chicken, turkey, etc.

drunk
1 *(adj)* If a person is **drunk**, they have had too much alcohol to drink, and cannot control themselves.
2 *(n)* a person who often gets drunk. **drunkard** *(n)*.

dry dries drying dried; drier driest
1 *(v)* to take the moisture out of something.
2 *(adj)* not wet.
3 *(adj)* dull, or boring. *A dry speech.*

dry-clean dry-cleaning
dry-cleaned *(v)* to clean clothes with special chemicals in order to remove stains. **dry-cleaner** *(n)*.

DTP *short for* **desktop publishing**.

dual
1 *(adj)* double.
2 **dual carriageway** *(n)* a road with a dividing strip between traffic travelling in opposite directions.

dubious *(dyoo-bee-us) (adj)* If you are **dubious** about something, you are not sure about it. **dubiously** *(adv)*.

duchess *(n)* the wife or widow of a duke, or a woman with the rank which is equal to a duke.

duck ducking ducked
1 *(n)* a water bird.
2 *(v)* to bend low to avoid something.

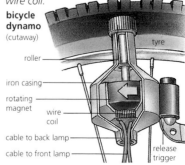

wood ducks
male
female

due
1 *(adj)* If something is **due**, it is expected to arrive or happen. **duly** *(adv)*.

2 *(adj)* suitable. *Please handle these books with due care.* **duly** *(adv)*.
3 If something happens **due to** something else, it happens because of it.

duel *(n)* a sword or gun fight between two people, fought according to strict rules.

duet *(n)* a piece of music or a song performed by two people.

duke *(n)* a nobleman. In Britain, a duke is the highest rank of male peer.

dull duller dullest
1 *(adj)* not bright.
2 *(adj)* not clever.
3 *(adj)* boring.

dumb dumber dumbest
1 *(adj)* not able to speak.
2 *(adj) (informal)* stupid.

dummy dummies
1 *(n)* a rubber teat given to a baby to suck.
2 *(n)* an imitation person or object.

dump dumping dumped
1 *(v)* to leave something thoughtlessly or roughly. *Don't dump your bag there!*
2 *(n)* a place where unwanted things can be left. *A rubbish dump.*

dune *(n)* a sand hill made by the wind, near the sea, or in a desert.

dung *(n)* the solid waste products of large animals.

dungeon *(n)* a prison, usually underground. *See* **castle**.

duplicate duplicating duplicated *(v)* to make an exact copy of something. **duplicate** *(n)*.

during *(prep)* within a particular time. *Please call during the morning.*

dusk *(n)* the time of day after sunset when it is nearly dark.

dust dusting dusted
1 *(n)* particles of dirt, fluff, etc. that gather on surfaces.
2 *(v)* to remove dust from surfaces with a cloth. **duster** *(n)*.

duty *(joo-tee)* duties
1 *(n)* the things a person must do or ought to do. *A soldier's duty.*
2 *(n)* tax charged on goods brought into a country.
3 If you are **on duty**, you are at work.

duvet *(doo-vay) (n)* a thick, padded cover for a bed, filled with feathers or other light material.

DVD *(n)* a disc that looks like a CD and stores sound, information and moving pictures. The initials DVD stand for digital versatile disc. *Is that film on DVD yet?* **DVD player** *(n)*.

dwarf dwarves dwarfing dwarfed
1 *(n)* a very small person, animal, or plant. **dwarf** *(adj)*.
2 *(v)* to make something else seem very small.

dwell dwelling dwelt *or* dwelled *(v) (old-fashioned)* to live in a place.

dwindle dwindling dwindled *(v)* to become smaller or less.

dye dying dyed
1 *(n)* a substance used to change the colour of something.
2 *(v)* If someone **dyes** something, they change its colour by soaking it in dye.

dynamic *(adj)* energetic and good at getting things done. **dynamism** *(n)*.

dynamite *(n)* an explosive.

dynamo *(n)* a machine for converting the power of a turning wheel into electricity. Some bicycle lights are powered by a dynamo. *As the bicycle wheel turns, the roller makes the magnet inside the dynamo rotate, creating a moving magnetic field. Electricity is produced as the magnetic field sweeps over the wire coil.*

bicycle dynamo *(cutaway)*
tyre
roller
iron casing
rotating magnet
wire coil
cable to back lamp
cable to front lamp
release trigger

dyslexia *(dis-lex-ee-a) (n)* If you have dyslexia, you find reading and spelling difficult because you confuse the order of letters. **dyslexic** *(adj)*.

Ee

eager (adj) keen and enthusiastic. **eagerness** (n), **eagerly** (adv).

eagle (n) a large bird of prey which often nests in mountainous areas.

Philippine eagle

ear (n) the part of the body used for hearing. *Sound waves travel down the ear canal and hit the ear drum, making it vibrate. These vibrations are transferred to the cochlea where they are changed to electrical signals and sent to the brain.*

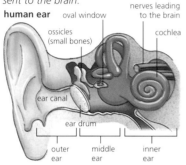

human ear

nerves leading to the brain
oval window
ossicles (small bones)
cochlea
ear canal
ear drum
outer ear   middle ear   inner ear

earl (n) a nobleman. In Britain, an earl is a male peer of middle rank.

early earlier earliest
1 (adj) before the usual time. *An early start.* **earliness** (n), **early** (adv).
2 (adj) near the beginning of a period of time. *An early 20th-century house.*

earn earning earned
1 (v) to work to receive money. **earner** (n), **earnings** (plural n).
2 (v) to work to achieve a result. *You have earned your reward.*

earnest (adj) serious and keen. **earnestly** (adv).

earth
1 Earth (n) the planet on which we live. *The diagram shows the different layers of the Earth.* **earthly** (adj).
2 (n) soil. **earthy** (adj).
3 (n) the hole where a fox lives.
4 (n) a wire through which electricity can pass into the ground. **earth** (v).

Earth (cutaway)

solid inner core
liquid outer core
mantle
crust

earthquake (n) a violent shaking of the Earth, caused by a movement of rock plates at the Earth's surface. *See* **fault**.

easel (n) a folding wooden stand for a painting.

east
1 (n) one of the four main points of the compass, the direction from which the Sun rises. **east** (adj), **east** (adv).
2 (adj) An **east** wind blows from the east. **easterly** (adj).
3 (adj) to do with, or existing in the east. *The east coast.* **eastern** (adj).

Easter (n) the Christian festival in which people celebrate the resurrection of Jesus Christ.

easy easier easiest
1 (adj) If something is **easy**, it does not require much effort or ability. **easiness** (n), **easily** (adv).
2 (adj) comfortable and relaxing. *An easy chair.* **ease** (n).

eat eating ate eaten
1 (v) to take in food through your mouth.
2 If something is being **eaten away**, it is being destroyed slowly.

eavesdrop eavesdropping eavesdropped (v) to listen in secret to someone's conversation.

ebb ebbing ebbed
1 (v) When the tide **ebbs**, it goes out and the sea level goes down. **ebb** (n).
2 (v) to get weaker. *The wounded tiger's strength ebbed away.*

ebony
1 (n) a very hard, black wood.
2 (n) a deep black colour. **ebony** (adj).

eccentric (ek-sen-trik)
1 (adj) odd, or strange. **eccentrically** (adv).
2 (n) someone with odd habits. *An eccentric professor.*

echo echoes echoing echoed (v) When a sound **echoes**, it repeats several times, because its sound waves have met a large surface and bounced back. **echo** (n).

éclair (ek-lair) (n) a finger-shaped cake made from sweet pastry, filled with cream and usually covered with chocolate.

eclipse
1 (n) In an **eclipse of the Moon**, the Earth comes between the Sun and the Moon, so that all or part of the Moon's light is blocked out.
2 (n) In an **eclipse of the Sun**, the Moon comes between the Sun and the Earth, so that all or part of the Sun's light is blocked out.

ecology
1 (n) the study of the relationship between plants, animals, and their environment. **ecologist** (n).
2 (n) the study of how human activity affects the Earth. This is also known as human ecology. **ecologist** (n), **ecological** (adj), **ecologically** (adv).

e-commerce (ee-kom-urs) (n) e-commerce is the general name for business carried out on the Internet.

economical (adj) not wasteful. *Our car is very economical on petrol.*

economics (singular n) the study of the way money is made and used in a society. **economist** (n).

economy economies
1 (n) the way that a country runs its industry, trade, and finance.
2 When you **make economies**, you do things differently to save money. **economize** (v).
3 (n) An **economy pack** contains a large quantity of something at a low price.

ecosystem (ee-koh-sis-tem) (n) a self-contained community of creatures, plants, and their environment. *If part of an ecosystem is destroyed, other parts may be affected.*

ecstasy ecstasies
1 (n) a feeling of great happiness. **ecstatic** (adj), **ecstatically** (adv).
2 (n) a drug which creates a short-term effect of pleasure and extreme energy, followed by great exhaustion.

eczema (ex-ma) (n) a skin disease that makes the skin dry, rough, and itchy.

eddy eddies (n) a circular current in a liquid. **eddy** (v), **eddying** (adj).

edge edging edged
1 (n) a boundary.
2 (v) to move very slowly and carefully. *We edged our way along the ledge.*
3 If you are **on edge**, you are nervous or anxious. **edgy** (adj).

edgeways
1 (adv) sideways.
2 If you cannot get **a word in edgeways** in a discussion, people do not give you a chance to speak.

edible (adj) fit to be eaten. *Only pick the edible mushrooms!*

edit editing edited
1 (v) to check a piece of writing for mistakes and cut it down if it is too long.
2 (v) to cut and put together pieces of film or videotape to make a film, television programme, etc.

edition *(n)* a version of a book or newspaper, printed at a particular time. *A new paperback edition.*

editor
1 *(n)* the person in charge of a newspaper or magazine.
2 *(n)* someone who checks the contents of a book and gets it ready to be published.

educate educating educated *(v)* to give people knowledge or a skill.

education *(n)* the process of gaining knowledge and skills. educational *(adj)*.

eel *(n)* a long, thin, snake-like fish. *The electric eel stuns its prey with a strong electric shock.*

electric eel

eerie eerier eeriest *(adj)* strange and frightening. eerily *(adv)*.

effect *(n)* the result or consequences of something.

effective *(adj)* If something or someone is **effective**, they do their job very well. effectively *(adv)*.

effervescent
1 *(adj)* An **effervescent** liquid is very fizzy. effervescence *(n)*.
2 *(adj)* An **effervescent** person is very lively. effervescence *(n)*.

efficient *(adj)* If someone or something is **efficient**, they work very well and do not waste time or energy. efficiency *(n)*, efficiently *(adv)*.

effluent (off-loo-ent) *(n)* waste water and sewage.

effort *(n)* If you make an **effort**, you try hard. effortless *(adj)*.

e.g. the initials of the Latin phrase *exempli gratia*, which means "for example"

egg
1 *(n)* an oval or rounded object produced by female birds, reptiles, and fish, in which their young develop. *Also see* **chicken**.
2 *(n)* a cell created within a woman's body which, when fertilized, grows into a baby.

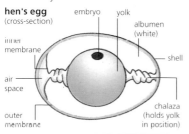

hen's egg
(cross-section)

embryo | yolk
inner membrane
air space
albumen (white)
shell
chalaza (holds yolk in position)
outer membrane

egocentric *(adj)* If you are **egocentric**, you are far more interested in yourself than in others. egocentricity *(n)*.

eiderdown (eye-der-down) *(n)* a warm bed cover filled with feathers or some other stuffing.

Eid-ul-Adha *(n)* a Muslim festival during the last month of the Islamic year when many Muslims make a pilgrimage to Mecca. Some Muslims celebrate the festival by sacrificing animals.

Eid-ul-Fitr *(n)* the Muslim festival to celebrate the end of the Ramadan period of fasting.

either
1 *(conj)* **Either** can be used to indicate a choice. *You can either stay or go.*
2 *(pronoun)* one of two. *Take either of them.* either *(adj)*.
3 *(adv)* also, or similarly. *If Tom's not going, I won't either.*

eject ejecting ejected
1 *(v)* to push something out. *Press this button to eject the tape.*
2 *(v)* to throw someone out. *We ejected the troublemakers from the meeting.*
3 *(v)* When pilots **eject** from their planes, they are thrown out of the cockpit by a special seat.

ejector seat

spur (breaks through plane canopy)
protective helmet with safety visor
oxygen mask
quick-release harness
lightweight seat (contains rocket motors, parachutes, and survival pack)
leg restraint line
life raft (inflates on contact with water)

elaborate elaborating elaborated
1 (el-**ab**-or-ut) *(adj)* complicated and detailed. *An elaborate pattern.* elaborately *(adv)*.
2 (el-**ab**-or-ate) *(v)* to give more details. *Please elaborate on your plans.*

elapse elapsing elapsed *(v)* When time **elapses**, it passes.

elastic *(n)* a rubbery material which stretches. elasticity *(n)*.

elated *(adj)* very pleased and excited. elation *(n)*.

elbow *(n)* the joint that connects the upper and lower parts of your arm.

elder *(adj)* older. *My elder sister.*

elderly *(adj)* old.

elect electing elected *(v)* to choose someone or decide something by voting. election *(n)*.

electrician *(n)* someone who installs electrical systems and mends electrical machines.

electricity *(n)* a form of energy caused by moving electrons, that is used for lighting, heating, and making machines work. electric *(adj)*, electrical *(adj)*.

electrocute electrocuting electrocuted *(v)* to kill or injure someone by giving them a severe electric shock. electrocution *(n)*.

electrode *(n)* a conductor through which an electric current can flow into or out of a gas or liquid. *See* **sparking plug**.

electrolyte *(n)* a soluble substance that conducts electricity.

electromagnet *(n)* a magnet which works by electricity.

electron *(n)* one of the microscopic parts of an atom. Electrons carry electrical energy. *See* **atom**.

electronic *(adj)* **Electronic** machines are worked by minute amounts of electricity produced by electrons. They contain transistors, silicon chips, or valves which control an electric current. *Computers, televisions, and radios are all electronic.* electronically *(adv)*.

electronic mail *(n)* messages sent by one computer to another.

electronics
1 *(singular n)* the study of minute electrical currents, by creating circuits with electronic components.
2 *(singular n)* the technology that makes electronic machines work.

elegant *(adj)* graceful and stylish. elegance *(n)*, elegantly *(adv)*.

element
1 *(n)* In chemistry, an **element** is a substance that cannot be split into a simpler substance. *Oxygen, copper, and carbon are elements.*
2 *(n)* one of the simple, basic parts of something. *Claude taught me the elements of cooking.*
3 *(n)* a wire or coil in an electrical heater, toaster, etc. that heats up when electricity passes through it. *See* **iron**.
4 the elements *(plural n)* the weather.

elementary *(adj)* simple, or basic.

elephant *(n)* a large mammal with a long trunk and ivory tusks, that lives in Africa or India.

elephants

African elephant   Indian elephant

elevate elevating elevated
1 *(v)* to lift something up.
2 *(v)* to promote someone to an important job or status. **elevation** *(n)*, **elevated** *(adj)*.

elevator
1 *(n)* *(US)* a machine that carries people or goods between different levels of a building (lift, *UK*).
2 *(n)* the moveable part of a tail plane, used to alter the angle of flight of an aircraft. *See* **aircraft**.

elf elves *(n)* a small, magical, mischievous person described in legends and fairy stories. **elfin** *(adj)*.

eligible
1 *(adj)* If you are **eligible** for something, like a job, you have the right qualifications for it. **eligibility** *(n)*.
2 *(adj)* An **eligible** man or woman is a suitable person for someone to marry.

eliminate eliminating eliminated
1 *(v)* to get rid of someone or something. **elimination** *(n)*.
2 *(v)* When a person or a team is **eliminated** from a competition, they cannot take part in it any more. **elimination** *(n)*.

elite *(el-eet)* *(n)* a group of people who have special advantages and privileges. **elitism** *(n)*, **elite** *(adj)*.

ellipse *(n)* an oval shape. **elliptical** *(adj)*.

elocution *(n)* the art of speaking clearly.

elongate elongating elongated
1 *(v)* to make something longer or stretch it out.
2 **elongated** *(adj)* long and thin.

elope eloping eloped *(v)* When a young man and woman **elope**, they run away from their homes to get married. **elopement** *(n)*.

eloquent *(el-oh-kwent)* *(adj)* An **eloquent** person speaks easily and interestingly. **eloquence** *(n)*.

else
1 *(adv)* other, or different. *They have gone somewhere else.*
2 *(adv)* more. *Tell me if you need anything else.*

elsewhere *(adv)* somewhere else.

elusive *(adj)* very hard to find or catch. **elusiveness** *(n)*, **elusively** *(adv)*.

e-mail *short for* **electronic mail**.

embankment
1 *(n)* a long, low, earth bank, built to carry a railway, road, etc.
2 *(n)* a high bank at the sides of a river, built to stop it from flooding.

embargo embargoes *(n)* an official order forbidding something from happening.

embark embarking embarked
1 *(v)* to go on board a ship or aeroplane, ready for a journey.
2 *(v)* to start something that will take a long time to finish. *Tanya has embarked on a massive art project.*

embarrass embarrasses embarrassing embarrassed *(v)* If something **embarrasses** you, it makes you feel awkward and uncomfortable. *Ron blushes when he is embarrassed.* **embarrassment** *(n)*.

embezzle embezzling embezzled *(v)* to steal money secretly from the organization that you work for. **embezzlement** *(n)*.

emblem *(n)* a symbol, or a sign. *The emblem of our club is a spider.*

embrace embracing embraced *(v)* to hug someone. **embrace** *(n)*.

embroider embroidering embroidered *(v)* to sew a picture or a design on to cloth. **embroidery** *(n)*.

embroidery stitches

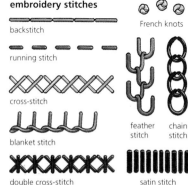

backstitch
running stitch
cross-stitch
blanket stitch
double cross-stitch
French knots
feather stitch
chain stitch
satin stitch

embryo *(em-bree-oh)* *(n)* an unborn baby in the very early stage of development in its mother's womb.

emerald
1 *(n)* a bright green precious stone.
2 *(n)* a bright green colour. **emerald** *(adj)*.

emerge emerging emerged
1 *(v)* If you **emerge** from somewhere, you come out into the open. **emergence** *(n)*.
2 *(v)* to become known. *News is emerging of a serious road accident.*

emergency emergencies *(n)* a sudden and dangerous situation that must be dealt with quickly.

emigrate emigrating emigrated *(v)* to leave your own country in order to live in another one. **emigrant** *(n)*, **emigration** *(n)*.

eminent *(adj)* well-known and respected. *An eminent surgeon.* **eminence** *(n)*, **eminently** *(adv)*.

emir *(n)* a ruler in some Muslim countries, known as emirates.

emission
1 *(n)* the release of something, like chemicals, into the air.
2 **emissions** *(plural n)* substances released into the air.

emit emitting emitted *(v)* to release or send out something, such as heat, light, or sound. *The spaceship emitted a strange beeping sound.*

emotion *(n)* a strong feeling, such as happiness, love, anger, or grief.

emotional
1 *(adj)* to do with your feelings. *Emotional problems.*
2 *(adj)* When someone becomes **emotional**, they show their feelings, especially by crying. **emotionally** *(adv)*.

emperor *(n)* the male ruler of an empire.

emphasize *or* **emphasise** emphasizing emphasized *(v)* If you **emphasize** something, you make it stand out clearly because you think it is important. **emphasis** *(n)*, **emphatic** *(adj)*.

empire
1 *(n)* a group of countries that all have the same ruler. *The Roman Empire.*
2 *(n)* a large group of companies controlled by one person.

employ employing employed
1 *(v)* to pay someone to work for you. **employer** *(n)*, **employment** *(n)*.
2 *(v)* to use something. *You can employ an electric whisk to beat the eggs.*

employee *(n)* a person who works for someone or some organization and is paid by them.

empress empresses *(n)* the female ruler of an empire, or the wife of an emperor.

empty empties emptying emptied; emptier emptiest
1 *(adj)* If a container is **empty**, there is nothing inside it.
2 *(v)* to take the contents out of a container.
3 *(adj)* without meaning or purpose. *An empty promise.* **emptiness** *(n)*.
4 *(n)* an empty bottle or can.

emulsion
1 *(n)* a mixture of two liquids in which the particles of one liquid spread out in the other liquid, but do not dissolve. *When oil and vinegar are mixed, they form an emulsion.*
2 *(n)* a type of paint, used on inside walls.

enable enabling enabled *(v)* to make it possible for someone to do something. *Telescopes enable people to see the stars more clearly.*

enamel
1 *(n)* a shiny, glass-like substance that is used to coat and protect metal, pottery, and glass. **enamelled** *(adj)*.
2 *(n)* the hard, white surface of your teeth. *See* **tooth**.

enchanted *(adj)* A place or thing that is **enchanted** has been put under a magic spell or seems magical. *An enchanted castle.*

enchanting *(adj)* delightful and lovely. **enchanted** *(adj)*, **enchantingly** *(adv)*.

enclose enclosing enclosed
1 *(v)* to put a fence or wall around an area. **enclosure** *(n)*.
2 *(v)* to put something in an envelope or package with a letter. **enclosure** *(n)*.

encore *(on-kor)* *(n)* an extra item added to the end of a performance because the audience has been applauding so much.

encounter *(n)* an unexpected or difficult meeting. **encounter** *(v)*.

encourage encouraging encouraged *(v)* to give someone confidence by praising or supporting them. **encouragement** *(n)*, **encouraging** *(adj)*.

encyclopedia *(en-sy-klo-pee-dee-a)* or **encyclopaedia** *(n)* a book or set of books with information about many different subjects, arranged in alphabetical order. **encyclopedic** *(adj)*.

end ending ended
1 *(n)* the last part of something.

2 *(n)* one of the two points furthest from the middle of an object.
3 *(v)* to finish something.

endanger endangering endangered *(v)* to be dangerous to someone or something. *Pollution can endanger wildlife.* **endangered** *(adj)*.

endangered species *(n)* a type of animal that is in danger of becoming extinct. *The blue whale is an endangered species.*

endless *(adj)* Something **endless** has no end, or seems to have no end.

endure
1 *(v)* If you **endure** something unpleasant or painful, you put up with it. **endurance** *(n)*.
2 *(v)* If something **endures**, it lasts for a long time. **enduring** *(adj)*.

enemy enemies
1 *(n)* someone who hates you and wants to harm you.
2 *(n)* the country or army that you are fighting against in a war.

energetic *(adj)* strong and active. **energetically** *(adv)*.

energy energies
1 *(n)* the strength to do active things without getting tired.

2 *(n)* power from coal, electricity, and other sources which makes machines work and produces heat.
3 *(n)* In physics, **energy** is the ability of something to do work. It is measured in joules.

engaged
1 *(adj)* If two people are **engaged**, they have decided that they will get married. **engagement** *(n)*.
2 *(adj)* If a telephone number or public toilet is **engaged**, it is in use.
3 *(adj)* If someone is **engaged** in doing something, they are busy and occupied doing it.

engine
1 *(n)* a machine that changes an energy source, such as petrol, into movement. *In the petrol engine shown here, electrical sparks from the sparking plugs ignite the compressed petrol and air mixture in the cylinders which burns rapidly and pushes the pistons down in turn. The fast-moving pistons turn the crankshaft which produces a twisting effect that turns the wheels. Also see* **jet engine**.
2 *(n)* the front part of a train that pulls all the carriages.
See **steam locomotive**.

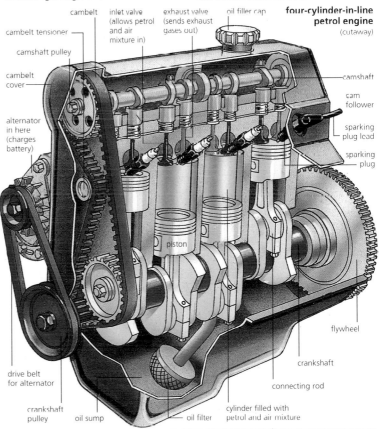

four-cylinder-in-line petrol engine (cutaway)

cambelt
inlet valve (allows petrol and air mixture in)
exhaust valve (sends exhaust gases out)
oil filler cap
cambelt tensioner
camshaft pulley
cambelt cover
alternator in here (charges battery)
camshaft
cam follower
sparking plug lead
sparking plug
piston
flywheel
crankshaft
connecting rod
drive belt for alternator
crankshaft pulley
oil sump
oil filter
cylinder filled with petrol and air mixture

engineer engineering engineered
1 (n) someone who is trained to design and build machines, vehicles, bridges, roads, etc. **engineering** (n).
2 (v) to make something happen by using a clever plan. *Don engineered a meeting between the two rivals.*

English
1 (adj) from England, or to do with England.
2 (n) the main language spoken in Britain, the USA, Australia, Canada, and many other countries.

engrave engraving engraved (v) to cut a design or letters into a metal or glass surface. **engraver** (n), **engraving** (n).

engrossed (adj) If you are engrossed in something, you give it all your attention. **engrossing** (adj).

engulf engulfing engulfed (v) to cover or swallow up someone or something. *A huge wave engulfed the swimmers.*

enigma (n) a mystery, or a puzzle. **enigmatic** (adj).

enjoy enjoying enjoyed (v) to get pleasure from doing something. **enjoyment** (n), **enjoyable** (adj), **enjoyably** (adv).

enlarge enlarging enlarged (v) to make something bigger. *We want to enlarge this photo.* **enlargement** (n).

enlist enlisting enlisted
1 (v) to join the army, navy, or air force.
2 (v) If you enlist someone's help, you get them to help you.

enormous (adj) extremely large. **enormity** (n), **enormously** (adv).

enough (n) as much as is needed. **enough** (adv).

enquire see **inquire**.

enquiry see **inquiry**.

enrage enraging enraged (v) to make someone angry. *Lucinda's unhelpful comments enrage me!*

enrich enriches enriching enriched (v) to improve the quality of something by adding good things to it. *You can enrich soil with fertilizer.* **enrichment** (n), **enriching** (adj).

enrol enrolling enrolled (v) When you enrol in a club, class, or school, you put your name on a list because you want to join. **enrolment** (n).

ensemble (on-*som*-bul) (n) a group of musicians or actors who often perform together.

ensue ensuing ensued (v) to happen next. *A furious argument ensued.* **ensuing** (adj).

ensure ensuring ensured (v) to make certain that something happens. *Please ensure that you lock the door.*

enter entering entered
1 (v) to go into a place.
2 (v) to say that you want to take part in a competition, race, or exam.
3 (v) to type a small amount of information into a computer, or write it in a book.

enterprise (n) something that you try to do that is new and difficult.

enterprising (adj) Someone who is enterprising has lots of good ideas and is brave enough to try things that are new and difficult.

entertain entertaining entertained
1 (v) to amuse and interest someone. **entertainer** (n), **entertainment** (n), **entertaining** (adj).
2 (v) to invite people to your home for a meal. *We're entertaining friends tonight.*

enthusiastic (adj) If you are enthusiastic about something, you are very keen to do it or like it very much. **enthusiasm** (n), **enthusiast** (n).

entice enticing enticed (v) to tempt someone to do something. **enticement** (n), **enticing** (adj).

entire (adj) whole. **entirely** (adv).

entrance entrancing entranced
1 (*en-trunss*) (n) the way into a place.
2 (*en-transs*) (v) to give someone a feeling of wonder and pleasure. **entrancing** (adj).

entrant (n) someone who takes part in a competition, race, or exam.

entrepreneur (n) someone who starts businesses and is good at finding new ways to make money. **entrepreneurial** (adj).

entrust entrusting entrusted (v) If you entrust someone with something valuable or important, you give it to them to look after for you.

entry entries
1 (n) a way into a place.
2 (n) a picture, story, answer, etc. that you send into a competition.
3 (n) a small piece of information in a dictionary, diary, computer, etc.

envelop (*en-vel-erp*) enveloping enveloped (v) to cover or surround something completely. *The house was soon enveloped in flames.*

envelope (*en-ver-lope* or *on-ver-lope*) (n) a paper cover for a letter or card.

enviable (adj) If someone has something enviable, you would like to have it yourself.

envious (adj) If you are envious, you wish that you could have something that someone else has. **enviously** (adv).

environment
1 (n) the natural world of the land, sea, and air. *We must protect the environment.* **environmentalist** (n), **environmental** (adj), **environmentally** (adv).
2 (n) all the things that influence your life, such as the area where you live, your family, and the things that happen to you. *Some children never have a secure home environment.*

environmentally friendly (adj) Products are environmentally friendly if they are made of substances that do not damage the natural environment.

envy envies envying envied (v) to wish that you could have something that someone else has. **envy** (n).

enzyme (n) a protein in the bodies of humans and animals which speeds up chemical reactions, without being changed itself. *Enzymes help to digest food.*

epic
1 (n) a long story, poem, or film about heroic adventures and great battles. **epic** (adj).
2 (adj) heroic, or impressive. *An epic voyage of exploration.*

epidemic (n) When there is an epidemic, an infectious disease spreads quickly to many people.

epigram (n) a short, witty saying. **epigrammatic** (adj).

epilepsy (n) a disease of the brain that causes a person to have sudden blackouts or fits. **epileptic** (n), **epileptic** (adj).

epilogue (n) a short speech or piece of writing added to the end of a play, story, or poem.

episode
1 (n) one of the programmes in a television or radio serial.
2 (n) an event or set of events in your life. *I don't want to talk about that embarrassing episode!*

epitaph (n) a short description of someone who has died, written on their gravestone.

equal equalling equalled
1 *(adj)* to be the same as something else in size, value, or amount. **equally** *(adv)*.
2 *(v)* If you **equal** what someone else has done, you do as well as them.

equality *(n)* the same rights for everyone. *Racial equality.*

equation *(n)* a mathematical statement that one set of numbers or values is equal to another set of numbers or values, for example, $4 \times 4 = 16$ or $3x + 2y = 13$.

equator *(n)* an imaginary line around the middle of the Earth, halfway between the North and South Poles. *The equator is marked by a red line on this picture.*
equatorial *(adj)*.

equator

equestrian *(adj)* to do with horse riding. *Equestrian events.*

equilateral *(adj)* An equilateral triangle has sides of equal length. *See* **shape**.

equilibrium *(n)* balance.

equinox equinoxes *(n)* one of the two days in the year when day and night last exactly the same length of time all over the world.

equip equipping equipped *(v)* to provide someone with all the things that they need

equipment *(n)* the tools and machines that you need for a particular purpose.

equivalent *(adj)* If one thing is **equivalent** to another, it is the same as the other in amount, value, or importance. **equivalent** *(n)*.

era *(n)* a period of time in history. *The Jurassic era.*

eradicate eradicating eradicated *(v)* to get rid of something completely, especially something bad like disease, crime, or poverty. **eradication** *(n)*.

erase erasing erased
1 *(v)* to rub something out with a rubber.
2 *(v)* to wipe out something stored in a computer or recorded on a tape.

eraser *(n)* a small piece of rubber used for removing pencil mistakes.

erect erecting erected
1 *(adj)* standing upright. **erection** *(n)*, **erectly** *(adv)*.
2 *(v)* to put up a structure. *This building was erected in 1982.* **erection** *(n)*.

erode eroding eroded *(v)* When something is **eroded**, it is gradually worn away by water or wind.

erosion *(n)* the gradual wearing away of a substance by water or wind. *Soil erosion.*

erotic *(adj)* to do with sexual love.

errand *(n)* If someone sends you on an **errand**, they ask you to go somewhere nearby to take a message or to deliver or collect something.

erratic *(adj)* If something is **erratic**, it does not follow a regular pattern. *Erratic behaviour.* **erratically** *(adv)*.

error *(n)* a mistake.

erupt erupting erupted.
1 *(v)* When a volcano **erupts**, it throws out rocks, hot ash, and lava with great force. **eruption** *(n)*.
2 *(v)* to start happening suddenly. *Fighting erupted on the streets.*
3 *(v)* If someone **erupts**, they suddenly become very angry.

escalator *(n)* a moving staircase. *This diagram of an escalator shows how a moving belt of steps is controlled by a drive wheel.*

drive wheel
for handrail

belt
(links
drive
wheels)

drive wheel
for steps

upper track

returning steps

rising steps

lower track
(supports
wheels)

moving handrail

escalator
(cutaway)

wheel
(runs along track)

escape escaping escaped
1 *(v)* to break free from a place where you have been kept by force. **escape** *(n)*.
2 *(v)* to avoid something. *We escaped the rush hour traffic.*
3 *(v)* to leak out of a crack or hole in something. *Gas was escaping from the pipe.* **escape** *(n)*.

escort escorting escorted *(v)* to go somewhere with someone, especially to protect them. **escort** *(n)*.

especially *(adv)* specially, or mainly. *Crispin is especially good at singing. Alex loves sport, especially tennis.* **especial** *(adj)*.

Esperanto *(n)* an artificial language invented in the 19th century and intended to be a world language.

espionage *(n)* spying.

essay *(n)* a piece of writing about a particular subject.

essential
1 *(adj)* vital and important. *It is essential that you read the instructions before you begin.* **essentially** *(adv)*.
2 *(n)* something you really need and cannot do without. *Do make sure that you bring the essentials listed below.*

establish establishes establishing established
1 *(v)* to set up a business, society, or organization. **establishment** *(n)*.
2 *(v)* to settle somewhere. *We feel established in our new house now*
3 *(v)* to confirm that something is true or correct. *The detectives established that the crime took place at night*

estate
1 *(n)* a large area of land owned by one person.
2 *(n)* an area of land with houses, factories, or offices on it.
3 *(n)* all the money, property, and other assets that someone leaves behind when they die.

estate agent *(n)* someone whose job is selling houses or land for people.

esteem *(n)* If you hold someone in **esteem**, you respect and admire them. **esteem** *(v)*, **esteemed** *(adj)*.

estimate
estimating estimated
1 *(ess-tim-ate) (v)* to work something out roughly.
2 *(ess-tim-ut) (n)* a rough guess or calculation about an amount, distance, cost, etc.

estuary *(est-yur-ee)* **estuaries** *(n)* the wide part of a river where it joins the sea.

etc. an abbreviated form of the Latin phrase *et cetera*, which means "and the rest". Etc. is used at the end of lists.

eternal *(adj)* lasting for ever. **eternally** *(adv)*.

ethnic *(adj)* to do with different racial groups. **ethnically** *(adv)*.

EU *(n)* a group of countries in Europe which have special trade and political agreements with each other. EU stands for European Union.

euro *(yoor-oh)* *(n)* the currency of some of the countries in the EU.

European *(adj)* from Europe, or to do with Europe. **European** *(n)*.

euthanasia *(yooth-an-ay-zee-a)* *(n)* the painless killing of someone who is suffering from an incurable or painful disease, or who is very old. Euthanasia is against the law in Britain.

evacuate evacuating evacuated *(v)* to move away from an area because it is dangerous. *Will everybody evacuate the building, please!* **evacuation** *(n)*.

evade evading evaded
1 *(v)* to keep away from someone, or to keep out of their way.
2 *(v)* to avoid something you should do or respond to. *Shona keeps evading the question.* **evasive** *(adj)*.

evaluate evaluating evaluated *(v)* to decide how good or how valuable something is, after thinking carefully about it. **evaluation** *(n)*.

evangelical *(adj)* An evangelical Christian tells people about the Christian gospel.

evaporate evaporating evaporated
1 *(v)* When a liquid **evaporates**, it changes into a vapour. **evaporation** *(n)*.
2 *(v)* to become less and then completely disappear. *Neal's confidence evaporated when he walked into the crowded room.*

even evening evened
1 *(adj)* An **even** number can be divided exactly by two.
2 *(adj)* equal. *An even score.* **evenly** *(adv)*.
3 *(adj)* smooth and level. *An even surface.*
4 *(adv)* in spite of. *Even if it takes all day, I'll complete the course.*
5 *(adv)* surprisingly. *We all enjoyed the film, even Sarah.*

6 **even out** *(v)* If you **even things out**, you make them more equal.

evening *(n)* the time of day between the late afternoon and the early part of the night.

event
1 *(n)* something that happens, especially something interesting or important. **eventful** *(adj)*.
2 *(n)* one of the activities, such as a race, that is held during a sports competition.

eventually *(adv)* finally, or at last. **eventual** *(adj)*.

ever
1 *(adv)* at any time. *Have you ever tried hang-gliding?*
2 *(adv)* all the time. *Ever grateful.*

evergreen *(n)* a bush or tree which has green leaves all the year round. **evergreen** *(adj)*.

everlasting *(adj)* never-ending.

every *(adj)* all the people or things in a group. *Every day of the week.*

everybody *(pronoun)* all people.

everyday *(adj)* usual, or normal. *An everyday event.*

everyone *(pronoun)* all people.

everything *(pronoun)* all things.

everywhere *(adv)* in all places.

evict evicting evicted *(v)* to force someone to move out of their home. **eviction** *(n)*.

evidence *(n)* information and facts that help to prove something or make you believe that something is true.

evident *(adj)* clear and obvious. **evidently** *(adv)*.

evil *(adj)* wicked and cruel. **evil** *(n)*.

evolution
1 *(n)* the gradual development of animals and plants over thousands of years in order to fit in better with their environment. **evolve** *(v)*, **evolutionary** *(adj)*.
2 *(n)* a gradual change into a different form. **evolve** *(v)*.

ewe *(n)* a female sheep.

exact *(adj)* perfectly correct and accurate. **exactness** *(n)*, **exactly** *(adv)*.

exaggerate exaggerating exaggerated *(v)* to make something seem bigger, better, more important, etc. than it really is. **exaggeration** *(n)* **exaggerated** *(adj)*.

exam *(n)* an official test that you take to show how much you know about a subject. Exam is short for examination.

examination
1 *(n)* See **exam**.

2 *(n)* a careful check, or an inspection. *A medical examination.*

examine examining examined
1 *(v)* to look carefully at something. *The detectives examined the evidence.*
2 *(v)* When doctors **examine** you, they check your body carefully to see what is wrong with you.
3 *(v)* to test someone in an exam. **examiner** *(n)*.

example
1 *(n)* something typical of a larger group of things. *The wallaby is an example of a marsupial.*
2 *(n)* a model for others to follow. *Felicity is an example to the rest of the class.*
3 If you **make an example** of someone, you punish them as a warning to other people.

exasperate exasperating exasperated *(v)* If someone or something **exasperates** you, they make you very annoyed. **exasperation** *(n)*, **exasperating** *(adj)*.

excavate excavating excavated *(v)* to dig in the earth, either in order to put up a building or to discover ancient remains. **excavation** *(n)*, **excavator** *(n)*.

exceed exceeding exceeded
1 *(v)* to be greater or better than something else. *The holiday exceeded my wildest dreams.*
2 *(v)* to do more than is allowed or expected. *Drivers who exceed the speed limit will be fined.*

excel *(ex-sel)* excelling excelled *(v)* If you **excel** at something, you do it extremely well. *Gaby excels at ice-skating.*

excellent *(adj)* very good indeed. **excellence** *(n)*, **excellently** *(adv)*.

except *(prep)* apart from. *Everyone except Hannah went home.* **except** *(conj)*.

exception
1 *(n)* something that is not included in a general rule or statement. *Jasper hates girls, with just a few exceptions.*
2 If someone **takes exception** to something, they are offended or annoyed by it.

exceptional *(adj)* outstanding, or rare. *Bryony shows exceptional talent for drawing.*

excerpt *(n)* a short piece taken from a longer book, film, or piece of music.

excess excesses
1 *(n)* too much of something. **excess** *(adj)*.
2 **in excess of** more than.

3 If you do something **to excess**, you do it too much.

excessive *(adj)* too much. *Augustus always eats an excessive amount.* **excessively** *(adv)*.

exchange exchanging exchanged
1 *(v)* to give one thing and receive another. *We exchanged presents. They exchanged glances.* **exchange** *(n)*.
2 *(n)* a place where people meet to buy and sell things. *The Stock Exchange.*
3 *(n)* the place where all the telephone calls in an area are connected.
4 **exchange rate** *(n)* a comparison of currencies throughout the world. You use the exchange rate to calculate how much money you will receive when you exchange one currency for another.

Exchequer *(n)* the British government department in charge of collecting taxes and paying out public money.

excite exciting excited *(v)* If something **excites** you, it makes you eager and interested. **excitement** *(n)*, **excited** *(adj)*, **exciting** *(adj)*.

exclaim exclaiming exclaimed *(v)* to say something loudly, especially because you are surprised or excited. **exclamation** *(n)*.

exclamation mark *(n)* the punctuation mark (!) used after an expression of surprise, excitement, or other strong feeling.

exclude excluding excluded
1 *(v)* If you **exclude** something, you leave it out. *The list excludes prices.* **excluding** *(prep)*.
2 *(v)* to stop someone joining or taking part in something. **exclusion** *(n)*.

excrete excreting excreted *(v)* to pass solid waste matter out of your body. **excretion** *(n)*, **excretory** *(adj)*.

excruciating *(adj)* extremely painful. **excruciatingly** *(adv)*.

excursion *(n)* a short journey, often to a place of interest.

excuse excusing excused
1 *(ex-kuze)* *(v)* If you **excuse** someone for doing something, you forgive them. **excusable** *(adj)*.
2 *(ex-kuse)* *(n)* a reason you give to explain why you have done something wrong.
3 *(ex-kuze)* *(v)* to give someone permission not to do something. *The instructor excused Lydia from games because of her injured toe.*

execute executing executed
1 *(v)* to kill someone as a punishment for a crime. **execution** *(n)*.
2 *(v)* If you **execute** a plan or order, you put it into action.

executive *(n)* someone who has a senior job in a company and is involved in planning its future.

exempt *(adj)* If you are **exempt** from something, you do not have to take part in it. **exemption** *(n)*, **exempt** *(v)*.

exercise exercising exercised
1 *(n)* physical activity that you do to keep fit and healthy.
2 *(v)* to make your body work hard, for example, by playing sport, in order to keep fit and healthy.
3 *(n)* a piece of work that you do in order to practise a skill. *Piano exercises.*

exhale exhaling exhaled *(v)* to breathe out. **exhalation** *(n)*.

exhaust exhausting exhausted
1 *(v)* If something **exhausts** you, it makes you very tired. **exhaustion** *(n)*, **exhausted** *(adj)*, **exhausting** *(adj)*.
2 *(v)* to use something up completely. *The explorers had almost exhausted their food supplies.*
3 *(n)* the waste gases produced by the engine of a motor vehicle.
4 *(n)* the pipe at the back of a motor vehicle from which waste gases from the engine are sent out.

exhibit exhibiting exhibited *(v)* to show something to the public. **exhibit** *(n)*, **exhibitor** *(n)*.

exhibition *(n)* a public display of works of art, historical objects, etc.

exhilarating *(adj)* very exciting and thrilling. **exhilaration** *(n)*.

exile exiling exiled *(v)* to send someone away from their own country and order them not to return. **exile** *(n)*.

exist existing existed
1 *(v)* to live, or to be real. *Did King Arthur exist?* **existence** *(n)*.
2 *(v)* to have just enough food to stay alive. *We existed on berries and water.*

exit exiting exited
1 *(v)* to leave, or to go out. **exit** *(n)*.
2 *(n)* the way out of a place.

exorcize or **exorcise** exorcizing exorcized *(v)* to make an evil spirit leave a person or a place. **exorcism** *(n)*, **exorcist** *(n)*.

exotic
1 *(adj)* from a foreign, tropical country. *An exotic plant.*
2 *(adj)* strange and fascinating. *An exotic perfume.*

expand expanding expanded *(v)* to increase in size. **expansion** *(n)*.

expanse *(n)* a very large area. *A vast expanse of desert stretched ahead.*

expect expecting expected
1 *(v)* to think that something will happen. *I expect it will rain.*
2 *(v)* to wait for someone to arrive. *We're expecting visitors.*
3 *(v)* to think that something ought to happen. *Aunt Jane expects you to behave perfectly.* **expectation** *(n)*.
4 *(informal)* If a woman is **expecting**, she is pregnant.

expedition
1 *(n)* a long journey for a special purpose, such as exploring.
2 *(n)* a short trip to do something enjoyable. *A shopping expedition.*

expel expelling expelled
1 *(v)* If someone is **expelled** from a school, they have to leave because they have behaved badly. **expulsion** *(n)*.
2 *(v)* to send or force something out. *You expel air from your lungs.*

expenditure *(n)* the amount of money that a person, a company, or a country spends.

expense
1 *(n)* the spending of money, time, energy, etc. *Never mind the expense!*
2 **expenses** *(plural n)* money spent on something to do with a job, which is paid back later. *Travelling expenses.*

expensive *(adj)* costing a lot of money. **expensively** *(adv)*.

experience experiencing experienced
1 *(v)* If you **experience** something, it happens to you.
2 *(n)* something that happens to you.
3 *(n)* the knowledge and skill that you gain by doing something. *Do you have any experience of sailing?* **experienced** *(adj)*.

experiment experimenting experimented
1 *(n)* a scientific test to try out a theory or to see the effect of something. **experiment** *(v)*.
2 *(v)* to try something new. **experiment** *(n)*.

expert *(n)* someone who is very skilled at something or knows a lot about a particular subject. **expertise** *(n)*, **expert** *(adj)*.

expire expiring expired
1 *(v)* When a ticket, licence, etc. **expires**, it reaches the end of the time when it can be used. **expiry** *(n)*.
2 *(v)* to die.

explain explaining explained
1 (v) to make something clear so that it is easier to understand.
explanation (n), **explanatory** (adj).
2 (v) to give a reason for something. *Please explain why you are so late.*
explanation (n).

explode exploding exploded (v)
If something explodes, it blows apart with a loud bang and great force.

exploit exploiting exploited
1 (ex-*ployt*) (v) to treat someone unfairly, usually by not paying them enough for their work.
exploitation (n).
2 (ex-*ployt*) (n) a brave or daring deed.

explore exploring explored
1 (v) to travel in order to discover what a place is like. **exploration** (n), **explorer** (n).
2 (v) If you **explore** an idea or possibility, you discuss it or think about it carefully. **exploratory** (adj).

explosion
1 (n) a sudden and noisy release of energy.
2 (n) a sudden increase or growth. *A population explosion.*

explosive
1 (n) a substance that can blow up.
2 (adj) able or likely to explode. **explosively** (adv).
3 (adj) If a situation is **explosive**, it is very dangerous.

export exporting exported (v)
to send goods to another country to be sold there. **export** (n).

expose exposing exposed
1 (v) to uncover something so that people can see it.
2 (v) to reveal the truth about someone or something.
3 (v) to let light fall on to a photographic film.

exposure
1 (n) the harmful effect of very cold weather or water on someone's body. *The survivors from the shipwreck were suffering from exposure.*
2 (n) a piece of film which produces a photograph when it is exposed to the light. *This film has 36 exposures.*
3 (n) the length of time that a photographic film is exposed to light.

express expresses expressing expressed
1 (v) to show what you feel or think by saying, doing, or writing something. *Harriet expressed her happiness in a little dance.*
2 (n) a fast train that stops at only a few stations.
3 (adj) very fast. *Express delivery.*

expression
1 (n) the act of showing your feelings. *Self-expression.*
2 (n) the look on someone's face. *A puzzled expression.*
3 (n) a phrase that has a particular meaning. *Where does the expression "lock, stock, and barrel" come from?*

exquisite (adj) very beautiful and delicate. *An exquisite piece of embroidery.* **exquisitely** (adv).

extend extending extended
1 (v) to make something longer or bigger. *We are going to extend our house at the back.* **extension** (n).
2 (v) to stretch out. *Our garden extends right down to the stream.*

extensive
1 (adj) spreading over a wide area.
2 (adj) including a lot of things. *An extensive choice of desserts.*

extent (n) the size, level, or scale of something. *What is the extent of the damage?*

exterior (n) the outside of something, especially a building. **exterior** (adj).

exterminate exterminating exterminated (v) to kill large numbers of people or animals. **extermination** (n).

external (adj) on the outside. **externally** (adv).

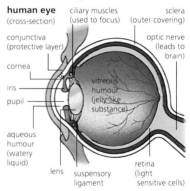
dodo

extinct
1 (adj) If a type of animal or flower is **extinct**, it has died out. *The dodo was a large, flightless bird that lived on the island of Mauritius and became extinct in the 18th century.* **extinction** (n).
2 (adj) If a volcano is **extinct**, it has stopped erupting.

extinguish extinguishes extinguishing extinguished
1 (v) to put out a flame, fire, or light.
2 (v) to put an end to a feeling or belief. *Nothing could extinguish Romeo's love for Juliet.*

extra
1 (adj) more than the usual amount. *An extra helping of chips.* **extra** (adv).
2 (n) someone with a very small part in a film, usually in a crowd scene.

extract extracting extracted
1 (ex-*trakt*) (v) to take or pull something out. **extraction** (n).
2 (ex-*trakt*) (n) a short section taken from a book, piece of music, etc.

extraordinary (adj) very unusual, or remarkable. **extraordinarily** (adv).

extraterrestrial
1 (adj) to do with, or coming from outer space. *Extraterrestrial messages.*
2 (n) a creature from outer space.

extravagant (adj) If you are **extravagant**, you spend too much money, or are wasteful in the way you use things. **extravagance** (n), **extravagantly** (adv).

extreme
1 (adj) very great. *Extreme happiness.* **extremely** (adv).
2 (adj) furthest, or outermost. *We reached the extreme edge of the wood.* **extremity** (n).

extrovert (n) someone who enjoys being with other people and is lively and talkative. **extrovert** (adj).

exuberant (ex-yoo-ber-ent) (adj) very cheerful and lively. **exuberance** (n), **exuberantly** (adv).

eye eyeing eyed
1 (n) one of the two organs in your head that you use for seeing.
2 (n) the small hole in a needle.
3 (v) to look carefully at someone or something. *Bert eyed the parrot suspiciously.*
4 If you have an **eye for something**, you can judge how good it is. *Sue has an eye for a bargain.*

human eye (cross-section)

ciliary muscles (used to focus)
sclera (outer covering)
conjunctiva (protective layer)
optic nerve (leads to brain)
cornea
iris
pupil
vitreous humour (jelly-like substance)
aqueous humour (watery liquid)
lens
suspensory ligament
retina (light sensitive cells)

eyebrow (n) the line of hair that grows above each of your eyes.

eyelash eyelashes (n) one of the short, curved hairs that grow on the edge of your eyelids.

eyelid (n) the upper or lower fold of skin that covers your eye when it is closed.

eyesight (n) the ability to see.

eyewitness eyewitnesses (n) someone who has seen something take place and can describe what happened.

eyrie (ear-ee) (n) the nest of an eagle or some other bird of prey, built high on trees, mountains, or cliffs.

Ff

fable (n) a story that teaches a lesson. Fables are often about animals. *Aesop's fables.*

fabric (n) cloth, or material.

fabulous
1 (adj) wonderful, or marvellous.
2 (adj) existing only in stories and legends. *Fabulous creatures.* **fabulously** (adv).

face facing faced
1 (n) the front of your head, from your forehead to your chin. **facial** (adj).
2 (n) a side or surface of something. *A mountain face. A clock face.*
3 (v) to look towards something. *Our flat faces the park.* **facing** (adj).
4 (v) to meet or tackle something. *Robin faced many dangers.*

facility facilities
1 (n) a service provided for people to use and enjoy, such as a sports centre, park, etc.
2 (n) the ability to do something easily. *Daisy has a facility for drawing.*

fact
1 (n) a piece of information that is true. **factual** (adj), **factually** (adv).
2 **in fact** (adv) actually.

factor
1 (n) one of the things that helps to produce a result. *Cosmo's speed was a factor in his success.*
2 (n) a whole number that can be divided exactly into a larger number. *2, 3, 4, and 6 are factors of 12.*

factory factories (n) a building where things are made in large numbers, using machines.

fad (n) (informal) a temporary fashion or interest.

fade fading faded
1 (v) to become paler in colour.
2 (v) to become gradually weaker. *Hope is fading among the survivors.*

faeces (fee-sees) (plural n) the solid waste matter that people and animals pass out of their bodies.

Fahrenheit (adj) measured on a temperature scale on which water boils at 212° and freezes at 32°.

fail failing failed
1 (v) If you **fail** an exam or test, you do not pass it. **fail** (n).
2 (v) If you **fail** to do something, you do not do it. **failure** (n).
3 **without fail** (adv) definitely, or every single time.

failing (n) a fault or weakness in someone or something.

faint fainting fainted; fainter faintest
1 (adj) weak. *A faint sound.* **faintness** (n), **faintly** (adv).
2 (v) to become dizzy and lose consciousness for a short time.
3 (adj) A **faint** chance or idea is a very slight one.
4 **faint-hearted** (adj) timid and not at all confident.

fair fairer fairest
1 (adj) reasonable and equal. *Fair treatment.* **fairness** (n), **fairly** (adv).
2 (adj) **Fair** hair is light yellow.
3 (adj) quite good. **fairly** (adv).
4 (n) an outdoor entertainment with rides, amusements, and stalls. **fairground** (n).

fairy fairies
1 (n) a magical creature like a tiny person with wings, found in fairy stories.
2 **fairy lights** (n) small, coloured lights that are used to decorate Christmas trees.
3 **fairy story** or **fairy tale** (n) a children's story about magic, fairies, giants, witches, etc.

faith
1 (n) trust and confidence in someone or something. *Our coach has lots of faith in our team.*
2 (n) a religion.

faithful (adj) loyal and trustworthy. **faithfulness** (n), **faithfully** (adv).

fake faking faked
1 (v) to make a copy of something and pretend that it is genuine. *Mia faked her boss's signature.*
2 (n) a copy of something that is made to fool people. *This painting is not by Raphael, but it's a clever fake.* **fake** (adj).

falcon

falcon (n) a bird of prey that catches small birds in flight. In the traditional practice of falconry, falcons are trained to return with their prey to their owner, or falconer. *This young falcon stands on the falconer's gloved fist, and wears a leg strap and leash, which will be removed later.*

fall falling fell fallen
1 (v) to drop downwards to the ground. **fall** (n).

2 (v) to decrease, or to become lower. *The temperature has fallen.* **fall** (n).
3 (v) to become. *After a while, Yves fell asleep.*
4 (v) to happen. *Night fell.*
5 (n) (US) the season between summer and winter, when it gets colder, the days get shorter, and the leaves fall from the trees (autumn, UK).
6 (v) If two people **fall out**, they quarrel with each other.
7 (v) If something **falls through**, it fails to happen.

fallow (adj) Land that is **fallow** has been ploughed, but not planted with crops so that it can improve in quality.

false
1 (adj) not true, or not correct. *False information.* **falsely** (adv).
2 (adj) not real. *False eyelashes.*

fame (n) being famous. *Terry longs for fame.* **famed** (adj).

familiar
1 (adj) If something is **familiar**, it is well known or easily recognized. *A familiar saying.*
2 (adj) If you are **familiar** with something, you know it well. *Quentin is familiar with all Shakespeare's plays.* **familiarity** (n).

family families
1 (n) a group of people related to each other, especially parents and their children.
2 (n) a group of related animals or plants. *The leopard and the jaguar are members of the cat family.*
3 **family tree** (n) a chart that shows how the members of a family are related over many generations.

famine (n) a serious shortage of food in a country.

famished (adj) If you are **famished**, you are very hungry.

famous (adj) If someone is famous, they are well known to many people.

fan
1 (n) an enthusiastic supporter of a sport, pop group, etc.
2 (n) a machine or an object that you use to blow or wave air on to you, in order to keep cool. **fan** (v).

leaf or mount   stick   guard
Japanese fan

fanatic (n) someone who is wildly enthusiastic about a belief, a cause, or an interest. *Lee is a football fanatic.* **fanatical** (adj), **fanatically** (adv).

fancy

fancy fancies fancying fancied; fancier fanciest
1 *(adj)* highly decorated, or elaborate.
2 *(v) (informal)* If you **fancy** something, you would like to do it or have it. *I fancy some lunch.*
3 *(v) (informal)* If you **fancy** someone, you are attracted to them.

fancy dress *(n)* If you wear **fancy dress**, you dress up as someone else, usually for a party.

fang *(n)* a long, pointed tooth.

fantastic
1 *(adj)* too strange to be believable. **fantastically** *(adv)*.
2 *(adj)* extremely good. **fantastically** *(adv)*.

fantasy fantasies
1 *(n)* something that you imagine happening, but which is not likely to happen in real life. **fantasize** *(v)*.
2 *(n)* a very imaginative story.

far farther farthest *or* further furthest
1 *(adv)* at or to a great distance. *Have you travelled far?*
2 *(adv)* very much. *I far prefer cycling to walking.*
3 *(adj)* opposite, or distant. *Kim was waving on the far side of the river.*

farce
1 *(n)* a funny play in which there are many silly misunderstandings.
2 *(n)* a ridiculous situation. **farcical** *(adj)*.

fare
1 *(n)* the cost of travelling on a bus, train, plane, etc.
2 *(n) (old-fashioned)* food and drink.

Far East *(n)* the countries of eastern Asia such as China and Japan.

farewell *(interject)* goodbye. **farewell** *(n)*.

far-fetched *(adj)* hard to believe.

farm farming farmed
1 *(v)* to grow crops and rear animals. **farmer** *(n)*, **farming** *(n)*.
2 *(n)* land and buildings used for growing crops or rearing animals. *The picture shows a range of machinery used on a farm.* **farm** *(adj)*.

fascinate fascinating fascinated *(v)* If someone or something **fascinates** you, you are really interested and excited by them. **fascination** *(n)*.

fascism *(fash-izm) (n)* a way of organizing a country according to extreme right-wing and nationalist principles, with a powerful dictator and only one political party. **fascist** *(n)*.

fashion
1 *(n)* a style of clothing that is popular at a certain time. **fashionable** *(adj)*.
2 *(n)* a way of doing things.

20th-century fashions

1900s　1910s　1920s　1930s　1940s　1950s　1960s

fast fasting fasted; faster fastest
1 *(adj)* quick. **fast** *(adv)*.
2 *(v)* to give up eating food for a time. *Muslims fast during Ramadan.* **fast** *(n)*.
3 *(adv)* firmly, or tightly. *Kit's head was stuck fast between the railings.*
4 *(adj)* ahead of the right time. *My watch is five minutes fast.*
5 *(adj)* **Fast** colours or dyes do not run or fade when you wash them.

fasten fastening fastened *(v)* to tie or join something firmly. **fastener** *(n)*, **fastening** *(n)*.

fast food *(n)* food, such as burgers and pizzas, that is prepared and served quickly by restaurants.

fat fatter fattest
1 *(adj)* overweight, or plump. **fatness** *(n)*, **fatten** *(v)*.
2 *(n)* the soft substance in the body of a person or animal that helps to keep them warm. **fatty** *(adj)*.
3 *(n)* **Fats** are found in foods such as meat, milk, and cheese. They give you energy and are stored in your body to keep you warm.
4 *(adj)* big, or thick. *A fat dictionary.*

fatal
1 *(adj)* causing death. *A fatal accident.* **fatally** *(adv)*.
2 *(adj)* likely to have important, and usually bad, results. *A fatal decision.*

fatality fatalities *(n)* a death caused by an accident, a war, or another form of violence.

fate
1 *(n)* the force that some people believe controls events and decides what happens to people.
2 *(n)* Your **fate** is what will happen to you.

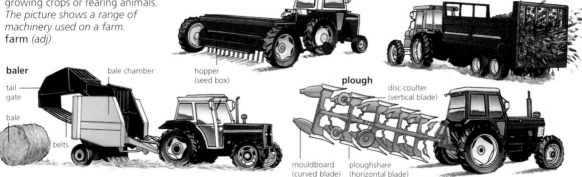

seed drill
hopper (seed box)

muck spreader
vertical beater

baler
bale chamber
tail gate
bale
belts

plough
disc coulter (vertical blade)
mouldboard (curved blade)
ploughshare (horizontal blade)

Some words that begin with a "f" sound are spelt "ph"

fateful *(adj)* important because it has a strong, usually unpleasant, effect on future events. *I remember the fateful day I first met Archie.* **fatefully** *(adv).*

father *(n)* a male parent. **fatherhood** *(n),* **fatherly** *(adj).*

fathom fathoming fathomed
1 *(v)* If you cannot **fathom** something, you cannot understand it.
2 *(n)* a unit for measuring the depth of water. 1 fathom = 1.8m or 6ft.

fatigue *(fat-eeg) (n)* great tiredness.

faucet *(faw-set) (n) (US)* a piece of equipment used to control the flow of a liquid (tap, *UK).*

fault faulting faulted
1 *(n)* something wrong. *A mechanical fault.* **faulty** *(adj).*
2 *(n)* a weakness in someone's character. *Everyone has some faults.*
3 *(n)* If something is your **fault**, you are to blame for it.
4 *(v)* to criticize, or to find a mistake in something. *I can't fault your plan.*
5 *(n)* a large crack in the Earth's surface that can cause earthquakes. *The picture shows a tear fault, like the San Andreas fault in California, USA, where parts of the Earth's crust have pulled in opposite directions.*

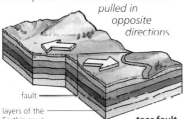

fault

layers of the Earth's crust

tear fault

fauna *(n)* the animal life of a particular area. *Woodland fauna.*

favour favouring favoured
1 *(n)* something helpful or kind that you do for someone.
2 *(v)* to like one thing or person best. *Dad always favours Johnny!*
3 If you are **in favour of** something, you agree with it or support it.

favourite
1 *(n)* the person or thing that you like best. **favourite** *(adj).*
2 *(n)* the person, team, or animal that is expected to win a race.

favouritism *(n)* unfair kindness shown to one person more than others.

fawn
1 *(n)* a young deer.
2 *(n)* a light brown colour. **fawn** *(adj).*

fax faxes *(n)* a copy of a letter, document, etc. sent along a telephone line, using a special machine. **fax** *(v).*

fear fearing feared
1 *(n)* the feeling you have when you are in danger or you expect something bad to happen. **fearful** *(adj).*
2 *(v)* to be afraid of something or someone.
3 *(v)* to be worried about something. *I fear we're going to be late again.*

fearless *(adj)* very brave and not afraid. **fearlessly** *(adv).*

fearsome *(adj)* frightening. *A fearsome monster.*

feasible *(adj)* If something is feasible, it can be done. **feasibility** *(n),* **feasibly** *(adv).*

feast *(n)* a large meal for a lot of people on a special occasion. **feast** *(v).*

feat *(n)* an amazing achievement.

feather *(n)* one of the light, fluffy parts that cover a bird's body. **feathered** *(adj).* Also see **bird**.

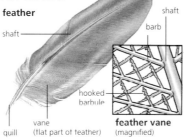

feather

shaft

shaft

barb

hooked barbule

quill

vane (flat part of feather)

feather vane (magnified)

feature featuring featured
1 *(n)* Your **features** are the different parts of your face.
2 *(n)* an important part or quality of something. *My new computer has several useful features.* **feature** *(v).*
3 *(v)* to use someone as one of the main stars in a film.
4 *(n)* a newspaper article or part of a television programme that deals with a particular subject. *A music feature.*

federal *(adj)* If a country has a federal government, it is made up of several states that are controlled by a central government but also have their own government and make their own laws. **federalism** *(n),* **federalist** *(n).*

fed up *(adj) (informal)* If you are **fed up**, you are bored, or unhappy about something.

fee *(n)* the amount of money that someone charges for a service.

feeble feebler feeblest *(adj)* very weak. **feebly** *(adv).*

feed feeding fed
1 *(v)* to give food to a person or an animal.
2 *(v)* When babies or animals **feed**, they eat.

3 *(n)* food for animals.
4 *(v)* to put something, for example coins or information, into a machine. *Jan fed all the data into her computer.*

feedback
1 *(n)* comments and reactions to something. *I'd like some feedback on these ideas.*
2 *(n)* the loud, piercing noise made when the sound produced by an amplifier goes back into it.

feel feeling felt
1 *(v)* to touch something with your fingers, or to experience something touching you. *Jess felt the sun on her face.*
2 *(v)* to have a certain emotion or sensation. *Maddy felt angry.* **feeling** *(n).*
3 *(v)* to think, or to have an opinion. *Barney felt that he had been badly treated.* **feeling** *(n).*

feign *(rhymes with pain)* feigning feigned *(v)* to pretend. *Bob feigned illness so that he could miss the test.*

feisty *(fy-stee) (adj) (informal)* If you are **feisty**, you are lively and able to stand up for yourself.

feline *(adj)* to do with cats.

fell felling felled *(v)* to cut something down or make something fall. *The gardener felled the tree. The wrestler felled his opponent.*

fellow
1 *(n) (old-fashioned)* a man, or a boy.
2 *(adj)* belonging to the same class or group. *I like my fellow students.*

felon *(n)* someone who has committed a serious crime. **felony** *(n).*

felt
1 *(n)* a thick cloth made of wool or other fibres pressed together.
2 **felt-tip** *(n)* a colouring pen with a felt nib.

female *(n)* a person or animal of the sex that can give birth to babies or lay eggs. **female** *(adj).*

feminine
1 *(adj)* to do with women.
2 *(adj)* Someone who is **feminine** has qualities that are supposed to be typical of women. **femininity** *(n).*
3 *(adj)* belonging to one of the classes or genders of nouns in French, Latin, and other languages.

feminist *(n)* someone who believes strongly that women ought to have the same opportunities and rights that men have. **feminism** *(n),* **feminist** *(adj).*

fen *(n)* an area of flat, low, marshy land.

Some words that begin with a "f" sound are spelt "ph".

fence fencing fenced
1 (n) a wooden or wire barrier built to separate two areas of land.
fencing (n), fence (v).
2 (v) to fight with long, thin swords or foils, as a sport. fencer (n), fencing (n).
3 If you sit on the fence, you are undecided and so avoid taking either side in an argument.

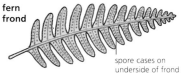

fencing

mask

foil

fend fending fended
1 (v) If you fend for someone, you take care of them.
2 (v) If you fend off someone who is attacking you, you defend yourself.

fender (n) a low guard put around a fireplace to stop coal, etc. falling into the room.

ferment fermenting fermented (v) When a drink, such as beer or wine, ferments, a chemical change takes place which makes the sugar in it turn into alcohol. fermentation (n).

fern (n) a plant with feathery leaves, or fronds, and no flowers, that usually grows in damp places.

fern
frond

spore cases on underside of frond

ferocious (adj) very fierce and savage. ferocity (n), ferociously (adv).

ferret (n) a small, fierce mammal, often used for catching rabbits.

ferry ferries ferrying ferried
1 (n) a boat or ship that regularly carries people across a stretch of water.
2 (v) to carry people or things from one place to another.

fertile
1 (adj) able to have babies. fertility (n).
2 (adj) Land that is fertile is good for growing lots of crops and plants. fertility (n).

fertilize or **fertilise** fertilizing fertilized
1 (v) When an egg or a plant is fertilized, sperm joins with the egg, or pollen comes into contact with the reproductive part of the plant, so that reproduction begins. fertilization (n).

2 (v) to put a substance, such as manure, on land to make it richer and make crops grow better. fertilizer (n).

fervent (adj) If someone is fervent about something, they believe in it passionately. fervently (adv).

festival
1 (n) a time when people celebrate something, such as a holy day.
2 (n) an organized set of artistic or musical events, often held at the same time each year. An opera festival.

festive (adj) cheerful and lively because there is something to celebrate. A festive mood.

festoon festooning festooned (v) to cover something with decorations.

fetch fetches fetching fetched
1 (v) to go to get something or somebody.
2 (v) to be sold for a particular price. That lamp should fetch a good price.

fetching (adj) attractive, or pretty.

fête (rhymes with late) (n) an outdoor event with games, stalls, and things for sale, usually held to raise money for charity.

fetus or **foetus** (feet-uss) fetuses (n) a baby or animal before it is born, at the stage when it is developing in its mother's womb. See pregnant.

feud (rhymes with chewed) (n) a bitter quarrel between two people or families that lasts for a long time. feud (v).

feudalism (n) the medieval system in which people were given land and protection by the landowner, and in return, worked and fought for him. This diagram shows how feudalism worked, with the king at the head of the system, and people at every level of society owing loyalty to the lord above them. feudal (adj).

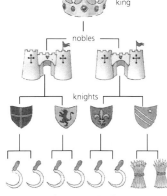

feudal system

king

nobles

knights

peasants (free men and serfs or villeins)

fever
1 (n) If someone has a fever, they have a high temperature. feverish (adj).
2 (n) great excitement or agitation. feverish (adj).

few fewer fewest (adj) not many. few (n).

fez fezzes (n) a round, flat-topped, red hat, worn by some Muslim men.

fiancé (fee-on-say) (n) If a man and woman are engaged to be married, he is her fiancé.

fiancée (fee-on-say) (n) If a man and woman are engaged to be married, she is his fiancée.

fiasco (n) a complete failure.

fib fibbing fibbed (v) to tell a small lie. fib (n), fibber (n).

fibre
1 (n) a fine thread of cloth.
2 (n) a part of foods such as cereals and vegetables, which passes through the body, but is not digested. Fibre helps you to digest food. fibrous (adj).

fibreglass (n) material made from fine threads of glass, used in buildings, cars, boats, etc.

fibre optics (singular n) the passing of light through extremely thin glass or plastic tubes, or fibres. Fibre optics is used in operations and for sending telephone signals.

fickle (adj) Someone who is fickle changes their mind very often. fickleness (n).

fiction (n) stories that are made up. fictional (adj).

fiddle fiddling fiddled
1 (v) to keep touching or playing about with something.
2 (v) (informal) to cheat. Nora fiddled her expenses. fiddle (n).
3 (n) (informal) a violin. fiddler (n).

fiddly (adj) If something is fiddly, it is awkward to do because it is very small or very complicated.

fidget fidgeting fidgeted (v) to keep moving because you are bored or uneasy. fidgety (adj).

field fielding fielded
1 (n) a piece of land, sometimes used for growing crops or playing sports.
2 (v) In games like cricket and baseball, the team that is fielding tries to catch the ball and get the batting team out.
3 (n) an area of study or interest. Robin is an expert in the field of ornithology.

fielder (n) someone who fetches or catches the ball in games like cricket and baseball.

field trip (n) If you go on a **field trip**, you travel somewhere with your school to study something in its natural environment.

fiend (rhymes with leaned) (n) a wicked person, or a devil. **fiendish** (adj), **fiendishly** (adv).

fierce fiercer fiercest (adj) violent, or aggressive. **fierceness** (n), **fiercely** (adv).

fiery fierier fieriest
1 (adj) like fire, or to do with fire.
2 (adj) very emotional. A fiery temper.

fiesta (fee-est-a) (n) a holiday or religious festival, especially in Spain and Latin America.

fight fighting fought
1 (v) to attack someone and try to hurt them. **fight** (n).
2 (v) to have an argument. **fight** (n).
3 (n) a determined attempt to achieve something. The speaker invited us to join the fight against poverty.

fighter
1 (n) someone who fights, such as a boxer or soldier.
2 (n) an aeroplane used in a war.

figure figuring figured
1 (n) a written number.
2 (n) a person's shape. Marilyn has a wonderful figure.
3 (n) a person. A well-known figure.
4 **figure out** (v) to understand or solve something.

file filing filed
1 (n) a box or folder for papers or documents.
2 (v) to put papers or documents away in a file.
3 (n) a tool used to make things smooth. **file** (v). See **woodwork**.
4 **computer file** (n) a set of data held in a computer.
5 **single file** (n) a line of people one behind the other.

fill filling filled
1 (v) to make something full.
2 (v) If you **fill in a form**, you answer all the questions on it.
3 (v) If you **fill in** for someone, you do their job while they are away.

fillet (n) a piece of meat or fish with the bones taken out. **fillet** (v).

filling
1 (n) a substance that a dentist puts into holes in your teeth to prevent more decay.
2 (n) the food inside a sandwich, pie, cake, etc.

filling station (n) a garage where you can buy petrol.

filly fillies (n) a young female horse.

film filming filmed
1 (n) a story shown on television or at the cinema.
2 (n) a roll of light-sensitive material, that you use in a camera to take photographs.
3 (v) to record something with a camera or camcorder.
4 (n) a very thin layer of something. A film of dirt.

filter filtering filtered
1 (n) a device that cleans liquids or gases as they pass through it. See **aquarium**.
2 (v) to put something through a filter.

filth
1 (n) dirt. **filthiness** (n), **filthy** (adj).
2 (n) rudeness. Don't talk filth! **filthiness** (n), **filthy** (adj).

fin
1 (n) a flap-like shape on the body of a fish, used for steering it through the water. See **fish**.
2 (n) a small, triangular-shaped structure on an aircraft, boat, etc., used to help with steering. See **aircraft**.
3 **fins** (plural n) long, flat attachments that you fit on your feet to help you swim underwater. See **scuba diving**.

final (adj) last. **finally** (adv).

finalize or **finalise** finalizing finalized (v) to finish making arrangements. Have you finalized the dates for your trip?

finance
1 (n) money, or the management of money. An expert in finance. **financial** (adj), **financially** (adv).
2 (v) to provide money for something.
3 **finances** (plural n) the amount of money that an individual or a company has. Our finances are rather low at the moment.

find finding found
1 (v) to discover, or to come across something.
2 **find out** (v) to learn about something or someone.
3 (n) a valuable or important discovery. This restaurant is a real find!

findings (plural n) the results of an inquiry or a court case.

fine fining fined; finer finest
1 (adj) very good, or excellent. A fine painting.
2 (adj) okay, or all right.
3 (adj) not rainy. A fine day.
4 (adj) thin, or delicate.

5 (v) to demand some money as a punishment for doing something wrong. **fine** (n).

finger fingering fingered
1 (n) one of the long parts of your hand that you can move.
2 (n) an object shaped like a finger. A chocolate finger.
3 (v) to touch something lightly with your fingers. Ted fingered the fishing rod longingly.

fingerprint (n) the print made by the pattern of curved lines on your fingertips.

finicky (adj) fussy, especially about food. A finicky eater.

finish finishes finishing finished
1 (v) to end or complete something.
2 (n) the end of something, such as a race.

finite (ty-nyte) (adj) limited, or with an end. **finitely** (adv).

fiord see **fjord**.

fir (n) a pointed, evergreen tree with needle-like leaves and cones.

fire firing fired
1 (n) flames, heat, and light produced by burning.
2 (v) to shoot a gun or other weapon.
3 (v) to sack someone from their job.

fire extinguisher (n) a metal case containing chemicals and water, that you use to put out a fire. When you squeeze the handle of a foam and water fire extinguisher, the piercer punctures the canister which releases carbon dioxide gas. The gas pushes on the surface of the water and detergent mixture, forcing it up the tube, through the hose and out of the spray nozzle, in a jet of foam and water.

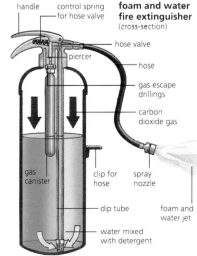

handle — control spring for hose valve — **foam and water fire extinguisher** (cross-section)

hose valve
piercer
hose
gas escape drillings
carbon dioxide gas
gas canister
clip for hose
spray nozzle
dip tube
foam and water jet
water mixed with detergent

fireproof *(adj)* If something is fireproof, it is made from materials that will not catch fire.

firetrap *(n)* a building that would be hard to escape from if it caught fire.

firework *(n)* a container, filled with gunpowder and other chemicals, that makes bangs and coloured sparks when it is lit.

firm firmer firmest
1 *(adj)* strong and solid. *A firm bed.*
2 *(adj)* definite and not easily altered. *A firm manner.* **firmly** *(adv)*.
3 *(n)* a business, or a company.

first
1 *(n)* a person, or a thing that acts or happens earliest. *Adam was the first to leave the party.*
2 *(adj)* earliest in time. *Michaela took the first bus.*
3 *(adv)* before something else. *Guy always gets to school first.*
4 *(adj)* most important. *The first team.* **firstly** *(adv)*.

first aid *(n)* medical help that is given to someone immediately after an accident.

fish fish *or* fishes; fishes fishing fished
1 *(n)* an animal that lives in water and has scales, fins, and gills. *The fish shown below is a female perch. Also see* **gill**.
2 *(v)* to try to catch fish. **fishing** *(n)*. *See* **angling**.
3 *(v)* If you **fish** for information, you try to discover something in an indirect way.

fist *(n)* a tightly closed hand.

fit fitting fitted; fitter fittest
1 *(adj)* healthy and strong. **fitness** *(n)*.
2 *(v)* to be the right size or shape. *This skirt doesn't fit.*
3 *(n)* a sudden, uncontrollable attack of something. *A fit of giggles.*
4 *(adj)* good enough. *Fit for the job.*
5 *(n)* If someone has an epileptic **fit**, they suddenly become unconscious and their muscles become tense.

fitting
1 *(adj)* right, or suitable. *Some people think it is fitting to wear dark colours at funerals.*
2 **fittings** *(plural n)* furnishings, such as carpets, curtains, and equipment.

fix fixes fixing fixed
1 *(v)* to mend something.
2 *(v)* to decide on something. *Shall we fix a date for the party?*
3 *(v)* to attach something to another thing. *Fix the photograph to the wall.*
4 *(n)* *(informal)* If you are **in a fix**, you are in an awkward situation.

fixation *(n)* an obsession, or something that you think about a great deal. *Jonathan has a fixation about his height.*

fixture
1 *(n)* a sports match or event.
2 *(n)* an object that is fitted into a house, such as a bath or cupboard.

fizz fizzes fizzing fizzed *(v)* to bubble and hiss. **fizzy** *(adj)*.

fizzle fizzling fizzled *(v)* *(informal)* If something **fizzles out**, it gradually gives up after a good start.

flag *(n)* a piece of cloth with a pattern on it, that is a symbol of a country, organization, etc.

international flags

United Nations   Olympic Games

International Red Cross   European Union

flair *(n)* natural skill or ability. *Jamie has a flair for cooking.*

flak
1 *(n)* anti-aircraft fire.
2 *(n)* *(informal)* opposition and criticism.

flake flaking flaked
1 *(n)* a small, thin piece of something. *Large flakes of paint fell off the door.*
2 *(v)* If something **flakes**, small, thin pieces of it peel off. **flaky** *(adj)*.
3 **flake out** *(v)* *(informal)* to fall asleep or collapse.

flamboyant *(adj)* bold, showy, and brightly coloured.

flame
1 *(n)* a tongue of fire. **flaming** *(adj)*.
2 **flame-coloured** *(adj)* deep orangey-red.

flamingo flamingos *or* flamingoes *(n)* a pink, long-legged bird with webbed feet.

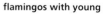

flammable *(adj)* likely to catch fire. *Flammable material.*

flamingos with young

flank flanking flanked
1 *(n)* the side of an animal, between its ribs and hips.
2 *(v)* to be at the side of someone or something. *The king was flanked by attendants.*

flannel
1 *(n)* woven, woollen fabric.
2 *(n)* a small square of cloth, used to wash your face.

flap flapping flapped
1 *(v)* to move up and down. *The bird flapped its wings.*
2 *(v)* to swing loosely. *The sail flapped in the breeze.*

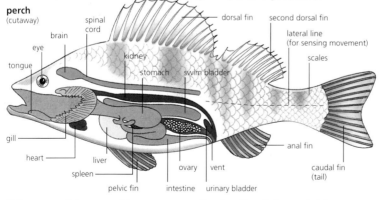

perch (cutaway)
spinal cord
brain
eye
tongue
kidney
stomach   swim bladder
dorsal fin   second dorsal fin
lateral line (for sensing movement)
scales
gill
heart
liver
spleen
ovary   vent
pelvic fin   intestine   urinary bladder
anal fin
caudal fin (tail)

fisherman fishermen *(n)* someone who catches fish for a job or as a sport.

fishmonger *(fish-mung-gur)* *(n)* someone who sells fish.

fishy fishier fishiest
1 *(adj)* tasting or smelling of fish.
2 *(adj)* *(informal)* strange and suspicious. *A fishy story.*

fjord *or* **fiord** *(fee-ord)* *(n)* a narrow channel of sea that runs inland between high cliffs. Fjords were formed in the Ice Age by glaciers.

flab *(n)* extra fat on your body. **flabbiness** *(n)*, **flabby** *(adj)*.

flabbergasted *(adj)* *(informal)* stunned and surprised.

flaccid *(flass-id)* *(adj)* soft and limp.

3 (n) something attached on one side only. *The flap of an envelope.*
4 (n) a hinged part on an aircraft wing, used to control the way that the aircraft rises and falls. *See* **aircraft**.
5 (n) (informal) a state of panic.

flapjack (n) a sweet, sticky cake made from oats and syrup.

flare flaring flared
1 (n) a bright flame used as an emergency signal.
2 (v) If something **flares up**, it suddenly becomes stronger or more violent.

flash flashes flashing flashed
1 (n) a short burst of light.
2 (v) to shine brightly, in bursts.
3 (n) a short burst of something. *A flash of inspiration. A news flash.*
4 (v) to show something briefly. *Emily flashed a smile at the sailor.*

flashback (n) a part of a book or film that tells you what happened earlier.

flashy flashier flashiest (adj)
If something is **flashy**, it is showy and expensive. *Todd wears very flashy clothes.*

flask
1 (n) a narrow-necked bottle, used in a science laboratory. *See* **apparatus**.
2 (n) a container which is insulated so that it keeps liquids hot or cold. *See* **vacuum flask**.

flat flatter flattest
1 (adj) level, or smooth. *A flat surface.*
2 (adj) not high. *Flat shoes.*
3 (adj) emptied of air. *A flat tyre.*
4 (adj) very definite. *A flat refusal.*
5 (n) a set of rooms for living in, usually on one floor of a building.
6 (adj) In music, a **flat** note is lower in pitch than the usual note. *B flat is a semitone lower than B.*
7 (adj) In a musical score, a **flat** sign shows that the next note is flat. *See* **notation**.

flatter flattering flattered
1 (v) to praise someone, especially when you want a favour. flatterer (n), flattery (n).
2 (adj) If something, like a piece of clothing, is **flattering**, it makes you look good.

flaunt flaunting flaunted (v)
to show something off confidently. *The duchess flaunted her diamonds.*

flavour flavouring flavoured
1 (n) taste. flavoured (adj), flavourless (adj).
2 (v) to add taste to food. *Flavour the stew with herbs and pepper.* flavouring (n).

flaw (n) a fault, or a weakness. flawed (adj), flawless (adj).

flea
1 (n) a small, jumping and biting insect that lives on the blood of people or animals.
2 flea market (n) a street market selling old clothes and other second-hand items.

flea
(magnified)

fleck (n) a spot, or a tiny patch of something. *A fleck of soot landed on Carl's white shirt.* flecked (adj).

fledgling (n) a young bird.

flee fleeing fled (v) to run away from danger.

fleece (n) a sheep's woolly coat. fleecy (adj).

fleet (n) a group of vehicles, such as ships or trucks.

fleeting (adj) not lasting long. *A fleeting glance.* fleetingly (adv).

flesh
1 (n) the soft part of your body, made up of fat and muscle. fleshy (adj).
2 (n) the meat of an animal, or the part of a fruit or vegetable that you can eat.

flex flexes flexing flexed
1 (n) the wire that joins a piece of electrical equipment to the plug.
2 (v) to bend or stretch something. *Tarzan flexed his muscles.*

flexible (adj) able to bend or change. *A flexible plastic ruler. Francis is flexible about Saturday's arrangements.* flexibility (n), flexibly (adv).

flick flicking flicked
1 (v) to move with a quick, sudden movement. *Pete flicked a pea off the table.* flick (n).
2 the flicks (plural n) (slang) the cinema.

flicker flickering flickered (v)
If something **flickers**, it moves unsteadily. *The flame flickered in the wind.* flicker (n).

flight
1 (n) flying, or the ability to fly.
2 (n) a journey by aircraft.
3 If you **take flight**, you run away. flight (n).

flimsy flimsier flimsiest (adj) thin, or weak. *Flimsy material.* flimsiness (n), flimsily (adv).

flinch flinches flinching flinched (v) to make a quick movement away from a source of pain. *Di flinched as the nurse approached with a needle.*

fling flinging flung (v) to throw something violently.

flint (n) a hard, blackish-grey stone, used in prehistoric times for making tools and weapons.

flip flipping flipped
1 (v) to toss or move something quickly. *Egon flipped the pancakes.*
2 (v) (informal) If someone **flips**, they suddenly become angry or excited.

flippant (adj) careless and not serious. *A flippant comment.* flippancy (n), flippantly (adv).

flipper
1 (n) one of the broad, flat limbs of a sea creature, such as a seal or dolphin, that help it to swim. *See* **dolphin**.
2 flippers (plural n) long, flat attachments that you fit on your feet to help you swim.

flirt flirting flirted
1 (v) If you **flirt** with someone, you talk to them in a teasing, sexy way. flirt (n), flirtatious (adj).
2 (v) If you **flirt** with an idea, you consider it, but not very seriously.

float floating floated
1 (v) to rest on water or air.
2 (v) to move lightly and easily.
3 (n) a small object attached to the end of a fishing line, which shows when the fish is biting. *See* **angling**.
4 (n) a decorated truck that forms part of a procession.

flock flocking flocked
1 (n) a group of animals or birds. *A flock of sheep.*
2 (v) to gather in a crowd. *Hundreds of fans flocked to see the band.*

flog flogging flogged
1 (v) to beat someone with a whip or stick. flogging (n).
2 (v) (slang) to sell something.

flood flooding flooded
1 (v) When something, like a river, **floods**, it overflows with liquid beyond its normal limits. flood (n).
2 (v) to overwhelm, or come in large amounts. *The charity was flooded with offers of help.*

floodlight (n) a strong light, used to light up buildings or sports grounds.

floor
1 (n) the flat surface that you walk on inside a building.
2 (n) a storey in a building. *The skyscraper has over 40 floors.*

flop flopping flopped
1 (v) to fall limply. floppy (adj).
2 (n) (informal) a failure.

floppy disk (n) a flexible magnetic disk that stores computer data. Floppy disks are also called diskettes. *See* **computer**.

Some words that begin with a "f" sound are spelt "ph".

flora *(n)* the plant life of a particular area. *Woodland flora.*

floral *(adj)* flowery. *Floral curtains.*

florist *(n)* someone who sells flowers.

flotsam *(n)* objects from a shipwreck found floating in the sea or washed up on the shore.

flounder floundering floundered
1 *(v)* to struggle through water, snow, mud, etc.
2 *(v)* to have difficulties in coping with something. *Luke is floundering with his maths.*
3 *(n)* a flat fish.

flour *(n)* powder made from ground wheat, corn, etc., that you use for cooking and baking. **floury** *(adj)*.

flourish flourishes flourishing flourished
1 *(v)* to grow and succeed. *Our new computer club is flourishing.*
2 *(v)* to wave something around in order to show it off. **flourish** *(n)*.

flout flouting flouted *(v)* If you flout the rules, you break them deliberately.

flow flowing flowed *(v)* to move along smoothly like a river. **flow** *(n)*.

flow chart *(n)* a diagram that shows how something develops, stage by stage.

flower flowering flowered
1 *(n)* the coloured part of a plant which produces seeds or fruit.
2 *(v)* to blossom or produce flowers.
3 *(n)* a plant which has flowers.

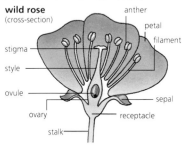

wild rose
(cross-section)

anther
petal
filament
stigma
style
ovule
sepal
ovary
receptacle
stalk

flu *(n)* an illness that gives you a high temperature and makes you feel weak. Flu is short for influenza.

fluctuate fluctuating fluctuated *(v)* to change all the time. *Petrol prices keep fluctuating.* **fluctuation** *(n)*.

fluent *(adj)* able to speak smoothly and clearly, especially in another language. **fluency** *(n)*, **fluently** *(adv)*.

fluff fluffing fluffed
1 *(n)* small, soft clumps of material that come off carpets, clothes, etc.
2 *(v)* When a bird **fluffs** its feathers, it shakes them out.

fluid
1 *(n)* a flowing substance, either a liquid or gas.
2 *(adj)* flowing, or liquid. **fluidity** *(n)*.

fluke
1 *(n)* a lucky accident.
2 *(n)* part of the tail of a sea creature, such as a whale or dolphin. *See* **dolphin**.

fluorescent
1 *(adj)* giving out a bright light. *Fluorescent lighting.* **fluorescence** *(n)*.
2 *(adj)* A **fluorescent** colour is so bright that it seems to give out light when a light is shone on it.

fluoride *(n)* a chemical put in toothpaste and water to prevent tooth decay.

flush flushes flushing flushed *(v)* to flood something with water as a way of cleaning it. **flush** *(n)*.

flushed *(adj)* If you are **flushed**, your face has become red. **flush** *(n)*.

fluster flustering flustered *(v)* to confuse or rush someone.

flutter fluttering fluttered
1 *(v)* to wave or flap rapidly. *The flag fluttered in the breeze.*
2 *(n)* If you are **in a flutter** about something, you are excited and nervous about it.

fly flies flying flew flown
1 *(v)* to travel through the air.
2 *(n)* an insect with wings. *See* **insect**.
3 flies *(plural n)* a flap on trousers covering a zip or buttons.
4 *(v)* to move fast, or to do something fast. *Time just flew by.*

fly fishing *(n)* a type of fishing using flies made from fur, feathers, etc. that are attached to a hook which the fish swallows. *The picture shows examples of four types of fly used in fly fishing for trout: a dry fly, which represents an adult fly; a wet fly, which imitates a hatching fly; a nymph, which trout mistake for a fly larva; and a lure, which attracts the trout just by its colour or brightness.*

trout-fishing flies

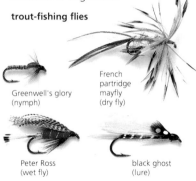

Greenwell's glory
(nymph)

French
partridge
mayfly
(dry fly)

Peter Ross
(wet fly)

black ghost
(lure)

flying saucer *(n)* a saucer-shaped flying object, believed by some to be a spacecraft from another planet.

flyover *(n)* a bridge that carries one road over another.

foal foaling foaled
1 *(n)* a young horse.
2 *(v)* to give birth to a young horse.

foam foaming foamed
1 *(n)* a mass of small bubbles.
2 *(v)* to make bubbles.
3 *(n)* a soft, spongy material, often used to stuff toys or furniture.

focus focuses *or* foci; focuses focusing focused
1 *(v)* to adjust your eyes or a camera lens so that you can see something clearly. *I focused my camera carefully before I took the picture.*
2 *(v)* to concentrate on something or somebody. *Let's focus on your problems.*
3 *(n)* the centre of a picture, or the centre of attention. **focal** *(adj)*.

fodder *(n)* food for cows and horses.

foe *(n)* an enemy.

foetus *see* **fetus**.

fog *(n)* a very thick mist of water droplets in the air. **foggy** *(adj)*.

foghorn *(n)* a loud siren used to warn ships in foggy weather.

foil foiling foiled
1 *(n)* thin, silvery sheets of metal.
2 *(v)* to prevent someone from carrying out a plan. *The police foiled the robbers' plot.*
3 *(n)* a sword used in fencing. *See* **fence**.

fold folding folded
1 *(v)* to bend something over on itself. *Henry folded the sheets.*
2 *(n)* a small, fenced area for sheep.
3 *(v)* If a company **folds**, it collapses and stops trading.

folder *(n)* a cardboard cover used for keeping papers.

foliage *(n)* leaves.

folk folk *or* folks
1 *(n)* people, especially your family.
2 *(adj)* traditional, and belonging to the ordinary people. *Folk music.*

folklore *(n)* the stories, customs, and knowledge of ordinary people, that are passed down to their children.

follow following followed
1 *(v)* to go behind someone. *The police car followed us.*
2 *(v)* to come after. *December follows November.*
3 *(v)* to be guided by someone or something. *Harvey always follows the latest trends.* **follower** *(n)*.

following

following
1 *(prep)* next, or coming after something. *Following the dinner, there will be a dance.*
2 *(adj)* next, or after. *The following year.*
3 *(n)* If someone has a following, they are very popular.

folly follies
1 *(n)* foolishness.
2 *(n)* a foolish act.
3 *(n)* a building with no real purpose. *The folly in the picture is on the Isle of Wight, England.*

folly

fond fonder fondest *(adj)* If you are fond of someone or something, you like them very much. **fondness** *(n)*, **fondly** *(adv)*.

fondle fondling fondled *(v)* to touch or stroke gently. *Nancy fondled the kitten.*

font *(n)* a large, stone bowl used in a church to hold the water for baptisms.

food *(n)* substances that people, animals, and plants take in to stay alive and grow.

food chain *(n)* a group of animals and plants which are dependent on each other, since each one feeds on the one below them in the chain. *The food chain shown here has one producer and several levels of consumers.*

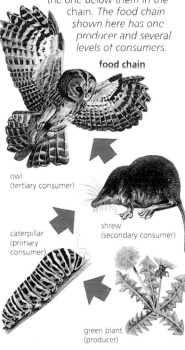

food chain

owl
(tertiary consumer)

shrew
(secondary consumer)

caterpillar
(primary consumer)

green plant
(producer)

food web *(n)* the complex network of food chains in an ecosystem.

fool

fool fooling fooled
1 *(n)* a silly person. **foolishness** *(n)*, **foolish** *(adj)*.
2 *(v)* to trick someone. *The dealer fooled Josie into buying a fake watch.*

foolproof *(adj)* Something that is foolproof is very simple to use, and cannot easily go wrong.

foot feet
1 *(n)* one of the two parts of your body that you walk on.
2 *(n)* the bottom, or the lower end of something. *The foot of the bed.*

football
1 *(n)* an outdoor ball game played by two teams who try to score goals. Soccer, rugby football, and American football are all types of football. *The picture shows an American football player with part of his clothing cut away.* **footballer** *(n)*.
2 *(n)* the ball used to play football.

American football player

leather football

shoulder pad

helmet

face mask

chin strap

chest plate

shirt

hip pad

towel

girdle shell

knee-length pants

thigh pad

knee pad

elastic tape (protects ankles)

sock

studded shoe

footnote *(n)* a note at the bottom of a page.

forage foraging foraged *(v)* to go in search of food. *The outlaws foraged for berries in the wood.*

forbid forbidding forbade forbidden *(v)* to tell someone not to do something. **forbidden** *(adj)*.

forbidding *(adj)* unfriendly, or off-putting. **forbiddingly** *(adv)*.

force forcing forced
1 *(v)* If you force someone to do something, you make them do it. **forceful** *(adj)*, **forcefully** *(adv)*.
2 *(n)* strength, or power.

3 *(n)* In physics, a force is any action that alters the shape or the movement of an object.
4 *(n)* an army, or other team of people. *The police force.*

forceps *(plural n)* an instrument, like tongs, used for holding or lifting, especially in operations.

ford *(n)* a shallow part of a stream or river that you can cross on foot or in a vehicle. **ford** *(v)*.

forecast forecasting forecast or forecasted *(v)* to say what you think will happen in the future. *The weatherman forecasts rain for tomorrow.* **forecast** *(n)*, **forecaster** *(n)*.

foreground *(n)* the part of a picture that is in front of the main subject. *This painting has a cottage in the foreground.*

forehead *(n)* the top part of your face between your hair and your eyes.

foreign
1 *(adj)* to do with, or coming from another country. **foreigner** *(n)*.
2 *(adj)* If something is foreign to you, it is strange or unnatural.

forensic *(adj)* using science to help investigate or solve crimes. A forensic investigation uses scientific information such as fingerprints, blood tests, handwriting analysis, etc.

foresee foreseeing foresaw foreseen *(v)* to expect or predict that something will happen. **foresight** *(n)*, **foreseeable** *(adj)*.

forest *(n)* a large area thickly covered with trees. **forested** *(adj)*.

forever *(adv)* always, or continually. *Matt is forever asking questions.*

forfeit forfeiting forfeited
1 *(n)* a penalty. *If you lose the game, you have to pay a forfeit.*
2 *(v)* to give up the right to something. *If you are late, you will forfeit your place in the team.*

forge forging forged
1 *(v)* to make illegal copies of paintings, money, etc. **forger** *(n)*, **forgery** *(n)*.
2 *(v)* If you forge ahead, you move forward or make progress.
3 *(n)* a blacksmith's shop.

forget forgetting forgot forgotten *(v)* If you forget something, you do not remember it. **forgetfulness** *(n)*, **forgetful** *(adj)*.

forgive forgiving forgave forgiven *(v)* to pardon someone, or to stop blaming them for something. **forgiveness** *(n)*, **forgiving** *(adj)*.

Some words that begin with a "f" sound are spelt "ph".

fork forking forked

1 (n) an instrument with prongs, used for eating, or for working in a garden.
2 (n) a place where a road, river, tree, etc. branches in two or more directions. fork (v), forked (adj).
3 (v) If you **fork out** for something, you pay for it reluctantly.

fork-lift truck (n) a vehicle with two prongs, or forks, at the front, used for lifting and carrying loads. *When the driver operates the controls on this fork-lift truck, the cylinder rises and chains pull up the carriage and the forks, which carry the load.*

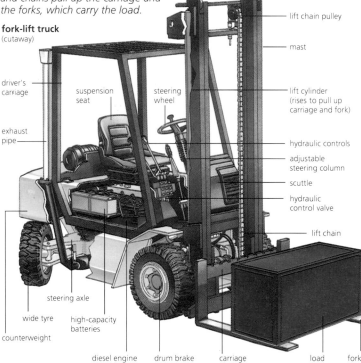

fork-lift truck
(cutaway)

lift chain pulley

mast

driver's carriage

suspension seat

steering wheel

lift cylinder (rises to pull up carriage and fork)

exhaust pipe

hydraulic controls

adjustable steering column

scuttle

hydraulic control valve

lift chain

steering axle

wide tyre

high-capacity batteries

counterweight

diesel engine   drum brake   carriage   load   fork

forlorn (adj) sad, or lonely.
forlornly (adv).

form forming formed

1 (n) shape. *The monster took on a human form.* formless (adj).
2 (n) a type, or a kind. *Which form of travel do you prefer?*
3 (v) to make up or create something. *The lines formed a rectangle.*
4 (n) a class at school.
5 (n) a piece of paper with questions to be filled in.
6 If you are **in good form**, you are fit and cheerful.

formal

1 (adj) official. *We're waiting for formal permission, before we make any plans.* formally (adv).
2 (adj) proper and not casual. *Formal clothes.* formally (adv).

format formatting formatted

1 (v) to prepare a computer disk to be used.
2 (n) the shape or style of something. *The new magazine has a bolder, larger format than the old one.*

formation

1 (n) the process of making something. *We are studying the formation of crystals.*
2 (n) a pattern, or a shape. *Look at that wonderful cloud formation!*

former

1 (n) the first of two things that you have been talking about. *I am fond of spiders and snakes, but I really prefer the former.*
2 (adj) previous, or earlier. *Our former house.* formerly (adv).

formidable (adj) difficult, or frightening. *A formidable challenge.* formidably (adv).

formula formulas *or* formulae

1 (n) a rule in science or maths that is written with numbers and symbols.
2 (n) a suggested set of actions. *What's your formula for success?*

formulate formulating formulated (v) If you **formulate** a theory, you work out an idea and then state it clearly.

forsake forsaking forsook

forsaken (v) to abandon or give up someone or something.

fort

1 (n) a building like a castle, which is strongly built to survive attacks.
2 If you **hold the fort**, you look after things for someone else while they are away.

forte (for-tay)

1 (n) Your **forte** is your strong point.
2 (adv) loudly. Forte is an Italian word, used as an instruction in music.

forthcoming

1 (adj) coming soon. *Forthcoming attractions.*
2 (adj) If someone is not very **forthcoming**, they do not say much.

fortify fortifies fortifying fortified

1 (v) to make a place stronger against attack. *The soldiers fortified the castle's defences.* fortification (n).
2 (v) If you **fortify** yourself, you make yourself feel better and stronger. *The climbers fortified themselves with hot soup.*

fortnight (n) a two-week period.
fortnightly (adj), fortnightly (adv).

fortress fortresses (n) a castle or town that is strengthened against attack.

fortunate (adj) lucky.
fortunately (adv).

fortune

1 (n) chance, or good luck.
2 (n) a large amount of money.
3 (n) fate, or destiny.

forward

1 forward *or* forwards (adv) toward the front, or ahead. *We crept forward cautiously.* forward (adj).
2 (adj) toward the future. *I am looking forward to the holidays.*
3 (n) a player in football, hockey, etc. who plays in an attacking position and tries to score goals.

fossil (n) the remains or trace of an animal or a plant from millions of years ago, preserved as rock. *Examples of different types of fossils are shown in this picture.* fossilized (adj).

fossils

echinoderm

gastropod

ammonite   brachiopod   trilobite

foster fostering fostered
1 (v) to encourage or develop something. *The new club fostered a sense of community..*
2 (v) to look after a child who is not your own, without becoming its legal parent.

foul fouling fouled; fouler foulest
1 (adj) very dirty, or disgusting.
2 (v) to make something dirty or unpleasant.
3 (n) an action in sport that is against the rules. **foul** (v).

found founding founded (v) to set up or start something, such as a school. **founder** (n).

foundation
1 (n) the base or basis of something.
2 foundations (plural n) solid structures on which a building is built. *See* **building**.

foundry foundries (n) a workshop for melting and shaping metal.

fountain (n) a shower of water, pumped up through an ornament or a statue into a pool.

fountain pen (n) a pen with a nib that is supplied with ink from a container inside the pen.

fowl fowl or fowls (n) a bird, such as a chicken or duck, that is kept for its eggs or meat.

fox foxes (n) a kind of wild dog, with large, pointed ears, and a bushy tail.

fox

foyer (foy-ay) (n) the entrance hall of a cinema, theatre, or hotel.

fractal (n) a mathematically produced pattern whose parts, when magnified, exactly resemble the whole.

fraction
1 (n) a part of a whole number. ½, ¾, and ⅛ are all fractions.
2 (n) a small amount. *Polly bought the painting for a fraction of its real value.* **fractional** (adj), **fractionally** (adv).

fracture fracturing fractured (v) to break or crack something, especially a bone. **fracture** (n).

fragile (adj) delicate or easily broken.

fragment (frag-ment) (n) a small piece of something. **fragment** (frag-ment) (v).

fragrant (adj) sweet-smelling. **fragrance** (n).

frail frailer frailest (adj) feeble and weak. **frailty** (n).

frame framing framed
1 (n) a basic structure over which something is built. *Our house has a timber frame.*
2 (n) a border that surrounds something. *A picture frame.*
3 (v) to put something in a frame.
4 (v) (informal) If someone **frames** an innocent person, they make them seem guilty by giving false information about them.

framework (n) the structure of a building or other object.

franc (n) the main unit of money in France, Belgium, and Switzerland.

frank franker frankest (adj) open and honest. **frankness** (n), **frankly** (adv).

frantic (adj) wildly anxious, or wildly excited. **frantically** (adv).

fraud
1 (n) If you practise **fraud**, you gain money by tricking people. **fraudulent** (adj), **fraudulently** (adv).
2 (n) If someone is a **fraud**, they pretend to be something they are not.

freak
1 (adj) very unusual. *Freak weather conditions.*
2 (n) an unnatural or strange person or animal.
3 (n) (informal) someone who is very enthusiastic about something. *A health freak.*

freckle (n) a small, light brown spot on your skin, caused by the sun. **freckled** (adj), **freckly** (adj).

free freeing freed; freer freest
1 (adj) If a person or animal is **free**, they can do what they like. **freely** (adv).
2 (v) If you **free** a person or animal, you let them go from a prison or cage.
3 (adj) If something is **free**, it does not cost anything.

freedom (n) the right to do and say what you like.

freelance (adj) If you are a freelance worker, you do not earn a salary, but are paid for each job that you do. **freelancer** (n).

free-range (adj) Free-range animals are allowed to feed and wander freely.

freeway (n) (US) a main road with several lanes.

freeze freezing froze frozen
1 (v) to become solid or icy at a very low temperature. *Water freezes at 0°C.* **freezing** (adj).
2 (v) to stop still because you are frightened.

freezer (n) a large refrigerator which is kept very cold so that you can store food in it for several months.

freight (frate) (n) goods or cargo carried by trains, ships, planes, etc.

freighter (fray-ter) (n) a plane or ship that carries goods.

frenzy frenzies (n) If you are in a frenzy, you are wildly excited or angry about something. **frenzied** (adj).

frequency frequencies
1 (n) the number of times that something happens. *The frequency of road accidents has increased.*
2 (n) the number of radio waves per second of a radio signal. *High frequency radio signals.*

frequent frequenting frequented
1 (free-kwent) (adj) common, or happening often. **frequently** (adv).
2 (free-kwent) (v) to visit somewhere often or regularly. *Mark frequents the local park.*

fresco frescos or frescoes (n) a painting made on a wall or ceiling while the plaster is still wet. *This ancient Minoan fresco shows a bull-leaping ritual.*

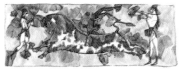

fresco

fresh fresher freshest
1 (adj) clean, or new. **freshly** (adv).
2 (adj) not frozen, or not tinned. *Fresh fruit.*
3 (adj) cool. *A fresh sea breeze.*

freshwater (adj) to do with, or living in water that does not contain salt. *Freshwater fish.*

fret fretting fretted
1 (v) to worry or get annoyed about something. **fretfulness** (n), **fretful** (adj), **fretfully** (adv).
2 (n) one of the bars on the fingerboard of a stringed musical instrument, such as a guitar. *See* **guitar**.

friction
1 (n) the force which slows objects down when they rub against each other.
2 (n) disagreement, or arguing.

fridge short for **refrigerator**.

friend (n) someone whom you enjoy being with and know well. **friendship** (n).

friendly friendlier friendliest (adj) kind and helpful. **friendliness** (n).

frieze *(freez) (n)* a decorated strip, usually along the top of a wall.

fright
1 *(n)* a sudden feeling of fear. *I had a fright when you jumped out on me.*
2 *(informal)* If someone **looks a fright**, they look messy or shocking. *Callum looks a fright in his mum's old hat.*

frighten frightening frightened *(v)* to scare someone. **frightening** *(adj)*.

frightful *(adj)* terrible, or shocking. **frightfully** *(adv)*.

frill *(n)* a ruffled strip of material or paper, used as decoration. **frilly** *(adj)*.

fringe fringing fringed
1 *(n)* the hair that hangs over your forehead.
2 *(v)* to form an edge or border. *Bluebells fringed the path.* **fringe** *(n)*.

frisk frisking frisked
1 *(v)* to play in a lively way. **frisky** *(adj)*, **friskily** *(adv)*.
2 *(v) (informal)* to search someone for weapons, drugs, etc.

frivolous *(adj)* silly and light-hearted. **frivolously** *(adv)*.

frog *(n)* a small, greenish-brown amphibian with long back legs that it uses for jumping. Frogs live on land, but lay their eggs in water. *The pictures below show the life cycle of the common frog. Also see* **rainforest**.

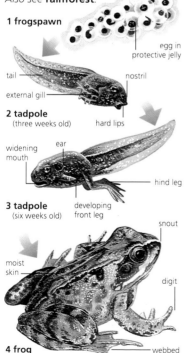

1 frogspawn

egg in protective jelly

tail

nostril

external gill

2 tadpole
(three weeks old)

hard lips

widening mouth

ear

hind leg

3 tadpole
(six weeks old)

developing front leg

snout

moist skin

digit

4 frog
(adult male)

webbed foot

frogman frogmen *(n)* someone who swims underwater using diving equipment, to investigate things, like wrecks. *A police frogman was called in to search the river.*

frolic frolicking frolicked *(v)* to play happily. *The children frolicked in the sun.* **frolic** *(n)*.

frond *(n)* a large, divided leaf on a plant such as a fern or palm. *See* **fern**.

front
1 *(n)* the part of something that faces forwards. **front** *(adj)*.
2 *(n)* the place where armies are fighting.
3 *(n)* the edge of a mass of cold or warm air.
4 If you **put up a front**, you pretend to feel or think something.

frontier *(n)* the border between two countries.

frost frosting frosted
1 *(n)* powdery ice that forms on things in freezing weather.
2 *(v)* If something **frosts up**, it becomes covered with frost. *The windscreen frosted up overnight.*
3 *(n)* weather with a temperature below freezing point.

frostbite *(n)* If someone suffers from frostbite, parts of their body, such as their fingers, toes, or ears, are damaged by extreme cold. **frostbitten** *(adj)*.

frosting *(n) (US)* a sweet, sugar coating used to decorate cakes (icing, *UK*).

frosty frostier frostiest
1 *(adj)* covered with frost.
2 *(adj)* very cold, because there is a frost. *Frosty weather.*
3 *(adj)* If someone is **frosty**, they are unfriendly. **frostiness** *(n)*, **frostily** *(adv)*.

froth *(n)* lots of small bubbles on top of a liquid. **froth** *(v)*, **frothy** *(adj)*.

frown frowning frowned *(v)* to move your eyebrows together and wrinkle your forehead, usually as a sign that you are annoyed. *Dad frowned when he saw the broken window.* **frown** *(n)*.

frozen
1 *(adj)* If something, like food, is frozen, it has been made so cold that all the water in it has turned into ice.
2 *(adj)* extremely cold. *My hands are frozen.*

frugal *(adj)* If you are **frugal**, you are very careful not to waste anything. **frugality** *(n)*, **frugally** *(adv)*.

fruit fruit *or* fruits
1 *(n)* an edible part of a plant or tree, containing seeds. **fruity** *(adj)*.
2 *(n)* the result of something. *This book is the fruit of many years' hard work.*

fruit

melon

pear

peach

apple

nectarine

apricot

plum

grapes

cherries

grapefruit

orange

lemon

lime

kumquat

strawberry

raspberry

cranberries

blackberry

gooseberry

redcurrants

elderberries

blackcurrants

pineapple

bananas

mango

fig

papaya

guava

prickly pear

tree tomato

litchi

kiwi fruit

star fruit

passion fruit

pomegranate

fruitful *(adj)* successful, or useful. **fruitfulness** *(n)*, **fruitfully** *(adv)*.

fruitless *(adj)* unsuccessful, or useless. **fruitlessly** *(adv)*.

fruit machine *(n)* a gambling machine that people operate in order to try to win money.

frustrate frustrating frustrated (v)
If something or someone **frustrates**
you, they prevent you from doing
something. **frustration** (n),
frustrated (adj), frustrating (adj).

fry fries frying fried (v) to cook food
in hot oil. **frying pan** (n).

fuel (n) something that is used as a
source of energy, such as coal, petrol,
or gas. **fuel** (v).

fugitive (n) someone who is running
away. The girl was a fugitive from an
unhappy home. fugitive (adj).

fulcrum fulcrums or fulcra (n)
the point at which something
balances or turns.

fulfil fulfilling fulfilled
1 (v) to carry out something.
Toni fulfilled her promise by paying
back all the money. fulfilment (n)
2 (v) If you fulfil a need, a wish, or an
ambition, you satisfy it. The club fulfils
a need for after-school activities.
fulfilment (n).

full fuller fullest
1 (adj) If something is **full**, there is no
room left inside it.
2 (adj) whole, or complete. I want a
full explanation. fully (adv).

full stop (n) the punctuation mark (.)
used to show that a sentence has
ended or a word has been shortened.

fumble fumbling fumbled (v)
to handle something uncertainly or
clumsily.

fume fuming fumed
1 (v) to be very angry. Hector was
fuming at Muriel's rudeness.
2 **fumes** (plural n) strong-smelling or
poisonous gas, smoke, or vapour
given off by something burning or by
chemicals.

function functioning functioned
1 (v) If something **functions**, it works.
2 (n) a purpose, role, or job.

functional (adj) If something is
functional, it is designed to work
well, rather than to look beautiful.

fund funding funded
1 (n) a store of money, or other
things. A fund of jokes.
2 (v) If someone **funds** something,
they give money to support it.

fundamental (adj) basic and
necessary. My father taught me the
fundamental principles of physics.
fundamentally (adv).

funeral (n) the ceremony held after
someone has died, at which the body
is buried or cremated.

funfair (n) an outdoor entertainment
with rides, amusements, and stalls.

fungus fungi or funguses (n)
a type of plant that has no leaves,
flowers, or roots. Mushrooms and
toadstools are both fungi. Many
fungi are extremely poisonous.

fungi

sulphur tuft
chanterelle
amethyst deceiver

Coriolus
versicolor
fly agaric
ink cap
orange peel
fungus
Russula
atropurpurea

funnel funnelling funnelled
1 (n) an open cone that narrows to a
tube, used for pouring liquids and
powders into narrow-necked
containers. See **apparatus**.
2 (v) to pour liquids and powders
through a funnel.
3 (n) a chimney on a ship.

funny funnier funniest
1 (adj) amusing. **funnily** (adv).
2 (adj) strange. There's a funny smell
in the kitchen. funnily (adv).

fur (n) the soft, hairy coat of an
animal. **furry** (adj).

furious (adj) extremely angry.
furiously (adv).

furlong (n) (old-fashioned)
a distance of 201m, or 220yds.

furnace (n) an extremely hot oven,
used to melt metal, glass, etc.
The picture shows how pure iron is
created from iron ore in a furnace.
Blasts of hot air and burning coke
raise the
temperature
of the iron
mixture to
melting point,
when it
separates into
pure iron
and waste
products,
or slag.

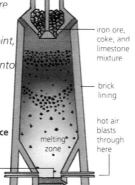

iron ore,
coke, and
limestone
mixture

brick
lining

hot air
blasts
through
here

blast furnace
(cross-section)

melting
zone

molten slag

tap for
molten iron

molten
iron

furnish furnishes furnishing
furnished
1 (v) to equip a room or house with
carpets, curtains, and furniture.
furnishings (plural n).
2 (v) to supply something. Can you
furnish any proof of your age?

furniture (n) large, movable things
such as chairs, tables, and beds which
are needed in a home.

furrow (n) the groove cut by a
plough when it turns over the soil.

further education (n) education
for people who have left school but
who are not at university.

furthermore (adv) in addition, or as
well.

furtive (adj) sly and cautious.
A furtive glance. **furtiveness** (n).

fury furies (n) violent anger.

fuse fusing fused
1 (v) to join two pieces of metal,
plastic, etc. by heating them.
2 (n) a safety device in electrical
equipment which cuts off the power
in an emergency. If too much current
is flowing in the circuit, the wire in the
fuse melts, or blows, and the circuit is
broken.
3 (v) If a piece of electrical equipment
fuses, the fuse blows.
4 (n) a string or wick leading from a
bomb, which is lit to make the bomb
explode.

fuselage (fyoo-zil-arj) (n) the body
of an aircraft.

fusion (n) the joining together of
two pieces of metal, plastic, etc.,
caused by heating.

fuss fusses fussing fussed
1 (v) to be unnecessarily worried or
excited about something. **fussy** (adj).
2 (n) more talk or activity than is
necessary. Carla always makes a fuss
about having visitors.

futile (adj) If an action is **futile**, it is
useless and a waste of time.
futility (n).

future (n) the time to come.
future (adj).

fuzz
1 (n) short, soft hair. **fuzzy** (adj).
2 **the fuzz** (n) (slang) the police.

Gg

gabble gabbling gabbled (v) If you gabble, you talk so fast that it is hard for people to understand you.

gadget (n) a small machine that does a particular job. *We have a gadget for slicing hard-boiled eggs.*

Gaelic (*gay-lik* or *gal-ik*) (n) the name of the traditional languages spoken by some people in Scotland, Ireland, and the Isle of Man.

gag gagging gagged
1 (v) to tie a piece of cloth around someone's mouth in order to stop them from talking.
2 (n) a piece of cloth used to stop someone making a noise.
3 (n) (informal) a joke.

gain gaining gained
1 (v) to get or win something.
2 (n) a profit, or an increase.
3 (v) If you **gain on** someone, you start to catch up with them.

gala (n) a special event or entertainment. *A swimming gala.*

galaxy galaxies (n) a group of stars and planets. **galactic** (adj).

gale (n) a very strong wind.

gallant (adj) brave and fearless. *A gallant knight.* **gallantly** (adv).

gall bladder (n) the organ in your body that stores bile from the liver. *See* **chicken, digestion**.

galleon (n) a sailing ship with three masts built in the 15th or 16th centuries.

gallery galleries
1 (n) a place where exhibitions of paintings, sculpture, photographs, etc. are held.
2 (n) an upstairs seating area, especially in large halls and theatres.

galley
1 (n) the kitchen on a boat or aircraft. *See* **aircraft, boat**.
2 (n) a long boat with oars, used in ancient times.

gallop galloping galloped (v) When a horse **gallops**, it runs as fast as it can. **gallop** (n).

gallows (singular n) a wooden frame used in the past for hanging criminals.

galore (adv) in large numbers. *There were rides galore at the fair.*

galoshes (plural n) waterproof shoes that fit over your ordinary shoes in order to protect them.

galvanize or **galvanise** galvanizing galvanized
1 (v) to coat steel or iron with zinc in order to stop it rusting.
2 (v) If you **galvanize** someone into action, you shock them into doing something.

gamble gambling gambled
1 (v) to bet money on a race, game, or something that might happen. **gambler** (n).
2 (v) to take a risk. *We gambled on the weather staying fine all day.*

game
1 (n) an activity with rules that can be played by one or more people. *A game of tennis. A computer game.*
2 (n) wild animals, including birds, that are hunted for sport and for food. *Pheasants and hares are both types of game.*
3 (adj) If you are **game**, you are willing to try something new or adventurous.

gamekeeper (n) someone whose job is to protect game, especially from poachers.

gamesmanship (n) If you practise **gamesmanship**, you try to beat your opponent by using methods that are not against the rules, but are tricky and surprising.

gammon (n) meat from the back leg or side of a pig.

gander (n) a male goose.

gang ganging ganged
1 (n) a group of people, usually with a leader.
2 (n) an organized group of criminals.
3 (v) If several people **gang up** on you, they all turn against you.

gangplank (n) a short bridge or piece of wood, used for walking on and off a boat.

gangrene (n) If someone has **gangrene**, their flesh rots, usually because the blood supply has been cut off.

gangster (n) a member of a criminal gang.

gangway
1 (n) a clear pathway between rows of seats, for people to walk down.
2 (n) a gangplank.

gaol *see* **jail**.

gap (n) a space between things.

gape gaping gaped
1 (v) to open your mouth wide, usually with surprise. *The children gaped at all the presents.*
2 (v) to split or hang open. *My shirt is gaping at the seams.*

3 (n) the part of a beak that opens. *See* **dolphin**.

garage
1 (n) a small building used for storing vehicles.
2 (n) a place where petrol is sold and vehicles are repaired.

garbage
1 (n) (US) unwanted things or waste material, usually from the home (rubbish, UK).
2 (n) (US) nonsense.

garbled (adj) If you receive a **garbled** message, it is mixed up and does not make sense.

garden (n) a place where flowers, vegetables, shrubs, etc. are grown. **gardener** (n), **gardening** (n), **garden** (v).

gargle gargling gargled (v) to move a liquid around your throat without swallowing it.

gargoyle (n) a grotesque stone head or figure, carved below the roof of old buildings, such as churches. Gargoyles were often used as waterspouts.

gargoyle

garish (*gair-ish*) (adj) brightly coloured and over-decorated. **garishly** (adv).

garland (n) a ring of flowers, often worn around the neck or on the head.

garlic
1 (n) a strong-smelling plant very like an onion.
2 (n) the strong-tasting bulb of the garlic plant, used crushed-up in cooking to add flavour to food.

garment (n) a piece of clothing.

garnish garnishes garnishing garnished (v) to decorate food with small amounts of other food or herbs. **garnish** (n).

garrison (n) a group of soldiers based in a town and ready to defend it. **garrison** (v).

garter (n) a piece of elastic worn around the top of socks or stockings to stop them slipping down.

gas gases or gasses
1 (n) an air-like substance that will spread to fill any space that contains it. *Hydrogen gas.* **gaseous** (adj). *See* **molecule**.
2 (n) a gas that is used as a fuel. Gas can be made from coal and can also be found underground.
3 (n) (US) a liquid fuel used in many vehicles. Gas is short for gasoline (petrol, UK).

gash gashes (n) a long, deep cut. *I've got a nasty gash on my knee.*

gasp gasping gasped (v) to take in breath suddenly because you are surprised or in pain. **gasp** (n).

gastric (adj) to do with the stomach. *Gastric juices.*

gate
1 (n) a frame or barrier that can be opened and closed.
2 (n) the number of people entering a sports ground for a match or event.

gateau (gat-oh) gateaux (n) a rich cake, usually containing cream.

gatecrash gatecrashes gatecrashing gatecrashed (v) to go to a party when you have not been invited. **gatecrasher** (n).

gather gathering gathered
1 (v) to collect or pick things. *We gathered blackberries from the bushes beside the road.*
2 (v) to come together in a group. *A large crowd gathered.*
3 (v) to discover or learn something. *I gather we're not welcome here.*
4 gathers (plural n) small folds in material. **gather** (v), **gathered** (adj).

gaudy (gaw-dee) gaudier gaudiest (adj) very brightly coloured and vulgar.

gauge (rhymes with page) gauging gauged
1 (v) to judge something, or make a guess about it. *We've tried to gauge people's reaction to the plan.*
2 (n) an instrument for measuring something. *A pressure gauge.*
3 (n) the distance between the two rails of a railway track.

gaunt (adj) unnaturally thin and bony.

gauntlet (n) a long, protective glove. In the past, gauntlets were worn by soldiers to prevent injury from weapons. *This pair of leather gauntlets was worn by a cavalryman in the 17th century.*

gauntlets

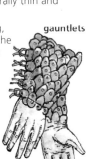

gauze (gawz)
1 (n) a very thin woven cloth, used as a bandage.
2 (n) a thin mesh of wire. *See* **apparatus**.

gay gayer gayest
1 (adj) homosexual, or lesbian.
2 (adj) (old-fashioned) happy and lively. **gaily** (adv).

gaze gazing gazed (v) to stare at something steadily. **gaze** (n).

gazetteer (n) an index of places at the back of a map or atlas.

gear
1 gears (plural n) a set of toothed wheels which fit together and pass on or change the movement of a machine. *This diagram shows how gears work. The arrows show the direction of movement.*
2 (n) equipment, or clothing.

gears

cogwheel

axle

tooth

gel (jel) (n) a thick, jelly-like substance. *Hair gel.*

gelatine (n) a clear, tasteless substance that you add to liquids to make them become solid.

gem (n) a precious stone, such as a diamond, ruby, or emerald.

gender
1 (n) the sex of a person or creature.
2 (n) All nouns have genders. The four genders are masculine, feminine, neuter (neither masculine nor feminine), and common (either masculine or feminine). In some languages, such as French and German, the gender of a noun changes the way that it is used.

gene (jeen) (n) one of the parts of the cells of all living things. Genes are passed from parents to children and control how you look and the way in which you grow. **genetic** (adj).

genealogy (jeen-ee-al-uh-jee) genealogies
1 (singular n) the study of family history. **genealogist** (n).
2 (n) the history of a family.

general
1 (adj) to do with everybody or everything. *General knowledge.* **generally** (adv).
2 (adj) not detailed, or not specialized.
3 (n) a very high-ranking army officer.

generation (n) all the people born around the same time.

generator (n) a machine which produces electricity.

generous (adj) People who are generous are happy to use their time and money to help others. **generosity** (n), **generously** (adv).

genetics (singular n) the study of the ways that personal characteristics are passed from one generation to another through genes. **genetic** (adj), **genetically** (adv).

genitals (plural n) the sex organs on the outside of the body.

genius (jee-nee-us) geniuses (n) an unusually clever or talented person.

genome (jee-nome) (n) all the DNA making up a living plant or animal. *Scientists are studying the human genome to help them learn more about human diseases.*

gentle gentler gentlest
1 (adj) not rough. **gentleness** (n), **gently** (adv).
2 (adj) kind and sensitive. **gentleness** (n), **gently** (adv).
3 (adj) not extreme. *A gentle slope.*

gentleman gentlemen
1 (n) a polite name for a man.
2 (n) a man with good manners.

genuine (jen-yoo-in)
1 (adj) real and not fake.
2 (adj) If someone is genuine, they behave in a natural way and do not pretend. **genuinely** (adv).

geography (n) the study of the Earth, including its people, resources, climate, and physical features. **geographer** (n), **geographical** (adj).

geology (n) the study of the Earth's layers of soil and rock. **geologist** (n), **geological** (adj).

geometric
1 (adj) to do with geometry.
2 (adj) A geometric shape is a regular shape, such as a circle, triangle, rectangle, or square.

geometry (n) the branch of mathematics which deals with lines, angles, shapes, etc. *The picture below shows a range of instruments used in geometry.*

geometry instruments

ruler

shape template

set square

compasses

protractor

Some words that begin with a "g" sound are spelt "gh".

geranium *(n)* a common garden plant with thick stems and red, pink, white, or purple flowers.

gerbil *(n)* a small, furry rodent with long feet and a long, tufted tail. Gerbils are often kept as pets.

gerbil with babies

geriatric *(adj)* to do with very old people. *A geriatric hospital.*

germ *(n)* a very small living organism that can cause disease.

German measles *(singular n)* a contagious illness which gives you a rash and a slight fever. It is not usually serious, except for pregnant women.

germinate germinating germinated *(v)* When seeds or beans germinate, they start to grow shoots and roots.

germinating bean

plumule (young shoot)

seed containing cotyledons (food stores)

radicle (young root)

1 radicle grows down

2 plumule breaks above ground

testa (seed case)

leaf

cotyledon

shoot

root

root hairs

3 testa is discarded

4 shoot sprouts leaves

gesticulate *(jes-tik-yoo-late)* gesticulating gesticulated *(v)* to indicate something by waving your hands about in an excited or angry way. *The chef was gesticulating wildly from the kitchen.* **gesticulation** *(n)*.

gesture gesturing gestured
1 *(v)* to move your head or hands in order to communicate a feeling. *The teacher gestured to Nikki that she should sit down.* **gesture** *(n)*.
2 *(n)* an action which shows a feeling. *I sent her flowers as a gesture of friendship.*

get getting got
1 *(v)* to obtain something. *Please get me a paper.*
2 *(v)* to own something. *Have you got a pet?*

3 *(v)* to become. *The pond got bigger.*
4 *(v)* to arrive somewhere. *At last, we got home.*
5 get by *(v)* to manage with very little money.
6 get at *(v)* to attack or annoy someone.
7 get off with *(v)* *(informal)* to start a relationship with someone.
8 get over *(v)* to recover from something.

getaway *(n)* a fast escape from a situation, especially a crime.

geyser *(gee-zer)* *(n)* a hole in the ground through which hot water and steam shoots up in bursts. *Geysers are found in volcanic areas, where water is heated to boiling point underground and then forced upwards.*

geyser

geyser

hot spring

crater-shaped nozzle

collecting chamber

narrow passageway

hot, cracked rocks

ghastly ghastlier ghastliest
1 *(adj)* *(informal)* very bad, or unpleasant. *A ghastly mistake.*
2 *(adj)* If you feel or look **ghastly**, you feel or look very ill.

ghetto ghettos *or* ghettoes *(n)* an area of a city where a group of poor people of the same race or colour live together.

ghost *(n)* a spirit of a dead person, believed to haunt people or places. **ghostly** *(adj)*.

GI *(n)* *(US)* an American soldier. GI is short for government issue.

giant
1 *(n)* In stories, a **giant** is a very large and strong creature.
2 *(adj)* very large. *Giant size.*

gibbet *(jib-it)* *(n)* a wooden frame used in the past for hanging criminals.

giddy giddier giddiest *(adj)* If you feel **giddy**, you feel dizzy and unsteady, because you are ill or excited. **giddiness** *(n)*, **giddily** *(adv)*.

gift
1 *(n)* a present.
2 *(n)* a special talent. *Vincent has a gift for painting.* **gifted** *(adj)*.

gig *(n)* *(informal)* a booking for a musician or band to play in public.

gigabyte *(n)* a unit used to measure the capacity of a computer's memory.

gigantic *(jy-gan-tik)* *(adj)* huge, or enormous. **gigantically** *(adv)*.

giggle giggling giggled *(v)* to laugh in a nervous, high-pitched way. **giggle** *(n)*, **giggly** *(adj)*.

gill *(n)* one of the two organs on the sides of a fish, through which the fish breathes. *The gill filaments are filled with blood. As water flows over them, oxygen from the water passes into the blood and carbon dioxide from the blood passes into the water. Also see* **fish**.

fish's gill

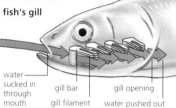

water sucked in through mouth

gill bar

gill filament

gill opening

water pushed out

gilt *(adj)* A **gilt** object is decorated with a thin coating of gold leaf or gold paint. **gild** *(v)*.

gimmick *(n)* something unusual, used to get people's attention. *The entertainer's gimmick was a flashing bow-tie.* **gimmicky** *(adj)*.

gin *(n)* a strong alcoholic drink made from grain and juniper berries.

ginger
1 *(n)* a plant root used to give a hot, spicy flavour to food and drink.
2 *(n)* a reddish-brown colour. **ginger** *(adj)*, **gingery** *(adj)*.

gingerly *(adv)* cautiously and carefully.

gingham *(n)* checked cotton cloth.

gipsy *see* **gypsy**.

giraffe *(n)* an African mammal with a very long neck and legs, and dark blotches on its skin. The giraffe is the tallest animal in the world.

giraffes

girl *(n)* a female child or young woman.

girlfriend *(n)* the girl or woman with whom a boy or man is having a romantic relationship.

girth *(n)* the measurement around something.

Some words that begin with a "g" sound are spelt "gh".
Some words that begin with a "gi" sound are spelt "gy" or "gui".

give giving gave given
1 *(v)* to hand over something to another person. *Give me that book!*
2 *(v)* to pay. *What will you give me for this beautiful vase?*
3 **give way** *(v)* to let someone else go in front of you.
4 **give in** *or* **give up** *(v)* to surrender, or stop trying.

glacier *(glass-ee-er) (n)* a huge mass of ice that flows down a mountain valley. As the glacier moves, it erodes rocks and deposits moraine.

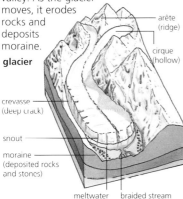

glacier

arête (ridge)

cirque (hollow)

crevasse (deep crack)

snout

moraine (deposited rocks and stones)

meltwater   braided stream

glad gladder gladdest
1 *(adj)* pleased or happy. **gladness** *(n)*, **gladden** *(v)*, **gladly** *(adv)*.
2 If you are **glad** of something, you are grateful for it.

gladiator *(n)* an ancient Roman warrior who fought against other gladiators or fierce animals in order to entertain the public. *The picture shows a fight between two types of gladiator, a retiarius, armed with a net and trident, and a murmillo, fighting with a dagger and shield. Also see* **amphitheatre**.

gladiators

glamorous *(adj)* attractive and exciting. **glamour** *(n)*.

glance glancing glanced
1 *(v)* to look at something very briefly. **glance** *(n)*.
2 *(v)* to hit something and slide off at an angle. *The ball glanced off the goalpost into the net.* **glancing** *(adj)*.

gland *(n)* an organ in the body which either produces natural chemicals or allows substances to leave the body. *Sweat glands.* **glandular** *(adj)*.

glandular fever *(n)* an infectious illness which gives you a sore throat, swollen glands, and a high temperature.

glare glaring glared
1 *(v)* to look at someone in a very angry way. **glare** *(n)*.
2 *(n)* very bright light which dazzles.

glaring *(adj)* very obvious. *A glaring error.* **glaringly** *(adv)*.

glass glasses
1 *(n)* a transparent material used in windows, bottles, etc. *The picture shows two 16th-century craftsmen blowing glass.*
2 *(n)* a container for drinking, made from glass.

glass-blowing

glasses *(plural n)* lenses set in frames, worn to improve your eyesight.

glaze glazing glazed
1 *(v)* to fit glass into a window.
2 *(n)* a thin coat of liquid painted on pottery before it is fired, to give it a shiny finish.
3 *(v)* If your eyes **glaze over**, they look fixed and glass-like because you are tired or bored. **glazed** *(adj)*

glazier *(n)* a person who fits glass into windows.

gleam gleaming gleamed *(v)* to shine. **gleam** *(n)*.

glee *(n)* enjoyment and delight. **gleeful** *(adj)*, **gleefully** *(adv)*.

glen *(n)* a narrow valley, usually in Scotland.

glide gliding glided *(v)* to move smoothly and easily. *The swan glided down the stream.*

glider *(n)* a very light aircraft, which flies by floating and rising on air currents instead of by engine power.

glider

glimmer glimmering glimmered *(v)* to shine faintly. **glimmer** *(n)*.

glimpse glimpsing glimpsed *(v)* to see something briefly. **glimpse** *(n)*.

glint glinting glinted *(v)* to sparkle, or to flash. **glint** *(n)*.

glisten glistening glistened *(v)* to shine in a sparkling way.

glitter glittering glittered *(v)* to sparkle with many tiny lights or reflections.

gloat gloating gloated *(v)* to delight in your own good luck, or in someone else's bad luck.

global warming *(n)* a gradual rise in the temperature of the Earth's atmosphere, caused by an increase in the greenhouse effect. *See* **greenhouse effect**.

globe
1 *(n)* a round model of the world.
2 *(n)* the world. **global** *(adj)*.
3 *(n)* anything shaped like a round ball. **globular** *(adj)*.

gloomy gloomier gloomiest
1 *(adj)* dull and dark. *A gloomy dungeon.* **gloom** *(n)*.
2 *(adj)* If you are **gloomy**, you feel sad and pessimistic. **gloom** *(n)*.

glory glories
1 *(n)* fame and admiration. *After the victory, the team enjoyed their glory.* **glorious** *(adj)*.
2 *(n)* a beautiful and impressive sight. *The glories of Venice.* **glorious** *(adj)*.

gloss *(n)* a shine on a surface. **glossy** *(adj)*.

glossary glossaries *(n)* A **glossary** explains the meaning of technical words and phrases used in a book.

glove *(n)* a warm or protective hand covering.

glow glowing glowed *(v)* If something **glows**, it gives off a steady light, often because it is hot. **glow** *(n)*, **glowing** *(adj)*.

glow-worm *(n)* a small beetle whose tail gives off a green glow in the dark. *See* **insect**.

glucose *(n)* a natural sugar found in plants which gives energy to living things.

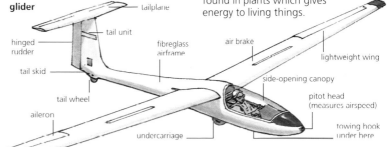

tailplane

tail unit

hinged rudder

fibreglass airframe

air brake

lightweight wing

tail skid

side-opening canopy

tail wheel

pitot head (measures airspeed)

aileron

undercarriage

towing hook under here

glue (n) a substance used to make one surface stick to another. **glue** (v).

glum glummer glummest (adj) gloomy and miserable. **glumly** (adv).

glutton (n) a very greedy person. gluttony (n), gluttonous (adj).

GM (adj) the initials **GM** stand for genetically modified. When plants or food are genetically modified, some of their genes are treated by scientists to change them in some way, such as making crops more resistant to insect pests.

gnarled (narld) (adj) twisted and lumpy with age. A gnarled oak tree.

gnash (nash) gnashing gnashed (v) If you **gnash** your teeth, you grind them together in anger or grief.

gnat (nat) (n) a small, winged insect which bites.

gnaw (naw) gnawing gnawed or gnawn (v) to keep biting something. The dog gnawed at the bone.

gnome (nome) (n) In folk and fairy stories, **gnomes** are dwarf-like old men.

go goes going went gone
1 (v) to move away from or towards a place. I'm going home.
2 (v) to work properly. This machine won't go.
3 (v) to become. The class went quiet.
4 (v) If you are **going** to do something, you will do it in the future.
5 (v) to have a place, or to belong. Where do the plates go?
6 (n) a turn. It's my go at batting.

goal
1 (n) something that you aim for. Shelagh's goal is to run for Ireland.
2 (n) a frame with a net into which you aim a ball in sports such as soccer and basketball.
3 (n) When you score a **goal** in a game, you send the ball into or through a net, and win points.

goalkeeper (n) a player who defends the goal in various sports. See **ice hockey, soccer**.

goat (n) a farm animal with horns and a beard, reared mainly for its milk.

gobble gobbling gobbled (v) to eat food quickly and greedily.

goblet (n) an old-fashioned drinking container with a stem and a base, usually made from pottery or metal.

goblin (n) In fairy stories, **goblins** are small, unpleasant, ugly creatures.

God (n) In Christianity, Islam, and Judaism, **God** is the creator and ruler of the universe.

god (n) a supernatural being that is worshipped.

goddess goddesses (n) a female supernatural being that is worshipped. This picture shows some ancient Egyptian gods and goddesses.

Egyptian gods and goddesses

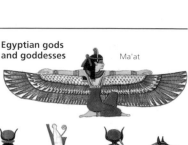

Ma'at

Re   Amun   Osiris   Isis   Horus   Hathor   Anubis

godparent (n) someone who promises their support for a child when the child is baptized into the Christian religion.

goggles (plural n) special glasses that fit tightly round your eyes to protect them. Swimming goggles.

go-kart (n) a very low, small, open vehicle, built for racing.

gold
1 (n) a precious metal used to make jewellery, and sometimes for money.
2 (n) a warm, yellow colour.
gold (adj), golden (adj).

goldfish goldfish or goldfishes (n) an orange-coloured fish, often kept in ponds and aquariums.

golf (n) a game in which players use clubs to hit a small, white ball round a special course. This picture shows four types of clubs used for playing golf: a wood for striking the ball long distances; an iron for medium to short-range shots; a wedge for lifting the ball high in the air; and a putter for tapping the ball into the hole on the green. **golfer** (n), **golfing** (n).

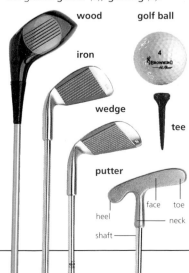

wood   golf ball

iron

wedge

tee

putter

face   toe
heel   neck
shaft

gondola (n) a light boat with high pointed ends, used on the canals of Venice. Gondolas are moved through the water by a gondolier using a single oar.

gong (n) a disc of metal that makes a hollow, echoing sound when it is hit with a hammer.

good
better best
1 (adj) of high quality, or deserving praise. A good teacher. A good book.
2 (adj) kind, or virtuous. A good deed.
3 (adj) suitable. A good fit.
4 (adj) well-behaved. Marigold is such a good girl!
5 (adj) fit and well. I'm feeling good.
6 (adj) If something is **good** for you, it improves your health or behaviour.

gondola

goodbye (interject) a word said to someone who is leaving.

goods (plural n) a general name for things which are sold or things which someone owns. Leather goods.

gooey gooier gooiest (adj) (informal) sticky. **gooeyness** (n).

goose geese (n) a large, long-necked bird with webbed feet. See **bird**.

goose pimples (plural n) tiny bumps on your skin which appear when you are cold or frightened.

gore goring gored
1 (n) (old-fashioned) blood that flows from a wound.
2 (v) If someone is **gored** by a bull, they are pierced by its horns.

gorge gorging gorged
1 (n) a deep valley with steep, rocky sides. See **river**.

2 (v) If you **gorge** yourself, you stuff yourself with food.

gorgeous (adj) really beautiful, or attractive.

gorilla (n) a very large, strong ape with dark fur, that comes from Africa.

gorse (n) a prickly, evergreen shrub with bright yellow flowers.

gory gorier goriest (adj) If something is **gory**, it involves a lot of blood. A gory film.

gospel
1 (n) one of the first four books in the New Testament of the Bible. The gospels describe the life and teachings of Jesus Christ.
2 If you take something as **gospel**, you believe it to be completely true.

gossip gossiping gossiped (v) to talk with enjoyment about other people's personal lives. **gossip** (n), **gossipy** (adj).

Gothic (adj) in the style of art or architecture used in Western Europe between the 12th and 16th centuries. Gothic buildings have pointed arches and windows. See **arch**.

govern governing governed (v) to control a country, organization, etc. using laws or rules. **governor** (n).

government
1 (n) the people who rule or govern a country or state.
2 (n) the control and administration of a country, state, or organization. **governmental** (adj), **governmentally** (adv).

gown
1 (n) (old-fashioned) a woman's dress.
2 (n) a loose robe worn by judges, lawyers, university teachers, etc.

GP (n) a family doctor, who treats common illnesses and refers patients to specialist doctors if necessary. GP is short for general practitioner.

grab grabbing grabbed (v) to take hold of something suddenly and roughly. I grabbed the handrail as I tripped on the stairs.

grace
1 (n) an elegant way of moving. Anna moves with a dancer's grace. **graceful** (adj), **gracefully** (adv).
2 (n) pleasant behaviour. Edward accepted my apology with grace. **gracious** (adj), **graciously** (adv).
3 (n) a short prayer of thanks before or after a meal.

grade
1 (n) a mark given for work done in school, college, etc. I got grade A for maths. **grade** (v).

2 (n) quality. Top grade eggs.
3 (n) (US) a class or year in a school.

grade school (n) (US) a school for children aged between five and twelve.

gradient (n) a slope, or the steepness of a slope.

gradual (adj) If something is **gradual**, it takes place slowly but steadily. **gradually** (adv).

graffiti (plural n) things that people write or draw on the walls of public buildings.

graft grafting grafted
1 (v) to plant a shoot from one plant into a slit in another, so that they grow as one. **graft** (n).
2 (v) to take the skin from one part of the body to help repair an injury to another part. Surgeons grafted skin from Dean's leg to his burnt face. **graft** (n).
3 (v) (informal) to work hard.

grain
1 (n) the seed of a cereal plant.
2 (n) a general name for the product of cereal crops.
3 (n) a very small particle of salt, sand, sugar, etc.

grain crops

barley

rye

wheat

oats

grammar (n) the rules of writing or speaking a language. **grammatical** (adj).

grand grander grandest (n) large and impressive. **grandly** (adv).

grandchild grandchildren (n) You are the **grandchild** of your parents' parents.

grandparent (n) Your **grandparent** is the parent of one of your parents.

grandstand (n) a covered structure at a sports ground with seats for spectators.

grant granting granted
1 (v) to give something or allow something. We were granted permission to leave.
2 (n) a sum of money given by the government or other organizations for a special purpose. A study grant.
3 If you take something **for granted**, you do not appreciate it, or you assume that you will get it.

granulated sugar (n) coarsely ground white sugar.

grape (n) the small fruit that grows on a vine which can be eaten as it is, dried to make currants, raisins, etc., or crushed to make wine. See **fruit**.

grapefruit grapefruit or grapefruits (n) a large, yellow citrus fruit. See **fruit**.

grapevine
1 (n) a climbing plant on which grapes grow.
2 If you hear something **on the grapevine**, you hear news before most other people hear about it.

graph (rhymes with laugh) (n) a diagram which shows how two sets of numbers are related.

graphic
1 (adj) very realistic. Sonia told the story in graphic detail.
2 (adj) to do with art and design.

graphics
1 (plural n) the layout and pictures of a book or magazine.
2 (plural n) the pictures in a computer game. This game has terrible graphics.

grapple grappling grappled
1 (v) to wrestle with someone.
2 (v) If you **grapple** with a problem, you think hard about all the ways that it could be solved.

grasp grasping grasped
1 (v) to seize something and hold it tightly. **grasp** (n).
2 (v) to understand something. Have you grasped what I'm telling you? **grasp** (n).

grass grasses
1 (n) a green plant with long, thin, leaves that grows wild and is used for lawns. **grassy** (adj).
2 (n) (slang) marijuana.

grasshopper (n) a jumping insect with long back legs. A grasshopper sings to other grasshoppers by rubbing the hard veins on its front wings over the tiny teeth inside its back legs.

European grasshopper

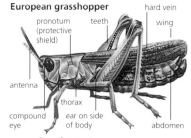

hard vein

pronotum (protective shield)

teeth

wing

antenna

thorax

compound eye

ear on side of body

abdomen

grassland (n) a large, open area of grass, often used for animals to graze on.

grate grating grated
1 (v) to shred food, such as cheese, into small, thin pieces.
2 (v) If something **grates** on you, it annoys you.
3 (n) a grid of metal bars in a fireplace.

grateful (adj) If you are **grateful** for something that you are given, you appreciate it and are thankful for it. **gratefully** (adv).

gratitude (n) a feeling of being glad and thankful.

grave graver gravest
1 (n) a place where a dead person is buried.
2 (adj) very serious. Grave danger. **gravely** (adv).
3 **gravestone** (n) a piece of carved stone that marks someone's grave.
4 **graveyard** (n) a piece of land, often near a church, where dead people are buried.

gravel (n) small, loose stones used for paths and roads.

gravity
1 (n) the force that pulls things down towards the surface of the Earth and stops them from floating away into space.
2 (n) seriousness.

gravy (n) a hot, savoury sauce, served with meat and usually made from the juices of cooked meat.

graze grazing grazed
1 (v) to scrape the surface off your skin. **graze** (n).
2 (v) When animals **graze**, they eat grass that is growing in a field.

grease
1 (n) an oily substance found in animal fat, and in hair and skin. **greasy** (adj).
2 (n) a thick, oily substance used on machines to help the parts move easily. **grease** (v), **greasy** (adj).

great greater greatest
1 (adj) very big or large. **greatly** (adv).
2 (adj) very important and famous. A great man. **greatness** (n).
3 (adj) very good, or wonderful. We had a great time.

greedy greedier greediest (adj) If you are **greedy**, you want more of something than you need. **greed** (n), **greedily** (adv).

green greener greenest
1 (n) the colour of grass or leaves. **green** (adj).
2 (adj) Someone who is **green** is concerned with protecting the environment.
3 (n) an area of grass in a public place. The village green.

4 (n) an area of ground used for an activity or sport. A bowling green.

greenhouse (n) a glass building used for growing plants.

greenhouse effect (n) the warming of the atmosphere around the Earth, caused by gases such as carbon dioxide, which collect in the atmosphere and prevent the Sun's heat from escaping.

greenhouse effect

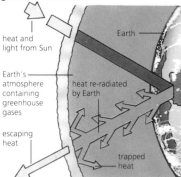

heat and light from Sun

Earth

Earth's atmosphere containing greenhouse gases

heat re-radiated by Earth

escaping heat

trapped heat

greenhouse gases (plural n) gases such as carbon dioxide, methane, and CFCs that are found in the Earth's atmosphere and help to hold heat in.

greet greeting greeted
1 (v) to say something friendly or welcoming to someone when you meet them. **greeting** (n).
2 (v) to react to something in a particular way. Harriet greeted the news with horror.

grenade (n) a small bomb that is thrown by hand or fired from a rifle.

grey (n) the colour between black and white, like the colour of the sky on a rainy day. **grey** (adj).

grid
1 (n) a set of straight lines that cross each other at right angles to form a regular pattern of squares.
2 **national grid** (n) the network of wires and cables through which electricity is supplied to all parts of the country.

gridiron (n) (US) a playing field marked out for American football.

grief (n) a feeling of great sadness.

grievance (n) If you have a **grievance**, you have a real or imagined reason to feel angry or annoyed about something.

grieve grieving grieved (v) to feel very sad, usually because someone whom you love has died.

grill grilling grilled
1 (n) the part of a cooker that heats food from above.
2 (v) to cook food under a grill.
3 (v) (informal) to ask someone lots of detailed questions in order to find out information.

grim grimmer grimmest (adj) gloomy, stern, and unpleasant. A grim expression. **grimly** (adv).

grime (n) thick dirt. **grimy** (adj).

grin grinning grinned (v) to give a large, cheerful smile. **grin** (n).

grind grinding ground (v) to crush something into a powder.

grip gripping gripped
1 (v) to hold something very tightly. **grip** (n).
2 (v) If something **grips** you, it holds your attention completely because it is so exciting. **gripping** (adj).

gristle (n) a tough substance, sometimes found in meat.

grizzle grizzling grizzled (v) to keep on whining and complaining.

groan groaning groaned (v) to make a long, low sound, showing that you are in pain or are unhappy. **groan** (n).

grocer (n) someone who owns a shop selling food and household goods.

groin (n) the hollow between the top of your leg and your stomach.

groom grooming groomed
1 (n) someone who looks after horses.
2 (v) to brush and clean an animal, such as a horse. **grooming** (n).
3 (n) a man who is about to get married or has just been married.

grooming kit for horses

hoof oil

sponges

dandy-brush

body brush

currycomb

mane comb

sweat scraper

stable rubber

hoof pick

water brush

groove (n) a long cut in the surface of something.

grope groping groped (v) to feel about with your hands for something that you cannot see.

gross gross; grosser grossest
1 (adj) unpleasantly big and ugly.
2 (adj) The **gross** amount is the total amount, with nothing taken away.
3 (adj) very rude and bad-mannered.
4 (adj) very bad. A gross error. **grossly** (adv).
5 (n) a group of 144 things.

grotesque (grow-tesk) (adj) unnatural and horrible. **grotesquely** (adv).

grotty grottier grottiest (adj) (slang) unpleasant and unattractive.

ground
1 (n) the surface of the Earth.
2 (n) a piece of land used for playing a game or sport.
3 **grounds** (plural n) reason, or cause. What grounds do you have for accusing me?
4 **grounds** (plural n) the land surrounding a large building or group of buildings.

grounded
1 (adj) If an aircraft is **grounded**, it cannot fly.
2 (adj) (informal) If you are **grounded**, you are not allowed to go out.

group grouping grouped
1 (n) a number of things that go together or are similar in some way.
2 (v) to put things into groups, or to make a group.
3 (n) a number of musicians who play or sing together.

grove (n) (poetic) a small group of trees. An olive grove.

grovel grovelling grovelled (v) to be unnaturally humble and polite to someone because you are afraid of them or because you think that they are very important.

grow growing grew grown
1 (v) to increase in size, length, or amount.
2 (v) to plant something and look after it so that it lives and gets bigger.
3 (v) to become. Simon grew lazier and lazier.
4 (v) If something **grows on** you, you gradually start to like it.

growl growling growled (v) When an animal **growls**, it makes a low, deep noise, usually because it is angry.

grown-up (n) an adult. **grown-up** (adj).

growth
1 (n) the process of growing. Here's a chart to measure your growth.
2 (n) a lump of body tissue either on or inside someone's body.

grub
1 (n) the young form of some insects, that looks like a short, white worm.
2 (n) (slang) food.

grubby grubbier grubbiest (adj) dirty. **grubbiness** (n).

grudge grudging grudged
1 (n) a feeling of anger towards someone who has hurt or insulted you in the past. Jon bore a grudge against Daniel for months.
2 (v) If you **grudge** someone something, you do not want them to have it. **grudging** (adj).

gruelling (adj) very demanding and tiring. A gruelling job.

gruesome (adj) Something that is **gruesome** is disgusting and horrible.

gruff gruffer gruffest (adj) rough and bad-tempered. A gruff voice. **gruffly** (adv).

grumble grumbling grumbled (v) to complain about something in a bad-tempered way.

grumpy grumpier grumpiest (adj) bad-tempered. **grumpily** (adv).

grunge (n) a type of American music and a way of dressing. Grunge music features loud guitar playing, and is influenced by heavy metal and punk. Grunge clothing is scruffy, and usually includes jeans and workboots.

grunt grunting grunted (v) to make a deep, gruff sound, like a pig. **grunt** (n).

guarantee
1 (n) a promise made by the makers of something that if it breaks or goes wrong within a certain time, they will mend or replace it for you. **guarantee** (v).
2 (n) a promise that something will definitely happen. **guarantee** (v).

guard guarding guarded
1 (v) to protect a person or place from attack.
2 (v) to watch a person carefully to prevent them from escaping.
3 (n) someone who protects or keeps watch over a person or place.
4 (n) a railway official who travels on a train and is in charge of passengers and goods.
5 (n) an object placed near another object to provide protection.
6 (v) If you **guard against** something, you try to stop it happening.

guardian
1 (n) someone who is not the parent of a child but who has the legal responsibility to look after them.
2 (n) someone who guards or protects something. **guardian** (adj).

guard's van (n) the last compartment on a train, kept for railway officials in charge of the train.

guerrilla (ger-il-er) (n) a member of a small army that fights an official army by launching surprise attacks. **guerrilla** (adj).

guess (gess) guesses guessing guessed
1 (v) to give an answer that may be right but which you cannot be sure about. I guessed at the answer instead of working it out. **guess** (n).
2 (v) (US) to think or believe something. I guess Karen will arrive shortly.

guest
1 (n) someone who has been invited to visit you or to stay in your home.
2 (n) someone staying in a hotel.

guide guiding guided
1 (v) to help someone, usually by showing them around a place, or by leading them across difficult country. **guide** (n).
2 (n) a book containing maps and information about a place. **guidebook** (n).
3 **guide-dog** (n) a dog trained to lead a blind person.
4 (n) a member of the Guide Association.

guillotine (gil-oh-teen)
1 (n) a large machine with a sharp blade, used in the past to behead criminals.
2 (n) an instrument with a sharp blade, used for cutting paper.

guilty guiltier guiltiest
1 (adj) If you are **guilty**, you have committed a crime or done something wrong. **guilt** (n).
2 (adj) If you feel **guilty**, you feel bad because you have done something wrong or have failed to do something. **guilt** (n), **guiltily** (adv).

guinea pig (gin-ee pig)
1 (n) a small mammal with smooth fur, short ears, and a very short tail. Guinea pigs are often kept as pets.
2 (n) a person who is used in an experiment.

guinea pig

guitar *(n)* a musical instrument with strings, which you pluck or strum with your fingers or a plectrum. *The vibrations of the strings on this electric guitar are transformed by the pick-ups into electrical impulses which are then amplified through a loudspeaker.* Also see **acoustic guitar**.

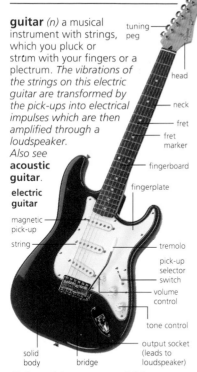

electric guitar

tuning peg

head

neck

fret

fret marker

fingerboard

fingerplate

magnetic pick-up

string

tremolo

pick-up selector switch

volume control

tone control

output socket (leads to loudspeaker)

solid body

bridge

Gujarati *(goo-jer-ar-tee)* *(n)* a language spoken in Gujarat, a state in Western India.

gulf
1 *(n)* a large area of sea that is partly surrounded by land. *The Persian Gulf.*
2 *(n)* a serious difference or disagreement between people.

gull *short for* **seagull**.

gullible *(adj)* If you are **gullible**, you believe anything that you are told and are easily tricked.

gully gullies *(n)* a long, narrow valley or ditch.

gulp gulping gulped
1 *(v)* to swallow something quickly and noisily.
2 *(n)* a large mouthful of drink.

gum
1 *(plural n)* Your **gums** are the areas of firm, pink flesh around the base of your teeth. *See* **tooth**.
2 *(n)* glue. **gum** *(v)*, **gummy** *(adj)*.
3 *(n)* See **chewing gum**.

gun gunning gunned
1 *(n)* a weapon that fires bullets through a long metal tube.
2 **gun down** *(v)* to shoot someone with a gun. *The sheriff gunned down the bandits.*

gunfire *(n)* the firing of guns.

gunpowder *(n)* a powder that explodes easily, used in fireworks and to fire some guns.

gunsmith *(n)* someone who makes and repairs guns.

gurgle gurgling gurgled
1 *(v)* When water **gurgles**, it makes a low, bubbling sound. **gurgle** *(n)*.
2 *(v)* to make a low, bubbling sound like gurgling water. *The baby gurgled happily.* **gurgle** *(n)*.

gush gushes gushing gushed
1 *(v)* When liquid **gushes**, it flows fast in large amounts. **gush** *(n)*.
2 *(v)* When a person **gushes**, they are embarrassingly sentimental or emotional. **gushing** *(adj)*.

gust *(n)* a sudden, strong blast of wind. **gusty** *(adj)*.

gut gutting gutted
1 *(plural n)* Your **guts** are the organs inside your body, especially your stomach and intestines.
2 *(v)* If a fire **guts** a building, it destroys the inside.
3 **guts** *(plural n)* *(informal)* courage.

gutter *(n)* a channel or length of tubing through which rain is drained away from a road or from the roof of a building. *See* **building**.

guzzle guzzling guzzled *(v)* to eat or drink something quickly and noisily.

gym
1 *(n)* a large room with special equipment for doing exercises and physical training. Gym is short for gymnasium.
2 *(n)* exercises to make your body strong and fit, usually done in a gym.

gymkhana *(n)* a sporting event at which horses and their riders take part in competitions.

gymnasium *see* **gym**.

gymnastics *(singular n)* physical exercises, often on bars or ropes, which involve difficult and carefully controlled body movements. **gymnast** *(n)*, **gymnastic** *(adj)*.

gypsy *or* **gipsy** *(jip-see)* gypsies *(n)* someone who usually lives in a caravan and travels from place to place.

gyrate *(jy-rate)* gyrating gyrated *(v)* to move round and round in a circle. **gyratory** *(adj)*.

gyroscope *(n)* a wheel which spins inside a frame and causes the frame to balance in any position. Gyroscopes are used to help keep ships and aircraft steady.

gyroscope

Hh

habit
1 *(n)* something that you do regularly, often without thinking about it.
2 *(n)* a piece of clothing, like a long loose dress, worn by monks and nuns.

habitable *(adj)* If a building is **habitable**, it is safe, warm, and clean enough to live in.

habitat *(n)* the place and conditions in which a plant or an animal lives naturally.

habitually *(adv)* usually, or normally. *Tootsie is habitually optimistic.* **habitual** *(adj)*.

hack hacking hacked
1 *(v)* to chop or cut something roughly.
2 *(v)* If you **hack** into a computer system, you manage to get information from it illegally. **hacker** *(n)*.
3 *(n)* a long, steady ride on horseback.

haemoglobin *or* **hemoglobin** *(hee-mer-glow-bin)* *(n)* a substance found in your red blood cells, which contains iron and carries oxygen around your body.

haemophilia *or* **hemophilia** *(hee-mer-fil-ee-a)* *(n)* If people suffer from **haemophilia**, their blood does not clot, so they bleed severely when they cut themselves. **haemophiliac** *(n)*.

haemorrhage *or* **hemorrhage** *(hem-er-ij)* *(n)* severe bleeding, usually inside someone's body.

haggard *(adj)* Someone who is **haggard** looks thin, tired, and worried.

haggis *(n)* a Scottish food made from the chopped heart, liver, kidneys, etc. of a sheep, mixed with oatmeal and boiled in a bag made from a sheep's stomach.

haggle haggling haggled *(v)* to argue, usually about the price of something.

haiku *(hy-koo)* *(n)* a short Japanese poem in three parts.

hail hailing hailed
1 *(v)* When it **hails**, small pieces of frozen rain fall from the sky. **hail** *(n)*.
2 *(v)* to attract someone's attention. *Travis hailed a taxi.*

hair *(n)* the mass of fine, soft strands that grow on your head or body, or on the body of an animal.

haircut (n) When you have a haircut, someone cuts and styles your hair.

hairdresser (n) someone who cuts and styles people's hair.

hairgrip (n) a piece of bent wire with sides that press together to hold your hair in place.

hair-raising (adj) very frightening.

hairy hairier hairiest
1 (adj) covered in hair.
2 (adj) (slang) dangerous and frightening.

halal (n) meat that has been produced and prepared according to the rules of the Muslim religion. halal (adj).

half halves
1 (n) one of two equal parts of something.
2 (adv) partly, or not completely. The meal was only half-cooked.

half term (n) a short holiday in the middle of a school term.

half-time (n) a short break in the middle of a game, such as football or hockey.

hall
1 (n) an area of a house just inside the front door.
2 (n) a large room used for meetings or other public events.

hallelujah (hal-ay-loo-ya) (interject) a word used to express joy and thanks to God.

Halloween or **Hallowe'en** (n) the evening before All Saints Day, believed in the past to be the night when witches and ghosts were active.

hallucinate (hal oo sin ate) hallucinating hallucinated (v) to see something in your mind that is not really there. hallucination (n).

halo (hay-low) haloes (n) a circle of light, around the heads of angels and holy people in paintings.

halt halting halted (v) to stop. halt (n).

halve halving halved
1 (v) to cut or divide something into two equal parts.
2 (v) to reduce something so that there is only half as much as there was. We have halved the cast for our school play.

ham (n) the meat from the upper part of a pig's leg, that has been salted and sometimes smoked.

hamburger
1 (n) a round, flat piece of minced meat, usually served in a bread roll.

2 (n) (US) minced meat.

hamlet (n) a very small village.

hammer hammering hammered
1 (n) a tool with a metal head on a handle, used for hitting things, such as nails. hammer (v).
2 (v) to hit something hard. Elsa hammered at the door.

hammock (n) a piece of strong cloth or net that is hung up by each end and used as a bed.

hamper hampering hampered
1 (n) a large box or basket used for carrying food, especially on a picnic.
2 (v) to make it difficult for someone to do something. Nina's high-heeled shoes hampered her running.

hamster (n) a small animal like a mouse, with no tail, often kept as a pet. Hamsters have pouches in their cheeks for storing food.

hamster

hand handing handed
1 (n) the part of your body on the end of your arm that you use for picking things up, writing, eating, etc.
2 (v) to pass or give something to someone. Hand me the salt.
3 (n) a set of cards that you hold in your hand during a game of cards.
4 (n) one of the pointers on a clock. The minute hand.
5 If you give someone a hand, you help them.

handbag (n) a bag in which people carry their money and other small things.

handbook (n) a book that gives you information or advice.

handcuffs (plural n) metal rings joined by a chain, that are fixed around prisoners' wrists to prevent them from escaping. handcuff (v).

handful
1 (n) the amount of something that you can hold in your hand.
2 (n) a small number of people or things.
3 (n) (informal) If someone is a handful, they are difficult to cope with.

handicap
1 (n) If someone has a handicap, they are disabled in some way. handicapped (adj).
2 (n) something that makes it difficult for you to do something. Laurie's platform shoes were a great handicap in the race.

3 (n) a disadvantage given to the more skilful competitors in a sport, in order to make the competition more equal. A golf handicap.

handicraft (n) a skill, such as pottery or sewing, that involves making things with your hands.

handkerchief (n) a small square of cloth that you use for blowing your nose.

handle handling handled
1 (n) the part of an object that you use to carry, move, or hold that object. A door handle.
2 (v) to pick something up and hold it in your hands in order to look at it carefully. Please handle the goods with care.
3 (v) to deal with someone or something. Katy is very good at handling tricky situations.

handlebars (plural n) the bar at the front of a bicycle or motorcycle that you use to steer. See **bicycle**.

handshake (n) a way of greeting someone by taking their hand and shaking it.

handsome (adj) attractive, or good looking.

handstand (n) When you do a handstand, you balance on your hands, with your feet up in the air.

handwriting (n) the style you use for forming letters and words when you write. Archibald has very neat handwriting.

handy handier handiest
1 (adj) useful and easy to use.
2 (adj) skilful. Sasha is handy with a power drill.
3 (adj) close by. Is there a cloth handy?

hang hanging hung or hanged
1 (v) to fix something somewhere by attaching the top of it and leaving the bottom free. Hang your coat on this hook.
2 (v) to kill someone by putting a rope around their neck and then taking the support from under their feet. The past tense and past participle of this sense of the verb is "hanged".
3 **hang up** (v) to end a telephone conversation by putting down the receiver.
4 **hang out** (v) (informal) to spend a lot of time in a place.

hangar (n) a large building where aircraft are kept.

hanger (n) a piece of specially shaped wood, metal, or plastic used for hanging up clothes.

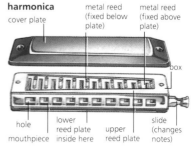

hang-glider

anti-luff line (keeps glider stable)
keel
king post
leading edge
harness
tension adjustment cord
nylon hang loop
rigging wire
batten
instrument cluster (includes variometer, altimeter, and airspeed indicator)
polyester sail
parachute
control frame
control bar

hang-glider (n) an aircraft like a giant kite, with a harness for a pilot hanging below it. *The pilot controls the hang-glider by moving his body.* hang-gliding (n).

hangover (n) a headache and a feeling of sickness that you get after drinking too much alcohol.

hang-up (n) (informal) If you have a hang-up about something, you worry about it all the time.

hanker hankering hankered (v) to wish or long for something. hankering (n).

Hanukkah or **Chanukah** (hah-ner-ker) (n) the Jewish festival of lights, when Jews remember the purification of the Temple. *At Hanukkah, Jews light candles on a menorah, or branched candlestick.*

menorah

haphazard (adj) disorganized. *The papers were scattered over the floor in a haphazard manner.* haphazardly (adv).

happen happening happened
1 (v) to take place, or to occur.
2 (v) If you happen to do something, you have the chance or luck to do it. *Ned happened to arrive just as the bus was leaving.*

happy happier happiest
1 (adj) pleased and contented. happiness (n), happily (adv).
2 (adj) lucky, or fortunate. *Meeting Bob in town was a happy coincidence.*

harangue (huh-rang) haranguing harangued (v) to talk loudly or crossly to someone. harangue (n).

harass harasses harassing harassed (v) to pester or annoy someone. harassment (n).

harbour harbouring harboured
1 (n) a place where ships shelter or unload their cargo.

2 (v) to look after someone secretly.

hard harder hardest
1 (adj) firm and solid. *A hard bed.* hardness (n).
2 (adj) difficult. *A hard exam.* hardness (n).
3 (adj) strong or powerful. *Hard drugs.*
4 (adj) tough and brave.

hardboard (n) stiff board made from pressed wood pulp.

hard copy (n) a printed version of a document created by a computer.

hard disk (n) a disk inside a computer, used for storing large amounts of data. See **computer**.

harden hardening hardened
1 (v) to become harder, or to make something harder.
2 (v) to become tough and unfeeling. *The emperor hardened himself against the complaints of his subjects.* hardened (adj).

hardly (adv) scarcely, or only just. *I could hardly wait to open my gifts.*

hardship (n) difficulty, or suffering.

hardware
1 (n) tools and other household equipment.
2 (n) computer equipment, such as a printer or VDU.

hardwood (n) strong, hard wood from deciduous trees, such as oak, beech, or ash.

hardy hardier hardiest (adj) If a person, an animal, or a plant is hardy, they are tough and can survive in very difficult conditions.

hare (n) a mammal like a large rabbit, with long, strong back legs. *Male and female hares often box together before they mate.*

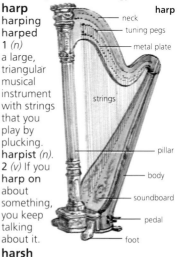

hares boxing

harm harming harmed (v) to injure or hurt someone or something. harm (n), harmful (adj).

harmonica (n) a small musical instrument, played by blowing out and drawing in your breath through the mouthpiece. *Harmonicas contain two sets of reeds fixed to reed plates above and below the mouthpiece. The reeds are left free at one end so that they can vibrate and produce notes when air passes over them.*

harmonica
cover plate
metal reed (fixed below plate)
metal reed (fixed above plate)
box
hole
mouthpiece
lower reed plate inside here
upper reed plate
slide (changes notes)

harmony harmonies
1 (n) agreement. *The team worked in harmony.* harmonious (adj).
2 (n) a pleasant-sounding set of musical notes played at the same time. harmonious (adj).

harness harnesses harnessing harnessed
1 (n) a set of leather straps on a horse, used to control it. See **tack**.
2 (n) an arrangement of straps, used to keep someone safe. *A climbing harness.* See **rock climbing**.
3 (v) to control and use something. *We can now create electricity by harnessing the Sun's energy.*

harp
harping harped
1 (n) a large, triangular musical instrument with strings that you play by plucking. harpist (n).
2 (v) If you harp on about something, you keep talking about it.

harp
neck
tuning pegs
metal plate
strings
pillar
body
soundboard
pedal
foot

harsh harsher harshest
1 (adj) unpleasant, or cruel. *A harsh punishment.* harshly (adv).

2 (adj) A **harsh** noise sounds rough and loud. **harshly** (adv).

harvest harvesting harvested
(v) to collect or gather up crops. The picture shows the main parts of a combine harvester, which is used to harvest crops such as wheat, barley, and peas. Wheat is gathered and cut by the header, and carried to the threshing drum and beater to separate the grain from the straw. The straw then travels along straw walkers, where more grain is collected and the waste is unloaded. The grain is cleaned in the cleaning shoe and stored in the grain tank, ready for unloading. **harvest** (n).

hatch
hatches
hatching
hatched
1 (v) When an egg **hatches**, a baby bird, reptile, or fish breaks out of it.
2 (n) a covered hole in a floor, door, wall, or ceiling. A serving hatch.

turtles hatching

hatchback (n) a car with a rear door that opens upwards.

2 (v) If something **haunts** you, you keep worrying about it. Laura was haunted by the memory of the child's face. **haunting** (adj).
3 (n) a place you have visited often.

have having had
1 (v) to own or possess something. I have a new bicycle.
2 (v) to experience or enjoy something. Let's have some fun!
3 (v) to receive or get something. Did you have some lunch?

combine harvester (cutaway)

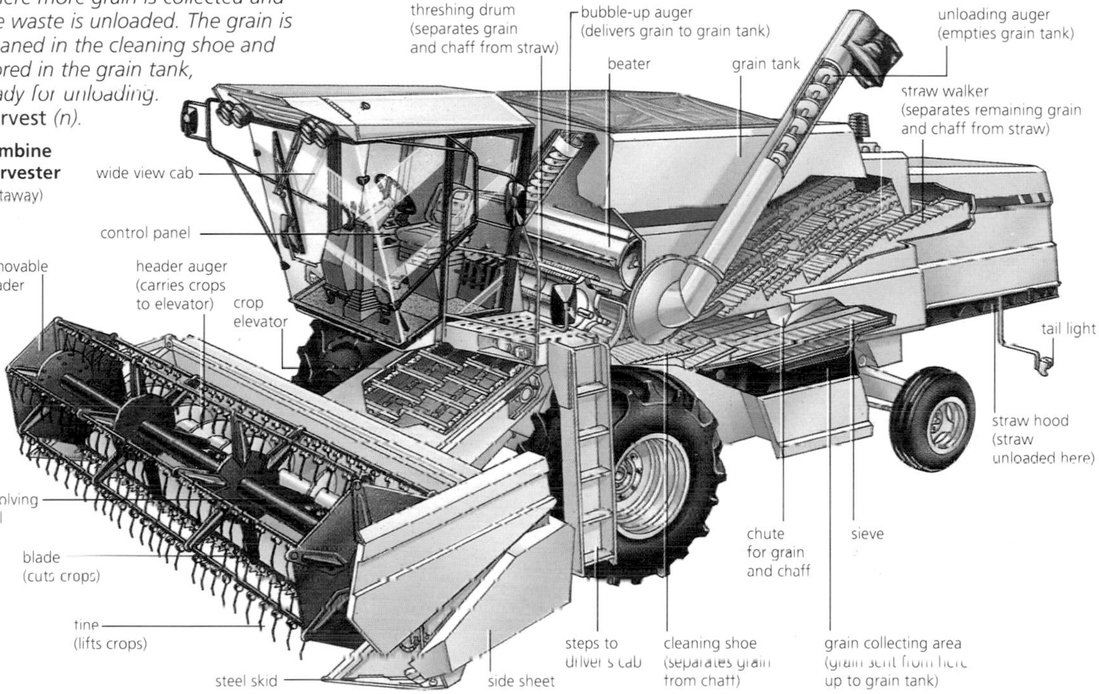

threshing drum (separates grain and chaff from straw)
bubble-up auger (delivers grain to grain tank)
beater
grain tank
unloading auger (empties grain tank)
straw walker (separates remaining grain and chaff from straw)
wide view cab
control panel
removable header
header auger (carries crops to elevator)
crop elevator
tail light
straw hood (straw unloaded here)
revolving reel
blade (cuts crops)
tine (lifts crops)
steel skid
side sheet
steps to driver's cab
cleaning shoe (separates grain from chaff)
chute for grain and chaff
sieve
grain collecting area (grain sent from here up to grain tank)

hash hashes
1 (n) small pieces of meat and vegetables cooked together.
2 (n) (informal) a mess. Barney made a hash of his exams.
3 (n) (slang) a form of the drug cannabis. Hash is short for hashish.

hassle hassling hassled
1 (v) (informal) If someone **hassles** you, they annoy you by going on about something.
2 (n) (informal) a nuisance. It was a real hassle having to get up so early.

hasty hastier hastiest (adj) quick, or hurried. A hasty decision. **haste** (n), **hasten** (v), **hastily** (adv).

hat
1 (n) an item of clothing that you wear on your head.
2 hat trick (n) three successes in a row, such as three goals in a row in a football match.

hatchet (n) a small axe.

hate hating hated (v) to dislike or detest someone or something. **hate** (n), **hatred** (n).

hateful (adj) horrible.

haughty haughtier haughtiest (adj) If you are **haughty**, you are very proud and look down on other people. **haughtily** (adv).

haul hauling hauled
1 (v) to pull something with difficulty. Pandora hauled the sack of potatoes into the shed.
2 (n) a distance to be travelled. The flight between London and Sydney is a long haul.
3 (n) a quantity of something that is caught. A big haul of fish.

haunt haunting haunted
1 (v) If a ghost **haunts** a place, it visits it often. **haunted** (adj).

haven
1 (n) a harbour.
2 (n) a safe place.

havoc (n) great damage and chaos. The floods have wreaked havoc.

hawk (n) a bird of prey, with a hooked beak and sharp claws, that eats other birds and small animals.

hay (n) grass which is dried and fed to farm animals.

hay fever (n) an allergy to pollen or grass that makes you sneeze, makes your eyes water, and can make you wheeze.

haystack (n) a large pile of hay.

hazard hazarding hazarded
1 (n) a danger, or a risk. A fire hazard. **hazardous** (adj).
2 (v) to risk or take a chance on something. I'll hazard a guess at the answer.

haze (n) tiny specks of smoke, dust, or moisture in the air that prevent you from seeing a long way.

hazel
1 (n) a tree that produces hazelnuts.
2 (n) a greenish-brown colour.
hazel (adj).

hazy hazier haziest
1 (adj) misty. hazily (adv).
2 (adj) If you have a **hazy** memory of something, it is vague and unclear.

head heading headed
1 (n) the top part of your body where your brain, eyes, and mouth are.
2 (n) the person in charge. head (adj).
3 (n) the top, or the front of something. The head of the queue.
4 (v) to lead something. Horatio headed the expedition.
5 (v) to move towards something. We headed for the exit.

headache (n) a pain in your head.

headdress headdresses (n) a head covering. This headdress was worn by Native Americans as a sign of their bravery in wars and raids.

Native American headdress

tufts of dyed horsehair
brow band
ermine strip
eagle feathers
downy feathers
skullcap of buffalo skin

heading (n) words written as a title above a section of writing.

headlice (plural n) tiny insects that live and breed in human hair.

headline
1 (n) the title of a newspaper article, printed in large type.
2 headlines (plural n) the most important items in a news broadcast.

headmaster (n) a man who is in charge of a school.

headmistress headmistresses (n) a woman who is in charge of a school.

headphones (plural n) small speakers that you wear over your ears.

headquarters headquarters (n) the place from which an organization is run.

headway (n) If you make headway, you go forwards or make progress.

heal healing healed (v) to cure someone, or make them healthy. healer (n), healing (n).

health
1 (n) strength and fitness.
2 (n) the state or condition of your body. Aunt Agnes is in poor health.

health food (n) food that is natural and good for you.

healthy healthier healthiest
1 (adj) If you are **healthy**, you are fit and well. healthiness (n).
2 (adj) Something that is **healthy** makes you fit. A healthy diet.

heap heaping heaped
1 (n) a pile. heaped (adj).
2 (v) to pile up.
3 (n) (informal) something that is old and broken-down.

hear hearing heard (v) to sense sounds through your ears. hearing (n).

hearing aid (n) a small piece of equipment that people wear in or behind their ears to help them hear.

hearsay (n) things you are told but have not actually seen or experienced.

hearse (rhymes with curse) (n) a car that carries a coffin to a funeral.

heart
1 (n) the organ in your chest that pumps blood around your body.
2 (n) courage, or enthusiasm.
3 (n) love and affection. You have won my heart.
4 (n) the centre of something. The heart of the city.
5 If you learn something **off by heart**, you memorize it.
6 hearts (plural n) one of the four suits in a pack of cards, with a red heart-shaped symbol.

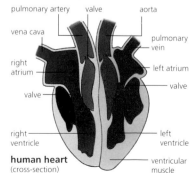

pulmonary artery   valve   aorta
vena cava
right atrium
pulmonary vein
left atrium
valve
valve
right ventricle
left ventricle
human heart (cross-section)
ventricular muscle

heart attack (n) If someone has a heart attack, they collapse because their heart has started to beat irregularly.

heartbroken (adj) If you are heartbroken, you are extremely sad.

hearth (n) the area in front of a fireplace.

heartless (adj) cruel and unkind. heartlessness (n), heartlessly (adv).

hearty heartier heartiest
1 (adj) cheerful and enthusiastic. heartiness (n), heartily (adv).
2 (adj) A **hearty** meal is large and filling.

heat heating heated
1 (n) great warmth.
2 (v) to warm or cook something.
3 (n) passion. In the heat of the argument, I lost my self-control. heated (adj), heatedly (adv).
4 (n) a stage in a competition. Callum got through to the third heat.
5 **heat wave** (n) unusually hot weather that lasts for a few days.

heath (n) a large, wild area of grasses, ferns, and heather.

heathen
1 (n) someone who does not believe in one of the main world religions.
2 (n) (old-fashioned) someone who is uncivilized.

heather (n) a small, spiky bush with pink, purple, or white flowers.

heave heaving heaved
1 (v) to lift, pull, push, or throw something with great effort.
2 (v) to go up and down. Gloria's chest heaved with emotion.

heaven
1 (n) a wonderful place where God is believed to live and where good people are believed to go after they die.
2 (n) a marvellous place, thing, or state. It was heaven to be on holiday. heavenly (adj).
3 the heavens (plural n) the sky.

heavy heavier heaviest
1 (adj) weighing a lot. heaviness (n), heavily (adv).
2 (adj) great in amount or force. Heavy fighting. Heavy rain. heaviness (n), heavily (adv).
3 (adj) (slang) serious and hard to cope with. A heavy film.

heavy metal (n) a type of music with a strong beat, featuring loud electric guitars and drums.

heckle heckling heckled (v) to interrupt a speaker by making rude comments. heckler (n).

hectic (adj) very busy. hectically (adv).

hedge (n) a border made from bushes.

hedgehog (n) a small mammal, covered with spikes, that comes out at night.

hedgehogs

hedgerow (n) a row of bushes.

heel
1 (n) the back part of your foot.
2 (n) something that supports the back part of your foot. *Sukie loves shoes with high heels.*

hefty heftier heftiest (adj) (informal) large, or powerful. *Neal used to be slim, but now he's really hefty.* **heftily** (adv).

heifer (heff-er) (n) a young cow that has not had a calf

height
1 (n) a measurement of how high something is.
2 (n) the most important or greatest point of something. *Sadie thinks that her new hat is the height of fashion.*

heighten heightening heightened (v) to make something higher or stronger. *The painting looked wonderful after Pablo had heightened its colours.*

heir (air) (n) someone who has been, or will be, left money, property, or a title. *The heir to the throne.*

heiress (air-ess) heiresses (n) a girl or woman who has been, or will be, left money, property, or a title.

heirloom (air-loom) (n) something precious that is owned by a family and handed down from one generation to the next.

helicopter (n) an aircraft with large, rotating blades on top, which can take off and land vertically. *The picture shows a Schweizer 300C helicopter.*

helicopter

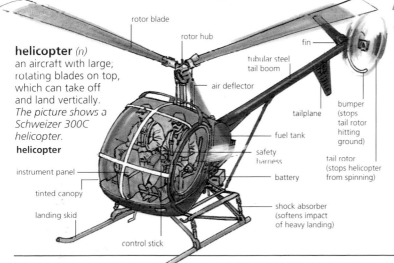

rotor blade
rotor hub
fin
tubular steel tail boom
air deflector
bumper (stops tail rotor hitting ground)
tailplane
fuel tank
tail rotor (stops helicopter from spinning)
safety harness
battery
instrument panel
tinted canopy
landing skid
shock absorber (softens impact of heavy landing)
control stick

hell
1 (n) a place of suffering and misery, where evil people are believed to go after they die.
2 (n) a very unpleasant place, thing, or state. *It was hell having to work such long hours.* **hellish** (adj).

hello (interject) a word said to somebody when you meet them.

helm
1 (n) the wheel or handle used to steer a boat. **helmsman** (n).
2 If someone is **at the helm** of something, they are in charge of it.

helmet (n) a hard hat that protects your head.

help helping helped
1 (v) to assist.
2 (n) assistance. **helper** (n).

helpful (adj) friendly and willing to help. **helpfulness** (n), **helpfully** (adv).

helping (n) a portion of food.

helpless (adj) If you are **helpless**, you cannot look after yourself. **helplessness** (n), **helplessly** (adv).

hem hemming hemmed
1 (n) to fold over an edge of material and sew it down. **hem** (n).
2 (v) If you are **hemmed in**, you are surrounded and cannot get out.

hemisphere (n) one half of a sphere, especially of the Earth. *France is in the Earth's northern hemisphere.*

hemoglobin see **haemoglobin**.

hemophilia see **haemophilia**.

hemorrhage see **haemorrhage**.

hemp (n) a plant whose fibres are used to make rope and sacks.

hen
1 (n) a bird kept for its eggs and its meat. See **chicken**.
2 (n) a female bird.

hence
1 (adv) for this reason.
2 (adv) (old-fashioned) from this place.

heptathlon (n) a competition for women, made up of seven athletic events.

heraldry (n) the study of coats of arms and family histories. *The picture shows some patterns and symbols used in heraldry.*

heraldry

cross   chevron   bend

fleur-de-lys   lion rampant   lion passant

herb (n) a plant used in cooking or medicine. **herbalist** (n), **herbal** (adj).

herbs

rosemary
bay
dill
sage
mint
basil
thyme
parsley

herbivore (n) an animal that eats plants rather than meat. *Rabbits are herbivores.* **herbivorous** (adj).

herd herding herded
1 (n) a large group of animals.
2 (v) to make people or animals move together as a group. *We were all herded into a tiny room.*

here
1 (adv) to, at or in this place. *Please come here.*
2 (adv) at this point in time. *Here the music gets louder.*

hereditary *(adj)* If something is hereditary, it is passed from parent to child. *A hereditary disease.*

heretic *(n)* someone whose views are unacceptable to religious leaders or to people in authority. **heresy** *(n)*.

heritage *(n)* valuable or important traditions, buildings, etc. that belong to a country or a family.

hermit *(n)* someone who has chosen to live totally alone.

hero heroes
1 *(n)* a brave or good person. **heroism** *(n)*, **heroic** *(adj)*.
2 *(n)* the main character in a book, play, film, etc.

heroin *(n)* a very powerful drug. Heroin is dangerously addictive and illegal.

heroine
1 *(n)* a brave or good girl or woman.
2 *(n)* the main female character in a book, play, film, etc.

heron *(n)* a long-legged bird, with a long, thin beak, that lives near water.

herself *(pronoun)* her and nobody else. *Emily has hurt herself.*

hesitate hesitating hesitated *(v)* to pause before you do something. *Zoë hesitated before diving into the river.* **hesitation** *(n)*, **hesitant** *(adj)*.

hessian *(n)* thick, rough cloth, used for making sacks or covering walls.

hexagon *(n)* a shape with six straight sides. **hexagonal** *(adj)*. See **shape**.

heyday *(n)* Someone's **heyday** is the best or most successful period in their life.

hibernate hibernating hibernated *(v)* When animals **hibernate**, they spend the winter in a deep sleep in which their heartbeat, temperature, and breathing rate become very low. Animals hibernate to survive low temperatures and lack of food. **hibernation** *(n)*.

hiccup *or* **hiccough**
1 *(n)* a sudden sound in your throat, caused by a spasm in your chest.
2 *(n)* *(informal)* a small delay or problem. *A technical hiccup.*

hide hiding hid hidden
1 *(v)* to go where you cannot be seen.
2 *(v)* to keep something secret or concealed. *Julia managed to hide her disappointment.*
3 *(n)* an animal's skin that is used to make leather.

hideous *(adj)* ugly, or horrible. **hideousness** *(n)*, **hideously** *(adv)*.

hieroglyphics *(hi-ra-glif-iks)* *(plural n)* writing used by ancient Egyptians, made up of pictures and symbols. *The hieroglyphics shown below were used to represent both objects and letters or sounds.*

hieroglyphics

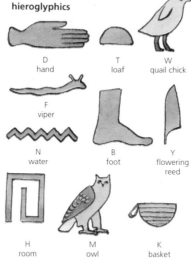

D hand	T loaf	W quail chick
F viper		
N water	B foot	Y flowering reed
H room	M owl	K basket

high higher highest
1 *(adj)* Something that is **high** is a great distance from the ground. *A high mountain.* **high** *(adv)*.
2 *(adj)* measuring from top to bottom. *The tree was 30m high.*
3 *(adj)* more than the normal level or amount. *High prices.* **highly** *(adv)*.
4 *(adj)* *(informal)* If you feel **high**, you are very excited.
5 **high tide** *(n)* the time when the sea is furthest up the beach.

higher education *(n)* education at college or university.

highlands *(plural n)* areas with mountains or hills. **highland** *(adj)*.

highlight highlighting highlighted
1 *(v)* to draw attention to something.
2 *(n)* the best or most interesting part of something.
3 *(v)* to mark important words using a pen with brightly coloured ink.
4 **highlights** *(plural n)* fair streaks in your hair.

highwayman highwaymen *(n)* a robber, usually on horseback, who used to stop travellers on the road and steal from them.

hijack hijacking hijacked *(v)* If someone **hijacks** a plane or other vehicle, they take control of it and force its pilot or driver to go somewhere. **hijacker** *(n)*, **hijacking** *(n)*.

hike *(n)* a long walk in the country. **hiker** *(n)*, **hiking** *(n)*, **hike** *(v)*.

hilarious *(adj)* very funny. **hilarity** *(n)*.

hill *(n)* a raised area of land that is smaller than a mountain. **hilly** *(adj)*.

hiker
rucksack
woollen hat (prevents heat loss)
scarf
waterproof jacket
map case
overtrousers
thermal glove
hiking boot
gaiter

himself *(pronoun)* him and no one else. *Justin has hurt himself.*

hinder hindering hindered *(v)* If someone or something **hinders** you, they make things difficult for you.

Hindi *(n)* a language spoken in northern India.

Hinduism *(n)* the main religion of India. Hindus have lots of gods, and believe that they live many lives in different bodies. *This bronze statue represents Shiva, one of the main gods in Hinduism.* **Hindu** *(n)*.

Shiva

hinge hingeing hinged
1 *(n)* a movable metal joint on a window or door. **hinged** *(adj)*.
2 *(v)* to depend on something. *My future hinges on your decision.*

hint
1 *(n)* a clue, or a helpful tip. **hint** *(v)*.
2 *(n)* a trace, or a tiny amount. *There's a hint of garlic in this soup.*

hip *(n)* the part of your body between your thighs and your waist.

hip-hop *(n)* a type of American rap music.

hippie *or* **hippy** hippies *(n)* a name for someone who does not live or dress in a conventional way. Hippies often live in groups.

hippopotamus hippopotamuses *or* hippopotami *(n)* a large African mammal with short legs and thick skin, that lives near water.

Some words that begin with a "hi" sound are spelt "hy"

hire hiring hired *(v)* to rent something or employ someone for a short time. *We hired a car for the day.*

hire-purchase *(n)* a way of paying for something in several small amounts over a period of time.

Hispanic *(adj)* coming from, or to do with Spanish or Portuguese-speaking countries. **Hispanic** *(n).*

hiss hisses hissing hissed *(v)* to make a "ssss" noise like a snake, especially to show that you do not like something or someone. *We hissed at the villains in the play.* **hiss** *(n).*

historic *(adj)* important in history. *The historic first landing on the moon.*

history histories
1 *(n)* the study of past events. **historian** *(n)*, **historical** *(adj)*, **historically** *(adv).*
2 *(n)* a description of past events. *I'm reading a history of the Wild West.*

hit hitting hit
1 *(v)* to smack or strike something with your hand, a bat, etc. **hit** *(n).*
2 *(v)* to knock or bump into something. *The stone hit the window.*
3 *(v)* to have a bad effect on someone or something. *The factory was hit by the recession.*
4 *(n)* a successful song, play, etc.
5 *(v) (informal)* If you **hit it off** with someone, you get on well with them.

hitch hitches hitching hitched
1 *(v)* to join something to a vehicle. *They hitched the trailer to the van.*
2 *(n)* a problem. *There's been a hitch in our plans, so we can't come.*
3 *(n)* a kind of knot. See **knot.**
4 *(slang)* If you **get hitched**, you marry someone.

hitchhike hitchhiking hitchhiked *(v)* to travel by getting lifts in other people's vehicles. *It can be very dangerous to hitchhike.* **hitchhiker** *(n).*

hi-tech or **high-tech** *(adj)* If something is **hi-tech**, it is very sophisticated and uses the latest technology. Hi-tech is short for high-technology.

hither
1 *(adv) (old-fashioned)* to or towards this place. *Come hither!*
2 If you run **hither and thither**, you run in lots of different directions.

HIV
1 *(n)* a virus that can lead to AIDS. HIV stands for human immunodeficiency virus.
2 If someone is **HIV positive**, they have the HIV virus and may develop AIDS.

hive *(n)* a box for keeping bees so that their honey can be collected. *The queen bee lays her eggs in the brood box and honey is stored in the supers. The honey-filled supers are collected from the hive by beekeepers.* Also see **honeycomb.**

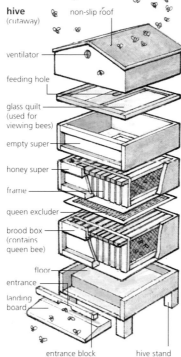

hive (cutaway)
non-slip roof
ventilator
feeding hole
glass quilt (used for viewing bees)
empty super
honey super
frame
queen excluder
brood box (contains queen bee)
floor
entrance
landing board
entrance block
hive stand

hoard hoarding hoarded *(v)* to collect and store things. **hoard** *(n)*, **hoarder** *(n).*

hoarding *(n)* a high fence or board where posters are displayed.

hoarse hoarser hoarsest *(adj)* A **hoarse** voice is rough or croaky.

hoax *(rhymes with pokes)* hoaxes *(n)* a trick, or a practical joke.

hobble hobbling hobbled *(v)* to walk with difficulty, because you are in pain or are injured.

hobby hobbies *(n)* something that you enjoy doing in your spare time.

hockey *(n)* a game played with sticks and a ball, by two teams aiming to score goals.

hoe *(n)* a gardening tool with a long handle and a thin blade, used for weeding and loosening earth. **hoe** *(v).*

hoist hoisting hoisted
1 *(v)* to lift something heavy, usually with a piece of equipment.
2 *(n)* a piece of equipment used for lifting heavy objects.

hold holding held
1 *(v)* to carry, support, or keep something. *Hold the cup carefully.* **holder** *(n).*
2 *(v)* to contain something, or be able to contain it. *This mug holds a pint.*
3 *(v)* to organize or arrange something. *We are holding a party.*
4 *(n)* the part of a ship where the cargo is stored.

hole
1 *(n)* a hollow place, or a gap.
2 *(n)* an animal's burrow.
3 *(n) (informal)* an unpleasant or dirty place. *Sidney's flat is a hole.*

holiday *(n)* time away from school or work, especially a trip away from home.

hollow hollowing hollowed
1 *(adj)* If something is **hollow**, it has an empty space inside it. **hollow** *(n).*
2 **hollow out** *(v)* If you **hollow** something out, you take its insides out.

holly *(n)* an evergreen tree or bush with prickly leaves and red berries.

hologram *(n)* an image made by laser beams that looks three-dimensional.

holster *(n)* a holder for a pistol, worn on a belt.

holy holier holiest *(adj)* to do with or belonging to God or a god.

Holy Communion *(n)* a Christian service in which people eat bread and drink wine in memory of the death and resurrection of Jesus Christ.

home
1 *(n)* Your **home** is where you live or belong.
2 If you **feel at home** with something or someone, you feel comfortable with them.

homesick *(adj)* If you are **homesick**, you miss your home and family.

homicide *(n)* murder.

homoeopathy
(home-ee-op-ath-ee) (n) a way of treating illness by giving people very small amounts of drugs that produce the same symptoms as the illness. **homoeopathic** *(adj)*

homosexual *(adj)* Someone who is **homosexual** has sexual feelings for a person of the same sex. **homosexual** *(n)*, **homosexuality** *(n).*

honest *(adj)* An **honest** person is truthful and will not lie or steal. **honesty** *(n)*, **honestly** *(adv).*

honey *(n)* a sweet, sticky, golden-brown substance made by bees. See **hive, honeycomb.**

honeycomb (n) a wax structure made by bees and used by them to store honey, pollen, and eggs. A honeycomb consists of many rows of six-sided cells. *The picture shows the different functions of the cells in a honeycomb. For the first six days, the brood cells are unsealed so the worker bees can feed the growing larvae. Then the bees seal the cells and the larvae change into pupae which develop into bees. Also see* **hive**.

honeycomb

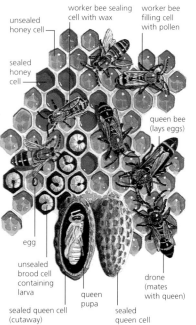

worker bee sealing cell with wax
worker bee filling cell with pollen
unsealed honey cell
sealed honey cell
queen bee (lays eggs)
egg
unsealed brood cell containing larva
queen pupa
drone (mates with queen)
sealed queen cell
sealed queen cell (cutaway)

honeymoon (n) a holiday that a husband and wife take together after their wedding.

honour honouring honoured
1 (n) Someone's **honour** is their good reputation and the respect that other people have for them.
2 (v) to give praise or an award. *The mayor honoured Kim for her bravery.*
3 (v) to keep an agreement. *Both parties must honour the contract.*

honourable
1 (adj) An **honourable** action is good and deserves praise.
2 (adj) If someone is **honourable**, they keep their promises.

hood
1 (n) the part of a jacket or coat that goes over your head. **hooded** (adj).
2 (n) the folding roof or cover of a car, pram, etc.
3 (n) (US) the cover for a car's engine (bonnet, UK).

hoof hooves or hoofs (n) the hard covering over the foot of a horse, deer, etc. *See* **horse**.

hook
1 (n) a curved piece of metal or plastic, used to catch or hold something.
2 (n) a punch in boxing, made with the elbow bent. *A right hook.*

hooked
1 (adj) curved. *A hooked nose.*
2 (adj) (slang) If you are **hooked** on something, you like it a lot, or are addicted to it.

hooligan (n) a noisy, violent person who makes trouble. **hooliganism** (n).

hoop (n) a large ring. **hooped** (adj).

hooray see **hurray**.

hoot hooting hooted (v) to make a sound like an owl or a car horn.

hop hopping hopped
1 (v) to jump, especially on one leg. **hop** (n).
2 (v) (informal) to get into or out of a vehicle. *Hop in the car!*
3 **hops** (plural n) the dried seed cases of hop plants, that are used to make beer.

hope hoping hoped
1 (v) to wish for or expect something. **hopeful** (adj), **hopefully** (adv).
2 (n) a feeling of expectation or confidence. *I have plenty of hope for the future.* **hopefulness** (n), **hopeful** (adj), **hopefully** (adv).

hopeless
1 (adj) without hope. *A hopeless case.* **hopelessness** (n), **hopelessly** (adv).
2 (adj) bad, or lacking in skill. *You're hopeless at map reading!* **hopelessness** (n), **hopelessly** (adv).

horde (n) a large, noisy, moving crowd of people or animals.

horizon
1 (n) the line where the sky and the Earth or sea seem to meet.
2 (n) the limit of your experience or opportunities. *Travel broadens your horizons.*

horizontal (adj) flat and parallel to the ground. *A horizontal line.* **horizontally** (adv).

hormone (n) Your **hormones** are chemicals made in your body that affect the way that you grow and develop. **hormonal** (adj).

horn
1 (n) a hard, bony growth on the head of some animals. **horned** (adj).
2 (n) the hard, bony substance that horns and hooves are made from.
3 (n) a musical instrument that you blow. *A French horn. See* **brass**.
4 (n) a machine that gives a signal by making a hooting sound. *A car horn.*

horoscope (n) a prediction about your life, based on the position of the stars and planets when you were born.

horrible (adj) very unpleasant. **horribly** (adv).

horrid (adj) nasty, or unkind.

horrific (adj) shocking.

horrify horrifies horrifying horrified (v) If something **horrifies** you, you are shocked and disgusted by it. **horrifying** (adj), **horrifyingly** (adv).

horse
1 (n) a large, strong animal with hooves, that people ride or use to pull coaches, carriages, ploughs, etc. *The picture shows a male Anglo-Arab horse.*
2 (n) a piece of gymnastics apparatus that you jump over.

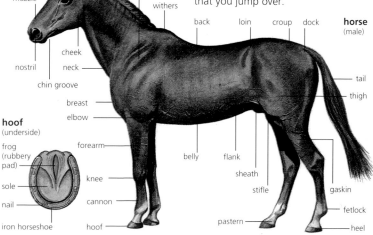

forelock
muzzle
mane
shoulder
withers
cheek
nostril
neck
chin groove
breast
elbow
hoof (underside)
frog (rubbery pad)
forearm
sole
nail
iron horseshoe
knee
cannon
hoof
back
loin
croup
dock
horse (male)
tail
thigh
belly
flank
sheath
stifle
pastern
gaskin
fetlock
heel

Some words that begin with a "h" sound are spelt "wh".

human   h

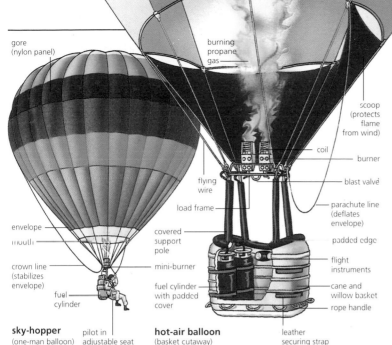

gore
(nylon panel)

burning
propane
gas

scoop
(protects
flame
from wind)

coil

burner

blast valve

flying
wire

load frame

parachute line
(deflates
envelope)

padded edge

flight
instruments

cane and
willow basket

rope handle

envelope

mouth

covered
support
pole

mini-burner

crown line
(stabilizes
envelope)

fuel cylinder
with padded
cover

fuel
cylinder

sky-hopper
(one-man balloon)

pilot in
adjustable seat

hot-air balloon
(basket cutaway)

leather
securing strap

horsepower (n) an old-fashioned unit for measuring engine power.

horticulture (n) the growing of fruit, vegetables, and flowers. horticultural (adj).

hose hosing hosed
1 (n) a long rubber or plastic tube through which liquids or gases travel.
2 (v) to wash or water something or someone with a hose. *Stop hosing your brother!*

hospice (n) a hospital that provides special care for people who are dying.

hospitable (adj) friendly and welcoming. hospitality (n).

hospital (n) a place where you receive medical treatment and are looked after when you are ill.

host
1 (n) an organizer of an event. host (v).
2 (n) a large number. *The audience asked a host of questions.*

hostage (n) someone held prisoner and threatened by an enemy, as a way of demanding money or other conditions.

hostel (n) a building where people can stay, usually at low cost.

hostess hostesses (n) a female organizer of an event.

hostile (adj) unfriendly, or angry. *A hostile crowd.* hostility (n).

hot hotter hottest
1 (adj) having a high temperature.
2 (adj) very spicy and strong-tasting.
3 (adj) recent, or exciting. *Hot news.*

hot-air balloon (n) an aircraft that consists of an enormous bag filled with hot air or gas, and a basket for carrying passengers.

hot dog (n) a sausage in a long bread roll.

hotel (n) a place where you pay to stay overnight and have meals.

hotline
1 (n) a telephone line used for a special purpose, such as ordering goods. *A customer hotline.*
2 (n) a direct telephone link between heads of government, to be used in an emergency.

hot-water bottle (n) a rubber container for hot water, used to warm a bed.

hound hounding hounded
1 (n) a dog. *A foxhound.*
2 (v) to chase or pester somebody. *Ziggy was hounded by journalists.*

hour (n) a unit of time equal to 60 minutes. hourly (adv).

house housing housed
1 (n) a building where people live.
2 (v) If you **house** someone or something, you find a place for them to live or to be.
3 If something in a restaurant is **on the house**, it is free.

houseboat (n) a boat that people live on, with cooking and sleeping areas.

household
1 (n) all the people who live together in a house. householder (n).

2 (adj) belonging to, or to do with a house or family. *We all share the household chores.*

housework (n) work done to keep a house clean and tidy.

hovel (n) a small, dirty house or hut.

hover hovering hovered
1 (v) to stay in one place in the air.
2 (v) to linger, or be uncertain. *Horace hovered in the doorway.*

hovercraft (n) a vehicle that can travel over land and water, supported by a cushion of air.

however
1 (adv) in whatever way, or to whatever extent. *You have to go, however much you hate it.*
2 (adv) on the other hand. *We can't come on Friday. However, we could manage Saturday.*

howl howling howled (v) to cry like a dog or wolf in pain. howl (n).

HQ short for **headquarters**.

hub
1 (n) the centre of a wheel. See **bicycle**.
2 (n) the centre of an organization or activity. *London was the hub of the British Empire.*

huddle huddling huddled (v) to crowd together in a tight group. *We huddled together against the cold.*

hue (n) a colour, or a shade of a colour.

huff (n) If you are **in a huff**, you show that you are upset in a childish, sulky way.

hug hugging hugged (v) to hold someone tightly in a loving or caring way. hug (n).

huge huger hugest (adj) enormous, or gigantic. *A huge amount of money.*

hulk
1 (n) the remains of a wrecked ship.
2 (n) a large, clumsy person. hulking (adj).

hum humming hummed
1 (v) to sing with your mouth closed. hum (n).
2 (v) to make a steady, buzzing noise. hum (n).

human
1 human or human being (n) a person. human (adj).
2 (adj) natural and understandable. *It was only human for Amy to get angry when her bike was stolen.*
3 (plural n) When people campaign for **human rights**, they fight for everyone's right to have justice, fair treatment, and free speech.

humane *(adj)* kind and merciful. **humanely** *(adv)*.

humanitarian *(adj)* to do with helping people and relieving suffering. *Humanitarian aid for refugees.*

humanities *(plural n)* non-science subjects, such as literature, history, and art.

humanity
1 *(n)* all human beings.
2 *(n)* kindness and sympathy.

humble humbler humblest *(adj)* modest and not proud. **humbly** *(adv)*.

humdrum *(adj)* A **humdrum** life is dull and filled with routine events.

humid *(adj)* warm and damp. **humidity** *(n)*.

humiliate humiliating humiliated *(v)* to make someone look or feel totally foolish and undignified. **humiliation** *(n)*.

humility *(n)* If you show **humility**, you are not proud and you recognize your own faults.

hummingbird *(n)* a very small, brightly coloured tropical bird that makes a humming sound when it flaps its wings rapidly. *This violet-cheeked hummingbird is sticking its long beak into a flower so that it can suck up nectar through its hollow tongue.*

hummingbird

humour humouring humoured
1 *(n)* the general name for things that make people laugh or smile. **humorous** *(adj)*.
2 *(n)* If you have a **sense of humour**, you are quick to appreciate the funny side of life. **humorous** *(adj)*.
3 *(v)* If you **humour** someone, you keep them happy by agreeing with them or doing what they want.

hump humping humped
1 *(n)* a small hill, or a large lump.
2 *(v)* (slang) to carry something heavy or awkward. *The porter humped our luggage up the stairs.*

humus *(n)* rich earth made from rotting vegetable and animal matter.

hunch hunches hunching hunched
1 *(v)* to lower your head into your shoulders and lean forward.
2 *(n)* an idea that is not backed by much reason or proof. *I had a hunch that I would hear some good news.*

hungry hungrier hungriest *(adj)* wanting food. **hunger** *(n)*, **hungrily** *(adv)*.

hunk
1 *(n)* a large piece of bread, cheese, meat, etc.
2 *(n)* (slang) an attractive man.

hunt hunting hunted
1 *(v)* to search for something. *Lisa hunted for her watch.*
2 *(v)* to chase foxes or other wild animals for sport. **hunt** *(n)*, **hunter** *(n)*, **hunting** *(n)*.

hurdle hurdling hurdled
1 *(n)* a small fence that you jump over in a running event. *The sequence below shows a hurdler clearing a hurdle.* **hurdler** *(n)*, **hurdling** *(n)*.
2 *(v)* to jump over something.
3 *(n)* an obstacle.

hurdling

hurl hurling hurled *(v)* to throw something very strongly.

hurray or **hooray** or **hurrah** *(interject)* a word used when people cheer.

hurricane *(n)* a violent storm.

hurry hurries hurrying hurried
1 *(v)* to do things as fast as possible.
2 When you are **in a hurry**, you do everything very quickly and often impatiently. **hurried** *(adj)*.

hurt hurting hurt
1 *(v)* to cause pain.
2 *(v)* to be in pain.
3 *(v)* to upset somebody by doing or saying something unkind. **hurtful** *(adj)*.

hurtle hurtling hurtled *(v)* to move at great speed.

hydrofoil

husband *(n)* the male partner in a marriage.

hush hushes hushing hushed
1 *(n)* a sudden period of quietness. *A hush fell on the audience as the curtain went up.*
2 *(interject)* be quiet! *Hush!*
3 **hush up** *(v)* to keep something secret.
4 **hush-hush** *(adj)* (informal) very secret and confidential.

husk *(n)* the outer casing of seeds or grains.

husky huskies; huskier huskiest
1 *(adj)* A **husky** voice sounds low and hoarse. **huskiness** *(n)*, **huskily** *(adv)*.
2 *(n)* a strong dog with a furry coat, bred to pull sledges in arctic conditions.

hustle hustling hustled *(v)* to push someone roughly in order to make them move. *The guard hustled the prisoners out of the room.*

hut
1 *(n)* a small, primitive house.
2 *(n)* a wooden shed.

hutch hutches *(n)* a wooden cage for rabbits or other small pets.

hybrid *(n)* a plant or an animal that has been bred from two different species.

hydrant *(n)* an outdoor water tap for use in emergencies.

hydraulic *(hi-drol-ik)* *(adj)* Hydraulic machines work by power that is created by liquid being forced through pipes under pressure. **hydraulics** *(singular n)*.

hydroelectricity *(n)* electricity that is made from energy produced by running water. **hydroelectric** *(adj)*.

hydrofoil *(n)* a boat with ski-like attachments at the front and back, which lift the hull out of the water once the boat is travelling fast.

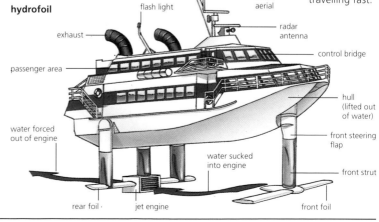

radio aerial
flash light
radar antenna
control bridge
exhaust
passenger area
hull (lifted out of water)
water forced out of engine
front steering flap
water sucked into engine
front strut
rear foil
jet engine
front foil

hydrogen (n) a colourless gas that is lighter than air and catches fire easily. *Hydrogen combines with oxygen to make water.*

hydrometer (n) an instrument used to measure the density of a liquid.

hyena (n) a wild animal, like a dog, that eats the flesh of dead animals and has a shrieking howl.

hygienic (hi-jee-nik) (adj) clean and free enough from germs not to be a health risk. **hygiene** (n), **hygienically** (adv).

hymn (him) (n) a song of praise to God.

hype (n) extravagant claims made about something in order to promote it. **hype** (v).

hyperactive (adj) If someone is hyperactive, they are abnormally restless and lively. **hyperactivity** (n).

hypermarket (n) a very large self-service store, usually on the outskirts of a town.

hyphen (hi-fern) (n) the punctuation mark (-) used to separate the parts of a word made from two or more parts, for example, "easy-going" and "full-time". **hyphenation** (n), **hyphenate** (v).

hypnotize or **hypnotise** hypnotizing hypnotized (v) to put someone into a trance. **hypnotism** (n), **hypnotist** (n).

hypochondriac (hi-per-kon-dree-ak) (n) someone who continually thinks that they are ill or will become ill. **hypochondria** (n)

hypocrite (hip-oh-krit) (n) someone who pretends to believe or feel something that is different from their true beliefs or feelings. **hypocrisy** (n), **hypocritical** (adj), **hypocritically** (adv).

hypodermic (n) a hollow needle used for giving injections.

hypotenuse (n) the side opposite the right angle of a right-angled triangle.

hypothermia (n) If someone is suffering from hypothermia, they have become dangerously cold.

hypothesis hypotheses (n) an idea about the way that a scientific investigation or experiment will turn out.

hysterical (adj) If someone is hysterical, they are very emotional and out of control, because they are very excited, frightened, or angry. **hysteria** (n), **hysterically** (adv).

Ii

ice icing iced
1 (n) frozen water. **ice** (v), **icy** (adj).
2 (v) If someone **ices** a cake, they cover it with a sweet coating.

ice age (n) a very early period of time when a large part of the world was covered with ice.

iceberg (n) a huge mass of ice floating in the sea.

ice cream (n) a sweet, frozen food made from milk or cream.

ice hockey (n) a team game played with sticks and a flat disc called a puck, by skaters aiming to score goals.

ice hockey goalkeeper — helmet, mask, team shirt (left side cutaway), arm and chest protector with built-in shoulder floater, trapper (catching glove), blocker (stick glove), goal stick, puck, strap-on goal pad, skate

ice-rink (n) a place where people skate on a prepared surface of ice.

ice-skate ice-skating ice-skated (v) to move around on ice, wearing high-sided boots with blades on the bottom. **ice skate** (n).

ice-skating movements — bunny jump, stag jump, death spiral, revolutions in the air

icicle (n) a long, thin stem of ice, formed from dripping water which has frozen.

icing (n) a sugar coating used to decorate cakes.

icon or **ikon**
1 (n) a picture of Jesus or a saint found in some Eastern churches such as the Greek and Russian Orthodox churches: *This icon was painted by a Russian artist in the early 13th century.*
2 (n) one of several small pictures on a computer screen, representing programs or functions that you can use.

icon

icy icier iciest
1 (adj) very cold, or covered with ice.
2 (adj) unfriendly. *An icy stare.*

ID short for **identification**.

idea (n) a thought, or a plan.

ideal
1 (adj) very suitable, or perfect. *Hamsters make ideal pets.*
2 (n) the situation you would most like to see. *My ideal is world peace.* **idealistic** (adj).

identical (adj) exactly alike. **identically** (adv).

identification (n) something that proves who you are. *A driving licence is often used for identification.*

identify identifies identifying identified (v) to recognize something or somebody.

identity identities (n) Your **identity** is who you are.

idiom (n) a commonly used expression or phrase that means something different from what it appears to mean. For example, if you catch someone "red-handed", it does not mean that their hands are red.

idiot (n) a foolish person. **idiotic** (adj), **idiotically** (adv).

idle idler idlest
1 (adj) lazy. **idleness** (n), **idly** (adv).
2 (adj) not active. *The factory stood idle during the strike.*

idol
1 (n) someone or something that is worshipped as a god.
2 (n) someone whom other people love and admire. *A pop idol.*

i.e. an abbreviation of the Latin phrase *id est*, which means "that is", and is used to explain something further. *It's the penultimate shop, i.e. the one before last.*

if *(conj)* a word used to show that something will happen on condition that another thing happens first. *I will pay you if you work hard.*

igloo *(n)* the traditional, dome-shaped house of the Inuit people, made of blocks of ice or hard snow.

ignite igniting ignited *(v)* to set fire to something.

ignition *(n)* the electrical system of a vehicle which uses power from a battery to start the engine.

ignorant
1 *(adj)* uneducated, or not knowing about many things. **ignorance** *(n)*, **ignorantly** *(adv)*.
2 *(adj)* not knowing about something. *I was completely ignorant of Barney's intentions.* **ignorance** *(n)*.

ignore ignoring ignored *(v)* to take no notice of something. *Jessica ignored their rude comments.*

ikon *see* **icon**.

ill worse worst
1 *(adj)* sick. **illness** *(n)*.
2 *(adj)* bad. *Did you suffer any ill effects after your accident?*

illegal *(adj)* against the law. **illegally** *(adv)*.

illegible *(adj)* If your handwriting is **illegible**, it is very difficult to read.

illegitimate
1 *(adj)* An **illegitimate** child is born to parents who are not married. **illegitimacy** *(n)*.
2 *(adj)* against the law, or unacceptable.

illiterate *(adj)* not able to read and write. **illiteracy** *(n)*.

illogical *(adj)* Something **illogical** is not reasonable and does not make sense. **illogically** *(adv)*.

illuminate illuminating illuminated
1 *(v)* to light up something, like a building. **illuminated** *(adj)*.
2 *(v)* to make something clearer and easier to understand. **illuminating** *(adj)*.
3 *(v)* In the Middle Ages, manuscripts were **illuminated** by adding pictures and decoration to the text. *The letter*

"L", shown here, comes from a manuscript which was illuminated by monks. **illumination** *(n)*, **illuminated** *(adj)*.

illusion *(n)* something which appears to exist, but does not. **illusory** *(adj)*.

illustration
1 *(n)* a picture in a book, magazine, etc. **illustrator** *(n)*, **illustrate** *(v)*, **illustrative** *(adj)*.
2 *(n)* an example. *Keri gave lots of illustrations of her brother's stupidity.* **illustrate** *(v)*.

image
1 *(n)* a picture in a book, on a television screen, etc.
2 *(n)* a picture that you have in your mind of something or someone. *I have an image of my ideal house.*
3 *(n)* Your **image** is the way that you appear to other people.
4 *(n)* When writers use an **image**, they describe something in terms of something else, for example, "The dragon's eyes were like pits of fire."

imagery *(n)* descriptive language used by writers in poems, stories, etc. *Similes and metaphors are both types of imagery.*

imagine imagining imagined *(v)* to picture something in your mind. **imagination** *(n)*, **imaginary** *(adj)*.

imbecile *(im-ber-seel)* *(n)* an idiot.

imitate imitating imitated *(v)* to copy or mimic someone or something. **imitation** *(n)*.

immature
1 *(adj)* young and not fully developed. **immaturity** *(n)*.
2 *(adj)* If someone is **immature**, they behave in a silly, childish way. **immaturity** *(n)*, **immaturely** *(adv)*.

immediately *(adv)* now, or at once. **immediate** *(adj)*.

immense *(adj)* huge, or enormous. **immensity** *(n)*, **immensely** *(adv)*.

immerse immersing immersed
1 *(v)* to cover something completely in a liquid. **immersion** *(n)*.
2 *(v)* If you are **immersed** in something, you are completely involved in it. **immersion** *(n)*.

immigrant *(n)* someone who comes from abroad to live permanently in a country. **immigration** *(n)*, **immigrate** *(v)*.

imminent *(adj)* about to happen.

immiscible *(adj)* **Immiscible** liquids cannot be properly mixed or blended together. *Oil and water are immiscible.*

immobilize *or* **immobilise** immobilizing immobilized *(v)* to make it impossible for someone or something to move. *The accident immobilized Ella for weeks.*

immoral *(adj)* unfair, wrong, or wicked. **immorality** *(n)*.

immune *(adj)* protected against a disease. **immunity** *(n)*, **immunize** *(v)*.

impact
1 *(n)* the action of one thing hitting another.
2 *(n)* the effect that something has on people. *Our first visit to the theatre had a great impact on me.*

impair impairing impaired *(v)* to damage something, or to make something less effective. *The constant gunfire impaired the soldiers' hearing.* **impairment** *(n)*.

impartial *(adj)* fair, or not favouring one person or point of view over another. **impartiality** *(n)*, **impartially** *(adv)*.

impatient
1 *(adj)* in a hurry, or unable to wait. **impatience** *(n)*, **impatiently** *(adv)*.
2 *(adj)* easily annoyed. *Dad gets impatient with quarrelling children.* **impatience** *(n)*, **impatiently** *(adv)*.

imperfect
1 *(adj)* faulty, or not perfect. **imperfection** *(n)*, **imperfectly** *(adv)*.
2 *(adj)* The **imperfect** form of a verb is used to describe actions which continue, for example, "I was running, I am running, I will be running".

imperial
1 *(adj)* to do with an empire. *In the 19th century, Britain had strong imperial ambitions.*
2 *(adj)* The **imperial** system of measurement is the non-metric system which uses such units as feet, pints, and ounces. *See page 284.*

impersonal
1 *(adj)* lacking in warmth and feeling. *The captain had a cold, impersonal manner.*
2 *(adj)* to do with people generally, rather than with one particular person.

impersonate impersonating impersonated *(v)* to pretend to be someone else, either seriously or for fun. **impersonation** *(n)*, **impersonator** *(n)*.

impertinent *(adj)* rude and cheeky. **impertinence** *(n)*.

impetuous *(adj)* Someone who is **impetuous** does things suddenly, without thinking first. **impetuously** *(adv)*.

implement implementing implemented
1 *(n)* a tool, or an utensil.
2 *(v)* to put something, like a plan or an idea, into action. **implementation** *(n)*.

implication

1 (n) something that happens as a result of something else, and which is sometimes not foreseen. *Having girls in our gang has many implications.*
2 (n) something suggested, but not actually said. *Mum has not said "yes", but the implication is that we can go.*

imply implies implying implied (v) to suggest or mean something without actually saying it.

impolite (adj) If someone is impolite, they are rude and have bad manners. **impolitely** (adv).

import (im-port) importing imported (v) to bring foreign goods into your own country to be sold. **import** (im-port) (n).

important

1 (adj) Something **important** is worth taking seriously and can have a great effect. *An important choice.* **importance** (n), **importantly** (adv).
2 (adj) An **important** person is powerful and holds a high position.

impossible (adj) If something is impossible, it cannot be done or cannot happen. **impossibility** (n), **impossibly** (adv).

impostor (n) someone who pretends to be someone that they are not.

impractical (adj) not sensible, or not useful. *An impractical plan.*

impress impresses impressing impressed
1 (v) to make people think highly of you. **impressive** (adj).
2 (v) If you **impress** something on someone, you make it very clear to them.

impression

1 (n) an idea, or a feeling. *I had the impression that Sid didn't like me.*
2 (n) an imitation of someone or something. *Tom did his impression of a seal.*
3 If something or someone **makes an impression** on you, they have a strong effect on you.

impressionable (adj) If someone is impressionable, they are easily influenced by other people.

imprison imprisoning imprisoned (v) to put someone in prison or lock them up. **imprisonment** (n).

improve improving improved (v) to get better, or to make something better. **improvement** (n).

improvise improvising improvised
1 (v) to do the best you can with what is available. *We improvised a shelter from some old blankets.*

2 (v) When actors or musicians **improvise**, they make up words or music as they perform. **improvisation** (n).

impudent (adj) rude, cheeky, and outspoken. *An impudent remark.* **impudence** (n), **impudently** (adv).

impulse (n) a sudden desire to do something. **impulsive** (adj), **impulsively** (adv).

inaccurate (adj) not very precise, or not correct. **inaccuracy** (n), **inaccurately** (adv).

inadequate (adj) not enough or not good enough. **inadequately** (adv).

inappropriate (adj) unsuitable for the time, place, etc. *Sara's shoes are inappropriate for hiking.* **inappropriately** (adv).

inarticulate (adj) not able to express yourself very clearly in words.

inaudible (adj) not loud enough to be heard. **inaudibility** (n), **inaudibly** (adv).

inborn (adj) If a skill or quality is inborn, you inherit it from your parents and it is natural to you.

Inc. (US) an abbreviation for **incorporated company**. An incorporated company is one where, if the company goes bankrupt, the people who own shares in it only lose the value of those shares.

incapable (adj) If you are incapable of doing something, you are unable to do it.

incense (n) a substance which is burnt to give off a sweet smell.

incentive (n) something that encourages you to make an effort. *The prospect of winning a prize was an incentive to work hard.*

incessant (adj) nonstop or continuous. *Incessant noise.* **incessantly** (adv).

incident (n) an event, or something which happens.

incidentally (adv) by the way. **incidental** (adj).

incision (n) a neat cut made by a knife or blade.

incite inciting incited (v) If you incite someone to do something, you provoke them or urge them to do it.

incline inclining inclined
1 (in-kline) (v) to lean, or to slope. **incline** (in-kline) (n).
2 If you are **inclined to** do something, you like to do it, or you tend to do it. *Rowena is inclined to avoid exercise.* **inclination** (n).

include including included (v) to contain something or someone as part of something else. *The shopping list includes food for supper. We included Abigail in our plans.*

inclusive (adj) including and covering everything. *The rent is inclusive of bills.*

incoherent (adj) unclear, or not logical. **incoherently** (adv).

income

1 (n) the money that someone earns or receives regularly.
2 **income tax** (n) the portion of your earnings that is paid to the government to help run the country.

incompatible (adj) If people or objects are incompatible, they cannot live together or be used together. **incompatibility** (n).

incompetent (adj) If you are incompetent at something, you cannot do it very well or effectively. **incompetence** (n), **incompetently** (adv).

incomplete (adj) not finished, or not complete. **incompletely** (adv).

incomprehensible (adj) impossible to understand. **incomprehensibly** (adv).

inconceivable (adj) impossible to believe or imagine. **inconceivably** (adv).

inconclusive (adj) not clear, or not certain. *Inconclusive results.* **inconclusively** (adv).

inconsiderate (adj) Someone who is inconsiderate does not think about other people's needs and feelings. **inconsiderately** (adv).

inconspicuous (adj) Something that is inconspicuous cannot be seen easily. **inconspicuously** (adv).

inconvenient (adj) If something is inconvenient, it is awkward and causes difficulties. **inconvenience** (n), **inconveniently** (adv).

incorporate incorporating incorporated (v) When you incorporate something into another thing, you make it a part of that thing. *We've incorporated a new song into our show.* **incorporation** (n).

incorrect (adj) wrong. **incorrectly** (adv).

increase increasing increased (v) to grow in size or number. **increase** (n), **increasingly** (adv).

incredible (adj) unbelievable, or amazing. *The beanstalk grew to an incredible height.* **incredibly** (adv).

incriminate incriminating incriminated *(v)* to show that someone is guilty of a crime or other wrong action.

incubator
1 *(n)* a container in which premature babies are kept safe and warm while they grow larger and stronger.
2 *(n)* a container in which eggs are kept warm until they hatch.
incubation *(n)*, incubate *(v)*.

incurable *(adj)* A person with an incurable disease cannot be made better.

indecent *(adj)* rude, or shocking. indecency *(n)*, indecently *(adv)*.

indeed *(adv)* certainly.

indefinite
1 *(adj)* not clear.
2 **indefinite article** the grammatical term for "a", "an", or "some", used before a noun.

indent *(in-dent)* indenting indented *(v)* to start a line of writing or typing a few spaces in from the margin. indent *(in-dent) (n)*.

independent
1 *(adj)* free from the control of other people or things. independence *(n)*, independently *(adv)*.
2 *(adj)* If someone is independent, they do not want or need much help from other people.
independence *(n)*, independently *(adv)*.

indestructible *(adj)* If something is indestructible, it cannot be destroyed. indestructibly *(adv)*.

index indexes *or* indices
1 *(n)* an alphabetical list that shows you where to find words or pictures.
2 *(n)* Your **index finger** is the one nearest to your thumb.

indicate indicating indicated
1 *(v)* to show, or to prove something. *The report indicates that the company is losing money at a rapid rate.* indication *(n)*, indicative *(adj)*.
2 *(v)* to signal. *Drivers should always indicate before turning.* indication *(n)*, indicator *(n)*.

indifferent
1 *(adj)* If someone is indifferent to something, they are not interested in it. *Amelia was indifferent to where we went.* indifference *(n)*.
2 *(adj)* poor in quality. *Toby produced an indifferent piece of work.*

indigestion *(n)* If you have indigestion, your stomach hurts because you are having difficulty in digesting food.

indignant *(adj)* If you are indignant, you are upset and annoyed because you feel that something is not fair. indignation *(n)*, indignantly *(adv)*.

indirect *(adj)* not straightforward. *An indirect route.* indirectly *(adv)*.

indispensable *(adj)* If someone or something is indispensable, they are essential and cannot be replaced. indispensably *(adv)*.

indistinguishable *(adj)* When two things are indistinguishable, you cannot tell them apart. *The twins are virtually indistinguishable.*

individual
1 *(adj)* single and separate. *Slowly, I got to know the individual members of the group.* individually *(adv)*.
2 *(n)* a person. *A strange individual.*
3 *(adj)* unusual, or different. *Ricky has a very individual hairstyle.*
individually *(adv)*.

indoors *(adv)* inside a building.

indulge indulging indulged
1 *(v)* to let someone have their own way. *Nathan's grandparents indulge him dreadfully.* indulgence *(n)*, indulgent *(adj)*.
2 *(v)* If you indulge in something, you allow yourself to enjoy it.

industrial *(adj)* to do with businesses and factories. *The industrial area of the city.* industrially *(adv)*.

industry industries *(n)* the business of making things or providing services in order to earn money.

inefficient *(adj)* If someone or something is inefficient, they do not work very well and they waste time and energy. inefficiency *(n)*, inefficiently *(adv)*.

inequality inequalities *(n)* the treatment of people or things in an unequal or unfair way.

inert
1 *(adj)* lifeless and unmoving.
2 *(adj)* An inert gas does not react with other chemicals.

inertia
1 *(n)* a lazy, tired feeling.
2 *(n)* The inertia of an object is its resistance to any change in motion. Inertia makes it hard to get something moving when it is still and hard to make something stop when it is moving.

inevitable *(adj)* If something is inevitable, it will certainly happen. inevitability *(n)*, inevitably *(adv)*.

inexpensive *(adj)* cheap. inexpensively *(adv)*.

inexperienced *(adj)* An inexperienced person has had little practice in doing something.

inexplicable *(adj)* If something is inexplicable, it cannot be explained. inexplicably *(adv)*.

infamous *(in-fer-muss) (adj)* If someone or something is infamous, they have a very bad reputation.

infant
1 *(n)* a young child or baby. infancy *(n)*.
2 *(n)* In Britain, an infant is a schoolchild aged between four and seven years.

infantry infantries *(n)* the part of an army that fights on foot.

infatuated *(adj)* If you are infatuated with someone, you like them so much that you stop thinking clearly and sensibly about your relationship. infatuation *(n)*.

infection *(n)* an illness caused by germs. infect *(v)*.

infectious
1 *(adj)* An infectious disease is spread from one person to another by germs in the air or on objects.
2 *(adj)* If a mood is infectious, it spreads easily. *Infectious laughter.*

infer inferring inferred *(v)* to draw a conclusion from something that somebody says or does. *We inferred from Tim's absence that he wanted to leave our gang.* inference *(n)*.

inferior *(adj)* If something is inferior to something else, it is not as good. inferiority *(n)*.

infertile
1 *(adj)* unable to have babies. infertility *(n)*.
2 *(adj)* Land that is infertile is useless for growing crops and plants. infertility *(n)*.

infested *(adj)* If an object or a building is infested, it is full of animal or insect pests. infestation *(n)*, infest *(v)*.

infiltrate infiltrating infiltrated *(v)* to join an organization secretly, in order to spy on it or damage it in some way. infiltration *(n)*.

infinite *(in-fin-it) (adj)* endless. *Infinite possibilities.* infinitely *(adv)*.

infinitive *(n)* the basic form of a verb, for example, "to run", "to be", "to write".

infirm *(adj)* weak, or ill. infirmity *(n)*.

infirmary infirmaries *(n)* a hospital.

inflammable *(adj)* An inflammable substance can catch fire easily.

inflatable (adj) An inflatable object can be filled with air or blown up. *The picture shows an inflatable life raft with its safety equipment.* **inflatable** (n).

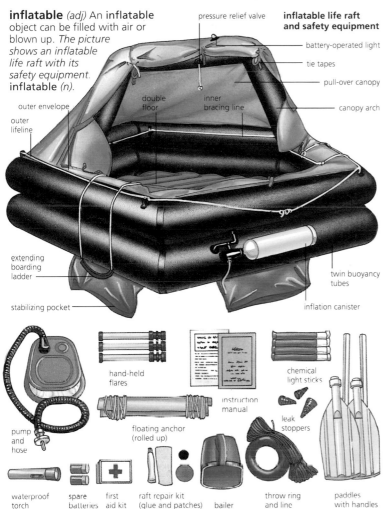

inflatable life raft and safety equipment

- pressure relief valve
- battery-operated light
- tie tapes
- pull-over canopy
- canopy arch
- inner bracing line
- double floor
- outer envelope
- outer lifeline
- extending boarding ladder
- stabilizing pocket
- twin buoyancy tubes
- inflation canister
- pump and hose
- hand-held flares
- floating anchor (rolled up)
- instruction manual
- chemical light sticks
- leak stoppers
- waterproof torch
- spare batteries
- first aid kit
- raft repair kit (glue and patches)
- bailer
- throw ring and line
- paddles with handles

inflate inflating inflated (v) to make something expand by blowing air into it.

inflation (n) a widespread rise in prices. **inflationary** (adj).

inflexible (adj) not able to bend, or not able to change. **inflexibility** (n), **inflexibly** (adv).

inflict inflicting inflicted (v) to cause suffering to somebody or something. *The bombing inflicted severe damage on the town.*

influence influencing influenced (v) to have an effect on someone or something. **influence** (n).

influenza see **flu**.

inform informing informed
1 (v) to tell someone something. *Lee informed me that he was leaving.*
2 (v) If you **inform on** a criminal, you give the police information about them. **informer** (n).

informal (adj) relaxed, easy-going, and casual. *An informal party.* **informality** (n), **informally** (adv).

information (n) facts and knowledge.

information technology (n) the use of computers and other electronic equipment to produce, store, or communicate information.

informative (adj) If something or someone is **informative**, they provide useful information.

infrequent (adj) not happening very often. **infrequently** (adv).

infuriate infuriating infuriated (v) If someone or something **infuriates** you, they make you very angry. **infuriating** (adj), **infuriatingly** (adv).

ingenious (in-jee-nee-us) (adj) clever and original. *An ingenious plan.* **ingenuity** (n), **ingeniously** (adv).

ingredient (n) one of the items that something is made from, especially an item of food in a recipe.

inhabit inhabiting inhabited (v) If you **inhabit** a place, you live there. **inhabitant** (n).

inhale inhaling inhaled (v) to breathe in. **inhalation** (n).

inhaler (n) a container from which you take medicine by breathing it in through your mouth.

inherit inheriting inherited
1 (v) to receive money, property, or a title from someone who has just died. **inheritance** (n).
2 (v) If you **inherit** a particular characteristic, it is passed down to you from one of your parents.

inhuman (adj) cruel and brutal. **inhumanity** (n).

initial
1 (adj) first, or at the beginning. *My initial reaction to seeing the ghost was to scream.* **initially** (adv).
2 (n) the first letter of a name.

initiative (in-ish-er-tiv) (n) If you use your **initiative**, you do what is necessary without other people telling you what to do. **initiate** (v).

inject injecting injected (v) to use a needle and syringe to put medicine into someone's body. **injection** (n).

injure injuring injured (v) to hurt or harm someone.

injury injuries (n) damage, or harm.

injustice
1 (n) unfairness.
2 (n) an unfair situation or action. *You did me an injustice when you called me a liar.*

ink (n) a coloured liquid used for writing and printing. **inky** (adj).

inland (adj) away from the sea. *The hotel is five miles inland.*

inmate (n) someone who has to live in a prison, long-stay hospital, or other institution.

inn (n) a pub, or a small hotel.

inner
1 (adj) inside, or nearest the centre. *A bicycle tyre has an inner tube.*
2 (adj) private. *Nobody can know your inner thoughts.*

innings (singular n) a team's or a player's turn to bat in cricket.

innocent
1 (adj) not guilty. **innocence** (n), **innocently** (adv).
2 (adj) not knowing about something. *Ella was innocent of her aunt's plans.* **innocence** (n), **innocently** (adv).

innovation (n) a new idea, or an invention. **innovate** (v), **innovative** (adj).

inoculate inoculating inoculated (v) to inject a weak form of a disease into someone's body, so that they become protected against it. **inoculation** (n).

inpatient (n) someone who stays in hospital while being treated.

input
1 (n) something that is contributed or put into something else. *Our team has really benefited from Graeme's input.*
2 (n) information fed into a computer. **input** (v).

inquest (n) an official investigation to find out why someone has died. *The police held an inquest after the accident.*

inquire or **enquire** inquiring inquired (v) to ask about somebody or something. *Rupert inquired about the times of the trains.* **inquiring** (adj), **inquiringly** (adv).

inquiry or **enquiry** inquiries (n) a study, or an investigation, especially an official one.

inquisitive (adj) questioning, or curious. **inquisitiveness** (n), **inquisitively** (adv).

insane (adj) mad. **insanity** (n), **insanely** (adv).

insanitary (adj) dirty and likely to cause disease.

inscribe inscribing inscribed
1 (v) to carve or engrave letters on a surface. **inscribed** (adj).
2 (v) to write a special message or dedication in a book.

inscription (n) a carved, engraved, or specially written message. *There are inscriptions under most statues.*

insect (n) a small creature, usually with three pairs of legs, two pairs of wings, three main sections to its body, and no backbone. *The picture below shows a selection of insects.*

insecticide (n) a chemical used to kill insects.

insecure
1 (adj) unsafe, or not fastened properly. *These door locks are very insecure.* **insecurely** (adv).
2 (adj) anxious and not confident. *Polly felt very insecure among so many strangers.* **insecurity** (n).

insensitive (adj) thoughtless and unsympathetic to other people's feelings. **insensitivity** (n), **insensitively** (adv).

insert inserting inserted
1 (v) (in-sert) to put something carefully inside something else. *Insert a coin in the slot.* **insertion** (n).
2 (n) (in-sert) something that is put inside something else. *This magazine has an insert on mountain bikes.*

inside
1 (n) the interior or inner part of something. **inside** (adj).
2 (prep) in less than. *We were back home inside an hour.*
3 (prep) within. *Put it inside the bag.*
4 (adv) into. *He went inside the house.*

insight (n) If you have **insight** into something or somebody, you understand something about them that is not obvious.

insignificant (adj) not important. **insignificance** (n), **insignificantly** (adv).

insincere (adj) Someone who is **insincere** is not genuine, or not honest. **insincerity** (n), **insincerely** (adv).

insipid (adj) dull, or tasteless.

insist insisting insisted (v) If you insist on something, you demand it very firmly. *Sally insisted on wearing her jeans.* **insistence** (n), **insistent** (adj).

insolent (adj) insulting and rude. **insolence** (n), **insolently** (adv).

insoluble
1 (adj) A substance that is **insoluble** will not dissolve.
2 (adj) A problem that is **insoluble** cannot be solved.

insomnia (singular n) If you have insomnia, you often find it very hard to sleep. **insomniac** (n).

inspect inspecting inspected (v) to look at something very carefully. **inspection** (n).

inspector
1 (n) someone who checks or examines things. *Ticket inspector.*
2 (n) a senior officer in the British police force.

insects

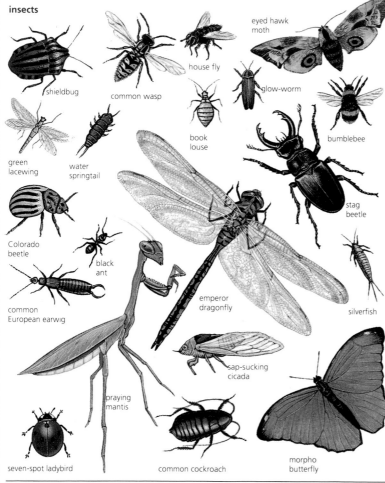

eyed hawk moth

house fly

glow-worm

shieldbug

common wasp

book louse

bumblebee

green lacewing

water springtail

Colorado beetle

black ant

stag beetle

common European earwig

emperor dragonfly

silverfish

praying mantis

sap-sucking cicada

seven-spot ladybird

common cockroach

morpho butterfly

inspire inspiring inspired (v) to influence and encourage someone to do something. *The rock concert inspired me to take guitar lessons.* inspiration (n), inspiring (adj).

install installing installed (v) to put something in place, ready to be used. *We have had a new computer installed in our classroom.* installation (n).

instalment
1 (n) If you pay for something by instalments, you pay for it in regular, small amounts over a period of time.
2 (n) one part of a serialized story.

instance (n) an example. *Nancy gave me several instances of when I had offended her.*

instant
1 (n) a moment. *It was over in an instant.* instantaneous (adj), instantaneously (adv).
2 (adj) happening straightaway. *Instant results.* instantly (adv).

instead (adv) in place of. *Bill went to the party instead of Ben.*

instep (n) the top of your foot, between your toes and your ankle.

instinct
1 (n) behaviour that is natural rather than learnt. *Ducks swim by instinct.*
2 (n) If you have an instinct about something, you know or feel something without being told about it. *I had an instinct that she was not telling the truth.* instinctive (adj), instinctively (adv).

institute instituting instituted
1 (v) to begin, set up, or found. *The headmaster instituted an inquiry into the missing money.*
2 (n) an organization set up to promote or represent the interests of a particular cause or group of people.

institution
1 (n) a large organization where people live or work together, such as a hospital or college. institutional (adj).
2 (n) a well-established custom or tradition. *Weekend barbecues have become an institution in our family.*

instruct instructing instructed
1 (v) to give an order. *The captain instructed his crew to set sail.* instruction (n).
2 (v) to teach a subject or skill. *Ginger instructed me in tap-dancing.* instruction (n), instructor (n).

instructions (plural n) written or spoken words telling you what to do or how to do something

instrument
1 (n) a tool used for delicate or scientific work. *Surgical instruments.*
2 (n) an object that you use to make music. *The picture shows a range of musical instruments from around the world.* instrumentalist (n).

musical instruments

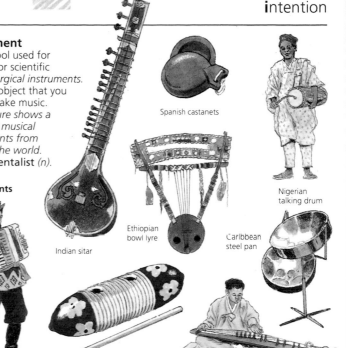

Spanish castanets

Nigerian talking drum

Ethiopian bowl lyre

Caribbean steel pan

Indian sitar

Russian accordion

Mexican reso

Korean kayagŭm

insufficient (adj) not enough, or not adequate. insufficiently (adv).

insulate insulating insulated (v) to cover something with material in order to stop heat or electricity escaping from it. insulation (n), insulating (adj).

insulin (n) a hormone produced in your pancreas which regulates the amount of sugar that you have in your body. People who have diabetes need to be given insulin.

insult insulting insulted (v) to say or do something rude and upsetting to somebody. insult (n), insulting (adj).

insurance (n) When you take out insurance, you pay money to a company which agrees to pay you in the event of sickness, fire, accident, etc. insure (v), insured (adj).

intact (adj) unharmed, or complete. *Fortunately, our books survived the flood intact.*

intake
1 (n) the amount of people or things that are taken in. *Our college has a high intake of music students.*
2 (n) the act of taking something in. *A sharp intake of breath.*

integrate integrating integrated (v) to combine several things or people into one whole. *People of many nationalities have been integrated into our community.* integration (n).

integrity (n) If someone has integrity, they are honest and stick to their principles.

intellectual
1 (adj) involving thought and reason. *Bethan enjoys intellectual puzzles.*
2 (n) someone who spends most of their time thinking and studying.

intelligent (adj) Someone who is intelligent is clever and quick to understand, think, and learn. intelligence (n), intelligently (adv).

intelligible (adj) If something is intelligible, it can be understood. intelligibly (adv).

intend intending intended (v) If you intend to do something, you mean to do it.

intense (adj) very strong. *Intense heat. Intense happiness.* intensity (n), intensely (adv).

intensify intensifies intensifying intensified (v) to make something more powerful or concentrated. *The police intensified their search.* intensification (n).

intent
1 (adj) If you are intent on doing something, you are determined to do it. *Biff is intent on going to college.*
2 (n) an aim, or a purpose.

intention (n) the thing that you mean to do. *It's my intention to win this race.* intentional (adj).

interactive *(adj)* An interactive computer program allows users to make choices in order to control and change it in some ways. **interact** *(v)*.

intercept intercepting intercepted *(v)* to stop the movement of something or someone from one place to another. *The goalkeeper intercepted the ball.* **interception** *(n)*.

intercom *(n)* a microphone and speaker system which allows you to listen and talk to someone in another room or building.

interest interesting interested
1 *(v)* If something **interests** you, you want to know more about it. **interest** *(n)*, **interesting** *(adj)*.
2 *(n)* an additional amount of money paid by someone who borrows money, or paid to someone who invests money. Interest is usually an agreed percentage of the amount borrowed or invested.

interfere interfering interfered *(v)* to involve yourself in a situation that has nothing to do with you. **interfering** *(adj)*.

interference
1 *(n)* involvement in something that has nothing to do with you. *I can't stand any more interference from our neighbours!*
2 *(n)* When you get **interference** on your television or radio, something interrupts the signal, so you cannot see or hear the programme properly.

intergalactic *(adj)* between galaxies. *Intergalactic space travel.*

interior *(n)* the inside of something, especially a building. **interior** *(adj)*.

interjection *(n)* a word used as a greeting, or to express surprise, pain, or delight. *"Ah!", "oh!", and "hello!" are all interjections. See page 3.*

intermediate *(adj)* in between two things, or in the middle. *There are three swimming classes: beginners, intermediate, and advanced.*

intermission *(n)* *(US)* a short break in a film, play, or concert (interval, UK).

intermittent *(adj)* stopping and starting. *Intermittent rain.* **intermittently** *(adv)*.

internal *(adj)* happening or existing inside someone or something. *An internal examination.* **internally** *(adv)*.

international *(adj)* involving different countries. *International trade.* **internationally** *(adv)*.

Internet *(n)* a network that connects millions of computers around the world. The Internet is also known as the Net.

interpret interpreting interpreted
1 *(v)* to decide what something means. *I interpreted Jim's wave as a sign of friendship.* **interpretation** *(n)*.
2 *(v)* If someone **interprets** for two people who each speak a different language, they translate for them. **interpreter** *(n)*.

interrogate interrogating interrogated *(v)* to question someone thoroughly. **interrogation** *(n)*.

interrupt interrupting interrupted
1 *(v)* to stop something happening for a short time. *Vicky interrupted our game.* **interruption** *(n)*.
2 *(v)* to start talking before someone else has finished talking. *Don't interrupt me!* **interruption** *(n)*.

interval *(n)* a time between events or parts of a play, concert, show, etc.

intervene intervening intervened
1 *(v)* If you **intervene** in a situation, you get involved in it in order to change what is happening. *Bobby intervened to prevent his brothers from fighting.* **intervention** *(n)*.
2 *(v)* If a period of time **intervenes** between events, it comes between them. **intervening** *(adj)*.

interview *(n)* a meeting when someone is asked questions. *A job interview.* **interview** *(v)*.

intestines *(plural n)* the very long tube through which food passes when it is digested, after it leaves your stomach. **intestinal** *(adj)*. *See* **digestion**.

intimate *(adj)* Friends who are **intimate** are very close and share their feelings with one another. **intimacy** *(n)*, **intimately** *(adv)*.

intimidate intimidating intimidated *(v)* to frighten someone into doing something. **intimidation** *(n)*.

intolerable *(adj)* If something is **intolerable**, you cannot bear it. **intolerably** *(adv)*.

intolerant *(adj)* People who are **intolerant** get unreasonably angry when other people think or behave in a different way from them. **intolerance** *(n)*, **intolerantly** *(adv)*.

intransitive *(adj)* Intransitive verbs stand on their own and do not need an object. *The verbs "to laugh", "to sneeze", and "to frown" are all intransitive.*

intrepid *(adj)* An intrepid person is courageous and bold.

intricate *(adj)* detailed and complicated. *An intricate pattern.* **intricacy** *(n)*, **intricately** *(adv)*.

intrigue intriguing intrigued
1 *(v)* to fascinate or puzzle someone. *Kit's story intrigued me.* **intriguing** *(adj)*.
2 *(v)* to plot secretly. **intrigue** *(n)*.

introduce introducing introduced
1 *(v)* to bring people together for the first time and tell each one the other's name.
2 *(v)* to bring in something new. *The company are introducing a new product.*

introduction
1 *(n)* Your **introduction** to something is your first experience of it. *I can still remember my introduction to rock climbing.*
2 *(n)* the act of introducing one person to another.
3 *(n)* the opening words of a book, speech, etc. **introductory** *(adj)*.

introvert *(n)* someone who keeps their thoughts and feelings to themselves and is quite shy. **introverted** *(adj)*.

intrude intruding intruded *(v)* to force your way into a place or situation where you are not wanted or invited. **intruder** *(n)*, **intrusion** *(n)*.

intuition *(n)* a feeling about something that cannot be explained logically. *My intuition tells me that you will win this race.* **intuitive** *(adj)*.

Inuit *(n)* a person or a race of people from the Arctic north of Canada, America, and Greenland. Inuits are also known as Eskimos. *This Inuit is fishing through a hole in the ice.* **Inuit** *(adj)*.

Inuit

inundate inundating inundated
1 *(v)* to flood. *The village was inundated by flood water.*
2 *(v)* to overwhelm someone with a large quantity of something. *We were inundated with presents.*

invade invading invaded *(v)* to send armed forces into another country in order to take it over. **invader** *(n)*, **invasion** *(n)*.

invalid
1 *(in-va-lid) (n)* someone who is disabled, or who is seriously ill.
2 *(in-val-id) (adj)* If a ticket, library card, etc. is **invalid**, it cannot be used for some reason.

invaluable *(adj)* very useful indeed.

invent inventing invented
1 *(v)* to think of an original machine, device, idea, etc. **invention** *(n)*, **inventor** *(n)*.
2 *(v)* to make something up.
Leon invented a story to explain why he was soaking wet. **invention** *(n)*.

invertebrate *(n)* a creature without a backbone. **invertebrate** *(adj)*.

inverted commas *(n)* signs, (") or ('), used in writing to show that someone is speaking. Inverted commas are sometimes called speech marks or quotation marks.

invest investing invested
1 *(v)* to give or lend money to something, like a company, in the belief that you will be rewarded in the future. **investment** *(n)*, **investor** *(n)*.
2 *(v)* to give time or effort to something. *I've invested a lot of time in practising the trumpet.*

investigate investigating investigated *(v)* If you **investigate** something, like a crime, you find out as much as possible about it. **investigation** *(n)*, **investigative** *(adj)*.

invincible *(adj)* unbeatable.

invisible *(adj)* Something that is **invisible** cannot be seen. **invisibility** *(n)*, **invisibly** *(adv)*.

invite inviting invited *(v)* to ask someone to do something, or to go somewhere. *We've invited Horace home for tea.* **invitation** *(n)*.

invoice *(n)* a written request for payment after you have done a job or sold something.

involve involving involved *(v)* to include something as a necessary part. *The project involves field work.*

involved
1 *(adj)* If you are **involved** in something, you take a part in it. *I was one of the people involved in the play.*
2 *(adj)* complicated. *Involved work.*

inward or inwards *(adv)* towards the inside.

ion *(n)* an electrically-charged atomic particle.

IQ *(n)* a measure of a person's intelligence. The initials IQ stand for intelligence quotient.

irate *(adj)* angry, or very annoyed.

iron
1 *(n)* a strong, hard metal used to make things like gates and railings. Iron is also found in some foods and is used by your body to make blood.
2 *(n)* a piece of electrical equipment with a handle and a heated surface, used to smooth creases out of clothing. *This picture shows the main parts inside a steam iron.* **iron** *(v)*.

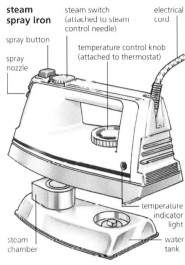

steam spray iron
steam switch (attached to steam control needle)
electrical cord
spray button
temperature control knob (attached to thermostat)
spray nozzle
temperature indicator light
steam chamber
water tank
hole for steam control needle
element
thermostat (controls temperature of element)
electrical connector
sole plate with steam-release holes under here

Iron Age *(n)* a period of history which began about 1,000BC, when iron was first used to make tools and weapons. *In the Iron Age, most people in Western Europe were farmers living in small settlements, like the one reconstructed in this picture.*

Iron Age settlement

thatched roof
hut (for storage or cooking)
living quarters
animal enclosure
look-out platform
granary on stilts
fencing
bank for defence
ditch for defence
gateway

ironic
1 *(adj)* If a situation is **ironic**, the opposite happens to what you would expect. *It was ironic that the clumsiest boy in the class should become a famous ballet dancer.* **irony** *(n)*, **ironically** *(adv)*.
2 *(adj)* mildly sarcastic. *"A fine job you made of that!" said Rosa, with an ironic smile.* **irony** *(n)*.

irrational
1 *(adj)* not sensible, or not logical. **irrationally** *(adv)*.
2 *(adj)* unreasonable, or insane. **irrationally** *(adv)*.

irregular
1 *(adj)* not regular in shape, timing, or size, etc. *An irregular hexagon. An irregular bus service.* **irregularly** *(adv)*.
2 *(adj)* not following the normal pattern. *It's most irregular to come to school in slippers!* **irregularity** *(n)*.

irrelevant *(adj)* If something is **irrelevant**, it has nothing to do with a particular subject. *The story contained many irrelevant details.* **irrelevance** *(n)*, **irrelevantly** *(adv)*.

irresistible *(adj)* too tempting to resist. *The fudge cake was irresistible.* **irresistibly** *(adv)*.

irresponsible *(adj)* reckless and not capable of taking responsibility. **irresponsibly** *(adv)*.

irrigate irrigating irrigated *(v)* to supply water to crops by digging channels and laying pipes. **irrigation** *(n)*.

irritable *(adj)* Someone who is **irritable** is bad-tempered and grumpy. **irritably** *(adv)*.

irritate irritating irritated (v)
If something or someone **irritates** you, they make you annoyed. **irritation** (n), **irritating** (adj), **irritatingly** (adv).

Islam (n) the religion based on the teachings of Mohammed. Muslims believe that Allah is God and that Mohammed is his prophet. Their religion is based on prayer, fasting, charity, and pilgrimage. **Islamic** (adj).

island (n) land surrounded on all sides by water.

isolate isolating isolated
1 (v) to keep someone or something separate, or on their own. *Polly was isolated because she had a highly infectious illness.* **isolation** (n).
2 (v) to discover and identify something. *We've isolated the fault in your computer program.*

isosceles (eye-soss-il-eez) (adj) An **isosceles** triangle has two equal sides. *See* **shape**.

ISP (n) An **ISP** is a company that provides a service linking individual computers to the Internet. The initials ISP stand for Internet Service Provider.

issue issuing issued
1 (v) to send out, or to give out. *Our group has issued a leaflet.*
2 (n) an edition of a newspaper or magazine.
3 (n) the main topic for debate or decision.

IT short for **information technology**.

italic (n) a sloping form of print, used to emphasize certain words or to make them stand out. The word *italic* is printed in italic. **italic** (adj).

itch itches itching itched (v) If your skin **itches**, it is uncomfortable and you want to scratch it. **itch** (n), **itchy** (adj).

item (n) one of a number of things. *An item of clothing.*

itinerary itineraries (n) a detailed plan of a journey.

itself (pronoun) it and nothing else. *This machine works by itself.*

ivory
1 (n) the natural substance from which elephants' tusks are made.
2 (n) a creamy-white colour. **ivory** (adj).

ivy ivies (n) an evergreen climbing or trailing plant, which has pointed leaves.

ivy

---

jab jabbing jabbed
1 (v) to poke somebody with something sharp. *Katy jabbed her elbow into my ribs.*
2 (n) (informal) an injection. *A flu jab.*

jabber jabbering jabbered (v) to talk in a fast and excitable way that is hard to understand.

jack
1 (n) a tool used to raise a vehicle off the ground for repair.
2 (n) a picture playing card with a value between that of a ten and a queen. The jack is sometimes called the knave.

jackal (n) a kind of wild dog, found in Africa and Asia, that feeds off the dead bodies of other animals.

jacket
1 (n) a piece of clothing worn on the top half of your body, with a front opening and long sleeves.
2 (n) a covering. *A book jacket.*

jackknife jackknifing jackknifed (v) When an articulated truck **jackknifes**, the trailer swings around at right angles to the direction of travel and the driver loses control.

jacuzzi (ja-koo-zee) (n) a large bath with underwater jets of water which massage your skin.

jade
1 (n) a green, semiprecious stone, used for making ornaments and jewellery. *The picture shows a jade death mask, made by the Mayas, an ancient civilization of Central America.*

jade death mask

2 (n) a bluish-green colour. **jade** (adj).

jaded (adj) If you are **jaded**, you are very tired and lacking in energy.

jagged (jag-ed) (adj) uneven and sharp. *A jagged edge.*

jaguar (n) a large wild cat, similar to a leopard, found in South and Central America.

jaguar

---

jail or **gaol**
1 (n) a prison. **jailer** (n).
2 **jailbird** (n) a prisoner, or a criminal who often breaks the law.

jam jamming jammed
1 (n) a sweet, sticky food, made from boiled fruit and sugar.
2 (n) a situation in which things cannot move. *A traffic jam.*
3 (v) to squeeze or wedge something into place. *Alvin jammed his bag into the locker.*
4 (n) (informal) a difficult situation.
5 (informal) When musicians have a **jam session**, they make up music as they play together. **jam** (v).

jangle jangling jangled (v) to make a loud, unpleasant, ringing sound.

janitor (n) (US) someone whose job is to look after a school or some other public building (caretaker, UK).

jar jarring jarred
1 (n) a small, glass container with an airtight lid.
2 (v) to jolt or shake something or someone. *The fall jarred my knee.*
3 (v) If something **jars on you**, it makes you feel uncomfortable or annoyed.

jargon (n) words used by people in a particular business or activity, that other people cannot easily understand. *Computer jargon.*

jaundice (n) a disease, usually of the liver, which turns the skin yellow.

jaunt (n) a short pleasure trip or outing.

jaunty jauntier jauntiest (adj) giving a carefree and self-confident impression. *Sophie wore her cap at a jaunty angle.* **jauntily** (adv).

javelin (n) a pointed, light, metal spear, thrown in an athletics event.

jaw jawing jawed
1 (n) one of the two bones between your nose and your chin that hold your teeth. *See* **skeleton**.
2 (n) the lower part of your face.
3 (v) (slang) to talk for a long time in a boring way.

jaywalk jaywalking jaywalked (v) to cross a street carelessly, taking no notice of traffic or signals. **jaywalker** (n).

jazz (n) a lively, rhythmical type of music in which players often make up their own tunes.

jazzy jazzier jazziest (adj) (informal) Something that is **jazzy** is very noticeable, and often has bright colours and a strong pattern. *Rod wore a very jazzy shirt.*

jealous *(adj)* If you are **jealous** of someone, you want what they have. **jealousy** *(n)*, **jealously** *(adv)*.

jeans *(plural n)* casual trousers made of denim, worn by both sexes.

jeep *(n)* an open vehicle, used for driving over rough country.

jeer jeering jeered *(v)* to make fun of someone in a loud, unpleasant way. **jeeringly** *(adv)*.

Jehovah *(n)* a name for God in the Old Testament.

jello *(n)* *(US)* a fruit-flavoured dessert made with gelatine, that is boiled and then allowed to set (jelly, *UK*).

jelly jellies
1 *(n)* a fruit-flavoured dessert, made with gelatine, that is boiled and then allowed to set.
2 *(n)* *(US)* a sweet, sticky food, made from boiled fruit and sugar (jam, *UK*).
3 *(n)* a clear, semi-solid substance found, for example, surrounding the eggs in frogspawn. *See* **frog**.

jellyfish jellyfish *or* jellyfishes *(n)* a sea creature with a jelly-like body and trailing tentacles. *The picture shows how a jellyfish has its mouth in the centre, with feelers or arms stretching out from it*

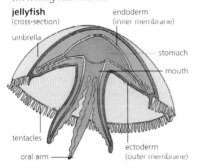

jellyfish
(cross-section)

umbrella

endoderm
(inner membrane)

stomach

mouth

tentacles

oral arm

ectoderm
(outer membrane)

jeopardy *(jep-er-dee)* *(n)* If someone's job or life is **in jeopardy**, it is in danger or is threatened in some way. **jeopardize** *(v)*.

jerk jerking jerked *(v)* to move suddenly, or to pull something suddenly and sharply. **jerky** *(adj)*.

jersey *(n)* a knitted piece of clothing that you wear on the top half of your body.

jest *(n)* a joke, or something said in fun. **jest** *(v)*.

jester *(n)* an entertainer at a court in the Middle Ages.

jet
1 *(n)* a high-pressure stream of liquid or gas.
2 *(n)* an aircraft powered by jet engines.

jet engine *(n)* an engine that creates the forward thrust needed to move an aircraft, boat, etc. by sucking in air or water, and forcing it out at the rear. *The picture shows a turbofan jet engine, which is used on many aircraft. Air is sucked in by the fan, squeezed by the compressors, then mixed with fuel and burnt in the combustion chamber. The gases produced in the chamber are forced out through a series of turbines which drive the compressors and the fan. Also see* **hydrofoil**.

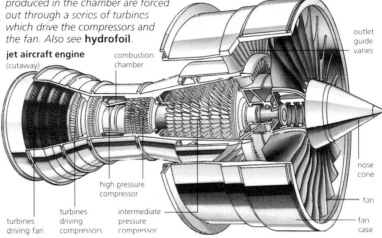

jet aircraft engine
(cutaway)

combustion chamber

outlet guide vanes

nose cone

fan

fan case

high pressure compressor

turbines driving fan

turbines driving compressors

intermediate pressure compressor

jet lag *(n)* a feeling of tiredness and confusion after a long flight from a different time zone.

jetsam *(n)* part of a ship's cargo that is thrown or lost overboard.

jettison jettisoning jettisoned *(v)* to throw overboard, or to throw out something which you no longer need.

jetty jetties *(n)* a structure built out into the sea to give shelter from the waves. Boats moor and unload beside jetties.

Jew
1 *(n)* someone who belongs to the race of people descended from the ancient tribes of Israel.
2 *(n)* someone who practises the religion of Judaism.

jewel *(n)* a precious stone, such as a diamond, ruby, or emerald.

jewellery *(n)* ornaments that you wear, such as rings, bracelets, and necklaces, made of jewels, gold, etc.

Jewish *(adj)* to do with Jews or with the religion of Judaism.

jigsaw *(n)* a wooden or cardboard puzzle made up of pieces of a picture that have been cut up and have to be put back together.

jingle
1 *(n)* a tinkling sound made by the movement of small bells, keys, etc. jingle *(v)*.

2 *(n)* a simple song used to advertise a product.

jinx jinxes *(n)* something that is supposed to bring bad luck. *Our computer seems to have a jinx.*

job
1 *(n)* a task.
2 *(n)* the work that somebody does for a living.

jockey jockeying jockeyed
1 *(n)* someone who rides horses in races.
2 *(v)* If you **jockey for position** with someone, you try to beat them at something, often by unfair actions.

jocular *(adj)* cheerful and amusing.

jodhpurs *(jod-pers)* *(plural n)* trousers that you wear for horse riding. Jodhpurs are loose around the top part of the leg and tight below the knee.

joey *(n)* *(Australian)* *(informal)* a young kangaroo that is carried in its mother's pouch.

jog jogging jogged
1 *(v)* to run at a slow, steady pace. jogger *(n)*, jogging *(n)*.
2 *(v)* to knock something by accident.
3 *(v)* If something **jogs your memory**, it reminds you of something.

join joining joined
1 *(v)* to fasten or tie two things together. join *(n)*.
2 *(v)* to come together with something or someone. *Please join us for supper.*
3 *(v)* to become a member of a club or group.
4 **join up** *(v)* to become a member of the army, navy, or air force.

joiner *(n)* someone who makes wooden furniture and house fittings, such as door frames. **joinery** *(n)*.

Some words that begin with a "j" sound are spelt with a "g".

joint
1 *(adj)* done or shared by two or more people. *A joint effort.* **jointly** *(adv).*
2 *(n)* a large piece of meat.
3 *(n)* a place where two bones meet, for example, your knee or elbow. There are four main types of joint in your body: fixed; sliding; hinge; and ball-and-socket. *This diagram of a human hip joint shows how the ball at the top of the femur fits into the socket of the pelvis.*

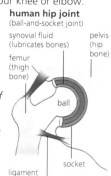

human hip joint
(ball-and-socket joint)

synovial fluid
(lubricates bones)

pelvis
(hip bone)

femur
(thigh bone)

ball

socket

ligament
(joins bones together)

joke joking joked *(v)* to say funny things or play tricks on people in order to make them laugh. **joke** *(n).*

jolly jollier jolliest
1 *(adj)* happy and cheerful.
2 *(adv)* very. *Jolly good!*

jolt jolting jolted
1 *(v)* to move roughly. *The cart jolted along the track.* **jolt** *(n).*
2 *(v)* to bump into or knock someone or something. **jolt** *(n).*

jot jotting jotted *(v)* to write something down quickly. *I've jotted down some ideas.*

joule *(rhymes with fool) (n)* a unit for measuring energy or work done.

journal
1 *(n)* a diary in which you write what you have done each day.
2 *(n)* a serious magazine.

journalist *(n)* someone who collects information and writes articles for newspapers and magazines. **journalism** *(n),* **journalistic** *(adj).*

journey *(n)* a trip from one place to another. **journey** *(v).*

joust *(n)* a contest between two knights, riding horses and armed with lances. *The picture shows a medieval joust.* **joust** *(v).*

jousting knights

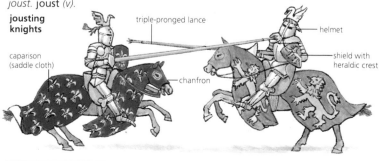

caparison
(saddle cloth)

triple-pronged lance

chanfron

helmet

shield with heraldic crest

jovial *(adj)* Someone who is **jovial** is cheerful and enjoys talking and laughing with other people. **jovially** *(adv).*

joy
1 *(n)* a feeling of great happiness.
2 *(n) (informal)* good luck, or success. *I asked my dad for some money, but I didn't have any joy.*

joyful *(adj)* very happy. **joyfulness** *(n),* **joyfully** *(adv).*

joyride *(n)* a ride in a stolen car for the thrill of it. **joyrider** *(n),* **joyriding** *(n).*

joystick *(n)* a lever used to control movement in a computer game or in an aircraft.

jubilant *(adj)* very happy and delighted. *Josh was jubilant about winning the race.* **jubilation** *(n),* **jubilantly** *(adv).*

jubilee *(n)* a big celebration to mark the anniversary of a special event.

Judaism *(n)* the religion of the Jewish people, based on the law of Moses. Jews believe that they are God's chosen people. *The picture shows the symbol of Judaism, the six-pointed star of David.*

star of David

judge judging judged
1 *(v)* to hear cases in a law court and decide how a guilty person should be punished. **judge** *(n).*
2 *(v)* to decide who is the winner of a competition. **judge** *(n).*
3 *(v)* to form an opinion about someone or something. *After meeting Nat, I judged him to be honest.*

judgment *or* judgement
1 *(n)* the ability to decide or judge something.
2 *(n)* a decision made by a judge.
3 *(n)* an opinion of something or someone.

judicial *(joo-dish-al) (adj)* to do with a court of law or a judge.

judicious *(joo-dish-uss) (adj)* sensible and wise. *A judicious decision.* **judiciously** *(adv).*

judo *(n)* a sport in which two people fight each other using controlled movements, and each tries to throw the other to the ground. *This sequence shows a basic forward throw in judo, called Harai goshi.*

judo
(forward throw)

jug *(n)* a container with a lip for pouring liquids.

juggernaut *(n)* a very large lorry.

juggle juggling juggled *(v)* to keep a set of balls, clubs, or other objects moving through the air by repeatedly throwing them up and catching them again, one after another. **juggler** *(n).*

juggling equipment

balls

clubs

juice *(n)* liquid that comes out of fruit, vegetables, or meat. **juicy** *(adj).*

jukebox jukeboxes *(n)* a machine that plays records when you put coins into it.

jumble jumbling jumbled
1 *(v)* to mix things up so that they are untidy and not well organized. **jumble** *(n).*
2 *(singular n)* second-hand clothes and other objects that are sold at a jumble sale.
3 **jumble sale** *(n)* a sale of second-hand clothes and other objects, usually to raise money for charity or other good causes.

jumbo
1 *(adj)* very large. *A jumbo packet.*
2 **jumbo jet** *(n) (informal)* a very large jet aircraft that can carry hundreds of passengers. *See* **aircraft**.

jump jumping jumped
1 *(v)* to leap, or to spring. **jump** *(n).*
2 *(n)* an object that you jump over. *The horse fell at the last jump.*
3 *(v)* If you **jump at** something, you accept it eagerly.

Kk

jumper
1 *(n)* a knitted piece of clothing that you wear on the top half of your body.
2 *(n) (US)* a sleeveless dress, usually worn over a shirt or sweater (pinafore dress, *UK*).

jump jet *(n)* a jet aircraft that takes off and lands by going straight up and down, instead of using a runway.

jump leads *(n)* a set of wires that are used to connect the batteries of two cars so that one can be started using the other's battery.

jump rope *(n) (US)* a length of rope used for skipping (skipping rope, *UK*).

junction *(n)* a place where roads or railway lines meet or join each other.

jungle *(n)* a thick, tropical forest.

junior
1 *(adj)* not very important in rank or position. *A junior manager.*
2 *(n)* someone who is younger than someone else.
3 *(adj)* for young children. *A junior encyclopedia*
4 *(n)* In Britain, a **junior** is a schoolchild aged between eight and eleven years

junk
1 *(singular n)* things that are worthless or useless. *My room is full of junk!*
2 *(n)* a Chinese sailing boat with square sails and a flat bottom. *Junks have been used for trading for hundreds of years.*
3 **junk food** *(n)* food that is not good for you because it contains a lot of fat, sugar, and chemical additives.
4 **junk mail** *(n)* advertising leaflets and letters that you receive without having asked for them.

junkie *(n) (informal)* a drug addict.

jury juries *(n)* a group of people at a trial who decide whether the person accused of a crime is innocent or guilty.

just
1 *(adj)* fair and right. *A just decision.* justly *(adv).*
2 *(adv)* exactly. *I'm sure I put the book just there.*
3 *(adv)* very recently. *I'm afraid that Humphrey has just left.*

justice
1 *(n)* fairness and rightness.
2 *(n)* the system of laws and punishments in a country.
3 **Justice of the Peace** *(n)* someone who gives judgments in local British courts of law. Justices of the Peace are also known as JPs.

justify justifies justifying justified *(v)* If you **justify** an action, you give a reason or explanation to show that it is necessary and acceptable. *How can you justify stealing my pen?* justification *(n).*

jut jutting jutted *(v)* to stick out. *The cliff jutted into the sea.*

juvenile
1 *(n)* a young person who is not yet an adult, according to the law.
2 *(adj)* involving or concerning young people who are not yet adults, according to the law.
3 *(adj)* childish. *Juvenile behaviour.*
4 **juvenile delinquent** *(n)* a young person who breaks the law juvenile delinquency *(n)*

juxtapose juxtaposing juxtaposed *(v)* to place things side by side. juxtaposition *(n).*

kaleidoscope *(n)* a tube through which you see changing patterns made by mirrors and pieces of coloured glass. kaleidoscopic *(adj).*

kangaroo *(n)* a large Australian marsupial that carries its young in a pouch.

karaoke *(ka-ree-yoh-kee) (n)* an entertainment in which people sing the words of popular songs while a machine plays the backing music.

karate *(ka-rah-tee) (n)* a sport in which two people fight each other using controlled movements, especially kicking with their feet and chopping with their hands.

kayak *(ky-ak) (n)* a covered, narrow boat in which you sit and move through the water by paddling with a double-bladed paddle.

curved paddle blade
safety helmet
buoyancy aid
kayak
shaft
spraydeck (keeps water out)
deck

kebab *(n)* small pieces of meat or vegetables, cooked on a skewer.

keel keeling keeled
1 *(n)* a long bar along the bottom of a boat that holds it together. *See* **ship**.
2 **keel over** *(v) (informal)* to fall over in one smooth, steady movement.

keen keener keenest
1 *(adj)* enthusiastic and eager. *Kim is keen to join the team.* keenness *(n).*
2 If you are **keen on** someone or something, you like them very much.
3 *(adj)* able to notice things easily. *A keen sense of smell.*

keep keeping kept
1 *(v)* to have something and not get rid of it. *Let's keep these books.*
2 *(v)* to stay the same. *We ran around to keep warm.*
3 *(v)* to continue doing something. *Dottie kept laughing at me.*
4 *(n)* a strong tower in a castle. *See* **castle**

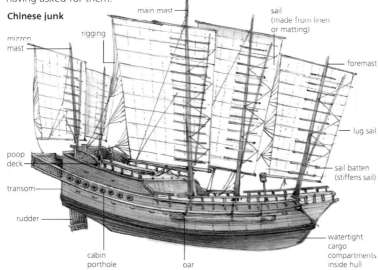

Chinese junk

main mast
sail (made from linen or matting)
rigging
mizzen mast
foremast
poop deck
lug sail
transom
sail batten (stiffens sail)
rudder
cabin porthole
oar
watertight cargo compartments inside hull

Some words that begin with a "k" sound are spelt with a "c".

keeper (n) someone who looks after an animal, a park, or a museum collection.

keg (n) a small barrel.

kennel
1 (n) a small hut for a dog to sleep in.
2 **kennels** (plural n) a place where dogs are looked after while their owners are away.

kerb (n) the line of stones or concrete along the edge of a pavement. See **road**.

kerosene (n) (US) a liquid that is burnt to give light or heat (paraffin, UK).

ketchup (n) a thick tomato sauce.

kettle (n) a container with a handle and a spout, used for boiling water.

key
1 (n) a shaped piece of metal used for opening a lock, starting a car, etc.
2 (n) one of the buttons on a computer or typewriter.
3 (n) one of the black and white bars that you press on a piano.
4 (n) a scale of musical notes based around one particular note. A tune in the key of F.

keyboard
1 (n) the set of keys on a computer, typewriter, piano, etc.
2 (n) An **electronic keyboard** has keys like a piano, and controls to produce other sounds, and is worked by electricity.

khaki (kah-kee) (n) a yellowish-brown colour, used especially for soldiers' uniforms. **khaki** (adj).

kibbutz (kib-ootz) kibbutzim (n) a small community in Israel in which all the people live and work together.

kick kicking kicked
1 (v) to hit something with your foot. **kick** (n).
2 (n) (informal) a feeling of excitement. Dan gets a kick out of driving fast.
3 **kick off** (v) to start a football match by kicking the ball. **kick-off** (n).

kid kidding kidded
1 (n) a young goat.
2 (n) (informal) a child.
3 (v) (informal) to tell someone something untrue, as a joke.

kidnap kidnapping kidnapped (v) to capture someone and keep them as a prisoner until certain demands are met. **kidnapper** (n).

kidney (n) Your kidneys are the organs in your body that remove waste matter from your blood and turn it into urine. See **organ**.

kill killing killed (v) to end the life of a person or animal.

kiln (n) a very hot oven, used to bake objects made of clay until they are hard and dry.

kilohertz kilohertz (n) a unit for measuring the frequency of radio signals.

kilojoule (kil-uh-jool) (n) a unit for measuring energy or work done. 1 kilojoule = 1,000 joules.

kilowatt (n) a unit for measuring electrical power. 1 kilowatt = 1,000 watts.

kilt (n) a pleated, tartan skirt worn by Scottish men as part of a traditional costume.

kimono (n)
a long, loose dress with wide sleeves and a sash, worn by Japanese women.

kin (plural n) people related to you.

kind kinder kindest
1 (adj) friendly, helpful, and generous. **kindness** (n), **kindly** (adv).
2 (n) a type, or a sort.

kindergarten (n) a school or class for preschool children.

kindle kindling kindled
1 (v) to make something start to burn. The campers quickly kindled a fire.
2 (v) to get something started. Our visit to the castle kindled my interest in history.

kindling (n) small, thin pieces of wood used for starting fires.

kinetic (adj) to do with movement, or caused by movement. Kinetic energy. **kinetically** (adv).

king
1 (n) a man from a royal family who is the ruler of his country.
2 (n) a chesspiece that can move one square in any direction. See **chess**.
3 (n) a playing card with a picture of a king on it.

kingdom
1 (n) a country that has a king or queen as its ruler.
2 (n) a part of the natural world. The animal kingdom.

kimono

date eri
(separate collar)

eri
(collar)

obi-jime
(cord)

obi
(sash)

kimono

tabi
(split-toed
socks)

zori
(sandals)

kingfisher (n) a small, brightly coloured bird which lives near water and catches fish for food. Kingfishers have a shrill whistle.

kingfisher

kiosk (n) a small stall from which sweets, newspapers, magazines, etc. are sold.

kip (n) (slang) If you have a **kip**, you have a short sleep. **kip** (v).

kiss kisses kissing kissed (v) to touch someone with your lips to greet them or to show that you like or love them. **kiss** (n).

kit
1 (n) the clothes and equipment that you need to play a sport. Football kit.
2 (n) a collection of parts that you fix together to make something. A model aeroplane kit.

kitchen (n) a room in which food is prepared and cooked.

kite (n) a frame covered with paper or material which is flown in the wind, attached to a long piece of string. The picture shows a stunt kite, which can be made to perform turns, dips, and loops.

stunt kite

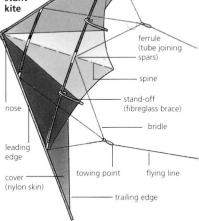

cross spar

ferrule
(tube joining
spars)

spine

stand-off
(fibreglass brace)

bridle

nose

leading edge

cover
(nylon skin)

towing point

flying line

trailing edge

kitten (n) a young cat.

kitty kitties (n) an amount of money contributed by everyone in a group and then used to buy something.

kiwi (kee-wee)
1 (n) a bird from New Zealand that cannot fly.
2 (n) (informal) a name for someone who comes from New Zealand.

knack (nak) (n) an ability to do something difficult or tricky.

Some words that begin with a "k" sound are spelt with a "c".

knave *(nave)*
1 *(n)* one of the three picture playing cards, with a value between that of a ten and a queen. The knave is sometimes called the jack.
2 *(n)* *(old-fashioned)* a dishonest man or boy.

knead *(need)* kneading kneaded *(v)* When you **knead** dough, you punch it and stretch it to make it smooth.

knee *(nee)* *(n)* the joint between your upper and lower leg, which you bend when you walk.

kneel *(neel)* kneeling knelt *(v)* to bend your legs and put your knees on the ground. *Please kneel down!*

knickers *(nik-ers)* *(plural n)* pants worn by women and girls.

knife *(nife)* knives knifing knifed
1 *(n)* a tool with a sharp blade, used for cutting things.
2 *(v)* to stab someone with a knife.

knight *(nite)*
1 *(n)* In medieval times, a **knight** was a warrior who fought on horseback. A king or noble would give a knight land and in return the knight would fight for him. **knightly** *(adj)*. *Also see* **feudalism, joust**
2 *(n)* a man who has been given the title "Sir" as a reward for service to his country. **knighthood** *(n)*, **knight** *(v)*
3 *(n)* a chesspiece with a horse's head that has to move in an L-shape, three squares at a time. *See* **chess**.

plume (ostrich feathers)
chanfron
helmet
visor
sword
gorget
pauldron
breastplate
skirt
vambrace
gauntlet
cuisse
poleyn
greave
sabaton
barding
coat of arms
mounted knight
caparison

knit *(nit)* knitting knitted
1 *(v)* to make a piece of clothing out of wool, using a pair of long, pointed needles. **knitting** *(n)*.
2 *(v)* When a bone **knits**, it heals after it has been broken.

knob *(nob)*
1 *(n)* a small, round handle on a drawer or door.
2 *(n)* a control button on a machine.

knock *(nok)* knocking knocked
1 *(v)* to bang or hit something. *Knock the nails into the wall with a hammer.* **knock** *(n)*.
2 **knock out** *(v)* to make someone unconscious.

knocker *(nok-er)* *(n)* a piece of metal attached to a door that you use to knock on the door.

knot *(not)* knotting knotted
1 *(n)* a fastening made by looping and twisting string or rope together.
2 *(v)* to make a knot in a piece of string or rope.
3 *(n)* a hard spot in a piece of wood where a branch joined the main trunk.
4 *(n)* a unit for measuring the speed of a ship or aircraft.

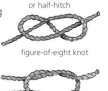

knots
overhand knot or half-hitch
figure-of-eight knot
reef knot or square knot
double carrick bend
sheet bend

know *(noh)* knowing knew known *(v)* to be familiar with a person, place, or piece of information.

knowledge *(nol-ij)* *(singular n)* the things that someone or everyone knows.

knowledgeable or **knowledgable** *(nol-ij-ab-ul)* *(adj)* If you are **knowledgeable**, you know a lot. *Al is knowledgeable about art.*

knuckle *(nuk-el)* *(n)* one of the joints where your fingers join your hand.

koala *(n)* an Australian mammal that looks like a small bear and lives in trees.

kookaburra *(n)* an Australian bird that makes a loud, cackling sound, like the sound of someone laughing.

Koran or **Qur'an** *(n)* the holy book of Islam.

kosher *(adj)* Kosher food is food that has been prepared according to the laws of the Jewish religion.

L l

label labelling labelled
1 *(n)* a piece of paper, cloth, plastic, etc. that is attached to something and gives information about it.
2 *(n)* a word or phrase explaining something. *Picture labels.*
3 *(v)* to attach a label to something, or give something a label.

laboratory laboratories *(n)* a room containing special equipment for people to use in scientific experiments.

labour labouring laboured
1 *(v)* to work hard. **labour** *(n)*.
2 *(n)* people employed to do work, especially physical work. *Part-time labour.*
3 *(n)* the work of giving birth to a baby.
4 **Labour Party** *(n)* one of the main political parties in Britain, which believes in social equality and the importance of the welfare state.

lace lacing laced
1 *(n)* thin material made from cotton or silk, with a pattern of small holes and delicate stitches. *This picture shows the equipment used to make lace.* **lacy** *(adj)*.
2 **laces** *(plural n)* long pieces of thin cord used to tie shoes.
3 *(v)* to tie something together with a lace. *Lace up your shoes.*

lace-making
pillow
lace
pins
bobbin
pricking (pattern)
threads

lack lacking lacked
1 *(v)* to be without something that you need. *The refugees lack food.*
2 *(n)* If there is a **lack** of something, people do not have enough of it.

lacrosse *(n)* a ball game for two teams, in which each player has a long stick with a small net on the end. The players run with the ball, pass it to each other, and aim to score goals.

rubber ball
lacrosse stick
frame
throwing bar
cordbag
side wall
ball stop
leather lace
lightweight aluminium handle

Some words that begin with a "k" sound are spelt with a "c".

lad (n) a boy or young man.

ladder
1 (n) a metal, wooden, or rope structure that you use to climb up and down. Ladders are made from two long, side pieces linked by a series of cross-pieces, called rungs.
2 (n) a long tear in a pair of tights or stockings. **ladder** (v).

laden (adj) carrying a lot of things. *Matt arrived laden with presents.*

ladle (n) a large, deep spoon with a long handle, used for serving soup, casseroles, etc. **ladle** (v).

lady ladies
1 (n) a polite name for a woman.
2 **Lady** (n) a title used by a woman who has either earned the title herself, as a reward for service to her country, or who is married to a Lord or a man with the title "Sir".

lag lagging lagged
1 (v) to cover water pipes with a thick material to stop them from freezing in cold weather. **lagging** (n).
2 (v) If you **lag behind** other people, you do not keep up with them.

lager (lar-ger)
1 (n) a kind of light, pale beer.
2 **lager lout** (n) (slang) a young man who gets drunk and then behaves in a noisy, violent way.

lagoon (n) a large pool of seawater separated from the sea by a bank of sand.

laid-back (adj) (informal) very relaxed and calm.

lair (n) a place where a wild animal rests and sleeps.

lake (n) a large area of fresh water surrounded by land.

lamb
1 (n) a young sheep.
2 (n) meat from a young sheep.

lame lamer lamest
1 (adj) Someone who is **lame** has an injured leg and so is unable to walk properly. **lameness** (n), **lamely** (adv).
2 (adj) weak, or unconvincing. *A lame excuse.* **lamely** (adv).

lament lamenting lamented
1 (n) a sad song, especially one about someone's death.
2 (v) to feel or show great sadness.

lamp (n) a light that uses gas, oil, or electricity.

lance (n) a long spear used in the past by soldiers riding horses. *See **joust**.*

land landing landed
1 (n) the part of the Earth's surface that is not covered by water.

2 (v) to come down from the air to the ground. *The plane landed safely.*
3 (v) (informal) to succeed in getting something. *I've landed a place in the team.*
4 (informal) If you are **landed with** something, you have been given something difficult or unpleasant to deal with.

landfill (n) rubbish and waste that is buried under the ground in large holes.

landing
1 (n) an area of floor at the top of a staircase.
2 **landing strip** (n) a strip of ground which aircraft use for taking off and landing.

landlady landladies
1 (n) a woman who rents out a room, house, or flat.
2 (n) a woman who owns or runs a pub.

landlord
1 (n) a man who rents out a room, house, or flat.
2 (n) a man who owns or runs a pub.

landmark
1 (n) an object in a landscape that can be seen from a long way away.
2 (n) an important event in someone or something's development. *Leaving home was a landmark in Finn's life.*

landscape
1 (n) a large area of land that you can view from one place.
2 **landscape gardening** (n) the designing, shaping, and planting of a garden in an attractive way.

landslide
1 (n) a sudden fall of earth and rocks down the side of a mountain or hill.
2 (n) an election victory in which the winner gains many more votes than anyone else.

lane
1 (n) a narrow road or street.
2 (n) one of the strips marked on a main road, that is wide enough for a single line of vehicles.
3 (n) one of the strips, each wide enough for one person, into which a race track or swimming pool is divided.

language
1 (n) the words that people use to talk and write to each other.
2 (n) a set of signs, symbols, or movements used to express meaning. *Sign language.*

lanky lankier lankiest (adj) Someone who is **lanky** is very tall and thin. **lankiness** (n).

lantern (n) a candle with a protective frame around it. *Lanterns can be made from paper, like the ones shown here, or from glass and metal.*

Japanese lanterns

lanyard (n) a cord worn around your neck to which you can attach a whistle or compass. *See **compass**.*

lap lapping lapped
1 (n) the flat area formed by the top part of your legs when you are sitting down. *Why don't you sit on my lap?*
2 (n) the distance around a running track.
3 (v) When water **laps** against something, it moves gently against it.
4 (v) When an animal **laps up** a drink, it flicks the liquid up into its mouth with its tongue.

lapel (n) part of the collar of a coat or jacket, that folds back over your chest.

lapse
1 (n) a small mistake or failure. *Kay has been dieting hard, with a slight lapse over Christmas.* **lapse** (v).
2 (n) the passing of time. *After a lapse of two years, Jo-Jo returned.*

laptop (n) a portable computer that is so small and light you can use it on your lap.

lard (n) solid, white fat used in cooking.

larder (n) a cupboard or small room in which food is stored.

large larger largest
1 (adj) big. **largeness** (n).
2 If a person or an animal is **at large**, they are free. *There's a tiger at large in the town.*

largely (adv) mostly.

lark
1 (n) a small, brown bird that flies very high in the sky and has an attractive song.
2 (n) (informal) something silly that you do for fun or as a joke. **lark** (v).

larva larvae (n) an insect at the stage of development between an egg and a pupa. *See **caterpillar**.*

laryngitis (la-rin-jy-tuss) (n) a swelling of the throat caused by an infection.

larynx (la-rinx) (n) the top of your windpipe, which holds your vocal cords.

lasagne (laz-an-ya) (n) an Italian dish made from layers of pasta and meat or vegetables, covered with a cheese sauce.

laser
1 (n) a machine that makes a very narrow, powerful beam of light which can be used for light shows, for cutting things, or for medical operations. The word laser stands for light amplification by stimulated emission of radiation.
2 **laser beam** (n) a concentrated beam of light, made by a laser. Laser beams are used to read compact discs. *See* **compact disc**.

lash lashes lashing lashed
1 (n) a stroke with a whip.
2 (v) to tie things together very firmly using rope.
3 (n) one of the small hairs growing around your eyes.
4 **lash out** (v) to hit someone suddenly and angrily.

lass lasses (n) a girl or young woman.

lasso (lass-oo) lassos or lassoes (n) a length of rope with a large loop at one end, which can be thrown over an animal to catch it. **lasso** (v).

last lasting lasted
1 (adj) coming at the end or after everything else. *Jane was the last one to leave.* **lastly** (adv).
2 (adj) most recent. *I saw Dominic last week.*
3 (v) to go on for a particular length of time. *The film will last for 90 minutes.*

lasting (adj) Something that is lasting keeps going for a long time.

latch latches latching latched
1 (n) a lock or fastening for a door. **latch** (v).
2 If you leave a door **on the latch**, you close it, but do not lock it.
3 (v) If you **latch on** to someone or something, you become very attached to them and dependent on them.

latchkey
1 (n) a key that opens a door with a latch.
2 **Latchkey children** have to let themselves in when they return from school because there is nobody at home.

late later latest
1 (adj) When someone or something is late, they come after the expected time. **lateness** (n).
2 (adj) near the end of a period of time. *The late 20th century.*
3 (adj) no longer alive. *The late Elvis Presley.*

latecomer (n) someone who arrives late.

lately (adv) recently.

latent (adj) existing, but not yet very obvious or very strong. *A latent talent.*

lateral
1 (adj) on or towards the side. *A lateral root.* **laterally** (adv).
2 **lateral thinking** (n) the ability to think about problems in an unusual and not obvious way.

lather (n) a mass of white bubbles formed when soap is mixed with water.

Latin (n) the language of the Ancient Romans.

latitude (n) the position of a place, measured in degrees north or south of the equator. **latitudinal** (adj).

latter
1 (n) the second of two things just mentioned. *I like apples and pears, but I prefer the latter.*
2 (adj) later. *It snowed during the latter part of our holiday.*

lattice (n) a pattern of crossed lines, with diamond-shaped spaces in between them. **latticed** (adj).

laugh laughing laughed (v) When you **laugh**, you make a sound to show that you think that something is funny. **laugh** (n), **laughter** (n).

laughable (adj) If someone or something is **laughable**, they are ridiculous and cannot be taken seriously.

launch launches launching launched
1 (v) to put a large ship into the water for the first time. **launch** (n).
2 (v) to send a rocket up into space. **launch** (n).
3 (v) to start or introduce something new. *The charity launched a new fundraising campaign.* **launch** (n).
4 (n) a large motorboat.
5 **launch pad** (n) a place where rockets leave the ground to go into space.

launderette (n) a place where you pay to use washing machines and spin-dryers.

laundry laundries
1 (n) clothes, towels, and sheets that are being washed or are about to be washed.
2 (n) a place where washing is done.

laurel
1 (n) an evergreen bush with smooth, shiny leaves.
2 (n) a wreath made from bay or laurel leaves, given to heroes and poets in Ancient Rome.
3 If you **rest on your laurels**, you rely on your past achievements and do not try any more.

lavatory lavatories (n) a toilet.

lavender
1 (n) a plant with pale purple flowers that has a pleasant smell.
2 (n) a pale purple colour, the colour of lavender flowers. **lavender** (adj).

lavish lavishes lavishing lavished
1 (adj) generous, or extravagant. *Lavish gifts.* **lavishly** (adv).
2 (v) If you **lavish** attention, money, care, etc. on someone, you give them a lot of it.

law
1 (n) a rule made by the government that must be obeyed.
2 (n) a statement or principle in science, maths, etc. *The law of gravity.*

law-abiding (adj) If you are law-abiding, you obey the laws of a country.

law court (n) a place where it is decided whether someone is guilty or innocent of a crime.

lawful (adj) permitted by the law. **lawfulness** (n), **lawfully** (adv).

lawn (n) a piece of grass, usually next to a house.

lawn mower (n) a machine that people use to cut grass.

lawyer (n) someone who advises people about the law and speaks for them in court.

lax (adj) relaxed, or not strict.

laxative (n) a medicine or food that you eat to help you empty your bowels. **laxative** (adj).

lay laying laid
1 (v) to put, or to place. *Lay the clothes on the bed.*
2 (v) to produce an egg.
3 (adj) A **lay** person is not a priest.

layabout (n) (informal) a lazy person.

lay-by
1 (n) In Britain, a **lay-by** is a place by the side of the road where drivers can park.
2 (n) (Australian) a way of paying for something in several small amounts, over a period of time.

layer (n) a thickness of something. *Layers of paint.* **layered** (adj).

lay-off (n) a situation in which people are temporarily sent home from work because there is not enough for them to do.

layout (n) the pattern or design of something. *The layout of a book.*

lazy lazier laziest (adj) If you are lazy, you do not want to work or exercise. **laziness** (n), **laze** (v), **lazily** (adv).

lead leading led
1 *(rhymes with bead)* (v) to show someone the way, usually by going in front of them. **leader** (n).
2 *(rhymes with bead)* (v) to be in charge. **leader** (n), **leadership** (n).
3 *(rhymes with bed)* (n) a soft, grey metal.
4 *(rhymes with bead)* (n) a suggestion, or a clue. *The police have been given several new leads.*
5 *(rhymes with bead)* (n) a long strip attached to a collar, that you use to hold and control a dog.

leaf leaves
1 (n) a flat and usually green part of a plant or tree, that grows out from a stem, twig, branch, etc.
The cross-section of a leaf, below, shows the palisade cells, where light is converted to food in a process called photosynthesis, and the mesophyll cells, where respiration takes place.
leafy (adj).
2 (n) a page of a book.

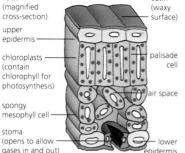

leaf
(plane tree)

vein
(carries water, minerals, and food)

upper epidermis
(protective layer of cells)

apex
(leaf point)

midrib

margin
(outer edge)

lower epidermis
(covered with tiny holes called stomata)

petiole
(stem)

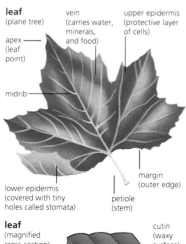

leaf
(magnified cross-section)

cutin
(waxy surface)

upper epidermis

chloroplasts
(contain chlorophyll for photosynthesis)

palisade cell

air space

spongy mesophyll cell

stoma
(opens to allow gases in and out)

lower epidermis

leaflet (n) a printed, and usually folded, piece of paper that gives information, or advertises something. **leaflet** (v).

league *(leeg)* (n) a group of people, countries, or teams who have a shared interest or activity. *A football league.*

leak leaking leaked
1 (v) If a container **leaks**, it lets liquid or gas escape from it. **leak** (n), **leaky** (adj).
2 (v) If a liquid or gas **leaks**, it escapes through a hole or crack in a container. **leak** (n).
3 (v) If a story or information is **leaked**, somebody tells it to someone else who is not meant to know it. **leak** (n).

lean leaning leant or leaned; leaner leanest
1 (v) to bend towards or over something. *The mother leant over her baby.*
2 (v) to slope. *Look how that wall leans!*
3 (v) to rest your body against something for support.
4 (adj) slim and muscular.
5 (adj) If meat is **lean**, it has very little or no fat.

leaning (n) If you have a **leaning** towards something, you are interested in it or good at it.

leap leaping leapt or leaped (v)
to jump, or to jump over something. **leap** (n).

leap year (n) a year that has 366 days, caused by adding an extra day in February. A leap year comes every fourth year.

learn learning learnt or learned
1 (v) to gain knowledge or a skill.
2 (v) to discover some news. *I learnt that Abdul was going away.*

lease (n) an agreement that you sign when you rent a flat, land, etc.

leash leashes (n) a long strip attached to a collar, that you use to hold and control a dog.

least
1 (n) the smallest amount. *Of all the children, Sue eats the least.* **least** (adj).
2 (adv) less than anything else. *Turnip is my least favourite vegetable.*
3 **at least** as a minimum. *We need at least another week's holiday.*

leather (n) animal skin that is treated and used to make shoes, bags, and other goods. **leathery** (adj).

leave leaving left
1 (v) to go away. *We're leaving for France tomorrow.*
2 (v) to let something stay or remain. *Leave the dishes, I'll do them later.*
3 (n) time away from work.
4 **leave behind** (v) If you **leave** something **behind**, you forget to bring it.
5 **leave out** (v) If you **leave** something **out**, you do not include it.

lecture
1 (n) a talk given to a class or an audience in order to teach them something. **lecturer** (n), **lecture** (v).
2 (n) a telling-off that lasts a long time. **lecture** (v).

ledge (n) a narrow shelf. *A window ledge. A mountain ledge.*

leek (n) a long, white vegetable with green leaves at one end. *See* **vegetable**.

leer (n) an unpleasant grin. **leer** (v).

left
1 (adj) This page is on the **left** hand side of the book. **left** (n), **left** (adv).
2 In politics, people **on the left** support the equal distribution of wealth and workers' rights.

left-handed (adj) If you are **left-handed**, you use your left hand to write. **left-hander** (n).

leftovers (plural n) food that has not been eaten, and can be used for another meal.

left-wing (adj) If you are **left-wing**, you believe in the equal distribution of wealth and in workers' rights. **left wing** (n), **left-winger** (n).

leg
1 (n) the part of your body between your hip and foot.
2 (n) one of the parts that support a chair, table, etc.
3 (n) A **leg** of a journey is one part or stage of it.
4 *(informal)* If you **pull someone's leg**, you make fun of them by telling them something untrue.

legacy legacies (n) money or property that has been left to someone in a will.

legal
1 (adj) to do with the law. *Legal documents.*
2 (adj) lawful, or allowed by law. **legally** (adv).

legend
1 (n) an old, well-known story. **legendary** (adj).
2 (n) If someone is a **legend**, they are very famous. **legendary** (adj).

leggings (plural n) close-fitting, stretchy trousers.

legible (adj) If handwriting or print is **legible**, it can be read easily. **legibility** (n), **legibly** (adv).

legion
1 (n) part of the Roman army.
2 (n) a large body of soldiers or ex-soldiers. *The foreign legion.*
3 (adj) very many, or numerous. *Melissa's faults are legion.*

legislation *(singular n)* laws. *The government has introduced new traffic legislation.* **legislate** *(v).*

legitimate
1 *(adj)* lawful, or acceptable. **legitimately** *(adv).*
2 *(adj)* A **legitimate** child is born to parents who are married.

leisure
1 *(n)* free time when you do not have to work. **leisure** *(adj).*
2 **leisurewear** *(n)* clothing for relaxing in, or for sport.
3 **leisure centre** *(n)* a building where you can take part in enjoyable activities such as swimming, badminton, etc.

leisurely *(adj)* unhurried. *We enjoyed a long, leisurely breakfast.*

lemon *(n)* a yellow citrus fruit with a thick skin. *See* **fruit.**

lemonade *(n)* a sweet, fizzy drink that is sometimes lemon-flavoured.

lend lending lent *(v)* to let someone have something for a short time.

length
1 *(n)* the distance from one end of something to the other.
2 *(n)* the time that something lasts. *Do you know the length of this film?* **lengthy** *(adj).*

lengthen lengthening lengthened *(v)* to make something longer.

lengthways *(adv)* in the direction of the longest side. *Fold the paper lengthways.*

lenient *(lee-nee-ent) (adj)* gentle and not strict. **leniently** *(adv).*

lens lenses
1 *(n)* the part of your eye that focuses light. *See* **eye.**
2 *(n)* a piece of curved glass or plastic in a pair of glasses or in a camera, telescope, etc. Lenses bend light rays so that you can focus a camera or see things magnified through a telescope. *The diagram shows how concave and convex lenses make light rays bend in different ways. Also see* **telescope.**

lenses

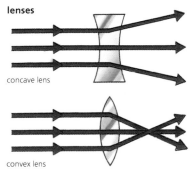

concave lens

convex lens

Lent *(n)* the 40 days before Easter in the Christian church's year. *Some people give up certain luxuries for Lent.*

lentil *(n)* a small, dried seed that can be cooked and eaten. Lentils can be green, orange, or brown.

leopard *(lep-erd) (n)* a large wild cat with a spotted coat, found in Africa and Asia.

leopard

leotard *(lee-oh-tard) (n)* a tight, one-piece garment worn for dancing or exercise.

lesbian *(adj)* Women who are lesbian have sexual feelings for other women. **lesbian** *(n),* **lesbianism** *(n).*

less
1 *(adj)* smaller, or in smaller quantities. *There is less fat in margarine than in butter.* **less** *(adv).*
2 *(prep)* minus. *We bought it for the sale price, less ten per cent discount.*

lessen lessening lessened *(v)* to get smaller in size, strength, importance, etc. *The noise lessened as the teacher approached the classroom.*

lesson
1 *(n)* a set period in school when pupils are taught, or a session when a skill is taught.
2 *(n)* an experience that teaches you something. *Juggling with peaches turned out to be a messy lesson.*

let letting let
1 *(v)* to allow, or to permit something.
2 *(v)* to rent out a house, land, etc.
3 **let down** *(v)* If you **let someone down,** you disappoint them by not doing something that you promised.
4 *(v)* If you are **let off** a punishment or duty, you no longer have to undergo it or do it.

lethal *(adj)* If something is **lethal,** it can kill. **lethally** *(adv).*

letter
1 *(n)* a sign that is part of an alphabet and is used in writing. *The letter A.*
2 *(n)* a message that you write to someone, or receive from someone.

lettering *(n)* letters written in a certain style. *Italic lettering.*

lettuce *(n)* a green, leafy salad vegetable. *See* **vegetable.**

leukaemia *or* **leukemia** *(loo-kee-mee-a) (n)* a serious disease in which the blood makes too many white cells.

level levelling levelled
1 *(adj)* flat and smooth. **level** *(v).*
2 *(adj)* equal. *The scores are level.*
3 *(n)* a height. *Eye level. Sea level.*
4 *(n)* a standard, or a grade. *Advanced level study.*
5 *(v)* If something **levels out,** it stops rising or falling and stays the same.

level crossing *(n)* In Britain, a **level crossing** is a place where a road and railway cross at the same level.

lever *(lee-ver)*
1 *(n)* a bar that you use to lift an object, by placing one end under the object and pushing down on the other end. **leverage** *(n),* **lever** *(v).*
2 *(n)* a handle that you use to make a machine work.

liable
1 *(adj)* likely *Judy is liable to get angry when she hears the news.*
2 *(adj)* If you are **liable** for something that you have done, you are responsible for it by law. **liability** *(n).*

liar *(n)* someone who tells lies.

libel *(n)* an untrue written statement about another person that is damaging to them. **libellous** *(adj).*

liberal
1 *(adj)* tolerant, especially of other people's ideas. **liberalism** *(n).*
2 *(adj)* generous. *A liberal helping of cream.*

Liberal Democrats *(n)* one of the main political parties in Britain, who believe in following a middle way between the policies of the Conservative and Labour parties.

liberate liberating liberated *(v)* to set someone free. **liberation** *(n).*

liberated *(adj)* Someone who is **liberated** has been set free, or feels free. **liberation** *(n).*

liberty liberties *(n)* freedom.

library libraries *(n)* a place where you can go to read or borrow books. **librarian** *(n).*

lice *(plural n)* small insects without wings, that live on animals or people.

licence *(n)* a document giving permission for you to do something or own something. *A driving licence.*

license licensing licensed *(v)* If someone is **licensed** to do something, such as sell alcohol, they have official permission to do it.

lichen *(ly-ken or lit-chen) (n)* a flat, moss-like plant that grows on stones, trees, etc.

Himalayan lichen

lick licking licked
1 *(v)* to pass your tongue over something. **lick** *(n)*.
2 *(v)* to touch something lightly. *Small waves licked the shore.*

lid *(n)* a top, or a cover.

lie lying lay lain *or* lying lied
1 *(v)* to say something that is not true. The past tense of this sense of the verb is "lied".
2 *(n)* a statement that is untrue.
3 *(v)* to get into, or to be in, a flat, outstretched position.
4 *(v)* to be, or to be placed somewhere. *The village lies in a deep valley.*

lieutenant *(lef-ten-ent) (n)* a junior officer in the army or navy.

life lives
1 *(n)* Your **life** is the time from your birth until your death.
2 *(n)* liveliness and cheerfulness. *I feel full of life today!*

lifeguard *(n)* someone who is trained to save swimmers in danger.

life jacket *(n)* a jacket that will keep you afloat if you fall into water.

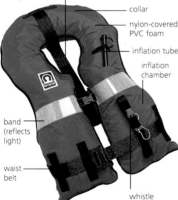

life jacket
back strap
collar
nylon-covered PVC foam
inflation tube
inflation chamber
band (reflects light)
waist belt
whistle

lifestyle *(n)* a way of living. *Rodney has a very glamorous lifestyle.*

lift lifting lifted
1 *(v)* to raise something or someone.
2 *(n)* a machine that carries people or goods between floors of a building.
3 *(n)* a ride, especially in a car.

light lighting lighted *or* lit; lighter lightest
1 *(v)* to start something burning.
2 *(v)* to make something bright and visible.

3 *(n)* brightness, for example, from the sun or a lamp.
4 *(adj)* not dark. *Light blue.*
5 *(n)* an object that gives out light, such as a torch or lamp.
6 *(adj)* weighing little. **lightness** *(n)*.
7 *(adj)* gentle. **lightly** *(adv)*.
8 **light up** *(v)* to make something bright. *A smile lit up Bill's face.*

lighthouse *(n)* a tower, set in or near the sea, with a flashing light that guides ships or warns them of danger.

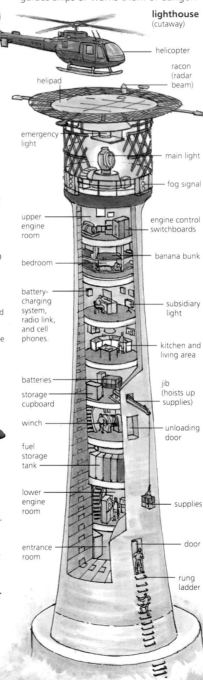

lighthouse
(cutaway)
helicopter
racon (radar beam)
helipad
emergency light
main light
fog signal
upper engine room
engine control switchboards
banana bunk
bedroom
battery-charging system, radio link, and cell phones.
subsidiary light
batteries
kitchen and living area
jib (hoists up supplies)
storage cupboard
winch
unloading door
fuel storage tank
lower engine room
supplies
entrance room
door
rung ladder

lightning *(n)* flashes of electricity in the sky, usually with thunder.

lightweight
1 *(adj)* not heavy. *A lightweight coat.*
2 *(adj)* not important, or not serious.

light year *(n)* a unit for measuring distance in space. A light year is the distance that light travels in one year.

like liking liked
1 *(v)* to enjoy or be pleased by something or someone. **liking** *(n)*.
2 *(prep)* similar to. *I want a hat like yours.*
3 *(prep)* typical of. *It's just like Daisy to be late.*
4 *(adj)* similar. *The twins are as like as two peas.*

likely likelier likeliest *(adj)* probable. **likelihood** *(n)*.

likewise *(adv)* also, or in the same way. *I'll dance if you do likewise.*

limb
1 *(n)* an arm or a leg.
2 *(n)* a branch of a tree.

limber limbering limbered
1 *(v)* When you **limber up**, you stretch your muscles before exercising.
2 *(adj)* *(US)* supple and flexible.

lime
1 *(n)* a green citrus fruit, shaped like a lemon. *See* **fruit**.
2 *(n)* a white substance or powder, used to make cement and as a fertilizer on fields.

limelight *(n)* If you are **in the limelight**, you are the centre of attention.

limerick *(n)* a nonsense verse made up of five lines that rhyme in a particular way.

limestone *(n)* a rock that contains calcium carbonate and from which lime is made.

limit limiting limited
1 *(n)* an edge, or a boundary. **limitless** *(adj)*, **limitlessly** *(adv)*.
2 *(v)* to keep within a certain area or amount. *I've limited myself to three cups of tea a day.* **limitation** *(n)*.

limited
1 *(adj)* small and unable to increase.
2 *(n)* A **limited edition** of a book, picture, etc. may be valuable because it is one of only a small number.
3 *(n)* A **limited company** is one where people who own shares in it lose only the value of those shares if the company goes bankrupt.

limp limping limped; limper limpest
1 *(v)* to walk in an uneven way, usually because of an injury. **limp** *(n)*.

2 (adj) floppy and not firm. *A limp handshake.* **limply** (adv).

line lining lined
1 (n) a long, narrow mark.
2 (n) a row of people or words.
3 (n) a piece of string, rope, etc.
4 (v) to make a lining for something.
5 (n) an attitude, or an approach to something. *My dad takes a firm line on discipline.*

linen (n) cloth made from the flax plant, used to make clothes and household items, such as tablecloths and tea towels.

linesman linesmen (n) an official who decides if the ball has gone over the line, in games such as football and tennis. See **soccer**.

linger lingering lingered (v) to stay, or to wait around. *The fans lingered outside the theatre.* **lingering** (adj).

linguist (n) someone who studies foreign languages, or someone who speaks them well.

lining (n) a piece of material sewn inside something. *Humphrey's jacket has a patterned lining.*

link linking linked
1 (n) one of the separate rings that make up a chain.
2 (n) a connection between things or people.
3 (v) to join objects, ideas, or people together.

lino (n) a smooth, shiny material used as a floor covering. Lino is short for linoleum.

linocut (n) a print made from a block of lino with a pattern or picture cut into it.

lint (n) soft material used for covering wounds.

lion (n) a large, wild cat with a mane, found in Africa and Asia

lip
1 (n) Your **lips** are the pink edges of your mouth.
2 (n) the edge or rim of a cup or hole.
3 (n) (slang) cheek, or rude talk.

lip-read lip-reading lip-read (v) When deaf people **lip-read**, they watch someone's lips while they are talking in order to understand what they are saying. **lip-reading** (n).

liquid (n) a wet substance that you can pour. **liquid** (adj).

liquid-crystal display (n) a way of showing numbers and letters on clocks, calculators, etc. Different parts of a grid of liquid crystals reflect light as electronic signals are sent to them. See **calculator**.

liquidize or **liquidise** liquidizing liquidized (v) to make solid food into a liquid. **liquidizer** (n).

liquor (lik-er) (n) strong alcoholic drink, such as whisky, gin, or vodka.

liquorice (lik-er-iss or lik-er-ish) (n) a black substance that comes from a plant root, and is used to make sweets.

lira (leer-a) lire (n) the main unit of money in Italy and Turkey.

lisp (n) a way of talking in which you say 'th' instead of 's'. **lisp** (v).

list listing listed
1 (v) to set down words, numbers, etc. in a line. **list** (n).
2 (v) When a ship **lists**, it leans to one side.

listen listening listened (v) to pay attention so that you can hear something. **listener** (n).

literacy (n) the ability to read and write. **literate** (adj).

literally (adv) If you take someone literally, you believe their exact words.

literature (n) books, especially novels, plays, and poems. **literary** (adj).

litmus (n) a substance that turns red when touched by an acid, and blue when touched by an alkali. Litmus comes in paper or liquid form

litter
1 (n) rubbish that is left scattered around. **litter** (v).
2 (n) a group of kittens, piglets, puppies, etc. born at the same time to one mother.
3 **litter tray** (n) an indoor toilet for a cat or other pet.

little littler littlest
1 (adj) small in size. *A little girl.*
2 (n) a small amount of something. *I'll have just a little.*
3 (adj) not much. *We have little time.*

live living lived
1 (rhymes with give) (v) to be alive. *Some cats live for 20 years.*
2 (rhymes with five) (adj) alive or living. *You can buy live chickens in the market.*
3 (rhymes with give) (v) to have your home somewhere. *Josie lives in Chicago.*
4 (rhymes with five) (adj) broadcast as it is happening.
5 (rhymes with five) (adj) If an electrical appliance is **live**, it is carrying electricity which can give you a shock.
6 (rhymes with five) (adj) unexploded. *A live cartridge.*

livelihood (n) the way that you make money to support yourself.

lively livelier liveliest (adj) active and full of life. **liveliness** (n).

liver
1 (n) the organ in your body that cleans your blood. Your liver also produces bile which helps to digest food. See **digestion**, **organ**.
2 (n) You can eat the **liver** of some animals, such as pigs.

livestock (n) animals kept on a farm, such as horses, sheep, and cows.

living
1 (adj) alive now.
2 (n) money to live. *Joe earns his living by painting.*

living room (n) a lounge, or a sitting room.

lizard (n) a small reptile with a long body and a tail. *The picture shows parts of a lizard and a range of different lizards.*

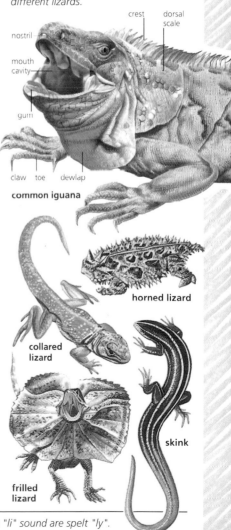

crest
dorsal scale
nostril
mouth cavity
gum
claw   toe   dewlap
common iguana

horned lizard

collared lizard

frilled lizard

skink

Some words that begin with a "li" sound are spelt "ly".

llama *(n)* a South American mammal, kept for its wool and meat.

load loading loaded
1 *(n)* something that is carried, especially something heavy.
2 *(v)* to put things on to or into something. *Bobby loaded the car with camping equipment.*
3 *(v)* to put a bullet into a gun, a film into a camera, or a program into a computer.
4 *(plural n) (informal)* If you have **loads** of something, you have a lot of it.

loaf loaves; loafing loafed
1 *(n)* bread baked in a shape.
2 *(n)* food that has been cooked in a loaf-shaped tin. *Meat loaf.*
3 *(v)* If you **loaf around**, you are lazy and do very little.

loafer
1 *(n)* someone who is lazy and does not do much.
2 *(n)* a flat, slip-on, leather shoe.

loam *(n)* loose, rich soil made of sand, clay, and rotted vegetable and animal material. **loamy** *(adj)*.

loan loaning loaned
1 *(v)* to lend something to someone.
2 *(n)* an amount of money that you borrow.

loathe loathing loathed *(v)* to hate or dislike someone or something. *Tabitha loathes school cabbage.* **loathing** *(n)*.

loathsome *(adj)* very unpleasant or disgusting. *A loathsome monster.*

lob lobbing lobbed *(v)* to throw or hit a ball high into the air. **lob** *(n)*.

lobby lobbies
1 *(n)* a hall in a large building.
2 *(n)* a group of people who try to persuade politicians to act or vote in a certain way. **lobby** *(v)*.

lobster *(n)* a sea creature with a shell, ten legs, and a long body. Lobsters can be eaten, and turn pink when they are cooked.

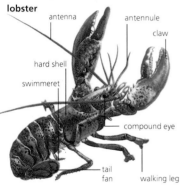
lobster
antenna
antennule
claw
hard shell
swimmeret
compound eye
tail
fan
walking leg

local
1 *(adj)* near your house, or to do with the area where you live. *A local newspaper.* **locally** *(adv)*.
2 *(n) (informal)* Someone's **local** is a pub where they often go to drink.

locality localities *(n)* an area, or a neighbourhood.

locate locating located
1 *(v)* to find out where something is.
2 If something is **located** in a particular place, you will find it there.

location
1 *(n)* the place or position where someone or something is.
2 If a film or television programme is made **on location**, it is filmed out of the studio.

loch *(n)* a Scottish lake.

lock locking locked
1 *(n)* a part of a door, box, etc. that you can open and shut with a key.
2 *(v)* to fasten something with a key.
3 *(n)* a part of a canal with gates at each end where boats are raised or lowered to different water levels.
4 **locks** *(plural n) (poetic)* hair. *Curly locks.*

locker *(n)* a small cupboard that can be locked, where you can leave your belongings.

locket *(n)* a piece of jewellery which women wear on a chain around their necks, and which often contains a photograph.

locksmith *(n)* someone who makes and mends locks and keys.

locomotive *(n)* a railway engine. *See* **steam locomotive**.

locust *(n)*
an insect similar to a grasshopper, which eats and destroys crops. Locusts fly in swarms of up to 2000 million.

locust

lodge lodging lodged
1 *(n)* a small house or place where you can stay.
2 *(v)* If you **lodge** with someone, you stay in their house and usually pay them money.
3 *(v)* If something **lodges** somewhere, it gets stuck there.
4 *(n)* a beaver's home. *See* **beaver**.

lodger *(n)* somebody who pays to live in a room in someone else's house. **lodgings** *(n)*.

loft *(n)* a room in the roof of a building.

lofty loftier loftiest
1 *(adj)* very high and imposing. *A lofty building.*
2 *(adj)* distant and haughty. **loftily** *(adv)*.

log logging logged
1 *(n)* a part of a tree that has been chopped down or has fallen down.
2 *(n)* a record kept by the captain of a ship. **log** *(v)*.
3 *(n)* a written record of something. *Liza kept a log of her progress.* **log** *(v)*.
4 *(v)* When you **log on** or **log in** to a computer, you begin to use it by entering a name or a password.
5 *(v)* When you have finished using a computer, you **log off** or **log out**.

logic *(n)* careful and correct reasoning. **logical** *(adj)*, **logically** *(adv)*.

logo *(loh-go) (n)* a symbol that represents a particular company or organization.

loiter *(loy-ter)* loitering loitered *(v)* to stand around, usually because you have nothing to do.

loll lolling lolled
1 *(v)* to sit or stand in a lazy, sloppy way. *Wayne lolled on the sofa.*
2 *(v)* to hang loosely. *The wolf's tongue lolled out of its mouth.*

lollipop *(n)* a sweet on a stick.

lolly lollies
1 *(n)* an iced sweet on a stick.
2 *(n) (slang)* money.

lonely lonelier loneliest
1 *(adj)* If you are **lonely**, you are sad because you are by yourself. **loneliness** *(n)*.
2 *(adj)* far from other people or things. *A lonely farmhouse.*

long longing longed; longer longest
1 *(adj)* more than the average length, distance, time, etc. *A long walk.* **long** *(adv)*.
2 *(adj)* from one end to the other. *The footpath was about two miles long.*
3 *(adj)* taking a lot of time. *Is the film very long?*
4 *(v)* If you **long for** something, you want it very much. **longing** *(n)*.

longitude *(n)* the position of a place, measured in degrees east or west of a line that runs through the Greenwich Observatory in London, England. **longitudinal** *(adj)*.

long-range
1 *(adj)* to do with the future. *Long-range plans.*
2 *(adj)* designed to travel a long way. *Long-range missiles.*

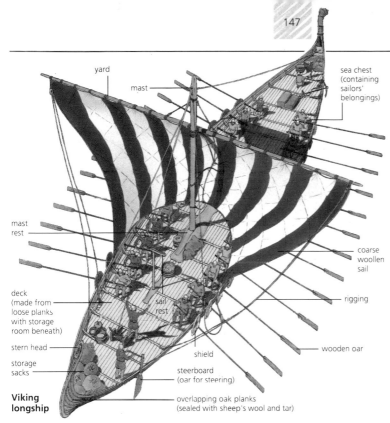

yard

mast

sea chest (containing sailors' belongings)

mast rest

deck (made from loose planks with storage room beneath)

coarse woollen sail

sail rest

rigging

stern head

storage sacks

shield

wooden oar

steerboard (oar for steering)

Viking longship

overlapping oak planks (sealed with sheep's wool and tar)

longship (n) a long, narrow ship, with many oars and a sail, used especially by the Vikings. The Vikings used longships to carry warriors to new lands.

long-sighted (adj) If you are long-sighted, you can see things more clearly when they are far away.

long-term (adj) to do with a long period of time. Long-term plans.

long-winded (adj) unnecessarily long and boring.

loo (n) (informal) a toilet.

loofah (n) a rough sponge that you wash yourself with in the bath.

look looking looked
1 (v) to use your eyes to see things.
2 (v) to seem or appear. It looks as if the weather will be bad all week.
3 (n) a glance or expression on someone's face. An angry look.
4 (v) If you **look after** something or someone, you take care of them.
5 (v) If you **look down on** someone, you think that you are better than they are.
6 (v) If you **look forward** to something, you wait for it eagerly.
7 (v) If you **look up** something, you try to find out about it in a book.

lookout (n) someone who keeps watch for something. We posted a lookout outside our den.

loom looming loomed
1 (v) to appear in a sudden or frightening way. Suddenly, a tall figure loomed out of the shadows.
2 (n) a machine used for weaving cloth. The picture shows a woman working on a traditional Bangladeshi backstrap loom.

loom

loop (n) a curve or circle in a piece of string, rope, etc. loop (v).

loose looser loosest
1 (adj) not fitting tightly. Loose trousers. **loosely** (adv).
2 (adj) not firm. A loose tooth. **loosely** (adv).
3 (adj) not contained, or not bound together. Loose papers. **loosely** (adv).

loosen loosening loosened
1 (v) to make something less tight.
2 (v) If you **loosen up**, you become less shy and more relaxed.

loot looting looted
1 (v) to steal from shops or houses in a riot or war. **looter** (n).
2 (n) stolen money or valuables.

lopsided (adj) unbalanced, or with one side heavier than the other.

lord
1 (n) a nobleman. **lordly** (adj).
2 Lord (n) a title used by a man who is a member of the aristocracy or who has earned the title as a reward for service to his country.
3 Lord (n) a title for God or Jesus.

lorry lorries (n) a large motor vehicle used for carrying goods by road. See **truck**.

lose losing lost
1 (v) If you **lose** something, you do not have it any more.
2 (v) to be beaten or defeated in a game, argument, etc.

loss losses
1 (n) the losing of something. The loss of a friend.
2 (n) something that is lost.

lot
1 (n) a large number or amount.
2 (n) a group of objects that are sold together at an auction.
3 If you **draw lots**, a group of you pick objects, such as straws, to decide who will do something.

lotion (n) a cream that you put on your skin or hair.

lottery lotteries (n) a competition in which you buy tickets with the aim of winning a prize.

loud louder loudest
1 (adj) noisy, or producing a lot of sound. **loud** (adv), **loudly** (adv).
2 (adj) very bright and colourful.

loudspeaker (n) a machine that turns electrical signals into sounds. See **speaker**.

lounge lounging lounged
1 (v) to sit around lazily.
2 (n) a comfortable room for sitting in.

love loving loved
1 (v) to like someone or something very much. **love** (n).
2 If you are **in love** with someone, you are passionately fond of them.
3 If you **make love**, you have sexual intercourse with someone. **lover** (n).
4 (n) in tennis, a score of no points.

lovely lovelier loveliest
1 (adj) If someone is lovely, they are beautiful to look at, or have a very attractive personality. **loveliness** (n).
2 (adj) enjoyable. We had a lovely day.

low lower lowest
1 (adj) not high. A low table.
2 (adj) A low sound is quiet and soft, or deep in pitch.
3 (adj) If someone feels low, they are depressed or ill.
4 low tide (n) the time when the sea is furthest down the beach.

lower lowering lowered
1 (v) to move something down.
2 (adj) not as high as something else.
3 (adj) **Lower case** letters are small, and not capital letters.

loyal (adj) Someone who is **loyal** supports their friends and does not betray or desert them. **loyalty** (n), **loyally** (adv).

LSD (n) a strong drug that makes people see frightening, dream-like things. LSD is illegal in Britain and in many other countries.

Ltd short for **limited**.

lubricate lubricating lubricated (v) to add oil or grease to the parts of a machine, so that it runs more smoothly. **lubricant** (n), **lubrication** (n).

luck
1 (n) something that happens to someone by chance. *Bingo is a game of luck.*
2 (n) good fortune, or good things that happen to you that have not been planned. *Wish me luck!*

lucky luckier luckiest
1 (adj) Someone who is **lucky** is fortunate and good things seem to happen to them.
2 (adj) Something that is **lucky** happens by chance and is fortunate. **luckily** (adv).
3 (adj) A **lucky** number, charm, etc. is one that you think will bring you luck.

ludicrous (loo-dik-russ) (adj) ridiculous or foolish. **ludicrously** (adv).

lug lugging lugged (v) to move something heavy.

luggage (n) cases and bags that you take with you when you travel.

lukewarm
1 (adj) slightly warm.
2 (adj) not keen, or not enthusiastic.

lull lulling lulled
1 (n) a short pause or break during a period of fighting or activity.
2 (v) to make someone feel peaceful, safe, or sleepy. *The sound of the waves on the shore lulled Fay to sleep.*

lullaby lullabies (n) a gentle song sung to send a baby to sleep.

lumber lumbering lumbered
1 (v) to move around heavily and clumsily. *We could hear Theodore lumbering about upstairs.*
2 (n) sawn-up wood or timber.
3 If you are **lumbered** with an unpleasant job or duty, you have been left to deal with it.

luminous (adj) shining, or glowing in the dark. **luminously** (adv).

lump
1 (n) a mass of solid matter. *A lump of pastry.*
2 (n) a swelling. *Look at this lump on my head!*

lunar (adj) to do with the Moon. *A lunar eclipse.*

lunatic
1 (n) (informal) a foolish and annoying person. **lunacy** (n), **lunatic** (adj).
2 (n) an insane person.

lunch lunches (n) the meal that you eat in the middle of the day. **lunch** (v).

lung (n) Your **lungs** are the two organs inside your chest that you use to breathe. See **organ**, **respiration**.

lunge lunging lunged (v) to move forward quickly and suddenly. **lunge** (n).

lurch lurches lurching lurched
1 (v) to move in an unsteady, jerky way. *The train lurched to a halt.*
2 If someone **leaves you in the lurch**, they leave you in a difficult situation, without any help.

lure luring lured
1 (v) to attract someone or some creature and perhaps lead them into a trap.
2 (n) something that attracts you to a particular place. *I can never resist the lure of the sea.*

lurid
1 (adj) vivid and glowing. *A lurid yellow.*
2 (adj) sensational and shocking. *Lurid newspaper stories.*

lurk lurking lurked (v) to wait around secretly. *The robbers lurked behind the house.*

luscious (lush-uss) (adj) delicious and attractive. **lusciously** (adv).

lush (adj) growing thickly and healthily. *Lush vegetation.*

lust lusting lusted (v) If you **lust** after someone or something, you want or desire them very strongly. *Magnus has always lusted after power.* **lust** (n), **lustful** (adj).

luxury luxuries
1 (n) something expensive which you do not really need, but which is enjoyable to have. **luxury** (adj).
2 If you live **in luxury**, you are surrounded by expensive and beautiful things that make your life very comfortable and pleasant. **luxurious** (adj).

lyric
1 (n) a short poem that expresses strong feelings, especially love.
2 **lyrics** (plural n) the words of a song.

Mm

macabre (mak-ah-br) (adj) gruesome and frightening.

macaroni or **maccaroni** (n) short tubes of pasta. See **pasta**.

Mach (mak) (n) a unit for measuring an aircraft's speed. Mach 1 is the speed of sound.

machete (ma-shett-ee) (n) a heavy knife with a broad blade.

machine
1 (n) a piece of equipment made up of moving parts, that is used to do a job.
2 **machine gun** a gun that can fire bullets very quickly without needing to be reloaded.

machinery (singular n) a group of machines, or the parts of a machine.

macho (mat-show) (adj) (slang) If men or boys are **macho**, they act in an exaggeratedly masculine way.

mackerel mackerel or mackerels (n) a shiny, bluish, sea fish that can be eaten.

mackintosh mackintoshes (n) a coat that keeps you dry in the rain.

mad madder maddest
1 (adj) insane. **madness** (n).
2 (adj) very foolish.
3 (adj) (informal) very angry.
4 (adj) (informal) If you are **mad** about someone or something, you like them very much. **madly** (adv).
5 **mad cow disease** (n) an informal name for **BSE**.

madam (n) a formal name for a woman, used in speaking and writing. *Can I help you, madam? Dear Madam.*

Mafia (n) a criminal organization, founded in Sicily, and responsible for many illegal activities worldwide.

magazine
1 (n) a thin book, that is published regularly, and contains news, articles, photographs, advertisements, etc.
2 (n) the part of a gun that holds the cartridges.

maggot (n) the larva of certain flies, such as the bluebottle and the housefly.

magic
1 (n) In stories, **magic** is the power to make impossible things happen. **magical** (adj), **magically** (adv).
2 (n) clever tricks done to entertain people. **magician** (n).

magistrate (n) someone who acts as a judge in less serious law cases.

magnet (n) a piece of metal that attracts iron or steel. Magnets have two ends, or poles, a north pole and a south pole. *The diagram illustrates a law of magnetism: the like poles of two magnets repel each other, while the unlike poles attract each other.* magnetism (n), magnetic (adj).

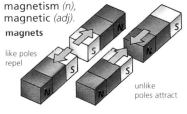

magnets
like poles repel
unlike poles attract

magnificent (adj) very impressive or beautiful. magnificently (adv).

magnify magnifies magnifying magnified
1 (v) to make something appear larger so that it can be seen more easily. magnification (n), magnified (adj).
2 (v) to make something seem greater or more important than it really is. *Sophie always magnifies her problems.*
3 **magnifying glass** (n) a glass lens that makes things look bigger.

magnitude (n) the size or importance of something. *Once she had seen the mess, Tara realized the magnitude of her task.*

magpie (n) a black and white bird with a large beak. Magpies often collect shiny objects.

mahogany (n) a hard, dark, reddish-brown wood.

maid
1 (n) a female servant, especially in a hotel.
2 (n) (poetic) a young, unmarried woman.

maiden
1 (n) (poetic) a young, unmarried woman.
2 (n) A woman's **maiden name** is the surname that she has before she marries.
3 (n) A **maiden voyage** or flight is the first one made by a particular ship or plane.

mail
1 (n) letters and parcels sent by post. mail (v).
2 (n) armour made by joining together small metal rings. See **centurion**.
3 (n) If you buy something by **mail order**, you order it and pay for it and then the item is posted to you.

maim maiming maimed (v) to injure someone so badly that part of their body is damaged for life.

main
1 (adj) largest, or most important.
2 **mains** (plural n) the large pipes or wires that supply water, gas, or electricity to a building.

mainframe (n) a large and very powerful computer to which other smaller computers are connected.

mainly
1 (adv) most importantly. *I mainly like swimming.*
2 (adv) almost completely. *The film was mainly rubbish.*
3 (adv) usually. *Mainly, I go straight home after school.*

maintain maintaining maintained
1 (v) to keep a machine or building in good condition. maintenance (n).
2 (v) to continue to say that something is so. *Tarquin maintains that he is innocent.*
3 (v) to continue something and not let it come to an end. *We have always maintained a close friendship.*
4 (v) to give money to support somebody. maintenance (n).

maisonette (n) a flat on two floors.

maize (n) a crop plant that produces sweetcorn.

majesty majesties
1 (n) dignity and grandeur. majestic (adj), majestically (adv).
2 (n) The formal title for a king or queen is **His Majesty** or **Her Majesty**.

major
1 (adj) important, or serious. *A major disaster.*
2 (n) an army officer.
3 (n) In music, a **major scale** has a semitone between the third and fourth and the seventh and eighth notes.

majority majorities
1 (n) more than half of a group of people or things. *The majority of students came by bike.*
2 (n) the number of votes by which someone wins an election.
3 (n) When someone reaches their **majority**, they become an adult by law.

make making made
1 (v) to build or produce something. *My mum makes great cakes.*
2 (v) to do something. *Wallis made two phone calls.*
3 (v) to cause something to happen. *The view made Jules feel dizzy.*
4 (v) to add up to. *Six and five make eleven.*
5 (n) the name of the company that makes a particular type of product. *What make is your bicycle?*

makeshift (adj) A makeshift object is made from whatever is available and is only meant to be used for a short time.

make-up (n) the coloured powders and creams that women and actors put on their faces. *The picture shows two examples of the dramatic make-up used in Japanese Kabuki theatre.*

Kabuki make-up

malaria (mal-*air*-ee-a) (n) a tropical disease that people get from mosquito bites.

male (n) a person or animal of the sex that fertilizes the female. male (adj).

malicious (mal-*ish*-uss) (adj) hurting other people deliberately. *Malicious gossip.* malice (n), maliciously (adv).

malignant
1 (adj) nasty and evil. *The villain gave a malignant grin.* malignantly (adv).
2 (adj) A **malignant** growth or disease is dangerous because it tends to spread very fast.

mall (rhymes with all) (n) (US) a large, covered shopping centre.

malleable (mal-ee-ab-ul) (adj) If a substance is **malleable**, it is easily moulded into different shapes.

malnutrition (n) illness caused by not having enough food or by eating the wrong kind of food.

malt (n) dried grain, usually barley, used for making whisky and milky drinks. malted (adj).

maltreat maltreating maltreated (v) to treat a person or an animal cruelly. maltreatment (n).

mammal (n) an animal that feeds its young on its own milk. *Human beings, cows, mice, and dolphins are all examples of mammals.*

mammoth
1 (n) an extinct animal, like a large elephant, with long, curved tusks. Mammoths lived in the Ice age.
2 (adj) very large. *This is a mammoth task!*

woolly mammoth

man men; manning manned
1 (n) an adult, male human being. **manhood** (n), **manly** (adj).
2 (n) the human race.
3 (v) to be in charge of equipment. *We need some people to man the phones.*

manage managing managed
1 (v) to be in charge of a shop, business, etc. *Terry manages a small electrical company.* **management** (n).
2 (v) to be able to do something that is difficult or awkward. *Can you manage to carry all those bags?*

manager
1 (n) someone in charge of a shop, business, etc. or in charge of a group of people at work. **managerial** (adj).
2 (n) someone who handles the business affairs of a pop group, film star, football team, etc.

mane (n) the long, thick hair on the head and neck of a lion or horse. *See* **horse**.

manger (n) a container from which cattle and horses eat.

mangle mangling mangled
1 (v) to crush and twist something. *The car was completely mangled in the crash.* **mangled** (adj).
2 (n) an instrument used in the past for squeezing the water out of wet clothes.

manhole (n) a covered hole in the ground, leading to sewers or underground pipes.

maniac (may-nee-ak) (n) someone who is mad, or someone who acts in a wild or violent way. **maniacal** (adj).

manicure (n) a treatment for your hands and fingernails.

manipulate manipulating manipulated
1 (v) to use your hands in a skilful way. *Karen manipulated the plane's controls expertly.*
2 (v) to influence people in a clever way so that they do what you want them to do. **manipulation** (n), **manipulative** (adj).

mankind (n) the human race.

man-made (adj) Something that is man-made is made by people and not produced naturally. *Nylon is a man-made fibre.*

manner
1 (n) the way in which you do something. *Look at the manner in which Garth uses his paintbrush.*
2 (n) the way that someone behaves. *Kate has a very gentle manner.*
3 **manners** (plural n) polite behaviour.

manoeuvre (man-oo-ver) manoeuvring manoeuvred
1 (n) a difficult movement that needs skill. *The pilots performed a series of breathtaking manoeuvres.*
2 (v) to move something carefully into a particular position.
3 When an army is **on manoeuvres**, a large number of soldiers, tanks, etc. are moved around an area in order to train them for battle.

manor (n) a large, old country house surrounded by land.

mansion (n) a large, grand house.

manslaughter (n) the crime of killing someone, without planning it in advance.

mantelpiece (n) a wooden or stone shelf above a fireplace.

manual
1 (adj) worked by hand. *A manual typewriter.* **manually** (adv).
2 (n) an instruction book that tells you how to do something.
3 **manual work** (n) physical work.

manufacture manufacturing manufactured
1 (v) to make something with machines in a factory. **manufacture** (n), **manufacturer** (n).
2 (v) to invent something, or make something up. *Eric manufactured a reason for his strange appearance.*

manure (n) animal waste put on land to improve the quality of the soil and to make crops grow better.

manuscript
1 (n) the original handwritten or typed pages of a book, poem, piece of music, etc., before it is printed.
2 (n) a handwritten document. *A medieval manuscript.*

many more most
1 (adj) great in number. **many** (pronoun).
2 **how many?** what number?

Maori (mauw-ree) **Maori** or **Maoris** (n) one of the native people of New Zealand who lived there before the Europeans arrived. *This Maori, wearing traditional costume and make-up, is performing a dance of celebration at a festival.* **Maori** (adj).

Maori

map mapping mapped
1 (n) a detailed plan of an area, showing features such as towns, roads, rivers, mountains, etc.
2 (v) to make a map of a place.
3 (v) If you **map out** something, you plan it.

maple (n) a tree with large, five-pointed leaves. Maples are grown for their wood and their sap, which is used to make syrup.

marathon
1 (n) a running race of approximately 26 miles (42km), that is run along roads.
2 (n) something that lasts for a long time. *The final tennis set was a real marathon.*

marble
1 (n) a hard stone with coloured patterns in it, used for building and making sculptures.
2 **marbles** (singular n) a children's game, in which small glass balls, called marbles, are rolled along the ground.

march marches marching marched
1 (v) When soldiers **march**, they walk together with regular steps.
2 (n) a piece of music to which you can march.
3 (v) to walk somewhere quickly and in a determined way. *Bravely, Camilla marched up to the headmaster.*
4 (n) a large group of people walking together in order to protest or express their opinion about something. **march** (v).

mare (n) an adult, female horse.

margarine (n) a yellow fat, similar to butter, that is usually made from vegetable oil.

margin
1 (n) the long, blank space that runs down the edge of a page.
2 (n) a difference between two amounts, especially a small one. *Algernon won the election by a very narrow margin.* **marginal** (adj).

marijuana (ma-roo-whah-nah) (n) a form of the drug cannabis that people smoke to give them a feeling of pleasure. Marijuana is illegal in Britain and many other countries.

marina (n) a small harbour where boats, yachts, etc. are kept.

marine
1 (adj) to do with the sea. *Marine life.*
2 (n) a soldier trained to serve both at sea and on land.

mark marking marked
1 (n) a small scratch or stain on something. **mark** (v).
2 (v) to put a mark on something, especially to show who something belongs to or where things are.
3 (n) a number or letter put on a piece of work to show how good it is. **mark** (v).

4 (v) to keep very close to an opposing player, in a game like football or hockey, in order to prevent them from getting the ball or from scoring.
5 (n) the main unit of money in Germany. Mark is short for deutschmark.

market
1 (n) a group of stalls, usually in the open air, where things are sold.
2 If a product is **on the market**, it is available and can be bought.

market research (n) When a person or company does **market research**, they collect information about the products that people buy and what people want and need.

marksman marksmen (n) someone who is expert at shooting with a gun.

marmalade (n) a jam made from oranges or other citrus fruit and usually eaten on toast for breakfast.

maroon marooning marooned
1 (v) If someone is **marooned** somewhere, they are stuck and cannot leave. *The sailors were marooned on a desert island.*
2 (n) a dark, reddish-brown colour. maroon (adj).

marquee (mar-kee) (n) a large tent used for parties and fêtes.

marriage (n) the relationship between a husband and wife.

married (adj) Someone who is married has a husband or wife.

marrow
1 (n) the soft substance inside your bones. See **bone**.
2 (n) a large, long, green vegetable. See **vegetable**.

marry marries marrying married
1 (v) When people **marry**, they go through a ceremony in which they promise to spend their lives together.
2 (v) to perform a marriage ceremony.

marsh marshes (n) an area of wet, low-lying land. marshy (adj).

marshal marshalling marshalled
1 (n) an official who helps to organize a public event, such as a concert.
2 (v) to gather together a group of people or things and arrange them in a sensible order. *The general marshalled his troops.*
3 (n) (US) a police officer in charge of a district.

marshmallow (n) a soft, spongy sweet.

marsupial (mar-soo-pee-ul) (n) a kind of mammal. Female marsupials carry their young in their pouches. *Kangaroos and koalas are marsupials.*

martial (mar-shall)
1 (adj) to do with war or soldiers.
2 **martial arts** (plural n) styles of fighting or self-defence that come from the Far East, for example, judo and karate.
3 **martial law** (n) government by the army.

martyr (mar-ter) (n) someone who is killed or made to suffer, because of their beliefs. **martyrdom** (n).

marvel marvelling marvelled (v) If you **marvel** at something, you are filled with surprise and wonder.

marvellous (adj) very good indeed. marvellously (adv).

marzipan (n) a sweet, almond-flavoured paste, used on cakes.

mascara (n) a substance put on eyelashes to colour them and make them look thicker.

mascot (n) something that is supposed to bring good luck, such as an animal or a toy.

masculine
1 (adj) to do with men.
2 (adj) Someone who is **masculine** has qualities that are supposed to be typical of men. **masculinity** (n).
3 (adj) belonging to one of the main classes or genders of nouns in French, Latin, and other languages.

mash mashes mashing mashed (v) to crush food after it has been cooked.

mask masking masked
1 (n) a covering worn over the face to hide, protect, or disguise it. *This mask, made in Tami Island, New Guinea, would have been worn by a boy at a special ceremony to celebrate his adulthood.* masked (adj).
2 (v) to cover something up or disguise it. *The aniseed masked the taste of the poison.*

mask

mason (n) someone who cuts and carves stone for buildings, gravestones, etc.

masonry (n) stone used in a building.

mass masses
1 (n) a large number of people or things together.
2 (n) In physics, the **mass** of an object is the amount of physical matter that it contains. *Mass is measured in grams or ounces.*
3 the **masses** (plural n) the ordinary people. *This show is designed to appeal to the masses.*
4 (adj) Mass-produced things are made in very large quantities, usually by machine.

massacre (mass-er-ker) (n) the killing of a very large number of people, often in battle. **massacre** (v).

massage (mass-arj) massaging massaged (v) to rub someone's body with your fingers in order to loosen their muscles, or to help them relax. massage (n).

massive (adj) huge and bulky. massively (adv).

mass media (plural n) a general word for different forms of communication that reach a large number of people. Television, radio, and newspapers are all mass media.

mast (n) a tall pole that stands on the deck of a boat and supports its sails. See **dinghy**, **ship**.

master mastering mastered
1 (v) If you **master** a subject or skill, you become very good at it.
2 (n) a name for a male teacher in some secondary schools.

mastermind masterminding masterminded (v) If you **mastermind** a course of action, you plan it and control the way that it is carried out.

masterpiece (n) a brilliant piece of art, literature, music, etc.

mat (n) a thick pad of material, used for covering a floor, wiping your feet, protecting a table, etc.

matador (n) a bullfighter.

match matches matching matched
1 (n) a sports game in which one person or team plays another.
2 (v) If two things **match**, they go well together. matching (adj).
3 (n) a small, thin stick of wood with a chemical tip which is struck to produce a flame.
4 (v) to put two people or teams in opposition to each other. *The brothers are matched in the first round.*

mate mating mated
1 (v) When male and female animals **mate**, they have sexual intercourse in order to reproduce. mating (n).
2 (n) the male or female partner of a couple or pair.
3 (n) (informal) a friend.

material
1 (n) the substances from which something is made. *What materials do you need to build a house?*
2 (n) cloth, or fabric.

materialistic *(adj)* People who are **materialistic** are only concerned with money and possessions. **materialism** *(n)*.

maternal *(adj)* to do with being a mother. *Maternal feelings.*

maternity
1 *(n)* motherhood.
2 **maternity leave** *(n)* time that a woman is allowed away from her job to have a baby.
3 **maternity ward** *(n)* a large room in a hospital for women who have just had or are about to have a baby.

mathematics *(singular n)* the study of numbers, quantities, and shapes. **mathematical** *(adj)*.

maths *short for* **mathematics**.

matinée *(mat-in-ay)* *(n)* an afternoon performance of a play or showing of a film.

matrimony *(n)* a general name for marriage. **matrimonial** *(adj)*.

matrix *(may-trix)* **matrices** *(n)* In maths, a **matrix** is a rectangular chart with figures set out in columns and rows.

matt *(adj)* not shiny. *Matt paint.*

matter mattering mattered
1 *(n)* things or materials. *Undigested matter. Printed matter.*
2 *(n)* something that needs to be dealt with. *Let's sort this matter out now.*
3 *(v)* If something **matters**, it is important.

mattress mattresses *(n)* a soft, thick pad, usually containing springs, that you put on the base of a bed to sleep on.

mature maturer maturest
1 *(adj)* adult, or fully grown. **maturity** *(n)*, **mature** *(v)*.
2 *(adj)* behaving in a sensible, adult way. *Edmund is very mature for his age.* **maturity** *(n)*, **maturely** *(adv)*.
3 *(adj)* ripe. *A mature cheese.* **mature** *(v)*.

maul mauling mauled *(v)* to handle someone or something in a rough and possibly damaging way.

mausoleum *(maw-za-lee-um)* *(n)* a large tomb.

mauve *(rhymes with stove)* *(n)* a light purple colour. **mauve** *(adj)*.

maximum *(n)* the greatest possible amount, or the upper limit. *Two hours is the maximum allowed for the test.* **maximum** *(adj)*.

maybe *(adv)* perhaps.

mayhem *(n)* a situation of confusion or violent destruction.

mayonnaise *(n)* a creamy sauce made from egg yolks, oil, and vinegar.

mayor *(n)* the leader of a town, city, or district council.

maze *(n)* a complicated network of paths or lines, made as a puzzle to find your way through. *The picture shows the maze at Colonial Williamsburg, Virginia, USA, which is based on a 17th-century maze at Hampton Court, England.*

maze
(aerial view)

meadow *(n)* a field of grass, often used for animals to graze in.

meal *(n)* food which is served and eaten, usually at a particular time of day. Breakfast and lunch are meals.

mean meaning meant; meaner meanest
1 *(v)* to intend to do something. *I mean to go skating tomorrow.*
2 *(v)* to try to convey a message. *What does this poem mean?*
3 *(adj)* not generous. **meanness** *(n)*, **meanly** *(adv)*.
4 *(adj)* unkind or unfair. *A mean trick.* **meanness** *(n)*, **meanly** *(adv)*.
5 *(n)* an average. *The mean of 3, 5, and 10 is 6.*

meaning
1 *(n)* the idea behind something spoken or written.
2 *(n)* the importance or significance of something. *What is the meaning of life?*

meantime *(n)* the time in between. *We leave early tomorrow morning. In the meantime, let's get some sleep!*

meanwhile *(adv)* at the same time. *George went to explore. Meanwhile, Hattie ate all the picnic.*

measles *(n)* an infectious disease causing a fever and a rash.

measure measuring measured
1 *(v)* to find out the size, capacity, weight, etc. of something. **measurement** *(n)*.

2 *(n)* an action intended to achieve a result. *What measures can we take to fight crime?*

meat *(n)* the edible flesh of an animal.

mechanic *(n)* someone who is skilled at operating or mending machinery.

mechanical *(adj)* operated by machinery. *A mechanical toy.* **mechanically** *(adv)*.

mechanics *(singular n)* a part of physics which deals with the way that forces affect still or moving objects.

mechanism *(n)* the system of moving parts inside a machine.

medal *(n)* a piece of metal, shaped like a coin, star, or cross, which is given to someone for being brave, or for service to their country, or as a prize for sporting achievement.

media *(plural n)* a general name for different forms of communication with people, such as television, radio, and newspapers.

mediaeval *see* **medieval**.

medical
1 *(adj)* to do with health treatment. *Medical advice.* **medically** *(adv)*.
2 *(n)* *(informal)* an examination by a doctor. Medical is short for medical examination.

medicine
1 *(n)* a substance, usually liquid, used in treating illness. **medicinal** *(adj)*.
2 *(singular n)* the treatment of illness. *You must study medicine in order to become a doctor.*

medieval *or* **mediaeval** *(adj)* to do with the Middle Ages, the period of history between approximately AD1000 and AD1450.

mediocre *(mee-dee-oh-ker)* *(adj)* of average or less than average quality. **mediocrity** *(n)*.

meditate meditating meditated
1 *(v)* to think very deeply about something. *Felix meditated on the meaning of life.* **meditation** *(n)*.
2 *(v)* to relax the mind and body by a regular programme of mental exercise. **meditation** *(n)*.

medium media *or* mediums
1 *(adj)* average, or middle. *Kevin is of medium height.*
2 *(n)* the method by which something is communicated. *This art course will teach you to use a variety of media.*
3 *(n)* Mediums claim to make contact with the spirits of the dead.

meek meeker meekest *(adj)* quiet, humble, and obedient. **meekly** *(adv)*.

meet meeting met
1 *(v)* to come face to face with someone or something.
2 *(v)* to come together. *The paths met.*

meeting *(n)* an arranged event in which people come together, often to discuss something.

megabyte *(n)* a unit used to measure the capacity of a computer's memory.

melancholy *(adj)* very sad. melancholy *(n)*, melancholic *(adj)*.

mellow mellowing mellowed; mellower mellowest
1 *(adj)* soft, warm, and gentle. *Mellow colours.*
2 *(v)* If someone mellows, they become gentler and more relaxed.

melodramatic *(adj)* If someone is melodramatic, they talk and behave in an exaggerated way and make a fuss about small things.

melody melodies *(n)* a tune. melodic *(adj)*.

melon *(n)* a large, rounded, juicy fruit. See **fruit**.

melt melting melted *(v)* When a substance melts, it changes from a solid to a liquid because it has become hotter.

member
1 *(n)* someone who belongs to a club, group, family, etc. membership *(n)*.
2 Member of Parliament *(n)* someone elected by the people of a district to represent them in parliament.

membrane *(n)* a very thin layer of tissue or skin, that lines or covers certain organs or cells. See **cell**, **egg**.

memo *(n)* a brief message sent by one person to another person in the same organization. Memo is short for memorandum.

memorable *(adj)* easily remembered, or worth remembering.

memorize *or* **memorise** memorizing memorized *(v)* to learn something by heart.

memory memories
1 *(n)* the power to remember things.
2 *(n)* something that you remember from the past. *Happy memories.*
3 *(n)* the part of a computer in which information is stored.

menace
1 *(n)* a threat, or a danger. menacing *(adj)*.
2 *(n)* *(informal)* a nuisance.

mend mending mended *(v)* to repair something which is broken.

meningitis *(men-inj-eye-tiss) (n)* a serious disease that causes the membranes surrounding the brain to become very swollen.

menstruate menstruating menstruated *(v)* When a woman or girl menstruates, blood comes from her womb, about once a month. menstruation *(n)*.

mental *(adj)* to do with the mind. *Mental arithmetic.* mentally *(adv)*.

mention mentioning mentioned *(v)* to speak briefly about something. mention *(n)*.

menu
1 *(n)* a list of foods served in a café, restaurant, etc.
2 *(n)* a list of choices shown on a computer screen.

mercenary mercenaries
1 *(n)* a soldier who is paid to fight for a foreign army.
2 *(adj)* If someone is mercenary, they are mainly interested in making money.

merchandise *(singular n)* a general name for goods which are bought or sold, usually in large quantities.

merchant
1 *(n)* someone who sells goods for profit, especially someone who trades with foreign countries.
2 *(n)* A country's merchant navy is made up of the ships and crew that carry cargo for that country.

mercury *(n)* a poisonous, silvery, liquid metal. Mercury is used in some thermometers.

mercy mercies *(n)* If you show mercy to someone, you are kind to them and do not punish them. merciful *(adj)*, mercifully *(adv)*.

merely *(adv)* only, or simply. *Don't blame me, I'm merely the messenger.* mere *(adj)*.

merge merging merged *(v)* When two things merge, they join together to form a whole.

merger *(n)* the act of making two businesses, teams, etc. into one.

merit
1 *(n)* If something has merit it is good. merit *(v)*.
2 *(n)* the good points or qualities of a person or thing.

mermaid *(n)* In stories, a mermaid is a sea creature with the upper body of a girl and the tail of a fish.

merry merrier merriest
1 *(adj)* cheerful, or joyful.
2 *(adj)* *(informal)* slightly drunk.

mesh meshes *(n)* a network of wire, rope, etc.

mess messes messing messed
1 *(n)* a dirty or untidy state or thing. *My room is a mess!* messy *(adj)*, messily *(adv)*.
2 *(n)* a confused and disorganized state or thing. *My life is a mess!*
3 mess up *(v)* If you mess something up, you make it dirty or untidy, or you make it go wrong.
4 *(n)* In the armed forces, a mess is a room in which soldiers, sailors, airmen, etc. can eat, drink, and relax.

message
1 *(n)* information sent to someone else. *A secret message.*
2 *(n)* the meaning of something, like a book or film.

messenger *(n)* someone who carries a message.

metal *(n)* a chemical substance, such as iron, copper, or silver, which is usually hard and shiny, is a good conductor of heat and electricity, and can be melted and formed into shapes. metallic *(adj)*.

metaphor *(n)* a way of describing something as though it were something else, for example, "The princess is a shining jewel, and her father is a raging bull."

meteorite *(n)* a remaining part of a meteoroid which falls to Earth.

meteoroid *(n)* a small piece of rock from space which enters the Earth's atmosphere and burns up, giving a "shooting star" effect.

meteorology *(n)* the study of the Earth's atmosphere and, in particular, its climate and weather. meteorologist *(n)*, meteorological *(adj)*.

meter *(n)* an instrument for measuring the quantity of something, especially the amount of something that has been used. *An electricity meter.* meter *(v)*.

method *(n)* a way of doing something.

methodical *(adj)* careful, logical, and well-organized. methodically *(adv)*.

meticulous *(adj)* very careful and precise. meticulously *(adv)*.

metric *(adj)* The metric system of measurement is based on units of ten. Metres, litres, and kilograms are all metric measurements. See page 284.

metronome *(n)* a device that produces a regular beat which helps musicians to keep time as they play.

miaow miaowing miaowed
(v) to make a noise like a cat.
miaow (n).

microbe (n) a germ or other
living thing that is too small to be
seen without a microscope.

microchip (n) a minute piece of
silicon with electronic circuits
printed on it, used in computers
and other electronic equipment.
See **chip**.

microcomputer (n) a very
small computer, usually
without an internal memory.

microlight (n) a very light
aircraft with large,
fabric-covered wings
and a passenger
compartment hanging
underneath them.
Microlights are
powered by a
small engine.

microlight

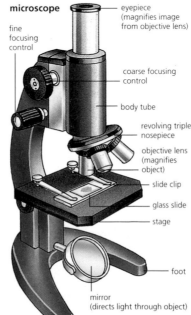

sail

leading
edge

sail
batten

nose

keel fin

pylon

base tube

front
strut

keel

compression
strut

engine

fuel
tank

trike

washout rod

pusher
propeller

wheel spat

tandem
cockpit

nose
wheel

microorganism (n) a living thing
that is too small to be seen without a
microscope. *Bacteria and viruses are
microorganisms.*

microphone (n) an instrument that
changes sound into an electric
current, to make the sound louder,
record it, or transmit it to radio or
television stations. *When sound waves
enter the diaphragm inside a moving
coil microphone, they make it vibrate.
These vibrations are transferred to a
wire coil which moves inside a
magnet, producing a constantly
changing electric current. The current
is sent down wires to an amplifier, or
to recording or transmitting
equipment.*

protective grille

thin metal
diaphragm

coil of wire fixed
to diaphragm

electrical wires
leading to
amplifier

magnet

handle

**moving coil
microphone**
(cutaway)

microprocessor (n) the central
processing unit of a microcomputer.

microscope (n) an instrument with
powerful lenses that magnifies very
small things so that they look large
enough to be seen and studied.

microscope

fine
focusing
control

eyepiece
(magnifies image
from objective lens)

coarse focusing
control

body tube

revolving triple
nosepiece

objective lens
(magnifies
object)

slide clip

glass slide

stage

foot

mirror
(directs light through object)

microscopic (adj) too small to be
seen without a microscope.

microwave
1 (n) a high frequency
electro-magnetic wave.
2 **microwave oven** (n) an oven which
cooks food very quickly by beaming
microwaves into it. The microwaves
make the moisture in the food vibrate
and become hot and this heat is
passed through the food so that it
cooks.

midday (n) noon, or 12 o'clock in
the middle of the day. **midday** (adj).

middle
1 (adj) central, or halfway between
two extremes. **middle** (n).
2 If you are **in the middle** of doing
something, you are involved in doing
it. *I'm in the middle of watching this
programme.*

middle-aged (adj) Someone who is
middle-aged is between 40 and 60
years old.

Middle Ages (n) the period of
history between approximately
AD1000 and AD1450.

Middle East (n) the hot countries of
Western Asia between the eastern
end of the Mediterranean Sea and
India. Israel, Iraq, and Iran are all in
the Middle East.
Middle Eastern (adj).

midge (n) a tiny, winged insect that
bites.

midnight (n) 12 o'clock in the
middle of the night. **midnight** (adj).

midway (adv) halfway. *The car
broke down midway between Sydney
and Canberra.*

midwife midwives (n) a nurse
trained to help when a baby is being
born. **midwifery** (n).

might (n) strength, or force.
mighty (adj), **mightily** (adv).

migraine (n) a very bad headache
which makes you feel sick.

migrate migrating migrated (v)
When birds **migrate**, they fly at a
particular time of year to live in
another region. **migration** (n),
migratory (adj).

mild milder mildest
1 (adj) Someone who is **mild** is gentle
and not aggressive. **mildness** (n),
mildly (adv).
2 (adj) moderate and not too harsh.
Mild weather. **mildness** (n),
mildly (adv).

mildew (n) a thin coating of mould
that can grow on damp cloth, paper,
etc. **mildewed** (adj).

militant *(adj)* Someone who is militant is prepared to fight or to be very aggressive in support of a cause in which they believe. **militancy** *(n)*, **militantly** *(adv)*.

military *(adj)* to do with soldiers and the armed forces. *A military hospital.*

militia *(mil-ish-a)* *(n)* a group of soldiers recruited in an emergency.

milk milking milked
1 *(n)* the white liquid produced by female mammals to feed their young. People drink milk from cows and goats. **milky** *(adj)*.
2 *(v)* to take milk from a cow or other animal.
3 **milk tooth** *(n)* one of your first teeth that falls out and is replaced by a permanent tooth.

mill
1 *(n)* a building containing machinery for grinding grain into flour. **mill** *(v)*. *See* **windmill**.
2 *(n)* a large factory with machinery for processing textiles, wood, paper, etc. *A cotton mill.*
3 *(n)* a small machine used for grinding something into powder. *A pepper mill.* **mill** *(v)*.

millennium millenniums *or* millennia *(n)* a period of a thousand years. **millennial** *(adj)*.

millet *(n)* a cereal crop with tiny seeds, grown especially in India.

million
1 *(n)* a thousand thousands (1,000,000).
2 *(n)* *(informal)* a great many.

millionaire *(n)* someone whose money and property is worth at least a million pounds or dollars.

milometer *(n)* an instrument used for counting how many miles a vehicle has travelled.

mime *(n)* a form of acting in which actions are used instead of words. **mime** *(v)*.

mimic mimicking mimicked *(v)* to imitate someone else's speech or actions. **mimic** *(n)*.

minaret *(n)* the tall, thin tower of a mosque, from which Muslims are called to prayer.

mince mincing minced
1 *(v)* to cut or chop meat or similar substances into very small pieces.
2 *(n)* finely chopped meat.
3 **mince pie** *(n)* a sweet, pastry tart made from mincemeat.

mincemeat *(n)* a sweet mixture of finely chopped dried fruit, spices, etc., used in pies and tarts.

mind minding minded
1 *(n)* the part of you that thinks, remembers, dreams, etc.
2 *(v)* to care, or to be bothered about something. *Do you mind what she says about you?*
3 *(v)* to look after something or somebody. **minder** *(n)*.
4 *(v)* to watch out for something. *Mind the step!*

mine mining mined
1 *(adj)* belonging to me.
2 *(v)* to dig up minerals from below the ground. **mine** *(n)*, **miner** *(n)*.
3 *(n)* a bomb placed in the ground or in the sea.

mineral
1 *(n)* a substance found in the earth, that can be obtained by mining. Iron, salt, and diamonds are all minerals. **mineral** *(adj)*.
2 **mineral water** *(n)* water that has mineral salts and gases dissolved in it. Mineral water can be still or fizzy.

minerals

diamond

gold

copper

silver

sulphur

pyrite

malachite

turquoise

mingle mingling mingled *(v)* to mix together. *The guests mingled happily.*

miniature *(min-it-cher)* *(adj)* a small version of something bigger. *A miniature radio.* **miniaturize** *(v)*

minibeast *(n)* an insect or other small creature.

minibus minibuses *(n)* a small bus that can usually carry between eight and sixteen passengers.

minidisc *(n)* a miniature compact disc that stores sound. The short name for minidisc is MD. **minidisc player** *(n)*.

minimize *or* **minimise** minimizing minimized
1 *(v)* to make something as small as possible. *Charlotte minimized the risk of getting lost by taking a map.*
2 *(v)* to make something seem as unimportant or insignificant as possible. *When we told Mum what had happened, we minimized the danger.*

minimum *(n)* the smallest possible amount, or the lowest limit. *We need a minimum of six people to play this game.* **minimum** *(adj)*.

miniskirt *(n)* a very short skirt.

minister
1 *(n)* a clergyman. **ministry** *(n)*.
2 *(n)* someone in charge of a government department. *The Minister for Health.* **ministry** *(n)*, **ministerial** *(adj)*.

minnow *(n)* a tiny freshwater fish.

minor
1 *(adj)* less important, or less serious. *We will deal with minor matters after the main issues have been discussed.*
2 *(n)* someone under adult age.
3 *(n)* In music, a **minor scale** has a semitone between the second and third notes.

minority minorities
1 *(n)* a small number or part within a bigger group. *Only a minority were against the proposal.*
2 *(n)* a group of people of a particular race or religion living among a larger group of a different race or religion.

minstrel *(n)* a medieval musician and poet.

mint
1 *(n)* a strongly-scented plant with leaves that are used for flavouring. *See* **herb**.
2 *(n)* a peppermint-flavoured sweet.
3 *(n)* a place where coins are manufactured. **mint** *(v)*.

minus
1 *(prep)* In maths, a **minus** sign (-) is used in a subtraction sum. *6 minus 4, or 6 - 4 = 2.*
2 *(prep)* *(informal)* without. *I went to school minus my sandwiches.*

minute minuter minutest
1 *(min-it)* *(n)* a unit of time equal to 60 seconds.
2 *(my-newt)* *(adj)* very small indeed. **minutely** *(adv)*.
3 **minutes** *(min-its)* *(plural n)* the written record of what was said at a meeting.

miracle *(mir-ak-ul)* *(n)* a remarkable and unexpected event. **miraculous** *(adj)*, **miraculously** *(adv)*.

mirage (*mir-ahj*) (*n*) something that you think you see in the distance, such as water, which is not really there. Mirages are caused by light refracting off hot surfaces.

mirror (*n*) a very shiny surface which reflects the image of whatever is in front of it. **mirror** (*v*).

misbehave misbehaving misbehaved (*v*) to behave badly.

miscalculate miscalculating miscalculated (*v*) to work something out incorrectly, or to judge a situation wrongly. **miscalculation** (*n*).

miscarriage
1 (*n*) When a pregnant woman has a miscarriage, the baby dies in her womb, usually early in the pregnancy. **miscarry** (*v*).
2 **miscarriage of justice** (*n*) a failure of the legal system to come to the right decision or verdict.

miscellaneous (*miss-el-ay-nee-uss*) (*adj*) assorted, or of different types. *The drawer was full of miscellaneous socks, but I couldn't find a pair.* **miscellany** (*n*).

mischief (*n*) playful, mildly naughty behaviour that may cause annoyance to others. **mischievous** (*adj*), **mischievously** (*adv*).

misconduct (*n*) dishonest, irresponsible, or immoral action by someone in a position of responsibility.

miser (*my-zer*) (*n*) a very mean person who spends as little as possible in order to hoard money. **miserly** (*adj*).

miserable (*adj*) sad, unhappy, or dejected. **misery** (*n*), **miserably** (*adv*).

misfit (*n*) someone or something not suited to the people or situation around them.

misfortune
1 (*n*) an unlucky event.
2 (*n*) bad luck.

misguided (*adj*) If you are misguided, you have the wrong idea about something. **misguidedly** (*adv*).

mishap (*n*) an unfortunate accident.

mislay mislaying mislaid (*v*) to lose something for a short while, because you have put it in a place where you cannot find it.

mislead misleading misled (*v*) to give someone the wrong idea about something. **misleading** (*adj*), **misleadingly** (*adv*).

misprint (*n*) a mistake in a book, newspaper, etc. where the letters have been printed wrongly.

miss misses missing missed
1 (*v*) to fail to hit something.
2 (*v*) to fail to catch, see, do, etc. *Gurdit missed the train by seconds.*
3 (*v*) to be unhappy because someone or something is not with you. *I missed my brother when he went away.*
4 **Miss** (*n*) a title given to a girl or an unmarried woman.

missile (*n*) a weapon which is thrown or shot at a target. *An atomic missile.*

misspell misspelling misspelled *or* misspelt (*v*) to spell something wrongly.

mist (*n*) a cloud of water droplets in the air. **misty** (*adj*).

mistake mistaking mistook mistaken
1 (*n*) an error, or a misunderstanding.
2 (*v*) to believe that someone is somebody different. *I always mistake Tracey for her sister.*

mistletoe (*n*) an evergreen plant that grows as a parasite on trees. Mistletoe has white berries and is often used as a Christmas decoration.

mistletoe

mistreat mistreating mistreated (*v*) to treat something roughly or badly. **mistreatment** (*n*).

mistress mistresses (*n*) a name for a female teacher in some schools.

mistrust mistrusting mistrusted (*v*) to be suspicious of someone. **mistrust** (*n*).

misunderstanding
1 (*n*) a failure to understand. **misunderstand** (*v*).
2 (*n*) a disagreement between two people.

misuse (*miss-yooze*) misusing misused (*v*) to use something in the wrong way. **misuse** (*miss-yuce*) (*n*).

mix mixes mixing mixed (*v*) to combine or blend different things. *Mix all the ingredients together.*

mixture (*n*) something made from things mixed together.

moan moaning moaned
1 (*v*) to complain in a dreary way.
2 (*v*) to make a low, sad sound, usually because you are in pain or are unhappy. **moan** (*n*).

mob (*n*) a large and dangerous crowd of people.

mobile
1 (*adj*) able to move or be moved. *A mobile crane.* **mobility** (*n*).

2 (*n*) a decoration made of several things balanced at different heights and hanging from a central thread.

mobile phone (*n*) a telephone that you can carry around with you.

mock mocking mocked
1 (*v*) to make fun of someone in an unpleasant way. **mockery** (*n*).
2 (*adj*) false, or imitation. *A mock battle.*
3 (*n*) a practice examination.

model
1 (*n*) a small version of a real-life object, made to scale. *A model railway.*
2 (*adj*) perfect, or ideal. *A model child.*
3 (*n*) someone who poses for an artist or a photographer. **model** (*v*).
4 (*n*) a particular type of product. *This car is the very latest model.*

modem (*n*) a piece of electronic equipment used to send information between computers by telephone.

moderate
1 (*adj*) not extreme. *Moderate speed.* **moderation** (*n*), **moderately** (*adv*).
2 (*adj*) of average or below average quality. *My exam results were only moderate.*

modern (*adj*) up-to-date, or new in style. *Modern architecture.*

modernize *or* **modernise** modernizing modernized (*v*) to make something more modern or up to date. **modernization** (*n*).

modest (*adj*) People who are modest are not boastful about their abilities or achievements. **modesty** (*n*), **modestly** (*adv*).

modify modifies modifying modified (*v*) to alter something slightly. **modification** (*n*).

module (*n*) a separate, independent section that can be linked to other parts to make something larger.

Mohammed *or* **Muhammad** (*n*) the founder of the Islamic religion. Muslims believe that Mohammed is God's main prophet.

moist (*adj*) damp and slightly wet. **moisture** (*n*), **moisten** (*v*).

mole
1 (*n*) a small, furry, mammal that digs tunnels and lives underground.
2 (*n*) a small growth on the skin.

mole

molecule (n)
the smallest part of
a substance that
can exist on its
own. Molecules are
usually made of
two or more atoms
bonded together.

molecules

molecules in a solid

*The diagrams show
how molecules are
tightly packed in
solids, loosely linked
in liquids, and
widely spaced in
gases. This means
that solids usually
keep their shape,
liquids can flow,
and gases can
spread out easily.*

molecules in a liquid

molecules
in a gas

molecular (adj).

molest molesting molested
1 (v) to disturb, annoy, or interfere
with someone.
2 (v) to abuse or attack someone
sexually. **molester** (n).

mollusc (n) a creature with a soft
body and no spine, usually protected
by a shell. *Snails, clams, and oysters
are all molluscs.*

mollycoddle mollycoddling
mollycoddled (v) to look after
someone too carefully.

molten (adj) Molten metal is so hot
that it has melted to become a liquid.

moment
1 (n) a very brief period of time. *I only
saw the rocket for a moment.*
momentary (adj),
momentarily (adv).
2 If something is happening **at the
moment**, it is happening now.

monarch (n) a ruler, such as a king
or queen, who has usually inherited
his or her position. **monarchy** (n).

monastery monasteries (n) a group
of buildings where monks live and
work. **monastic** (adj).

money monies (n) the coins and
notes which people use to buy things.
monetary (adj).

mongrel (n) a dog of mixed breed.

monitor monitoring monitored
1 (v) to keep a check on something
over a period of time.
2 (n) the visual display unit of a
computer. See **computer**.
3 (n) a television screen used in a
studio to show what is being recorded
or transmitted.

monk (n) a man who lives in a
religious community and has promised
to devote his life to God.

monkey (n) an animal like a small
ape, usually with a tail.

monocle (n) a glass lens worn to
improve the eyesight of one eye.

monogram (n) a design made from
two or more letters, usually someone's
initials. **monogrammed** (adj).

monologue (mon-oh-log) (n) a long
speech by one person.

monopolize or **monopolise**
monopolizing monopolized (v)
to keep something all to yourself.
*Cuthbert monopolized the
conversation so we couldn't get a
word in edgeways!*

monopoly monopolies (n)
the complete control of something,
especially a service or the supply of a
product.

monorail (n) a railway that runs on
one rail, usually high off the ground.

monotonous (adj) If something is
monotonous, it goes on and on in a
dull and boring way. **monotony** (n),
monotonously (adv).

monsoon (n) a season of torrential
rain and strong winds in India and
other Asian countries.

monster
1 (n) In stories, a **monster** is a large,
fierce, or horrible creature.
2 (n) a very wicked person.
3 (adj) (informal) huge.
A monster packet of cereal.

monstrous
1 (adj) extremely large, terrible, or
strange. *A monstrous creature.*
monstrosity (n), **monstrously** (adv).
2 (adj) wrong and wicked. *Monstrous
behaviour.* **monstrously** (adv).

month (n) a four-week period.
monthly (adj), **monthly** (adv).

monument
1 (n) an old, important statue,
building, etc. *An ancient monument.*
2 (n) a statue, building, etc. that is
meant to remind people of an event
or a person. *A war monument.*

monumental (adj) very large, or
very important. **monumentally** (adv).

mood
1 (n) Your **mood** is the way that you
are feeling.
2 If you are **in a mood**, you feel sulky
or bad tempered.

moody moodier moodiest
1 (adj) cross, or unhappy.
moodily (adv).
2 (adj) A moody person has frequent
changes of mood or feelings.
moodiness (n)

moon
1 (n) a satellite of a planet. *Mars has
two moons.*
2 **Moon** (n) the satellite that moves
around the Earth once each month
and reflects light from the Sun.
*The first diagram below shows how
the Moon moves around the Earth,
while the second identifies the
different phases of the Moon as they
are seen from the Earth during the
course of a month.*

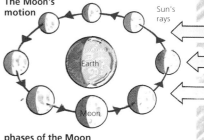
**The Moon's
motion**
Sun's
rays
Earth
Moon

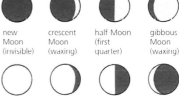
phases of the Moon

new
Moon
(invisible)

crescent
Moon
(waxing)

half Moon
(first
quarter)

gibbous
Moon
(waxing)

full
Moon

gibbous
Moon
(waning)

half-Moon
(last
quarter)

crescent
Moon
(old Moon)

moonlight moonlighting moonlit
1 (n) the light of the Earth's moon
that you can see at night.
moonlit (adj).
2 (v) (informal) to work at a second
job, usually at night, and often
secretly.

moor mooring moored
1 (n) an open, grassy area, often
covered with heather. **moorland** (n).
2 (v) If you **moor** a boat, you tie it up
or anchor it. **moorings** (n).

mop mopping mopped
1 (n) a long stick with a sponge or a
bundle of cloth or string at one end,
used to clean floors.
2 (v) to clean a floor, or soak up liquid
with a mop, cloth, or sponge.

mope moping moped (v) to be
miserable and depressed.

moral
1 (adj) to do with right and wrong.
*Carl faced the moral dilemma of
saying nothing or telling the truth.*
morality (n), **morally** (adv).
2 (plural n) Your **morals** are your
standards of behaviour.
3 (n) the lesson taught by a story

morale (mor-ahl) (n) hope, or confidence. *The prisoners kept up their morale by telling jokes.*

morbid (adj) Someone who is morbid is very interested in death and gruesome things. **morbidly** (adv).

more most
1 (adj) greater in number, size, etc. more (n), more (adv).
2 **more or less** roughly, or nearly.

moreish (adj) (slang) If a food is moreish, you want more of it.

morning (n) the time of day between dawn and midday.

morose (adj) gloomy and bad-tempered.

Morse code (n) a way of sending messages that uses light or sound in a pattern of dots and dashes to represent letters. *This picture shows the word "morse" in Morse code.*

■■ ■■ ■■■■ ●■■● ●●● ●

M   O   R   S   E

morsel (n) a small piece of food.

mortal
1 (adj) unable to live forever. *All humans are mortal.* **mortality** (n).
2 (n) a human being.
3 (adj) deadly, or causing death. *A mortal wound.* **mortally** (adv).

mortar
1 (n) a mixture of lime, sand, water, and cement that is used for building.
2 (n) a deep bowl used, with a pestle, for crushing things.

mortgage (n) a loan from a building society or bank to buy a house.

mortuary mortuaries (n) a room or building where dead bodies are kept until their funerals.

mosaic (moh-zay-ik) (n) a pattern or picture made up of small pieces of coloured stone or glass. *This Ancient Roman mosaic represents a Byzantine empress.*

mosaic

Moslem see **Muslim**.

mosque (mosk) (n) a building used by Muslims for worship. See **architecture**.

mosquito (moss-kee-toe) mosquitoes or mosquitos (n) a small insect which sucks blood from animals and humans. Mosquitoes can spread diseases such as malaria.

sucking tube

mosquito

moss mosses (n) a small, furry, green plant that grows on wet soil or stone. Mosses do not have roots, flowers, or fruit, but reproduce by producing spores. **mossy** (adj). See **spore**.

mostly (adv) mainly, or usually.

motel (n) a roadside hotel for motorists.

moth (n) an insect like a butterfly, that usually flies at night. *The emperor moth is found in Europe and Asia.*

emperor moth (male)

mother (n) a female parent. **motherhood** (n), **motherly** (adj).

motion motioning motioned
1 (n) movement. *The motion of the boat made me feel sick.*
2 (v) to tell someone something through movement. *The teacher motioned Spud to sit down.*
3 (n) a suggestion made at a meeting.

motivate motivating motivated (v) to encourage someone to do something. *The coach tried to motivate his team to win.* **motivation** (n), **motivated** (adj).

motive (n) a reason for doing something.

motocross (n) cross-country motorcycle racing.

motor motoring motored
1 (n) a machine that changes electrical energy into mechanical energy to produce movement. See **engine**.
2 (adj) to do with cars or engines. *Motor mechanics.*
3 (v) to drive. **motoring** (n).

motorbike (n) (informal) a motorcycle.

motorcycle (n) a two-wheeled vehicle with an engine. *The picture shows a Yamaha TDM850 motorcycle.*

motorcycle

tail cover
rear direction indicator
grab bar
brake light
pillion (passenger seat)
rear mudguard
pillion footrest (folded-up)
rider's seat
shock absorber
fuel tank
twist-grip throttle
speedometer
windscreen
cowl (covering)
headlight
front direction indicator
radiator
brake cable
front mudguard
front fork (contains spring)
front brake calliper
lightweight, three-spoke wheel
disc brake
rear fender
swing arm
exhaust silencer
exhaust pipe
brake pedal
rider's footrest
crank case
clutch and gearbox
exhaust down pipe
twin-cylinder engine

Some words that begin with a "mor" sound are spelt "mau".

motorist *(n)* a car driver.

motorway *(n)* a wide road with several lanes for fast, long-distance traffic.

mottled *(adj)* If something is mottled, it is covered with patches of different colours.

motto mottos *or* mottoes *(n)* a short sentence that is meant to guide your behaviour. Some families have a motto as part of their coat of arms. *See* **coat of arms**.

mould moulding moulded
1 *(v)* to model or shape something. *Mould the clay into a cat shape.*
2 *(n)* a hollow container that you can pour liquid into, so that it sets in that shape. *A jelly mould.*
3 *(n)* a furry fungus that grows on old food or damp walls.
mouldiness *(n)*, mouldy *(adj)*

moult moulting moulted *(v)* When a bird or animal **moults**, its outer covering of fur, feathers, or skin comes off so that a new one can grow.

mound *(n)* a hill, or a pile.

mount mounting mounted
1 *(v)* to get on, or to climb up. *Sheila mounted her horse.* **mount** *(n)*.
2 *(v)* to rise, or to increase. *Excitement mounted as the great day drew near.*
3 *(v)* to put a picture or photograph in a frame. **mount** *(n)*.
4 *(n)* a mountain.

mountain
1 *(n)* a very high piece of land, higher than a hill.
2 *(n)* a large amount of something. *A mountain of work.*

mountain bike *(n)* a strong bicycle with many gears that can be ridden on rough or hilly ground. *See* **bicycle**.

mountaineer *(n)* someone who climbs mountains.
mountaineering *(n)*.

mourn mourning mourned *(v)* to be very sad and grieve for someone who has died.
mourner *(n)*, mourning *(n)*.

mournful *(adj)* sad and miserable. **mournfully** *(adv)*.

mouse mice
1 *(n)* a small, furry animal with a long tail.
2 *(n)* a small control box that you use to move the cursor on your computer screen. *See* **computer**.

harvest mouse

mousse (rhymes with goose)
1 *(n)* a cold food made with beaten egg whites, that tastes light and fluffy. *Chocolate mousse.*
2 *(n)* a substance that you use to style your hair.

moustache *(n)* the hair on a man's top lip.

mousy *or* **mousey**
1 *(adj)* Mousy hair is light brown.
2 *(adj)* quiet and shy. **mousily** *(adv)*.

mouth mouthing mouthed
1 *(n)* the part of your face that you use for eating and talking.
2 *(n)* the entrance to a cave or river.
3 *(v)* If you **mouth** words, you move your lips but do not make any sound.

mouth organ *(n)* a small musical instrument that you play by blowing out and drawing in your breath. Mouth organ is another name for harmonica. *See* **harmonica**.

move moving moved
1 *(v)* to change place or position.
2 *(n)* a step, or a movement.
3 *(v)* If you are **moved** by something, such as a film or piece of music, it makes you feel emotional.
moving *(adj)*.

movement
1 *(n)* a change from one place or position to another.
2 *(n)* a group of people who have joined together to support a cause. *The peace movement.*
3 *(n)* one of the main parts of a long piece of classical music.

movie *(n)* *(informal)* a film.

mow mowing mowed mown *(v)* to cut grass, corn, etc. **mower** *(n)*.

MP *(n)* someone elected by the people of a district to represent them in parliament. The initials MP stand for Member of Parliament.

mph The initials **mph** stand for miles per hour. *This car's top speed is 130mph.*

Mr *(miss-ter)* *(n)* a title put in front of a man's name. *Mr Roland Brown.*

Mrs *(miss-iz)* *(n)* a title put in front of a married woman's name. *Mrs Clare White.*

Ms *(miz)* *(n)* a title put in front of a woman's name which does not indicate whether she is married or unmarried. *Ms Anna Black.*

much
1 *(adv)* greatly. *It's much too expensive. Much to my surprise, Tom turned up for work.* **much** *(adj)*.
2 *(n)* a large amount of something. *I don't eat much.*

muck mucking mucked
1 *(n)* dirt, or mess. **mucky** *(adj)*.
2 **muck out** *(v)* to clean out an animal's home.
3 **muck about** *(v)* *(slang)* to act in a silly way.
4 **muck up** *(v)* *(slang)* to spoil something, or to make a mess of it.

mucus *(mew-kuss)* *(n)* a slimy substance made in some parts of your body, such as your nose.
mucous *(mew-kuss)* *(adj)*.

mud *(n)* earth that is wet and sticky. **muddy** *(v)*, **muddy** *(adj)*.

muddle muddling muddled
1 *(v)* to mix things up, or to confuse them. **muddled** *(adj)*.
2 *(n)* a mess or confusion.

muesli *(myooz-lee)* *(n)* a breakfast cereal made from grain, dried fruit, and nuts.

muffin
1 *(n)* a round, flat bun, usually eaten toasted.
2 *(n)* *(US)* a round, sweet cake.

muffle muffling muffled *(v)* to make a sound quieter or duller. *Hannah stuffed a handkerchief into her mouth to muffle her laughter.*

mug mugging mugged
1 *(n)* a large cup with a handle. Mugs often have straight sides.
2 *(v)* *(informal)* to attack someone and try to steal their money. **mugger** *(n)*.

muggy muggier muggiest *(adj)* If the weather is **muggy**, it is warm and damp. **mugginess** *(n)*.

Muhammad *see* **Mohammed**.

mule *(n)* an animal produced by mating a female horse with a male donkey.

multicultural *(adj)* involving or made up of people from different races or religions. *A multicultural community.* **multiculturally** *(adv)*.

multilingual *(adj)* using several different languages. *A multilingual guidebook.* **multilingually** *(adv)*.

multimedia *(adj)* combining different media, such as sound, pictures, and text. *A multimedia computer game.* **multimedia** *(n)*.

multiple
1 *(adj)* made up of many parts or things. *Theresa suffered multiple injuries.*
2 *(n)* a number into which a smaller number can go an exact number of times. *10 and 15 are multiples of 5.*
3 A **multiple-choice** test gives a number of answers for each question, from which you have to choose one.

multiple sclerosis (n) a serious disease which causes loss of feeling in parts of the body.

multiply multiplies multiplying multiplied
1 (v) to grow in number or amount. *The weeds keep multiplying.*
2 (v) to add the same number to itself several times. *If you multiply 3 by 4, you get 12.* **multiplication** (n).

multiracial (adj) involving people of different races. *A multiracial school.* **multiracially** (adv).

multistorey (adj) A multistorey building has several floors.

multitude
1 (n) a crowd of people.
2 (n) a large number of things. *The new club offers a multitude of activities.* **multitudinous** (adj).

mum (n) an informal name for your mother.

mummy mummies
1 (n) an informal name for your mother.
2 (n) a dead body that has been preserved with special salts and resins and wrapped in cloth so that it will last for a very long time. The Ancient Egyptians placed the mummies of their rulers in elaborate coffins. *This illustration shows Tutankhamun's mummy and the three coffins that surrounded it. The large picture shows the second coffin in more detail.* **mummify** (v), **mummified** (adj).

mumps (n) an infectious illness that makes the glands in your neck swell up.

munch munches munching munched (v) to chew or crunch food.

mundane (adj) boring and ordinary.

mural (n) a wall painting.

murder murdering murdered (v) to kill someone. **murder** (n), **murderer** (n).

murky murkier murkiest (adj) dark, dirty, and gloomy.

murmur murmuring murmured
1 (v) to talk very quietly. **murmur** (n).
2 (v) to make a quiet, low, continuous sound. *The wind murmured in the trees.* **murmur** (n).

muscle
1 (n) one of the parts of your body that causes movement. Your muscles are attached to your skeleton and pull on your bones to make them move. *The diagram shows the muscles that move your arm.*
2 (n) strength, or power. *This job needs muscle.*

upper arm muscles
biceps (contract to bend arm)
tendons (attach muscle to bone)
triceps (contract to straighten arm)

museum (n) a place where interesting objects are displayed for people to look at.

mushroom mushrooming mushroomed
1 (n) a type of plant that has no leaves, flowers, or roots. Many mushrooms can be eaten.
2 (v) to grow quickly, or to spread. *New housing estates have mushroomed around the village.*

music
1 (n) a pleasant arrangement of sounds, played on instruments or sung.
2 (n) printed or written signs or notes that represent musical sounds. *Can you read music?* See **notation**.

musical
1 (adj) If you are **musical**, you are very interested in music, or you can play an instrument well. **musically** (adv).
2 (adj) to do with music. *Musical instruments.*
3 (n) a play or film which includes singing and dancing.

musical instrument (n) an instrument on which you can play music. See **brass**, **percussion**, **strings**, **woodwind**.

musician (n) someone who plays or composes music.

musk (n) a strong scent produced by some deer and used in perfume.

musket (n) an old-fashioned gun. **musketeer** (n).

Muslim or **Moslem** (n) someone who follows the religion of Islam. **Muslim** (adj).

mussel (n) a type of shellfish that you can eat. Mussels have hinged shells and soft, orangey-coloured bodies. *In order to feed, mussels pump seawater through their bodies.*

mussel
shell or valve
hinge
water passed out here
water drawn in here

must
1 (v) to have to do something. *I must go before the rain starts.*
2 (v) to be definitely doing something. *He must be lying.*
3 (n) something that you need. *This book is a must.*

mustard (n) a hot and spicy food flavouring, usually eaten with meat.

muster mustering mustered
1 (v) to assemble in a group. *The pupils mustered in the playground.*
2 (v) to gather something together. *Fatima mustered all her strength for the final lap.*

mummy and coffins of Tutankhamun

vulture goddess
flail
cobra goddess
gold inlaid with coloured glass
striped royal headdress
crook
outer coffin (wood covered with plaster and gold foil)
second coffin (wood covered with plaster and gold foil)
third coffin (solid gold)
mummy with solid gold portrait mask
layers of linen sheet soaked in preserving resins
coffin bases

musty mustier mustiest *(adj)*
If something or somewhere is **musty**, it smells of damp and mould. **mustiness** *(n)*.

mutant *(n)* a living thing that has developed different characteristics because of a change in its parents' genes. **mutation** *(n)*, **mutate** *(v)*.

mute
1 *(adj)* silent, or unable to speak. **mutely** *(adv)*.
2 *(n)* someone who cannot speak.
3 *(n)* something that can be fitted to a musical instrument to make it play less loudly.

mutilate *(myoo-til-ate)* mutilating mutilated *(v)* to injure or damage someone or something. **mutilation** *(n)*.

mutiny mutinies *(n)* a revolt against someone in charge, especially in the army or navy. **mutineer** *(n)*, **mutiny** *(v)*, **mutinous** *(adj)*.

mutter muttering muttered *(v)* to say something quietly so that people cannot hear you properly.

mutton *(n)* meat from a sheep.

mutual *(adj)* shared, or joint. *A mutual friend.* **mutually** *(adv)*.

muzzle
1 *(n)* an animal's nose and mouth. *See* **dog, reindeer**.
2 *(n)* a cover for an animal's mouth which stops it biting. **muzzle** *(v)*.
3 *(n)* the open end of a gun's barrel. *See* **blunderbuss**.

myriad *(mir-ee-ad)* *(n)* a large number. *As we entered the hall, we were dazzled by a myriad of lights.*

myself *(pronoun)* me and nobody else. *I have hurt myself.*

mysterious *(adj)* puzzling and intriguing. *A mysterious stranger.* **mysteriously** *(adv)*.

mystery mysteries
1 *(n)* something that is puzzling or hard to understand.
2 *(n)* a story containing a puzzle which has to be solved. *A murder mystery.*

mystify mystifies mystifying mystified *(v)* to puzzle or confuse someone. **mystification** *(n)*.

myth
1 *(n)* an old story or legend, especially one about gods and heroes. **mythology** *(n)*, **mythical** *(adj)*.
2 *(n)* a false idea that many people believe.

mythology mythologies *(n)* a set of stories that have been made up about subjects like the ancient gods and heroes. **mythological** *(adj)*.

Nn

nag nagging nagged *(v)* to try to persuade someone to do something by speaking about it constantly. **nag** *(n)*.

nail
1 *(n)* the hard covering at the end of your fingers and toes.
2 *(n)* a small piece of pointed metal that you hammer into something. **nail** *(v)*.

naïve *(ny-eve)* *(adj)* If you are **naïve**, you are not very experienced, and may believe or trust people too much. **naïvety** *(n)*, **naïvely** *(adv)*.

naked *(adj)* bare, or uncovered. **nakedness** *(n)*, **nakedly** *(adv)*.

name
1 *(n)* what a person or a thing is called. *What is your name?* **name** *(v)*.
2 *(n)* a reputation. *Wayne made his name as a singer.*

nanny nannies
1 *(n)* someone trained to look after young children in their home.
2 *(n)* an informal name for your grandmother.
3 **nanny goat** *(n)* a female goat.

nap napping napped *(v)* to sleep for a short time. **nap** *(n)*.

nape *(n)* the back of your neck.

napkin *(n)* a square piece of cloth that you use to protect your clothes at mealtimes.

nappy nappies *(n)* paper tissue padding or cloth put around a baby's bottom.

narcotic *(n)* a drug which makes you sleepy or unable to feel pain.

narrate narrating narrated *(v)* to tell a story. **narration** *(n)*, **narrator** *(n)*.

narrative
1 *(n)* a story, or an account of something that has happened.
2 *(adj)* telling a story. *Narrative verse.*

narrow narrower narrowest
1 *(adj)* thin, or not wide. **narrowness** *(n)*, **narrow** *(v)*, **narrowly** *(adv)*.
2 *(adj)* If you have a **narrow** escape, you only just get away. **narrowly** *(adv)*.
3 If you are **narrow-minded**, you stick to your own ideas and do not want to listen to new ones.

narrow boat *(n)* a canal boat.

nasal *(adj)* to do with your nose.

nasty nastier nastiest
1 *(adj)* disgusting, or unpleasant. *A nasty taste.*
2 *(adj)* cruel, or unkind. **nastily** *(adv)*.

nation *(n)* a large group of people who live in the same part of the world and often share the same language, customs, etc. **national** *(adj)*, **nationally** *(adv)*.

nationalist *(n)* someone who is proud of their country, or who fights for its independence. **nationalism** *(n)*, **nationalistic** *(adj)*.

nationality nationalities *(n)* Your **nationality** is the nation or country to which you belong. *Sam has American nationality.*

nationalize *or* **nationalise** nationalizing nationalized *(v)* If an industry is **nationalized**, its ownership is transferred from a private company to the government. **nationalization** *(n)*.

native
1 *(n)* someone born in a particular place. *Barry is a native of Australia.* **native** *(adj)*.
2 **native country** *(n)* the country where you were born.

Nativity
1 *(n)* the birth of Jesus Christ.
2 **nativity play** *(n)* a play telling the story of the birth of Jesus Christ.

NATO *(n)* a group of countries, including Britain and the USA, which help each other to defend themselves. NATO stands for North Atlantic Treaty Organization.

natural
1 *(adj)* found in nature, or to do with nature. **naturally** *(adv)*.
2 *(adj)* normal, or usual. *It's only natural to need a rest after a long run.* **naturally** *(adv)*.
3 *(adj)* In music, a **natural** note is one that is not sharp or flat. The natural notes on a piano are the white ones.
4 *(adj)* In a musical score, a **natural** sign shows that the next note is natural. *See* **notation**.

natural history *(n)* the study of animals and plants.

naturalist *(n)* someone who studies animals and plants.

nature
1 *(n)* everything in the world that is not made by people, such as plants, animals, the weather, etc.
2 *(n)* Your **nature** is your character.

naughty naughtier naughtiest *(adj)* badly-behaved, or disobedient. **naughtiness** *(n)*, **naughtily** *(adv)*.

Some words that begin with a "na" sound are spelt "kna" or "gna"

nausea *(nor-zee-er)* *(n)* a feeling of sickness. **nauseous** *(adj)*.

nautical
1 *(adj)* to do with ships and sailing.
2 **nautical mile** *(n)* a unit for measuring distance at sea.
1 nautical mile = 1853m.

naval *(adj)* to do with a navy or warships.

navel *(n)* the small, round hollow in your stomach, where your umbilical cord was attached when you were born.

navigate navigating navigated *(v)* to travel in a ship, plane, or other vehicle, using maps, compasses, etc. to guide you. *The sextant was used to navigate at sea in the 18th and 19th centuries. It helped the navigator to work out his position on a map by measuring the angle between the Sun and the horizon, or the angle between stars.* **navigation** *(n)*, **navigator** *(n)*.

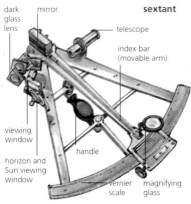

sextant
dark glass lens
mirror
telescope
index bar (movable arm)
viewing window
handle
horizon and Sun viewing window
vernier scale
magnifying glass

navy navies
1 *(n)* the ships and sailors that defend a country at sea.
2 **navy blue** *(n)* a very dark blue colour. **navy blue** *(adj)*.

nb the initials of the Latin phrase *nota bene*, which means "note well". The initials nb are used to make people take notice of something important.

near nearing neared
1 *(prep)* close to. *Alex lives near me.* **nearness** *(n)*, **near** *(adj)*, **near** *(adv)*.
2 *(v)* to come closer to something. *The train neared the station.*

nearby *(adj)* near, or close by. *The nearby shops sell most basic items.* **nearby** *(adv)*.

nearly *(adv)* almost, or not quite. *We are nearly home.*

neat neater neatest
1 *(adj)* tidy and orderly. *A neat bedroom.* **neatness** *(n)*, **neatly** *(adv)*.

2 *(adj)* simple and pleasing. *A neat solution.* **neatly** *(adv)*.
3 *(adj)* A **neat** drink is not mixed with anything else.

necessary *(adj)* If something is **necessary**, you have to do it or have it. **necessity** *(n)*, **necessarily** *(adv)*.

neck necking necked
1 *(n)* the part of your body that joins your head to your shoulders.
2 *(n)* a narrow part of something. *The neck of the bottle.*
3 *(v)* *(informal)* to kiss.

necklace *(n)* a piece of jewellery worn around your neck.

nectar *(n)* a sweet liquid that bees collect from flowers and turn into honey.

need needing needed
1 *(v)* to want something urgently. *The refugees need food and shelter.*
2 *(n)* something that you have to have. *I have few needs.*
3 *(v)* to have to do something. *I need to practise for the concert tomorrow.*

needle needling needled
1 *(n)* a thin, pointed piece of metal, with a hole for thread at one end, used for sewing.
2 *(n)* a long, thin, pointed rod, used for knitting.
3 *(n)* a thin, hollow tube with a sharp end that doctors use for giving injections or taking blood.
4 *(n)* a pointer on an instrument such as a compass. *See* **compass**.
5 *(v)* *(informal)* If someone **needles** you, they annoy you.

needless *(adj)* If something is **needless**, it is not necessary. **needlessly** *(adv)*.

negative
1 *(adj)* giving the answer "no". *I asked James if he wanted to come, but his reply was negative.*
2 *(adj)* If someone is **negative**, they are against lots of things and are unhelpful. **negatively** *(adv)*.
3 *(n)* a photographic film, used to make prints, which shows light areas as dark, and dark areas as light.
4 *(adj)* A **negative** number is less than zero.

neglect neglecting neglected
1 *(v)* to fail to look after someone or something. **neglectful** *(adj)*.
2 *(n)* If a person, building, etc. is suffering from **neglect**, they have not been looked after properly.

negotiate negotiating negotiated *(v)* to bargain or discuss something, so that you can come to an agreement. **negotiation** *(n)*, **negotiator** *(n)*.

negro negroes *(n)* a black person who comes from Africa or is descended from Africans.

neigh *(nay)* neighing neighed *(v)* to make the sound that a horse makes. **neigh** *(n)*.

neighbour *(n)* someone who lives next door to you or near to you.

neighbourhood *(n)* Your **neighbourhood** is the local area around your house.

neither *(adj)* not either. *Neither of my brothers likes custard.* **neither** *(pronoun)*.

neon *(n)* a gas which glows when an electric current is passed through it. Neon is used in lights and signs.

nephew *(n)* Someone's **nephew** is their brother's or sister's son.

nerve
1 *(n)* Your **nerves** are the thin fibres that send messages between your brain and other parts of your body, so that you can move and feel.
2 *(n)* courage and calmness. *You need lots of nerve to be a lion tamer.*
3 *(n)* *(informal)* cheek, or rudeness. *Harry's got a nerve, answering back like that!*
4 *(plural n)* *(informal)* If someone suffers from **nerves**, they are worried or frightened.

nervous
1 *(adj)* easily upset or frightened. **nervousness** *(n)*, **nervously** *(adv)*.
2 *(adj)* to do with the nerves. *The human nervous system.*
3 *(n)* If someone has a **nervous breakdown**, they become very depressed and feel that they cannot cope with their problems.

nest nesting nested
1 *(n)* a place built by birds and many other animals to lay their eggs and bring up their young. *Wasps' nests are built by a queen wasp from chewed-up wood mixed with saliva. The queen lays her eggs in the cells and the eggs develop into worker wasps that enlarge and strengthen the nest.*
2 *(v)* to make a nest or home.

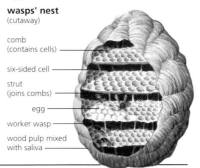

wasps' nest
(cutaway)
comb (contains cells)
six-sided cell
strut (joins combs)
egg
worker wasp
wood pulp mixed with saliva

Some words that begin with a "n" sound are spelt "kn" or "gn".

nestle nestling nestled (v) to settle into a comfortable position. *The baby nestled against her mother's shoulder.*

net
1 (n) material made from fine threads or ropes that are knotted together with holes between them.
2 (n) a bag made from net material and attached to a pole, that you use to catch fish, butterflies, etc.
3 (n) A **net amount** of money is the amount left after everything necessary, such as tax, has been taken away.
4 (n) The **net weight** of something is its weight without packaging.
5 **The Net** (n) a network that connects millions of computers around the world. The Net is short for the Internet.

netball (n) a game played by two teams, in which goals are scored by throwing a ball through a high net.

nettle (n) a weed that stings you if you touch it.

network
1 (n) a large number of lines, forming a criss-cross pattern.
2 (n) a system of things that are connected to each other. *A computer network.* **network** (v).
3 (n) a group of people who exchange professional or social information with each other. **networking** (n).

neurotic (adj) If someone is neurotic, they are very scared or worried, usually about something imaginary. **neurotically** (adv).

neuter neutering neutered
1 (adj) neither masculine nor feminine.
2 (adj) In some languages, such as German, nouns that are neither masculine nor feminine are **neuter**.
3 (v) If you **neuter** an animal, you remove its sex organs so that it cannot reproduce. **neutered** (adj).

neutral
1 (adj) If a country or a person is neutral in a war or an argument, they do not support either side. **neutrality** (n), **neutrally** (adv).
2 When a car is **in neutral**, the gears are not transmitting any power.
3 (adj) Neutral colours are pale and not bright. *Beige is a neutral colour.*
4 (adj) In chemistry, a **neutral** substance is neither an acid nor an alkali.

neutralize or **neutralise**
neutralizing neutralized (v) to stop something from working or from having an effect. *The medicine quickly neutralized the poison.*

neutron (n) one of the extremely small parts of an atom that has no electrical charge. See **atom**.

never (adv) at no time, or not ever.

nevertheless (adv) in spite of that, or yet. *Titus was cold and hungry. Nevertheless, he kept on walking.*

new newer newest
1 (adj) just made, or just begun.
2 (adj) different or strange. *New ideas.*
3 **new age** (adj) to do with spiritual and mystical ideas and beliefs.

news (singular n) fresh or recent information or facts.

newsagent (n) a person or shop that sells newspapers, magazines, etc.

newspaper (n) several sheets of folded paper containing news reports, articles, letters, etc. Newspapers are usually published daily.

newt (n) a small creature with short legs and a long tail that lives on land but lays its eggs in water.

marbled newt

newton
(n) a unit for measuring force.

next
1 (adj) immediately following. *We'll catch the next train.* **next** (adv).
2 (adj) nearest. *Bruno's desk is next to mine.* **next** (adv).
3 **next door** in or at the nearest house, building, etc.

nib (n) the part of a pen through which ink flows.

nibble nibbling nibbled (v) to bite something gently, or to take small bites of something. **nibble** (n).

nice nicer nicest (adj) pleasant, or good. **nicely** (adv).

niche (neesh)
1 (n) a hollow place in a wall.
2 (n) the environment to which an animal or a plant has adapted, or to which it belongs.

nickname (n) a name that you give to a friend. **nickname** (v).

nicotine (n) a poisonous and addictive substance found in tobacco.

niece (n) Someone's **niece** is their brother's or sister's daughter.

night (n) the time between sunset and sunrise, when it is dark.

nightie (n) (informal) a loose dress that girls or women wear in bed.

nightingale (n) a small bird that sings beautifully.

nightly (adv) happening every night. *The doctor visits nightly.* **nightly** (adj).

nightmare (n) a frightening or unpleasant dream or situation.

nil (n) nothing, or zero.

nimble nimbler nimblest (adj) If you are **nimble**, you move quickly and lightly. **nimbly** (adv).

nip nipping nipped (v) to pinch somebody sharply. **nip** (n).

nipple (n) one of the two small, raised parts on a person's chest.

nitrogen (n) a colourless gas which makes up about four-fifths of the Earth's air.

nits (plural n) eggs laid by lice.

no
1 (interject) a word used to refuse something. *"No, I won't!"*
2 (adj) not any. *There was no hope.*

no. short for **number**.

noble nobler noblest
1 (adj) A **noble** family is aristocratic and of high rank. **nobility** (n), **nobleman** (n), **noblewoman** (n).
2 (adj) If someone is **noble**, they act in a way that is good and unselfish. **nobility** (n), **nobly** (adv).

nobody nobodies
1 (pronoun) not a single person. *There was nobody there.*
2 (n) If a person is described as a **nobody**, they are not considered to be important.

nocturnal
1 (adj) to do with the night, or happening at night. *A nocturnal journey.* **nocturnally** (adv)
2 (adj) A **nocturnal** animal is active at night. *Badgers and owls are nocturnal animals.*

nod nodding nodded (v) to move your head up and down, especially to say yes. **nod** (n).

noise (n) a sound, especially a loud or unpleasant one. **noisiness** (n).

noisy noisier noisiest (adj) loud. **noisily** (adv).

nomad (n) a member of a tribe that wanders around, instead of living in one place. *The picture shows the camp of some Bedouin nomads.* **nomadic** (adj).

nomads

Some words that begin with a "n" sound are spelt "kn", "gn", or "pn".
Some words that begin with a "ni" sound are spelled "ny".

nominate nominating nominated
(v) to suggest that someone would be the right person to do a job.
I nominate George as our team leader.
nomination (n).

none (pronoun) not one, or not any.
none (adj), none (adv).

nonetheless (adv) in spite of that.
Harriet fell off her horse three times. Nonetheless, she completed the course. nonetheless (conj).

nonfiction (n) writing that gives information about real things, people, and events, rather than made-up stories. nonfiction (adj).

nonsense (n) If something is nonsense, it is silly or has no meaning. nonsensical (adj).

nonstop (adj) without any stops or breaks. *A nonstop flight to Los Angeles.* nonstop (adv).

noodles (plural n) very thin pasta in long pieces that you can put in soups, Chinese dishes, etc.

noon (n) twelve o'clock in the middle of the day.

no one or **no-one** (pronoun) not a single person. *There was no one in the park.*

noose (n) a large loop at the end of a piece of rope, which closes up as the rope is pulled.

normal (adj) usual and ordinary.
normality (n), normally (adv).

north
1 (n) one of the four main points of the compass, the direction on your right when you face the setting Sun in the northern hemisphere. north (adj), northern (adj), north (adv).
2 (adj) A **north** wind blows from the north. northerly (adv).
3 North Pole (n) the very cold part of the Earth in the far north.

nose nosing nosed
1 (n) the part of your face that you use when you smell and breathe.
2 (n) the pointed part at the front of some aircraft. See **aircraft**.
3 (v) If a ship, car, etc. noses forwards, it moves very slowly.

nostalgic (adj) People who are nostalgic like to think about the past and are sad because things have changed since then. nostalgia (n).

nostril (n) Your nostrils are the two holes in your nose through which you breathe and smell.

nosy nosier nosiest (adj) (informal) Someone who is nosy is too interested in things that do not concern them. nosily (adv).

notation (n) a series of signs or symbols used to represent elements in a system, such as music or maths.
An example of music notation is shown below.

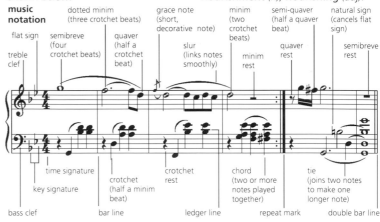

note noting noted
1 (n) a short letter or message..
2 (n) a piece of paper money.
3 (n) a musical sound or the symbol that represents it. See **notation**.
4 (v) to notice a fact and pay attention to it. *Please note the price increase.*
5 (v) to write something down.
I've noted your name in my book.

notebook
1 (n) a small pad or book of paper, used for writing notes.
2 (n) a very small, portable computer.

nothing
1 (pronoun) not anything at all.
There was nothing in the cupboard.
2 (pronoun) not anything important.
I did nothing all weekend.

notice noticing noticed
1 (v) to see or become aware of something. *Did you notice the smell?*
noticeable (adj), noticeably (adv).
2 (n) a written message put in a public place to tell people about something.
3 If someone **hands in their notice**, they tell their employer that they will be leaving their job.

notify notifies notifying notified
(v) to tell someone about something officially or formally. notification (n).

notorious (adj) If someone or something is **notorious**, they are well known for something bad. *The school is notorious for bullying.*

nought (rhymes with sort) (n) the number 0, or zero.

noun (n) a word that refers to a person or thing. *"Dog", "happiness", and "France" are all nouns.*
See page 3.

nourish (nuh-rish) nourishes nourishing nourished (v) to give a person, animal, or plant enough food to keep them strong and healthy.
nourishment (n), nourishing (adj).

novel
1 (n) a book that tells a story.
novelist (n).
2 (adj) new and interesting.
A novel idea.

novelty novelties (n) something new, interesting, and unusual.
novelty (adj).

novice (n) a beginner, or someone who is not very experienced.

nowhere (adv) not any place.
There was nowhere to hide.

nuclear (new-klee-ur)
1 (adj) to do with the splitting of atoms. *Nuclear physics.*
2 nuclear power (n) power created by the splitting of atoms.
3 nuclear weapon (n) a weapon which uses the power created by splitting atoms.
4 nuclear reactor (n) a large machine that produces nuclear power in a power station.

nucleus nuclei
1 (n) the central part of an atom, made up of neutrons and protons.
See **atom**.
2 (n) the central part of a cell, that contains the chromosomes.
See **cell**.

nude
1 (adj) naked. nudist (n), nudity (n).
2 (n) a naked human figure, especially one in a painting or sculpture.

nudge nudging nudged (v) to give someone or something a small push, often with your elbow. nudge (n).

nuisance (new-sunss) (n) someone or something that annoys you and causes problems for you.

Some words that begin with a "no" sound are spelt "kno" or "gno".

numb *(num) (adj)* unable to feel anything. **numbness** *(n)*, **numb** *(v)*.

number numbering numbered
1 *(n)* a word or sign used for counting and doing sums.
2 *(v)* to give a number to something. *Isla numbered the cards from 1 to 10.*
3 *(v)* to amount to a number. *The crowd numbered at least 300.*

numeral *(n)* a written sign that represents a number. *Roman numerals. Arabic numerals.*

numerate *(adj)* If you are numerate, you can understand basic arithmetic. **numeracy** *(n)*.

numerator *(n)* In fractions, the numerator is the number above the line, which shows how many parts of the denominator are taken.

numerical *(adj)* to do with numbers. *Numerical order.* **numerically** *(adv)*.

numerous *(adj)* many. *Tracey's tapes are too numerous to count.*

nun *(n)* a woman who lives in a Christian religious community and has promised to devote her life to God.

nurse nursing nursed
1 *(n)* someone who looks after people who are ill, usually in a hospital.
2 *(v)* to look after someone who is ill

nursery nurseries
1 *(n)* a room where very young children sleep and play.
2 *(n)* a place where babies and very young children are looked after while their parents are at work.
3 *(n)* a place where you can buy plants and seeds.
4 nursery rhyme *(n)* a short poem for very young children.
5 nursery school *(n)* a school for children aged three to five years old.

nut
1 *(n)* a fruit with a hard shell that grows on trees. **nutty** *(adj)*.
2 *(n)* a small piece of metal with a hole in the middle that screws on to a bolt and holds it in place.

nutritious *(nyoo-trish-uss) (adj)* Food that is nutritious contains substances that your body can use to help you stay healthy and strong. **nutrition** *(n)*, **nutritiously** *(adv)*.

nylon *(n)* a light, man-made fibre, used to make tights, fishing line, etc.

nymph
1 *(n)* In ancient Greek and Roman stories, a nymph is a spirit of nature.
2 *(n)* a young form of an insect, such as a grasshopper, which changes into an adult by repeatedly shedding its skin.

Oo

oaf *(n)* a clumsy and rude person.

oak *(n)* a large, hardwood tree that produces acorns.

OAP *(n)* an old person who receives a pension. The initials OAP stand for old age pensioner.

oar *(n)* a wooden pole with a flat blade at one end, used for rowing a boat.

oasis *(oh-ay-siss)* oases *(n)* a place in a desert where there is water, and where plants and trees grow.

oath
1 *(n)* a serious, formal promise.
2 *(n)* a swear word.

oats *(plural n)* a cereal plant that is used to make porridge. *See* **grain**.

obedient *(adj)* If you are obedient, you do what you are told to do. **obedience** *(n)*, **obediently** *(adv)*.

obese *(adj)* very fat. **obesity** *(n)*.

obey obeying obeyed *(v)* to do the things that someone tells you to do.

object objecting objected
1 *(ob-jekt) (n)* something that you can see and touch, but is not alive.
2 *(ob-jekt) (n)* the thing that you are trying to achieve. *The object of this game is to get the ball into the net.*
3 *(ob-jekt) (n)* The object of a verb is the noun that receives the action of the verb and usually comes after it. *In the sentence "Jemima thumped Barney", Barney is the object of the verb "to thump".*
4 *(ob-jekt) (v)* If you object to something, you dislike or disagree with it. **objection** *(n)*, **objector** *(n)*.

objectionable *(adj)* unpleasant and likely to offend people.

objective
1 *(adj)* based on facts, not on feelings or opinions. *An objective report.* **objectivity** *(n)*, **objectively** *(adv)*.
2 *(n)* an aim that you are working towards. *Our objective is to produce a pollution-free car.*

obligation *(n)* something that it is your duty to do. *There's no obligation to stay.* **obligatory** *(adj)*.

oblige obliging obliged
1 *(v)* If you are obliged to do something, you have to do it.
2 *(v)* to do someone a favour. *We needed transport, so Mum obliged by driving us there.* **obliging** *(adj)*, **obligingly** *(adv)*.

obliterate obliterating obliterated *(v)* to destroy something completely.

oblong *(n)* a shape with four straight sides and four right angles, that is longer than it is wide.

obnoxious *(adj)* very unpleasant. **obnoxiously** *(adv)*.

obscene obscener obscenest *(adj)* indecent and shocking. **obscenity** *(n)*, **obscenely** *(adv)*.

obscure obscuring obscured; obscurer obscurest
1 *(adj)* not well known. **obscurity** *(n)*.
2 *(adj)* not easy to understand.
3 *(v)* to make it difficult to see something. *The pillar obscured our view of the stage.*

observant *(adj)* If you are observant, you are good at noticing things. **observantly** *(adv)*.

observatory observatories *(n)* a building containing telescopes and other scientific instruments for studying the sky and the stars.

observe observing observed
1 *(v)* to watch someone or something carefully. *The police have been observing the house all week.* **observation** *(n)*.
2 *(v)* to notice something by looking or watching. *I observed that Henry had torn his trousers.* **observation** *(n)*.
3 *(v)* to make a remark. *Warren observed that the train was late again.* **observation** *(n)*.

obsess obsesses obsessing obsessed *(v)* If something obsesses you, you think about it all the time. **obsession** *(n)*, **obsessive** *(adj)*.

obsolete *(adj)* out of date and no longer used.

obstacle *(n)* something that gets in your way or prevents you from doing something.

obstinate *(adj)* If someone is obstinate, they are stubborn and unwilling to change their mind. **obstinacy** *(n)*, **obstinately** *(adv)*.

obstreperous *(adj)* If someone is obstreperous, they resist in a rough and noisy way. **obstreperously** *(adv)*.

obstruct obstructing obstructed
1 *(v)* to block a road or path. *Fallen trees obstructed the road.* **obstruction** *(n)*, **obstructive** *(adj)*.
2 *(v)* to prevent something from happening, or to make something difficult. *Max obstructed all attempts to make him tidy his room.* **obstruction** *(n)*, **obstructive** *(adj)*.

obtain obtaining obtained *(v)* to get, or to be given something.

166

obtuse
1 *(adj)* If someone is **obtuse**, they are slow to understand things.
2 *(adj)* An **obtuse** angle is an angle of between 90° and 180°.

obvious
(adj) If something is **obvious**, it is easy to see or understand. **obviously** *(adv)*.

occasion
1 *(n)* a time when something happens. *Zucas had been to London on several occasions.*
2 *(n)* a special or important event.

occasional
(adj) happening sometimes. *Occasional visits.* **occasionally** *(adv)*.

occupation
1 *(n)* a job. **occupational** *(adj)*.
2 *(n)* something that you enjoy doing in your free time. *Football is Gary's favourite occupation.*
3 *(n)* the taking over and controlling of a country or an area by an army.

occupy occupies occupying occupied
1 *(v)* to live in a building, room, etc. *Who occupies this house?* **occupant** *(n)*, **occupier** *(n)*.
2 *(v)* to keep someone busy and happy. *The boys were occupied for hours on the computer.*
3 *(v)* If an army **occupies** a country or an area, it captures it and takes control of it.

occur occurring occurred
1 *(v)* to happen. *When did the accident occur?* **occurrence** *(n)*.
2 *(v)* If something **occurs to you**, you suddenly think of it.

ocean
(oh-shun) (n) one of the large areas of water on the Earth's surface. *This map shows the five main oceans of the world.*

o'clock
(adv) a word you use when saying what the time is. O'clock is short for "of the clock". *It's 3 o'clock.*

octagon
(n) a shape with eight straight sides. **octagonal** *(adj)*. See **shape**.

octahedron
(n) a solid shape with eight, usually triangular, faces. See **shape**.

octave
(n) the eight note gap in a musical scale between a note and the next note of the same name above or below it.

octopus octopuses
(n) a sea creature with a soft body and eight long tentacles that it uses for catching its prey.

octopus
eye (adapted for underwater light)
sucker mantle (body)
tentacle
light-sensitive skin (changes colour for camouflage)
mouth under here
siphon (squirts ink)

odd odder oddest
1 *(adj)* strange and difficult to explain or understand. **oddly** *(adv)*.
2 *(adj)* An **odd** number cannot be divided exactly by two. *1, 13, 47, and 895 are all odd numbers.*
3 *(adj)* not matching. *Odd socks.*

odds
(plural n) the probability of something happening. *The odds are that Toyah will win the race.*

ode
(n) a poem praising something. *Ode to a nightingale.*

odour
(oh-der) (n) a smell.

oesophagus
(ee-sof-uh-guss) **oesophagi** *(n)* the tube in your body that carries food from your throat into your stomach. See **anatomy**, **digestion**.

off
1 *(prep)* away from a place. *Take those books off the table.* **off** *(adv)*.
2 *(adv)* not switched on. *Someone has turned off the computer.*
3 If food has **gone off**, it has gone bad and can no longer be eaten.

offence
1 *(n)* a crime.
2 If you **cause offence**, you upset someone.
3 If you **take offence**, you feel upset by something that someone has done or said.

offend offending offended
1 *(v)* to upset someone.
2 *(v)* to commit a crime. **offender** *(n)*.

offensive
1 *(adj)* If someone or something is **offensive**, they are unpleasant and upset people. **offensively** *(adv)*.
2 *(n)* an attack, usually a military one.
3 *(adj)* attacking. *The army took offensive action.*

offer offering offered
1 *(v)* to ask someone if they would like something. *Can I offer you some cake?* **offer** *(n)*.
2 *(v)* to say that you are willing to do something for someone. *I offered to take the message.* **offer** *(n)*.

offering
(n) something that is offered to God or to a god.

offhand
1 *(adj)* abrupt, or casual.
2 *(adj)* without preparation. *I don't know the answer offhand.*

office
1 *(n)* a room or building in which people work, usually sitting at desks.
2 *(n)* an important, powerful position. *The office of Prime Minister.*

officer
(n) someone who is in charge of other people, especially in the armed forces or the police.

official
1 *(adj)* If something is **official**, it has been approved by someone in authority. *There will be an official inquiry into the accident.* **officially** *(adv)*.
2 *(n)* someone who holds an important position in an organization. *A government official.*

off-licence (n) In Britain, an off-licence is a shop which sells alcoholic drinks.

off-peak (adj) happening when there is less activity or demand. Off-peak travel.

off-putting (adj) (informal) discouraging or disturbing.

offside (adj) If a player is offside in a game such as football, they have broken the rules of the game by moving too far forward, ahead of the ball. offside (adv).

offspring (plural n) an animal's young, or a human's children.

often (adv) many times.

ogre (oh-ger) (n) a fierce, cruel giant in fairy stories.

oh (interject) a word used to express surprise, disappointment, or pain.

ohm (rhymes with dome) (n) a unit for measuring how much resistance a substance gives to the flow of electricity through it.

oil oiling oiled
1 (n) a thick, smooth liquid. Different types of oil are used for heating buildings, for cooking, and for making machines run smoothly. oily (adj).
2 (v) to cover something with oil. You should oil your bicycle chain regularly.
3 oils (plural n) artists' paints containing oil. See artist.

oil rig (n) a large platform used as a base for drilling for oil under the sea or under the ground. The picture shows the Kittiwake oil rig in the North Sea.

okay or **OK**
1 (adj) (informal) all right.
2 (informal) When you say okay, you mean that you agree.

old older oldest
1 (adj) Someone who is old has lived for a long time.
2 (adj) Something that is old has existed or been used for a long time.
3 (adj) from an earlier time. A meeting of old pupils of the school.

old age
1 (n) the time when a person is old.
2 old age pension (n) an amount of money paid regularly by the government to retired people.

old-fashioned (adj) no longer fashionable or popular.

olive (n) a small black or green savoury fruit that is eaten whole or crushed for its oil.

omen (n) a sign or warning about something that will happen in the future.

ominous (adj) If something is ominous, it makes you feel that something bad is going to happen. An ominous silence. ominously (adv).

omit omitting omitted
1 (v) to leave something out. Hans omitted a line from the song. omission (n).
2 (v) If you omit to do something, you do not do it. Rupert omitted to eat his breakfast. omission (n).

omnibus omnibuses (n) a collection of stories, books or television programmes, that were previously published or shown separately.

omnivore (n) an animal that eats plants and meat. omnivorous (adj).

once
1 (adv) one time. I've only been to London once.
2 (adv) in the past. This country was once covered by ice.
3 (conj) after something has happened. I'll tell you all about it once we get home.
4 at once immediately. Take those muddy shoes off at once!

one-way
1 (adj) Traffic can only travel in one direction down a one-way street.
2 (adj) A one-way ticket allows you to travel to a place but not back again.

onion (n) a round vegetable with a strong smell and taste. See vegetable.

on-line
1 (adj) If you are on-line, you are connected to the Internet.
2 (adj) On-line information is kept in computer documents that are available to people using the Internet.

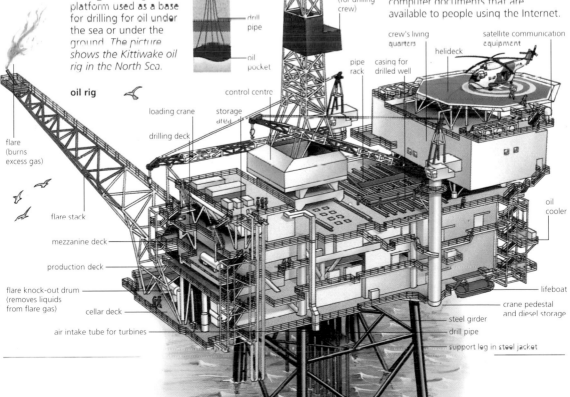

sea bed
(cross section)

rig
sea
sea bed
drill pipe
oil pocket

derrick
(drilling tower)

monkey board
(for drilling crew)

crew's living quarters
helideck
satellite communication equipment

pipe rack
casing for drilled well

oil cooler

control centre

oil rig

loading crane
storage area
drilling deck

flare (burns excess gas)

flare stack

mezzanine deck

production deck

flare knock-out drum
(removes liquids from flare gas)

cellar deck

air intake tube for turbines

lifeboat

crane pedestal and diesel storage

steel girder

drill pipe

support leg in steel jacket

only

1 *(adv)* not more than, or just. *There were only three people in the shop.*
2 *(adj)* with nothing or no one else. *Maria was the only person there.*
3 *(conj)* but. *We would have got here earlier, only the car broke down.*
4 *(n)* An **only child** has no brothers or sisters.

onomatopoeia

(on-oh-mat-er-pee-er) (n) a word that sounds like the thing it describes. *"Pop" and "sizzle" are examples of onomatopoeia.*

onward *or* onwards *(adv)* forward.
We've lived here from 1987 onward.

ooze *oozing oozed (v)* to flow out slowly. *Mud oozed from my shoes.*

opaque *(oh-pake) (adj)* not clear enough to see through. *The water in the stream was muddy and opaque.*

open

1 *(adj)* not shut. **open** *(v)*.
2 *(adj)* not covered, or not enclosed. *Open land. Open air.*
3 *(adj)* If you are **open** about something, you are honest about it. **openness** *(n)*, **openly** *(adv)*.
4 *(v)* to start, or to begin. *The story opens in a wild wood.*
5 *(n)* If you have an **open mind**, you are able to accept new ideas.

opening

1 *(n)* a hole or a space in something. *A small opening in the hedge.*
2 *(adj)* coming at the beginning. *The opening lines of a play.* **opening** *(n)*.
3 *(n)* a chance. *This part could give you an opening into show business.*

opera *(n)* a play in which the words are sung. **operatic** *(adj)*.

operate *operating operated*

1 *(v)* to make something work. *Damian soon learnt how to operate the time machine.*
2 *(v)* to cut open someone's body in order to repair a damaged part or remove a diseased part.

operation

1 *(n)* an event that has been carefully planned and involves a lot of people. *A massive security operation.*
2 If something is **in operation**, it is working.
3 *(n)* the cutting open of someone's body in order to repair a damaged part or remove a diseased part.

operator

1 *(n)* someone who works a machine.
2 *(n)* someone who works on a telephone switchboard, connecting calls and dealing with problems.

opinion

1 *(n)* the ideas and beliefs that you have about something. *What's your opinion on co-education?*
2 **opinion poll** *(n)* a way of finding out what people in general think about something, by questioning a selection of people.

opponent *(n)* someone who is against you in a fight or a game.

opportunity *opportunities (n)*
a chance to do something. *Carla's job gives her the opportunity to travel.*

oppose *opposing opposed (v)*
to be against something and try to prevent it from happening. *Orlando is opposed to whaling.*

opposite

1 *(prep)* If something is **opposite** you, it is facing you. **opposite** *(adj)*.
2 *(adj)* completely different. *Sue ran off in the opposite direction when she saw me.* **opposite** *(n)*.

opposition

1 *(n)* When there is **opposition** to something, people are against it. *There was a lot of opposition to the plans for a new supermarket.*
2 *(n)* the person or team that you play against in a match or competition.
3 the **Opposition** *(n)* the main political party that is not in power.

oppress *oppresses oppressing oppressed*

1 *(v)* to treat people in a cruel, unjust, and hard way. **oppression** *(n)*, **oppressor** *(n)*, **oppressive** *(adj)*.
2 *(v)* If something **oppresses** you, it makes you feel worried or weighed down. **oppressive** *(adj)*.

opt *opting opted*

1 *(v)* to choose to have or do something. *Lydia opted to learn German.*

2 opt out *(v)* to choose not to take part in something.

optical

1 *(adj)* to do with eyes or eyesight.
2 optical illusion *(n)* something that you think you see which is not really there.

optician *(n)* someone who tests your eyesight and supplies glasses and contact lenses.

optimistic *(adj)* People who are **optimistic** always believe that things will turn out well and successfully. **optimism** *(n)*, **optimist** *(n)*.

option *(n)* something that you can choose to do.

optional *(adj)* If something is **optional**, you can choose whether or not to have it or do it.

oral

1 *(adj)* to do with your mouth. *Oral hygiene.* **orally** *(adv)*.
2 *(n)* a spoken exam or test. *A French oral.*
3 *(adj)* to do with speaking. **orally** *(adv)*.

orange

1 *(n)* the colour of carrots, or a mixture of red and yellow. **orange** *(adj)*.
2 *(n)* a round fruit with a thick, orange skin and sweet, juicy flesh. *See* **fruit**.

orbit *orbiting orbited*

1 *(n)* the invisible path followed by an object circling a planet or the Sun. **orbital** *(adj)*.
2 *(v)* to travel around a planet or the Sun.

orchard *(n)* a field or farm where fruit trees are grown.

orchestra *(n)* a large group of musicians who play their instruments together. *The diagram below shows the positions of the main instruments in a symphony orchestra, which usually plays classical music.*

symphony orchestra

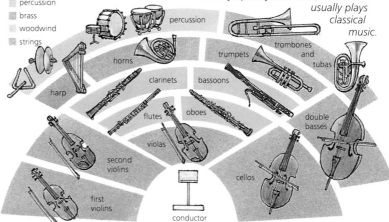

- percussion
- brass
- woodwind
- strings

percussion, trombones and tubas, trumpets, horns, clarinets, bassoons, harp, flutes, oboes, violas, second violins, cellos, double basses, first violins, conductor

orchid *(or-kid) (n)* a plant with colourful and often unusually shaped flowers. *The Vanda tricolor orchid shown here grows in Southeast Asia.*

orchid

ordeal *(n)* a very difficult and testing experience.

order ordering ordered
1 *(v)* to tell someone that they have to do something. **order** *(n)*.
2 *(v)* to ask for something in a restaurant. **order** *(n)*.
3 *(v)* to ask a manufacturer or a shop to get you something. *I've ordered a new television.*
4 *(n)* neatness. *Priscilla loves order.* **orderly** *(adv)*.
5 *(n)* good behaviour. *Can we have some order in this classroom?*
6 If you put things **in order**, you arrange them so that each thing is in the right place.
7 If an object is **out of order**, it is broken and does not work.
8 *(informal)* If a person is **out of order**, they are behaving badly.

ordinary *(adj)* normal, or usual. **ordinarily** *(adv)*.

ore *(n)* a rock which contains metal. *Iron ore.*

organ
1 *(n)* a large musical instrument with one or more keyboards and pipes of different lengths. **organist** *(n)*.
2 *(n)* a part of the body that does a particular job. *The diagram shows the main human organs used for breathing, and for digesting and excreting food. The kidneys are shown separately because they are positioned behind the intestines.*

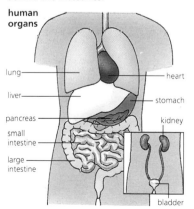
human organs
lung
heart
liver
stomach
pancreas
kidney
small intestine
large intestine
bladder

organic
1 *(adj)* using only natural products and no chemicals, pesticides, etc. *Organic farming.* **organically** *(adv)*.

2 *(adj)* to do with living things and their organs.

organism *(n)* a living plant or animal.

organization or **organisation**
1 *(n)* a large company, charity, or other group.
2 *(n)* the task of planning and running something. *We left the organization of the party to Jeffrey.*

organize or **organise** organizing organized
1 *(v)* to plan and run an event. **organizer** *(n)*.
2 *(v)* to arrange things neatly and in order. *Look how well Celia has organized the books on her shelves!*

orgy *(or-jee)* orgies *(n)* a wild party, with too much eating, drinking, etc.

oriental *(adj)* belonging to, or coming from the countries of the Far East, especially Japan and China. **Orient** *(n)*.

orienteering *(n)* a sport in which people have to find their way across rough country as fast as they can, using a map and compass.

origami *(n)* the Japanese art of paper folding. *This picture shows an example of origami.*

origami bird

origin *(n)* the point where something began. *What was the origin of this argument?*

original
1 *(adj)* first, or earliest. *Who were the original settlers in Australia?* **originally** *(adv)*.
2 *(adj)* new and imaginative. *What an original idea!* **originality** *(n)*.
3 *(n)* a work of art that is not a copy. **original** *(adj)*.

originate originating originated *(v)* to begin from somewhere or something. *This drawing originated from a doodle.* **origination** *(n)*.

ornament *(n)* a small, attractive object that you use to decorate a room. **ornamental** *(adj)*.

ornate *(adj)* richly decorated. **ornately** *(adv)*.

ornithology *(n)* the study of birds. **ornithologist** *(n)*.

orphan *(n)* a child whose parents are both dead. **orphaned** *(adj)*.

orphanage *(n)* a place where orphans live and are looked after.

orthodontist *(n)* someone who straightens uneven teeth.

orthodox
1 *(adj)* Orthodox views and beliefs are ones that are accepted by most people. **orthodoxy** *(n)*.
2 *(adj)* Members of a religion are described as **orthodox** if they believe in its older, more traditional teachings.

orthopaedic *(or-thoh-pee-dik) (adj)* to do with the branch of medicine that deals with bones.

osmosis *(oz-moh-sis) (n)* the process by which a solvent passes through a membrane from a less concentrated solution to a more concentrated solution, until they reach the same level of concentration.

ostrich ostriches *(n)* a large African bird that cannot fly. *See* **bird**.

other
1 *(adj)* not the one that you have just mentioned. **other** *(pronoun)*.
2 others *(pronoun)* the rest. *Where are the others?*

otherwise
1 *(conj)* or if not. *Catch a bus from the station. Otherwise, take a taxi.*
2 *(adv)* apart from that. *We didn't have very good seats, but otherwise the concert was excellent.*

otter *(n)* a furry mammal that lives near water and eats fish.

otter

ouch *(owtch) (interject)* a cry of pain.

ought *(ort) (v)* If you ought to do something, you should do it.

our *(pronoun)* belonging to us.

ourselves *(pronoun)* us and no one else.

oust *(owst)* ousting ousted *(v)* to force someone out of a position or job. *Hamish has been ousted as captain of the team.*

out
1 *(adv)* not in. *I called round but you were out.*
2 *(adv)* no longer burning, or no longer alight. *The fire went out.*
3 *(adv)* no longer taking part in a game. *You will be out if you get a question wrong.*
4 *(adv)* aloud. *Pandora called out for help.*
5 *(adv)* not correct. *My calculations were wildly out.*

Some words that begin with an "or" sound are spelt "au' or "aw".

170

outback *(n)* the remote areas of Australia, away from the cities.

outbreak *(n)* a sudden start of something, such as disease or war.

outburst *(n)* a sudden pouring out of strong emotion. *An outburst of anger.*

outcast *(n)* someone who is not accepted by other people.

outcome *(n)* the result of something. *The outcome of the vote is hard to predict.*

outcry outcries *(n)* If there is an outcry about something, a lot of people complain loudly about it.

outdo outdoes outdoing outdid outdone *(v)* If you **outdo** someone, you do something better than they do.

outdoors *(adv)* outside, or in the open air. outdoor *(adj)*.

outer
1 *(adj)* on the outside, or furthest from the middle. *The outer edge.*
2 **outer space** *(n)* space beyond the Earth's atmosphere.

outfit
1 *(n)* a set of clothes.
2 *(n)* *(informal)* a group, company, or organization. *A printing outfit.*

outgoing *(adj)* Someone who is outgoing is very sociable and friendly.

outgrow outgrowing outgrew outgrown *(v)* to grow too big or too old for something.

outing *(n)* a short trip somewhere for pleasure.

outlaw outlawing outlawed
1 *(n)* *(old-fashioned)* a criminal, especially in the Wild West.
2 *(v)* to forbid something by law.

outlay *(n)* money spent on something.

outlet
1 *(n)* a pipe or hole that lets out liquid or gas.
2 *(n)* a shop where a company's products can be bought.
3 *(n)* an activity that lets you express your feelings.

outline
1 *(n)* the line which shows the edge of something.
2 *(n)* the basic points or ideas about something. *Give me an outline of the film's plot.*

outlook
1 *(n)* your general attitude to things. *Yasmin has a very positive outlook.*
2 *(n)* the way that something is likely to develop. *The weather outlook.*

outnumber outnumbering outnumbered *(v)* to be larger in number than another group. *Girls outnumber boys on this course by four to one.*

outpatient *(n)* someone who goes to a hospital for treatment, but does not stay there.

outpost *(n)* a remote fort or settlement.

output
1 *(n)* the amount produced by a person, machine, or business.
2 *(n)* information produced by a computer. output *(v)*.

outrageous *(adj)* very shocking, or offensive. outrage *(n)*, outrageously *(adv)*.

outright
1 *(adj)* totally, or completely. *The outright winner.*
2 *(adv)* instantly. *Kirk was dismissed outright for stealing.*

outset *(n)* the start, or the beginning. *I knew from the outset that the show would be a success.*

outside
1 *(adv)* out of a building, or in the open air. outside *(prep)*.
2 *(n)* the surface of something or the part that surrounds the rest of it. *The outside of the box was painted pink.* outside *(adj)*.
3 **outside chance** *(n)* a very small chance.

outskirts *(plural n)* the outer edges of a town.

outspoken *(adj)* If you are outspoken, you express your views strongly and clearly, especially when you are criticizing someone.

outstanding
1 *(adj)* extremely good. *An outstanding performance.*
2 *(adj)* not yet paid, or not yet dealt with. *An outstanding bill.*

outward
1 *(adj)* appearing on the surface. *Philip's outward appearance was calm, but really he was very nervous.* outwardly *(adv)*.
2 *(adj)* going away from a place. *An outward journey.*
3 **outwards** *(adv)* towards the outside. *Stand facing outwards.*

outwit outwitting outwitted *(v)* to gain an advantage over someone by being cleverer than them.

oval *(n)* a shape like an egg. oval *(adj)*.

ovary ovaries *(n)* the female organ that produces eggs.

ovation *(n)* loud applause and cheering.

oven *(n)* a closed space where you cook food.

over
1 *(prep)* above, or on top of something. *The shelf over the bed.*
2 *(prep)* across. *Rachel stepped over the line.*
3 *(prep)* more than. *Over 12 years old.*
4 *(adv)* leaning, or falling down. *John fell over.*
5 *(adv)* finished. *The match was over in two hours.*
6 *(adv)* remaining. *I shared out the sweets, and still had three over.*
7 If you **get over** an illness or an experience, you recover from it and are no longer ill or upset.

overall *(adv)* generally, or considering everything. *Overall, I think the party was a success.* overall *(adj)*.

overalls
1 *(plural n)* a piece of clothing worn over your clothes to protect them when you are doing a dirty job.
2 *(plural n)* *(US)* loose trousers with shoulder straps and a panel covering the chest (dungarees, *UK*).

overarm *(adv)* throwing or hitting with your arm above your shoulder. *Rex served overarm.* overarm *(adj)*.

overbearing *(adj)* very dominating or bossy.

overboard *(adv)* over the side of a boat. *The pirate fell overboard.*

overcast *(adj)* An overcast sky has dark clouds.

overcome overcoming overcame overcome
1 *(v)* to defeat or deal with something, such as a feeling or problem. *I must overcome my fear of spiders.*
2 *(v)* If someone is **overcome** by smoke, emotion, guilt, etc. they are so strongly affected by it that they are made unconscious or helpless.

overdose *(n)* a quantity of a drug that is large enough to kill you or make you seriously ill.

overdraft *(n)* an amount of money that someone takes out of their bank when they do not have any money in their account. overdrawn *(adj)*.

overdue *(adj)* late. *My library books are overdue.*

overflow overflowing overflowed
1 *(v)* to flow over the edges of something. *The bath overflowed.*
2 *(n)* a pipe or hole through which water can flow out of a bath, sink, etc. when it becomes too full.

overgrown *(adj)* An overgrown garden is covered with weeds because it has not been looked after.

overhaul overhauling overhauled *(v)* to examine carefully all the parts of a piece of equipment and make any repairs that are needed. **overhaul** *(n)*.

overhead
1 *(adj)* above your head. *Overhead lighting.* **overhead** *(adv)*.
2 **overheads** *(plural n)* regular business costs, such as wages, rent, telephone bills, heating, and lighting.

overhear overhearing overheard *(v)* to hear what someone else is saying when they do not know that you are listening.

overjoyed *(adj)* If you are overjoyed, you are extremely happy.

overlap overlapping overlapped *(v)* to cover part of something else. *Arrange the roof tiles so that they overlap. Our holiday dates overlap.*

overleaf *(adv)* on the next page.

overload overloading overloaded
1 *(v)* to give something or someone too much to carry or too much work to do. **overload** *(n)*.
2 *(v)* to send too much electricity through something so that it breaks down. **overload** *(n)*.

overlook overlooking overlooked
1 *(v)* to fail to notice something. *Daisy overlooked the extra costs.*
2 *(v)* to be able to look down on something from a window or room. *Our room overlooked the beach.*
3 *(v)* to choose to ignore something wrong that someone has done. *I overlooked Jude's rude remarks.*

overly *(adv)* very, or excessively. *Oliver is always overly cautious.*

overnight
1 *(adv)* during the night. *We stayed overnight at a small hotel.* **overnight** *(adj)*.
2 *(adv)* suddenly. *Toby's fortunes changed overnight.*

overpass overpasses *(n)* (US) a bridge that carries one road over another (flyover, UK).

overpower overpowering overpowered
1 *(v)* to defeat someone, because you are stronger than they are.
2 *(v)* If something **overpowers** you, it affects you very strongly. *I was overpowered by the disgusting smell.*

overrated *(adj)* If you think that something is **overrated**, you think that it is not really as good as many people say it is.

overrule overruling overruled *(v)* If someone in authority **overrules** a decision, they say that the decision was wrong and has to be changed.

overrun overrunning overran overrun
1 *(v)* to spread all over a place in large numbers. *The town was overrun with rats.*
2 *(v)* If something **overruns**, it goes on for longer than it was meant to.

overseas *(adj)* to or from other countries. *Overseas visitors.* **overseas** *(adv)*.

oversleep oversleeping overslept *(v)* to sleep for longer than you intended.

overtake overtaking overtook overtaken *(v)* to go past another moving vehicle in order to get in front of it.

overthrow overthrowing overthrew overthrown *(v)* to defeat a leader or ruler and remove them from power by force. **overthrow** *(n)*.

overtime *(n)* time spent working beyond normal working hours.

overture *(n)* a piece of music played at the start of a musical, opera, or ballet.

overturn overturning overturned
1 *(v)* to turn something over so that it is upside down, or on its side.
2 *(v)* to reverse a decision that someone else has made.

overweight *(adj)* too fat, or too heavy.

overwhelm overwhelming overwhelmed
1 *(v)* to defeat someone completely.
2 *(v)* to have a very strong effect. *I was overwhelmed by the applause.* **overwhelming** *(adj)*.

overwork overworking overworked *(v)* to work too hard.

ovulation *(n)* the production of eggs from the ovaries.

owe owing owed
1 *(v)* to have to pay money to someone, especially money that you have borrowed.
2 *(v)* to have a duty to do something for someone in return for something that they have done for you. *I owe you a favour.*
3 *(v)* to be grateful to someone for giving you something. *My sister owes her life to the brave firemen.*
4 **owing to** because of. *The bus was late owing to roadworks.*

owl *(n)* a bird with large eyes, that hunts at night. *The tawny owl, shown below, is found throughout Europe.*

swivelling neck

tawny owl

forward-facing eye

hooked beak

talon

own owning owned
1 *(adj)* belonging to you. *My own pen.*
2 *(v)* to possess, or to have something. **owner** *(n)*.
3 *(v)* If you **own up** to something, you confess that you have done something wrong.
4 **on your own** alone and by yourself.

ox oxen *(n)* a large, horned mammal, often used for carrying things or for pulling carts.

oxygen *(n)* a colourless gas found in the air, that humans and animals need in order to breathe.

oxymoron *(n)* a short phrase in which the words seem to contradict each other, for example, "a wise fool".

oyster *(n)* a flat, edible shellfish that occasionally contains a pearl. See **pearl**.

ozone
1 *(n)* a form of oxygen that can be poisonous in large quantities.
2 **ozone layer** *(n)* a layer of ozone high above the Earth's surface that blocks out some of the Sun's harmful rays. *Recently, scientists have discovered a hole in the ozone layer above Antarctica, probably caused by the use of chemicals, such as CFCs. In this satellite picture, the hole in the ozone layer is coloured orange. Also see **atmosphere**.*

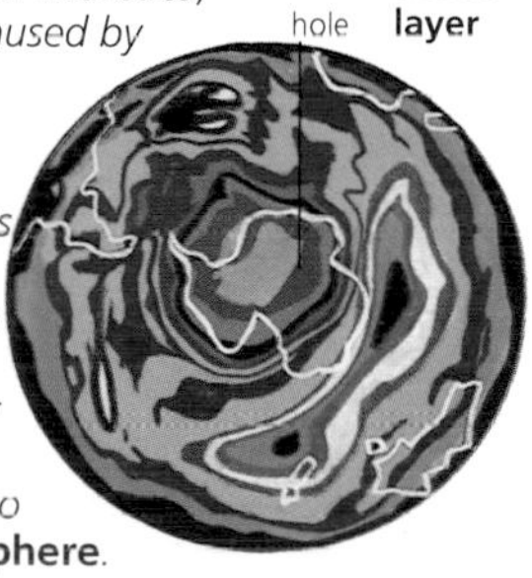

ozone layer

hole

Pp

pace pacing paced
1 *(n)* a step, or a stride.
2 *(n)* a rate of speed. *A rapid pace.*
3 *(v)* to walk backwards and forwards.
Archie paced up and down the hall.

pacemaker *(n)* a machine put into someone's body to help their heart beat more regularly.

pacifist *(n)* someone who strongly believes that war and violence are wrong, and who will not fight. pacifism *(n)*.

pacify pacifies pacifying pacified *(v)* If you **pacify** someone, you make them feel calmer.

pack packing packed
1 *(v)* to put objects into a box, case, bag, etc. packing *(n)*.
2 *(v)* to fill a space tightly. *A vast crowd packed the stadium.*
3 *(n)* a collection of objects. *A pack of cards.*
4 *(n)* a group of wild animals. *A pack of wolves.*
5 *(n)* a bundle, or a load.

package
1 *(n)* a parcel.
2 *(n)* a computer program that can do several related things. *A desktop publishing package.*
3 **package deal** *(n)* an offer which includes several things that must all be taken together.
4 **package holiday** *(n)* a holiday where the travel, hotel, etc. are included in the price and are arranged for you.

packaging *(n)* the wrapping on things that you buy.

packet *(n)* a small container or package. *A packet of seeds.*

pact *(n)* an agreement, often between two countries.

pad padding padded
1 *(n)* a wad of soft material, used to absorb liquid, give protection, etc. *See* **cricket**.
2 *(v)* to cover something with soft material.
3 *(v)* to walk around softly. *Barney padded along the corridor.*
4 *(n)* sheets of paper fastened together.

padding
1 *(n)* stuffing.
2 *(n)* extra words put into a speech or piece of writing to make it longer.

paddle paddling paddled
1 *(v)* to walk in shallow water.
2 *(n)* a short, wide oar, used to propel some boats. paddle *(v)*.
See **inflatable, kayak.**

paddle steamer *(n)* a boat which is propelled by large, revolving paddle wheels that are powered by a steam engine.

paddle steamer

paddock *(n)* a small field where horses can be kept.

paddy field *(n)* a wet field where rice is grown.

paddy field

padlock *(n)* a lock with a curved metal bar that you can fix on to things.

paediatrician *(pee-dee-a-trish-un)* *(n)* a doctor who is trained to treat children's illnesses. paediatrics *(n)*.

paedophile *(pee-doh-file)* *(n)* an adult who is sexually attracted to children. paedophilia *(n)*

page
1 *(n)* a sheet of paper in a book, newspaper, etc.
2 *(n)* In the past, **pages** were young, boy servants. Nowadays, a page is a boy attendant at a wedding.

pageant *(paj-ent)* *(n)* a public show where people walk in processions or act out historical scenes. pageantry *(n)*.

pager *(n)* a small, electronic machine that people such as doctors carry, so that they can be contacted easily.

pail *(n)* a bucket.

pain
1 *(n)* a feeling of physical hurt or of great unhappiness.
2 **pains** *(plural n)* effort, or trouble. *Grant took great pains over his essay.*

painful *(adj)* If something is **painful**, it hurts you physically or makes you very unhappy. painfully *(adv)*.

painkiller *(n)* a pill or medicine that you take to stop pain.

painstaking *(adj)* careful and thorough. painstakingly *(adv)*.

paint painting painted
1 *(n)* a liquid that you use to colour surfaces.
2 *(v)* to use paint to make a picture or cover a surface. painter *(n)*, painting *(n)*.

pair *(n)* two things that match or go together. pair *(v)*.

palace *(n)* a large, splendid house or building. palatial *(adj)*.

palate
1 *(n)* the roof of your mouth.
2 *(n)* a person's sense of taste.

pale paler palest *(adj)* light or whitish in colour. paleness *(n)*.

palette
1 *(n)* a flat board that you use to mix paints on, with a hole for your thumb. *See* **artist**.
2 **palette knife** *(n)* a thin, rounded, flexible knife, used for painting or cooking. *See* **artist**.

palindrome *(n)* a word or sentence that reads the same backwards as forwards. *The names Hannah, Bob and Otto are palindromes.*

pallid *(adj)* If you are **pallid**, you have a pale face or skin.

palm
1 *(n)* the flat surface on the inside of your hand.
2 *(n)* a tall, tropical tree with large leaves at the top.

palmistry *(n)* the practice of telling people's fortunes from the lines on their palms. palmist *(n)*.

palmtop *(n)* a computer that is small enough to be held in one hand. Another name for a palmtop is a hand-held.

pampas
1 *(n)* a huge, treeless plain in South America.
2 **pampas grass** *(n)* a type of tall, feathery grass.

pamper pampering pampered *(v)* to spoil yourself or someone else with food, kindness, etc.

pamphlet *(n)* a small, thin booklet.

pan panning panned
1 *(n)* a round, metal container, used for cooking.
2 *(v)* to look for gold by washing earth in a pan or sieve.
3 *(v)* to move a camera, in order to follow an action. *The cameraman panned in on the speeding car.*

pancake *(n)* a thin, flat cake, made from batter and fried in a pan.

pancreas *(n)* a gland near your stomach which makes a fluid that helps you to digest food. *See* **digestion**.

panda *(n)* an animal like a bear that lives in China. *The picture shows a giant panda eating a bamboo shoot.*

giant panda

pane *(n)* a sheet of glass in a window or door.

panel
1 *(n)* a flat piece of wood or other material. **panelling** *(n)*.
2 *(n)* a board with controls or instruments on it.
3 *(n)* a group of people chosen to do something, such as judge a competition. **panellist** *(n)*.

pang *(n)* a brief pain or feeling of emotion. *A pang of regret.*

panic
1 *(n)* a feeling of terror or fright. **panic** *(v)*, **panicky** *(adj)*.
2 If you are **panic-stricken**, you are struck with a sudden fear.

pannier
1 *(n)* a basket hung on an animal, such as a donkey.
2 *(n)* a bag hung beside the rear wheel of a bicycle.

panorama *(n)* a wide view of an area. **panoramic** *(adj)*.

pansy **pansies** *(n)* a small garden flower, usually coloured purple, yellow, or white.

pant **panting** **panted** *(v)* to breathe quickly and loudly because you are out of breath.

panther *(n)* a leopard, especially the black leopard.

pantomime *(n)* a traditional Christmas play, based on a fairy tale, with songs and jokes.

pantry **pantries** *(n)* a small room in or near a kitchen, where food or crockery is kept.

pants
1 *(plural n)* underwear that covers your bottom.
2 *(plural n)* *(US)* a piece of clothing with two legs that covers the lower part of your body (trousers, *UK*).

panty-hose *(plural n)* *(US)* a close-fitting garment that covers the hips, legs, and feet (tights, *UK*).

paper **papering** **papered**
1 *(n)* thin material usually made from wood pulp.
2 *(n)* a newspaper.
3 *(n)* part of an exam.
4 *(v)* to put wallpaper up, or cover something with paper.

paperback *(n)* a book with a paper cover.

paperweight *(n)* a heavy, often decorative object, used for holding down papers.

paperwork *(n)* writing, such as reports, that is part of someone's job.

papier mâché *(pap-ee-ay mash-ay)* *(n)* the art of making models, pots, etc. out of pieces of paper that have been soaked in glue.

papyrus *(pa-pye-russ)* **papyri** *(n)* paper made from the papyrus plant, which grew in ancient Egypt.

parable *(n)* a fable or story that has a moral or religious lesson.

parachute *(pa-ra-shoot)* *(n)* a large piece of cloth fastened to thin ropes, that is used to drop people or loads safely from aeroplanes. **parachutist** *(n)*, **parachute** *(v)*.

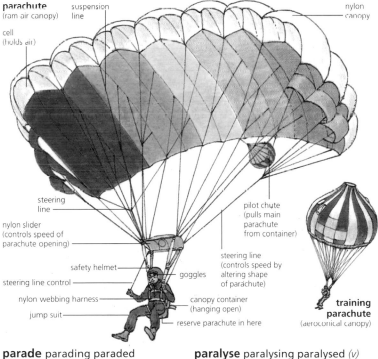

parachute (ram air canopy)
suspension line
cell (holds air)
nylon canopy
steering line
nylon slider (controls speed of parachute opening)
pilot chute (pulls main parachute from container)
safety helmet
goggles
steering line (controls speed by altering shape of parachute)
steering line control
nylon webbing harness
canopy container (hanging open)
jump suit
reserve parachute in here
training parachute (aeroconical canopy)

parade **parading** **paraded**
1 *(n)* a procession of people, decorated trucks, and musicians.
2 *(v)* If you **parade** something, you show it off.
3 *(n)* a row of shops.

paradise *(n)* a wonderful place, or heaven.

paradox **paradoxes** *(n)* an idea which seems to contradict itself, but which is true. **paradoxical** *(adj)*.

paraffin *(n)* a liquid that is burnt to give light or heat in a lamp or stove.

paragliding *(n)* the sport of cross-country parachuting, using a special parachute shaped like flexible wings. **paraglider** *(n)*, **paraglide** *(v)*.

paragraph *(n)* a short passage in a piece of writing which begins on a new line.

parallel
1 *(adj)* If two lines are **parallel**, they stay the same distance from each other.
2 *(n)* If a situation has a **parallel**, there is another situation very similar to it. **parallel** *(v)*.
3 If electrical parts are connected in **parallel**, each one can receive power even when the others are not being used.

parallelogram *(n)* a flat, four-sided shape with opposite sides that are equal and parallel. *See* **shape**.

paralyse **paralysing** **paralysed** *(v)* to make someone or something lose power, feeling, or movement. **paralysis** *(n)*.

paraphernalia *(n)* numerous pieces of equipment, belongings, etc.

paraphrase paraphrasing
paraphrased (v) If you **paraphrase**
speech or writing, you say or write it
again in a different way to make it
clearer. **paraphrase** (n).

paraplegic (pa-ra-plee-jik) (n)
someone who has no feeling or
movement in the lower part of their
body. **paraplegic** (adj).

parasite
1 (n) an animal or plant that gets its
food by living on or inside another
animal or plant. *Leeches are parasites
that use suckers to attach themselves
to people or animals, and then feed
on their blood.* **parasitic** (adj).
2 (n) someone who lives on other
people's money without doing
anything to earn it.

leech

sucker
under
here

muscular body
(contracts and expands
to make leech move)

parasol (n) a type of umbrella that
shades you from the sun.

paratroops (plural n) soldiers who
are carried by aeroplane and dropped
by parachute. **paratrooper** (n).

parcel (n) a package, or something
wrapped up in paper. **parcel** (v).

parched (adj) very dry or thirsty.

parchment
1 (n) heavy, paper-like material,
made from the skin of sheep or
goats, and used for writing on.
2 (n) very good quality
writing paper.

pardon pardoning
pardoned
1 (v) to forgive or excuse
someone, or to release
them from punishment.
2 (interject) You say **pardon** as a
polite way of asking someone to
repeat what they have said.
3 (interject) You say **pardon** after you
have done something rude, such as
burping, as a way of saying sorry.

parent (n) a mother or father.
parenthood (n), **parental** (adj).

parenthesis parentheses
1 (n) an extra phrase or explanation in
brackets.
2 (n) one of a pair of round brackets
( ) used to mark off an extra phrase or
explanation.

parish parishes
1 (n) an area that has its own church.
2 **parish council** (n) a group of
people who look after village affairs.

parishioner (n) someone who lives
in a parish.

park parking parked
1 (n) a large garden, or a piece of
ground for public use.
2 (v) to leave a car in a parking place
or on the side of a street.

parking meter (n) a machine that
you put money into, in order to pay
for parking on the street.

parliament (n) the group of people
who have been elected to make the
laws of a country.
parliamentary (adj).

parody parodies (n) a funny
imitation of a piece of writing, song,
speech, etc. **parody** (v).

parole (n) the early release of a
prisoner on condition that they
behave well. **parole** (v).

paroxysm (par-ox-ism) (n) a sudden
violent fit of something. *A paroxysm
of laughter. A paroxysm of pain.*

parrot
1 (n) a tropical bird with a curved beak
and brightly coloured feathers. Parrots
can learn to repeat
things that are said
to them. *The
parrot shown here
comes from the
South American
rainforest.*
2 (n) someone who
repeats or imitates
words without
understanding what
they mean. **parrot** (v).

**scarlet
macaw**

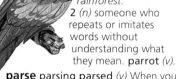

parse parsing parsed (v) When you
parse a sentence, you identify its
subject and object, and, sometimes,
the parts of speech of its words.

parsnip (n) a pale yellow root
vegetable. *See* **vegetable**.

parson (n) a priest, or a vicar.
parsonage (n).

part parting parted
1 (n) a portion, or a piece.
2 (n) a character or role in a play or
film. *Nat played the part of Hamlet.*
3 (v) to separate, or to divide. *We
parted at the crossroads.*
4 (v) If you **part with** something, you
give it away.

part exchange (n) If you buy
something by **part exchange**, you
give something you own as part of the
payment. **part exchange** (v).

partial (par-shal)
1 (adj) Someone who is **partial**
favours one person or side more than
another. **partiality** (n).

2 (adj) not complete. *The holiday was
only a partial success.* **partially** (adv).
3 If you are **partial to** a particular
food or drink, you are especially fond
of it. **partiality** (n).

participate participating
participated (v) to join in or share in
an activity or event. **participant** (n),
participation (n).

participle (n) a form of a verb. The
English language has two participles,
the present, for example, "playing",
and the past, for example, "played".
Participles can sometimes be used as
adjectives, for example, "shining",
"crumpled", "swollen".

particle
1 (n) an extremely small thing or part
of something.
2 **particle physics** (singular n)
the study of the behaviour of the
minute parts of atoms.

particular
1 (adj) individual, or special. *I want
this particular painting.*
2 (adj) Someone who is **particular** is
very fussy about small things.
3 (n) a fact, or a detail. *Please send me
some particulars about the course.*
4 **in particular** especially. *All the rides
are fun, but there's one in particular
that you must try.* **particularly** (adv).

parting
1 (n) a line in your hair where it is
combed in two directions.
2 (n) a separation. *An emotional
parting.*

partly (adv) not completely.

partner
1 (n) one of two or more people who
do something together. *Business
partners. Dancing partners.*
partnership (n).
2 (n) a husband, wife, or permanent
companion.

part of speech parts of speech (n)
a term, such as noun, verb, adjective,
etc., that describes a word's type and
function. *See page 3.*

part-time (adj) If you have a
part-time job, you work for a few
hours or a few days each week.
part-timer (n), **part time** (adv).

party parties
1 (n) an organized occasion with
music, games, entertainment, etc.
when people enjoy themselves in a
group. **party** (v).
2 (n) a group of people working
together. *A search party.*
3 (n) an organized group of people
with similar political beliefs, who try to
win elections. *The Green Party.*

pass passes passing passed
1 *(v)* to go past someone or something. *Pass the park and then turn left.*
2 *(v)* to give something to somebody. *Pass the salt, please.*
3 *(v)* to kick, throw, or hit a ball to someone in your team in a sport or game. pass *(n).*
4 *(v)* to succeed in a test or exam. pass *(n).*
5 *(n)* a crossing-place over a mountain.
6 **pass away** *(v)* to die.
7 **pass out** *(v)* to faint.

passage
1 *(n)* a corridor.
2 *(n)* a short section in a book or piece of music.
3 *(n)* a journey by ship or aeroplane.

passenger *(n)* someone who travels in a car or other vehicle and is not the driver.

passer-by passers-by *(n)* someone who happens to be going past.

passion *(n)* a very strong feeling of anger, love, hatred, etc.

passionate *(adj)* If you are passionate about something or someone, you have strong feelings about them. **passionately** *(adv).*

passive
1 *(adj)* If you are passive, you let things happen to you and do not react when you are attacked. **passively** *(adv).*
2 *(adj)* A passive verb is one where the verb's subject has something done to it rather than doing the action itself. *In the sentence, "The ball was kicked", the verb is passive, but in "I kicked the ball", the verb is active.*
3 **passive smoking** *(n)* the breathing in of smoke from other people's cigarettes.

Passover *(n)* an important Jewish festival in the spring, in memory of the way that God rescued the Israelites from slavery in Egypt.

passport *(n)* an official booklet which proves who you are, and allows you to travel abroad.

password *(n)* a secret word that you need to know to get into a building or computer system.

past
1 *(n)* the period of time before the present. past *(adj).*
2 *(adj)* finished, or ended.
3 *(adj)* previous. *I've drawn on my past experience in my new job.*
4 *(prep)* by, after, or beyond. past *(adv).*

5 *(n)* The **past participle** is the form of a verb used to show that something happened before the present. For example, "bought" is the past participle of "buy" and "played" is the past participle of "play".

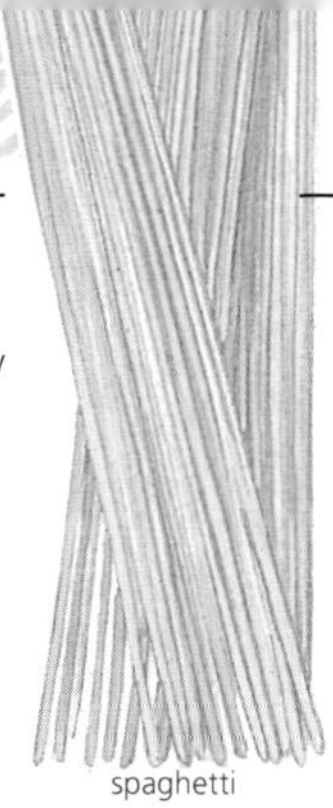

pasta *(n)* a food made from flour, eggs, and water, that is made into shapes. *The picture shows a selection of different types of pasta.*

pasta

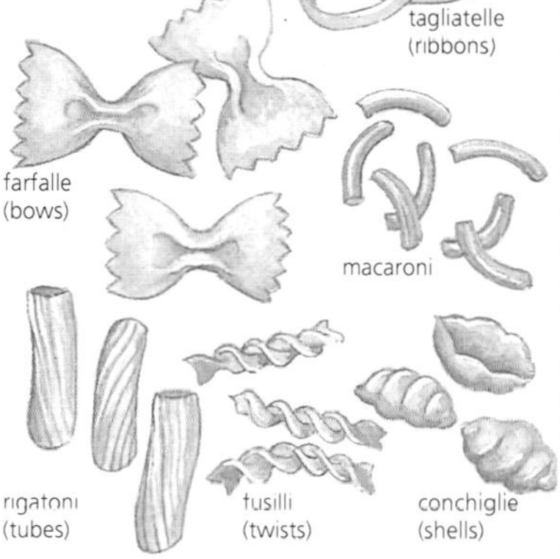

spaghetti

tagliatelle
(ribbons)

farfalle
(bows)

macaroni

rigatoni
(tubes)

fusilli
(twists)

conchiglie
(shells)

paste pasting pasted
1 *(n)* a soft, sticky mixture that you can spread. *Wallpaper paste. Fish paste.*
2 *(v)* to stick with glue.

pastel
1 *(n)* a chalky crayon.
2 *(adj)* soft and light in colour.

pasteurized *or* **pasteurised** *(adj)* Milk that is pasteurized has been boiled to kill bacteria. **pasteurize** *(v).*

pastor *(n)* a church minister or priest in charge of a congregation.

pastoral
1 *(adj)* to do with the countryside.
2 *(adj)* **Pastoral** care is help with religious or personal matters.

pastry pastries
1 *(n)* a dough that is rolled out and used for pies.
2 *(n)* a small cake made from pastry.

pasture *(n)* grazing land for animals.

pasty pasties; pastier pastiest
1 *(pas-tee) (n)* a small pie, usually filled with meat and vegetables.
2 *(pay-stee) (adj)* If you look pasty, you have a white or dull complexion.

pat patting patted
1 *(v)* to tap or stroke something gently with your hand. *Candida patted the baby donkey.* pat *(n).*
2 If you give someone a **pat on the back**, you praise them and say that they have done well.

patch patches patching patched
1 *(v)* to put a piece of material on something in order to mend it. patch *(n).*
2 *(n)* a small, odd-shaped part of something, such as an area of white fur on a black dog.
3 *(n)* a piece of ground. *A vegetable patch.*
4 *(n)* a short period of time. *Raisa is going through a bad patch.*

patchwork *(n)* patterned fabric, made by sewing small patches of different material together.

patchy patchier patchiest *(adj)* uneven. *Patchy fog made the road dangerous.*

pâté *(pa-tay) (n)* a soft paste, usually made of meat or fish, that is spread on toast, crackers, etc.

patent patenting patented
1 *(v)* If you invent something, you can patent it to stop other people copying your idea. patent *(n).*
2 *(adj)* obvious, or open. *Leo told a patent lie.* **patently** *(adv).*
3 **patent leather** *(n)* very shiny leather used for shoes.

paternal *(adj)* to do with being a father. **paternally** *(adv).*

path *(n)* a track, or a route. **pathway** *(n).*

pathetic *(adj)* feeble, or useless. **pathetically** *(adv).*

patience
1 *(n)* If you have patience, you can put up with difficult things and are able to wait calmly.
2 *(n)* a card game for one player.

patient
1 *(adj)* If you are patient, you are good at putting up with things and can wait calmly. **patiently** *(adv).*
2 *(n)* someone who is receiving medical treatment.

patio
1 *(n)* a paved area next to a house, used for sitting outside.
2 **patio doors** glass doors which open out on to a patio.

patisserie *(n)* a shop where you can buy cakes and pastries.

patriot *(n)* someone who loves their country and is prepared to fight for it. **patriotism** *(n),* **patriotic** *(adj).*

patrol patrolling patrolled
1 (v) to walk or travel around an area in order to protect it or to keep watch on people. *Police are patrolling the neighbourhood carefully.*
2 (n) a group of soldiers, ships, etc. that protect and watch an area.

patron (pay-tron)
1 (n) a customer of a shop, or someone who supports a theatre, artist, writer, etc. patronage (pat-ron-ij) (n).
2 patron saint (n) a saint who is believed to look after a particular country or group of people.

patronize or **patronise** patronizing patronized
1 (v) to talk down to someone or act as though you are better than them.
2 (v) If you **patronize** a shop, restaurant, etc. you go there regularly.

patter pattering pattered
1 (v) to make light, quick, patting sounds. *The rain pattered on my umbrella.* patter (n).
2 (n) fast talk. *A magician's patter.*

pattern
1 (n) an arrangement of colours, shapes, etc. on paper or material.
2 (n) a model that you can copy from. *A dress pattern.*
3 (n) If things follow a **pattern**, they happen in a similar way.

pause pausing paused (v) to stop for a short time. pause (n).

pavement
1 (n) a raised path beside a street.
2 (n) (US) a paved street or road.

pavilion (n) a building at a sports ground where players can get changed, rest, wash, eat, etc.

paw (n) the foot of an animal, such as a dog or cat.

pawn pawning pawned
1 (v) to leave a valuable item at a shop called a pawnbroker's, in return for money. The item is returned to you if you repay your debt, or is sold if you fail to do so.
2 (n) the smallest piece on a chessboard. *See* **chess**.

pay paying paid
1 (v) to give money for something. payment (n).
2 (v) to be worthwhile, or to be advantageous. *It pays to be polite.*
3 (v) to give or offer something. *Hattie paid me a compliment.*
4 (v) to suffer. *Ed paid for his mistake.*
5 (n) wages, or salary.

PC
1 (n) the initials for personal computer.

2 (n) the initials for police constable.
3 (adj) (informal) Someone who is **PC** makes a great effort not to offend minority groups, women, etc. The initials PC stand for politically correct.

PE (n) a lesson at school in which you do sports, gymnastics, etc. The initials PE stand for physical education.

pea (n) a small, green vegetable which grows in a pod. *See* **vegetable**.

peace
1 (n) calm and quiet. peaceful (adj), peacefully (adv).
2 (n) a period without war. peacetime (n).

peach peaches (n) a soft fruit with a furry skin and a stone at its centre. *See* **fruit**.

peacock (n) a large, blue and green bird with long tail-feathers.

peacock

peak
1 (n) the top of something, such as a mountain.
2 (n) the highest or best point. *Carlton reached the peak of his career when he won the gold medal.* peak (v).
3 (n) the curved, front part of a cap.

peal pealing pealed (v) When bells **peal**, they ring.

pear (n) a juicy fruit that gets narrower towards its stalk. *See* **fruit**.

pearl (n) a small, round, whitish object that grows inside oysters and other shellfish and is used to make jewellery.

oyster

mother-of-pearl lining   pearl   oyster shell

peasant
1 (n) someone who works on a small piece of land.
2 (n) In medieval times, **peasants** were agricultural labourers who worked for their local lord.

peat (n) dark brown, partly decayed vegetable matter that can be used as fuel or compost.

pebble (n) a small, round stone. pebbly (adj).

peck pecking pecked
1 (v) When a bird **pecks** at something, it strikes it or picks it up with its beak.
2 (n) (informal) a quick kiss. *Aunt Doris gave me a peck on the cheek.* peck (v).

peckish (adj) (informal) hungry.

peculiar
1 (adj) strange, or odd. peculiarly (adv).
2 peculiar to belonging to, or exclusive to. *Koalas are peculiar to Australia.* peculiarity (n), peculiarly (adv).

pedal pedalling pedalled
1 (n) a lever on a bicycle, car, piano, etc. that you push with your foot.
2 (v) to make something work or move by using a pedal or pedals.

peddle peddling peddled (v) to travel around selling things, especially drugs. peddler (n).

pedestal (n) a base for a statue.

pedestrian
1 (n) someone who travels on foot.
2 pedestrian crossing (n) a place for people to cross the road safely.
3 pedestrian precinct (n) a shopping area which cars are not allowed to enter.

pedlar (n) (old-fashioned) In the past, pedlars travelled around selling things. *See* **castle**.

peel peeling peeled
1 (n) the tough outer skin of a fruit.
2 (v) to remove the peel of a fruit.
3 (v) to come off. *I got so sunburnt that the skin on my back peeled.*

peep peeping peeped (v) to glance or look secretly at something. peep (n).

peer peering peered
1 (v) to look hard at something which is difficult to see.
2 (n) a nobleman. peerage (n).
3 (plural n) Your **peers** are people of similar age and type to you.

peg (n) a thin piece of wood, metal, or plastic, used to hold things down or hang things up. peg (v).

pelican (n) a large water bird with a pouch below its beak where it holds the fish that it catches.

pelican

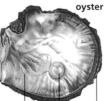

pellet
1 (n) a small, rounded piece of something, such as food or screwed-up paper.
2 (n) a small lead ball fired from a gun.
3 (n) Many birds make **pellets**, which are parcels of things that they cannot digest. Pellets are made in the bird's stomach and then regurgitated, or coughed up.

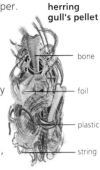

herring gull's pellet — bone — foil — plastic — string

pelt pelting pelted
1 (v) to throw something very hard.
2 (v) to rain very hard. It's pelting down outside.
3 (n) an animal's skin or fur.

pen penning penned
1 (n) an instrument used for writing with ink.
2 (n) a small, fenced area for sheep, cattle, etc.
3 (v) (old-fashioned) to write.

penalize or penalise penalizing penalized (v) to make someone suffer a punishment for something that they have done wrong.

penalty penalties
1 (n) a punishment.
2 (n) an advantage won in a game when the opposing side breaks a rule.

pence (n) Pence is a plural of penny. This costs 50 pence.

pencil (n) an instrument used for drawing and writing, made from a stick of graphite in a wood casing.

pendant (n) a piece of jewellery that hangs on a chain around the neck.

pendulum (n) a weight in some clocks which moves from side to side and helps to keep the clock ticking regularly.

penetrate penetrating penetrated (v) to go inside something or through something. The nail penetrated Nick's shoe. penetration (n).

pen friend (n) someone, usually from abroad, who exchanges letters with you.

penguin (n) a seabird of the Antarctic region that cannot fly, and which uses its wings as flippers for underwater swimming. See polar.

penicillin (n) a drug that kills bacteria and helps to fight some diseases.

peninsula (n) a piece of land that sticks out into the sea, and is surrounded on three sides by water. The map shows the North American state of Florida, which is a peninsula. peninsular (adj).

Florida

peninsula

penis penises (n) the male organ used for urinating and sexual intercourse.

penitent (adj) extremely sorry. penitence (n).

penknife penknives (n) a small knife with blades that fold into a case. This penknife is a Swiss army knife.

penknife — large blade — wood saw — scissors — can-opener — small blade — bottle opener — reamer (pierces holes) — corkscrew — case — wire stripper — screwdriver

pen name (n) a public name used by a writer.

penniless (adj) If you are **penniless**, you have absolutely no money.

penny pennies or pence (n) the smallest unit of money in Britain.

pension (n) an amount of money paid regularly to someone who has retired from work. pensioner (n).

pentagon (n) a five-sided shape. pentagonal (adj). See shape.

penultimate (adj) next to last. "This" is the penultimate word in this sentence.

people (plural n) human beings.

pepper
1 (n) a spicy powder used to flavour food. peppery (adj).
2 (n) a hollow vegetable, usually red, green, or yellow. See vegetable.

peppermint
1 (n) a herb often used in flavouring.
2 (n) a peppermint-flavoured sweet.

per
1 (prep) in each, or for each. There's enough for three sweets per person.
2 per annum (adv) each year.
3 per capita (adj) for each person.
4 per cent (n) one in every hundred. Ten per cent of a hundred is ten.

perceive perceiving perceived (v) to notice something, or to understand a situation.

percentage (n) a fraction or proportion of something, expressed as a number out of a hundred. The symbol for percentage is %.

perceptive (adj) If you are perceptive, you are quick to notice things or understand situations.

perch perches perching perched
1 (n) a place where a bird stands.
2 (v) to sit or stand on the edge of something, often high up.
3 (n) an edible, freshwater fish. See fish.

percussion (n) musical instruments which are played by being hit or shaken. The picture shows some small percussion instruments. percussionist (n).

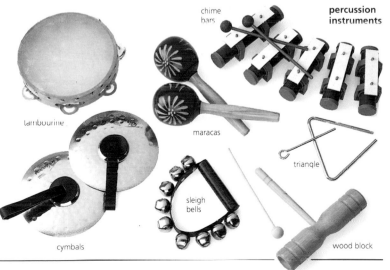

percussion instruments — chime bars — tambourine — maracas — triangle — sleigh bells — cymbals — wood block

perennial
1 (n) a flower which blooms every year.
2 (adj) happening repeatedly. *A perennial problem.* **perennially** (adv).

perfect perfecting perfected
1 (*pur-fect*) (adj) without any faults. **perfection** (n), **perfectly** (adv).
2 (*pur-fect*) (v) to succeed, with effort, in making something work well. *After much practice, Callum perfected his juggling act.*

perforated (adj) Perforated paper has many small holes punched in it, usually so that a section can be torn off easily. **perforation** (n).

perform performing performed
1 (v) to do something, or to carry something out.
2 (v) to give a show in public.

performance (n) the public acting of a play, showing of a film, etc.

perfume (n) a liquid put on your skin to make you smell pleasant.

perhaps (adv) possibly.

peril (n) serious danger. **perilous** (adj), **perilously** (adv).

perimeter
1 (n) the outside edge of an area.
2 (n) the distance around the edge of a shape or an area.

period
1 (n) a length of time. *Ewan left the room for a short period.*
2 (n) the monthly flow of blood from the womb of a girl or woman.
3 (n) (US) the punctuation mark (.) used to show that a sentence has ended or that a word has been abbreviated (full stop, UK).

periodical
1 (adj) happening at intervals. **periodically** (adv).
2 (n) a journal or magazine that is published regularly.

periphery peripheries (n) the outside edge of something.

periscope (n)
a vertical tube with prisms at each end that allows you to see something from a position a long way below it. Periscopes are used in submarines. *The diagram shows how a periscope works.*

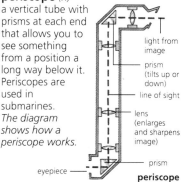

light from image

prism (tilts up or down)

line of sight

lens (enlarges and sharpens image)

prism

eyepiece

periscope

perish perishes perishing perished
1 (v) to die.
2 (v) If a substance, such as food or rubber, **perishes**, it becomes rotten.

perk perking perked
1 (n) (informal) an extra advantage that comes from doing a particular job. *One of the perks of working in this café is the free food.*
2 (v) If you **perk up**, you become more cheerful. **perky** (adj).

perm (n) a process in which hair is treated with chemicals to give it curls or waves which last for several months. Perm is short for permanent wave.

permanent (adj) lasting for a long time or for ever. **permanence** (n), **permanently** (adv).

permeate permeating permeated (v) to spread or pass through something. *A delicious smell permeated the house.*

permissible (adj) If something is permissible, it is allowed.

permission (n) If you give permission for something, you say that it can happen.

permissive (adj) Someone who is permissive is very tolerant and allows freedom where others would not. **permissiveness** (n).

permit permitting permitted
1 (*pur-mit*) (v) to allow something.
2 (*pur-mit*) (n) a written statement giving permission for something.

permutation (n) one of the ways in which a series of things can be arranged or put in order. *There are six permutations of the numbers 1, 2, and 3: 123, 132, 213, 231, 312, and 321.*

perpendicular (n) a line at right angles to another line, or vertical to the ground. **perpendicular** (adj).

perpetual (adj) never-ending, or unchanging. **perpetually** (adv).

perplex perplexes perplexing perplexed (v) to make someone puzzled and slightly worried. **perplexity** (n), **perplexed** (adj).

persecute persecuting persecuted (v) to treat someone cruelly and unfairly because you are prejudiced against them. **persecution** (n).

persevere persevering persevered (v) If you **persevere** at something, you keep on trying and do not give up. **perseverance** (n).

persist persisting persisted (v) to keep on doing something. **persistence** (n), **persistent** (adj).

person
1 (n) an individual human being.
2 If you do something **in person**, you do it yourself.
3 In grammar, the **first person** refers to "I" or "we"; the **second person** refers to "you"; the **third person** refers to "he", "she", "it", or "they"

personal (adj) to do with one person only. *This letter is personal and private.* **personally** (adv).

personal computer (n) a small computer that can stand on a desk or table and can be used at home.

personality personalities
1 (n) the type of character that someone has. *Fiona has a very outgoing personality.*
2 (n) a famous person. *A show business personality.*

personal stereo (n) a small cassette or disc player with headphones, that you can carry around.

perspective
1 (n) a particular way of looking at a situation. *I enjoyed the trip, but from Guy's perspective, it was a disaster.*
2 If a picture is **in perspective**, distant objects are drawn smaller than nearer ones so that the view looks exactly as someone would see it.

perspire perspiring perspired (v) to sweat. **perspiration** (n).

persuade persuading persuaded (v) to make someone do something, by telling them reasons why they should do it. **persuasion** (n), **persuasive** (adj).

perturb perturbing perturbed (v) to worry or confuse somebody. *Harry's questions perturbed me.*

perverse (adj) deliberately unreasonable and stubborn. **perversity** (n).

pervert (*per-vert*) (n) someone who behaves in an unacceptable, disgusting, or harmful way, particularly in sexual matters. **perverted** (*per-ver-ted*) (adj).

peseta (*per-say-ter*) (n) the main unit of money in Spain.

pessimistic (adj) People who are pessimistic are gloomy and always think that the worst will happen. **pessimism** (n), **pessimist** (n), **pessimistically** (adv).

pest
1 (n) an insect that destroys or damages flowers, fruit, or vegetables.
2 (n) any creature that causes serious interference to human activity.
3 (n) a persistently annoying person.

pester pestering pestered *(v)* to keep annoying other people, often by asking or telling them something again and again.

pesticide *(n)* a chemical used to kill pests, usually insects.

pestle *(pess-ul) (n)* a short stick with a thick, rounded end, used to crush things in a bowl called a mortar.

pet petting petted
1 *(n)* a tame animal kept for company or pleasure.
2 *(n)* somebody's favourite person or thing. *Teacher's pet.*
3 *(v) (US)* to stroke or pat an animal in a gentle, loving way.

petal *(n)* one of the coloured, outer parts of a flower head. See **flower**.

petition *(n)* a letter, signed by many people, asking those in power to change their policy or actions.

petrified *(adj)* If you are **petrified**, you are unable to move because you are so frightened.

petrol *(n)* a liquid fuel used in many vehicles.

petticoat *(n)* a thin garment worn underneath a skirt or dress. See **underclothes**.

petty pettier pettiest *(adj)* trivial and unimportant. *Petty criticisms*

pH *(n)* a measure of how acidic or alkaline a substance is. The initials pH stand for potential of hydrogen. *Acids have pH values under seven and alkalis have pH values over seven.*

phantom *(n)* a ghost.

Pharaoh *(fair-oh) (n)* one of the kings of ancient Egypt.

Pharaoh

pharmacist *(n)* a trained person who prepares and sells drugs and medicines. **pharmacy** *(n)*.

phase phasing phased
1 *(n)* a stage in someone or something's growth or development. *Bertie is going through a quarrelsome phase.*
2 phase in *(v)* to start something gradually.
3 phase out *(v)* to stop something gradually.

pheasant
(fez-ant) (n)
a large bird with a long tail that is shot for sport and for food.

pheasant

phenomenal *(fin-om-in-al) (adj)* amazing, or astonishing. *The group's first album was a phenomenal sucess.* **phenomenally** *(adv)*.

phenomenon *(fin-om-in-on)* **phenomena** *(n)* something very unusual and remarkable.

philosophical *(fil-oss-off-ik-al)*
1 *(adj)* to do with philosophy.
2 *(adj)* If you are **philosophical**, you accept difficulties and problems calmly. **philosophically** *(adv)*.

philosophy *(fil-oss-off-ee)*
1 *(n)* the study of ideas about human life. **philosopher** *(n)*.
2 *(n)* A person's **philosophy** is their set of basic ideas and beliefs on how life should be lived.

phlegm *(flem) (n)* the thick substance that you cough up when you have a cold.

phobia *(n)* an overpowering fear of something. **phobic** *(adj)*.

phone short for **telephone**.

phonetically *(adv)* If something is spelt **phonetically**, it is spelt using special symbols to represent sounds.

phonetics *(singular n)* the study of the sounds used in speaking.

photo short for **photograph**.

photocopier *(n)* a machine that copies documents instantly.

photocopy photocopies *(n)* a copy of a document made by a photocopier. **photocopy** *(v)*.

photo finish photo finishes *(n)* a very close end to a race, where a photograph has to be studied to decide who has won.

photofit *(n)* a portrait made by the police to trace someone suspected of a crime. The photofit is put together from features which a witness thinks are most like those of the suspect.

photogenic *(foh-toh-jen-ik) (adj)* If someone is **photogenic**, they look very good in photographs. **photogenically** *(adv)*.

photograph *(n)* a picture taken by a camera on film and then developed on paper.

photography *(n)* the creation of pictures by exposing a film inside a camera to light. *The single-lens reflex camera shown below is used in professional and amateur photography. The reflex mirror sends light from the lens through the pentaprism to the viewfinder, so you see the same image that falls on the film. When you press the shutter release button, the mirror swings up, the shutter opens, and light hits the film.* **photographer** *(n)*, **photographic** *(adj)*.

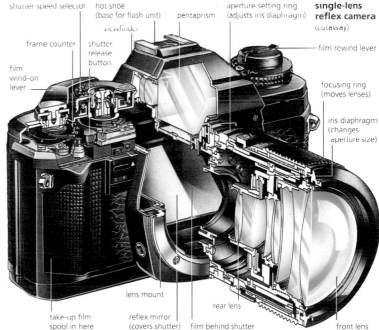

shutter speed selector
hot shoe (base for flash unit)
viewfinder
pentaprism
aperture setting ring (adjusts iris diaphragm)
single-lens reflex camera (cutaway)
frame counter
shutter release button
film wind-on lever
film rewind lever
focusing ring (moves lenses)
iris diaphragm (changes aperture size)
lens mount
take-up film spool in here
reflex mirror (covers shutter)
film behind shutter
rear lens
front lens

photosynthesis *(n)* a chemical process by which green plants make their food. Plants use energy from the Sun to turn water and carbon dioxide into food, and give off oxygen as a waste product.

phrase *(n)* a group of words that have a meaning, but do not form a sentence.

physical
1 *(adj)* to do with the body. *Physical education.* **physically** *(adv)*.
2 *(adj)* to do with the shape and appearance of things. *Physical geography.* **physically** *(adv)*.

physics *(singular n)* the scientific study of energy, movement, heat, sound, light, etc. **physicist** *(n)*.

physiotherapy *(n)* treatment for damaged muscles and joints, using exercise and massage. **physiotherapist** *(n)*.

piano
1 *(n)* a large keyboard instrument which produces musical sounds when padded hammers strike tuned strings. **pianist** *(n)*.
2 *(adv)* softly. Piano is an Italian word, used as an instruction in music.

grand piano
(lid removed)

- bass bridge (transmits vibrations of strings to soundboard)
- wooden soundboard (amplifies sound)
- overstringing
- iron frame
- hitch pins
- treble strings
- bass strings

grand piano and pianist

music stand
lid
pedal
piano case

- treble bridge (transmits vibrations of strings to soundboard)
- dampers
- bearing bar
- wrest plank
- tuning pins or wrest pins
- keyboard

pick picking picked
1 *(v)* to choose, or to select. *Pick a number.*
2 *(v)* to collect, or to gather. *Have you picked all the strawberries?*
3 *(n)* a tool with pointed metal ends, used for breaking up earth or stones.

4 *(v)* If you **pick at** something, you take little bits off it.
5 *(v)* If someone **picks on** you, they keep criticizing you.

picket picketing picketed *(v)* to stand outside a place of work, making a protest and sometimes trying to prevent people from entering. **picket** *(n)*, **picketer** *(n)*.

pickle pickling pickled
1 *(v)* to preserve food in vinegar or in salt water.
2 *(n)* a mixture of chopped, cooked vegetables and spices, often eaten with cold meals.
3 *(n)* *(informal)* a difficult situation.

pickpocket *(n)* someone who steals from people's pockets or bags.

pick-up *(n)* a small truck with an open back.

picky pickier pickiest *(adj)* *(informal)* fussy, or choosy. *A picky eater.*

picnic picnicking picnicked
1 *(n)* a packed meal taken away from home to be eaten out-of-doors.
2 *(v)* to eat a picnic. **picnicker** *(n)*.

pictorial *(adj)* using pictures. *A pictorial guide.* **pictorially** *(adv)*.

picture picturing pictured
1 *(n)* an image of something, for example, a painting, photograph, or sketch.
2 *(v)* to imagine something. *I pictured Jim as tall, dark, and handsome.* **picture** *(n)*.

picturesque *(pik-chur-esk)* *(adj)* If a place or view is **picturesque**, it is beautiful to look at.

pie *(n)* a pastry case filled with meat, fruit, etc. and baked in an oven.

piece piecing pieced
1 *(n)* a bit or section of something.
2 *(n)* something written or made. *A piece of embroidery.*
3 **piece together** *(v)* to put pieces together, or to put facts together.

pier
1 *(n)* a platform of metal and wood extending into the sea. Piers often have entertainments on them.
2 *(n)* a pillar supporting a bridge.

pierce piercing pierced *(v)* to make a hole in something. *Piers has had his ear pierced.*

piercing *(adj)* very loud and shrill. *A piercing scream.*

pig
1 *(n)* a farm animal with a blunt snout, which is kept for its meat.
2 *(n)* *(informal)* a greedy and disgusting person.

pigeon *(n)* a common, grey bird, sometimes used for racing or for carrying messages.

pigeon

piggy-back *(n)* If someone gives you a **piggy-back**, they carry you on their shoulders or on their back.

pigment *(n)* a substance that gives colour to something. There is pigment in paints and in your skin.

pigsty pigsties
1 *(n)* a shelter and yard where pigs are kept.
2 *(n)* a very untidy and often dirty place. *Your bedroom is a pigsty!*

pigtail *(n)* a length of hair that has been divided into three and plaited together.

pile
1 *(n)* a heap or mound of something. **pile** *(v)*.
2 **pile-up** *(n)* *(informal)* a serious road crash involving several vehicles.

pilfer pilfering pilfered *(v)* to steal small things. **pilferer** *(n)*.

pilgrim *(n)* someone who goes on a journey to worship at a holy place. **pilgrimage** *(n)*.

pill
1 *(n)* a small, solid tablet of medicine.
2 **the pill** *(n)* *(informal)* a pill that women take daily to prevent them from becoming pregnant.

Some words that begin with a "pi" sound are spelt "py".

pillar *(n)* a column which supports part of a building. See **column**.

pillow *(n)* a large, soft cushion on which you rest your head when you are lying in bed.

pillowcase *(n)* a fabric cover that you put over a pillow to keep it clean.

pilot piloting piloted
1 *(n)* someone who flies an aircraft.
2 *(n)* someone who steers a ship in and out of port.
3 *(v)* to control or guide something.
4 *(adj)* done as an experiment. *A pilot television programme.* pilot *(n)*.

pimple *(n)* a small, raised spot on the skin. pimply *(adj)*.

pin pinning pinned
1 *(n)* a thin, pointed piece of metal, usually used to join material together.
2 *(v)* to join things together with a pin *Please can you pin up the hem of my dress.*
3 *(v)* to hold something or someone firmly in position. *I pinned a notice on the board. Sophia pinned me against the wall.*

pinafore
1 *(n)* a piece of clothing that you wear to protect your clothes when you are cooking, painting, etc.
2 pinafore dress *(n)* a sleeveless dress, usually worn over a shirt or sweater.

pinball *(n)* a game in which you shoot small balls around a number of obstacles on a table.

pincer *(pin-ser)*
1 *(n)* the pinching claw of a shellfish, such as a crab. See **crab**.
2 pincers *(plural n)* a tool for gripping and pulling things, especially for pulling out nails.

pinch pinches pinching pinched
1 *(v)* to squeeze someone's skin painfully between your thumb and index finger. pinch *(n)*.
2 *(n)* a small amount of something *A pinch of salt.*
3 *(v) (informal)* to steal something. *Someone's pinched my bike!*

pine pining pined
1 *(n)* a tall, straight, evergreen tree, with cones and needles rather than leaves.
2 *(v)* If you pine for someone, you feel very sad because you are separated from them.

pineapple *(n)* a large, tropical fruit with yellow flesh and a tough skin. See **fruit**.

ping pong see **table tennis**.

pink *(n)* a pale red colour. pink *(adj)*.

pins and needles *(singular n)* *(informal)* a pricking, tingling feeling that you get when some of the blood supply to part of your body has been cut off.

pinstripe *(n)* a fabric with a very narrow stripe.

pioneer
1 *(n)* someone who explores unknown territory and settles there.
2 *(n)* one of the first people to work in a new and unknown area. *The Wright brothers were pioneers of flight.* pioneer *(v)*.

pious *(py-uss) (adj)* Someone who is pious practises their religion faithfully and seriously. piety *(n)*, piously *(adv)*.

pip
1 *(n)* the small, hard seed of a fruit.
2 *(n)* a short, high sound, such as the ones used as time signals on the radio.

pipe piping piped
1 *(n)* a tube, usually used to carry liquids.
2 *(v)* to send something along pipes, tubes, or wires.
3 *(n)* a tube with a bowl on the end of it, used for smoking tobacco. Pipes are usually wooden.
4 *(n)* a tube with holes in it, used as a musical instrument or as part of an instrument. *The picture shows some panpipes from Peru.*
5 piped music *(n)* music that is sent through wires all over a building.

panpipes

pipeline
1 *(n)* a large pipe that carries water, gas, oil, etc. over long distances.
2 If something is in the pipeline, it is being planned

piping
1 *(n)* a system of pipes.
2 *(n)* a thin, pipe-like line of decoration on a cake, chair, etc.
3 *(adj)* very high or shrill. *A piping voice.*
4 If food is piping hot, it is very hot indeed.

pirate pirating pirated
1 *(n)* someone who attacks and steals from ships at sea. piracy *(n)*.
2 *(v)* If someone pirates a tape, computer game, etc. they make illegal copies from the original version and sell them. pirated *(adj)*.

pistol *(n)* a small handgun.

pit pitting pitted
1 *(n)* a hole in the ground.

2 *(n)* a small dip.
3 *(n)* a coal mine.
4 *(v)* If two people are pitted against each other, they are made to compete with each other.
5 the pits *(n)* the place where racing cars pull in for fuel and repairs during a race.
6 *(slang)* If something is the pits, it is terrible.

pitch pitches pitching pitched
1 *(n)* an area of grass on which a sport is played.
2 *(n)* the level of a musical note.
3 *(v)* When you pitch a tent, you put it up.
4 *(v)* to throw something, especially a baseball.

pitcher
1 *(n)* an open-topped water container like a large jug.
2 *(n) (US)* the person who throws the ball at the batter in a baseball game.

pitchfork *(n)* a long-handled fork with two prongs, used for lifting hay.

pitfall *(n)* a hidden danger or difficulty.

pitiful
1 *(adj)* causing or deserving pity. *The lost children were in a pitiful state.* pitifully *(adv)*.
2 *(adj)* useless, or worthless. *This essay is a pitiful effort!* pitifully *(adv)*.

pitiless *(adj)* If someone is pitiless, they show no pity or mercy. pitilessly *(adv)*.

pity pities pitying pitied *(v)* If you pity someone, you feel sorry for them. pity *(n)*, pityingly *(adv)*.

pivot *(n)* the central point on which something turns or balances. pivot *(v)*.

pixie or **pixy** *(n)* a small elf or fairy in legends and fairy stories.

pizza *(n)* a flat, round base of dough, baked with toppings of cheese, tomatoes, and other foods.

placard *(n)* a poster, nameplate, or notice.

placate placating placated *(v)* to make someone calm or happy, often by giving them something that they want.

place placing placed
1 *(n)* a particular area or position.
2 *(v)* to put something somewhere, deliberately and carefully. *Kim placed the goldfish bowl out of harm's way.*
3 *(v)* to remember. *I know I've met you somewhere, but I can't place you.*
4 If something is in place, it is in its proper position.

Some words that begin with a "pi" sound are spelt "py".

placid (*plass-id*) (*adj*) Someone who is **placid** is calm and even-tempered. **placidly** (*adv*).

plague (*playg*) plaguing plagued
1 (*n*) a serious disease which spreads quickly to many people.
2 (*v*) If something **plagues** you, you are troubled and annoyed by it. *The explorers were plagued by flies.*

plaice plaice (*n*) a flat sea fish that can be eaten.

plaid (*rhymes with bad*) (*n*) cloth with a pattern of checks of different colours and sizes, usually made in Scotland.

plain plainer plainest
1 (*adj*) ordinary in appearance, and not fancy or beautiful.
2 (*n*) a large, level area of land.
3 (*adj*) simple and straightforward. *Just give me the plain facts.*
4 **plain clothes** (*n*) ordinary clothes, rather than uniform. *The police wore plain clothes.* **plain-clothes** (*adj*).

plaintive (*adj*) sad and mournful. *A plaintive cry.* **plaintively** (*adv*).

plait (*rhymes with bat*) (*n*) a length of hair that has been divided into three and twisted together. **plait** (*v*), **plaited** (*adj*).

plan planning planned
1 (*v*) to work out how you will do something. **plan** (*n*).
2 (*v*) If you **plan** to do something, you intend to do it. *I planned to go shopping today.*
3 (*n*) a diagram used in the construction of something.
4 (*n*) a map of a room, building, or small area.

plane
1 (*n*) a machine with wings and an engine, that flies through the air. Plane is short for aeroplane. *See* **aircraft**.
2 (*n*) a tool used for smoothing wood. **plane** (*v*). *See* **woodwork**.
3 (*n*) a flat surface. *A dice has six planes.*

planet (*n*) one of the nine, round objects circling the Sun. *This picture shows the planets of the solar system in their correct order, but not drawn to scale.* **planetary** (*adj*).

plank (*n*) a long, flat strip of wood used, for example, for floorboards.

plankton (*n*) a general name for the minute animals and plants which live in water.

plant
planting
planted
1 (*n*) a living organism that often contains a green pigment called chlorophyll, which allows it to capture energy from the Sun. Many land plants have stems, roots, and leaves. *Also see* **flower**.
2 (*v*) to put plants or seeds in the ground so that they can grow.
3 (*v*) to put something in a secret place. *Terrorists planted a bomb in the store.*
4 (*n*) a factory, laboratory, or power station. *A chemical plant.*
5 (*n*) large industrial machinery or buildings.

plantation
1 (*n*) a farm in a hot country where coffee, tea, rubber, etc. are grown.
2 (*n*) a place where a large number of trees or bushes have been planted.

plaque (*plak* or *plahk*)
1 (*n*) a plate with words inscribed on it, usually on a wall in a public place.
2 (*n*) the coating made from food, bacteria, and saliva that forms on your teeth and can cause tooth decay.

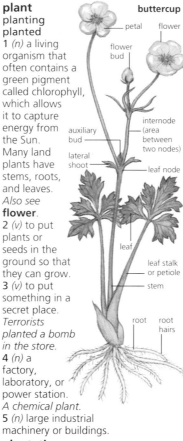

buttercup — petal — flower — flower bud — internode (area between two nodes) — auxiliary bud — lateral shoot — leaf node — leaf — leaf stalk or petiole — stem — root — root hairs

plaster plastering plastered
1 (*n*) a substance made of lime, sand, and water, used by builders to put a smooth finish on walls.
2 (*n*) a sticky bandage that you put on a skin wound.
3 (*v*) to spread something thickly on a surface. *Joe plastered his hair with gel.*
4 **plaster cast** (*n*) a hard, white case that holds the parts of a broken bone together until it mends.

plastic (*n*) a man-made substance that is light and strong and can be moulded into different shapes.

plastic surgery (*n*) operations on skin and body tissue. Plastic surgery can be used to repair damage or to improve someone's appearance.

plate
1 (*n*) a flat dish for food.
2 (*n*) a flat sheet of glass or metal.
3 (*n*) an illustration in a book.
4 (*n*) one of the sheets of rock which make up the Earth's outer crust. *The map shows the eight main plates that make up the Earth's surface, sometimes known as continental plates.*

continental plates

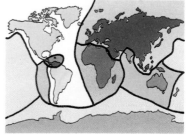

■ Eurasian plate   □ Nazca plate
■ African plate   □ Pacific plate
□ American plate   ■ Antarctic plate
■ Caribbean plate   ■ Indian-Australian plate

plateau (*plat-oh*) plateaus or plateaux (*n*) an area of high, flat land.

platform (*n*) a flat, raised structure on which people or things can stand. *A station platform.*

planets

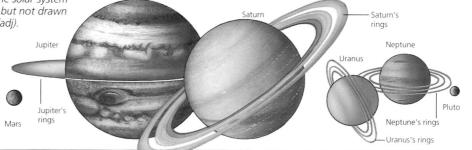

Saturn — Saturn's rings — Neptune — Uranus — Pluto — Neptune's rings — Uranus's rings — Jupiter — Jupiter's rings — Mercury — Venus — Earth — Mars — Sun

platinum *(n)* a very valuable, silvery-white metal.

platypus platypuses *(n)* an Australian mammal with webbed feet and a broad bill.

platypus

plausible *(plaw-zib-ul)* *(adj)* believable. *Gus gave a plausible reason for being so late.* plausibly *(adv)*.

play playing played
1 *(v)* to take part in a game or other enjoyable activity.
2 *(n)* a story that is acted, usually in the theatre.
3 *(v)* to make music on an instrument. *Lesley plays the saxophone.*
4 *(v)* to take part in a sport.
5 *(v)* to act a part in a play.

playground *(n)* a surfaced, fenced, outdoor area, often with swings, slides, etc. where children can play.

playroom *(n)* a room in which children can play.

playtime *(n)* a time between lessons when schoolchildren can play.

playwright *(n)* someone who writes plays.

plc *(n)* the initials for public limited company. A public limited company is one whose shares can be bought by members of the public. If the company goes bankrupt, the shareholders lose only the value of their shares.

plea *(n)* a strongly felt, emotional request. *A plea for mercy.*

plead pleading pleaded
1 *(v)* If you **plead** with someone, you beg them to do something.
2 *(v)* to say whether you are guilty or not guilty in a court. *I plead guilty.*

pleasant pleasanter pleasantest *(adj)* enjoyable and likable. *We spent a pleasant afternoon by the river.* pleasantly *(adv)*.

please pleasing pleased
1 *(v)* to satisfy, or to give pleasure. *Your present pleased me greatly.*
2 *(interject)* You say **please** when you ask for something politely. *Please may I have some cake?*

pleasure *(n)* a feeling of enjoyment or satisfaction. **pleasurable** *(adj)*.

pleat *(n)* one of a series of parallel folds in a piece of clothing, such as a skirt. **pleated** *(adj)*.

plectrum plectra or plectrums *(n)* a small piece of metal or plastic used to pluck the strings of guitars, etc.   **plectra**

pledge pledging pledged *(v)* to make a firm promise. **pledge** *(n)*.

plentiful *(adj)* existing in large amounts. *Food was plentiful at the feast.* plentifully *(adv)*.

plenty *(n)* a great number, or a large amount. *There's plenty of space.*

pliable *(ply-ab-ul)*
1 *(adj)* If an object or material is **pliable**, it can be bent easily.
2 *(adj)* If a person is **pliable**, they can be influenced easily.

plight *(n)* a situation of great danger or hardship. *Everyone is horrified by the terrible plight of the refugees.*

plimsoll or **plimsole**
1 *(n)* a soft, canvas shoe with a rubber sole, often worn for sports or PE.
2 **Plimsoll line** *(n)* a line on the side of a ship that indicates how heavily loaded it is permitted to be.

plod plodding plodded *(v)* to walk or work in a slow and deliberate way.

plot plotting plotted
1 *(v)* to make a secret plan. **plot** *(n)*.
2 *(n)* a small area of land. *A building plot.*
3 *(n)* the story of a novel, film, play, etc.
4 *(v)* to mark out something, like a graph, or a route on a map.

plough *(rhymes with cow)* ploughing ploughed
1 *(n)* a piece of farm equipment pulled by an animal or a tractor and used to turn over soil before seeds are sown. *The picture below shows a wooden model of an Ancient Egyptian plough. Also see* **farm**.
2 *(v)* to turn over soil using a plough.
3 *(v)* If you **plough through** something, you work hard to get through it.

Egyptian plough

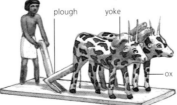

plough   yoke

ox

pluck plucking plucked
1 *(v)* to pick fruit or flowers.
2 *(v)* to play notes on a stringed instrument, by pulling on the strings with your fingers or with a plectrum.

3 *(v)* to pull feathers out of a bird.
4 *(n)* courage and bravery.
plucky *(adj)*, **pluckily** *(adv)*.

plug plugging plugged
1 *(n)* an object pushed into a hole to block it. *A bath plug.* **plug** *(v)*.
2 *(n)* an electrical connector.
3 *(v)* *(informal)* to gain publicity for something by talking about it, usually on radio or television.

plug-in *(n)* a computer program that can be added to a Web browser and allows you to see and use extra information on a Web site. You can use plug-ins to play high-quality sound, watch videos and view animations.

plum *(n)* a small, soft fruit with a purple, yellow, or red skin. *See* **fruit**.

plumage *(plew-mij)* *(n)* a bird's feathers.

plumbing *(plum-ing)* *(n)* the system of water pipes in a building. **plumber** *(n)*.

plump plumper plumpest *(adj)* slightly fat, or rounded in shape.

plunder plundering plundered *(v)* to use violence in order to steal things, usually during a battle. **plunder** *(n)*.

plunge plunging plunged
1 *(v)* to dive into water. **plunge** *(n)*.
2 *(v)* to push something into water.
3 *(v)* to slope steeply. *The cliffs plunged to the sea.*
4 *(v)* to do something suddenly. *We plunged into action.*

plural *(n)* the form of a word that is used for two or more of something. *The plural of child is children.*

plus
1 In maths, a **plus** sign (+) is used in an addition sum. *6 plus 4 equals 10, or 6 + 4 = 10.*
2 *(prep)* in addition to. *Celia has a husband plus three children to feed.*

plywood *(n)* board made from thin sheets of wood glued together.

p.m. the initials of the Latin phrase *post meridiem* which means "after midday". *School finishes at 4 p.m.*

pneumatic *(new-mat-ik)*
1 *(adj)* filled with air. *Pneumatic tyres.*
2 *(adj)* operated by compressed air. *A pneumatic drill.*

pneumonia *(new-moan-ee-a)* *(n)* a serious lung disease which makes breathing very difficult.

poach poaches poaching poached
1 *(v)* to catch fish or animals illegally on someone else's land. **poacher** *(n)*.
2 *(v)* to cook eggs, fish, etc. by heating them gently in liquid.

pocket pocketing pocketed
1 (n) a pouch sewn on to or into clothing and used for carrying things.
2 (v) to take something secretly. *Clive pocketed the money and ran.*
3 (n) a small area. *The army met pockets of resistance on their way.*

pocket money (n) spending money that parents regularly give to their children.

pod (n) a long case that holds the seeds of certain plants. *A pea pod.*

podgy podgier podgiest (adj) slightly fat.

poem (n) a piece of writing set out in short lines, often with a noticeable rhythm and some words that rhyme.

poetry (n) a general word for poems. *Do you write poetry?* **poet** (n).

point pointing pointed
1 (v) to show where something is, especially by using your index finger.
2 (n) the sharp end of something. *A pencil point.*
3 (n) the main purpose behind something that is said or done. *The point of the presentation was to get people thinking.*
4 (n) a specific place or stage. *Don't go beyond this point.*
5 (n) a unit for scoring in a game.
6 (v) to aim at someone or something. *Don't point that gun at me!*
7 (v) If you **point out** something, you draw attention to it or explain it.
8 **points** (plural n) railway lines which can be moved to send a train on to a different track.

point-blank (adj) very close indeed. *They shot at point-blank range.*

pointless (adj) If something is pointless, it has no realistic purpose. *It's pointless to take your bikini on an Arctic expedition.* **pointlessly** (adv).

poise (rhymes with boys) poising poised (v) to be balanced. *The glass was poised on the edge of the table.*

poised (adj) If you are **poised**, you are self-confident and find it easy to talk to people. **poise** (n).

poison (n) a substance that can kill or harm someone if it is swallowed or breathed in. **poison** (v), **poisonous** (adj).

poke poking poked (v) to prod sharply with a finger or pointed object. **poke** (n).

poker (n) a long, metal tool used for stirring up a fire.

poky or **pokey** pokier pokiest (adj) (informal) very small and cramped. *A poky house.*

polar (adj) belonging to the icy regions, known as the Arctic and the Antarctic, around the North and South Poles.

polar regions and polar wildlife

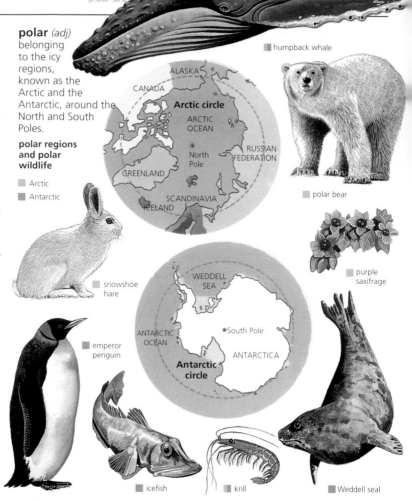

humpback whale

ALASKA
CANADA
Arctic circle
ARCTIC OCEAN
North Pole
RUSSIAN FEDERATION
GREENLAND
SCANDINAVIA
ICELAND

■ Arctic
■ Antarctic

polar bear

purple saxifrage

snowshoe hare

WEDDELL SEA
•South Pole
ANTARCTIC OCEAN
ANTARCTICA
Antarctic circle

emperor penguin

■ icefish   ■ krill   ■ Weddell seal

pole
1 (n) a long, smooth piece of wood, metal, plastic, etc.
2 (n) one of the two points on the Earth's surface that are furthest away from the equator. *The North Pole. The South Pole.* See **polar**.
3 (n) one of the two opposite ends of a magnet. See **magnet**.
4 If two people or things are **poles apart**, they are very different.

pole vault (n) a jump over a high bar, using a flexible pole. *The picture sequence shows an athlete performing a pole vault.* **pole-vault** (v).

pole vault

fibreglass pole
vaulting box

police (pol-eess) policing policed
1 (plural n) the people whose job is to make sure that the law is obeyed. **policeman** (n), **policewoman** (n).
2 (v) to use police officers to protect and guard people and property.

bar

policy policies (n) a general plan of action. *A traffic policy.*

polio (n) an infectious virus which affects the brain and spine and which can cause paralysis. Polio is short for poliomyelitis.

polish polishes polishing polished
1 (v) to rub something in order to make it shine. polish (n).
2 (n) a cleaning substance used to make things shine.

polished (adj) If you give a polished performance, you are well rehearsed and perform confidently.

polite politer politest (adj) well behaved and courteous to other people. politeness (n), politely (adv).

politician (n) someone involved in the government of a country, such as an MP or a congressman.

politics (n) the debate and activity involved in governing a country. political (adj), politically (adv).

poll
1 (n) a counting of votes in an election.
2 (n) a survey of people's opinions or beliefs.

pollen
1 (singular n) fine grains found inside flowers. Pollen contains fertilizing cells and is transferred to other plants by the wind or by insects.
2 pollen count (n) a measurement of the level of pollen in the air, which indicates how badly people with hay fever may be affected.

willow
water lily
yarrow
pollen grains (magnified)

pollinate pollinating pollinated (v) to transfer pollen from one flower to another in order to fertilize the flower. pollination (n).

polling station (n) a building where people go to vote in elections.

pollution (n) damage to the environment caused by human activities. Pollution includes the harmful effects of noise and light. pollute (v).

polo (n) a game played on horseback by two teams of three or four players who try to hit a small ball through goal posts, using long, wooden mallets.

polyester (n) an artificial substance used to make plastic products and fabric for clothes.

polygamy (n) If someone practises polygamy, they have several wives or husbands at once. polygamous (adj).

polygon (n) a flat shape with many sides.

polystyrene (n) a light, stiff plastic often used to make disposable cups and packing materials.

polythene (n) a light, flexible plastic used to make bags.

polyunsaturates (n) soft animal and vegetable fats and oils, thought to be healthier for you than other fats. polyunsaturated (adj).

pompous (adj) full of self importance. pompously (adv).

pond (n) a small, enclosed pool of fresh water.

ponder pondering pondered (v) to think about things carefully.

pond-skater (n) an insect with a long, narrow body and very long, thin legs that it uses to walk on the surface of ponds.

pond-skater

pondweed (n) a general name for plants that grow in freshwater ponds and slow streams.

pong (n) (informal) an unpleasant smell. pong (v).

pony ponies (n) a small horse.

ponytail (n) a bunch of hair that is tied with a band and hangs behind the head.

pony trekking (n) If you go pony trekking, you ride ponies across the countryside for pleasure.

poodle (n) a breed of dog with long, curly hair.

pool pooling pooled
1 (n) a small area of still water.
2 (n) a swimming pool.
3 (n) a game in which you use a stick, called a cue, to hit coloured balls into pockets on a table. *Pool is similar to snooker but is played on a smaller table.*
4 (v) If people pool their money, ideas, etc. they put them together to be shared.

pools (n) a competition in which people win money if they guess the results of certain football matches correctly.

poor poorer poorest
1 (adj) If you are poor, you do not have much money.
2 (adj) low in quality or standard. *Poor eyesight.*
3 (adj) unfortunate, and provoking sympathy. *Poor Alex!*

poorly
1 (adv) badly. *The room was poorly lit.*
2 (adj) ill. *Sadie is poorly today.*

pop popping popped
1 (v) to make a small bang or bursting sound. pop (n).
2 (n) (informal) a sweet, fizzy drink such as lemonade.
3 pop music (n) modern, popular music with a strong, and often fast, beat. pop (n).
4 (n) an informal name for your father.
5 (v) (informal) to go somewhere or put something somewhere quickly. *Gary has just popped out. Laura popped a mint into her mouth.*

popcorn (n) grains of maize that are heated until they swell up and burst.

Pope (n) the head of the Roman Catholic Church.

poppadom or **poppadum** (n) a large, round, crispy disc, made from flour and spices, and served with Indian meals.

poppy poppies (n) a flower with large, colourful petals. Poppies have seedcases with tiny holes for the seeds to escape from when they are shaken by the wind.
common poppy
dried seedcase
flower
seeds

popular (adj) liked or enjoyed by many people. popularity (n), popularly (adv).

populated (adj) If a place is populated, it has people living there.

population
1 (n) the people who live in a place.
2 (n) the number of people who live in a place.

porcelain (por-ser-lin) (n) very fine china, often used to make ornaments or cups and saucers. *This 18th-century figure of Madame de Pompadour was made in porcelain at the Meissen factory in Germany.*
porcelain figure

porch porches
1 (n) a covered area around a doorway.
See **building**.
2 (n) (US) a raised platform around the outside of a house.

porcupine (n) a rodent covered with long, sharp spines.

Malaysian porcupine

pore (n) one of the tiny holes in your skin through which you sweat.
See **skin**.

pork (n) meat from a pig..

pornography (n) magazines, videos, etc. that are intended to be sexually exciting in a way that many people find obscene and offensive. **pornographic** (adj).

porous (adj) Something that is porous lets liquid or gas through it.

porridge (n) a breakfast food made by boiling oats in milk or water.

port
1 (n) a town with a harbour.
2 (n) the left side of a ship or aircraft. port (adj).
3 (n) a strong, sweet red wine.

portable (adj) able to be carried easily.

portcullis portcullises (n) a heavy grating in the entrance to a castle that was used as an extra defence. This cutaway view of a castle gatehouse shows how the portcullis and drawbridge were raised and lowered.

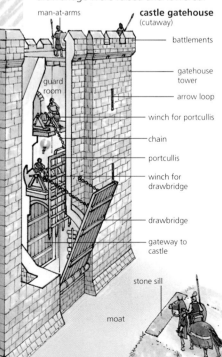

man-at-arms

castle gatehouse (cutaway)

battlements

gatehouse tower

guard room

arrow loop

winch for portcullis

chain

portcullis

winch for drawbridge

drawbridge

gateway to castle

stone sill

moat

porter (n) someone who carries luggage for people at a railway station or hotel.

portion (n) a part, or a piece.

portrait
1 (n) a drawing, painting, or photograph of a person.
2 (n) a description of something.

portray portraying portrayed
1 (v) to show or describe someone or something in a certain way. The author portrays Hetty as an eccentric. portrayal (n).
2 (v) to act a part in a play or film. portrayal (n).

pose posing posed
1 (v) to keep your body in a particular position so that you can be photographed, painted, or drawn. pose (n).
2 (v) to pretend to be someone else in order to deceive people. The thieves posed as policemen.
3 (v) If you **pose a question**, you ask it.

posh posher poshest
1 (adj) (informal) upper-class. A posh accent.
2 (adj) (informal) very smart and expensive. A posh hotel.

position positioning positioned
1 (n) the place where something is.
2 (v) to put something in a particular place. Position the pictures carefully.
3 (n) the way in which someone is standing, sitting, or lying.
4 (n) your place in a race or competition.
5 (n) a particular job. I'm applying for the position of nanny.

positive
1 (adj) sure, or certain. I'm positive that I left my pencil case here. positively (adv).
2 (adj) hopeful and optimistic. Dolly has a positive approach to life.
3 (adj) A **positive** number is more than zero.

possession
1 (n) something that you own. possess (v).
2 If something is **in your possession**, you own it or have it.

possessive
1 (adj) If someone is **possessive**, they want to keep someone or something for themselves and do not want to share them with other people.
2 (n) the form of a noun or pronoun that shows that something belongs to it. In "This ball is mine" and "Tom's bat", "mine" and "Tom's" are possessives. **possessive** (adj).

possible (adj) If something is possible, it might happen or might be true. **possibility** (n), **possibly** (adv).

post posting posted
1 (n) a long, thick piece of wood, concrete, or metal that is fixed in the ground.
2 (n) a particular job that someone has. Mr Jarvis holds the post of station master.
3 (v) to send a letter or parcel from one place to another.
4 (singular n) the letters and parcels that you send or receive.
5 **post office** (n) the place where people go to buy stamps, send parcels, receive pensions, etc.

postage (n) the cost of sending a letter or parcel by post.

postcard (n) a card, usually with a picture on one side, that you send by post.

postcode (n) the set of numbers and letters at the end of an address, used to help sort letters, parcels, etc. more quickly.

poster (n) a large, printed picture or notice that can be put up on a wall.

postman postmen (n) a man who delivers letters and parcels.

postmark (n) an official mark on a letter to show when and where it was posted.

postpone postponing postponed (v) to put something off until later. We postponed the match because of rain. **postponement** (n).

postscript (n) a short message, beginning "ps", which is added to the end of a letter, after your signature.

posture (n) the position of your body when you stand, sit, or walk.

postwoman postwomen (n) a woman who delivers letters and parcels.

posy posies (n) a small bunch of flowers.

pot potting potted
1 (n) a round container used for cooking or storing food.
2 (n) a container made of clay, especially one used for growing plants.
3 (n) (slang) marijuana.
4 (v) to hit a ball into a pocket in snooker, pool, or billiards. Sean has potted the black.

potato potatoes (n) a round root vegetable. See **vegetable**.

potent (adj) powerful, or strong. A potent drug. **potency** (n), **potently** (adv).

potential

1 *(n)* Your **potential** is what you are capable of achieving in the future. **potential** *(adj)*, **potentially** *(adv)*.
2 *(n)* If an idea, place, etc. has **potential**, you think that you can develop it into something better.

pothole

1 *(n)* a deep hole that leads to underground caves.
2 *(n)* a hole in the surface of a road.

potholing *(n)* the sport of climbing down potholes and exploring underground caves. **potholer** *(n)*.

potter pottering pottered

1 *(n)* someone who makes objects out of clay, such as bowls, plates, vases, etc. *The picture shows a potter working at her wheel.*
2 *(v)* to be occupied in a leisurely way. *Pandora pottered around the house all day.*

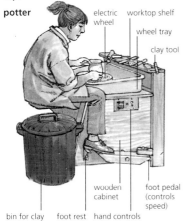

potter

electric wheel · worktop shelf
wheel tray
clay tool
wooden cabinet · foot pedal (controls speed)
bin for clay · foot rest · hand controls

pottery potteries

1 *(n)* objects made of baked clay, such as bowls, plates, vases, etc.
2 *(n)* a place where clay objects are made.

potty potties; pottier pottiest

1 *(n)* a type of bowl that very young children use instead of a toilet.
2 *(adj)* *(informal)* slightly mad.

pouch pouches

1 *(n)* a small leather or fabric bag.
2 *(n)* a flap of skin in which kangaroos and other marsupials carry their young.

poultry *(plural n)* farmyard birds kept for their eggs and meat.

pounce pouncing pounced *(v)*
to jump on something suddenly and grab hold of it.

pound pounding pounded

1 *(n)* the main unit of money in Britain.

2 *(n)* a unit of weight, equal to 0.454kgs. *See page 284.*
3 *(v)* to keep hitting something noisily and with force. *The rain pounded on the roof.*
4 *(n)* an enclosure, especially one for lost bicycles or stray dogs.

pour pouring poured

1 *(v)* to make liquid flow out of a jug, bottle, etc.
2 *(v)* to rain heavily.
3 *(v)* to move somewhere quickly and in large numbers. *People poured out of the stadium on to the street.*

pout pouting pouted *(v)* to push out your lips because you are cross or disappointed about something. **pout** *(n)*.

poverty *(n)* the state of being poor. *The refugees lived in dreadful poverty.*

powder powdering powdered

1 *(n)* tiny grains of a solid substance. **powdery** *(adj)*.
2 *(v)* to cover something with powder. *Gloria powdered her nose.*

power

1 *(n)* control over other people or things. **powerful** *(adj)*, **powerless** *(adj)*.
2 *(n)* the ability or authority to do something.
3 *(n)* great force, or great strength. **powerful** *(adj)*, **powerfully** *(adv)*.
4 *(n)* electricity or other forms of energy.
5 power cut *(n)* a temporary stoppage in the electricity supply.
6 power station *(n)* a place where electricity is produced.

practicable *(adj)* able to be done successfully. *Is it practicable to do all this work today?* **practicably** *(adv)*.

practical

1 *(adj)* to do with experience or action rather than with theory and ideas. *Do you have any practical experience of teaching?*
2 *(adj)* If someone is **practical**, they are good at making and doing things with their hands.
3 *(adj)* sensible and useful. *Brown is a practical colour for a carpet.*
4 *(n)* a lesson or exam in which you do something, rather than reading or writing about it. *A chemistry practical.*

practical joke *(n)* a humorous trick played on someone.

practically

1 *(adv)* almost. *It's practically impossible to get there by public transport.*
2 *(adv)* in a sensible way. *Abby tackled the job very practically.*

practice

1 *(n)* the regular repetition of an action in order to improve it. *Piano practice.*
2 *(n)* a custom or habit. *How old is the practice of sending birthday cards?*
3 *(n)* the business of a doctor or lawyer.
4 in practice *(adv)* what really happens when you do something rather than what is meant to happen.

practise practising practised

1 *(v)* to do something over and over again so that you improve.
2 *(v)* If someone **practises** a religion, they follow its teachings and attend its services or ceremonies.
3 *(v)* to work as a doctor or lawyer. *Giles practises medicine in Glasgow.*
4 *(v)* to put something into action. *Practise what you preach.*

prairie *(n)* a large area of grassland in North America.

praise praising praised

1 *(v)* to say good things about someone because you admire them or think that they have done something well. **praise** *(n)*.
2 *(v)* to thank and worship God. **praise** *(n)*.

pram *(n)* a four-wheeled vehicle for a baby that you push along.

prance prancing pranced

1 *(v)* to leap in a lively way.
2 *(v)* When horses **prance**, they walk quickly with high steps.

prank *(n)* a trick played on someone.

prawn *(n)* a small shellfish that you can cook and eat. Prawns are pale pink when cooked.

pray praying prayed

1 *(v)* to talk to God, either out loud or silently. **prayer** *(n)*.
2 *(v)* to hope very much that something happens. *We're praying that it will be sunny tomorrow.*

preach preaches preaching preached

1 *(v)* to give a religious talk to people, especially during a church service. **preacher** *(n)*.
2 *(v)* to tell other people what they should do. *I wish my mum would stop preaching at me!*

precarious *(adj)* unsafe and risky. *The glass was perched in a precarious position on the edge of the table.* **precariously** *(adv)*.

precaution *(n)* something that you do in order to prevent something dangerous or unpleasant from happening. *Let's take a first aid kit as a precaution.* **precautionary** *(adj)*.

precede (pree-seed) preceding preceded (v) If one thing **precedes** something else, it comes before it. *A short cartoon preceded the main film.* preceding (adj).

precinct (pree-sinkt)
1 (n) a shopping area in a town, where traffic is not allowed.
2 (n) (US) an area in a city that is the responsibility of a particular police station.

precious (presh-uss)
1 (adj) rare and valuable.
2 (adj) very special to you. *Precious memories.*
3 precious stone (n) a valuable mineral, often used in jewellery.

precipice (n) a steep cliff face.

precis (pray-see) precis (n) a short summary of a longer piece of writing.

precise (adj) exact, accurate, and neat. precision (n), precisely (adv).

precocious (prek-oh-shuss) (adj) Precocious children are very advanced for their age.

predator (n) an animal that hunts and kills other animals. predatory (adj).

predecessor
1 (n) someone who had your job or position before you.
2 (n) an ancestor.

predicament (n) an awkward or difficult situation.

predict predicting predicted (v) to say what you think will happen in the future. prediction (n).

predominate predominating predominated (v) to be greater in power or number than others. *Girls predominate in our class.* predominance (n), predominant (adj).

preen preening preened (v) When birds **preen** themselves, they clean and arrange their feathers with their beaks.

preface (pref-uss) (n) an introduction at the front of a book.

prefect (n) a school pupil who has special duties and responsibilities.

prefer preferring preferred (v) to like one thing better than another. *I prefer oranges to apples.* preference (n).

prefix prefixes (n) a part of a word added at its beginning that changes the word's meaning. "Sub", "un", and "re" are all prefixes. *The prefix "pre", which means "before", is used in "prehistoric" and "premeditated"*

pregnant (adj) A woman who is pregnant has a baby growing in her womb. *This diagram of a pregnant woman's womb shows a baby ready to be born.* pregnancy (n).

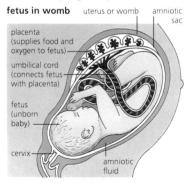

fetus in womb   uterus or womb   amniotic sac
placenta (supplies food and oxygen to fetus)
umbilical cord (connects fetus with placenta)
fetus (unborn baby)
cervix
amniotic fluid

prehistoric (adj) belonging to a time very long ago before history was written. prehistory (n).

prejudice
1 (n) a fixed and unreasonable opinion. prejudiced (adj).
2 (n) unfair behaviour that results from having fixed opinions about something or some people. *There are still too many cases of racial prejudice.*

preliminary (adj) preparing the way for what comes later. *We were given a preliminary talk before the course started.* preliminary (n).

premature (adj) happening or coming early. *A premature baby.* prematurely (adv).

premeditated (adj) planned in advance. *A premeditated attack.*

premier (prem-ee-er)
1 (adj) leading, top, or principal. *America's premier rock group.*
2 (n) the leader of a government.

premiere (prem-ee-air) (n) the first public performance of a film or play.

premises (plural n) a building and the land that belongs to it. *A burglar was seen entering the premises.*

premium
1 (n) money that is paid to take out an insurance policy.
2 If something is **at a premium**, it is rare and valued very highly.

premonition (n) a feeling that something bad is going to happen.

preoccupied (adj) If you are preoccupied, your thoughts are completely taken up with something. preoccupation (n).

prep
1 (n) (informal) homework. Prep is short for preparation.

2 prep school (n) In Britain, prep schools are private schools for pupils up to the age of thirteen. Prep school is short for preparatory school.

prepare preparing prepared (v) to get ready. preparation (n).

preposition (n) a word showing the position of things or people in relation to each other. "On", "beside" and "with" are prepositions. See page 3.

preposterous (adj) ridiculous and absurd. preposterously (adv).

preschool (adj) to do with children who are too young to go to school. *Preschool education.*

prescribe prescribing prescribed
1 (v) to say what should be done. *Mum prescribed a trip to the cinema to make us feel better.*
2 (v) When doctors prescribe medicine for a patient, they decide what drugs they should take and write an order, or prescription, to a chemist.

prescription (n) an order for drugs written by a doctor to a chemist.

presence (n) being in a place. *We would appreciate your presence at our party.*

present presenting presented
1 (prez-ent) (adj) If someone is present in a place, they are there.
2 (prez-ent) (n) the time now.
3 (priz-ent) (v) to give someone a gift or prize in a formal way.
4 (prez-ent) (n) something that you buy or make to give to somebody.
5 (priz-ent) (v) to introduce something, such as a television programme. presenter (n).
6 (n) The present participle of a verb ends with "ing" and is used to form some tenses, for example, "I am cooking" and "Harry will be cooking tomorrow." It can also be used as an adjective, as in "a thriving business", or as a noun, as in "Their singing gave me a headache."

presentation
1 (n) the formal giving of a prize or present. *At the end of term, we had a presentation for our teacher.*
2 (n) the way that something is produced and the way that it looks. *Your work is good but your presentation is atrocious!*

presently (adv) soon, or shortly.

preserve preserving preserved
1 (v) to protect something so that it stays in its original state. preservation (n).
2 (v) to treat food so that it does not go bad. preservative (n).
3 (n) jam. Apricot preserve.

preside presiding presided (v)
to be in charge of something.
Rodney presided over the meeting.

president
1 (n) the elected head of state of a
republic. *These portraits of American
presidents are carved out of rock at
Mount Rushmore in the USA.*
presidency (n), **presidential** (adj).
2 (n) the head of a society or
organization.

Mount Rushmore,
USA

George   Thomas   Theodore   Abraham
Washington Jefferson   Roosevelt   Lincoln

press presses pressing pressed
1 (v) to push firmly. *Press the button
to open the door.* **pressure** (n).
2 (v) to persuade strongly. *We pressed
Eddie into taking a role in the play.*
3 (v) to smooth out the creases in
clothes with an iron.
4 (n) a machine for printing
5 **the press** (n) a general name for
newspapers and the people who
produce them.

pressing (adj) urgent, or needing
immediate attention. *I must dash, I
have a pressing appointment.*

press stud (n) a fastener for
clothing, made up of a small knob
that pushes into a hole.

press-up or **push-up** (n)
an exercise in which you lie on the
floor and raise your body off it by
pushing with your arms.

pressure
1 (n) the force with which you press
on something. *Apply pressure here.*
2 (n) the force with which a liquid or
gas pushes against something.
Water pressure.
3 (n) strong influence. *Ulrika is under
pressure to finish her work.*

pressurize or **pressurise**
pressurizing pressurized
1 (v) to make someone do something.
Mabel pressurized me into staying.
2 (v) to seal off an aircraft cabin,
diving chamber, etc. so that the air
pressure inside stays the same as the
pressure at the Earth's surface.

prestige (press-teej) (n) the good
reputation and high status that comes
from being successful, powerful, rich,
etc. **prestigious** (adj).

presumably (adv) probably.

presume presuming presumed
1 (v) to think that something is true
without being certain. *I presume that
you like chocolate.*
2 (v) to dare. *Don't presume to tell me
what to do!* **presumption** (n).

pretend pretending pretended (v)
to try to make people believe that
things are different from the way they
really are. **pretence** (n).

pretext (n) a false reason. *Joe went
to the pub on the pretext of taking
the dog for a walk.*

pretty prettier prettiest
1 (adj) attractive and pleasing to look
at. **prettiness** (n), **prettily** (adv).
2 (adv) (informal) quite. *A pretty bad
film.*

prevail prevailing prevailed
1 (v) to succeed despite difficulties.
2 (v) to be common or usual. *Poverty
and crime prevail in many inner cities.*
prevalent (adj).

prevent preventing prevented (v)
to stop something from happening.
prevention (n).

preventative medicine (n)
health education or treatment that is
intended to stop people developing
disease and illness.

preview (n) a showing of a play or
film before it is released for public
viewing.

previous (adj) former, or happening
before. *I like this school more than my
previous one.* **previously** (adv).

prey (rhymes with tray) prey;
preying preyed
1 (n) a creature that is hunted and
eaten by other animals. **prey** (v).
2 (v) When an animal **preys on**
another animal, it hunts it and then
eats it.

price pricing priced
1 (n) the amount that you have to pay
for something.
2 (v) to give something a price.

priceless (adj) If something is
priceless, it is too valuable for anyone
to say how much it is worth.

prick pricking pricked (v) to make a
small hole in something with a sharp
point. **prick** (n).

prickle (n) a sharp point, for
example, on a rose bush. **prickly** (adj).

pride
1 (n) a feeling of satisfaction in
something that you do. *Zara takes
pride in her work.*
2 (n) a too high opinion of your own
importance and cleverness.

priest (n) a religious leader who
takes services in a church, temple, etc.

prim primmer primmest (adj)
Someone who is **prim** is very formal
and hates anything rough or rude.

prima donna
1 (n) a female opera star.
2 (n) (informal) someone who is
demanding and often bad-tempered.

primarily (adj) chiefly, or mainly.

primary
1 (adj) most important, chief, or main.
2 (adj) first, or earliest.
Primary education.

primary colours (n) In painting, the
primary colours are red, yellow, and
blue, which can be mixed to make all
the other colours.

primary school (n) In Britain, a
primary school is a school for
children aged from five to eleven, or
five to nine.

primate
1 (n) any member of the group of
intelligent mammals that includes
humans, apes, and monkeys.
2 (n) an archbishop.

prime (adj) of first importance or
quality. *Prime Minister. Prime beef.*

Prime Minister (n) the leader of a
government in some countries.

prime number (n) a number that
can be divided only by itself or by 1.
7, 13, and 29 are all prime numbers.

primeval (pry-mee-vul) (adj)
belonging to the earliest period of the
Earth.

primitive
1 (adj) simple, and not highly
developed or civilized. *The primitive
tribes of Amazonia.*
2 (adj) uncivilized, basic, and crude.
*Conditions at the hostel were very
primitive.*

prince (n) the son of a king or queen.

princess princesses (n) the daughter
of a king or queen, or the wife of a
prince.

principal
1 (adj) most important, chief, or main.
principally (adv).
2 (n) the head of a college or other
organization.

principle
1 (n) a scientific rule or truth.
2 (n) a basic rule which governs your
behaviour. *It's against Rollo's
principles to eat meat.*
3 If you agree to someone's plan **in
principle**, you are happy with the
general idea, but not necessarily with
the details.

print printing printed
1 *(v)* to produce words or pictures on a page with a machine that uses ink. *Colour pictures are usually printed by combining four colours of ink on white paper. This is called four-colour printing. The picture below has been magnified so that you can see how it is made up of millions of overlapping dots of black, yellow, cyan (blue), and magenta (red).* **printer** *(n)*.
2 *(v)* to write using letters that do not join up.
3 *(n)* a photograph, or a printed copy of a painting.

printed picture

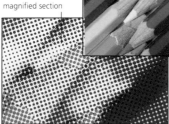

magnified section

print-out *(n)* a printed copy of information stored in a computer.

prior *(adj)* earlier. *Pogo can't come because of a prior engagement.*

priority priorities *(n)* something that is more important than other things.

prise prising prised *(v)* to force something open, using a lever.

prism *(n)* a clear glass or plastic shape that bends light or breaks it up into the colours of the spectrum. Prisms usually have a triangular ends. *See* **periscope**, **shape**, **spectrum**.

prison *(n)* a building where people are forced to stay, usually as punishment for a crime.

private
1 *(adj)* If something is **private**, it belongs to or concerns one person, organization, etc. and no one else. *Private possessions.* **privacy** *(n)*.
2 *(adj)* secret. *Private thoughts.* **privately** *(adv)*.
3 *(n)* a soldier of the lowest rank.

private school *(n)* a school where parents pay for their children's education.

privatize *or* **privatise** privatizing privatized *(v)* to sell or hand over a government-funded public industry or organization to private individuals or companies. **privatization** *(n)*.

privilege *(n)* a special advantage given to a person or a group of people. **privileged** *(adj)*.

prize prizing prized
1 *(n)* a reward for winning a game or competition.
2 *(v)* to value something very much. *I prize my freedom.* **prized** *(adj)*.

pro
1 *(adj)* If you are **pro** something, you are in favour of it.
2 *(n)* a shortened form of the word professional, often used in sport. *A golf pro.*
3 **pros and cons** advantages and disadvantages.

probable *(adj)* likely, or expected to happen. *It's probable that Yves will win.* **probability** *(n)*, **probably** *(adv)*.

probation
1 *(n)* If someone is **on probation** at work, they are having a trial period. **probationary** *(adj)*.
2 *(n)* If an offender is put **on probation** for a crime that they have committed, they are supervised for a certain time by a probation officer.

probe probing probed *(v)* to examine or explore something very carefully. **probe** *(n)*.

problem
1 *(n)* a difficult situation that needs to be sorted out or overcome.
2 *(n)* a puzzle or question to be solved. *A maths problem.*

procedure *(pro-see-dure) (n)* a way of doing something. *Follow the usual procedure for leaving the building.*

proceed proceeding proceeded
1 *(v)* to move forward, or to carry on.
2 *(plural n)* The **proceeds** of an event are the sums of money that it raises.

process processes processing processed
1 *(pro-sess) (n)* an organized series of actions that produce a result. *We studied the process of making rubber.* **processing** *(n)*.
2 *(pro-sess) (v)* When food is **processed**, it is treated and changed from its original state. **processing** *(n)*, **processed** *(adj)*.
3 *(pro-sess) (v)* to take part in a procession.

procession *(n)* a number of people walking or driving along a route as part of a public festival, religious service, etc.

proclaim proclaiming proclaimed *(v)* If someone **proclaims** something, they announce it publicly. **proclamation** *(n)*.

procrastinate procrastinating procrastinated *(v)* to put off something that you have to do. **procrastination** *(n)*.

prod prodding prodded *(v)* to poke something or someone. *I prodded Mitch to wake him up.* **prod** *(n)*.

prodigy *(prod-ij-ee)* prodigies *(n)* Child **prodigies** are extraordinarily clever or talented for their age.

produce producing produced
1 *(prod-yuce) (v)* to make something. *This factory produces cars.*
2 *(prod-yuce) (n)* things that are produced or grown for eating. *Dairy produce.*
3 *(prod-yuce) (v)* to bring something out for people to see. *Ginger produced a mouse from his pocket.*
4 *(prod-yuce) (v)* to be in charge of putting on a play or making a film. **producer** *(n)*.

product
1 *(n)* something that is manufactured or made by a natural process.
2 *(n)* the result that you get when you multiply two numbers. *15 is the product of 3 and 5.*

production
1 *(n)* the process of manufacturing or growing something.
2 *(n)* a play, opera, show, etc.
3 **production line** *(n)* a system of manufacturing in which the product moves along slowly while different things are added or done to it.

productive *(adj)* making a lot of products, or producing good results. *A productive meeting.* **productivity** *(n)*.

profession
1 *(n)* a job for which you need special training or study. *Medicine, teaching, and law are all professions.*
2 *(n)* something that you state openly. *A profession of love.*

professional
1 *(n)* a member of a profession, for example, a doctor, teacher, or lawyer. **professional** *(adj)*.
2 *(n)* someone who is paid for doing something that many others do as amateurs. *A soccer professional.* **professional** *(adj)*.
3 *(adj)* If somebody is **professional** at something, they are expert at it. **professionally** *(adv)*.

professor *(n)* the head and principal teacher of a university department.

proficient *(prof-ish-ent) (adj)* If you are **proficient** at doing something, you are able to do it properly and skilfully. **proficiency** *(n)*, **proficiently** *(adv)*.

profile
1 *(n)* the outline of someone's face, seen from the side.

2 (n) a brief account of someone's life or progress. *Pupil profiles.* **profile** (v).

profit (n) the money made by selling something, after the cost of making it or buying it has been taken away. profit (v), profitable (adj).

profound (adj) very deeply felt or thought. *Profound sadness.* profoundly (adv).

program programming programmed
1 (n) a series of instructions written in a special code that controls the way that a computer works.
2 (v) to give computers or other machines instructions to make them work. programming (n).

programme
1 (n) a television or radio show.
2 (n) a schedule, or a list of events.
3 (n) A theatre or concert programme is a pamphlet that gives you information about the performance.

programmer (n) someone whose job is to program a computer.

progress progresses progressing progressed
1 (v) to move forward, or to improve slowly. *How are you progressing with your fitness programme?* progress (n), progression (n).
2 If something is in progress, it is happening. *Roadworks are in progress all this week.*

prohibit prohibiting prohibited (v) to stop or ban something officially. prohibition (n).

project projecting projected
1 (proj-ekt) (n) a scheme, or a plan.
2 (proj-ekt) (n) a study of something, worked over a period of time. *We are starting a project on the Romans.*
3 (pro-jekt) (v) to stick out. *The branch projected into the road.* projecting (adj).
4 (pro-jekt) (v) to show an image on a screen. projector (n).
5 (pro-jekt) (v) to throw something forwards. projectile (n).
6 (pro-jekt) (v) to look ahead, or to forecast. *The company has projected a loss for next year.*
7 (pro-jekt) (v) If you project your voice, you make it carry a long way.

projection
1 (n) something that sticks out. *We noticed a strange projection behind the curtain.*
2 (n) a forecast, or a prediction.
3 (n) A **map projection** is a way of representing the globe on a flat page. *Mercator's projection.*

projector (n) a piece of equipment which shows slides or film on a screen.

prolific (adj) very productive, or producing a large quantity. *A prolific writer.*

prologue (pro-log) (n) a short speech or piece of writing which introduces a play, story, or poem.

prolong prolonging prolonged (v) to make something last longer.

promenade (n) a paved road or path that runs beside the beach at a seaside resort.

prominent
1 (adj) very easily seen. *The windmill is a prominent landmark.*
2 (adj) famous, or important. *A prominent politician.* prominence (n).

promise promising promised
1 (v) to say definitely that you will do something. promise (n).
2 (n) Someone who shows **promise** seems likely to do well in the future. promising (adj).

promote promoting promoted
1 (v) to move someone to a more important job. promotion (n).
2 (v) If a sports team is **promoted**, it moves to a higher league. promotion (n).
3 (v) to make the public aware of something or someone. *Merlin is busy promoting his latest book.* promotion (n).

prompt prompting prompted; prompter promptest
1 (adj) very quick and without delay. *A prompt answer.* promptly (adv).
2 (v) to remind actors of their lines, when they have forgotten them during a play. prompt (n).

prone
1 (adj) vulnerable, or easily affected by something harmful. *Dakita is prone to colds in the winter.*
2 (adj) lying flat or face-down.

prong (n) one of the sharp points of a fork.

pronoun (n) a word that is used in place of a noun. "I", "me", "her", and "it" are all pronouns. *See page 3.*

pronounce pronouncing pronounced
1 (v) to say words in a particular way. *How do you pronounce "psychic"?*
2 (v) to make a formal announcement. *The mayor pronounced the fair open.*

pronunciation
(pro-nun-see-ay-shun) (n) the way in which a word is pronounced.

proof (n) evidence that something is true. *Do you have proof of your age?*

prop propping propped
1 (v) to support something that would otherwise fall down. *Bob propped the ladder against the wall.* prop (n).
2 (n) In theatre, films, etc. a **prop** is any item that the actors need to carry or use. Prop is short for property.

propaganda (singular n) biased information, used to present a certain viewpoint.

propel propelling propelled (v) to drive or push something forward. *The aircraft was propelled by twin jet engines.* propulsion (n).

propellant (n) a chemical or fuel that propels something. See **aerosol**.

propeller (n) a set of rotating blades which provide force to move a vehicle through water or air.

proper
1 (adj) accepted, or right. *Is this the proper way to sit?* properly (adv).
2 (adj) real. *I want a proper explanation, not a made-up story.*
3 (adj) correct in behaviour. *Claudia is very prim and proper.* properly (adv).

proper noun (n) A **proper noun** is the name of a particular person, place, time, etc., such as "Jane", "New York", "Wednesday". Proper nouns start with a capital letter.

property properties
1 (n) the things that you own. *Whose property is this pen?*
2 (n) buildings and land belonging to someone. *Two fierce dogs guarded the property.*

prophesy (prof-ess-eye) prophesies prophesying prophesied (v) to predict that something will happen in the future. prophecy (prof-ess-ee) (n).

prophet (prof-it) (n) someone who predicts what will happen in the future.

proportion
1 (n) a part of something. *A large proportion of the class supported me.*
2 (n) the amount of something in relation to other things. *The proportion of boys to girls in the school is growing.* proportional (adj), proportionally (adv).
3 If something is **in proportion** to something else, it is the correct size in relation to it. *Edna has a large nose, but it is in proportion to the rest of her features.*
4 (plural n) The **proportions** of something are its measurements or size.

propose proposing proposed
1 (v) to suggest a plan or an idea. *Candy proposed that we all went swimming.* proposal (n).
2 (v) to ask someone to marry you. proposal (n).

propulsion (n) the force by which a plane, rocket, etc. is pushed along. *Jet propulsion.*

prose (n) writing that is in ordinary lines, not in verse.

prosecute prosecuting prosecuted (v) to accuse someone in a court of law. prosecution (n).

prospect
1 (n) something in the future that you look forward to or dread.
2 (n) a view, or a scene.

prospectus prospectuses (n) a brochure giving information about a school, company, etc.

prosper prospering prospered (v) to be successful, or to thrive. prosperity (n), prosperous (adj).

protect protecting protected (v) to guard or shelter something. protection (n), protective (adj).

protein (pro-teen) (n) a substance found in foods such as meat, cheese, eggs, and lentils. Humans and animals need protein in their diet.

protest protesting protested
1 (pro-test) (v) to object to something strongly and publicly.
2 (pro-test) (n) a demonstration or a statement against something.

Protestant (prot-iss-tant) (n) a Christian who does not belong to the Roman Catholic or Orthodox church.

proton (n) one of the microscopic parts of an atom that carries a positive electrical charge. See **atom**.

protoplasm (n) a jelly-like substance that makes up the living matter of all cells.

prototype (n) the first version of a new invention, used for experiment and development. *The prototype shown below, called the Renault Racoon, has four hydraulic legs for travelling over difficult terrain and two hydrojets which enable it to travel over water.* prototype (adj).

prototype car

protractor (n) a semicircular instrument, used for measuring angles, and usually made of transparent plastic. See **geometry**.

protrude protruding protruded (v) to stick out, or to jut out. *The rocks protruded into the sea.*

proud prouder proudest
1 (adj) pleased with what you or someone else has achieved.
2 (adj) A proud person thinks too highly of their own importance or abilities.

prove proving proved (v) to show that something is true. *The experiment proved our hypothesis.*

proverb (n) a wise, old saying.

provide providing provided
1 (v) to supply the things that someone needs. provision (n).
2 provided (conj) on condition that, or as long as. *I will go swimming provided that you come too.*

province (n) a district, or a region of a country.

provision
1 (n) the act of providing something.
2 provisions (plural n) groceries and other household goods.

provisional (adj) If something is provisional, it is temporary or not yet definite. *A provisional driving licence.* provisionally (adv).

provoke provoking provoked (v) to annoy someone and make them angry. provocation (n), provocative (adj).

prowess (n) skill, or bravery. *Zita's prowess on the ski slopes is legendary.*

prowl prowling prowled (v) to move around quietly and secretly, like an animal looking for food.

proximity (n) nearness.

prudent (adj) If you are prudent, you are cautious and think carefully before you do something. prudence (n), prudently (adv).

prune pruning pruned
1 (n) a dried plum.
2 (v) to cut off branches from a tree or bush, in order to make it grow more strongly.

pry pries prying pried (v) If you pry, you look into other people's business in a nosy way.

ps short for **postscript**.

psalm (sahm) (n) a sacred song or poem, especially one from the Book of Psalms in the Bible.

pseudonym (syoo-doh-nim) (n) a name that you use which is not your own. Many writers use pseudonyms.

psychiatrist (sy-ky-a-trist) (n) a doctor who is trained to treat mental illness. psychiatry (n), psychiatric (adj).

psychic (sy-kik) (adj) Someone who is psychic can use their mind in an unusual way, for example, to tell what people are thinking or to predict the future. psychic (n).

psychologist (sy-kol-oj-ist) (n) someone who studies people's minds and the ways that people behave. psychology (n), psychological (adj).

psychopath (sy-koh-path) (n) someone who has something wrong with their character, so that they are violent or dangerous. psychopathic (adj).

pto The letters pto, written at the bottom of a page, stand for please turn over.

pub (n) a place where adults can go to drink alcohol. Pub is short for public house.

puberty (pew-ber-tee) (n) the time when your body changes from a child's to an adult's.

public
1 (adj) to do with people. *Public opinion.*
2 (adj) If something is public, it belongs to, or can be used by everybody. *Public transport.* publicly (adj).
3 the public (n) people in general.

publican (n) someone who runs a pub.

publication
1 (n) The publication of a book or magazine is the production and distribution of it, so that people can buy it.
2 (n) a book, or a magazine.

publicity (n) information that tells you about a person or an event. *The film received a lot of publicity in the newspapers.*

publicize or **publicise** publicizing publicized (v) If you publicize an event, you make it known to as many people as possible.

public opinion (singular n) the views or beliefs of people in general.

public school
1 (n) In Britain, public schools are schools where parents pay for their children's education.
2 (n) (US) a school run by the state, providing free education.

publish publishes publishing published (v) to produce and distribute a book, magazine, etc., so that people can buy it. **publisher** (n), **publishing** (n).

pucker puckering puckered (v) to wrinkle, or to fold. **pucker** (n).

pudding
1 (n) a sweet food served at the end of a meal.
2 (n) a sponge or suet mixture cooked with fruit or meat. A treacle pudding.

puddle (n) a small pool of rainwater or other liquid.

puff puffing puffed
1 (v) to blow or breathe out something, such as smoke or steam. **puff** (n).
2 **puff up** (v) to swell up. **puffy** (adj).
3 **puff pastry** (n) pastry made in thin layers, that puffs up when it is cooked.

puffin (n) a black and white sea bird whose beak becomes brightly coloured in the mating season.

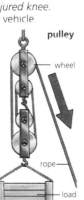
puffin

pugnacious (adj) If someone is pugnacious, they are fond of fighting or quarrelling. **pugnaciously** (adv).

pull pulling pulled
1 (v) to move something towards you. **pull** (n).
2 (v) If you **pull out** of something, you stop doing it. Adam pulled out of the team because of an injured knee.
3 **pull up** (v) to stop a vehicle.

pulley
1 (n) a wheel with a grooved rim in which a rope or chain can run, used to lift loads more easily.
2 (n) a lifting machine made from a rope or chain and a set of linked pulleys. The diagram shows how a pulley is used to lift a heavy load.

pulley
wheel
rope
load

pullover (n) a knitted piece of clothing that you wear on the top half of your body.

pulp (n) a soft, crushed mass of something, such as fruit, vegetables, or wood. **pulp** (v).

pulpit (n) a raised, enclosed platform in a church where a priest stands to preach.

pulsate pulsating pulsated (v) to beat or vibrate regularly. Rock music pulsated through the house.

pulse
1 (n) a bean, pea, or lentil seed.
2 (n) a steady beat or throb, especially the pumping of blood through your body. **pulse** (v).

puma (pyoo-ma) (n) a wild cat, found in America.

pumice stone (n) a piece of light, greyish rock, used for rubbing away hard skin.

pummel pummelling pummelled (v) to punch someone or something repeatedly.

pump pumping pumped
1 (n) a machine that forces liquids or gases from one container into another. A bicycle pump. A water pump.
2 (v) to empty or fill a container using a pump.
3 **pumps** (plural n) flat, slip-on shoes, often made of canvas.
4 (v) If you **pump** someone for information, you keep asking them questions.

pumpkin (n) a very big, round, orange fruit that grows on the ground. People often carve faces in pumpkins at Halloween.

pumpkin

pun (n) a joke based on a word that has two meanings. **pun** (v).

punch punches punching punched
1 (v) to hit something or someone with your fist. **punch** (n).
2 (n) a drink made from fruit juice, spices, and usually alcohol.
3 (n) a metal tool used for making holes. **punch** (v).
4 **punch line** (n) the last line of a joke or story, that makes it funny or surprising.

punctual (adj) If you are punctual, you arrive at the right time. **punctuality** (n), **punctually** (adv).

punctuation
1 (n) marks that you use in writing to divide up sentences, to show that someone is speaking, or to show questions, etc. **punctuate** (v).
2 **punctuation mark** (n) a written mark such as a comma, exclamation mark, full stop, etc.

puncture (n) a hole in a ball, tyre, etc., made by a sharp object. **puncture** (v)

pungent (adj) If something is pungent, it tastes or smells strong or sharp. A pungent drink.

punish punishes punishing punished (v) If you **punish** someone, you make them suffer for committing a crime, or for behaving badly. **punishment** (n).

Punjabi (poon-jar-bee) (n) a language spoken in the Punjab, a state of India.

punk
1 (n) a style of music and dress that was popular in the 1970s. Punks used razor blades and safety pins for decoration, and had brightly coloured hair.
2 **punk rock** (n) loud, fast music played by punk bands in the 1970s.

punt (n) a boat with a flat bottom, that you push along with a long pole. **punt** (v).

puny punier puniest (adj) small and feeble. **puniness** (n), **punily** (adv).

pupa pupae or pupas (n) an insect at the stage of development between a larva and an adult. See **caterpillar**.

pupil
1 (n) someone who is being taught, especially a schoolchild.
2 (n) the round, black part of your eye, that lets light travel through it. See **eye**.

puppet (n) a toy in the shape of a person or an animal, that you control by pulling strings that are attached to it, or by moving your hand inside it.

puppy puppies
1 (n) a young dog.
2 **puppy fat** (n) extra weight which children lose as they grow older.

purchase purchasing purchased
1 (v) to buy something. **purchaser** (n).
2 (n) something that has been bought.

pure purer purest (adj) clean and not mixed with anything else. Pure gold. **purity** (n).

purée (pyoor-ay) (n) liquidized or sieved food. **purée** (v).

purge purging purged (v) to clean something out by getting rid of unwanted things. **purge** (n).

purify purifies purifying purified (v) to make someone or something pure. **purification** (n).

purple (n) the colour of blackcurrant juice. **purple** (adj).

purpose
1 (n) a reason, or an intention. **purposeful** (adj), **purposely** (adv).
2 **on purpose** deliberately.

purr purring purred
1 (v) When a cat **purrs**, it makes a low sound in its throat to show pleasure. purr (n).
2 (v) to make a low sound like a cat. *The limousine purred up the drive.*

purse pursing pursed
1 (n) a small container in which people keep their money.
2 (v) If you **purse your lips**, you press them together.

pursue (per-syoo) pursuing pursued
1 (v) to follow or chase something.
2 (v) to continue something. *We'll pursue this argument later.*

pursuit (per-syoot)
1 (n) an activity, or an occupation. *Leisure pursuits.*
2 If you are **in pursuit of** someone, you are trying to catch them.

pus (n) a thick, yellowish liquid that comes out of an infected wound.

push pushes pushing pushed
1 (v) to move something away from you. push (n).
2 (v) to press yourself forward. *We pushed through the crowd.*
3 (v) to try to force someone to do something. *Harry's father pushed him into a medical career.*

push-up see **press-up**.

put putting put
1 (v) to place, lay, or move something.
2 (v) to express in words. *How can I put this so that you'll understand?*
3 **put down** (v) to kill an animal because it is very ill.

4 **put off** (v) If you **put something off**, you delay doing it.
5 **put off** (v) If you **put someone off** something, you stop them liking it.
6 **put up** (v) If you **put someone up**, you let them sleep overnight at your house.

putrid (pyoo-trid) (adj) decaying and foul-smelling.

putt (rhymes with but) putting putted (v) to tap a golf ball into the hole on a green. putt (n), putter (n).

putty putties (n) a paste that sets hard, used to fix windows into frames.

puzzle puzzling puzzled
1 (n) a game or activity for which you have to think hard in order to solve problems. *A crossword puzzle.*
2 (n) something or someone that is hard to understand.
3 (v) If something **puzzles** you, it makes you confused or unsure. puzzled (adj).

pyjamas (plural n) a shirt and trousers that you wear in bed.

pylon (n) a tall, metal tower that supports electricity cables.

pyramid
1 (n) a solid shape with triangular sides that meet at the top. Most pyramids have a square base and four sides. See **shape**.
2 (n) an ancient Egyptian stone monument where Pharaohs and their treasure were buried. *The picture shows a reconstruction of how a pyramid was built and a cutaway view of the Great Pyramid at Giza in Egypt.*

Qq

quack quacking quacked (v) When ducks **quack**, they make a sharp, loud sound. quack (n).

quad
1 (n) one of four children born at almost the same time to one mother. Quad is short for quadruplet.
2 (n) an open square with buildings around it, in a school or college. Quad is short for quadrangle.

quadrant (n) a quarter of a circle or a quarter of the circumference of a circle.

quadrilateral (n) a flat shape with four straight sides. quadrilateral (adj).

quadruped (n) a four-footed animal. *Horses are quadrupeds.*

quadruple quadrupling quadrupled
1 (v) to multiply something by four.
2 (adj) four times as big, or four times as many.

quagmire (n) a wet and boggy area of ground.

quail quailing quailed
1 (n) a small bird that is hunted for sport and for food.
2 (v) If you **quail**, you feel or look afraid. *Kylie quailed as the monster drew nearer.*

quaint quainter quaintest (adj) charming and old-fashioned. *A quaint little fishing village.* quaintness (n), quaintly (adv).

quake quaking quaked
1 (v) to shake and tremble with fear.
2 (n) (informal) an earthquake.

qualification
1 (n) a skill or ability that makes you able to do something.
2 (n) a certificate which shows that you have certain skills or abilities.

qualify qualifies qualifying qualified
1 (v) to reach a level or standard that allows you to do something. *Winning the match qualified us to play in the final.*
2 (v) to change or limit the meaning of something. *Victoria qualified the statement, "Boys are stupid", by adding the word "most".*

quality qualities
1 (n) The **quality** of something is how good or bad it is. *You can tell it is a cheap video by its poor quality.*

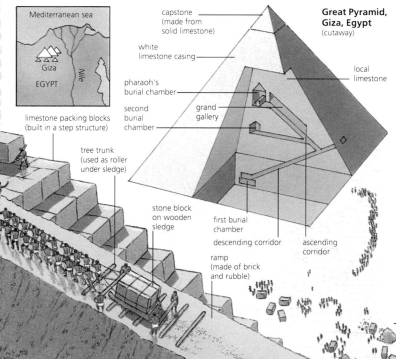

Mediterranean sea
Giza
EGYPT
Nile

capstone (made from solid limestone)

white limestone casing

pharaoh's burial chamber

second burial chamber

grand gallery

Great Pyramid, Giza, Egypt (cutaway)

local limestone

limestone packing blocks (built in a step structure)

tree trunk (used as roller under sledge)

stone block on wooden sledge

first burial chamber

descending corridor

ascending corridor

ramp (made of brick and rubble)

2 (n) a special characteristic of someone or something. *Elina has all the right qualities to be a nurse.*

qualm (*rhymes with arm*) (n) a feeling of worry or uneasiness. *I had serious qualms about flying.*

quandary (*kwon-dree*) quandaries (n) If you are **in a quandary** about something, you are confused, and do not know what to do about it.

quantity quantities (n) an amount or number.

quarantine (n) When an animal is put **in quarantine**, it is kept away from other animals in case it has a disease. quarantine (v).

quarrel quarrelling quarrelled
1 (v) to argue, or to disagree. quarrelsome (adj).
2 (n) an argument.

quarry quarries
1 (n) a place where stone, slate, etc. is dug from the ground. quarry (v).
2 (n) a person or an animal that is being chased or hunted.

quarter
1 (n) one of four equal parts quarter (v).
2 (n) a part of a town. *The Latin quarter in Paris is famous for its artists.*
3 quarters (*plural n*) lodgings or rooms where people live.

quartet (n) a piece of music that is played or sung by four people.

quartz (n) a hard mineral that comes in many different forms and colours. Quartz is used to make very accurate clocks, watches, and electronic equipment.

quartz crystal

quash quashes quashing quashed
1 (v) to put down a rebellion.
2 (v) to reject an idea or a decision. *The appeal court quashed the conviction.*

quaver quavering quavered
1 (v) to shake, or to tremble. *Desmond's voice quavered because he was so nervous.*
2 (n) a musical note representing half of one beat. *See* **notation**.

quay (*key*) (n) a place where boats can stop to load or unload.

queasy queasier queasiest (adj) If you feel **queasy**, you feel sick and uneasy. queasiness (n).

queen
1 (n) a woman from a royal family, who is the ruler of her country.
2 (n) the wife of a king.

3 (n) a large bee, wasp, or ant, that can lay eggs. *See* **honeycomb**.
4 (n) a playing card with a picture of a queen on it.
5 (n) the most powerful chesspiece, that can move in any direction. *See* **chess**.

queer queerer queerest (adj) odd, or strange. queerly (adv).

quell quelling quelled (v) to stop, or to become calm. *My fears were quelled when I saw someone I knew.*

quench quenches quenching quenched
1 (v) If you **quench** a fire, you put it out.
2 (v) If you **quench** your thirst, you drink until you are no longer thirsty.

query (*kweer-ee*) queries querying queried
1 (n) a question or doubt about something.
2 (v) to ask questions about something because you think there has been some mistake. *May I query that statement?*

quest (n) a long search.

question questioning questioned
1 (n) a sentence that asks something.
2 (n) a problem, or something that needs to be talked about. *We need to tackle the question of bullying.*
3 (v) to ask questions.
4 (v) to be doubtful about something. *I question the truth of that claim.*

question mark (n) the punctuation mark (?), used in writing to show that a sentence is a question.

questionnaire (n) a list of questions that someone asks you, in order to find out your opinions.

queue (*kyoo*) queueing queued
1 (n) a line of people waiting for something.
2 (v) to wait in a line of people.

quibble quibbling quibbled (v) to argue about unimportant things. quibble (n).

quiche (*keesh*) (n) a savoury dish made of pastry and filled with eggs, cheese, vegetables, etc.

quick quicker quickest
1 (adj) fast. quicken (v), quick (adv), quickly (adv).
2 (adj) clever and lively.
3 (n) the skin under your nails.

quicksand (n) loose, wet sand that you can sink into.

quiet quieter quietest
1 (adj) not loud. *Everyone spoke in quiet voices.* quietness (n), quieten (v), quietly (adv).

2 (adj) peaceful and calm. *We spent a quiet afternoon by the river.* quietness (n), quietly (adv).

quill
1 (n) the long, hollow, central part of a bird's feather.
2 (n) one of the long, pointed spines on a porcupine. *See* **porcupine**.
3 quill pen (n) a pen made from a bird's feather, with its quill cut to form a nib.

nib
quill pen

quilt (n) a warm, usually padded covering for a bed.

quilted (adj) If material is **quilted**, it is padded and sewn in lines.

quintet (n) a piece of music that is played or sung by five people.

quip (n) a witty or clever remark.

quit quitting quit *or* quitted
1 (v) to stop doing something. *Dad has promised to quit smoking.*
2 (v) to leave something. *Donovan decided to quit his job.*

quite
1 (adv) rather, or fairly. *The concert was quite good.*
2 (adv) completely. *Have you quite finished?*

quiver quivering quivered
1 (v) to tremble or vibrate. quiver (n).
2 (n) a case for arrows.

quiz quizzes quizzing quizzed
1 (n) a test or game where you have to answer questions.
2 (v) to question someone closely.

quota (n) a fixed amount or share of something. *Our class already has its quota of books.*

quotation
1 (n) a sentence or short passage from a book, play, speech, etc. which is repeated by somebody else.
2 (n) a written estimate of how much a job will cost.

quotation mark (n) the punctuation mark (") or (') used in writing to show where speech begins and ends or used to highlight certain words.

quote quoting quoted
1 (v) to repeat words that were spoken or written by someone else. quote (n).
2 (v) to estimate or guess how much a job will cost. quote (n).

quotient (*kwo-shent*) (n) the number that you get when you divide one number by another. *3 is the quotient of 12 and 4.*

Qur'an *see* **Koran**.

Rr

rabbi *(rab-eye) (n)* a Jewish religious leader.

rabbit *(n)* a small, long-eared, furry mammal that lives in a burrow. *See* **angora**.

rabble *(n)* a noisy crowd of people.

rabies *(ray-beez) (n)* a fatal disease that makes dogs and other animals go mad. **rabid** *(rab-id) (adj)*.

raccoon *or* **racoon** *(n)* a mammal with a black and white face and a ringed tail, that lives in North America.

race racing raced
1 *(n)* a test of speed. *A running race.* **race** *(v)*.
2 *(n)* one of the major groups into which human beings can be divided. People of the same race come from the same part of the world and share the same physical characteristics, such as skin colour.
3 *(v)* to run or move very fast.

race relations *(plural n)* the way that people of different races get on together when they live in the same community.

racial
1 *(adj)* to do with a person's race. *What is your racial origin?*
2 *(adj)* to do with different races. *Racial harmony.*

racist *(ray-sist) (adj)* Someone who is racist thinks that some races are better than others, and treats people of other races unfairly or cruelly. **racism** *(n)*, **racist** *(n)*.

rack racking racked
1 *(n)* a framework for holding things or for hanging things from. *A plate rack. A clothes rack.*
2 *(n)* an instrument of torture, used to stretch the body of a victim.
3 *(v)* If you **rack your brains**, you think very hard. *I racked my brains to remember his name.*

racket
1 **racket** *or* **racquet** *(n)* a stringed bat that you use in tennis, squash, and badminton. *See* **badminton**.
2 *(n)* a very loud noise.
3 *(n)* a dishonest activity. *The police exposed a drugs racket.*

racoon *see* **raccoon**.

racquet *see* **racket**.

radar
1 *(n)* Planes and ships use **radar** to find solid objects by reflecting radio waves off them. Radar stands for radio detecting and ranging.
2 **radar trap** *(n)* a system using radar equipment that is set up by the police to catch speeding drivers.

radial *(adj)* spreading out from the centre.

radiant
1 *(adj)* bright and shining. **radiance** *(n)*.
2 *(adj)* Someone who is **radiant** looks very healthy and happy.

radiate radiating radiated
1 *(v)* to spread out from the centre.
2 *(v)* to send out something strongly. *Mario radiates confidence.*

radiation
1 *(n)* the sending out of rays of light, heat, etc.
2 *(n)* particles that are sent out from a radioactive substance.

radiator
1 *(n)* a metal container through which hot water or steam circulates, sending out heat into a room.
2 *(n)* a metal device through which water circulates to cool a vehicle's engine. *See* **car**, **racing car**.

radical
1 *(adj)* If a change is **radical**, it is thorough and has important and far-reaching effects. **radically** *(adv)*.
2 *(adj)* Someone who is **radical** believes in extreme political change. **radical** *(n)*.

radio radioing radioed
1 *(n)* a piece of equipment that you use to listen to sounds sent by electrical waves. **radio** *(adj)*.
2 *(v)* to send a message using a radio.

radioactive *(adj)* If an object is **radioactive**, it gives off strong, usually harmful rays. **radioactivity** *(n)*.

radiography *(n)* the process of taking X-ray photographs of people's bones, organs, etc. **radiographer** *(n)*.

radish radishes *(n)* a small red and white vegetable that you eat in salads. *See* **vegetable**.

radium *(n)* a radioactive element sometimes used to treat cancer.

racing car *(n)* a car designed to race at very high speeds. *The picture shows a cutaway view of a Camel Benetton Ford B193B Formula I racing car.*

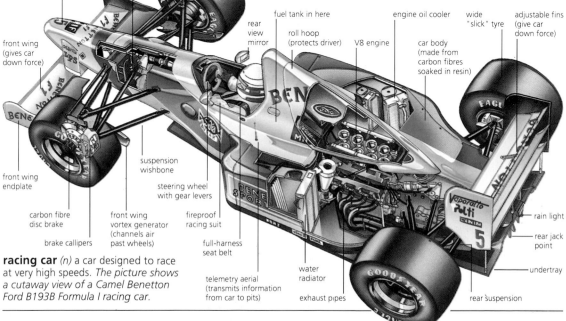

racing car (cutaway)

nose cone
driver's pedals
front wing (gives car down force)
front wing endplate
carbon fibre disc brake
brake callipers
front wing vortex generator (channels air past wheels)
suspension wishbone
steering wheel with gear levers
fireproof racing suit
full-harness seat belt
telemetry aerial (transmits information from car to pits)
rear view mirror
fuel tank in here
roll hoop (protects driver)
V8 engine
engine oil cooler
wide "slick" tyre
adjustable fins (give car down force)
car body (made from carbon fibres soaked in resin)
water radiator
exhaust pipes
rain light
rear jack point
undertray
rear suspension

radius *(ray-dee-uss)* radiuses or radii
1 *(n)* a straight line drawn from the centre of a circle to its outer edge. *See* **circle**.
2 *(n)* a bone in your lower arm. *See* **skeleton**.
3 *(n)* a circular area around a thing or a place. *Most of my friends live within a radius of a mile from my house.*

raffle *(n)* a way of raising money, by selling tickets and then giving prizes to people with winning tickets. **raffle** *(v).*

raft rafting rafted
1 *(n)* a floating platform, often made from logs tied together.
2 *(v)* to travel by raft. **rafting** *(n).*
3 *(n)* an inflatable rubber craft with a flat bottom. *The picture shows an inflatable raft travelling through fast-moving water.*

white-water rafting

rag
1 *(n)* a piece of old cloth.
2 **rags** *(plural n)* very old, torn clothing.

rage raging raged
1 If you are **in a rage**, you are very angry.
2 *(v)* to be violent or noisy. *The wind raged around the house.*

ragged *(rag-ed) (adj)* old, torn, and scruffy. **raggedly** *(adv).*

raid
1 *(n)* a sudden attack on a place. **raider** *(n),* **raid** *(v).*
2 *(n)* a sudden visit by the police to search for criminals, drugs, etc. **raid** *(v).*

rail
1 *(n)* a fixed bar or metal track.
2 *(n)* the railway. *Thomas loves travelling by rail.* **rail** *(adj).*

railing *(n)* a metal bar that is a part of a fence.

railway
1 *(n)* a train track.
2 *(n)* a system of transport using trains.

rain raining rained
1 *(n)* water that falls from clouds. **rain** *(v),* **rainy** *(adj).*
2 *(v)* to fall like rain.

rainbow *(n)* an arch of different colours caused by sunlight shining through raindrops. *See* **spectrum**.

rainfall *(n)* the amount of rain that falls in one place in a certain time.

rainforest *(n)* a thick, tropical forest where a lot of rain falls. *The map shows the main rainforests of the world, and is surrounded by examples of rainforest wildlife.* **rainforest** *(adj).*

rainforests and rainforest wildlife

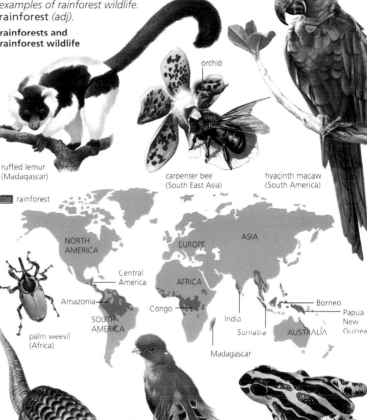

rainforest

orchid

ruffed lemur (Madagascar)

carpenter bee (South East Asia)

hyacinth macaw (South America)

NORTH AMERICA

EUROPE

ASIA

Central America

AFRICA

Amazonia

Congo

India

Borneo

Papua New Guinea

SOUTH AMERICA

Sumatra

AUSTRALIA

palm weevil (Africa)

Madagascar

pangolin (Africa)

golden cock-of-the-rock (South America)

arrow-poison frog (South America)

raise raising raised
1 *(v)* to lift something up. *Raise your glasses for a toast.*
2 *(v)* If you **raise** money, you collect it for a particular cause or charity.
3 *(v)* to look after children or young animals until they are adults. *Martha has raised five sons.*

raisin *(n)* a dried grape.

rake raking raked
1 *(n)* a garden tool with metal teeth, used to level soil or to collect leaves, grass cuttings, etc.
2 *(v)* to use a rake. *Bernard is raking up leaves.*
3 *(v) (informal)* If you **rake it in**, you make a lot of money.

rally rallies
1 *(n)* a large meeting. *A political rally.*
2 *(n)* In racket games, such as tennis, a **rally** is a long exchange of shots.

ram ramming rammed
1 *(n)* a male sheep.
2 *(v)* to crash into something deliberately.
3 *(v)* to push something into a space. *Kitty rammed her clothes into the bag.*
4 **ram-raid** *(v)* to drive a vehicle into a shop front in order to steal from that shop. **ram-raider** *(n),* **ram-raiding** *(n).*

RAM *(n)* the part of a computer's memory which is lost when you switch the computer off. The initials RAM stand for random access memory.

Ramadan *(n)* the ninth month of the Islamic year when Muslims must not eat between sunrise and sunset.

ramble rambling rambled
1 (v) to go on a long, country walk for pleasure. **ramble** (n), **rambler** (n).
2 (v) to speak for a long time in a way that is hard to follow.

rambling (adj) badly planned, or out of control. *A rambling house. A rambling speech.*

ramp
1 (n) a man-made slope linking one level with another.
2 (n) a ridge across a road, designed to reduce the speed of vehicles.

rampage (n) If you go **on the rampage**, you rush about in a noisy and destructive way. **rampage** (v).

rampant (adj) wild and unrestrained. *Rampant weeds.*

rampart (n) the surrounding wall or embankment of a fort or castle.

ramshackle (adj) rickety, or likely to fall apart. *A ramshackle cottage.*

ranch ranches (n) a large farm for cattle, usually in North America. **rancher** (n).

rancid (adj) Rancid food tastes sour because it has gone bad.

rand (n) the main unit of money in South Africa.

random
1 (adj) without any fixed plan or order. *Juan grabbed a random selection of clothes.* **randomly** (adv).
2 If you do something **at random**, you do it without any plan or purpose.

range ranging ranged
1 (n) a collection or number of things.
2 (v) to vary between one extreme and the other. *The dogs ranged in size from tiny pekes to enormous wolfhounds.* **range** (n).
3 (n) the distance that a bullet or rocket can travel.
4 (n) an area of open land used for a special purpose. *A cattle range.*
5 (n) a long chain of mountains.
6 (v) to wander over a large area. *Cattle ranged over the plains.*
7 (n) a cooking stove.

ranger (n) someone in charge of a wildlife park or forest.

rank
1 (n) an official position or job level. *Cyril rose to the rank of colonel.*
2 (n) a line of people or things. *A taxi rank.*
3 (n) social class. *People of all ranks supported the cause.*

ransack ransacking ransacked (v) to search a place wildly, usually looking for things to steal.

ransom (n) money that is demanded before someone can be set free.

rant ranting ranted (v) to talk or shout in a loud and angry manner.

rap rapping rapped
1 (v) to hit something sharply and quickly. **rap** (n).
2 (n) a type of music where words are spoken in a rhythmical way with a musical backing. **rap** (v).

rape raping raped
1 (v) to force someone to have sexual intercourse. **rapist** (n).
2 (n) a bright yellow plant, used for cattle feed and oil.

rapid (adj) quick and speedy. **rapidity** (n), **rapidly** (adv).

rapier (n) a long, double-edged sword, often used in duels in the 16th and 17th centuries. *This rapier was made in Italy in the 16th century.*

knuckle guard

rapier

hilt   steel inlaid with gold

double-edged steel blade

guard for thumb and forefinger

rare rarer rarest
1 (adj) not often seen, or unusual. **rarity** (n), **rarely** (adv).
2 (adj) Rare meat is very lightly cooked.

rascal (n) a usually friendly name for someone who is very mischievous.

rash rashes; rasher rashest
1 (n) spots or red patches on your skin, caused by an allergy or illness.
2 (adj) If you are **rash**, you act quickly, without thinking first. **rashly** (adv).

rasher (n) a thin slice of bacon.

rasp rasping rasped
1 (n) a coarse file used for smoothing metal or wood.
2 (v) to speak in a harsh voice.

raspberry raspberries (n) a small red, soft fruit. *See* **fruit**.

rat
1 (n) a long-tailed rodent like a large mouse. Rats sometimes spread disease.
2 (n) (informal) a disloyal or treacherous person.
3 **rat race** (n) very stressful competition for success at work.

rat

rate rating rated
1 (n) the speed at which something happens. *Rhonda spends money at an alarming rate.*
2 (n) a charge, or a fee. *Maurice charges very high rates for his work.*
3 (n) standard, or quality. *Sasha gave a first-rate performance.*
4 (v) to value someone or something. *Dillon's fellow runners rate him highly.* **rating** (n).

rather
1 (adv) fairly, or quite. *It's rather a long way to walk.*
2 (adv) more willingly. *I'd rather be at the seaside than at school.*

ratio (ray-shee-oh) (n) the proportion of one thing to another, expressed in its simplest terms. *In a group with 15 girls and 5 boys, the ratio of girls to boys is 3 to 1.*

ration (n) a limited amount, or a share. *No more chocolate for you today, you've already had your ration!* **rationing** (n), **ration** (v).

rational
1 (adj) sensible and logical. *We made a rational decision to turn the two small shops into one.* **rationally** (adv).
2 (adj) calm, reasonable, and sane. *Rational behaviour.* **rationally** (adv).

rattle rattling rattled
1 (v) to make a rapid series of short, sharp noises. **rattle** (n).
2 (n) a baby's toy.

rattlesnake (n) a poisonous snake from North and South America with a tail that rattles as it vibrates.

rattlesnake

rattle

raucous (raw-kus) (adj) harsh, or loud. **raucously** (adv).

rave raving raved
1 (v) to speak in a wild, uncontrolled way.
2 (v) (informal) to be very enthusiastic about something.
3 (n) a type of party with fast, rhythmic, electronic music and flashing lights.

raven (n) a large, black bird of the crow family.

raven

Some words that begin with a "r" sound are spelt "wr".

ravenous *(adj)* very hungry.

ravine *(n)* a deep, narrow valley with steep sides.

raw rawer rawest
1 *(adj)* Food that is **raw** has not been cooked or processed.
2 **raw materials** *(n)* the basic things used to make something.

ray
1 *(n)* a strong line of light, radiation, etc
2 *(n)* a type of fish with a flat body, large wing-like fins, and a long tail.

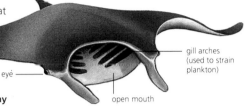

poisonous spine

gill arches (used to strain plankton)

eye

pectoral fin

giant devil ray

open mouth

razor *(n)* an instrument with a blade, used to shave hair from the skin.

reach reaches reaching reached
1 *(v)* to stretch out to something with your hand. *Can you reach the top shelf?*
2 *(v)* to extend, or to go as far as. *Our garden reaches down to the river.*
3 *(v)* to arrive somewhere. *We eventually reached the summit.*

react reacting reacted
1 *(v)* to respond to something that happens. *The firemen reacted quickly to the alarm.* **reaction** *(n)*.
2 *(v)* If one substance **reacts** with another, a chemical change takes place in one or both of the substances as they are mixed together. **reaction** *(n)*.

reactionary *(adj)* If someone is **reactionary**, they are against change and want to keep things as they are. **reactionary** *(n)*.

reactor *(n)* a large machine in which nuclear energy is produced.

read reading read
1 *(v)* to look at written or printed words and understand what they mean.
2 *(v)* to understand some form of communication. *Hilary can read my mind.*

readily *(adv)* easily, or willingly.

ready readier readiest *(adj)* If you are **ready**, you are prepared, or you are in a position to start.

real
1 *(adj)* true and not imaginary. *The real story isn't quite so dramatic.* **reality** *(n)*.
2 *(adj)* genuine and not artificial. *A real diamond.*

realistic
1 *(adj)* very like the real thing. *A realistic model.* **realism** *(n)*, **realistically** *(adv)*.
2 *(adj)* sensible, practical, or correct. *I will only pay a realistic price for the bike.* **realistically** *(adv)*.
3 *(adj)* If you are **realistic**, you view things as they really are. *Frannie is realistic about her chances of winning.* **realistically** *(adv)*.

reality realities
1 *(n)* truth, or the actual situation. *Being a model looks glamorous, but the reality is not much fun.*
2 *(n)* a fact of life that must be faced. *After the holiday, we must return to the reality of work.*

realize or **realise** realizing realized *(v)* to become aware that something is true. *Randall realized that he hadn't been working hard enough.* **realization** *(n)*.

really
1 *(adv)* actually, or in reality. *Are the rumours really true?*
2 *(adv)* very. *I'm really happy.*

reap reaping reaped
1 *(v)* to cut a crop for harvest.
2 *(v)* If you **reap** the reward for something you have done, you experience the results of it.

reappear reappearing reappeared *(v)* to come into sight again. **reappearance** *(n)*.

rear rearing reared
1 *(v)* to breed and bring up young animals.
2 *(v)* to care for and educate children.
3 *(n)* the back of something. **rear** *(adj)*.
4 *(v)* If a horse **rears**, it rises up on its back legs.

rearrange rearranging rearranged *(v)* to arrange things differently.

reason reasoning reasoned
1 *(n)* the cause of something, or the motive behind someone's action.
2 *(v)* to think in a logical way. *Aaron reasoned that it would be quicker to walk.* **reason** *(n)*.
3 *(v)* If you **reason** with someone, you try to persuade them that what you suggest is sensible.

reasonable
1 *(adj)* fair. *Your offer seems reasonable to me.* **reasonably** *(adv)*.
2 *(adj)* sensible. *Hal won't make a fuss, he's always very reasonable.* **reasonably** *(adv)*
3 *(adj)* moderate, or quite good. *The weather was reasonable.* **reasonably** *(adv)*

reassure reassuring reassured *(v)* to calm someone and give them confidence. **reassurance** *(n)*.

rebel *(reb-ul)* *(n)* someone who fights against a government or people in authority. **rebel** *(rib-ell)* *(v)*, **rebellious** *(rib-ell-ee-uss)* *(adj)*.

rebellion
1 *(n)* armed resistance against a government.
2 *(n)* an organized protest against people in authority.

rebuke rebuking rebuked *(v)* to tell someone off. **rebuke** *(n)*.

recall recalling recalled
1 *(v)* to remember something. *I can still recall the day I met you.*
2 *(v)* to order someone to return. *The witness was recalled to the stand.*

recap recapping recapped *(v)* *(informal)* to repeat the main points of what has been said. Recap is short for recapitulate. **recap** *(n)*.

recede receding receded
1 *(v)* to go back. *The tide receded.* **receding** *(adj)*
2 *(v)* to fade gradually. *Hopes of rescue receded as night fell.*
3 *(v)* When a man's hair **recedes**, he becomes more and more bald at the front. **receding** *(adj)*.

receipt *(re seet)* *(n)* a piece of paper acknowledging that money or goods have been received.

receive receiving received *(v)* to get or to accept something.

receiver
1 *(n)* the part of a telephone that you hold in your hand.
2 *(n)* a piece of equipment for receiving radio or television signals.

recent *(adj)* happening, made, or done a short time ago. **recently** *(adv)*.

reception
1 *(n)* the way in which something or someone is received. *The play was given a frosty reception. The reception on our television is very bad.*
2 *(n)* a formal party.
3 *(n)* the place in a building where people go as they arrive and where inquiries are answered. **receptionist** *(n)*.

Some words that begin with a "r" sound are spelt "wr".

recess recesses
1 *(n)* a break from work for rest or relaxation.
2 *(n)* a part of a room set back from the main area.

recession *(n)* a time when a country produces fewer goods and more people become unemployed.

recipe *(ress-ip-ee)* *(n)* a set of instructions for preparing and cooking food.

recipient *(n)* a person who receives something. *The recipient of the first prize wins a holiday in Barbados.*

recital *(n)* a musical performance by a single performer or by a small group of musicians.

recite reciting recited *(v)* to say aloud something that you have learned by heart. **recitation** *(n)*.

reckless *(adj)* If you are reckless, you are careless about your own and other people's safety. **recklessly** *(adv)*.

reckon reckoning reckoned
1 *(v)* to calculate or count up. **reckoning** *(n)*.
2 *(v)* to think, or to have an opinion. *I reckon that our team will win.*

reclaim reclaiming reclaimed
1 *(v)* to get back something that is yours. *Maud reclaimed her jewels from the safe.*
2 *(v)* to make land suitable for farming, etc., by clearing it or draining it. **reclamation** *(n)*.

recline reclining reclined *(v)* to lean or lie back.

recognize *or* **recognise**
recognizing recognized *(v)* to see someone and know who they are. **recognition** *(n)*, **recognizable** *(adj)*, **recognizably** *(adv)*.

recollect recollecting recollected *(v)* to remember, or to recall. **recollection** *(n)*.

recommend recommending recommended *(v)* to suggest something or someone because you think that they are good. *My uncle recommended my piano teacher.* **recommendation** *(n)*.

reconcile reconciling reconciled
1 *(v)* to bring back together people who have fallen out with each other. **reconciliation** *(n)*.
2 *(v)* to decide to put up with something. *I reconciled myself to working over the holidays.*

reconsider reconsidering reconsidered *(v)* to think again about a previous decision.

reconstruction
1 *(n)* the rebuilding of something that has been destroyed. **reconstruct** *(v)*.
2 *(n)* the careful piecing together of past events. **reconstruct** *(v)*.

record recording recorded
1 *(rik-ord)* *(v)* to write down information so that it can be kept. **record** *(n)*.
2 *(rik-ord)* *(v)* to put music or other sounds on to a tape or disc. **recording** *(n)*.
3 *(rek-ord)* *(n)* If you set a **record** in something like a sport, you do it better than anyone has ever done before.

recorder
1 *(n)* a machine for recording sounds on magnetic tape.
2 *(n)* a woodwind musical instrument. You play the recorder by blowing into the mouthpiece and covering holes with your fingers to make different notes.

mouthpiece

lip

window

head joint

descant recorder

fingerhole

middle joint or barrel

double hole

foot joint

recover recovering recovered
1 *(v)* to get better after an illness or difficulty. **recovery** *(n)*.
2 *(v)* to get back something that has been lost or stolen. **recovery** *(n)*.

recreation
(rek-ree-ay-shun) *(singular n)* the games, sports, hobbies, etc. that people do for pleasure in their spare time. *What do you do as recreation?* **recreational** *(adj)*.

recruit *(re-kroot)* *(n)* someone who has recently joined a business, or an organization such as the armed forces. **recruitment** *(n)*, **recruit** *(v)*.

rectangle *(n)* a four-sided shape with two pairs of equal, parallel sides and four right angles. **rectangular** *(adj)*. See **shape**.

rectify rectifies rectifying rectified *(v)* to put something right.

recuperate recuperating recuperated *(v)* to recover slowly from an illness or injury. **recuperation** *(n)*.

recur recurring recurred
1 *(v)* to happen again. *The same problem recurs every time I use the computer.* **recurrence** *(n)*, **recurrent** *(adj)*.
2 *(v)* In a division sum, if a number in the answer **recurs**, it keeps occurring. For example, $10 \div 3 = 3.33333...$ or 3.3 recurring.

recycle recycling recycled *(v)* to process used items, such as glass bottles, newspapers, and aluminium cans, so that they can be reused to make new products. **recyclable** *(adj)*.

red *(n)* the colour of blood. **red** *(adj)*.

redeem redeeming redeemed
1 *(v)* to save, or to rescue. *Glen redeemed our reputation by scoring three goals.* **redemption** *(n)*.
2 *(v)* to claim back or exchange something. *Caroline redeemed her tokens for a set of drinking glasses.*

red herring *(n)* something that diverts people unnecessarily from what they should be doing.

red tape *(n)* rules, regulations, and paperwork that make it difficult to get things done.

reduce reducing reduced *(v)* to make something smaller or less. *Todd is trying to reduce his weight.* **reduction** *(n)*.

redundant *(adj)* no longer needed, especially for a job. *When the pit closed, the miners were made redundant.* **redundancy** *(n)*.

reed
1 *(n)* a plant with long, thin, hollow stems, that grows in or near water.
2 *(n)* a piece of thin cane or metal in the mouthpiece of some musical instruments, such as a clarinet, oboe, or saxophone. When you blow over or through the reed, it vibrates and makes a sound. See **woodwind**.

reef
1 *(n)* a line of rocks or coral close to the surface of the sea. *The picture shows part of the Great Barrier Reef near Queensland, Australia.*
2 **reef knot** *(n)* a strong double knot. See **knot**.

reef

reek reeking reeked *(v)* to smell strongly of something unpleasant. *The room reeked of tobacco smoke.*

reel reeling reeled
1 *(n)* a cylinder on which thread, film, etc. is wound. See **angling**.
2 *(v)* to stagger around unsteadily. *The drunkard reeled into a lamppost.*
3 *(n)* a type of folk dance.
4 *(v)* If you **reel off** something, you say it very fast.

ref *short for* **referee**.

refectory refectories *(n)* a communal dining hall. *A school refectory.*

refer referring referred
1 *(v)* If you **refer to** a book, you look in it for information.
2 *(v)* If you **refer to** something while talking or writing, you mention it.
3 *(v)* to pass a question or a problem on to someone else. *My doctor has referred me to a specialist.*

referee
1 *(n)* someone who supervises a sports match or game and makes sure that the players obey the rules.
2 *(n)* someone who provides a statement about a person's character and abilities.

reference
1 *(n)* a mention of someone or something. *There was a reference to you in the speech.*
2 *(n)* a written statement about someone's character and abilities. *You will need references for this job.*
3 *(n)* a book, magazine, etc. that you use in order to produce a piece of work. *Please list your references at the end of your essay.*

reference book *(n)* a book that you use to find information. *Encyclopedias and dictionaries are reference books.*

referendum referendums *or* **referenda** *(n)* a vote by the people of a country on a very important question.

refill refilling refilled *(v)* to fill something again. **refill** *(n)*.

refine refining refined *(v)* to purify something, like sugar or oil.

refined *(adj)* A **refined** person is very polite and has elegant manners and tastes.

refinery refineries *(n)* a factory where raw materials are purified. *Oil refineries turn crude oil into petrol and other products.*

refit refitting refitted *(v)* to repair something, or to supply it with new parts or equipment.

reflect reflecting reflected
1 *(v)* to show an image of something on a shiny surface. **reflection** *(n)*.
2 *(v)* When rays of light or heat are **reflected**, they bounce off an object. *The diagram below shows how a light ray is reflected when it hits a mirror.*
3 *(v)* to think carefully. *Arthur reflected on the meaning of life.* **reflection** *(n)*.

reflection

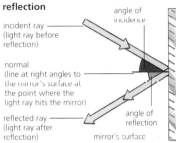

incident ray (light ray before reflection)

normal (line at right angles to the mirror's surface at the point where the light ray hits the mirror)

reflected ray (light ray after reflection)

angle of incidence

angle of reflection

mirror's surface

reflective
1 *(adj)* acting like a mirror.
2 *(adj)* thoughtful. **reflectively** *(adv)*.

reflex reflexes
1 *(n)* an automatic and instinctive action. *Blinking is a reflex.* **reflex** *(adj)*.
2 *(adj)* A **reflex** angle is an angle between 180° and 360°.

reform reforming reformed *(v)* to improve something that is unsatisfactory. *Buster is trying to reform his behaviour.* **reform** *(n)*.

refract refracting refracted *(v)* When a light ray or sound wave is **refracted**, it changes direction because it has travelled from one medium into another. *The diagram shows how a light ray is refracted as it moves from air into glass and then back into the air.* **refraction** *(n)*.

refraction

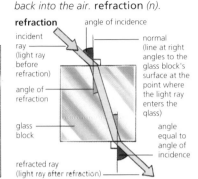

incident ray (light ray before refraction)

angle of refraction

glass block

refracted ray (light ray after refraction)

angle of incidence

normal (line at right angles to the glass block's surface at the point where the light ray enters the glass)

angle equal to angle of incidence

refrain refraining refrained
1 *(v)* to stop yourself from doing something. *Please refrain from standing on the seats.*
2 *(n)* a regularly repeated chorus or song.

refresh refreshes refreshing refreshed *(v)* If something **refreshes** you, it makes you feel fresh and strong again. **refreshing** *(adj)*.

refreshments *(plural n)* drink and small amounts of food.

refrigerator *(n)* a very cold cabinet used for storing food and drink. *Refrigerators are kept cool by a special substance called refrigerant that circulates constantly. The diagram shows how refrigerant evaporates inside the refrigerator, drawing heat away from the food, and condenses outside it, sending out the heat that it has gained.* **refrigeration** *(n)*, **refrigerate** *(v)*.

evaporator (turns refrigerant liquid into vapour which draws heat from freezer compartment)

freezer compartment

rubber seal

expansion valve (decreases pressure of refrigerant)

condenser (turns refrigerant vapour into liquid which sends out heat)

cooling fin

compressor (increases pressure of refrigerant and pumps it around the condenser and evaporator)

thermostat (controls compressor)

expanded polystyrene (insulates refrigerator)

plastic inner case

metal outer case

refrigerator (cutaway)

electrical lead

refuel refuelling refuelled *(v)* to take on more fuel.

refuge *(n)* a place of shelter and safety.

refugee *(n)* a homeless person who has been forced to leave their home because of war, persecution, or natural disaster.

refund refunding refunded *(v)* to give money back to the person who paid it. **refund** *(n)*.

refuse refusing refused
1 *(rif-yooz)* *(v)* to say you will not do something or accept something. **refusal** *(n)*.
2 *(ref-yuce)* *(n)* rubbish, or waste.

regal *(adj)* to do with or fit for a king or queen. **regally** *(adv)*.

regard regarding regarded
1 *(v)* to have an opinion about something. *Douglas regards politicians with contempt.* **regard** *(n)*.
2 *(plural n)* If someone sends you their **regards**, they send you their best wishes.

regarding *(prep)* about, or concerning.

regardless *(adj)* without considering anything or anyone else. *Nina drove at high speed, regardless of the other drivers.* **regardlessly** *(adv)*.

regatta *(n)* a series of races for rowing or sailing boats.

reggae *(reg-ay)* *(n)* a type of rhythmic pop music which came from the West Indies.

regiment *(n)* a large army unit under the command of a colonel.

region *(n)* a large area or district. **regional** *(adj)*, **regionally** *(adv)*.

register registering registered
1 *(n)* a book in which names or official records are kept. *A class register.* **registration** *(n)*.
2 *(v)* to enter something on an official list. *All cars must be registered.* **registration** *(n)*.
3 *(n)* the range of notes produced by a musical instrument or a voice.
4 *(v)* to show an emotion. *Aaron's face registered dismay.*

register office or **registry office** *(n)* In Britain, a **register office** is a place where births and deaths are recorded, and where people can get married.

regret regretting regretted *(v)* to be sad or sorry about something. **regret** *(n)*, **regretful** *(adj)*.

regrettable *(adj)* If something is **regrettable**, it is unfortunate and you wish that it had not happened.

regular
1 *(adj)* usual, or normal. *This is my regular route home.* **regularly** *(adv)*.
2 *(adj)* happening at predictable times. *Regular meals.* **regularity** *(n)*, **regularly** *(adv)*.
3 *(adj)* even, or steady. *A regular pattern. A regular heartbeat.* **regularity** *(n)*, **regularly** *(adv)*.

regulate regulating regulated *(v)* to control or adjust something. *My watch needs regulating.*

regulation
1 *(n)* an official rule.
2 *(n)* the act of controlling or adjusting something.

regurgitate *(re-gurj-it-ate)* regurgitating regurgitated *(v)* to bring food from the stomach back into the mouth. *Many birds regurgitate food and feed it to their young.*

rehearse *(re-herss)* rehearsing rehearsed *(v)* to practise for a public performance. **rehearsal** *(n)*.

reign *(rain)* reigning reigned *(v)* to rule as a king or queen. **reign** *(n)*.

reimburse *(re-im-burss)* reimbursing reimbursed *(v)* to pay someone back the money they have had to spend on your behalf. *The company will reimburse your train fare.* **reimbursement** *(n)*.

reindeer reindeer *(n)* a deer that lives in Arctic areas. *Both the male and female reindeer have large, branching antlers.*

reindeer
(male)
— antler

— muzzle

— pouch

reinforce reinforcing reinforced *(v)* to strengthen something. *Concrete bridges are reinforced by metal rods.*

reinforcement
1 *(n)* something that strengthens.
2 **reinforcements** *(plural n)* extra troops sent to strengthen a fighting force.

reject rejecting rejected
1 *(re-jekt)* *(v)* to refuse to accept something. *Julius rejected all offers of help.* **rejection** *(n)*.

2 *(ree-jekt)* *(n)* something or someone that is not wanted or accepted. *I've sorted out my collection of tapes and thrown all the rejects away.*

rejoice rejoicing rejoiced *(v)* to be very happy about something.

relapse relapsing relapsed *(v)* to fall back or return to the position that you were in before. *Megan gave up chocolate for a month, but now she's relapsed.* **relapse** *(n)*.

relate relating related
1 *(v)* If things **relate** to each other, there is a connection between them. *All these questions relate to the same thing.*
2 *(v)* If people **relate** to each other, they get on well together.
3 *(v)* to tell a story.

related *(adj)* If you are **related** to someone, you are part of their family.

relation
1 *(n)* a connection between things.
2 *(n)* a member of your family.

relationship
1 *(n)* the way in which two people get on together.
2 *(n)* the way in which things are connected.

relative
1 *(n)* a member of your family.
2 *(adj)* compared with others. *Poor people in the West live in relative luxury compared with people in the Third World.*

relatively *(adv)* compared with others. *A 50 year old seems relatively young in a room full of pensioners.*

relax relaxes relaxing relaxed
1 *(v)* to rest and take things easy. **relaxation** *(n)*.
2 *(v)* to become less tense and anxious. **relaxation** *(n)*.
3 *(v)* to make something less strict. *The new headmaster has relaxed the discipline at our school.*

relay relaying relayed
1 *(ree-lay)* *(n)* a team race in which members of the team take it in turn to run, passing a baton from one runner to the next.
2. *(re-lay)* *(v)* to pass a message on to someone else.

release releasing released
1 *(v)* to free something or someone. **release** *(n)*.
2 *(v)* If a record, film, etc. is **released**, it is issued for the first time. **release** *(n)*.

relegate relegating relegated *(v)* If a sports team is **relegated**, it is moved to a lower league.

relent relenting relented (v)
to become less strict or more merciful. I was meant to stay in all day, but in the end Mum relented.

relentless (adj) unceasing and determined. Aled practises the trumpet with relentless enthusiasm. **relentlessly** (adv).

relevant (adj) If something is relevant, it is directly concerned with what is being discussed or dealt with. **relevance** (n).

reliable (adj) trustworthy, or dependable. **reliability** (n), **reliably** (adv).

relic (n) something that has survived from the distant past.

relief
1 (n) a feeling of freedom from pain or worry. It's such a relief to know that you're safe!
2 (n) aid given to people in special need. Famine relief.
3 relief map (n) a map which shows the areas of high and low ground by shades of colour.

relieve relieving relieved
1 (v) to ease someone's trouble or pain.
2 (v) If you **relieve** someone, you take over a duty from them.

religion
1 (n) belief in God or gods. **religious** (adj).
2 (n) the practice of your belief through worship, obedience, and prayer. **religious** (adj).

relish relishes relishing relished
1 (v) to enjoy something greatly
2 (n) a sauce. Tomato relish.

reluctant (adj) If you are **reluctant**, you do not want to do something. **reluctance** (n), **reluctantly** (adv).

rely relies relying relied (v) If you rely on somebody or something, you need and trust them. I had to rely on my friends to help me. **reliant** (adj).

remain remaining remained (v) to be left behind or left over.

remainder (n) the amount left over.

remains
1 (plural n) things left over. What shall I do with the remains of my lunch?
2 (plural n) a body after death.
3 (plural n) the ruins of ancient buildings. Have you seen the Roman remains at Bath?

remark remarking remarked (v) to make a comment about something. **remark** (n).

remarkable (adj) unusual and worth noticing. **remarkably** (adv).

remedial (adj) intended to help someone with a learning problem or physical difficulty. Remedial maths.

remedy remedies remedying remedied
1 (n) a cure for an illness.
2 (n) the answer to a problem.
3 (v) to put something right. Bill remedied the problem with the radio.

remember remembering remembered
1 (v) to keep something in your mind. I'll always remember Marco.
2 (v) to bring something to mind. Try to remember the answer.

remind reminding reminded (v) to make someone remember something. Please remind me to lock the door. **reminder** (n).

reminisce (rem-in-iss) reminiscing reminisced (v) to think or talk about the past and things that you remember. **reminiscence** (n).

remnant (n) a piece or part of something that is left over. A remnant of material.

remorse (n) a strong feeling of guilt and regret about something that you have done. **remorseful** (adj), **remorsefully** (adv).

remote remoter remotest (adj) far away, isolated, or distant. **remoteness** (n), **remotely** (adv).

remote control (n) a system by which machines can be operated from a distance, usually by radio signals or by an infra-red beam. **remote-controlled** (adj).

remove removing removed (v) to take something away. **removal** (n).

Renaissance (n) the flowering of art and learning in Europe, between the 14th and 16th centuries, inspired by a revival of interest in the ancient Greeks and Romans. This picture is based on the pen and ink "Study for the Head of Leda", by Leonardo da Vinci, one of the leading artists of the Italian Renaissance.

Italian Renaissance drawing

rendezvous (ron-day-voo) rendezvous (n) an arranged place and time for a meeting. **rendezvous** (v).

renew renewing renewed
1 (v) to replace something old with something new. **renewal** (n).
2 (v) to start something again.

3 (v) to extend the period of a library loan, club membership, etc. **renewal** (n).

renewable energy (n) power from sources, such as wind, waves, and the Sun, that can never be used up.

renovate renovating renovated (v) to restore something to good condition, or to make it more modern. **renovation** (n).

renowned (adj) famous, or well known. **renown** (n).

rent (n) money paid by a tenant to the owner of a house, flat, etc. in return for living in it. **rent** (v).

rental (n) the hiring of equipment, such as televisions, cars, or machinery.

repair repairing repaired (v) to make something work again, or to put back together something that is broken. **repair** (n).

repay repaying repaid (v) to pay back money or something else. Please repay the money you owe. I repaid her visit. **repayment** (n).

repeat repeating repeated (v) to say or do something again. **repeat** (n), **repetition** (n).

repel repelling repelled
1 (v) to drive away. The army repelled the enemy forces
2 (v) to disgust someone.

repellent
1 (adj) disgusting. A repellent smell.
2 (n) a chemical that keeps insects and other pests away.

repent repenting repented (v) to be deeply sorry for the bad things that you have done. **repentance** (n), **repentant** (adj).

repertoire (rep-er-twar) (n) the collection of songs, jokes, stories, etc. that an entertainer performs in public.

repetition (n) the repeating of words or actions. **repetitious** (adj), **repetitive** (adj).

replace replacing replaced
1 (v) to put one thing or person in place of another. **replacement** (n).
2 (v) to put something back where it was.

replay replaying replayed
1 (re-play) (n) a second match between two teams or players, when the first match has ended in a draw. **replay** (re-play) (v).
2 (re-play) (v) to play back a tape in order to see or hear something again. **replay** (re-play) (n).

replica (n) an exact copy of something. **replicate** (v)

Some words that begin with a "r" sound are spelt "wr".

reply replies replying replied *(v)* to give an answer or a response. reply *(n)*.

report reporting reported
1 *(v)* to give a written or spoken account of things that have happened. report *(n)*.
2 *(v)* If you **report** someone, you make an official complaint about them.
3 *(v)* to appear for duty. *Please report for work on Monday morning.*

reporter *(n)* someone who reports the news for radio, television, or a newspaper.

represent representing represented
1 *(v)* to act on behalf of someone else.
2 *(v)* to stand for something. *On a map, water is usually represented by the colour blue.* representation *(n)*.

representative *(n)* someone who is sent on behalf of someone else. *A sales representative.*

repress represses repressing repressed
1 *(v)* If you **repress** an emotion, like anger, you keep it under control and do not show it. repressed *(adj)*.

2 *(v)* to keep people under very strict control. *The Emperor repressed his people.* repression *(n)*, repressed *(adj)*.

reprieve *(rip-reeve)* reprieving reprieved *(v)* to postpone or cancel a punishment, especially a death sentence. reprieve *(n)*.

reprimand reprimanding reprimanded *(v)* to tell someone off formally. reprimand *(n)*.

reprisal *(n)* an act of revenge.

reproach reproaches reproaching reproached *(v)* to blame someone, or to show that you disapprove of them. *Annie reproached me for forgetting her birthday.* reproach *(n)*.

reproduce reproducing reproduced
1 *(v)* to make a copy of something. reproduction *(n)*.
2 *(v)* When animals **reproduce**, they breed and produce babies. reproduction *(n)*.

reptile *(n)* a cold-blooded animal with a scaly skin, that lays eggs. Lizards, crocodiles, snakes, turtles, and tortoises are all reptiles. *The picture shows a range of reptiles from around the world.* reptilian *(adj)*.

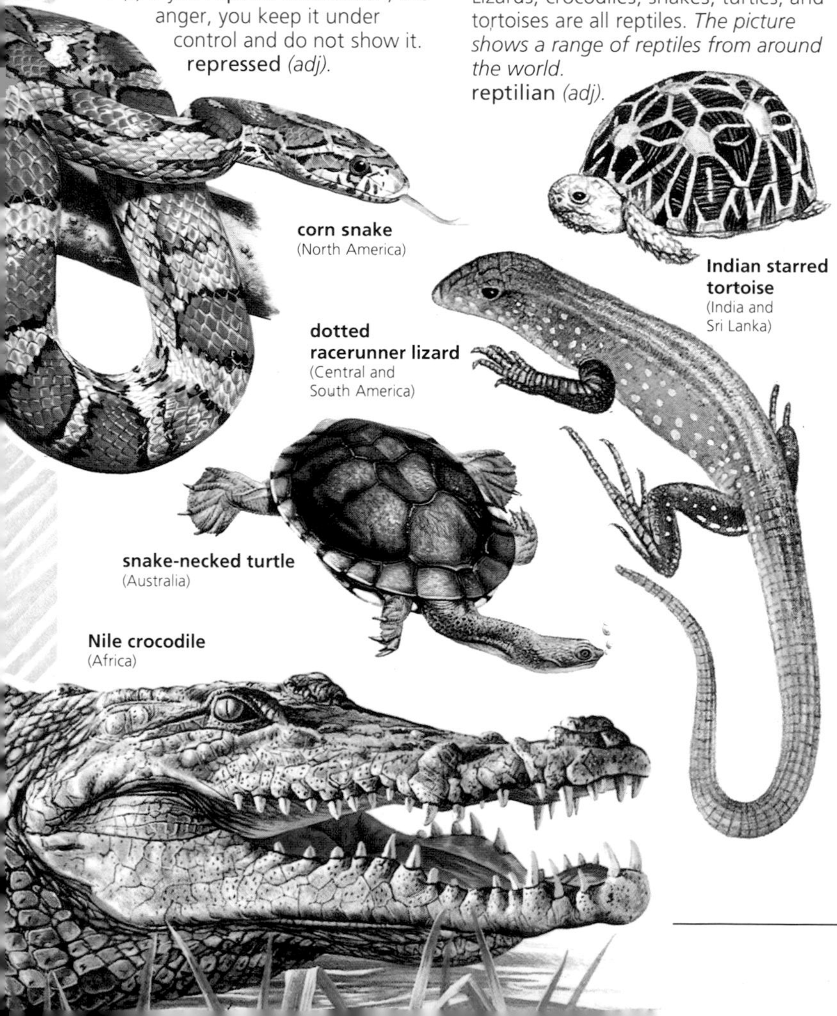

corn snake
(North America)

dotted racerunner lizard
(Central and South America)

Indian starred tortoise
(India and Sri Lanka)

snake-necked turtle
(Australia)

Nile crocodile
(Africa)

republic *(n)* a country or state that elects its government and does not have a king or queen. *The leader of a republic is the president.*

republican
1 *(adj)* to do with a republic, or in favour of a republic.
2 Republican Party *(n)* the name of one of the two main political parties in the USA.

repugnant *(adj)* very unpleasant and disgusting. *Melissa found the job of cleaning out the pigsties totally repugnant.* repugnance *(n)*.

repulse repulsing repulsed
1 *(v)* to drive, or to force back. *The crew repulsed the alien's attack.*
2 *(v)* to reject something. *Mel repulsed my offer of help.*

repulsive *(adj)* very ugly, or disgusting. *A repulsive monster.* repulsively *(adv)*.

reputable *(adj)* reliable and trustworthy. *Always buy electrical equipment from a reputable dealer.* reputably *(adv)*.

reputation *(n)* the opinion that other people have of you. *Abdul has a reputation for hard work.*

repute *(n)* fame.

reputed *(adj)* supposed to be, or thought to be. *Dominic is reputed to be very good at chess.* reputedly *(adv)*.

request requesting requested
1 *(v)* to ask for something politely. *Visitors are requested not to take photographs.*
2 *(n)* something that you ask for. *That's a very strange request!*
3 request stop *(n)* a bus stop where people have to ask the driver to stop or have to hold out their arm as the bus approaches.

requiem *(rek-wee-em)*
1 *(n)* a church service where prayers are said for someone who has died.
2 *(n)* a piece of music composed in memory of a dead person, often a musical setting of the requiem service.

require requiring required
1 *(v)* to need something. *Do you require anything to eat?*
2 *(v)* If someone **requires** you to do something, you must do it.

requirement *(n)* something that you need to do or have. *The ability to swim 50m is a requirement of this sailing course.*

reread rereading reread *(v)* to read something again. *Kerry reread the train timetable anxiously.*

rescue helicopter

radar scanner
hydraulic rescue winch
winch operator
cabin door
rotor hub
rotor blade
tail rotor
tail plane
engine under here
engine air intake duct
viewing window
rotor hub
dual pilot cockpit
tail wheel
waterproof floor
footstep
crash resistant fuel system
landing lights
steel lifeline
exhaust
winchman
inflation canister
undercarriage
stretcher
immersion suit
flotation bag
(used for water landing)
boat-shaped hull

rescue
rescuing rescued
1 (v) to save someone who is in danger or is trapped somewhere. **rescue** (n), **rescuer** (n).
2 **rescue helicopter** (n) a specially-equipped helicopter used to rescue people on land and at sea. *The picture shows a Sea King rescue helicopter.*

research researches researching researched (v) to study and find out about a subject, usually by reading a lot of books about it, or by doing experiments. **research** (n).

resemble resembling resembled (v) to be or look like somebody or something. *Lucy resembles her Great Aunt Matilda.* **resemblance** (n).

resent resenting resented (v) to feel hurt or angry about something that has been done or said to you. *I resent being treated as an idiot.* **resentment** (n), **resentful** (adj).

reservation
1 (n) an area of land set aside for native people. *A Native American reservation.*
2 (n) a booking. *Do you have a reservation for this flight?*
3 (plural n) If you have **reservations** about something, you feel doubtful about it.

reserve reserving reserved
1 (v) to arrange for something to be kept for you. *Harvey reserved a seat on the train.*
2 (n) an extra member of a team who plays if one of the team is injured or cannot play.
3 (n) a protected place where animals can live and breed safely. *A nature reserve.*

reserved
1 (adj) If a seat, table, or room is **reserved**, it is kept for someone to use later.
2 (adj) Someone who is **reserved** behaves in a quiet, shy way and does not show their feelings much.

reservoir (rez-er-vwar) (n) a natural or artificial lake used for storing a large amount of water.

residence (n) the place where somebody lives, especially someone important or wealthy.

resident (n) someone who lives in a particular place. *The village residents.* **residential** (adj).

residue
1 (n) remains, or leftovers. **residual** (adj).
2 (n) a substance that is left after combustion or evaporation.

resign (riz-ine) resigning resigned
1 (v) to give up a job. **resignation** (rez-ig-nay-shun) (n).
2 (v) If you **resign yourself** to something, you accept it without complaining or worrying about it. *I've resigned myself to losing.* **resignation** (n), **resigned** (adj).

resist resisting resisted
1 (v) to refuse to accept something. *Jessie resisted all offers of help.*
2 (v) to fight back. *The villagers resisted the advancing army.*
3 (v) to stop yourself doing something that you would like to do. *I resisted the temptation to tickle Theobald's feet.*

resistance
1 (n) fighting back. *Resistance is useless. We must surrender!*
2 (n) the ability of a substance or an electrical circuit to oppose an electrical current passing through it. *Resistance is measured in ohms.*

resolution (n) a promise to yourself that you will try hard to do something. *New Year resolutions.*

resolve resolving resolved
1 (v) to decide that you will try hard to do something. *Shane resolved to find a part time job.* **resolve** (n).
2 (v) to deal with a problem or difficulty successfully. *We need to resolve this misunderstanding quickly.*

resort resorting resorted
1 (n) a place where people go on holiday. *A skiing resort.*
2 (v) If you **resort to** something, you turn to it because you do not have any other choices.
3 If you do something **as a last resort**, you do it because everything else has failed to work.

resource (n) something valuable or useful to a place or person. *North Sea oil is one of Britain's most valuable resources.* **resourceful** (adj).

respect respecting respected
1 (v) to admire and have a high opinion of someone.
2 (n) a feeling of admiration or consideration for someone that makes you take them seriously.
3 (n) a detail or particular part of something. *I liked Guy's plan in many respects.*

respectable
1 (adj) If someone is **respectable**, they behave in a decent way that does not offend anyone. **respectably** (adv).
2 (adj) reasonably good. *Bonzo got a respectable score.*

respiration *(n)* breathing, or the process of taking in oxygen and sending out carbon dioxide.
The diagram shows the main organs used in respiration. Air is drawn into the lungs and travels to the alveoli where oxygen from the air passes into the blood. Carbon dioxide from the blood passes into the alveoli and is breathed out.

human respiration system

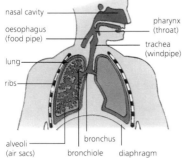

nasal cavity
oesophagus (food pipe)
lung
ribs
pharynx (throat)
trachea (windpipe)
alveoli (air sacs)
bronchus
bronchiole
diaphragm

respond responding responded
1 *(v)* to reply. **response** *(n)*.
2 *(v)* to react to something. *Rosie did not respond to her brother's taunts.*

responsibility responsibilities
1 *(n)* a duty. *It's my responsibility to provide tea.*
2 If you **take responsibility** for something bad that has happened, you agree that you are to blame for it.

responsible
1 *(adj)* If someone is **responsible** for something, they have to do it and it is their fault if it goes wrong.
2 *(adj)* If a person is **responsible**, they are sensible and can be trusted. **responsibly** *(adv)*.

rest resting rested
1 *(v)* to relax, or to sleep. **rest** *(n)*.
2 *(n)* the others, or the remaining part of something. *I came first and beat all the rest.*
3 *(v)* to lean on something. *Rest your rackets against the wall.*
4 *(v)* to stop and stay in one place. *The spotlight rested on his face.*
5 *(n)* a period of silence in a piece of music. *See* **notation**.

restaurant *(n)* a place where people pay to eat meals.

restless *(adj)* If someone is **restless**, they find it hard to keep still or to concentrate on anything. **restlessness** *(n)*, **restlessly** *(adv)*.

restore restoring restored
1 *(v)* to repair something that has been damaged.
2 *(v)* to give or bring something back. *Please restore the pen to its owner.*

restrain restraining restrained *(v)* to prevent someone from doing something. *We managed to restrain Harry from eating another ice cream.* **restraint** *(n)*.

restrained *(adj)* If someone is **restrained**, they are very quiet and controlled.

restrict restricting restricted *(v)* to keep something within limits. *Please restrict yourselves to one cake each.* **restriction** *(n)*, **restricted** *(adj)*.

rest room *(n)* *(US)* a polite word for toilet.

result resulting resulted
1 *(n)* something that happens because of something else. *The result of our efforts was a delicious meal.*
2 *(v)* If one thing **results in** something else, it causes it.
3 *(n)* a final score or mark. *Football results.*

resume resuming resumed *(v)* to start doing something again after a break. *We will resume our discussion after lunch.*

Resurrection *(n)* In the Christian religion, the **Resurrection** is Christ's coming back to life three days after his death.

resuscitate *(re-suss-it-ate)* resuscitating resuscitated *(v)* to make someone conscious again after they have stopped breathing. **resuscitation** *(n)*.

retail retailing retailed
1 *(v)* to sell goods to the public.
2 The **retail price** of goods is the price at which they are sold in the shops.

retailer *(n)* someone who sells goods to the public, usually in a shop.

retain retaining retained *(v)* to keep something. *Please retain your receipt.* **retention** *(n)*.

retaliate retaliating retaliated *(v)* to do something unpleasant to someone because they have done something unpleasant to you. **retaliation** *(n)*, **retaliatory** *(adj)*.

retard retarding retarded *(v)* to slow down. *The children's poor diet retarded their growth.* **retarded** *(adj)*.

retch *(retch or reach)* retches retching retched *(v)* When you **retch**, you feel your throat and stomach move as if you are going to be sick. **retch** *(n)*.

reticent *(ret-i-sent)* *(adj)* If someone is **reticent**, they are unwilling to tell people what they know or feel. **reticence** *(n)*.

retire retiring retired
1 *(v)* to give up work, usually because of your age. **retirement** *(n)*, **retired** *(adj)*.
2 *(v)* to leave a sports competition, usually because you have been injured.
3 *(v)* to go to a quieter place. *The jury has retired to consider its verdict.*
4 *(v)* *(old-fashioned)* to go to bed.

retort retorting retorted
1 *(v)* to answer someone quickly and sharply. **retort** *(n)*.
2 *(n)* a glass container with a round body and a long neck, used in a laboratory.

retrace retracing retraced *(v)* to go back over something. *I retraced my steps to see if I had missed the turning.*

retreat retreating retreated
1 *(v)* to move back or withdraw from a difficult situation. **retreat** *(n)*.
2 *(n)* a quiet place where you can go to think or be alone.

retrieve retrieving retrieved *(v)* to get or bring something back. *Franny retrieved her umbrella from the lost property office.* **retrieval** *(n)*.

return returning returned
1 *(v)* to go back. *It's time to return home.* **return** *(n)*.
2 *(v)* to give or send something back. *Please return my book.* **return** *(n)*.
3 **in return** in exchange for something, or as a payment for something.
4 **return match** *(n)* a second match between two teams who have already played each other once.
5 **return ticket** *(n)* a ticket that allows you to travel to a place and back again.

reunion *(n)* a meeting between people who have not seen each other for a long time.

reusable *(adj)* If something is **reusable**, it can be used again rather than being thrown away.

rev revving revved
1 *(v)* *(informal)* to make an engine run quickly and noisily.
2 **revs** *(plural n)* *(informal)* the speed at which an engine turns. Revs is short for revolutions per minute.

reveal revealing revealed *(v)* to allow something to be seen or known. *Carmen would not reveal the whereabouts of her secret hiding place.* **revealing** *(adj)*.

revel revelling revelled *(v)* If you **revel in** something, you enjoy it very much.

Some words that begin with a "r" sound are spelt "wr".

revelation *(n)* a very surprising fact that is made known to people.

revenge *(n)* action that you take to pay someone back for harm that they have done to you or to your friends.

revenue *(n)* the money that a government makes from taxes.

reverberate reverberating reverberated *(v)* to echo loudly and repeatedly. *Jo's screams reverberated around the cave.* reverberation *(n)*.

reverence *(n)* great respect and admiration. reverent *(adj)*, reverently *(adv)*.

reverse reversing reversed
1 *(n)* the opposite. *You may think this is fun, but in fact it's quite the reverse.*
2 *(v)* to turn something round or inside out. *Reverse the order of these numbers. You can reverse this jacket.* reversible *(adj)*.
3 *(v)* to move a vehicle backwards. *Reverse the car into the parking space.*
4 *(v)* to cancel something. *The verdict was reversed by the appeal court.* reversal *(adj)*.

revert reverting reverted *(v)* to go back to the way things were. *Despite her resolutions, Gina soon reverted to her old habits.* reversion *(n)*.

review reviewing reviewed
1 *(n)* a piece of writing that gives an opinion about a new book, play, film, etc. reviewer *(n)*, review *(v)*.
2 *(v)* to study something carefully in order to see whether changes are necessary. *We will review the budget each year.* review *(n)*.
3 *(v)* *(US)* to look at your school work and try to learn it before an exam (revise, *UK*).

revise revising revised
1 *(v)* to look at your school work and try to learn it before an exam. revision *(n)*.
2 *(v)* to change and correct something, usually in order to bring it up to date. *The new city guide has been thoroughly revised.* revision *(n)*.

revive reviving revived
1 *(v)* to bring someone back to consciousness after they have been unconscious.
2 *(v)* to bring something back into use. *We've revived a play from the 1950s.* revival *(n)*.

revolt revolting revolted
1 *(v)* to fight against authority. revolt *(n)*.
2 *(v)* If something revolts you, you find it horrible and disgusting.

revolting *(adj)* disgusting.

revolution
1 *(n)* a violent uprising by the people of a country, intended to change its political system. revolutionary *(n)*, revolutionary *(adj)*.
2 *(n)* a very large, important change. revolutionary *(adj)*.
3 *(n)* one complete turn of a wheel.

revolutionize or **revolutionise** revolutionizing revolutionized *(v)* to change something totally. *The introduction of the printing press revolutionized communication.*

revolve revolving revolved
1 *(v)* to turn round and round in a circle.
2 *(v)* If something revolves around a person or thing, that person or thing is the most important part of it. *Hester's life revolves around television.*

revolver *(n)* a small handgun that can fire several shots before it needs to be reloaded.

reward *(n)* something that you receive as a present for doing something good or useful. reward *(v)*.

rewarding *(adj)* If something is rewarding, it gives you pleasure and satisfaction. *A rewarding job.*

rheumatism *(room-at-izm) (n)* a disease that causes the joints and muscles to become stiff and painful. rheumatic *(room-at-ik) (adj)*.

rhinoceros rhinoceroses or rhinoceros *(n)* a large, heavy mammal that comes from Africa and Asia and has one or two large horns on its nose. *The picture shows a rhinoceros with a cattle egret and two oxpeckers on its back.*

rhinoceros

rhizome *(rye-zome) (n)* the thick stem of some plants that grows just under the ground, and from which roots and leaves grow.

rhombus *(rom-buss)* rhombuses or rhombi *(n)* a shape that has four straight sides of equal length but does not have right angles. *See* **shape**.

rhubarb *(roo barb) (n)* a plant with long red or green stems that can be cooked and eaten.

rhyme *(rime)* rhyming rhymed
1 *(v)* If words rhyme, they end with the same sound. *Seat rhymes with beat and feet.* rhyme *(n)*.
2 *(n)* a short poem.

rhythm *(rith-um) (n)* a regular beat in music, poetry, or dance. rhythmic *(adj)*, rhythmical *(adj)*, rhythmically *(adv)*.

rib
1 *(n)* one of the curved bones which protect your lungs. *See* **skeleton**.
2 *(n)* the main vein of a leaf. *See* **leaf**.

ribbon *(n)* a long, thin piece of material used for tying up hair, or for decorating a present.

rice *(n)* a kind of tall grass that is grown in flooded fields and whose seeds can be cooked and eaten. *See* **paddy field**.

rich riches; richer richest
1 *(adj)* Someone who is rich has a lot of money and possessions.
2 *(adj)* If something is rich in a particular thing, it contains a lot of it. *Milk is rich in calcium.* richly *(adv)*.
3 *(adj)* Food that is rich contains a lot of fat or sugar and makes you feel full very quickly.
4 riches *(plural n)* great wealth.

rickety *(adj)* old, weak, and likely to break. *A rickety chair.*

ricochet *(rick-oh-shay)* ricocheting ricocheted *(v)* If a stone or bullet ricochets, it hits a wall or other hard surface and flies off in a different direction.

rid ridding rid
1 *(v)* to remove something that is unwanted. *I must rid myself of this ridiculous costume.*
2 If you get rid of something, you throw it away.

riddle *(n)* a question that seems to make no sense, but which has a clever answer.

ride riding rode ridden
1 *(v)* to sit on a horse, bicycle, or motorcycle and travel along on it. rider *(n)*.
2 *(n)* a journey on a horse, bicycle, or motorcycle, or in a car or other vehicle.

ridge
1 *(n)* a narrow, raised piece of land.
2 *(n)* a narrow, raised strip on something. ridged *(adj)*.

ridicule ridiculing ridiculed *(v)* to make fun of someone or something. ridicule *(n)*.

ridiculous *(adj)* extremely silly or foolish. ridiculously *(adv)*.

riding hat (n) a hard hat that you wear to protect your head when riding a horse.

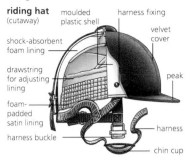

riding hat (cutaway)
moulded plastic shell
harness fixing
shock-absorbent foam lining
velvet cover
drawstring for adjusting lining
peak
foam-padded satin lining
harness
harness buckle
chin cup

rifle (n) a long-barrelled gun that you hold against your shoulder as you fire it.

rig rigging rigged
1 (n) a large structure on land or in the sea, used to drill for oil or gas under the ground. See **oil rig**.
2 (v) to control something dishonestly. *Natalie rigged the competition so that she came first.*
3 (v) If you **rig up** something, you make it quickly from whatever you can find. *We rigged up a tent from broom handles and sheets.*

rigging (n) the ropes on a boat or ship which support and control the sails. See **junk**.

right
1 (adj) This page faces the **right** hand side of the book. right (n), right (adv).
2 (adj) correct. *I got the answers right.*
3 (adj) good, fair, and acceptable. *It's not right to be cruel to animals.*
4 (adv) exactly. *We managed to park right outside the cinema.*
5 (n) something that the law allows you to have or do. *The right to vote.*
6 In politics, people **on the right** support capitalism, free enterprise, and firm law and order.

right angle (n) an angle of 90°, like one of the angles of a square.

righteous
1 (adj) Someone who is **righteous** does not do anything that is bad or against the law. righteousness (n).
2 (adj) with good reason. *When I saw the mess in my room, I was filled with righteous indignation.*

right-handed (adj) If you are **right-handed**, you use your right hand to write. right-hander (n).

right-wing (adj) If you are **right-wing**, you believe in capitalism, free enterprise, and firm law and order.

rigid (rij-id)
1 (adj) stiff and difficult to bend. rigidity (n), rigidly (adv).
2 (adj) very strict and difficult to change. *A rigid rule.* rigidly (adv).

rim (n) the outside or top edge of something. *The jug has a blue rim.*

rind (n) the outer layer on cheese, bacon, and some fruits. *Lemon rind.*

ring ringing rang rung
1 (n) a circle. *Put a ring around the correct answer.* ring (v).
2 (n) a thin band worn on your finger as a piece of jewellery.
3 (v) When a bell **rings**, it makes a musical sound.
4 (v) to telephone someone. ring (n).
5 (n) the area in which a boxing or wrestling match takes place.

ringleader (n) the leader of a group of people who commit crimes or do things that are wrong.

ringlet (n) a long, tight curl of hair.

rink (n) an indoor area with a specially prepared surface that is used for ice-skating or roller-skating.

rinse rinsing rinsed
1 (v) to wash something in clean water without using any soap. rinse (n).
2 (n) a special liquid that you can put on your hair to colour it slightly.

riot rioting rioted (v) If people **riot**, they behave in a noisy, violent, and usually uncontrollable way. riot (n), riotous (adj).

rip ripping ripped
1 (v) to tear something. rip (n).
2 **rip off** (v) (slang) If someone **rips you off**, they sell you a faulty product or charge you an unfair amount of money for something. rip-off (n).

ripe riper ripest (adj) ready to be harvested, picked, or eaten. *Ripe fruit.* ripeness (n), ripen (v).

ripple
1 (n) a very small wave on the surface of a lake, pond, etc. ripple (v).
2 (n) a small wave of sound. *A ripple of laughter.*

rise rising rose risen
1 (v) to go or move upwards. *The balloon rose slowly into the air.*
2 (v) to stand up.
3 (v) to increase. *Prices rose dramatically last year.* rise (n).
4 (n) the process by which a person, country, etc. becomes more powerful. *The rise of the British Empire.*

risk risking risked (v) to do something that might cause something unpleasant to happen. *Joel risked his life to rescue the kitten.* risk (n), risky (adj).

ritual (n) a set of actions that are always performed in the same way as part of a religious ceremony or social custom. ritual (adj), ritually (adv).

rival rivalling rivalled
1 (n) someone whom you are competing against. rivalry (n), rival (adj).
2 (v) to be as good as something or someone else. *No team can rival us at ice hockey.*

river (n) a large stream of fresh water that flows into a lake or sea. *The picture shows how a river develops and changes as it flows from its source to its mouth.*

river
mountains or hills
river source
stream feeding river
tributary (river joining larger river)
river valley
spur (hill crossing river valley)
rapids (fast-moving water)
gorge (deep river valley cut through rock)
waterfall
braided stream
pool
meander cliff
flood plain
meander (loop)
ox-bow lake (lake formed from cut-off meander)
river mouth or estuary
delta (area where river splits into channels)

Some words that begin with a "r" sound are spelt "rh" or "wr".

rivet riveting riveted
1 *(n)* a strong metal bolt that is used to fasten pieces of metal together. rivet *(v)*.
2 *(v)* If you are **riveted** by something, you find it so interesting that you cannot stop watching it or listening to it. riveting *(adj)*.

road *(n)* a wide path with a smooth surface on which vehicles travel.

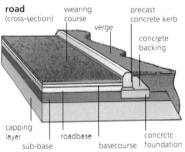

road (cross-section)　wearing course　verge　precast concrete kerb　concrete backing
capping layer　roadbase　basecourse　concrete foundation
sub-base

roadworks *(plural n)* repair work being done to a road.

roadworthy *(adj)* A car that is roadworthy is in good enough condition to be driven on the roads. roadworthiness *(n)*.

roam roaming roamed *(v)* to wander around without any particular purpose. *I roamed the streets until dark.* roam *(n)*.

roar roaring roared *(v)* to make a loud, deep noise. *The lion roared. The crowd roared.* roar *(n)*.

roaring *(adj)* If you do a **roaring** trade, you sell a lot of things.

roast roasting roasted
1 *(v)* to cook meat or vegetables in a hot oven. roast *(adj)*.
2 *(n)* a joint of meat that has been cooked in a hot oven.
3 *(v)* to be very hot. *We were roasted by the sun.* roasting *(adj)*.

rob robbing robbed *(v)* to steal something from somebody. robber *(n)*.

robbery robberies *(n)* the crime of stealing money or goods.

robe *(n)* a piece of clothing like a long, loose coat.

robin *(n)* a bird with a red breast. *The American robin is much larger than the European robin.*

European robin

American robin

robot *(n)* a machine that is programmed to do jobs that are usually performed by a person. robotic *(adj)*.

robotic arm *(n)* an electronically-controlled mechanical arm, that can use tools and work like a human arm. *The arrows on this picture of a robotic arm show the six directions in which it can move. Also see* **space shuttle, underwater.**

waist　shoulder　elbow　wrist　welding tool
robotic arm

robotics *(singular n)* the science and study of making and using robots.

robust *(adj)* strong. *A robust bicycle. A robust child.* robustly *(adv)*.

rock rocking rocked
1 *(n)* the very hard substance of which the Earth is made.
2 *(n)* a large stone.
3 *(v)* to move gently backwards and forwards or from side to side.
4 *(n)* a hard sweet, shaped like a long stick, usually sold at the seaside.
5 **rock music** *(n)* pop music with a very strong beat and a simple tune.

rock climbing *(n)* the sport of climbing steep rock faces, usually with the help of ropes and other equipment. *The picture shows a climber with various pieces of equipment that are used in rock climbing*

rock climbing
helmet
chock inserted in crack
karabiner or krab (clip)
sit harness
chocks and nuts on ropes (for inserting in cracks)
nylon tape
rope (attached to fellow climber)
rock boot

rockery rockeries *(n)* an area of a garden where small plants are grown amongst rocks and stones.

rocket rocketing rocketed
1 *(v)* to increase very quickly. *The price of oil has rocketed.*
2 *(n)* a firework that shoots high into the air and then explodes.
3 *(n)* a vehicle shaped like a long tube with a pointed end, that can travel very fast through the air. Rockets are used for space travel and for carrying missiles. *See* **space shuttle.**

rock'n'roll *(n)* a kind of dance music with a strong beat and a simple tune. Rock'n'roll is short for rock and roll. rock'n'roll *(adj)*.

rod *(n)* a long, thin pole.

rodent *(n)* a mammal with large, sharp front teeth that it uses for gnawing things. *Rats, beavers, and squirrels are all rodents.*

rodeo *(n)* an entertainment in which cowboys show off their skills, such as riding untamed horses and catching cattle with lassos.

rodeo rider

roe
1 *(n)* a type of small deer.
2 *(n)* a mass of eggs or sperm found inside a fish and often eaten as food.

rogue *(rohg)* *(n)* a dishonest person.

role
1 *(n)* the job or purpose of a person or thing. *Gavin's role is to supervise the workers.*
2 *(n)* the part that a person acts in a play. *Julian played the role of Hamlet.*

roll rolling rolled
1 *(v)* to move along by turning over and over. *The ball rolled down the hill.*
2 *(v)* to make something into the shape of a ball or tube.
3 *(n)* something that has been made into the shape of a tube. *A roll of wallpaper. A Swiss roll.*
4 *(v)* to flatten something by pushing a rounded object over it. *Roll the pastry. Roll the lawn.*
5 *(n)* a small round loaf of bread to be eaten by one person.
6 *(n)* a continuous, deep, vibrating sound. *A roll of thunder.*
7 **roll up** *(v)* (informal) to come along. *A large crowd rolled up for the match.*

roller
1 *(n)* an object shaped like a tube, that can turn round and round and is used in machines. *An ink roller.*
2 *(n)* a small plastic tube that you wind hair around to make it curl.

rollerblade *(n)* an ankle-length boot with a row of wheels on its base, that you skate around on. Rollerblades are also known as in-line skates. **rollerblading** *(n)*, **rollerblader** *(n)*.

rollerblade

foam lining
buckle
boot shell
urethane wheel
SKI ROLLER
stopper   wheel axle   base plate

roller coaster *(n)* a fairground ride consisting of a train of carriages that travels fast over a track that rises, falls, and curves.

roller-skating *(n)* the sport of moving about on shoes or boots with wheels attached to them. **roller skate** *(n)*, **roller-skate** *(v)*.

ROM *(n)* permanent computer memory that can be read but not changed. The initials ROM stand for read-only memory.

romance
1 *(n)* a love affair.
2 *(n)* an exciting story, usually about love.
3 *(n)* mystery and excitement. *The romance of the East.*

Roman numerals *(n)* letters used by the Ancient Romans to represent figures. Roman numerals are sometimes used today, for example, on some clocks.

Roman numerals

I   II   III   IV   V   X
one two three four five ten

XL   L   XC   C   D   M
40   50   90   100   500   1,000

romantic
1 *(adj)* like a love story. *How romantic of Igor to send you roses!*
2 *(adj)* like a fairy story. *A romantic castle.*

romp romping romped *(v)* to play in a noisy and energetic way. *The boys love romping in the sea.* **romp** *(n)*.

roof
1 *(n)* the covering on the top of a building

2 *(n)* the top part of something. *The roof of your mouth. The roof of a car.*

roof rack *(n)* a frame placed on top of a car, for carrying luggage.

rook
1 *(n)* a large, black bird like a crow, that lives in a big group called a rookery.
2 *(n)* a chesspiece, also known as a castle, that can move in straight lines, across the board but not diagonally. *See* **chess**.

room
1 *(n)* one of the separate parts of a house or building, with its own door and walls.
2 *(n)* enough space for something. *Is there room for us all to go in your car?*

roost roosting roosted
1 *(n)* a place where birds rest or build their nests.
2 *(v)* When birds **roost**, they settle somewhere for the night.

rooster *(n)* a fully-grown male chicken.

root rooting rooted
1 *(n)* the part of a plant that grows under the ground. *Water and dissolved foods are absorbed from the soil through root hairs and travel up the roots to the plant's stem through xylem and phloem vessels.*
2 *(v)* to form roots. *I took some plant cuttings, but they didn't root.*
3 *(plural n)* Your **roots** are where your family comes from, where you grew up, and where you feel that you belong.

rope *(n)* a strong, thick cord, made from twisted fibres.

rose
1 *(n)* a garden flower that usually has a sweet smell and grows on bushes with thorns.
2 *(n)* a light pink colour. **rose** *(adj)*.

rosette *(n)* a large, round badge with ribbons attached to it, worn to show that you have won something, or that you support a particular person, team, or political party.

plant root
(cutaway)

phloem
(carries dissolved foods)
root hair
xylem
(carries water)
cortex
(root tissue)
root cap

Rosh Hashanah *or* **Rosh Hashana** *(n)* the Jewish New Year.

rostrum *(n)* a raised platform for a speaker or conductor.

rosy rosier rosiest
1 *(adj)* pink. *Rosy cheeks.*
2 *(adj)* hopeful. *A rosy future.*

rot rotting rotted *(v)* When something **rots**, it becomes weak and starts to break up because it is old or damp. **rot** *(n)*.

rota *(n)* a list of people who take it in turns to do a job.

rotary *(adj)* turning round and round, or rotating. *This mowing machine has a rotary action.*

rotate rotating rotated
1 *(v)* to turn round and round like a wheel. **rotation** *(n)*.
2 *(v)* to do things or use things in a fixed order, one after the other. **rotation** *(n)*.

rotten
1 *(adj)* Food that is **rotten** has gone bad and cannot be eaten.
2 *(adj)* If floorboards, furniture, etc. are **rotten**, they have become weak and have started to break up.
3 *(adj)* *(informal)* very bad, or unpleasant. *A rotten trick.*

rough *(ruff)* roughing roughed; rougher roughest
1 *(adj)* A **rough** surface is not smooth, but has dents or bumps in it.
2 *(adj)* Someone who is **rough** is not gentle or polite and may fight with people. **roughly** *(adv)*.
3 *(adj)* *(informal)* difficult and unpleasant. *Moira had a rough time in her last job.*
4 *(adj)* vague, or not exact. *I've got a rough idea of where Rupert lives.* **roughly** *(adv)*.
5 *(adj)* **Rough** work is work that you do as preparation for the final version.
6 *(v)* *(informal)* If you **rough it**, you manage without the usual comforts of home.

roughage *(ruff-ij)* *(n)* the fibre found in foods such as cereals and vegetables, which passes through the body but is not digested. Roughage helps you to digest food.

round rounder roundest
1 *(adj)* shaped like a circle or ball.
2 *(prep)* on all sides of something. *We have a fence round our garden.*
3 *(prep)* going in a circle. *We circled round the tree.*
4 *(adj)* returning to a place. *A round trip from London to New York.*
5 *(n)* a series of visits made by a postman, milkman, doctor, etc.

6 *(n)* a set of matches or games in a competition.

7 *(n)* a simple song in which people start singing one after another, so that they are singing different parts of the song at the same time.

roundabout
1 *(n)* a road junction where vehicles must go round in a circle to join the road that they want

2 *(n)* a round, revolving platform in a playground, that children can ride on.

rounders
(singular n) a ball game in which players score points by hitting a ball and then running round four posts called bases.

rouse rousing roused
1 *(v)* to wake someone up.

2 *(v)* to make someone feel interested or excited. **rousing** *(adj)*.

route
(root) *(n)* the set of roads or paths that you follow to get from one place to another.

routine
(root-een)
1 *(n)* a regular way of doing things.

2 *(adj)* Something that is **routine** is normal and not at all difficult or unusual.

row rowing rowed
1 *(rhymes with low)* *(n)* a line of people or things, side by side.

2 *(rhymes with low)* *(v)* to use oars in order to move a boat through water. **row** *(n)*.

3 *(rhymes with cow)* *(n)* an angry argument or quarrel. **row** *(v)*.

4 *(rhymes with cow)* *(n)* a dreadful noise

rowdy rowdier rowdiest *(adj)*
wild and noisy. *Don't play such rowdy games!* **rowdiness** *(n)*, **rowdily** *(adv)*.

rowlock
(rol-uk) *(n)* a curved piece of metal on the side of a rowing boat, used for holding the oar in place while you row.

royal
(adj) to do with a king or queen, or a member of their family. **royalty** *(n)*.

RSVP
the initials of the French phrase *Répondez s'il vous plaît*, which means "please reply". RSVP is often written at the bottom of an invitation.

rub rubbing rubbed
1 *(v)* to press one thing against another and move them backwards and forwards. *Finnigan rubbed his chin thoughtfully.*

2 *(v)* If you **rub out** pencil marks, you use a rubber to remove them from the paper.

3 *(v)* *(informal)* If you **rub it in**, you keep telling someone about their mistakes.

rubber
1 *(n)* a substance made from the juice of a rubber tree, or produced artificially. Rubber is strong, elastic, and waterproof, and is used for making things like tyres, balls, and boots. *The picture shows liquid rubber, or latex, being collected by a method called tapping.*

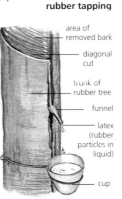

rubber tapping

area of removed bark

diagonal cut

trunk of rubber tree

funnel

latex (rubber particles in liquid)

cup

2 *(n)* a small piece of rubber used for rubbing out pencil marks.

rubbish
1 *(n)* things that you throw away because they are not useful or valuable.

2 *(n)* nonsense. *Don't talk rubbish!*

rubble
(n) broken bricks and stones. *All that was left of their house was a pile of rubble.*

ruby rubies
(n) a dark red precious stone.

rucksack
(n) a large bag that you carry on your back when you are walking or climbing. See **hike**

rudder
(n) a hinged plate, attached to the back of a boat or aeroplane, and used for steering. See **aircraft**, **dinghy**, **ship**.

rude ruder rudest *(adj)*
not polite. **rudeness** *(n)*, **rudely** *(adv)*

ruffian
(n) a violent person

ruffle ruffling ruffled
1 *(v)* to disturb something that was smooth so that it becomes uneven or messy. *She ruffled his hair.*

2 *(v)* to make someone feel annoyed or worried. *Ziggy's questioning really ruffled me.*

rug
1 *(n)* a thick mat, made from wool or other fibres.

2 *(n)* a small blanket.

rugby
or **rugger** *(n)* a game played by two teams with an oval-shaped ball which they can kick, pass, or carry.

rugged
(rug-id)
1 *(adj)* wild and rocky. *Rugged countryside.*

2 *(adj)* tough and strong. *I have always admired Kirk's rugged good looks.*

rugger
see **rugby**.

ruin ruining ruined
1 *(v)* to spoil something completely. **ruin** *(n)*.

2 *(n)* a building that has been destroyed or very badly damaged.

3 *(v)* to make someone lose all their money. *Geoffrey was almost ruined by the legal costs of the case.*

rule ruling ruled
1 *(n)* an official instruction that tells you what you must or must not do.

2 *(v)* to govern a country, or to have power over it.

3 *(n)* the time during which a person rules a country.

4 *(v)* to make an official decision or judgement. *The judge ruled that the father should be allowed to see his children.* **ruling** *(n)*.

5 If you do something **as a rule**, you usually do it.

6 rule out *(v)* If you **rule something out**, you decide that it is not possible.

ruler
1 *(n)* a long, flat piece of wood, plastic, or metal that you use for measuring and drawing straight lines.

2 *(n)* someone who rules a country.

rum
(n) a strong alcoholic drink made from sugar cane.

rumble rumbling rumbled *(v)*
to make a low, rolling noise like the sound of thunder. **rumble** *(n)*.

rummage
(rum-ij) rummaging rummaged *(v)* to look for something by moving things around in an untidy or careless way. *Ned rummaged in his backpack for a toffee.*

rumour
(n) something that lots of people are saying although it may not be true.

rump
(n) the back part of an animal, above its hind legs.

run running ran run
1 *(v)* to move quickly, using your legs. **run** *(n)*.

2 *(v)* to take someone somewhere in a car. *Shall I run you home?*

3 *(v)* to function, or to work. *Most lorries run on diesel.*

4 *(v)* to be in charge of something. *Octavia runs a small business.*

5 *(n)* a point in a game of cricket.

6 *(n)* a small enclosure for animals. *A chicken run.*

7 *(v)* If you **run away**, you escape from a place or leave it secretly.

8 *(v)* If you have **run out of** something, you have used it all and have none left.

9 If someone is **run over**, they are hit by a car or other vehicle.

runaway

1 (n) a child who has run away from home.
2 (adj) out of control. *A runaway train.*
3 (adj) very easy. *A runaway victory.*

rung (n) one of the horizontal bars on a ladder.

runner

1 (n) someone who runs in a race.
2 (n) a rod or bar on which something slides.

runner-up runners-up (n) the person or team that comes second in a race or competition.

runny runnier runniest

1 (adj) If something is runny, it flows, or moves like a liquid. *Runny paint.*
2 (adj) If you have a runny nose, mucus is dripping from it.

runway (n) a strip of land that aircraft use for taking off and landing.

rural (adj) to do with the countryside or farming.

rush rushes rushing rushed

1 (v) to go somewhere quickly, or to do something quickly. *Eddie rushed to the shop before it shut.* rush (n).
2 rushes (plural n) tall plants with rounded stems that grow in damp places.

rust rusting rusted

1 (n) the reddish-brown substance that can form on iron and steel when they get wet. rusty (adj).
2 (v) to become covered with rust. *The door hinges have rusted.*

rustle rustling rustled

1 (v) When leaves, papers, etc. rustle, they make a soft, crackling sound as they move together gently.
2 (v) to steal horses or cattle. rustler (n), rustling (n).
3 (v) (informal) If you rustle up something, you provide it quickly. *Russell rustled up some supper.*

rut

1 (n) a deep, narrow track made in the ground by wheels.
2 (n) If someone is in a rut, they do the same sort of thing all the time.

ruthless (adj) Someone who is ruthless is cruel and has no pity. ruthlessness (n), ruthlessly (adv).

rye

1 (n) a cereal grown in cold countries and used to make flour and whisky.
2 (n) (US) a dark brown bread made from rye flour.

Ss

Sabbath (n) the weekly day of rest in some religions. The Jewish Sabbath is Saturday, while the Christian Sabbath is Sunday.

sabotage (*sab-er-tahj*) (n) deliberate damage intended to cause difficulties for an enemy, employer, etc. saboteur (n), sabotage (v).

sabre (*say-bur*)
1 (n) a heavy sword with a curved blade.
2 sabre-toothed tiger (n) an extinct big cat with very long, sabre-shaped fangs.

sabre-toothed tiger

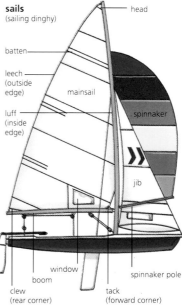

sack

sacking sacked
1 (n) a large bag made from strong cloth, used for carrying coal, potatoes, flour, etc.
2 (v) If an employer sacks someone, the employer tells them that they no longer have a job and must leave. sack (n).

sacred (*say-krid*) (adj) holy, or connected with religion. *Sacred music.*

sacrifice sacrificing sacrificed

1 (n) the killing of an animal or person as an offering to a god. sacrifice (v), sacrificial (adj).
2 (v) to give up something important or enjoyable for a good reason. *I sacrificed my supper so that we could go to the play.* sacrifice (n).

sacrilege (*sak-ril-ij*) (n) disrespect for something holy or very important. sacrilegious (adj).

sad sadder saddest

1 (adj) unhappy. sadness (n), sadden (v), sadly (adv).
2 (adj) Something which is sad makes you feel unhappy. *Sad news.*

saddle saddling saddled

1 (n) a leather seat on the back of a horse, on which a rider sits. See **tack**.
2 (n) a seat for a bicycle.

3 (v) If someone saddles you with an unpleasant job or responsibility, they leave you to deal with it.

safari (n) an expedition to see or to hunt large wild animals.

safe safer safest

1 (adj) If something is safe, it is not in danger of being harmed or stolen. safety (n), safely (adv).
2 (adj) not dangerous, or not risky. *Is this ladder safe?*
3 (n) a strong box in which you can lock away money or valuables.

safeguard safeguarding safeguarded

1 (v) to protect something.
2 (n) a law or regulation that is meant to protect something.

sag sagging sagged (v) to hang down or sink down. *The bed sagged in the middle.*

sage

1 (n) a herb whose leaves are often used in cooking. See **herb**.
2 (adj) wise. *A sage remark.*
3 (n) a wise person.

sail sailing sailed

1 (n) a large sheet of strong cloth, such as canvas, that makes a boat or ship move when it catches the wind. *The picture below shows the main parts of the sails on a sailing dingy. Also see* **ship**.
2 (v) to travel in a boat or ship. sailing (n).
3 (v) When a boat or ship sails, it starts out on a voyage.
4 (n) an arm of a windmill. See **windmill**.

sails
(sailing dinghy)

head

batten

leech
(outside edge)

mainsail

luff
(inside edge)

spinnaker

jib

window

boom

spinnaker pole

clew
(rear corner)

tack
(forward corner)

sailboard *(n)* a flat board with a mast and sail fixed to it, used for windsurfing. *See* **windsurfing**.

sailor *(n)* someone who works on a ship as a member of the crew.

saint
1 *(n)* a man or woman honoured by the Christian church, because of their very holy life. The short form of Saint is St. *The picture shows a painting of Saint Peter from a 13th-century manuscript.*
2 *(n)* a very good and kind person. **saintly** *(adj)*.

Saint Peter

sake *(n)* If you do something for someone else's **sake**, you do it in order to help or please them.

salad
1 *(n)* a mixture of raw vegetables.
2 *(n)* a mixture of cold foods. *Rice salad. Fruit salad.*

salamander
1 *(n)* an amphibian, similar to a newt, which lives on land but breeds in water.
2 *(n)* In myths and legends, a salamander is a newt-like creature that lives in fire.

poison-secreting skin

salamander

salary salaries *(n)* the money someone is paid for their work, usually once a month.

sale
1 *(n)* a time when goods are sold at cheaper than usual prices.
2 *(n)* the act of selling something. *How's the sale of your house going?*
3 **for sale** available for people to buy.
4 **on sale** available in the shops.

saliva *(n)* the liquid in your mouth that keeps it moist and helps you to swallow and begin to digest food.

salmon salmon *(n)* a large fish with a silvery skin and pink flesh. *Salmon can leap up to three metres in order to jump a waterfall.*

Atlantic salmon

saloon
1 *(n)* a car with a hard roof and a separate boot.
2 *(n)* (US) a bar where people can buy and drink alcoholic drinks.

salt
1 *(n)* a common, white substance, found in sea water and under the ground, and used for adding flavour to food. **salty** *(adj)*.
2 *(n)* a chemical compound formed from an acid and a metal.
3 If you take something with **a pinch of salt**, you do not believe that it is really true.

salute saluting saluted
1 *(v)* When soldiers **salute**, they raise their hand to their forehead as a sign of respect. **salute** *(n)*.
2 *(v)* to praise or honour someone for something that they have done. *The school saluted Jill for her bravery.*

salvage salvaging salvaged *(v)* to rescue something from a shipwreck, fire, etc.

salvation *(n)* the state of being saved from evil, harm, or destruction.

same *(adj)* exactly alike, or not different.

sample sampling sampled
1 *(n)* a small amount of something that shows what the whole of it is like. *The doctor took a blood sample.*
2 *(v)* to try a small amount of something in order to see if you like it. *Gerald sampled the cheese before buying it.*

samurai *(sam-yoo-rye)*
samurai *(n)* a Japanese warrior. *This samurai is defending himself from attack with his naginata, a long rod with a curved blade at the end.*

samurai

iron helmet

neck guard

enemy arrow

katana (long, curved sword)

armour of leather scales

wakizashi (short sword)

naginata

sanction sanctioning sanctioned
1 *(v)* to allow something, or to give approval to something.

2 **sanctions** *(plural n)* punishment for breaking the law or for unacceptable behaviour. *One country sometimes applies sanctions against another country, by refusing to trade with them.*

sanctuary sanctuaries
1 *(n)* a holy place.
2 *(n)* a place where someone who is being hunted can be safe.
3 *(n)* a place where birds or animals are protected.

sand sanding sanded
1 *(n)* the tiny grains of rock which make up beaches and deserts. **sandy** *(adj)*.
2 *(v)* to smooth or polish a surface with sandpaper or a sanding machine.

sandal *(n)* a light, open shoe with straps that go over your foot.

sandbag *(n)* a sack filled with sand, used as protection against flood water, bullets, or explosions.

sandpaper *(n)* paper with grains of sand stuck to it that you rub over surfaces to make them smooth.

sandwich sandwiches *(n)* two pieces of bread around a filling of cheese, meat, or some other food.

sandwich course *(n)* a programme of study which includes a period of work in business or industry.

sane saner sanest
1 *(adj)* Someone who is **sane** has a healthy mind. **sanity** *(n)*, **sanely** *(adv)*.
2 *(adj)* sensible, or not at all crazy. *We can rely on Janet to make a sane decision.* **sanity** *(n)*, **sanely** *(adv)*.

sanitary
1 *(adj)* clean and free from germs.
2 **sanitary towel** *(n)* a pad of soft material that some women and girls wear during their periods.

sanitation *(n)* a system for protecting people from dirt and disease, for example, by a clean water supply and sewage disposal.

sap sapping sapped
1 *(n)* the liquid in the stems of plants.
2 *(v)* to weaken something gradually. *Hunger had sapped Ali's strength.*

sapling *(n)* a young tree.

sapphire *(saf-fire)* *(n)* a bright blue precious stone.

sarcastic *(adj)* If you are **sarcastic**, you say the opposite of what you really mean as a way of criticizing or mocking someone. **sarcasm** *(n)*, **sarcastically** *(adv)*.

sardine *(n)* a small sea fish, often sold in tins as food.

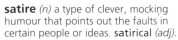

sari *(sah-ree) (n)*
a long piece of light
material, worn draped
around the body. Saris
are worn mainly by
Indian women and girls.
*The picture shows an
Indian woman wearing
a sari.*

sari

sarong *(sa-rong) (n)*
a piece of cloth wrapped
around the the body like
a skirt or dress, originally
worn by Malaysian men
and women.

sash sashes
1 *(n)* a strip of material worn around
the waist or diagonally across the
chest.
2 **sash window** *(n)* a window with
two frames that can slide up or down.

satchel *(n)* a leather bag for school
books carried over the shoulder or on
the back.

satellite
1 *(n)* a machine that is sent into orbit
around the Earth. *The picture shows
the main parts of a communications
satellite which receives and sends
television and telephone signals.*
2 *(n)* a moon or other natural object
that moves in orbit around a planet.
See **moon**.

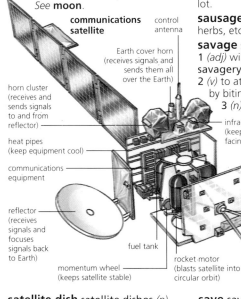

communications
satellite

control
antenna

Earth cover horn
(receives signals and
sends them all
over the Earth)

horn cluster
(receives and
sends signals
to and from
reflector)

heat pipes
(keep equipment cool)

communications
equipment

reflector
(receives
signals and
focuses
signals back
to Earth)

fuel tank

momentum wheel
(keeps satellite stable)

rocket motor
(blasts satellite into
circular orbit)

infra-red Earth sensor
(keeps satellite
facing Earth)

mirrored
radiator wall
(keeps equipment
cool)

thruster nozzle
(adjust position
of satellite in
orbit)

solar array drive
mechanism
(rotates solar panels
to face Sun)

satellite dish satellite dishes *(n)*
a dish-shaped receiver for television
signals sent by satellite. Satellite dishes
are usually attached to outside walls.

satellite television *(n)* television
programmes that are transmitted by
satellite and received by a satellite
dish.

satire *(n)* a type of clever, mocking
humour that points out the faults in
certain people or ideas. **satirical** *(adj)*.

satisfaction *(n)* a feeling of
contentment, because you have done
something that you wanted to do or
have done something well.

satisfactory *(adj)* good enough.
satisfactorily *(adv)*.

satisfy satisfies satisfying satisfied
1 *(v)* to please someone by doing
enough or giving them enough.
*The pizzas soon satisifed the hungry
children.* **satisfied** *(adj)*.
2 *(v)* to convince someone that
something is true. *Jackson's alibi
satisfied the police.*

saturate saturating saturated
1 *(v)* to make something very wet.
saturated *(adj)*.
2 *(v)* to fill something so full that there
is not room for anything else.
saturation *(n)*, saturated *(adj)*.

sauce *(n)* a thick liquid served with
food.

saucepan *(n)* a metal cooking pot
with a handle and, sometimes, a lid.

saucer *(n)* a small, curved plate that
is placed under a cup.

sauna *(sor-nah) (n)* a room filled with
steam where people sit and sweat a
lot.

sausage *(n)* minced meat, bread,
herbs, etc. in a tube of thin skin.

savage savaging savaged
1 *(adj)* wild and vicious. *A savage dog.*
savagery *(n)*, savagely *(adv)*.
2 *(v)* to attack a person or an animal
by biting or scratching them.
3 *(n)* an uncivilized person.

save saving
saved
1 *(v)* to rescue
someone or something
from danger.
2 *(v)* If something **saves** time,
space, energy, etc., it does not
waste it.

3 *(v)* to keep money to use in the
future rather than spending it now.
4 *(v)* to stop a ball from going into the
goal. **save** *(n)*.

savings *(n)* money that you have
saved.

savoury *(adj)* Food that is **savoury**
has a salty or spicy flavour, not a
sweet one.

saw sawing sawed sawn
1 *(n)* a tool with a toothed blade, used
for cutting wood.
2 *(v)* to cut something with a saw.

sawdust *(n)* the powder that you
get when you saw wood.

saxophone *(n)* a musical
instrument made of
brass, often played
in jazz and
dance bands.
saxophonist *(n)*.

crook

ligature
(holds reed)

mouthpiece

alto saxophone

key rods

upper stack key

body

lower stack key

lower
octave key

spatula key

bell

say saying said
1 *(v)* to speak.
What did you say?
2 *(v)* to mean
something. *What
does that sign say?*
3 If you **have a say** in something, you
are one of the people involved in
deciding it.

saying *(n)* a well-known phrase that
gives advice.

scab *(n)* the hard covering that forms
over a wound when it is healing.

scaffold *(n)* a raised wooden
platform on which criminals were
executed.

solar array panel
(generates electricity
from Sun)

solar sailing flap
(helps control
satellite's
position)

thermal
blanket cover
(layers of
protective foil)

scaffolding *(n)* the structure of metal poles and wooden planks that workmen stand on when they are working on a building.

scald scalding scalded *(v)* to burn yourself with very hot liquid. scald *(n)*, scalding *(adj)*.

scale scaling scaled
1 *(n)* one of the small, hard pieces of skin that cover the body of a fish, snake, or other reptile. scaly *(adj)*.
2 *(n)* a series of numbers, units, etc. that are used to measure something. *The Richter scale measures the strength of Earth movements.*
3 *(n)* a series of musical notes going up or down in order.
4 *(n)* the relationship between the measurements on a map or model and the actual measurements.
5 scales *(plural n)* an instrument used for weighing things.
6 *(v)* to climb up something *Joel scaled the mountain.*

scallop *(n)* a shellfish with two hinged shells or valves. Scallops move around by opening and closing their valves rapidly.

queen scallop
eye
gill
tentacles
shell or valve
adductor muscle (holds shells together when closed)
barnacle growing on shell

scalp *(n)* the skin on the top of your head where your hair grows. *See* **brain**.

scalpel *(n)* a small, sharp knife used by surgeons.

scamper scampering scampered *(v)* to run somewhere with short, quick steps. *The squirrel scampered along the branch.*

scan scanning scanned
1 *(v)* to look through a book or piece of writing because you are searching for something. *Max scanned the letter for news of this brother.*
2 *(v)* to look carefully along something. *We scanned the horizon for ships.*

scanner
1 *(n)* a machine used by medical staff to view inside a patient's body. scan *(n)*, scan *(v)*.
2 *(n)* a machine used to copy pictures or text from paper onto a computer. scan *(n)*, scan *(v)*.

scandal
1 *(n)* gossip about someone's dishonest or immoral behaviour.
2 *(n)* something that you think is disgraceful. scandalous *(adj)*.

scanty scantier scantiest *(adj)* not enough, or not big enough. *We had only scanty information.*

scapegoat *(n)* someone who is made to take all the blame for something.

scar *(n)* a mark left on your skin by an old cut or wound. scar *(v)*.

scarce *(adj)* Something that is scarce is hard to find because there is so little of it. *Fresh water is scarce on the island.* scarcity *(n)*.

scarcely *(adv)* hardly. *I've scarcely seen Susie today.*

scare scaring scared *(v)* to frighten a person or an animal. scare *(n)*, scared *(adj)*, scary *(adj)*.

scarecrow *(n)* a model of a person, put in a field to frighten birds away from crops.

scarf scarfs or scarves *(n)* a strip of material worn round your neck or head.

scarlet *(n)* a bright red colour. scarlet *(adj)*.

scatter scattering scattered
1 *(v)* to throw things over a wide area. *We scattered the seed over the earth.*
2 *(v)* to run off in different directions.

scatterbrained *(adj)* If you are scatterbrained, you are always forgetting things

scavenge scavenging scavenged *(v)* to search among rubbish for food or something useful. scavenger *(n)*.

scene *(seen)*
1 *(n)* a view, or a picture. *Fleur paints country scenes.*
2 *(n)* a part of a play or film where the events all happen in the same place.
3 *(n)* the place where something happens. *The ambulance rushed to the scene of the accident.*
4 *(n)* *(informal)* an area of interest or activity. *Efra is very interested in the jazz scene.*
5 If you **make a scene**, you get very angry with someone in public.

scenery *(seen-er-ee)* sceneries
1 *(n)* the natural countryside of an area, such as trees, hills, and lakes.
2 *(n)* the painted boards and curtains that are used on stage as the background to a play, opera, or ballet.

scenic *(seen-ik)* *(adj)* A scenic place has beautiful surrounding countryside.

scent *(sent)* scenting scented
1 *(n)* a pleasant smell. *The scent of roses.* scented *(adj)*.
2 *(n)* a liquid that you can put on your skin to make you smell pleasant.
3 *(n)* an animal's smell.
4 *(v)* If you **scent** danger or victory, you start to feel that it will happen.

sceptical *(adj)* If you are sceptical about something, you doubt whether it is really true. sceptic *(n)*, scepticism *(n)*, sceptically *(adv)*.

schedule *(shed-yool)* scheduling scheduled
1 *(n)* a plan, programme, or timetable.
2 *(v)* If you **schedule** an event, you plan it for a particular time.

scheme *(skeem)* scheming schemed
1 *(n)* a plan, or an arrangement.
2 *(v)* to plan or plot something, especially something secret or dishonest. schemer *(n)*, scheming *(adj)*.

scholar *(skol-er)*
1 *(n)* a student who has won a scholarship.
2 *(n)* a very clever and learned person.

scholarship *(n)* a prize that pays for you to go to a school or college.

school
1 *(n)* a place where children go to be taught.
2 *(n)* a group of fish or other sea creatures. *A school of porpoises.*

science *(n)* the study of nature and the physical world by testing, experimenting, and measuring. Biology, physics, and chemistry are all types of science. scientist *(n)*, scientific *(adj)*, scientifically *(adv)*.

science fiction *(n)* stories about life in the future, or life on other planets.

scissors *(plural n)* a sharp tool with two blades, used for cutting paper, material, etc.

scoff scoffing scoffed
1 *(v)* to be scornful and mocking about someone or something. *Nat scoffed at the idea of ballet lessons.*
2 *(v)* *(informal)* to eat very fast and greedily. *Lisa scoffed her lunch.*

scold scolding scolded *(v)* to tell someone off.

scone *(n)* a round bun, often eaten with butter.

scoop scooping scooped
1 *(v)* to lift or pick up something. *Jasper scooped up a handful of snow.*
2 *(n)* a spoon, especially a serving spoon.
3 *(n)* a story in a newspaper that other papers do not have.

scooter
1 (n) a type of child's bicycle, with two wheels and a flat board, which you stand on with one foot, while pushing on the ground with the other foot.
2 (n) a small motorcycle.

scope (n) the range of opportunity that something gives. *There is plenty of scope for improving this garden.*

scorch scorches scorching scorched
1 (v) to burn something slightly, usually with an iron. scorch (n).
2 (v) to dry something up. *The blazing sun scorched the earth.*
3 (adj) If the weather is **scorching**, it is extremely hot.

score scoring scored
1 (v) to get a goal or win a point in a game.
2 (n) the number of points or goals that each team wins in a game.
3 (n) a written piece of music.
4 (v) to cut a line or lines in a surface.
5 (n) twenty. *Seth lived for four score years.*
6 scores (plural n) a large number. *I've received scores of letters.*

scorn (n) a strong feeling of contempt and superiority. *Gwen poured scorn on my idea of becoming a doctor.* scornful (adj).

scorpion (n) a creature like a long spider, with a poisonous sting in its tail.

tail — **Sahara scorpion**
pedipalp (sensitive pincer)
sting
abdomen
walking leg

scoundrel (n) someone who cheats and lies.

scour scouring scoured
1 (v) to clean something by rubbing it hard. scourer (n).
2 (v) to search an area thoroughly. *Police scoured the building for clues.*

scourge (skurj) (n) a cause of great harm and suffering.

scout scouting scouted
1 (n) a soldier sent ahead of the main army to find the enemy.
2 (v) to look for something. *We scouted around for firewood.*
3 (n) a member of the Scout Association.

scowl scowling scowled (v) to make an angry face. scowl (n).

scrabble scrabbling scrabbled (v) to dig or scratch in the ground with your hands or feet, usually in order to find something.

scraggy scraggier scraggiest (adj) skinny and lean. scragginess (n).

scramble scrambling scrambled
1 (v) to climb over rocks or hills.
2 (v) to rush or struggle to get somewhere. scramble (n).
3 (v) to mix up sounds or words.
4 scrambled egg (n) a mixture of eggs and milk, cooked in a pan.

scrap scrapping scrapped
1 (n) a small piece of paper, food, etc.
2 (n) metal from old cars or machines.
3 (v) to get rid of something. *We had to scrap our plans due to the weather.*
4 (v) (informal) to fight, or to quarrel. scrap (n).

scrapbook (n) a book in which you stick pictures, newspaper cuttings, etc.

scrape scraping scraped
1 (v) to clean, peel, or scratch something with a sharp object. scrape (n).
2 (n) (informal) an awkward situation. *Miranda's always getting into scrapes.*
3 (v) If you **scrape through** an examination, you only just pass it.

scratch scratches scratching scratched
1 (v) to make a mark or a cut. scratch (n).
2 (v) to rub a part of you that itches. scratch (n), scratchy (adj).
3 (informal) If you do something **from scratch**, you start from the beginning.
4 (informal) If something is **not up to scratch**, it is not good enough.

scrawl scrawling scrawled (v) to write in a quick, careless way. scrawl (n).

scream screaming screamed
1 (v) to cry out loudly, or to shriek. scream (n).
2 (n) (informal) a very funny thing or person. *Zak's such a scream!*

scree (n) small stones covering an area on a mountain side.

screech screeches screeching screeched (v) to make a high, unpleasant sound. *The car screeched to a halt.* screech (n).

screen screening screened
1 (n) a wall, or a barrier. screen (v).
2 (n) the front of a television set or computer monitor, or the white surface that films are shown on.
3 (v) to test someone, to see if they have a disease. screening (n).

screw screwing screwed
1 (n) a metal fastener like a nail, with a groove in its head and a spiral thread.
2 (v) to fasten something with screws.
3 (v) If you **screw on** a lid, you turn or twist it.
4 (v) If you **screw up** paper or material, you make it into a ball, ready to be thrown away.

screwdriver (n) a tool with a flat tip that fits into the head of a screw, in order to turn it. See **tool**.

scribble scribbling scribbled
1 (v) to write carelessly or quickly. scribble (n).
2 (v) to make meaningless marks with a pencil, pen, or crayon. scribble (n).

scribe (n) A **scribe** was someone who copied books by hand, before printing was invented. *The picture shows a statue of an Ancient Egyptian scribe.*

Egyptian scribe

script
1 (n) an alphabet. *There are several different Indian scripts.*
2 (n) the written version of what an actor or broadcaster says.

scripture (n) religious writing, especially the Bible.

scroll scrolling scrolled
1 (n) a rolled-up piece of paper or parchment with writing on it. *The picture shows a Hebrew scroll made of parchment.*
2 (v) to move the text on a computer screen up and down so that you can see more of it.

scroll

scrounge scrounging scrounged (v) (informal) to get things free from people by asking for them. *Can I scrounge a sandwich from you?*

scrub scrubbing scrubbed
1 (v) to clean something by rubbing it hard with a brush.
2 (n) low bushes or short trees that cover a piece of ground.

scruffy scruffier scruffiest (adj) shabby and untidy. scruffily (adv).

scrum (n) a group of rugby players pushing to get the ball.

scrupulous (screw-pyoo-luss) (adj) careful and exact. *Tobia is scrupulous about money.* scrupulously (adv).

scrutinize or **scrutinise** scrutinizing scrutinized (v) to examine something closely. scrutiny (n).

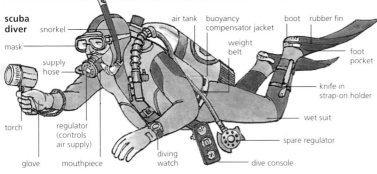

scuba diver
snorkel
mask
supply hose
torch
regulator (controls air supply)
glove
mouthpiece
diving watch
air tank
buoyancy compensator jacket
weight belt
knife in strap-on holder
wet suit
spare regulator
dive console
boot
rubber fin
foot pocket

scuba diving *(n)* underwater swimming, with an air tank on your back that is connected to your mouth by a hose. Scuba stands for self-contained underwater breathing apparatus. **scuba diver** *(n)*.

scuffle *(n)* a small fight. **scuffle** *(v)*.

scull sculling sculled
1 *(n)* an oar.
2 *(v)* to row in a small, light boat.

sculpture
1 *(n)* something carved or shaped out of stone, wood, metal, etc. *This sculpture by Henry Moore is called "Recumbent Figure".*
2 *(n)* the art or work of making sculpture. **sculptor** *(n)*, **sculpt** *(v)*.

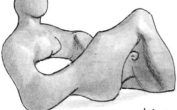
sculpture

scum *(n)* a layer of dirty froth on top of a liquid.

scurf *(n)* small flakes of dead skin on your scalp or in your hair.

scurry scurries scurrying scurried *(v)* to hurry, or to run with short, quick steps.

scuttle scuttling scuttled
1 *(v)* to dash.
2 *(n)* a coal bucket.
3 *(v)* to make a hole in a ship so that it sinks.

scythe
handle
blade
grass nail (prevents grass from sticking to blade)

scythe *(sythe)* *(n)* a tool with a large, curved blade, used for cutting grass or crops. **scythe** *(v)*.

sea *(n)* a large area of salt water.

seafarer *(n)* a sailor, or someone who travels by sea. **seafaring** *(adj)*.

seafood *(n)* fish or shellfish that are eaten as food.

seagull *(n)* a large, grey or white bird that is commonly seen near the sea.

sea horse *(n)* a fish with a head shaped like a horse's head and a long, curling tail.

sea horse

seal sealing sealed
1 *(n)* a sea mammal with small flippers that breeds on land. *See* **polar**.
2 *(v)* to close something up. *We've sealed up the old well.* **seal** *(n)*.
3 *(n)* a stamp, pressed into wax, used to make a document official, or to close up a letter or an envelope.

sea level *(n)* the average level of the surface of the sea, which is used to measure land heights. *This mountain is 2,000ft above sea level.*

sea lion *(n)* a sea mammal, like a seal, but with sticking-out ears and large flippers.

sea lion
flipper

seam
1 *(n)* a line of sewing that joins two pieces of material.
2 *(n)* a band of a different kind of rock between layers of other rock. *A coal seam.*

seaplane *(n)* an aircraft that can take off and land on water.

search searches searching searched *(v)* to explore or examine something closely. **search** *(n)*.

search engine *(n)* a computer program on the Internet that finds Web sites containing particular words that you type into your computer.

searching *(adj)* deep and thorough. *Searching questions.*

searchlight *(n)* a large, powerful light that can be turned in a particular direction.

search warrant *(n)* an order from a court that allows the police to go into a building to look for things or people.

seashell *(n)* the shell of a sea creature, such as a mussel or cockle.

seashore *(n)* the sandy or rocky land next to the sea.

seasick *(adj)* If you are seasick, you feel ill because of the rolling movement of a boat or ship.

seaside *(n)* the coast, especially at a holiday resort.

season seasoning seasoned
1 *(n)* a time of the year. The four seasons are spring, summer, autumn, and winter. **seasonal** *(adj)*.
2 *(v)* to add flavour to food with salt, spices, etc.
3 If a food is **in season**, it is fresh and easily available.

seasoning *(n)* herbs and spices that are added to food to give it more flavour.

seat seating seated
1 *(n)* a place where you can sit.
2 *(v)* to sit. *Jack seated himself on the arm of the sofa.*
3 *(v)* to have room for people to sit down. *This table seats six.*

seat belt *(n)* a belt that you wear across your lap and chest in a car or plane to make you safer. *See* **car**.

seaweed *(n)* a type of algae that grows in the sea. *The picture shows examples of brown, green, and red seaweed growing underwater.*

seaweed
serrated wrack
sugar kelp
thongweed
sea lettuce
dulse

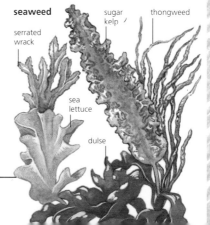

secateurs *(sek-er-terz)* *(plural n)* strong scissors that you use in the garden for cutting and pruning.

secluded *(adj)* quiet and private. *The farm is in a secluded valley.* **seclusion** *(n).*

second seconding seconded
1 *(adj)* next, or after the first. **second** *(adv),* **secondly** *(adv).*
2 *(v)* If you **second** a proposal at a meeting, you support it. **seconder** *(n).*
3 *(n)* a sixtieth of a minute.

secondary
1 *(adj)* to do with the second stage of something. *Secondary education.*
2 *(adj)* less important. *A secondary problem.* **secondarily** *(adv).*

secondary school *(n)* In Britain, a secondary school is a school for pupils aged 11 or 13 upwards.

second-hand *(adj)* If something is second-hand, it has belonged to another person first.

secondment *(n)* If someone is **on secondment**, they are doing a different job for a short time.

second-rate *(adj)* not very good.

secret
1 *(n)* a mystery, or something that only a few people know.
2 *(adj)* not known by many people. **secrecy** *(n),* **secretly** *(adv).*
3 **in secret** privately.

secret agent *(n)* a spy, or someone who obtains secret information.

secretary secretaries
1 *(n)* someone whose job is to type letters, answer the telephone, keep records, and do other office work for an employer. **secretarial** *(adj).*
2 *(n)* a government minister or representative. *The Home Secretary.*

secrete secreting secreted
1 *(v)* to produce a liquid. *Some snakes secrete poison.* **secretion** *(n).*
2 *(v)* to hide. *The spy secreted the secret message in the heel of his shoe.*

section
1 *(n)* a part or division of something. *The tail section of an aeroplane.*
2 *(n)* a drawing or plan that shows a slice through an object.

sector
1 *(n)* a part of a circle made by drawing two straight lines from the centre to different places on the circumference. See **circle**.
2 *(n)* a part of a business, or an area of trade. *The marketing sector.*

secure securing secured
1 *(adj)* If you feel **secure**, you feel safe and sure of yourself. **security** *(n).*

2 *(adj)* safe, firmly closed, or well-protected. **security** *(n),* **securely** *(adv).*
3 *(v)* If you **secure** something, you make it safe, especially by closing it tightly.

sedan *(n)* *(US)* a covered car for four or more people (saloon, *UK*).

sedate sedating sedated
1 *(adj)* calm and unhurried. *We strolled along at a sedate pace.* **sedately** *(adv).*
2 *(v)* to make someone calm or sleepy, especially by giving them medicine. **sedation** *(n).*

sedative *(n)* a drug that makes you quiet and calm.

sediment
1 *(n)* solid pieces that settle at the bottom of a liquid.
2 *(n)* **Sedimentary rock** is formed by layers of material in the ground being pressed together. **sedimentation** *(n).*

seduce seducing seduced *(v)* If you **seduce** someone, you tempt or persuade them to do something, especially to have sex. **seduction** *(n),* **seductive** *(adj),* **seductively** *(adv).*

see seeing saw seen
1 *(v)* to use your eyes, to look at, or to notice something or someone.
2 *(v)* to understand, or to recognize. *I see what you mean.*
3 *(v)* If you **see about** something, you deal with it or think it over.
4 *(v)* If you **see through** someone or something, you are not deceived or tricked by them.
5 *(v)* If you **see a job through**, you continue doing it right to the end.

seed *(n)* a small, hard object that grows into a plant. See **germinate**.

seedling *(n)* a young plant that has been grown from a seed.

seek seeking sought *(v)* to look for something, or search for something.

seem seeming seemed *(v)* to appear to be, or to give the impression of being. *They seem to be happy.*

seep seeping seeped *(v)* to flow or trickle slowly. *Some water has seeped through the ceiling.* **seepage** *(n).*

seethe seething seethed
1 *(v)* If a liquid **seethes**, it bubbles or boils.
2 *(v)* to be very angry or excited. **seething** *(adj).*

segment
1 *(n)* a piece of something. *Lucy divided the orange into segments.*

2 *(n)* a part of a circle made by drawing a straight line across it.

segregate segregating segregated *(v)* to keep groups of people apart from each other. **segregation** *(n),* **segregated** *(adj).*

seize *(seez)* seizing seized
1 *(v)* to take something quickly or by force. *Molly seized a rolling pin.*
2 *(v)* If a machine **seizes up**, it jams or stops working.

seizure *(seez-yur)* *(n)* A **seizure** is a sudden attack of illness.

seldom *(adv)* rarely. *We seldom see our neighbours.*

select selecting selected
1 *(v)* to pick or choose. **selector** *(n).*
2 *(adj)* carefully chosen and exclusive. *Sir Hugh has a house in the select part of town.*

selective *(adj)* If you are **selective**, you choose carefully.

self selves *(n)* your individual nature or personality.

self-catering *(adj)* If you go on a self-catering holiday, you do your own cooking.

self-centred *(adj)* thinking only about yourself.

self-confident *(adj)* If you are self-confident, you know that you are all right, and that you can do things well. **self-confidence** *(n),* **self-confidently** *(adv).*

self-conscious *(adj)* If you are self-conscious, you think that people are looking at you, and you worry about what they are thinking. **self-consciously** *(adv).*

self-control *(n)* control of yourself and your feelings. **self-controlled** *(adj).*

self-defence *(n)* the act of protecting yourself against an attacker.

self-employed *(adj)* If you are self-employed, you work for yourself, not an employer.

self-explanatory *(adj)* If something is self-explanatory, it does not need any further explanation. *These instructions are self-explanatory.*

selfish *(adj)* Someone who is **selfish** puts their own feelings and needs first. **selfishness** *(n),* **selfishly** *(adv).*

self-raising flour *(n)* flour containing baking powder, that makes cakes or bread rise.

self-respect *(n)* reasonable pride in yourself and your abilities. **self-respecting** *(adj).*

self-service (adj) If a shop or garage is **self-service**, you help yourself to what you want, and then pay for it at the check-out.

self-sufficient (adj) If a family or community is **self-sufficient**, they grow or make everything that they need themselves. **self-sufficiency** (n).

sell selling sold
1 (v) to give something in exchange for money. **seller** (n).
2 (v) to make someone believe or want something. *Sasha tried to sell us the idea of a Caribbean holiday.*

sellout (n) If a show is a **sellout**, all the tickets have been sold.

semaphore (n) a way of sending a message by signalling with your arms or with flags. *The picture shows the message SOS in semaphore.*

semaphore

S   O   S

semen (see-men) (n) the liquid produced by males, that carries sperm to fertilize the female's egg.

semicircle (n) half a circle. **semicircular** (adj).

semicolon (n) the punctuation mark (;) used to separate parts of a sentence.

semidetached (adj) A **semidetached** house is joined to another house on one side.

semifinal (n) a match to decide who will play in the final. **semifinalist** (n).

semitone (n) the smallest possible space, or interval, between two musical notes.

senate (sen-it) (n) a governing group or council. *The American Senate.* **senator** (sen-at-or) (n).

send sending sent
1 (v) to make someone or something go somewhere. *Send Tamara to the shop for a paper.* **sender** (n).
2 (v) If you **send for** something or someone, you make them come to you. *Let's send for some tea.*
3 **send up** (v) (informal) to copy and laugh at someone. *Cory hates it when her friends send up her accent.* **send-up** (n).

send off sending off sent off
1 (v) to make a player leave the sports field as a punishment.

2 (v) to write to ask for something. *We sent off for the free offer.*
3 **sendoff** (n) (informal) If you are given a **sendoff**, people gather to wish you well for a journey, new job, etc.

senile (adj) weak in mind and body because of old age. **senility** (n).

senior (adj) Someone who is **senior** to you is older or more important than you are. **seniority** (n)

senior citizen (n) an old person, especially a pensioner.

sensation
1 (n) a feeling. *Moira was so cold, she had no sensation in her toes.*
2 (n) something that causes a lot of excitement and interest. **sensational** (adj), **sensationally** (adv).

sense sensing sensed
1 (n) good judgement, or understanding. *Topsy has no sense.*
2 (n) the ability to feel or be aware of something. *A sense of direction.*
3 (n) Your five **senses** are sight, hearing, touch, taste, and smell.
4 (n) meaning. *I can't make sense of this story.*
5 (v) to feel or be aware of something. *I sensed that Gareth was angry.*

senseless
1 (adj) pointless, or without meaning. *What a senseless attack on an old man!* **senselessly** (adv).
2 (adj) unconscious.

sensible (adj) If you are **sensible**, you think carefully and do not do stupid or dangerous things. **sensibly** (adv).

sensitive
1 (adj) easily offended, or easily hurt. **sensitivity** (n), **sensitively** (adv).
2 (adj) aware of other people's feelings. **sensitivity** (n), **sensitively** (adv).
3 (adj) able to react to the slightest change. *Sensitive measuring equipment.* **sensitivity** (n), **sensitively** (adv).

sensor (n) an instrument that can detect changes in heat, sound, pressure, etc.

sentence
1 (n) a group of words that make sense. A sentence starts with a capital letter and ends with a full stop.
2 (n) a punishment given to a criminal in court. *A short prison sentence.* **sentence** (v).

sentimental (adj) to do with emotion, romance, or feelings. *This ring has sentimental value: it was my mother's.* **sentimentally** (adv)

sentry sentries (n) a soldier who stands guard.

separate separating separated
1 (sep-er-ate) (v) to part or divide something or some people. **separation** (n).
2 (sep-er-rut) (adj) different, individual, or not together. *The three children have separate bedrooms.* **separately** (adv).
3 (sep-er-ate) (v) If a husband and wife **separate**, they stop living together. **separation** (n).
4 **separates** (sep-er-ruts) (plural n) clothes, such as a skirt and blouse, that you can wear together or on their own.

septic (adj) infected with bacteria. *Maria's cut finger went septic.*

sequel (see-kwell) (n) a second book or film that continues the story from the first.

sequence (see-kwence) (n) a series of things that follow in order. *My life is a sequence of disasters.*

serene (adj) calm and peaceful. **serenity** (n), **serenely** (adv).

serf (n) a farm worker in medieval times who belonged to the lord of the manor. **serfdom** (n). See **feudalism**.

sergeant (sar-jent) (n) an officer in the armed forces or police force.

serial
1 (n) a story that is told in several instalments. *A television serial.* **serialization** (n), **serialize** (v).
2 (adj) Something that is **serial** happens in a row or in order.
3 (n) A **serial number** is a number that identifies a machine or other product.

series series
1 (n) a group of related things, that follow in order. *A series of lessons.*
2 (n) a number of television or radio programmes that are linked in some way. *A detective series.*
3 Electrical parts that are connected in **series** allow electricity to pass through them one after the other.

serious
1 (adj) solemn and thoughtful. **seriousness** (n), **seriously** (adv).
2 (adj) sincere, or not joking. *Are you serious about leaving school?* **seriousness** (n), **seriously** (adv).
3 (adj) very bad, or worrying. *A serious illness.* **seriousness** (n), **seriously** (adv).
4 (adj) important. *Stop messing about, this match is serious!* **seriousness** (n), **seriously** (adv).

sermon (n) a religious talk given during a church service.

serpent (n) (poetic) a snake. Serpents often represent evil in pictures and stories. *This Aztec pendant is made in the shape of a two-headed serpent.*

serpent pendant

serrated (adj) A serrated knife has teeth like a saw.

servant (n) someone who works in somebody else's house, doing housework, cooking, etc.

serve serving served
1 (v) to work for someone.
2 (v) to give someone food or help them in a shop.
3 (v) to begin play in games like tennis, by hitting the ball. **serve** (n).

server (n) a computer that provides a service for other computers in a network. The server may run the network, or provide a link to a printer or some other piece of equipment.

service
1 (n) The service in a shop, café, etc. is the way that you are looked after.
2 (n) a business or organization that provides you with something. *The police service.*
3 (n) a religious ceremony or meeting.
4 (n) a check on a car or machine to make sure that it is working properly. **service** (v).
5 services (plural n) an area next to a motorway where you can eat, rest, and fill up your vehicle with fuel.
6 services (plural n) the armed forces, such as the army, air force, or navy. **serviceman** (n), **servicewoman** (n).

serviette (n) a square piece of paper or material that you use to protect your clothes while eating.

session
1 (n) a period of time used for an activity. *A training sesssion.*
2 (n) a formal meeting. *A court session.*

set setting set
1 (n) a group of things that go together. *A chess set.*
2 (n) the scenery for a play or film.
3 (adj) ready. *Are we all set to leave?*
4 (adj) fixed. *We eat at set times.*
5 (v) to put, fix, or arrange. *Set the alarm for 6 a.m.*
6 (v) If a liquid **sets**, it becomes solid.

7 (v) When the Sun **sets**, it goes below the horizon.

setback (n) something that delays you or stops you making progress.

set square (n) a flat, triangular plastic shape that you use to draw angles. See **geometry**.

settee (n) a long, soft seat with arms and a back, and room for two or more people.

settle settling settled
1 (v) to sort out, decide, or agree on something. *We settled the argument by tossing a coin.*
2 (v) to make yourself comfortable. *Phillip settled down with a good book.*
3 (v) to go and live somewhere. **settler** (n).
4 (v) If you **settle in**, you get used to your new house, school, etc.
5 (v) If you **settle up**, you pay a bill or an account.

set up setting up set up
1 (v) to get something ready for use, or arrange it. *The film crew set up their cameras.*
2 (n) (informal) the way that something is organized or arranged.

sever severing severed (v) to cut or break something. *The two countries have severed all ties.*

several (adj) a small number of people, things, etc. *We have several umbrellas at home.* **several** (pronoun).

severe severer severest (adj) strict, harsh, or demanding. *Steve's Dad is very severe on him.* **severity** (n), **severely** (adv).

sew (so) sewing sewed sewn (v) to stitch using a needle and thread. **sewing** (n).

sewage (n) liquid and solid waste that is carried away in sewers and drains.

sewer (n) an underground pipe that carries away liquid and solid waste.

sewing machine (n) a machine for sewing very fast, worked by hand, foot, or electric motor.

sex sexes
1 (n) A person's **sex** is their identity as male or female. *The symbols used for the male and female sexes are shown here.*
2 (n) the instinct which causes two people to be physically attracted to each other. **sexual** (adj).
3 (n) the act of sexual intercourse.

male

female

sexist (adj) Someone who is **sexist** discriminates against members of one or the other sex. *It is sexist to assume that girls can't play football.* **sexism** (n), **sexist** (n).

sexual intercourse (n) an intimate physical act between a man and a woman, in which a man's penis enters a woman's vagina.

sexy sexier sexiest (adj) attractive in a sexual way. **sexily** (adv).

shabby shabbier shabbiest
1 (adj) worn, neglected, or in need of repair. *Shabby clothes.* **shabbiness** (n), **shabbily** (adv).
2 (adj) unfair, or mean. *That was a shabby trick Kit played on you.* **shabbily** (adv).

shack (n) a small, roughly built hut or house.

shackles (plural n) a pair of linked metal rings put around the wrists or ankles of a prisoner.

shade shading shaded
1 (v) to shelter something from the light. *A large hat shaded her face.* **shade** (n).
2 (n) an area that is sheltered from the light. *Come and sit in the shade.* **shady** (adj).
3 (n) a level of colour or meaning. *A lighter shade of blue. This poem has several shades of meaning.*
4 (v) to make part of a drawing darker than the rest. **shading** (n).

shadow shadowing shadowed
1 (n) a dark shape made by something blocking out light. **shadowy** (adj).
2 (v) to follow someone closely and watch them carefully, and usually secretly. *We shadowed the thieves all the way back to their den.*

shaft
1 (n) the long, narrow bar of a spear, arrow, or paddle. See **kayak**.
2 (n) a rotating bar that transmits power to wheels or a propeller.
3 (n) a thin beam of light.
4 (n) a hole in the earth through which you enter a mine.
5 (n) the central stem of a feather. See **feather**.

shaggy shaggier shaggiest (adj) Shaggy hair is long, rough, and uncombed.

shake shaking shook shaken
1 (v) to tremble, or to quiver.
2 (v) to take hold of something and move it quickly up and down. *Shake the bottle before opening.*

shaky shakier shakiest
1 (adj) unsteady and wobbly. *The calf stood up on shaky legs.*

2 (adj) not very good, or not very strong. *Tim's spelling is rather shaky.*

shallow shallower shallowest (adj) not deep. *Shallow water.*

sham (n) something that is not what it seems to be. **sham** (adj).

shambles (singular n) If something is a shambles, it is very badly organized and chaotic. *The match turned into a shambles after the crowd invaded the pitch.*

shame
1 (n) a feeling of guilt and sadness about something that you have done.
2 (n) a pity, or a sad thing to have happened. *It's a shame that Alexandra can't come tonight.*

shampoo (n) a soapy liquid used for washing hair, carpets, etc. **shampoo** (v).

shamrock (n) a small, green plant whose leaves are divided into three parts. The shamrock is the national emblem of Ireland.

shanty shanties (n) a song with a strong rhythm that was sung by sailors as they worked.

shantytown (n) an area of very poor, temporary housing.

shape shaping shaped
1 (n) the form or outline of something. *The picture shows a range of flat and solid shapes.*
2 (v) to mould something into a shape.
3 shape up (v) (informal) to develop. *The new team is shaping up well.*

share sharing shared
1 (v) to divide what you have between two or more people.
2 (n) the portion of something that you receive.

shares (plural n) the equal portions into which the overall value of a business is divided. People can pay money for shares in many companies, receiving in return regular, smaller amounts of money, based on how profitable the company is.

shark
1 (n) a large and often fierce sea fish with very sharp teeth.
2 (n) someone who cheats people.

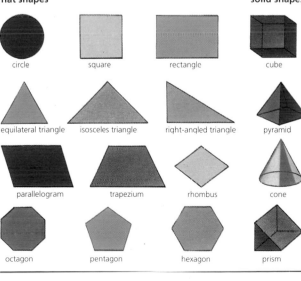

tiger shark

sharp sharper sharpest
1 (adj) A **sharp** edge is fine or pointed, and is likely to prick or cut.
2 (adj) quick-witted, or clever.
3 (adj) sudden and dramatic. *A sharp turn in the road.*
4 (adj) slightly sour. *Lemon juice tastes sharp.*
5 (adj) clearly outlined. *A sharp picture.*
6 (adv) exactly. *Be here at three o'clock sharp.*
7 (adj) In music, a sharp note is higher in pitch than the usual note. *C sharp is a semitone higher than C.*
8 (adj) cross and abrupt. **sharply** (adv).

shatter shattering shattered (v) to break into tiny pieces.

shattered
1 (adj) shocked and upset. *I was shattered by Pom's news.* **shattering** (adj).
2 (adj) (informal) extremely tired.

shave shaving shaved (v) to remove hair with a razor.

shawl (n) a piece of soft material, sometimes wrapped around a baby or worn by women over their shoulders.

sheaf sheaves (n) a bundle. *A sheaf of corn. A sheaf of papers.*

shear shearing sheared shorn
1 (v) to cut the fleece off a sheep. *The picture shows a farmer shearing a sheep with electric clippers.*
2 shears (plural n) a large cutting tool with two blades, used for cutting hedges, trimming grass, etc.

sheepshearing

sheath (n) a holder for a knife or dagger. *See **dagger**.*

shed shedding shed
1 (n) a small hut used for storing things.
2 (v) to let something fall or drop off. *Some reptiles shed their skin. Some trees shed their leaves. People shed tears.*

sheen (n) a shine on a surface.

sheep sheep (n) a farm animal kept for its wool and meat.

sheepdog (n) a working farm dog that rounds up sheep.

sheepish (adj) If someone looks sheepish, they look embarrassed or ashamed, often because they have done something foolish. **sheepishly** (adv).

sheer sheerer sheerest
1 (adj) extremely steep. *There was a sheer drop to the rocks below.*
2 (adj) total and complete. *Our holiday was sheer bliss.*
3 (adj) extremely thin and transparent. *Sheer stockings.*

sheet
1 (n) a large, thin, rectangular piece of cloth used to cover a bed.
2 (n) a thin, flat piece of paper, glass, metal, etc.

sheik or **sheikh** (shake) (n) the head of an Arab tribe, village, or family.

shelf shelves (n) a horizontal board on a wall or in a cupboard, used for storing things.

flat shapes

circle   square   rectangle

equilateral triangle   isosceles triangle   right-angled triangle

parallelogram   trapezium   rhombus

octagon   pentagon   hexagon

solid shapes

cube   tetrahedron

pyramid   octahedron

cone   cylinder

prism   dodecahedron

shell

shell
1 (n) a protective outer case. Nuts, tortoises, shellfish, and eggs all have shells.
2 (n) a type of bomb that is fired from a gun.

fighting conch

seashells

court cone

cowrie shell

scorpion spider conch

screw shell

shellfish shellfish (n) a sea creature with a shell, such as a crab, lobster, or mussel. Shellfish are usually edible.

shelter (n) a place where you can keep dry in wet weather, or stay safe from danger. **shelter** (v).

shelve shelving shelved
1 (v) to put something off for a while.
2 (v) to put something on a shelf or shelves.

shepherd (n) someone whose job is to look after sheep.

sheriff (n) the chief person in charge of enforcing the law in an American county.

sherry sherries (n) a strong wine.

shield shielding shielded
1 (n) a piece of armour, carried to protect your body from attack. *Soldiers used to carry shields in battle.*
2 (n) a protective barrier. *A heat shield.*
3 (v) to protect someone or something. *Henry shielded me from the bullies. The parasol shielded us from the sun.*

shift shifting shifted
1 (v) to move something heavy.
2 (n) a set period of several hours' continuous work. *A night shift.*

shimmer shimmering shimmered (v) to shine with a flickering light.

shin (n) the front part of your leg between your knee and ankle.

shine shining shone
1 (v) to give off a bright light.
2 (v) If someone **shines** at something, they are very good at it.

shingle (n) small, rounded pebbles.

Shinto (n) a Japanese religion which involves the worship of ancestors and the spirits of nature.

ship (n) a large boat used for sea travel. *The two pictures below show HMS Victory, the ship on which Admiral Nelson was killed in 1805, during the battle of Trafalgar. The cutaway view shows a reconstruction of life on board the Victory.*

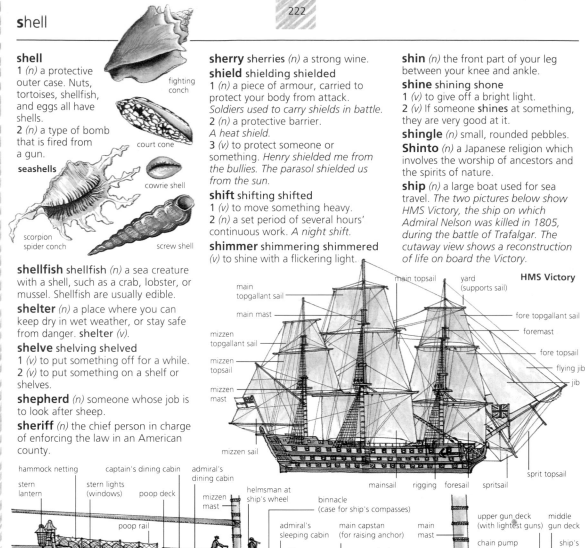

HMS Victory

main topgallant sail
main mast
mizzen topgallant sail
mizzen topsail
mizzen mast
mizzen sail
main topsail
yard (supports sail)
fore topgallant sail
foremast
fore topsail
flying jib
jib
sprit topsail
mainsail
rigging
foresail
spritsail

hammock netting
captain's dining cabin
admiral's dining cabin
stern lantern
stern lights (windows)
poop deck
mizzen mast
helmsman at ship's wheel
binnacle (case for ship's compasses)
poop rail
admiral's sleeping cabin
main capstan (for raising anchor)
main mast
upper gun deck (with lightest guns)
middle gun deck
quarter deck
chain pump (pumps out water)
ship's boat
captain's cabin
admiral's day cabin
officers' cabins
wardroom (officers' quarters)
lower gun deck (with heaviest guns)
orlop deck
rudder
hold
pintle strap
gudgeon strap
elm keel
officers' stores
gunpowder store
light room
powder monkey (fetches explosives)
shot locker
cable tier
stores
surgeon's cabin
water casks
hanging magazine
coiled anchor cable

shipshape *(adj)* clean, tidy, and in good order.

shipwreck
1 *(n)* the wrecking or destruction of a ship.
2 *(n)* the remains of a wrecked ship.

shipyard *(n)* a place where ships are built or repaired.

shirk shirking shirked *(v)* to avoid doing much work. **shirker** *(n)*.

shirt *(n)* a piece of clothing that you wear on the top half of your body. Shirts usually have a collar, sleeves, and buttons down the front.

shirty shirtier shirtiest *(adj) (slang)* cross, or annoyed. **shirtily** *(adv)*.

shiver shivering shivered *(v)* to shake with cold or fear. **shiver** *(n)*, **shivery** *(adj)*.

shoal
1 *(n)* a large group of fish swimming together.
2 *(n)* a stretch of shallow water.

shock shocking shocked
1 *(n)* a sudden, violent fright.
2 *(v)* to give someone a fright.
3 *(v)* to horrify and disgust someone. *The news of the motorway crash shocked us all.* **shocking** *(adj)*.
4 *(n)* the violent effect of an electric current passing through someone's body.
5 *(n)* a thick, untidy mass. *Jason has a shock of golden curls.*

shoddy shoddier shoddiest *(adj)* carelessly produced and of poor quality. **shoddiness** *(n)*.

shoe *(n)* an outer covering for the foot, often made of leather.

shoehorn *(n)* a narrow piece of plastic or metal that you use to help your heel slip easily into a shoe.

shoelace *(n)* a cord used for lacing up shoes.

shoot shooting shot
1 *(v)* to fire a gun. **shot** *(n)*.
2 *(v)* to make a film or video.
3 *(v)* to move very fast.
4 *(n)* a young plant that has just appeared above the surface, or a new part of a plant that is just beginning to grow. See **germinate**, **plant**.

shooting star *(n)* a meteoroid, or piece of rock from space, which burns up as it enters the Earth's atmosphere.

shop
1 *(n)* a place where goods are displayed and sold.
2 *(v)* to go to the shops in order to buy goods. **shopper** *(n)*, **shopping** *(n)*.

shop floor
1 *(n)* the area of a factory where the machines are operated.
2 *(n)* a general name for the workers in a factory.

shopkeeper *(n)* someone who runs a small shop.

shoplifter *(n)* someone who steals goods from a shop. **shoplifting** *(n)*.

shopsoiled *(adj)* Goods that are shopsoiled are dirty or slightly damaged because they have been on display in a shop.

shore *(n)* the edge of the land where it meets a sea, river, or lake.

short shorter shortest
1 *(adj)* less than the average length, distance, time, etc. *A short book.* **shortness** *(n)*, **short** *(adv)*.
2 If you are **short of** something, you have less of it than you need. *Henry is very short of money at the moment.*

shortage *(n)* When there is a shortage of something, there is not enough of it. *A food shortage.*

shortbread *(n)* a rich biscuit made with butter.

shortcoming *(n)* a failing, or a weak point in someone or something. *One of Marvin's shortcomings is that he is always late.*

shortening *(n)* butter, lard, or other fat used in baking.

shorthand *(n)* a system of writing symbols instead of words, used for very quick note-taking.

short-handed *(adj)* If you are short-handed, you do not have enough people to do a job.

shortly *(adv)* soon, or presently. *The train will be arriving shortly.*

short-range *(adj)* small in time or distance. *A short-range shot.*

shorts *(plural n)* short trousers, often worn for sports or as leisure wear.

short-sighted
1 *(adj)* If you are short-sighted, you cannot see things clearly when they are far away. **short-sightedness** *(n)*.
2 *(adj)* not aware of future consequences. *A short-sighted decision.* **short-sightedness** *(n)*.

short-tempered *(adj)* Someone who is short-tempered becomes angry very quickly and easily.

shot
1 *(n)* the firing of a gun.
2 *(n)* a photograph.
3 *(n)* a heavy metal ball thrown in an athletics event.
4 *(n) (informal)* an injection.
5 *(n) (informal)* an attempt. *Fiona had a shot at beating the record.*

shotgun *(n)* a gun with a long barrel that fires cartridges full of tiny pellets.

shot put *(n)* an athletics event in which you throw a heavy metal ball as far as possible. **shot-putter** *(n)*.

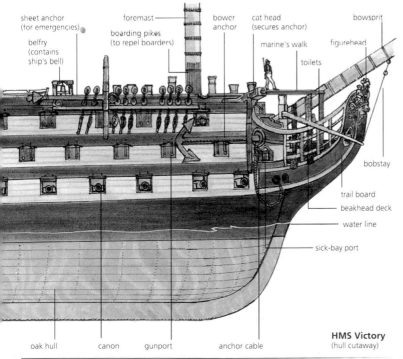

sheet anchor (for emergencies)

belfry (contains ship's bell)

foremast

boarding pikes (to repel boarders)

bower anchor

cat head (secures anchor)

marine's walk

figurehead

toilets

bowsprit

bobstay

trail board

beakhead deck

water line

sick-bay port

HMS Victory (hull cutaway)

oak hull   canon   gunport   anchor cable

shoulder *(n)* the part of your body between your neck and your arm.

shout shouting shouted *(v)* to call out loudly. **shout** *(n)*.

shove *(shuv)* shoving shoved *(v)* to push roughly. **shove** *(n)*.

shovel shovelling shovelled
1 *(n)* a type of spade with raised sides.
2 *(v)* to move things with a shovel or spade. *Mildred shovelled the snow off the path.*

show showing showed
1 *(v)* to let something be seen. *Show me the picture!*
2 *(v)* to explain, or to demonstrate. *Show me how to do it!*
3 *(v)* to guide or lead someone. *Let me show you to your seat.*
4 *(v)* to be visible. *That stain won't show.*
5 *(n)* a public performance, or an exhibition.

show business *(n)* the world of theatre, films, television, and other entertainments.

shower showering showered
1 *(n)* a brief fall of rain. **showery** *(adj)*.
2 *(v)* to fall in large numbers. *Leaves showered from the tree.*
3 *(v)* to give someone lots of things. *Rosie showered me with presents.*
4 *(n)* a piece of equipment that produces a fine spray of water for washing your body.
5 *(v)* to wash yourself under a shower.

showjumping *(n)* a sport in which horses and riders jump over fences. **show-jumper** *(n)*.

show-off *(n)* someone who behaves in a boastful way in order to impress people. **show off** *(v)*.

showroom *(n)* a large room used to display goods that are for sale. *A car showroom.*

shrapnel *(n)* small pieces of metal scattered by an exploding shell or bomb.

shred *(n)* a long, thin strip of cloth or paper that has been torn off something. **shred** *(v)*.

shredder *(n)* a machine for cutting used documents into tiny pieces so that no one can read them.

shrew *(n)* a small, insect-eating mammal with a long nose and small eyes. *The picture shows a white-toothed shrew with her young.*

shrewd shrewder shrewdest *(adj)* clever, experienced, and cunning in dealing with practical situations. **shrewdly** *(adv)*.

shriek shrieking shrieked *(v)* to cry out or scream in a shrill, piercing way. **shriek** *(n)*.

shrill shriller shrillest *(adj)* harsh, high-pitched, and piercing. *The shrill blast of a whistle.*

shrimp *(n)* a small, edible shellfish with a pair of claws and a long tail.

shrine *(n)* a holy building that often contains sacred relics.

shrink shrinking shrank shrunk
1 *(v)* If something **shrinks**, it becomes smaller, often after being wet. *My shirt has shrunk in the wash.*
2 *(v)* to move away because you are frightened. *The children shrank closer to the wall as the creature approached.*

shrivel shrivelling shrivelled *(v)* If something **shrivels**, it becomes smaller, often after drying in heat. **shrivelled** *(adj)*.

shrub *(n)* a small plant or bush with woody stems.

shrubbery shrubberies *(n)* an area where shrubs are planted.

shrug shrugging shrugged *(v)* to raise your shoulders to show doubt or lack of interest. **shrug** *(n)*.

shudder shuddering shuddered *(v)* to shake violently from cold or fear.

shuffle shuffling shuffled
1 *(v)* to walk slowly, hardly raising your feet from the floor.
2 *(v)* to mix together playing cards, papers, etc.

shun shunning shunned *(v)* to avoid someone or something. *Mo shunned any contact with the outside world.*

shunt shunting shunted *(v)* to move things from one place to another. *The engine shunted the carriages into a siding.*

shut shutting shut
1 *(v)* to block an opening, or close something with a door, lid, cover, etc. *Shut the door behind you, please.* **shut** *(adj)*.
2 **shut down** *(v)* to stop, or to close down. *The local factory has shut down.*

shutter
1 *(n)* a cover that protects the outside of a window and keeps out the light.
2 *(n)* the part of a camera which opens to expose the film to the light.

shuttle
1 *(n)* the part of a loom that carries threads from side to side.
2 *(n)* a bus or other form of transport that travels frequently between two places. **shuttle** *(v)*.
3 See **space shuttle**.

shy shying shied; shier shiest
1 *(adj)* If someone is **shy**, they are timid and do not enjoy meeting new people. **shyness** *(n)*.
2 *(v)* If a horse **shies**, it moves backwards or sideways suddenly, because it is frightened.

sibling *(n)* a brother, or a sister.

sick sicker sickest
1 *(adj)* unwell. **sickness** *(n)*.
2 If you are **sick**, you vomit.
3 *(adj)* *(informal)* If you are **sick of** something, you have had too much of it. *I'm sick of your crazy ideas, Leon.*
4 *(adj)* *(informal)* A **sick** joke makes fun of other people's suffering.

sicken sickening sickened *(v)* If something **sickens** you, it makes you feel shocked and disgusted. **sickening** *(adj)*.

sickly sicklier sickliest
1 *(adj)* If food is **sickly**, it makes you feel sick.
2 *(adj)* weak and often ill.

side siding sided
1 *(n)* a surface of a shape or an object.
2 *(n)* an outer part of something that is not the front or the back.
3 *(n)* a team. *Please play on our side.*
4 *(v)* If you **side** with someone, you support them in an argument.

sideboard *(n)* a piece of furniture with a large, flat surface and drawers or cupboards below. Sideboards are usually found in dining rooms.

sideburns *(plural n)* the hair that grows down the sides of a man's face.

side effect *(n)* an effect of taking a medicine besides the intended effect.

sideshow *(n)* a small entertainment at a fair.

sidetrack sidetracking sidetracked *(v)* to distract someone from what they are doing or saying.

sidewalk *(n)* *(US)* a raised path beside a street (pavement, *UK*).

sideways *(adv)* moving towards the side. **sideways** *(adj)*.

siding *(n)* a section of railway track used for storing or shunting carriages.

shrew with young

siege *(seej)* *(n)* the military action of surrounding a place, such as a castle or city, and waiting for its defenders to surrender.

siesta *(see-est-a)* *(n)* an afternoon rest, taken in hot countries.

sieve *(siv)* *(n)* a container with lots of very small holes in it, used for separating large from small pieces, or liquids from solids. **sieve** *(v)*.

sift sifting sifted
1 *(v)* to put substances through a sieve to get rid of lumps.
2 *(v)* to examine something carefully. *Police sifted through the evidence for clues.*

sigh *(rhymes with lie)* sighing sighed *(v)* to breathe out deeply, often to express sadness or relief. **sigh** *(n)*.

sight
1 *(n)* the ability to see. *Nancy lost her sight in an accident.*
2 *(n)* a view, or a scene. *The New York skyline is a marvellous sight.*

sightseer *(n)* someone who travels to see interesting places for pleasure. **sightseeing** *(n)*, **sightsee** *(v)*.

sign signing signed
1 *(n)* a symbol that stands for something. *A dollar sign. A minus sign.*
2 *(n)* a public notice giving information. *A road sign.*
3 *(v)* to write your name in your own way.
4 **sign language** *(n)* a way of communicating by using hands, not speech, used especially by deaf people. **sign** *(v)*.

signal
1 *(n)* a form of communication that does not use speech. *A railway signal.* **signal** *(v)*.
2 *(n)* Television and radio **signals** are pictures and sounds sent through the air by electrical pulses.

signature *(n)* the individual way that you write your name.

Shakespeare's signature

signature tune *(n)* the music that is always played at the beginning and end of a television or radio series.

significant *(adj)* important, or meaning a great deal. **significance** *(n)*, **significantly** *(adv)*.

signpost *(n)* a roadside sign giving directions.

Sikh *(seek)* *(n)* a member of an Indian religious sect that believes in a single god. **Sikhism** *(n)*.

silage *(n)* cut grass or hay that is stored in a large sealed container, called a silo, and used as animal feed.

silencer *(n)* an attachment that reduces noise from a vehicle exhaust or gun. *See* **motorcycle**.

silent *(adj)* absolutely quiet. **silence** *(n)*, **silently** *(adv)*.

silhouette *(sil-oo-ett)* *(n)* a dark outline seen against a light background.

silicon *(n)* a very common chemical element used to make microchips, transistors, etc.

silk *(n)* a soft, smooth fabric made from fibres produced by a silkworm. **silky** *(adj)*.

silkworm *(n)* a caterpillar that spins a cocoon of silk threads and then turns into a moth.

life cycle of a silkworm

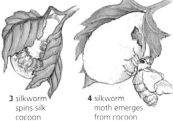

1 silkworm hatches

2 silkworm feeds and grows

3 silkworm spins silk cocoon

4 silkworm moth emerges from cocoon

silly sillier silliest *(adj)* foolish, or not sensible. **silliness** *(n)*.

silo
1 *(n)* a tower or pit for storing grain, grass for silage, etc.
2 *(n)* an underground shelter for a guided missile.

silt *(singular n)* the fine particles that are carried by running water and that settle on river beds.

silver
1 *(n)* a shiny, grey, precious metal used in jewellery and coins.
2 *(n)* coins made from silver or silver-coloured metal.
3 *(n)* the colour of silver. **silver** *(adj)*, **silvery** *(adj)*.

similar *(adj)* alike, or of the same type. **similarity** *(n)*, **similarly** *(adv)*.

simile *(sim-ill-ee)* *(n)* a way of describing something by comparing it with something else, for example, "Her eyes are like stars and her lips are like roses".

simmer simmering simmered
1 *(v)* to boil very gently.
2 **simmer down** *(v)* *(informal)* to calm down.

simple simpler simplest
1 *(adj)* easy, or not hard to understand or do. **simplicity** *(n)*, **simply** *(adv)*.
2 *(adj)* plain, and not fussy. *A simple meal.* **simplicity** *(n)*, **simply** *(adv)*.

simplify simplifies simplifying simplified *(v)* to make something easier or less complicated. **simplification** *(n)*.

simply
1 *(adv)* in a simple way.
2 *(adv)* absolutely. *Simply marvellous.*

simulator *(n)* a machine that allows you to experience what it is like to fly a plane, drive a speedboat, etc. by using computer technology, film, and mechanical movement.

simultaneous *(adj)* happening at the same time. **simultaneously** *(adv)*.

sin *(n)* bad behaviour that goes against moral and religious laws. **sinful** *(adj)*, **sinfully** *(adv)*.

since
1 *(conj)* from the time that. *I've lived here since I was three.*
2 *(conj)* as, or because. *Since you've been so helpful, we'll give you a treat.*

sincere *(sin-seer)* sincerer sincerest *(adj)* If you are **sincere**, you are honest and truthful in what you say and do. **sincerity** *(n)*, **sincerely** *(adv)*.

sinew *(sin-yoo)* *(n)* a tough fibre that connects a muscle to a bone.

sing singing sang sung *(v)* to make a musical noise with your voice. **singer** *(n)*.

singe singeing singed *(v)* to scorch or burn something at the tip or the surface.

single
1 *(adj)* individual, or only one.
2 *(adj)* unmarried.
3 *(adj)* one-way. *A single ticket to Chicago.*
4 *(n)* a tape or CD with one main song on it.

single-minded *(adj)* If you are **single-minded**, you concentrate on achieving one aim.

singular *(adj)* to do with one thing or one person.

sinister *(adj)* If something is **sinister**, it seems evil and threatening.

Some words that begin with a "si" sound are spelt "sci" , "ci", "sy", or "cy".

sink sinking sank sunk
1 (n) a basin with taps and a plughole, used for washing.
2 (v) to go down slowly. *The ship sank. Sophie sank to her knees.*
3 (v) to make a ship sink. **sinking** (n).

sinus (sy-nuss) sinuses (n) one of the hollow spaces in your skull at the top of your nose. See **brain**.

sip sipping sipped (v) to drink slowly in small amounts. **sip** (n).

siphon or **syphon** (sy-fun) (n) a tube through which liquid is drained upwards and then down to a lower level. **siphon** (v).

sir
1 (n) a formal name for a man, used in speaking and writing. *Can I help you, sir? Dear Sir.*
2 (n) the title given to a knight. *Have you met Sir Algernon Fortescue?*

sister (n) a girl or woman who has the same parents as you. **sisterly** (adj).

sit sitting sat
1 (v) to rest on your buttocks.
2 (v) If you **sit** an exam, you answer the questions in it.

site (n) the place where something is or happens. *The site of the battle.*

sitting room (n) a room in which people can sit and relax.

situation
1 (n) the circumstances which exist at a particular time. *The flood has produced a desperate situation.*
2 (n) the position of something. *The house is in a pleasant situation overlooking the sea.*

size (n) the measurement of how large or small something is.

sizeable (adj) quite large.

sizzle sizzling sizzled (v) to make a hissing noise, like sausages frying.

skate skating skated
1 (n) a boot with a blade on the bottom, used for moving across ice.
2 (v) to move smoothly across ice, wearing skates.

skateboard (n) a small board with wheels, that you stand on and ride.

skeleton (n) the framework of bones in a body.

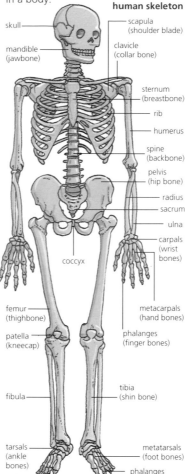

human skeleton

skull
mandible (jawbone)
scapula (shoulder blade)
clavicle (collar bone)
sternum (breastbone)
rib
humerus
spine (backbone)
pelvis (hip bone)
radius
sacrum
ulna
carpals (wrist bones)
coccyx
metacarpals (hand bones)
femur (thighbone)
patella (kneecap)
phalanges (finger bones)
fibula
tibia (shin bone)
tarsals (ankle bones)
metatarsals (foot bones)
phalanges (toe bones)

sketch sketches
1 (n) a quick, rough drawing of something. **sketch** (v).
2 (n) a short piece of acting that is usually humorous.

skewer (n) a long, metal pin for holding meat or vegetables while they are cooking.

ski (n) one of a pair of long, narrow runners which you fasten to boots, and use for travelling over snow. **skiing** (n).

skid skidding skidded
1 (v) to slide on a slippery surface.
2 (n) a runner on the bottom of a helicopter. See **helicopter**.

skill (n) an ability to do something well. **skilful** (adj), **skilled** (adj).

skim skimming skimmed
1 (v) to take something off the top of a liquid. **skimmed** (adj).
2 (v) to glide across a surface.

skin
1 (n) the outer covering of tissue on the bodies of humans and animals.
2 (n) the outer layer of a fruit or vegetable. *A banana skin.*

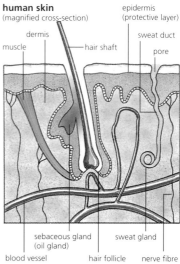

human skin (magnified cross-section)

epidermis (protective layer)
dermis
muscle
hair shaft
sweat duct
pore
sebaceous gland (oil gland)
sweat gland
blood vessel
hair follicle
nerve fibre

skinny skinnier skinniest (adj) very thin.

skip skipping skipped
1 (v) to jump over a turning rope.
2 (v) to move along in a bouncy way, hopping on each foot in turn.
3 (v) (informal) to leave something out deliberately. *I skipped the gory scenes in my book.*

skirt (n) a piece of clothing, worn by women and girls, that hangs from the waist.

skittles (singular n) a game in which you bowl a ball at bottle-shaped pieces of wood, called skittles.

ski boot and skis

upper shell
velcro adjustment strap
manual release for binding
adjusting catch
buckle
lower shell
binding (fixes boot to ski)
ski

ski (top view)
waist
side-cut (inward curve)
tip

ski (side view)
shovel
tail
camber (upward curve)
steel edge

Some words that begin with a "si' sound are spelt "ci", "cy", "sy", or "sci".

skive skiving skived (v) (informal) to avoid doing any work. **skiver** (n).

skull (n) the bony framework of your head. See **skeleton**.

skunk (n) a black and white mammal with a bushy tail. Skunks give off a foul smell when they are threatened.

skunk

sky skies (n) the upper atmosphere as seen from the Earth.

skydiving (n) parachute-jumping that involves stunts or formation work. This picture of skydiving shows a formation called a star. **skydiver** (n), **skydive** (v).

skydiving

skylight (n) a window in a roof.

skyscraper (n) a very tall building with many storeys.

slab (n) a large, flat block of stone, wood, or other heavy material.

slack slacker slackest
1 (adj) loose, or not tight. **slacken** (v).
2 (adj) not busy. In a recession, trade is slack for many shops.
3 (adj) If you are **slack** in your work, you do not try very hard at it.

slalom (slah-lum) (n) an event in which competitors ski downhill, between poles.

slalom skier

slam slamming slammed (v) to close something heavily and loudly. Jessica slammed the book shut.

slander (n) an untrue, spoken statement that damages someone's name or reputation. **slander** (v).

slang (n) words and expressions used by particular groups of people, but not in formal speech or writing.

slant slanting slanted
1 (v) to slope, or to be at an angle. My handwriting slants to the right.
2 (n) a point of view. These new facts give a very different slant to the story.

slap slapping slapped (v) to hit someone or something with the palm of your hand. **slap** (n).

slapdash (adj) Slapdash work is done carelessly and hurriedly.

slapstick (n) rough and noisy comedy, often performed by clowns.

slash slashes slashing slashed
1 (v) to make a sharp, sweeping cut in something with a knife or blade.
2 (v) to reduce something dramatically. The shop has slashed all its prices.

slate
1 (n) a blue-grey rock that can be split into thin pieces, and is often used for roofing.
2 (n) a roofing or flooring tile made from slate.

slaughter (slaw-ter) slaughtering slaughtered
1 (v) to kill animals for their meat.
2 (n) the brutal killing of large numbers of people.

slave slaving slaved
1 (n) someone who is forced to work for someone else, without being paid. **slavery** (n).
2 (v) to work very hard. I've slaved all day over my homework.

slay slaying slayed or slew slain (v) (poetic) to kill someone in a violent way. The knight slew the dragon.

sled or **sledge** (n) a vehicle with wooden or metal runners, used for travelling over snow and ice.

sledgehammer (n) a heavy hammer.

sleek sleeker sleekest (adj) smooth and shiny.

sleep sleeping slept (v) to rest in an unconscious state. **sleep** (n).

sleeper (n) one of the thick concrete or wooden cross-pieces that support a railway track.

sleeping bag (n) a padded bag in which you sleep, especially when you are camping.

sleepwalker (n) someone who walks in their sleep. **sleepwalk** (v).

sleepy sleepier sleepiest (adj) tired, or drowsy. **sleepiness** (n).

sleet (n) partly melted falling snow, or partly frozen rain.

sleeve (n) the part of a garment that covers your arm.

sleigh (slay) (n) a sled, usually pulled by horses or other animals. The picture shows a reindeer pulling a sleigh in Lapland.

sleigh

slender slenderer slenderest
1 (adj) slim or thin.
2 (adj) small and inadequate in amount. A slender income.

slice (n) a thin piece or wedge of food cut from a larger piece. **slice** (v).

slick slicker slickest
1 (adj) very fast, efficient, and professional. A slick performance.
2 (n) a pool of oil covering an area of water or road.

slide sliding slid
1 (v) to move smoothly over a surface. Amy is sliding down the banister.
2 (n) a transparency inside a frame, that you view on a projector screen.
3 (n) a small piece of glass on which you place a specimen, in order to view it under a microscope. See **microscope**.

slight slightest (adj) small, or not very important. A slight delay. **slightly** (adv).

slim slimmer slimmest
1 (adj) thin and graceful. **slim** (v).
2 (adj) very small. A slim chance.

slime (n) a slippery substance, such as mud. **slimy** (adj).

sling slinging slung
1 (n) a piece of cloth used to support an injured arm.
2 (v) (informal) to throw something in a rough way. Sling your bag on the top bunk.

slip slipping slipped
1 (v) to lose your balance on a slippery surface.
2 (v) to move quickly and easily. Georgia slipped away silently.
3 (n) a small mistake.
4 (n) a light garment worn under a skirt or dress.

slipper *(n)* a soft, light shoe that you wear indoors.

slippery *(adj)* smooth, oily, or wet, and very hard to grip on to.

slipshod *(adj)* careless and untidy.

slit slitting slit *(v)* to make a long, narrow cut in something. **slit** *(n)*.

slither slithering slithered *(v)* to slip and slide along like a snake.

sliver *(n)* a very thin piece or slice of something.

slog slogging slogged
1 *(v)* to work hard. **slog** *(n)*.
2 *(n)* a long, hard walk. **slog** *(v)*.
3 *(v)* to hit a ball hard.

slogan *(n)* an easily-remembered word or phrase used in advertising.

slop slopping slopped *(v)* to splash or spill liquid.

slope sloping sloped *(v)* to be at an angle. *The wall slopes to the left.*

sloppy sloppier sloppiest
1 *(adj)* wet or slushy. **sloppiness** *(n)*.
2 *(adj)* *(informal)* careless and untidy. *Sloppy work.* **sloppiness** *(n)*, **sloppily** *(adv)*.
3 *(adj)* *(informal)* very sentimental. *Sloppy love songs.*

slot
1 *(n)* a small, narrow space or groove in which something is fitted.
2 **slot machine** *(n)* a machine that gives out a product or provides amusement when a coin is put in its slot.

sloth *(rhymes with both)*
1 *(n)* a very slow-moving South American mammal with a shaggy coat.
2 *(n)* laziness. **slothful** *(adj)*.

three-toed sloth with baby

slouch slouches slouching slouched
1 *(v)* to sit, stand, or walk in a lazy way, with your shoulders and head drooping.
2 *(n)* *(slang)* a slow and lazy person. *Dan's no slouch at football.*

slovenly *(adj)* careless, untidy, and dirty. **slovenliness** *(n)*.

slow slower slowest
1 *(adj)* not fast. **slowness** *(n)*, **slowly** *(adv)*.
2 *(adj)* behind the right time. *My watch is five minutes slow.*

sludge *(n)* soft, thick mud.

slug
1 *(n)* a soft, slimy creature that is similar to a snail, but has no shell. A slug moves in a series of waves in which it lifts part of its sole and then puts it down further forward. The sole is covered with mucus for protection and to help it cling to surfaces.
2 *(n)* a bullet.

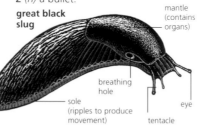

great black slug

mantle (contains organs)

breathing hole

sole (ripples to produce movement)

eye

tentacle

sluggish *(adj)* slow-moving and lacking in energy. **sluggishness** *(n)*.

slum *(n)* an overcrowded, poor, and neglected area of housing in a town or city.

slump slumping slumped
1 *(v)* to fall in a heavy or uncontrolled way. *Maurice slumped to the ground.*
2 *(n)* a time of decline in industry and trade, when demand for products is greatly reduced.

slur slurring slurred
1 *(v)* to pronounce words unclearly by running different sounds into one another.
2 *(n)* If something is a **slur** on your character, it is insulting or damaging.

slush *(singular n)* snow that has partly melted. **slushy** *(adj)*.

sly slier sliest *(adj)* crafty, cunning, and secretive. **slyly** *(adv)*.

smack smacking smacked *(v)* to hit someone with the palm of your hand as a punishment. **smack** *(n)*.

small smaller smallest
1 *(adj)* little, or tiny.
2 **small talk** conversation about unimportant things.

smart smarting smarted; smarter smartest
1 *(adj)* well-dressed, tidy, and clean. **smartness** *(n)*, **smartly** *(adv)*.
2 *(adj)* clever, or quick-thinking. **smartness** *(n)*.
3 *(v)* to sting, or to hurt.

smash smashes smashing smashed
1 *(v)* to break something into a lot of pieces by hitting or dropping it.
2 *(n)* a car crash.
3 *(n)* a tennis stroke in which you hit the ball downwards very hard.

smashing *(adj)* *(informal)* very good, or enjoyable. *A smashing party.*

smear smearing smeared
1 *(v)* to rub something sticky or greasy over a surface. **smear** *(n)*.
2 *(v)* to try to damage someone's reputation by telling untrue stories about them.

smell smelling smelled *or* smelt
1 *(v)* to sense through your nose. *I can smell dinner cooking.*
2 *(n)* an odour, or a scent.
3 *(v)* to give off a smell, especially an unpleasant one. *Your socks smell horrible!*
4 *(n)* the ability to notice smells. *Dogs have an excellent sense of smell.*

smelt smelting smelted *(v)* to heat rock containing metal so that the metal melts and can be removed.

smile smiling smiled *(v)* When you smile, your mouth widens and turns up at the corners to show that you are happy or amused. **smile** *(n)*.

smirk smirking smirked *(v)* to smile in an unpleasant way. **smirk** *(n)*.

smog *(n)* a mixture of fog and smoke that sometimes hangs in the air over cities and industrial areas.

smoke smoking smoked
1 *(n)* the mixture of gas and tiny particles that is given off when something burns. **smoky** *(adj)*.
2 *(v)* to give off smoke. *The bonfire was still smoking.*
3 *(v)* to hold a cigarette or cigar in your mouth and breathe in its smoke. **smoker** *(n)*, **smoking** *(n)*.
4 *(v)* to treat food by hanging it in smoke. **smoked** *(adj)*.

smooth smoothing smoothed; smoother smoothest
1 *(adj)* A smooth surface is even and flat, not rough or bumpy. *A smooth road.* **smoothness** *(n)*, **smooth** *(v)*.
2 *(adj)* happening easily, with no problems or difficulties. **smoothness** *(n)*, **smoothly** *(adv)*.
3 *(v)* to make things more even and flat. *Amy smoothed down her hair.*
4 *(adj)* Someone who is **smooth** seems too pleasant and confident.

smother *(smuth-er)* smothering smothered
1 *(v)* to cover someone's nose and mouth so that they cannot breathe.

2 (v) to cover something completely. *Al smothered his pudding with cream.*
3 (v) to protect someone too closely.

smoulder smouldering smouldered (v) If something smoulders it burns slowly, with no flames.

SMS message (n) a message that you type into your mobile phone and send to another person who reads it on the screen of their mobile phone. SMS stands for short messaging service.

smudge smudging smudged (v) to make a messy mark by rubbing ink, paint, etc. **smudge** (n).

smug smugger smuggest (adj) If you are smug, you are too pleased with yourself. **smugness** (n), **smugly** (adv).

smuggle smuggling smuggled
1 (v) to take goods into a country illegally. **smuggler** (n).
2 (v) to take something into or out of a place secretly.

snack (n) a small, light meal.

snag (n) a small problem or difficulty.

snail (n) a small creature with no legs, a soft, slimy body, and a shell on its back.

garden snail

snake (n) a long, thin reptile that has no legs and slithers along the ground. Some snakes have poisonous bites. *The diagram shows the internal organs of a snake. Also see* **adder**, **venom**.

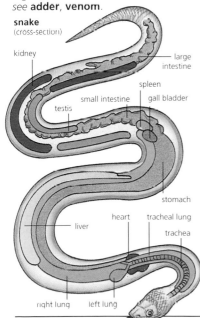

snake
(cross-section)

kidney

large intestine

spleen

small intestine · gall bladder

testis

stomach

heart · tracheal lung

liver

trachea

right lung · left lung

snap snapping snapped
1 (v) to break with a sudden, loud, cracking sound. *The twigs snapped beneath our feet.* **snap** (n).
2 (v) to try to bite someone. *The dog snapped at me.*
3 (v) to speak sharply and angrily to someone. **snappy** (adj).
4 (n) a card game.
5 (n) (informal) a photograph.
6 A **snap decision** is a decision that is made very quickly.

snapshot (n) a photograph taken with a simple camera.

snare snaring snared
1 (n) a trap for birds or animals.
2 (v) to catch a bird or an animal in a snare.
3 **snare drum** (n) a small drum, with strings or wires stretched across its base, that produces a rattling sound when hit. *See* **drum**.

snarl snarling snarled
1 (v) If an animal snarls, it shows its teeth and makes a growling sound.
2 (v) to say something angrily.

snatch snatches snatching snatched
1 (v) to take or grab something roughly.
2 (n) a small part. *I overheard snatches of their conversation.*

sneak sneaking sneaked
1 (v) to move quietly and secretly. *Melissa sneaked up on me from behind.* **sneaky** (adj), **sneakily** (adv).
2 (v) (informal) If someone sneaks on you, they tell a person in charge that you have done something wrong. **sneak** (n).

sneaker (n) a soft, casual shoe with a rubber sole.

sneer sneering sneered (v) to smile in an unpleasant, mocking way. **sneer** (n).

sneeze sneezing sneezed (v) to push out air through your nose and mouth suddenly, often because you have a cold. **sneeze** (n).

sniff sniffing sniffed
1 (v) to breathe in strongly and often noisily, through your nose. **sniff** (n).
2 (v) to smell something. **sniff** (n).

sniffle sniffling sniffled (v) (informal) to breathe noisily through your nose, usually because you have a cold.

snigger sniggering sniggered (v) to laugh quietly or secretly.

snip snipping snipped (v) to cut something using small, quick scissor cuts. **snip** (n).

sniper (n) someone who shoots at people while staying hidden. **snipe** (v).

snivel snivelling snivelled (v) to cry or complain in a noisy, whining way.

snob (n) someone who looks down on people who are not rich and powerful. **snobbery** (n).

snooker (n) a game in which players use long cues to knock coloured balls across a table and into pockets. *This picture shows a snooker table at the beginning of a game.*

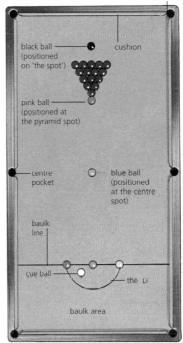

snooker table

corner pocket

black ball (positioned on 'the spot')

cushion

pink ball (positioned at the pyramid spot)

centre pocket

blue ball (positioned at the centre spot)

baulk line

cue ball

the D

baulk area

snoop snooping snooped (v) (informal) to look around somewhere secretly. **snooper** (n).

snooty snootier snootiest (adj) (informal) If someone is snooty, they look down on people who are not as rich and powerful as they are.

snooze snoozing snoozed (v) (informal) to sleep lightly for a short time, usually during the day. **snooze** (n).

snore snoring snored (v) to breathe noisily through your mouth while you are asleep. **snore** (n).

snorkel (n) a tube that you use to breathe through when you are swimming underwater. **snorkelling** (n). *See* **scuba diving**.

snort snorting snorted (v) to breathe out air noisily through your nose. **snort** (n).

snout (n) the nose and mouth of a pig or similar animal.

snow snowing snowed
1 (n) light flakes of ice that fall from the sky when it is very cold.
2 (v) When it snows, snow falls from the sky. **snowy** (adj).

snowflake
(magnified)

snowball snowballing snowballed
1 (n) snow pressed into a ball.
2 (v) If something **snowballs**, it grows rapidly. *Once we started inviting friends, the party snowballed.*

snowplough snowploughing snowploughed
1 (n) a vehicle used to push snow off a road or railway line.
2 (v) When you **snowplough** in skiing, you go down the slope slowly with the tips of your skis pointing inwards and the ends pointing out.

snub snubbing snubbed
1 (v) to behave in a rude, unfriendly way towards someone. **snub** (n).
2 **snub nose** a small, turned-up nose.

snuff (n) powdered tobacco used for sniffing. *Snuff was very popular in the 18th century.*

snuffle snuffling snuffled (v) to breathe noisily and with difficulty.

snug snugger snuggest (adj) warm, cosy, and comfortable. *The cottage was warm and snug.* **snugly** (adv).

snuggle snuggling snuggled (v) to sit or lie close to someone or something, so that you are warm and comfortable.

soak soaking soaked
1 (v) to put something in water and leave it there.
2 (v) When something **soaks up** liquid, it absorbs it or takes it in.

soaking (adj) very wet.

soap (n) a substance that you rub on to your skin when you wash yourself. **soapy** (adj).

soap opera (n) a television series about the everyday lives of a group of people.

soar soaring soared
1 (v) to fly very high in the air.
2 (v) to rise or increase very quickly. *Inflation has soared to 10%.*

sob sobbing sobbed (v) to breathe in short bursts because you are crying. **sob** (n).

sober soberer soberest
1 (adj) not drunk.
2 (adj) careful and serious. *A sober warning.* **soberly** (adv).
3 (adj) **Sober** colours are dark and dull.

sob story sob stories (n) a sad tale about yourself, intended to make people feel sorry for you.

soccer (n) a game played by two teams of eleven players who try to score goals by kicking a ball into a net at each end of a pitch. *The picture shows half a soccer pitch with a team in 4.4.2. formation.*

sociable (adj) Someone who is sociable enjoys talking to people and spending time with them. **sociability** (n), **sociably** (adv).

social
1 (adj) to do with the way that people live together. *This neighbourhood has many social problems.* **socially** (adv).
2 (adj) to do with activities that you take part in with other people in your spare time. *Josca has an exciting social life.* **social** (n), **socially** (adv).
3 (adj) **Social** animals or insects live in groups rather than on their own.

socialism (n) a way of organizing a country, with the main industries owned by the government so that everyone can benefit from the money made by them. **socialist** (n), **socialist** (adj).

social security (n) money paid by the government to people who are unemployed, ill, or poorly paid.

social services (plural n) services provided by the government for people who have problems with health, childcare, housing, etc.

society societies
1 (n) all the people who live in the same country or area and share the same laws and customs.
2 (n) an organization for people who share the same interests. *Polly is a member of the local music society.*

sociology (n) the study of the ways in which people live together in different societies. **sociologist** (n), **sociological** (adj).

sock socking socked
1 (n) a piece of clothing that you wear on your foot.
2 (v) (slang) to hit someone very hard.

socket
1 (n) a hole or set of holes into which an electrical plug or bulb fits.
2 (n) a bone with a hole into which another bone fits. *See* **joint**.

soda
1 (n) a kind of fizzy water that can be mixed with alcoholic drinks or fruit juice.
2 (n) (US) a general word for fizzy drinks.

sodden (adj) extremely wet. *Flora fell in a pond and her clothes are sodden.*

sodium (n) a chemical found in salt.

sodium bicarbonate (n) a chemical substance used in baking to help cakes rise.

sofa (n) a long, soft seat with arms and a back, and room for two or more people.

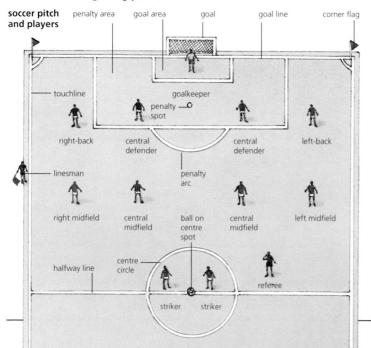

soccer pitch and players — penalty area — goal area — goal — goal line — corner flag

touchline — goalkeeper — penalty spot

right-back — central defender — central defender — left-back

linesman — penalty arc

right midfield — central midfield — ball on centre spot — central midfield — left midfield

halfway line — centre circle — referee

striker — striker

soft softer softest
1 *(adj)* Something that is **soft** is not stiff or hard, and is easily pressed or bent into a different shape. *A soft cushion.* **softness** *(n)*, **soften** *(v)*.
2 *(adj)* smooth and gentle to touch. *Babies have very soft skin.*
3 *(adj)* pleasantly quiet and gentle. *Soft music.* **softly** *(adv)*.
4 *(adj)* not strict or tough enough. *My Dad's so soft, he'll let me do anything.*
5 **soft drink** *(n)* a cold drink that does not contain alcohol.

softball *(n)* a type of baseball, played with a large, soft ball.

softhearted *(adj)* If someone is **softhearted**, they are very kind, sympathetic, and generous to others.

software *(n)* a general name for computer programs or the disks on which the programs are stored.

soggy soggier soggiest *(adj)* very wet and heavy.

soil soiling soiled
1 *(n)* ground or earth in which plants grow.
2 *(v)* If you **soil** something, you make it dirty or stained.

solar *(adj)* to do with the Sun. *A solar eclipse.*

solar energy *(n)* energy from the Sun that can be used for heating, lighting, etc. *Solar panels, like the one shown below, are fixed to roofs and use solar energy to produce hot water.*

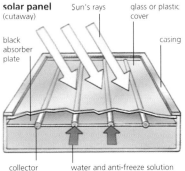

solar panel (cutaway)

Sun's rays

glass or plastic cover

black absorber plate

casing

collector circuit pipe

water and anti-freeze solution flows through collector circuit pipes into heat store

solar system *(n)* the Sun and the planets that move around it. In our solar system there are nine planets, many moons, and also asteroids and comets, all of which move around the Sun. *See* **planet**.

solder soldering soldered *(v)* to join pieces of metal together by putting a small amount of hot, liquid metal between them, which hardens as it cools.

soldier soldiering soldiered
1 *(n)* someone who is in the army. **soldierly** *(adj)*.
2 *(v)* If you **soldier on**, you keep doing something difficult.

soldiers

Roman legionary

11th-century knight

15th-century knight

17th-century cavalryman

18th-century Prussian musketeer

19th-century US private

sole
1 *(n)* the underneath part of the foot.
2 *(n)* a kind of flat sea fish.
3 *(adj)* only. *I was the sole survivor.* **solely** *(adv)*.

solemn *(adj)* very serious. **solemnity** *(n)*, **solemnly** *(adv)*.

solicitor *(n)* someone who is trained to give people advice about the law and to prepare legal documents.

solid
1 *(adj)* hard and firm. *The water had frozen solid.* **solidity** *(n)*.
2 *(adj)* not hollow. *A solid chocolate egg.*

solidarity *(n)* agreement between a group of people that they will work or fight together to achieve something.

solidify solidifies solidifying solidified *(v)* to become hard and firm.

solidly
1 *(adv)* firmly and strongly. *This house is very solidly built.*
2 *(adv)* without interruption. *Alma worked solidly for two hours.*

solitary
1 *(adj)* If someone is **solitary**, they spend a lot of time alone.
2 *(adj)* single. *There was not one solitary person on the beach.*
3 **solitary confinement** *(n)* a punishment in which a prisoner is put in a cell alone and is not allowed to see or talk to anybody.

solo *(n)* a piece of music that is played or sung by one person. **soloist** *(n)*.

soluble *(adj)* A substance that is **soluble** can be dissolved in liquid.

solution
1 *(n)* the answer to a problem or difficulty.
2 *(n)* a liquid that has something dissolved in it.

solve solving solved *(v)* to find the answer to a problem.

solvent
1 *(n)* a liquid that makes other substances dissolve.
2 If someone practises **solvent abuse**, they breathe in fumes from glue or other substances in order to experience strange feelings. Solvent abuse is very dangerous.

sombre *(som-bur) (adj)* dark and gloomy. *Karl is in a sombre mood.*

some
1 *(adj)* a number of things, or an amount of something. *There were some children in the park. Would you like some cake?*
2 *(pronoun)* a certain number of people or things. *Some of us are going abroad.*

somebody *(pronoun)* someone.

somehow *(adv)* in some way. *Somehow, the rabbit managed to wriggle free.*

someone *(pronoun)* a person. *Someone has taken my pen!*

somersault *(n)* When you do a **somersault**, you tuck your head into your chest and roll over forwards on the ground or in the air. **somersault** *(v)*.

something *(pronoun)* a thing. *There's something moving in the bushes.*

sometime *(adv)* at some time in the past or the future. *I'll do my homework sometime tomorrow.*

sometimes *(adv)* at some times but not at others. *Gertrude sometimes has a nap in the afternoon.*

somewhere (adv) to or in some place. *My aunt lives somewhere in Ohio.*

son (n) Someone's **son** is their male child.

sonar (n) a piece of equipment that is used on ships to calculate how deep the water is, or where underwater objects are. It works by sending sound waves through the water and listening for when they bounce back off something. Sonar stands for sound navigation ranging.

sonar

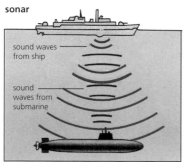

sound waves from ship

sound waves from submarine

sonata (n) a piece of music for one or two instruments.

song
1 (n) a piece of music with words for singing.
2 (n) the musical sounds made by a bird.

sonic
1 (adj) to do with sound waves.
2 **sonic boom** (n) the loud noise produced by an aeroplane when it breaks through the sound barrier and flies faster than the speed of sound.

sonnet (n) a poem with 14 lines and a fixed pattern of rhymes.

soon sooner soonest
1 (adv) in a short time. *I'll visit you soon.*
2 If you would **sooner** do something, you would prefer to do that thing.

soot (n) black powder that is produced when something is burnt, and that often collects in chimneys. **sooty** (adj).

soothe soothing soothed
1 (v) to make someone less angry or upset. *Fran tried to soothe the screaming baby.* **soothing** (adj).
2 (v) to make something less painful. *This cream should soothe your rash.* **soothing** (adj).

sophisticated (sof-iss-tik-ate-id)
1 (adj) People who are **sophisticated** have a lot of knowledge and experience of social life, fashion, and culture. **sophistication** (n).

2 (adj) A **sophisticated** machine is cleverly designed and able to do difficult or complicated things. **sophistication** (n).

sopping (adj) extremely wet.

soprano
1 (n) a high singing voice. **soprano** (adj).
2 (n) a woman or young boy with a soprano voice.

sorbet (sor-bay) (n) a frozen dessert, rather like ice cream, made with fruit, sugar, and sometimes beaten egg whites. *Lemon sorbet.*

sorcerer (sor-ser-er) (n) someone who performs magic by calling up evil spirits. **sorcery** (n).

sordid
1 (adj) dishonest and shameful.
2 (adj) dirty and messy. *A sordid room.*

sore sorer sorest
1 (adj) painful. **soreness** (n).
2 (n) an area of infected, painful skin on your body. *A cold sore.*

sorrow (n) great sadness. **sorrowful** (adj), **sorrowfully** (adv).

sorry sorrier sorriest
1 (interject) a word that you say when you feel unhappy or upset because you have done something wrong or because someone is suffering. **sorry** (adj).
2 (adj) If you feel **sorry** for someone, you have sympathy and compassion for them.
3 If someone or something is in a **sorry state**, they are in very bad condition.

sort sorting sorted
1 (n) a type, or a kind. *What sort of dog is that?*
2 (v) to arrange things into groups.
3 (v) If you **sort out** a problem, you deal with it and solve it.

SOS (n) a signal sent out by a ship or plane to say that it is in difficulty and in need of urgent help. The initials SOS stand for save our souls. *See* **semaphore.**

soul
1 (n) your spirit, which many people believe lives on after you have died.
2 (n) a person. *You mustn't tell another soul.*

sound sounding sounded
1 (n) something that you hear.
2 (v) If a horn or bell **sounds**, it makes a noise.
3 (v) to give an impression. *Your holiday sounds wonderful.*
4 (adj) reliable, practical, or strong. *A sound idea.* **soundly** (adv).

sound barrier (n) When an aircraft goes through the **sound barrier**, it meets a sudden increase in the force of the air against it because it has passed the speed of sound.

sound effects (plural n) noises that accompany a play or film to make it more realistic.

soundproof (adj) A **soundproof** room does not let any sound in or out of it. **soundproof** (v).

soundtrack (n) the recorded sound for a film.

soup (n) a liquid food made with vegetables, meat or fish.

sour
1 (adj) Something that is **sour** has a bitter taste. **sourness** (n).
2 (adj) bad-tempered. *Eustace has a very sour expression.* **sourness** (n), **sourly** (adv).

source
1 (n) the place, person, or thing from which something comes. *We must find the source of the problem.*
2 (n) the place where a stream or river starts.
3 (n) someone or something that provides information.

south
1 (n) one of the four main points of the compass, the direction to your left when you face the setting Sun, in the northern hemisphere. **south** (adj), **southern** (adj), **south** (adv).
2 (adj) A **south** wind blows from the south. **southerly** (adj).
3 **South Pole** (n) the very cold part of the Earth in the far south. *See* **polar.**

souvenir (soo-ven-ear) (n) an object that you keep to remind you of a place, event, etc.

sou'wester (n) a waterproof hat with a wide brim at the back to keep your neck dry.

sovereign (sov-rin) (n) a king or queen.

sow sowing sowed sown or sowed
1 (rhymes with go) (v) to put seeds into the ground so that they will grow.
2 (rhymes with how) (n) a female pig.

soya (n) a kind of bean that can be cooked and eaten, or made into milk, oil, or flour to be used in cooking.

space
1 (n) an empty or available area. *We'll need lots of space for dancing.*
2 (n) the universe beyond the Earth's atmosphere.

spacecraft (n) a vehicle that travels in space.

space shuttle (n) a spacecraft made up of four parts (the orbiter, the external fuel tank, and two booster rockets), which separate after the launch. The orbiter returns to Earth. *This picture shows a cutaway view of a space shuttle and shows how the parts separate.*

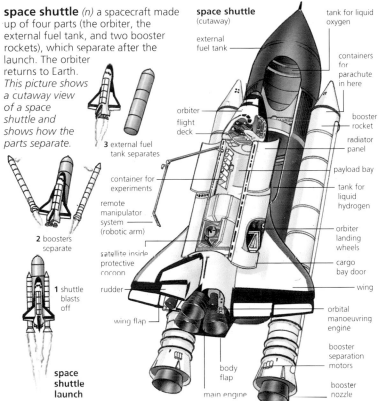

space shuttle (cutaway)

tank for liquid oxygen

external fuel tank

containers for parachute in here

orbiter flight deck

booster rocket

radiator panel

payload bay

tank for liquid hydrogen

orbiter landing wheels

cargo bay door

wing

orbital manoeuvring engine

booster separation motors

booster nozzle

main engine

body flap

wing flap

rudder

satellite inside protective cocoon

remote manipulator system (robotic arm)

container for experiments

3 external fuel tank separates

2 boosters separate

1 shuttle blasts off

space shuttle launch

spacesuit (n) the protective clothing that an astronaut wears in space. *See* **astronaut**.

spacious (adj) very large. *A spacious kitchen.*

spade
1 (n) a tool with a flat blade and a long handle, used for digging.
2 **spades** (plural n) one of the four suits in a pack of cards, with a black symbol like a heart with a stalk.

spaghetti (n) long, thin strings of pasta. *See* **pasta**.

span
1 (n) Your **span** is the distance between your little finger and thumb when your hand is outstretched.
2 (n) The **span** of something is its length from one end to the other. **span** (v).
3 (n) a length of time. **span** (v).

spank spanking spanked (v) to smack someone as a punishment.

spanner (n) a tool used for tightening and loosening nuts. *See* **tool**.

spare sparing spared
1 (adj) free for extra use. *Spare time. A spare tyre.*

2 (v) to make something available. *Can you spare me a few minutes?*
3 (v) to let someone live instead of killing them.

spark sparking sparked
1 (n) a red-hot speck caused by fire, electricity, or friction. **spark** (v).
2 **spark off** (v) to make something happen. *The concert sparked off my interest in music.*

sparking plug (n) one of the parts of a petrol engine that supplies an electrical spark to ignite the petrol and air mixture in a cylinder. Sparking plugs are screwed into the cylinders and connected to the distributor, which supplies the current to create the spark. *Also see* **engine**.

sparking plug

ceramic insulator (prevents electrical current from escaping)

terminal nut (attached to lead from distributor)

plug thread (screws into cylinder head)

plug body

centre electrode (spark crosses from here to side electrode)

side electrode

sparkle sparkling sparkled (v) to shine with lots of flashing points of light. **sparkle** (n).

sparrow (n) a small, brown bird.

spasm (n) a short, sudden attack of pain or emotion. *A spasm of laughter.*

spatula
1 (n) a kitchen utensil with a broad, flat blade, used for lifting and stirring food.
2 (n) an instrument with a flat blade, used by doctors and scientists. *See* **apparatus**.

spawn (n) the eggs produced by fish and amphibians. *See* **frog**.

speak speaking spoke spoken (v) to talk, or to say words.

speaker
1 (n) somebody who gives a speech in public.
2 (n) a piece of equipment that turns electrical signals into sound, usually attached to a stereo system. Speaker is short for loudspeaker. *The diagram shows a cutaway view of a speaker. Electrical signals from a stereo system flow into the coil of wire, creating a magnetic force that makes the coil move backwards and forwards, towards and away from the magnet. The moving coil makes the cone vibrate and produce sounds.*

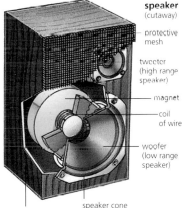

speaker (cutaway)

protective mesh

tweeter (high range speaker)

magnet

coil of wire

woofer (low range speaker)

speaker cone (made from paper or plastic)

cabinet

spear (n) a long, pointed weapon that used to be thrown in battle.

special
1 (adj) extraordinary and important. *A special day.* **specially** (adv).
2 (adj) particular. *You need a special badge to get into the exhibition.*

specialist (n) an expert at one particular job. **specialism** (n).

speciality specialities (n) the thing that you are particularly good at. *Simon's speciality is cooking.*

specialize *or* **specialise**
specializing specialized *(v)*
to concentrate on one thing that you
are good at or interested in.
Alice specializes in medieval art.

species *(spee-sheez)* **species** *(n)*
one of the groups into which animals
and plants are divided, according to
their characteristics. *The domestic dog
is a species of mammal.*

specific *(adj)* particular, definite, or
individually named. *Hilda insists on a
specific type of tea.* **specifically** *(adv).*

specification *(n)* detailed
information and instructions about
something that is to be built or made.

specify specifies specifying
specified *(v)* to mention something in
an exact way. *Please specify which
course you would like to attend.*

specimen *(n)* a sample, or an
example. *Please supply a specimen of
your signature.* **specimen** *(adj).*

speck *(n)* a minute piece of
something, like dust or dirt.

speckled *(adj)* covered with small,
irregular marks. *A speckled egg.*

spectacle *(n)* a remarkable and
dramatic sight. *The firework show was
quite a spectacle.*

spectacles *(plural n)* lenses set in
frames which are worn to improve
your eyesight.

spectacular
1 *(adj)* remarkable and dramatic to
look at. *A spectacular waterfall.*
2 *(n)* a show that contains dramatic
effects and acts.

spectator *(n)* someone who watches
an event. **spectate** *(v).*

spectre *(spek-tur) (n)* a ghost.
spectral *(adj).*

spectrum spectra
1 *(n)* a wide range of things or ideas.
2 *(n)* the range of colours that is
revealed when light shines through a
prism or through drops of water.
When white light travels through a
prism it is bent or refracted. Since
each of the colours in light travels at a
slightly different speed, they each
bend at a different angle and spread
out in a spectrum.

spectrum

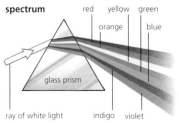

red · yellow · green

orange · blue

glass prism

ray of white light · indigo · violet

speculate speculating speculated
1 *(v)* to wonder or guess about
something when you do not know all
the facts. **speculation** *(n).*
2 *(v)* to buy shares on the stock
market or to put money into other
projects that carry some risk.
speculation *(n).*

speech speeches
1 *(n)* the ability to speak.
2 *(n)* a talk given to a group of people.

speechless *(adj)* unable to speak.
Dad was speechless with rage.

speed speeding sped *or* speeded
1 *(n)* the rate at which something
moves.
2 *(v)* to travel very fast, or to travel
faster than is allowed.
3 *(n)* quickness of movement.

speedometer *(n)* an instrument in a
vehicle that shows you how fast you
are travelling.

spell spelling spelt *or* spelled
1 *(v)* to write or say the letters of a
word in their correct order.
2 *(n)* a period of time, usually a short
one. *A spell of silence.*
3 *(n)* words that are supposed to have
magical powers.

spelunking *(US)* If you **go
spelunking**, you explore caves
(caving, *UK*). **spelunker** *(n).*

spend spending spent
1 *(v)* to use money to buy things.
2 *(v)* If you **spend** time or energy, you
use it.

sperm *(n)* one of the reproductive
cells from a male that is capable of
fertilizing eggs in a female.

sphere *(sfear) (n)* a ball or globe
shape. **spherical** *(sfe-rik-al) (adj).*

sphinx

sphinx *(sfinks)* sphinxes *(n)*
a mythical monster with a woman's
head and a lion's body. *The picture
above shows the statue of the sphinx
at Giza, in Egypt.*

spice *(n)* a substance with a
distinctive smell or taste, used to
flavour foods. *The picture shows a
range of spices.*

spices

cloves

powdered
turmeric

paprika

caraway
seeds

nutmeg

cinnamon
sticks

allspice · cumin seeds

spider *(n)* an eight-legged creature
like an insect, that weaves a web to
trap flies for food. *This picture shows
a selection of spiders from around the
world.*

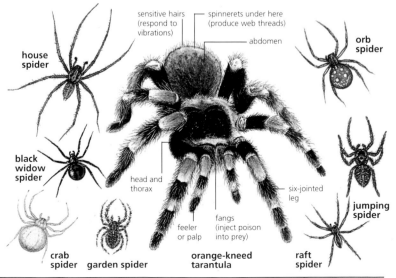

sensitive hairs
(respond to
vibrations)

spinnerets under here
(produce web threads)

abdomen

orb
spider

house
spider

black
widow
spider

head and
thorax

six-jointed
leg

jumping
spider

feeler
or palp

fangs
(inject poison
into prey)

crab
spider · garden spider

orange-kneed
tarantula

raft
spider

spike *(n)* a sharp point. **spiky** *(adj)*.

spill spilling spilt *or* spilled *(v)* If you spill something, you let the contents of a container fall out accidentally.

spin spinning spun
1 *(v)* to turn round fast on the spot.
2 *(v)* to create a thread by twisting fine fibres together. *The picture shows a spinning jenny, a machine invented in the 18th century, that could spin up to eight threads at once.*

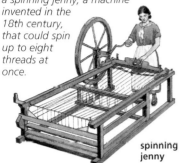

spinning jenny

spinach *(n)* a dark green, leafy vegetable. *See* **vegetable**.

spindly spindlier spindliest *(adj)* long, thin, and rather weak.

spin-dryer *(n)* a machine which extracts moisture from clothes by spinning them round very fast.

spine
1 *(n)* the backbone. **spinal** *(adj)*. *See* **skeleton**.
2 *(n)* part of a book's cover that joins the front and the back. *See* **book**.

spinster *(n)* a woman who has never been married.

spiral *(adj)*
A **spiral** pattern winds around in circles like a spring. *The chambers inside a nautilus shell are arranged in a spiral pattern.* **spiral** *(n)*, **spiral** *(v)*.

nautilus shell
(cutaway)

spire *(n)* the pointed cone on top of some church towers. *See* **cathedral**.

spirit
1 *(n)* the part of a person that is not physical and is expressed in their deepest thoughts and feelings.
2 *(n)* enthusiasm and determination in a person or group of people. *We shared a spirit of hope.* **spirited** *(adj)*.
3 *(n)* a ghost, or a being with no physical form.
4 *(n)* a strong alcoholic drink such as whisky, gin, or vodka.
5 **spirit level** *(n)* an instrument used for checking whether a surface is level. *See* **woodwork**.

spiritual *(adj)* to do with beliefs, thoughts, and feelings, and not physical things. **spiritually** *(adv)*.

spiritualism *(n)* communication with the spirits of dead people. **spiritualist** *(n)*.

spit spitting spat *or* spit *(v)* to force saliva out of your mouth.

spite
1 *(n)* deliberate nastiness. **spiteful** *(adj)*, **spitefully** *(adv)*.
2 **in spite of** without taking notice of. *Ingrid went swimming in spite of the rain.*

splash splashes splashing splashed *(v)* to scatter liquid. **splash** *(n)*.

splendid *(adj)* impressive, excellent, or very good. **splendidly** *(adv)*.

splint *(n)* a piece of wood, plastic, or metal, used to support a broken or damaged limb.

splinter *(n)* a thin, sharp piece of wood, glass, metal, etc. **splinter** *(v)*.

split splitting split
1 *(v)* to break something into separate pieces.
2 *(n)* a crack.
3 *(v)* If a couple **splits up**, they stop going out together or living together.

splutter spluttering spluttered
1 *(v)* to speak with difficulty, usually because you are upset.
2 *(v)* If an engine **splutters**, it makes choking and spitting noises because it is not working properly.

spoil spoiling spoilt *or* spoiled
1 *(v)* to ruin or wreck something.
2 *(adj)* If children are **spoilt**, their parents have allowed them to have their own way too often.

sponge
1 *(n)* a sea animal with a rubbery, absorbent skeleton. The skeletons of sponges are often used for washing and cleaning.
2 *(n)* soft material, filled with holes, used for washing and cleaning. **sponge** *(v)*, **spongy** *(adj)*.
3 *(n)* a light cake.

sponsor sponsoring sponsored *(v)* to give money to people who are doing something worthwhile, often for charity. **sponsorship** *(n)*.

spontaneous *(adj)* without previous thought or planning. **spontaneity** *(n)*, **spontaneously** *(adv)*.

spool *(n)* a reel on which film, tape, thread, etc. is wound.

spoon *(n)* a piece of cutlery, used for eating desserts, soups, etc.

spoor *(n)* the trail left behind by an animal.

spore *(n)* a cell produced by non-flowering plants such as fungi, mosses, and ferns, which develops into a new plant. *The picture shows some moss spore cases. When the cases open, the spores are spread by the wind.* *Also see* **fern**.

moss spore cases

sporran *(n)* a small, leather pouch, worn in front of the kilt as part of the traditional Scottish highland dress.

sport *(n)* a general name for games involving physical activity. Sports can be played professionally, or for pleasure.

spot spotting spotted
1 *(n)* a small mark that is usually round. **spotted** *(adj)*.
2 *(n)* a sore, red place on the skin. **spotty** *(adj)*.
3 *(n)* a place, or a location. *This looks a good spot for a picnic.*
4 *(v)* to notice something. *Angelina has spotted a friend.*

spotless *(adj)* absolutely clean. **spotlessly** *(adv)*.

spotlight *(n)* a powerful light used to light up a small area.

spouse *(n)* a husband, or a wife.

spout spouting spouted
1 *(n)* a tube through which liquid is poured, for example, the spout of a kettle.
2 *(v)* *(informal)* to talk about something in a boring, pompous way.

sprain spraining sprained *(v)* to injure a joint by twisting it. *Liza sprained her ankle when she fell.*

sprawl sprawling sprawled
1 *(v)* to sit or lie with your arms and legs spread out carelessly.
2 *(v)* to spread out in all directions. *The city sprawled for miles.*

spray spraying sprayed *(v)* to scatter liquid in very fine drops. **spray** *(n)*.

spread spreading spread
1 *(v)* to unfold, or to stretch out. *Hilary spread out the map on the table. Joel spread his arms wide.*
2 *(v)* to cover a surface with something. *We spread the bread with peanut butter.* **spread** *(n)*.
3 *(v)* to scatter, or to make known. *Spread the news.*

sprightly sprightlier sprightliest *(adj)* lively and energetic.

spring springing sprang sprung
1 (n) the season between winter and summer, when it becomes warmer and leaves grow on the trees.
2 (v) to jump suddenly. *The lion sprang at the antelope.*
3 (n) a coil of metal which moves back to its original position after being compressed or pushed down.
4 (n) a place where water rises up from underground and becomes a stream.

springboard (n) a flexible board that people jump on in order to increase their height or force in diving or gymnastics. *The picture shows a diver using a springboard.*

springboard jump

spring-clean spring-cleaning spring-cleaned (v) to clean a house thoroughly, concentrating on the places that do not get cleaned often. **spring-cleaning** (n).

sprinkle sprinkling sprinkled (v) to scatter liquid or powder in small amounts. *Sprinkle the top of the dish with grated cheese.*

sprint sprinting sprinted
1 (v) to run fast. *Gerry sprinted to the shops.*
2 (n) a very fast race run over a short distance. **sprinter** (n), **sprint** (adj).

sprint start

sprocket (n) a wheel with a toothed edge, usually driven by a chain. *See* **bicycle**.

sprout sprouting sprouted
1 (v) When a plant **sprouts**, it starts to grow and produce shoots or buds.
2 (n) a round, green vegetable. *See* **vegetable**.

spur spurring spurred
1 (n) a spike or spiked wheel on the heel of a rider's boot, used to make their horse go more quickly.
2 **spur on** (v) If something **spurs you on**, it encourages or motivates you.

spurt spurting spurted
1 (v) When liquid **spurts**, it flows or gushes suddenly. **spurt** (n).

2 (n) a sudden burst of energy, growth, or speed.

spy spies spying spied
1 (v) to watch something closely from a hidden place.
2 (n) someone who secretly collects information about an enemy. **spy** (v).

squabble (n) a childish argument or quarrel. **squabble** (v).

squad (n) a small group of people involved in the same activity, such as soldiers or football players.

squalid (adj) dirty and unpleasant.

squander squandering squandered (v) to spend money wastefully.

square squaring squared
1 (n) a shape with four equal sides and four right angles. *See* **shape**.
2 (v) to multiply a number by itself. *4 squared equals 16.*
3 **square root** (n) the number that, when multiplied by itself, gives a particular number. *5 is the square root of 25.*

squash squashes squashing squashed
1 (v) to crush or flatten something.
2 (n) a racket game played by two people who hit a small rubber ball against the walls of an enclosed court.
3 (n) a concentrated fruit drink.
4 (n) a large, pumpkin-like vegetable. *See* **vegetable**.

squash court

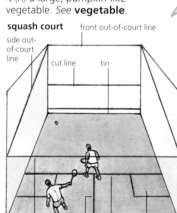

front out-of-court line
side out-of-court line
cut line   tin
back out-of-court line   half court line   short line   service box

squat squatting squatted
1 (v) to crouch with your knees bent.
2 (v) to live, without permission, in an empty house that does not belong to you. **squat** (n), **squatter** (n).
3 (adj) short and broad.

squawk squawking squawked (v) to make a loud, harsh cry like the noise of a parrot. **squawk** (n).

squeak squeaking squeaked (v) to make a short, high-pitched sound like the noise of a mouse. **squeak** (n).

squeal squealing squealed (v) to make a shrill, high-pitched sound, usually because you are frightened or in pain. **squeal** (n).

squeamish (adj) easily sickened or shocked. **squeamishly** (adv).

squeeze squeezing squeezed
1 (v) to press something firmly together from opposite sides. **squeeze** (n).
2 (v) to force something into or through a space. *We squeezed into the bus.* **squeeze** (n).

squid (n) a sea creature with a long, soft body and ten tentacles. *Squids swim by squirting water out of their bodies with great force.*

lateral fin
body
eye (adapted for underwater light)
light-sensitive skin (changes colour for camouflage)
tentacle

squid

long tentacle for grasping prey

claw with suckers

squint squinting squinted
1 (v) If you squint at something, you nearly close your eyes in order to see it more clearly.
2 (n) Someone who has a squint has eyes which look in different directions from one another.

squire
1 (n) the chief landowner in a country district.
2 (n) In medieval times, a squire was a young nobleman who accompanied and helped a knight.

squirm squirming squirmed
1 (v) to wriggle about uncomfortably.
2 (v) to feel uncomfortable because you are embarrassed or ashamed.

squirrel (n) a tree-climbing rodent with a bushy tail. *The grey squirrel shown here is found in Europe and North America.*

grey squirrel

squirt squirting squirted (v) to send out a stream of liquid. *Misha turned on the hose and squirted her brothers.* squirt (n).

squishy squishier squishiest (adj) (informal) soft and soggy.

St. see **saint**.

stab stabbing stabbed
1 (v) to wound someone by piercing their skin with a knife or other sharp instrument. stab (n).
2 (informal) If you **make a stab** at something, you try to do it.

stable
1 (n) a building or a part of a building where a horse is kept.
2 stables (n) a place where horses are kept for use in riding lessons.
3 (adj) firm and steady. *Before you climb the ladder, check that it is stable.* stability (n), stabilize (v).
4 (adj) safe and secure. *The children had a stable upbringing.* stability (n).

staccato (sta-kah-toh) (adv) When you play notes **staccato**, you make them short and separate.

stack stacking stacked (v) to pile things up, one on top of another. stack (n).

stadium stadiums or stadia (n) a sports ground surrounded by rows of seats for spectators.

staff
1 (plural n) the people who work in an organization. *The school staff.*
2 (n) (old-fashioned) a thick, wooden stick.

stag
(n) an adult male deer. *The picture shows a stag roaring. Stags roar to one another in the mating season in order to compete for females.*

red deer stag

stage staging staged
1 (n) a period of development. *Our plans are still at an early stage.*
2 (n) a level of progress. *You have done so well that you can move to the next stage.*
3 (n) an area where plays and concerts are performed.
4 (v) to organize a public performance or event. *Our school is staging a play.*
5 If you **go on the stage**, you become an actor.

stagecoach stagecoaches (n) a horse-drawn vehicle, used in the past to carry passengers and mail for long distances. Stagecoaches travelled in stages and were supplied with fresh horses at each stage.

stagecoach

stage-manage stage-managing stage-managed (v) to organize a play, concert, or other event. stage manager (n).

stage-struck (adj) Someone who is stage-struck thinks that the theatre is very glamorous, and wants to become an actor.

stagger staggering staggered
1 (v) to walk or stand unsteadily.
2 If you are **staggered** by something, you are astonished and amazed.
3 (v) When you **stagger** events, you time them so that they do not happen at the same time. *The guards staggered their breaks.*

staggering (adj) amazing, or astonishing. *Hugo bought the house for a staggering amount of money.*

stagnant (adj) Stagnant water cannot flow and is dirty and smelly.

stagnate stagnating stagnated
1 (v) When water **stagnates**, it changes colour, and becomes stale and often smelly.
2 (v) If a situation or person **stagnates**, they remain the same for a long time, when they should be changing. stagnation (n).

staid (adj) If someone is **staid**, they are not lively and do not like change.

stain staining stained
1 (n) a mark on something that is hard to remove.
2 (v) to make a mark that is hard to remove from something. *The paint stained my coat.*
3 (n) colouring used on wood.

stained glass (n) coloured pieces of glass, held together by lead strips. Stained glass is often used in church windows. *The picture shows a stained glass window from Chartres Cathedral in France.*

stainless steel (n) a type of steel that does not rust or tarnish.

stairs (plural n) steps that allow you to walk from one level of a building to another. staircase (n).

stake staking staked
1 (n) a thick, pointed post that can be driven into the ground.
2 (v) to bet. *Jim staked his money on the race.*
3 (n) If you have a **stake** in something, you are involved in it or you have put money into it.
4 If something is **at stake**, it is at risk.

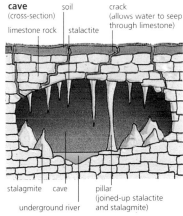

stained glass

stalactite (n) a thin piece of rock, shaped like an icicle, which hangs from the roof of a cave. Stalactites are made from calcium minerals, dissolved in dripping water, which have slowly solidified. *The picture below shows stalactites in a cave.*

cave (cross-section)   soil   **crack** (allows water to seep through limestone)

limestone rock   stalactite

stalagmite   cave   pillar (joined-up stalactite and stalagmite)

underground river

stalagmite (n) a piece of rock which sticks up from the floor of a cave. Stalagmites are made from calcium minerals, dissolved in dripping water, which have slowly solidified. *The picture above shows stalagmites in a cave.*

stale staler stalest (adj) no longer fresh. *Stale cake.*

stalemate (n) a situation in an argument or game of chess, in which neither side can win.

stalk *(stork)* **stalking stalked**
1 *(n)* the long, main part of a plant from which the leaves, flowers, and fruit grow.
2 *(n)* a thin branch that holds a leaf, flower, or fruit.
3 *(v)* to follow slowly and quietly. *The leopard stalked its prey.*
4 *(v)* to walk in a proud, stiff way. *Harvey stalked out of the room in a temper.*

stall **stalling stalled**
1 *(v)* When a car **stalls**, its engine stops suddenly.
2 *(n)* a table from which things are sold in a market or jumble sale.
3 *(n)* a section in a stable or barn where one animal is kept.
4 *(v)* to delay doing something until later.
5 *(plural n)* In a theatre, the **stalls** are the seats on the ground floor.

stallion *(n)* a male horse.

stamina *(n)* the energy to keep doing something for a long while. *You need stamina for long-distance running.*

stammer **stammering stammered**
(v) If you **stammer** when you speak, you repeat the first sound of a word before you manage to say the whole word. **stammer** *(n)*.

stamp **stamping stamped**
1 *(n)* a small piece of paper that you stick on a letter or parcel to show that you have paid for it to be sent. **stamp** *(v)*.

penny black, Britain, 1840

2 *(n)* an object used to print a mark on paper. You press the stamp first on to an ink pad and then on to paper. **stamp** *(v)*.
3 *(v)* to bang your foot down.

Japan, 1956

stamps

USSR, 1959

USA, 1969

Australia 1994

stampede **stampeding stampeded**
(v) When people or animals **stampede**, they suddenly rush somewhere wildly. **stampede** *(n)*.

stand **standing stood**
1 *(v)* to be on your feet with your body upright.

2 *(v)* to put something somewhere. *Stand the vase on the table.*
3 *(v)* to continue unchanged. *My offer still stands.*
4 *(n)* an object on which you put things. *A music stand.*
5 *(n)* a covered area for spectators at a sports ground.
6 *(n)* a small, outdoor shop. *A hot dog stand.*
7 **stand for** *(v)* to represent. *The initials US stand for United States.*
8 *(v)* If you **cannot stand** something, you hate it or are unable to bear it.
9 *(v)* If you **stand by** someone, you support them when they are in trouble.
10 *(v)* If something **stands out**, it can be seen or noticed easily.

standard
1 *(adj)* usual, or average. *What is the standard fare?*
2 *(n)* a way of judging or measuring how good something is. *Standards of grammar seem to be falling.*
3 **standard lamp** *(n)* a lamp on a tall base that stands on the floor.

stand-by *(n)* something or someone that is ready to be used if needed.

stand-in *(n)* someone who takes the place of another person when that person cannot be there. **stand in** *(v)*.

standstill *(n)* If something comes to a **standstill**, it stops completely.

stanza *(n)* one of the groups of lines into which a poem is divided. Another name for stanza is verse.

staple
1 *(n)* a small piece of wire which is punched through sheets of paper to hold them together. **stapler** *(n)*, **staple** *(v)*.
2 *(adj)* A **staple** food is the main food eaten in a country. **staple** *(n)*.

star **starring starred**
1 *(n)* a ball of burning gases in space, seen from the Earth as a tiny point of light in the sky at night. **starry** *(adj)*.
2 *(n)* a shape with several points, usually five or six.
3 *(n)* a well-known actor or entertainer.
4 *(v)* to take the main part in a film or play.

starboard *(n)* the right-hand side of a ship or aircraft. **starboard** *(adj)*.

starch **starches**
1 *(n)* a substance found in such foods as potatoes, bread, and rice. Starch is very filling and gives you energy.
2 *(n)* a substance used for making cloth stiff. **starch** *(v)*.

stare **staring stared** *(v)* to look at someone or something for a long time without moving your eyes. **stare** *(n)*.

starfish **starfish** *(n)* a star-like sea creature with five or more arms.

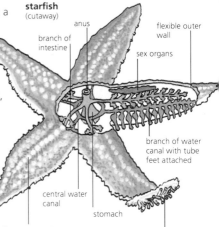

starfish (cutaway)

anus
flexible outer wall
branch of intestine
sex organs
branch of water canal with tube feet attached
central water canal
stomach
arm with spines and pincers to attack enemies
water-filled podium or tube foot

stark **starker starkest**
1 *(adj)* bare and plain. *A stark landscape. The stark truth.*
2 *(adj)* completely, or totally. *The emperor was stark naked.*

start **starting started**
1 *(v)* to set something in motion, or to be set in motion.
2 *(n)* the beginning of something.
3 *(v)* to jump in surprise.
4 *(n)* an advantage at the beginning of a race. *You can have a 20m start.*

startle **startling startled** *(v)* to surprise someone and make them jump. **startled** *(adj)*, **startling** *(adj)*.

starve **starving starved** *(v)* to suffer or die from hunger. **starvation** *(n)*.

starving
1 *(adj)* suffering or dying from hunger.
2 *(adj)* *(informal)* very hungry.

state **stating stated**
1 *(v)* to say something clearly. *Please state your name.*
2 *(n)* the government of a country. *Affairs of state.*
3 *(n)* an area within a country that makes its own laws. *The State of Texas.*
4 *(n)* the way that something is, or the condition that something or someone is in. *Your room is in a terrible state. Betty is in a state of confusion.*
5 *(informal)* If someone is **in a state**, they are upset.
6 **state-of-the-art** *(adj)* very advanced and up to date. *A state-of-the-art computer system.*

statement
1 *(n)* something that is said formally.
2 *(n)* a list of all the amounts paid into and out of a bank account.

stay staying stayed
1 *(v)* to remain where you are.
2 *(v)* to spend time somewhere. *We didn't stay long at the party.*
3 *(n)* a period of time spent somewhere as a visitor. *Have you had an enjoyable stay?*

steam locomotive *(n)* an engine powered by steam and used for pulling trains. *The steam produced by this steam locomotive forces the pistons to move. The pistons drive the connecting rods and crank rods which are connected to the driving wheels.*

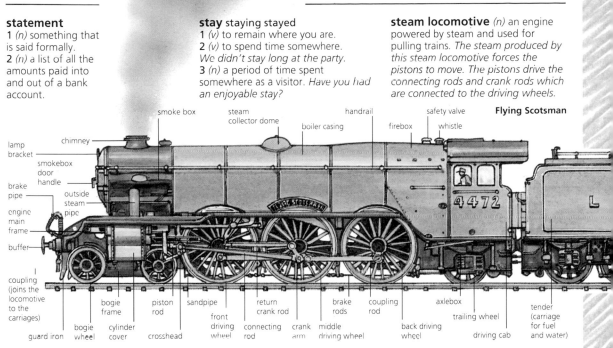

Flying Scotsman

Labels: smoke box; steam collector dome; handrail; safety valve; whistle; boiler casing; firebox; chimney; lamp bracket; smokebox door handle; brake pipe; outside steam pipe; engine main frame; buffer; coupling (joins the locomotive to the carriages); guard iron; bogie wheel; bogie frame; cylinder cover; piston rod; crosshead; sandpipe; front driving wheel; connecting rod; return crank rod; crank arm; brake rods; middle driving wheel; coupling rod; back driving wheel; axlebox; trailing wheel; driving cab; tender (carriage for fuel and water); 4472

static
1 *(adj)* not moving, or not changing. *A static caravan. A static situation.*
2 *(n)* electricity that is produced by friction. Static is short for static electricity.
3 *(n)* the crackling noises that you hear when static electricity in the air causes interference to a radio or television signal.

station
1 *(n)* a place where trains or buses stop. *A bus station.*
2 *(n)* a building used as the base for a police force, ambulance service, or fire brigade.
3 *(n)* a radio or television channel.

stationary *(adj)* at rest, or not moving.

stationery *(n)* writing materials, such as paper, envelopes, and pens.

statistic *(n)* a fact or a piece of information, expressed as a number or percentage. **statistical** *(adj)*, **statistically** *(adv)*.

statue *(n)* a model of a person or animal made from metal, stone, etc.

status statuses *(n)* a person's rank or position in society.

statute *(n)* a rule, or a law.

stave staving staved *or* stove
1 *(n)* the set of five lines on which music is written. *See* **notation**.
2 **stave off** *(v)* If you **stave something off**, you manage to keep it away

steady steadies steadying steadied; steadier steadiest
1 *(adj)* continuous and not changing much. *Steady progress.* **steadily** *(adv)*.
2 *(adj)* not moving about, or not shaking. *A steady hand.*
3 *(v)* to stop something moving about or shaking.
4 *(adj)* sensible and dependable.

steak *(n)* a thick slice of meat or fish.

steal stealing stole stolen
1 *(v)* to take and keep something that does not belong to you.
2 **steal away** *(v)* to leave quietly.

stealthy *(rhymes with wealthy)* stealthier stealthiest *(adj)* secret and quiet. *We crept away with stealthy steps.* stealth *(n)*, stealthily *(adv)*.

steam steaming steamed
1 *(n)* the vapour formed when water boils.
2 *(v)* When glass **steams up**, it gets covered with condensation.
3 *(informal)* If you **let off steam**, you release your stored-up energy or feelings.
4 *(informal)* If you **run out of steam**, you have no more energy left.

steam-engine *(n)* an engine powered by steam. Coal or wood burnt in a boiler produces hot air that travels in pipes through a water tank. As the water in the tank boils, it creates steam. Steam is forced into cylinders where it pushes pistons to operate machinery.
See **steam locomotive**.

steamroller *(n)* a steam-driven vehicle used to flatten road surfaces.

steel
1 *(n)* a hard, strong metal made mainly from iron.
2 **steel band** *(n)* a group that plays music on drums made from oil barrels. *See* **instrument**.

steep steeping steeped; steeper steepest
1 *(adj)* sharply sloping up or down. *A steep hill.* **steeply** *(adv)*.
2 *(adj)* sharp, or rapid. *A steep drop in student numbers.*
3 *(v)* to soak something in a liquid.
4 If something is **steeped** in something, it is full of it.

steeple *(n)* a church tower with a spire.

steeplechase *(n)* a cross-country horse race over fences, water jumps, ditches, etc.

steer steering steered *(v)* to make a vehicle go in a particular direction.

steering wheel *(n)* the wheel in a vehicle used to control its direction.

stem stemming stemmed
1 *(n)* the long, main part of a plant, from which the leaves, flowers, and fruit grow. *See* **plant**.
2 *(v)* If something **stems from** a place or thing, it comes from it. *The quarrel stemmed from a misunderstanding.*
3 *(v)* to stop something from flowing or spreading. *The rescue team tried to stem the flow of oil from the tanker.*

stench stenches (n) a strong, unpleasant smell.

stencil (n) a piece of card, plastic, or metal with a design cut out of it, which can be painted over to transfer the design on to a surface. **stencil** (v).

stencilling equipment

stencil brush

oiled stencil card

stencilled design

step stepping stepped
1 (v) to move your foot forward and put it down. **step** (n).
2 (n) the sound of someone walking. *Can you hear steps behind you?*
3 (n) one of the flat surfaces on a staircase.
4 (n) one of the things that you need to do in order to make or achieve something. *This recipe is in six steps.*
5 (informal) If someone says that you should **watch your step**, they are telling you to be careful.

stepfamily stepfamilies (n) the family of your stepfather or stepmother.

stepfather (n) the man who is married to your mother, but is not your father.

stepmother (n) the woman who is married to your father, but is not your mother.

stereo
1 (n) sound that comes from two different directions at the same time. Stereo is short for stereophonic.
2 (n) a CD player, cassette player, or radio with stereo speakers.

stereotype (n) a simplified idea of a person or thing. *We've created a teenage stereotype for this advertising campaign.* **stereotypical** (adj).

sterile
1 (adj) free from germs.
2 (adj) unable to have babies.

sterilize or **sterilise** sterilizing sterilized (v) to clean something so thoroughly that you make it free from germs. **sterilization** (n).

sterling (n) the currency of Great Britain.

stern sterner sternest
1 (adj) serious and severe. *Paula gave me a stern look.*

2 (n) the back end of a ship.

steroid (n) a chemical substance found naturally in your body. Steroids are sometimes taken as a drug by athletes to build up their strength, but their use is usually banned.

stethoscope (n) a Y-shaped tube connected to two earpieces, used by a doctor to listen to a patient's heartbeat or breathing.

eartip

ear tube

non-chill rim

double leaf spring

stainless steel chest piece

plastic tubing

stethoscope

stew
1 (n) meat and vegetables, cooked slowly in liquid. **stew** (v).
2 If you are **in a stew** about something, you are upset and worried about it. **stew** (v).

steward
1 (n) a man who looks after passengers on an aeroplane or ship.
2 (n) someone who helps to direct people at a large public event, such as a race or concert.

stewardess stewardesses (n) a woman who looks after passengers on an aeroplane or ship.

stick sticking stuck
1 (n) a long, thin piece of wood.
2 (n) a long, thin piece of something. *A stick of seaside rock.*
3 (v) to glue or fasten one thing to another. **sticky** (adj).
4 (v) to push something with a point into something else. *Fran stuck a needle into her finger.*

5 (v) If something **sticks**, it becomes fixed in a particular position. *This door keeps sticking.*
6 (v) If someone **sticks** to an idea, friend, etc. they support them and do not give them up.
7 (v) (informal) If you **stick up** for someone, you support them.

sticker (n) a sticky paper or plastic badge that you can attach to things.

stick insect (n) an insect with a long body that looks like a twig.

stiff stiffer stiffest
1 (adj) difficult to bend or turn. **stiffen** (v), **stiffly** (adv).
2 (adj) If you feel **stiff**, your muscles hurt because you have overworked them.

3 (adj) difficult, or severe. *A stiff exam.*
4 (adj) formal and distant.

stifle stifling stifled
1 (v) If you **stifle** a cough, sneeze, or yawn, you close your mouth to prevent it from being noticed.
2 (n) a knee joint in some animals. *See dog.*

stigma
1 (n) a mark of shame or embarrassment.
2 (n) the part of a flower which receives the pollen when the flower is pollinated. *See flower.*

stile (n) a wooden step used to climb over a wall or fence.

still stiller stillest
1 (adj) not moving. *Stand still!*
2 (adv) even now. *Are you still here?*
3 (adj) not fizzy. *Still orange drink.*
4 (adv) however.

stimulate stimulating stimulated
1 (v) If someone or something **stimulates** you, they fill you with exciting new ideas. **stimulating** (adj).
2 (v) to encourage something to grow or develop.

sting stinging stung
1 (n) the sharp part of an insect, animal, or plant that can pierce your skin and leave some poison in it. **sting** (v). *See scorpion.*
2 (v) to hurt with a sharp or throbbing pain. *My eyes are stinging.*

stingray (n) a flat-bodied fish that has large, wing-like fins and a long tail with poisonous spines.

stingray

stingy (stin-jee) stingier stingiest (adj) very mean. **stingily** (adv).

stink stinking stank stunk
1 (v) to have an unpleasant smell. **stink** (n).
2 (v) (slang) to be very bad. *Robyn's plan stinks!*

stir stirring stirred
1 (v) to mix a liquid by moving a spoon or stick round and round in it.
2 (v) to move slightly.
3 If you **cause a stir**, you make people excited about something.

stitch stitches stitching stitched
1 (v) to make loops of thread or wool in sewing or knitting. **stitch** (n). *See embroidery.*

2 *(v)* to close up a wound by sewing with thread. **stitch** *(n)*.
3 *(n)* a sudden, sharp pain in your side, caused by exercise.
4 *(informal)* If you are **in stitches**, you cannot stop laughing.

stock stocking stocked
1 *(v)* If a shop **stocks** a product, it keeps a supply of the product to sell.
2 *(n)* all the products that a factory, warehouse, or shop has to sell.
3 *(n)* a liquid used in cooking, made from the juices of meat or vegetables.
4 *(v)* If you **stock up** on something, you buy a large supply of it.

stockbroker *(n)* someone whose job is buying and selling stocks and shares in companies for other people.

stock car *(n)* a car driven in rough races in which the cars crash into one another on purpose

stocking *(n)* a close-fitting garment that covers your leg.

stockist *(n)* a shop that keeps a supply of a particular product.

stockpile stockpiling stockpiled *(v)* to build up a large supply of food or weapons that you can use in the future.

stocks
1 *(plural n)* a heavy, wooden frame with holes in it, used in the past to hold criminals by their ankles. *The picture shows some medieval stocks.*
2 *(plural n)* If you have **stocks** in a company, you have invested money in it, and receive regular smaller amounts in return, based on how profitable the company is.

stocks

stocky stockier stockiest *(adj)*
A stocky person is short, broad, and strong. **stockily** *(adv)*.

stodgy stodgier stodgiest *(adj)*
Stodgy food is very heavy and filling.

stoke stoking stoked *(v)* to put more fuel on a fire in order to keep it burning.

stomach
1 *(n)* the part of the body where food is digested. *See* **digestion**, **organ**.
2 *(n)* the front part of your body, just below your waist.

stone
1 *(n)* a small piece of rock, usually found on the ground. **stony** *(adj)*.

2 *(n)* a hard material used for building, making sculptures, etc.
3 *(n)* a hard seed found in the middle of a fruit such as a cherry or peach.
4 *(n)* a unit of weight equal to 14lbs, or 6.35kg. *See page 284*

Stone Age *(n)* a very early period in human history, when people used stone to make tools and weapons.

stone circle *(n)* a circle of large, tall stones put up in prehistoric times. *The picture shows Stonehenge, a prehistoric stone circle in Wiltshire, England.*

Stonehenge

sarsen stone

lintel (horizontal stone)

stoned *(adj) (slang)* If you are stoned, you are very drunk or drugged.

stool *(n)* a small seat with no back.

stoop stooping stooped
1 *(v)* to bend down low.
2 *(v)* to walk, sit, stand, etc. with your head and shoulders bent forwards. **stoop** *(n)*.

stop stopping stopped
1 *(v)* When something **stops**, it comes to an end. *The music stopped.*
2 *(v)* If you **stop** something, you put an end to it or do not do it any more.
3 *(v)* to be no longer moving or working. *My watch has stopped.*
4 *(n)* one of the places on a route where a bus or train picks up passengers.
5 *(n)* If you **stop** or **stop up** a hole, you fill it or plug it.

stopper *(n)* a piece of cork or plastic that fits into the top of a test tube, jar, or bottle, in order to close it.

stopwatch *(n)* a watch that you can start and stop at any time, used for timing races.

storage *(n)* If you put something in **storage**, you put it in a place where it can be kept until it is needed. **storage** *(adj)*.

store storing stored
1 *(v)* to put things away until they are needed.

2 *(v)* to keep information on a computer, by saving it as a computer file.
3 *(n)* a place where things are kept.
4 *(n)* a large shop with many departments.

storey storeys *or* stories *(n)* one layer or floor of a building.

stork *(n)* a large bird with long, thin legs and a long bill.

storm storming stormed
1 *(n)* a period of bad weather with strong wind and rain, and sometimes thunder and lightning. **stormy** *(adj)*.
2 *(n)* a show of strong and angry feelings. *A storm of protest.* **stormy** *(adj)*.
3 *(v)* to attack somewhere suddenly. *The army stormed the castle.*
4 *(v)* If you **storm out**, you rush out of a place angrily

story stories
1 *(n)* a spoken or written account of someone's life or adventures.
2 *(n)* a lie. *Are you telling stories?*

stout stouter stoutest
1 *(adj)* quite fat.
2 *(adj)* strong and thick. *Stout boots.*

stove *(n)* a piece of equipment used for cooking or for heating a room.

stowaway *(n)* someone who hides in a plane, ship, or other vehicle, because they want to escape secretly or cannot afford a ticket.

straggle straggling straggled *(v)* to follow slowly behind a group of people. **straggler** *(n)*.

straight straighter straightest
1 *(adj)* not bent, or not curved.
2 *(adj)* level, or neat. *Put your hat straight.* **straighten** *(v)*.
3 *(adj)* honest, or correct. *A straight answer.*
4 *(adv)* immediately. *Gus arrived straight after me.*

straightaway *(adv)* at once.

straightforward
1 *(adj)* simple and uncomplicated. *The operation was straightforward.*
2 *(adj)* honest, or to the point. *John gave a straightforward answer.*

strain straining strained
1 *(n)* stress, or tension. **strained** *(adj)*.
2 *(v)* If you **strain** a muscle in your body, you damage it by pulling it or overusing it. **strain** *(n)*.
3 *(v)* If you **strain** to do something, you try very hard to do it.
4 *(v)* If you **strain** a mixture, you pour it through a sieve or colander, to separate the solids from the liquid. **strainer** *(n)*, **strained** *(adj)*.

strait

1 (n) a narrow strip of water between two seas or two countries.

The picture shows the Strait of Gibraltar between Spain and Morocco.

2 If you are in dire straits, you are in trouble.

strait

strand

1 (n) one of the threads or wires that are twisted together to form a rope.

2 (n) a single hair.

stranded

1 (adj) washed up on a shore. A stranded whale.

2 (adj) If you are stranded somewhere, you are stuck there and cannot get away.

strange stranger strangest (adj)

odd, unusual, or unfamiliar. strangeness (n), strangely (adv).

stranger

1 (n) someone you do not know.

2 (n) someone in a place where they have not been before. I am a stranger in this city.

strangle strangling strangled (v)

to kill someone by squeezing their throat so that they cannot breathe. strangler (n), strangulation (n).

strap strapping strapped

1 (n) a strip of leather or material, used to fasten things together.

2 (v) to fasten things, or hold things in place with straps.

strategy strategies (n) a clever plan

for winning or achieving something. strategic (adj), strategically (adv).

straw

1 (n) dried stalks of corn, wheat, etc.

2 (n) a thin, hollow tube through which you can drink.

strawberry strawberries (n) a soft,

red fruit. See **fruit**.

stray straying strayed

1 (v) to wander away, or to get lost. stray (adj).

2 (n) a lost cat or dog.

streak streaking streaked

1 (n) a stripe of colour. streaky (adj).

2 (v) to move very fast. The sprinter streaked past us.

stream streaming streamed

1 (n) a small river.

2 (n) a long line of moving people, cars, etc.

3 (n) a class of schoolchildren who are at the same level in their work.

4 (v) to move or flow fast.

streamer (n) a long, thin strip of

coloured paper, used as a decoration.

streamlined (adj) If a car, plane, or

other vehicle is **streamlined**, it is designed so that it can cut through air or water very quickly and easily. See **aerodynamic**.

street

1 (n) a road with houses or other buildings along it.

2 (n) (informal) If you have street cred, you are fashionable and popular. Cred is short for credibility.

streetwise (adj) If you are

streetwise, you know how to survive in towns or cities without getting into trouble.

strength

1 (n) If you have strength, you are physically strong. strengthen (v).

2 (n) Someone's strengths are their good points, or the things that they can do well.

strenuous (stren-yoo-uss) (adj)

Something that is **strenuous** needs a lot of energy or effort. strenuously (adv).

stress stresses stressing stressed

1 (n) worry, strain, or pressure. stressful (adj).

2 (v) If you stress something, you show that it is important. stress (n).

stretch stretches stretching stretched

1 (v) to make something bigger, longer, or greater.

2 (v) to reach out with your arms. stretch (n).

3 (v) to extend, or to spread out. The path stretches for miles.

4 (n) a period of time, especially time spent in a prison.

5 stretch out (v) to lie full length.

stretcher (n) a narrow bed made of

canvas stretched between two poles, and used for carrying an injured person.

strict stricter strictest

1 (adj) If someone is strict, they make you obey the rules and behave properly. strictness (n), strictly (adv).

2 (adj) complete, or total. This trick needs strict concentration. strictly (adv).

stride striding strode stridden (v)

to walk with long steps. stride (n).

strife (n) trouble, or arguing.

strike striking struck

1 (v) to hit or attack someone or something. strike (n).

2 (v) When a clock strikes, it chimes to show the time.

3 (v) to make an impression on someone. Simon struck me as silly.

4 (v) If you strike a match, you light it.

5 (v) When people strike, they refuse to work because of an argument or disagreement with their employer. strike (n).

striker

1 (n) a soccer player who plays in an attacking position. See **soccer**.

2 (n) someone who is on strike.

striking (adj) unusual, or noticeable

in some way. strikingly (adv).

string stringing strung

1 (n) a thin cord or rope.

2 (n) a thin wire on a musical instrument such as a guitar. string (v).

3 (v) to put a row of objects on a piece of string or wire. Natasha was stringing beads to make a necklace.

4 string out (v) If you string something out, you stretch or lengthen something. We strung out the game until bedtime.

strings (plural n) the section of an

orchestra that is made up of stringed instruments, such as violins and cellos. The picture shows the main parts of a violin, and other instruments in the section of an orchestra, called the strings.

viola

double bass

scroll

tuning peg

violin

fingerboard

horse hair

neck

wooden stick

string

cello

purfling (curved band)

f hole (sound hole)

bridge

table or belly

bow

chin rest

tailpiece

strip stripping stripped
1 *(v)* to take something off.
Jo stripped the wallpaper off the wall.
2 *(v)* to undress. **stripper** *(n)*.
3 *(n)* a narrow piece of paper, material, etc.
4 *(n)* the clothes that a football team wears. *Our team has a new strip.*

stripe *(n)* a band of colour.
striped *(adj)*, **stripy** *(adj)*.

strive striving strove striven *(v)* to make a great effort to do something. *Strive to do your best.*

strobe *(n)* a light that keeps flashing on and off very quickly.

stroke stroking stroked
1 *(n)* a hit. *A backhand stroke. A stroke of lightning.*
2 *(v)* to pass your hand gently over something. *You may stroke the kitten.* **stroke** *(n)*.
3 *(n)* When someone has a **stroke**, a part of their brain is damaged, which sometimes causes part of their body to be paralysed.
4 *(n)* a line drawn by a pen or brush.
5 *(n)* a method of moving in swimming or rowing.

stroll *(n)* a short, relaxed walk. **stroll** *(v)*.

strong stronger strongest
1 *(adj)* powerful, or having great force. *A strong wind.* **strongly** *(adv)*.
2 *(adj)* hard to break. *A strong shelf.* **strongly** *(adv)*.
3 *(adj)* full of taste, spices, alcohol, etc. *A strong curry.* **strongly** *(adv)*.

stronghold *(n)* a fortress, or a place that is well defended.

stroppy stroppier stroppiest *(adj)* *(informal)* quarrelsome and unhelpful. **stroppiness** *(n)*, **stroppily** *(adv)*.

structure
1 *(n)* the organization of something, or the way that it is made up. **structure** *(v)*, **structural** *(adj)*.
2 *(n)* a building, or something that has been put together. **structural** *(adj)*.

struggle struggling struggled
1 *(v)* If you **struggle** with someone, you fight or wrestle with them. **struggle** *(n)*.
2 *(v)* If you **struggle** with something, you find it difficult to do. **struggle** *(n)*.

strum strumming strummed *(v)* to play a guitar, banjo, etc. by brushing your fingers over the strings.

strut strutting strutted
1 *(v)* to walk proudly and stiffly with your chest pushed out.
2 *(n)* a wooden or metal supporting bar. *See* **hydrofoil**.

stub stubbing stubbed
1 *(n)* a short end of something, such as a pencil or cigarette. **stubby** *(adj)*.
2 *(v)* to hurt your toe by banging it against something.
3 **stub out** *(v)* to put a cigarette out.

stubble
1 *(n)* short, spiky pieces of corn or wheat, left in a field after harvesting. **stubbly** *(adj)*.
2 *(n)* the short hair that grows on a man's face if he does not shave. **stubbly** *(adj)*.

stubborn *(adj)* obstinate, or determined not to give way. **stubborness** *(n)*, **stubbornly** *(adv)*.

stuck-up *(adj)* *(informal)* conceited and snobbish.

stud
1 *(n)* a small, round piece of metal, such as a fastener or an earring.
2 *(n)* one of the short pegs on the bottom of football or hockey boots, which give extra grip.
3 *(n)* a farm where horses are kept for breeding.

student *(n)* someone who is studying, especially in a college or university.

studio
1 *(n)* a room in which an artist or a photographer works.
2 *(n)* a place where films, tapes, CDs, etc. are made.

studious *(stew-dee-us)* *(adj)* If you are studious, you like to study, and work carefully. **studiousness** *(n)*, **studiously** *(adv)*.

study studies studying studied
1 *(n)* an office or room where someone works.
2 *(v)* to spend time learning a subject or skill. **study** *(n)*.
3 *(v)* to examine something carefully. *Amanda studied the football results.*

stuff stuffing stuffed
1 *(n)* a substance, or a material.
2 *(v)* to fill something tightly. *James stuffed his pockets with conkers.*
3 *(v)* to put something into something else. *Don't forget to stuff the turkey.*
4 If you are **stuffed up**, you have a cold and cannot breathe through your nose.

stuffing *(n)* a filling, especially a mixture of chopped food that you cook inside a chicken, pepper, etc.

stuffy stuffier stuffiest
1 *(adj)* A **stuffy** room has stale air in it. **stuffiness** *(n)*.
2 *(adj)* A **stuffy** person is prim and easily shocked. **stuffily** *(adv)*.

stumble stumbling stumbled
1 *(v)* to trip up, or to walk in an unsteady way.
2 *(v)* to make mistakes when you are talking or reading aloud.

stump
1 *(n)* the part that is left when a tree is cut down.
2 *(n)* one of the three wooden sticks of a cricket wicket. *See* **cricket**.

stumpy stumpier stumpiest *(adj)* short and thick. *A stumpy crayon.*

stun stunning stunned *(v)* If you are stunned, you are shocked, dazed, or knocked out.

stunning *(adj)* beautiful, or amazing. **stunningly** *(adv)*.

stunt stunting stunted
1 *(n)* a dangerous trick or act.
2 *(v)* to stop the proper growth of something. **stunted** *(adj)*.
3 **publicity stunt** *(n)* a trick to get public attention for a company, organization, event, etc.
4 *(n)* A **stunt man** takes the place of an actor to perform the dangerous actions in a film.

stupendous *(adj)* very good, or very big. **stupendously** *(adv)*.

stupid stupider stupidest *(adj)* silly, or unintelligent. **stupidity** *(n)*, **stupidly** *(adv)*.

sturdy sturdier sturdiest *(adj)* strong and firm. *A sturdy tree.*

stutter stuttering stuttered *(v)* If you **stutter** when you speak, you repeat the first sound of a word before you manage to say the whole word. **stutter** *(n)*.

sty sties
1 *(n)* a pen in which pigs live.
2 **sty** or **stye** *(n)* a red, painful swelling on your eyelid.

style styling styled
1 *(n)* a way of doing something, such as writing, dressing, building, etc.
2 *(n)* If you do something with **style**, you do it smartly or elegantly. **stylish** *(adj)*, **stylishly** *(adv)*.
3 *(v)* to arrange or design something. *The model's hair was styled by Philippe of Paris.* **style** *(n)*.
4 *(n)* the part of a flower which extends from the ovary and supports the stigma. *See* **flower**.

subaqua *(sub-ak-wa)* *(adj)* to do with underwater sports, such as scuba diving. *Subaqua swimming.*

subconscious *(n)* part of your mind that influences you without your being aware of it. **subconsciously** *(adv)*.

subcontinent (n) a large area of land that is smaller than a continent. *The Indian subcontinent.*

subdivide subdividing subdivided (v) to divide something into smaller, even parts. *I cut the apple in half, then subdivided each half into quarters.* subdivision (n).

subdued
1 (adj) unusually quiet and restrained.
2 (adj) not bright. *Subdued lighting.*

subject subjecting subjected
1 (sub-jekt) (n) the topic of a book, newspaper article, conversation, etc.
2 (sub-jekt) (n) an area of study, such as geography or mathematics.
3 (sub-jekt) (n) A **subject** of a king or queen is someone who lives in their country.
4 (sub-jekt) If you are **subject to** something, you are likely to be affected by it. *Laura is subject to terrible colds.*
5 (sub-jekt) (v) If you **subject** someone to something, you force them to suffer it. *Our neighbours subjected us to loud music all night.*

subjective (adj) to do with opinions rather than actual facts. *Donna's essay on animal rights was purely subjective.* subjectively (adv).

submarine (n) a ship that can travel under the water for long periods.

submerge submerging submerged (v) to put something under water.

submit submitting submitted
1 (v) to hand in, or put something forward. *Have you submitted your essay? Can I submit a plan to the committee?* submission (n).
2 (v) to agree to obey something. *I submitted to their decision.* submission (n).

subordinate
1 (adj) less important.
2 (n) someone who is low in rank, and can be told what to do.

subscribe subscribing subscribed
1 (v) to pay money regularly for a paper or magazine. subscriber (n), subscription (n).
2 (v) to give money to a charity or an appeal.

subsequent (adj) coming after, or following. *Felix lost the first match, but played better in subsequent ones.* subsequently (adv).

subside subsiding subsided
1 (v) If the ground **subsides**, it caves in or sinks down. subsidence (n).
2 (v) to become less. *Gradually, the noise subsided.*

subsidiary (adj) minor, or less important. *A subsidiary role.*

subsidy subsidies (n) money that a government or organization contributes in order to make goods cheaper. subsidize (v).

substance
1 (n) a material. Objects, powders, and liquids are all substances.
2 (n) the important part of something. *The substance of an argument.*

substantial (adj) solid, large, or important. substantially (adv).

substitute (n) something or someone used instead of another, such as a footballer who plays when another player is injured. substitution (n), substitute (v).

subtitle
1 (n) the second, less important title of a book, film, etc.
2 subtitles (plural n) the translated words that appear on the screen when a foreign film is shown.

subtle (sut-ul) subtler subtlest
1 (adj) delicate, or not easy to notice. *A subtle flavour.* subtly (adv).
2 (adj) using clever or disguised methods. *A subtle plan.* subtlety (n), subtly (adv).

subtract subtracting subtracted (v) to take one number away from another. *If you subtract four from six, you are left with two.* subtraction (n).

suburb (n) an area of housing at the edge of a large town or city. suburbia (n), suburban (adj).

subway
1 (n) a covered path for pedestrians under a road or railway.
2 (n) (US) an underground railway network (underground, UK).

succeed (suk-seed) succeeding succeeded
1 (v) to manage to do something. *Bill succeeded in fixing the car.*
2 (v) to take over from someone in an important position. *Travis succeeded his father as company director.*
3 (v) to do well, or to get what you want. success (n), successful (adj).

succulent (suk-yu-lent) (adj) juicy. *A succulent peach.* succulence (n).

suck sucking sucked
1 (v) to draw something into your mouth, using your tongue and lips. *George still sucks his thumb.* suck (n).
2 (v) to pull strongly. *The vacuum cleaner sucked up my ring.*

suction (n) the creation of a vacuum, so that air or liquid is sucked in, or so that two surfaces stick together.

sudden (adj) quick, or unexpected. suddenness (n), suddenly (adv).

sue suing sued (v) If you **sue** someone, you take them to court to make them pay for the harm that they have done to you.

suede (swayd) (n) soft leather with a smooth, velvet-like surface.

suet (n) a dry fat that is used in cooking.

suffer suffering suffered
1 (v) to experience something bad, such as unhappiness or pain. sufferer (n), suffering (n).
2 (v) If you **suffer** from an illness, you get it often, or have it for a long time. *Jacob suffers from hay fever.*

sufficient (suf-ish-unt) (adj) If something is **sufficient**, it is enough or adequate. *We left sufficient food for the cats while we were away.* sufficiently (adv).

suffix suffixes (n) a group of letters added at the end of a word, to create a new but related word. For example, "ness", "ly" and "ful" are all suffixes. *The suffix "ness" is used in "sadness" and "happiness".*

suffocate suffocating suffocated
1 (v) If someone **suffocates**, they die because they cannot breathe. suffocation (n).
2 (v) to stop someone breathing, so that they die.

sugar
1 (n) a sweet substance that comes from plants and is used in foods and drinks. sugary (adj).
2 sugar beet (n) a root vegetable from which sugar is produced.
3 sugar cane (n) a tall, tropical plant that has sugar in its stems.

sugar beet

suggest suggesting suggested (v) to put something forward as an idea or a possibility. *I suggested going to China for our next holiday.* suggestion (n).

suicide (soo-iss-ide) (n) If someone commits **suicide**, they kill themselves. suicidal (adj), suicidally (adv).

suit suiting suited
1 (n) a set of smart, matching clothes, usually a man's jacket and trousers.
2 (n) one of the four types of playing card in a pack of cards. The four suits are clubs, diamonds, hearts, and spades.
3 (v) to be acceptable and convenient. *Does Wednesday suit you?*

4 *(v)* If a hairstyle or an outfit **suits** you, it makes you look good.

suitable *(adj)* If something is **suitable**, it is right for a particular purpose. **suitability** *(n)*, **suitably** *(adv)*.

suitcase *(n)* a container used for carrying clothes when you travel.

suite *(sweet)*
1 *(n)* a set of matching furniture.
2 *(n)* a set of rooms in a hotel.

sulk sulking sulked *(v)* If you **sulk**, you are angry and silent. **sulk** *(n)*, **sulky** *(adj)*.

sullen *(adj)* gloomy, silent, and bad-tempered. **sullenly** *(adv)*.

sulphur *(sul-fur)*
1 *(n)* a yellow chemical element, used in gunpowder and matches. See **mineral**.
2 **sulphur dioxide** *(n)* a poisonous gas found in some industrial waste, that causes air pollution.

sultan *(n)* an emperor or ruler of a Muslim country.

sultana
1 *(n)* a small, brown, dried fruit, made from grapes.
2 *(n)* the wife or daughter of a sultan.

sultry sultrier sultriest
1 *(adj)* If the weather is **sultry**, it is hot and humid. **sultriness** *(n)*.
2 *(adj)* If a person is **sultry**, they are passionate or sexy. **sultriness** *(n)*.

sum summing summed
1 *(n)* an amount of money.
2 *(n)* an arithmetic problem.
3 *(v)* If you **sum up**, you go through the main points of what has been said, in order to reach a conclusion.
4 **sum total** *(n)* the whole, or the final amount. *What is the sum total of your savings?*

summary summaries *(n)* a short statement of the main points of something that has been said or written. **summarize** *(v)*.

summer *(n)* the season between spring and autumn, when the weather is warmest. **summery** *(adj)*.

summit
1 *(n)* the top of a mountain.
2 *(n)* a meeting of leaders from different countries.

summon summoning summoned
1 *(v)* to call or request someone to come. *Summon the next witness.*
2 *(v)* If you **summon up** courage, you make a great effort to be brave.

summons summonses *(n)* an order to appear in court. **summons** *(v)*.

sun sunning sunned
1 **Sun** *(n)* the star that the Earth moves around, and that gives us light and warmth. See **planet**.
2 *(n)* light and warmth from the Sun. *Don't stay too long in the sun.*
3 *(v)* If you **sun** yourself, you sit or lie in the sunlight.

Sun
(cutaway)

corona
(outer part of
Sun's atmosphere)

chromosphere
(thin layer of gases)

photosphere
(Sun's surface)

sunspot
(cooler patch
on Sun's
surface)

convection
zone
(carries heat
outwards)

prominence
(gas stream)

radiation zone
(transmits heat
from Sun's core)

sunbathe sunbathing sunbathed *(v)* to sit or lie in sunlight in order to make your body suntanned.

sunburn *(n)* sore, red skin caused by staying in sunlight too long. **sunburnt** *(adj)*.

sundial *(n)* an instrument that shows the time by using the Sun's light. A pointer casts a shadow that moves slowly around a flat, marked dial.

sundial

sunglasses *(plural n)* dark glasses that protect your eyes from sunlight.

sunrise *(n)* the time in the morning when the Sun appears above the horizon.

sunset *(n)* the time in the evening when the Sun sinks below the horizon.

sunshine *(n)* the light from the Sun.

sunstroke *(n)* an illness, caused by staying in hot sunlight for too long, that gives you a fever and a headache.

suntan *(n)* If you have a **suntan**, your skin is brown because you have been in hot sunlight. **suntanned** *(adj)*.

super *(adj)* very good.

superb *(adj)* excellent, or magnificent. **superbly** *(adv)*.

superficial *(soo-per-fish-ul)*
1 *(adj)* on the surface. *A superficial cut.* **superficially** *(adv)*.
2 *(adj)* not deep, or not thorough. *My interest in music is only superficial.* **superficially** *(adv)*.

superfluous *(soo-per-floo-uss)* *(adj)* more than is needed or wanted. *A superfluous remark.*

superintendent
1 *(n)* someone in charge of something. *A swimming pool superintendent.*
2 *(n)* a senior police officer.

superior
1 *(adj)* better. *Daisy thinks that butter is superior to margarine.*
2 *(n)* someone who is in a more important position than you.
3 *(adj)* If someone acts in a **superior** way, they behave as if they are better than other people. **superiority** *(n)*.

superlative *(soo-per-la-tiv)*
1 *(adj)* **Superlative** adjectives and adverbs are used to describe the greatest or highest degree of things or actions. "Biggest" is the superlative of "big" and "most quickly" is the superlative of "quickly". **superlative** *(n)*.
2 *(adj)* very good. **superlatively** *(adv)*.

supermarket *(n)* a large shop that sells food and other household items.

supernatural *(adj)* If something is **supernatural**, it involves things that natural laws cannot explain, such as ghosts. **supernaturally** *(adv)*.

supersonic *(adj)* faster than the speed of sound. *The picture shows Concorde, which flies at supersonic speeds.*

Concorde

superstitious *(adj)* People who are **superstitious** are afraid that something bad will happen if they do not follow certain rules. **superstition** *(n)*.

supervise supervising supervised *(v)* to watch over, and be in charge of, someone while they do something. *Mum usually supervises my homework.* **supervision** *(n)*.

supper
1 *(n)* an evening meal.
2 *(n)* a snack that you eat before you go to bed.

supple suppler supplest (adj) If you are **supple**, you can move or bend your body easily. **suppleness** (n).

supplement supplementing supplemented
1 (n) an additional piece. This newspaper has a colour supplement. **supplementary** (adj).
2 (v) to add to something. Rhonda supplements her diet with extra vitamins.

supplies (plural n) food and equipment taken on an expedition.

supply supplies supplying supplied (v) to provide someone with what they want or need. Ali supplies me with magazines. **supply** (n), **supplier** (n).

support supporting supported
1 (v) to hold something up in order to keep it from falling. **support** (n).
2 (v) to help and encourage someone. **support** (n), **supportive** (adj).
3 (v) to believe in someone or something. Sally supports the Green Party. **support** (n), **supporter** (n).

suppose supposing supposed (v) to think that something is true, or to expect something. I suppose you're right. I suppose that Justin will be late.

suppress suppresses suppressing suppressed
1 (v) to stop something happening. The dictator suppressed the revolution. **suppression** (n).
2 (v) to hide or control something. Carly tried to suppress her giggles.

supreme (adj) the greatest, best, or most powerful. **supremacy** (n), **supremely** (adv).

sure surer surest (adj) certain and definite. Are you sure that he's here?

surf surfing surfed
1 (n) the spray produced by waves as they break on the shore.
2 (v) to ride on breaking waves, using a surfboard. **surfer** (n), **surfing** (n).
3 (v) to move from one Web site to another on the Internet. **surfing** (n).

surfing

surface surfacing surfaced
1 (n) the outer face or top of something.
2 (v) to come to the surface, or to appear. The submarine surfaced when it was hit. The lost coins surfaced after several years.

surfboard (n) a light, narrow board which surfers stand on to ride breaking waves. See **surf**.

surge surging surged (v) to rush forward or upward. The crowd surged forward as the gate was opened. **surge** (n).

surgeon (sur-jun) (n) a doctor who performs operations.

surgery (sur-jer-ee) surgeries
1 (n) a place where you go to see a doctor, dentist, vet, etc.
2 (n) medical treatment that involves cutting the patient open and repairing, removing, or replacing body parts. **surgical** (adj).

surly surlier surliest (adj) If someone is **surly**, they are bad-tempered and unfriendly.

surname (n) a person's last name or family name.

surpass surpasses surpassing surpassed (v) to do better than you have done before. Today, Patrick surpassed his previous record.

surplus (adj) spare, or more than what is needed. The charity shop is asking for any surplus clothes.

surprise surprising surprised (v) to do or say something unexpected. Alvin's outburst surprised us all. **surprise** (n), **surprising** (adj).

surrender surrendering surrendered (v) to give up, or to admit that you are beaten in a fight or battle. **surrender** (n).

surround surrounding surrounded (v) to be on every side of something. Robin Hood and his men surrounded Nottingham Castle.

surroundings (plural n) the things around something or someone. People work better in cheerful surroundings.

survey surveying surveyed
1 (sur-vay) (n) a report on what people think about something. We are producing a survey of reactions to the new shopping centre.
2 (sur-vay) (v) to look at the whole of a scene or situation. Mum surveyed the mess with horror.
3 (sur-vay) (v) to measure an area in order to make a map or plan. **survey** (sur-vay) (n), **surveyor** (n).

survive surviving survived (v) to stay alive, especially after some dangerous event. Only one passenger survived the car crash. **survival** (n), **survivor** (n).

sushi

sushi (soo-shee) (n) a Japanese food made from raw fish or seafood, pressed into rice. The picture shows sushi packed in bamboo leaves.

suspect suspecting suspected
1 (suss-pekt) (v) to think that someone should not be trusted. **suspicion** (n).
2 (suss-pekt) (v) to think that something is wrong with a situation. The doctor suspected something more serious than flu. **suspicion** (n), **suspect** (suss-pekt) (adj).
3 (suss-pekt) (n) someone thought to be responsible for a crime.

suspend suspending suspended
1 (v) to hang something downwards. Phoebe suspended a banner from her bedroom window.
2 (v) to stop something for a short time. Work was suspended for the holidays.
3 (v) to punish someone by stopping them taking part in an activity for a short while. Sophie was suspended from school for a week. **suspension** (n).

suspenders (plural n) elastic straps attached to a belt and worn to hold up women's stockings.

suspense (n) an anxious and uncertain feeling, caused by having to wait to see what happens.

suspicious
1 (adj) If you feel **suspicious**, you think that something is wrong. **suspicion** (n).
2 (adj) If something is or looks **suspicious**, it makes people think that something is wrong.

sustain sustaining sustained
1 (v) to keep something going. Crispin sustained a conversation with his cat for over ten minutes.
2 (v) If something **sustains** you, it gives you energy. The hot soup sustained the walkers for hours.
3 (v) to suffer something. Tracey sustained some nasty bruises.

swagger swaggering swaggered (v) to walk or act in a conceited way.

swallow swallowing swallowed
1 (v) to make food or drink pass down your throat.
2 (n) a migrating bird with long wings and a forked tail.

swallow

swamp (n) an area of wet, marshy ground.

swan *(n)* a water bird with white feathers, webbed feet, and a long neck. *The picture shows a female swan with her young.*

swan and cygnets

swank swanking swanked *(v)* *(informal)* to show off. *Shona was swanking about her new bike.* **swanky** *(adj)*.

swap or **swop** swapping swapped *(v)* to exchange one thing for another. **swap** *(n)*.

swarm swarming swarmed
1 *(v)* When bees **swarm**, they fly together in a thick mass. **swarm** *(n)*.
2 *(adj)* If a place is **swarming** with people, it is very crowded.

swarthy swarthier swarthiest *(adj)* A **swarthy** person has dark skin.

swastika *(n)* the emblem of the Nazi party during Hitler's rule in Germany.

swat swatting swatted *(v)* to kill a fly with a quick blow.

sway swaying swayed *(v)* to move or swing from side to side. *The corn swayed in the wind.*

swear swearing swore sworn
1 *(v)* to use rude words.
2 *(v)* to make a formal, solemn promise. *I swear to tell the truth.*

sweat sweating sweated *(v)* When you **sweat**, you let out moisture through the pores in your skin, because you are hot or anxious. **sweat** *(n)*.

sweater *(n)* a knitted piece of clothing that you wear on the top half of your body.

sweatshirt *(n)* a collarless, casual top with long sleeves.

sweep sweeping swept
1 *(v)* to clean up somewhere, using a brush.
2 *(v)* to move rapidly and forcefully. *The duchess swept into the room.*
3 *(n)* someone whose job is to sweep chimneys.

sweeping *(adj)* Something that is **sweeping** affects many things or people. *Sweeping changes in the firm have resulted in many job losses.*

sweet sweeter sweetest
1 *(n)* a small piece of food, made with sugar or chocolate.

2 *(adj)* Food that is **sweet** has a sugary flavour, not a savoury one.
3 *(adj)* pleasant, or cute. **sweetly** *(adv)*.

sweetcorn *(n)* the juicy, yellow seeds of the maize plant, that are eaten as a vegetable.

swell swelling swelled swollen
1 *(v)* to grow fatter. *Jake's knee swelled where he had knocked it.* **swollen** *(adj)*.
2 *(adj)* *(US)* wonderful.

sweltering *(adj)* When the weather is **sweltering**, it is very hot indeed. **swelter** *(v)*.

swerve swerving swerved *(v)* to change direction quickly, usually to avoid something.

swift swifter swiftest
1 *(adj)* fast, or rapid. **swiftness** *(n)*, **swiftly** *(adv)*.
2 *(n)* a migrating bird with long, narrow wings, similar to a swallow. *See* **bird**.

swig swigging swigged *(v)* *(informal)* to drink in large gulps, usually from a bottle, flask, etc.

swim swimming swam swum *(v)* to propel yourself through water, using your arms and legs. **swimmer** *(n)*.

swimsuit *(n)* a costume worn by a woman or girl when she goes swimming.

swindle swindling swindled *(v)* to cheat someone out of something, especially money. **swindle** *(n)*, **swindler** *(n)*.

swine swine
1 *(n)* *(old-fashioned)* a pig.
2 *(n)* a very unpleasant person.

swing swinging swung
1 *(v)* to move from side to side.
2 *(n)* a piece of play equipment that you sit on and move backwards and forwards.
3 *(n)* the amount by which votes move from one party to another. *There was a swing of 20% against the government.*

swing-wing *(adj)* A swing-wing aircraft has movable wings that can be swept back after takeoff to allow the plane to fly faster.

swipe swiping swiped
1 *(v)* *(informal)* to hit something or somebody hard. **swipe** *(n)*.
2 *(v)* to run a plastic credit card through the groove of a machine which reads it.
3 *(v)* *(slang)* to steal something. *Max swiped my chocolate!*

swirl swirling swirled *(v)* to move in circles. *The water swirled around the plughole.*

switch switches switching switched
1 *(v)* to exchange one thing for another.
2 *(v)* to change from one thing to another. *Miles switched courses.*
3 *(v)* to turn on a piece of electrical equipment. **switch** *(n)*.

switchboard *(n)* the control centre for a telephone system, where an operator can put calls through to different people and places.

swivel swivelling swivelled *(v)* to turn or rotate on the spot.

swoop swooping swooped *(v)* When a bird **swoops**, it pounces on another creature by flying downwards suddenly

swop *see* **swap**.

sword *(sord)* *(n)* a weapon with a handle and a long, sharp blade. Swords were used in the past for man-to-man fighting and are still used in ceremonies such as coronations.

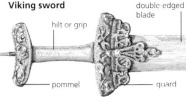

Viking sword — double-edged blade — hilt or grip — pommel — guard

swot swotting swotted
1 *(v)* *(informal)* to study very hard, often for an examination.
2 *(n)* *(informal)* a name that other people give to someone who studies extremely hard.

syllable *(n)* one of the sounds in a word. *The word America has four syllables: A-me-ri-ca.*

syllabus syllabuses or syllabi *(n)* a programme of work that must be covered for a particular subject or exam.

symbol *(n)* a design or object that represents something else. *A dove is a symbol of peace.* **symbolic** *(adj)*, **symbolically** *(adv)*.

symmetrical *(adj)* One half of a **symmetrical** shape exactly mirrors the other. **symmetry** *(n)*, **symmetrically** *(adv)*.

symmetrical shapes

sympathy sympathies
1 (n) the understanding and sharing of other people's troubles. *After her accident, Polly's friends gave her lots of sympathy.* **sympathize** (v), **sympathetic** (adj), **sympathetically** (adv).
2 If you are **in sympathy** with somebody's aims or actions, you agree with them and support them.

symphony symphonies (n) a long piece of music for an orchestra, usually in four parts, called movements. **symphonic** (adj).

symptom (n) something that shows that you have an illness. *A rash is one of the symptoms of measles.*

synagogue (sin-a-gog) (n) a building used by Jews for worship.

synchronize or **synchronise** (sin-kron-ize) synchronizing synchronized (v) to make things happen at exactly the same time. *Let's synchronize our watches before we arrange a meeting time.* **synchronization** (n).

syncopate syncopating syncopated (v) to stress beats in a piece of music that are not normally stressed. **syncopation** (n).

synonym (sin-oh-nim) (n) a word that means the same, or nearly the same, as another word. *Rapid is a synonym of quick.*

synopsis synopses (n) a brief summary of a longer piece of writing.

syntax (n) the rules of grammar that govern the way that words are put together to make phrases and sentences.

synthesizer or **synthesiser** (n) an electronic keyboard instrument that can make a variety of sounds, and can imitate other musical instruments.

synthetic (adj) Something that is synthetic is man-made or artificial. **synthetically** (adv).

syphon see **siphon**.

syringe (n) a tube with a plunger and a hollow needle, used for giving injections and taking blood samples.

syrup (n) a sweet, sticky, substance made from sugar. *Maple syrup.* **syrupy** (adj).

system
1 (n) a group of things which exist or work together in an organized way. *The Solar System. A heating system.*
2 (n) a way of organizing or arranging things. *The education system.* **systematic** (adj), **systematically** (adv).

Tt

tab
1 (n) a small piece of paper, metal, etc. that you can hold or pull. *Most drink cans have ring tabs.*
2 (informal) If you **keep tabs on** someone, you watch them closely to see what they are doing.
3 (informal) If you **pick up the tab**, you pay the bill in a café or restaurant.

tabby tabbies (n) a cat with a grey or brownish-yellow striped coat. See **cat**.

tabernacle (tab-er-nak-ul)
1 (n) a building used for worship.
2 (n) a container or shrine for holy objects.

table
1 (n) a piece of furniture with a flat top resting on legs.
2 (n) a chart showing figures or information.
3 **table manners** (n) the way you behave when you are eating.
4 **tables** (plural n) lists of numbers multiplied by other numbers.

tablecloth (n) a piece of material used to protect or decorate a table.

tablespoon (n) a large spoon that you use as a measure in cooking, or to serve food. **tablespoonful** (n).

tablet
1 (n) a small, solid piece of medicine that you swallow.
2 (n) a piece of stone with writing carved on it.

table tennis (n) a game for two or four players, who hit a small, light ball over a low net on a table, using round bats.

tabloid (n) a newspaper printed on small pages, with large headlines and lots of pictures. **tabloid** (adj).

taboo (adj) If a subject is **taboo**, you may upset or offend people if you talk about it. *Death is a taboo subject in some societies.* **taboo** (n).

tabular (adj) set out in the form of a table or chart. *Please present your results in tabular form.* **tabulate** (v).

tacit (tass-it) (adj) If something is **tacit**, it is understood or agreed without being stated. *My parents have given their tacit agreement to my staying up late.* **tacitly** (adv).

taciturn (adj) If someone is **taciturn**, they are quiet and shy and do not talk much. **taciturnly** (adv).

tack tacking tacked
1 (n) a small, sharp nail. **tack** (v).
2 (v) to attach or fix something using tacks. *We tacked a picture to the wall.*
3 (v) If you **tack** material, you sew it loosely before doing it neatly. **tack** (n).
4 (v) to sail in a zig-zag course against the wind. **tack** (n).
5 (n) equipment that you need to ride a horse, such as a saddle and bridle. *The picture shows the main parts of a bridle and saddle. The horse on the right wears the western-style tack which is popular in the USA.*

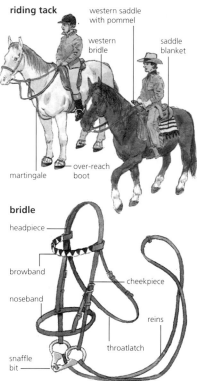

riding tack

western saddle with pommel
western bridle
saddle blanket
martingale
over-reach boot

bridle
headpiece
browband
cheekpiece
noseband
snaffle bit
throatlatch
reins

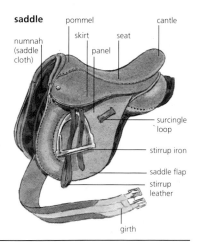

saddle
numnah (saddle cloth)
pommel
skirt
seat
panel
cantle
surcingle loop
stirrup iron
saddle flap
stirrup leather
girth

tackle tackling tackled
1 (v) If you **tackle** someone in a ball game, you try to get the ball away from them. **tackle** (n).
2 (v) to deal with a problem or difficulty. *We must tackle the litter problem.*
3 (n) the equipment that you need to do something. *Fishing tackle.*

tacky tackier tackiest
1 (adj) slightly sticky. *The paint is still tacky on this door.*
2 (adj) (informal) If something is tacky, it looks cheap and tasteless. *The shop was full of tacky ornaments.*

tact (n) If you handle a person or situation with **tact**, you are sensitive and do not upset anyone. **tactful** (adj), **tactfully** (adv).

tactics (plural n) plans or methods to win a game or battle. **tactical** (adj), **tactically** (adv).

tag tagging tagged
1 (n) a label. *A price tag.*
2 (n) a children's chasing game.
3 (v) If you **tag along** with someone, you go with them. *Henry wasn't part of the gang; he just tagged along.*

tail tailing tailed
1 (n) the long part at the end of an animal's body.
2 (n) something that is like a tail. *We joined the tail of the procession.*
3 (v) (informal) If you **tail** someone, you follow them closely. **tail** (n).
4 (v) If something **tails off**, it gets less or weakens. *Misha's enthusiasm for the project has started to tail off.*

tailor tailoring tailored
1 (n) someone who makes or alters clothes, especially men's suits.
2 (v) to design or alter something so that it suits someone perfectly. *The computer company will tailor the system to suit our needs.*

take taking took taken
1 (v) to move or carry something. *Take your plate into the kitchen.*
2 (v) to get, seize, or capture something. *Ken's taken my pen!*
3 (v) to accept something. *Do you take credit cards?*
4 (v) to use something. *The camera takes most types of film.*
5 (v) If you **take after** someone in your family, you look like them or have the same characteristics as them.
6 **take in** (v) (informal) If somebody **takes you in**, you believe the lies that they tell you.

takeaway
1 (n) a restaurant selling meals that you take and eat somewhere else.

2 (n) a meal that you buy from a takeaway restaurant.

takeoff (n) the beginning of a flight, when the aircraft leaves the ground. **take off** (v).

takeover (n) If there is a **takeover** of a company, another company buys enough shares in it to control the company. **take over** (v).

takings (plural n) money received from customers in a shop, café, etc.

talcum powder (n) a fine, white powder that you can use to dry your body or to make it smell nice.

tale
1 (n) (old-fashioned) a story.
2 (n) a lie, or a complaint about someone. *Don't tell tales!*

talent (n) an ability, or a skill. **talented** (adj).

talk talking talked
1 (v) to speak.
2 (n) a conversation.
3 (n) a speech, or a lecture.

talkative (adj) If you are talkative, you talk a lot.

tall taller tallest (adj) high, or higher than usual. *A tall tree. A tall woman.*

tally tallies tallying tallied
1 (n) a count, or a record. *Keep a tally of what I owe you.*
2 (v) to add up or match. *These figures don't quite tally.*

talon (n) a sharp claw.

tame tamer tamest
1 (adj) A **tame** animal is not wild, and can live with people. **tame** (v).
2 (adj) not very exciting. **tamely** (adv).

tamper tampering tampered (v) to interfere with something, so that it becomes damaged or broken.

tampon (n) a plug of soft material that some women and girls wear inside their vagina to absorb the flow of blood during their periods.

tan tanning tanned
1 (n) a light, yellow-brown colour.
2 (n) If you have a **tan**, your skin has become darker because you have been out in the sun a lot. **tan** (v).
3 (v) Animal skin is **tanned** to make it into leather. **tanner** (n), **tannery** (n).

tandem (n) a bicycle for two people.

tandoori (n) an Indian method of cooking meat, bread, etc. by baking it in a clay oven.

tangent
1 (n) a straight line that touches the edge of a curve in one place. *See* **circle**.

2 If you **go off at a tangent**, you start talking about something different from the main discussion.

tangerine (n) a small, sweet orange, that you can peel easily.

tangle tangling tangled (v) to make things twisted and muddled. **tangle** (n).

tank
1 (n) a large container for liquid or gas. *See* **aquarium**.
2 (n) an armoured vehicle used by soldiers. *See* **armoured vehicle**.

tanker (n) a ship or lorry that carries gas or liquid. *The picture shows an oil tanker.*

pipes for cleaning cargo tanks
bridge
helipad
lifeboat
living accommodation, engine room, and control rooms
pipes for loading ballast water
anchor
oil tanker

tantrum (n) a fit of temper.

tap tapping tapped
1 (n) a piece of equipment used to control the flow of a liquid.
2 (v) to hit or knock something gently. **tap** (n).
3 (v) to listen to a telephone conversation, using a secret device. **tap** (n).
4 **tap-dancing** (n) dancing with shoes that have metal plates on their soles, that make a clicking noise. **tap-dancer** (n), **tap-dance** (v).

tape taping taped
1 (n) a thin strip of material, paper, plastic, etc. *A name tape.*
2 (v) to record sound or pictures on audio or video tape.
3 (n) a long piece of magnetic ribbon used for recording sound or pictures, usually contained in a plastic case or cassette. *The picture shows an audio tape.*

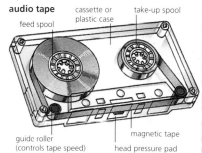

audio tape
cassette or plastic case
take-up spool
feed spool
guide roller (controls tape speed)
magnetic tape
head pressure pad

tape measure *(n)* a long, thin strip of material or steel, marked in centimetres or inches so that you can measure things with it.

taper tapering tapered
1 *(v)* to become narrower at one end.
2 **taper off** *(v)* to become gradually smaller.
3 *(n)* a wooden strip or thin candle used for carrying a flame. *We lit the candles with a taper.*

tape recorder *(n)* an electrical machine that you use to play or record music or sound. **tape-record** *(v)*.

tapestry tapestries *(n)* a heavy piece of cloth with pictures or patterns woven into it. *The picture shows a tapestry being sewn.*

tapestry

single canvas (made from hemp or linen thread)

tapestry wool

tapestry needle with rounded head

tar *(n)* a thick, black, sticky substance, used for making roads.

tarantula *(n)* a large, hairy, poisonous spider. *See* **spider**.

target targeting targeted
1 *(n)* something that you aim at or attack. **target** *(v)*.
2 *(n)* a round object marked with circles, which an archer aims his arrows at.
3 *(v)* If you **target** something, you concentrate on it. *The publicity campaign is targeting a very young audience.*

tariff
1 *(n)* a tax on imports and exports.
2 *(n)* a list of prices in a hotel or restaurant.

tarmac *(n)* a mixture of tar and small stones that is used on road surfaces. *Tarmac is short for Tarmacadam.* **tarmac** *(v)*.

tarnish tarnishes tarnishing tarnished *(v)* If something **tarnishes**, it becomes duller or less bright.

tarpaulin *(n)* a heavy, waterproof sheet.

tart tarter tartest
1 *(n)* an open fruit pie or pastry. *An apple tart.*
2 *(adj)* If food is **tart**, it tastes sour or sharp. **tartness** *(n)*.
3 *(adj)* A **tart** reply is unkind or sarcastic. **tartly** *(adv)*.

tartan *(n)* woollen cloth patterned with squares of different colours. Tartan is used especially for Scottish kilts.

task *(n)* a job, or a duty.

task force *(n)* a team, especially of soldiers, formed to deal with a problem.

tassel *(n)* a bunch of threads tied at one end, used as a decoration on clothing, furniture, etc. **tasselled** *(adj)*.

taste tasting tasted
1 *(n)* Your sense of **taste** tells you what food you are eating.
2 *(n)* The **taste** of a food is whether it is sweet, sour, bitter, salty, etc. *This diagram of a human tongue shows the areas where different tastes are detected most strongly.* **taste** *(v)*, **tasty** *(adj)*.
3 *(n)* If you have good **taste**, you make good choices of furnishings, clothes, etc. **tasteful** *(adj)*.
4 *(v)* to try a bit of food or drink to see if you like it. **taste** *(n)*.

areas of taste (human tongue)

bitter

sour

sour

salt sweet and sour

tattered *(adj)* old and torn, or scruffy. *Tattered jeans.*

tattoo *(n)* a picture or words that have been permanently printed on somebody's skin, using ink and needles. **tattooist** *(n)*, **tattoo** *(v)*.

tatty tattier tattiest *(adj)* shabby and worn out. **tattily** *(adv)*.

taunt taunting taunted *(v)* to try to make someone angry or upset by teasing them. *The gang taunted George with jokes about his size.* **taunt** *(n)*.

taut *(adj)* stretched tight. *A taut rope.*

tavern *(n)* *(old-fashioned)* a pub, or an inn.

tawny *(n)* a light, sandy-brown colour. **tawny** *(adj)*.

tax taxes *(n)* money that has to be paid to the government for public services. **taxation** *(n)*, **tax** *(v)*.

taxi taxiing taxied
1 *(n)* a car with a driver who you pay to take you where you want to go.
2 *(v)* When planes **taxi**, they move along the ground.

taxing *(adj)* If something is **taxing**, it is demanding and puts a strain on you. *A taxing job.*

tea
1 *(n)* a drink made from the leaves of a tea plant. *The picture shows tea leaves being picked on a hillside plantation in Southern India.*
2 *(n)* a light afternoon meal.
3 *(n)* an evening meal, or supper.

tea-picking

teach teaches teaching taught *(v)* to give a lesson, or show someone how to do something. *Joel taught me how to swim.* **teacher** *(n)*.

team teaming teamed
1 *(n)* a group of people who work together or play a sport together. *A hockey team.* **teamwork** *(n)*.
2 *(v)* If two people **team up**, they join together to do something.

tear tearing tore torn
1 *(rhymes with dear)* *(n)* a drop of liquid that comes from your eye. **tearful** *(adj)*.
2 *(rhymes with dare)* *(n)* a rip in a piece of paper or material.
3 *(rhymes with dare)* *(v)* to pull one part of something away from the rest. *Ben has torn his trousers.*
4 *(rhymes with dare)* *(v)* to move very fast. *Louise tore down the street.*

tease teasing teased *(v)* to mock someone by saying unkind things to them.

teaspoon *(n)* a small spoon that you use for stirring drinks, or as a measure in cooking. **teaspoonful** *(n)*.

teat
1 *(n)* a nipple of an animal, from which its babies can suck milk.
2 *(n)* a rubber top for a baby's bottle, with a small hole in the top of it.

technical
1 *(adj)* to do with science, machines, industry, etc. **technically** *(adv)*.
2 *(adj)* using words that only experts understand. *Once we started to talk about computers, the conversation became very technical.*

technician *(n)* someone who looks after scientific equipment, or does practical laboratory work.

technique *(tek-neek)* *(n)* a skilful way of doing something.

technology technologies *(n)* the use of science to do practical things. **technological** *(adj)*.

teddy bear

teddy bear
(n) a stuffed toy bear made from soft, furry material. *The teddy bear shown here was made in the Steiff factory in Germany.*

teddy bear

tedious *(tee-dee-us) (adj)* long and boring. **tediously** *(adv).*

teeming *(adj)* If a place is **teeming**, it is full of people or animals.

teenage *(adj)* to do with people aged from 13 to 19. **teenager** *(n).*

teens *(plural n)* the years between 13 and 19. *Tanya is in her teens.*

teepee *see* **tepee**.

tee shirt *see* **T-shirt**.

teeth *(plural n)* the white, bone-like structures in your mouth that you use for biting and chewing food. *The diagram shows a lower set of adult teeth.*

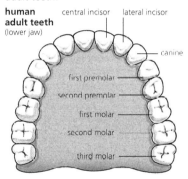

human adult teeth (lower jaw)

central incisor   lateral incisor

canine

first premolar

second premolar

first molar

second molar

third molar

teething
1 *(adj)* If a baby is **teething**, new teeth are coming through its gums.
2 **teething troubles** *(plural n)* the temporary problems that you may experience when you start a new job or activity.

teetotal *(adj)* If a person is **teetotal**, they never drink alcohol. **teetotaller** *(n).*

telecommunications
(plural n) the sending of messages by telephone, satellite, radio, etc. *See* **satellite**.

telegram *(n)* a message that is written down and sent by radio or electrical signals. Telegrams usually give urgent news or congratulations.

telegraph *(n)* a way of sending messages using radio or electrical signals. **telegraph** *(v).*

telemetry *(n)* the use of radio waves to transmit and record information from a measuring instrument.

telepathy *(tel-ep-ath-ee) (n)* If you use **telepathy**, you send your thoughts to someone else without speaking, writing, or making signs. **telepathic** *(telly-path-ik) (adj).*

telephone *(n)* a machine which uses electrical wires and radio waves to enable you to speak to someone far away. **telephone** *(v).*

electrical signals from radio waves enter here

electron gun

electrically-charged focusing plate (controls position of beams on fluorescent screen)

vacuum

constantly moving electron beams (invisible until they hit phosphor strips)

glass cathode-ray tube

reinforced glass screen

telephoto lens *(n)* a camera lens that makes things that are far away look closer and larger.

telescope *(n)* a tube-shaped instrument which makes things that are far away look closer and larger. Telescopes are used especially for looking at stars. *The picture shows a refractor telescope and a diagram of how the light travels through it.* **telescopic** *(adj).*

television
1 *(n)* a piece of equipment with a screen, that receives and shows moving pictures with sound. *This simplified diagram shows how moving pictures are produced inside the cathode-ray tube of a television. Radio waves are converted into electrical signals which make beams of electrons sweep continuously across a fluorescent screen. As the beams hit the screen's phosphor strips, they create constantly changing dots of coloured light, which the viewer sees as moving images.*
2 *(n)* the sending of sounds and moving pictures along radio waves to be picked up by a television set.

trinitron mask (directs electron beams on to phosphor strips)

fluorescent screen of phosphor strips (strips glow when hit by electron beams)

television (cathode-ray tube cutaway)

tell telling told
1 *(v)* to speak to someone.
2 *(v)* to show something. *The red light tells you to stop.*
3 *(v)* to recognize, or be certain. *It was hard to tell who it was in the dark.*
4 **tell off** *(v)* If you **tell someone off**, you scold them because they have done something wrong.

temper *(n)* an angry or impatient mood.

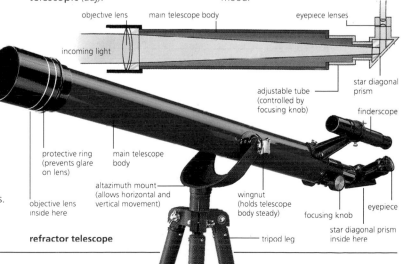

objective lens   main telescope body   eyepiece lenses

incoming light

star diagonal prism

adjustable tube (controlled by focusing knob)

finderscope

protective ring (prevents glare on lens)

main telescope body

altazimuth mount (allows horizontal and vertical movement)

objective lens inside here

wingnut (holds telescope body steady)

focusing knob

eyepiece

star diagonal prism inside here

tripod leg

refractor telescope

temperament (n) your nature, or your personality. *Laura has a very calm temperament.*

temperamental
1 (adj) excited, unpredictable, or moody. *A temperamental artist.*
2 (adj) caused by your temperament. **temperamentally** (adv).

temperate (adj) If an area has a **temperate** climate, it has neither very high nor very low temperatures.

temperature
1 (n) a measure of how cold or hot something is.
2 (n) If you have a **temperature**, your body is hotter than normal because you are ill.

tempest (n) (poetic) a violent storm.

template (n) a shape or pattern that you draw or cut around to make the same shape in paper, metal, material, etc. See **geometry**.

temple (n) a building used for worship. *This reconstruction of the Parthenon, a temple dedicated to the Goddess Athene, shows how it would have looked in the 5th century BC.*

tempo (n) the speed or timing of a piece of music.

temporary (adj) If something is **temporary**, it lasts for only a short time. **temporarily** (adv).

tempt tempting tempted
1 (v) If you **tempt** someone, you make them want something by telling them how good it is. **tempting** (adj).

2 (v) If you are **tempted**, you are attracted to doing something wrong.

temptation
1 (n) the act of being tempted. *Try to resist temptation.*
2 (n) something that you want to have or do, although you know it is wrong. *That cake is such a temptation!*

tenant (n) someone who rents a room, house, office, etc.

tend tending tended
1 (v) If something **tends** to happen, it often or usually happens.
2 (v) If you **tend** a person, animal, or plant, you take care of it.

tendency tendencies (n) If you have a **tendency** to do something, you often or usually do it.

tender
1 (adj) sore, or sensitive. *Sal's bruises were still tender.* **tenderness** (n).
2 (adj) soft. *A tender steak.* **tenderness** (n).
3 (adj) gentle and kind. *A tender kiss.* **tenderness** (n), **tenderly** (adv).

tendon (n) a strong, thick cord that joins a muscle to a bone. See **muscle**.

tenor
1 (n) a male singing voice that is quite high. **tenor** (adj).
2 (n) a singer with a tenor voice.

tenpin bowling (n) an indoor game in which you roll a large, heavy ball at a group of wooden objects, called pins, in order to try to knock them all down.

tense tenser tensest
1 (adj) If you are **tense**, you are nervous or worried. *Miriam is always tense before an exam.* **tenseness** (n), **tensely** (adv).
2 (adj) stretched tight and stiff. *Your muscles will be tense if you don't warm up before a game.* **tenseness** (n), **tense** (v).
3 (n) a form of a verb that shows whether an action happened in the past, is happening in the present, or will happen in the future.

tension
1 (n) the tightness or stiffness of a rope, wire, etc. *After you've put up your tent, test the tension of all the guy ropes.*
2 (n) a feeling of worry, nervousness, or suspense. *Tension mounted as the boxers entered the ring.*
3 (n) If there is **tension** between two people, there is difficulty or strain in their relationship.

tent (n) a shelter made of nylon or cloth, supported by poles and ropes.

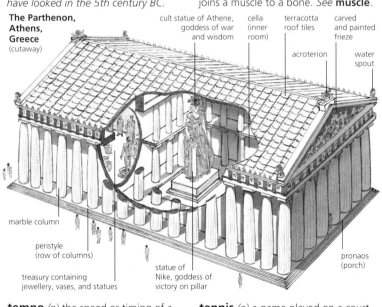

The Parthenon, Athens, Greece (cutaway)

cult statue of Athene, goddess of war and wisdom
cella (inner room)
terracotta roof tiles
carved and painted frieze
acroterion
water spout
marble column
peristyle (row of columns)
treasury containing jewellery, vases, and statues
statue of Nike, goddess of victory on pillar
pronaos (porch)

ridge tent
ridge pole under here
adjuster
pole spindle
upright pole
guy rope
door
peg
sewn-in groundsheet
inner tent
hooded flysheet

tentacle (n) one of the long, flexible limbs of some animals such as octopuses and squids. Tentacles are used for moving and feeling. See **jellyfish**, **octopus**, **slug**, **squid**.

tentative (adj) hesitant, or unsure. *Giles made a tentative attempt to join in the game.* **tentatively** (adv).

tenterhooks If you are on **tenterhooks**, you are in suspense, waiting for something to happen.

tenuous (ten-yoo-uss) (adj) not very important, or not very significant. **tenuously** (adv).

tennis (n) a game played on a court by two or four players who use rackets to hit a ball over a net.

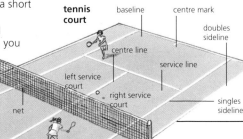

tennis court
baseline
centre mark
doubles sideline
centre line
service line
left service court
right service court
singles sideline
net

tepee *or* **teepee**
(*n*) a round tent made from animal skins or canvas, used by Native Americans.

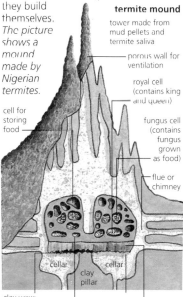

tepee

opening for smoke to escape

travois (for carrying tepee and other goods)

stitched and painted buffalo hide

tepid (*adj*) slightly warm.

term
1 (*n*) a part of the school year. **termly** (*adv*).
2 (*n*) a length of time. *The job is for a limited term of eight months.*
3 (*n*) a word. *Musical terms.*
4 **terms** (*plural n*) the conditions of an agreement.

terminal
1 (*n*) a building where passengers arrive and leave. *An airport terminal.*
2 (*n*) a computer keyboard and screen linked to a network.
3 (*adj*) If someone has a **terminal** illness, they cannot be cured and will die from it. **terminally** (*adv*).

terminate terminating terminated (*v*) to stop, or to end. *The train terminates here.*

termite (*n*) an ant-like insect that destroys wood. Termites live together in colonies inside large mounds that they build themselves. *The picture shows a mound made by Nigerian termites.*

termite mound

tower made from mud pellets and termite saliva

porous wall for ventilation

royal cell (contains king and queen)

fungus cell (contains fungus grown as food)

flue or chimney

cell for storing food

cellar   cellar

clay pillar

clay vanes (allow water to evaporate to cool the cellar)

nursery cell (contains eggs and larvae)

clay plate (absorbs water)

terrace
1 (*n*) a row of houses joined together. **terraced** (*adj*).
2 (*n*) a flat area next to a house, café, etc. where you can sit.
3 **terraces** (*plural n*) wide steps where you stand to watch a match.

terracotta (*n*) a type of clay used for ornaments, pots, or roofs.

terrain (*n*) ground, or land.

terrapin (*n*) a water reptile with webbed feet and a shell. *The picture shows a diamondback terrapin that comes from Florida, USA.*

terrapin

terrestrial (*adj*) to do with the Earth, or living on the Earth.

terrible (*adj*) very bad, shocking, or awful. **terribly** (*adv*).

terrific
1 (*adj*) very good, or enjoyable.
2 (*adj*) very great. *Rod set off at terrific speed.* **terrifically** (*adv*).

terrify terrifies terrifying terrified (*v*) to frighten someone very much. **terrifying** (*adj*), **terrifyingly** (*adv*).

territory territories (*n*) an area of land, especially land that belongs to someone. **territorial** (*adj*).

terror
1 (*n*) great fear.
2 If you are **terror-struck**, you are so frightened that you cannot do anything.

terrorist (*n*) someone who uses violence, for example, bombing or hijacking, for political reasons. **terrorism** (*n*).

terrorize *or* **terrorise** terrorizing terrorized (*v*) to frighten someone very much.

terse terser tersest (*n*) brief and abrupt. *When I asked Aunt Agatha her age, she gave a very terse reply.*

tertiary (*adj*) third in order.

tessellate tessellating tessellated (*v*) When shapes tessellate, they fit together exactly, without leaving gaps. *The picture shows how hexagons tessellate.* **tessellated** (*adj*).

tessellating shapes

test testing tested
1 (*n*) a set of questions or actions that check your knowledge or skill. **test** (*v*).
2 (*n*) a medical examination or check-up. *A blood test.* **test** (*v*).
3 (*v*) to try something out. *Esther tested the new recipe.* **test** (*n*).

testicle (*test-ik-ul*) (*n*) one of the two glands behind a man's penis that produce sperm.

testify testifies testifying testified (*v*) to state the truth, or to give evidence in a court of law.

testimony testimonies (*n*) a statement given by a witness who is under oath, in a court of law.

test match test matches (*n*) a cricket or rugby match played between teams from different countries.

test pilot (*n*) a pilot who flies new aeroplanes in order to test them.

test tube
1 (*n*) a small, thin, glass tube used in a science laboratory. *See* **apparatus**.
2 **test-tube baby** (*n*) a baby that develops from an egg which has been fertilized outside the mother's body, but which then grows normally inside her womb.

tetanus (*n*) a serious disease caused by bacteria getting into a cut or wound. Tetanus makes your muscles, and especially your jaw, become stiff.

tether tethering tethered
1 (*v*) to tie up an animal so that it cannot move far. **tether** (*n*).
2 If you are **at the end of your tether**, you have run out of patience.

text
1 (*n*) the main section of writing in a book, rather than the pictures or index.
2 (*n*) a textbook.

textbook (*n*) a book used at school or college as part of a course.

text message (*n*) a message that you type into your mobile phone and send to another person who reads it on the screen of their mobile phone.

textile (*n*) a fabric or cloth.

texture (*n*) the feel of something, such as its roughness or smoothness.

thank thanking thanked
1 (*v*) to tell someone that you are grateful for what they have done.
2 **thanks** (*plural n*) spoken or written words showing that you are grateful.

thankful (*adj*) glad, or grateful. *Helena was thankful for a decent meal.* **thankfully** (*adv*)

thatch thatches *(n)* straw or reeds used for making roofs. *The picture shows some features of a roof made of thatch.* **thatch** *(v)*, **thatched** *(adj)*.

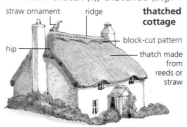

straw ornament   ridge   **thatched cottage**

hip

block-cut pattern

thatch made from reeds or straw

thaw thawing thawed
1 *(v)* to become soft or liquid after being frozen. *Leave the turkey to thaw overnight.*
2 *(n)* a time when snow and ice melt because the weather has become warmer.

theatre
1 *(n)* a place where you go to watch plays, shows, etc.
2 *(n)* a part of a hospital where surgeons operate.

theatrical
1 *(adj)* to do with the theatre. *Theatrical costumes.*
2 *(adj)* If something is **theatrical**, it is intended to create a dramatic effect.

theft *(n)* the crime of stealing. *Kit is being punished for theft.*

their *(pronoun)* belonging to them. *Have the girls brought their books?* **theirs** *(pronoun)*.

them *(pronoun)* the things, people, etc. just mentioned. *Owen and Aled will be here soon, so look out for them.*

theme *(theem)*
1 *(n)* the subject of a speech, book, film, etc.
2 *(n)* a melody, or a tune.
3 **theme park** *(n)* a park with rides and attractions, based on a subject, such as the Wild West.

themselves *(pronoun)* them and no one else. *The children dressed themselves.*

then
1 *(adv)* at that time. *I didn't know Pandora then.*
2 *(adv)* afterwards. *Eat first, then talk.*
3 *(adv)* as a result. *If you stay up late, then you'll be tired tomorrow.*

theology theologies *(n)* the study of religion and religious beliefs. **theological** *(adj)*.

theorem *(n)* a statement, especially in maths, that can be proved to be true. *Pythagoras' theorem.*

theory *(rhymes with weary)* theories
1 *(n)* an idea that is intended to explain something.
2 *(n)* the rules and principles of a subject, rather than its practice. **theoretical** *(adj)*.
3 If something should happen in **theory**, you expect it to happen, but it may not. **theoretically** *(adv)*.

therapy therapies *(n)* a treatment for illness, for example, physiotherapy, art therapy, and speech therapy. **therapist** *(n)*.

there
1 *(adv)* to, in, or at that place. *Let's not go there again!*
2 *(pronoun)* The word **there** is often used as a subject in sentences. *There is a man outside. There has been some mistake.*

therefore *(adv)* as a result. *Stanley is ill, therefore Joe must take his place.*

therm *(n)* a unit for measuring heat, especially heat from burning gas.

thermal
1 *(adj)* to do with heat, or holding in heat. *Thermal underwear.*
2 *(n)* a rising current of warm air.

thermometer *(n)* an instrument used to measure temperature. *The picture shows a clinical thermometer, which is used to measure body temperature. The bulb is usually placed under the tongue, and as the mercury heats up it expands and rises up the capillary tube.*

clinical thermometer

glass capillary tube

scale in Celsius and Fahrenheit

triangular glass stem (acts as a magnifying glass)

mercury

constriction in tube (prevents mercury returning to bulb)

thin-walled glass bulb

thermostat *(n)* a device connected to a radiator, iron, etc. that switches off the heat when the temperature gets too high. *See* **refrigerator**.

thesaurus *(thi-saw-russ)* thesauruses *or* thesauri *(n)* a book containing lists of words with similar or related meanings.

these *(plural pronoun)* the things here, or the things being talked about. **these** *(adj)*.

thesis theses *(n)* an idea to be debated or proved.

they
1 *(pronoun)* the people, animals, or things being talked about.
2 *(pronoun)* people in general. *They say that it will snow.*

thick thicker thickest
1 *(adj)* wide, fat, or dense. *Thick walls. Thick soup.* **thickness** *(n)*, **thicken** *(v)*, **thickly** *(adv)*.
2 *(adj) (informal)* stupid.

thicket *(n)* a thick growth of plants, bushes, or small trees.

thief thieves *(n)* someone who steals things. **thieve** *(v)*, **thieving** *(adj)*.

thigh *(n)* Your **thigh** is the top part of your leg, between your knee and your hip.

thin thinner thinnest *(adj)* not fat, not thick, or not dense. *A thin cat. A thin sauce.* **thinness** *(n)*, **thin** *(v)*, **thinly** *(adv)*.

thing
1 *(n)* an object, idea, or event.
2 **things** *(plural n)* belongings. *Don't leave your things here.*

think thinking thought
1 *(v)* to use your mind. *Try to think of the answer.* **thinker** *(n)*.
2 *(v)* to have an idea or opinion. *Will thinks girls are silly.*

third
1 *(n)* one of three equal parts.
2 *(adj)* If you come **third** in a race, you finish behind two other people. **thirdly** *(adv)*.

Third World *(n)* the poorer, developing countries of the world.

thirst
1 *(n)* a need for liquid. **thirst** *(v)*.
2 *(n)* a longing for something. *Jesse has a great thirst for adventure.* **thirst** *(v)*.

thirsty thirstier thirstiest *(adj)* If you are **thirsty**, you want to drink something. **thirstily** *(adv)*.

this *(pronoun)* the thing here, or the thing being talked about. **this** *(adj)*.

thistle *(n)* a wild plant with prickly leaves and purple flowers.

spear thistle

thorax thoraxes
1 *(n)* the part of your body between your neck and your stomach.
2 *(n)* the part of an insect's body between its head and its abdomen. *See* **beetle**.

thorn *(n)* a sharp point on the stem of a plant, such as a rose.

thorny thornier thorniest
1 *(adj)* covered with thorns.
2 *(adj)* difficult. *A thorny problem.*

thorough *(adj)* If you are **thorough**, you do a job carefully and completely. **thoroughness** *(n)*, **thoroughly** *(adv)*.

thoroughfare *(n)* a road or path which is open at both ends. *Is there a thoroughfare through the woods?*

those *(plural pronoun)* the people or things there. *The purple boots are all right, but I prefer those in the window.* **those** *(adj)*.

though
1 *(conj)* even if, or despite the fact that. *I'm still hungry, though I've just had breakfast.*
2 *(adv)* nevertheless. *He's quite friendly; I don't like him, though.*

thought
1 *(n)* an idea.
2 If you are **deep in thought**, you are thinking hard about something.

thoughtful
1 *(adj)* serious, or involving a lot of thought. *A thoughtful essay.*
2 *(adj)* A **thoughtful** person considers other people's feelings and needs. **thoughtfully** *(adv)*.

thoughtless *(adj)* A **thoughtless** person does not consider other people's feelings and needs. **thoughtlessly** *(adv)*.

thrash thrashes thrashing thrashed
1 *(v)* to beat with a stick or a whip.
2 *(v)* to beat someone thoroughly in a game. *Gemma always thrashes me at tennis.* **thrashing** *(n)*.
3 *(v)* If you **thrash out** an idea or a problem, you talk about it until something is decided.

thread threading threaded
1 *(n)* a strand of cotton, silk, etc. used for sewing.
2 *(v)* to pass a thread through something, like the eye of a needle, or a set of beads.
3 *(n)* the raised, spiral ridge around a screw.

threadbare *(adj)* If your clothes are **threadbare**, they are old and worn out.

threaten threatening threatened *(v)* If someone or something **threatens** you, it frightens you or puts you in danger. **threat** *(n)*.

three-dimensional or **3-D** *(adj)* solid, or not flat. Cubes and spheres are three-dimensional shapes.

thresh threshes threshing threshed *(v)* to separate the grain of a crop, like wheat, from the chaff and straw. *The picture shows 19th-century farmers threshing by hand, by beating the corn with flails. Nowadays, most farmers use combine harvesters to thresh their crops.*
Also see **harvest**.

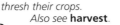

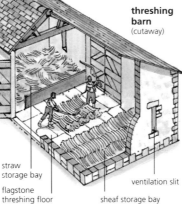

threshing barn (cutaway)

straw storage bay

flagstone threshing floor

ventilation slit

sheaf storage bay

threshold
1 *(n)* the base of a doorway.
2 *(n)* the beginning of something. *We are on the threshold of a great adventure!*

thrifty thriftier thriftiest *(adj)* Someone who is **thrifty** does not waste money, food, supplies, etc. **thrift** *(n)*.

thrill *(n)* a feeling of excitement and pleasure. **thrill** *(v)*, **thrilling** *(adj)*.

thriller *(n)* an exciting story about mystery, danger, or crime.

thrive thriving thrived *(v)* to do well and flourish. *Roses thrive in our garden. Yasmin is thriving at her new school.* **thriving** *(adj)*.

throat
1 *(n)* the front of your neck.
2 *(n)* the passage that runs from your mouth into your stomach or lungs.

throb throbbing throbbed *(v)* to beat in a regular way. *The drumbeat throbbed in my ears.* **throb** *(n)*.

throne
1 *(n)* an elaborate chair for a king or queen. *This picture from the Bayeux tapestry shows Harold Godwinsson seated on his throne, as King of England.*
2 If someone **comes to the throne**, they become king or queen.

throng *(n)* a large crowd of people. **throng** *(v)*.

throne

throttle throttling throttled
1 *(v)* If you **throttle** someone, you squeeze their throat so that they cannot breathe.
2 *(n)* a valve in a vehicle's engine that opens to let fuel, or fuel and air, flow into it.

through
1 *(prep)* from one end or side to the other. *Lily squeezed through the crowd.* **through** *(adv)*.
2 *(prep)* by way of, or because of. *Elsa got the job through a friend.*
3 *(adv)* completely. *Jacques was wet through.* **through** *(adj)*.

throughout *(prep)* all the way through. *Chickenpox spread throughout the school.* **throughout** *(adv)*.

throw throwing threw thrown
1 *(v)* to make something move, especially through the air. *Dean threw the ball.* **throw** *(n)*.
2 *(v)* *(informal)* If something **throws** you, it confuses you.
3 **throw away** *(v)* to get rid of something.
4 **throw up** *(v)* *(informal)* to vomit.

thrush thrushes
(n) a garden bird with a brown back and a spotted breast.

song thrush

thrust thrusting thrust
1 *(v)* to push something suddenly and hard. **thrust** *(n)*.
2 *(n)* The **thrust** of an argument is its main point.

thud *(n)* a noise like the sound of a heavy object falling on the ground. **thud** *(v)*.

thug *(n)* a violent person.

thumb thumbing thumbed
1 *(n)* the short, thick digit that you have on each hand.
2 *(v)* to turn over the pages of a book.
3 *(v)* *(informal)* If you **thumb a lift**, you hitchhike.

thumbtack *(n)* *(US)* a small pin with a flat, round head used for fastening paper on noticeboards, walls, etc. (drawing pin, UK).

thump thumping thumped
1 *(v)* to hit someone or something with your fist. **thump** *(n)*.
2 *(n)* a dull sound. *The paper landed on the mat with a thump.* **thump** *(v)*.

thunder thundering thundered
1 *(n)* the loud, rumbling sound that you hear during a storm.
2 *(v)* to make a loud noise like thunder. *The trucks thundered past.*

thwart thwarting thwarted *(v)*
If you **thwart** somebody's plans, you prevent them from happening.

tiara *(n)* a piece of jewellery like a small crown.

tick ticking ticked
1 *(n)* the sound that a clock or watch makes. **tick** *(v)*.
2 *(n)* a mark that someone makes to show that an answer is correct or that something has been done. **tick** *(v)*.
3 *(n)* a very small insect that lives on the skin of some animals.
4 **tick off** *(v)* *(informal)* If you **tick** someone **off**, you tell them off.

ticket *(n)* a printed piece of paper or card that proves that you have paid to do something. *A train ticket.*

tickle tickling tickled *(v)* to keep touching or poking someone gently, often causing them to laugh or feel irritated. **ticklish** *(adj)*.

tiddlywinks *(plural n)* a game in which each player tries to flick plastic counters into a cup.

tide *(n)* the constant change in sea level, caused by the pull of the Sun and the Moon. **tidal** *(adj)*.

tidings *(plural n)* *(poetic)* news.

tidy tidier tidiest *(adj)* neat, or in proper order. **tidiness** *(n)*, **tidy** *(v)*.

tie ties tying tied
1 *(v)* to join two pieces of string, cord, etc. together with a knot.
2 *(n)* a long piece of fabric which is worn knotted around the collar of a shirt.
3 *(n)* a situation in which two people finish level in a competition. *There was a tie for second place.* **tie** *(v)*.

tie-break or **tiebreaker** *(n)* a special game played to decide the result of a match or competition when the players have won the same number of points.

tier *(teer)* *(n)* one of several levels, placed one above the other, for example, a row of seats in a theatre or a layer of a wedding cake. **tiered** *(adj)*.

tiger *(n)* a large, striped, wild cat found in Asia.

tiger
and cubs

tight tighter tightest
1 *(adj)* fitting closely, or fastened closely. *Tight jeans.* **tighten** *(v)*, tightly *(adv)*.
2 *(adj)* fully stretched. **tighten** *(v)*.
3 *(adj)* *(informal)* mean with money.
4 *(adj)* *(informal)* drunk.

tightrope *(n)* a stretched, high wire on which circus performers balance.

tights *(plural n)* a close-fitting garment that covers your hips, legs, and feet.

tile *(n)* a small, flat piece of baked clay, cork, slate, etc., often used for covering floors, roofs, or walls. *The picture shows a baked clay, or ceramic, tile.* **tile** *(v)*.

Dutch ceramic tile

till tilling tilled
1 *(prep)* until. *Wait till I call for you.*
2 *(n)* a drawer or box in a shop, used to hold money, and often part of a cash register.
3 *(v)* to plough the soil ready for planting crops.

tilt tilting tilted *(v)* to lean to one side. **tilt** *(n)*.

timber *(n)* cut wood used for furniture making, building, etc.

time timing timed
1 *(n)* the passing of seconds, minutes, hours, etc.
2 *(n)* a particular moment shown on a clock or watch. *What is the time now?*
3 *(n)* a particular period. *A time of great happiness.*
4 *(v)* to measure how long something takes. *I'll time you while you run.*
5 *(v)* to choose the moment for something. *Harry timed his entrance perfectly.*

timetable *(n)* a printed chart of the times when events, lessons, travel departures, etc. are planned to happen. **timetable** *(v)*.

timid *(adj)* shy and easily frightened. **timidly** *(adv)*.

tin
1 *(n)* a silvery metal used to make alloys and food cans.
2 *(n)* a food can.

tinge *(tinj)*
1 *(n)* a very small amount of added colour. *White with a tinge of pink.*
2 *(n)* a slight feeling. *Indra's smile had a tinge of sadness to it.*

tingle tingling tingled *(v)* to sting, prick, or tickle. **tingle** *(n)*.

tinker tinkering tinkered *(v)* to work at or fiddle with something, with the aim of repairing it or improving it.

tint *(n)* a small amount of added colour. **tint** *(v)*, **tinted** *(adj)*.

tiny tinier tiniest *(adj)* very small, or minute.

tip tipping tipped
1 *(v)* to make something lean or fall over.
2 *(v)* to lean, or to fall over.
3 *(n)* the thin end of something. *The tip of a snooker cue.*
4 *(n)* a useful hint.
5 *(n)* a sum of money given, in addition to the bill, to a waitress, taxi driver, etc. as thanks for their services.
6 *(n)* a rubbish dump.

tiptoe tiptoeing tiptoed *(v)* to walk quietly, without putting your heels down.

tire tiring tired
1 *(v)* to make someone tired, or to become tired and weak. **tired** *(adj)*.
2 *(v)* to become bored. *I soon tired of Terry's chatter.*

tiresome *(adj)* boring, irritating, or annoying. **tiresomely** *(adv)*.

tissue *(tish-yoo or tiss-yoo)*
1 *(n)* soft, thin paper used for wiping, wrapping, etc.
2 *(n)* a mass of cells which form the flesh and muscle of a living creature.

title
1 *(n)* the name of a book, film, etc.
2 *(n)* the very first part of a person's name, for example, Miss, Mrs, Mr.
3 *(n)* a special name, showing a high position in society, for example, Sir, Dame, Lord, Lady. **titled** *(adj)*.

toad *(n)* an amphibian like a frog, but with a rougher skin, that lives mainly on land. *The male midwife toad carries strands of eggs wrapped around its back legs for several weeks before depositing them in a pond to hatch.*

midwife toad

toadstool *(n)* a usually posionous fungus with a rounded top on a stalk.

toast toasting toasted
1 *(n)* grilled bread. **toast** *(v)*.
2 *(v)* to drink in honour of someone. *Let's toast the bride and bridegroom.* **toast** *(n)*.

tobacco *(n)* the chopped, dried leaves of the tobacco plant, smoked in pipes, cigars, and cigarettes.

Some words that begin with a "ti" sound are spelt "ty".

toboggan tobogganing toboganed
1 (n) a small sledge.
2 (v) to travel by toboggan, especially downhill.

today
1 (n) on this day. I'm going out today.
2 (n) nowadays, or at the present time. Today, most adults in the western world can read and write.

toddler (n) a young child who has just learned to walk.

toe (n) one of the five digits at the end of your foot.

toffee (n) a chewy sweet made from boiled sugar and butter.

toga (n) a piece of clothing worn by Ancient Romans. It was wrapped around the body and over the left shoulder.

toga

together (adv) with another person or thing. The boys arrived together.

toil toiling toiled (v) to work very hard and continuously. **toil** (n).

toilet
1 (n) a large bowl with flushing water, used for disposing of urine and faeces.
2 (n) a room or building containing toilets.

token
1 (n) a small, physical object used to represent something larger, or to show someone's feelings. Roderick gave Sue a ring as a token of his love.
2 (n) a card or piece of paper that can be exchanged for goods or services. A book token.

tolerate tolerating tolerated (v) If you **tolerate** something, you put up with it or endure it. It is difficult to tolerate rude people. **tolerant** (adj).

toll tolling tolled
1 (v) to ring a bell, usually in a slow, solemn way.
2 (n) a charge for using a private road or bridge.
3 If something **takes its toll**, it results in serious damage or suffering. Famine has taken its toll in Ethiopia.

tomahawk (n) a war axe used by Native Americans. This decorated tomahawk was used by the Shawnee people.

tomahawk

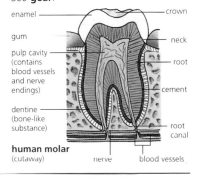

tomato tomatoes (n) a sweet, red fruit, often eaten in salads.

tomb (n) a grave, usually for an important person. The picture shows the tomb of Robert Curthose, Duke of Normandy, in Gloucester Cathedral, England.

tomb

tomboy (n) a girl who enjoys activities usually associated with boys, such as climbing trees or playing football.

tombstone (n) a carved block of stone which marks the place where someone is buried.

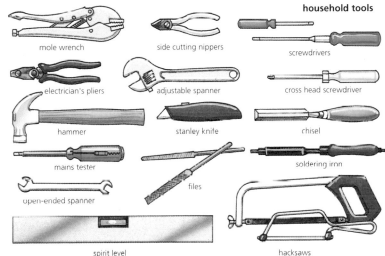

mole wrench

side cutting nippers

household tools

screwdrivers

electrician's pliers

adjustable spanner

cross head screwdriver

hammer

stanley knife

chisel

mains tester

soldering iron

open-ended spanner

files

spirit level

hacksaws

tomorrow (n) the day after today.

tone
1 (n) the way that something sounds.
2 (n) the general atmosphere of a place or situation. The tone of our conversation was cheerful.
3 (n) In music, a **tone** is an interval between two notes that is equal to two semitones.
4 (n) a shade of a colour. A pink tone.

tongs (plural n) a tool with two connected arms, used for picking up things.

tongue (tung) (n) a flap of muscle in your mouth, used for tasting, eating, and talking. See **taste**.

tongue twister (n) a sentence or verse that is very hard to say fast, for example, "Red leather, yellow leather."

tonic
1 (n) something that makes you feel better. Our seaside trip was a real tonic.
2 (n) a slightly bitter-tasting mineral water, that is often mixed with alcoholic drinks.

tonight (n) this evening or night.

tonsillitis (n) a disease that makes your tonsils infected and painful.

tonsils (plural n) two flaps of soft tissue in your throat at the back of your mouth.

too
1 (adv) as well, or in addition. Is Janey coming too?
2 (adv) very, extremely, or more than enough. The heavy metal band was too noisy for Granny.

tool (n) a piece of equipment that you use to do a particular job.

tooth teeth
1 (n) one of the white, bone-like structures in your mouth, used for biting and chewing food. Also see **teeth**.
2 (n) one of a row of sticking out parts on a saw, comb, cogwheel, etc. See **gear**.

enamel

crown

gum

neck

pulp cavity (contains blood vessels and nerve endings)

root

dentine (bone-like substance)

cement

root canal

human molar (cutaway)

nerve

blood vessels

top topping topped
1 (n) the highest point of something.
2 (adj) very good, or best. *A top singer.*
3 (n) a covering, or a lid. *A bottle top.*
4 (n) a piece of clothing for the upper part of your body.
5 (v) to be the best, or to lead. *Fred topped the class in spelling.*

top-heavy (adj) If something is top-heavy, it is heavier towards the top, and therefore likely to fall over.

topic
1 (n) the subject of a discussion, study, lesson, etc.
2 (n) an extended study on a particular subject, usually in a primary school.

topical (adj) relevant now, or in the news at present.

topple toppling toppled (v) to fall over, usually from a height.

Torah (n) the sacred scroll in a Jewish synagogue, on which is written in Hebrew the books of Genesis, Exodus, Leviticus, Numbers, and Deuteronomy.

torch torches
1 (n) a battery-powered light that you can carry with you.
2 (n) a piece of wood dipped in wax or fat, used to light buildings in medieval times.

toreador (toh-ree-a-dor) (n) a bullfighter mounted on a horse.

torment tormenting tormented
1 (tor-ment) (v) to upset or annoy someone deliberately.
2 (tor-ment) (n) great pain.

tornado tornados *or* tornadoes (n) a windstorm that swirls in a circle.

torpedo torpedoes (n) an underwater missile that explodes when it hits something.

torrent (n) a large mass of flowing or falling water. **torrential** (adj).

torso (n) the part of your body between your neck and your waist.

tortoise (n) a slow-moving reptile with a shell and thick, scaly skin. *The giant tortoise in the picture is allowing finches to crawl over its body in search of parasites.*

giant tortoise

torture torturing tortured (v) to cause someone extreme pain. torture (n).

Tory Tories (n) a nickname for a member of the British Conservative Party. **Tory** (adj).

toss tosses tossing tossed
1 (v) to throw something upwards.
2 (v) to throw something away casually.

total
1 (n) the result of an addition or multiplication sum. *Add up these figures and give me the total.* total (v).
2 (adj) complete and utter. *The party was a total surprise.* totally (adv).

totem pole (n) a carved pole that acts as a sacred emblem for a tribe or family of Native Americans. *The painted totem pole shown here is in Stanley Park, Vancouver, Canada.*

totem pole

totter tottering tottered (v) to sway and stagger.

toucan (too-kan) (n) a brightly coloured tropical bird which has a huge beak.

toucan

touch touches touching touched
1 (v) to make contact with something, using your hands or other areas of your body.
2 (v) to make gentle contact with another object. *The ship touched the quay as it docked.*
3 Your **sense of touch** is your ability to feel things with your fingers, or with other parts of your body.
4 If you **keep in touch** with someone, you contact them regularly, by telephone, letter, etc.

touchdown (n) the moment when an aircraft or a spacecraft lands.

touching (adj) Something that is touching appeals to your emotions. touchingly (adv).

touchline (n) the line marking the side of a pitch in sports such as soccer and rugby. See **soccer**.

touchy touchier touchiest (adj) irritable and easily annoyed. touchiness (n).

tough (tuff) tougher toughest
1 (adj) strong and difficult to damage, either physically or mentally. *Tough boots. A tough personality.*
2 (adj) difficult. *A tough decision.*

toupee *or* **toupet** (too-pay) (n) a piece of false hair, usually used to disguise a man's baldness.

tour
1 (n) a journey round a set route, often for sightseeing. tour (v).
2 When a band or team go **on tour**, they go to different places to play.

tourist (n) someone who travels and visits places for pleasure. tourism (n).

tournament
1 (n) a competition for players of sports, chess, cards, etc. *A tennis tournament.*
2 (n) In the Middle Ages, tournaments were events where knights jousted against each other. See **joust**.

tourniquet (tor-nik-ay) (n) a very tight bandage or band put round a wounded limb to stop the flow of blood.

tow towing towed (v) to pull something behind you, usually with a rope, chain, etc. *The breakdown truck towed the car away.* tow (n).

towards *or* **toward** (prep) in the direction of. *Oswin marched towards the door.*

towel (n) a thick, soft, absorbent cloth for drying yourself.

tower towering towered
1 (n) a tall structure that is thin in relation to its height. *The picture shows the Leaning Tower of Pisa in Italy.*
2 (v) to be very tall and dominant. *The skyscraper towered over the houses.*

tower

town *(n)* a place with houses, shops, offices, schools, etc. where many people live.

towpath *(n)* a path beside a canal or river.

toxic *(adj)* poisonous. **toxin** *(n)*.

toy toying toyed
1 *(n)* an object that children play with.
2 *(v)* If you **toy** with something, you play with it in a half-hearted, unenthusiastic way.

trace tracing traced
1 *(v)* to find out where something or somebody is.
2 *(v)* to draw over the outline of a shape. **tracing** *(n)*.
3 *(n)* a visible sign that something has happened or that someone has been somewhere. *Traces of blood.*

tracks
brown hare
pigeon
reindeer
fox
brown bear

track tracking tracked
1 *(n)* the marks left behind by a moving animal or person.
2 *(n)* a path, or route.
3 *(n)* a course used for races. *A greyhound track.*
4 *(v)* to follow someone or something. **tracking** *(n)*.

track and field *(n)* competitive athletic sports that involve running, jumping, or throwing. *The picture shows the standard layout of a stadium used for track and field.* **track-and-field** *(adj)*.

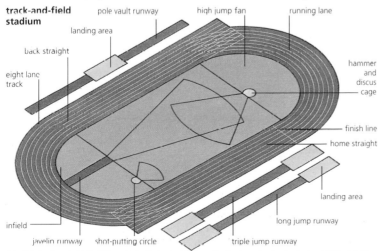

track-and-field stadium
pole vault runway, landing area, back straight, eight lane track, infield, javelin runway, shot-putting circle, high jump fan, running lane, hammer and discus cage, finish line, home straight, landing area, long jump runway, triple jump runway

tracksuit *(n)* a loose trousers and top, usually worn for sports.

traction engine *(n)* a large, slow, steam-powered vehicle, used in the 19th and early 20th century to pull heavy loads.

tractor *(n)* a powerful vehicle used on farms. Tractors are often used to pull farm machinery or heavy loads. *Also see* **farm**.

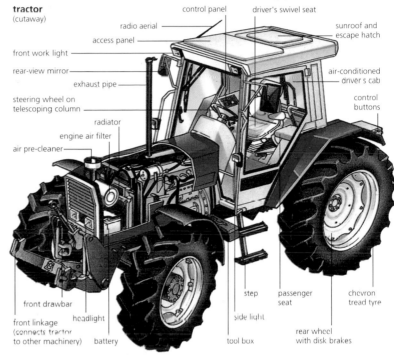

tractor (cutaway)
control panel, driver's swivel seat, sunroof and escape hatch, radio aerial, access panel, air-conditioned driver's cab, front work light, rear-view mirror, control buttons, exhaust pipe, steering wheel on telescoping column, radiator, engine air filter, air pre-cleaner, chevron tread tyre, step, passenger seat, side light, rear wheel with disk brakes, front drawbar, front linkage (connects tractor to other machinery), headlight, battery, tool box

trade trading traded
1 *(n)* the business of buying and selling things. **trader** *(n)*, **trade** *(v)*.
2 *(n)* a particular job or craft. *Bob's trade is thatching.*
3 *(v)* to exchange one thing for another. *We've started a club to trade computer games.*

trademark *(n)* a name, sign, or design that shows that a product is made by a particular company.

trade union *(n)* an organized group of workers, set up to help improve working conditions and pay. **trade unionist** *(n)*.

tradition *(n)* a custom that has been passed down from generation to generation. **traditional** *(adj)*.

traffic trafficking trafficked
1 *(n)* moving vehicles. *Heavy traffic.*
2 *(v)* to buy and sell drugs or other goods illegally. **trafficking** *(n)*.

traffic jam *(n)* a line of vehicles that can hardly move because there are so many cars on the road

traffic lights *(n)* a set of lights that controls traffic on roads.

traffic warden *(n)* someone whose job is to check that vehicles are parked legally

tragedy tragedies
1 *(n)* a serious play with a sad ending.
2 *(n)* a very sad event.

trail trailing trailed
1 *(n)* a track or path for people to follow.
2 *(v)* to follow someone, in order to check up on them.
3 *(v)* to follow slowly behind others.

trailer
1 *(n)* a vehicle that is towed by a car or truck and used to carry things.
2 *(n)* a short piece of film used to advertise a film or programme to be shown in the future.
3 *(n) (US)* a mobile home.

train training trained
1 *(n)* a string of railway carriages pulled by an engine. *The train shown below is a French TGV Atlantic, which is powered by electricity from overhead wires.*
2 *(v)* to learn how to do something, such as a job. **training** *(n)*.
3 *(v)* to teach a person or animal how to do something.
4 *(v)* to practise and prepare for a sports event. **training** *(n)*.
5 *(n)* the long piece of fabric that trails behind a bride's dress.

train
(cutaway)

passenger
carriage

motor ventilator

main transformer
(changes high voltage
from overhead wires
to lower working
voltage)

auxiliary energy supply unit
(alternative energy source)

pantograph
(carries electric current to
train from overhead wires)

freon tank
(stores gas
to cool motor)

traction motor
(drives wheels)

bogie
(wheeled support
for traction motor)

motor ventilation system

brake rheostat
(controls braking)

driver's cab

windscreen
wiper

light

railway track

trainer
1 *(n)* someone who helps a person or an animal become fit enough to compete in a sport.
2 *(n)* a light shoe with a thick sole, designed to be used for sport.

traitor *(n)* someone who betrays their country or friends by working for an enemy.

tram *(n)* a large vehicle that carries passengers. Trams run on rails laid in roads and are usually powered by electricity from overhead wires.

tramp tramping tramped
1 *(v)* to go for a long walk. *We tramped through the countryside.* **tramp** *(n)*.
2 *(v)* to walk or tread with heavy steps. **tramp** *(n)*.
3 *(n)* someone who does not have a permanent home.

trample trampling trampled *(v)* to damage something by walking all over it.

trampoline *(n)* a piece of canvas attached to a frame by elastic rope or springs. Trampolines are used for jumping on, either for sport or for pleasure. **trampolining** *(n)*.

trance *(n)* If you are **in a trance**, you are conscious, but not really aware of what is happening around you.

tranquil *(tran-kwil) (adj)* calm and peaceful. **tranquillity** *(n)*.

transaction *(n)* a business deal. **transact** *(v)*.

transatlantic
1 *(adj)* crossing the Atlantic Ocean. *A transatlantic telephone call.*
2 *(adj)* on or from the other side of the Atlantic. *A transatlantic fashion.*

transfer transferring transferred
1 *(trans-fur) (v)* to move a person or thing from one place to another. *I transferred the ball to my right hand.* **transfer** *(trans-fur) (n)*.
2 *(trans-fur) (n)* a small picture or design that can be stuck to another surface by rubbing or ironing.

transform transforming transformed *(v)* to make a great change in something. *Meeting Alphonso has transformed my life.* **transformation** *(n)*.

transformer *(n)* a piece of equipment that changes the voltage of an electric current.

transfusion *(n)* the injection of blood from another person into the body of someone who is injured or ill.

transient *(adj)* lasting for a short time only. **transience** *(n)*.

transistor
1 *(n)* a small electrical component that controls the flow of a current.
2 *(n) (informal)* a small, portable radio.

transit If goods are **in transit**, they are being moved from one place to another.

transition *(n)* a change from one situation to another.

transitive *(adj)* A transitive verb usually needs an object in order to make sense. *The verbs "to hit", "to pull", and "to cut" are all transitive.*

translate translating translated *(v)* to put something into another language. **translation** *(n)*, **translator** *(n)*.

translucent *(adj)* A translucent substance is not clear, like glass, but will let the light through. *Frosted glass is translucent.* **translucency** *(n)*.

transmit transmitting transmitted
1 *(v)* to send something from one place or person to another. *Did you transmit my fax message?* **transmission** *(n)*.
2 *(v)* to send out radio or television signals. *The programme will be transmitted next Friday.* **transmission** *(n)*, **transmitter** *(n)*.

transparency transparencies *(n)* a photographic slide.

transparent
1 *(adj)* A transparent substance is clear, like glass, and lets light through.
2 *(adj)* obvious, or clear. *The woman was a transparent liar.*

transpiration *(n)* the process by which plants lose moisture into the atmosphere. **transpire** *(v)*.

transplant transplanting transplanted
1 *(trans-plant) (v)* to remove something, like a plant, and put it somewhere else.
2 *(trans-plant) (n)* a surgical operation in which a diseased organ, such as a kidney, is replaced by a healthy one.

transport transporting transported
1 *(trans-port) (v)* to move people and goods from one place to another.
2 *(trans-port) (singular n)* all types of vehicles that carry people or goods.

trap trapping trapped *(v)* to capture a person or an animal by using some sort of trick or bait. **trap** *(n)*.

trap door *(n)* a horizontal door in a floor or ceiling.

trapeze *(trap-eez) (n)* a bar hanging from two ropes, used by circus performers and gymnasts.

trapezium trapeziums *or* trapezia
(n) a four-sided shape with one pair of
opposite parallel sides. *See* **shape**.

trash
1 *(singular n) (US)* things that you
have thrown away because they are
not useful or valuable (rubbish, *UK*).
2 *(singular n) (US)* nonsense
(rubbish, *UK*).

traumatic *(adj)* If something is
traumatic, it is shocking and very
upsetting. **trauma** *(n)*.

travel travelling travelled *(v)* to go
from one place to another. **travel** *(n)*.

travel agent *(n)* a person or
company that organizes travel and
holidays for its customers.
travel agency *(n)*.

traveller
1 *(n)* someone who is travelling or
who travels regularly.
2 *(n)* a travelling sales representative.
3 *(n)* someone who lives in a van or
mobile home and travels around,
often in a group.

trawler *(n)* a fishing boat that drags
a large, bag-shaped net through the
water. **trawl** *(v)*.

tray *(n)* a flat board used for carrying
food and drinks.

treacherous *(tretch-er-uss) (adj)*
dangerous, or not to be trusted.
A treacherous character.
A treacherous path.
treacherously *(adv)*.

treacle *(n)* a sweet, sticky syrup
made from sugar.

tread treading trod trodden
1 *(v)* to put your foot down on the
ground. *I have trodden in something
rather nasty.*
2 *(n)* the ridges on a tyre or on the
sole of a shoe that help to prevent
slipping.

treason *(n)* the crime of betraying
your country, for example, by spying
for another country.

treasure treasuring treasured
1 *(n)* very precious and valuable
objects, such as gold and jewels.
2 *(v)* to love and value very highly
something that you have or own.
I treasure my independence.
treasure *(n)*, **treasured** *(adj)*.

treasurer *(n)* the person who looks
after the money for an organization,
club, etc.

treasury treasuries
1 *(n)* a place where treasure is stored.
See **temple**.
2 *(n)* the funds of an organization,
government, etc.

treat treating treated
1 *(v)* to deal with people or things in a
certain way. *In China, old people are
treated with great respect.*
treatment *(n)*.
2 *(v)* Doctors **treat** people to try to
cure them of illness. **treatment** *(n)*.
3 *(v)* to process something in order to
change it in some way. *Sewage is
treated with chemicals to make it
harmless.* **treatment** *(n)*.
4 *(v)* to give someone a special gift, or
take someone somewhere special.
*Uncle Bonzo treated us to tea at a
smart hotel.* **treat** *(n)*.

treaty treaties *(n)* a formal
agreement between two or more
countries.

treble
1 *(adj)* three times as big, or three
times as many.
2 *(adj)* high-pitched. *A treble recorder.*
3 *(n)* a boy's singing voice that is very
high.

tree *(n)* a large, woody plant with a
trunk, roots, branches, and leaves.
See **trunk**.

trek trekking trekked *(v)* to walk a
long way, often in difficult conditions.
trek *(n)*.

trellis trellises *(n)* a criss-cross
framework of thin strips of wood,
used to support growing plants.

tremble trembling trembled *(v)*
to shake, especially from fear or
excitement.

tremendous
1 *(adj)* huge, or enormous.
A tremendous explosion.
tremendously *(adv)*.
2 *(adj)* very good, or excellent. *We had
a tremendous time surfing.*
tremendously *(adv)*.

tremor *(n)* a shaking movement.
*Earth tremors are very common in the
earthquake belt.*

trench trenches *(n)* a long, thin
channel dug in the earth.

trend
1 *(n)* the general direction in which
things are changing. *Recently, there
has been a trend towards smaller
families.*
2 *(n)* the latest fashion. *The trend this
season is for shorter skirts.*
trendy *(adj)*.

trespass trespasses trespassing
trespassed
1 *(v)* to enter someone's private
property without permission.
trespasser *(n)*.
2 *(n) (old-fashioned)* a sin.

tress tresses *(n) (poetic)* a lock of
hair.

trial
1 *(n)* a test. *Athletes have to do a trial
if they want to join the team.*
2 *(n)* the examination of someone
who appears in court accused of a
criminal offence.

trial bike *(n)* a light, strong
motorcycle built for cross-country
racing and riding.

triangle
1 *(n)* a three-sided shape.
triangular *(adj)*. *See* **shape**.
2 *(n)* a triangular percussion
instrument. You play the triangle by
striking it with a metal rod.
See **percussion**.

tribe *(n)* a group of people who
share the same ancestors, customs,
and laws. **tribal** *(adj)*.

tribunal *(n)* a law court.

tributary tributaries *(n)* a stream or
river that flows into a larger stream or
river. *See* **river**.

tribute If you pay **tribute to**
someone or something, you praise
them.

trick tricking tricked
1 *(v)* If you **trick** someone, you make
them believe something that is not
true. *Kevin tricked me into believing
that he was related to the Queen.*
trick *(n)*.
2 *(n)* a clever and entertaining act.
A magic trick.

trickle trickling trickled *(v)* to flow
very slowly in small quantities. *Water
trickled constantly from the tap.*
trickle *(n)*.

tricky trickier trickiest *(adj)* difficult,
or awkward. *A tricky situation.*

tricycle *(n)* a three-wheeled cycle.

trifle
1 *(n)* a dessert made from layers of
sponge cake, fruit, jelly, custard, and
cream.
2 *(n)* something that is not very
important. **trifling** *(adj)*.

trigger triggering triggered
1 *(n)* the lever on a gun that you pull
to fire it. *See* **blunderbuss**.
2 *(v)* to cause something to happen,
as a reaction. *The man's arrest
triggered riots in the streets.*

trim trimming trimmed; trimmer
trimmest
1 *(v)* to cut small pieces off something
in order to improve its shape.
trim *(n)*.
2 *(adj)* slim and shapely. *A trim
waistline.*

trimming

1 (n) something used as a decoration.

2 trimmings (plural n) the things that go with something. *Roast turkey and all the trimmings.*

trio

1 (n) a group of three things or people.

2 (n) a piece of music that is played or sung by three people.

trip tripping tripped

1 (v) to stumble, or to fall over.

2 (n) a journey, or a visit. *A trip to the zoo.* **tripper** (n).

triple tripling tripled

1 (v) to make something three times as big or three times as many. **triple** (adj).

2 (adj) made up of three parts. *The triple jump involves a hop, a step, and a jump.*

triplet (n) one of three children born to the same mother at almost the same time.

tripod (n) a three-legged stand used to support a camera or other piece of equipment. *See* **apparatus**.

trireme (try-reem) (n) an ancient Greek warship, propelled by oars.

triumph (n) a victory, or a great achievement. **triumph** (v), **triumphant** (adj).

trivial (adj) If something is **trivial**, it is not very important. *Don't bother me with such trivial questions.* **trivia** (plural n), **trivialize** (v).

trolley

1 (n) a two or four-wheeled cart used for carrying things. *A shopping trolley.*

2 (n) a table on wheels.

troop trooping trooped

1 (n) an organized group of soldiers, scouts, etc.

2 (v) to move in a group. *Sid and his friends trooped through the house.*

trophy (troh-fee) trophies (n) a prize or award.

tropic

1 (n) one of the lines of latitude that are 23.5° north and south of the equator, and are called the Tropic of Cancer and the Tropic of Capricorn.

2 the tropics (plural n) the extremely hot area between the Tropic of Cancer and the Tropic of Capricorn.

tropical (adj) to do with, or living in the hot, rainy area of the tropics.

tropical fish tropical fish (n) fish that originally come from the tropics. Tropical fish are often kept as pets in aquariums.

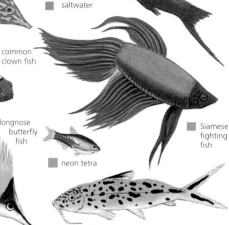

tropical fish
■ freshwater
■ saltwater

■ swordtail

■ common clown fish

■ Siamese fighting fish

■ neon tetra

■ multispotted catfish

trot trotting trotted (v) When a horse **trots**, it moves briskly at a pace between a walk and a canter. **trot** (n).

trouble troubling troubled

1 (n) a difficult or dangerous situation. **troublesome** (adj).

2 (v) to disturb or worry someone. *The letter troubled Perdita.*

3 If you **take the trouble** to do something, you make an effort to do it.

4 (v) to bother someone by asking them for help.

trough (troff) (n) a long, narrow container from which animals can drink or feed.

trousers (plural n) a piece of clothing with two legs that covers the lower part of your body.

trout trout (n) an edible, freshwater fish.·

trowel

1 (n) a tool with a small, curved blade used for planting and other light garden work.

2 (n) a tool with a flat, diamond-shaped blade, used for laying cement, filling holes in plaster, etc.

truant

1 (n) a pupil who stays away from school without permission. **truancy** (n).

2 If pupils **play truant**, they stay away from school without permission.

truce (n) a temporary agreement to stop fighting.

truck

1 (n) a large motor vehicle used for carrying goods by road. *The picture shows an articulated truck, which is made up of a cab and a trailer, linked by a flexible joint.*

2 (n) a large container used for carrying goods by rail.

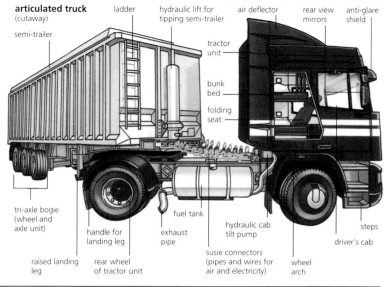

articulated truck (cutaway)

semi-trailer

ladder

hydraulic lift for tipping semi-trailer

air deflector

rear view mirrors

anti-glare shield

tractor unit

bunk bed

folding seat

tri-axle bogie (wheel and axle unit)

raised landing leg

handle for landing leg

rear wheel of tractor unit

fuel tank

exhaust pipe

susie connectors (pipes and wires for air and electricity)

hydraulic cab tilt pump

wheel arch

driver's cab

steps

■ spotted grouper

■ French angelfish

■ longnosed filefish

■ yellow longnose butterfly fish

trudge trudging trudged *(v)* to walk slowly and heavily. *We trudged through the mud.*

true truer truest *(adj)* accurate, or correct. **truly** *(adv)*.

truncheon *(n)* a thick, rounded stick used by the police in violent situations.

trundle trundling trundled
1 *(v)* to move along on wheels or rollers. *The bus trundled up the hill.*
2 *(v)* *(informal)* to walk slowly.

trunk
1 *(n)* the main stem of a tree. Tree trunks contain xylem and phloem vessels which transport fluids up and down the tree. *In the section of a tree trunk below, you can see the rings of xylem, or sapwood, that are created each year.*
2 *(n)* a large case or box, used for storage or for carrying clothes on a long journey.
3 *(n)* the upper part of your body, not including your head and arms.
4 *(n)* the long nose of an elephant.
5 *(n)* *(US)* the place, usually at the back of a car, where luggage can be carried (boot, *UK*).
6 **trunks** *(plural n)* close-fitting shorts worn by men or boys for swimming.

tree trunk (section)   annual ring   bark covering layers of phloem

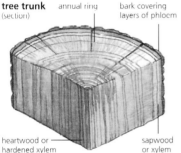

heartwood or hardened xylem   sapwood or xylem

trust trusting trusted *(v)* If you **trust** someone, you believe that they are honest and reliable. **trust** *(n)*.

trustworthy *(adj)* honest, reliable, and able to be trusted. **trustworthiness** *(n)*.

truth *(n)* the real facts. **truthful** *(adj)*, **truthfully** *(adv)*.

try tries trying tried
1 *(v)* to attempt to do something, or to do the best you can. **try** *(n)*.
2 *(v)* to examine someone accused of a criminal offence in a court of law.
3 *(n)* If you score a **try** in rugby, you touch the ball down behind your opponent's try line.

trying *(adj)* If a person is **trying**, they make you feel annoyed and impatient.

tsar *see* **czar**.

T-shirt *or* **tee shirt** *(n)* a light, cotton garment, usually with short sleeves and a round neck.

tub
1 *(n)* a plastic container used for storing foods. *A tub of ice cream.*
2 *(n)* *(old-fashioned)* a large, wide container, used for bathing in, or for washing clothes.

tubby tubbier tubbiest *(adj)* Tubby people are short and slightly fat. **tubbiness** *(n)*.

tube
1 *(n)* a long, hollow cylinder. *The poster came rolled in a tube.*
2 **the tube** *(n)* the nickname for London's underground railway system.

tuber *(n)* a rounded root of a plant such as a potato.

tubular *(adj)* shaped like a tube.

tuck tucking tucked
1 *(v)* to fold or push something into a restricted space. *Tuck the sheets in well.*
2 *(n)* a small fold sewn in material.
3 *(v)* *(informal)* If you **tuck in** to your food, you eat it enthusiastically. **tuck-in** *(n)*.
4 **tuck shop** *(n)* a shop in a school where sweets, crisps, etc. are sold.

tuft *(n)* an upright bunch of hair, grass, feathers, etc. **tufted** *(adj)*.

tug tugging tugged
1 *(v)* to pull hard. **tug** *(n)*.
2 **tug** *or* **tugboat** *(n)* a small, powerful boat that tows large ships.
3 **tug of war** *(n)* a contest between two teams, each at one end of a rope, who try to pull each other over a centre line.

tuition *(tew-ish-un)* *(n)* training or teaching, often given to a single person or to a small group.

tumble tumbling tumbled
1 *(v)* to fall, often with a rolling motion.
2 **tumble dryer** *(n)* a machine which dries clothes by tossing them around in hot air.

tumbler *(n)* a tall glass with straight sides.

tummy tummies *(n)* *(informal)* your stomach.

tumour *(n)* a swelling or lump caused by the abnormal growth of a mass of new cells.

tumult *(n)* loud noise and confusion. *The king's commands could not be heard in the tumult of the battle.* **tumultuous** *(adj)*.

tuna tuna *or* tunas *(n)* a large, edible sea fish. Cooked tuna flesh is brownish in colour.

tundra *(n)* the cold areas of northern Europe and Asia where there are no trees and the soil under the surface is permanently frozen.

tune tuning tuned
1 *(n)* a series of musical notes, arranged in a pattern. **tuneful** *(adj)*.
2 *(v)* to adjust a radio, the pitch of a musical instrument, etc.
3 **in tune** producing the right notes. *Can you sing in tune?*

tunic *(n)* a loose, sleeveless garment.

tuning fork *(n)* a piece of metal with two prongs, used for tuning musical instruments. When struck, it vibrates with a particular note.

tunnel *(n)* an underground passage. *The picture below shows cutaway sections of the Channel Tunnel. The tunnel runs under the sea bed between Cheriton, near Folkestone, in England, and Coquelles, near Calais, in France.* **tunnel** *(v)*.

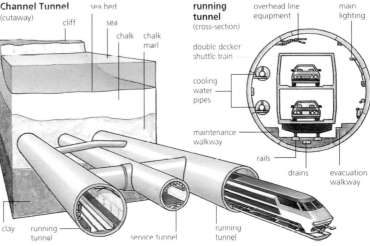

Channel Tunnel (cutaway)   sea bed   cliff   sea   chalk   chalk marl

clay   running tunnel   service tunnel   running tunnel

running tunnel (cross-section)   overhead line equipment   main lighting

double decker shuttle train

cooling water pipes

maintenance walkway

rails

drains   evacuation walkway

turban (n) a man's headdress, made from a long cloth wound round the head. Some Muslims, Hindus, and Sikhs wear turbans.

turbine (n) an engine driven by water, steam, or gas which passes through the blades of a wheel and makes it revolve. See **jet engine**.

turbo (adj) A turbo or turbo-charged engine has high-pressure air forced into its cylinders by a turbine, to produce extra power.

turbofan (n) a type of aircraft engine in which a large fan, driven by a turbine, pushes air into the hot exhaust at the rear of the engine, giving extra power. See **jet engine**.

turbulent (adj) wild, confused, or unpredictable. Turbulent waters.

turf (n) the surface layer of grass and earth on a lawn or sports pitch.

turkey
1 (n) a large, flightless bird, usually reared for its meat. The picture shows a North American wild turkey.
2 (n) (slang) a hopeless or useless person or thing.

wild turkey

turmoil (n) violent confusion. The class was in turmoil.

turn turning turned
1 (v) to change direction. Turn left at the junction. **turn** (n).
2 (v) to spin, or to revolve. Turn the wheel.
3 (v) to change appearance or state. The liquid turns into a vapour when heated.
4 (v) to move a switch, tap, etc. in order to control the supply of something. Turn down the volume.
5 (n) If it is your **turn** to do something, it is your chance or duty to do it.
6 (n) A good **turn** is a helpful action.
7 **turn down** (v) If you **turn something down**, you refuse it.
8 (v) If someone **turns up**, they appear.
9 **turn on** (v) (slang) If something **turns you on**, it makes you enthusiastic and excited. **turn-on** (n).

turnip (n) a round, white root vegetable.

turnstile (n) a revolving gate that only goes one way round, and controls admission to a sports ground, theme park, etc.

turntable (n) a circular, revolving surface. Turntables of different sizes can be used for playing records or turning engines.

turpentine (n) a mixture of tree resin and oil, used in paint and medicines.

turquoise (tur-kwoyz)
1 (n) a bluish-green, semiprecious stone. See **mineral**.
2 (n) a bluish-green colour. **turquoise** (adj).

turtle (n) a water reptile with flippers and a large shell. The shell of the matamata turtle looks like a dead leaf.

matamata turtle

tusk (n) one of the pair of long, curved, pointed teeth of an elephant, walrus, etc.

tussle tussling tussled (v) to fight or wrestle vigorously. **tussle** (n).

tutor (n) a teacher, usually one who teaches people individually or in small groups. **tutorial** (n).

tutu (n) a short ballet skirt made of several stiff layers of net.

tuxedo (n) (US) a man's dinner jacket with silk lapels, worn with a bow tie for formal occasions. Tuxedo is often shortened to tux.

TV short for **television**.

tweezers (plural n) small pincers used for pulling out hairs or for picking up very small objects.

twice (adv) two times.

twig twigging twigged
1 (n) a small, thin branch.
2 (v) (informal) to realize or understand something.

twilight (n) the time of day when the Sun has just set and it is beginning to get dark.

twin twinning twinned
1 (n) one of two children born to the same mother at almost the same time.
2 (adj) one of a matching pair. Twin beds.
3 If a town is **twinned** with a town in another country, the two towns exchange visits and organize events together.

twinge (twinj) (n) a sudden pain or unpleasant feeling. A twinge of arthritis. A twinge of regret.

twinkle twinkling twinkled (v) to shine and sparkle. The stars twinkle in the sky. **twinkle** (n).

twirl twirling twirled (v) to turn or spin round and round. **twirl** (n).

twist twisting twisted
1 (v) to turn, or to bend. Roderick twisted the top off the jar. The road twisted through the mountains.
2 (v) to wind two strands of something together.

twitch twitches twitching twitched (v) to make small, jerky movements. **twitch** (n), **twitchy** (adj).

type typing typed
1 (n) a kind, or a sort. What type of car do you have?
2 (v) to write something using a typewriter or computer.
3 (n) printed letters and numbers. This picture shows two kinds of type. Serif has a small line, or serif, at the end of each letter's main strokes. Sans serif has no serifs.

type

serif

type

sans serif

typewriter (n) a machine that prints letters and numbers when you press keys with your fingers.

typhoid (ty-foyd) (n) a serious, infectious disease that causes fever, diarrhoea, and sometimes death. It is caused by germs in food or water.

typhoon (ty-foon) (n) a violent, tropical storm.

typical
1 (adj) Something that is **typical** has the usual features that you associate with that kind of thing. A typical English village. **typically** (adv).
2 (adj) If someone does something that is **typical**, they behave in their usual way. It's typical of Toby to forget my birthday! **typically** (adv).

typist (n) someone who uses a typewriter or computer to write things.

tyrant (n) someone who rules other people in a cruel and unkind way. **tyranny** (n), **tyrannical** (adj).

tyre (n) a circle of rubber around the rim of a wheel. Tyres are usually filled with air.

Uu

udder *(n)* the bag-like part of a cow, sheep, etc. that hangs down near its back legs and produces milk.

UFO *(n)* a strange object seen flying in the sky, that is believed by some people to be a spaceship from another planet. UFO is short for unidentified flying object.

ugly uglier ugliest
1 *(adj)* If something or someone is ugly, they are unattractive and unpleasant to look at.
2 *(adj)* dangerous and violent. *There were ugly scenes as police and demonstrators clashed.*

ulcer *(ul-ser) (n)* a sore area, either on your skin or inside your mouth or stomach.

ultimate
1 *(adj)* last, or final. **ultimately** *(adv).*
2 *(adj)* original, or basic. *The Sun is the ultimate source of all our energy.* **ultimately** *(adv).*
3 *(n)* the greatest, or the best. *This car is the ultimate in speed and luxury.*

ultimatum *(n)* a final warning.

ultrasound *(n)* sound that is of too high frequency for the human ear to hear it. Ultrasound waves are used in medical scans.

ultraviolet light *(n)* light that cannot be seen by the human eye, which is given off by the Sun and causes your skin to tan.

umbilical cord *(n)* the tube that connects an unborn baby to its mother's body and through which it gets oxygen and food.
See **pregnant**.

umbrella *(n)* a frame with a circular cloth stretched over it that you hold over your head to protect you from the rain.

umpire *(n)* someone who makes sure that a cricket or tennis match is played according to the rules.

unable *(adj)* If you are **unable** to do something, you cannot do it.

unacceptable *(adj)* If something is unacceptable, it is not good enough to be allowed or accepted.

unaccustomed *(adj)* If you are unaccustomed to something, you are not used to it.

unadulterated *(adj)* If a substance is unadulterated, it has not had anything extra added to it.

unaided *(adj)* If you do something unaided, you do it on your own without any help.

unanimous *(yoo-nan-im-uss) (adj)* agreed by everyone. *A unanimous decision.* **unanimously** *(adv).*

unapproachable *(adj)* Someone who is unapproachable is not friendly, or is not easy to get to know.

unarmed *(adj)* Someone who is unarmed is not carrying any weapons.

unauthorized *or* **unauthorised** *(adj)* If something is unauthorized, it is done without official permission.

unavoidable *(adj)* If something is unavoidable, it is impossible to prevent. **unavoidably** *(adv).*

unaware *(adj)* If you are unaware of something, you do not know that it exists or is happening.

unbalanced
1 *(adj)* Something that is unbalanced cannot balance and falls over.
2 *(adj)* Someone who is unbalanced is slightly mad.
3 *(adj)* A piece of writing or a speech that is unbalanced puts forward only one side of an argument.

unbearable *(adj)* If something is unbearable, it is so bad or unpleasant that you cannot stand it.

unbelievable *(adj)* If something is unbelievable, it is so strange, surprising, or wonderful that you find it hard to accept that it is true.

unbending *(adj)* If someone is unbending, they are very firm and will not change their mind.

unburden unburdening unburdened *(v)* If you unburden yourself, you get rid of a load or a worry. *Jerome unburdened himself by confessing what he had done.*

uncanny *(adj)* very strange and difficult to explain or understand. **uncannily** *(adv).*

uncertain *(adj)* If you are uncertain about something, you are not sure about it. **uncertainty** *(n).*

uncivilized *or* **uncivilised**
1 *(adj)* not yet civilized or educated. *An uncivilized tribe.*
2 *(adj)* Uncivilized behaviour is rude and rough.

uncle *(n)* the brother of your father or mother, or the husband of your aunt.

uncomfortable
1 *(adj)* If you are uncomfortable, you do not feel relaxed in your body or your mind. **uncomfortably** *(adv).*

2 *(adj)* Something that is uncomfortable makes you feel uneasy or unhappy. *An uncomfortable situation.*

uncomplimentary *(adj)* If someone says uncomplimentary things about you, they are insulting or rude.

uncompromising *(adj)* If you are uncompromising, you refuse to change your mind. **uncompromisingly** *(adv).*

unconditional *(adj)* not depending on anything else. *Maxine has an unconditional college place.* **unconditionally** *(adv).*

unconfirmed *(adj)* not yet known to be true. *Unconfirmed rumours.*

unconscious
1 *(adj)* not awake, or unable to see, hear, think, etc. because you have fainted or been knocked out.
2 *(adj)* unaware of something. *George was unconscious of the fact that the bus was leaving.*

uncontrollable *(adj)* Something that is uncontrollable cannot be stopped or controlled. **uncontrollably** *(adv).*

uncooperative *(adj)* If you are uncooperative, you refuse to help people or do things for them.

uncouth *(adj)* rough and rude.

uncover uncovering uncovered
1 *(v)* to take a cover off something.
2 *(v)* to reveal something. *The investigation uncovered a major fraud.*

undaunted *(adj)* If you are undaunted, you are not put off by dangers or difficulties.

undecided *(adj)* If you are undecided about something, you have not made up your mind about it.

undeniable *(adj)* Something that is undeniable is certainly true. **undeniably** *(adv).*

under
1 *(prep)* below or beneath something. *The key is under the doormat.*
2 *(prep)* less than a number or amount. *Children under 12 will not be admitted.*
3 *(prep)* If you have people under you, you give them orders.

underarm *(adv)* throwing with your arm swinging under your shoulder. **underarm** *(adj).*

undercarriage *(n)* the part of an aircraft, including the wheels, which supports it when it is on the ground. *See* **aircraft**.

underclothes *(plural n)* clothes that you wear under your other clothes. *The picture shows European underclothes from four centuries.*

underclothes

| 1580s: body and farthingale | 1600s: stays and petticoat | 1800s: crinoline, petticoat, and drawers | 1900s: united garment | 1950s: long bra and corset |

underdog *(n)* a person or team that is expected to be the loser in a situation or competition.

underestimate underestimating underestimated
1 *(v)* to think that something is not as good or as great as it really is. *Freddie feels that his mother underestimates his talents.*
2 *(v)* to make a guess which is too low. *Kieran underestimated the amount of food we would need.*

underfoot *(adv)* under your feet, or on the ground. *It's slippery underfoot.*

undergo undergoes undergoing underwent undergone *(v)* to experience or suffer something. *Dan underwent a serious operation.*

underground
1 *(adj)* below the ground. *An underground stream.* **underground** *(adv)*.
2 *(adj)* secret and often illegal. *An underground organization.*

3 *(n)* a railway system in which the trains travel through tunnels below the ground. *The London Underground.*

undergrowth *(n)* bushes and plants that grow in a thick mass under trees, usually in a wood or forest.

underline underlining underlined
1 *(v)* to draw a line under a word or sentence.
2 *(v)* to stress how important something is.

undermine undermining undermined *(v)* to weaken something gradually.

underneath *(prep)* under or below something. **underneath** *(adj)*.

undernourished *(adj)* Someone who is undernourished is weak and unhealthy through lack of food.

underpants *(plural n)* pants worn by men or boys.

underpass underpasses *(n)* a road or path that passes underneath another road.

underprivileged *(adj)* Someone who is **underprivileged** is poor and does not have the opportunities that most people have.

understand understanding understood
1 *(v)* to know what something means or how something works. *Luke understands engines.*
2 *(v)* to know what someone is like or why they behave in the way that they do. *I can understand why you're so happy.* **understanding** *(adj)*.
3 *(v)* to believe that something is true. *I understand that Drew's family is moving to Melbourne.*

understandable
1 *(adj)* easy to grasp or understand.
2 *(adj)* easy to sympathize with. *It's understandable that Justin's upset.* **understandably** *(adv)*.

undertake undertaking undertook undertaken *(v)* If you **undertake** something, you agree to do a particular job. **undertaking** *(n)*.

undertaker *(n)* someone whose job is to arrange funerals and prepare dead bodies to be buried or cremated.

underwater *(adj)* living or happening under the surface of water. *The picture shows a submersible and a remote operated vehicle (ROV), which are both used for underwater exploration.* **underwater** *(adv)*.

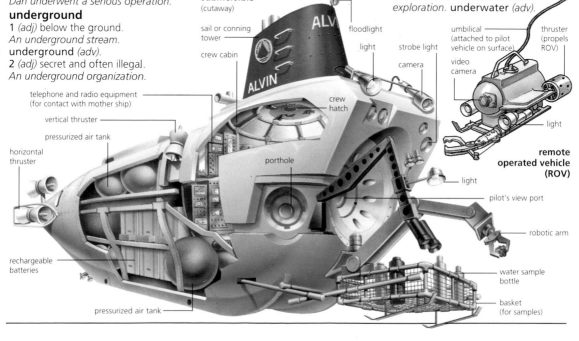

submersible
(cutaway)

sail or conning tower

floodlight

light

strobe light

camera

crew cabin

telephone and radio equipment
(for contact with mother ship)

vertical thruster

pressurized air tank

horizontal thruster

crew hatch

porthole

rechargeable batteries

pressurized air tank

light

pilot's view port

robotic arm

water sample bottle

basket
(for samples)

umbilical
(attached to pilot vehicle on surface)

thruster
(propels ROV)

video camera

light

remote operated vehicle (ROV)

underwear *(singular n)* clothes that you wear next to your skin, under your other clothes. See **underclothes**.

underworld
1 *(n)* the secret world of criminals.
2 *(n)* In legends, the Underworld is the place under the ground where the spirits of dead people live.

undesirable *(adj)* unpleasant.

undeveloped
1 *(adj)* An **undeveloped** country is poor and does not have many modern industries.
2 *(adj)* **Undeveloped** land does not have buildings on it.

undo undoes undoing undid undone
1 *(v)* to untie or unfasten something.
2 *(v)* to remove or destroy the effects of something.

undress undresses undressing undressed *(v)* to take off your clothes.

unearth unearthing unearthed
1 *(v)* to dig something up.
2 *(v)* to find something after searching for it. *At last, I unearthed my pen.*

uneasy *(adj)* If you feel **uneasy** about something, you feel slightly worried or unhappy about it. **uneasiness** *(n)*, **uneasily** *(adv)*.

unemployed *(adj)* Someone who is **unemployed** does not have a paid job. **unemployment** *(n)*.

unequal *(adj)* not the same as something else in size, value, or amount. **unequally** *(adv)*.

uneven
1 *(adj)* not flat, or not smooth.
2 *(adj)* not regular, or not consistent. *An uneven essay.* **unevenly** *(adv)*.

uneventful *(adj)* not interesting, or not exciting.

unexpected *(adj)* Something that is **unexpected** is surprising because you did not think it would happen. **unexpectedly** *(adv)*.

unfair unfairer unfairest *(adj)* not reasonable, or not right. **unfairly** *(adv)*.

unfaithful
1 *(adj)* not loyal, or not trustworthy. **unfaithfully** *(adv)*.
2 *(adj)* Someone who is **unfaithful** to their partner has a sexual relationship with someone else.

unfamiliar
1 *(adj)* not well-known, or not easily recognized. *The room was full of unfamiliar people.*
2 *(adj)* If you are **unfamiliar** with something, you do not know it well.

unfit
1 *(adj)* not healthy, or not strong.
2 *(adj)* not suitable, or not good enough. *The king was unfit to rule.*

unfold unfolding unfolded
1 *(v)* to open something that was folded. *I unfolded the letter.*
2 *(v)* When a story or plan **unfolds**, more of it becomes known.

unforgettable *(adj)* so good, bad, etc. that you will never forget it.

unforgivable *(adj)* If someone does something **unforgivable**, they do something so bad that you cannot forgive them. **unforgivably** *(adv)*.

unfortunate
1 *(adj)* unlucky. *An unfortunate accident.* **unfortunately** *(adv)*.
2 *(adj)* If you say that something was **unfortunate**, you mean that you wish it had never happened.

unfriendly unfriendlier unfriendliest *(adj)* unkind, or unhelpful. **unfriendliness** *(n)*.

ungrateful *(adj)* If you are **ungrateful** for something, you are not thankful for it and do not appreciate it. **ungratefully** *(adv)*.

unhappy unhappier unhappiest *(adj)* miserable, or upset. **unhappiness** *(n)*, **unhappily** *(adv)*.

unhealthy unhealthier unhealthiest
1 *(adj)* unfit, or not well.
2 *(adj)* Something that is **unhealthy** makes you unfit. *An unhealthy diet.*

unhygienic *(adj)* unclean, and not free from germs. *It's unhygienic to prepare food without washing your hands first.*

unicorn *(n)*
an imaginary animal like a horse with one straight horn growing from its forehead. *This unicorn comes from a series of tapestries called "The Lady and the Unicorn", made in about 1500.*

unicorn

unicycle *(n)* a cycle with only one wheel.

unidentified *(adj)* If something is **unidentified**, no one knows what it is. **unidentifiable** *(adj)*.

uniform
1 *(n)* a special set of clothes worn by all the members of a school, army, or organization. **uniformed** *(adj)*.
2 *(adj)* Things that are **uniform** are all the same, and not different or changing in any way. *The houses were all of uniform height.* **uniformity** *(n)*, **uniformly** *(adv)*.

unify unifies unifying unified *(v)* to bring together different people or groups in order to form a larger group. **unification** *(n)*.

unimportant *(adj)* Something that is **unimportant** will not have a great effect and does not need to be taken seriously.

uninhabited *(adj)* If a place is **uninhabited**, no one lives there.

unintelligible *(adj)* If something is **unintelligible**, it cannot be understood. **unintelligibly** *(adv)*.

unintentional *(adj)* Something that is **unintentional** is done by accident, not deliberately. **unintentionally** *(adv)*.

uninterested *(adj)* If you are **uninterested** in something, you do not want to know about it.

union
1 *(n)* an organized group of workers set up to help improve work conditions and pay.
2 *(n)* the joining together of two or more things or people.

unique *(yoo-neek) (adj)* If something is **unique**, it is the only one of its kind. **uniquely** *(adv)*.

unisex *(adj)* able to be used by both men and women. *Unisex clothing.*

unison *(n)* If people say or do something **in unison**, they say or do it together.

unit
1 *(n)* a single, complete thing.
2 *(n)* a group of people who work together to do a job. *An army unit.*
3 *(n)* a piece of furniture that fits together with others of the same type. *Kitchen units.*
4 *(n)* an amount used as a standard of measurement. *A gram is a unit of weight.*

unite uniting united *(v)* If people **unite**, they join together or work together to achieve something. **unity** *(n)*.

universal
1 *(adj)* Something that is **universal** applies to everyone or everything. *This film has universal appeal.* **universally** *(adv)*.
2 **universal indicator** *(n)* a solution or a piece of paper that turns a different colour to show how acidic or alkaline a substance or solution is.

universe *(n)* everything in space, including the Earth, Sun, Moon, and stars.

university universities *(n)* a place where people can study for degrees or do research.

unjust *(adj)* not fair, or not right. unjustly *(adv)*.

unkempt *(adj)* untidy and neglected.

unkind unkinder unkindest *(adj)* unfriendly, unhelpful, and not generous. unkindly *(adv)*.

unknown *(adj)* unfamiliar, or not known about. *An unknown planet.*

unless *(conj)* except, or if not. *I can't come unless someone gives me a lift.*

unlike *(prep)* If one thing is unlike another, the two things are very different.

unlikely unlikelier unlikeliest *(adj)* not probable.

unlimited *(adj)* If there is an unlimited amount of something, you can have or use as much of it as you want.

unload unloading unloaded *(v)* to remove things from a container or vehicle.

unlock unlocking unlocked *(v)* to unfasten something with a key.

unlucky unluckier unluckiest
1 *(adj)* Someone who is unlucky is unfortunate and bad things seem to happen to them.
2 *(adj)* Something that is unlucky happens by chance and is unfortunate. unluckily *(adv)*.
3 *(adj)* An unlucky number, date, etc. is one that you think will bring you bad luck.

unmistakable *(adj)* If someone or something is unmistakable, they are very individual and cannot be confused with someone or something else. unmistakably *(adv)*.

unnatural
1 *(adj)* unusual, or not normal. *An unnatural sound.* unnaturally *(adv)*.
2 *(adj)* false, or not sincere. *Stan sounded nervous and unnatural.* unnaturally *(adv)*.

unnecessary *(adj)* If something is unnecessary, you do not need to do it or have it. unnecessarily *(adv)*.

unobserved *(adj)* unseen, or unnoticed.

unofficial
1 *(adj)* not approved by someone in authority. *An unofficial report.*
2 *(adj)* informal. *An unofficial visit.*

unpack unpacking unpacked *(v)* to take objects out of a box, case, etc.

unpleasant *(adj)* horrible, or not likable. unpleasantly *(adv)*.

unplug unplugging unplugged *(v)* to remove a plug from an electric socket.

unpopular *(adj)* not liked or enjoyed by many people.

unpredictable *(adj)* If something or someone is unpredictable, you do not know what they will do or say next. unpredictably *(adv)*.

unprepared *(adj)* not ready for something.

unprovoked *(adj)* If an action is unprovoked, no one has done anything to cause it or encourage it.

unravel unravelling unravelled
1 *(v)* to unwind a tangled mass of string, wool, etc.
2 *(v)* to search for and discover the truth about a complex situation. *The detectives unravelled the mystery.*

unreasonable *(adj)* not fair. *The film star's demands were totally unreasonable.* unreasonably *(adv)*.

unrecognizable or **unrecognisable** *(adj)* If someone or something is unrecognizable they have totally changed so that you do not immediately know who or what they are.

unreliable *(adj)* Something or someone who is unreliable cannot be depended on or trusted.

unrest *(n)* disturbance and trouble.

unrestricted *(adj)* without rules or restrictions. *This ticket gives you unrestricted use of the pool.*

unripe *(adj)* not yet ready to be harvested, picked, or eaten.

unrivalled *(adj)* better than anything else.

unroll unrolling unrolled *(v)* to open out something that is rolled up. *We unrolled our sleeping bags.*

unruly unrulier unruliest *(adj)* badly-behaved and disobedient.

unscathed *(adj)* not hurt. *The driver survived the crash unscathed.*

unscrupulous *(adj)* Unscrupulous people have few principles and are not concerned about whether their actions are right or wrong. unscrupulously *(adv)*.

unseen *(adj)* hidden, or not able to be seen.

unsettle unsettling unsettled *(v)* to disturb someone, or to make someone feel uneasy.

unsightly *(adj)* ugly and unpleasant to look at.

unskilled *(adj)* An unskilled worker has no particular skill or training.

unstable
1 *(adj)* not firm, or not steady.
2 *(adj)* An unstable person has rapid changes of mood and behaviour.

unsteady *(adj)* shaky, or wobbly. unsteadily *(adv)*.

unstuck
1 *(adj)* If something has come unstuck, it is not glued together any more.
2 *(informal)* If your plans come unstuck, you are not able to carry them out.

unsuccessful *(adj)* If you are unsuccessful, you do not do well, or do not get what you want. unsuccessfully *(adv)*.

unsuitable *(adj)* not right for a particular purpose. *Clive was wearing unsuitable clothes for the expedition.* unsuitability *(n)*, unsuitably *(adv)*.

unsure *(adj)* not certain, or not definite. *Katie is unsure about the future.*

unthinkable *(adj)* If something is unthinkable it is out of the question and cannot be considered.

untidy untidier untidiest *(adj)* not neat. untidiness *(n)*, untidily *(adv)*.

untie untying untied *(v)* to undo knots or bows.

until *(conj)* up to the time that. *You can stay until tomorrow.*

unto *(prep)* *(old-fashioned)* to.

untold *(adj)* too great to be counted or worked out. *Untold damage.*

untouched
1 *(adj)* not handled by anyone.
2 *(adj)* left alone, or ignored. *The thieves took the money, but left the jewellery untouched.*

untrue *(adj)* false, or incorrect.

unused *(adj)* An unused item has never been used.

unusual *(adj)* strange, abnormal, or odd. unusually *(adv)*.

unwaged *(adj)* without a paid job.

unwanted *(adj)* If something is unwanted, you do not need or want it.

unwelcome *(adj)* If someone or something is unwelcome, they are not gladly received or accepted.

unwell *(adj)* ill, or poorly.

unwieldy *(adj)* difficult to hold, or hard to manage. *An unwieldy parcel.*

unwilling *(adj)* reluctant, or not keen to do something. **unwillingly** *(adv)*.

unwind unwinding unwound
1 *(v)* to undo something that has been wound up. *Tina unwound the hose.*
2 *(v)* to relax and become less worried or tense. *Ann plays sport to unwind.*

unworthy *(adj)* not deserving, or below standard. *The beer crate made an unworthy seat for the President.*

unwrap unwrapping unwrapped
(v) to take the packaging or outer layer off something.

up *(prep)* from a lower to a higher place. **upward** *(adj)*, **up** *(adv)*.

upbeat *(adj)* *(informal)* optimistic and cheerful.

upbringing *(n)* the way that a child is raised or brought up.

update updating updated
1 *(v)* to give someone the latest information. *Please update us on your plans.* **update** *(n)*.
2 *(v)* to change something in order to include the latest style or information. *We are updating our catalogue.*

upgrade upgrading upgraded
1 *(v)* to improve something. *Jamal upgraded his computer by adding extra memory.*
2 *(v)* to promote someone to a better or more important job.

upheaval *(n)* a big change or disturbance. *Moving house was a great upheaval for us all.*

uphill *(adj)* sloping upwards.

upholstery *(n)* the stuffing, covering, etc. that is put on furniture.

upkeep *(n)* the work or cost of looking after something or someone.

up-market *(adj)* Goods that are up-market are expensive and of high quality.

upon *(adv)* on.

upper *(adj)* higher. *An upper window.*

upper case *(adj)* Upper case letters are capital letters.

upright
1 *(adj)* standing up, or standing straight. **upright** *(adv)*.
2 *(adj)* honest and fair. *An upright citizen.*
3 *(n)* a vertical post.

uprising *(n)* a rebellion, or a revolt.

uproar *(n)* shouting, noise, and confusion. *The lesson ended in uproar.* **uproarious** *(adj)*.

uproot uprooting uprooted
1 *(v)* to take a plant out of the earth.
2 *(v)* to move someone from where they are settled in their home or work.

upset upsetting upset
1 *(v)* to make someone unhappy or distressed. **upset** *(adj)*.
2 *(v)* to overturn something. *Sinead upset the milk.*
3 *(v)* to make someone feel ill. *Oysters always upset me.*

upside down
1 *(adv)* the wrong way up.
2 *(adv)* in a confused or untidy condition. *The thieves turned the place upside down.*

upstairs *(adv)* to or on a higher floor.

uptight
1 *(adj)* *(informal)* tense, or anxious.
2 *(adj)* *(informal)* unable to express your feelings easily.

up-to-date *(adj)* If something is up-to-date, it contains the most recent information or is in the latest style.

urban *(adj)* to do with, or living in towns or cities. *Urban wildlife.*

Urdu *(n)* a language spoken in Pakistan and India.

urge urging urged
1 *(v)* to encourage or persuade someone strongly. *Dad urged me to try harder.*
2 *(n)* a strong wish or need to do something. *Todd felt a sudden urge to throw something.*

urgent *(adj)* If something is urgent, it needs very quick or immediate action. **urgency** *(n)*, **urgently** *(adv)*.

urinate *(yoor-in-ate)* urinating urinated *(v)* to pass urine from your body. **urination** *(n)*.

urine *(yoor-in)* *(n)* the liquid waste that people and animals pass out of their bodies.

URL *(n)* the series of letters (and sometimes numbers) that you type into your computer to enable a browser to find a particular Web site or page. URL stands for uniform resource locator. Another name for URL is Web address.

urn
1 *(n)* a vase used as an ornament or as a container for the ashes of a dead person. *The picture shows an urn made in Ancient Greece.*
2 *(n)* a large, insulated container, used for serving tea or coffee and for keeping them hot.

urn

usage
1 *(n)* the way that something is used or treated. *Careless usage.*
2 *(n)* the way that a language is spoken and written. *English usage.*

use using used
1 *(yooz)* *(v)* to do a job with something. *I used a penknife to cut through the wrapping.*
2 *(yooce)* *(n)* the action of using something. *I'm sure I can find a use for your present. Put away the tools after use.*
3 *(yooz)* *(v)* If you use someone, you take advantage of them in order to get something that you want.
4 **use up** *(yooz)* *(v)* If you use something up, you finish it.

used
1 *(yoozed)* *(adj)* already made use of. *A used car.*
2 *(yoost)* If you are used to something, you know it well.
3 *(yoost)* If you used to do something, you did it in the past.

useful *(yooce-ful)* *(adj)* Something that is useful is helpful and can be used a lot. **usefulness** *(n)*.

useless *(yooce-less)*
1 *(adj)* Something that is useless cannot be used or is not helpful.
2 *(adj)* *(informal)* not very good. *I'm useless at French.*

user-friendly *(adj)* If a machine is user-friendly, it is easy to use.

usher *(n)* someone who shows people to their seats in a court, at a wedding, etc. **usher** *(v)*.

usherette *(n)* a woman who takes tickets and shows people to their seats at a cinema or theatre.

usual *(adj)* normal, or regular. **usually** *(adv)*.

utensil *(n)* a tool or container, often one used in the kitchen.

utmost *(n)* the most, or the greatest possible. *The government said they would do their utmost to help the refugees.* **utmost** *(adj)*.

utter uttering uttered
1 *(v)* to speak, or to make some sort of sound from your mouth. *Petrova uttered a low moan.* **utterance** *(n)*.
2 *(adj)* complete, total, or absolute. *The play was an utter disaster.* **utterly** *(adv)*.

U-turn
1 *(n)* a U-shaped turn made by a vehicle, in order to change its direction.
2 *(n)* a complete reversal of policy or attitude. *A government U-turn.*

Vv

vacant
1 (adj) empty, or not occupied.
A vacant house.
2 (adj) available. *This job is vacant.*
vacancy (n).
3 (adj) If someone looks **vacant**, they have a blank expression on their face.

vacate vacating vacated (v)
to leave, or to make somewhere empty. *Hotel guests should vacate their rooms by 10 a.m.*

vacation
1 (n) a break between university or college terms.
2 (n) (US) time away from school or work, especially a trip away from home (holiday, UK).

vaccinate vaccinating vaccinated
(v) to protect someone against a disease, usually by giving them an injection. vaccination (n).

vaccine (vak-seen) (n) a substance injected or given by mouth to protect someone from disease.

vacuum
(vak-yoom) (n)
a sealed space
from which all air
or gas has been
emptied.

vacuum
cleaner (n)
a machine that
sucks up dirt
from carpets,
furniture, etc.

vacuum flask
(n) a container
that keeps liquids
hot or cold. The
vacuum between
its two glass
walls prevents
heat or cold
escaping.

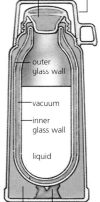

vacuum flask
(cross-section)

stopper   cup

outer
glass wall

vacuum

inner
glass wall

liquid

body   tip protector

vagina (vaj-eye-na) (n) the passage leading from the womb, through which babies are born.

vague (vayg) vaguer vaguest (adj) not clear, or not definite. *I have only vague memories of Miranda.*

vain vainer vainest
1 (adj) If someone is **vain**, you are too proud of yourself, especially of the way that you look.
2 (adj) unsuccessful, or futile. *Bik made a vain attempt to stop the bus.*

valiant (adj) brave, or courageous. valiantly (adv).

valid
1 (adj) sensible and acceptable. *You can leave early only if you have a valid reason.* validity (n).
2 (adj) acceptable, or legal. *To travel on the train, you need a valid ticket.*

valley (n) an area of low ground between two hills, usually containing a river.

valour (n) (poetic) bravery, or courage.

valuable
1 (adj) Something that is **valuable** is worth a lot of money, or is very important in some other way. *A valuable jewel. Valuable information.*
2 valuables (plural n) possessions that are worth a lot of money.

value valuing valued
1 (n) what something is worth. *What is the value of this watch?*
2 (v) to think that something is important. *I value Posy's friendship greatly.*
3 (v) to assess how much something is worth. *The auctioneer valued the paintings before the sale.*
4 (plural n) People's **values** are their beliefs and ideas about what is most important in life.

valve (n) a type of tap that controls the flow of fluid, air, etc. See **engine**, **heart**.

vampire (n) In folk tales and horror stories, a **vampire** is a corpse with fangs that rises from its grave to drink the blood of human victims.

van (n) a closed vehicle for carrying goods. *A delivery van.*

vandal (n) someone who needlessly damages or destroys other people's property. vandalism (n), vandalize (v).

vane
1 (n) A **weather vane** is a pointer that swings around to show the direction of the wind.
2 (n) the flat part of a bird's feather. See **feather**.

vanilla (n) the pod or bean of a tropical orchid, used for flavouring ice cream, cakes, etc.

vanilla

vanilla
orchid

vanilla
pods

vanish vanishes vanishing vanished (v) to disappear suddenly.

vanity (n) a feeling of extreme pride and conceit.

vapour (n) a gas, usually one that has been changed from a liquid or solid. *Water vapour is visible as clouds, mist, or steam.*

variable
1 (adj) likely to change. *Variable weather.* variability (n).
2 (n) In maths, a **variable** is a value, given to a symbol, such as x or y, that may change.

variation (n) a change in something.

variety varieties
1 (n) a selection of different things.
2 (n) a different type of the same thing. *A new variety of rose.*

various
1 (adj) several. *I have various hobbies.*
2 (adj) different. *The cakes were many and various.*

varnish varnishes (n) a clear coating that you paint on wood to protect it and give it a shiny finish.
varnish (v).

vary varies varying varied
1 (v) to change or be different. *Mimi's handwriting varies depending on her mood.*
2 (v) If you **vary** something, you make changes to it.

vase (n) an ornamental container, often used for flowers. *The picture shows an Art Deco style enamelled vase, made in the 1930s.*

vase

vast vaster vastest (adj) huge in area or extent. *The vast Sahara Desert. Polly has a vast fund of jokes.*
vastness (n), vastly (adv).

VAT (n) a British tax added to the cost of many types of goods. The initials VAT stand for value-added tax.

vault vaulting vaulted
1 (v) to leap over something, using your hands or other support.
vault (n).
2 (n) an underground burial chamber.

VDU (n) the screen of a computer and the keyboard connected to it. The initials VDU stand for visual display unit. See **computer**.

veal (n) the meat from a calf.

veer veering veered (v) to change direction. *The wind veered from east to north-east.*

vegan (vee-gan) (n) someone who does not use or eat any animal products. veganism (n), vegan (adj).

vegetable (n) a plant grown to be used as food. Vegetables are usually eaten with savoury foods. *The picture shows a variety of different vegetables.*

vegetables

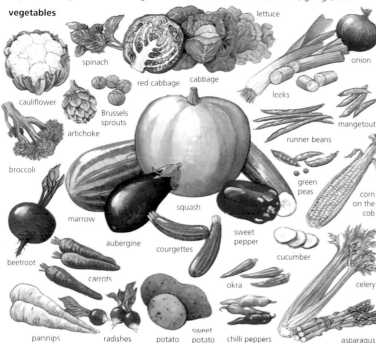

lettuce
onion
cabbage
red cabbage
spinach
leeks
cauliflower
Brussels sprouts
artichoke
mangetout
runner beans
broccoli
green peas
corn on the cob
marrow
squash
aubergine
courgettes
sweet pepper
cucumber
beetroot
carrots
okra
celery
parsnips
radishes
potato
sweet potato
chilli peppers
asparagus

vegetarian (n) someone who does not eat meat or fish.
vegetarianism (n), **vegetarian** (adj).

vegetation (n) plant life of all types.

vehement (vee-uh-ment) (adj) If you are vehement about something, you express your feelings about it very strongly. **vehemence** (n), **vehemently** (adv).

vehicle (vee-ik-ul) (n) something in which people or goods are carried from one place to another. Vehicles can range in size and power from a sledge to an express train.

veil (vale) (n) a fine piece of material worn by women to hide their faces.

vein (vane) (n) one of the tubes through which blood is carried back to the heart from other parts of the body. See **circulation**.

vellum
1 (n) fine parchment, made from the skin of a calf, lamb, etc.
2 (n) very high quality writing paper.

velocity (vel-oss-it-ee) **velocities** (n) speed. *The velocity of the rocket is 3,000mph.*

velvet
1 (n) a soft, thick fabric made from cotton or silk. **velvety** (adj).

2 (n) the soft skin on the growing antler of a deer. See **antler**.

vendetta (n) a long-running feud between two families, gangs, etc.

vending machine (n) a coin-operated machine from which you can buy food, drink, or other products.

venetian blind (n) an indoor blind made from thin strips that can be raised or tilted to alter the amount of light coming in.

vengeance (n) action that you take to pay someone back for harm that they have done to you or to your friends or family.

venom (n) poison produced by some snakes and spiders and injected through their fangs into their victims' bodies. *This diagram of a snake's jaws shows where its venom is stored.*

snake's jaws

fang
upper jaw
flexible muscle (allows jaw bones to separate)
venom sac
lower jaw

vent venting vented
1 (n) an opening through which waste can escape.
2 (n) the shaft of a volcano through which smoke and lava escapes. See **volcano**.

3 (v) If you **vent** your feelings, you show them in an obvious way.

ventilate ventilating ventilated (v) to let fresh air into a place and to send stale air out. **ventilation** (n).

ventriloquism (n) the art of speaking without moving your lips so that your words seem to come from somewhere else, for example, from a dummy's mouth. **ventriloquist** (n).

venture venturing ventured
1 (v) to put yourself at risk by doing something daring or dangerous. *The explorers ventured bravely into the dense jungle.*
2 (n) a project which is rather risky.

venue (ven-yoo) (n) a place where an event is held.

veranda or **verandah** (n) a raised platform around the outside of a house, often with a roof.

verb (n) a word that describes what someone or something does, thinks, or feels. "Sing", "have", and "come" are all verbs. See **page 3**.

verbal
1 (adj) to do with words. *A verbal reasoning test.*
2 (adj) spoken. *Verbal abuse.*
3 (adj) to do with verbs.

verdict
1 (n) the decision of a judge or jury on whether someone is guilty or not guilty.
2 (n) a decision, or an opinion. *What's your verdict on my chicken casserole?*

verge verging verged
1 (n) land at the side of a road, often with grass on it.
2 If you are **on the verge** of doing something, you will do it soon. *Hector is on the verge of leaving.*
3 (v) to be very near to something. *Ophelia's behaviour was verging on madness.*

verify verifies verifying verified (v) to confirm, or to back up something. *Roberta verified that what the witness said was true.* **verification** (n), **verifiable** (adj).

verruca (ver-oo-kuh) **verrucae** or **verrucas** (n) a small, hard, and sometimes painful growth, usually on the sole of the foot.

versatile (adj) talented or useful in many ways. *A versatile entertainer. A versatile tool.* **versatility** (n).

verse
1 (n) one part of a poem or song, made up of several lines.
2 (n) a general name for poetry.

version
1 (n) one way of expressing something. *Holly gave her version of what had happened.*
2 (n) a revised form or model of a book, car, piece of software, etc.

versus (prep) against. *Today's match is USA versus Canada.*

vertebra vertebrae (n) one of the bones that make up your spine.

vertebrate (n) a creature with a backbone. *Humans, elephants, and snakes are all vertebrates.* vertebrate (adj).

vertex vertexes or vertices
1 (n) the highest point of something.
2 (n) the point where two lines meet to form an angle.

vertical (adj) upright and perpendicular to the ground. *A vertical post.* vertically (adv).

very
1 (adv) to a great extent, much, or most. *I am very pleased to see you.*
2 (adj) exact. *You're the very person I wanted to see.*

vessel
1 (n) a general name for a ship.
2 (n) (old-fashioned) a container for liquids.

vest
1 (n) a piece of underwear worn on the top half of your body.
2 (n) (US) a short, light, sleeveless jacket, often worn under the jacket of a suit (waistcoat, UK).

vestige (vest-ij) (n) a trace of something. *There's a vestige of truth in what Bill says.*

vet vetting vetted
1 (n) someone who is trained to treat sick animals. Vet is short for veterinary surgeon.
2 (v) to check that someone can be trusted. *We have vetted every member of our gang.*

veteran
1 (n) someone with a lot of experience of something.
2 (n) a soldier who has returned from war.
3 veteran car (n) a car made before 1919, especially one made before 1905.

veterinary
1 (adj) to do with the treatment of animals.
2 veterinary surgeon see **vet**.

veto (vee-toe) vetoes vetoing vetoed (v) If someone **vetoes** something, they use their power to put a stop to a plan. veto (n).

vex vexes vexing vexed (v) to annoy or irritate somebody. vexation (n), vexatious (adj).

VHF (n) the waveband most commonly used for high-frequency reception of radio signals, also known as the FM band. The initials VHF stand for very high frequency.

via (prep) by way of. *This train goes to Edinburgh via York.*

viable (adj) workable, or capable of succeeding. *A viable plan.* viability (n).

viaduct (n) a large bridge that carries a railway or road across a valley.

vibrant (adj) bright, or lively. *Vibrant colours. A vibrant personality.* vibrancy (n), vibrantly (adv).

vibrate vibrating vibrated (v) to shake rapidly. vibration (n).

vicar (n) a priest in the Church of England.

vicarage (n) a vicar's house.

vice
1 (n) immoral or criminal behaviour.
2 (n) a tool that holds an object between two jaws so that you can work on it.

vice-captain (n) a deputy who helps the captain and takes over duties when the captain is unable to act.

vice president (n) a deputy who helps the president and takes over duties when the president is unable to act.

vice versa (adv) a Latin phrase meaning "the other way round" *You help me and vice versa.*

vicinity (vis-in-it-ee) vicinities (n) the area near a particular place. *After the robbery, the police sealed off all the roads in the vicinity.*

vicious (adj) bad-tempered, aggressive, and violent. viciousness (n), viciously (adv).

victim (n) someone who suffers or is killed because of something or someone else. *There were many victims of the air crash.*

victimize or **victimise** victimizing victimized (v) to pick someone out for unfair treatment. victimization (n).

victor (n) the winner in a battle or contest.

victory victories (n) a win in a battle or contest. victorious (adj), victoriously (adv).

video videoing videoed
1 (v) to record sound and pictures on to a tape. video (adj).

2 (n) a machine for playing video tapes. Video is short for video cassette recorder.
3 (n) a pre-recorded video tape.

video tape (n) magnetic tape on which sound and pictures are recorded.

vie vying vied (v) If you **vie** with someone, you compete with them. *The brothers vied for attention.*

view viewing viewed
1 (n) what you can see from a certain place. *The view from my window.*
2 (v) to look at something to see if you want to buy it. *May we view the house next weekend?* viewing (n).
3 (n) what you think about something. *What are your views on whaling?*

vigilant (adj) watchful and alert. vigilance (n), vigilantly (adv).

vigorous (adj) energetic, lively, or forceful. *Vigorous exercise. A vigorous speech.* vigour (n), vigorously (adv).

Viking (n) one of the Scandinavian peoples who invaded England and parts of northern Europe between the 8th and 11th centuries. See **longship**.

vile viler vilest (adj) horrible and disgusting. vileness (n).

villa
1 (n) In Ancient Roman times, a **villa** was a country house, usually built around a courtyard and including farm buildings.
2 (n) a large house set in a garden, usually in Mediterranean countries.

village (n) a small group of houses and other buildings in the countryside. villager (n).

villain (vill-un) (n) a wicked person, often an evil character in a play. villainous (adj).

villein (vill-ayn) (n) a farm worker in medieval times who belonged to the lord of the manor. See **feudalism**.

vindictive (adj) Someone who is **vindictive** is unforgiving and wants revenge. vindictiveness (n), vindictively (adv).

vine (n) a climbing plant on which grapes grow.

vinegar (n) a sour-tasting liquid, made from fermented wine, cider, etc. and used to flavour food.

vineyard (vin-yard) (n) an area of farmland where grapes are grown.

vintage (vin-tij)
1 (n) the wine produced in a particular year.
2 (adj) very good, or the best of its kind. *Yehudi gave a vintage performance.*

3 **vintage car** *(n)* a car made between 1919 and 1930.

violate violating violated
1 *(v)* to break a promise, a rule, or a law. **violation** *(n)*.
2 *(v)* to treat a person or place with no respect. **violation** *(n)*.

violence *(n)* the use of physical force to hurt or kill. **violent** *(adj)*, **violently** *(adv)*.

violet *(n)* a bluish-purple colour. **violet** *(adj)*.

violin *(n)* a musical instrument with four strings, played with a bow. See **strings**.

VIP *(n)* a famous or important person The initials VIP stand for very important person.

viper *(n)* an adder. See **adder**.

virgin
1 *(n)* someone who has never had sexual intercourse.
2 *(adj)* untouched, or in its natural state. *Virgin snow.*

virile *(adj)* Someone who is **virile** has qualities that are supposed to be typical of men. **virility** *(n)*.

virtually *(adv)* nearly, or almost. *We have virtually finished.* **virtual** *(adj)*.

virtual reality *(n)* an environment created by a computer which seems real to the person who experiences it.

virtue *(n)* a good quality. *Patience is a virtue.* **virtuous** *(adj)*, **virtuously** *(adv)*.

virtuoso *(n)* a highly skilled performer, especially a musician.

virulent
1 *(adj)* If a disease is **virulent**, it is very severe or harmful. **virulence** *(n)*, **virulently** *(adv)*.
2 *(adj)* **Virulent** criticism is very severe or bitter. **virulence** *(n)*, **virulently** *(adv)*.

virus viruses
1 *(n)* an organism that multiplies in body cells, often causing disease. See **AIDS**.
2 *(n)* the disease caused by a virus.
3 *(n)* hidden instructions within a computer program, designed to damage data or destroy a computer system.

visa *(vee-zer)* *(n)* a document giving permission for someone to enter a foreign country.

visible *(adj)* Something that is **visible** is able to be seen. *The island was visible on the horizon.* **visibility** *(n)*, **visibly** *(adv)*.

vision
1 *(n)* sight. *Eagles have excellent vision.*
2 *(n)* something that you see in a dream or trance, which is often strange or beautiful.
3 *(n)* the ability to think ahead.

visit visiting visited *(v)* to go to see people or places. **visit** *(n)*, **visitor** *(n)*.

visual
1 *(adj)* to do with seeing. *A visual guide.* **visually** *(adv)*.
2 *(n)* an image, or a picture.

visualize or **visualise** visualizing visualized *(v)* to picture something or to see something in your mind. **visualization** *(n)*.

vital *(adj)* essential, or absolutely necessary. **vitally** *(adv)*.

vitality *(n)* energy and liveliness. *Puppies are usually full of vitality.*

vitamin *(n)* one of the substances in food that is necessary for good health. *Vitamin C helps to protect you against colds.*

vivacious *(adj)* A **vivacious** person has a lively personality. **vivacity** *(n)*, **vivaciously** *(adv)*.

vivid *(adj)* very bright, clear, or realistic. *A vivid dream. Vivid colours.* **vividness** *(n)*, **vividly** *(adv)*.

vivisection *(n)* the use of live animals for scientific and medical research.

vocabulary vocabularies *(n)* the range of words that a person uses and understands. *Caspar has a very wide vocabulary.*

vocal
1 *(adj)* to do with the voice.
2 *(adj)* If someone is **vocal** they are outspoken and often express their opinions. **vocally** *(adv)*.
3 *(plural n)* On a tape, CD, etc. the **vocals** are the parts that are sung.

vocalist *(n)* a singer

vocation
1 *(n)* a strong feeling that you want to do a particular job.
2 *(n)* a job or profession, especially one that needs special training. **vocational** *(adj)*.

vociferous *(vo-sif-er-us)* *(adj)* If someone is **vociferous**, they are noisy and talkative and insist on being heard. **vociferously** *(adv)*.

vodka *(n)* a strong alcoholic drink made from rye.

vogue *(vohg)* If something is in **vogue**, it is the current fashion.

voice voicing voiced
1 *(n)* the power to speak and sing. *Lois has lost her voice.*
2 *(n)* the sound produced when you speak or sing. *Minnie has a high voice.*
3 *(v)* When you **voice** an opinion, you express it. **voice** *(n)*.

void
1 *(n)* an empty space. *The spaceship careered into the void.*
2 *(adj)* If a result is declared **void**, it does not count any more.

volatile
1 *(adj)* A **volatile** chemical evaporates very easily or is unstable in some other way. **volatility** *(n)*.
2 *(adj)* Someone who is **volatile** has rapid mood changes.

volcano volcanoes *(n)* a mountain with vents through which molten lava, ash, cinders, and gas erupt, sometimes violently. Volcanoes occur along the boundaries of the Earth's plates, where molten rock is forced upwards from magma reservoirs. Some volcanoes are extinct, others are dormant, and a few are active. *This picture shows a cutaway view of an erupting volcano.*

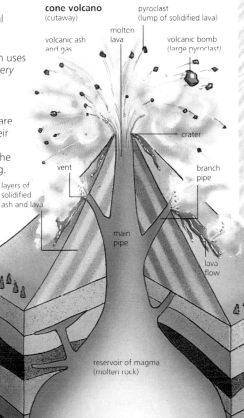

cone volcano (cutaway)

pyroclast (lump of solidified lava)

molten lava

volcanic ash and gas

volcanic bomb (large pyroclast)

crater

vent

branch pipe

layers of solidified ash and lava

main pipe

lava flow

reservoir of magma (molten rock)

volley *(n)* a shot in games, such as tennis and soccer, where the ball is hit or kicked before it can bounce.

volleyball *(n)* a six-a-side game in which teams use their hands to hit a large ball over the net, and try to make it hit the ground on their opponent's side.

volt *(n)* a unit of electrical force. Volts are used to measure voltage.

voltage *(n)* the force of an electrical supply, expressed in volts. *12 volts is the voltage of most car batteries.*

volume
1 *(n)* the amount of space taken up by a three-dimensional shape, such as a box or room. To work out the volume of an object, you multiply its length by its width by its breadth.
2 *(n)* the degree of sound produced by a radio, a pop group, etc.
3 *(n)* a large book, often one of a series. *This encyclopedia has 12 volumes.*

voluntary
1 *(adj)* willing and unforced. *A voluntary decision.*
2 **voluntary work** *(n)* unpaid work, usually done to help others.

volunteer volunteering volunteered *(v)* to offer to do a job. **volunteer** *(n)*.

vomit vomiting vomited *(v)* When you **vomit**, you bring up food from your stomach through your mouth. **vomit** *(n)*.

vote voting voted *(v)* to make a choice in an election or other poll, usually by marking a paper or raising your hand. **vote** *(n)*.

voucher *(n)* a piece of paper which can be exchanged for goods or services. *A gift voucher.*

vow vowing vowed *(v)* to make a serious and important promise.

vowel *(n)* one of the letters a, e, i, o, and u. Y is also a vowel in words like gymnastics, but a consonant in words like yo-yo.

voyage *(n)* a sea journey. **voyager** *(n)*.

vulgar
1 *(adj)* rude, or coarse. **vulgarity** *(n)*.
2 **vulgar fraction** *(n)* a fraction shown by numbers above and below a line, such as ¼ and ½, rather than by a decimal point, such as 0.25 and 0.5.

vulnerable *(adj)* If someone or something is **vulnerable**, they are in a weak position and likely to be hurt or damaged in some way. **vulnerability** *(n)*, **vulnerably** *(adv)*.

Ww

wad *(wod)* *(n)* a thick pad, or a bundle. *A wad of banknotes.*

waddle waddling waddled *(v)* to walk awkwardly, swaying from side to side. *The geese waddled into the farmyard.*

wade wading waded *(v)* to walk through water.

wader
1 *(n)* a wading bird.
2 *(n)* a thigh-length, waterproof boot, used for fishing in deep water.

wafer *(n)* a thin, light, crispy type of biscuit.

waffle waffling waffled
1 *(n)* a type of square pancake, sometimes eaten with syrup.
2 *(v)* *(informal)* to speak in a long-winded, rambling way. **waffle** *(n)*.

wag wagging wagged *(v)* to move something from side to side. *Fido wagged his tail.*

wage waging waged
1 **wage** *or* **wages** *(n)* the money someone is paid for their work.
2 *(v)* If you **wage** a campaign or a war, you start it and carry on with it.

waggle waggling waggled *(v)* to move from side to side. *Trevor can waggle his ears.*

wagon
1 *(n)* a horse-drawn cart.
2 *(n)* a railway truck.

wail wailing wailed *(v)* to let out a long cry of sadness or distress. **wail** *(n)*.

waist *(n)* the middle part of your body, between your hips and your ribs, where your body narrows.

waistcoat *(n)* a short, light, sleeveless jacket, often worn under the jacket of a suit.

wait waiting waited
1 *(v)* to pause, or to stop doing something for a period of time.
2 *(v)* If you **wait on** someone, you serve them food and drink in a restaurant.

waiter *(n)* a man who serves people with food and drink in a restaurant or bar.

waiting room *(n)* a room where people sit and wait for something, such as a train or an appointment.

waitress waitresses *(n)* a woman who serves people with food and drink in a restaurant or bar.

wake waking woke woken
1 *(v)* to become fully conscious after being asleep. *Dora woke with a start when the door banged.*
2 *(v)* to rouse someone from their sleep. *My dog woke me up.*
3 *(n)* the trail left by a moving boat.

walk walking walked
1 *(v)* to move along on your feet. **walker** *(n)*.
2 *(n)* a journey on foot.
3 *(v)* *(informal)* If you **walk all over** somebody, you take advantage of them.

walking stick *(n)* a stick held by someone to help them to walk.

walkover *(n)* *(informal)* a very easy victory in a sports match, especially one gained because an opponent is unfit to play.

wall *(n)* a solid structure that separates two areas or supports a roof.

wallaby wallabies *(n)* a small type of kangaroo.
red-necked wallaby

wallet *(n)* a pouch for holding money, usually made of leather.

wallop walloping walloped *(v)* *(informal)* to hit someone very hard, usually as a punishment. **wallop** *(n)*.

wallow wallowing wallowed
1 *(v)* to roll about in mud or water.
2 *(v)* If you **wallow in** something, you enjoy it greatly.

wallpaper *(n)* patterned or coloured paper that is stuck in strips to a wall in order to decorate a room.

walrus walruses *(n)* a large sea animal from the Arctic with long tusks and flippers.

waltz waltzes *(n)* a ballroom dance with a regular 1-2-3 beat. **waltz** *(v)*.

wand *(rhymes with pond)* *(n)* a thin stick that is supposed to have magical powers.

walruses

Some words that begin with a "w" sound are spelt "wh".

wander wandering wandered
1 (v) to walk around without going in any particular direction. **wander** (n).
2 (v) to move around. *Don't let your eyes wander.*

wane waning waned
1 (v) to get smaller or less. *As the job progressed, Jem's enthusiasm waned.*
2 (v) When the Moon **wanes**, it appears to get smaller. *See* **moon**.

wangle wangling wangled (v)
(informal) to gain something by crafty or dishonest methods. *I managed to wangle a front row seat.*

want wanting wanted
1 (v) to feel that you would like something. *I want a chocolate.* **want** (n).
2 (v) to need something. *What Gerry wants is a good meal.* **want** (n).

war
1 (n) fighting between opposing forces.
2 (n) a struggle against something. *A war against hunger.*

ward warding warded
1 (n) a large room in a hospital where patients are looked after.
2 (n) a young person who is under the care of a guardian.
3 **ward off** (v) to prevent something from attacking or hurting you. *I'm trying to ward off a cold.*

warden (n) someone in charge of a building where people stay, such as a youth hostel, old people's home, or study centre.

warder (n) someone who works in a prison, dealing with prisoners and maintaining security.

wardrobe
1 (n) a tall cupboard used for storing clothes.
2 (n) a collection of clothes or theatrical costumes.

warehouse (n) a large building used for storing goods.

warfare (n) a general term for the fighting of wars. *Jungle warfare.*

warlike (adj) hostile, aggressive, or likely to start a war.

warm warming warmed; warmer warmest
1 (adj) fairly hot. **warmth** (n).
2 (v) to increase the temperature of something.
3 (adj) very friendly. *We were given a warm welcome.* **warmth** (n), **warmly** (adv).
4 (v) If you **warm up** before a sports match, you exercise gently to prepare yourself for it. **warm-up** (n).

5 (v) When an engine **warms up**, it starts to run smoothly.

warm-blooded (adj)
Warm-blooded animals have a body temperature that remains approximately the same, whatever their surroundings.

warn warning warned (v) If you **warn** someone, you tell them about a danger or a bad thing that might happen. **warning** (n).

warp warping warped (v) If an object **warps**, it gets twisted or bent by heat or dampness.

warrant (n) an official piece of paper that gives permission for something. *A search warrant.*

warren (n) a group of underground tunnels where rabbits live.

warrior (n) a soldier, or someone who fights. *See* **samurai**.

warship (n) a ship with guns on it, used in war. *See* **ship**.

wart (rhymes with port) (n) a small, hard lump on your skin. **warty** (adj).

wary wariest wariest (adj) cautious and careful. *Desmond is always very wary of dogs.* **wariness** (n), **warily** (adv).

wash washes washing washed
1 (v) to clean something with water, soap, etc. **wash** (n).
2 (n) the trail of disturbed water behind a moving boat.
3 (v) When you **wash up**, you clean the plates, cutlery, etc. after a meal.
4 (v) If the sea **washes up** something, it leaves it on the shore.

washable (adj) If a material is **washable**, you can wash it without damaging it.

washer (n) a plastic or metal ring that fits under a bolt or screw to give a tighter fit or to prevent a leak.

washing
1 (n) clothes that are going to be washed, or have been washed.
2 **washing-up** (n) the plates, cutlery, etc. that need cleaning after a meal.

washing machine (n) a machine that washes clothes.

wasp (n) a flying insect that has black and yellow stripes and can sting. *See* **insect**, **nest**.

wastage (n) loss. *You'll need three metres of fabric, allowing for wastage.*

waste wasting wasted
1 (v) If you **waste** something, you use it wrongly or throw it away when you do not need to. *Don't waste your time.* **waste** (n).

2 (n) rubbish, or something left over and not needed. *Chemical waste.* **waste** (adj).
3 (v) If someone **wastes away**, they get thinner and weaker because of illness or starvation.

wasteful (adj) If you are **wasteful**, you use things up needlessly and do not think about saving them. **wastefulness** (n), **wastefully** (adv).

wasteland (n) land that is not used for anything.

watch watches watching watched
1 (n) a small clock, usually worn on your wrist.
2 (v) to look at something. *Alma was watching the television news.*
3 (v) to notice, or to be careful about something. *Watch what you're doing with those scissors!*

water watering watered
1 (n) a colourless liquid that you can drink
2 (v) to pour water on something. *Can you water the plants?*
3 (v) If your mouth **waters**, you see or smell food and feel hungry.
4 (v) If your eyes **water**, tears come from them.
5 **water down** (v) If you **water something down**, you make it weaker, usually by adding water.

watercolours (plural n) paints that are mixed with water, not oil. *See* **artist**.

water cycle (n) the constant movement of the Earth's water. Plants transpire, and water from rivers and oceans evaporates, making water vapour. This vapour rises, forms clouds and then falls as rain, hail, or snow. Some water enters plants and soil and the rest runs off into rivers and oceans.

water cycle

rain, hail, or snow

water vapour

cloud

river

waterfall (n) water from a stream or river that falls down over rocks.

watering can (n) a metal or plastic container with a handle and a long spout, used for watering plants.

waterlogged (adj) If something is **waterlogged**, it is completely flooded or filled with water. *A waterlogged football pitch.*

Some words that begin with a "w" sound are spelt "wh".

water main *(n)* a large supply pipe that carries water under the ground.

watermark *(n)* a mark in paper that you can see when you hold it up to the light.

waterproof *(adj)* If something is waterproof, it keeps water out.

water-ski water-skiing water-skied *(v)* to travel on skis over water, towed by a boat. water-skier *(n)*, water-skiing *(n)*.

watertight *(adj)* If something is watertight, it is completely sealed so that water cannot enter.

water vapour *(n)* the gas produced when water evaporates.

watt *(n)* a unit of electrical power. wattage *(n)*.

wave waving waved
1 *(v)* to move your hand, for example when you are saying hello or goodbye to someone. **wave** *(n)*.
2 *(v)* to move something from side to side in the air. *The fairy godmother waved her magic wand.* **wave** *(n)*.
3 *(n)* a moving ridge on the surface of water, especially the sea.
4 *(n)* a curl in your hair. **wavy** *(adj)*.
5 *(n)* a vibration of energy that travels through air or water, for example, sound waves or radio waves.

wavelength
1 *(n)* the distance between one wave of light, sound, etc. and another.
2 *(n)* the size of wavelength that a radio station uses to transmit its programmes.
3 *(informal)* If you are **on the same wavelength** as someone, you think in the same way as they do.

waver wavering wavered *(v)* to be uncertain or unsteady. *Nada never wavered in her determination to win.*

wax waxes waxing waxed
1 *(n)* a substance made from fats or oils, and used to make crayons, polish, and candles. **waxy** *(adj)*.
2 *(v)* to put wax polish on something, such as a car.
3 *(v)* When the moon **waxes**, it appears to get larger. *See* **moon**.

way
1 *(n)* a direction. *Which way is north?*
2 *(n)* a road or route. *Do you know the way home?*
3 *(n)* a method or style of doing something. *Is this the right way to spell your name?*
4 **ways** *(plural n)* habits, or customs.

WC *(n)* a toilet. The initials WC stand for water closet.

weak weaker weakest
1 *(adj)* not powerful, or not having much force. **weakness** *(n)*, **weaken** *(v)*, **weakly** *(adv)*.
2 *(adj)* easy to break.
3 *(adj)* lacking taste. *Weak tea.*
4 Your **weak points** are the things that you are not very good at.

weakling *(n)* a weak person or animal.

wealthy wealthier wealthiest *(adj)* Someone who is **wealthy** has a lot of money or property. **wealth** *(n)*.

wean weaning weaned
1 *(v)* When you **wean** babies, you start giving them other food instead of their mother's milk.
2 *(v)* If you **wean someone off** something, you help them to give it up gradually.

weapon *(n)* something that can be used for fighting, such as a sword or a gun. **weaponry** *(n)*.

wear wearing wore worn
1 *(v)* to be dressed in something, or to have something attached to you. *Rosie wore a red brooch.* **wearer** *(n)*.
2 *(n)* clothes. *Boys' wear.*
3 *(n)* the gradual damage done to something by constant use. *My coat is showing signs of wear.*
4 **wear out** *(v)* If an activity **wears you out**, it makes you very tired.
5 *(v)* If you **wear out** your clothes, you make them ragged and useless.
6 **wear away** *(v)* to destroy something slowly, bit by bit.
7 **wear off** *(v)* to become less *The effects of the painkiller have worn off.*

weary wearier weariest *(adj)* very tired, or exhausted. **weariness** *(n)*, **wearily** *(adv)*.

weather weathering weathered
1 *(n)* the state of the atmosphere, for example, how hot or cold it is and whether it is raining, snowing, etc.
2 *(v)* If wood or stone **weathers**, it changes after being outside for a long time.
3 *(v)* If you **weather** a storm or a crisis, you get through it.

weather-beaten *(adj)* Something that is **weather-beaten** is damaged or worn by the weather.

weather forecast *(n)* a prediction about the weather for the next few days.

weave weaving wove *or* weaved woven *or* weaved
1 *(v)* to make cloth, baskets, etc. by passing threads or strips over and under each other. **weaver** *(n)*.

2 *(v)* to move from side to side in order to get through something. *Dan wove his way through the crowd.*

web
1 *(n)* a very fine net of sticky threads, made by a spider to catch flies and other insects.
2 **The Web** *(n)* a collection of linked pages stored on computers all over the world, which people can look at by using the Internet. The Web is short for the World Wide Web.

webbed *(adj)* Animals with **webbed** feet have skin connecting their toes, which helps them to swim.

Web page *(n)* a computer document on the World Wide Web.

Web site *(n)* a collection of linked Web pages on the World Wide Web, set up by an individual or an organization. Web site is sometimes shortened to site.

wedding *(n)* a marriage ceremony.

wedge
1 *(n)* a piece of food, wood, etc. that is thin at one end and thick at the other. *A wedge of cheese.*
2 *(v)* If you **wedge** something, you fix it tightly, or force it into a space. *Wedge open the door.*

wee *(adj)* very small, or tiny.

weed weeding weeded
1 *(n)* a wild plant, growing in a garden or a field.
2 *(v)* If you **weed** your garden, you pull the weeds out.

week *(n)* a period of seven days, usually from Sunday to Saturday. weekly *(adj)*.

weekday *(n)* one of the five working days of the week, from Monday to Friday.

weekend *(n)* Saturday and Sunday.

weep weeping wept *(v)* to cry because you feel very sad or very emotional. **weepy** *(adj)*.

weigh weighing weighed
1 *(v)* to measure how heavy or light someone or something is, on scales or on a weighing machine.
2 *(v)* If you **weigh up** an idea or a situation, you think about it carefully.
3 *(v)* If you are **weighed down**, you have too much to carry.

weight
1 *(n)* Someone or something's **weight** is how heavy they are.
2 *(n)* a heavy object. *This backpack is a weight!*
3 *(n)* a heavy object that people lift as an exercise to make their muscles stronger.

Some words that begin with a "w" sound are spelt "wh".

weightlifting (n) a sport in which people lift weights to show how strong they are. **weightlifter** (n).

weir (rhymes with fear) (n) a wall built across a river to control the flow of water.

weird (adj) strange, or mysterious. **weirdness** (n), **weirdly** (adv).

welcome welcoming welcomed
1 (v) If you **welcome** someone, you greet them in a friendly way. **welcome** (n), **welcoming** (adj), **welcome** (interject).
2 (adj) If something is **welcome**, you like it or are glad to have it. **welcome** (v).

weld welding welded (v) to join two pieces of metal by heating them and then fixing them together. **welder** (n).

welfare (n) Someone's **welfare** is their state of health, happiness, and comfort.

welfare state (n) a system in which the government uses money from taxes to pay for education, health care, and social services.

well
1 (adv) If you do something **well**, you do it successfully.
2 (adv) thoroughly. *Wash your hands well.*
3 (adj) healthy. *You're looking well.*
4 (n) a hole from which you can draw water or oil from under the ground.
5 (interject) You say **well** at the start of a sentence to show surprise or doubt. *Well, look who's here! Well, I'm not sure about that.*

wellbeing (n) health and happiness.

wellington (n) a rubber boot that you wear in the rain.

well-known (adj) known by many people. *A well-known fact.*

well-off (adj) If someone is **well-off**, they are wealthy or rich.

west
1 (n) one of the four main points of the compass, the direction in which the Sun sets. **west** (adj), **west** (adv).
2 (adj) A **west** wind blows from the west. **westerly** (adv).

western
1 (adj) to do with the west of a country or the west of the world. *Western Australia. Western civilization.*
2 (n) a cowboy film, set in the western part of the USA.

wet wetting wet or wetted; wetter wettest
1 (adj) covered with, or full of liquid.

2 (v) to make something wet. *Wet the cloth before you wipe those shelves.*

wetland (n) marshy land.

whack (n) a hard hit. **whack** (v).

whale
1 (n) a large sea mammal, shaped like a fish. Whales take air into their lungs, but live in water.
2 (informal) When you have a **whale of a time**, you really enjoy yourself.

killer whale

dorsal fin

flipper

tail fluke

whaler
1 (n) someone who hunts whales for their meat and oil. **whaling** (n).
2 (n) a boat used to catch whales.

wharf (worf) wharfs or wharves (n) a place where boats and ships can be loaded or unloaded.

what
1 (adj) The word **what** is used in questions to discover more about something. *What music do you like?*
2 (pronoun) the thing or things that. *I heard what you said.*
3 (adj) The word **what** is used to emphasize how great, small, strange, etc. something or someone is. *What a surprise! What an idiot!*

whatever
1 (pronoun) anything that. *Wear whatever you like.*
2 (pronoun) what. *Whatever have you done that for?*

wheat (n) a cereal plant, whose grain is used for making flour. *See* **grain**.

wheel wheeling wheeled
1 (n) a circular object which turns on an axle, used to work machinery or move a vehicle.
2 (v) to push something on wheels. *Wheel your bicycle up the hill.*

wheelbarrow (n) a small cart with one wheel at the front, often used in gardens.

wheelchair (n) a chair on wheels for people who are ill, injured or disabled.

wheelie (n) (informal) If you do a **wheelie** on a bicycle or motorcycle, you ride with the front wheel off the ground.

wheeze wheezing wheezed (v) to breathe with difficulty, making a whistling noise in your chest. **wheeziness** (n), **wheezy** (adj).

when
1 (conj) at the time that. *I told Jake the news when I saw him yesterday.*
2 (adv) The word **when** is used to ask about the time that something happened. *When was Dickens born?*

whenever (conj) at any time. *We'll eat whenever you're hungry.*

where
1 (conj) at the place that. *I visited the house where my friend lives.*
2 (adv) The word **where** is used to ask about the place or position of something. *Where is Emma?*

whereabouts
1 (adv) roughly where. *Whereabouts in New York did you stay?*
2 (n) the place where someone or something is. *I'm afraid we don't know Billy's whereabouts.*

whereas (conj) but. *My parents eat meat, whereas I am a vegetarian.*

wherever (conj) to any place. *We'll go wherever you suggest.* **wherever** (adv).

whether (conj) if. *I wonder whether it will rain.*

whey (n) When you separate milk to make cheese, the watery part is **whey**.

which
1 (adj) The word **which** is used to ask about a choice of things. *Which dress shall I wear?*
2 (pronoun) You use **which** to show what you mean. *It's the house which has a red door.*

whichever (pronoun) any, or no matter which. *You can have whichever you want.*

whiff (n) a smell in the air.

while
1 (n) a period of time. *It was a long while before I ate noodles again.*
2 **while** or **whilst** (conj) during the time that. *Can you feed my gerbil while I am away?*
3 (conj) in contrast to. *Hannah likes skating while I prefer swimming*

whim *(n)* a sudden idea or wish, which is often rather silly.

whimper whimpering whimpered *(v)* to make weak, crying noises. whimper *(n)*.

whine whining whined
1 *(v)* to make a long, drawn-out sound that is sad or unpleasant.
2 *(v)* to complain or moan about something in an irritating way.

whinge whingeing whinged *(v)* *(informal)* to whine, or to complain.

whip whipping whipped
1 *(n)* a long piece of leather used for hitting people or animals. whip *(v)*.
2 *(v)* to move something suddenly. *Callum whipped the present behind his back.*
3 *(v)* to beat cream, eggs, etc. until they are stiff.

whirl whirling whirled
1 *(v)* If something **whirls**, it moves around quickly. *Leaves were whirling across the playground.*
2 *(n)* a fast or confused movement. *A whirl of activity.*
3 *(informal)* If you **give something a whirl**, you try it out.

whirlwind
1 *(n)* a wind like a cyclone, that moves in a tall column and goes round and round very fast.
2 *(adj)* very quick or sudden. *A whirlwind tour of Europe.*

whisk whisking whisked
1 *(n)* a metal tool that you use for beating eggs or cream. whisk *(v)*.
2 *(v)* to move something quickly or suddenly. *Our plates were whisked away before we finished eating.*

whisker *(n)* one of the long, stiff hairs near the mouth of some animals.

whisky whiskies *(n)* a strong, alcoholic drink made from barley or rye.

whisper whispering whispered *(v)* to talk very quietly, or to make a soft sound. whisper *(n)*.

whistle whistling whistled
1 *(n)* an instrument that makes a high, loud sound when you blow it.
2 *(v)* to blow air through your lips to make a sound or a tune. whistle *(n)*.
3 *(v)* to move very fast with a whistling sound. *The train whistled past.*

white whiter whitest
1 *(n)* the colour of snow. white *(adj)*.
2 *(adj)* If your skin is **white**, it is pale in colour.
3 *(adj)* If coffee or tea is **white**, it has milk in it.
4 *(n)* The **white** of an egg is the part around the yolk. *See* **egg**.

whitewash *(n)* a mixture of lime and water, used for painting walls white. whitewash *(v)*.

whizz whizzes whizzing whizzed *(v)* to move very fast, often with a buzzing sound.

who *(hoo)*
1 *(pronoun)* The word **who** is used to ask questions about people. *Who is that man?*
2 *(pronoun)* The word **who** is used to show which person you are talking about, or to give more information about someone. *The woman who lives next door. I visited my granny, who wasn't very well.*

whoever *(hoo-ev-er)*
1 *(pronoun)* anyone at all, or no matter who. *Whoever made this mess will have to tidy it up.*
2 *(pronoun)* who. *Whoever could that be at the door?*

whole *(hole)*
1 *(adj)* the total amount of something. *I've eaten a whole loaf of bread.*
2 *(adj)* complete, or not broken. *I'd rather have a whole biscuit than a broken one.*
3 *(n)* the entire thing, or all the parts of something. *Two halves make a whole.*

wholefood *(hole food) (n)* food that has been processed as little as possible, such as brown rice.

wholemeal *(hole-meel) (adj)* Wholemeal flour has all the grain left in it.

wholesale *(hole-sayl) (adv)* When shopkeepers buy things **wholesale**, they buy them cheaply in large quantities, in order to sell them in their shops. wholesaler *(n)*.

wholesome *(hole-sum) (adj)* healthy, or good for you. *A wholesome diet.*

wholly *(hoe-lee) (adv)* completely. *I am wholly to blame for the mess.*

whooping cough *(hoo-ping koff) (n)* an infectious disease that makes children cough violently and breathe in a noisy way.

whose *(hooz)*
1 *(pronoun)* The word **whose** is used to ask who something belongs to. *Whose skateboard is this?*
2 *(pronoun)* The word **whose** is used to indicate the person or thing that you are talking about. *That's the girl to whose party I've been invited.*

why *(adv)* The word **why** is used to ask about the reason for something. *Why did you leave?* why *(conj)*.

wick *(n)* the twisted cord running through a candle, which you light.

wicked *(adj)* very bad, cruel, or evil. wickedness *(n)*, wickedly *(adv)*.

wicket
1 *(n)* a set of three stumps, with two bails resting on them, used in cricket. *The batsman stands in front of the wicket and the bowler aims at it. See* **cricket**.
2 *(n)* the strip of ground between two wickets.
3 *(n)* the act of a batsman being got out in cricket.

wide wider widest
1 *(adj)* from one side to the other, or from edge to edge. *This room is seven metres wide.*
2 *(adj)* large from side to side. *A wide tunnel.* widen *(v)*.
3 *(adj)* covering a large number of things. *We stock a wide range of magazines.* widely *(adv)*.

widespread *(adj)* happening in many places, or among many people. *There is widespread concern about global warming.*

widow *(n)* a woman whose husband has died, and who has not married again. widowed *(adj)*.

widower *(n)* a man whose wife has died, and who has not married again. widowed *(adj)*.

width *(n)* the distance from one side of something to the other. *What is the width of this carpet?*

widthways *(adv)* in the direction of the widest side. *Fold the paper widthways.*

wife *(n)* the female partner in a marriage.

wig *(n)* a covering of false hair, made to fit someone's head.

wiggle wiggling wiggled *(v)* to make small movements from side to side or up and down. wiggly *(adj)*.

wild wilder wildest
1 *(adj)* natural and not tamed by humans. *Wild flowers.* wildness *(n)*.
2 *(adj)* uncontrolled, often in an angry way. *Mum went wild when she saw the mess.* wildly *(adv)*.

wilderness wildernesses *(n)* an area of wild, uninhabited land, such as a desert.

wildlife *(n)* wild animals and plants.

wilful
1 *(adj)* deliberate. *Wilful damage.* wilfully *(adj)*.
2 *(adj)* Someone who is **wilful** is determined to have their own way. wilfulness *(n)*.

will

1 *(n)* written instructions stating what should happen to someone's property and money when they die.

2 *(n)* Your **will** is your determination to do something. *Efra has an amazing will to succeed.*

willing *(adj)* People who are **willing** are eager and pleased to offer their help. **willingness** *(n)*, **willingly** *(adv)*.

willow *(n)* a tree with thin, hanging branches, often found near water.

wilt wilting wilted

1 *(v)* If a plant **wilts**, it begins to droop.

2 *(v)* If a person **wilts**, they become tired through lack of energy or food.

wimp *(n)* *(informal)* a feeble or cowardly person. **wimpish** *(adj)*.

win winning won

1 *(v)* to come first in a contest. **win** *(n)*, **winner** *(n)*.

2 *(v)* to gain or deserve something. *Julius won his brother's respect.*

wince wincing winced *(v)* to twitch or flinch because you are in pain. **wince** *(n)*.

winch winches *(n)* a cable wound around a rotating drum, that you use for pulling or hoisting things. **winch** *(v)*. See **portcullis**, **rescue**.

wind winding wound

1 *(rhymes with pinned)* *(n)* moving air. **windy** *(adj)*.

2 *(rhymes with kind)* *(v)* to wrap something round something else. *Verity wound her scarf several times around her neck .*

3 *(rhymes with kind)* *(v)* to twist and turn. *The road wound up the mountainside.*

4 *(rhymes with kind)* *(v)* to turn the key of a clock.

5 **wind up** *(rhymes with kind)* *(v)* *(slang)* If you **wind someone up**, you deliberately make them more and more annoyed. **wind-up** *(n)*.

winded *(adj)* If you are **winded**, you are out of breath because of exercise or a sudden hit in the stomach.

windfall

1 *(n)* fruit that has been blown off a tree.

2 *(n)* a sudden piece of good fortune, usually an unexpected gain of money.

wind instrument *(n)* an instrument played by blowing, for example, the trombone, harmonica, and clarinet. See **brass**, **harmonica**, **woodwind**.

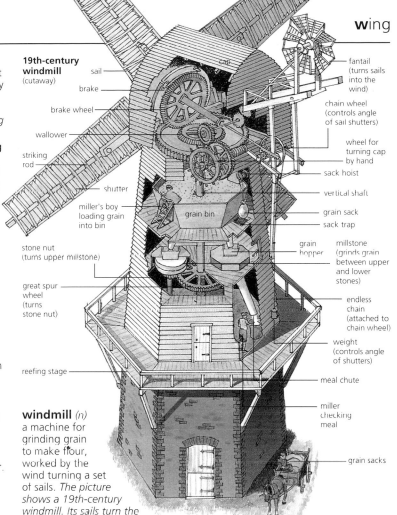

19th-century windmill (cutaway)

- sail
- brake
- brake wheel
- wallower
- striking rod
- shutter
- miller's boy loading grain into bin
- stone nut (turns upper millstone)
- great spur wheel (turns stone nut)
- reefing stage
- cap
- fantail (turns sails into the wind)
- chain wheel (controls angle of sail shutters)
- wheel for turning cap by hand
- sack hoist
- vertical shaft
- grain bin
- grain sack
- sack trap
- grain hopper
- millstone (grinds grain between upper and lower stones)
- endless chain (attached to chain wheel)
- weight (controls angle of shutters)
- meal chute
- miller checking meal
- grain sacks

windmill *(n)* a machine for grinding grain to make flour, worked by the wind turning a set of sails. *The picture shows a 19th-century windmill. Its sails turn the wallower which is connected by a series of shafts and cogwheels to the greater spur wheel, which turns the millstones to grind grain into flour.*

window *(n)* a transparent piece of glass within a wall.

window-shopping If you go window-shopping, you look in shop windows but do not buy anything.

windpipe *(n)* the tube that links the lungs with the nose and mouth. See **respiration**.

windscreen *(n)* the window of strengthened glass in front of the driver of a vehicle. See **car**.

windsurfing *(n)* the sport of sailing by standing on a board with a flexible mast and a sail, and holding on to a curved boom. *This picture of windsurfing at sea shows a windsurfer riding a wave called a rollercoaster.* **windsurfer** *(n)*.

windsurfing

windswept *(adj)* exposed, and blown by the wind.

wind turbine *(n)* a machine with blades shaped like propellers that uses energy from the wind to make electricity.

wind turbines

wine *(n)* an alcoholic drink made from the juice of grapes.

wing

1 *(n)* one of the feather-covered limbs of a bird, that the bird flaps in order to fly. See **bird**.

2 *(n)* an outer part or extension of something. *The new wing of the hospital will be opened next month.*

3 *(n)* a wing-like structure on an aircraft that makes it able to fly.

4 **wings** *(plural n)* the side of a theatre stage which cannot be seen by the audience.

Some words that begin with a "w" sound are spelt "wh".

wingspan (n) the distance between the outer tips of the wings of a bird or an aircraft.

wink winking winked (v) to close one eye briefly as a signal or a friendly gesture.

winner
1 (n) a person or team that wins a contest.
2 (n) (informal) an excellent idea or plan.

winter (n) the season between autumn and spring, when the weather is coldest. **wintry** (adj).

wipe wiping wiped
1 (v) to clear or clean a surface with your hand or a cloth, using a sweeping motion.
2 (v) to rub something in order to clean it. *Wipe the dishes.*
Wipe your feet.
3 (v) to remove something. *Wipe that smile off your face!*
4 **wipe out** (v) to destroy something totally. *The earthquake wiped out the whole village.*

wire wiring wired
1 (n) a long, thin, flexible piece of metal. Wire can be used to pull or support things, or to conduct an electrical current.
2 **wire up** (v) to connect electrical wires to equipment. *Marco wired up the new cooker.*

wireless (n) (old-fashioned) a radio.

wiry wirier wiriest
1 (adj) tough and stiff. *Wiry hair.*
2 (adj) A **wiry** person is thin but tough.

wisdom (n) knowledge, experience, and understanding.

wise wiser wisest (adj) Wise people know what is right to say and do in different situations. **wisely** (adv).

wish wishes wishing wished
1 (v) to think or say that you would like something. **wish** (n).
2 (v) to hope for something for somebody else. *I wish you a happy New Year!*

wisp (n) a small and delicate piece of something. *A wisp of hair.*
A wisp of smoke. **wispy** (adj).

wit
1 (n) the ability to say clever and funny things.
2 (n) someone who can say clever and funny things.
3 (n) the ability to think quickly and clearly.
Doyle had the wit to find an escape route.

witch witches (n) a woman with magical powers.

with (prep) attached to, or accompanying. *Chicken with fried noodles.*

withdraw withdrawing withdrew withdrawn
1 (v) to remove, or to take away something. *Sadie withdrew the cash from her bank. Alex withdrew his support for the project.* **withdrawal** (n).
2 (v) to drop out, or to go away. *Lee withdrew from the team because of injury.*

withdrawn (adj) A withdrawn person is very shy and quiet.

wither withering withered
1 (v) When something **withers**, it shrivels up because it has lost moisture.
2 (adj) A **withering** look or remark is a very scornful one.

withhold withholding withheld (v) to keep something back, or to refuse to give something. *My parents withheld their permission for a party.*

within (prep) inside. *Within the cave was a dragon. I want you back within the next ten minutes.* **within** (adv).

without (prep) If you are **without** something, you do not have it.

withstand withstanding withstood (v) to bear or to stand something. *The sea wall withstood the pounding of the waves.*

witness witnesses (n) someone who sees something happen and who may be called to give evidence in court. **witness** (v).

witty wittier wittiest (adj) Someone who is **witty** says or writes humorous things. **wittily** (adv).

wizard (n) a man or male creature with magical powers.

wobble wobbling wobbled (v) to move from side to side in an unsteady manner. *The cups wobbled on the tray.* **wobbly** (adj).

woe (n) great sadness or grief. **woeful** (adj), **woefully** (adv).

wolf wolves (n) a wild, flesh-eating mammal, that looks like a large dog and hunts in a pack.

Asiatic wolf

woman (n) an adult, female human being. **womanhood** (n), **womanly** (adv).

womb (woom) (n) the part of a woman in which a baby develops before it is born. *See* **pregnant**.

wombat (n) a short-legged marsupial that makes burrows.

wombat

wonder wondering wondered
1 (v) to think about something in a casual or curious way. *I wonder whether it is time for tea.*
2 (v) to be amazed at something. *We wondered at Linda's ability to talk nonstop for hours.* **wonder** (n).

wonderful
1 (adj) amazing, splendid, or magnificent. *The Himalayan mountains were a wonderful sight.*
2 (adj) extremely pleasant. *It was wonderful to see Hugh again.* **wonderfully** (adv).

wood
1 (n) the substance that forms the trunk and branches of a tree. **wooden** (adj).
2 (n) an area of trees that is smaller than a forest. **wooded** (adj).

woodland (n) land covered mainly by trees.

woodlice (plural n) small, insect-like creatures which feed on rotten wood and are found in damp, shaded places. The singular of woodlice is woodlouse.

great spotted woodpecker

woodpecker
(n) a brightly coloured bird that lives in woodland and can drill through bark and wood with its bill.

Some words that begin with a "w" sound are spelt "wh".

oboe   flute   piccolo   bassoon

cor anglais

clarinet

barrel joint

ligature

mouthpiece
containing reed

top of
upper joint

key

fingerhole

middle joint

bell joint

woodwind (n)
The **woodwind**
section of an orchestra
is made up of instruments
that you blow into, that were
originally made of wood.
*The illustration above shows a
clarinet, with its main parts labelled,
and five other instruments from the
woodwind section of an orchestra.*

woodwork
1 *(n)* things made out of wood.
An exhibition of woodwork.
2 *(n)* the craft of making things from
wood. *The picture shows a range of
tools used for woodwork.*
woodworking *(adj)*.

woodworking tools

steel rule

tenon saw

coping saw

junior
hacksaw

bradawl

screwdriver

smoothing
plane

hand
drill

mitre box

sandpaper
and block

bench hook

g-cramp

files

mallet

wool (n) the
hair of a sheep,
spun into a thread
for knitting, weaving,
etc. **woollen** *(adj)*.

word
1 *(n)* a group of spoken or written
sounds, that have a meaning.
2 *(n)* an order. *Jump when I give the
word!*

3 *(n)* news, or a message. *Is there any
word from London?*
4 If you **give your word**, you promise
something.

word processing *(n)* the use of a
computer and software to type and
print documents. Words are viewed
on screen and can easily be changed,
copied, and stored.
word processor *(n)*.

work working worked
1 *(v)* to study, or to do a job.
work *(n)*.
2 *(v)* to function properly. *Does your
computer work?*
3 *(n)* a piece of music, painting,
sculpture, etc. *A work of art.*
4 *(v)* If you **work out** a puzzle, you
solve it by thinking hard.
5 *(v)* When you **work out** in a gym,
you do physical exercise.

workable *(adj)* If a plan is
workable, it can be carried out.

worker *(n)* someone who is
employed to do a job.

workman workmen *(n)* a man who
does manual work.

workshop
1 *(n)* a room, shed, or other building
where things are made or mended.
2 *(n)* a group of people who meet to
discuss, learn about, or practise a
particular skill. *A writer's workshop.*

world
1 *(n)* the planet Earth.
2 *(n)* an area of activity. *The world of
sport.*

worldly worldlier worldliest
1 *(adj)* concerned with the world of
money and material things, rather
than with spiritual or religious matters.
worldliness *(n)*.
2 *(adj)* used to the way that people
behave.

worldwide *(adj)* to do with, or
reaching most parts of the world.

World Wide Web *(n)*
a collection of
linked pages stored
on computers all over
the world, which
people can look
at by using the
Internet.

worm *(n)*
a small
creature that
lives in the
soil. Worms
have long, thin,
soft bodies and
no backbones.

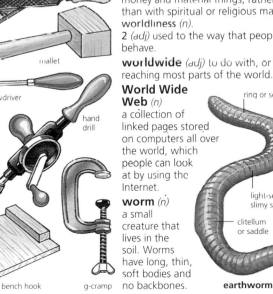

ring or segment

light-sensitive
slimy skin

clitellum
or saddle

head

earthworm

Some words that begin with a "w" sound are spelled "wh".

worn *(adj)* Something that is **worn** is old and less useful because it has been used a lot. *Worn tyres can be very dangerous.*

worry worries worrying worried
1 *(v)* to be anxious or uneasy about something. **worrier** *(n)*, **worrying** *(adj)*, **worryingly** *(adv)*.
2 *(n)* something that makes you anxious. *Callum is a worry to his mum.*

worse *(adj)* less good. *Your handwriting is worse than mine.*

worship worshipping worshipped
1 *(v)* to express your love and devotion to God or a god. **worship** *(n)*.
2 *(n)* a church service.
3 *(v)* If you **worship** someone, you think that they are wonderful.

worst *(adj)* worse than anything else. *Carl's handwriting is the worst I've ever seen.*

worth
1 *(adj)* having a certain value. *This painting is worth a fortune.* **worth** *(n)*.
2 *(adj)* deserving, or good enough for. *It's worth going to the sale for the bargains.*

worthless *(adj)* If something is **worthless**, it has no value or is useless. **worthlessness** *(n)*.

worthwhile *(adj)* useful and valuable. *Learning French is a worthwhile activity.*

worthy worthier worthiest *(adj)* deserving. *I'm happy to give money to a worthy cause.*

wound *(n)* an injury in which the skin is cut, usually caused by an accident, violence, etc. **wound** *(v)*.

wraith *(rayth)* *(n)* a ghost or ghostlike figure.

wrangle wrangling wrangled *(v)* to argue or debate in a noisy or angry way. **wrangle** *(n)*.

wrap wrapping wrapped *(v)* to cover something in paper, material, etc. in order to protect it.

wrapper *(n)* the protective material in which something is wrapped. *A sweet wrapper.*

wrath *(roth)* *(n)* anger.

wreak *(reek)* wreaking wreaked *(v)* to cause, or to inflict. *The bull wreaked havoc in the china shop.*

wreath *(reeth)*
1 *(n)* a circle of flowers or leaves worn on the head. *A laurel wreath.*
2 *(n)* an arrangement of flowers, leaves, etc. in memory of the dead.

wreck wrecking wrecked
1 *(v)* to destroy or ruin something completely.
2 *(n)* something that has been ruined, for example, a ship.

wreckage *(n)* the broken remains at the site of a crash or explosion.

wrench wrenches wrenching wrenched
1 *(v)* to pull something suddenly and forcefully. *I wrenched open the door.*
2 *(n)* an adjustable tool for gripping and pulling nuts, bolts, etc.

wrestle wrestling wrestled
1 *(v)* to fight by gripping an opponent and trying to throw them to the floor.
2 *(v)* If you **wrestle** with a problem, you try to solve it by thinking very hard.

wrestling *(n)* a sport in which you fight according to rules. *The picture shows the ancient Japanese sport of Sumo wrestling.* **wrestler** *(n)*.

Sumo wrestling

wretch wretches
1 *(n)* a miserable and unfortunate person. **wretched** *(adj)*.
2 *(n)* a mean and unpleasant person.

wriggle wriggling wriggled *(v)* to twist and turn.

wring wringing wrung *(v)* to squeeze the moisture from wet material by twisting it with both hands.

wrinkle *(n)* a crease or line in someone's skin or in material.

wrist *(n)* the joint that connects your hand and your arm.

write writing wrote written
1 *(v)* to put down letters, words, or numbers on paper or another surface, using a pen, pencil, etc.
2 *(v)* to compose poetry, prose, music, etc. **writer** *(n)*.
3 *(v)* If someone **writes off** a car in a crash, it is a total wreck and cannot be repaired. **write-off** *(n)*.

writhe writhing writhed *(v)* to twist about. *Sammy writhed in agony.*

writing
1 *(n)* anything that has been written. *Who did this writing on the wall?*
2 *(n)* literature, stories, poems, etc.

wrong
1 *(adj)* incorrect, or not right. *Wrong answers.* **wrongly** *(adv)*.
2 *(adj)* bad and sinful. *It is wrong to steal.* **wrong** *(n)*, **wrongful** *(adj)*.

WWW *(n)* WWW is short for World Wide Web.

Xmas see **Christmas**.

x-ray
1 *(n)* a beam of energy that can pass through solid things. **x-ray** *(adj)*.
2 *(n)* a photograph of the inside of a person's body, taken using x-rays. *The picture shows an x-ray of a hand.* **x-ray** *(v)*.

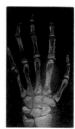

x-ray

xylophone *(zy-luh-fone)* *(n)* a musical instrument with wooden bars of different sizes, which are struck to give different notes.

yacht *(rhymes with dot)*
1 *(n)* a large sailing boat, used for pleasure or for racing. **yachting** *(n)*.
2 *(n)* a large, luxury motor cruiser.

yak *(n)* a long-haired ox from Tibet.

yaks

yank yanking yanked *(v)* to pull something sharply and strongly. **yank** *(n)*.

yap yapping yapped *(v)* to bark repeatedly, with short, high-pitched sounds.

yard
1 *(n)* an enclosed area with a hard surface, usually next to a building.
2 *(n)* a unit of measurement. See page 284.
3 *(n)* (US) an area of grass surrounding or next to a house.

yardstick *(n)* a standard used to judge things or people. *I judge comedians by the yardsick of whether they make me laugh.*

yarn
1 *(n)* a very long strand of wool or cotton, used for sewing, knitting, etc.
2 *(informal)* If someone **spins a yarn**, they tell a long and exaggerated story.

yashmak *(n)* a veil worn by some Muslim women to cover all of their face except for their eyes.

yawn yawning yawned
1 *(v)* to open your mouth wide and breathe in, often because you are tired or bored. **yawn** *(n)*.
2 *(v)* to make a wide opening or gap. *A huge gulf yawned between the two rocks.*

year *(n)* a period of 365 days, or 366 days in a leap year, which is the time that it takes the Earth to circle the Sun once.

yearn *(rhymes with burn)* yearning yearned *(v)* to wish or long for something very strongly. **yearning** *(n)*.

yeast *(n)* a yellow fungus used to make bread and to ferment alcoholic drinks.

yell yelling yelled *(v)* to shout or scream very loudly. **yell** *(n)*.

yellow *(n)* the colour of lemons or butter. **yellow** *(adj)*.

yelp yelping yelped *(v)* When a dog yelps, it makes a sharp, high-pitched cry, showing that it is in pain. **yelp** *(n)*.

yen
1 *(n)* the main unit of money in Japan.
2 *(n)* *(informal)* If you have a **yen** for something, you want it very much.

yes *(interject)* a word used to show agreement.

yesterday *(n)* the day before today.

yet
1 *(adv)* so far. *I haven't received an answer yet.*
2 *(adv)* up to now. *You're not allowed out yet.*
3 *(adv)* still, or even. *There were yet more surprises in store.*
4 *(conj)* but. *Celia passed all her exams yet couldn't find a job.*

yield yielding yielded
1 *(v)* to produce something. *The field yielded 90 tons of potatoes.* **yield** *(n)*.
2 *(v)* to surrender. *Yield, Sir Jasper!*

yodel yodelling yodelled *(v)* to sing in a voice that changes rapidly between high and low sounds. Yodelling is popular in Switzerland. **yodeller** *(n)*.

yoga *(n)* a system of exercises and meditation that helps people to become mentally relaxed and physically fit. Yoga came originally from Hindu teachings.

yogurt *or* **yoghurt** *(n)* a slightly sour-tasting food prepared from milk curdled by bacteria.

yoke *(n)* a wooden frame attached to the necks of oxen to link them together for ploughing. *See* **plough**.

yolk *(rhymes with poke)* *(n)* the yellow part of an egg. If the egg is fertilized, the protein and fat from the yolk nourish the developing embryo. *See* **egg**.

Yom Kippur *(n)* a Jewish holy day when Jews fast all day, to mark the Day of Judgement.

yonder *(adj)* *(old-fashioned)* over there. **yonder** *(adv)*.

you
1 *(pronoun)* the person or people that someone is talking to.
2 *(pronoun)* anyone, or people in general. *You never know.*

young younger youngest
1 *(adj)* Someone who is **young** has lived for a short time.
2 *(adj)* Something that is **young** has existed for a short time. *A young country.*
3 *(plural n)* the offspring of an animal.

youngster *(n)* a young person.

your *(pronoun)* belonging to you.

yourself yourselves *(pronoun)* you and nobody else. *Help yourself to some food.*

youth
1 *(n)* the time of life when a person is young.
2 *(n)* a young male person, usually aged between 13 and 18.
3 **youth hostel** a place where people can stay very cheaply while on holiday. Youth hostels are usually used by young people.

yo-yo *(n)* a toy consisting of a string wound around a flat reel. You loop the string over your finger and flick the reel up and down on the string.

yuletide *(n)* *(old-fashioned)* the Christmas season.

yuppy yuppies *(n)* a slightly insulting word for a young person with a well-paid job and an expensive lifestyle. Yuppy stands for young, upwardly-mobile professional.

zany zanier zaniest *(adj)* humorous in an unusual, crazy way. **zanily** *(adv)*.

zap zapping zapped *(v)* *(slang)* to shoot someone, usually in a game.

zeal *(zeel)* *(n)* enthusiasm and eagerness. **zealous** *(zel-uss)* *(adj)*.

zebra *(n)* an African wild animal, similar to a horse, with black and white stripes on its body.

zebras

zebra crossing *(n)* a pedestrian crossing marked by flashing orange lights and broad white stripes painted on the road.

zero *(n)* nothing, nought, or nil.

zest
1 *(n)* enthusiasm and liveliness.
2 *(n)* the outer skin of a citrus fruit.

zigzag *(n)* a line with sharp, diagonal turns. **zigzag** *(v)*.

zimmer frame *(n)* a light, metal frame with four legs, used by old people to support them as they walk.

zinc *(n)* a bluish-white metal that is used in some alloys and for coating metals so that they will not rust.

zip zipping zipped
1 *(n)* a fastener for fabrics. A zip consists of two strips of metal or plastic teeth which link when pulled together. **zip** *(v)*.
2 *(v)* to move fast.

zip code *(n)* *(US)* the set of numbers and letters at the end of an address, used to help sort letters, parcels, etc, more quickly (postcode, UK).

zodiac *(n)* a circular, imaginary belt in the sky which includes the path of the Sun, the Moon, and the planets. The zodiac is divided into twelve equal parts whose names are the names of constellations. The names, or signs, of the zodiac are used in astrology.

zombie
1 *(n)* a dead body brought back to life by supernatural power.
2 *(n)* *(informal)* someone who seems lifeless or dull.

zone *(n)* an area that is separate from other areas and used for a special purpose. *A conservation zone.*

zoo *(n)* a place where animals are kept for people to see or study them.

zoology *(n)* the study of animals. **zoologist** *(n)*, **zoological** *(adj)*.

zoom zooming zoomed *(v)* to move very fast. *Rod zoomed off on her bike.*

COUNTRIES AND NATIONALITIES

If a nationality is not given with the country, you refer to people from that country as a citizen of .....

Afghanistan - *Afghan*
Albania - *Albanian*
Algeria - *Algerian*
Andorra - *Andorran*
Angola - *Angolan*
Antigua and Barbuda
Argentina - *Argentine*
Armenia - *Armenian*
Australia - *Australian*
Austria - *Austrian*
Azerbaijan - *Azerbaijani*
Bahamas - *Bahamian*
Bahrain - *Bahraini*
Bangladesh - *Bangladeshi*
Barbados - *Barbadian*
Belarus - *Belarussian*
Belgium - *Belgian*
Belize - *Belizean*
Benin - *Beninese*
Bhutan - *Bhutanese*
Bolivia - *Bolivian*
Bosnia Herzegovina
Botswana
Brazil - *Brazilian*
Brunei
Bulgaria - *Bulgarian*
Burkina-Faso - *Burkinian*
Burma - *Burmese*
Burundi
Cambodia - *Cambodian*
Cameroon - *Cameroonian*
Canada - *Canadian*
Cape Verde - *Cape Verdean*
Central African Republic
Chad - *Chadian*
Chile - *Chilean*
China - *Chinese*
China (Taiwan) - *Nationalist Chinese*
Colombia - *Colombian*
Comoros -*Comoran*
Congo - *Congolese*
Costa Rica - *Costa Rican*
Croatia - *Croat*
Cuba - *Cuban*
Cyprus - *Cypriot*
Czech Republic - *Czech*
Denmark - *Dane*
Djibouti - *Djiboutian*
Dominica - *Dominican*
Dominican Republic
Ecuador - *Ecuadorian*
Egypt - *Egyptian*
El Salvador - *Salvadorean*
Equatorial Guinea - *Equatorial Guinean*
Eritrea - *Eritrean*
Estonia - *Estonian*
Ethiopia - *Ethiopian*
Fiji
Finland - *Finn*
France - *Frenchman, Frenchwoman*
Gabon - *Gabonese*
Gambia, The - *Gambian*
Georgia - *Georgian*
Germany - *German*
Ghana - *Ghanaian*
Greece - *Greek*

Grenada - *Grenadian*
Guatemala - *Guatemalan*
Guinea - *Guinean*
Guinea-Bissau
Guyana - *Guyanese*
Haiti - *Haitian*
Honduras - *Honduran*
Hungary - *Hungarian*
Iceland - *Icelander*
India - *Indian*
Indonesia - *Indonesian*
Iran - *Iranian*
Iraq - *Iraqi*
Ireland, Republic of
Israel - *Israeli*
Italy - *Italian*
Ivory Coast
Jamaica - *Jamaican*
Japan - *Japanese*
Jordan - *Jordanian*
Kazakhstan - *Kazakh*
Kenya - *Kenyan*
Kiribati
Korea, North - *North Korean*
Korea, South - *South Korean*
Kuwait - *Kuwaiti*
Kyrgyzstan - *Kyrgyz*
Laos - *Laotian*
Latvia - *Latvian*
Lebanon - *Lebanese*
Lesotho
Liberia - *Liberian*
Libya - *Libyan*
Liechtenstein
Lithuania - *Lithuanian*
Luxembourg - *Luxembourger*
Macedonia - *Macedonian*
Madagascar
Malawi - *Malawian*
Malaysia
Maldives - *Maldivian*
Mali - *Malian*
Malta - *Maltese*
Marshall Islands - *Marshall Islander*
Mauritania - *Mauritanian*
Mauritius - *Mauritian*
Mexico - *Mexican*
Micronesia - *Micronesian*
Moldava - *Moldavan*
Monaco - *Monegasque*
Mongolia - *Mongolian*
Morocco - *Moroccan*
Mozambique - *Mozambican*
Namibia - *Namibian*
Nauru - *Nauruan*
Nepal - *Nepalese*
Netherlands - *Dutchman, Dutchwoman*
New Zealand - *New Zealander*
Nicaragua - *Nicaraguan*
Niger
Nigeria - *Nigerian*
Norway - *Norwegian*
Oman - *Omani*
Pakistan - *Pakistani*
Panama - *Panamanian*
Papua New Guinea - *Papua New Guinean*
Paraguay - *Paraguayan*
Peru - *Peruvian*
Philippines, The - *Filipino, Filipina*
Poland - *Pole*

Portugal - *Portuguese*
Qatar - *Qatari*
Romania - *Romanian*
Russia - *Russian*
Rwanda
St Kitts and Nevis
St Lucia - *St Lucian*
St Vincent - *Vincentian*
San Marino
Sao Tome and Principe
Saudi Arabia - *Saudi Arabian*
Senegal - *Senegalese*
Seychelles
Sierra Leone - *Sierra Leonean*
Singapore - *Singaporean*
Slovakia - *Slovak*
Slovenia - *Slovene*
Solomon Islands - *Solomon Islander*
Somalia - *Somali*
South Africa - *South African*
Spain - *Spaniard*
Sri Lanka
Sudan - *Sudanese*
Surinam - *Surinamer*
Swaziland - *Swazi*
Sweden - *Swede*
Switzerland - *Swiss*
Syria - *Syrian*
Tajikistan - *Tajik*
Tanzania - *Tanzanian*
Thailand - *Thai*
Togo - *Togolese*
Tonga -*Tongan*
Trinidad and Tobago
Tunisia - *Tunisian*
Turkey - *Turk*
Turkmenistan - *Turkmen*
Tuvalu - *Tuvaluan*
Uganda - *Ugandan*
Ukraine - *Ukrainian*
United Arab Emirates
United Kingdom
United States *American*
Uruguay - *Uruguayan*
Uzbekistan - *Uzbek*
Vanuatu
Vatican City
Venezuela - *Venezuelan*
Vietnam -*Vietnamese*
Western Samoa - *Western Samoan*
Yemen - *Yemeni*
Yugoslavia, Republic of -*Yugoslav*
Zaire - *Zairean*
Zambia - *Zambian*
Zimbabwe - *Zimbabwean*

DAYS OF THE WEEK

Monday	Friday
Tuesday	Saturday
Wednesday	Sunday
Thursday	

MONTHS OF THE YEAR

January	July
February	August
March	September
April	October
May	November
June	December

MEASUREMENTS

Length

METRIC
1 millimetre (mm)
1 centimetre (cm) = 10mm
1 metre (m) = 100cm
1 kilometre (km) = 1,000m

IMPERIAL
1 inch (in)
1 foot (ft) = 12in
1 yard (yd) = 3ft
1 mile = 1,760yd

Volume

METRIC
1 millilitre (ml)
1 centilitre (cl) = 10ml
1 litre (l) = 100cl
1 kilolitre (kl) = 1,000l

IMPERIAL
1 fluid ounce (fl oz)
1 pint (pt) = 20fl oz
1 quart = 2pt
1 gallon (gal) = 8pt

Weight

METRIC
1 milligram (mg)
1 gram (g) = 1,000mg
1 kilogram (kg) = 1,000g
1 tonne (t) = 1,000kg

IMPERIAL
1 ounce (oz)
1 pound (lb) = 16oz
1 stone = 14lb
1 hundredweight (cwt) = 112lb
1 ton = 20cwt

Area

METRIC
1 square cm (cm^2)
1 square m (m^2) = 10,000cm^2
1 hectare = 10,000m^2
1 square kilometre (km^2) = 100 hectares

IMPERIAL
1 square inch (in^2)
1 square foot (ft^2) = 144in^2
1 square yard (yd^2) = 9ft^2
1 acre = 4,840yd^2
1 square mile = 640 acres

NUMBERS

1 - one	16 - sixteen
2 - two	17 - seventeen
3 - three	18 - eighteen
4 - four	19 - nineteen
5 - five	20 - twenty
6 - six	21 - twenty-one
7 - seven	30 - thirty
8 - eight	40 - forty
9 - nine	50 - fifty
10 - ten	60 - sixty
11 - eleven	70 - seventy
12 - twelve	80 - eighty
13 - thirteen	90 - ninety
14 - fourteen	100 - hundred
15 - fifteen	1000 - thousand

INDEX OF PICTURE LABELS

THE USBORNE SCHOOL
ILLUSTRATED
THESAURUS

Contents

What is a thesaurus?

A thesaurus is a book which gives lists of words with similar meanings. This thesaurus will help you choose the best words for your writing.

Is there a more exciting word for "new"?

If you know the word that you need, but want to say it in a more interesting way, your thesaurus will provide you with a list of alternative words, or "synonyms", for that word.

Your thesaurus can help you avoid using the same word over and over again. Really overused words, such as "nice" and "good", have panels with synonyms arranged in lists to help you make the right choices.

POSTC

Dear Lucy,
I'm having a really ~~nice~~ *fantastic* time in Nice.
I have a ~~nice~~ *breathtaking* view from my window.
The food is ~~nice~~ *scrumptious* and the weather has been ~~nice~~ *glorious* too!
Love Anna X

This thesaurus contains illustrated panels on lots of different subjects to give you ideas for writing and to help get your imagination working. You can see a list of panels on the page opposite.

A night in the forest

Slowly darkness enveloped the... The sky was star-studded and... I stood still and listened carefully hedgehog snuffled about in the u... an owl hooted and in the di... siren began to wail.

Shadowy shapes of b... flutte... silvery in the moonlig... badge...

You can also use your thesaurus to find a word that you know, but just can't remember.

What's that word that means "noise" and begins with "d"?

Looking at an entry

headword All headwords are arranged in alphabetical order.

part of speech shows the part that the word plays in a sentence. Look at the **Guide to parts of speech** on the page facing this one.

opposite gives an opposite word or words.

number introduces each new meaning of the word.

list of synonyms gives you a choice of alternative words, with the most suitable ones first. Most of the synonyms fit exactly into the example sentence, so you can try out each one until you find the word you like.

You may not recognize all the synonyms in a list. Always use a dictionary to check unfamiliar words.

frantic
(adj) You'll be frantic when you hear the news. beside yourself, at your wits' end, desperate, panic-stricken, distraught, hysterical, overwrought, worked up, frenzied.
OPPOSITE: calm.

fraud
1 *(n) Dodgy Dave is guilty of fraud.* swindling, cheating, deception, sharp practice, double-dealing, embezzlement, trickery.
2 *(n) (informal) That man is a fraud.* impostor, phoney *(informal)*, fake, cheat, con man *(informal)*, swindler, double-dealer, charlatan, quack *(doctor)*.

example sentence or **phrase** demonstrates how the word is used and helps you to find the meaning that you want.

word-use label shows that a word is informal, slang or old-fashioned. Informal words are not normally used in formal or official writing. Word-use labels also show when a word is plural or if it should only be used in a certain situation.

What's in your thesaurus?

chameleon

List of panels

leaping goalkeeper

staring eyes

treasure-island

spicy stir-fry

jester

perplexed

sorcerer's castle

Other helpful features

word lists give groups of related words for you to choose from. Some of these lists are illustrated.

song
(n) TYPES OF SONG: anthem, aria, ballad, calypso, canon, carol, chant, folk song, hymn, jingle, love song, lullaby, madrigal, nursery rhyme, pop song, psalm, round, sea shanty, serenade, spiritual.

cross-references point you to the headword where you will find the list of words you want. The number shows you which meaning you need to look for.

> **prod** *see* **poke** 2.

cross-references to panels direct you to a range of related words in an illustrated panel.

castle
(n) fortress, fort, stronghold, citadel, palace, chateau.
❖ *Also see* **medieval life**.

> If you can't find the word you want, look for a similar word. For example, for "slowly", look up "slow"

Guide to parts of speech

noun *(n)* Nouns give the name of a person, animal or thing. They tell you who or what a sentence is about. "Sofa" and "happiness" are nouns.
Some nouns, such as "ruins", which are normally used in the plural form, have a label *(plural n)*.

pronoun *(pronoun)* Pronouns refer to a person or thing without naming it. They act like nouns. "We" and "it" are pronouns.

adjective *(adj)* Adjectives are descriptive words which tell you more about a person or thing. They are used with nouns and pronouns. "Huge" and "busy" are adjectives.

verb *(v)* Verbs are action words. They tell you what someone or something does, thinks or feels. "Destroy" and "imagine" are verbs.

adverb *(adv)* Adverbs tell you how, when, where or why something happens. They are used with verbs. "Suddenly" and "sadly" are adverbs.

preposition *(prep)* Prepositions show where people or things are, or what relation they have to each other. "Under" and "near" are prepositions.

phrase *(phrase)* This thesaurus also contains phrases which are made up of several parts of speech. "Fall in love with" and "take advantage of" are phrases.

noun ——— Chloë

and

pronoun ——— I

verb ——— clambered

adverb ——— cautiously

preposition ——— up

the

adjective ——— craggy

noun ——— cliff.

Choosing and using words

You can transform your writing by choosing interesting words. Try to avoid repeating the same words and use your thesaurus to find exciting alternatives.

Before you start to write, think carefully about the effect you want to create. The examples on this page will give you ideas for using words in different ways.

Creating atmosphere

To make a scene really come to life, try to use all your senses to describe what you see, hear, smell and feel.

Fire swept through the forest, devouring everything in its path. Flames licked around the blackened trees and lit up the night sky with a weird orange glow. Branches snapped and crackled in the blaze and the air was thick with the acrid smell of smoke.

Conveying action and excitement

Lots of verbs (action words) and short sentences will give your writing a sense of speed and drama.

Buzz dived for the ball; grabbed it and raced off. Bouncing the ball in front of him, he dodged and swerved up the court. Suddenly he stopped, took aim and shot. It was a goal! The crowd roared with delight. Buzz had saved the match.

Describing people

Make your characters interesting and convincing by describing their features, their expressions, their build and the way they move. Details of hair and clothing will help to create a realistic picture.

A burly figure strode along the quay, his crimson frockcoat flapping in the breeze. Where his left hand should have been, a silver hook gleamed from under a lacy cuff. One eye was hidden by a black patch, but the other glittered greedily. Beneath his tangled beard, his mouth looked thin and cruel and a deep scar ran across his weather-beaten cheek.

WANTED
Dead or Alive

Writing conversation

To make a conversation sound natural, think about the way people talk in real life. Try to find different ways of saying "said" (see panel on page 415) and begin a new line whenever a different person starts to speak.

Poppy inquired

Is that a love letter?

It's none of your business!

Ben snapped

"Is that a love letter?" inquired Poppy, nosily, leaning over Ben's shoulder. "It's none of your business!" snapped Ben, blushing furiously. "Now clear off and leave me alone!"
"Is it to Sophie?" she continued. Ben was silent. "Because, if so, I'm sure she'll be very happy..." Poppy tailed off, miserably. "Sophie? No way!" Ben retorted. He took a deep breath. "It's actually to you."

Starting a story

There are lots of different ways to begin a story. You can introduce a character, or set a scene, or even jump straight in with an exciting piece of action or an intriguing conversation. A really dramatic opening will grab your readers' attention and make them want to read on.

Thump!
A large, scaly, orange dragon landed at Todd's feet. "Excuse me," said Todd, stepping carefully over its tail. "You're blocking the pavement."
"Not for long!" cried the dragon. "Come on, there isn't a moment to lose. We might already be too late!"

Ending a story

You can finish a story by tidying everything up, but sometimes it's fun to leave a mystery unsolved.

It was time to leave Netherfield Manor. Of course it wasn't haunted, it was just a creaky, draughty old house. As I fumbled for my key, I glanced in the hall mirror. Was it just the reflection of the candle flame or was there someone there, calling to me? I locked the door behind me and walked away for ever.

A a

abandon
1 *(v) When the river flooded, we had to abandon our homes.* leave, desert, leave behind, vacate, quit, evacuate.
2 *(v) Rain forced us to abandon the match.* discontinue, stop, scrap, give up.

ability
1 *(n) I know I have the ability to do better.* potential, capacity, power, capability.
2 *(n) Pablo has great ability in art.* skill, talent, expertise, flair, aptitude.

able
(adj) Vikram is an able tennis player. capable, competent, proficient, accomplished, practised, skilled, skilful, expert, gifted, talented, clever.

abnormal *see* **strange** 1.

abolish
(v) The government wants to abolish smoking in public places. stamp out, put an end to, do away with, eradicate, wipe out, get rid of, eliminate, stop.

about
(adv) Jo has about 20 hats! approximately, roughly, around, more or less, close to, nearly, approaching, nearing.
OPPOSITE: exactly.

abroad
(adv) Mum is abroad this week. overseas, out of the country, in a foreign country.

abrupt
1 *(adj) My ride came to an abrupt end.* sudden, rapid, swift, hasty, unexpected, surprising, unanticipated, unforeseen.
OPPOSITES: gradual, slow.
2 *(adj) Alice gave an abrupt reply.* curt, blunt, brusque, brisk, terse, snappy, direct.

absent *see* **away** 1.

absent-minded
(adj) Professor Peabody is so absent-minded. forgetful, scatterbrained, vague, dreamy, distracted, preoccupied, inattentive, lost in thought.

absolute
(adj) That goal was absolute magic! pure, sheer, complete, total, utter, perfect.

absolutely
(adv) This is absolutely ridiculous! completely, totally, altogether, utterly, perfectly, positively, thoroughly, entirely.

absorb
1 *(v) Use a cloth to absorb the water.* soak up, mop up, suck up, drink up.
2 *(v) I can't absorb all this information at once. See* **take in**.
3 *(v) This book will absorb you for hours.* enthral, captivate, engross, fascinate, rivet.

absorbing *see* **fascinating**.
absurd *see* **ridiculous**.

abuse
1 *(v) Don't abuse your computer.* misuse, ill-treat, damage, harm, manhandle.
2 *(v) It's wrong to abuse animals.* ill-treat, maltreat, be cruel to, harm, hurt, injure, beat, batter, molest.
3 *(n) I've had enough of this abuse.* rudeness, insults *(plural)*, attacks *(plural)*, character assassination, invective, ridicule, derision, slander *(spoken)*, libel *(written)*, cursing, swearing.

accelerate *see* **speed up** 1.

accept
1 *(v) I hope you will accept this gift.* take, receive, welcome.
OPPOSITES: reject, refuse.
2 *(v) I can't accept this behaviour!* allow, tolerate, put up with *(informal)*, take, stand, bear.
3 *(v) I hope you can accept our plan.* agree to, approve, consent to, go along with, resign yourself to, submit to.
OPPOSITE: reject.

accident
1 *(n) Our holiday consisted of one accident after another.* mishap, disaster, misfortune, calamity, catastrophe, blow.
2 *(n) There's been an accident on the motorway. See* **crash** 2.
3 *(n) I broke the plate by accident.* mistake, bad luck.
4 *(n) We met by accident.* chance, coincidence, luck, fluke, serendipity.

accidental
(adj) An accidental meeting. chance, unexpected, unintentional, unplanned, unforeseen, casual, fluky *(informal)*.

accompany *see* **go with** 1.
accomplish *see* **achieve**.

account
(n) A written account. report, record, description, narrative, explanation, statement, diary, journal, log, history.

accurate
1 *(adj) Accurate measurements.* exact, precise, correct, spot-on *(informal)*, strict, unerring, faultless, careful, meticulous.
OPPOSITES: approximate, rough.
2 *(adj) An accurate newspaper report.* correct, factual, true, truthful, faithful.
OPPOSITES: inaccurate, false.

accuse
(v) I don't want to accuse you of stealing. blame you for, charge you with, denounce you for, take you to task for.

ache
(v) My knee is starting to ache. hurt, throb, pound, be painful, be sore, smart.

achieve
(v) See what you can achieve in an hour. accomplish, manage, bring about, do, complete, finish, carry out.

achievement
(n) Climbing the mountain was a great achievement. accomplishment, attainment, feat, triumph, exploit, success.

act
1 *(v) Hugh loves to act in his own plays.* perform, appear, take part, star, play.
2 *(v) Act your age!* behave.
3 *(v) This medicine should act quickly.* work, take effect, react, function.
4 *(n) Saving Fido was a courageous act.* deed, feat, action, undertaking, enterprise, exploit, effort, move, step, operation, accomplishment, achievement.
5 *(n) Rosie's shyness is just an act.* pose, pretence, show, sham, front, façade, mask, cover-up, fake, counterfeit.

action
1 *(n) That was a brave action. See* **act** 4.
2 *(n) The film was packed with action.* activity, drama, excitement, adventure, movement, energy, incident.

active
1 *(adj) Gran is very active.* lively, sprightly, energetic, sporty, vigorous, nimble, spry.
OPPOSITES: sluggish, slow.
2 *(adj) Sally has an active life.* busy, full, energetic, bustling, action-packed.
OPPOSITES: sedentary, idle.
3 *(adj) Marco is an active member of the group.* enthusiastic, hard-working, energetic, involved, committed, dedicated.

activity
1 *(n) The classroom was full of activity.* action, movement, bustle, hustle and bustle, life, commotion.
2 *(n) Football is my favourite leisure activity.* pursuit, occupation, pastime, interest, hobby, project, undertaking.

actor, actress
*(n) performer, player, film star, star, lead, supporting actor, character actor, bit player, extra, starlet, dramatic artist.

adapt
1 *(v) I want to adapt my bike so it can go faster.* modify, alter, adjust, convert, remodel, reconstruct, rebuild, change.
2 *(v) Dan plans to adapt his book for TV.* alter, change, modify, tailor, edit, rewrite.
3 *(v) It's hard to adapt to life in a new country.* acclimatize, adjust, get used, accustom yourself, fit in.

adaptable *see* **flexible** 3.

add
1 *(v) Add one more name to the list.* append, attach, tack on *(informal)*, include, insert, affix.
2 *(v) Add these figures together. See* **add up** 1.

addict
1 *(n) A drug addict.* user *(informal)*, junkie *(informal)*, crack-head *(slang)*.
2 *(n) A computer addict.* enthusiast, fanatic, devotee, freak *(informal)*, buff *(informal)*, nut *(slang)*, fiend *(informal)*.

addicted

addicted
1 *(adj) Alice is addicted to computer games.* hooked on, obsessed by, crazy about, devoted to.
2 *(adj) Ziggy is addicted to drugs.* hooked on, dependent on.

additional *see* **extra**.

add up
1 *(v) Add up these figures.* add, count up, tot up, total, reckon up, find the sum of.
2 *(v) How much does my bill add up to?* amount to, come to, total.
3 *(v) I'm not sure that our story will add up.* make sense, sound convincing, ring true, hold water, be plausible.

adequate
1 *(adj) Do you have adequate supplies for your voyage?* sufficient, enough, ample.
OPPOSITES: inadequate, insufficient.
2 *(adj) Your work is adequate, but nothing more.* satisfactory, fair, passable, acceptable, tolerable, good enough, O.K. *(informal)*, all right, so-so *(informal)*.
OPPOSITE: unsatisfactory.

adjust
1 *(v) Are you starting to adjust to your new life?* adapt, acclimatize, get used, accustom yourself, reconcile yourself.
2 *(v) We need to adjust our TV.* tune, retune, regulate, fix, fiddle with *(informal)*.
3 *(v) Adjust the straps until they fit tightly.* alter, change, move, fiddle with *(informal)*.

admire
1 *(v) I do admire Uncle Jim.* respect, look up to, think highly of, rate *(slang)*, approve of, idolize, revere, appreciate, value.
OPPOSITE: despise.
2 *(v) Let's all admire Gary's new car.* praise, marvel at, wonder at, delight in.

admirer
(n) Do you have an admirer? fan, follower, devotee, supporter, disciple, suitor, lover, wooer, worshipper.

admiring
(adj) An admiring glance. appreciative, adoring, approving, delighted, devoted.
OPPOSITES: scornful, disdainful.

admission
1 *(n) Admission to the concert is free.* entrance, entry, admittance, access.
2 *(n) Burglar Beryl made an admission of guilt. See* **confession**.

admit
1 *(v) How many pupils will the school admit?* accept, take in, give a place to, allow in, receive, welcome.
OPPOSITE: exclude.
2 *(v) You must admit that you're lying.* confess, own up, acknowledge, concede, accept, recognize, grant.
OPPOSITE: deny.

adolescence
(n) Dad remembers his adolescence with affection. teenage years *(plural)*, teens *(plural)*, youth, puberty.

adolescent
(n) teenager, youngster, youth, juvenile.

adopt
1 *(v) Let's adopt Fran's idea.* take up, follow, accept, go in for, support, endorse.
OPPOSITE: reject.
2 *(v) Will you adopt this injured duck?* take in, befriend, foster, parent, take under your wing.

adorable
(adj) An adorable little kitten. lovable, appealing, endearing, charming, delightful, sweet, cute, cuddly, winsome.
OPPOSITES: revolting, repellent.

adore
1 *(v) Juliet, I adore you. See* **love** 1.
2 *(v) (informal) I adore fudge. See* **like** 1.

adult
1 *(n) Wait until you're an adult.* grown-up.
OPPOSITE: child.
2 *(adj) Rosie seems very adult.* mature, grown-up, experienced, sensible.
OPPOSITES: immature, childish.

advance
1 *(v) The army began to advance.* move forward, move onward, press on, proceed, progress, approach, come near, bear down.
OPPOSITES: retreat, withdraw.
2 *(v) I hope to advance rapidly this term. See* **improve** 1.
3 *(v) The money will help to advance research.* promote, further, develop, boost, accelerate.
OPPOSITES: hinder, obstruct.
4 *(v) Please advance me some money.* lend, loan.
5 *(n) This is a major advance in space technology.* development, step, improvement, breakthrough.
OPPOSITE: setback.

advanced
1 *(adj) An advanced new computer system.* modern, up-to-date, state-of-the-art, progressive, sophisticated.
OPPOSITES: out of date, obsolete.
2 *(adj) Advanced maths.* complicated, complex, higher, difficult, hard.
OPPOSITES: elementary, basic.

advantage
1 *(n) A good memory is an advantage if you want to learn a language.* asset, help, benefit, bonus, boon, blessing.
OPPOSITES: disadvantage, handicap.
2 **take advantage of** *see* **take advantage of**.

adventure
1 *(n) Crossing the rapids was a great adventure.* feat, escapade, experience, exploit, enterprise, undertaking, venture.
2 *(n) Amanda longed for adventure.* excitement, drama, thrills *(plural)*, thrills and spills *(plural)*, danger.

adventure words

adventures can be...
action-packed	incredible
amazing	intriguing
astonishing	nail-biting
baffling	nerve-racking
dangerous	perilous
exciting	perplexing
exhilarating	puzzling
extraordinary	remarkable
fascinating	scary *(informal)*
frightening	strange
hair-raising	terrifying
hazardous	thrilling

adventure clues
ancient manuscript	last will and testament
chart	map
cryptic message (message in code)	newspaper cutting
cypher (code)	parchment scroll
diary	photograph
footprints	riddle
inscription	sealed letter
	secret symbols
	tape recording

cryptic message

penknife

equipment for adventures
binoculars	rope ladder
camera	rucksack
codebook	survival kit
compass	torch
magnifying glass	vine cutters
map	water bottle
notebook	
penknife	

compass

binoculars

LOST CITY

in the city you see...
bridge
canal
city walls
courtyard
lake
market place
mosaic pavement
palace
pyramid
river
temple
tombs
winding streets

courtyard

the city is...
ancient
beautiful
deserted
fabled
forbidding
forgotten
hidden
legendary
magnificent
mysterious
remote
ruined
sinister
undiscovered
unexplored

temple

plan of labyrinth

under the lost city
cavern
dead end
labyrinth
  (network of tunnels)
maze
pillar
sealed passage
secret entrance
stone steps
tunnel
underground chamber
underground passage
underground waterway

the tunnels under the city are...
airless
bewildering
claustrophobic
confusing
creepy (informal)
crooked
dark
disorientating
endless
meandering
musty
narrow
shadowy
silent
stuffy
tortuous
twisting
winding

underground passage

TEMPLES AND TOMBS

in the temples and tombs you see...
burial chamber
carved symbols
coffin
corridor
engravings
flaming torch
gilded shrine
gilded throne
hidden entrance
hieroglyphics
  (picture writing)
mummy
  (embalmed body)

pillar
sacrificial altar
sarcophagus
  (stone coffin)
shrine
skull rack
staircase
statue
stone slab
stone tablet
treasure chamber
tunnel
wall painting

hieroglyphics

sarcophagus

statue

the temple is...
awe-inspiring
colossal
crumbling
immense
imposing
magnificent
majestic
massive
monumental
towering
vast

inside the temple it is...
cool
dim
dingy
eerie
gloomy
menacing
murky
mysterious
sinister
smoky

treasures of the tombs
amulet (lucky charm)
armlet
bowl
bracelet
chalice
  (drinking cup)
coin
dagger
diadem
  (light crown)
flagon (jug)
goblet
golden casket
golden mask
helmet
idol
jewelled collar
medallion
necklace
pendant
shield
sword

golden mask

goblet

dagger

necklace

coins

Also see **fantasy words, ghosts & hauntings, jungle, pirates & shipwrecks, space adventure, treasure words.**

adventurous
1 *(adj) Gerry is an adventurous climber.*
See **daring**.
2 *(adj) Kit loves adventurous holidays.*
exciting, challenging, dangerous, risky.

advertise
(v) Let's advertise our play in the paper.
publicize, announce, draw attention to,
plug *(informal)*, promote, push.

advertisement
(n) advert *(informal)*, ad *(informal)*, plug
(informal), announcement.
TYPES OF ADVERTISEMENT: blurb *(book
jacket)*, brochure, classified advertisement
(newspaper), commercial *(TV and radio)*,
display, flier, hand-out, leaflet, notice,
placard, poster, promotion, publicity stunt,
sandwich board, small ad *(newspaper)*
(informal).

advice
*(n) I need some advice on how to mend
my bicycle.* suggestions *(plural)*, hints
(plural), tips *(plural)*, guidance, help.

advise
(v) I advise that you try again. suggest,
recommend, urge, counsel, encourage.

affair
1 *(n) I'll handle this; it's my affair.*
business, concern, problem, responsibility.
2 *(n) Kurt's disappearance was a strange
affair.* business, occurrence, event,
incident, episode, matter, case.
3 *(n) Romeo and Juliet had a passionate
affair.* love affair, romance, relationship,
attachment, involvement, liaison.
4 *(n) The party was a grand affair.*
occasion, event, do *(informal)*, function.

affect
(v) The weather can affect my mood.
influence, have an effect on, have an
impact on, sway, alter, change, transform.

affection
(n) Kate looked at her mum with affection.
fondness, tenderness, warmth, devotion,
love, liking, friendship.

affectionate see **loving**.

afford
(v) I can't afford a new pair of jeans. pay
for, spare the money for, meet the cost of,
find the cash for, bear the expense of.

afraid see **scared** 1, 2.

age
1 *(n) We're studying the Elizabethan age.*
period, era, days *(plural)*, time, epoch.
2 *(v) We all age as time passes.* grow old,
decline, deteriorate, fade, grow older,
grow up, mature, come of age.
3 **ages** *(plural n) I haven't seen Hugo for
ages.* a long time, a long while, weeks
(plural), months *(plural)*, years *(plural)*,
aeons *(plural)*, yonks *(plural) (informal)*.

aggravate
1 *(v) Complaining will only aggravate the
problem.* make worse, worsen, magnify,
intensify, heighten, exacerbate.

2 *(v) (informal) Practical jokes aggravate
Mrs Badger.* See **annoy** 1.

aggressive
*(adj) Roger is so aggressive; he's always
starting fights.* quarrelsome, belligerent,
pugnacious, argumentative, antagonistic,
provocative, hostile, violent.
OPPOSITES: submissive, friendly.

agile
*(adj) Monkeys are agile in their
movements.* nimble, lithe, sprightly,
acrobatic, lively, supple, limber, flexible.
OPPOSITES: awkward, stiff.

agitated
(adj) The long wait made me feel agitated.
uneasy, edgy, restless, fidgety, nervous,
worked up, anxious, perturbed, unnerved,
disconcerted, troubled, worried.
OPPOSITES: calm, serene.

agonizing
(adj) An agonizing pain. excruciating,
racking, stabbing, shooting, piercing,
searing, acute, intense, unbearable.

agony
1 *(n) When he broke his ankle, Marvin
was in agony.* pain, torment, distress,
paroxysms *(plural)*.
2 *(n) Parting from Peter was agony.*
misery, torture, torment, anguish.

agree
1 *(v) Do you agree that this is a good film?*
acknowledge, admit, accept, recognize.
OPPOSITE: deny.
2 *(v) Let's agree a date to play tennis.* fix,
decide on, arrange, settle on, arrive at.
3 *(v) I wish you two would agree!*
get on, see eye to eye, be united, concur.
OPPOSITES: disagree, quarrel.
4 **agree with** *(v) I agree with animal
rights.* See **support** 3.
5 **agree with** *(v) Does your version of
events agree with mine?* correspond to,
coincide with, match, fit, conform to, tally
with, square with.
OPPOSITE: differ from.
6 **agree to** *(v) I hope that Nat will agree
to our plan.* consent to, accept, go along
with, comply with, assent to, approve.

agreement
(n) The two sides reached an agreement.
understanding, consensus, settlement,
arrangement, deal *(informal)*, bargain,
contract, pact, truce, treaty.

aid
1 *(n) Many countries offered aid to victims
of the earthquake.* help, assistance, relief,
support, backing, a helping hand.
2 *(v) The money we raise will aid starving
children.* See **help** 3.

aim
1 *(n) My aim is to become a pilot.*
ambition, goal, target, intention, plan,
objective, wish, dream, hope, aspiration.
2 *(v) I aim to be famous one day.* intend,
plan, mean, want, wish, aspire, propose.

3 *(v) Aim the arrow at the bull's-eye.*
point, direct, line up with, zero in on.

aimless
*(adj) Amy wandered around in an aimless
way.* pointless, purposeless, futile,
haphazard, random, rambling, desultory.
OPPOSITE: purposeful.

air
1 *(n) The kite soared high into the air.* sky,
atmosphere, heavens *(plural)*, ether.
2 *(n) The air felt cool on my face.* fresh air,
breeze, wind, draught, breath of air.
3 *(n) The house had an air of mystery.*
appearance, look, atmosphere, feeling,
sense, aura, mood, impression.

aircraft
(n) plane, aeroplane,
flying machine
(old-fashioned).
TYPES OF AIRCRAFT:
airliner, airship,
biplane, bomber, cargo
plane, executive jet,
fighter, glider, hang-
glider, helicopter, hot-air
balloon, jet, jumbo jet, jump
jet, microlight, reconnaissance
plane, rescue helicopter,
seaplane, stealth bomber,
supersonic jet, tanker, triplane.
❖ Also see **journey words**.

*hot-air
balloon*

airport
(n) aerodrome, airfield, heliport.

airy
(adj) The room was light and airy. fresh,
well-ventilated, draughty, spacious, open.
OPPOSITE: stuffy.

alarm
1 *(n) If you hear the alarm, run for cover!*
siren, bell, buzzer, signal, warning, alert.
2 *(n) Seb shrank back in alarm.* dismay,
panic, consternation, fear, fright, terror.
3 *(v) This news may alarm you.* startle,
frighten, scare, worry, panic, unnerve, put
the wind up *(informal)*, upset, disturb,
distress, shock, dismay.
OPPOSITE: reassure.

alert
1 *(adj) You seem very alert this morning.*
wide-awake, sharp, quick, perceptive,
attentive, on the ball *(informal)*, on your
toes, lively, quick off the mark *(informal)*.
OPPOSITES: lethargic, slow.
2 *(adj) The guards stayed alert all night.*
See **awake**.
3 *(v) Alert the police!* See **warn** 1.

alien
1 *(n) An alien stepped from the
spacecraft.* extraterrestial, space creature.
2 *(adj) The new school seemed alien to
me.* See **strange** 3.

alike
(adj) The twins look alike. identical, the
same, similar, like peas in a pod *(informal)*.
OPPOSITE: different.

alive
1 *(adj) Our rabbits are still alive.* living, breathing, alive and kicking, in the land of the living *(informal)*, surviving, flourishing. OPPOSITE: dead.
2 *(adj) There are no dinosaurs alive today.* living, existing, in existence. OPPOSITE: extinct.

alley
(n) alleyway, backstreet, passage, lane.

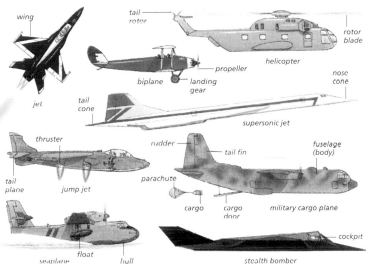

wing
tail rotor
rotor blade
helicopter
propeller
nose cone
biplane
landing gear
jet
tail cone
supersonic jet
thruster
rudder
tail fin
fuselage (body)
tail plane
jump jet
parachute
cargo
cargo door
military cargo plane
seaplane
float
hull
cockpit
stealth bomber

allow
1 *(v) Will your dad allow you to go?* give you permission, permit, let, authorize, give you leave, give you the green light, give you the go-ahead *(informal)*. OPPOSITE: forbid.
2 *(v) Mrs Badger will not allow talking in class.* permit, tolerate, stand for *(informal)*, put up with *(informal)*, endure, sanction. OPPOSITES: forbid, prohibit.

allowance
1 *(n) Each refugee had an allowance of food.* share, portion, ration, measure, amount, quota, allocation.
2 *(n) A clothes allowance.* grant, subsidy.

all right
1 *(adj) Is it all right to come in?* O.K. *(informal)*, permitted, in order, acceptable.
2 *(adj) I had an accident but I'm all right.* O.K. *(informal)*, unharmed, uninjured, safe, safe and sound, healthy, well.
3 *(adj) The food was all right.* adequate, acceptable, satisfactory, average, fair, O.K. *(informal)*, reasonable, tolerable, passable.

ally
(n) America was an ally of Britain in World War II. partner, associate, colleague, friend, helper. OPPOSITE: enemy.

almost *see* **nearly.**

alone
1 *(adj) Are you alone in the house?* on your own, by yourself, unaccompanied, unattended, solitary, solo.
2 *(adj) After my friends left, I felt alone.* lonely, solitary, isolated, friendless, forlorn, abandoned, forsaken, deserted, desolate.

aloof *see* **cold 4.**

a lot *see* **many.**

also
(adv) too, as well, besides, in addition, additionally, furthermore, on top of that.

alter
1 *(v) Let's alter our plans. See* **change 1.**
2 *(v) I need to alter my trousers.* adjust, take in, take up, let out, let down, shorten, lengthen, remodel, revamp, transform.

alternative
1 *(adj) Let's try an alternative plan.* different, other, substitute, back-up.
2 *(n) Do I have an alternative?* choice, option, fall-back.

always
1 *(adv) Fifi is always late.* consistently, invariably, without exception, regularly, repeatedly, unfailingly, constantly, continually, perpetually, forever. OPPOSITES: never, rarely.
2 *(adv) I will love you always.* forever, forever and ever, evermore, eternally, unceasingly, until the end of time.

amaze *see* **astonish.**

amazed *see* **astonished.**

amazement
(adj) Tiggy looked at me in amazement. astonishment, surprise, shock, confusion, bewilderment, wonder, admiration.

amazing
(adj) Arthur made an amazing discovery. astonishing, incredible, remarkable, extraordinary, unusual, startling, astounding, staggering, stunning, breathtaking, miraculous, phenomenal, electrifying, sensational *(informal)*.

ambition
1 *(n) My ambition is to become a pilot. See* **aim 1.**
2 *(n) Joel has plenty of ambition.* drive, enthusiasm, eagerness, enterprise, get-up-and-go *(informal)*, oomph *(informal)*.

ambitious
(adj) An ambitious businessman. go-getting *(informal)*, pushy *(informal)*, go-ahead, forceful, purposeful, enterprising. OPPOSITE: unambitious.

ammunition
(n) TYPES OF AMMUNITION: blank cartridge, bullet, cannonball, cartridge, grenade, missile, rocket, rubber bullet, shell, shot, shrapnel.

amount
1 *(n) We bought a large amount of jelly babies.* quantity, number, supply.
2 *(n) The reservoir holds a large amount of water.* quantity, volume, mass, expanse.
3 *(n) What was the final amount that you raised?* sum, total, grand total, sum total.
4 **amount to** *(v) Lord Lucre's savings amount to millions. See* **add up 2.**

amuse
1 *(v) I think this joke will amuse you.* make you laugh, tickle you *(informal)*, cheer you up, raise a smile.
2 *(v) This game will amuse you for hours.* entertain, keep you amused, occupy, absorb, engross, interest, fascinate. OPPOSITE: bore.

amusement
1 *(n) The joke caused much amusement.* laughter, hilarity, mirth, merriment. OPPOSITES: boredom, sadness.
2 *(n) What do you do for amusement?* fun, pleasure, entertainment, enjoyment, interest, recreation, leisure, pastime, sport.

amusing
1 *(adj) An amusing joke. See* **funny 1.**
2 *(adj) An amusing game of cards. See* **entertaining.**

analyse
(v) Let's analyse the situation. examine, think through, investigate, study, consider, review, inquire into, scrutinize, evaluate.

ancient
1 *(adj) How did people live in ancient times?* early, past, bygone, olden *(old-fashioned)*, primeval, prehistoric, primitive. OPPOSITES: modern, recent.
2 *(adj) Our school buildings are ancient.* old, aged, archaic, antiquated, timeworn, out of date, old-fashioned, outmoded, antediluvian, out of the ark *(informal)*. OPPOSITES: modern, state-of-the-art.

Ancient Egypt

Ancient Egypt

travel in Ancient Egypt
barge
cargo boat
chariot
donkey
ferry
funeral barge
palanquin
  (carrying chair)
sledge
trading ship

palanquin

chariot

royal barge

funeral barge

pharaoh's cabin

steering oar

Egyptian pastimes
board games
boat trips
dancing
fencing
fishing
hunting
music
storytelling
water tournaments
wrestling

hunting

some Egyptian people
architect
astronomer
craftsman
dancer
embalmer
farmer
magician
musician
nobleman
pharaoh (king)
physician (doctor)
priest
priestess
queen
scribe
slave
soldier
soothsayer (prophet)
tax collector
tomb-builder
vizier (chief minister)

scribe

Egyptian clothes and jewellery

crown
flail
crook
fan
cone of perfumed fat
plaited wig
jewelled headdress
cape
belt
bead collar
skirt
royal apron
slave
sandal
pharaoh
ankh
scarab beetle
amulets (lucky charms)
queen
robe
pleated kilt
pectoral
anklet
nobleman
ring
pendant

inside a royal burial chamber
canopic jar (container for
  internal organs)
gilded throne
gold coffin
hieroglyphs (picture writing)
mummy (embalmed body)
painted coffin
painted statue
portrait mask
sarcophagus
  (stone coffin)

painted coffin

canopic jars

Egyptian pyramid

The Great Pyramid at Giza (cutaway)

capstone
pharaoh's burial chamber
chamber
shaft
chamber
grand gallery
mortuary temple
corridor

Ancient Greece

Greek gods and goddesses

Aphrodite (goddess of love and beauty)

Apollo (god of the sun, music and poetry)

Artemis (goddess of hunting and the moon)

Athene (goddess of wisdom and war)

Hera (queen of the gods)

Hermes (messenger of the gods)

Pluto (god of the underworld)

Poseidon (god of the sea)

Zeus (king of the gods)

Athene

Zeus

Aphrodite

some Greek people

actor
architect
aristocrat (landowner)
artist
citizen (free man)
craftsman
doctor
dramatist

fortune teller
freed slave
historian
magistrate
merchant
musician
philosopher
poet
politician

priest
priestess
sailor
scholar
sculptor
slave
soldier
soothsayer (prophet)
teacher

Greek philosopher Aristotle

Greek clothes and jewellery

headband

himation (wrap)

diadem (gold headband)

necklace

chiton (robe made from one length of cloth)

girdle (belt)

bracelet

himation (wrap)

bronze helmet

brooch

cuirass (breast and back plate)

tunic

short sword

thigh-length tunic

round shield

chlamys (short cloak)

bronze greave (shin guard)

leather sandal

Greek pastimes

athletics
board games
chariot racing
cottabos (wine throwing)
dinner parties
gymnastics
hunting
music
poetry
politics
religious festivals
theatre

theatrical masks

musician with lyre

discus

Olympic Games

boxing
chariot racing
horse racing
pentathlon (running, wrestling, long jump, discus and javelin)
running
wrestling

running

javelin

wrestling

Greek city

Acropolis (area for temples and sanctuaries)

agora (public square)
altar
city gate
city wall
council chamber
court of justice

gymnasium (training ground)
market stall
monument
odeon (concert hall)
public baths
shops
stadium
temple
theatre
treasury

Acropolis at Athens

Greek temple

treasury

statue of the goddess Athene

The Parthenon at Athens (cutaway)

inner chamber

sculpted frieze

column

walkway

porch

anger
1 (n) *Mum turned purple with anger.*
rage, fury, wrath, indignation, annoyance,
exasperation, irritation, outrage.
2 (v) *Your giggles will anger Mrs Badger.*
infuriate, enrage, madden, incense, rile,
annoy, exasperate, irritate, provoke.
OPPOSITES: pacify, placate.

angry
(adj) *Dad was angry that I hadn't told the
truth.* furious, livid, irate, incensed, fuming,
seething, raging, enraged, mad (informal),
apoplectic, cross, annoyed, indignant.

animal
(n) *A wild animal.* creature, beast.

announce
1 (v) *I heard the head announce that the
trip was cancelled.* state, declare, give out,
reveal, disclose, make known, make public.
2 (v) *Will you announce the next act in the
talent show?* introduce, present, lead into.

announcement
(n) *Did you hear the announcement?*
notice, statement, message, bulletin,
communication, advertisement, report,
declaration, disclosure.

announcer
(n) presenter, broadcaster, anchorman,
newsreader, newscaster, commentator,
master of ceremonies, town crier.

annoy
1 (v) *Doesn't your brother annoy you?*
irritate, exasperate, infuriate, get on your
nerves (informal), madden, provoke, rile,
bug (informal), rub you up the wrong way,
aggravate (informal), needle (informal), get
to (informal), get up your nose (slang),
nark (slang), get on your wick (slang).
2 (v) *Don't annoy Dad when he's busy.*
disturb, bother, trouble, pester, hassle
(informal), badger, harass, worry.

annoyed
(adj) *Kim was annoyed that she hadn't got
her own way.* irritated, exasperated, cross,
indignant, displeased, vexed, riled, miffed
(informal), peeved (informal), piqued.
OPPOSITE: pleased.

annoying
(adj) *Are you being deliberately annoying?*
irritating, infuriating, maddening,
exasperating, aggravating (informal),
tiresome, trying, irksome, troublesome.

anonymous
1 (adj) *The writer wishes to remain
anonymous.* nameless, unnamed,
unidentified, unknown, unacknowledged,
uncredited, incognito.
2 (adj) *An anonymous letter.* unsigned.

answer
1 (v) *You didn't answer my question.* reply
to, respond to, react to, acknowledge.
OPPOSITE: ask.
2 (v) *"Never!" I heard Luke answer.* reply,
respond, retort, return, rejoin, retaliate.
OPPOSITES: ask, inquire.

3 (n) *Kay gave no answer to my question.*
reply, response, reaction, comeback
(informal), acknowledgment, rejoinder.
OPPOSITE: question.
4 (n) *What is the answer to this problem?*
solution, explanation, key.

answer back
(v) *Don't answer back!* talk back, argue,
contradict, be cheeky, be impertinent.

anticlimax see **letdown**.

antisocial
(adj) *Antisocial behaviour.* disruptive,
anarchic, rebellious, uncooperative,
offensive, disagreeable, hostile, disorderly,
unruly, antagonistic.

anxiety see **worry** 3.

anxious
1 (adj) *Sally is anxious about her exams.*
worried, apprehensive, concerned,
nervous, tense, uneasy, edgy, on edge,
uptight (informal), jittery (informal),
troubled, agitated, perturbed, fretful,
fearful, distressed, overwrought.
OPPOSITES: calm, confident.
2 (adj) *We are anxious to get started.*
See **eager** 2.

apathetic see **indifferent**.

apologetic see **sorry** 1.

apologize
(v) *You ought to apologize for breaking
the window.* say sorry, say you are sorry,
make an apology, express regret, be
penitent about, ask forgiveness, beg
pardon, eat humble pie.

apology
(n) *Mum accepted my apology.* expression
of regret, confession, explanation, excuse,
plea, defence, justification.

appalling see **dreadful** 1, 2, 3.

apparent see **obvious**.

appeal
1 (n) *A charity appeal.* campaign.
2 (n) *Burglar Beryl made an appeal for
mercy.* plea, request, cry, call, petition.
3 (v) *We will have to appeal for more
volunteers.* ask, put in a plea, beg, plead,
call, request, petition, canvass.
4 **appeal to** (v) *This film will appeal to
young children.* interest, delight, attract,
fascinate, captivate, enthral, enchant,
charm, please.
OPPOSITES: bore, repulse, alienate.

appealing see **charming**.

appear
1 (v) *We watched the ship appear over the
horizon.* come into view, come into sight,
emerge, loom, materialize, surface.
OPPOSITES: disappear, vanish.
2 (v) *What time did you appear at the
party?* arrive, turn up, show up (informal),
roll up (informal), come.
OPPOSITES: leave, depart.
3 (v) *Do you appear in the play?* feature,
figure, perform, act, take part, play a part.

4 (v) *You appear fit and well.* look, seem,
give the impression of being.
5 (v) *The next issue of "Rap Weekly" will
appear on Monday.* come out, be
published, become available, come on the
market, hit the shops (informal).

appearance
1 (n) *Can you describe Samantha's
appearance?* looks (plural), bearing,
demeanour, figure, image, expression, air.
2 (n) *Ed gives the appearance of being
confident.* impression, illusion, outward
appearance, show, semblance, pretence.
OPPOSITE: reality.
3 (n) *The sudden appearance of rain
spoiled the barbecue.* arrival, advent,
coming, presence.
OPPOSITE: disappearance.

appearance words

tall	thin	strong
lanky	bony	athletic
leggy	emaciated	beefy
towering	gaunt	(informal)
	lanky	brawny
short	lean	broad-
diminutive	scraggy	shouldered
dumpy	scrawny	burly
little	skeletal	hulking
petite	skinny	muscular
pint-sized	spare	powerful
(informal)	spindly	sinewy
small	waiflike	stocky
squat		strapping
tiny	**slim**	sturdy
	dainty	thickset
fat	elfin	well-built
chubby	lithe	wiry
corpulent	slender	
flabby	slight	**weak**
heavy	svelte	anaemic
hefty	sylphlike	delicate
obese	trim	feeble
overweight	willowy	fragile
paunchy		frail
plump	**curvy**	puny
podgy	bosomy	sickly
portly	busty	weedy
potbellied	buxom	(informal)
stout	curvaceous	wimpish
tubby	shapely	(informal)
weighty	voluptuous	
		upright
		erect
		straight
		straight-
		backed
		unbending

*hulking
sumo
wrestler*

appetite
(n) *Indiana has an appetite for adventure.* taste, thirst, hunger, need, desire, passion, liking, longing, craving, yearning, hankering, eagerness, zest.
OPPOSITES. dislike, aversion.

appetizing *see* **delicious.**

applaud
(v) *The audience are sure to applaud.* clap, cheer, whistle, give you a standing ovation, give you a big hand *(informal)*, put their hands together, ask for an encore.
OPPOSITES: boo, heckle.

apply
1 (v) *Apply the lotion twice a day.* use, smear on, put on, rub in, spread on, administer, cover with.

*sylphlike
ballerina*

hunched	smart
bent	dapper
bowed	neat
crooked	spruce
drooping	tidy
slouching	well-dressed
stooping	well-groomed

young	messy
boyish	bedraggled
girlish	dishevelled
youthful	scruffy
	shabby
old	tatty
aged	unkempt
elderly	untidy

graceful	fashionable
agile	chic
dignified	trendy *(informal)*
elegant	smart
lithe	stylish
poised	up-to-date

clumsy	unfashionable
awkward	dowdy
blundering	old-fashioned
bumbling	
gangling	sophisticated
gauche	classy *(slang)*
gawky	debonair
lumbering	elegant
shambling	glamorous
uncoordinated	refined
ungainly	suave

*wiry
gymnast*

Also see **faces & features,
hair & hairstyles.**

2 (v) *This comment could apply to you.* refer, relate, be relevant, be applicable, be pertinent, have a bearing on, pertain.
3 **apply for** (v) *Did you apply for the job?* make an application for, put in for, try for, inquire after, request.
4 **apply yourself** (v) *You need to apply yourself to your work. See* **concentrate** 2.

appointment
(n) *I have an appointment at four o'clock.* engagement, meeting, date, rendezvous, interview, consultation *(medical).*

appreciate
1 (v) *I will always appreciate your help.* value, be grateful for, be thankful for, be appreciative of, be obliged to you for, be indebted to you for, welcome.
OPPOSITE: be ungrateful for.
2 (v) *Aunt Bertha will never appreciate pop music.* enjoy, approve of, admire, think much of, think highly of, rate *(slang),* understand.
OPPOSITE: despise.
3 (v) *Do you appreciate how long it took to make this meal? See* **realize.**

apprehensive *see* **anxious** 1.

approach
1 (v) *The army began to approach.* draw near, come closer, move nearer, edge nearer, bear down, near, advance, push forward, catch up.
OPPOSITES: move away, back off.
2 (v) *I intend to approach Dad about my pocket money.* speak to, talk to, tackle, sound out, appeal to, make a proposal to.
3 (v) *I'm not sure how to approach this essay.* tackle, set about, go about, start, begin, embark on, make a start on.

approachable *see* **friendly.**

appropriate *see* **suitable** 1, 2.

approve
1 (v) *The chairman must approve the plan first.* accept, agree to, authorize, pass, endorse, consent to, give the go-ahead to *(informal),* rubber-stamp *(informal).*
2 **approve of** (v) *I hope you'll approve of what I've done.* be pleased with, like, applaud, admire, think highly of, have a good opinion of, appreciate, respect.
OPPOSITE: disapprove of.

approximately *see* **about.**

area
1 (n) *I have a lot of friends in this area.* district, neighbourhood, locality, part of the world, region, vicinity.
2 (n) *The fire destroyed a large area of forest.* expanse, stretch, patch, tract.

arena
(n) *A sports arena.* stadium, ground, field, ring, pitch, bowl, oval, rink.

argue
1 (v) *My brothers argue all the time.* quarrel, squabble, bicker, row, fight, fall out *(informal),* disagree, wrangle.
OPPOSITES: agree, get on.

2 (v) *My cousins argue that eating animals is wrong.* claim, assert, declare, maintain, insist, reason, hold, contend.

argument
1 (n) *We had an argument over who should pay.* row, quarrel, squabble, disagreement, dispute, difference of opinion, clash, fight, tiff *(informal),* bust-up *(informal),* set-to *(informal).*
OPPOSITE: agreement.
2 (n) *The argument about violence on TV continues.* debate, discussion, controversy.
3 (n) *Your argument is very convincing.* reasoning, logic, evidence, defence, justification, case, reasons *(plural),* grounds *(plural).*

armed
1 (adj) *The robber is armed.* carrying weapons, armed to the teeth.
OPPOSITES: unarmed, defenceless.
2 (adj) *The soldiers were armed with swords.* equipped, fitted out, supplied, provided, issued.

helmet
visor
*cuirass
(breast and
back plate)*
gauntlet
*cuisse
(thigh
guard)*
*greave
(shin guard)*
*suit of
armour*

armour
(n) protection.
TYPES OF ARMOUR: body armour, bulletproof vest, chain mail, flak jacket, plate armour, riot shield, suit of armour.

aroma *see* **smell** 1.

arrange
1 (v) *Would you arrange these ornaments for me?* display, set out, put out, tidy, position, line up, align, put in order.
2 (v) *Can you arrange these words in alphabetical order?* sort, group, organize, set out, rank, classify, categorize, collate.
3 (v) *Let's arrange a party.* organize, plan, fix up, set up, prepare, schedule.

arrangement
1 (n) *The arrangement is that we use the gym on Tuesdays.* agreement, understanding, deal *(informal),* set-up *(informal),* system, plan, scheme.
2 (n) *What a beautiful arrangement of flowers!* display, array, show.

arrest
(v) *The police decided to arrest Burglar Beryl.* take into custody, detain, apprehend, catch, capture, seize, haul in, collar *(informal),* run in *(informal),* pick up *(informal),* nab *(informal),* nick *(slang).*

arrive

1 (v) *When do you think Tracy will arrive?* appear, turn up, show up (informal), come, roll up (informal), get here, put in an appearance, show (informal).
OPPOSITES: leave, depart.
2 (v) *When will we arrive in New York?* land, touch down, dock, berth, disembark.
OPPOSITES: leave, take off, set sail.

arrogant see **proud** 2.

art

1 (n) *Lysander is studying art.* the visual arts (plural), design, fine art, art history.
TYPES OF ART: architecture, carving, computer art, drawing, engraving, etching, graphics, illustration, installation art, mosaic making, painting, photography, printing, sculpture, stained glass, tapestry. *Also see* **drawing**, **painting**.
2 (n) *We admired the potter's art.* See **skill**.

article

1 (n) *There's an interesting article in the newspaper.* item, feature, story, report, write-up, piece, column, exclusive, scoop (informal), editorial, leader.
2 (n) *What's that odd-looking article on the table?* object, thing, item.

artificial

1 (adj) *Lycra is an artificial fibre.* synthetic, man-made, manufactured.
OPPOSITE: natural.
2 (adj) *Artificial pearls are cheaper than real ones.* imitation, fake, simulated, synthetic, sham, mock, pseudo (informal).
OPPOSITES: genuine, natural.
3 (adj) *Araminta gave me an artificial smile.* insincere, forced, false, feigned, affected, phoney (informal), put-on.
OPPOSITES: genuine, sincere.

ascend see **rise** 1.

ash

(n) *The ash from the volcano glowed red-hot.* cinders (plural), embers (plural).

ashamed

(adj) *Ben looked ashamed that he'd lost his temper.* guilty, conscience-stricken, sorry, mortified, embarrassed, shamefaced, sheepish, red-faced, repentant, remorseful, rueful, abashed, chastened, humiliated.
OPPOSITE: unrepentant.

ask

1 (v) *Jon wants to ask if his answer is right.* inquire, enquire, query, question.
OPPOSITES: reply, answer.
2 (v) *The police want to ask Burglar Beryl about the robbery.* question, interrogate, cross-examine, quiz, grill (informal), pump, give the third degree to.
3 (v) *Wait for the doctor to ask you into the surgery.* invite, summon, order, bid.
4 ask for (v) *Jo decided to ask for more pocket money.* request, appeal for, beg for, plead for, demand, call for, claim, press for, petition for, apply for.

5 ask for (v) *You did rather ask for that punch on the nose!* deserve, bring on yourself, provoke, cause, encourage.

asleep

(adj) *Dad's asleep on the sofa.* sleeping, fast asleep, sound asleep, dozing, snoozing (informal), napping, having a kip (slang), slumbering (old-fashioned), crashed out (slang), dead to the world (informal).
OPPOSITE: awake.

assault see **attack** 2, 4, 5.

assemble

1 (v) *Mrs Badger told us to assemble in the hall.* See **meet** 3.
2 (v) *The workers began to assemble the car.* construct, build, put together, manufacture, piece together.
OPPOSITES: dismantle, take apart.

assembly see **meeting** 2.

assertive

1 (adj) *You should try to be more assertive.* confident, self-assured, firm, decisive, positive, emphatic, forceful.
OPPOSITE: passive.
2 (adj) *Pat is becoming too assertive.* domineering, overbearing, aggressive, opinionated, dogmatic, forceful, strong-willed, pushy (informal).
OPPOSITE: submissive.

assistance see **help** 5.

assistant

(n) helper, deputy, second-in-command, right-hand man or woman, henchman (informal), subordinate.

associate

1 (v) *Don't associate with those boys! See* **mix** 3.
2 (v) *I always associate that smell with school dinners.* connect, identify, link, lump together, relate to.

assorted see **mixed** 1.

assortment see **mixture** 1.

assume

(v) *I assume you like chocolate.* presume, take it for granted, expect, suppose, imagine, suspect, believe, guess (informal).

assure

(v) *Can you assure me that I won't be in danger?* promise, give your word, swear, guarantee, reassure, convince, persuade.

astonish

(v) *Marvello the Magician will astonish you with his tricks.* amaze, astound, stun, stagger, leave you speechless, startle, surprise, dazzle, take your breath away, leave you open-mouthed, wow (slang).

astonished

(adj) *I was astonished to hear the news.* amazed, astounded, stunned, staggered, surprised, startled, taken aback, shocked, flabbergasted (informal), dumbfounded, gobsmacked (slang), thunderstruck.

astonishing see **amazing**.

astound see **astonish**.

astronaut

(n) spaceman, spacewoman, cosmonaut (Russian), space traveller, shuttle crew member. ❖ *Also see* **space adventure**.

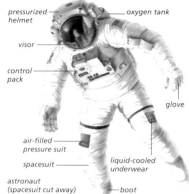

pressurized helmet — oxygen tank — visor — control pack — glove — air-filled pressure suit — spacesuit — liquid-cooled underwear — boot
astronaut (spacesuit cut away)

athletics

(n) track and field events (plural), games (plural).
TYPES OF ATHLETICS EVENT: cross-country, decathlon, discus, hammer throw, heptathlon, high jump, hurdles, javelin, long jump, marathon, pentathlon, pole vault, relay, running, shot put, sprint, steeplechase, triple jump, walking.
❖ *Also see* **sport words**.

atmosphere

1 (n) *The spaceship blasted into the atmosphere.* air, sky, heavens (plural), space, ether.
2 (n) *There was a strange atmosphere at the party.* feeling, mood, ambience, air, aura, vibrations (plural) (informal), vibes (plural) (slang).

atrocious see **dreadful** 1, 2, 3.

attach

(v) *Attach the pieces together.* fasten, join, fix, link, connect, stick, pin, tie, secure.
OPPOSITES: detach, separate.

attack

1 (v) *The soldiers will attack the city by night.* invade, storm, charge, strike, fall upon, descend on, bombard, raid, rush.
OPPOSITES: defend, protect.
2 (v) *The robbers threatened to attack the guard.* assault, beat up (informal), mug (informal), jump on, set on, set about, lay into (informal), put the boot in (slang).
3 (v) *The newspapers often attack the government.* criticize, find fault with, blame, slate (informal), have a go at (informal), lay into (informal), snipe at, get at, harangue, censure, berate.
OPPOSITE: defend.
4 (n) *The commanders planned their attack.* assault, charge, invasion, offensive, strike, raid, sortie, foray, onslaught, bombardment, blitz (air raid).
OPPOSITE: defence.

5 *(n) We were shocked by the attack on the old lady.* assault, mugging *(informal)*.
6 *(n) Lord Lucre was upset by the newspaper's attack.* criticism, slating *(informal)*, censure, tirade, onslaught, character assassination, denigration.
7 *(n) Joseph had an attack of coughing.* fit, bout, spell, outbreak.

attempt *see* **try** 1, 2.

attend
1 *(v) Are you planning to attend the club meeting?* go to, be present at, be at, turn up for, put in an appearance at, show up at *(informal)*.
2 attend to *(v) Please attend to your work. See* **concentrate** 2.
3 attend to *(v) The doctor will attend to you now. See* **see to**.

attic
(n) loft, roof space, garret *(old-fashioned)*.

attitude
1 *(n) What's your attitude towards fox-hunting?* opinion of, view on, reaction to, position on, point of view on, perspective on, stance on, thoughts on *(plural)*.
2 *(n) I don't like your attitude.* approach, outlook, manner, behaviour, disposition, frame of mind, mood, air, demeanour.

attract
(v) This window display is bound to attract customers. draw, pull *(informal)*, bring in, entice, lure, seduce, tempt, appeal to, interest, fascinate, captivate, enchant.
OPPOSITES: repel, drive away, put off.

attractive
(adj) Sam is really attractive. good-looking, handsome, pretty, striking, stunning *(informal)*, beautiful, gorgeous, fetching *(informal)*, charming, enchanting, alluring
OPPOSITES: unattractive, ugly.

audible
(adj) Jon's yells were audible all over the school. easy to hear, clear, loud, distinct, detectable, perceptible.
OPPOSITE: inaudible.

audience
(n) crowd, spectators *(plural) (sport)*, viewers *(plural) (TV)*, listeners *(plural) (radio)*, congregation *(religious meeting)*.

author *see* **writer**.

authority
1 *(n) Do you have authority to use this computer? See* **permission**.
2 *(n) The headteacher has authority over us.* power, control, command, influence.

authorize *see* **approve** 1

automatic
1 *(adj) An automatic machine.* automated, mechanized, mechanical, computerized, programmable, push-button, robotic.
OPPOSITES: manual, hand-operated.
2 *(adj) An automatic gesture.* instinctive, involuntary, unconscious, spontaneous, unthinking, mechanical, reflex.
OPPOSITES: conscious, deliberate.

available
1 *(adj) There are still some seats available. See* **free** 3.
2 *(adj) There is lots more food available.* to hand, on tap, at your disposal, obtainable, ready, handy, convenient, accessible.
OPPOSITE: unavailable.

avenue *see* **road**.

average
1 *(adj) Brownchester is an average small town.* ordinary, typical, everyday, normal, standard, run-of-the-mill, commonplace, unremarkable, unexceptional.
OPPOSITES: unusual, extraordinary.
2 *(adj) The meal was average.* mediocre, middling, so-so *(informal)*, not bad, tolerable, passable, fair, indifferent.
OPPOSITES: outstanding, exceptional.

avoid
1 *(v) I think that Sasha is trying to avoid me.* keep away from, steer clear of, hide from, evade, elude, shun, ignore.
2 *(v) Josh managed to avoid doing the washing-up.* get out of, escape, evade, dodge, wriggle out of, duck out of *(informal)*, shirk, sidestep.

awake
(adj) The guards stayed awake all night. wide-awake, alert, aware, conscious, wakeful, watchful, vigilant, attentive, on the lookout, on guard, on the alert.
OPPOSITE: asleep.

award
1 *(v) Who will award the prizes on Sports Day? See* **present** 5
2 *(n) Finn won an award for his poem. See* **prize** 1.

aware of
1 *(adj) Patsy was aware of the danger.* conscious of, mindful of, sensitive to, heedful of, alive to, wise to *(slang)*.
OPPOSITES: unaware of, oblivious to.
2 *(adj) Are you aware of the rules about school uniform?* familiar with, acquainted with, conversant with, knowledgeable about, clued-up on *(informal)*
OPPOSITES: unaware of, ignorant of.

away
1 *(adj) Nathan is away today.* absent, not here, not present, off.
2 *(adj) Our neighbours are away.* not here, not at home, on holiday, abroad.

awe
1 *(n) I looked at the painting with awe.* wonder, amazement, astonishment, admiration, reverence, respect.
2 *(n) We gazed at the monster with awe.* dread, fear, horror, terror, alarm.

awful *see* **dreadful** 1, 2, 3.

awkward
1 *(adj) Penny is so awkward; she's always dropping things.* clumsy, uncoordinated, butter-fingered *(informal)*, ham-fisted *(informal)*, inept, bungling, all thumbs.
OPPOSITE: dexterous.

2 *(adj) The robot moved with awkward steps.* clumsy, uncoordinated, ungainly, stiff, jerky, gawky, lumbering, blundering, ungraceful, inelegant, gauche.
OPPOSITE: graceful.
3 *(adj) This parcel is a really awkward shape.* inconvenient, difficult, unwieldy, unmanageable, cumbersome, bulky, troublesome.
OPPOSITES: convenient, handy.
4 *(adj) Nina is being deliberately awkward.* difficult, uncooperative, unhelpful, perverse, obstinate, stubborn, stroppy *(informal)*, bolshie *(informal)*, bloody minded *(informal)*, impossible *(informal)*.
OPPOSITES: cooperative, obliging.
5 *(adj) This is a really awkward problem to solve.* difficult, tricky, perplexing, baffling, thorny, troublesome, problematic
OPPOSITE: straightforward.
6 *(adj) Gus found himself in an awkward situation.* difficult, tricky, delicate, embarrassing, uncomfortable, unpleasant, ticklish, problematic, sticky *(informal)*, cringe-making *(informal)*, compromising.

babble *see* **prattle**.

baby
(n) infant, child, newborn child, babe *(old-fashioned)*, sprog *(slang)*, rug rat *(slang)*.

babyish *see* **childish**.

back
1 *(n) Jed has hurt his back.* spine, spinal column, backbone, vertebrae *(plural)*.
2 *(n) I sat at the back of the bus.* rear, rear end, far end, tail end, end, stern *(ship)*.
OPPOSITE: front.
3 *(adj) The horse kicked its back legs in the air.* hind, rear.
OPPOSITES: fore, front.
4 *(v) Jack began to back along the ledge.* retreat, move back, reverse, backtrack.
OPPOSITE: advance.
5 *(v) Jo will back my idea. See* **support** 3.

background
1 *(n) Tell me a bit about your background.* upbringing, education, family history, family circumstances *(plural)*, experience, qualifications *(plural)*, credentials *(plural)*.
2 *(n) Choose a dramatic background for your picture.* backdrop, setting, backcloth, scene, surroundings *(plural)*, context.

back out
(v) You can't back out now - I need you! drop out, pull out, resign, withdraw, get cold feet, chicken out *(informal)*.

back up
(v) Will you back me up if I tell the truth? support, side with, stand by, stand up for, stick up for *(informal)*, vouch for.

bad

bad a bad person	a bad accident	a bad smell	bad work	bad weather	Smoking is bad for you.	I feel bad about what I have done.
corrupt	appalling	disgusting	abysmal	awful	damaging	ashamed
criminal	catastrophic	foul	awful	dismal	dangerous	awful
crooked	disastrous	horrible	diabolical	dreadful	detrimental	conscience-
(informal)	dreadful	loathsome	*(informal)*	dreary	harmful	stricken
depraved	horrendous	nasty	dreadful	filthy	risky	contrite
dishonest	horrific	nauseating	inadequate	foul	unhealthy	dreadful
evil	nasty	offensive	inferior	murky		embarrassed
immoral	serious	repulsive	poor	nasty	After you left	guilty
sinful	terrible	revolting	substandard		I felt bad.	mortified
villainous	tragic	sickening	unacceptable	Overeating	awful	red-faced
wicked		unpleasant	unsatisfactory	makes you	blue	regretful
	a bad film	vile		feel bad.	depressed	remorseful
a bad child	abysmal		a bad mood	dreadful	down	rueful
badly behaved	appalling	bad food	angry	ill	dreadful	sad
cheeky	atrocious	decayed	bad-tempered	nauseous	glum	shamefaced
difficult	diabolical	mildewed	cross	off colour	low	sheepish
disobedient	*(informal)*	mouldy	grouchy	poorly	melancholy	sorry
mischievous	dire *(informal)*	off	*(informal)*	*(informal)*	miserable	terrible
naughty	lousy *(slang)*	putrid	grumpy	queasy	sad	uncomfortable
rebellious	pathetic	rancid	irritable	rotten *(informal)*	unhappy	uneasy
rude	*(informal)*	rotten	peevish	sick	wretched	upset
uncooperative	rotten *(informal)*	sour	ratty *(informal)*	terrible		
unruly	terrible	spoiled	sulky	unwell		

badge
(n) I sewed the badge on to my sweater.
emblem, crest, logo, symbol, insignia.

badger *see* pester.

bad-tempered
(adj) Dad gets bad-tempered when we're late. irritable, cross, short-tempered, grumpy, grouchy *(informal)*, ratty *(informal)*, crabby, crotchety *(informal)*, cantankerous, snappy, touchy, fractious, peevish, testy, morose, surly.
OPPOSITE: good-humoured.

baffle *see* puzzle 2.

bag
(n) TYPES OF BAG: backpack, basket, briefcase, carrier bag, handbag, holdall, knapsack, rucksack, sack, satchel, shopping bag, shoulder bag, sports bag, suitcase.

baggy *see* loose 1.

baking *see* hot 1.

balance
1 *(v) Can you balance a ball on your nose?* support, keep steady, steady, poise.
2 *(v) Try to make the scales balance.* even up, be equal, be level, counterbalance, reach equilibrium, be steady, stabilize.

ball
1 *(n) A ball of fire.* sphere, globe, orb.
2 *(n) A masked ball.* dance, party.

ban
(v) The judge decided to ban Dave from driving. prohibit, bar, prevent, stop, disqualify.
OPPOSITES: permit, authorize.

band
1 *(n) My skirt has a blue band round the bottom.* stripe, strip, line, ribbon.
2 *(n) Fasten the bundle with a leather band.* strap, strip, thong, belt, hoop.
3 *(n) William has a large band of friends.* See **group** 3.
4 *(n) Let's listen to the band.* group, ensemble, orchestra

jazz band   sousaphone   piano   trumpet

trombone   banjo   drums   clarinet

bang
1 *(n) I heard a loud bang from the science lab.* explosion, blast, crash, thud, thump, boom, pop, report.
2 *(v) Don't bang your head on that shelf!* See **hit** 2.

banish
(v) The king decided to banish the magician. exile, send away, expel, cast out, outlaw, throw out, deport.
OPPOSITES: admit, welcome.

bank
1 *(n) We walked along the river bank.* side, shore, edge, embankment, brink.
2 *(n) We climbed a grassy bank.* mound, slope, embankment, knoll, ridge, rise, hill.

bankrupt
(adj) Flash Frank is bankrupt. ruined, insolvent, broke *(informal)*.
OPPOSITE: solvent.

banquet
(n) The king laid on a magnificent banquet. feast, dinner, spread *(informal)*, meal.

bar
1 *(n) A metal bar.* rod, pole, post, stake, railing, girder, crowbar, jemmy.
2 *(n) A bar of chocolate.* slab, block, piece, hunk, chunk.
3 *(n) We had drinks in a local bar.* pub, inn, wine bar, public house, tavern.*(old-fashioned)*, boozer *(informal)*.
4 *(v) Don't bar my way!* block, obstruct.

bare
1 *(adj) The boys were bare to the waist.* naked, stripped, undressed, unclothed, uncovered, nude, exposed.
OPPOSITES: dressed, clothed.
2 *(adj) The room was completely bare.* unfurnished, empty, vacant, stripped.
OPPOSITES: full, cluttered.
3 *(adj) We climbed the bare hillside.* bleak, barren, desolate, windswept, exposed.
4 *(adj) Give me a bare outline of what happened.* basic, simple, straightforward, plain, stark, bald, unembellished, unvarnished, unadorned.
OPPOSITE: elaborate.

barely *see* hardly.

bargain
1 *(n) Ann has found a bargain.* good deal, good buy, special offer, reduction, discount, steal *(informal)*, snip *(informal)*.

2 (n) The two sides made a bargain. deal (informal), agreement, arrangement, pact, contract, settlement, treaty.
3 (v) You have to bargain for food in the market. haggle, barter, negotiate.

bark
(v) The dog began to bark. yap, woof, growl, snarl, howl, yelp, bay, bow-wow.

barrel
(n) cask, keg, tub, vat, drum.

base
1 (n) The base of the statue is cracked. bottom, foot, foundation, plinth, stand, pedestal, support.
OPPOSITE: top.
2 (n) All troops must return to their base. headquarters (plural), camp, station, quarters (plural), billet, garrison, base camp, starting point.
3 (v) Base your essay on your own experience. model, ground, construct, build, develop from, derive from.

bash (informal) see **hit** 1, 2, 4.

basic
1 (adj) What are the basic points in your essay? fundamental, key, central, underlying, main, chief, essential.
2 (adj) I'm learning basic Italian. elementary, simple, easy, rudimentary.
OPPOSITE: advanced.

bath
1 (n) Fill the bath with water. tub.
2 (n) Matt had a bath after the match. soak, wash, scrub, sponge down, shower.

bathe
1 (v) Is it safe to bathe here? See **swim** 2.
2 (v) Bathe your feet in warm water. soak, immerse, douse, dip, wash, cleanse.

batter
(v) Don't batter the door like that! pound, hammer, thump, bash (informal), beat, pummel, thrash, smash, buffet

battered
1 (adj) A battered old suitcase. worn-out, beaten-up, scruffy, damaged, squashed, scarred, dilapidated, weather-beaten.
2 (adj) Claude emerged battered from the fight. bruised, beaten, hurt, injured, bleeding, wounded, scarred.

battle
1 (n) The battle was long and bloody. fight, conflict, struggle, skirmish, confrontation, clash, combat, campaign, siege, dogfight, shoot-out, rebellion.
2 (v) Carl had to battle to win the game. struggle, fight, strive.

bay
(n) The yacht sheltered in the bay. cove, estuary, inlet, natural harbour

beach
1 (n) Let's go to the beach today. seaside, coast, seashore, shore. ❖ Also see **sea & seashore, seaside words**.
2 (n) We played tennis on the beach. sand, sands (plural), shingle.

beam
1 (v) The sight of his new bike made Ben beam. grin, smile, grin from ear to ear.
2 (n) A beam of sunlight shone through the curtains. ray, shaft, streak, stream, gleam, glimmer, glow.
3 (n) Don't remove that beam or the ceiling will collapse. plank, support, joist, girder, rafter, timber, prop, brace, spar.

bear
1 (v) Can you bear my weight? take, support, carry, shoulder.
2 (v) I can't bear the noise! See **stand** 4.

beast
1 (n) A wild beast. animal, creature.
2 (n) A beast with two heads. See **monster** 1.

beastly (informal) see **mean** 6.

beat
1 (v) Teachers used to beat their pupils. hit, strike, thrash, cane, whip, flog, belt (slang), clout (informal), wallop (informal), thump, batter, birch.
2 (v) I'm bound to beat you at chess. defeat, thrash, get the better of, hammer (informal), slaughter (informal), clobber (informal), wipe the floor with (informal), lick (informal), blow you out of the water (informal), run rings round (informal), triumph over.
3 (v) The suspense made my heart beat fast. pound, thump, hammer, bang, palpitate, pulsate, pulse.
4 (v) Beat the egg whites until they are stiff. whisk, whip, stir, mix, blend.
5 (n) This song has a very strong beat. rhythm, pulse, stress, accent.

beat up
(v) (informal) Don't let Bozo beat you up. assault, attack, batter, lay into (informal), knock you about, rough you up (informal), beat the living daylights out of (informal), work you over (slang), duff you up (slang), put the boot in (slang).

beckon see **signal** 2.

become
(v) This caterpillar will become a butterfly. turn into, change into, develop into, grow into, be transformed into.

bed
(n) TYPES OF BED: air bed, berth, bunk bed, camp bed, cot, cradle, divan, double bed, four-poster bed, futon, hammock, single bed, sofa bed, water bed.

beg
1 (v) The poor woman had to beg for food. scrounge (informal), ask, cadge.
2 (v) I'll beg Dad to let us go. plead with, implore, entreat, beseech (old-fashioned).

begin
1 (v) Let's begin! start, get started, get going, get moving, get the show on the road (informal), take the plunge (informal), start the ball rolling, kick off (informal).
OPPOSITE: stop.
2 (v) It's time to begin our work. start, set about, commence, embark on.
OPPOSITE: finish.
3 (v) Don't begin an argument. start, provoke, initiate, trigger off, spark off, cause, instigate, incite.
OPPOSITE: end.
4 (v) When did life on earth begin? start, appear, originate, come into being, come into existence, emerge, arise, burst forth.
OPPOSITES: cease, end.

beginner
(n) I'm just a beginner. novice, learner, fledgling, greenhorn, new recruit.

beginning
1 (n) I was there at the beginning of the project. start, birth, outset, onset, starting point, commencement, inception, origin.
OPPOSITES: end, conclusion.
2 (n) We've missed the beginning of the film. start, opening, introduction, kickoff (informal), prologue (play), preface (book).
OPPOSITES: end, conclusion.

beautiful a beautiful woman	beautiful weather	beautiful music	beautiful scenery
alluring	brilliant	bewitching	awe-inspiring
attractive	delightful	captivating	breathtaking
dazzling	fabulous	enchanting	glorious
fetching	(informal)	entrancing	impressive
(informal)	fair	exquisite	incredible
good-looking	fine	glorious	magnificent
gorgeous	glorious	haunting	marvellous
lovely	gorgeous	heavenly	picturesque
pretty	lovely	(informal)	spectacular
radiant	magnificent	inspiring	striking
ravishing	marvellous	lovely	stunning
striking	perfect	magnificent	(informal)
stunning	superb	poignant	superb
(informal)	wonderful	sublime	wonderful

behave

behave
1 (v) *I'm sure you'll behave sensibly.* act, conduct yourself, acquit yourself.
2 (v) *When will you learn to behave?* be polite, remember your manners, mind your manners, control yourself.
OPPOSITES: misbehave, be rude.

behind
(adv) *Nat is behind with his project.* late, behind schedule, overdue.
OPPOSITE: ahead.

believable
(adj) *Your story is not believable.* credible, plausible, convincing, possible, probable, likely, conceivable, trustworthy.
OPPOSITES: unbelievable, implausible.

believe
1 (v) *It's hard to believe your story.* trust, accept, credit, feel convinced by, have faith in, be certain of, be sure of, swallow (informal), buy (informal), count on, fall for.
2 (v) *I used to believe that girls were stupid.* think, be convinced, feel, consider, be of the opinion, be certain.
3 (v) *I believe this is for me.* think, assume, guess (informal), presume, suppose, imagine, reckon, gather, suspect.

bellow *see* **shout**.

belongings *see* **things**.

bend
1 (v) *The road should bend just here.* turn, curve, twist, wind, swerve, veer.
2 (v) *Can you bend this metal rod?* twist, flex, curve, shape, wind, loop, contort, buckle, warp.
3 (v) *Bend down to get through the tunnel.* stoop, crouch, bow, lean, squat.
4 (n) *Watch out for the bend!* curve, turn, corner, twist, hairpin bend, loop, zigzag.

bendy *see* **flexible** 1.

bent
1 (adj) *A bent bicycle wheel.* twisted, buckled, crooked, warped, contorted.
OPPOSITE: straight.
2 (adj) (slang) *A bent cop. See* **corrupt** 1.

best
1 (adj) *Jon is the best runner in the team.* finest, top, foremost, leading, outstanding, unrivalled, unsurpassed, supreme.
OPPOSITE: worst.
2 (adj) *What's the best thing to do?* right, correct, most appropriate, most suitable, most fitting.
OPPOSITE: worst.

bet *see* **gamble** 1, 2.

betray
1 (v) *I hope your friend won't betray you.* deceive, be disloyal to, stab you in the back (informal), inform on, give you away, double-cross, sell you out (informal), sell you down the river (informal).
2 (v) *Don't betray the one you love.* deceive, be unfaithful to, cheat on (informal), two-time (informal).
3 (v) *Try not to betray your true feelings.* reveal, show, give away, expose, lay bare, let slip, blurt out, indicate.

better
1 (adj) *There's a better way of doing that.* preferable, easier, more effective, more appropriate, more acceptable.
OPPOSITE: worse.
2 (adj) *Are you better now?* fully recovered, well, fit, cured, on the mend, fitter, stronger, back on your feet.
OPPOSITE: worse.

beware of
(v) *Beware of falling rocks.* watch out for, look out for, be careful of, keep clear of, steer clear of, be on your guard against.

bewildered *see* **confused**.

biased
(adj) *A biased magazine article.* one-sided, unfair, prejudiced, distorted, slanted.
OPPOSITES: impartial, unbiased.

bicycle
(n) bike, cycle, pushbike, two-wheeler, mountain bike, racing bike, touring bike, BMX (motocross bicycle), tandem.

bill
(n) *Send me the bill.* account, invoice, statement, reckoning, charge.

billow
1 (v) *We watched the sails billow in the wind.* swell, bulge, fill out, balloon, puff out.
2 (v) *As the storm approached, the waves began to billow.* swell, rise, surge, roll, heave.

bind *see* **tie** 1.

bird
(n) fowl, feathered friend (informal), cock (male), hen (female), chick, nestling, fledgling.
TYPES OF BIRD: bird of paradise, blackbird, budgerigar, canary, chaffinch, chicken, cockatoo, crane, crow, cuckoo, dove, duck, eagle, emu, falcon, finch, flamingo, goose, grouse, gull, hawk, heron, hummingbird, jackdaw, jay, kingfisher, kiwi, kookaburra, lark, macaw, magpie, mina bird, moorhen, nightingale, ostrich, owl, parakeet, parrot, partridge, peacock, pelican, penguin, pheasant, pigeon, puffin, quail, raven, robin, rook, seagull, sparrow, starling, stork, swallow, swift, thrush, tit, toucan, turkey, turtledove, vulture, woodpecker, wren.

big

a big person	a big building	a big mountain	a big bag	a big bang
beefy (informal)	enormous	enormous	bulky	almighty (informal)
burly	huge	high	capacious	colossal
fat	immense	huge	enormous	deafening
heavy	large	lofty	heavy	ear-splitting
hefty	massive	massive	huge	enormous
obese	roomy	towering	large	loud
overweight	spacious		mammoth	mighty
stout	tall	a big helping of pudding	voluminous	resounding
strapping	towering			terrific
tall	vast	ample	a big wardrobe	tremendous
towering		enormous	capacious	
	a big monster	generous	enormous	a big decision
a big desert	colossal	huge	huge	critical
enormous	elephantine	jumbo (informal)	immense	crucial
extensive	enormous	large	large	grave
huge	gigantic	liberal	massive	important
immense	ginormous (informal)	mammoth	sizable	major
vast	hulking	mega (informal)	a big sister	momentous
gigantic blue whale	humongous (informal)	mountainous	elder	serious
		substantial	grown-up	significant
			older	weighty

bird words

claw
dazzling
bird of
paradise

hovering
tern

tail feathers

crown

beak

diving
kingfisher

bird moves

circle	plummet
dart	plunge
dive	pounce
drop	preen
flit	rise
float	roost
flutter	sail
fly	skim
glide	soar
hop	splash
hover	strut
land	swim
paddle	swoop
peck	take off
perch	waddle

bird sounds

cackle	honk
call	hoot
caw	peep
chatter	pipe
cheep	quack
chirp	screech
chirrup	shriek
coo	sing
crow	squawk
cry	trill
gabble	tweet
gaggle	twitter
gobble	warble
hiss	whistle

a bird's feathers can be...

bedraggled	gleaming
colourful	iridescent
dazzling	ruffled
downy	smooth
dull	speckled

wing

throat

breast

warbling
blackbird

---

bit
1 *(n) I'd love a bit of cheese.* piece, lump, chunk, hunk, block, slab, wedge, slice, morsel, scrap, fragment, crumb.
2 *(n) Would you like a bit of my orange?* piece, share, segment, section, part, portion, slice.
3 *(n) I'll be there in a bit. See* **moment** 1.

bitchy *(informal) see* **spiteful**.

bite
1 *(v) Bite on this apple.* chew, nibble, gnaw, chomp, crunch.
2 *(v) That insect might bite.* sting, nip.
3 *(v) Can I have a bite of your biscuit?* nibble, taste, bit, piece, mouthful, morsel.

biting *see* **cold** 2.

bitter
1 *(adj) This drink has a bitter taste.* sour, sharp, tart, acid, vinegary, pungent, acrid.
OPPOSITE: sweet.
2 *(adj) Does Jo's success make you feel bitter?* resentful, sore, embittered, begrudging, aggrieved, sour, jealous, envious, put out, wounded, hurt.
OPPOSITES: glad, grateful.
3 *(adj) The girls had a bitter row.* fierce, angry, violent, heated, acrimonious, vicious, savage.
4 *(adj) I have bitter memories of that time.* painful, agonizing, unhappy, distressing, heartbreaking, poignant, bittersweet.
OPPOSITES: happy, pleasant.
5 *(adj) The wind was bitter. See* **cold** 2.

bizarre *see* **strange** 1.

black
(adj) Count Dracula wore a black cloak. coal-black, jet-black, pitch-black, inky, sable, ebony, raven *(hair)*.

blame
1 *(v) I blame you for starting this row.* hold you responsible, accuse you of, charge you with, condemn, reproach, criticize, find fault with, censure.

2 *(n) Max accepted the blame for the incident.* responsibility, liability, censure, criticism, rap *(slang)*, stick *(informal)*.

bland
1 *(adj) A bland sauce.* mild, tasteless, flavourless, insipid, weak, nondescript.
OPPOSITES: tasty, spicy.
2 *(adj) A bland speech.* dull, boring, uninspiring, uninteresting, unexciting, humdrum, flat, monotonous, tedious.
OPPOSITES: exciting, stimulating.

blank
1 *(adj) Take a blank sheet of paper.* clean, empty, new, unused, unmarked, bare.
2 *(adj) Marcus looked blank when I questioned him.* vacant, glazed, at a loss, uncomprehending, flummoxed, puzzled, bewildered, confused, at sea.

blaze *see* **burn** 1, 2.

bleak
1 *(adj) We surveyed the bleak landscape.* bare, barren, exposed, windswept, desolate, deserted.
2 *(adj) The future looks bleak.* grim, depressing, gloomy, dismal, hopeless, dreary, forbidding, sombre.
OPPOSITES: hopeful, bright.

blend *see* **mix** 1.

blind
1 *(adj) Great Grandma is blind.* unable to see, sightless, visually impaired.
2 *(adj) How could I be so blind?* unaware, blinkered, unobservant, unsuspecting, insensitive, inattentive, heedless, dim, stupid, inconsiderate, thoughtless.
OPPOSITES: aware, sensitive.

blissful *see* **heavenly** 2.

blizzard
(n) snowstorm. ❖ *Also see* **ice**, **frost** & **snow**.

blob
(n) A blob of cream. drop, spot, dollop *(informal)*, splodge.

block
1 *(n) Please will you move this block of stone?* slab, lump, piece, chunk, hunk, mass, brick, cube, wedge.
2 *(v) Leaves sometimes block our drainpipe.* clog, stop up, obstruct, choke, fill, bung up.
3 *(v) Don't try to block my progress.* bar, obstruct, impede, interfere with, check, hinder, thwart, prevent, halt, stop.

bloke *(informal) see* **man** 1, 2.

blond, blonde
1 *(adj) James is blond; Jenny is blonde too.* fair-haired, golden-haired, fair, tow-headed, flaxen-haired *(old-fashioned)*.
2 *(adj) Millie has blonde hair.* fair, golden, ash-blonde, platinum-blonde, strawberry-blonde, honey-coloured, straw-coloured, sandy, yellow, peroxide-blonde, bleached, flaxen *(old-fashioned)*.

bloodthirsty *see* **savage** 2.

bloody
1 *(adj) A bloody wound.* bleeding, gory.
2 *(adj) A bloody shirt.* bloodstained, blood-soaked, blood-spattered.
3 *(adj) A bloody fight.* gory, fierce, ferocious, savage, violent, vicious.

bloom *see* **flower** 1, 2.

blot
1 *(n) My work was spoilt by a large blot of ink.* spot, blotch, smear, smudge, blob, splodge, splotch, patch.
2 *(n) That shed is a blot on the landscape.* blemish, eyesore, flaw, scar.

blotchy
(adj) Nancy's face looks blotchy. mottled, spotty, patchy, blemished.

blow
1 *(v) Blow on the paint to make it dry.* breathe, puff, huff, breathe out, exhale.
2 *(v) The leaves began to blow around.* whirl, flutter, waft, swirl, flap, whisk.
3 *(n) Bozo is recovering from a blow on the head.* bang, knock, bump, hit, smack, whack, bash *(informal)*, thump, punch, wallop *(informal)*, belt *(informal)*.
4 *(n) Losing the match was a real blow.* disappointment, disaster, catastrophe, calamity, setback, upset, misfortune, bombshell, shock, tragedy.

blow up
1 *(v) This bomb may blow up without any warning.* explode, detonate, go off.
2 *(v) The soldiers were ordered to blow up the bridge.* bomb, dynamite, destroy, blast.
3 *(v) You need to blow up your bicycle tyres.* inflate, pump up.
4 *(v) (informal) Please don't blow up when you see the mess. See* **lose your temper**.

blue
1 *(n)* SHADES OF BLUE: aquamarine, azure, cobalt, cornflower, cyan, forget-me-not, indigo, navy, powder blue, royal blue, sapphire, sky blue, turquoise, ultramarine.
2 *(adj) Kim is feeling blue. See* **depressed**.

blunt

1 *(adj) This blade is blunt.* not sharp, unsharpened, dull, rounded.
OPPOSITE: sharp.
2 *(adj) Carl's blunt comment upset me.* frank, candid, forthright, direct, tactless, insensitive, outspoken, curt, brusque, rude.
OPPOSITES: tactful, polite.

blurred

(adj) Without my glasses, everything is blurred. out of focus, fuzzy, hazy, misty, foggy, unclear, indistinct, faint.
OPPOSITES: clear, sharp, in focus.

blush

(v) I wish I wouldn't blush whenever I'm embarrassed. go red, go pink, redden, colour, turn scarlet, turn crimson, flush.

boast

(v) Don't boast about your success. brag, show off *(informal)*, crow, swank *(informal)*, swagger, exaggerate, blow your own trumpet, sing your own praises.

boastful

(adj) Leah is so boastful; she's always showing off. conceited, bigheaded *(informal)*, swollen-headed *(informal)*, cocky, vain, puffed up, arrogant.
OPPOSITES: modest, self-effacing.

boat

(n) ship, vessel, craft.
TYPES OF BOAT: aircraft

Ancient Greek galley

carrier, barge, battleship, cabin cruiser, canoe, catamaran, clipper, coracle, cruise liner, cruiser, destroyer, dhow, dugout, ferry, fishing boat, freighter, frigate, galleon, galley, gondola, houseboat, hovercraft, hydrofoil, hydroplane, inflatable dinghy, junk, kayak, launch, lifeboat, liner, man o' war, minesweeper, motorboat, narrow boat, paddle steamer, powerboat, punt, raft, rowing boat, sailing boat, sailing dinghy, schooner, skiff, speedboat, steamship, supertanker, tanker, trawler, trireme, tug, warship, yacht.
❖ *Also see*
journey words.

pennant   *yard*   *15th-century galleon*

topsail

mast

mizzen sail

foresail   *mainsail*

bowsprit   *poop deck*

stern

prow   *rudder*

deck   *hull*

19th-century paddle steamer

paddle wheel

bridge   *radio aerial*

radar antenna

hull

passenger area

funnel   *strut*

bridge

lifeboat   *helipad*

tanker   *foil*   *hydrofoil*

body

1 *(n) Jason has a muscular body.* build, physique, figure, frame, form, torso, trunk.
PARTS OF THE BODY: OUTSIDE: Adam's apple, ankle, arm, armpit, back, breast, buttock, calf, cheek, chest, chin, ear, elbow, eye, face, finger, foot, forehead, genitals *(plural)*, groin, hand, head, heel, hip, jaw, knee, knuckle, leg, limb, lip, midriff, mouth, navel, neck, nipple, nose, nostril, scalp, shin, shoulder, stomach, thigh, thumb, toe, waist, wrist. INSIDE: abdomen, adenoid, anus, aorta, appendix, artery, bladder, bone, bowel, brain, cartilage, colon, diaphragm, duodenum, eardrum, epiglottis, gall bladder, gland, gum, heart, intestine, kidney, larynx (voice box), ligament, liver, lung, muscle, nerve, oesophagus (gullet), ovary, pancreas, rectum, rib, sinew, spine, spleen, stomach, tendon, throat, tongue, tonsil, trachea (windpipe), uterus (womb), vein, vocal cords *(plural)*. Also see **bone**.
2 *(n) The police found a body in the woods.* dead body, corpse, remains *(plural)*, stiff *(slang)*.

bog

(n) marsh, marshland, peat bog, fen, swamp, quagmire, wetlands *(plural)*.

boil

(v) Wait for the water to boil. come to the boil, bubble, simmer, seethe, steam.
OPPOSITE: freeze.

boiling *see* **hot** 1, 2, 3.
boisterous *see* **rowdy**.

bold

1 *(adj) A bold knight.* intrepid, daring, audacious, brave, courageous, fearless, adventurous, heroic, valiant *(old-fashioned)*, gallant *(old-fashioned)*.
OPPOSITES: cowardly, fearful.
2 *(adj) A bold reply. See* **cheeky**.
3 *(adj) Bold colours.* bright, strong, vivid, striking, loud, eye-catching, conspicuous.
OPPOSITES: pale, unobtrusive.

bolshie *(informal) see* **awkward** 4.

bolt

1 *(v) Please bolt the door. See* **lock** 1.
2 *(v) Burglar Beryl tried to bolt when she saw the police. See* **run away**.

bomb

1 *(n) The soldiers made the bomb safe.* explosive, device.
TYPES OF BOMB: atom bomb, car bomb, depth charge, grenade, H-bomb (hydrogen bomb), incendiary device (firebomb), land mine, letter bomb, mine, napalm bomb, nuclear bomb, petrol bomb, time bomb.
2 *(v) Terrorists tried to bomb the building. See* **blow up** 2.

bone

(n) TYPES OF BONE: backbone, clavicle (collarbone), cranium (skull), femur (thighbone), mandible (jawbone), patella (kneecap), pelvis (hipbone), rib, scapula (shoulder blade), sternum (breastbone), tibia (shinbone), vertebra.

bony *see* **thin** 1.

boo

(v) When the villain appeared, we all began to boo. jeer, heckle, catcall, hiss.
OPPOSITES: cheer, applaud.

book

1 *(n) A best-selling book.* title, publication, work, paperback, hardback, volume.
2 *(n) Write your ideas in your book.* jotter, notebook, notepad, pad, exercise book.
3 *(v) We need to book a room in advance.* reserve, organize, arrange, order, secure.

booty *see* **loot** 1.

border

1 *(n) We crossed the border into Germany.* frontier, boundary, borderline.
2 *(n) My writing paper has a blue border.* edge, margin, surround, frame.
3 *(n) Susie's skirt has a red border.* edging, hem, trimming, frill, fringe.

bore

1 *(v) This film will bore you.* send you to sleep, bore you to death, bore you to tears, bore you out of your mind, leave you cold *(informal)*, turn you off *(informal)*, pall on, tire, weary.
OPPOSITES: interest, fascinate.
2 *(v) The miners had to bore deep into the rock.* drill, penetrate, tunnel, mine.
3 *(n) Shopping can be a bore.* drag *(informal)*, yawn *(informal)*, turn-off *(informal)*, nuisance, bother, pain *(informal)*, pain in the neck *(informal)*.

bored
(adj) Learning endless facts can make you feel bored. bored to death, bored to tears, bored out of your mind, fed up *(informal)*, switched off *(informal)*, indifferent, apathetic, weary, listless, jaded, restless.
OPPOSITES: interested, fascinated.

boring
(adj) A boring job. dull, tedious, uninteresting, monotonous, repetitive, routine, humdrum, unvaried, mind-numbing, unexciting, uninspiring, dreary.
OPPOSITES: interesting, fascinating.

borrow
(v) Can I borrow some paper? have, use, scrounge *(informal)*, cadge, have the loan of, touch you for *(slang)*.
OPPOSITE: lend.

boss
(n) (informal) employer, manager, supervisor, director, gaffer *(informal)*.

bossy
(adj) My sister is so bossy; she's always ordering me around. domineering, overbearing, dictatorial, high-handed, imperious, autocratic, tyrannical, bullying
OPPOSITES: meek, submissive.

bother
1 *(v) I don't want to bother you, but I need a lift.* trouble, disturb, put you out, impose on, inconvenience, pester, hassle *(informal)*, harass, nag.
2 *(v) Doesn't it bother you that someone's been in your room?* worry, concern, upset, annoy, irritate, trouble, disturb, perturb, distress, alarm, dismay.
3 *(v) Dad didn't seem to bother about the mess.* mind, care, be bothered, be concerned, be worried, object to.
4 *(n) Our new car has given us a lot of bother.* See **trouble** 1.

bottom
1 *(n) The bottom of the statue was set in concrete.* foot, base, foundation, pedestal, plinth, support.
OPPOSITE: top.
2 *(n) What's that muck on the bottom of your shoe?* sole, underside, underneath.
3 *(n) Joe slipped and fell on his bottom.* behind *(informal)*, backside *(informal)*, bum *(slang)*, rear, rear end, posterior, rump.
4 *(n) The submarine sank to the bottom of the sea.* depths *(plural)*, bed, floor.

boulder see **rock** 1.

bounce
1 *(v) We watched the kangaroos bounce across the plain.* bound, spring, leap, jump.
2 *(v) Can you make this ball bounce off the wall?* rebound, ricochet.

bouncy
1 *(adj) A bouncy diving board.* springy, flexible, bendy, elastic, resilient, rubbery.
OPPOSITES: rigid, stiff.
2 *(adj) A bouncy girl. See* **lively** 1.

bound see **leap** 1, 3.

box
(n) TYPES OF BOX: carton, case, casket, chest, coffer, coffin, crate, jewellery box, lunch box, matchbox, shoe box, trunk.

boy
(n) lad, youth, schoolboy, young man.

brain
(n) Crosswords exercise your brain. mind, intellect, brains *(plural) (informal)*, powers of reasoning *(plural)*, brainpower, grey matter *(informal)*, intelligence.

brainy *(informal)* see **clever** 1.

branch
1 *(n) A branch of a tree.* bough, limb, twig, stem, sprig.
2 *(n) A branch of a bank.* division, local office, department, section, subdivision.

brash
(adj) A brash salesman. over-confident, cocky, assertive, aggressive, pushy *(informal)*, bumptious, swaggering, self-important, boastful, bigheaded *(informal)*.
OPPOSITES: timid, retiring.

brave
(adj) A brave knight. courageous, fearless, intrepid, plucky, gutsy *(informal)*, heroic, valiant *(old-fashioned)*, gallant *(old-fashioned)*, daring, bold, lion-hearted.
OPPOSITES: cowardly, fearful.

bravery see **courage**.

break
1 *(v) Don't break that plate!* smash, shatter, smash to smithereens, crack, splinter, chip, fracture *(bone)*.
2 *(v) That branch could break at any moment.* crack, snap, split, splinter, give way, come away, disintegrate, fragment.
3 *(v) Don't break my radio!* damage, ruin, wreck, destroy, bust *(informal)*.
4 *(v) If you break the rules, you'll be in trouble.* disobey, disregard, defy, flout, infringe, violate.
OPPOSITES: obey, abide by.
5 *(n) The break from revision will do you good.* rest, breather *(informal)*, time off, time out, breathing space, respite.
6 *(n) Cross when there's a break in the traffic.* lull, gap, let-up *(informal)*, interval, pause, interruption.

breakable see **fragile**.

break down
1 *(v) I hope the car doesn't break down.* stop, stop working, conk out *(informal)*, die, seize up, go kaput *(informal)*.
2 *(v) Anji will break down when she hears the news.* go to pieces, collapse, lose control, be overcome, crack up *(informal)*, fall apart *(informal)*.

break-in
(n) Police are investigating the break-in. burglary, forced entry, robbery, theft, raid.

break up
1 *(v) The yacht hit the rocks and began to break up.* disintegrate, break into pieces, break apart, smash up, splinter, shatter.

2 *(v) When will school break up? See* **end** 6.
3 *(v) Justin thinks his parents may break up. See* **separate** 3.

breasts
(plural n) Pam has large breasts. bust, bosom, chest, boobs *(plural) (slang)*.

breathe
(v) Don't forget to breathe! take a breath, inhale, exhale, take a gulp of air.

breathless
(adj) Giles was breathless after his run. out of breath, out of puff, panting, gasping, wheezing, winded.

breed
1 *(v) Jamie's rabbits have started to breed.* reproduce, multiply, produce young.
2 *(n) What breed of cat do you like best?* See **kind** 3.

breezy see **windy** 1.

bribe
1 *(v) Burglar Beryl tried to bribe the police.* buy off, influence, corrupt, pay off *(informal)*, grease the palm of *(slang)*.
2 *(n) Beryl offered the judge a bribe.* incentive, tip, pay-off *(informal)*, backhander *(slang)*, sweetener *(slang)*.

bridge
(n) footbridge, flyover, overpass, viaduct, aqueduct, ropebridge, drawbridge.

brief
1 *(adj) Dad gave a brief account of the accident. See* **short** 2.
2 *(adj) We paid a brief visit to Aunt Bertha. See* **short** 3.
3 *(v) The coach will brief you before the match.* instruct, give you the facts, inform, fill you in *(informal)*, put you in the picture *(informal)*, give you the lowdown *(informal)*, prepare, prime, advise.

bright
1 *(adj) A bright light.* dazzling, blinding, glaring, shining, blazing, beaming, intense, brilliant, radiant, incandescent.
OPPOSITES: dull, dim.
2 *(adj) Bright colours.* vivid, bold, vibrant, intense, rich, brilliant, glowing, luminous, fluorescent, loud, glaring, gaudy, garish.
OPPOSITES: dull, pale.
3 *(adj) Bright weather.* sunny, clear, fair, cloudless, pleasant.
OPPOSITES: dull, cloudy.
4 *(adj) A bright student. See* **clever** 1.
5 *(adj) A bright future. See* **hopeful** 2.

brilliant
1 *(adj) A brilliant diamond.* dazzling, sparkling, glittering, scintillating, flashing, shining, glistening, shimmering, gleaming, lustrous, bright, flashy, showy.
OPPOSITE: dull.
2 *(adj) A brilliant child.* gifted, talented, accomplished, bright, clever, intelligent, brainy *(informal)*, precocious, exceptional.
OPPOSITES: stupid, slow.
3 *(adj) A brilliant party. See* **fantastic** 3.

bring

1 *(v) A boat will bring supplies from the mainland.* fetch, carry, take, deliver, transport, ferry, convey, transfer.
2 *(v) Did someone bring you home?* See **take** 3.
3 *(v) Hooligans bring trouble.* cause, create, produce, provoke, give rise to, lead to, result in, generate, attract.

bring up

1 *(v) It's hard to bring up children on your own.* raise, rear, look after, support, care for, nurture, educate, train.
2 *(v) Stop leaping about or you'll bring up your lunch.* See **vomit**.
3 *(v) Don't bring up the subject of homework.* See **mention** 2.

brisk

1 *(adj) Will walked at a brisk pace.* quick, fast, swift, rapid, spanking *(informal)*, speedy, energetic, vigorous, sprightly.
OPPOSITES: leisurely, sluggish.
2 *(adj) Mrs Badger has a brisk manner.* businesslike, no-nonsense, crisp, decisive, bustling, lively, bright.
OPPOSITE: lethargic.

bristly *see* **hairy** 2.

brittle *see* **fragile**.

broad

1 *(adj) Lawrence surveyed the broad stretch of desert.* wide, vast, large, extensive, expansive, sweeping, boundless.
OPPOSITE: narrow.
2 *(adj) This shop sells a broad range of magazines.* wide, extensive, large, varied, comprehensive, wide-ranging, all-embracing, unlimited, encyclopedic.
OPPOSITES: narrow, limited.
3 *(adj) Chloë gave a broad description of the thief.* See **general** 2.

broad-minded *see* **tolerant** 1.

broke

(adj) (informal) Flash Frank will be broke if his business fails. penniless, bankrupt, ruined, insolvent, poverty-stricken, impoverished, destitute, stony-broke *(slang)*, skint *(slang)*, strapped for cash *(slang)*, cleaned out *(slang)*.
OPPOSITES: solvent, flush *(informal)*.

broken

1 *(adj) This bone is broken.* fractured, cracked, chipped, shattered, smashed, crushed, splintered, snapped, severed.
2 *(adj) Our washing machine is broken.* out of order, faulty, defective, broken-down, inoperative, damaged, on the blink *(slang)*, clapped out *(informal)*, bust *(informal)*, kaput *(informal)*.
3 *(adj) Since his business failed, Frank is a broken man.* demoralized, dispirited, discouraged, humbled, humiliated, crushed, ruined, beaten, defeated.
4 *(adj) The tourist spoke in broken English.* halting, faltering, disjointed, hesitating, stammering, imperfect.

broken-down *see* **broken** 2.

brown

1 *(n) SHADES OF BROWN:* beige, bronze, buff, chocolate, cinnamon, cocoa, coffee, copper, donkey brown, dun, fawn, ginger, hazel, khaki, russet, rust, sepia, tan, terracotta, umber.
2 *(adj) Brown hair.* dark, brunette, mousy, sandy, tawny, chestnut, auburn, coppery.
3 *(adj) Brown skin.* See **tanned**.

bruise

1 *(n) Darren has a bruise on his forehead.* black mark, shiner *(informal)*, bump, swelling, lump, contusion.
2 *(v) Be careful not to bruise your shins.* bump, bang, bash *(informal)*, knock, hit, injure, hurt, mark, make black and blue.

brush

1 *(n) Where's the brush?* broom, floor brush, scrubbing brush, clothes brush.
2 *(v) I must brush my hair.* comb, tidy, straighten, neaten, untangle, smooth.
3 *(v) Please brush the floor.* sweep, clean.

brutal *see* **savage** 2.

bubble

1 *(v) The sauce began to bubble.* See **boil**.
2 *(v) Look at the lemonade bubble.* fizz, sparkle, effervesce, foam, froth.
3 *(n) A bubble of paint ran down the tin.* bead, globule, drop, droplet, blob, blister.
4 **bubbles** *(plural n) Soap bubbles.* suds *(plural)*, lather, foam, froth.

bubbly

1 *(adj) Bubbly lemonade.* See **fizzy**.
2 *(adj) A bubbly personality.* See **lively** 1.

buckle

1 *(v) Buckle the straps on your rucksack.* fasten, do up, secure, close, clip, clasp.
2 *(v) The collision made my bicycle wheel buckle.* crumple, warp, twist, fold, bend, bulge, become contorted, collapse.

budge

(v) Rick found a good seat and wouldn't budge. move, shift, stir, give way.

bug

1 *(n) There's a bug hiding under that stone.* insect, creepy-crawly *(informal)*.
2 *(n) (informal) This bug is making me feel sick.* virus, infection, germ.
3 *(n) (informal) There's a bug in my computer program.* error, fault, defect, failing, flaw, virus, gremlin, malfunction, snarl-up *(informal)*.
4 *(v) (informal) The detectives decided to bug Beryl's phone calls.* tap, listen in on, monitor, eavesdrop on.
5 *(v) (informal) Rodney's jokes really bug me.* See **annoy** 1.

build

1 *(v) It took Dad ages to build the shed.* construct, put up, erect, assemble, put together, make, knock together *(informal)*.
OPPOSITES: demolish, dismantle.
2 *(n) Ed has a muscular build.* frame, body, physique, figure, form, shape.

building

(n) structure, edifice, construction, premises *(plural)*, pile *(informal)*.

buildings can be...

austere	graceful	outlandish
awe-inspiring	hideous	plain
beautiful	historic	rambling
crumbling	imposing	ruined
dazzling	impressive	simple
elaborate	lofty	solemn
exotic	magical	stark
flamboyant	magnificent	striking
futuristic	majestic	sumptuous
gleaming	massive	towering
glittering	monstrous	ugly
	ornate	vast

MOSQUE

outside a mosque
cupola (small dome)
dome
onion dome
minaret
outer wall

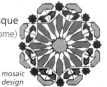

mosaic design

inside a mosque

ablution fountain (washing fountain)
arcade (row of arches)
calligraphy (decorative writing)
carpets
courtyard
enamel tiles
jali (latticed screen)
kiblah (wall facing Mecca)
mihrab (niche showing direction of Mecca)
minbar (pulpit)
mosaics
pointed arch
prayer hall
women's section

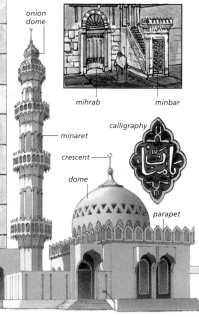

onion dome

mihrab

minbar

calligraphy

minaret

crescent

dome

parapet

PALACE

outside a palace

balcony
balustrade
  (ornamental railing)
colonnade
  (row of columns)
courtyard
parapet (low wall
  along roof)

portico
  (covered
  entrance)
terrace
tower
turret
wing

inside a palace

ballroom
banqueting hall
bedroom
boudoir
  (lady's bedroom
  or sitting room)
chapel

corridor
drawing room
dressing room
entrance hall
grand staircase
great hall
hall of mirrors
kitchens
laundry
library
long gallery
music room
nursery
portrait gallery
servants' quarters
spiral staircase
state apartment
stateroom
throne room

inside the palace rooms

carved frieze
chandelier
gilt stucco
  (gold plasterwork)
marble floor
painted ceiling
panelled wall
parquet floor
  (polished
  wooden floor)
sculpture
tapestry
wall hanging

column

colonnade

hall of mirrors

parapet

ornamental pool

gilt stucco

painted ceiling

CHURCH

outside a church

belfry (bell tower)
buttress (support)
carving
flying buttress
gargoyle
lancet window
  (narrow, pointed
  window)
lead roof
pinnacle
porch
rose window
  (large, round window)
spire
stained-glass window
steeple
tower
weather vane

inside a church

aisle
altar
arch
carving
chancel
  (area for
  altar and
  choir)

choir screen
choir stalls
  (seats for choir)
column
crypt
  (underground
  burial
  chamber)

effigy (statue)
font
lectern (stand
  for Bible)
nave
  (main area)
organ loft
pew
pillar
pulpit
side chapel
tiled floor
tomb
transept
  (side wing)

painted carving

pinnacle

belfry

stained-glass window

lead roof

organ

altar

choir stalls

pulpit

lectern

aisle

pew

font

buttress

transept

SKYSCRAPER

outside a skyscraper

balcony
bronze glass
fire escape
helipad
navigation light
plaza
  (paved forecourt)
radio mast
reflective glass
roof garden
scenic lift
tinted glass

inside a skyscraper

atrium (central hall)
entrance lobby
escalator
express lift
fountain
mezzanine floor
  (halfway level
  between ground
  and first floor)
observation platform
open-plan office
penthouse suite
revolving restaurant
shopping mall
underground
  car park

plaza

atrium

Also see **Ancient Egypt, Ancient Greece, houses & homes, medieval life, Roman life.**

build-up
(n) After all the build-up, the concert was disappointing. hype, publicity, promotion, advertising, ballyhoo (informal), fuss.

build up
1 (v) Jet has managed to build up a huge collection of CDs. amass, assemble, accumulate, collect, put together, construct, create, establish.
2 (v) Jet aims to build up her collection even further. See **increase** 3.
3 (v) Don't let the noise build up any more. See **increase** 2.

bulging
1 (adj) The monster had bulging eyes. protruding, sticking out, popping out, bug.
2 (adj) My bag is bulging. bursting at the seams, straining at the seams, overstuffed, swollen, distended.

bulky
(adj) A bulky parcel. large, enormous, massive, unwieldy, unmanageable, cumbersome, hulking, heavy, weighty.

bullet
(n) shot, slug, pellet, rubber bullet.

bully
1 (v) I didn't mean to bully you. intimidate, frighten, terrorize, push you around (slang), browbeat, torment, persecute, tyrannize, bulldoze (informal), bludgeon.
2 (n) I tried to escape from the bully. bully boy, tormentor, persecutor, tyrant, tough, thug, heavy (slang).

bump
1 (n) Guy has a bump on his knee. lump, swelling, bulge.
2 (n) Ed fell out of bed with a bump. thud, thump, crash, bang, jolt, smack, clunk.
3 (v) Don't bump your head! See **hit** 2.
4 (v) We watched the jeep bump across the field. bounce, jolt, rattle, jerk.

bump into see **crash into**.

bumpy
1 (adj) A bumpy track. rough, uneven, potholed, rutted, pitted, lumpy.
OPPOSITES: smooth, even.
2 (adj) A bumpy ride. rough, bouncy, bone-breaking, jolting, jerky, jarring.
OPPOSITE: smooth.
3 (adj) A bumpy sea crossing. rough, choppy, stormy, turbulent.
OPPOSITE: smooth.

bunch
1 (n) Romeo clutched a bunch of flowers. bouquet, posy, spray, arrangement.
2 (n) I've lost a bunch of papers. set, bundle, collection, sheaf, batch, stack, heap, pile, group, number, quantity, mass, clump, cluster, assortment.
3 (n) (informal) A bunch of people watched the juggler. See **crowd** 1.

bundle
1 (n) A bundle of papers. sheaf, bunch, batch, pile, bale, heap, stack, group, collection, mass, package, packet.

2 (v) Please bundle these newspapers together. tie, bind, fasten, pack, roll, heap.
3 (v) Did you see the kidnappers bundle a man into their car? shove, push, hustle, hurry, rush, thrust, throw.

bung
(v) (slang) Bung your trainers in the wardrobe. throw, shove (informal), sling (informal), dump, stick (informal), put, plonk, drop, stuff.

bungle see **make a mess of**.

burglar
(n) housebreaker, robber, thief, cat burglar, intruder, ram raider (informal).

burglary
1 (n) Beryl was arrested for burglary. housebreaking, robbery, stealing, theft, breaking and entering, ram raiding (informal).
2 (n) Police are investigating the burglary. See **break-in**.

burn
1 (v) The forest could burn for days. blaze, be on fire, be in flames, be alight, be ablaze, smoulder, glow, smoke.
2 (v) Matilda watched the candle burn. flicker, glow, blaze, flare, flash.
3 (v) We need to burn this garden rubbish. set fire to, incinerate, set alight, set on fire, reduce to ashes, ignite, kindle.
4 (v) If the iron is too hot it will burn your top. singe, scorch, char, sear, scald (liquid).
5 (v) My skin is starting to burn. go red, go pink, redden, blister, peel, sting, smart, tingle, prickle.

burning
1 (adj) We watched the burning coals. blazing, flaming, glowing, fiery, red-hot, smouldering, sizzling, smoking.
2 (adj) A burning smell came from the science lab. smoky, pungent, acrid.
3 (adj) Jan has a burning desire to change the world. passionate, intense, ardent, fervent, all-consuming, deep, sincere, earnest, raging, frenzied, frantic.

burp
(v) (informal) belch, bring up wind.

burst
1 (v) Our pipes might burst. crack, split, break, break open, rupture, fracture, explode, shatter, disintegrate, tear apart.
2 (v) Shall I burst this balloon? pop, puncture, prick, pierce, stab.
3 (v) Don't burst into the room like that! rush, charge, barge (informal), crash, dash.
4 (n) Dan had a sudden burst of energy. spurt, surge, rush.

bury
(v) Pirate Peg plans to bury the treasure in her garden. conceal, hide, stow away, stash (informal), secrete, cover up.

bus
(n) We travelled by bus. coach, double-decker, minibus, charabanc (old-fashioned), omnibus (old-fashioned).

bush
(n) Hide behind this bush! shrub, hedge, shrubbery, plant.

bushy
(adj) Bushy hair. thick, shaggy, wiry, bristly, fuzzy, frizzy, tangled, unruly, luxuriant.

business
1 (n) A computer business. See **firm** 6.
2 (n) This company has a lot of business with Japan. trade, commerce, trading, buying and selling, dealings (plural), transactions (plural).
3 (n) It's my business how I spend my money. See **affair** 1.

businessman, businesswoman
(n) executive, tycoon, financier, industrialist, trader, entrepreneur, manager, director.

bust
1 (n) This T-shirt is too tight round the bust. chest, bosom, breasts (plural).
2 (adj) (informal) My radio is bust. See **broken** 2.

busy
1 (adj) You always seem to be busy. occupied, fully occupied, active, bustling about, on the go (informal), up to your eyes (informal), working, hard at work, slaving away, on duty.
OPPOSITES: idle, at a loose end.
2 (adj) Jem is busy doing her homework. hard at work, involved in, engaged in, occupied with, absorbed in, engrossed in, preoccupied with.
3 (adj) We stayed in a busy seaside resort. bustling, lively, buzzing, humming (informal), crowded, swarming, teeming, hectic, frenetic.
OPPOSITES: quiet, sleepy.

butt in see **interrupt** 1.

buy
(v) Let's buy a TV. purchase, get, acquire, invest in (informal), obtain, pay for.
OPPOSITE: sell.

by accident
(phrase) Timmy hit me by accident. accidentally, by mistake, by chance, unintentionally, inadvertently, unwittingly.

cadge see **scrounge**.

café
(n) snack bar, coffee shop, tea shop, restaurant, buffet, cafeteria.

cake
(n) gateau, sponge cake, layer cake, fruitcake, swiss roll, gingerbread, cupcake, bun, pastry, éclair, doughnut.

calamity see **disaster**.

cautious

calculate *see* **figure out** 1.

call
1 *(v) Did you call for help?* shout, yell, cry, cry out, scream, holler *(informal)*, bellow.
2 *(v) Call the boys to come in for tea.* summon, order, instruct, invite, assemble, rally, gather, collect, muster.
3 *(v) What shall we call our gang? See* **name** 1.
4 *(v) I'll call you later. See* **phone** 1.
5 *(v) Can I call this morning?* drop in *(informal)*, come round, visit, pop in *(informal)*, look in *(informal)*, stop by, pay you a visit, look you up.
6 **call for** *(v) Did Ali call for the parcel?* come for, collect, fetch, pick up.

callous
(adj) Bozo is so callous about other people's feelings. uncaring, unfeeling, heartless, hardhearted, cold, cruel, unsympathetic, insensitive, thick-skinned.
OPPOSITES: caring, sympathetic.

calm
1 *(adj) The sea was calm.* still, smooth, motionless, tranquil, unruffled, glassy.
OPPOSITES: rough, choppy.
2 *(adj) Claire always seems so calm.* serene, peaceful, untroubled, placid, tranquil, unflustered, relaxed, laid-back *(informal)*, self-possessed, cool, composed, level-headed, unflappable *(informal)*.
OPPOSITES: agitated, frantic.
3 *(v) Heather tried to calm the crying baby.* soothe, settle, quieten, pacify, hush.

camouflage *see* **disguise** 1, 3.

cancel
(v) Let's cancel the match. call off, scrap, drop, ditch *(slang)*, abandon, write off.

capable *see* **able**.

capture *see* **catch** 2.

car
(n) motorcar, motor, vehicle, automobile *(old-fashioned)*, wheels *(plural)* *(informal)*, banger *(informal)*.
TYPES OF CAR: classic car, convertible, estate, family car, hatchback, limousine, off-road vehicle, people carrier, racing car, rally car, saloon, sports car, stretch limo *(informal)*, veteran car, vintage car

care
1 *(v) You should care about the future.* mind, be concerned, concern yourself, be bothered, be interested in, worry.
2 *(n) Act with care. See* **caution**.
3 **care for** *(v) Can you care for my rat while I'm away? See* **look after**.

career *see* **job** 2.

careful
1 *(adj) Neesha always does careful work.* painstaking, meticulous, methodical, well-organized, neat, accurate, thoughtful.
OPPOSITES: careless, slapdash.
2 *(adj) Be careful crossing the road.* wary, attentive, alert, cautious, on your guard, observant, watchful.

careless
1 *(adj) Careless work.* slapdash, sloppy *(informal)*, scrappy, untidy, shoddy, slipshod, rushed, disorganized, inaccurate.
OPPOSITES: careful, meticulous.
2 *(adj) Careless actions.* thoughtless, inconsiderate, negligent, irresponsible.
OPPOSITES: careful, considerate.

carry
1 *(v) Carry your luggage to the car.* take, bring, transfer, move, shift, cart, lug, haul, hump *(informal)*, ferry, transport, deliver.
2 *(v) Can you carry my weight?* support, bear, take, hold, shoulder, sustain.

carry on *see* **continue** 1, 2, 3.

carry out
(v) We must carry out our plan. execute, accomplish, complete, carry through, fulfil.

carve
(v) Try to carve a figure. sculpt, hew, chisel, whittle, form, shape, engrave, etch.

case
1 *(n) I'll carry your case.* suitcase, bag, holdall, trunk, luggage, baggage.
2 *(n) Put that away in its case.* container, holder, wrapper, cover, box, cabinet.

castle
(n) fortress, fort, stronghold, citadel, palace, chateau. ❖ *Also see* **medieval life**.

casual
1 *(adj) A casual manner.* nonchalant, blasé, informal, free and easy, offhand, careless, relaxed, laid-back *(informal)*.
2 *(adj) Casual clothes.* informal, leisure, comfortable, ordinary, everyday, sporty.

cat
(n) pussy *(informal)*, pussycat *(informal)*, puss *(informal)*, moggy *(informal)*, kitten, tomcat *(male)*, tom *(male)*, mouser.
TYPES OF CAT: Burmese, chinchilla, long-haired cat, Manx, Persian, short-haired cat, Siamese, tabby, tortoiseshell

catastrophe *see* **disaster**.

catch
1 *(v) Catch the ball.* grab, seize, grasp, clutch, snatch, get, intercept.
2 *(v) The police are trying to catch a thief.* capture, seize, trap, snare, arrest, nick *(slang)*, nab *(informal)*, collar *(informal)*.
3 *(v) I don't want to catch another cold.* get, contract, pick up, develop, go down with, succumb to, get infected with.
4 *(n) What's the catch?* snag, drawback, disadvantage, hitch, trap, trick.

catching
(adj) Is this disease catching? infectious, contagious.

catty *(informal) see* **spiteful**.

cause
1 *(v) This decision may cause problems.* create, produce, lead to, bring about, give rise to, generate, start, trigger off, spark off, stir up, provoke, make.
2 *(n) What was the cause of the problem?* root, source, reason for, origin.
3 *(n) Please support this cause.* campaign, movement, project, enterprise, charity.

caution
(n) Act with caution. care, attention, watchfulness, vigilance, forethought.

cautious
1 *(adj) A cautious swimmer.* careful, wary, unadventurous.
OPPOSITES: careless, reckless.
2 *(adj) A cautious reply.* guarded, careful, cagey *(informal)*, noncommittal, discreet, circumspect.
OPPOSITES: careless, unguarded.

pouncing Siamese

playful kittens

cat words

cat moves

claw	paw
creep	pounce
crouch	prowl
curl up	scratch
dash	slink
dive	sprawl
drop	spring
leap	stalk
nuzzle	stretch
pad	

cat sounds

caterwaul	
rough	
hiss	
mew	
miaow	
purr	
screech	
spit	
squeak	
yelp	
yowl	

a cat's coat can be...

bedraggled, flea-bitten, fluffy, mangy, matted, shaggy, shiny, silky, sleek, smooth, soft

a cat can seem...

adventurous	independent
affectionate	inquisitive
alert	lazy
aloof	mischievous
contented	playful
crazy	quizzical
curious	supercilious
dignified	timid
friendly	wild

muzzle
chest
sleek tabby

ruff
frill

fluffy long-haired cat

cave

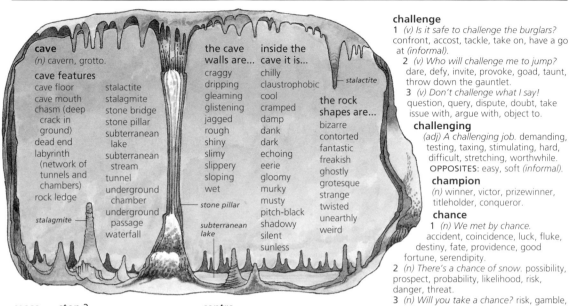

cave
(n) cavern, grotto.

cave features
cave floor
cave mouth
chasm (deep
    crack in
    ground)
dead end
labyrinth
    (network of
    tunnels and
    chambers)
rock ledge

stalactite
stalagmite
stone bridge
stone pillar
subterranean
    lake
subterranean
    stream
tunnel
underground
    chamber
underground
    passage
waterfall

stalagmite —

the cave walls are...
craggy
dripping
gleaming
glistening
jagged
rough
shiny
slimy
slippery
sloping
wet

— stone pillar

inside the cave it is...
chilly
claustrophobic
cool
cramped
damp
dank
dark
echoing
eerie
gloomy
murky
musty
pitch-black
shadowy
silent
sunless

subterranean lake

— stalactite

the rock shapes are...
bizarre
contorted
fantastic
freakish
ghostly
grotesque
strange
twisted
unearthly
weird

---

cease see **stop** 3.

ceaseless
(adj) I can't stand this ceaseless noise.
constant, continual, incessant, never-ending, nonstop, continuous, everlasting, endless, unending, unceasing, perpetual, relentless, persistent, interminable.
OPPOSITES: occasional, intermittent.

celebrate
1 *(v) Do you celebrate St Patrick's Day?*
observe, commemorate, keep, mark.
2 *(v) You should celebrate on your birthday.* enjoy yourself, party *(informal)*, whoop it up *(informal)*, live it up *(informal)*, make merry, paint the town red *(informal)*.

celebration
(n) The celebration lasted all weekend.
festivity, merrymaking, revelry, jollification, festivities *(plural)*, party, shindig *(informal)*, bash *(informal)*, rave *(slang)*, feast, carnival, gala, jubilee, festival.

celebrity
(n) Jason has become a TV celebrity. star, personality, idol, superstar, VIP (very important person), big name, big shot *(informal)*, megastar.

cellar
(n) basement, vault, crypt *(church)*.

cemetery
(n) graveyard, burial ground, churchyard.

central
1 *(adj) The central part of the city.* inner, middle, innermost, interior, core, focal.
OPPOSITE: outer.
2 *(adj) The central point of an argument.*
main, key, focal, pivotal, principal, major, dominant, leading, most important, chief, basic, fundamental, essential.

centre
1 *(n) Drive to the centre of the city.*
middle, heart, midpoint.
OPPOSITES: edge, outskirts *(plural)*.
2 *(n) This office is the centre of our operation.* hub, heart, focal point, nerve centre, core, focus, nucleus, crux.

ceremony
(n) Is there a ceremony to mark the end of term? event, function, gathering, celebration, do *(informal)*, service, ritual.

certain
1 *(adj) Chas was certain he had seen a ghost.* sure, positive, in no doubt, confident, convinced, satisfied, assured, persuaded, definite.
2 *(adj) The detectives need certain proof.*
definite, absolute, conclusive, undeniable, unquestionable, indisputable, irrefutable, clear, unmistakable, reliable.
3 *(adj) Is it certain that Dad will lose his job?* definite, settled, guaranteed, inevitable, unavoidable, inescapable, inexorable, sure, fixed, destined, fated.
4 *(adj) The shop is closed on certain days.*
specific, particular, special, individual, established, fixed, set.

chain
1 *(n) A chain of disasters. See* **series**.
2 **chains** *(plural n) The prisoners were kept in chains.* irons *(plural)*, shackles *(plural)*, fetters *(plural)*, handcuffs *(plural)*, manacles *(plural)*, leg irons *(plural)*.

chair
(n) seat.
TYPES OF CHAIR: armchair, deck chair, dining chair, easy chair, office chair, reclining chair, rocking chair, sun lounger, swivel chair, throne.

challenge
1 *(v) Is it safe to challenge the burglars?*
confront, accost, tackle, take on, have a go at *(informal)*.
2 *(v) Who will challenge me to jump?*
dare, defy, invite, provoke, goad, taunt, throw down the gauntlet.
3 *(v) Don't challenge what I say!*
question, query, dispute, doubt, take issue with, argue with, object to.

challenging
(adj) A challenging job. demanding, testing, taxing, stimulating, hard, difficult, stretching, worthwhile.
OPPOSITES: easy, soft *(informal)*.

champion
(n) winner, victor, prizewinner, titleholder, conqueror.

chance
1 *(n) We met by chance.*
accident, coincidence, luck, fluke, destiny, fate, providence, good fortune, serendipity.
2 *(n) There's a chance of snow.* possibility, prospect, probability, likelihood, risk, danger, threat.
3 *(n) Will you take a chance?* risk, gamble, leap in the dark.
4 *(n) You will have another chance to win soon.* opportunity, occasion, time, turn.
5 *(adj) It was a chance meeting.*
accidental, coincidental, unexpected, unintentional, unplanned, unforeseen, random, casual, fluke, fortuitous.

change
1 *(v) We must change our plans.* alter, revise, amend, modify, adapt, vary, reform.
2 *(v) I want to change my room.* alter, rearrange, transform, make over, redo, reorganize, remodel, revamp.
3 *(v) The frog began to change into a prince.* turn, be transformed, morph *(informal)*, mutate, metamorphose, transmute, become.
4 *(v) Can I change this jumper for a smaller one?* exchange, swap, switch, trade, substitute, replace with.
5 *(v) Let's change our direction.* switch, alter, shift, reverse.
6 *(n) There's been a change in Guy's attitude.* shift, switch, alteration, transformation, turnaround, sea change, reversal, metamorphosis.
7 *(n) This is a pleasant change.* variation, departure, diversion, break, novelty.
8 *(n) I need some change for the bus.*
coins *(plural)*, small change, loose change, cash, coppers *(plural)*, silver.

change your mind
(phrase) Why don't you change your mind and stay? revise your opinion, think better of it, think twice, reconsider, rethink.

chaos
(n) There was chaos in the classroom.
confusion, disorder, pandemonium, bedlam, turmoil, uproar, tumult, anarchy.

chaotic
(adj) The office was chaotic. disorganized, jumbled, muddled, topsy-turvy, shambolic *(informal)*, out of control, riotous, anarchic.

character
1 *(n) Marie has a very gentle character.* personality, nature, temperament, disposition, make-up.
2 *(n) Yves is a strange character.* person, individual, type *(informal)*, sort *(informal)*.
3 *(informal) Eddie's a real character!* individual, eccentric, clown, comic, case *(informal)*, oddball *(informal)*.
4 *(n) This village has a special character.* quality, atmosphere, feel, personality.

characteristic
(n) Untidiness is a characteristic of many teenagers. quality, attribute, trait, feature, peculiarity, idiosyncrasy, mark, property.

charge
1 *(n) What is the charge for entering the museum?* cost, fee, price, rate, payment.
2 *(v) The troops began to charge the enemy.* attack, storm, assault, rush at.
3 *(v) The police will charge Beryl with burglary.* accuse of, indict, prosecute for.

charm
1 *(n) Oz has a mysterious charm.* appeal, charisma, allure, magnetism, fascination.
2 *(n) A wizard's charm. See* **spell**.
3 *(n) A lucky charm.* amulet, talisman.
4 *(v) Kamala will charm you with her singing.* delight, captivate, enchant, bewitch, beguile, fascinate, mesmerize.

charming
(adj) A charming smile. appealing, attractive, enchanting, captivating, winning, bewitching, engaging, irresistible, disarming, fetching *(informal)*.

chart
(n) Study this chart. plan, map, table, diagram, graph, blueprint.

chase
(v) Fido loves to chase Pickles. run after, pursue, follow, tail, hunt, stalk, trail.

chat *see* **talk** 1, 5, 6.

chatter *see* **prattle**.

chatterbox
(n) (informal) Sophie is a real chatterbox! gossip, chatterer, prattler, motormouth *(slang)*, windbag *(slang)*.

chatty
(adj) (informal) Zoë sent me a chatty letter. gossipy, newsy, friendly, informal.

cheap
1 *(adj) This CD is cheap.* inexpensive, reasonable, moderately priced, good value, economical, cut-price, reduced.
OPPOSITE: expensive.
2 *(adj) This cheap furniture won't last.* poor-quality, inferior, shoddy, trashy, tacky *(informal)*, tawdry, rubbishy, crappy *(slang)*, crummy *(slang)*, worthless.
OPPOSITES: high-quality, superior.
3 *(adj) What a cheap trick! See* **mean** 6.

cheat
1 *(v) Watch out for Dodgy Dave or he'll cheat you.* trick, swindle, con *(informal)*, screw *(informal)*, sting *(informal)*, bamboozle *(informal)*, dupe, do *(informal)*, fleece, rip you off *(slang)*, take you for a ride *(informal)*, pull a fast one on *(slang)*, hoodwink, defraud.
2 *(v) Don't cheat in this test.* break the rules, bend the rules, copy, crib *(informal)*.
3 *(n) That man's a cheat.* swindler, con man *(informal)*, rogue, shark *(informal)*, double-dealer, double-crosser, fraud *(informal)*, crook *(informal)*, impostor.

check
(v) Check your bike carefully before you set off. examine, inspect, check out, test, try out, give it the once-over *(informal)*, look over, scrutinize.

checkup
(n) A medical checkup. examination, medical *(informal)*, physical *(informal)*.

cheeky
(adj) I've had enough of your cheeky comments! impertinent, impudent, rude, saucy, bold, insolent, disrespectful, insulting, pert, fresh *(informal)*, forward.
OPPOSITES: polite, respectful.

cheer
(v) When we heard the score, we all began to cheer. applaud, clap, whoop, whistle, yell, stamp, give a standing ovation.

cheerful
(adj) Sally is always cheerful. happy, good-humoured, cheery, light-hearted, jolly, sunny, chirpy *(informal)*, perky, merry, bright, breezy, buoyant, optimistic.
OPPOSITES: miserable, depressed.

cheer up
1 *(v) Try to cheer up.* perk up *(informal)*, buck up *(informal)*, take heart, rally, brighten, snap out of it *(informal)*.
2 *(v) How can I cheer you up?* encourage, comfort, buck you up *(informal)*, give you new heart, buoy you up, jolly you along *(informal)*, gladden, hearten.

chest
1 *(n) A person's chest.* ribcage, breast *(old-fashioned)*
2 *(n) A storage chest.* trunk, box, crate, container, case, strongbox, coffer, casket.

chew
(v) Chew your food thoroughly. munch, crunch, chomp, gnaw, grind up, nibble.

chief
1 *(adj) Amy was the chief bridesmaid.* principal, senior, head, leading, main.
2 *(adj) What is your chief reason for leaving? See* **main**.

child
(n) kid *(informal)*, youngster, young person, boy, girl, little one, nipper *(informal)*, brat, kiddywink *(informal)*, sprog *(slang)*, infant, toddler, tot, tiny tot, adolescent, teenager, juvenile, minor.

childish
(adj) Childish behaviour. infantile, juvenile, immature, babyish, puerile, foolish, silly.

chilly
1 *(adj) A chilly morning.* cold, icy, frosty, crisp, cool, nippy, fresh, raw, wintry.
OPPOSITE: warm.
2 *(adj) A chilly response.* cool, frosty, unfriendly, aloof, standoffish, cold, hostile.
OPPOSITES: friendly, warm.

chip
1 *(n) My mug has a chip in it.* nick, crack, split, flaw, notch, scratch, dent, gash.
2 *(n) I knocked a chip off the table.* splinter, sliver, shaving, flake, piece, fragment, chunk, wedge.

choice
1 *(n) Do I have a choice?* option, alternative, vote, say, voice.
2 *(n) There was a wide choice of desserts.* selection, range, variety, array, assortment.
3 *(n) Have you made your choice?* selection, pick, decision, preference.

choke
1 *(v) The thick smoke made us choke.* gasp, gag, retch, cough, suffocate.
2 *(v) The villain tried to choke his victim.* strangle, throttle, garrotte, suffocate, smother, stifle, overwhelm, overpower.
3 *(v) Leaves often choke the stream.* block, clog, stop up, obstruct, dam, bung up, constrict, congest.

choose
1 *(v) I think we should choose Bill as our captain.* select, pick, elect, appoint, decide on, opt for, settle on, fix upon.
2 *(v) You may choose to walk alone.* decide, prefer, opt, elect, see fit, wish, resolve, make up your mind, determine.

choosy *(informal) see* **fussy**.

chop
1 *(v) Can you chop this log in two?* split, cut, cleave, hew, hack, slice, divide, sever.
2 *(v) Chop the carrots finely.* chop up, cut up, slice, dice, cube, mince.

choppy
(adj) A choppy sea. rough, ruffled, stormy, squally, turbulent, heaving.
OPPOSITES: smooth, calm.

chore *see* **task**.

chubby *see* **plump**.

chuck *(informal) see* **throw** 1.

chuckle *see* **giggle**.

chuffed *(slang) see* **pleased**.

chunk
(n) A chunk of cheese. block, hunk, slab, lump, wedge, slice, wodge *(informal)*.

circle
1 *(n) Draw a circle.* ring, loop, disc, hoop, band, round shape, circular shape.
2 *(v) The road will circle the city.* surround, enclose, encircle, ring, skirt, hem in, orbit.
3 *(v) Watch the dancers circle round the room. See* **whirl**.

city

city		on the pavement you can see...	people may...	the traffic may be...	you can shop at...	the city may be...
(n) metropolis, town.		beggar	brush past	at a standstill	boutique	bewildering
city sights	**city streets**	busker	crowd	bumper-to-	chain store	bustling
art gallery	alley	bus stop	dawdle	bumper	covered market	busy
bridge	avenue	entertainer	hurry	chock-a-block	department	buzzing
cathedral	backstreet	flower seller	jostle	crawling	store	congested
cinema	boulevard	fruit stall	loiter	slow-moving	kiosk	crowded
city hall	crescent	lamppost	mill about	snarled up	open-air	dirty
concert hall	cul-de-sac	litter	rush	solid	market	dynamic
fountain	flyover	newspaper	wander	tailed back	shopping mall	exciting
hotel	lane	vendor	window-shop		supermarket	grimy
ice rink	one-way street	pedestrian	**city transport**	**traffic sounds**		high-tech
leisure complex	passage	police officer	bicycle	beep	**you can eat**	historic
library	plaza	road sweeper	bus	chug	**and drink at...**	lively
mosque	ring road	shopper	car	growl	bistro	noisy
museum	square	street artist	open-topped	honk	burger bar	overwhelming
nightclub	subway	tourist	bus	hum	café	packed
opera house	(underground		taxi	purr	coffee shop	polluted
park	passage)		tram	roar	pavement café	pulsing
skyscraper			tube	screech	pub	run-down
sports stadium		*city skyline*	underground	squeal	restaurant	shabby
temple				toot	snack bar	smart
theatre				wail	tea shop	smoggy
tower					wine bar	smoky
block						spectacular
						throbbing

Also see **building**.

---

claim

1 (v) I've come to claim my money.
demand, ask for, collect, pick up, request.
2 (v) I still claim that I was right. insist,
maintain, argue, assert, affirm, declare.

clammy see **damp** 3.

clap see **applaud**.

class

(n) Which class are you in at school?
form, group, set, stream, year, level.

clean

1 (v) I must clean everything in my room.
wash, wipe, mop, scrub, scour, sponge,
dust, soap, sweep, vacuum, cleanse,
launder, rinse, disinfect.
2 (adj) Everything in my room is clean.
spotless, immaculate, squeaky-clean, fresh,
sanitary, hygienic, unsoiled, unstained,
washed, laundered, swept, scrubbed,
scoured, dusted, disinfected.
OPPOSITES: dirty, soiled.
3 (adj) You must only drink clean water.
pure, uncontaminated, unpolluted,
purified, sterile, clear, unadulterated.
OPPOSITES: polluted, contaminated.
4 (adj) Use a clean sheet of paper. blank,
new, empty, unused, unmarked, fresh.

clear

1 (adj) A clear stream. transparent, limpid,
pure, crystal clear, crystalline.
OPPOSITES: muddy, cloudy.

2 (adj) A clear signal. definite, plain,
distinct, recognizable, unmistakable.
OPPOSITES: unclear, confusing.
3 (adj) Clear writing. legible, bold, neat.
OPPOSITE: illegible.
4 (adj) A clear day. See **fine** 3.
5 (adj) A clear outline. clean, clear-cut,
definite, distinct, sharp, well-defined.
OPPOSITE: fuzzy.
6 (adj) A clear voice. audible, distinct,
penetrating, piercing.
OPPOSITES: indistinct, muffled.
7 (adj) A clear argument. clear-cut,
coherent, simple, straightforward, easy
to follow, unambiguous, lucid.
OPPOSITES: confusing, complicated.
8 (adj) A clear space. See **empty** 1.
9 (v) I must clear this rubbish from my
room. get rid of, remove, empty, strip,
unload, unpack, disentangle.
10 (v) I wish the mist would clear.
disappear, evaporate, melt away, lift.

clear up

1 (v) Clear up the kitchen. See **tidy** 3.
2 (v) Let's clear up this problem. sort out,
settle, resolve, clarify, unravel, put right.
3 (v) I hope your cold will clear up soon.
go away, disappear, get better.

clever

1 (adj) A clever student. intelligent, bright,
able, quick, brainy (informal), smart, gifted,
talented, capable, knowledgeable.

2 (adj) A clever trick. cunning, crafty,
ingenious, shrewd, smart, slick, inventive.

cliff

(n) precipice, rockface, crag, escarpment.
❖ Also see **sea & seashore**.

climax

(n) The climax of Jackson's career was
winning the gold medal. high point, high
spot, highlight, culmination, crowning
point, pinnacle, peak.

climb

1 (v) We tried to climb the mountain.
scale, clamber up, go up, ascend, shin up.
OPPOSITES: descend, go down.
2 (v) I think prices will climb. See **rise** 3.
3 (v) The road began to climb. See **rise** 4.

cling on to see **hold on to**.

clip see **fasten** 2.

clog see **block** 2.

close

1 (v) Close the gate. See **shut** 1.
2 (adj) Bill and Ben are close friends.
See **intimate** 1.
3 (adj) The match was close.
evenly matched, well-matched,
hard-fought, neck and neck.
4 close to (adj) I live close
to the park. See **near** 1.

cloth see
material.

clothes *(plural n)* clothing, garments *(plural)*, gear *(informal)*, togs *(plural)* *(informal)*, get-up *(informal)*, dress, costume, attire *(old-fashioned)*.

trousers and shorts
bermuda shorts
chinos
corduroys
culottes
cut-offs
cycling shorts
drainpipes
dungarees
flannels
flares
jeans
jodhpurs
knickerbockers
leggings
palazzo pants
pedal pushers
plus fours
ski pants

waistband

chinos

culottes

palazzo pants

suits
boiler suit
dress suit
lounge suit
morning suit
overalls
pinstripe suit
safari suit
sailor suit
shell suit
three-piece suit
tracksuit
trouser suit

three-piece suit

safari suit

tops
blouse
body
camisole top
cardigan
crew-neck jumper
cropped top
lumberjack shirt
polo-neck jumper
polo shirt
pullover
rugby shirt
smock
sweater
sweatshirt
tanktop
T-shirt
turtleneck jumper
vest top
V-neck jumper
waistcoat

blouse

cropped top

camisole top

skirts
flared skirt
gathered skirt
kilt
miniskirt
pleated skirt
puffball skirt
sarong
split skirt
straight skirt
tiered skirt
wrapover skirt

puffball skirt

wrapover skirt

pinafore dress

dresses
ball gown
cocktail dress
gym slip
kimono
maternity dress
minidress
pinafore
sari
shift dress
sundress

shift dress

fabrics
acrylic
cashmere
chiffon
corduroy
cotton
crushed velvet
denim
fur
jersey
lamé
leather
lycra
satin
silk
suede
taffeta
tweed
velvet
wool

patterns
checked
floral
gingham
paisley
polka dot
striped
tartan

gingham

floral

tartan

some clothes have...
beads
embroidery
flounces
frills
fringes
ruffles
sequins
tassels
tiers

sequin

bead

coats and jackets
anorak
blazer
bomber jacket
cagoule
cape
cloak
combat jacket
dinner jacket
double-breasted jacket
duffle coat
fleece
fur coat
greatcoat
mackintosh
overcoat
raincoat
shawl
sports jacket
tail coat
trench coat
waxed jacket

double-breasted jacket

collar

lapel

trench coat

accessories
bag
belt
bow tie
braces
cravat
cummerbund
gloves
jewellery
sash
scarf
shoes
tie

clothes can look...
baggy
casual
chic
clingy
comfortable
daring
dashing
drab
elegant
fashionable
feminine
figure-hugging
flamboyant
flattering
floating
flowing
formal
frilly
frumpy
fun
fussy
glamorous
glittering
neat
old-fashioned
outrageous
practical
revealing
roomy
scruffy
see-through
severe
skintight
slinky
smart
sophisticated
sporty
tight-fitting

clothes can be...
backless
cropped
fitted
flared
gathered
padded
pleated
ribbed
sleeveless
strapless
tailored
tapered

Also see **hat, jewellery, shoe.**

cloudy
1 *(adj) A cloudy sky.* overcast, hazy, grey, dull, gloomy, dismal, dark, leaden, heavy, thundery, threatening, sunless, starless.
OPPOSITES: clear, cloudless.
2 *(adj) Cloudy water.* murky, muddy, milky, opaque.
OPPOSITES: clear, transparent.

club
(n) Please join our club! group, society, organization, association, circle, clique, company, league, union, federation.

clue
(n) This clue may help solve the crime. lead, pointer, information, evidence, tip-off, suggestion, hint, sign, key, idea.

clumsy *see* awkward 1, 2.

clutch *see* grip.

clutter
1 *(n) Tidy up this clutter! See* mess 1.
2 *(v) Don't clutter the lounge with your comics.* litter, mess up, strew, make untidy.

coach
1 *(n) We travelled by coach. See* bus.
2 *(n) We've got a new tennis coach.* instructor, trainer, teacher, tutor, mentor.
3 *(v) Who'll coach the team? See* train 4.

coarse
1 *(adj) Coarse material.* rough, scratchy, bristly, prickly, hairy, thick, homespun.
OPPOSITES: fine, soft.
2 *(adj) Coarse jokes. See* crude.

coast *see* shore.

coat
1 *(n) Put on your coat.* ❖ *See* clothes.
2 *(n) An animal's coat keeps it warm in winter.* fur, hair, fleece, wool, pelt, hide.
3 *(n) Apply a coat of varnish. See* layer 1.

coax *see* persuade.

cocky *see* conceited.

coil *see* loop 1, 2.

cold
1 *(adj) It was a cold winter's day.* chilly, freezing, frosty, icy, crisp, nippy, raw, bitter, bleak, perishing *(informal)*, wintry.
OPPOSITES: warm, balmy.
2 *(adj) A cold wind blew in off the sea.* chill, icy, freezing, bitter, keen, biting, cutting, piercing, penetrating, arctic.
OPPOSITES: warm, balmy.
3 *(adj) I'm cold!* chilly, freezing, frozen, frozen stiff, perishing *(informal)*, chilled to the bone, shivering, numbed.
OPPOSITES: warm, hot.
4 *(adj) Mr Steel is a rather cold person.* distant, remote, aloof, reserved, unfriendly, standoffish, impersonal, unemotional, unfeeling, unsympathetic, uncaring.
OPPOSITES: warm, friendly.

collapse
1 *(v) Let's hope the roof doesn't collapse.* fall in, cave in, give way, subside, tumble down, crumble, disintegrate, fall to pieces, fall apart, crumple, buckle.

2 *(v) Jenny may collapse when she hears the bad news.* faint, pass out, lose consciousness, keel over, swoon *(old-fashioned)*, break down, go to pieces.
3 *(n) The collapse of Communism.* fall, ruin, downfall, destruction, break-up.

collect
1 *(v) Fran has started to collect old comics.* save, keep, accumulate, amass, pile up, gather together, stockpile, hoard.
2 *(v) We'll collect you from the station.* fetch, come and get, pick you up, call for.
3 *(v) A crowd began to collect around the juggler.* gather, assemble, congregate, converge, cluster, flock, concentrate, mass.
OPPOSITES: disperse, scatter.

collection
(n) Melissa has a collection of stamps. set, assortment, array, hoard, mass, pile, stack.

collision *see* crash 2.

colossal *see* huge.

colour
1 *(n) That colour of blue suits you.* shade, tone, tint, tinge, hue.
2 *(v) Colour the background green.* paint, shade, tint, dye, stain, tinge, colourwash.

colourful
(adj) A colourful shirt. brightly coloured, bright, vivid, vibrant, multicoloured, gaudy, jazzy *(informal)*, psychedelic.
OPPOSITES: dull, colourless.

column
1 *(n) A stone column. See* pillar.
2 *(n) A column of people. See* line 3.
3 *(n) A newspaper column. See* article 1.

combine
(v) Let's combine the teams to create a winning side. merge, put together, pool, mix, unite, join, integrate, amalgamate.
OPPOSITES: separate, divide.

come
1 *(v) The enemy will come under cover of darkness.* approach, advance, move closer, draw near, close in, bear down.
OPPOSITE: go.
2 *(v) Please come on time. See* arrive 1.
3 **come to** *(v) Stop when you come to the lights.* reach, get to, arrive at, get as far as.

comedy
(n) light entertainment, humour, fun.
TYPES OF COMEDY: black comedy, clowning, farce, improvisation, pantomime, parody, revue, satire, sitcom (situation comedy), sketch, skit, slapstick, spoof *(informal)*, stand-up comedy.

come in *see* enter 1.

come round
1 *(v) Please come round soon. See* call 5.
2 *(v) We waited anxiously for Jo to come round after her fall.* come to, regain consciousness, revive, recover, wake up.

come up
(v) Did any problems come up? crop up *(informal)*, arise, occur, emerge, happen.

comfort
1 *(v) Gina tried to comfort her sobbing sister.* console, soothe, calm, reassure, encourage, cheer up, sympathize with.
2 *(n) Lord Lucre enjoys a life of comfort.* ease, contentment, wellbeing, cosiness, luxury, affluence, opulence.
OPPOSITE: hardship.

comfortable
1 *(adj) A comfortable sofa.* comfy *(informal)*, soft, squashy, well-padded, well-cushioned, cosy, snug, roomy.
OPPOSITE: uncomfortable.
2 *(adj) Comfortable clothes.* comfy *(informal)*, loose-fitting, roomy, baggy, sloppy, stretchy, snug, casual, sporty.
OPPOSITES: uncomfortable, tight-fitting.

command *see* order 1, 3.

comment
1 *(v) Beth was quick to comment that I looked better.* remark, point out, mention, observe, note, say.
2 *(n) Ben made a nasty comment about my hair.* remark, observation, statement.

commit
(v) Beryl may commit another crime. carry out, perpetrate, execute, be guilty of.

common
1 *(adj) Red buses are a common sight in London.* normal, familiar, usual, everyday, frequent, regular, daily, ordinary, routine, commonplace, run-of-the-mill, standard.
OPPOSITES: rare, uncommon.
2 *(adj) There's a common theory that chocolate gives you spots. See* popular 3.
3 *(adj) Araminta says I'm common.* coarse, uncouth, vulgar, crude, rough, yobbish *(informal)*, loutish, ill-bred, inferior.
OPPOSITES: refined, well-bred.

communicate
1 *(v) Please communicate this message.* convey, pass on, relay, spread, transmit.
2 *(v) We try to communicate regularly.* be in touch, make contact, talk, converse, speak, correspond, write, e-mail.

company
1 *(n) I enjoy Orlando's company.* friendship, companionship.
2 *(n) We have company for dinner.* guests *(plural)*, visitors *(plural)*, callers *(plural)*.
3 *(n) An electronics company. See* firm 6.

compare
1 *(v) Compare your results with mine.* check against, contrast, set against.
2 **compare with** *(v) This restaurant can compare with any in the area.* equal, rival, match, measure up to, bear comparison with, hold a candle to *(informal)*.

compete
1 *(v) Are you going to compete on Sports Day?* take part, participate, join in, enter, be a contestant, be in the running.
2 *(v) Six teams will compete for the cup.* contend, vie, battle, fight, rival each other.

competent *see* able.

competition
1 *(n) Who won the competition?* contest, championship, tournament, match, game, race, event, challenge, rally, quiz.
2 *(n) There's a lot of competition for places at the school.* rivalry, one-upmanship *(informal)*, opposition.

competitive
1 *(adj) Tony is so competitive.* ambitious, pushy *(informal)*, aggressive, combative.
2 *(adj) We live in a competitive society.* dog-eat-dog, cutthroat, aggressive.

competitor
(n) Are you a competitor in this race? contestant, contender, challenger, participant, entrant, runner, candidate.

complain
(v) I'm tired of hearing you complain. criticize, find fault, make a fuss, protest, grumble, moan, grouse, whine, whinge *(informal)*, gripe *(informal)*, carp, groan *(informal)*, beef *(slang)*, bellyache *(slang)*.

complaint
(n) Please see the manager with your complaint. grievance, criticism, objection, protest, grouse, gripe *(informal)*.

complete
1 *(adj) Do you have the complete set?* See **whole**.
2 *(adj) The match was a complete disaster.* absolute, total, utter, unqualified, out-and-out, outright, thoroughgoing, perfect.
3 *(v) We must complete our project today* See **finish** 1.

completely see **absolutely**.

complex
(n) Nathan has a complex about being short. obsession, fixation, phobia, preoccupation, hang-up *(informal)*.

complicated
(adj) Complicated directions. complex, involved, elaborate, convoluted, intricate, difficult, perplexing, puzzling.
OPPOSITES: simple, straightforward.

compliment
(n) Freddie's compliment made me blush. flattering remark, praise, admiration, tribute, flattery, congratulations *(plural)*.

compose see **write** 2.

compromise
(v) We couldn't agree, so we had to compromise. make concessions, meet halfway, make a deal *(informal)*, strike a balance, find the middle ground, give and take, find a solution.

compulsory
(adj) At my school, wearing uniform is compulsory. obligatory, required, mandatory, necessary, stipulated.
OPPOSITE: optional.

computer
(n) TYPES OF COMPUTER: hand-held, laptop, mainframe, notebook, palmtop, PC (personal computer), server, word processor, work station.

(n) PARTS OF A COMPUTER: CD-ROM (compact disc with read only memory), CD-ROM drive, CD-writer, CPU (central processing unit), disk drive, floppy disk, hard disk, keyboard, memory expansion card, modem, monitor, mouse, printer, scanner, screen, sound card, speaker, VDU (visual display unit).

con
1 *(n) (informal) This offer is a real con!* swindle, cheat, con trick *(informal)*, rip-off *(slang)*, swiz *(informal)*, scam *(slang)*.
2 *(v) (informal) Dodgy Dave will con you out of your money.* See **cheat** 1.

conceal see **hide** 1, 2, 3.

conceited
(adj) Jack is so conceited; he's always boasting. vain, bigheaded *(informal)*, swollen-headed *(informal)*, puffed up, proud, arrogant, self-important, self-satisfied, boastful, cocky, bumptious.
OPPOSITES: modest, self-effacing.

concentrate
1 *(v) Do you find it hard to concentrate?* focus your thoughts, focus your attention, pay attention, stop your mind wandering.
2 **concentrate on** *(v) Concentrate on your work.* keep your mind on, focus on, give your full attention to, apply yourself to, attend to.

concern
1 *(v) This decision will concern you all.* affect, involve, apply to, relate to, be relevant to, be of interest to, matter to.
2 *(v) Don't let this problem concern you.* See **worry** 2.
3 *(n) Granny's illness has caused us a lot of concern.* See **worry** 3.
4 *(n) Show some concern for your sister!* consideration, care, sympathy, regard.
5 *(n) This mess is not my concern.* affair, business, responsibility, problem.

conclusion
1 *(n) We had to leave before the conclusion.* See **end** 1.
2 *(n) After all that thinking, what's your conclusion?* decision, judgment, verdict, opinion, deduction, answer, solution.

condemn
1 *(v) Don't condemn Ziggy for being different.* criticize, blame, denounce, censure, reproach, damn, slam *(slang)*.
2 *(v) The judge decided to condemn Burglar Beryl.* See **convict** 1.

condescending
(adj) Araminta is so condescending; she looks down on everyone. patronizing, superior, supercilious, disdainful, snobbish, snooty *(informal)*, toffee-nosed *(slang)*.

condition
1 *(n) Are you in good condition?* health, shape, trim, nick *(informal)*, form.
2 *(n) Our school is in a dreadful condition.* state, state of repair, order, situation, position, predicament, plight.

3 **conditions** *(plural n) The conditions in the prison were terrible.* circumstances *(plural)*, surroundings *(plural)*, environment, situation, way of life.

confess
1 *(v) Did Beryl confess that she was guilty?* admit, own up, acknowledge, concede, declare, reveal, disclose, blurt out, confide.
2 *(v) If you broke the window you should confess.* own up, accept responsibility, plead guilty, come clean *(informal)*, make a clean breast of it, spill the beans *(informal)*.

confession
(n) A confession of guilt. admission, acknowledgment, declaration, profession.

confide in
(v) You can confide in me; I won't tell a soul. open your heart to, unburden yourself to, tell your secrets to, tell all to *(informal)*, trust, have confidence in.

confident
1 *(adj) Izzy is confident in new situations.* self-confident, self-assured, poised, self-possessed, composed, assertive, fearless.
OPPOSITES: diffident, insecure.
2 *(adj) I'm confident that it will be sunny.* certain, sure, convinced, positive, optimistic, hopeful.
OPPOSITE: doubtful.

confidential see **private** 2.

confirm
(v) Sid's actions confirm my suspicions about him. bear out, verify, prove, substantiate, corroborate, validate, back up, support, strengthen, reinforce.

confiscate
(v) Mrs Badger will confiscate that comic. seize, remove, take away, impound.

confront
(v) Are you brave enough to confront Bozo? face, face up to, stand up to, resist, oppose, defy, challenge, tackle, accost.

confuse
1 *(v) Complicated instructions confuse me.* bewilder, perplex, baffle, puzzle, muddle, flummox, faze, mystify, bemuse.
2 **confuse with** *(v) I often confuse you with your twin brother.* mistake you for, mix you up with, take you for.

confused
(adj) Don't speak so fast; it makes me feel confused. bewildered, dazed, muddled, disorientated, befuddled, at sixes and sevens, at sea, perplexed, baffled, flummoxed, nonplussed, puzzled.

confusing
(adj) These instructions are confusing. baffling, bewildering, perplexing, mystifying, puzzling, misleading, ambiguous, unclear, complicated.
OPPOSITES: clear, straightforward.

confusion
(n) A scene of total confusion met my eyes. chaos, turmoil, muddle, disorder, disarray, disorganization, jumble, clutter, shambles.

congratulate
(v) *I'll be the first to congratulate you if you win.* shake your hand, pat you on the back *(informal)*, compliment, praise, offer you good wishes, wish you joy.
OPPOSITE: commiserate with.

conjurer *see* **magician** 2.

connect
1 (v) *Connect the cable to the television.* join, attach, link up, fix, fasten, secure.
OPPOSITE: disconnect.
2 (v) *I always connect that smell with school dinners. See* **associate** 2.

connection
(n) *Is there a connection between air pollution and asthma?* link, correlation, relationship, association, tie-in, parallel.

conquer
1 (v) *The army managed to conquer their enemy.* defeat, beat, overcome, subdue, overthrow, overpower, triumph over, crush, thrash, rout, vanquish, subjugate.
2 (v) *I'm trying to conquer my fear of flying.* overcome, get the better of, quell, subdue, master, rise above.

conscience
(n) *Dodgy Dave has no conscience when it comes to lying.* scruples *(plural)*, misgivings *(plural)*, qualms *(plural)*, principles *(plural)*, standards *(plural)*, morals *(plural)*, ethics *(plural)*, sense of right and wrong.

conscientious
(adj) *Oliver is conscientious about his work.* diligent, careful, meticulous, thorough, painstaking, dedicated, hard-working.
OPPOSITES: careless, slack.

conscious
1 (adj) *Fergus bumped his head, but remained conscious.* aware, awake, alert, compos mentis, with it *(informal)*.
OPPOSITES: unconscious, out cold.
2 (adj) *Annie made a conscious decision to stay out late. See* **deliberate**.

consequence *see* **result** 1.

consider
1 (v) *Consider the consequences before you take action.* think about, weigh up, give thought to, reflect on, examine, contemplate, ponder, mull over, chew over, turn over in your mind.
2 (v) *I consider fox-hunting to be wrong.* believe, regard, judge, deem, hold, think.

considerate *see* **thoughtful** 1.

consistent
1 (adj) *Toby is a consistent worker.* steady, dependable, reliable, predictable, stable, unchanging, unvarying, unfailing.
2 (adj) *The reports are consistent on this point.* compatible, in agreement, the same, matching, all of a piece.

consist of
(v) *The new maths course will consist of ten different modules.* be made up of, be composed of, comprise, include, contain, involve, incorporate.

console *see* **comfort** 1.

conspicuous *see* **noticeable**.

conspiracy *see* **plot** 1.

constant
1 (adj) *I can't stand this constant noise.* continuous, continual, incessant, never-ending, nonstop, ceaseless, perpetual, relentless, unremitting, interminable, unending, unceasing, persistent.
OPPOSITES: intermittent, occasional.
2 (adj) *Mum drove at a constant speed.* steady, even, consistent, uniform, fixed, unchanging, unvarying, invariable.
OPPOSITES: erratic, varying.

constantly
(adv) *Fifi talks constantly.* all the time, nonstop, continuously, continually, incessantly, without stopping, night and day, endlessly, unceasingly, relentlessly, perpetually, interminably, always.
OPPOSITES: occasionally, now and then.

construct *see* **build** 1.

consult
(v) *I'd like to consult you before I make up my mind.* ask, ask your advice, speak to, confer with, discuss something with, compare notes with, refer to, turn to.

contact
(v) *I must contact Mandy.* get in touch with, get hold of, communicate with, reach, ring, call, phone, speak to, write to, e-mail, text, fax.

contain
1 (v) *What does this file contain?* hold, include, consist of, comprise, incorporate.
2 (v) *I couldn't contain my laughter.* control, restrain, hold in, keep in, keep back, suppress, stifle, curb, check.

contaminate
(v) *Industrial waste can contaminate the water supply.* pollute, make impure, poison, infect, taint, dirty, foul, blight.
OPPOSITES: purify, decontaminate.

contemplate
1 (v) *This is a good spot to contemplate the view. See* **look at** 3.
2 (v) *I need to contemplate what I should do next. See* **consider** 1.
3 (v) *Ziggy loves to sit cross-legged and contemplate. See* **think** 4.

contemporary *see* **modern**.

contempt *see* **scorn** 2.

contented
(adj) *I feel quite contented about how things have turned out.* content, pleased, satisfied, gratified, glad, happy, cheerful, relaxed, at ease, comfortable, serene.
OPPOSITES: discontented, dissatisfied.

contents
(plural n) *The contents of a book.* content, subject matter, subject, theme, topic, sections *(plural)*, chapters *(plural)*.

contest *see* **competition** 1.

contestant *see* **competitor**.

continual *see* **constant** 1.

continually *see* **constantly**.

continue
1 (v) *We must continue walking.* keep, keep on, carry on, go on, persevere with, stick at, persist in.
2 (v) *This storm could continue for hours.* last, carry on, drag on, go on, persist.
3 (v) *You can continue your painting next week.* carry on with, return to, resume, proceed with, take up, pick up where you left off, start again, recommence.

continuous *see* **constant** 1.

continuously *see* **constantly**.

contract
1 (v) *This metal pipe will contract if you cool it.* get smaller, get shorter, get narrower, shrink, reduce, narrow, tighten, compress, draw in, close up.
OPPOSITE: expand.
2 (n) *Be sure you understand the contract before you sign.* agreement, settlement, arrangement, deal *(informal)*, bargain, transaction, commitment, pact, lease.

contradict
(v) *Don't contradict what I say!* argue with, dispute, disagree with, deny, challenge, oppose, object to.
OPPOSITES: agree with, support.

contrast
1 (v) *Contrast these two photos to see how Jack has changed.* compare, set side by side, set one against the other.
2 (v) *Your explanations contrast radically. See* **differ** 1.
3 (n) *Notice the contrast between the two pictures. See* **difference**.

contribute
1 (v) *Please contribute generously to the school fund. See* **give** 2.
2 **contribute to** (v) *Fine weather will contribute to a successful barbecue.* lead to, play a part in, add to, be conducive to, be partly responsible for, help.
OPPOSITE: detract from.

control
1 (v) *It's the headteacher's job to control the school's affairs.* manage, be in charge of, be in control of, direct, govern, run, administer, supervise, oversee, preside over, look after, deal with, handle, be in the driver's seat, hold the purse strings.
2 (v) *Try to control your giggles.* keep under control, keep in check, hold back, contain, restrain, curb, suppress, subdue.
3 (n) *Who has control over these men?* command, charge, authority, power, management, supervision, supremacy.

controversial
(adj) *The referee's decision was controversial.* contentious, open to question, questionable, debatable, arguable, disputed, widely discussed.
OPPOSITE: noncontroversial.

convalesce *see* **recover** 1.

convenient
1 *(adj) A convenient shop. See* **handy** 2.
2 *(adj) A convenient date. See* **suitable** 2.

conventional
1 *(adj) Black is the conventional colour to wear to a funeral.* standard, customary, usual, normal, correct, proper, orthodox.
OPPOSITES: unconventional, unorthodox.
2 *(adj) Jet thinks her parents are too conventional.* conservative, traditional, conformist, unadventurous, stuffy, strait-laced, rigid, bourgeois.
OPPOSITE: unconventional.

conversation *see* **talk** 5, 6.

convert
1 *(v) I want to convert my bike so it can take a passenger. See* **adapt** 1.
2 *(v) Don't worry; I'm not trying to convert you.* change your mind, persuade, convince, reform, re-educate.

convict
1 *(v) The judge decided to convict Burglar Beryl.* find guilty, declare guilty, condemn, sentence.
OPPOSITE: acquit.
2 *(n) A convict has escaped from prison.* prisoner, jailbird, con *(slang)*, criminal, offender, felon.

convince
(v) How can I convince you that I'm right? prove to, satisfy, assure, persuade, talk you round, bring you round, win you over.

convincing
1 *(adj) That's quite a convincing argument.* powerful, persuasive, plausible, credible, telling, cogent, conclusive.
OPPOSITES: unconvincing, weak.
2 *(adj) Our team had a convincing win.* decisive, conclusive, impressive, definite.
OPPOSITES: unconvincing, inconclusive.
3 *(adj) Ella gave a convincing impression of Mrs Badger. See* **realistic** 2.

cook
(v) Dad offered to cook lunch. make, prepare, rustle up *(informal)*, concoct, put together, heat up, warm up.
WAYS TO COOK: bake, barbecue, boil, braise, broil, casserole, deep-fry, fry, grill, microwave, poach, roast, sauté, scramble, simmer, steam, stew, stir-fry, toast.

cool
1 *(adj) A cool breeze blew in off the sea.* fresh, refreshing, chilly, cold, nippy.
OPPOSITE: warm.
2 *(adj) Stay cool in a crisis. See* **calm** 2.
3 *(adj) Araminta gave us a cool welcome.* lukewarm, unenthusiastic, offhand, half-hearted, unemotional, apathetic, indifferent, reserved, chilly, aloof, distant, standoffish, unfriendly, unwelcoming.
OPPOSITES: warm, friendly.
4 *(adj) (informal) Jet looks cool in those clothes. See* **fashionable**.
5 *(adj) (informal) What a cool idea! See* **great** 9.

6 *(v) Cool the mixture.* chill, refrigerate.
OPPOSITES: warm up, heat.

cooperate
(v) Let's all cooperate to get the job done fast. work together, pull together, join forces, help each other, collaborate, work as a team, pitch in, pool resources, unite.
OPPOSITE: compete.

cooperative
(adj) Oscar was very cooperative about the move. obliging, accommodating, helpful, supportive, willing.

cope
1 *(v) Life is hard but I'm sure you'll cope.* manage, survive, get by *(informal)*, muddle through, struggle through, win through, hold your own, rise to the occasion.
2 **cope with** *(v) Alex has a lot to cope with.* deal with, handle, contend with, bear, endure, grapple with, wrestle with.

copy
1 *(n) Pirate Peg made a copy of the map.* duplicate, replica, photocopy, carbon copy, facsimile, transcript, tracing.
2 *(n) This painting is a copy; the original is in Paris.* reproduction, replica, print, imitation, fake, forgery, counterfeit, sham.
3 *(v) Selena decided to copy her friend's work.* duplicate, reproduce, photocopy, print, crib *(informal)*, forge, counterfeit.
4 *(v) Donna can copy Aunt Bertha's voice.* imitate, mimic, impersonate, ape, echo.

cord
(n) string, rope, twine, cable, line.

core *see* **centre** 2.

corner
1 *(n) The car took the corner too fast.* bend, turn, curve, hairpin bend, turning, junction, intersection.
2 *(n) Find a dark corner to hide.* nook, niche, recess, cranny, crevice, hole, hideaway, hide-out, hidey-hole *(informal)*.
3 *(v) The police managed to corner the thieves. See* **trap** 2.

corny
1 *(adj) (slang) A corny joke.* unfunny, old, familiar, tired, stale, clichéd, hackneyed.
2 *(adj) (slang) A corny love song. See* **sentimental** 2.

corpse *see* **body** 2.

correct
1 *(adj) Is this the correct answer? See* **right** 1.
2 *(adj) What's the correct way to address a king?* right, proper, conventional, standard, acceptable, appropriate, fitting.
OPPOSITES: wrong, inappropriate.
3 *(v) Please correct your spelling mistakes.* put right, rectify, amend, remedy, improve.
4 *(v) Mrs Badger will correct your work. See* **mark** 7.

correspond
1 *(v) Our stories must correspond or no one will believe us.* match, agree, tally, be consistent, coincide, square.

2 *(v) My cousin and I try to correspond regularly.* write, exchange letters, communicate, be in touch, be in contact.

corridor
(n) passage, passageway, hallway, aisle.

corrode *see* **wear away**.

corrupt
1 *(adj) A corrupt official.* dishonest, crooked *(informal)*, bent *(slang)*, bribable, fraudulent, unscrupulous, untrustworthy.
2 *(v) Can violence on television corrupt children?* lead astray, be a bad influence on, warp, brutalize, deprave, pervert.

cost
1 *(v) How much will a new TV cost?* come to, set you back *(informal)*, sell for, fetch, go for, be worth.
2 *(n) Can we afford the cost of a room in this hotel? See* **price** 1.

costume
(n) Your costume is perfect for the fancy-dress party. outfit, get-up *(informal)*, garb, gear *(informal)*, clothes *(plural)*, dress, attire *(old-fashioned)*, period costume, national costume, uniform, livery.

cosy
(adj) A cosy cottage. snug, comfortable, comfy *(informal)*, homely, warm, secure.

cough
(n) Have you taken anything for that cough? tickle in your throat, hacking cough, bark, frog in your throat.

count
1 *(v) Let's count how much money we've made.* count up, add up, tot up, calculate, reckon up, total, tally.
2 *(v) Your result won't count if you're disqualified.* matter, mean anything, count for anything, amount to anything, signify, be taken into consideration, carry weight.

count on *see* **depend on** 1, 2.

country
1 *(n) A European country.* nation, state, land, kingdom, realm *(old-fashioned)*, republic, principality, people *(plural)*.
2 *(n) A house in the country.* countryside, rural area, green belt, farmland, outback *(Australia)*, bush *(Australia)*, backwoods *(plural)*, wilds *(plural)*, sticks *(plural)* *(informal)*, back of beyond.

couple
1 *(n) We're a couple now.* twosome, pair, item *(informal)*, duo, married couple, husband and wife, girlfriend and boyfriend, partners *(plural)*.
2 **a couple of** *(phrase) I need a couple of nails.* two, two or three, a few, several.

courage
(n) The rescuers showed great courage. bravery, fearlessness, guts *(plural)* *(informal)*, heroism, valour *(old-fashioned)*, gallantry, nerve, pluck, spirit, grit, bottle *(slang)*, boldness, daring, audacity.
OPPOSITE: cowardice.

courageous *see* **brave**.

course
1 (n) *I'm having a course of tennis lessons.* series, sequence, programme.
2 (n) *Are you taking the new maths course?* syllabus, programme, module, curriculum, classes (plural), lessons (plural), lectures (plural).
3 (n) *We worked out the ship's course.* route, path, bearings (plural), direction.

court
(n) *Beryl's case will be tried in a court.* law court, high court, crown court, magistrates' court, county court.

cover
1 (v) *Cover the statue with a cloth.* drape, wrap, cloak, veil, swathe, shroud, envelop, curtain, clothe, spread over, lay over.
OPPOSITE: uncover.
2 (v) *Use this scarf to cover your face.* shield, protect, hide, conceal, veil, shade, screen, obscure, mask, disguise.
OPPOSITE: expose.
3 (v) *A sprinkling of snow began to cover the ground.* carpet, blanket, cloak, coat.
4 (v) *This book should cover all you need to know.* contain, include, incorporate, encompass, embrace, deal with, examine, consider, describe, survey.
5 (v) *This should cover your train fare.* pay for, be enough for, be sufficient for, meet.
6 (n) *Is there a cover for this? See* **top** 2.
7 (n) *Do you need a cover for your bed?* duvet, bedspread, quilt, blanket, rug, sheet, eiderdown, coverlet (old-fashioned).
8 (n) *We ran for cover.* shelter, protection, refuge, safety, sanctuary.
9 (n) *The troops need some cover.* protection, support, covering fire.
10 (n) *Beryl dropped her cover to reveal her true identity.* disguise, front, mask, pretence, façade, cover-up, smoke screen.

cover up
(v) *It's no use trying to cover up your mistake.* conceal, hide, hush up, keep secret, suppress, cover your tracks, keep it under your hat.

cowardly
(adj) *Sir Lancelittle was too cowardly to attack the dragon.* timid, fearful, scared, afraid, spineless, faint-hearted, chicken (informal), yellow (informal), weak-kneed (informal), nervous, anxious.
OPPOSITES: brave, courageous.

cower
(v) *Don't cower in the corner!* cringe, grovel, skulk, crouch, shrink, quail, tremble, shiver, flinch.

crack
1 (n) *This plate has a crack in it.* split, chip, break, fracture, flaw.
2 (n) *The explorers squeezed through a crack in the rock.* chink, cleft, slit, crevice, cranny, fissure, rift, split, rent, gash.
3 (n) *I heard a loud crack.* snap, bang, crackle, smack, pop.
4 (v) *Don't crack the plate. See* **break** 1.

5 (v) *Let's crack this problem. See* **solve**.
6 (v) *Mel may crack under pressure.* crack up (informal), break down, go to pieces, fall apart (informal), collapse, lose control.

cracked
(adj) *A cracked mug.* chipped, split, broken, crazed, flawed, damaged.

crackle see **crack** 3.

crack up (informal) see **crack** 6.

craft
(n) *A craft exhibition.* handicraft, art.

crafty see **cunning**.

cram
1 (v) *Don't cram so many chocolates into your mouth!* stuff, jam, ram, shove, force, pack, squash, squeeze, press, crowd.
2 (v) (informal) *Celia is trying to cram for her exams. See* **study** 1.

cramped
(adj) *This room is so cramped!* tiny, small, narrow, confined, constricting, oppressive, claustrophobic, crowded, overcrowded.
OPPOSITES: spacious, roomy.

crash
1 (n) *The tray landed with a tremendous crash.* bang, clatter, thump, thud, clang, clash, clunk, boom, din, racket.
2 (n) *There's a crash in the high street.* collision, accident, smash, smash-up (informal), pile-up (informal), multiple pile-up (informal), prang (informal).
3 (v) *We watched the tower crash to the ground.* fall, topple, plunge, collapse, hurtle, clatter, overbalance.
4 (v) *Dad is scared that Leo will crash his car.* smash, smash up (informal), bump, prang (informal), write off (informal), total (slang), wreck, trash (slang).
5 (v) *Frank's firm may crash. See* **fail** 4.

crash into
(v) *Don't crash into me.* bump into, collide with, career into, barge into (informal).

crave see **long** 3.

crawl
1 (v) *You'll have to crawl along this ledge.* go on all fours, go on your hands and knees, worm your way, edge, inch, creep, slither, wriggle, drag yourself, squirm.
2 (v) *The car began to crawl forwards.* creep, edge, inch, move at a snail's pace.
3 (v) *Trust Calvin to crawl to the teacher.* grovel, toady, suck up (informal), butter up, flatter, fawn, pander.

craze
(n) *What's the latest craze?* trend, fashion, fad, thing (informal), novelty, mania, passion, enthusiasm, excitement.

crazy see **mad** 2, 3, 5.

creak
(v) *Listen to the gate creak!* squeak, grind, grate, scrape, screech, squeal, rasp.

cream
(n) SHADES OF CREAM: buttermilk, ivory, off-white, oyster, pearl.

creamy
(adj) *A creamy sauce.* smooth, rich, thick, velvety, buttery.

crease
1 (v) *Don't crease your dress!* crumple, crush, rumple, wrinkle, pucker, ruck up, scrunch up, screw up.
2 (n) *There's a crease in this material.* fold, tuck, pleat, wrinkle, pucker, crumple.

create
1 (v) *Callum plans to create a model village.* make, build, construct, produce, devise, design, develop, dream up, invent, concoct, fabricate, form, bring into being.
2 (v) *This decision may create problems. See* **cause** 1.

creation
(n) *We're learning about the creation of the universe.* origin, birth, dawning, beginning, formation, shaping, genesis.

creative
(adj) *Ben's written work is very creative.* imaginative, inventive, inspired, original.

creature
(n) *An odd creature.* animal, beast, being.

credible see **believable**.

creep
1 (v) *The snail began to creep along the path.* crawl, slither, inch, wriggle, worm, squirm, glide, dawdle, go at a snail's pace.
2 (v) *Emma tried to creep past her sleeping sister.* slip, sneak, steal, tiptoe, sidle, edge, inch, slink.
3 (n) (slang) *Calvin is such a creep!* toady, groveller, bootlicker (informal), sneak, telltale.

creepy (informal) see **spooky**.

crest
1 (n) *Our pet cockatoo has a scarlet crest.* plume, tuft, comb, topknot.
2 (n) *We climbed to the crest of the hill.* summit, top, peak, brow, ridge, crown.

crime
1 (n) *Crime is increasing.* lawbreaking, misconduct, delinquency, corruption, villainy, wrongdoing, foul play, vice.
2 (n) *What crime did Beryl commit?* offence, misdeed, misdemeanour, violation, wrong, atrocity, outrage, trespass, felony (old-fashioned).
TYPES OF CRIME: abduction, armed robbery, arson, assassination, assault, attempted murder, blackmail, breaking and entering, bribery and corruption, burglary, conspiracy to murder, criminal damage, drink-driving, drug pushing, drug trafficking, extortion, forgery, fraud, GBH (grievous bodily harm), hijacking, hit and run, hold-up, indecent assault, joyriding, kidnapping, looting, manslaughter, money laundering, mugging (informal), murder, poaching, racial attack, ram raiding (informal), shoplifting, smuggling, speeding, trespassing, rape, robbery, terrorism, theft, vandalism.

crime and detection

listening device

criminals
accomplice (helper)
con (*slang*)
crook (*informal*)
culprit
delinquent
felon
mastermind
offender
ringleader
villain

criminal weapons
automatic pistol
blunt instrument
crowbar
flick knife
jemmy (crowbar)
revolver
sawn-off shotgun

crowbar

criminals use...
balaclava
car bomb
explosives
false
 numberplates
gag
gelignite
getaway car
skeleton key
stocking mask
stolen car

crimes can be...
amateurish
bloodthirsty
brutal
bungled
daring
gruesome
ingenious
premeditated
unprovoked
vicious
violent
well-executed

detectives and investigators
criminal psychologist
detective
forensic expert
 (expert in medicine
 and crime)
handwriting expert
pathologist
 (doctor who examines
 dead bodies)
plain-clothes officer
police constable
private eye (*informal*)
private investigator
sleuth
undercover agent
WPC (woman police
 constable)

photographic evidence

THE INVESTIGATION

investigators use...
bug (listening device)
criminal record
identity parade
inside information
Photofit picture
strip-search
tip-off

types of evidence
blood stains
DNA profile
eyewitness account
fingerprints
footprints
forensic evidence
 (medical evidence)
photographic evidence
security camera pictures
tyre tracks

investigators...
act on a hunch
analyse the
 crime scene
deduce the
 time of death
dig up evidence
draw a blank
ferret out clues
find the culprit
follow a lead
investigate
 a crime
keep tabs
 on suspects
prove a
 theory
pursue their
 inquiries
solve a case

torch

magnifying glass

fingerprint

DNA profile

DNA

THE INTERROGATION

interrogators...
cross-examine
give suspects the
 third degree
grill (*informal*)
interview
pressurize
probe
pump
put the screws on
 (*informal*)
question
quiz
tape interviews

suspects...
betray an accomplice
clam up (*informal*)
come clean (*informal*)
confess
crack under pressure
give a statement
grass (*slang*)
inform on the ringleader
put up a front
refuse to cooperate
spill the beans (*informal*)
supply an alibi
volunteer information

interview tape

criminal record

THE CHASE

trackers use...
border check
decoy
helicopter
megaphone
patrol car
police cordon
roadblock

searchlight
search warrant
siren
sniffer dog
speed camera
two-way radio
unmarked car

trackers...
chase
corner
shadow
stake out a
 building
stalk
surround
tail
track down
trap

WANTED

Photofit picture

police cordon

AB 42873

Also see **crime, criminal**.

criminal
(*n*) TYPES OF CRIMINAL: assassin, bandit, blackmailer, bomber, burglar, computer hacker, drug dealer, forger, gangster, gunman, hijacker, hit man (*slang*), joyrider, kidnapper, mugger (*informal*), murderer, pickpocket, poacher, rapist, robber, shoplifter, swindler, terrorist, thief, vandal.

cringe
(*v*) Dad's jokes make me cringe. wince, flinch, shudder, quail, blush, blench, recoil.

crisis
1 (*n*) If this pipe bursts, we'll have a crisis. problem, emergency, disaster, catastrophe, panic, alarm, predicament, mess.

2 (*n*) The meeting reached a crisis. turning point, climax, critical stage, moment of truth, crunch (*informal*), culmination, crux.

crisp
1 (*adj*) A crisp cracker. crispy, crunchy, brittle, hard, dry, crumbly.
OPPOSITES: soft, soggy.
2 (*adj*) A crisp winter's day. See **cold** 1.

critical
1 (*adj*) Critical remarks. scathing, derogatory, disapproving, disparaging, censorious, nit-picking (*informal*), nagging, niggling, uncomplimentary, hypercritical.
OPPOSITES: complimentary, flattering.
2 (*adj*) A critical decision. See **vital**.

criticize
1 (*v*) I'll try not to criticize you. find fault with, knock (*informal*), snipe at, pick on, censure, denigrate, disparage, pick holes in, nitpick (*informal*), cast aspersions on, slate (*informal*), pan (*informal*), bad-mouth (*slang*), slag you off (*slang*).
OPPOSITES: praise, compliment.
2 (*v*) Please criticize this poem. analyse, review, evaluate, discuss, assess, comment on, give your opinion of.

croak
(*v*) Your cold is making you croak. speak huskily, speak hoarsely, have a frog in your throat, rasp, wheeze, squawk, caw (*bird*).

crooked

crooked
1 *(adj) A crooked path.* winding, twisting, curving, zigzag, meandering, tortuous. OPPOSITE: straight.
2 *(adj) A crooked branch. See* **twisted** 1.
3 *(adj) That poster is crooked.* tilted, at an angle, slanting, sloping, askew, skewwhiff *(informal)*, lopsided, off-centre. OPPOSITES: straight, level.
4 *(adj) (informal) Don't get involved in Dave's crooked deals.* dishonest, criminal, illegal, corrupt, fraudulent, unscrupulous, dodgy *(informal)*, dubious, questionable, shady *(informal)*, underhand, deceitful. OPPOSITES: honest, legal.

cross
1 *(adj) Liz is cross that she wasn't invited.* annoyed, indignant, put out, disgruntled, upset, offended, peeved *(informal)*, miffed *(informal)*, irritated, piqued, vexed, cheesed off *(slang)*, hacked off *(slang)*, in a bad mood, sulky, in a huff. OPPOSITES: pleased, contented.
2 *(adj) Dad was really cross when I broke the CD player. See* **angry**.
3 *(adj) Aunt Bertha always seems so cross. See* **bad-tempered**.
4 *(v) How will we cross the desert?* get across, travel across, journey across, traverse, cut across, ford *(river)*.
5 *(v) The new bridge will cross the railway line.* span, pass over, stretch across, bridge.
6 *(v) Where do the two streets cross?* intersect, meet, join, converge, crisscross.

cross out
(v) Cross out my name from the list. strike out, delete, rub out, scratch out, erase.

crouch
(v) Let's crouch behind this bush. squat, bend down, hunker down, duck, kneel, stoop, hunch over, cower.

crowd
1 *(n) A crowd of people gathered in the square.* group, bunch *(informal)*, gang, cluster, knot, throng, horde, mass, flock, swarm, mob, pack, army, crush, rabble, multitude, collection, company, assembly.
2 *(v) We watched the fans crowd into the stadium.* swarm, flock, throng, stream, surge, pile, push, shove, jostle, elbow, pack, squeeze, squash, press, cram, jam.

crowded
(adj) The stadium was crowded. packed, jam-packed, full, overcrowded, congested, overflowing, swarming, thronging, cramped, full to bursting.

crown
(n) The queen wore a glittering golden crown. coronet, diadem, tiara, circlet.

crucial *see* **vital**.

crude
(adj) Crude jokes. coarse, vulgar, rude, uncouth, crass, tasteless, indecent, dirty, smutty, bawdy, lewd, obscene, offensive. OPPOSITES: polite, sophisticated.

cruel
1 *(adj) A cruel murder.* brutal, vicious, savage, barbaric, bloodthirsty, sadistic, cold-blooded, callous, heartless, ruthless, pitiless, inhuman, diabolical, fiendish. OPPOSITES: kind, gentle.
2 *(adj) A cruel remark.* hurtful, unkind, spiteful, malicious, vicious, cutting, heartless, callous, hardhearted, unfeeling. OPPOSITE: kind.

crumb
(n) A crumb of food. morsel, bit, fragment, scrap, shred, speck, grain, particle, atom.

crumble
(v) The old castle will crumble if it isn't repaired. disintegrate, collapse, fall apart, fall to pieces, break up, fall into decay, go to rack and ruin.

crumple *see* **crease** 1, 2.

crunch
(v) Don't crunch your carrot so noisily! munch, chomp, chew, gnaw, champ.

crush
1 *(v) Try not to crush the strawberries.* squash, squeeze, bruise, flatten, pulp, mash, mangle, pulverize.
2 *(v) Crush the biscuits into little pieces.* grind, pound, smash, crumble, pulverize, shatter, crunch, break.
3 *(v) Don't crush your skirt. See* **crease** 1.

cry
1 *(v) Todd began to cry when he heard the news.* weep, sob, shed tears, blubber, snivel, whimper, wail, howl, bawl.
2 *(v) Gina tried to cry for help. See* **call** 1.
3 *(n) I heard a cry.* call, shout, scream, shriek, yell, screech, squeal, yelp, howl.

cuddle
(v) Henry loves to cuddle his bunny. hug, snuggle up to, fondle, caress, embrace, nestle against, hold, clasp.

cunning
(adj) A cunning plan. crafty, wily, devious, sneaky, artful, tricky, deceitful, sly, shrewd, clever, ingenious, subtle.

cup
(n) TYPES OF CUP: beaker, chalice, coffee cup, goblet, mug, tankard, teacup, trophy.

cure
(v) Will this ointment cure my rash? heal, make better, clear up, put right, help, treat, ease, relieve, alleviate, remedy. OPPOSITES: aggravate, make worse.

curious
1 *(adj) I'm curious to know what really happened.* interested, intrigued, puzzled, burning with curiosity, inquisitive. OPPOSITES: incurious, indifferent.
2 *(adj) Curious neighbours. See* **nosy**.
3 *(adj) A curious hat. See* **strange** 1.

curl
1 *(n) A curl of hair.* wave, coil, kink, ringlet, corkscrew, twist, spiral, lock.
2 *(v) Did you curl your hair yourself?* crimp, kink, coil, wave, perm, frizz.

3 *(v) The snake began to curl round my leg.* coil, wind, loop, spiral, twist, twine, twirl, writhe, snake, curve, bend.

curly
(adj) Curly hair. curling, wavy, frizzy, fuzzy, curled, crimped, permed, corkscrew. OPPOSITE: straight.

current
(adj) Marcie likes to keep up with current fashions. present-day, contemporary, modern, up-to-date, up-to-the-minute, popular, fashionable, happening *(informal)*, existing, prevailing. OPPOSITES: past, out of date.

curse
1 *(v) Please don't curse! See* **swear** 1.
2 *(n) Duncan let out a curse.* oath, swearword, obscenity, expletive, profanity.
3 *(n) The wizard put a curse on the village.* jinx, spell, malediction, the evil eye.

curt *see* **abrupt** 2.

curve *see* **bend** 1, 2, 4.

curved
(adj) A curved surface. bent, rounded, arched, bowed, bulging, convex, concave. OPPOSITES: flat, level.

custom
(n) Kissing under the mistletoe is a popular custom. tradition, practice, convention, institution, procedure, ritual, ceremony.

cut
1 *(v) How did you cut your finger?* gash, slash, slit, nick, graze, lacerate, wound.
2 *(v) We need to cut some wood for the fire. See* **chop** 1.
3 *(v) Will you cut my hair?* trim, clip, crop, snip, shape, layer, shave.
4 *(v) We must cut that low branch.* trim, prune, clip, lop off, hack off, mow *(grass)*.
5 *(v) Don't cut your name in the desk!* carve, gouge, score, scratch, chisel, engrave, inscribe, chip, notch, whittle.
6 *(v) You need to cut this essay.* shorten, trim, prune, abridge, condense, abbreviate, summarize, précis.
7 *(v) Is it a good idea to cut violent films for TV?* edit, censor, clean up, sanitize.
8 *(v) Supermarkets may cut their prices. See* **reduce** 1.
9 *(n) Zina has a cut on her leg.* gash, nick, slash, scratch, graze, laceration, wound.
10 *(n) We expect a cut in prices. See* **decrease** 1.

cute *see* **sweet** 3.

cutting
1 *(adj) A cutting remark.* hurtful, scathing, barbed, sarcastic, caustic, acerbic, vicious, malicious, spiteful, vitriolic, wounding.
2 *(adj) A cutting wind. See* **cold** 2.

cut up *see* **chop** 2.

cynical
(adj) Cyril has a cynical approach to life. sceptical, negative, pessimistic, mocking, ironic, sneering, suspicious, distrustful. OPPOSITES: positive, optimistic, trusting.

Dd

dab
1 *(v) Dab some lotion on that itchy bite.* pat, daub, dot, smear, stroke, wipe, tap.
2 *(n) You've got a dab of paint on your nose.* drop, spot, speck, blob, smudge.

dabble
1 *(v) If you dabble about in the stream you'll get wet.* paddle, splash, slosh *(informal)*, wade, wallow.
2 **dabble in** *(v) Sylvie likes to dabble in astrology.* dip into, play at, toy with, trifle with, tinker with, potter about with.

daft *(informal)* see **silly** 1, 2.

dainty
1 *(adj) A dainty ballerina.* graceful, petite, small-boned, trim, elegant, pretty.
OPPOSITES: clumsy, ungainly.
2 *(adj) Dainty stitching.* neat, delicate, fine, exquisite.
OPPOSITES: clumsy, coarse.

dam
(n) If the dam bursts the valley will be flooded. barrier, barrage, dyke, wall, barricade, embankment.

damage
1 *(n) The hurricane caused widespread damage.* destruction, devastation, havoc, ruin, harm, injury, suffering, loss.
2 *(v) Vandals damage other people's property.* spoil, deface, wreck, destroy, ruin, vandalize, abuse, harm, mar, tamper with, play havoc with, devastate.
3 *(v) Reading in poor light can damage your eyesight.* harm, impair, weaken, strain, injure, hurt.

damaging see **harmful** 1.

damp
1 *(adj) Damp ground.* moist, dewy, wet, soggy, sodden, sopping, waterlogged.
OPPOSITE: dry.
2 *(adj) A damp day on the moor.* wet, drizzly, rainy, misty, foggy, dank.
OPPOSITE: dry.
3 *(adj) A damp day in the jungle.* humid, muggy, clammy, steamy, sticky, sweaty.
OPPOSITE: dry.
4 *(adj) A damp cave. See* **dank**.

dance
1 *(n) Alexander is interested in dance.* dancing, choreography.
2 *(n) I went to the dance with Carl.* disco, discotheque, rave *(slang),* hop *(informal),* ball, barn dance, dinner-dance.
3 *(v) Let's dance!* bop *(informal),* boogie *(slang),* jive, rock, move to the music, take the floor, trip the light fantastic.
4 *(v) Mo began to dance about when she heard the news.* leap, jump, skip, prance, bounce, hop, caper, romp, frolic, cavort.

---

dance words

types of dance
ballet
ballroom dancing
belly dancing
break dancing
contemporary dance
country dancing
disco dancing
flamenco dancing
folk dancing
formation dancing
hip-hop
jazz dance
Latin American dancing
limbo dancing
line dancing
morris dancing
old-time dancing
rock 'n' roll
square dancing
tap

ballroom dances
cha-cha-cha
foxtrot
jive
quickstep
rumba
samba
tango
waltz

contemporary dance

dancers can be...
acrobatic
agile
athletic
balletic
clumsy
dainty
elegant
energetic
expressive
exuberant
graceful
lithe
lively
lumbering
nimble
poised
rhythmic
skilful
sprightly
stately
supple

break dancing

folk dances
highland fling
hornpipe
jig
reel

other dances
cancan
conga
jitterbug
minuet
polka
salsa
twist

dancers may...
boogie *(slang)*
bop *(informal)*
dart
glide
gyrate
hop
jiggle
jive
jump
kick
leap
pogo
prance
rock
shuffle
skip
slide
spin
spring
stomp *(informal)*
stretch
strut
sway
swing
swirl
swivel
teeter
totter
twirl
twist
whirl
wiggle

ballroom dancing

jazz dance

grand jeté

ballet words
arabesque
ballerina
choreographer (dance creator)
corps de ballet (group of dancers)
grand jeté (leap)

pas-de-deux (dance for two)
pirouette
prima ballerina (leading ballerina)
principal dancer
tutu (ballet dress)

arabesque

tap dancing

---

danger
1 *(n) There's a danger of snow.* risk, threat, chance, possibility.
2 *(n) Indiana encountered one danger after another.* hazard, threat, peril, risk, menace, pitfall, crisis.

dangerous
1 *(adj) Indiana set out on a dangerous expedition.* hazardous, perilous, risky, treacherous, hairy *(slang),* dicey *(informal).*
OPPOSITE: safe.
2 *(adj) That bridge looks dangerous.* precarious, unsafe, insecure, unstable, unreliable, dodgy *(informal),* shaky, rickety.
OPPOSITES: safe, secure.

3 *(adj) The robber is armed and dangerous.* violent, unpredictable, ruthless, desperate, threatening, menacing.
OPPOSITE: harmless.
4 *(adj) Acid is a dangerous substance.* hazardous, harmful, poisonous, toxic, noxious, deadly, destructive.
OPPOSITES: harmless, safe.

dangle
(v) Relax and let your arms dangle by your side. hang, hang down, swing, droop, trail, fall, flop, sway, flap.

dank
(adj) A dank cave. damp, wet, chilly, clammy, dripping, slimy.

dare

dare
1 (v) *Would you dare to sleep in a haunted house?* have the nerve, have the courage, be brave enough, risk, venture.
2 (v) *If you dare me to jump into the river I will!* challenge, defy, goad, taunt, provoke, throw down the gauntlet.
3 (n) *I did it for a dare.* challenge, bet.

daring
(adj) *A daring climber.* fearless, intrepid, adventurous, bold, audacious, plucky, brave, undaunted, daredevil, reckless, rash.
OPPOSITES: timid, cowardly.

dark
1 (adj) *A dark dungeon.* dim, dingy, pitch-dark, unlit, shadowy, murky, gloomy, dismal, drab, cheerless, grim, sombre.
OPPOSITES: bright, cheerful.
2 (adj) *A dark sky.* black, pitch-black, inky, jet-black, moonless, starless, sunless, cloudy, overcast, leaden, ominous.
OPPOSITES: bright, light.
3 (adj) *Dark hair.* brown, brunette, black, jet-black, raven, ebony, sable.
OPPOSITES: fair, blonde.
4 (adj) *Dark skin.* brown, black, swarthy, tanned, dusky, olive, sallow.
OPPOSITE: fair.

darkness
(n) *A figure vanished into the darkness.* dark, blackness, night, gloom, shadows (plural), shade, gathering gloom, dusk.

dart see **dash** 2.

dash
1 (v) *I must dash! See* **hurry** 1.
2 (v) *I saw a rabbit dash across the field.* run, race, tear, hurtle, sprint, dart, shoot, scoot, bolt, speed, flash, whiz (informal).

data
(n) information, facts (plural), figures (plural), details (plural), statistics (plural), info (informal), lowdown (informal).

date
1 (n) *I have a date with Paula on Saturday.* meeting, rendezvous, appointment, engagement, assignation.
2 (n) *Luke and Lucy have set a date for their wedding.* day, time, specific day.

daunting
(adj) *Facing the dragon was a daunting prospect for Sir Lancelittle.* alarming, unnerving, frightening, terrifying, intimidating, disconcerting, off-putting (informal), discouraging, disheartening.

dawdle
(v) *If you dawdle we'll be late.* delay, waste time, lag behind, go at a snail's pace, straggle, loiter, linger, dally, hang about.

dawn
1 (n) *We got up at dawn.* daybreak, sunrise, break of day, crack of dawn, first light, sunup, cockcrow.
OPPOSITES: dusk, sunset.
2 **dawn on** (v) *It didn't dawn on me until it was too late. See* **occur** 2.

day
1 (n) *Vampires sleep during the day.* daytime, daylight hours (plural), daylight.
OPPOSITE: night.
2 (n) *Luke and Lucy have decided on a day for their wedding.* date, time, specific day.
3 (n) *In my granddad's day there were no computers.* time, era, age, period, generation, heyday.

daydream
1 (v) *Sebastian likes to sit and daydream.* dream, stargaze, fantasize, imagine, muse.
2 (n) *I was in a daydream. See* **dream** 2.

dazed
1 (adj) *The blow from the ball left Leah dazed. See* **stunned** 1.
2 (adj) *Naresh felt dazed when he heard the news. See* **stunned** 2.
3 (adj) *I felt dazed with everyone shouting at once. See* **confused**.

dazzle
1 (v) *Bright lights dazzle me.* blind, confuse, daze, disorientate.
2 (v) *Marvello will dazzle you with his magic tricks. See* **astonish**.

dazzling
1 (adj) *A dazzling jewel. See* **brilliant** 1.
2 (adj) *A dazzling display of acrobatics. See* **spectacular**.

dead
1 (adj) *Queen Victoria is dead.* deceased, dead and buried, passed away, departed, gone, no more, perished.
OPPOSITES: alive, living.
2 (adj) *The man lay dead on the ground.* lifeless, inert, cold, rigid, stiff.
3 (adj) *The dodo is a dead species.* extinct, defunct, died out.
OPPOSITES: existing, living.
4 (adj) *My fingers feel dead. See* **numb**.
5 (adj) *At night the town is dead.* lifeless, deserted, quiet, boring, dull, uninteresting.
OPPOSITES: lively, buzzing.
6 (adj) *The radio is dead.* not working, useless, out of order, inoperative.
OPPOSITES: working, operational.

deadly
1 (adj) *Deadly fumes.* lethal, poisonous, toxic, noxious, dangerous, hazardous, venomous (snake), virulent (disease).
2 (adj) *A deadly wound.* lethal, fatal, mortal, death-dealing, terminal (illness).
3 (adj) *Deadly enemies.* mortal, bitter, hated, sworn, out-and-out, irreconcilable, remorseless, implacable, murderous.
4 (adj) *A deadly aim.* accurate, sure, true, unerring, unfailing, exact, precise.

deafening see **loud** 1.

deal
1 (n) (informal) *The businessmen made a deal.* arrangement, agreement, bargain, pact, contract, transaction.
2 (v) *Does Dodgy Dave still deal in second-hand cars?* trade, do business, buy and sell, stock, traffic (drugs).

3 (v) *It's your turn to deal the cards.* give out, dole out, distribute, hand out, divide.
4 **deal with** (v) *Can you deal with this problem?* handle, see to, take care of, tackle, cope with, manage, sort out.
5 **deal with** (v) *What issues will your essay deal with?* be about, be concerned with, have to do with, cover, consider, discuss, examine, explore, treat.

dear
1 (adj) *Lopa is a dear friend.* close, much-loved, intimate, valued, cherished, treasured, beloved, adored, bosom.
2 (adj) *That watch is much too dear. See* **expensive**.
3 (n) *What's the matter, dear?* darling, love, honey, pet, sweetheart, dearest, beloved (old-fashioned).

death
1 (n) *The death of the king saddened the nation.* passing, demise, loss, dying.
OPPOSITE: birth.
2 (n) *There's been a death in the family.* bereavement, loss.
3 (n) *The crash resulted in only one death.* fatality, casualty.

debate
1 (n) *We had a debate about the death penalty.* discussion, argument, dispute.
2 (v) *Nina was keen to debate the issue of animal rights. See* **discuss**.

debris
(n) *Rescuers sifted through the debris.* rubble, wreckage, remains (plural), ruins (plural), wreck, fragments (plural), pieces (plural), bits (plural), rubbish, litter, waste.

decay see **rot** 1, 2, 3.

deceitful
(adj) *A deceitful politician.* untruthful, untrustworthy, dishonest, insincere, hypocritical, two-faced, double-dealing, duplicitous, devious, underhand, tricky, sneaky, slippery, shifty, crafty, cunning, sly.
OPPOSITES: honest, truthful.

deceive
1 (v) *Keep your wits about you or Dodgy Dave will deceive you.* trick, fool, mislead, delude, pull the wool over your eyes, take you in (informal), dupe, hoodwink, double-cross, bamboozle (informal), kid (informal), cheat, swindle, con (informal), diddle (informal), take you for a ride (informal), pull a fast one on you (slang).
2 (v) *Don't deceive the one you love.* be unfaithful to, betray, cheat on (informal), two-time (informal).

decent
1 (adj) *Mum thinks this top is not decent.* respectable, presentable, seemly, proper, dignified, modest, fitting, appropriate, suitable, tasteful, fit to be seen.
OPPOSITES: indecent, improper.
2 (adj) *My bedroom is a decent size.* reasonable, adequate, acceptable, satisfactory, ample, sufficient, average.
OPPOSITES: inadequate, unsatisfactory.

3 *(adj) Mr Badger is a decent man.* good, kind, honest, honourable, trustworthy, thoughtful, helpful, obliging, generous, polite, courteous, respectable, upright.
4 *(adj) (informal) This band's really decent!* See **great** 9.

decide
1 *(v) Decide which book you want.* make up your mind, choose, select, pick, come to a decision about.
2 *(v) Once you decide to do something you should see it through.* make up your mind, make a decision, resolve, determine, commit yourself.
3 *(v) Let's decide the argument by tossing a coin.* settle, resolve, clinch, put an end to, clear up, sort out, end, conclude.

decipher
(v) Can you decipher this secret message? decode, work out, figure out *(informal)*, understand, read, interpret, translate, unravel, solve, crack, suss out *(slang)*.

decision
1 *(n) It's a hard decision to make.* choice.
2 *(n) The judge gave her decision.* verdict, judgment, ruling, conclusion, finding

decisive
1 *(adj) Our team won a decisive victory.* See **convincing** 2.
2 *(adj) Jon is a decisive person.* firm, strong-minded, forceful, purposeful, resolute, determined, definite, incisive.
OPPOSITES: indecisive, hesitant.

declare
(v) Declare your loyalty to the king - or die! announce, proclaim, profess, swear, state, make known, assert, affirm, confirm

decline
1 *(v) I'm afraid I'll have to decline your offer.* See **refuse** 1.
2 *(v) Pupil numbers are expected to decline.* See **decrease** 2.

decorate
1 *(v) It's my turn to decorate the tree.* trim, adorn, embellish, festoon, trick out.
2 *(v) I helped Dad to decorate the front room.* paint, paper, do up *(informal)*, spruce up, refurbish, renovate, revamp.

decoration
1 *(n) Hang this decoration on the Christmas tree.* ornament, bauble, trinket, streamer, tinsel, spangle, trimming.
2 *(n) Granny wore a plain dress with no decoration.* trimming, embroidery, frill, flounce, ruffle, fringe, tassel, frippery.

decorative
(adj) A decorative bow. ornamental, fancy, pretty, elaborate, ornate, nonfunctional.
OPPOSITES: functional, plain.

decrease
1 *(n) There has been a decrease in the number of crimes.* drop, fall, decline, reduction, cut, downturn, falling off, dwindling, lessening, slump, ebb.
OPPOSITE: increase.

2 *(v) Pupil numbers are expected to decrease.* fall, drop, decline, fall off, drop off, dwindle, lower, go down, tumble, slump, slide, plummet, plunge, nose-dive.
OPPOSITE: increase.
3 *(v) The wind began to decrease.* drop, subside, lessen, abate, let up, die down.
OPPOSITE: increase.
4 *(v) Decrease your speed.* See **reduce** 3.

decrepit see **dilapidated**.

dedicated
(adj) A dedicated nurse. committed, single-minded, enthusiastic, keen, devoted.

deed see **act** 4.

deep
1 *(adj) A deep crack opened up in the earth.* bottomless, yawning, gaping, fathomless, unfathomable, cavernous.
OPPOSITE: shallow.
2 *(adj) Our new carpet is a deep shade of blue.* dark, rich, strong, vivid, intense.
OPPOSITES: pale, light.
3 *(adj) The giant spoke in a deep voice.* low, low-pitched, bass, rich, booming, rumbling, resounding, resonant, sonorous.
OPPOSITES: high, high-pitched.
4 *(adj) Ned has a deep dislike of spiders.* profound, deep-seated, deep-rooted, intense, strong, extreme, heartfelt, fervent.

defeat
1 *(v) The soldiers were determined to defeat the enemy.* See **conquer** 1.
2 *(v) I hope we defeat the other team.* See **beat** 2.
3 *(n) The match ended in a defeat for our team.* beating, thrashing, pasting *(slang)*, drubbing, failure, setback, humiliation, disappointment, frustration.
OPPOSITES: victory, triumph.

defect see **fault** 1.

defence
(n) The police used shields as a defence against the rioters. protection, safeguard, guard, screen, shield, shelter, deterrent.

defenceless
(adj) Without weapons the soldiers were defenceless. vulnerable, open to attack, helpless, powerless, unprotected, unarmed, exposed, in danger.

defend
1 *(v) The soldiers did their best to defend the castle.* protect, guard, fortify, secure, safeguard, keep safe, shield, preserve, keep from harm, watch over, fight for.
2 *(v) Nathan tried to defend his point of view.* justify, explain, give reasons for, make a case for, argue for, vindicate.
3 *(v) Burglar Beryl has a lawyer to defend her.* speak for, plead for, support, back, stand up for, stick up for *(informal)*.

defiant
(adj) The defiant child refused to go to bed. disobedient, rebellious, insolent, truculent, recalcitrant, mutinous.
OPPOSITES: obedient, meek.

definite
1 *(adj) Is it definite that you can't come?* certain, sure, decided, settled, final, cut and dried *(informal)*, guaranteed, positive.
OPPOSITE: uncertain.
2 *(adj) Do you have any definite plans for the future?* specific, particular, explicit, precise, clear, clear-cut, clearly defined, set, fixed, confirmed, categorical.
OPPOSITES: vague, obscure.
3 *(adj) Your work shows a definite improvement.* marked, noticeable, obvious, distinct, unmistakable, pronounced, decided, perceptible, positive.
OPPOSITES: imperceptible, slight.

definitely
(adv) Carl is definitely the best-looking boy in the school. certainly, without doubt, undoubtedly, undeniably, unquestionably, beyond a shadow of a doubt, for certain, clearly, obviously, easily, far and away.

deformed
(adj) The monster was horribly deformed. misshapen, disfigured, contorted, bent, twisted, crooked, gnarled, maimed, mutilated, unsightly, grotesque, ugly.

defy
1 *(v) Rick doesn't dare to defy his parents.* disobey, disregard, fly in the face of, flout, challenge, confront, resist, stand up to.
OPPOSITES: obey, submit to.
2 *(v) I defy you to jump into the river.* See **dare** 2.

degrading
(adj) Living conditions in the prison were degrading. demeaning, humiliating, shameful, disgraceful, contemptible, debasing, dehumanizing, brutalizing.

dejected see **depressed**.

delay
1 *(v) If you delay any longer, you won't get a ticket.* wait, hesitate, hang around, stall, dither, pause, procrastinate, dawdle.
OPPOSITE: hurry.
2 *(v) I hope the traffic doesn't delay you.* hold you up, slow you down, keep you back, make you late, detain, keep you waiting, hamper, bog you down.
3 *(v) Mrs Badger agreed to delay the test for a week.* See **postpone**.
4 *(n) There was no delay on the journey.* hold-up, interruption, setback, stoppage.

delete
(v) Delete that word from your essay. remove, cut out, take out, omit, edit out, eradicate, scrub *(informal)*, erase, rub out, cross out, strike out, wipe.

deliberate
(adj) Anji took a deliberate risk. intentional, conscious, calculated, considered, studied, intended, planned, premeditated *(crime)*.
OPPOSITES: accidental, unintentional.

delicacy
(n) Caviar is a great delicacy. luxury, speciality, treat, gourmet food.

delicate

delicate
1 (adj) Delicate lace curtains. fine, dainty, exquisite, intricate, flimsy, fragile, gauzy, wispy, silky, gossamer, cobwebby.
OPPOSITES: coarse, tough.
2 (adj) A delicate child. frail, weak, sickly, ailing, unhealthy, feeble, peaky, unwell.
OPPOSITES: robust, healthy.
3 (adj) A delicate shade of blue. soft, subtle, subdued, gentle, muted, pastel.
OPPOSITES: strong, bright.
4 (adj) A delicate flavour. See **mild** 3.
5 (adj) A delicate situation. difficult, sensitive, tricky, sticky (informal), ticklish, dicey (informal), critical, precarious.
6 (adj) This situation needs delicate handling. careful, sensitive, tactful, discreet, diplomatic, kidglove.
OPPOSITES: tactless, indiscreet.

delicious
(adj) A delicious meal. tasty, appetizing, mouthwatering, scrumptious (informal), yummy (slang), delectable, luscious, flavoursome, moreish (informal).
OPPOSITES: unappetizing, revolting.

delight
1 (n) The birth of the baby caused great delight. See **happiness**.
2 (v) Gemma's singing will delight you. captivate, charm, thrill, enchant, enthral, entrance, entertain, amuse, please, cheer.

delighted see **pleased**.

delightful
1 (adj) We spent a delightful day by the river. See **lovely** 2.
2 (adj) Carrie is a delightful girl. charming, lovely, pleasant, agreeable, attractive, enchanting, engaging, bewitching.
OPPOSITES: unpleasant, disagreeable.

delirious
1 (adj) Without water, the travellers were soon delirious. light-headed, feverish, incoherent, raving, babbling, hallucinating, demented, deranged, crazy, irrational.
OPPOSITES: rational, clear-headed.
2 (adj) Maria was delirious about meeting Famous Fred. See **ecstatic**.

deliver
1 (v) A boat will deliver supplies to the island. bring, carry, take, transport, convey.
2 (v) Ahmed is in a hurry to deliver his invitations. distribute, give out, hand out, dish out (informal), send, post, dispatch.

demand
1 (v) I know Dad will demand an apology. insist on, expect, require, ask for, call for, request, press for.
2 (v) These problems demand urgent action. call for, require, need, necessitate. cry out for, want.

demanding
1 (adj) A demanding job. See **difficult** 2.
2 (adj) A demanding child. nagging, insistent, hard to please, fussy, impatient, fractious, clamorous.

demolish
(v) It didn't take long to demolish the building. knock down, pull down, tear down, destroy, dismantle, break down, wreck, flatten, level, raze to the ground, bulldoze, blow up, dynamite.

demonstrate
1 (v) Can you demonstrate how to make an omelette? show, illustrate, give an idea of, make clear, explain, describe, teach.
2 (v) Demonstrate your loyalty by voting for me. show, indicate, display, prove, confirm, express, testify to.
3 (v) We decided to demonstrate against the new road. protest, lobby, march, picket, hold a rally, hold a sit-in.

demonstration
1 (n) A demonstration of country dancing. display, exhibition, show, presentation, illustration, explanation, exposition.
2 (n) A demonstration against nuclear weapons. protest, demo (informal), march, rally, mass rally, sit-in, picket, parade.

demoralized see **discouraged**.

den
1 (n) The animal hid in its den. See **hole** 4.
2 (n) Bozo's gang has a den in the woods. hide-out, base, hiding place, hideaway, secret place, retreat, hang-out, haunt.

dense
1 (adj) Dense undergrowth. See **thick** 4.
2 (adj) Dense fog. See **thick** 5.
3 (adj) The crowd was so dense we couldn't move. solid, tightly packed, jam-packed, jammed together, crammed together, compacted, close-knit.
OPPOSITES: sparse, scattered.
4 (adj) Don't be so dense! See **stupid** 1.

dent
(v) I didn't mean to dent the car door. knock in, make a dent in, bash in (informal), push in, dint, buckle, crumple.

deny
1 (v) Burglar Beryl was quick to deny the charges. reject, declare untrue, dispute, contradict, disagree with, repudiate, refute, rebuff, disclaim.
2 (v) Your parents seem to deny you nothing. refuse, deprive you of, begrudge, forbid, withhold from you.

depart see **leave** 1.

department
(n) Which department does your dad work in? section, branch, division, segment.

dependable see **reliable** 1, 2.

depend on
1 (v) All Bethan's friends depend on her. rely on, count on, lean on, trust, have confidence in, turn to, confide in.
2 (v) You can depend on Tim being early. rely on, count on, bank on, be sure of, reckon on, calculate on, bet on.
3 (v) Our plans must depend on the weather. hang on, hinge on, turn on, be determined by, be subject to, rest on.

depressed
(adj) Jessica is feeling depressed. unhappy, sad, miserable, down, blue, low, glum, gloomy, down in the dumps (informal), dejected, downhearted, despondent, melancholy, discouraged, disheartened, dispirited, moody, morose, suicidal.
OPPOSITES: cheerful, happy.

depressing
1 (adj) This is such a depressing film. sad, gloomy, dreary, dismal, bleak, black, dark, morbid, sombre, melancholy, cheerless, heartbreaking, distressing, harrowing.
OPPOSITES: cheerful, happy.
2 (adj) It's depressing when you always lose. See **discouraging**.

derelict
(adj) A derelict cottage. dilapidated, tumbledown, ramshackle, run-down, crumbling, ruined, rickety, broken-down, neglected, abandoned, deserted.

descend
1 (v) The plane began to descend. go down, come down, drop, fall, sink, plummet, plunge, nose-dive, tumble.
OPPOSITES: ascend, climb.
2 (v) The road starts to descend here. go down, slope, drop, dip, fall, slant, incline.
OPPOSITES: ascend, rise, climb.

describe
1 (v) Ned was eager to describe how he caught the thief. relate, explain, report, outline, tell, give an account of, give details of, put into words, recount, narrate.
2 (v) How would you describe your sister? define, characterize, portray, label, depict.

description
1 (n) Write a description of your first day at this school. account, report, chronicle, narration, narrative, commentary.
2 (n) Write a detailed description of your brother. characterization, portrayal, depiction, pen portrait, sketch.

descriptive
(adj) A descriptive piece of writing. expressive, vivid, graphic, detailed, colourful, striking, imaginative.

desert
1 (v) Don't desert your friends. abandon, leave, forsake, turn your back on, walk out on (informal), leave in the lurch, leave high and dry, run out on (informal), cast off.
2 (v) The demoralized troops decided to desert. run away, abscond, make off, escape, bolt, turn tail, go AWOL (absent without leave), flee, fly, decamp, defect.
3 (n) The travellers were lost in the desert. wilderness, wasteland, wilds (plural).
4 (adj) Few plants can survive in desert conditions. dry, arid, moistureless, parched, hot, burning, barren, infertile.

deserted
(adj) A deserted farmhouse. abandoned, neglected, empty, vacant, uninhabited, unoccupied, isolated, desolate, lonely.

desert words

the sun is	the earth is...	you might see...	you might experience...	desert plants
blazing	arid (dry)	caravan	desert storm	cactus
blinding	barren	(group of	flash flood	date palm
burning	dusty	travellers)	sandstorm	grasses
dazzling	parched	dry riverbed	whirlwind	scrub
fiery	sandy	dust spiral		tumbleweed
glaring	scorched	gully	**you might**	
scorching	stony	(steep valley)	**become...**	**desert**
	sunbaked	mirage	blistered	**creatures**
the heat is...	windswept	(illusion	dehydrated	camel
blistering		of water)	delirious	desert rat
intense	**the rocks**	nomads	disorientated	lizard
oppressive	**are...**	(wandering	dizzy	locust
overpowering	cracked	tribesmen)	exhausted	rattlesnake
relentless	craggy	oasis	faint	scorpion
searing	crumbling	rock arch	famished	tarantula
sweltering	jagged	rock tower	footsore	vulture
	weathered	salt patch	parched	
		sand dune	sunburnt	
		water hole	weak	

date palm *oasis* *caravan*

grasses

scorpion

cracked rocks

desert rat

deserve

1 (v) Your painting must surely deserve a prize. warrant, merit, be worthy of, justify, be qualified for, be entitled to, win.
2 (v) You've worked hard enough to deserve a holiday. be entitled to, have a right to, earn.

design

1 (n) Rajesh is working on a design for a toy plane. drawing, sketch, plan, blueprint, draft, outline, diagram, model, prototype.
2 (n) I don't like the design on that wallpaper. pattern, motif, decoration.
3 (n) The design of this book cover is striking. layout, composition, format, style, arrangement, organization.
4 (n) Our car is the latest design. See **model** 2.
5 (v) Mel was asked to design a cover for the school magazine. draw up, devise, create, think up, dream up, conceive, originate, plan, draft, map out, sketch, outline, draw.

desirable

1 (adj) This house is in a desirable neighbourhood. attractive, popular, sought-after, fashionable, enviable, pleasant, appealing, agreeable, excellent, good, advantageous, in demand.
2 (adj) A desirable person. See **sexy** 1.

desire

1 (v) The genie will bring you anything you desire. wish for, want, fancy, set your heart on, long for, yearn for, hunger for, thirst for, hanker after, crave, covet, need.
2 (n) Sir Lancelittle had no desire for adventure. wish, appetite, thirst, hunger, craving, longing, hankering, yearning, urge, need.
3 (n) Cinderella's beauty filled the prince with desire. passion, ardour, love, lust, the hots (plural) (slang).
4 (n) The sight of the gold filled Pirate Peg with desire. See **greed** 2.

desolate

(adj) The wind howled across the desolate moor. bleak, barren, bare, windswept, wild, inhospitable, lonely, remote, isolated, empty, deserted, uninhabited.

despair

1 (v) The marooned sailors began to despair. lose hope, give up hope, lose heart, be discouraged, be despondent.
2 (n) Mirza tried to conquer her feelings of despair. desperation, hopelessness, dejection, despondency, depression, gloom, pessimism, misery, wretchedness, distress, anguish.
OPPOSITES: hope, optimism.

despairing see **desperate** 4

desperate

1 (adj) The travellers were desperate for water. in urgent need of, in want of.
2 (adj) Indiana made a desperate bid to escape. frantic, daring, death-defying, bold, audacious, determined, risky, dangerous, hazardous, reckless, rash, hasty, foolhardy, harebrained, madcap.
3 (adj) The climbers found themselves in a desperate situation. hopeless, impossible, perilous, precarious, dangerous, life-threatening, serious, critical, dire, drastic, appalling, dreadful, terrible, awful.
4 (adj) Juliet felt desperate when she saw that Romeo was dead. despairing, hopeless, distraught, grief-stricken, brokenhearted, heartbroken, inconsolable, distressed, wretched, anguished, suicidal.
OPPOSITES: hopeful, optimistic.

despise see **scorn** 1.

dessert

(n) What's for dessert? sweet, pudding, afters (plural) (informal).

destined

1 (adj) The expedition was destined to fail. doomed, bound, certain, meant, fated.
2 (adj) It was destined that we should fall in love. inevitable, unavoidable, inescapable, ordained, written in the stars, predestined, meant.

destiny see **fate** 1, 2.

destroy

1 (v) Earthquakes can destroy whole cities. wreck, devastate, demolish, ruin, flatten, level, wipe out, lay waste to, raze to the ground, wreak havoc on, ravage, smash, shatter.
2 (v) The soldiers were ordered to destroy the enemy. annihilate, wipe out, obliterate, exterminate, liquidate, kill, slay, slaughter, massacre, decimate, waste (informal).

destruction

(n) The earthquake caused widespread destruction. devastation, desolation, havoc, ruin, wreckage, damage.

detached

(adj) Try to remain detached; don't take sides. objective, disinterested, impartial, unbiased, unprejudiced, dispassionate, aloof, unemotional, unconcerned.

detail

1 (n) Check every detail of the plan. aspect, element, part, item, point, feature, particular, component.
2 details (plural n) Samir asked Mrs Badger for details about the French trip. information, particulars (plural), facts (plural), specifics (plural).

detailed

(adj) Bart gave a detailed account of the match. full, thorough, comprehensive, in-depth, exhaustive, complete, meticulous, precise, blow-by-blow, elaborate.
OPPOSITES: brief, general.

detective
(n) investigator, sleuth (informal), private detective, private investigator, private eye (informal). ❖ Also see **crime & detection**.

deteriorate see **get worse**.

determination
(n) Chris showed great determination in finishing the race. perseverance, tenacity, persistence, willpower, drive, resolve, single-mindedness, dedication, guts (plural) (informal), grit, spirit.

determined
1 (adj) Patsy is a very determined person. persistent, tenacious, single-minded, strong-willed, assertive, firm, gutsy (informal), obstinate, stubborn, dogged.
OPPOSITES: indecisive, weak-willed.
2 (adj) I don't want to go, but Nat is determined. resolved, immovable, insistent, set on it, bent on it, intent on it.
OPPOSITES: unsure, wavering.

detest see **hate** 1.

detour
(n) We took a detour to get home. diversion, indirect route, roundabout route, long way round, scenic route.

develop
1 (v) Nadia should develop once she starts her new school. mature, blossom, flourish, grow up, make progress, progress, grow, fill out, shoot up.
2 (v) Dad wants to develop his grocery business. See **expand** 2.
3 (v) Tom may develop a taste for modern art. acquire, pick up, cultivate, form.
4 (v) I might develop mumps. See **catch** 3.
5 (v) It's a good idea, but you need to develop it. enlarge on, elaborate on, expand, flesh out, pad out, fill out.

development
(n) We're studying the development of modern medicine. progress, advance, evolution, growth, improvement, spread, expansion, history, course.

devious see **cunning**.

devoted
1 (adj) Mo is a devoted friend. See **loyal**.
2 (adj) Sally is devoted to caring for sick animals. dedicated, committed.

devour see **eat** 2.

diagram
(n) Study this diagram. representation, figure, sketch, drawing, line drawing, outline, chart, plan, map, graph, table.

diarrhoea
(n) the runs (plural) (informal), the trots (plural) (informal), holiday tummy (informal), Delhi belly (informal), dysentery.

diary
1 (n) Jo keeps a diary to record her secret thoughts. journal, record, chronicle, log.
2 (n) Priscilla entered the meeting in her diary. personal organizer, appointments book, engagement book, calendar.

dictate
1 (v) You dictate and I'll take notes. read aloud, speak slowly, recite.
2 (v) I can't dictate what you should think. tell you, lay down the law about, decree, impose, direct, order, determine, ordain.

die
1 (v) Everyone must die eventually. expire, pass away, pass on, decease, snuff it (informal), kick the bucket (informal), bite the dust (informal), give up the ghost (informal), croak (slang).
2 (v) Soldiers sometimes die in battle. perish, fall, lose their lives, give their lives.
3 (v) Those flowers will die without water. wither, wilt, shrivel up, droop, fade.

diet
1 (v) I must diet to fit into this skirt. lose weight, slim, eat sparingly, fast.
2 (n) You need to go on a special diet. programme, regimen, regime, fast.
3 (n) Is this your usual diet? food, nutrition, nourishment, fare.

differ
1 (v) Our tastes in music tend to differ. be different, contrast, vary, conflict, diverge.
2 (v) Matt and I differ about which team is best. See **disagree** 1.

difference
(n) Note the difference in price between the two items. contrast, disparity, divergence, discrepancy, inconsistency.
OPPOSITE: similarity.

different
1 (adj) Mum and I have different opinions on clothes. differing, dissimilar, contrasting, conflicting, opposing, contradictory, clashing, incompatible.
OPPOSITES: similar, identical.
2 (adj) We stock a range of different chocolates. various, assorted, mixed, varied, miscellaneous, multifarious.
3 (adj) Try a different approach. new, fresh, other, original, changed, altered.
4 (adj) Every fingerprint is different. individual, distinct, unique, special, distinctive, separate, unrelated, personal.
5 (adj) With his purple hair, Ziggy is certainly different. See **unusual** 2.

difficult
1 (adj) A difficult maths problem. hard, tough, knotty (informal), advanced, complicated, complex, challenging, testing, baffling, thorny, puzzling.
OPPOSITES: easy, straightforward.
2 (adj) A difficult assault course. hard, challenging, demanding, testing, taxing, strenuous, tough, gruelling, exhausting, killing (informal), backbreaking, arduous.
OPPOSITES: easy, undemanding.
3 (adj) A difficult child. demanding, hard to please, fussy, fractious, unmanageable, uncooperative, unruly, obstreperous, bolshie (informal), stroppy (informal), wilful, awkward, obstinate, stubborn.
OPPOSITES: cooperative, undemanding.

4 (adj) A difficult situation. See **awkward** 6.

difficulty
1 (n) Gran has had a life full of difficulty. See **trouble** 2.
2 (n) Don't let this little difficulty put you off. problem, complication, obstacle, snag, stumbling block, hurdle, pitfall, hiccup (informal), hassle (informal), hindrance.

dig
1 (v) The climbers tried to dig a hole in the snow. scoop out, gouge out, hollow out, excavate, shovel, burrow, tunnel.
2 (v) Mum asked me to dig the flowerbed. turn over, fork over.
3 **dig up** (v) Pirate Peg began to dig up the treasure. unearth, excavate, uncover.

dignified
1 (adj) The duchess has a dignified manner. stately, solemn, formal, proud, lofty, majestic, upright, elegant, refined.
OPPOSITES: undignified, coarse.
2 (adj) Hetty gave a dignified reply. calm, composed, restrained, solemn, grave.
OPPOSITES: rude, unrestrained.

dilapidated
(adj) A dilapidated farmhouse. run-down, decaying, decrepit, ramshackle, tumbledown, neglected, crumbling, broken-down, rickety, shabby, uncared-for.
OPPOSITE: well-maintained.

dilute
(v) You need to dilute this sauce. water down, weaken, thin, add water to.
OPPOSITES: condense, thicken.

dim
1 (adj) A dim cave. dark, gloomy, murky, dingy, dull, poorly lit, ill-lit, shadowy.
OPPOSITES: bright, well-lit, sunny.
2 (adj) A dim figure in the mist. faint, indistinct, shadowy, pale, vague, hazy, fuzzy, bleary, blurred, ill-defined, misty.
OPPOSITES: clear, distinct.
3 (adj) Don't be so dim! See **stupid** 1.

din see **noise** 2.

dingy
(adj) A dingy attic. drab, dreary, dark, gloomy, ill-lit, shabby, grimy, cheerless.
OPPOSITES: bright, clean, cheerful.

dip
1 (n) Do you want a dip in the river? swim, bathe, dunk, splash, plunge, soaking, ducking.
2 (n) Watch out for that dip in the ground. hollow, depression, dent, hole, pit, incline, slope.
3 (v) Dip your mug in the stream. plunge, dunk, submerge, immerse, lower, rinse.
4 (v) The plane began to dip. See **drop** 2.

direct
1 (adj) Take the direct road. straight, shortest, undeviating, unswerving.
OPPOSITES: indirect, winding.
2 (adj) Take the direct train. nonstop, express, through.

d̦isguise

3 *(adj) You can rely on Nat to give a direct answer. See* **frank**.
4 *(adj) We need a direct response. See* **immediate**.
5 *(v) Greg will direct operations.* supervise, oversee, take charge of, control, run, manage, handle, lead, mastermind.
6 *(v) Let me direct you to the school.* show you the way, guide, point, lead, steer.

direction
(n) Which direction should we take? way, route, path, track, course, bearing.

directions
(plural n) Follow the directions carefully. instructions *(plural)*, guidelines *(plural)*, rules *(plural)*, recommendations *(plural)*, suggestions *(plural)*.

dirt
(n) We must get rid of all this dirt. grime, filth, muck, sludge, slime, mud, dust, crud *(informal)*, gunge *(informal)*, gunk *(informal)*, grot *(slang)*, mess, pollution.

dirty
1 *(adj) This room is really dirty.* filthy, grimy, mucky, grubby, squalid, sordid, foul, grotty *(slang)*, grungy *(slang)*, dusty, muddy, sooty, smoky, black, stained, soiled, spattered, streaked, insanitary.
OPPOSITES: clean, spotless.
2 *(adj) Don't tell dirty jokes.* blue, risqué, smutty, rude, filthy, indecent, crude, vulgar, obscene, pornographic.
OPPOSITES: clean, decent.
3 *(adj) George was sent off the pitch for dirty play. See* **foul** 5.
4 *(v) Try not to dirty your clothes.* soil, stain, muddy, mess up, make a mess of, muck up *(slang)*, smear, spatter, spot.

disabled
(adj) handicapped, incapacitated, infirm, paralysed, paraplegic, quadriplegic.
OPPOSITE: able-bodied.

disadvantage
(n) It's a disadvantage to live a long way from school. handicap, drawback, inconvenience, hindrance, nuisance, pain *(informal)*, hardship, fly in the ointment.
OPPOSITES: advantage, benefit.

disagree
1 *(v) We often disagree about which team is best.* argue, quarrel, row, squabble, bicker, fall out *(informal)*, clash, differ.
OPPOSITE: agree.
2 **disagree with** *(v) Why do you disagree with everything I say?* object to, take issue with, quarrel with, argue with, dispute, oppose, contradict.
OPPOSITE: agree with.
3 **disagree with** *(v) Do spicy meals disagree with you?* upset, make you ill, give you indigestion, cause you problems, bother, nauseate.

disagreement
1 *(n) We had a disagreement over who should pay. See* **argument** 1.

2 *(n) There's been a lot of disagreement about this matter.* conflict, dissent, division, difference of opinion, debate.
OPPOSITES: harmony, agreement.

disappear
(v) Slowly, the figure began to disappear. vanish, fade away, melt away, become invisible, vanish into thin air, leave no trace, dissolve, evaporate, dematerialize.
OPPOSITES: appear, materialize.

disappoint
(v) I'm sorry to disappoint you. let you down, dash your hopes, disillusion, disenchant, fail, fail to live up to your expectations, dishearten, sadden, dismay, displease, upset, frustrate, thwart.

disappointed
(adj) I felt disappointed when I learnt the truth. let down, dejected, despondent, crestfallen, downcast, disenchanted, disillusioned, saddened, discouraged, downhearted, miffed *(informal)*, fed up *(informal)*, disgruntled, dissatisfied.
OPPOSITES: satisfied, gratified.

disapprove
1 *(v) My parents disapprove when I play loud music.* object, protest, take exception.
OPPOSITE: approve.
2 **disapprove of** *(v) I disapprove of fox-hunting.* object to, take exception to, have a low opinion of, take a dim view of *(informal)*, frown on, condemn, deplore.
OPPOSITE: approve of.

disapproving *see* **critical** 1.

disaster
(n) We must try to avoid another disaster. catastrophe, calamity, tragedy, misfortune, mishap, accident, fiasco, cataclysm.

disastrous
(adj) The pilot made a disastrous mistake. catastrophic, fatal, tragic, terrible, devastating, horrendous, calamitous, grievous, ill-fated, unlucky, cataclysmic.
OPPOSITES: fortunate, lucky.

discipline
1 *(v) The coach will discipline the players.* train, instruct, school, drill, control.
2 *(v) If you break the rules, I will have to discipline you.* punish, penalize, reprimand, teach you a lesson, bring you into line, rebuke, chastise, chasten, correct, scold.
3 *(n) Good athletes need discipline.* self-discipline, self-control, strictness, firmness, routine, order, training.

discourage
(v) What can I do to discourage you from going? dissuade, deter, prevent, stop, talk you out of, put you off, advise you against.
OPPOSITE: encourage.

discouraged
(adj) We were discouraged by the bad news. disheartened, demoralized, dismayed, daunted, depressed, crushed, deterred, cowed, put off, unnerved.
OPPOSITES: encouraged, reassured.

discouraging
(adj) It's discouraging when you always lose. demoralizing, disheartening, depressing, disappointing, demotivating, dispiriting, daunting, off-putting *(informal)*.
OPPOSITES: encouraging, heartening.

discover
1 *(v) It didn't take me long to discover that Oz was lying.* find out, learn, become aware, realize, detect, spot, discern, work out, deduce, suss out *(slang)*, ascertain.
2 *(v) The explorers were lucky to discover the treasure. See* **find** 1.
3 *(v) The journalist was determined to discover the truth.* find out, uncover, bring to light, ferret out, dig up, expose, reveal.

discovery
(n) This is an amazing discovery. invention, find, revelation, innovation, breakthrough.

discreet
(adj) You can trust Tony; he's always discreet. careful, guarded, reserved, . cautious, tactful, diplomatic, prudent.
OPPOSITES: indiscreet, rash.

discrimination
(n) I hate discrimination of all kinds. prejudice, bigotry, unfairness, favouritism, bias, racism, sexism, chauvinism, ageism.
OPPOSITE: tolerance.

discuss
(v) Can we discuss this later? talk about, consider, debate, examine, exchange views on, argue about, confer about, go into, thrash out, argue the toss on *(informal)*.

discussion
(n) We had a discussion about where to go on holiday. conversation, debate, exchange of views, argument, talk, powwow, dialogue, conference.

disease *see* **illness** 1, 2.

disgrace
(n) Burglar Beryl has brought disgrace to her family. shame, embarrassment, humiliation, dishonour, scandal, ignominy.
OPPOSITES: honour, credit.

disgraceful
1 *(adj) Disgraceful behaviour.* appalling, shameful, scandalous, shocking, outrageous, disgusting, deplorable, despicable, contemptible, disreputable.
2 *(adj) A disgraceful defeat. See* **humiliating**.

disguise
1 *(n) I'll need a good disguise to get into the house.* cover, front, screen, façade, camouflage, alias.
2 *(n) Sally looks wonderful in her disguise.* fancy dress, costume, outfit, get-up *(informal)*, mask, veil, make-up, face paint.
3 *(v) The soldiers used bushes to disguise the tank.* camouflage, hide, cover up, conceal, screen, mask, shroud, veil.
4 *(v) Burglar Beryl decided to disguise herself as the milkman.* dress up as, pretend to be, impersonate, imitate.

disgust
1 *(n) The details of the crime filled me with disgust.* loathing, distaste, revulsion, repugnance, contempt, hatred, antipathy.
OPPOSITES: delight, approval.
2 *(v) Doesn't bad language disgust you?* sicken, revolt, appal, nauseate, turn your stomach, repel, offend, put you off.
OPPOSITES: delight, attract.

disgusted
(adj) Gran was disgusted by Mark's jokes. appalled, sickened, outraged, offended, scandalized, shocked, nauseated, repelled.
OPPOSITE: delighted.

disgusting
1 *(adj) A disgusting smell.* revolting, repulsive, nauseating, sickening, loathsome, offensive, obnoxious, foul, vile.
OPPOSITES: delightful, lovely.
2 *(adj) Disgusting behaviour.* appalling, obnoxious, offensive, odious, detestable, abominable, shocking, scandalous.
OPPOSITES: delightful, pleasing.

dishonest
(adj) A dishonest businessman. deceitful, fraudulent, lying, crooked *(informal),* bent *(slang),* immoral, untrustworthy, unscrupulous, corrupt, double-dealing, treacherous, slippery, shady *(informal),* tricky, wily, two-faced, hypocritical.
OPPOSITES: honest, truthful.

dishonesty
(n) Dad cannot stand dishonesty. deceit, deceitfulness, untruthfulness, insincerity, deviousness, lies *(plural),* cheating, double-dealing, sharp practice, fraud, hypocrisy.
OPPOSITES: honesty, truthfulness.

dish up
(v) Dad will dish up the vegetables. serve, serve up, dole out, give out, hand out.

disillusioned *see* **disappointed.**

disintegrate
1 *(v) The yacht hit the rocks and began to disintegrate. See* **break up** 1.
2 *(v) The wallpaper is starting to disintegrate.* crumble, rot, moulder away, decay, decompose, fall apart, fall to pieces.

dislike
1 *(v) I dislike bullies. See* **hate** 1.
2 *(n) George surveyed his broccoli with dislike.* distaste, displeasure, disgust, loathing, revulsion, repugnance, hatred, hostility, detestation, animosity.
OPPOSITES: liking, delight.

disloyal
(adj) A disloyal friend. false, unfaithful, two-faced, untrustworthy, treacherous.
OPPOSITES: loyal, faithful.

dismal
1 *(adj) Dismal weather. See* **dull** 1.
2 *(adj) A dismal story. See* **depressing** 1.

dismay
(n) I gazed at the mountain with dismay. alarm, apprehension, anxiety, trepidation, consternation, dread, distress, fear, horror.

dismiss
1 *(v) The boss may have to dismiss you.* give you notice, sack *(informal),* fire *(informal),* let you go, release, make you redundant, lay you off, give you your cards *(informal),* show you the door *(informal).*
2 *(v) Don't dismiss my idea without thinking about it first.* reject, discount, spurn, pooh-pooh *(informal),* disregard.

disobedient
(adj) A disobedient child. rebellious, uncooperative, defiant, badly behaved, disruptive, naughty, wilful, wayward, unruly, uncontrollable, unmanageable.
OPPOSITE: obedient.

disobey
1 *(v) Mum will be angry if you disobey her.* defy, refuse to obey, resist, rebel against, revolt against, go your own way.
OPPOSITE: obey.
2 *(v) Don't disobey the school rules.* break, flout, disregard, ignore, infringe, overstep.
OPPOSITE: obey.

disorganized
1 *(adj) Daisy is such a disorganized person.* scatterbrained, undisciplined, scatty *(informal),* muddleheaded, untogether *(slang),* shambolic *(informal),* chaotic.
OPPOSITE: well-organized.
2 *(adj) This essay is very disorganized.* jumbled, muddled, confused, chaotic, unstructured, unplanned, illogical, haphazard, unsystematic, unmethodical.
OPPOSITES: well-organized, clear.

display
1 *(n) We went to see the display.* demonstration, exhibition, presentation, show, array, pageant, spectacle, parade.
2 *(v) The makers were keen to display their products.* show, demonstrate, exhibit, present, unveil, reveal, show off, flaunt.

disprove
(v) Burglar Beryl's lawyer set out to disprove the charges. refute, prove false, discredit, invalidate, contradict.
OPPOSITE: prove.

disqualified
(adj) Our team is disqualified from the competition. banned, eliminated, debarred, out of the running, knocked out.

disrespectful
(adj) Don't be so disrespectful to your father! rude, impertinent, insolent, cheeky, impolite, impudent, irreverent, insulting.
OPPOSITE: respectful.

dissatisfied
(adj) I feel dissatisfied with the way I've been treated. displeased, unhappy, disgruntled, disappointed, discontented, fed up *(informal),* cheesed off *(slang).*
OPPOSITES: satisfied, contented.

dissolve
(v) Wait for the stock cube to dissolve. melt, break up, disintegrate, disperse, liquefy, soften, thaw, disappear.

distance
1 *(n) A short distance.* space, span, gap, interval, length, breadth, width.
2 *(n) A long distance.* stretch, extent, range, length, breadth, width.

distant
(adj) Distant lands. faraway, far-flung, far-off, remote, out-of-the-way, outlying.
OPPOSITES: nearby, neighbouring.

distinct
1 *(adj) A distinct signal. See* **clear** 2.
2 *(adj) A distinct outline. See* **clear** 5.
3 *(adj) A distinct voice. See* **clear** 6.
4 *(adj) The two companies are quite distinct.* different, separate, unconnected, dissimilar, distinguishable, detached.

distinguish
(v) Can you distinguish between frogs and toads? tell the difference, differentiate, discriminate, tell apart.

distort *see* **twist** 5.

distract
(v) Will it distract you if I watch television? put you off, disturb, bother, ruin your concentration, faze, disconcert, sidetrack, unsettle, worry, confuse, annoy.

distress
1 *(n) Your news caused me much distress.* pain, heartache, misery, anguish, torment, worry, anxiety, grief, agony, upset.
OPPOSITE: comfort.
2 *(v) This film might distress you. See* **disturb** 2.

distressing *see* **disturbing.**
distribute *see* **give out.**
distrust *see* **suspect** 1.

disturb
1 *(v) I don't want to disturb you while you're working.* bother, interrupt, distract, put you off, pester, hassle *(informal),* butt in on, annoy, trouble, disrupt.
2 *(v) It might disturb you to know the truth.* upset, alarm, distress, unsettle, worry, trouble, perturb, fluster, disconcert.

disturbed
1 *(adj) When I read your letter, I felt disturbed.* uneasy, worried, troubled, concerned, upset, distressed, alarmed, anxious, apprehensive, agitated, nervous.
2 *(adj) A disturbed teenager.* troubled, confused, unbalanced, neurotic, maladjusted, screwed up *(informal).*
OPPOSITE: well-adjusted.

disturbing
(adj) I found the film really disturbing. upsetting, distressing, worrying, unsettling, disquieting, troubling, perturbing, harrowing, alarming, frightening.

ditch
1 *(n) Henry fell into a ditch.* gully, trench, dyke, channel, hollow, pit, moat, drain.
2 *(v) (slang) Jason wants to ditch his girlfriend. See* **drop** 6.

dither *see* **hesitate.**

dot

dive
1 (v) We watched Alexis dive into the river. plunge, jump, leap, fall, belly-flop, plummet, go under.
2 (v) Suddenly, the plane began to dive. drop, sink, plunge, plummet, fall, descend, swoop, dip, nose-dive, tumble, submerge (submarine).
OPPOSITE: rise.
3 (v) The goalkeeper prepared to dive for the ball. lunge, pounce on, swoop on, fall upon, leap, jump.

diver
(n) frogman, scuba diver.

divide
1 (v) Where does the path divide? branch, fork, split, separate, diverge, subdivide.
2 (v) Can you divide this apple for me? cut up, halve, split, bisect.
3 (v) Let's divide the money between us. share, share out, split, distribute, dole out, deal out, allocate, allot, apportion, go halves, go fifty-fifty (informal).
4 (v) Please divide these papers into groups. See **sort** 3.

divine
(adj) A divine being. heavenly, celestial, holy, sacred, godlike, angelic, spiritual, supernatural, immortal, superhuman.

divorce
(v) Joe's parents have decided to divorce. split up, separate, part, break up.

dizzy
(adj) After her fall, Fran felt dizzy. giddy, faint, light-headed, woozy (informal), groggy (informal), reeling, weak at the knees, shaky, dazed, wobbly, unsteady.

do
1 (v) I have lots of things to do. undertake, carry out, get on with, achieve, accomplish, perform, complete, finish.
2 (v) Let's ask Mrs Bunn to do the teas. make, prepare, organize, handle, deal with, take care of, see to, manage, look after, arrange, be responsible for.
3 (v) This will do for our needs. be good enough, be adequate, be sufficient, suffice, be useful, be acceptable.
4 (v) Can you do this puzzle? solve, answer, complete, work out, figure out (informal), crack, find the solution to.
5 (v) You may do as you please. behave, act, live, lead your life, carry on.
6 (v) This may do some good. result in, cause, bring about, give rise to, lead to.
7 (v) William should do better at his new school. manage, get on, get along, cope, progress, advance, make out, fare.
8 (v) I must do my room. tidy, straighten up, sort out, organize, arrange, neaten.
9 (v) Sunita hopes to do drama at college. study, learn, take up, go in for.
10 (v) This car will do 130 miles per hour. travel at, go at, reach.
11 (v) (informal) Watch out for Dodgy Dave or he'll do you! See **cheat** 1.

dock
1 (n) We moored our boat at the dock. quay, wharf, jetty, harbour, landing stage.
2 (v) When will the boat dock? berth, moor, tie up, anchor, drop anchor.

doctor
(n) medical practitioner, medic (informal), doc (informal), quack (informal).
TYPES OF DOCTOR: anaesthetist, brain surgeon, consultant, GP (general practitioner), gynaecologist, homeopath, neurologist, obstetrician, orthopaedic surgeon, osteopath, paediatrician, plastic surgeon, psychiatrist, specialist, surgeon.

dodge
1 (v) I threw a pillow at Kevin, but he managed to dodge it. avoid, evade, escape, sidestep, swerve, duck, turn aside.
2 (v) Oz tries to dodge work. See **avoid** 2.

dodgy
1 (adj) (informal) Dave made a dodgy deal. See **crooked** 4.
2 (adj) (informal) That bridge looks dodgy. See **dangerous** 2.

dog
(n) hound, bitch (female), pup, puppy, mutt (informal), pooch (slang), mongrel, cur, canine, man's best friend.
TYPES OF DOG: Afghan hound, Alsatian, beagle, bloodhound, boxer, bulldog, Chihuahua, collie, corgi, dachshund, Dalmatian, Doberman, foxhound, Great Dane, greyhound, gundog, husky, Labrador, Pekingese, pointer, poodle, pug, retriever, Rottweiler, St Bernard, setter, sheepdog, spaniel, terrier, whippet, wolfhound.

dominate
1 (v) Do your big brothers dominate you? tyrannize, keep you under their thumb, rule, domineer over, boss you around (informal), take you over, have the whip hand over, take control of, monopolize.
2 (v) The skyscrapers dominate the city. tower over, overshadow, dwarf, look down on, loom over, soar above.

domineering see **bossy**.

donate see **give** 2.

done for
(adj) (informal) After the fight, Lee felt he was done for. finished, ruined, defeated, destroyed, dead, doomed, lost.

done in (informal) see **exhausted**.

doodle see **scribble** 2.

doomed
(adj) I'm afraid our love is doomed. cursed, ill-fated, fated, luckless, condemned, star-crossed, ill-omened, hopeless.

door
(n) doorway, entrance, entry, exit, gate, gateway, opening.

dope see **drug** 2, 3.

dopey
1 (adj) (informal) I felt dopey after my operation. groggy (informal), drowsy, woozy (informal), dazed, sleepy, muzzy, sluggish, lethargic, drugged.
2 (adj) (slang) Don't be so dopey! See **stupid** 1.

dot
(n) Remove that dot. spot, speck, fleck, mark, dab, blob, full stop, decimal point.

---

dog words

dog moves

bounce	frolic	race
bound	jump	romp
cower	leap	scamper
creep	loll	scrabble
cringe	lope	scratch
crouch	nuzzle	sprawl
flop	paw	spring
frisk	prowl	trot

shaggy Afghan hound

dog sounds

bark, bay, growl, howl, pant, snap, snarl, whimper, whine, yap, yelp, yowl

frisky puppies

a dog's coat can be...
coarse, curly, glossy, mangy, matted, rough, shaggy, shiny, silky, smooth, thick, wiry, woolly

a dog can be...
affectionate, aggressive, alert, docile, energetic, faithful, fierce, friendly, frisky, lively, loyal, obedient, playful, savage, submissive, timid, vicious, watchful

muzzle, shoulder, withers, flank, hindleg, foreleg, hock, alert Dalmatian, glossy dachshund

double

double
1 *(adj) Double railway tracks.* dual, twin, paired.
2 *(n) I've just seen your double.* twin, spitting image *(informal)*, lookalike, clone, counterpart.
3 *(v) We aim to double our numbers.* increase, multiply, expand, duplicate.

doubt
1 *(v) I'm starting to doubt if Oz will come.* be uncertain, be unsure, have doubts about, be dubious, wonder, question.
OPPOSITES: be sure, be certain.
2 *(v) I have reason to doubt your motives.* See **suspect** 1.
3 *(n) There's no doubt about Beryl's guilt.* uncertainty, question, debate, ambiguity.
OPPOSITE: certainty.
4 *(n) I have some doubt about your story.* suspicions *(plural)*, misgivings *(plural)*, reservations *(plural)*, qualms *(plural)*, scepticism, distrust, disbelief, incredulity.

doubtful
1 *(adj) It's doubtful whether the story is true.* uncertain, unclear, arguable, debatable, questionable, iffy *(informal)*.
OPPOSITES: certain, definite.
2 *(adj) Ellen was doubtful about her chances.* uncertain, dubious, unsure, unconvinced, hesitant, tentative.
OPPOSITES: confident, certain.

do up *(informal) see* **decorate** 2.

dowdy
(adj) Aunt Bertha wears such dowdy clothes. frumpy, drab, dreary, unattractive, unfashionable, old-fashioned, dull, dingy.
OPPOSITES: smart, fashionable.

down *see* **depressed**.

down-and-out *see* **homeless**.

down-to-earth
(adj) Roger has a down-to-earth approach. realistic, practical, hard-headed, no-nonsense, matter-of-fact, common-sense, sensible, sane, pragmatic.
OPPOSITES: unrealistic, impractical.

doze
(v) Granny likes to doze after lunch. snooze *(informal)*, catnap, sleep, take a nap, have forty winks *(informal)*, nod off *(informal)*, drop off *(informal)*, get some shuteye *(informal)*, have a kip *(slang)*.

drab
(adj) A drab bedsit. dreary, dingy, dismal, cheerless, gloomy, shabby, dull.
OPPOSITES: bright, cheerful.

drag
1 *(v) Drag that carpet over here.* pull, haul, tow, lug, tug, yank, trail, draw.
2 *(n) (informal) Shopping can be such a drag.* See **bore** 3.
3 **drag behind** *(v) Don't drag behind the others.* See **drop behind**.

drain
1 *(n) A drain for waste water.* ditch, pipe, sewer, trench, channel, gutter, drainpipe.

2 *(v) We watched the water drain away.* seep, ooze, trickle, ebb, leak, flow, escape.
3 *(v) Drain the water from the pond.* empty, draw off, siphon off, bleed, tap.

drama
1 *(n) We are staging a new drama.* See **play** 5.
2 *(n) Melissa wants to study drama.* acting, stagecraft, the theatre, the dramatic arts *(plural)*.
3 *(n) There was some drama in town.* crisis, incident, excitement, commotion, fuss, scene, turmoil, histrionics *(plural)*.

dramatic *see* **exciting**.

drastic
(adj) Drastic action is needed. radical, extreme, forceful, strong, serious, severe, desperate, rigorous, harsh, far-reaching.

draw
1 *(v) I want to draw a cat.* sketch, depict, portray, trace, outline, design, pen, pencil.
2 *(v) Draw a number from the bag.* pick, select, take out, pull out, choose, extract.
3 *(v) Horses draw carts.* See **pull**.
4 *(v) I think the teams will draw.* tie, finish equal, be neck and neck, be even, be level.
5 *(v) This game should draw a big crowd.* See **attract**.
6 *(n) The match ended in a draw.* tie, dead heat, stalemate, deadlock, impasse.
7 *(n) Are you entering the draw?* lottery, raffle, sweepstake, competition.

drawback *see* **disadvantage**.

drawing
(n) picture, study, design.
TYPES OF DRAWING: caricature, cartoon, charcoal drawing, comic strip, doodle, illustration, line drawing, pen-and-ink drawing, portrait, sketch, still life.

drawn *see* **haggard**.

draw on
(v) You can draw on your own experience for this story. make use of, use, employ, rely on, utilize, exploit, fall back on.

dread
1 *(v) There's no need to dread visiting the dentist.* fear, be afraid of, be apprehensive about, be scared of, shrink from, cringe at, shudder at, tremble at, flinch from, have cold feet, have butterflies in your stomach.
2 *(n) The sight of the monster filled Cedric with dread.* See **fear** 1.

dreadful
1 *(adj) A dreadful crime.* appalling, terrible, horrible, horrific, horrifying, horrendous, shocking, frightful, atrocious, awful, ghastly, vile, foul, hideous, gruesome, grisly, monstrous, sickening, harrowing, distressing, despicable, deplorable, unspeakable, tragic.
2 *(adj) A dreadful essay.* awful, terrible, atrocious, appalling, abysmal, abominable, diabolical *(informal)*, disgraceful, dire *(informal)*, deplorable, bad, lousy *(slang)*.
OPPOSITES: wonderful, excellent.

3 *(adj) Dreadful weather.* awful, terrible, horrible, atrocious, appalling, bad, foul, filthy, dirty, rough, miserable, dismal, murky, bleak, wet, rainy, stormy, wild.
OPPOSITES: wonderful, brilliant.

dream
1 *(n) I thought I could fly, but it was only a dream.* nightmare, daydream, fantasy, illusion, delusion, hallucination, speculation, vision.
2 *(n) You're in a dream again.* daydream, trance, daze, world of your own, reverie.
3 *(n) Eddie's dream is to be a star.* fantasy, hope, wish, desire, ideal, aspiration, ambition, goal, vision.
4 *(adj) This is my dream house.* ideal, perfect, fantasy.
5 *(v) Do you ever dream that you can fly?* imagine, fancy, fantasize, envisage, visualize, daydream, muse.
6 **dream up** *(v) Gita loves to dream up new recipes.* See **think up**.

dreamy
(adj) Daisy is so dreamy, she never knows where she is. absent-minded, airy-fairy, vague, faraway, abstracted, distracted.

dreary
1 *(adj) Dreary weather.* dull, depressing, dismal, gloomy, murky, bleak, grey, wet.
OPPOSITES: cheerful, bright.
2 *(adj) A dreary lesson.* See **boring**.

drenched *see* **soaking**.

dress
1 *(v) It's time to dress for the party.* get dressed, get changed, change, put your clothes on, dress up.
2 *(n) Poppy wore a red dress.* frock, gown, robe. ❖ Also see **clothes**.
3 *(n) Formal dress is required.* clothes *(plural)*, clothing, wear, gear *(informal)*, attire *(old-fashioned)*, costume, get-up *(informal)*, garments *(plural)*, togs *(plural)* *(informal)*, kit.

dress up
(v) It's time to dress up and go out. dress up to the nines *(informal)*, dress for dinner, put on your glad rags *(informal)*, tart yourself up *(slang)*, doll yourself up *(slang)*.

dribble
1 *(v) Look at Fido dribble!* drool, slobber, slaver, salivate, water at the mouth.
2 *(v) Don't let the syrup dribble out of the bottle.* trickle, drip, leak, ooze, seep, run.

drift
1 *(v) The boat began to drift downstream.* float, glide, sail, be carried, coast.
2 *(v) I love to drift around town.* See **wander** 1.
3 *(n) Zak fell into a drift of snow.* bank, mound, ridge, heap, pile, mass.

drill
1 *(v) Can you drill through this wood?* bore, pierce, penetrate, punch, puncture.
2 *(v) Our coach will drill us every day.* See **train** 4.

drink
1 *(v) Drink your milk.* sip, swallow, down, swig *(informal)*, gulp, guzzle, drain, knock back *(informal)*, quaff *(old-fashioned)*.
2 *(n) Bring some drink for the journey.* liquid, refreshment, beverage.
3 *(n) Supermarkets sell alcoholic drink.* liquor, spirits *(plural)*, booze *(informal)*, plonk *(informal)*, grog *(informal)*.
4 *(n) Take a drink from the bottle.* sip, swig *(informal)*, slug, swallow, gulp, suck.
5 *(n) Dodgy Dave went out for a drink.* tipple, tot, dram, booze-up *(slang)*.

drip
1 *(v) Look at the water drip from the ceiling!* trickle, splash, dribble, fall in drops, plop, leak, drop, seep, sprinkle, drizzle.
2 *(n) Clem could hear the steady drip of water.* dripping, trickle, dribble, splash.
3 *(n) (informal) Cyril is a real drip!* wimp *(informal)*, weed *(informal)*, wet *(informal)*, softy *(informal)*, mummy's boy *(informal)*, nerd *(slang)*, weakling.

drive
1 *(v) Let's drive home.* motor, travel, journey, go by car, ride.
2 *(v) Do you know how to drive this car?* handle, steer, control, operate.
3 *(v) How can I drive you to work harder?* force, spur you on, goad, push, compel, motivate, prompt, prod, incite, coerce, dragoon, oblige, urge, press.
4 *(n) We went for a drive in the car.* run, ride, spin *(informal)*, whirl *(informal)*, trip, journey, jaunt, outing, excursion.
5 *(n) Jacob has lots of drive.* ambition, determination, energy, push *(informal)*, motivation, enthusiasm, oomph *(informal)*.

drive out
(v) The king tried to drive out the sorcerer. banish, send away, send packing, cast out, throw out, expel, exile, evict, turf out *(informal)*, drum out, kick out *(informal)*.

droop
1 *(v) Don't let the scarf droop over your face.* hang down, sag, dangle, flop, trail.
2 *(v) The tulips are starting to droop.* wilt, go limp, sag, go floppy, hang down, flag, slump, wither, shrivel.

droopy *see* **floppy**.

drop
1 *(v) Don't drop that vase!* let go of, lose your grip on, let fall, let slip.
2 *(v) Suddenly the plane began to drop.* fall, sink, descend, dip, dive, plunge, plummet, tumble, nose-dive.
OPPOSITE: rise.
3 *(v) Prices may drop. See* **decrease** 2.
4 *(v) Can I drop my flute lessons?* give up, stop, discontinue, abandon, finish with.
5 *(v) We'll have to drop you from the team.* exclude, eliminate, leave you out of, kick you off *(informal)*, axe *(informal)*.
6 *(v) Holly decided to drop her boyfriend.* finish with, leave, dump *(informal)*, chuck *(informal)*, ditch *(slang)*, jilt.

7 *(n) A drop of paint ran down the tin.* droplet, bubble, globule, drip, bead, blob.
8 *(n) Add just a drop of sauce.* dash, spot, trace, dribble, bit, little, sprinkle, trickle, taste, pinch, soupçon, smidgen *(informal)*.
9 *(n) There's been a drop in crime. See* **decrease** 1.
10 *(n) The path led to a steep drop.* chasm, precipice, abyss, cliff, slope.

drop behind
(v) Try not to drop behind! fall behind, lag behind, straggle behind, trail behind, drag behind, dawdle, linger, loiter, dally, bring up the rear *(informal)*.

drop in *(informal) see* **call** 5.

drop off
1 *(v) Dad will drop you off at school.* set you down, let you off, leave, deposit.
2 *(v) (informal) Gran tends to drop off in front of the TV.* fall asleep, doze off, nod off *(informal)*, snooze *(informal)*, catnap, drowse, have forty winks *(informal)*.

drown
1 *(v) The pirates may drown if their ship sinks.* go under, go down, go to a watery grave, go to Davy Jones's locker.
2 *(v) The new reservoir will drown the village. See* **flood** 2.

drowsy *see* **sleepy** 1.

drug
1 *(n) Dr Dose wasn't sure which drug to prescribe.* medication, medicine, remedy, treatment, tonic, painkiller, antibiotic, tranquillizer, sedative, stimulant, antidepressant.
2 *(n) Cannabis is a type of drug.* narcotic, dope *(informal)*.
3 *(v) The vet had to drug the wild tiger.* dope, tranquillize, sedate, knock out, anaesthetize, put to sleep, inject.

drum
(v) Listen to the rain drum on the roof. beat, rap, tap, pound, thrum, reverberate.

drunk
1 *(adj) Dad said Dodgy Dave was drunk.* intoxicated, inebriated, tipsy, under the influence *(informal)*, tiddly *(informal)*, merry *(informal)*, legless *(informal)*, sozzled *(informal)*, paralytic *(informal)*, plastered *(slang)*, smashed *(slang)*, sloshed *(slang)*.
OPPOSITE: sober.
2 *(n) Dodgy Dave is a real drunk.* drunkard, alcoholic, hard drinker, heavy drinker, boozer *(informal)*, wino *(informal)*.
OPPOSITE: teetotaller.

dry
1 *(adj) The travellers crossed the dry desert.* arid, parched, dried up, barren, torrid, waterless, moistureless, scorched.
OPPOSITES: wet, humid.
2 *(adj) Lauren's dad has a dry sense of humour.* keen, sharp, shrewd, wry, ironic, laconic, sarcastic, deadpan, droll.
3 **dry up** *(v) Don't let the plants dry up.* wither, shrivel up, wilt, dehydrate, dry out.

duck
1 *(n) A duck paddled across the pond.* drake *(male)*, duckling.
2 *(v) You'll have to duck to avoid that beam.* stoop, bend down, lower your head, bob down, crouch down, dodge.
3 *(v) I'll duck you in the deep end!* dunk, push you under, submerge, plunge, dip, douse, immerse.

dull
1 *(adj) The sky has been dull all day.* cloudy, overcast, grey, gloomy, murky, leaden, dark, dismal, dreary, sunless.
OPPOSITES: bright, clear.
2 *(adj) Mrs Badger's lessons are never dull. See* **boring**.
3 *(adj) Aunt Bertha wears such dull colours.* drab, dreary, sombre, muted, subdued, dark, faded, colourless.
OPPOSITE: bright.
4 *(adj) Are you being deliberately dull? See* **stupid** 1.
5 *(adj) The prisoner stared with dull eyes.* lifeless, listless, expressionless, indifferent, apathetic, dead, blank, lacklustre.
OPPOSITES: bright, lively.

dumb
1 *(adj) I was dumb with fear.* speechless, unable to speak, tongue-tied, at a loss for words, silent, mute, mum.
2 *(adj) (informal) Don't be dumb! See* **stupid** 1.

dump
1 *(n) Take your rubbish to the dump.* tip, rubbish dump, rubbish tip, scrapheap, refuse centre, waste disposal site, junkyard, scrap yard, recycling centre.
2 *(n) (informal) This place is a dump.* hole *(informal)*, dive *(informal)*, tip *(informal)*, slum, pigsty, hovel, the pits *(informal)*.
3 *(v) Don't dump your bag on the floor.* drop, throw, plonk, sling *(informal)*, fling, toss, deposit, park *(informal)*.
4 *(v) (informal) You should dump that rubbish. See* **throw away** 1.
5 *(v) (informal) Holly decided to dump her boyfriend. See* **drop** 6.

dumpy
(adj) Mrs Bunn is a dumpy woman. squat, short, tubby, stubby, chubby, plump, stout, chunky, roly-poly, podgy, pudgy.
OPPOSITE: lanky.

dungeon
(n) The traitors were thrown into a dark dungeon. prison, cell, underground chamber, vault, lockup, pit.

dusk
(n) I must be home before dusk. nightfall, twilight, evening, sunset, sundown.
OPPOSITES: dawn, sunrise.

dust
1 *(n) The floor is covered in dust.* grime, dirt, grit, powder.
2 *(v) Dust the table.* wipe, clean, polish.
3 *(v) Dust the cake with icing sugar.* sprinkle, powder, cover, scatter.

dusty
1 *(adj) The attic was dusty.* dirty, grimy, grubby, filthy, mucky, sooty, unswept.
2 *(adj) The earth was dry and dusty.* crumbly, powdery, sandy, chalky, fine.

duty
1 *(n) It's my duty to tidy up.* responsibility, obligation, job, task, business, role, function, mission, vocation, calling.
2 *(n) Nigel worked late out of a sense of duty.* responsibility, loyalty, obligation, allegiance, obedience, respect, service.

dwindle
(v) Seth's strength began to dwindle. diminish, decline, weaken, decrease, lessen, shrink, wane, fade, peter out, ebb, sink, subside, abate, wither, disappear.
OPPOSITES: increase, strengthen.

dye
(v) Let's dye this shirt. colour, tint, stain.

dying
1 *(adj) The old man was dying.* declining, sinking, failing, fading fast, at death's door, breathing his last, expiring.
2 *(adj) (informal) I'm dying to know who won. See* **eager** 2.

dynamic
(adj) A dynamic salesperson. energetic, lively, vigorous, active, forceful, driving, go-getting *(informal)*, high-powered, go-ahead, zappy *(slang)*, aggressive.

Ee

eager
1 *(adj) An eager student.* enthusiastic, keen, interested, motivated, committed, zealous, diligent, hard-working.
OPPOSITES: apathetic, indifferent.
2 *(adj) Jade was eager to open her presents.* keen, impatient, bursting, dying *(informal)*, itching *(informal)*, anxious, longing, yearning, hungry, raring.
OPPOSITE: reluctant.

early
1 *(adv) I bet Kit will arrive early.* in good time, ahead of time, in advance, too soon.
OPPOSITE: late.
2 *(adj) An early manuscript.* old, ancient, primitive.
3 *(adj) Early humans hunted for food.* primitive, prehistoric, primeval, primordial.

earn
1 *(v) Nic is hoping to earn a lot of money.* make, bring in, obtain, gain, take home, rake in *(informal)*, collect, clear, gross, net.
2 *(v) You've worked hard enough to earn a holiday. See* **deserve** 2.
3 *(v) I want to earn a medal. See* **win** 2.

earnest *see* **serious** 1, 2.

earth
1 *(n) The earth is round.* world, globe, planet.
2 *(n) Dan dug up the earth.* ground, soil, land, clay, loam, topsoil, dirt, dust, turf.

---

earthquake
(n) earth tremor, quake *(informal)*.

earthquakes...	**you might see...**
destroy	chasms
devastate	cracks
flatten	crushed cars
ravage	debris
shatter	dust
smash	fallen trees
wreck	flames
	rubble
the earth may...	ruins
cave in	smoke
crack	trapped victims
gape	wreckage
jolt	
judder *(informal)*	**earthquake**
open up	**dangers**
quake	broken cables
quiver	burst dam
shake	burst water main
shift	collapsed bridge
subside	cracked pipes
tremble	falling masonry
vibrate	fire
yawn	flying glass
	gas explosion
buildings may...	landslide
buckle	tidal wave
collapse	
crack	**earthquake**
crumble	**words**
crumple	aftershock
disintegrate	epicentre
lurch	(earthquake
rock	centre)
shake	seismic wave
shudder	(shock wave)
sway	
tilt	
topple	
totter	*water*
tumble	*gushing*
wobble	*from burst*
	water main
rubble	
	chasm *crack*

---

easy
1 *(adj) The test was easy!* simple, straightforward, uncomplicated, a doddle *(informal)*, a piece of cake *(informal)*, child's play *(informal)*, a pushover *(slang)*.
OPPOSITES: hard, difficult.
2 *(adj) Declan thinks his new job is really easy.* undemanding, cushy *(informal)*, effortless, painless, light, soft *(informal)*.
OPPOSITES: hard, demanding.
3 *(adj) Lord Lucre has an easy life.* comfortable, carefree, untroubled, pleasant, relaxed, leisurely, contented, calm, tranquil, secure, affluent.
OPPOSITES: harsh, difficult, stressful.
4 *(adj) Dom's parents are too easy on him.* lenient with, lax with, indulgent towards, liberal with, tolerant towards.
OPPOSITES: hard, strict.

easy-going
(adj) Omar is so easy-going; nothing ever bothers him. even-tempered, placid, calm, relaxed, laid-back *(informal)*, carefree, happy-go-lucky, nonchalant, flexible, amenable, undemanding, tolerant.
OPPOSITES: uptight *(informal)*, intolerant.

eat
1 *(v) I need to eat.* have a meal, feed, dine, take food, take nourishment.
2 *(v) I can eat a huge amount.* consume, devour, swallow, put away, demolish.
WAYS TO EAT: bite, bolt, champ, chew, chomp, crunch, gnaw, gobble, gorge, grind, gulp, guzzle, lick, make a pig of yourself *(informal)*, munch, nibble, overeat, peck at, pick at, pig out *(slang)*, scoff *(informal)*, slurp *(informal)*, stuff yourself, suck, tuck into *(informal)*, wolf down.
3 *eat away (v) Eventually the sea will eat away the rocks. See* **wear away**.

eavesdrop
(v) I didn't mean to eavesdrop on your conversation. listen in, snoop, overhear, bug *(informal)*, tap.

eccentric
1 *(adj) Ziggy's behaviour is quite eccentric.* bizarre, peculiar, weird, strange, odd, unconventional, outlandish, quirky, idiosyncratic, cranky *(informal)*, wacky *(slang)*, off-the-wall *(slang)*, abnormal.
2 *(n) Professor Peabody is a real eccentric.* oddity, character *(informal)*, oddball *(informal)*, crank *(informal)*, crackpot *(informal)*, weirdo *(informal)*, nut *(slang)*.

echo
1 *(v) We heard the screams echo round the cave.* reverberate, ring, resound, sound, repeat.
2 *(v) Don't echo what I say. See* **repeat** 2.

ecstatic
(adj) I was ecstatic when I won. delighted, overjoyed, thrilled, elated, thrilled to bits *(informal)*, over the moon *(informal)*, on cloud nine *(informal)*, delirious, euphoric, in raptures, frenzied, hysterical.
OPPOSITES: wretched, dejected.

edge
1 *(n) Go to the edge of the field.* end, side, boundary, limit, perimeter, border, margin, kerb *(street)*, verge *(road)*, outskirts *(town)* *(plural)*.
OPPOSITES: centre, middle.
2 *(n) Theo filled the jug up to the edge.* rim, brim, lip
3 *(n) Lucy caught the edge of her skirt on a nail.* hem, border, fringe, edging, trimming, bottom.
4 *(n) The expedition is on the edge of disaster.* brink, threshold, verge, point.
5 *(v) Try to edge forwards.* inch, creep, ease, crawl, sidle, worm your way, work your way, steal, sneak, slink.

edgy *see* nervous.

education
(n) Your education must come first. schooling, teaching, tuition, training, instruction, coaching, drilling.

educational
(adj) An educational film. informative, instructive, edifying, enlightening, improving, cultural

eerie *see* spooky.

effect
1 *(n) One effect of the fire was to make us more careful.* result, consequence, outcome, upshot, aftereffect, side effect, knock-on effect, aftermath.
2 *(n) Going to France had a great effect on me.* influence, impact, impression.

efficient
1 *(adj) An efficient worker.* capable, competent, well-organized, businesslike, proficient, productive, effective, skilful.
OPPOSITES: inefficient, incompetent.
2 *(adj) An efficient business.* productive, cost-effective, streamlined, well-run, well-organized, economical, cost-cutting, energy-saving, timesaving.
OPPOSITES: inefficient, wasteful.

effort
1 *(n) Let's make an effort to break the record.* attempt, bid, try, endeavour, stab *(informal)*, shot *(informal)*, crack *(informal)*.
2 *(n) You must have put lots of effort into making this.* exertion, work, energy, power, force, muscle, labour, toil, trouble.

elaborate
1 *(adj) An elaborate ballgown.* extravagant, ornate, fancy, decorative, fussy, showy, ostentatious.
OPPOSITES: plain, simple.
2 *(adj) Elaborate plans. See* complicated.

elect *see* choose 1, 2.

elegant
1 *(adj) Mel looks elegant in that suit.* smart, sophisticated, stylish, chic *(female)*, debonair *(male)*, suave *(male)*, dashing, fashionable *(male)*, handsome *(male)*, poised.
2 *(adj) What an elegant room!* tasteful, stylish, exquisite, classical, beautiful, splendid, luxurious, sumptuous, stately.

embarrass
(v) Would it embarrass you if Dad wore his tank top? humiliate, make you uncomfortable, make you self-conscious, make you blush, mortify, shame, upset, distress, show you up *(informal)*.

embarrassed
(adj) Mr Plod felt embarrassed when his wig fell off. self-conscious, uncomfortable, humiliated, mortified, ashamed, red in the face *(informal)*, flustered, disconcerted.

embarrassing
(adj) This is such an embarrassing situation. awkward, humiliating, uncomfortable, mortifying, cringe-making *(informal)*, upsetting, distressing, compromising.

embrace *see* hug.

embroidery
(n) needlework, sewing, tapestry.

emerge
(v) Wait for the train to emerge from the tunnel. come out, appear, come into view, become visible, surface.

emergency
(n) If there's an emergency, ring for help. crisis, danger, difficulty, predicament, panic stations *(plural)* *(informal)*.

emotion *see* feeling 3.

emotional
1 *(adj) Letty is such an emotional person.* excitable, highly strung, temperamental, sensitive, sentimental, passionate, hot-blooded, intense, melodramatic.
OPPOSITE: unemotional.
2 *(adj) An emotional film. See* moving 2.

emphasize
(v) I must emphasize the importance of safety. stress, underline, highlight, play up, point out, lay emphasis on, lay stress on, insist on, press home, accentuate.
OPPOSITE: play down.

empty
1 *(adj) This cupboard is completely empty.* bare, clear, free.
OPPOSITES: full, stuffed.
2 *(adj) Dustin handed in an empty page. See* blank 1.
3 *(adj) The house next door is empty.* vacant, unoccupied, uninhabited, deserted, unfurnished, bare, free.
OPPOSITES: occupied, furnished.
4 *(adj) I wasted the day in empty pursuits.* meaningless, pointless, futile, purposeless, aimless, hollow, frivolous, worthless, trivial.
OPPOSITES: worthwhile, valuable.
5 *(v) Empty the rubbish into the bin.* tip, dump, unload, pour, clear, drain.

enchant
1 *(v) Erica will enchant you with her singing. See* delight 2.
2 *(v) The magician planned to enchant the princess.* bewitch, cast a spell on, charm, hypnotize, mesmerize.

enchanting *see* delightful 2.

encourage
1 *(v) I think this result will encourage you.* reassure, cheer you up, inspire, give you confidence, give you hope, spur you on, comfort, console, hearten, buoy you up.
OPPOSITES: discourage, demoralize.
2 *(v) We all turned out to encourage the team.* support, spur on, urge on, cheer, applaud, rally, rouse, egg on.
3 *(v) Parents should encourage their children to read.* urge, persuade, prompt, help, assist, aid.
OPPOSITES: discourage, dissuade.

encouraging
(adj) This is an encouraging result. reassuring, heartening, comforting, promising, favourable, satisfactory.
OPPOSITES: discouraging, demoralizing.

end
1 *(n) Let's wait until the end of the show.* finish, conclusion, completion, ending, close, finale, climax, final curtain *(theatre)*.
OPPOSITES: start, beginning, opening.
2 *(n) This is the end of the school grounds.* limit, boundary, edge, border, perimeter, margin.
3 *(n) Our expedition reached its end.* destination, goal, target, journey's end.
OPPOSITE: starting point.
4 *(n) Get to the end of the queue.* back, rear, tail, tail end.
OPPOSITES: front, head.
5 *(n) What caused the end of the Roman Empire?* fall, ruin, demise, destruction, collapse, death, dissolution, extinction.
OPPOSITES: birth, beginning.
6 *(v) When does school end for the summer?* stop, finish, close, break up, come to an end, cease, wind up.
OPPOSITES: start, open
7 *(v) Mrs Badger decided to end the lesson early.* finish, stop, bring to an end, conclude, wind up, break off, discontinue.
OPPOSITES: start, begin.

ending
(n) What a sad ending! end, conclusion, finish, resolution, finale, climax, outcome, upshot, result.
OPPOSITES: beginning, opening.

endless
1 *(adj) The desert seemed endless.* unending, never-ending, limitless, infinite, boundless, measureless.
2 *(adj) The city was invaded by an endless stream of tourists.* constant, continuous, never-ending, perpetual, nonstop, uninterrupted, incessant, interminable.

endure
1 *(v) I can't endure any more suffering.* bear, stand, put up with *(informal)*, tolerate, take, cope with, handle, suffer, go through, undergo, experience, stomach, swallow, brave, withstand, stick *(slang)*.
2 *(v) The poet's fame will endure for ever. See* live 4.

enemy

1 *(n) Japan was Britain's enemy in World War II.* opponent, foe, adversary, rival.
OPPOSITES: ally, friend.
2 **the enemy** *(n) Sir Blackheart has joined the enemy.* the other side, the opposition.

energetic

1 *(adj) Emma always seems so energetic.* lively, dynamic, active, full of life, full of beans *(informal)*, spirited, animated, vibrant, zippy *(informal)*, tireless.
OPPOSITES: lethargic, listless.
2 *(adj) Squash is an energetic sport.* strenuous, vigorous, fast-moving, active.

energy

1 *(n) I admire Marco's energy.* vitality, stamina, strength, vigour, drive, get-up-and-go *(informal)*, enthusiasm, liveliness, spirit, verve, zest, sparkle, exuberance, oomph *(informal)*.
2 *(n) Are you in favour of nuclear energy?* power, fuel.

enjoy

1 *(v) I enjoy cycling. See **like** 2.*
2 *(v) My parents enjoy good food.* love, appreciate, relish, take pleasure in, have a taste for, delight in, revel in, savour.
OPPOSITES: dislike, hate.
3 **enjoy yourself** *(v) Enjoy yourself at the party!* have a good time, have fun, have a laugh *(informal)*, have a ball *(informal)*, let your hair down, have the time of your life.

enjoyable

(adj) An enjoyable holiday. pleasant, delightful, fun, amusing, entertaining, pleasurable, lovely, great *(informal)*.

enlarge

(v) The council plans to enlarge the local sports field. extend, expand, make bigger, make larger, widen, lengthen, add to, develop, supplement, augment, blow up *(photograph)* *(informal)*, magnify *(image)*.
OPPOSITE: reduce.

enormous

(adj) Marcie eats an enormous amount of chocolate. huge, vast, massive, immense, colossal, gigantic, tremendous, prodigious, monstrous, mountainous, astronomic, stupendous, humongous *(informal)*, mammoth, monster.
OPPOSITES: tiny, minute.

enough

(adj) I think we have enough supplies for the journey. sufficient, adequate, ample, abundant, plenty of.
OPPOSITES: insufficient, inadequate.

enquire *see **ask** 1.*

enter

1 *(v) I let Mrs Badger enter in front of me.* go in, come in, move in, pass in.
OPPOSITE: leave.
2 *(v) Will you enter the competition?* take part in, participate in, sign up for, put your name down for, go in for, volunteer for, enrol in, be a competitor in.

3 *(v) Enter the results of the experiment in your notebook.* record, note down, write, take down, jot down, log, list, insert.

entertain

1 *(v) This game will entertain you while you're ill.* amuse, keep you amused, occupy, keep you occupied, cheer you up, divert, distract, delight, please, interest.
2 *(v) My parents like to entertain guests.* receive, invite, welcome, show hospitality to, play host to, wine and dine, put up.

entertaining

(adj) An entertaining novel. amusing, interesting, enjoyable, light-hearted, witty, funny, humorous, comical, hilarious, delightful, charming, enchanting.

entertainment *see **amusement** 2.*

enthralling *see **fascinating**.*

enthusiasm

(n) Tristan approaches his work with enthusiasm. eagerness, interest, relish, zest, excitement, keenness, passion, fervour, zeal, devotion, delight.
OPPOSITES: apathy, indifference.

enthusiastic

1 *(adj) Alice is an enthusiastic football fan.* keen, avid, eager, ardent, fervent, passionate, fanatical, zealous, mad keen *(informal)*, devoted, committed, earnest.
OPPOSITES: apathetic, half-hearted.
2 *(adj) Halim is always so enthusiastic.* positive, optimistic, exuberant, spirited, ebullient, lively, willing.
OPPOSITES: apathetic, indifferent.

entire *see **whole**.*

entrance

1 *(n) Don't block the entrance.* way in, entry, gateway, gate, doorway, door, drive, opening, access, approach.
OPPOSITE: exit.
2 *(n) Entrance to the museum is free.* admission, admittance, entry, access.
3 *(n) Famous Fred made a dramatic entrance.* entry, appearance, arrival.
OPPOSITE: exit.

envious

(adj) Toby looked envious when he saw my new bike. jealous, green with envy, green-eyed, resentful, grudging, covetous.

environment

1 *(n) I like to see animals in their natural environment.* surroundings *(plural)*, setting, habitat, location, territory, domain.
2 *(n) I can't work in this environment.* surroundings *(plural)*, situation, conditions *(plural)*, atmosphere.

envy

1 *(n) Toby was filled with envy when he saw my new bike.* jealousy, covetousness, desire, resentment, bitterness, discontent, the green-eyed monster *(informal)*.
2 *(v) It's pointless to envy other people's success.* be envious of, be jealous of, resent, begrudge, covet.

episode

1 *(n) Did you see the last episode of "WestEnders"?* instalment, part, section, scene, chapter.
2 *(n) I'd rather forget that embarrassing episode. See **event** 1.*

equal

1 *(adj) The boys are equal in their ability.* identical, alike, the same, comparable, evenly matched, evenly balanced, level, neck and neck, at level pegging *(informal)*.
2 *(adj) Two dozen is equal to 24.* equivalent, identical, the same as.
3 *(v) Two plus two will always equal four.* be equal to, make, add up to, total, amount to, correspond to, equate to.
4 *(v) We managed to equal the scores by half-time.* level, even up, balance, equalize.
5 *(v) Nothing can equal a steaming hot bath.* compare with, match, be as good as, match up to, touch, rival, measure up to, come near, hold a candle to *(informal)*.

equipment

(n) Do you have all your equipment for the expedition? gear, tackle, stuff, apparatus, tools *(plural)*, baggage, supplies *(plural)*.

erase

(v) Erase that word from your essay. remove, delete, rub out, wipe out, scratch out, cross out, strike out, cancel, expunge.

erode *see **wear away**.*

errand

(n) Mum gave me an errand to do in town. job, task, message, assignment, mission.

error *see **mistake** 1.*

escape

1 *(v) Burglar Beryl longs to escape from prison.* get away, run away, break loose, break free, break out of, bolt, abscond, scarper *(slang)*, do a bunk *(slang)*, do a runner *(slang)*, flit *(informal)*, flee, fly.
2 *(v) Don't let the oil escape from the barrel. See **leak** 2.*
3 *(v) Sid always tries to escape the washing-up.* avoid, evade, shirk, dodge, get out of, wriggle out of, duck *(informal)*.
4 *(v) Burglar Beryl plans to make her escape tonight.* getaway, break-out, flight.

essay

(n) I have to write an essay for homework. composition, piece, story, report, paper, extended essay, dissertation, review.

essential

(adj) Essential instructions. necessary, vital, crucial, indispensable, important, basic, fundamental, key.
OPPOSITES: inessential, unnecessary.

establish

1 *(v) Mum aims to establish a successful business.* set up, start, begin, found, get going, get off the ground *(informal)*, create, form, build, construct, originate.
2 *(v) I need to establish exactly what happened.* find out, ascertain, determine, confirm, prove, verify, authenticate.

estimate
1 (v) Try to estimate the cost of this dress. assess, evaluate, guess, judge, work out, calculate, reckon, weigh up, gauge.
2 (n) Annie supplied an estimate for her work. quotation, price, costing, valuation.

eternal
(adj) Eternal life. everlasting, endless, never-ending, without end, immortal, infinite, limitless, undying, timeless.
OPPOSITES: ephemeral, transitory.

even
1 (adj) An even surface. level, flat, smooth, horizontal, straight, flush.
OPPOSITES: uneven, rough, sloping.
2 (adj) An even flow of water. steady, regular, consistent, constant, unvarying, smooth, continuous, uninterrupted.
OPPOSITES: erratic, irregular.
3 (adj) The scores are even. level, equal, identical, all square, at level pegging (informal), tied, drawn, neck and neck.
OPPOSITE: unequal.

evening
(n) dusk, nightfall, twilight, sunset, sundown, gloaming (old-fashioned).

event
1 (n) I'd rather forget that unfortunate event. incident, episode, affair, business, matter, occasion, occurrence, experience.
2 (n) We've been planning this event for months. activity, do (informal), function, occasion, ceremony, entertainment.
3 (n) A sports event. See competition 1.

eventually see finally 1.

evidence
1 (n) The detectives need evidence. proof, confirmation, documentation, data.
2 (n) Is there any evidence of damage? indication, sign, trace, symptoms (plural).

evident see obvious.

evil
1 (adj) This evil deed must be punished. wicked, sinful, bad, diabolical, fiendish, villainous, vile, depraved, immoral, corrupt, atrocious, vicious, malicious, wrong.
OPPOSITES: good, virtuous.
2 (n) We must overcome evil. wickedness, sin, sinfulness, depravity, corruption, vice, immorality, villainy, wrongdoing, malice.
OPPOSITE: good.

exact
1 (adj) Are these measurements exact? See accurate 1.
2 (adj) At that exact moment, I sneezed. very, precise, specific, particular, actual.
3 (adj) An exact copy. faithful, identical, perfect, precise, strict, true, flawless.
OPPOSITE: rough.

exaggerate
(v) Jo tends to exaggerate her problems. overstate, overemphasize, magnify, overplay, dramatize, embellish, embroider, make too much of, play up, inflate.
OPPOSITES: play down, understate.

examination
1 (n) A school examination. exam, test, assessment, oral, practical.
2 (n) A medical examination. checkup, investigation, observation, inspection, test, scan, probe, once-over (informal).

examine
(v) Detectives will examine the evidence. look at, inspect, study, look into, go over, go through, sift through, scrutinize, survey, check, consider, weigh up, analyse, check out, investigate, explore, probe, test.

example
1 (n) This is an example of Finn's bad behaviour. instance, illustration, case, case in point, sample, specimen.
2 (n) Rosa has set an example for you to follow. model, pattern, standard, ideal.

exasperate see annoy 1.

excellent
(adj) An excellent film. superb, brilliant, fantastic (informal), wonderful, terrific (informal), marvellous, outstanding, great, first-class, first-rate, impressive, magnificent, splendid, fine, exceptional, superlative, remarkable, extraordinary, tremendous (informal), sensational (informal), stunning (informal).
OPPOSITES: terrible, inferior.

exception
(n) It's usually warm in July; this snow is an exception. rarity, freak, oddity, peculiarity, special case, quirk, anomaly, irregularity.

exceptional
1 (adj) This hot weather is exceptional for March. See unusual 1.
2 (adj) Your work is exceptional. See excellent.

exchange
(v) May I exchange this shirt for a bigger one? swap, change, switch, replace with, trade.

excited
(adj) Everyone was excited before the party. animated, worked up, wound up (informal), agitated, overwrought, high (informal), hyper (informal), restless, wild, feverish, frantic, frenzied, hysterical.

excitement
1 (n) Gemma was beside herself with excitement. eagerness, anticipation, exhilaration, enthusiasm, elation, agitation.
2 (n) I like films that are full of excitement. tension, suspense, thrills (plural), action, adventure, drama, kicks (plural) (informal).
3 (n) What's all the excitement about? commotion, fuss, activity, confusion, furore, hubbub, kerfuffle (informal).

exciting
(adj) An exciting film. thrilling, dramatic, exhilarating, electrifying, fast-moving, action-packed, cliffhanging, nail-biting, heart-stopping, spine-tingling, stirring, gripping, compelling, riveting.
OPPOSITES: boring, dull.

exclude
(v) If you try to spoil the game we'll exclude you. leave you out, ostracize, ignore, pass you over, leave you out in the cold (informal), shut you out, bar, ban, throw you out, kick you out (informal).

excruciating see agonizing.

excuse
1 (v) I can't excuse your behaviour. forgive, pardon, condone, make allowances for, overlook, ignore, tolerate.
2 (v) Dodgy Dave tried to excuse his actions. defend, justify, explain, vindicate, give reasons for.
3 (n) What's your excuse for arriving so late? reason, justification, grounds (plural), defence, alibi (legal), pretext.

exercise
1 (v) You'll get fat if you don't exercise. keep fit, work out, train, play sport, exert yourself, pump iron (slang).
2 (n) Exercise is good for you. activity, training, exertion, sport, games (plural), working out, pumping iron (slang), physical jerks (plural) (informal).

exhausted
(adj) After the race I was exhausted. tired out, worn out, ready to drop, shattered (informal), dead tired, weary, drained, dead beat (informal), done in (informal), whacked (informal), zonked (slang).

exhausting
(adj) An exhausting job. tiring, gruelling, arduous, strenuous, draining, punishing, backbreaking, killing (informal), difficult, hard, laborious, taxing, testing.

exhibition see display 1.

exhilarating see exciting.

expand
1 (v) Pipes expand when water freezes in them. swell, enlarge, increase in size, widen, thicken, lengthen, dilate, fill out.
OPPOSITES: contract, shrink.
2 (v) Dad wants to expand his business. develop, build up, extend, enlarge.
3 (v) It's a good idea, but you need to expand it. See develop 5.

expect
1 (v) I expect that Danni will arrive late. assume, presume, suppose, imagine, reckon, guess (informal), think, believe, envisage, anticipate, predict, foretell.
2 (v) Can we expect some improvement? look forward to, anticipate, look for, hope for, reckon on, bank on.
3 (v) Dad will expect an apology. insist on, demand, require, look for, call for, want.

expedition
(n) The explorers set out on an expedition. journey, voyage, trip, mission, quest, exploration, trek, safari, hike, tramp, tour.

expel
(v) The head may expel you from school. exclude, dismiss, ban, send you away, throw you out, turf you out (informal).

expensive
(adj) An expensive holiday. dear, pricey *(informal)*, costly, overpriced, exorbitant, extortionate, extravagant, steep *(informal)*.
OPPOSITES: cheap, inexpensive.

experience
1 *(n) What an amazing experience!* incident, occurrence, adventure, episode, affair, happening, event, ordeal.
2 *(n) For this job, you need the right experience.* skill, know-how *(informal)*, practical knowledge, training, background.
3 *(n) You will learn by experience.* doing, taking part, practice, participation, involvement, familiarity.
4 *(v) You may have to experience hardship.* undergo, suffer, endure, face, go through, live through, encounter, meet.

experienced
(adj) Bo is an experienced cook. practised, seasoned, skilled, accomplished, expert, proficient, competent, trained, qualified.
OPPOSITE: inexperienced.

experiment
1 *(n) Write up the results of your experiment.* investigation, practical, inquiry, test, trial, demonstration, research.
2 *(v) I love to experiment when I cook.* try things out, improvise, explore.

expert
1 *(n) We need an expert to mend our computer.* specialist, professional, consultant, authority, pro *(informal)*, pundit, boffin *(informal)*, anorak *(slang)*.
OPPOSITE: novice.
2 *(n) Dean is an expert at juggling.* master, genius, wizard, ace *(informal)*, virtuoso, past master, whiz *(informal)*, whiz kid *(informal)*, dab hand *(informal)*.
3 *(adj) An expert footballer.* See **skilful**.

explain
1 *(v) Can you explain what this means?* make clear, clarify, spell out, throw light on, elucidate, interpret, define, describe.
2 *(v) Please explain why you are late.* give an explanation for, give a reason for, account for, justify.

explode
(v) This bomb may explode without any warning. blow up, go off, detonate, erupt.

exploit *see* **take advantage of**.

explore
(v) Let's explore the castle. investigate, scout around, take a look around, check out *(informal)*, survey, reconnoitre, tour.

explorer
(n) discoverer, traveller, voyager.

explosion
(n) The explosion made the windows shake. blast, bang, boom, rumble, crash, detonation, report.

expose
1 *(v) Dad rolled up his trousers to expose his hairy legs.* See **reveal** 1.

2 *(v) The journalist was determined to expose the truth.* uncover, bring to light, make known, lay bare, unmask, reveal, disclose, divulge, leak, blow wide open *(slang)*, blow the whistle on *(informal)*.

express
1 *(v) Nasim was keen to express his views.* state, put into words, voice, make known, air, put across, communicate, point out, give vent to, articulate, verbalize.
2 *(adj) Take the express train.* high-speed, fast, nonstop, direct, through.

expression
1 *(n) Sim's face wore a strange expression.* look, appearance, aspect, air.
2 *(n) Where did you hear that expression?* word, phrase, saying, turn of phrase, idiom, term, choice of words, remark.

extend
1 *(v) Extend the elastic.* See **stretch** 1.
2 *(v) The desert seemed to extend for miles.* See **stretch** 4.
3 *(v) We plan to extend our house.* enlarge, build on to, add on to, make bigger, make larger, expand.

extinct
(adj) That species is extinct. dead, defunct, vanished, lost, died out, wiped out, gone.
OPPOSITES: surviving, extant.

extra
(adj) This extension will give us extra space. more, additional, further, added, spare, surplus, excess, leftover, superfluous.

extraordinary
1 *(adj) Carl's artistic talent is extraordinary.* exceptional, outstanding, unique, out of the ordinary, unprecedented, remarkable, amazing, phenomenal, unusual, rare.
OPPOSITES: unexceptional, ordinary.
2 *(adj) Ziggy wears some extraordinary clothes.* See **strange** 1.

extravagant
1 *(adj) Letty is so extravagant; she's always wasting money.* wasteful, careless with money, self-indulgent, lavish, imprudent.
OPPOSITES: thrifty, economical.
2 *(adj) What an extravagant gift!* lavish, costly, expensive, flashy, showy, over the top, overgenerous, excessive, immoderate, outrageous, OTT *(slang)*.

extreme
1 *(adj) Extreme pain.* severe, intense, acute, great.
2 *(adj) Extreme measures.* See **drastic**.
3 *(adj) Extreme political views.* fanatical, radical, uncompromising, unreasonable, hardline, way-out *(informal)*, outrageous, exaggerated, excessive, immoderate.
OPPOSITE: moderate.

extrovert
(adj) Kylie is so extrovert; she's the life and soul of the party. outgoing, lively, vivacious, bubbly, sociable, gregarious, friendly, confident, exuberant, animated.
OPPOSITES: introverted, withdrawn.

Ff

fabric *see* **material**.
fabulous *(informal) see* **fantastic** 3.
face
1 *(n) Burglar Beryl has a distinctive face.* features *(plural)*, appearance, countenance *(old-fashioned)*, mug *(slang)*, kisser *(slang)*.
2 *(n) Lisa made a horrible face.* scowl, grimace, frown, smirk, pout.
3 *(v) Our new house will face the sea.* overlook, look onto, look towards, front onto, be opposite.
4 *(v) The explorers will face many dangers.* encounter, experience, come up against, come across, meet, be confronted by.
5 *(v) I can't face this problem on my own.* deal with, cope with, face up to, tackle, confront, meet head-on, brave, get to grips with, come to terms with.

---

faces and features

faces	complexions	
angular	ashen	pasty
babyish	black	peaches-
chubby	blotchy	and-cream
craggy	bronzed	pimply
flabby	brown	pitted
fleshy	clear	radiant
gaunt	coarse	rosy
haggard	dark	rough
heart-shaped	delicate	ruddy
long	dusky	sallow
oval	fair	scarred
pinched	florid	shiny
plump	flushed	sickly
podgy	freckled	smooth
round	fresh	spotty
square	glowing	stubbly
strong-jawed	greasy	swarthy
triangular	healthy	tanned
	ivory	unshaven
	oily	wan
	olive	white
	pale	wrinkled
	pallid	

heart-shaped face

stubbly complexion

haggard face

fact

1 (n) *The fact is that pigs can't fly.* truth, reality, naked truth, actuality, certainty. OPPOSITE: fiction.

2 *facts (plural n) Give me the facts.* details (plural), particulars (plural), information, data, whole story, lowdown (informal), info (informal), gen (informal).

factual

(adj) *Write a factual account of your holiday.* true, accurate, true-to-life, truthful, honest, faithful, authentic, realistic, matter-of-fact, exact, precise, objective, unbiased, unvarnished. OPPOSITES: fictional, imaginary.

fade

1 (v) *I hope my shirt doesn't fade in the wash.* lose colour, become pale, become bleached, become washed out, whiten.

2 (v) *Bright sunlight will fade the carpet.* bleach, discolour, dull, whiten.

3 (v) *The light began to fade.* die away, wane, dwindle, fail, diminish, weaken, grow faint, dim, disappear, vanish.

fail

1 (v) *I bet I'll fail in the exam.* be unsuccessful, not pass, not make the grade (informal), not come up to scratch (informal), come to grief, come a cropper (informal), flunk (informal).
OPPOSITES: succeed, pass.

2 (v) *Henry's plan is bound to fail.* fall through, be unsuccessful, fall flat, misfire, miscarry, come to nothing, be frustrated, founder, flop (informal), fizzle out.
OPPOSITES: succeed, prosper.

3 (v) *I hope the engine doesn't fail.* cut out, give out, stop working, break down, die, conk out (informal), cease to function.

4 (v) *Flash Frank is afraid his business will fail.* collapse, crash, go bankrupt, go under, go to the wall, close down, go out of business, fold (informal), flop (informal), go bust (informal), go broke (informal).
OPPOSITES: succeed, prosper, thrive.

5 (v) *Aunt Bertha's eyesight is starting to fail.* deteriorate, weaken, decline, get worse, degenerate, go.
OPPOSITES: improve, strengthen.

6 (v) *I won't fail you.* let you down, disappoint, abandon, desert, forsake.

failing *see* **weakness** 1.

failure

1 (n) *The match ended in failure.* defeat, disaster, disappointment, frustration.
OPPOSITE: success.

2 (n) *The play was a failure.* disaster, fiasco, flop (informal), catastrophe, nonstarter, washout (informal).
OPPOSITE: success.

3 (n) *Cyril thinks he's a failure.* loser, no-hoper (informal), ne'er-do-well, non-achiever, disappointment, incompetent.
OPPOSITE: success.

4 (n) *The storm caused a power failure.* cut, loss, breakdown, stoppage, outage.

faint

1 (v) *Simone will faint when she sees all this blood.* pass out, black out, lose consciousness, keel over (informal), collapse, swoon (old-fashioned).

2 (adj) *Anjali felt faint after her run.* dizzy, giddy, light-headed, muzzy, woozy (informal), unsteady, weak, exhausted.

3 (adj) *There's a faint pink glow in the sky.* pale, soft, delicate, hazy, misty, vague
OPPOSITES: bright, distinct.

4 (adj) *Sarah spoke in a faint voice.* weak, feeble, low, soft, scarcely audible, hushed, whispered, subdued, muffled, muted.
OPPOSITES: loud, clear

fair

1 (adj) *Jenny has fair hair. See* **blonde** 2.

2 (adj) *Mrs Badger may be strict, but she is always fair.* just, impartial, even-handed, fair-minded, unbiased, unprejudiced, objective, open-minded.
OPPOSITES: unfair, unjust.

3 (adj) *I hope the weather will be fair tomorrow.* fine, dry, clear, bright, sunny, cloudless, favourable, clement
OPPOSITE: foul.

4 (adj) *Your work is fair.* adequate, satisfactory, acceptable, passable, reasonable, respectable, decent, not bad, all right, pretty good, average, middling, mediocre, tolerable, so-so (informal).

5 (n) *We went on lots of rides at the fair. See* **funfair**.

6 (n) *The school fair was a success.* fête, bazaar, sale, gala, carnival, festival.

7 (n) *Our village is putting on a craft fair.* exhibition, show, display, exhibit.

fairly *see* **quite** 1.

fairy

(n) pixie, elf, sprite, imp, brownie, leprechaun. ❖ *Also see* **fantasy words**.

faithful

1 (adj) *A faithful friend.* loyal, devoted, true, reliable, dependable, trustworthy, trusty, constant, staunch, unwavering.
OPPOSITES: disloyal, faithless.

2 (adj) *Is this a faithful account of the accident? See* **true** 2.

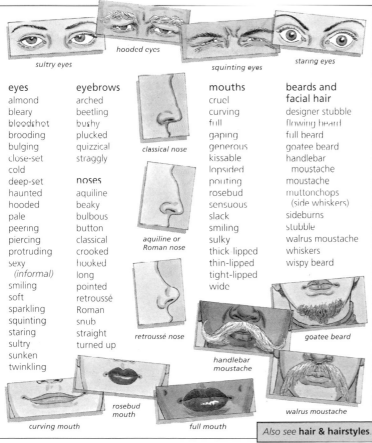

sultry eyes

hooded eyes

squinting eyes

staring eyes

eyes
almond
bleary
bloodshot
brooding
bulging
close-set
cold
deep-set
haunted
hooded
pale
peering
piercing
protruding
sexy
 (informal)
smiling
soft
sparkling
squinting
staring
sultry
sunken
twinkling

eyebrows
arched
beetling
bushy
plucked
quizzical
straggly

noses
aquiline
beaky
bulbous
button
classical
crooked
hooked
long
pointed
retroussé
Roman
snub
straight
turned up

classical nose

aquiline or Roman nose

retroussé nose

mouths
cruel
curving
full
gaping
generous
kissable
lopsided
pouting
rosebud
sensuous
slack
smiling
sulky
thick-lipped
thin-lipped
tight-lipped
wide

beards and facial hair
designer stubble
flowing beard
full beard
goatee beard
handlebar
 moustache
moustache
muttonchops
 (side whiskers)
sideburns
stubble
walrus moustache
whiskers
wispy beard

goatee beard

handlebar moustache

walrus moustache

rosebud mouth

curving mouth

full mouth

Also see **hair & hairstyles**.

fake

fake

1 *(n) This painting is a fake.* copy, forgery, imitation, reproduction, sham, counterfeit. OPPOSITE: original.
2 *(n) That man is a fake.* impostor, fraud *(informal)*, phoney *(informal)*, charlatan.
3 *(adj) Dodgy Dave deals in fake money.* counterfeit, forged, false, bogus, sham, phoney *(informal)*, imitation. OPPOSITES: genuine, authentic.
4 *(v) Carol tried to fake an attack of flu.* feign, put on, sham, simulate, counterfeit.

fall

1 *(v) Be careful you don't fall.* trip, slip, fall over, trip over, overbalance, stumble, go head over heels, come a cropper *(informal)*, tumble, collapse, fall in a heap.
2 *(v) The plane began to fall.* See **drop** 2.
3 *(v) Watch the leaves fall to the ground.* drift, float, waft, flutter, swirl, tumble.
4 *(v) The flood water started to fall.* sink, subside, recede, ebb, abate, lower. OPPOSITE: rise.
5 *(v) Pupil numbers are expected to fall.* See **decrease** 2.
6 *(n) Nat had a bad fall.* tumble, spill.
7 *(n) There has been a fall in the number of crimes* See **decrease** 1.
8 *(n) We're studying the fall of the Roman Empire.* See **collapse** 3.

fall apart *see* **disintegrate** 2.

fall asleep

(v) Gran tends to fall asleep in front of the TV. go to sleep, doze off, nod off *(informal)*, drop off *(informal)*. OPPOSITE: wake up.

fall in love with

(phrase) Could you ever fall in love with me? fall for, become fond of, lose your heart to, take a fancy to, become infatuated with, be smitten by, be bowled over by *(informal)*, become attached to.

fall out *(informal) see* **argue** 1.

fall over *see* **fall** 1.

fall through *see* **fail** 2.

false

1 *(adj) It's false to say that pigs can fly.* incorrect, untrue, wrong, inaccurate, mistaken, erroneous, misleading. OPPOSITES: true, correct.
2 *(adj) Dodgy Dave has a false passport.* See **fake** 3.
3 *(adj) Burglar Beryl uses a false name.* made-up, assumed, fictitious, invented, phoney *(informal)*, spurious, unreal. OPPOSITES: real, genuine.

familiar

1 *(adj) That's a familiar sight.* well-known, common, recognizable, everyday, normal, commonplace, routine, frequent, ordinary. OPPOSITES: unfamiliar, strange.
2 **familiar with** *(adj) Are you familiar with the rules of football?* acquainted with, knowledgeable about, conversant with, well up on, versed in, informed about.

family

1 *(n) Dad stayed at home to look after the family.* children *(plural)*, offspring, brood.
2 *(n) When did you last see your family?* relatives *(plural)*, relations *(plural)*, nearest and dearest, people *(plural)*, flesh and blood, kin, kith and kin.
3 *(n) Hugh comes from a noble family.* dynasty, clan, line, tribe, ancestors *(plural)*.

famous

(adj) A famous musician. well-known, world-famous, prominent, renowned, celebrated, legendary, notable, eminent, distinguished, leading, illustrious. OPPOSITES: unknown, obscure.

fan

1 *(n) Hanif is a computer fan.* fanatic, addict, enthusiast, buff *(informal)*, freak *(informal)*, fiend *(informal)*, nut *(slang)*.
2 *(n) Maisie is a fan of Famous Fred.* supporter, admirer, follower, groupie *(slang)*, devotee.

fanatical

1 *(adj) Sonia is a fanatical football supporter.* See **enthusiastic** 1.
2 *(adj) Dan holds fanatical views.* extreme, irrational, extremist, dogmatic, obsessive, radical, militant, bigoted, narrow-minded.

fancy

1 *(adj) A fancy vase.* See **decorative**.
2 *(v) I fancy a night out.* feel like, would like, could do with, feel the need for, want, long for, hanker after, yearn for.
3 *(v) (informal) Mel will really fancy you in that shirt.* go for, fall for, like the look of, be attracted to, take to, take a liking to, be captivated by, be crazy about *(informal)*, desire, lust after.

fantastic

1 *(adj) I saw a fantastic creature with two heads.* strange, peculiar, weird, odd, grotesque, outlandish, freakish, exotic, fabulous, fantastical, fairy-tale.
2 *(adj) (informal) I've put a fantastic amount of work into this project.* huge, enormous, massive, great, tremendous, terrific, overwhelming.
3 *(adj) (informal) I had a fantastic time.* great *(informal)*, wonderful, brilliant, excellent, terrific *(informal)*, marvellous, amazing *(informal)*, incredible *(informal)*, fabulous *(informal)*, superb, tremendous *(informal)*, smashing *(informal)*, sensational *(informal)*, mega *(slang)*, wicked *(slang)*. OPPOSITES: awful, terrible.

fantasy

1 *(n) I love reading tales of fantasy.* make-believe, imagination, invention, fiction.
2 *(n) It's just a fantasy; it isn't real.* dream, daydream, flight of fancy, figment of the imagination, illusion, hallucination, vision, delusion, apparition, invention, fabrication.
3 *(adj) Miranda lives in a fantasy world.* dream, imaginary, make-believe, pretend, unreal, fairy-tale.

fantasy words

fantasy characters
dwarf
elf
enchanter
enchantress
giant
gnome
goblin
healer
hobgoblin
king
knight
magician
maiden
mermaid
ogre
pixie
prince
princess
queen
seer (prophet)
sorcerer
sorceress
troll
warrior
witch
wizard
wood nymph

fantasy creatures
dragon
sea monster
serpent
unicorn
winged horse

wood nymph
ogre
unicorn
serpent
hobgoblin
dragon's lair

ENCHANTED FOREST

fantasy characters can be...

beautiful
bewitching
cruel
cunning
dazzling
enchanting
evil
fantastical
frightening
incredible
invisible
magical
malevolent
menacing
mesmerizing
monstrous
terrifying
unearthly
wonderful

sorcerers can...

bewitch
cast spells
change shape
enchant
enslave
entice
imprison
vanish

sorcerers use...

charms
curses
elixir
  (magic potion)
enchantment
incantations
  (magic spells)
magic ring
magic staff
sleeping potion
sorcery
spells
sword
talisman
  (lucky charm)
thunderbolt
wand

in the forest

creeper
dragon's lair
enchanted river
forest floor
glade (clearing)
magic stream
moss
path
poisoned pool
swamp
trailing ivy
undergrowth
vanishing lake
waterfall

heroes and heroines must...

accomplish a task
do battle
encounter danger
escape
go on a quest
outwit sorcerers
overcome evil
pursue
rescue
search
solve riddles
vanquish the enemy
withstand ordeals

the forest is...

ancient
bewitched
dank
dark
dense
gloomy
hushed
impenetrable
magical
misty
mysterious
shadowy
silent
strange
uninhabited

the trees are...

alive
decaying
gnarled
hostile
knotted
menacing
tangled
threatening
towering
twisted
watchful
wizened

fantasy clues

dream
inscription
legend
prophecy
revelation
riddle
runes
  (ancient
  writing)
sign
symbol
vision

SORCERER'S CASTLE

in the castle

battlements
dungeon
gatehouse
labyrinth
  (network of
  tunnels)
library
maze
moat
parapet
secret passage
spiral staircase
subterranean
  chamber
throne room
tower
treasure chamber
tunnel
turret
winding corridors

the castle is...

cloaked in mist
eerie
enchanted
forbidding
hidden
inaccessible
lonely
magnificent
menacing
mysterious
ominous

winged horse

sorcerer's castle

waterfall

elf

poisoned pool

troll

magic staff

sorcerer

sword

runes

pixie

talisman

Lizard Blood

Elixir of eternal life

magic potions

far

far
(adv) Have you travelled far? a long way, a great distance, a good way, miles.

faraway see **distant**.

far-fetched see **incredible** 1.

farm
(n) TYPES OF FARM: arable farm, croft (Scotland), dairy farm, fish farm, fruit farm, hill farm, hop garden, livestock farm, market garden, organic farm, pig farm, plantation (tropical countries), poultry farm, ranch (North America), sheep station (Australia, New Zealand), smallholding, stud farm (horse-breeding farm), vineyard.

farming
(n) agriculture.

fascinate
(v) This film will fascinate you. intrigue, enthral, engross, hold you spellbound, mesmerize, transfix, rivet, entrance, captivate, bewitch, tantalize.

fascinating
(adj) A fascinating story. intriguing, enthralling, compelling, gripping, riveting, engrossing, absorbing, spellbinding, mesmerizing, captivating, tantalizing.

fashion
1 (n) These new jeans are the latest fashion. style, trend, thing, look, cut, craze, fad, vogue, rage.
2 (n) Jake is interested in fashion. clothes (plural), clothes design, the rag trade (informal), the clothing industry, couture.

fashionable
(adj) Minty always wears fashionable clothes. the latest, up-to-date, trendy (informal), stylish, chic, smart, up-to-the-minute, modern, in, happening (informal), cool (informal), hip (slang).
OPPOSITES: unfashionable, frumpy.

fast
1 (adj) We had a fast tour of the castle. quick, rapid, swift, brisk, speedy, hasty, hurried, flying, breakneck.
OPPOSITES: slow, leisurely.
2 (adj) Flash Frank drives a fast car. speedy, nippy (informal), express (train), high-speed (train), supersonic (plane).
OPPOSITE: slow.
3 (adv) Rory finished his homework fast. quickly, rapidly, in no time, swiftly, speedily, hurriedly, hastily, in a flash, like a shot (informal), posthaste, pdq (slang).

fasten
1 (v) Fasten your bike to the railings. secure, attach, chain, lock, padlock, bolt, tie, lash, fix, clamp, screw.
OPPOSITES: unfasten, detach.
2 (v) Fasten these papers together. attach, secure, clip, clasp, staple, pin, tack, tie, bind, tape, fix, stick, paste.
OPPOSITES: unfasten, detach.
3 (v) Phil bent down to fasten his shoe. do up, tie, lace, knot, buckle, strap.
OPPOSITE: undo.

4 (v) My jeans won't fasten. close, button, zip up, meet.

fat
1 (adj) A fat man. overweight, obese, flabby, stout, large, corpulent, paunchy, portly, plump, podgy, pudgy, chubby, tubby, potbellied, beefy (informal).
OPPOSITE: thin.
2 (adj) A fat book. thick, weighty, bulky.
OPPOSITE: slim.

fatal
1 (adj) A fatal disease. deadly, lethal, terminal, killer, incurable, inoperable, malignant, mortal (wound).
OPPOSITES: harmless, minor.
2 (adj) The pilot made a fatal mistake. See **disastrous**.

fate
1 (n) Fate brought us together. destiny, providence, the stars (plural), fortune.
2 (n) Sir Lancelittle accepted his fate. destiny, doom, lot, future, end.

father
(n) dad (informal), daddy (informal), pop (informal), pa (informal), papa (informal), old man (informal), old boy (informal).

fatty
(adj) Chips are a fatty food. greasy, oily.

fault
1 (n) There's a fault in this computer program. flaw, defect, bug (informal), malfunction, mistake, error, inaccuracy, weakness, failing, shortcoming, snag.
2 (n) It's all my fault. responsibility.

faulty
(adj) Our new toaster is faulty. broken, not working, defective, out of order, inoperative, on the blink (informal), damaged, unusable, useless.

favourite
1 (adj) Who is your favourite singer? preferred, best-loved, most-liked, ideal.
2 (n) Benji is Mrs Badger's favourite. pet, darling, blue-eyed boy (informal).

fear
1 (n) Sir Lancelittle shrank back in fear. terror, dread, horror, fright, panic, trepidation, alarm, dismay, consternation, fear and trembling, awe.
2 (n) Paul has a fear of heights. horror, dread, terror, phobia about, thing about (informal), hang-up about (informal).
3 (n) My greatest fear is that I might fail. worry, concern, anxiety, doubt, suspicion.
4 (v) There's no need to fear going to the dentist. See **dread** 1.

fearless see **brave**.

feast
(n) banquet, dinner, slap-up meal (informal), spread (informal), nosh-up (slang), blowout (slang).

feat
(n) Crossing the rapids was an amazing feat. achievement, exploit, deed, act, stunt, accomplishment, performance.

feathers
(plural n) Birds' feathers. plumage, down.

feathery
(adj) The clouds looked feathery. wispy, fluffy, fleecy, downy.

feature
1 (n) Which feature of this book do you like best? aspect, detail, facet, side, characteristic, quality, attribute, point.
2 (n) Amit wrote a feature for the school magazine. See **article** 1.
3 (v) The film will feature an unknown actress. star, present, highlight, turn the spotlight on, give prominence to, promote.
4 **features** (plural n) Can you describe Beryl's features? See **face** 1.

fed up with
(adj) (informal) I'm fed up with your constant complaining. tired of, sick of (informal), sick and tired of (informal), weary of, bored with, browned off with (informal), cheesed off with (slang), hacked off with (slang), irritated by, irked by.

feeble
1 (adj) Hattie felt feeble after her illness. See **weak** 1.
2 (adj) Don't be so feeble! See **weak** 3.
3 (adj) That's a feeble excuse. weak, poor, lame, flimsy, unconvincing, implausible, pathetic, inadequate.
OPPOSITE: convincing.

feed
(v) It costs a lot to feed a family of four. provide for, cater for, give food to, nourish, sustain.

feel
1 (v) Feel the kitten's fur! touch, stroke, run your hands over, fondle, caress, handle, finger, paw (informal).
2 (v) You won't feel any pain. sense, be aware of, be conscious of, notice, perceive, experience, suffer, go through, undergo.
3 (v) Do my hands feel cold? seem, appear, strike you as.
4 (v) Dom tried to feel for the light switch. fumble, grope, feel around, explore.
5 (v) What do you feel about fox-hunting? See **think** 1.
6 **feel like** (v) I feel like a night out. See **fancy** 2.

feeling
1 (n) Veronica lost all feeling in her fingers. sensation, sense of touch, sensitivity, awareness.
2 (n) I have a feeling I've been here before. idea, funny feeling, hunch, notion, gut feeling (informal), suspicion, sneaking suspicion, inkling, sense, impression.
3 (n) Celia spoke with great feeling. emotion, passion, fervour, warmth, enthusiasm, sentiment, affection.
4 (n) There's a strange feeling in this room. See **atmosphere** 2.
5 **feelings** (plural n) It hurts my feelings when people laugh at me. self-esteem, ego, sensibilities (plural).

feelings

happy	sad	excited	annoyed	upset	surprised	worried
blissful	blue	eager	cross	dismayed	amazed	agitated
cheerful	dejected	enthusiastic	disgruntled	distraught	astonished	anxious
chirpy *(informal)*	depressed	feverish	exasperated	distressed	astounded	apprehensive
contented	despairing	frenzied	indignant	disturbed	dumbfounded	concerned
delighted	despondent	high *(informal)*	irritated	grieved	dumbstruck	distracted
ecstatic	doleful	hyper *(informal)*	miffed *(informal)*	hurt	flabbergasted	frantic
elated	down	hysterical	needled	pained	*(informal)*	fretful
euphoric	forlorn	overwrought	*(informal)*	shaken	gobsmacked	nervous
glad	gloomy	restless	vexed	shattered	*(slang)*	on edge
gleeful	glum	thrilled			incredulous	perturbed
jolly	grief-stricken	worked up	**angry**	**scared**	open-mouthed	tense
joyful	heartbroken		enraged	afraid	shocked	troubled
jubilant	low	**bored**	fuming	alarmed	speechless	uneasy
light-hearted	melancholy	apathetic	furious	frightened	staggered	
optimistic	miserable	fed up	incensed	horrified	startled	**confused**
overjoyed	mournful	*(informal)*	infuriated	panicky	stunned	baffled
perky	sorrowful	indifferent	irate	panic-stricken	stupefied	bewildered
pleased	tearful	jaded	livid	petrified	taken aback	dazed
rapturous	unhappy	listless	outraged	terrified	thunderstruck	disorientated
thrilled	wistful	weary	seething			fazed
						flummoxed
						flustered
						muddled
						mystified
						nonplussed
						perplexed
						puzzled

jubilant   *despondent*   *listless*   *livid*   *petrified*   *perplexed*

---

ferocious *see* **fierce** 1, 2.

fertile
(adj) A fertile field. fruitful, productive, rich, lush, well-manured, flourishing.
OPPOSITE: barren.

festival
(n) Our town is planning a festival to mark the end of the war. celebration, carnival, festivities *(plural)*, jamboree, fête, gala day, feast, holiday, jubilee, commemoration.

fetch
1 *(v) Would you fetch Dad's suit from the cleaner's?* go and get, get, collect, pick up, call for, go for, bring, carry, retrieve.
2 *(v) This painting will fetch a fortune.* sell for, go for, bring in, make, yield, earn.

feud *see* **quarrel** 3.

feverish
1 *(adj) You seem feverish; have you got a temperature?* hot, flushed, fevered, burning, shivery, trembling.
2 *(adj) The classroom was filled with feverish activity.* frenzied, frenetic, frantic, hectic, excited, agitated, restless.

few
(adj) Few people have walked on the moon. not many, hardly any, scarcely any, one or two, a handful of, a small number of, a couple of *(informal)*.
OPPOSITES: many, lots of.

fiasco *see* **failure** 2.

fictional *see* **imaginary** 1.

fiddle with
(v) Don't fiddle with your pencil case! fidget with, play with, toy with, finger, tinker with, tamper with, interfere with.

fidget
(v) Sit still and don't fidget! wriggle, squirm, jiggle, fiddle, jerk about, twitch, jitter *(informal)*, mess about.

fidgety
(adj) Waiting makes me fidgety. restless, nervous, nervy, on edge, edgy, jumpy, twitchy, jittery *(informal)*, uneasy, impatient, agitated, restive.

field
1 *(n) The cows are grazing in the field.* meadow, pasture, paddock, enclosure.
2 *(n) The players gathered on the sports field.* pitch, playing field, ground, arena.
3 *(n) Professor Peabody is an expert in the field of physics.* area, subject, sphere, discipline, department, domain.

fierce
1 *(adj) A fierce tiger.* ferocious, vicious, savage, wild, dangerous, fearsome, angry.
OPPOSITES: docile, tame.
2 *(adj) A fierce warrior.* ferocious, brutal, savage, violent, fearsome, cruel, ruthless, grim, bloodthirsty, menacing, threatening, barbaric, murderous, tigerish, wolfish.
OPPOSITES: gentle, kind.

3 *(adj) A fierce storm. See* **violent** 3.
4 *(adj) Fierce competition.* strong, intense, keen, cutthroat, relentless, furious.

fiery
1 *(adj) Fiery coals. See* **burning** 1
2 *(adj) A fiery personality.* hot-headed, passionate, impetuous, excitable, irritable, irascible, peppery, choleric, violent.
OPPOSITES: even-tempered, docile.

fight
1 *(v) The two armies prepared to fight.* do battle, take up arms, go to war, wage war, attack, mount an attack, cross swords, engage in hostilities, clash, struggle.
2 *(v) The boys began to fight in the playground.* brawl, scuffle, tussle, scrap *(informal)*, grapple, spar, wrestle, box.
3 *(v) We fight all the time. See* **argue** 1.
4 *(v) We will fight the decision to close our school.* oppose, contest, resist, campaign against, protest against, take a stand against, dispute, defy, object to.
5 *(n) Many soldiers were wounded in the fight.* conflict, battle, skirmish, encounter, confrontation, struggle, clash, combat, action, raid, war, hostilities *(plural)*.
6 *(n) There was a fight in the playground.* brawl, scuffle, tussle, punch-up *(informal)*, scrap *(informal)*, bust-up *(informal)*, set-to *(informal)*, free-for-all *(informal)*, riot.
7 *(n) I've had a fight with my sister. See* **argument** 1.

f

fight back

fight back
(v) *Should you fight back if someone punches you?* defend yourself, hit back, put up a fight, retaliate, give tit for tat.

figure
1 (n) *Our phone number starts with the figure 8.* number, digit, numeral, symbol.
2 (n) *Sasha has a slim figure.* build, frame, shape, physique, body.
3 (n) *I saw a dim figure in the mist.* shape, shadow, form, outline, silhouette.
4 (n) *Queen Victoria is a famous historical figure.* personality, character, person, personage, celebrity.

figure out
1 (v) (informal) *Can you figure out the cost?* work out, calculate, count up, add up, tot up, compute, reckon up.
2 (v) (informal) *I can't figure out these instructions.* See **understand** 2.

fill
1 (v) *Don't fill your bag with rubbish.* pack, stuff, cram, load, overload.
OPPOSITE: empty.
2 (v) *Can I fill your glass?* fill up, fill to the brim, replenish, refill, top up (informal).
OPPOSITES: empty, drain.
3 (v) *Fill the hole with earth.* close up, block up, bung up, plug, stop up, seal.
4 (v) *The scent of roses seemed to fill the air.* pervade, permeate, suffuse, saturate.

fill in
1 (v) *Please fill in this questionnaire.* complete, answer, fill out.
2 **fill in for** (v) *Can you fill in for James while he's ill?* See **stand in for**.
3 **fill you in on** (phrase) (informal) *Can I fill you in on what's happened?* update you on, bring you up to date with, give you the facts about, brief you about, inform you about, acquaint you with.

filling
(adj) *A filling meal.* satisfying, substantial, hearty, ample, heavy, stodgy, square.

film
1 (v) *A camera crew are going to film the wedding.* record on film, capture on film, photograph, take pictures of, make a film of, video, televise, shoot.
2 (n) *This book has been made into a film.* motion picture, movie (informal), picture.
TYPES OF FILM: action film, adventure film, animated film, black-and-white film, blockbuster, cartoon, comedy, detective film, disaster film, drama, epic, fantasy film, feature film, gangster film, horror film, martial arts film, musical, romantic film, sci-fi (science fiction) film, silent film, spoof (informal), 3-D film, thriller, war film, weepy (informal), Western. ❖ Also see **television & film**.
3 (n) *A film of dust.* See **layer** 1.

filthy see **dirty** 1, 2.

final
1 (adj) *The final episode.* See **last** 1.

2 (adj) *The referee's decision is final.* absolute, conclusive, decisive, indisputable, unalterable, irrevocable, definitive, definite.

finally
1 (adv) *Finally, the bus arrived.* eventually, at last, at long last, at length, at the last minute, in the end, ultimately.
2 (adv) *Finally, I'd like to thank you all for coming.* lastly, in conclusion, to conclude, to sum up, in summary.

find
1 (v) *Pirate Peg was lucky to find the treasure.* discover, come across, stumble upon, hit upon, spot, catch sight of, locate, uncover, unearth, turn up, chance upon.
2 (v) *Did you manage to find your pencil case?* locate, track down, trace, get back, recover, retrieve, regain.
OPPOSITES: lose, mislay.

find out see **discover** 1, 3.

fine
1 (adj) *That's a fine painting.* great, magnificent, splendid, superb, excellent, first-class, exceptional, outstanding, exquisite, beautiful, admirable, masterly, superior.
OPPOSITES: poor, second-rate.
2 (adj) *It's fine for you to come on Saturday.* all right, O.K. (informal), convenient, acceptable, satisfactory.
3 (adj) *The weather will be fine tomorrow.* dry, bright, sunny, fair, pleasant, clear, cloudless, clement.
OPPOSITES: bad, unpleasant.
4 (adj) *A fine crack appeared in the wall.* thin, narrow, hairline, threadlike.
OPPOSITES: wide, thick.
5 (adj) *The bride wore a veil of fine silk.* delicate, sheer, thin, lightweight, light, flimsy, floaty, translucent, transparent, gauzy, gossamer, chiffony, filmy, cobwebby, diaphanous.
OPPOSITES: heavy, thick.
6 (adj) *Granny collects fine china.* dainty, delicate, exquisite, elegant, fragile.
OPPOSITE: coarse.
7 (n) *Mum had to pay a fine for speeding.* penalty, charge.

finish
1 (v) *You must finish your project today.* complete, finalize, conclude, get done, round off, put the finishing touches to, bring to a close, end, wind up, wrap up (informal), sew up (informal).
OPPOSITES: start, begin.
2 (v) *When does school finish for the summer?* See **end** 6.
3 (v) *How quickly can you finish your dinner?* eat up, get through, polish off (informal), dispose of, consume, devour.
4 (n) *We waited to see the finish of the match.* See **end** 1.

finished
(adj) *I'm glad that job is finally finished.* completed, done, accomplished, wrapped up (informal), sewn up (informal), ended, over and done with, in the past.

fire
1 (n) *The fire could be seen for miles around.* blaze, flames (plural), inferno, conflagration.
2 (n) *The troops came under heavy fire.* gunfire, shelling, bombardment, sniping.
3 (v) *Watch the soldiers fire the rocket.* launch, let off, set off, trigger, discharge.
4 (v) (informal) *I hope the boss doesn't fire you.* See **dismiss** 1.
5 **on fire** (phrase) *Look! The forest is on fire!* blazing, burning, in flames, flaming, alight, ablaze, aflame.

fire words

fires...
blaze
burn
consume
damage
destroy
devastate
devour
dwindle
engulf
glow
grow
ignite
kindle
rage
rampage
ravage
raze to the ground
scorch
singe
smoke
smoulder
sweep

flames...
dance
dart
flash
flare
flicker
gleam
glitter
glow
leap
lick
play
shimmer

smoke...
belches
billows
blinds
chokes
coils
curls
envelops
obscures
spirals
suffocates
swirls
twists
wreathes

smoke smells...
acrid
bitter
pungent
sooty

you hear...
crack
crackle
hiss
murmur
pop
roar
rustle
snap
whisper

after the fire you see...
ashes
blackened walls
blistered paint
buckled iron
charred wood
debris
embers
gutted buildings
rubble
scorched earth
smouldering ruins

fireworks

types of firework

banger
cascade
Catherine wheel
firecracker
fountain
rocket
Roman candle
shooting star
sparkler

fireworks...

blaze
burst
cascade
dazzle
explode
fizzle out
flare
flash
flicker
glitter
rocket

shimmer
shoot
shower
sink
soar
sparkle
spin
spiral
spray
twirl
zoom

fireworks can be...

colourful
dazzling
deafening
ear-splitting
magical
multicoloured
spectacular
stunning
(informal)

you hear...

bang
crack
crackle
fizz
hiss
pop
scream
screech
splutter
squeal
thud
wail
whine
whistle
whiz
whoosh

firm

1 *(adj) The ground felt firm underfoot.* hard, solid, unyielding, resistant, rigid, compacted, compressed, frozen, stony.
OPPOSITE: soft.
2 *(adj) Make sure the ladder is firm.* steady, stable, secure, fixed, anchored, fastened, immovable, unshakable.
OPPOSITES: unsteady, wobbly.
3 *(adj) Do you have any firm plans for the future?* definite, fixed, settled, established, unalterable, unchangeable, inflexible.
OPPOSITES: vague, flexible.
4 *(adj) Ed and I are firm friends.* See **loyal**.
5 *(adj) Jess is firm in her ideas about animal rights.* adamant, resolute, inflexible, unbending, obstinate, unshakable, unfaltering, unwavering, unswerving.
OPPOSITES: wavering, irresolute.
6 *(n) Mum works for a big electronics firm.* company, business, organization, concern, corporation, conglomerate, multinational, outfit *(informal)*.

first

1 *(adj) The first computers seem very basic now.* earliest, original, initial, primitive.
OPPOSITE: latest.
2 *(adj) Read the first chapter for homework.* opening, introductory, initial.
OPPOSITES: last, closing.
3 *(adj) United play in the first division.* top, premier, highest, foremost, leading, main.
OPPOSITES: lowest, bottom.
4 *(adj) Rudi has mastered the first steps in ballet.* basic, elementary, rudimentary, primary, fundamental, key, cardinal.
5 *(adv) First, think of a title for your story.* firstly, first of all, to start with, to begin with, before anything else, in the first place, at the outset, beforehand.
OPPOSITES: last, lastly.

fish

(n) TYPES OF FISH: angelfish, brill, carp, catfish, clown fish, cod, eel, flounder, flying fish, goldfish, guppy, haddock, hake, halibut, herring, lamprey, mackerel, minnow, mullet, perch, pike, pilchard, piranha, plaice, ray, roach, salmon, sardine, sea horse, shark, skate, sole, sprat, stickleback, sturgeon, swordfish, tiddler *(informal)*, trout, tuna, whitebait, whiting.

fishy *(informal) see* **suspicious** 2.

fit

1 *(v) Do you think these jeans will fit?* be the right size, be big enough, be small enough, be the right shape.
2 *(v) Fit the parts of the puzzle together.* piece, put, join, connect, fix, place, lay, position, arrange.
3 *(v) The punishment should fit the crime.* suit, correspond to, match, be fitting for.
4 *(adj) Swimming keeps me fit.* healthy, in shape, in good shape, in good condition, in trim, toned up, strong, in good health.
OPPOSITES: unfit, out of shape.
5 *(adj) This video isn't fit for children.* See **suitable** 1.
6 *(n) Fido had a fit and died.* seizure, convulsion, attack, turn *(informal)*.
7 *(n) Den had a fit of coughing.* attack, bout, spell, outbreak, outburst.

fix

1 *(v) I need to fix my bike.* See **repair** 1.
2 *(v) Did you fix a date for the party?* agree on, decide on, set, settle, arrange, arrive at, establish, name, specify.
3 *(v) Fix the pieces together.* attach, join, link, fasten, connect, secure, stick, glue, paste, pin, nail, screw, bolt, tie, cement.
4 *(v) I must fix my hair.* tidy, neaten, arrange, see to, sort out, put in order.

5 *(v) (informal) The goalie tried to fix the result of the match.* rig, fiddle *(informal)*, manipulate, influence, set up *(informal)*.

fixed

1 *(adj) We have our meals at fixed times.* See **set** 7.
2 *(adj) Ed has very fixed views.* See **set** 8.
3 *(adj) Is my bike fixed yet?* mended, repaired, sorted, in working order, going.

fizzy

(adj) A fizzy drink. sparkling, bubbly, gassy, carbonated, effervescent, frothy, foaming.
OPPOSITES: still, flat.

flabby

(adj) Flabby thighs. flaccid, slack, fleshy, sagging, soft, unfirm, out of shape.

flag

(n) banner, standard, pennant, ensign.

flake

1 *(n) A flake of paint peeled off.* chip, sliver, shaving, peeling, wafer, fragment.
2 *(v) This paint is beginning to flake.* peel, peel off, blister, chip, fall off.

flame

(n) A flame of fire. tongue, flicker, blaze.

flaming *see* **burning** 1.

flap

1 *(v) Watch the bird flap its wings.* beat, flutter, flail, thrash, waggle, shake.
2 *(v) The sail began to flap in the breeze.* flutter, sway, wave, swish, swing, thrash about, flail about, whip around.
3 *(n) (informal) The chef was in a flap.* panic, state *(informal)*, tizzy *(informal)*, fluster, flutter, stew *(informal)*, sweat *(informal)*, dither.

flash

1 *(n) A flash of light lit up the sky.* blaze, flare, burst, streak, shaft, ray, glare, glint, gleam, flicker, sparkle, shimmer, glimmer.
2 *(n) Mehmet had a flash of inspiration.* burst, rush, surge, touch, sudden show.
3 *(v) I saw a light flash on the horizon.* flicker, flare, wink, blink, blaze, beam, gleam, glint, sparkle, twinkle, shimmer.
4 *(v) I saw a car flash past.* See **shoot** 3.

flashy *see* **vulgar** 2.

flat

1 *(adj) Find a flat surface to work on.* level, horizontal, even, smooth.
OPPOSITES: uneven, sloping, vertical.
2 *(adj) Oz lay flat on the ground.* stretched out, full length, prostrate, outstretched, prone, spread-eagled, reclining.
3 *(adj) You can't cycle with a flat tyre.* deflated, burst, punctured, blown out.
4 *(adj) After the show, the actors felt flat.* deflated, let down, low, down, dejected, despondent, depressed, dispirited.
OPPOSITES: high *(informal)*, elated.
5 *(adj) Cyril has a flat voice.* monotonous, boring, lifeless, unvarying, dull, lacklustre.
6 *(n) We live in a flat on the fifth floor.* apartment, bedsit, studio, penthouse, set of rooms, rooms *(plural)*, pad *(slang)*.

flatten

1 *(v) Please flatten this cloth.* smooth out, make flat, level, iron out, even out, press.
2 *(v) Someone should flatten those tower blocks. See* **demolish**.
3 *(v) Don't flatten the roses.* trample, squash, crush, compress, press down.

flatter

1 *(v) I always flatter you when I want something.* compliment, butter you up, praise, cajole, soft-soap *(informal)*, sweet-talk *(informal)*, play up to, suck up to *(informal)*, toady to, fawn on.
2 *(v) Those jeans really flatter your figure.* suit, set off, enhance, do something for, show to advantage.

flavour

1 *(v) You need to flavour this soup.* season, spice, ginger up, pep up.
2 *(n) This soup needs more flavour.* taste, zest, zing *(informal)*, seasoning, flavouring, savour, relish, piquancy.

flawless *see* **perfect** 1, 2.

fleck *see* **speck** 1.

flexible

1 *(adj) This rod is quite flexible.* pliable, bendy, supple, springy, pliant.
OPPOSITE: rigid.
2 *(adj) Our plans must be flexible.* open, fluid, adaptable, adjustable, elastic.
OPPOSITES: fixed, settled.
3 *(adj) Karen won't mind; she's very flexible.* adaptable, accommodating, amenable, open-minded, compliant.
OPPOSITE: inflexible.

flicker

(v) The flame began to flicker. blink, gutter, tremble, quiver, waver, glimmer, shimmer, flutter, glitter, sparkle, flash.

flimsy

1 *(adj) A flimsy chair.* weak, insubstantial, fragile, rickety, shaky, tottery, jerry-built.
OPPOSITES: sturdy, strong.
2 *(adj) Flimsy fabric. See* **fine** 5.
3 *(adj) A flimsy excuse. See* **feeble** 3.

flinch

(v) I always flinch at the sight of a needle. cringe, wince, draw back, recoil, cower, quail, shrink, baulk, shy away, start, jump.

fling *see* **throw** 1.

flippant

(adj) Don't make flippant remarks. cheeky, impertinent, glib, pert, offhand, frivolous, flip *(informal)*, disrespectful, irreverent.
OPPOSITES: serious, respectful.

flirt with

(v) Did Lydia flirt with you at the party? tease, chat you up *(informal)*, make eyes at, lead you on, make advances to, ogle.

float

1 *(v) The bottle started to float down the stream.* sail, drift, glide, slip, bob, swim.
2 *(v) I watched the balloon float through the air.* waft, sail, glide, drift, hover.

flood

1 *(v) I hope the river doesn't flood.* overflow, burst its banks, brim over.
2 *(v) The river may flood the valley.* engulf, swamp, submerge, drown, deluge, immerse, cover, fill.
3 *(v) I'll try not to flood you with letters.* swamp, overwhelm, inundate, deluge, shower, bog you down, snow you under.
4 *(n) Our village was cut off by the flood.* torrent, deluge, tide, flood water.
5 *(n) We received a flood of complaints.* torrent, stream, deluge, rush, mass, spate.

floor

(n) Our flat is on the second floor. storey, level, landing.

flop

1 *(v) Don't let your hood flop over your face.* fall, droop, hang, sag, dangle, flap, drop, collapse, slump, tumble, topple.
2 *(n) (informal) The play was a flop. See* **failure** 2.

floppy

(adj) Fido has floppy ears. droopy, sagging, dangling, limp, pendulous, flapping, soft, loose, flaccid, flabby.

flow

1 *(v) Watch the water flow over the rocks.* glide, stream, gush, rush, surge, pour, run, swirl, spill, cascade, sweep, course, trickle, ripple, drift, spurt, seep, ooze, leak.
2 *(v) Complaints have started to flow in.* flood, pour, stream, trickle.
3 *(n) There was a steady flow of water from the roof.* stream, cascade, flood, torrent, spurt, gush, surge, trickle, leak.

flower

1 *(n) What's your favourite flower?* bloom, blossom, plant.
TYPES OF FLOWER: bluebell, buttercup, carnation, chrysanthemum, cowslip, crocus, cyclamen, daffodil, dahlia, daisy, dandelion, forget-me-not, foxglove, freesia, geranium, hollyhock, hyacinth, iris, lily, lupin, marigold, nasturtium, orchid, pansy, passionflower, poppy, primrose, rose, snowdrop, sunflower, sweet pea, tulip, violet, wallflower, water lily.
2 *(v) Our tree will flower soon.* blossom, bloom, be in flower, produce flowers, burst into bloom.

flowing

(adj) A flowing robe. loose, swirling, floating, sweeping, trailing, cascading.

fluent

(adj) Max is a fluent public speaker. articulate, eloquent, polished, confident, natural, self-assured, glib, smooth-talking.
OPPOSITES: tongue-tied, hesitant.

fluffy

(adj) Fluffy baby animals. furry, fuzzy, woolly, fleecy, downy, feathery, soft.

fluid *see* **liquid** 1, 2.

fluke *see* **chance** 1, 5.

flushed

(adj) You look flushed. red, crimson, hot, red in the face, hot and bothered, feverish, flustered, burning, glowing, rosy.

flustered

(adj) All this attention makes me feel flustered. agitated, hot and bothered, disconcerted, rattled *(informal)*, ruffled, confused, fazed, unnerved, upset.

flutter *see* **flap** 1, 2, 3.

fly

1 *(v) Watch those birds fly!* soar, swoop, glide, flit, hover, circle, sail, coast, flutter, take to the air, take wing, take off.
2 *(v) See how the flags fly in the breeze.* flutter, wave, flap, swirl, stream, float.
3 *(v) The time seemed to fly by.* rush, race, whiz *(informal)*, zoom, hurtle, slip, roll.
4 *(v) Elliot is learning to fly a plane.* pilot, operate, control, navigate.
5 *(v) I must fly or I'll be late! See* **hurry** 1.

foam

1 *(n) The bowl was full of foam.* bubbles *(plural)*, froth, suds *(plural)*, lather, scum.
2 *(n) Fill the cushion with foam.* sponge.
3 *(v) The potion began to foam.* bubble, froth, fizz, effervesce, seethe, lather.

foggy

(adj) A foggy night. misty, smoggy, murky, hazy, cloudy, shadowy, soupy.

fold

1 *(v) Fold the cloth.* double over, turn over, bend, crease, pleat, tuck, gather.
2 *(n) There's a fold in this material.* pleat, gather, tuck, crease, wrinkle, crinkle.

follow

1 *(v) The detectives decided to follow Burglar Beryl.* pursue, go after, tail, trail, shadow, stalk, chase, track, hunt, hound.
2 *(v) Who will follow Lisa as captain?* come after, go after, succeed, take over from, take the place of, replace, supplant, supersede, step into the shoes of.
3 *(v) Follow these instructions.* obey, observe, pay attention to, comply with, be guided by, attend to, keep to, heed.
4 *(v) The lecture was hard to follow.* understand, keep up with, take in, comprehend, grasp, catch on to *(informal)*.

follower *see* **fan** 2.

fond

1 *(adj) A fond mother. See* **loving**.
2 *fond of (adj) Efra is fond of her boyfriend.* attached to, keen on, devoted to, in love with, stuck on *(slang)*, crazy about *(informal)*, mad about, besotted by.
3 *fond of (adj) Gus is fond of sweets.* keen on, partial to, crazy about *(informal)*, mad about, hooked on, addicted to.

food

(n) I need food. nourishment, sustenance, refreshment, provisions *(plural)*, rations *(plural)*, grub *(informal)*, nosh *(informal)*, tuck *(informal)*, victuals *(plural)*, fodder.

food and flavours

nice food is...	food can be...	food can feel...	food can taste...
appetizing	burnt	chewy	acid
delicious	charred	creamy	bitter
luscious	dry	crisp	bland
moreish	fatty	crumbly	fiery
(informal)	filling	crunchy	fruity
mouthwatering	fresh	glutinous	hot
scrumptious	healthy	(gluey)	insipid
(informal)	indigestible	gooey	(tasteless)
tasty	juicy	(informal)	peppery
yummy (slang)	lukewarm	greasy	salty
	mouldy	leathery	savoury
nasty food is...	nourishing	lumpy	sharp
disgusting	piping hot	mushy	sickly
foul	raw	oily	sour
inedible	rich	rubbery	spicy
nauseating	satisfying	runny	sugary
revolting	scalding	slimy	sweet
unappetizing	sizzling	sloppy	syrupy
vile	stale	smooth	tangy
yucky (slang)	steaming	soggy	tart
	stodgy	spongy	vinegary
	succulent	squashy	
	tepid	squidgy	
	undercooked	sticky	
	unhealthy	stringy	
	unsatisfying	tender	
	well-cooked	tough	
	wholesome	wobbly	

juicy grapes

gooey gateau

sticky jam tart

squidgy pizza

crisp lettuce

crunchy carrots

---

fool
1 (v) You can't fool me. See **deceive** 1.
2 (n) Dwayne's such a fool! See **idiot**.

fool around
(v) (informal) Don't fool around in class. clown around, act the fool, mess about (informal), lark about (informal), muck about (slang), waste time.

foolish see **silly** 1, 2.

forbid
(v) I love skating; please don't forbid it! ban, prohibit, rule out, veto, block.
OPPOSITES: allow, permit.

forbidden
(adj) Smoking is forbidden. not allowed, banned, prohibited, outlawed, taboo.
OPPOSITES: permitted, allowed.

force
1 (v) If you don't want to go, I won't force you. make, compel, pressurize, push, coerce, oblige, bring pressure to bear on, put the squeeze on (informal), dragoon.
2 (v) We had to force the lock. prise open, break open, wrench open, smash.
3 (n) You'll need lots of force to open this door. See **strength** 1.

foreign
1 (adj) Indy often travels to foreign lands. remote, distant, exotic, faraway, far-flung, unfamiliar, unknown, strange, alien.
OPPOSITE: native.
2 (adj) We have some foreign visitors. overseas, international.

foresee see **predict**.

forever see **always** 1, 2.

forgery see **fake** 1.

forget
1 (v) How could you forget my birthday? fail to remember, overlook, be oblivious to, lose track of, neglect, ignore.
OPPOSITE: remember.
2 (v) Try to forget this unfortunate incident. put out of your mind, pay no attention to, dismiss, discount, disregard.
OPPOSITES: remember, recall.
3 (v) Don't forget your lunch. go without, leave behind, fail to take, abandon.
OPPOSITE: remember.

forgetful
(adj) Professor Peabody is so forgetful! absent-minded, scatterbrained, vague, abstracted, dreamy, inattentive.

forgive
(v) I will forgive you for what you did. pardon, excuse, let you off, accept your apologies, exonerate, absolve.

forgiveness
(n) I need your forgiveness. pardon, mercy.

forlorn see **sad** 1.

form
1 (n) What form of music do you like? kind, type, sort, style, variety, manner.
2 (n) The enchanter took on the form of a serpent. See **shape** 3.
3 (n) What form are you in at school? See **class**.
4 (n) Please fill in this form. document, paper, sheet, questionnaire, application.
5 (n) I hope Linford is in good form. condition, shape, health, spirits (plural).
6 (v) It takes centuries for stalactites to form. develop, take shape, grow, come into existence, appear, materialize.
7 (v) Let's form a computer club. create, establish, set up, start, found, organize.

formal
1 (adj) The banquet will be a formal affair. dignified, stately, ceremonial, solemn, correct, proper, posh (informal), stiff.
OPPOSITES: informal, casual.
2 (adj) Please wear formal clothes. smart, dressed-up (informal), posh (informal), proper, correct, conventional.
OPPOSITE: casual.
3 (adj) You'll need formal permission to emigrate. official, lawful, proper, legal.

fortunate see **lucky** 1, 2.

fortune
1 (n) Lord Lucre's fortune is phenomenal. wealth, riches (plural), possessions (plural), assets (plural), inheritance, estate.
2 (n) Giles has won a fortune. huge amount, pile (informal), packet (informal), bundle (informal), millions (plural).
3 (n) We found the house by good fortune. See **luck** 1.

foul
1 (adj) A foul heap of rubbish. filthy, squalid, disgusting, revolting, nauseating, loathsome, repulsive, rotten, putrid, stinking, vile, sordid, grotty (slang).
2 (adj) Foul language. indecent, obscene, profane, blasphemous, filthy, offensive, smutty, lewd, crude, coarse, vulgar.
OPPOSITES: polite, decent, clean.
3 (adj) A foul crime. vile, horrible, monstrous, shocking, revolting, odious, sordid, despicable, contemptible, detestable, atrocious, abominable, wicked, villainous, evil, heinous, infamous.
4 (adj) Foul weather. rough, dirty, stormy, squally, rainy, foggy, drizzly, murky.
OPPOSITES: fair, fine.
5 (adj) Callum was sent off for foul play. unfair, rough, dirty, unsporting, violent, sneaky, unscrupulous, prohibited, illegal.
OPPOSITE: fair.

fragile

fragile
(adj) Fragile china. delicate, breakable, brittle, thin, weak, flimsy, insubstantial, frail, dainty.
OPPOSITES: strong, durable.

fragment *see* **piece** 2, 3.

frail
(adj) A frail old lady. delicate, weak, feeble, infirm, unsteady, vulnerable, puny.
OPPOSITES: strong, robust.

frank
(adj) A frank answer. plain, straight, direct, candid, forthright, honest, truthful, blunt, no-nonsense, upfront *(informal)*, sincere, open, outspoken, unreserved.
OPPOSITES: evasive, insincere.

frantic
1 *(adj) You'll be frantic when you hear the news.* beside yourself, at your wits' end, desperate, panic-stricken, distraught, hysterical, overwrought, worked up.
OPPOSITE: calm.
2 *(adj) The classroom was filled with frantic activity. See* **feverish** 2.

fraud
1 *(n) Dodgy Dave was sentenced for fraud.* swindling, cheating, deception, sharp practice, double-dealing, embezzlement, trickery, chicanery.
2 *(n) (informal) That man is a fraud.* impostor, phoney *(informal)*, fake, cheat, hoaxer, con man *(informal)*, swindler, double-dealer, charlatan, quack *(doctor)*.

freak
1 *(adj) Freak weather. See* **unusual** 1.
2 *(n) (informal) Nathan is a computer freak. See* **fan** 1.

free
1 *(adj) I'd like to go out tonight. Are you free?* available, uncommitted, footloose, fancy-free, off the leash *(informal)*, off the hook *(informal)*, at liberty.
OPPOSITES: busy, tied up.
2 *(adj) The prisoners longed to be free.* released, set free, set loose, unconfined, at liberty, unrestrained, on the loose.
OPPOSITES: imprisoned, confined.
3 *(adj) Is this seat free?* vacant, empty, unoccupied, unused, spare, available.
OPPOSITES: occupied, reserved, engaged.
4 *(adj) These tickets are free.* free of charge, complimentary, cost-free, gratis, on the house.
5 *(v) Let's campaign to free the hostages. See* **release** 1.
6 *(v) The judge decided to free Burglar Beryl. See* **release** 2.
7 *(v) Can you free the boot from your fishing line?* untangle, untie, extricate, undo, disentangle, disengage, clear.

freedom
(n) Pandora's parents allow her lots of freedom. independence, liberty, autonomy, leeway, licence, latitude, personal space, privileges *(plural)*.

freeze
1 *(v) I think the pond will freeze tonight.* ice up, ice over, go solid, harden, solidify.
2 *(v) Don't go outside; you'll freeze!* die of cold *(informal)*, be chilled to the bone, perish *(informal)*, go numb.
3 *(v) "Freeze, or I'll shoot!" said Arnie.* keep still, stay where you are, stand still, don't move a muscle, stand stock-still.

freezing *see* **cold** 1, 2, 3.

frenzied *see* **feverish** 2.

frenzy
(n) The news sent us into a frenzy. turmoil, uproar, furore, confusion, passion, rage, fury, fit, paroxysm, hysteria.

frequent
1 *(adj) A frequent problem.* persistent, recurrent, regular, repeated, continual, constant, incessant, oft-repeated.
2 *(adj) A frequent sight. See* **familiar** 1.

fresh
1 *(adj) This magazine needs some fresh ideas.* new, original, novel, innovative, creative, inventive, untried, unfamiliar, up-to-date, up-to-the-minute, modern.
OPPOSITES: stale, outdated.
2 *(adj) You should eat lots of fresh food.* natural, unprocessed, untreated, uncontaminated, uncooked, raw *(fruit, vegetables)*, freshly picked, freshly cooked.
OPPOSITES: processed, cooked, stale.
3 *(adj) Is this water fresh?* pure, drinkable, unpolluted, uncontaminated, running.
OPPOSITES: polluted, salty, stagnant.
4 *(adj) Start on a fresh sheet of paper.* clean, new, blank, empty, unused, spare.
OPPOSITES: used, full.
5 *(adj) Can you feel that fresh sea breeze?* cool, refreshing, brisk, bracing, invigorating, keen, chilly, nippy.

friend
(n) It's great to have a friend to talk to. mate *(informal)*, pal *(informal)*, chum *(informal)*, buddy *(informal)*, companion, comrade, soul mate, bosom friend, kindred spirit, confidant *(male)*, confidante *(female)*, crony, ally, well-wisher.
OPPOSITE: enemy.

friendly
(adj) Sasha is a friendly girl. warm, outgoing, sociable, chummy *(informal)*, matey *(informal)*, pally *(informal)*, companionable, hospitable, neighbourly, welcoming, open, approachable, warm-hearted, affectionate, sympathetic, kind-hearted, considerate, understanding, supportive, generous, helpful, convivial.
OPPOSITES: unfriendly, cold.

fright
1 *(n) I shrank back in fright. See* **fear** 1.
2 *(n) You gave me a fright. See* **scare** 3.
3 *(n) (informal) What a fright you look! See* **sight** 4.

frighten *see* **scare** 1, 2.

frightened *see* **scared** 1, 2.

frightening
(adj) What a frightening experience! scary *(informal)*, terrifying, petrifying, spine-chilling, hair-raising, bloodcurdling, horrifying, fearsome, ghastly, creepy *(informal)*, eerie, spooky *(informal)*, alarming, daunting, unnerving, sinister.
OPPOSITES: comforting, reassuring.

frilly
(adj) A frilly dress. flouncy, ruffled, ruched, flounced, lacy, frothy, fancy.

frisky
(adj) A frisky puppy. lively, playful, high-spirited, sprightly, bouncy, skittish, active.

frivolous
(adj) Frivolous remarks. empty-headed, foolish, fatuous, superficial, shallow, flippant, flip *(informal)*, silly, trivial, puerile, childish, inane, dizzy, giddy, pointless, worthless, insignificant, idle, trifling.
OPPOSITES: serious, sensible.

front
1 *(n) Put some people in the front of your painting.* foreground, forefront.
OPPOSITES: background, back.
2 *(n) Ivy grew up the front of the house.* face, façade, frontage.
OPPOSITES: rear, back.
3 *(n) Go to the front of the queue.* top, head, beginning.
OPPOSITES: end, back.
4 *(n) Dean's self-confidence is just a front.* pretence, show, mask, façade, cover, disguise, cover-up, sham, blind, screen.

frosty
1 *(adj) It's frosty this morning.* icy, freezing, hoary, crisp, wintry, keen, chilly, nippy, cold. ❖ *Also see* **ice**, **frost & snow**.
2 *(adj) Aunt Bertha gave a frosty reply.* cold, icy, chilly, glacial, unfriendly, cool, standoffish, stiff, aloof, discouraging.
OPPOSITES: warm, friendly.

frown
(v) Mum will frown at you if you snigger. scowl, glare, glower, grimace, look daggers, give you a dirty look, look stern.

frozen
1 *(adj) The roads are frozen.* icy, frosty, icebound, ice-covered, frozen solid.
2 *(adj) My nose is frozen.* freezing, numb, icy, chilled, dead, frostbitten, frozen solid.

fruit
(n) TYPES OF FRUIT: apple, apricot, avocado, banana, bilberry, blackberry, blackcurrant, blueberry, cherry, clementine, crab apple, cranberry, damson, date, elderberry, fig, gooseberry, grape, grapefruit, greengage, guava, kiwi fruit, kumquat, lemon, lime, loganberry, lychee, mandarin, mango, melon, nectarine, olive, orange, papaya, passion fruit, peach, pear, pineapple, plum, pomegranate, prickly pear, quince, raspberry, redcurrant, rhubarb, satsuma, star fruit, strawberry, tangerine, tomato, ugli fruit.

frustrated
(adj) I felt frustrated that I couldn't go to the party. disgruntled, vexed, annoyed, peeved *(informal)*, miffed *(informal)*, resentful, thwarted, foiled, disappointed, embittered, sick as a parrot *(informal)*.

full
1 *(adj) The box is full.* full up, filled, full to the brim, overflowing, packed, crammed, stuffed, jam-packed, chock-a-block, full to bursting, bursting at the seams, brimming over, chock-full, jammed, crowded, laden, loaded, teeming, swarming, well-stocked.
OPPOSITE: empty.
2 *(adj) I want a full explanation.* thorough, complete, detailed, comprehensive, exhaustive, unabridged, uncut, unedited.
OPPOSITES: incomplete, partial.
3 *(adj) Charlotte felt full after her lunch.* satisfied, well-fed, sated, satiated, gorged, stuffed *(informal)*, replete.
OPPOSITES: empty, hungry.

fun
1 *(n) Let's have some fun!* amusement, enjoyment, entertainment, fun and games *(plural)*, pleasure, recreation, diversion, distraction, high jinks *(plural)*, sport.
2 *(n) Oz is full of fun.* merriment, laughter, sparkle, high spirits *(plural)*, verve, zest, mirth, jollity, hilarity.
3 *(adj) The party was fun.*
See **enjoyable**.

funny
1 *(adj) A funny comedian.* amusing, comical, witty, humorous, hilarious, entertaining, satirical, ironic, droll, sarcastic, facetious, hysterical *(informal)*, side-splitting, absurd, ludicrous, laughable, farcical, ridiculous, riotous.
2 *(adj) A funny habit.* See **strange** 1.
3 *(adj) A funny noise.* See **strange** 2.

furious see **angry**.

furry
(adj) A furry creature. fluffy, fuzzy, hairy, woolly, fleecy.

fuss
(v) Don't fuss about petty details. worry, fret, get worked up, flap *(informal)*, be agitated, be in a stew *(informal)*, niggle.

fussy
(adj) Di is fussy about her food. particular, choosy *(informal)*, fastidious, hard to please, difficult, picky *(informal)*, finicky, pernickety *(informal)*, faddy *(informal)*.

future
(n) Your future looks bright. prospects *(plural)*, expectations *(plural)*, outlook.

fuzzy
1 *(adj) It's hard to control my fuzzy hair.* frizzy, fluffy, woolly, wiry, bushy.
2 *(adj) Without my glasses, everything looks fuzzy.*
See **blurred**.

funfair *(n)* fair, fairground, amusement park, theme park.

funfair rides
big dipper
big wheel
bumper cars
carousel
Dodgems
Ferris wheel
ghost train
helter-skelter
merry-go-round
roller coaster
simulator
swingboat

on a ride you...
bounce
bump
climb
crash
dive
drop
hang
hurtle
jerk
jolt
lurch
plummet
plunge
revolve
rock
slide
speed
spin
sway
swerve
swing
swoop
tilt
twist
whirl
zoom

rides can be...
exciting
exhilarating
hair-raising
nail-biting
scary *(informal)*
spine-tingling
stomach-churning
terrifying
thrilling

other amusements
amusement arcade
bouncy castle
coconut shy
fortune-teller
hall of mirrors
laser show
shooting gallery
skittles
slot machine
stall

people at a funfair...
gape
gasp
gaze
jostle
mill about
push
queue
scream
screech
shove
shriek
squeal
yell

funfair lights can be...
blazing
colourful
dazzling
flashing
glittering
magical
whirling

funfair music can be...
blaring
booming
jangling
pounding
rhythmic
strident
tinny

G g

gabble
(v) Don't gabble! I can't understand you. jabber, babble, rabbit on *(informal)*, rattle on, prattle, spout *(informal)*, blabber, gush.

gadget
(n) This gadget slices apples. device, tool, instrument, utensil, contraption, appliance, widget *(informal)*, gizmo *(slang)*, invention.

gaffe see **mistake** 2.

gain see **win** 2.

gale see **storm** 1.

gamble
1 *(v) If you gamble, you may lose.* bet, place a bet, have a flutter *(informal)*, speculate, take a risk, take a chance, try your luck, stick your neck out *(informal)*.
OPPOSITE: play safe.
2 **gamble on** *(v) Flash Frank loves to gamble on the horses.* bet on, put money on, back, have a flutter on *(informal)*.

game
1 *(n) Don't take it so seriously; it's only a game.* amusement, diversion, distraction, entertainment, romp, lark *(informal)*, prank, jest, joke, bit of fun.
2 *(n) Football is a popular game.* sport, pastime, recreation, entertainment, amusement, leisure activity.
3 *(n) When does the rugby game start?* match, competition, tournament, contest.

gang
(n) Can I join your gang? group, crowd, club, set, bunch *(informal)*, circle, crew *(informal)*, clique, posse *(informal)*, mob, team, squad.

gap
1 *(n) We found a gap in the wall.* hole, crack, opening, space, chink, crevice, cranny.
2 *(n) There will be a gap between each act.* interval, pause, break, rest, breathing space, lull, interlude, intermission.
3 *(n) Measure the gap between the two houses.* space, distance, interval.

gape see **stare** 1.

gaping
(adj) Beneath us stretched a gaping hole. yawning, cavernous, vast, wide, wide-open, enormous.

garden
(n) patch, plot, lawn, grounds *(plural)*, back yard, yard.

garish see **gaudy**.

gash see **cut** 1, 9.

gasp

gasp
1 *(v) This icy water will make you gasp.* catch your breath, gulp, splutter, choke.
2 *(v) Jogging makes me gasp. See* **pant**.

gate
(n) entrance, exit, gateway, doorway, way in, way out, door, opening, turnstile, stile.

gather
1 *(v) A crowd began to gather at the end of the pitch. See* **collect** 3.
2 *(v) I gather I'm next. See* **understand** 3.

gaudy
(adj) A gaudy tie. garish, loud, lurid, bright, glaring, flashy, vulgar, showy, tasteless.

gaunt
(adj) After their ordeal, the prisoners looked gaunt. haggard, wasted, scrawny, emaciated, sunken-cheeked, hollow-eyed, drawn, pinched, skeletal, cadaverous.

gaze *see* stare 1.

gear
1 *(n) Climbing gear. See* **equipment**.
2 *(n) (informal) Oz looks great in his party gear.* clothes *(plural)*, outfit, things *(plural)*, togs *(plural) (informal)*, strip *(sport)*.

general
1 *(adj) Untidiness is a general problem among teenagers.* common, widespread, normal, typical, everyday, usual, universal.
OPPOSITES: individual, unusual.
2 *(adj) Chloë gave a general outline of the story.* broad, rough, vague, loose, approximate, imprecise, sweeping.
OPPOSITES: precise, detailed.

generation
1 *(n) I get on best with people of my own generation.* age, age group, peer group.
2 *(n) Steam trains belong to a different generation.* era, age, time, period, epoch.

generous
(adj) Lord Lucre is generous with his money. open-handed, liberal, ungrudging, unstinting, free, lavish, magnanimous, kind, charitable, bountiful.
OPPOSITES: mean, stingy.

genius
(n) Imran is a genius at maths. mastermind, marvel, ace *(informal)*, whiz *(informal)*, brainbox *(slang)*, whiz kid *(informal)*, hotshot *(informal)*, prodigy *(child)*.

gentle
1 *(adj) Neesha has a gentle nature.* mild, sweet-tempered, peaceful, placid, tender, meek, docile, unassertive, kind.
OPPOSITES: violent, aggressive.
2 *(adj) The leaves stirred in the gentle breeze.* light, soft, faint, slight, mild, balmy, caressing.
OPPOSITES: strong, violent.
3 *(adj) Dad spoke to me in a gentle voice.* soft, soothing, quiet, low, reassuring.
OPPOSITES: harsh, loud.
4 *(adj) We cycled down a gentle slope.* gradual, slight, imperceptible, easy, steady.
OPPOSITES: steep, sudden.

5 *(adj) A gentle hint. See* **subtle** 2.

genuine
1 *(adj) Is that a genuine gold nugget?* real, actual, authentic, bona fide, true, veritable, solid, pure, natural, original *(art)*.
OPPOSITES: fake, imitation, artificial.
2 *(adj) Sophie's enthusiasm seems to be genuine. See* **sincere** 1.

gesture
1 *(n) I don't know what Sam's gesture means.* sign, signal, action, gesticulation.
2 *(v) I tried to gesture to you that the branch wasn't safe. See* **signal** 2.

get
1 *(v) Where did you get those jeans?* buy, get hold of, obtain, acquire, come by.
2 *(v) Please get me a chair. See* **fetch** 1.
3 *(v) When will we get our exam results?* receive, be given, hear, be told, be sent.
4 *(v) Oz hopes to get first prize.* win, gain, take, obtain, earn, achieve, attain, pick up.
5 *(v) It should get warmer in the afternoon.* become, grow, turn.
6 *(v) When did you finally get home?* arrive, come, reach, make it *(informal)*.
7 *(v) Shall I get supper?* make, prepare, fix *(informal)*, get ready, organize, cook.
8 *(v) I wish I could get you to go out with me.* persuade, convince, induce, coax, talk you into, wheedle you into, make, force.
9 *(v) I mustn't get a cold. See* **catch** 3.
10 *(v) I don't get what you mean. See* **understand** 1.
11 *(v) (informal) I'm going to get you for stealing my hat! See* **pay back** 2.

get across
1 *(v) How will we get across the desert? See* **cross** 4.
2 *(v) It's important to get your message across.* get over, put over, communicate, make clear, get through, bring home.

get at
1 *(v) I can't get at that shelf. See* **reach** 1.
2 *(v) Can you see what I'm trying to get at?* suggest, imply, lead up to, insinuate, convey, indicate, mean.
3 *(v) Why does everyone always get at me? See* **pick on**.

getaway *see* escape 4.

get away
1 *(v) Burglar Beryl tried to get away from the police. See* **escape** 1.
2 **get away with** *(v) Don't try to cheat; you won't get away with it.* get off scot-free, go unpunished, pull it off.

get back
1 *(v) What time did you get back? See* **return** 1.
2 *(v) Did you manage to get your pencil case back? See* **retrieve**.

get better
1 *(v) You must take your medicine if you want to get better. See* **recover** 1.
2 *(v) The situation can only get better. See* **improve** 2.

get even *(informal) see* get your own back.

get off
1 *(v) Don't get off until the bus stops.* get out, alight, disembark, dismount, exit.
2 *(v) (informal) Did you get off with Jo at the party?* make a date, get together, get lucky *(informal)*, make out *(informal)*.

get on
1 *(v) I wonder how I'll get on at my new school. See* **manage** 1.
2 *(v) The driver told us to get on.* get in, board, climb aboard, embark, enter.
3 *(v) Did you and Sarah get on?* get along, hit it off *(informal)*, become friends, make friends, see eye to eye, agree.

get out
(v) If there's a fire, get out as fast as you can! leave, clear out *(informal)*, escape, make your escape, exit, evacuate, free yourself, extricate yourself, break out.

get out of *see* avoid 2.

get over
1 *(v) It didn't take long for Alice to get over her illness.* recover from, get better from, shake off, convalesce, recuperate.
2 *(v) It can be hard to get over losing a friend.* recover from, survive, bounce back from, put behind you, forget.

get rid of
(v) Please get rid of that mouldy sandwich. throw away, dispose of, remove, bin, chuck *(slang)*, dump *(informal)*, ditch *(slang)*, do away with, discard.

get together *see* meet 3.

get up
(v) It's time to get up! get out of bed, rise and shine *(informal)*, wake up, surface *(informal)*, get dressed, rise, stand up.

get worse
(v) Your marks will get worse if you don't work harder. deteriorate, worsen, go downhill *(informal)*, take a turn for the worse, slip, slide, fall, slump, decline, lapse.
OPPOSITES: get better, improve.

get your own back
(phrase) (informal) Don't try to get your own back. take revenge, get your revenge, retaliate, get even *(informal)*, settle the score, be avenged, give tit for tat.

ghastly
1 *(adj) A ghastly crime. See* **horrible** 1.
2 *(adj) I saw a ghastly face in the moonlight.* deathly pale, ashen, spectral, deathlike, cadaverous, gruesome.

ghost
(n) Max says he saw a ghost on the stairs. spirit, spook *(informal)*, spectre, phantom, apparition, wraith, poltergeist, ghoul.

ghostly
1 *(adj) A ghostly sound. See* **spooky**.
2 *(adj) A ghostly figure.* ghostlike, spectral, phantom, wraithlike, shadowy, supernatural, unearthly, ghoulish.

ghosts and hauntings

ghosts and ghouls

apparition
banshee
bogeyman
ghost
ghoul
gremlin
phantom
poltergeist
  (mischievous spirit)
spectre
spirit
spook *(informal)*
vampire
werewolf
wraith
zombie

haunted house

panelled room

grand staircase

in a haunted house

attic
bats
candelabra
cellar
chains
cobwebs
fluttering curtains
four-poster bed
grandfather clock
grand staircase
guttering candles
library
locked door
looking glass
manacles
  (handcuffs)
mice
oak chest
panelled room
portrait
secret door
secret passageway
shadows
sliding panel
spiral staircase
stone steps
study
suit of armour
sword
tapestry
trap door
turret
west wing
winding corridor

ghosts and ghouls may...

appear
avenge (take
  revenge for)
beckon
creep
disappear
drift
flit
float
flutter
glide
glow
haunt
hover
loom
lurk
materialize
pace
pester
plague
possess
shimmer
skim
slide
slink
slither
stalk
sway
torment
trouble
vanish into
  thin air
waft
wander

ghostly sounds

bang
bump
cackle
chime
clank
clatter
clink
crash
creak
cry
grate
grind
groan
hammer
hoot
howl
knock
moan
murmur
mutter
rattle
rustle
scream
screech
shriek
sigh
sob
thud
wail
whisper

ghostly sounds can be...

bloodcurdling
chilling
creepy *(informal)*
disturbing
echoing
eerie
hair-raising
haunting
heart-stopping
high-pitched
lingering
long-drawn-out
melancholy
petrifying
piercing
reverberating
spine-chilling
uncanny
unearthly
unnerving
weird

haunted houses can be...

bleak
creepy *(informal)*
crumbling
cursed
derelict
deserted
dilapidated
forbidding
gloomy
grim
isolated
lonely
menacing
moonlit
mysterious
neglected
rambling
ramshackle
remote
spooky
  (informal)
swathed in mist
tumbledown
uninhabited

guttering candle

ghosts and ghouls may be...

anguished
ghastly
ghostly
ghoulish
grisly
grotesque
gruesome
horrifying
invisible
luminous
malevolent
mournful
restless
scary *(informal)*
shadowy
sinister
slimy
spectral
supernatural
tormented

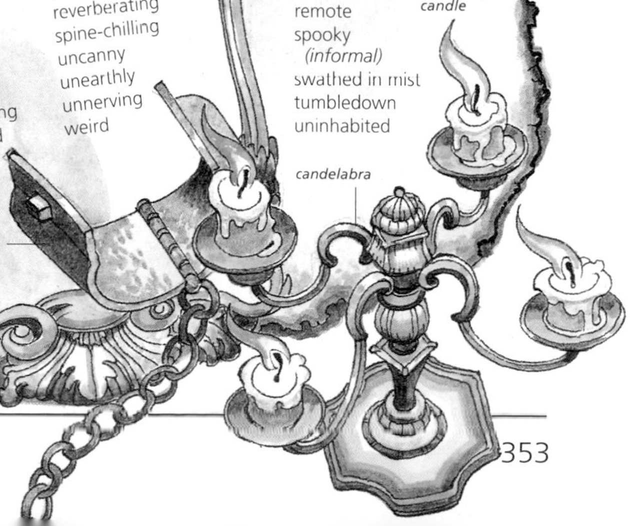

manacle

candelabra

giant
1 *(n) Jack dreamt about a fearsome giant.* ogre, monster, hulk, titan.
2 *(adj) Giant sale now on.* See **huge**.

gibberish see **nonsense** 1.

giddy see **dizzy**.

gift
1 *(n) Dad gave me this book as a gift.* See **present** 1.
2 *(n) Lord Lucre gave the school a generous gift.* donation, contribution, grant, hand-out, offering, bequest, legacy.
3 *(n) Mark has a gift for languages.* talent, aptitude, flair, ability, facility, knack, bent, genius, skill, expertise.

gifted see **talented** 1, 2.

gigantic see **huge**.

giggle
(v) You'll giggle when you see Dad in his tank top. titter, snigger, chuckle, chortle, laugh, cackle, snicker.

gimmick
(n) This toy is just a gimmick to make you buy the cereal. novelty, ploy, trick, stunt, publicity device, dodge, wheeze *(slang)*.

girl
(n) schoolgirl, lass, young woman, maiden *(old-fashioned)*, damsel *(old-fashioned)*.

gist
(n) Do you get the gist of what I'm saying? idea, general sense, drift, point, meaning, essence, substance, significance.

give
1 *(v) Give your ticket to the driver.* hand, pass, hand over, present, submit, deliver.
2 *(v) Lord Lucre offered to give some money to our fund.* donate, contribute, grant, award, present, allocate, make over, fork out *(slang)*, provide, supply, entrust, bestow, bequeath *(after death)*.
OPPOSITES: take away, receive.
3 *(v) A graph is a good way to give information.* communicate, convey, put across, display, show, set out, deliver, express, explain, demonstrate, impart.
4 *(v) Let's give a party!* throw, have, organize, arrange, put on, host, stage.
5 *(v) Please let me come; I won't give any trouble.* cause, make, create, produce.

give away see **betray** 1, 3.

give in
(v) Why don't you just give in and end the argument? give up, admit defeat, back down, climb down, throw in the towel, concede defeat, capitulate, surrender.

give out
(v) Mrs Badger asked me to give out the books. hand out, hand round, pass round, dish out *(informal)*, distribute, dole out, share out, circulate.
OPPOSITES: collect, take in.

give up
1 *(v) I'm determined to give up biting my nails.* See **stop** 3.

2 *(v) This assault course is tough, but I'm not going to give up.* give in, admit defeat, quit, lose heart, despair, drop out, throw in the towel, throw in the sponge, pack it in *(informal)*, call it a day *(informal)*.
3 *(v) Would you give up your pocket money for a good cause?* sacrifice, forfeit, relinquish, forgo, surrender, offer.

give way see **collapse** 1.

glad see **pleased**.

glamorous
1 *(adj) Helen looks glamorous in her ballgown.* dazzling, alluring, stunning *(informal)*, smart, elegant, sophisticated, snazzy *(informal)*, charming, enchanting, bewitching, entrancing, irresistible, captivating, sexy *(informal)*, seductive.
OPPOSITES: dull, dowdy.
2 *(adj) The party was a glamorous affair.* glittering, dazzling, glitzy *(slang)*, ritzy *(slang)*, colourful, fascinating, exciting.
OPPOSITES: humdrum, mundane.

glamour
(n) The glamour of Hollywood. glitter, dazzle, razzmatazz *(slang)*, razzle-dazzle *(slang)*, glitz *(slang)*, magic, fascination, allure, appeal, attraction, charm, elegance.

glance
1 *(n) Take a quick glance.* See **look** 4.
2 *(v) Would you glance at my homework?* See **look at** 2.

glare
(v) Aunt Bertha will glare at you if you interrupt. give you a hard stare, glower, look daggers, give you a dirty look, frown, scowl, give you a black look.

glaring
1 *(adj) Glaring headlights.* See **bright** 1.
2 *(adj) A glaring mistake.* See **obvious**.

glass
(n) Fill the glass to the brim. tumbler, wineglass, goblet, flute *(champagne)*.

gleam
1 *(v) As Aladdin rubbed the lamp, it began to gleam.* shine, glisten, glint, shimmer, glimmer, glow, sparkle, glitter, twinkle.
2 *(n) A gleam of light.* See **flash** 1.

gleaming see **shiny** 1, 2.

glide
1 *(v) I'd like to glide through the air like a bird.* float, drift, sail, soar, fly, coast, hover.
2 *(v) Watch me glide across the ice!* skate, slide, skim, sail, slip, skid.

glimmer see **gleam** 1.

glimpse
(n) I got a glimpse of something shiny in the grass. quick look, brief view, glance, peep, peek, sight, squint.

glint see **gleam** 1.

glisten see **gleam** 1.

glitter
1 *(v) The light made the diamonds glitter.* sparkle, shimmer, twinkle, glisten, shine, glint, gleam, glimmer, flash.

2 *(n) The glitter of the treasure dazzled me.* sparkle, brilliance, lustre, brightness.
3 *(n) Jodie is fascinated by the glitter of Hollywood.* See **glamour**.

gloat
(v) Don't gloat if you win. crow, brag, rub it in *(informal)*, boast, show off *(informal)*.

globe
1 *(n) The sun is a globe of fire.* See **ball** 1.
2 *(n) Indiana has travelled round the globe.* See **world** 1.

gloom
(n) When she heard the news, Emma was filled with gloom. melancholy, sorrow, sadness, unhappiness, despondency, dejection, misery, depression, despair, desolation, hopelessness, woe, pessimism.
OPPOSITES: happiness, delight.

gloomy
1 *(adj) It was a gloomy winter's day.* dismal, dreary, dull, dark, murky, cheerless, overcast, cloudy, sunless, dim, sombre.
OPPOSITES: bright, sunny.
2 *(adj) Wet weather makes me feel gloomy.* See **depressed**.

glorious
1 *(adj) A glorious victory.* magnificent, splendid, triumphant, heroic, honourable, famous, celebrated, renowned, illustrious.
OPPOSITES: shameful, humiliating.
2 *(adj) Glorious weather.* See **gorgeous** 3.

glossy
1 *(adj) Glossy paintwork.* shiny, shining, gleaming, bright, sparkling, shimmering, brilliant, smooth, polished, glazed.
OPPOSITES: dull, matt.
2 *(adj) Glossy hair.* shiny, shining, gleaming, sleek, silky, smooth, lustrous.
OPPOSITE: dull.

glow
1 *(n) I saw a strange glow in the sky.* light, gleam, glimmer, brightness, burning.
2 *(n) The wind will bring a glow to your cheeks.* bloom, blush, rosiness, pinkness, redness, flush.
3 *(v) We watched the coals glow in the hearth.* glimmer, burn, redden, smoulder.
4 *(v) These stickers glow in the dark.* shine, shimmer, gleam, glimmer, show up.

glowing
1 *(adj) Glowing coals.* See **burning** 1.
2 *(adj) Glowing colours.* See **bright** 2.
3 *(adj) A glowing complexion.* rosy, pink, healthy, radiant, reddish, ruddy, florid.
OPPOSITES: pale, wan.
4 *(adj) A glowing report.* complimentary, enthusiastic, ecstatic, rave *(informal)*.
OPPOSITES: critical, scathing.

glue see **stick** 5.

glum see **depressed**.

gnarled
(adj) Gnarled hands. twisted, misshapen, knobbly, knotted, distorted, contorted, weather-beaten, leathery, wrinkled.

gnash see **grind** 2.

gnaw
(v) *Carrots are nice to gnaw.* chew, bite, nibble, munch, crunch.

go
1 (v) *Do you want to go to London?* travel, journey, make your way, drive, fly, take the train, cycle, walk, motor, ride, sail, cruise, voyage, move.
2 (v) *It's time to go.* See **leave** 1.
3 (v) *The time seemed to go so quickly.* See **pass** 2.
4 (v) *Wind up the toy to make it go.* See **work** 4.
5 (v) *Where do these books go?* belong, stay, live *(informal)*, fit in, have a place.
6 (v) *Will this belt go round my waist?* reach, extend, stretch, fit.
7 (v) *Let's wait and see how things go.* work out, turn out, develop, unfold, progress, end up, pan out *(informal)*.
8 (v) *This cake will go mouldy if you don't eat it.* become, grow, turn, get.
9 (v) *If you use this cream, your rash will soon go.* See **go away** 3.
10 (v) *That chair will have to go.* be thrown away, be got rid of, be disposed of, be discarded, be chucked out *(informal)*, be dumped *(informal)*.
OPPOSITE: stay.
11 (v) *Granny's eyesight is beginning to go.* See **fail** 5.
12 (v) *Do these shorts and socks go?* match, go together, coordinate, complement each other, blend, harmonize.
13 (n) *(informal) Have a go!* See **try** 1.
14 (n) *(informal) Matty has lots of go.* energy, drive, vitality, get-up-and-go *(informal)*, oomph *(informal)*, push *(informal)*, vigour, life, spirit, verve.

go about
(v) *I'm not sure how to go about this task.* approach, tackle, begin, set about.

go after see **follow** 1, 2.

go-ahead *(informal)* see **permission**.

go ahead
(v) *We decided to go ahead without you.* start, begin, proceed, go on, continue.

goal see **aim** 1.

go along with
1 (v) *David asked me to go along with him.* See **go with** 1.
2 (v) *Let's hope Nat will go along with our plan.* See **agree** 6.

go away
1 (v) *Go away and leave me alone!* clear off *(informal)*, shove off *(informal)*, push off *(informal)*, get lost *(informal)*, scram *(informal)*, beat it *(slang)*, hop it *(slang)*.
OPPOSITES: come here, stay.
2 (v) *Do you have to go away so soon?* See **leave** 1.
3 (v) *I wish these spots would go away.* go, clear up, disappear, vanish, fade away, die down, melt away.
OPPOSITES: stay, appear.

go back see **return** 1, 2.

gobble
(v) *Don't gobble your food.* bolt, guzzle, gulp, scoff *(informal)*, wolf down, shovel down, devour, pig out on *(slang)*.

gobsmacked *(slang)* see **astonished**.

god
(n) deity, divine being, divinity, Creator.

go down
1 (v) *As we approached land, the plane began to go down.* See **descend** 1.
2 (v) *Prices are expected to go down.* See **decrease** 2.
3 (v) *I watched the sun go down over the sea.* See **set** 5.

go for
1 (v) *Did you see our goalie go for the ball?* reach for, stretch for, lunge for, dive for, clutch at, grab at, fetch, go and get.
2 (v) *I'm scared the dog might go for me.* attack, set upon, rush at, spring at.
3 (v) *Mel will really go for you in that shirt.* See **fancy** 3.

go in see **enter** 1.

golden
1 (adj) *Golden treasure.* gilded, gilt, shining, gleaming, brilliant.
2 (adj) *Golden hair.* See **blonde** 2.

gone
(adj) *All the food's gone.* finished, eaten, consumed, used up, done, missing, disappeared, vanished, lost.

good-looking see **attractive**.

gooey
(adj) *(informal) A gooey mixture.* sticky, squidgy, gluey, glutinous, tacky, syrupy.

go off
1 (v) *This bomb could go off at any moment.* See **explode**.
2 (v) *Don't go off without saying goodbye.* See **leave** 1.
3 (v) *(informal) This cheese will go off soon.* go mouldy, go bad, rot, decay, decompose, putrefy, go stale, go sour.
4 (v) *(informal) At present Tom likes the Howlers, but he'll soon go off them.* get bored with, tire of, go off them. get bored with, tire of, go sick of *(informal)*, take a dislike to, turn against.

go on see **continue** 1, 2.

go out
1 (v) *I just saw Samantha go out.* leave, walk out, walk off, depart, exit.
OPPOSITES: come in, enter.
2 (v) *It took ages for the fire to go out.* die down, be extinguished, be quenched.
OPPOSITES: kindle, ignite.

go out with
(v) *I don't want to go out with you any more.* see, go with, go steady with *(informal)*, date *(informal)*.

go over
(v) *Go over this topic carefully before the test.* look over, revise, review, read through, work through, study, examine, check, scan, skim.

good				
a good person	**a good deed**	**a good footballer**	**good work**	**a good excuse**
blameless	altruistic	accomplished	admirable	adequate
decent	(unselfish)	capable	careful	genuine
honest	caring	competent	commendable	legitimate
honourable	charitable	competent	competent	proper
just	considerate	expert	excellent	reasonable
kind	generous	fine	first-rate	satisfactory
law-abiding	helpful	first-class	pleasing	valid
moral	humane	gifted	satisfactory	
righteous	kind	proficient	sound	**good food**
saintly	thoughtful	skilful	splendid	appetizing
trustworthy		skilled	thorough	delicious
upright	**a good film**	talented		mouthwatering
virtuous	brilliant		**a good mood**	scrumptious
	excellent	**good weather**	buoyant	*(informal)*
a good child	fantastic	bright	carefree	tasty
angelic	*(informal)*	calm	cheerful	well-cooked
cooperative	great	clear	cheery	yummy
docile	impressive	cloudless	chirpy	*(informal)*
helpful	marvellous	fabulous	*(informal)*	
obedient	outstanding	*(informal)*	contented	**Fruit is good for you.**
obliging	sensational	fair	happy	beneficial
polite	*(informal)*	fine	jolly	healthy
well-behaved	superb	glorious	jovial	nourishing
well-mannered	terrific	mild	light-hearted	nutritious
willing	*(informal)*	sunny	optimistic	wholesome
	wonderful		positive	

gorgeous

gorgeous
1 *(adj) The queen wore a gorgeous diamond necklace.* magnificent, beautiful, splendid, superb, dazzling, glittering, stunning *(informal)*, brilliant, breathtaking, resplendent, opulent, sumptuous, showy. OPPOSITES: plain, ugly.
2 *(adj) You look gorgeous in that dress.* beautiful, lovely, stunning *(informal)*, dazzling, ravishing, attractive, sexy *(informal)*, drop-dead gorgeous *(slang)*. OPPOSITES: plain, unattractive.
3 *(adj) The weather was gorgeous.* glorious, wonderful, lovely, beautiful, marvellous, terrific *(informal)*, fantastic *(informal)*, superb, excellent, fine. OPPOSITE: awful.

go round
(v) Take the new road, if you want to go round the town. bypass, skirt, avoid, steer clear of, get round, make a detour round.

gory
(adj) This film contains some gory scenes. bloody, bloodthirsty, grisly, gruesome, brutal, violent, horrific, sickening, savage.

gossip
1 *(v) It's unkind to gossip about other people.* spread rumours, spread gossip, circulate rumours, spread stories, spread scandal, tittle-tattle, bad-mouth *(slang)*.
2 *(v) Don't gossip in class. See* **talk** 1.
3 *(n) Have you heard the gossip?* rumours *(plural)*, latest *(informal)*, scandal, tittle-tattle, hearsay, idle talk, dirt *(slang)*.
4 *(n) Mrs Bunn is a real gossip.* scandalmonger, gossipmonger, busybody, telltale, tattler, chatterbox *(informal)*.

go through
1 *(v) This arrow will never go through the dragon's skin. See* **pierce**.
2 *(v) I can't go through another day of this misery. See* **suffer** 3.
3 *(v) Try not to go through your pocket money so quickly.* spend, use up, exhaust, squander, fritter away, consume.

go under
1 *(v) Pirate Peg was scared her ship would go under.* sink, go down, be submerged.
2 *(v) Dad's firm may go under. See* **fail** 4.

go up *see* **rise** 1, 2.

govern
(v) Who will govern the country after the next election? rule, run, be in charge of, lead, control, administer, manage, conduct the affairs of, be in power over, direct, steer, command, preside over, reign over.

go with
1 *(v) Oz asked me to go with him to the party.* accompany, escort, go along with.
2 *(v) Does this top go with my skirt? See* **match** 2.

go without
(v) Could you go without chocolate, if you had to? do without, survive without, abstain from, deny yourself, go short of.

go wrong
1 *(v) Where did I go wrong in this maths question?* make a mistake, miscalculate, slip up *(informal)*, go astray, blunder.
2 *(v) Why do my brilliant ideas always go wrong?* turn out badly, end in disaster, come to grief, come to nothing, fail, misfire, fall flat, flop *(informal)*.

grab
1 *(v) I felt someone grab my arm.* clutch, seize, grip, clasp, grasp, catch hold of.
2 *(v) Burglar Beryl managed to grab the jewels. See* **snatch**.

graceful
1 *(adj) A graceful ballerina.* elegant, poised, supple, lithe, agile, nimble. OPPOSITES: clumsy, awkward.
2 *(adj) Graceful dance steps.* smooth, elegant, flowing, fluid, balletic. OPPOSITES: clumsy, awkward.

grade
1 *(n) I hope I get a good grade for my homework. See* **mark** 4.
2 *(n) Mum was promoted to a higher grade in the company. See* **level** 6.
3 *(v) Mrs Badger didn't have time to grade our tests.* assess, evaluate, classify, rate.

gradual
1 *(adj) There's been a gradual improvement in your work.* steady, continuous, progressive, systematic, step-by-step, slow, moderate, unspectacular. OPPOSITE: sudden.
2 *(adj) There's a gradual slope down to the river. See* **gentle** 4.

grand
1 *(adj) Lord Lucre lives in a grand mansion.* magnificent, imposing, impressive, splendid, superb, palatial, stately, sumptuous, opulent, luxurious. OPPOSITE: modest.
2 *(adj) The king made a grand entrance.* dignified, stately, majestic, regal.
3 *(adj) Our new neighbours seem very grand.* posh *(informal)*, upper class, upper crust *(informal)*, distinguished, aristocratic, haughty, high and mighty *(informal)*, lordly, imperious, pompous, pretentious. OPPOSITES: ordinary, common.

grapple
1 *(v) Indiana had to grapple with the monster. See* **struggle** 2.
2 *(v) I'm too tired to grapple with this problem now. See* **tackle** 2.

grasp
1 *(v) Grasp my hand so you don't fall! See* **grip**.
2 *(v) I don't quite grasp what you're saying. See* **understand** 1.
3 *(n) Winter held the country in its icy grasp.* grip, embrace, clasp, clutches *(plural)*, hold.
4 *(n) Rick has a good grasp of the subject.* understanding, comprehension, awareness, knowledge, mastery, grip, appreciation, perception, insight.

grass
1 *(n) Don't walk on the grass!* lawn, turf, green, pitch, playing field.
2 *(n) The cows roamed through the grass.* meadow, pasture, field.
3 *(v) (slang) Burglar Beryl didn't want to grass on her friends. See* **inform** 2.

grate
1 *(v) Please grate this carrot.* shred, mince.
2 *(v) I heard the door grate across the tiles.* scrape, grind, rasp, scratch, rub, creak, squeak.

grateful
(adj) I'm grateful for your help. thankful, appreciative of, obliged to you, indebted to you. OPPOSITE: ungrateful.

grave
1 *(n) We visited the grave of Queen Victoria.* burial place, tomb, sepulchre, burial chamber, mausoleum, crypt, vault.
2 *(adj) Mrs Badger looked grave as she gave us the news. See* **serious** 1.
3 *(adj) A grave problem. See* **serious** 3.
4 *(adj) A grave illness. See* **serious** 4.

graveyard
(n) cemetery, burial ground, churchyard.

graze
1 *(v) How did you graze your knee?* scrape, scratch, cut, skin, chafe.
2 *(v) Cows graze in fields.* feed, browse.

greasy
1 *(adj) I hate greasy chips.* fatty, oily.
2 *(adj) The mud made the path greasy. See* **slippery** 1.
3 *(adj) Flash Frank is such a greasy character. See* **slimy** 2.

great
1 *(adj) The explorers crossed a great stretch of desert.* immense, vast, large, huge, extensive, boundless, unlimited. OPPOSITES: small, short.
2 *(adj) A great boulder blocked the cave entrance.* large, huge, enormous, massive, immense, gigantic, colossal, stupendous, tremendous, mammoth, gargantuan. OPPOSITE: small.
3 *(adj) Clare's broken leg caused her great pain.* extreme, intense, considerable, acute, excessive, exceptional, inordinate. OPPOSITES: slight, little.
4 *(adj) This is a great day for the school.* important, significant, momentous, historic, red-letter. OPPOSITES: unimportant, insignificant.
5 *(adj) Anji is a great tennis player.* skilful, skilled, expert, first-class, ace *(informal)*, capable, proficient, able, talented, gifted, outstanding, impressive, crack *(slang)*. OPPOSITES: poor, terrible.
6 *(adj) Charles Dickens was a great writer.* remarkable, outstanding, exceptional, talented, gifted, superb, excellent, distinguished, illustrious, eminent, famous, celebrated, renowned, notable. OPPOSITES: second-rate, insignificant.

7 *(adj) Zoë is a great fan of Famous Fred.* devoted, enthusiastic, keen, zealous.
8 *(adj) Paris is one of the world's great cities. See* **major** 1.
9 *(adj) (informal) The party was really great.* excellent, superb, fantastic *(informal)*, terrific *(informal)*, tremendous *(informal)*, marvellous, decent *(informal)*, cool *(informal)*, mega *(slang)*, crucial *(slang)*, wicked *(slang)*, neat *(slang)*.

greed
1 *(n) Kevin's tummyache was the result of his greed.* greediness, gluttony, overeating, self-indulgence, piggishness, insatiability.
OPPOSITE: self-restraint.
2 *(n) The sight of the gold filled Pirate Peg with greed.* avarice, covetousness, desire, hunger, longing, craving, eagerness.
OPPOSITE: generosity.

greedy
1 *(adj) Don't be so greedy! Leave some ice cream for me!* gluttonous, self-indulgent, piggish, hoggish, insatiable, voracious.
OPPOSITES: self-restrained, abstemious.
2 *(adj) The greedy miser wouldn't share his money.* selfish, avaricious, grasping, covetous, rapacious, miserly, tightfisted, niggardly, money grubbing *(informal)*.
OPPOSITES: generous, unselfish.

green
1 *(n)* SHADES OF GREEN: acid green, apple green, bottle green, emerald, grass green, jade, khaki, lime green, Lincoln green, moss green, olive green, pea green, racing green, sage green, sea green.
2 *(adj) Daniel is interested in green issues.* environmental, ecological, conservationist.
3 *(adj) Unleaded petrol is supposed to be green.* environmentally friendly, non-polluting, eco-friendly, ecologically sound.
OPPOSITE: environmentally harmful.
4 *(adj) The cottage nestled in a green valley.* grassy, verdant, leafy, flourishing.
5 *(adj) Siân looked green when she saw my new bike. See* **envious**.

greet
(v) Mrs Badger was waiting to greet us as we arrived. welcome, say hello to, meet, receive, shake hands with, acknowledge, give a greeting to, salute, hail *(old-fashioned)*, nod to, wave to.

grey
1 *(n)* SHADES OF GREY: charcoal grey, dove grey, gunmetal, iron grey, pearl grey, pewter, silver, slate grey, smoke grey, steel grey.
2 *(adj) Winter days are often grey.* dull, cloudy, overcast, foggy, misty, murky, dark, dim, sunless, dreary, dismal, gloomy, drab, depressing, cheerless.
OPPOSITES: bright, sunny.
3 *(adj) Granddad's hair is grey.* silver, silvery, grizzled, greying, hoary, white.
4 *(adj) Cyril has such a grey personality.* colourless, anonymous, nondescript, dull, characterless, uninteresting.

5 *(adj) Natasha's face turned grey. See* **pale** 2.

grief
(n) Alice couldn't hide her grief when her dog died. sorrow, sadness, unhappiness, misery, dejection, distress, anguish, despair, heartache, pain, agony, suffering, regret, mourning, woe.
OPPOSITES: joy, delight.

grieve
(v) It's natural to grieve when someone dies. be sad, mourn, sorrow, weep, cry, sob, be heartbroken, pine, ache, mope, lament *(old-fashioned)*, go into mourning.
OPPOSITE: rejoice.

grim
1 *(adj) Mrs Badger looked grim as she gave us our test results.* serious, stern, sombre, severe, forbidding, formidable, fierce, cross, implacable, merciless.
OPPOSITES: cheerful, sympathetic.
2 *(adj) The witch's castle looked grim in the moonlight.* forbidding, menacing, ominous, sinister, bleak, gloomy.
OPPOSITES: pleasant, welcoming.
3 *(adj) This film contains some grim battle scenes.* grisly, gruesome, ghastly, shocking, harrowing, horrible, horrendous, hideous, frightful, appalling, unspeakable.
OPPOSITE: pleasant.

grimy *see* **dirty** 1.

grin *see* **smile** 1, 2.

grind
1 *(v) We need to grind some coffee.* crush, mill, pulverize, pound, powder, crumble, granulate, mash, smash, grate.
2 *(v) I hate it when you grind your teeth.* gnash, grate, rub together, scrape, grit.
3 *(n) (informal) I'm dreading the grind of revising.* hard work, slog, drudgery, chore, toil, sweat *(informal)*, exertion.

grip
(v) Grip my hand so you don't fall. grab, clutch, grasp, clasp, hold, hold on to, hang on to, seize, take hold of, clench.

gripe *(informal) see* **complaint**.

gripping *see* **fascinating**.

grisly *see* **gruesome**.

groan
1 *(v) I heard Bruno groan with pain.* moan, cry, murmur, whimper, sigh, whine.
2 *(v) (informal) My parents groan about the mess in my room. See* **complain**.

groggy *(informal) see* **dizzy**.

groom
1 *(n) I work as a groom at the local stables.* stableboy, stablegirl, stable lad, ostler *(old-fashioned)*.
2 *(v) Groom your pony regularly.* rub down, curry, brush, clean.

groove
(n) Make a groove in the wood. channel, cut, score, slot, track, scratch, hollow, trench, rut, trough, furrow, indentation.

grope
(v) I had to grope around in the dark for my key. fumble, feel, scrabble, pick, fish, search, hunt.

gross
(adj) (slang) That pink shirt is really gross. disgusting, revolting, vile, repulsive, foul, tasteless, tacky *(informal)*, naff *(slang)*, yucky *(slang)*.

grotesque
(adj) hideous, repulsive, ugly, misshapen, deformed, strange, bizarre, weird, outlandish, freakish, unnatural, monstrous.

a grotesque gargoyle

grotty
1 *(adj) (slang) Ziggy lives in a grotty flat.* horrible, disgusting, dingy, shabby, tatty, scruffy, run-down, dilapidated, seedy, dirty, filthy, grubby, squalid, sordid, stinking, crummy *(slang)*, scuzzy *(slang)*.
OPPOSITES: smart, attractive.
2 *(adj) (slang) I feel really grotty this morning. See* **rotten** 3.

ground
1 *(n) Lie flat on the ground!* floor, deck *(informal)*, earth.
2 *(n) Plant the seeds in the ground. See* **earth** 2.
3 *(n) The council is building a new football ground.* pitch, field, stadium, arena, park.
4 *(v) This storm could ground the ship.* run ashore, beach, wreck, shipwreck, strand.
5 *(v) (informal) Dad will ground you if you misbehave.* keep you in, forbid you to go out, confine you to the house, restrict.
6 grounds *(plural n) Lord Lucre's house is set in extensive grounds.* gardens *(plural)*, parkland, surroundings *(plural)*, estate, land, property, acres *(plural)*, fields *(plural)*.
7 grounds *(plural n) Bella has good grounds for complaint. See* **reason** 1.

group
1 *(v) Group round your team leaders.* gather, collect, get together, congregate, assemble, come together, cluster, crowd, get into groups.
OPPOSITES: split up, disperse.
2 *(v) Group the photos according to size. See* **sort** 3.
3 *(n) You're welcome to join our group.* gang, band, clique, posse *(informal)*, circle, set, bunch *(informal)*, crowd, crew *(informal)*, mob, club, community, party, company, meeting, gathering, assembly, society, association, organization.
4 *(n) A group of animals.* herd, horde, brood *(chicks)*, colony *(ants, rabbits)*, flock *(birds, sheep)*, gaggle *(geese)*, litter *(kittens, piglets, puppies)*, pack *(hounds, wolves)*, pride *(lions)*, school *(dolphins, whales)*, shoal *(fish)*, swarm *(insects)*.
5 *(n) A group of things.* bunch, bundle, cluster, clump, set, batch, assortment, collection, array, arrangement.

grovel
(v) *There's no need to grovel to Lord Lucre.* crawl, creep, toady, kowtow, bow and scrape, bootlick *(informal)*, fawn, suck up *(informal)*, curry favour with, ingratiate yourself with, humble yourself before.

grow
1 (v) *I hope I'll grow this year.* get bigger, get taller, fill out, shoot up.
OPPOSITES: shrink, get smaller.
2 (v) *Before our eyes, the puddle began to grow.* expand, get bigger, get larger, spread, swell, enlarge, increase, extend, stretch, fill out, widen, lengthen, deepen.
OPPOSITES: shrink, dwindle.
3 (v) *Mum hopes that her business will grow.* expand, develop, progress, advance, increase, prosper, flourish, boom, thrive.
OPPOSITES: contract, decline.
4 (v) *These seeds will grow in the spring.* germinate, sprout, bud, develop, spring up, shoot up, flourish, thrive.
5 (v) *We grow orchids in our greenhouse.* cultivate, produce, propagate, breed, raise, nurture, farm.
6 (v) *Eventually, Luke will grow more sensible.* become, get, come to be, turn.

grown-up *see* **adult** 1, 2.

growth
1 (n) *The rapid growth in technology has changed the world.* expansion, rise, increase, development, evolution, progress, advance, improvement.
OPPOSITE: decline.
2 (n) *There has been a marked growth in crime. See* **increase** 4.

grow up
(v) *The prince waited for the princess to grow up.* mature, develop, come of age, become an adult, reach adulthood.

grub
1 (n) *It's cruel to keep that grub in a jam jar.* caterpillar, maggot, larva.
2 (n) *(informal) I'm desperate for some grub. See* **food**.

grubby *see* **dirty** 1.

grudge
(n) *This grudge of yours will eat you up inside.* resentment, bitterness, grievance, hard feelings *(plural)*, spite, malice, ill will, envy, hatred, malevolence, venom, hostility, animosity, antipathy, dislike.

grudging
(adj) *Ellie gave me a grudging smile when I won.* reluctant, half-hearted, unenthusiastic, lukewarm, unwilling, ungracious, resentful, envious.
OPPOSITES: enthusiastic, wholehearted.

gruelling *see* **exhausting**.

gruesome
(adj) *A gruesome monster.* grisly, ghastly, ghoulish, horrible, hideous, loathsome, repulsive, monstrous, horrifying, frightful, fearful, terrible, dreadful, spine-chilling, hair-raising, macabre, grim.

gruff
1 (adj) *Uncle Arthur has a gruff voice.* husky, low, hoarse, croaky, rough, gravelly, harsh, rasping, throaty, guttural.
2 (adj) *Aunt Bertha has a gruff manner.* blunt, brusque, curt, abrupt, ungracious, crusty, crabby, grumpy, grouchy *(informal)*, crotchety *(informal)*, surly, bad-tempered.
OPPOSITES: gracious, pleasant.

grumble *see* **complain**.

grumpy
(adj) *Max gets grumpy when he's tired.* irritable, bad-tempered, grouchy *(informal)*, cross, ratty *(informal)*, crabby, crotchety *(informal)*, tetchy, peevish, surly, sullen, sulky, huffy, cantankerous.
OPPOSITES: good-humoured, cheerful.

grungy *(slang) see* **scruffy** 2.

guarantee *see* **promise** 1, 2.

guard
1 (v) *We must guard the house.* protect, keep watch over, safeguard, defend, patrol, police, mind, secure, shield.
2 (n) *A guard is on patrol.* watchman, lookout, sentinel, sentry *(army)*, warder *(prison)*, jailer *(prison)*, bodyguard, escort.

guess
1 (v) *Try to guess the weight of the doll.* estimate, hazard a guess at, have a stab at *(informal)*, work out, calculate, speculate about, predict, second-guess *(informal)*.
2 (v) *(informal) I guess I should go now. See* **think** 2.
3 (n) *Your guess was quite right.* estimate, conjecture, speculation, guesswork, guesstimate *(informal)*, prediction, shot in the dark, supposition, theory, hypothesis.

guest
(n) *Try to be polite in front of our guest.* visitor, caller, company.

guidance
(n) *You need guidance when choosing a career.* advice, counselling, direction, help, briefing, instruction, guidelines *(plural)*, pointers *(plural)*, tips *(plural)*, hints *(plural)*.

guide
1 (v) *Guide me to the nearest shelter.* lead, take, show, escort, accompany, direct, conduct, steer, shepherd.
2 (v) *Try to guide the ship into harbour.* steer, pilot, navigate, manoeuvre, direct.
3 (v) *You need someone to guide you as you choose a career.* advise, give you advice, counsel, give you direction, give you pointers, help, inform, instruct.
4 (n) *We followed the guide through the mountains.* leader, scout, escort, courier.
5 (n) *Use this as a guide when you do your drawing.* model, example, pattern, master, standard, benchmark, yardstick.

guilt
1 (n) *Gregory was tormented by guilt.* feelings of guilt *(plural)*, remorse, regret, shame, self-reproach, self-condemnation, guilty conscience, bad conscience.

2 (n) *The fingerprints proved Burglar Beryl's guilt.* culpability, responsibility, wrongdoing, misconduct, criminality.
OPPOSITE: innocence.

guilty
1 (adj) *Burglar Beryl was guilty.* to blame, at fault, responsible, culpable, convicted.
OPPOSITES: innocent, guiltless.
2 (adj) *Gregory felt guilty.* ashamed, conscience-stricken, guilt-ridden, filled with regret, remorseful, repentant, rueful, sheepish, shamefaced, hangdog.
OPPOSITES: unrepentant, unashamed.

gullible
(adj) *Letty is so gullible, she'd believe anything.* naive, trusting, easily taken in, unsuspecting, credulous, innocent, green.
OPPOSITES: suspicious, cynical.

gulp
1 (v) *Don't gulp your cola so quickly.* swallow, swig *(informal)*, knock back *(informal)*, down *(informal)*, swill, slurp *(informal)*, guzzle, toss off.
2 (v) *Don't gulp your food. See* **gobble**.
3 (v) *The icy water made me gulp. See* **gasp** 1.
4 (n) *A gulp of water might cure your hiccups.* mouthful, swallow, swig *(informal)*, slurp *(informal)*, draught.

gun
(n) firearm, artillery (heavy military guns).
TYPES OF GUN: airgun, automatic pistol, blunderbuss, cannon, handgun, howitzer, machine gun, mortar, musket, pistol, revolver, rifle, sawn-off shotgun, shotgun, stun gun, sub-machine-gun.

gunman
(n) armed robber, sniper, assassin, hit man *(slang)*, terrorist, gangster, killer, murderer.

gurgle
1 (v) *Can you hear the baby gurgle?* burble, crow, chuckle, laugh.
2 (v) *Listen to the stream gurgle over the stones.* babble, bubble, burble, splash, murmur, tinkle, ripple, lap, plash.

gush
(v) *Water began to gush from the pipe.* pour, cascade, stream, flow, flood, spurt, spout, squirt, splash, surge, overflow.

gust
(n) *A gust of wind blew my hat off.* puff, blast, flurry, rush, squall, gale, breeze.

gusty *see* **windy** 1.

gut
1 (n) *I have a pain in my gut.* stomach, belly, tummy *(informal)*, guts *(plural)*, insides *(plural) (informal)*, intestines *(plural)*, innards *(plural) (informal)*.
2 (adj) *(informal) I didn't think about it; it was a gut reaction.* instinctive, intuitive, spontaneous, involuntary, unthinking, natural, emotional, deep-seated.
3 **guts** *(plural n) (informal) It takes guts to face up to a bully. See* **courage**.

guzzle *see* **gobble**.

#

habit
1 *(n) Cindy has a habit of biting her nails.* practice, way, tendency, quirk, mannerism.
2 *(n) It's our habit to spend Christmas with Grandma.* custom, practice, tradition, routine, convention, procedure, rule.
3 *(n) Mum wants to kick her habit of smoking.* addiction to, dependence on, craving for, weakness for, obsession with, fixation with.

haggard
(adj) The rescued sailors looked haggard. drawn, drained, exhausted, worn out, tired out, thin, gaunt, hollow-cheeked, hollow-eyed, pinched, wasted, emaciated, all skin and bone *(informal)*, cadaverous.

haggle *see* bargain 3.

hair
1 *(n) Sharmila's hair reaches her waist.* locks *(plural)*, tresses *(plural)*, curls *(plural)*, mop *(informal)*, mane, shock, head of hair.
2 *(n) Craig is starting to get some hair on his chin.* whiskers *(plural)*, bristles *(plural)*, stubble, down, fuzz *(informal)*.
3 *(n) The animal's hair was matted.* fur, coat, wool, fleece *(sheep)*, mane *(horse)*.

hair-raising *see* frightening.

hairy
1 *(adj) A hairy animal.* furry, shaggy, long-haired, fleecy, woolly, fuzzy.
OPPOSITE: hairless.
2 *(adj) A hairy face.* bearded, whiskery, bristly, stubbly, unshaven, fuzzy.
OPPOSITE: clean shaven.

half-hearted
1 *(adj) I feel half-hearted about this plan.* lukewarm, unenthusiastic, apathetic, indifferent, unconcerned, unemotional, neutral, passive, uncommitted.
OPPOSITE: enthusiastic.
2 *(adj) The goalie made a half-hearted attempt to reach the ball.* listless, lacklustre, perfunctory, cursory, superficial.
OPPOSITES: wholehearted, determined.

hall
1 *(n) The dining room is at the far end of the hall.* hallway, entrance hall, lobby, foyer *(hotel, theatre)*, passage, corridor.
2 *(n) Over a hundred people gathered in the hall.* meeting hall, assembly hall, village hall, church hall, concert hall, auditorium, conference hall, exhibition hall.

halt *see* stop 1, 4, 9.

hammer
1 *(n) Len dropped the hammer on his foot.* mallet, sledgehammer, gavel.
2 *(v) Hammer this nail into the wood.* bang, drive, hit, knock, tap.

hamper *see* hinder 1.

hand
1 *(n) Raise your hand if you disagree.* fist, palm, paw *(informal)*, mitt *(slang)*.
2 *(n) I need a hand to move this table.* helping hand, help, assistance, aid.
3 *(n) The audience gave me a big hand.* clap, round of applause, ovation.
4 *(v) Hand your ticket to the bus driver.* give, hand over, pass, present, submit, offer, deliver, reach *(informal)*.

handcuffs
(plural n) cuffs *(plural) (informal)*, bracelets *(plural) (slang)*, manacles *(plural) (old-fashioned)*, fetters *(plural) (old-fashioned)*, shackles *(plural) (old-fashioned)*.

hand down
1 *(v) I hand down my clothes to my younger sister.* pass on, pass down, give.
2 *(v) Lord Lucre plans to hand down his fortune to his children.* leave, pass on, bequeath, will, transfer, give.

handicap
1 *(n) Deafness is a physical handicap.* disability, impairment.
2 *(n) It's a handicap to live a long way from school.* disadvantage, drawback, inconvenience, nuisance, obstacle, hindrance, impediment, stumbling block.
OPPOSITE: advantage.

---

hair and hairstyles

hair colours	hairstyles	you can have your hair...	hair can be...		other hair words
auburn	Afro	backcombed	bouncy	unkempt	
black	beehive	bleached	bushy	wavy	bald patch
blonde	bob	braided	coarse	wild	blue rinse
brown	braids	crimped	curly	windswept	fringe
carroty	bun	cropped	dishevelled	wiry	hair band
chestnut	bunches	dyed	fine	wispy	hair extension
coppery	chignon	flicked back	floppy		hairline
dark	cornrows	gelled	flowing		hairnet
fair	crew cut	hennaed	frizzy		hairpiece
flaxen	dreadlocks	highlighted	glossy		hair ribbon
(golden)	flat-top	layered	greasy		hair slide
ginger	French plait	permed	lank		parting
grey	hippy braids	plaited	limp		sideburns
greying	mohican	scraped back	matted		toupee (man's
mousy	pageboy	shaved	neat		hairpiece)
platinum	perm	slicked back	receding		wig
blonde	pigtail	streaked	shaggy		
raven (black)	plaits	tinted	shining		
red	ponytail	undercut	sleek		
sandy	pudding-bowl		smooth		
silver	quiff		spiky		
snowy	ringlets		straggly		
strawberry	short back		straight		
blonde	and sides		tangled		
white	skinhead		thinning		
	wedge		tousled		

braids

cornrows

beehive

chignon

quiff

bob

dreadlocks

mohican

hairpin

beads

hairgrip

gel

handicapped

handicapped *see* **disabled**.

handle
1 *(v) Be careful how you handle your guinea pig.* hold, pick up, touch, stroke, fondle, caress, feel, finger, paw *(informal)*.
2 *(v) This machine is easy to handle.* control, operate, manage, work, use, run, manoeuvre, drive, steer, manipulate.
3 *(v) Mrs Badger can handle our class.* deal with, manage, control, cope with.

hand out *see* **give out**.

handsome
(adj) Ryan is so handsome! attractive, good-looking, gorgeous, hunky *(informal)*.
OPPOSITES: ugly, unattractive.

handwriting *see* **writing**.

handy
1 *(adj) This gadget is really handy.* useful, practical, helpful, easy to use, user-friendly, convenient, well-designed, neat *(slang)*.
OPPOSITES: awkward, impractical.
2 *(adj) Do you have your ruler handy?* within easy reach, close at hand, nearby, accessible, convenient, available, ready.
OPPOSITES: inaccessible, out-of-the-way.

hang
1 *(v) I'd like the streamers to hang from the ceiling.* hang down, be suspended, dangle, swing, trail, drape, sway.
2 *(v) Look how the trees hang over the pond.* lean, bend, bow, droop, sag, loll.
3 *(v) Is this a good place to hang the picture?* put up, fix, pin up, nail, stick, hook, suspend, fasten, attach.
4 *(v) The eagle seemed to hang in the air.* See **hover**.

hang around
1 *(v) Is this where you like to hang around?* hang about, hang out *(informal)*, spend your time, loiter, linger, hang loose *(informal)*, frequent, haunt.
2 *(v) Don't hang around - we'll be late!* See **delay** 1.

hang on *see* **hold on** 1, 2.

hang-up
(n) (informal) I have a hang-up about flying. phobia, fear of, problem with, thing *(informal)*, mental block, inhibition.

happen
1 *(v) Anything could happen if you make a wish.* occur, take place, come about, come to pass *(old-fashioned)*, follow, result, transpire, come up, crop up *(informal)*.
2 *(v) Did you happen to see Vanessa?* chance, have the good fortune, have the luck, have the misfortune.
3 **happen to** *(v) What will happen to me if I fail my exams?* become of, befall.

happiness
(n) The thought of his holiday filled Mac with happiness. joy, delight, pleasure, contentment, bliss, glee, elation, ecstasy, jubilation, rejoicing, exuberance, euphoria, high spirits *(plural)*, rapture, merriment.
OPPOSITES: sadness, sorrow.

happy
1 *(adj) I feel happy.* cheerful, contented, in good spirits, light-hearted, jolly, joyful, jubilant, elated, ecstatic, euphoric, on cloud nine *(informal)*, over the moon *(informal)*, in seventh heaven, walking on air *(informal)*.
OPPOSITES: sad, miserable.
2 *(adj) I'm so happy you could come.* See **pleased**.
3 *(adj) We had a happy holiday.* blissful, heavenly, idyllic, jolly, merry, enjoyable.
OPPOSITE: miserable.

harass *see* **pester**.

harbour *see* **port**.

hard
1 *(adj) We tried to dig a hole, but the ground was too hard.* firm, solid, stony, rocky, unyielding, impenetrable, resistant, rigid, dense, compacted, frozen.
OPPOSITE: soft.
2 *(adj) This sum is hard!* See **difficult** 1.
3 *(adj) Gardening is such hard work.* exhausting, gruelling, strenuous, backbreaking, tough, killing *(informal)*, demanding, laborious, uphill, heavy.
OPPOSITES: easy, light.
4 *(adj) Barney has had a hard year.* difficult, tough, rough *(informal)*, unpleasant, painful, distressing, grim, unbearable, intolerable, disastrous, calamitous, dark, black.
OPPOSITES: easy, pleasant.
5 *(adj) The boxer suffered a hard blow to the head.* heavy, violent, powerful, driving, forceful, severe, strong, fierce, sharp.
OPPOSITES: gentle, light.
6 *(adj) Miss Blackheart is a hard woman.* hardhearted, heartless, unsympathetic, unfeeling, cold, callous, cruel, ruthless, pitiless, merciless, inflexible, unrelenting, stern, strict, brutal.
OPPOSITES: kind, softhearted.
7 *(adv) Greg works hard.* diligently, industriously, conscientiously, energetically, strenuously, vigorously, untiringly, persistently, doggedly, unceasingly, steadily, resolutely, furiously.

harden
(v) Wait for the mixture to harden. set, solidify, go hard, stiffen, freeze, jell, congeal, cake.
OPPOSITE: soften.

hardly
(adv) I hardly recognized you in that hat! scarcely, only just, barely, with difficulty.
OPPOSITE: easily.

hard-wearing
(adj) Hard-wearing fabric. tough, strong, sturdy, durable, long-lasting, rugged, resilient, stout.

hard-working
(adj) Libby is so hard-working! industrious, diligent, conscientious, energetic, tireless, productive, busy, indefatigable, keen.
OPPOSITES: lazy, workshy.

harm
1 *(v) Casper wouldn't harm anyone.* hurt, injure, ill-treat, abuse, wound, inflict pain on, inflict suffering on.
2 *(v) Reading in poor light can harm your eyesight.* See **damage** 3.
3 *(n) The fire caused a lot of harm.* See **damage** 1.
4 *(n) The rumours caused a lot of harm.* damage, distress, suffering, pain, ill feeling, mischief, upset, trauma.
OPPOSITE: benefit.

harmful
1 *(adj) Smoking is harmful.* damaging, bad for you, dangerous, detrimental, injurious.
OPPOSITES: beneficial, healthy.
2 *(adj) Bleach contains harmful substances.* See **dangerous** 4.

harmless
1 *(adj) This mixture is harmless.* safe, innocuous, nontoxic, nonpoisonous.
OPPOSITES: dangerous, deadly.
2 *(adj) It was just a bit of harmless fun.* gentle, innocent, inoffensive, innocuous, blameless, unobjectionable.
OPPOSITES: hurtful, offensive.

harrowing *see* **disturbing**.

harsh
1 *(adj) The commander spoke in a harsh voice.* grating, rasping, rough, strident, raucous, jarring, guttural, gruff, hoarse.
OPPOSITES: soft, gentle.
2 *(adj) Life in the prison was harsh.* hard, tough, austere, grim, Spartan, bleak, comfortless, brutal.
OPPOSITES: easy, comfortable.
3 *(adj) Aunt Bertha's criticisms were harsh.* severe, stern, unsparing, unkind, caustic, abrasive, stringent, ruthless, cruel.
OPPOSITES: gentle, compassionate.
4 *(adj) The station lights were harsh.* glaring, dazzling, garish, over-bright.
OPPOSITES: restful, subdued.

hassle
1 *(n) (informal) I got my ticket without any hassle.* bother, trouble, difficulty, fuss, inconvenience, problem, struggle.
2 *(v) (informal) I wish you wouldn't hassle me!* See **pester**.

hassled
(adj) (informal) After the shopping trip, Mum looked hassled. harassed, stressed, strained, uptight *(informal)*, worried, careworn, troubled, distraught, harried.
OPPOSITES: carefree, relaxed.

hasty
1 *(adj) You'll make mistakes if you're too hasty.* rash, impetuous, impulsive, impatient, hot-headed, reckless, foolhardy.
OPPOSITES: cautious, careful.
2 *(adj) The robbers made a hasty getaway.* See **fast** 1.
3 *(adj) I had a hasty glance at the paper.* quick, brief, rapid, hurried, fleeting, passing, cursory, perfunctory.
OPPOSITES: leisurely, thorough.

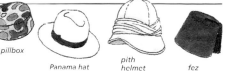

stetson

deerstalker

boater

pillbox

Panama hat

pith helmet

fez

trilby

cloche

hat
(n) headdress, headgear, head covering.
TYPES OF HAT:
balaclava, baseball cap, beanie, bearskin (soldier), beret, boater, bobble hat, bonnet, bowler, cap, cloche, coronet, crash helmet, crown, deerstalker, fez, hard hat, homburg, hunting cap, jockey cap, mitre (bishop), nightcap, Panama hat, peaked cap, pillbox, pith helmet, skullcap, sombrero, sou'wester, stetson, sunhat, tiara, top hat, trilby, turban, wimple (nun).

hate
1 (v) I hate bad language. detest, loathe, despise, cannot stand, cannot bear, have an aversion to, dislike, abhor, abominate.
OPPOSITES: love, adore.
2 (n) Miss Blackheart is full of hate. hatred, hostility, loathing, dislike, ill will, malice, venom, animosity, antagonism, vindictiveness, antipathy, enmity, rancour.
OPPOSITE: love.

haughty see **proud** 2.

haul see **pull**.

haunted
1 (adj) Do you think that Greystone Grange is haunted? visited by spirits, cursed, jinxed, ghostly, spooky (informal), eerie. ❖ Also see **ghosts & hauntings**.
2 (adj) I was haunted by the memory of Samantha's smile. obsessed, preoccupied, plagued, tormented, troubled, worried.

have
1 (v) I have six pets. own, possess, keep.
2 (v) How many chapters does your book have? contain, consist of, include, comprise, incorporate.
3 (v) You will have good and bad times in your life. experience, go through, live through, undergo, encounter, meet with, endure, enjoy, suffer.
4 (v) Everyone will have a prize. get, receive, be given, win, gain, obtain, acquire, secure, take.
5 (v) Let's have a party! See **give** 4.
6 (v) Let's have tea. eat, take, consume.
7 (v) Mum's going to have another baby. give birth to, produce, bring into the world, bear, deliver, bring up, raise.

have to
1 (v) I have to do my homework. must, should, ought to, have got to, need to.
2 (v) There's no escaping. You'll have to pay. be forced to, be compelled to, be made to, be obliged to, be required to.

havoc
(n) (informal) The pigs caused havoc in the pantry. chaos, confusion, mayhem, turmoil, upheaval, disruption, disorder.

haze
(n) I can hardly see you through the haze. mist, fog, murk, fumes (plural), clouds (plural), smog, smoke, dust.

hazy
1 (adj) It's so hazy I can hardly see. misty, foggy, smoky, cloudy, dim, smoggy.
OPPOSITES: clear, bright.
2 (adj) Without my glasses, everything looks hazy. See **blurred**.
3 (adj) I have a hazy memory of that weekend. See **vague** 2.

head
1 (n) I bumped my head. forehead, temple, skull, pate, cranium, crown, nut (slang), bonce (slang), block (slang).
2 (n) Why don't you use your head! brain, brains (plural) (informal), intelligence, intellect, common sense, wits (plural), reason, loaf (slang), noddle (informal).
3 (n) Our school has a new head. headteacher, principal, headmaster, headmistress.
4 (n) Dad is the head of his company. boss (informal), chief executive, director, president, chairman, MD (managing director), manager, chief, leader.
5 (n) The problem came to a head at the end of term. climax, crisis, critical point, turning point, crossroads, culmination.
6 (v) Who will head the team? See **lead** 2.

headache
(n) I've got a headache. splitting headache, migraine, sick headache, sore head.

head for
(v) Let's head for home. make for, aim for, go towards, make a beeline for, set off for.

heal
1 (v) Will this heal my rash? See **cure**.
2 (v) I hope your broken arm will heal soon. get better, mend, recover, improve, be cured, knit (bones).

health
(n) Exercise is good for your health. wellbeing, fitness, strength, constitution.

healthy
1 (adj) My parents have always been healthy. fit, well, in good shape, hale and hearty, strong, active, vigorous, bursting with health, blooming.
OPPOSITES: sickly, unwell.
2 (adj) Try to eat foods that are healthy. nutritious, wholesome, nourishing, good for you, healthgiving, beneficial.
OPPOSITES: unhealthy, harmful.

heap
1 (v) Heap the leaves together. See **pile** 2.
2 (n) A heap of papers. See **pile** 1.
3 heaps (plural n) (informal) Lord Lucre has heaps of money. See **plenty**.

hear
1 (v) Did you hear what I said? catch, pick up, listen to, pay attention to, take in, overhear, eavesdrop on, listen in on.
2 (v) I hear that you're leaving. See **understand** 3.

heart
1 (n) I like living in the heart of the city. See **centre** 1, 2.
2 (n) Andrew has a kind heart. nature, temperament, character, disposition.

heartbreaking
(adj) A heartbreaking story. heart-rending, tragic, distressing, harrowing, poignant, pitiful, agonizing, tear-jerking (informal).

heartless see **cruel** 1, 2.

hearty
1 (adj) We gave the explorers a hearty welcome. enthusiastic, effusive, friendly, warm, cordial, sincere, genuine, heartfelt, genial, unreserved, back-slapping.
OPPOSITES: cool, lukewarm.
2 (adj) After our walk, we'll need a hearty meal. substantial, filling, satisfying, sizable, nourishing, solid, square.
OPPOSITES: meagre, modest.

heat
1 (n) This heat is making me ill. warmth, high temperature, sultriness, hot weather, warm weather, heatwave, hot spell.
OPPOSITE: cold.
2 (v) I'll heat some soup for lunch. heat up, warm up, reheat, cook, make hot.
OPPOSITES: chill, cool.

heated see **passionate** 1.

heath see **moor** 1.

heave
1 (v) Heave the chest onto the deck. haul, lug, pull, lift, raise, hoist, tug.
2 (v) Heave the rubbish overboard. See **throw** 1.
3 (v) I'm going to heave! See **vomit**.

heaven
1 (n) Do you believe that there is a heaven? paradise, afterlife, hereafter, next world, life to come, life everlasting.
OPPOSITE: hell.
2 (n) Our holiday was pure heaven! bliss, delight, joy, ecstasy, paradise, happiness, seventh heaven.
OPPOSITES: hell (informal), misery.

heavenly
1 (adj) A heavenly messenger. divine, angelic, celestial, holy, blessed.
OPPOSITE: earthly.
2 (adj) (informal) A heavenly scent. glorious, exquisite, delightful, sublime, out of this world, blissful, divine (informal), gorgeous, wonderful.
OPPOSITES: vile, disgusting.

heavy

heavy
1 *(adj) I struggled with the heavy suitcase.*
weighty, bulky, unwieldy, cumbersome,
hefty, massive, top-heavy, immovable.
OPPOSITE: light.
2 *(adj) Ed is heavy for his age.* overweight,
hefty, large, beefy *(informal)*, stout, portly.
OPPOSITES: light, slight.
3 *(adj) Mrs Badger has a heavy workload.*
demanding, exhausting, gruelling, killing
(informal), taxing, onerous, tough,
backbreaking, arduous, intolerable.
OPPOSITES: light, undemanding.
4 *(adj) Heavy rain forced us to stay
indoors.* torrential, continuous, nonstop,
steady, unremitting, severe, penetrating.
OPPOSITE: light.
5 *(adj) The bush was heavy with berries.*
laden, weighed down, loaded, burdened.
6 *(adj) This film is too heavy for me.*
serious, deep, difficult, profound, dry.
OPPOSITES: lightweight, light-hearted.
7 *(adj) The sky was heavy before the
snowstorm.* leaden, louring, gloomy, dull,
overcast, threatening, oppressive.

hectic
(adj) The shops are hectic. busy, bustling,
chaotic, frenzied, frantic, frenetic.

heir, heiress
(n) Who is the heir to the throne? next in
line, successor, inheritor of.

hell
1 *(n) Do you believe that there is a hell?*
underworld, nether world, lower world,
infernal regions *(plural)*, inferno.
OPPOSITE: heaven.
2 *(n) (informal) Mum went through hell
worrying about Alice.* See **torture** 2.

help
1 *(v) I'd like to help you.* give you a hand,
assist, lend you a hand, be of use to, be of
assistance to, be helpful to, cooperate
with, collaborate with, support, advise,
give you moral support, back, stand by.
OPPOSITES: obstruct, hinder.
2 *(v) I'll help you if you get into trouble.*
rescue, save, come to your rescue, come to
your aid, save you from danger.
3 *(v) We raised money to help starving
children.* support, aid, assist, benefit.
4 *(v) Will this help my toothache?* cure,
relieve, ease, soothe, calm, make better,
alleviate, do a world of good for.
5 *(n) I'm grateful for my parents' help.*
support, assistance, backing, guidance,
advice, cooperation, friendship, aid,
encouragement, helping hand.

helpful
1 *(adj) Yusuf is always helpful.* obliging,
cooperative, supportive, kind, friendly,
considerate, caring, neighbourly.
OPPOSITES: unhelpful, uncooperative.
2 *(adj) Cam had some helpful suggestions.*
useful, constructive, practical, handy,
valuable, worthwhile, beneficial, positive.
OPPOSITES: useless, unhelpful.

helping
(n) Mo wants another helping of pudding.
portion, serving, plate, bowl, plateful,
bowlful, dollop *(informal)*, share, ration.

helpless
1 *(adj) Jon's injuries left him helpless.*
weak, feeble, incapacitated, disabled,
debilitated, paralysed, incapable,
bedridden, laid up *(informal)*, dependent.
2 *(adj) Without weapons the soldiers were
helpless.* powerless, impotent, useless,
ineffective, defenceless, unprotected,
vulnerable, exposed to danger.

herb
(n) TYPES OF HERB: basil, bay leaf, chives
(plural), coriander, dill, fennel, fenugreek,
marjoram, mint, oregano, parsley,
rosemary, sage, tarragon, thyme.

hero
1 *(n) Write about a sporting hero.*
champion, celebrity, star, superstar,
megastar, great man, great woman.
2 *(n) Famous Fred is my hero.* idol, role
model, ideal, shining example, heart-throb.
3 *(n) I'm playing the hero in the school
play.* lead, leading man, good guy
(informal), protagonist.
OPPOSITE: villain.

heroic
*(adj) Indiana has performed many heroic
deeds.* brave, courageous, daring,
adventurous, fearless, bold, intrepid,
death-defying, swashbuckling, gallant,
chivalrous, valiant *(old-fashioned)*.
OPPOSITES: cowardly, faint-hearted.

heroine
1 *(n) Miranda is my heroine.* idol, role
model, ideal, shining example.
2 *(n) I'm playing the heroine in the school
play.* lead, leading lady, protagonist.
OPPOSITE: villain.

hesitant
*(adj) Judd was hesitant at first, but in the
end he joined in.* tentative, cautious, wary,
unsure, uncertain, diffident, reluctant,
indecisive, half-hearted, wavering, timid.
OPPOSITES: decisive, resolute.

hesitate
(v) Don't hesitate; just do it! falter, dither,
delay, think twice, waver, hang back.

hidden
1 *(adj) Make sure that Mum's present is
hidden.* concealed, out of sight, covered
up, invisible, unseen, shrouded, veiled.
OPPOSITES: visible, exposed.
2 *(adj) Can you find the hidden message?*
secret, obscure, cryptic, coded, mysterious.

hide
1 *(v) Quick! It's time to hide!* take cover,
lie low, go into hiding, hole up *(informal)*,
go to ground, keep out of sight, find a
hiding place, conceal yourself, hide out.
2 *(v) Let's hide the present under these
clothes.* conceal, put out of sight, cover
up, bury, secrete, stow, stash *(informal)*.

3 *(v) It's hard to hide your feelings.*
conceal, disguise, cover up, mask, keep
secret, suppress, keep under your hat.
OPPOSITES: reveal, show.
4 *(v) The soldiers used bushes to hide the
tank.* See **disguise** 3.

hideous
1 *(adj) A hideous monster.* See **ugly** 1.
2 *(adj) A hideous crime.* See **horrible** 1.

high
1 *(adj) A high tower.* See **tall** 2.
2 *(adj) Your work is of high quality.*
excellent, outstanding, exceptional, top,
first-class, superior.
OPPOSITES: low, poor.
3 *(adj) Jo has a high voice.* high-pitched,
shrill, piercing, piping, soprano, treble.
OPPOSITES: low, deep.
4 *(adj) The price of the meal was rather
high.* excessive, steep *(informal)*,
exorbitant, extortionate, unreasonable.
OPPOSITES: low, reasonable.
5 *(adj) Lord Lucre moves in high society.*
distinguished, exalted, aristocratic, upper
class, eminent, leading, influential.
OPPOSITES: humble, lower class.
6 *(adj) (informal) We were all high after
the concert.* See **excited**.
7 *(adj) (informal) Ziggy was high after
taking drugs.* stoned *(slang)*, spaced out
(slang), on a trip *(informal)*, delirious.

highlight
1 *(n) Leonora's solo was the highlight of
the show.* high spot, climax, high point.
OPPOSITE: low point.
2 *(v) Use make-up to highlight your best
features.* emphasize, play up, draw
attention to, accentuate, set off, spotlight.
OPPOSITES: conceal, disguise.
3 *(v) The report will highlight the
importance of safety.* See **emphasize**.

highly strung
*(adj) Try not to upset Bo; she's very highly
strung.* nervous, excitable, temperamental,
easily upset, sensitive, twitchy, nervy
(informal), uptight *(informal)*, tense,
hypersensitive, neurotic, wired *(slang)*.

hijack
*(v) Terrorists have threatened to hijack the
plane.* seize, skyjack, take over,
commandeer, hold up, divert, waylay.

hike
1 *(v) We had to hike all the way home.*
walk, trek, tramp, backpack, trudge, slog,
march, ramble, plod, hoof it *(slang)*.
2 *(n) It's a short hike home.* See **walk** 3.

hilarious
(adj) The clowns were hilarious. side-
splitting, hysterical *(informal)*, uproarious,
riotous, funny, entertaining.

hill
1 *(n) Let's run to the top of the hill.*
hillside, mound, hillock, hummock, knoll,
dune, bank, peak, ridge, tor, fell.
2 *(n) This hill is too steep for our old van.*
slope, incline, rise, gradient.

hinder
1 *(v) That suitcase will hinder you terribly.* hamper, get in your way, slow you down, hold you up, delay, handicap, encumber.
2 *(v) If you want to go, I won't hinder you.* deter, stand in your way, hold you back, prevent, thwart, oppose, obstruct, curb.

hint
1 *(n) There was no hint that Megan was planning to leave.* clue, indication, suggestion, inkling, whisper, tip-off, intimation, insinuation, innuendo, allusion.
2 *(n) I've picked up a handy hint from this book.* tip, suggestion, piece of advice.
3 *(n) Is there a hint of garlic in the sauce?* trace, suggestion, touch, suspicion, whiff, tinge, dash, soupçon, taste.
4 *(v) I did hint that I wanted a bike.* imply, suggest, indicate, insinuate, let it be known, mention, signal, give you a tip-off.

hit
1 *(v) I hope Bozo won't hit you.* punch, thump, strike, belt *(slang)*, clobber *(slang)*, biff *(slang)*, whop *(informal)*, deck *(slang)*, clout *(informal)*, bash *(informal)*, wallop *(informal)*, sock *(slang)*, take a swipe at *(informal)*, beat you up *(informal)*, kick, knee, slap, smack, spank, beat, club, cosh, batter, pummel, hammer, jab, prod, poke.
2 *(v) Don't hit your head!* bump, bang, bash *(informal)*, knock, strike, whack, thump, smash, hurt.
3 *(v) Hit the ball hard* strike, slam, wham, whack, drive, smash, sock *(slang)*, knock, swat, swipe at *(informal)*, kick, head, punch, tap, volley, lob, putt *(golf)*.
4 *(v) I hope our car doesn't hit anything.* bump into, crash into, run into, collide with, smash into, bash into *(informal)*, knock, strike, bang into, meet head-on.
5 *(v) The bad weather will hit tourism this summer.* damage, affect, have an impact on, influence, make an impression on, leave its mark on, knock for six *(informal)*.
6 *(n) (informal) This film will be a hit. See* **success** 1.

hitch
(n) I'm sorry I'm late; there's been a hitch. problem, snag, complication, difficulty, hold-up, setback, hiccup *(informal)*, delay.

hoard
(v) Jamal loves to hoard his sweets. save, keep, hold on to, hang on to, save up, stockpile, store up, accumulate, amass, stack up, stash away *(informal)*, stow away, set aside, set by, squirrel away.

hoarse
(adj) My voice is hoarse from shouting. croaky, husky, rough, gruff, rasping, cracked, throaty, raucous, gravelly, harsh.

hobble
(v) These new shoes make me hobble. limp, shuffle, stumble, totter, stagger.

hobby
(n) Do you have a hobby? pastime, leisure activity, interest, pursuit, sideline.

hoist *see* **heave** 1.

hold
1 *(v) I want to hold the baby.* cuddle, embrace, hug, cradle, carry.
2 *(v) Hold my hand. See* **hold on to**.
3 *(v) I can't hold your weight.* carry, take, support, bear, sustain, shoulder.
4 *(v) The police will hold the suspect.* detain, confine, keep, remand in custody. OPPOSITES: release, let go.
5 *(v) We decided to hold a meeting.* call, organize, arrange, convene.
6 *(v) The hall will hold six hundred people.* seat, take, accommodate, contain, sit.
7 *(v) I hope this weather will hold until the weekend.* last, hold out, continue, hang on, carry on, stay, persist, keep up, endure.
8 *(n) Leya couldn't get a hold on the rock.* grip, foothold, footing, purchase.
9 *(n) Polly's parents have no hold over her.* control, authority, influence, power, clout.

hold back
(v) Try to hold back your giggles. keep back, control, check, suppress, stifle, smother, restrain, bite back.

hold on
1 *(v) Try to hold on until help comes.* hang on, hold out, keep going, persevere, stick it out *(informal)*, hang in there *(informal)*.
2 *(v) (informal) Hold on! I'm coming.* hang on *(informal)*, wait a minute, stay there, don't go away, hold the line *(telephone)*.

hold on to
(v) Hold on to my hand. hold, take, hang on to, grip, grasp, clasp, clutch, seize, cling on to, clench.

hold-up *see* **delay** 4.

hold up
1 *(v) I hope the traffic doesn't hold you up. See* **delay** 2.
2 *(v) These pillars hold up the roof. See* **support** 1.
3 *(v) The robbers planned to hold up the train.* rob, hijack, stick up *(slang)*, waylay.

hole
1 *(n) Don't fall into that hole!* pit, crater, trench, hollow, dip, depression, burrow, tunnel, pothole, abyss, shaft, excavation.
2 *(n) We found a hole in the wall.* gap, opening, cavity *(wall, tooth)*, crack, crevice, cranny, chink, fissure, slit, space.
3 *(n) There's a hole in my tyre.* puncture, slit, tear, split, cut, gash, rent, pinprick.
4 *(n) The creature returned to its hole.* lair, den, burrow *(rabbit)*, warren *(rabbit)*, earth *(fox)*, sett *(badger)*, cave, tunnel, nest.

holiday
1 *(n) You deserve a holiday.* break, rest, vacation, time off, leave.
2 *(n) Let's plan a holiday.* vacation, trip, tour, cruise, package holiday, self-catering holiday, camping holiday, beach holiday, skiing trip, adventure holiday, safari.
❖ *Also see* **journey words, mountain words, sea & seashore, seaside words**.

hollow
1 *(n) We found a hollow in the ground.* dip, depression, indentation, dent, recess, hole, crater, pit, cavity, trough, basin. OPPOSITES: rise, hill.
2 *(adj) The tube was hollow.* empty, unfilled, void, hollowed out, vacant. OPPOSITES: solid, filled.
3 *(adj) The drum made a hollow sound.* deep, low, echoing, reverberating, rumbling, muffled, muted, dull, dead.
4 *(adj) The prisoner had hollow cheeks.* sunken, caved-in, concave, deep-set *(eyes)*.
5 *(adj) I can't trust your hollow promises.* empty, meaningless, false, insincere. OPPOSITES: genuine, sincere.

holy
1 *(adj) A holy person.* saintly, pious, devout, God-fearing, religious, spiritual, virtuous, pure, godly.
2 *(adj) A holy place.* sacred, blessed, consecrated, sanctified, divine, hallowed *(old-fashioned)*.

home
(n) Is this your home? house, residence, pad *(slang)*, dwelling, dwelling place, domicile, abode *(old-fashioned)*, home town, birthplace, native land.
TYPES OF HOME: apartment, bedsit, bungalow, cabin, caravan, castle, chalet, chateau, cottage, council house, detached house, farmhouse, flat, high-rise flat, hostel, houseboat, hut, lodge, log cabin, maisonette, manor house, mansion, mill, mobile home, palace, prefabricated house, ranch, semi-detached house, shack, stately home, studio flat, tenement building, tent, terraced house, tower block, villa, windmill. ❖ *Also see* **houses & homes**.

homeless
(adj) You can't imagine what it's like to be homeless. destitute, down-and-out, outcast, abandoned, without a roof over your head, on the streets.

homely
(adj) Granny's cottage has a homely feel. cosy, comfortable, friendly, welcoming, snug, modest, unassuming, unpretentious, plain, simple. OPPOSITES: grand, pretentious.

honest
1 *(adj) I want an honest answer to my question.* truthful, sincere, straight, frank, candid, plain, direct, open, forthright, straightforward, upfront *(informal)*. OPPOSITES: false, insincere.
2 *(adj) Mr Badger wouldn't cheat; he's an honest man.* truthful, honourable, trustworthy, upright, moral, scrupulous, virtuous, law-abiding, principled. OPPOSITE: dishonest.
3 *(adj) I must find an honest way to earn money.* above board, legitimate, on the level *(informal)*, ethical, moral, legal, lawful, genuine, bona fide. OPPOSITES: dishonest, fraudulent.

honour
1 *(n) Mr Badger wouldn't cheat; he's a man of honour.* integrity, principle, high principles *(plural)*, honesty, morality, scruples *(plural)*, decency, virtue.
2 *(n) I will fight to defend my honour. See* **reputation**.
3 *(n) It's an honour to be chosen for the team.* privilege, credit, achievement, source of pride, compliment.

honourable *see* **honest** 2.

hooked *see* **addicted** 1, 2.

hooligan
(n) vandal, delinquent, yob *(informal)*, yobbo *(informal)*, thug, ruffian, roughneck *(slang)*, tough, rowdy, lout, lager lout.

hop *see* **skip** 1.

hope
1 *(v) We hope that we will arrive on time.* expect, anticipate, believe, trust.
2 *(v) I hope to be a star.* long, want, wish, yearn, aspire, intend, plan, expect, dream.
3 *(n) This result should give you some hope.* confidence, faith, optimism, belief, trust, assurance, expectations *(plural)*.
4 *(n) Cassandra's hope is to be a star. See* **wish** 1.
5 *(n) Try this door; it's our only hope.* chance, opportunity, prospect, possibility.

hopeful
1 *(adj) We are hopeful that we will win.* optimistic, confident, expectant.
OPPOSITES: pessimistic, despairing.
2 *(adj) The future looks hopeful.* promising, encouraging, heartening, reassuring, bright, rosy, favourable.
OPPOSITES: hopeless, grim.

hopeless
1 *(adj) The situation is hopeless.* beyond hope, beyond repair, beyond remedy, impossible, irredeemable, irreparable.
OPPOSITES: promising, hopeful.
2 *(adj) All our efforts proved to be hopeless.* futile, useless, pointless, worthless, in vain, worth nothing.
OPPOSITES: worthwhile, useful.
3 *(adj) The bad news made us feel hopeless. See* **pessimistic**.
4 *(adj) (informal) I'm hopeless at French.* useless *(informal)*, no good, clueless *(slang)*, incompetent, pathetic *(informal)*, rotten *(informal)*, lousy *(slang)*.
OPPOSITES: expert, proficient.

horrible
1 *(adj) We were shocked by the horrible crime.* dreadful, appalling, horrifying, horrific, horrendous, terrible, shocking, ghastly, vile, gruesome, grisly, monstrous, sickening, harrowing, awful, frightful, atrocious, hideous, loathsome, despicable.
2 *(adj) What a horrible meal!* revolting, disgusting, foul, nasty, awful, terrible, dreadful, horrid, vile, yucky *(slang)*, nauseating, stomach-turning, inedible.
OPPOSITES: lovely, delicious.

3 *(adj) Don't be so horrible to me!* mean, nasty, beastly *(informal)*, horrid *(informal)*, unkind, disagreeable, unpleasant, hateful, cruel, spiteful, vicious, offensive, hostile.
OPPOSITES: kind, considerate.

horrific *see* **horrible** 1.

horrified
(adj) Mum will be horrified when she hears the news. shocked, appalled, aghast, outraged, scandalized, disgusted, revolted, sickened, nauseated, offended.

horrify
1 *(v) The sight of the monster will horrify you. See* **scare** 1.
2 *(v) Your jokes will horrify Aunt Bertha. See* **shock** 2.

horror
(n) Ellie gazed at the scene in horror. shock, alarm, dismay, dread, fear, terror, fright, fear and trembling, disgust, loathing, revulsion, consternation, panic.

horse
(n) pony, stallion (male), mare (female), foal (baby), colt (young male), filly (young female), gelding (castrated male), mount, steed, nag *(informal)*, charger.
TYPES OF HORSE: carthorse, cob, dressage horse, driving horse, event horse, hunter, polo pony, racehorse, show horse.
COLOURS OF HORSE: bay, chestnut, dapple-grey, dun, grey, palomino, piebald, roan, skewbald.

hostile
(adj) Why are you so hostile? antagonistic, aggressive, anti *(informal)*, belligerent, unsympathetic, unfriendly, unwelcoming.
OPPOSITES: friendly, peaceable.

hot
1 *(adj) I can't stand this hot weather.* sweltering, baking, boiling; scorching, roasting, blistering, burning, blazing, searing, sultry, humid, steamy, torrid.
OPPOSITES: cold, freezing, icy.
2 *(adj) Be careful! This food is hot.* boiling, boiling hot, scalding, piping hot, steaming, sizzling, red-hot, bubbling.
OPPOSITES: cold, chilled.
3 *(adj) I feel hot.* flushed, feverish, sweaty, perspiring, boiling, boiling hot, overheated.
OPPOSITES: cold, freezing.
4 *(adj) Bozo has a hot temper.* fiery, violent, fierce, savage, flaming, impetuous.
OPPOSITES: mild, sweet.
5 *(adj) This curry has a hot taste.* spicy, peppery, fiery, piquant, sharp, strong, pungent, biting.
OPPOSITE: mild.

house
1 *(n) Is this your house?* home, residence, pad *(slang)*, dwelling, dwelling place, domicile, abode *(old-fashioned)*.
2 *(v) You need someone to house you.* take you in, put you up, give you a roof over your head, shelter, accommodate.

horse words

horse moves

amble	stride
bolt	stumble
buck	trek
canter	trot
gallop	walk
jump	
kick	**horse sounds**
leap	
pace	blow
plod	neigh
prance	puff
rear	snort
roam	whinny

a horse can look...
beautiful
dainty
elegant
graceful
muscular
powerful
solid
stocky
strong
sturdy

a horse's coat can be...
dull
glossy
mangy
matted
rough
shaggy
shiny
silky
sleek
smooth
tangled
thick
velvety

forelock   mane
neck   hindquarters
muzzle   withers
shoulder
breast
belly
hindleg
foreleg   fetlock
piebald

glossy bay

palomino

stocky pony

a horse can be...

alert	nervous
brave	nimble
calm	obedient
courageous	playful
docile	skittish
excitable	strong-willed
fractious	stubborn
friendly	surefooted
frisky	timid
gentle	tireless
good-natured	uncontrollable
hardy	well-behaved
highly strung	well-schooled
intelligent	well-trained
lively	wild

houses and homes

types of home

apartment
bedsit
bungalow
caravan
castle
cottage
council house
detached house
farmhouse
high-rise flat
hostel
houseboat
maisonette
mansion
mill
mobile home
semi-detached house
stately home
tenement building
terraced house
tower block
villa

homes can be made of...

brick
concrete
glass
slate
steel
stone
timber

homes can be...

half-timbered
ivy-covered
painted
pebble-dashed
plastered
thatched
timber-framed
whitewashed

half-timbered cottage

high-rise flats

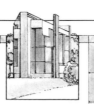
futuristic house

OUTSIDE THE HOME

homes may have...

balcony
bay window
casement window (hinged window)
chimney pots
dormer window (window in roof)
French windows
picture window
sash window (push-up window)
satellite dish
shutters
skylight
sliding doors
solar panel
TV aerial
window box

outside you may see...

crazy paving
creeper
drive
dustbin
fence
fire escape
flowerbed
flower tub
garage
garden
gate
graffiti
hedge
lawn
parking spaces
patio
railings
trellis
washing line

mobile home

INSIDE THE HOME

at the windows

bamboo blinds
faded curtains
floor-length curtains
net curtains
roller blinds
ruched curtains
tattered curtains
Venetian blinds
vertical blinds

homes can look...

dilapidated
drab
dreary
elegant
futuristic
gloomy
grand
imposing
modern
neat
neglected
palatial
pretty
quaint
rambling
ramshackle
shabby
tumbledown

on the floors

bare boards
carpet
cork tiles
flagstones
lino
marble floor
parquet floor
quarry tiles
rugs
rush matting
wooden floor

on the walls

bare plaster
ceramic tiles
damp patch
fancy border
flaking paint
gleaming paintwork
mould
peeling wallpaper
picture rail
wood panelling

homes can feel...

airy
chilly
cluttered
cosy
cramped
damp
dank
draughty
homely
lived-in
luxurious
musty
roomy
snug
spacious
stuffy
sunny
warm
welcoming

sash window

dormer window

casement window

---

hover
(v) The eagle seemed to hover in the air. hang, be suspended, float, drift, be poised, flutter.

howl
1 (v) The baby began to howl. bawl, wail, cry, scream, yell, shriek, caterwaul, bellow.
2 (v) Can you hear the wolves howl? bay, yelp, yowl.

huddle
1 (v) Let's huddle together to stay warm. bunch, cluster, squeeze, snuggle, nestle, cuddle, press, pack, crowd, herd, throng.
OPPOSITES: scatter, disperse.
2 (n) The players formed a huddle in the centre of the pitch. cluster, group, mass, crowd, pack, throng, jumble, heap.

huff see **mood** 2.

hug
(v) I long to hug you. take you in my arms, hold you close, cuddle, embrace, squeeze, hold, enfold, clasp, cling to.

huge
(adj) A huge building. enormous, immense, massive, vast, extensive, colossal, gigantic, monumental, mighty, lofty, towering, mammoth, giant, monstrous, monster, gargantuan, stupendous, ginormous (informal), humongous (informal).
OPPOSITES: tiny, minute.

hum
(n) Can you hear the hum of the engine? buzz, drone, murmur, purr, whir, throb, thrum, pulsing, vibration.

humble
1 (adj) Carl was humble about his success. See **modest** 1.
2 (adj) The emperor expects his subjects to be humble. meek, submissive, docile, respectful, polite, courteous, deferential, servile, slavish, subservient, obsequious.
OPPOSITES: proud, arrogant.
3 (adj) The woodcutter lived in a humble cottage. poor, simple, modest, ordinary, plain, unpretentious, lowly (old-fashioned), small, insignificant, unremarkable.
OPPOSITES: grand, ostentatious.

humid
(adj) It was humid in the jungle. sultry, muggy, steamy, sticky, clammy, close, sweltering, sweaty, damp, dank, misty.
OPPOSITES: dry, arid.

humiliate
(v) Your mum would never humiliate you in public. degrade, demean, put you down, make you feel small, take you down a peg (informal), make you eat humble pie, debase, deflate, disgrace, discredit, shame, make you ashamed, embarrass.

humiliating
(adj) A humiliating defeat. crushing, degrading, demeaning, ignominious, shameful, disgraceful, discreditable, embarrassing, mortifying, undignified.

humorous see **funny** 1.

h

hunger

(n) The refugees were dying of hunger. starvation, malnutrition, lack of food.

hungry

1 *(adj) After the match, we were all hungry.* ravenous, famished, starving *(informal)*, peckish *(informal)*, in need of food, half-starved, empty *(informal)*.
OPPOSITES: full, satisfied.
2 *(adj) Fred is hungry for success.* eager, longing, yearning, desperate, greedy.

hunt

1 *(v) Foxes hunt small animals.* prey on, stalk, track, trail, chase, pursue, hunt down, hound, capture, kill.
2 *(v) I must hunt for my tie. See* **search** 2.
3 *(n) The police organized a hunt for the escaped prisoner. See* **search** 3.

hurl *see* **throw** 1.

hurricane *see* **storm** 1.

hurry

1 *(v) We must hurry or we'll be late.* rush, be quick, get a move on *(informal)*, hurry up, lose no time, dash, fly, run, step on it *(informal)*, make haste *(old-fashioned)*.
OPPOSITES: dawdle, delay.
2 *(v) You can't hurry this process.* rush, hasten, speed up, accelerate, quicken.
OPPOSITES: slow down, delay.
3 *(n) Jessica left in a hurry.* rush, flurry, flap *(informal)*, commotion, bustle.

hurt

1 *(v) How did you hurt your arm?* injure, wound, bruise, cut, scratch, graze, scrape, burn, scald, sprain, break, damage.
2 *(v) My comment wasn't meant to hurt you.* hurt your feelings, upset, wound, distress, cause you pain, offend, grieve, sadden, sting, cut you to the quick.
3 *(v) This won't hurt.* be painful, be sore, sting, smart, burn, ache, throb, be tender.
4 *(adj) I felt hurt when Ben ignored me.* upset, wounded, saddened, distressed, cut to the quick, aggrieved, offended, put out.

hurtful

(adj) A hurtful remark. upsetting, distressing, offensive, unkind, cruel, nasty, spiteful, malicious, vicious, cutting, biting, scathing, wounding, sarcastic, withering.

hurtle *see* **speed** 4.

husky *see* **hoarse**.

hut

(n) The refugees lived in a tiny hut. shack, shelter, shed, cabin, hovel, shanty, den.

hype

1 *(n) After all the hype, the film was disappointing. See* **build-up**.
2 *(v) Famous Fred is trying to hype his new release. See* **promote** 2.

hypocritical

(adj) It's hypocritical of Burglar Beryl to condemn stealing. two-faced, insincere, deceitful, dishonest, duplicitous, phoney *(informal)*, inconsistent, self-righteous, sanctimonious, holier-than-thou.

hysterical

1 *(adj) You'll be hysterical when you hear the news.* frantic, frenzied, in a frenzy, berserk, beside yourself, distraught, overwrought, in a panic, out of control, wild, out of your mind, crazed.
2 *(adj) (informal) The comedy act was hysterical. See* **hilarious**.

I i

icy

1 *(adj) The weather was icy. See* **cold** 1, 2.
2 *(adj) The pavement was icy.* slippery, like glass, frosty, frozen over, treacherous, glassy, slippy *(informal)*.
3 *(adj) Aunt Bertha gave me an icy stare.* cold, chilly, frosty, glacial, frigid, stony, steely, hard, disapproving, withering, forbidding, hostile, unfriendly.
OPPOSITES: warm, friendly.

idea

1 *(n) The idea came to me in the bath.* thought, notion, inspiration, brainwave, plan, scheme, design, concept, theory, hypothesis, solution.

ice, frost and snow

ice, frost and snow words
black ice
blizzard
hail
hailstones
hoarfrost
icicles
Jack Frost
sheet ice
sleet
snowdrift
snowflakes
snowstorm
sub-zero temperatures

the wind is...
arctic
biting
bitter
chilling
freezing
glacial
icy
numbing
piercing
polar
raw
Siberian
stinging

the air feels...
bracing
chilly
crisp
fresh
frosty
invigorating
nippy

the ground is...
blanketed with snow
carpeted with snow
dusted with snow
frost-bound
frozen solid
hard
icy
slippery
slushy
sprinkled with snow
treacherous

the trees are...
bare
encrusted with ice
frost-covered
hoary
snow-covered
snow-laden

snow-laden trees

hoary leaves

snowflakes...
drift
eddy
float
settle
swirl
tumble
waft
whirl

snow...
blankets
buries
camouflages
drifts
envelops
muffles
shrouds
transforms

the snow is...
blinding
crisp
crunchy
dazzling
deep
fresh
frozen
glistening
glittering
melting
packed
powdery
slushy
soft
sparkling
thawing
untrodden

snowdrift

blizzard

in the snow you...
flounder
plod
sink in
slog
stomp *(informal)*
struggle
stumble
tramp
trudge
wade
wallow

frost...
coats
etches patterns
glistens
glitters
sparkles

the ice is...
brittle
cracked
crazed
glassy
gleaming
glinting
shiny
slippery
smooth

on the ice you...
glide
skate
skid
skim
slide
slip
slither

2 *(n) I had an idea that Aunt Bertha was angry.* feeling, notion, suspicion, hunch, inkling, sense, impression.
3 *(n) Give me an idea about what you'd like for your birthday.* clue, hint, indication, suggestion, inkling, intimation.
4 *(n) What was the idea of running off like that?* point, purpose, aim, object, intention, meaning, sense, use.
5 *(n) We all had the same idea about the film.* opinion, thoughts *(plural)*, view, viewpoint, feeling, attitude, impression, judgment, interpretation, conclusion.

ideal
1 *(adj) Edward is an ideal pupil.* model, perfect, faultless, exemplary, dream.
2 *(adj) This is the ideal time to buy a house.* best, perfect, right, most suitable, correct, most advantageous, optimum.
3 *(adj) In my ideal world it would always be summer.* imaginary, dream, fantasy, hypothetical, perfect, Utopian.

idealistic
(adj) Jamie has an idealistic view of life. unrealistic, romantic, over-optimistic, impractical, starry-eyed, perfectionist.
OPPOSITES: realistic, down-to-earth.

identical
(adj) These socks are identical. the same, matching, indistinguishable, similar, alike.
OPPOSITE: different.

identify
1 *(v) Can you identify these flowers?* recognize, name, put a name to, classify, catalogue, label.
2 *(v) Try to identify the differences between the two pictures.* See **spot** 1.
3 **identify with** *(v) Can you identify with the hero in the film?* relate to, sympathize with, feel for, empathize with, put yourself in the shoes of, see through the eyes of.

idiot
(n) Don't be such an idiot! fool, imbecile *(informal)*, nincompoop, twit *(informal)*, nitwit *(informal)*, numskull, dimwit *(informal)*, twerp *(informal)*, wally *(slang)*, prat *(slang)*, plonker *(slang)*, nerd *(slang)*, jerk *(slang)*, dork *(slang)*, airhead *(slang)*.

idiotic see **stupid** 1, 2.

idle *see* **lazy** 1.

idol
1 *(n) Who is your idol at the moment?* hero, heroine, heart-throb, pin-up *(slang)*, favourite, darling, ideal, star.
2 *(n) Indiana found a golden idol in the tomb.* image, statue, effigy, god.

idolize
(v) I idolize Famous Fred. adore, worship, hero-worship, look up to, admire, revere.

ignorant
1 *(adj) I'm totally ignorant about politics.* uninformed, unaware, unknowledgeable, clueless *(slang)*, unenlightened, naive, green, uneducated, unlearned, illiterate.
OPPOSITES: well-informed, educated.

2 *(adj) That was a very ignorant remark.* stupid, thoughtless, insensitive, shallow, superficial, crass, rude, crude, coarse.
OPPOSITES: intelligent, astute.
3 **ignorant of** *(adj) Ziggy is ignorant of the dangers of taking drugs.* unaware of, oblivious to, blind to, unfamiliar with, unacquainted with, in the dark about, unconscious of, ill-informed about.
OPPOSITES: aware of, conscious of.

ignore
1 *(v) Try to ignore Theo's nasty remarks.* take no notice of, pay no attention to, disregard, overlook, pass over, turn a deaf ear to, turn a blind eye to, be oblivious to.
OPPOSITES: pay attention to, heed.
2 *(v) If you try to spoil our game, we'll ignore you.* take no notice of, pay no attention to, send you to Coventry, shut you out, ostracize, shun, reject, snub, give you the cold shoulder *(informal)*, freeze you out *(informal)*, cut you dead *(informal)*.
OPPOSITE: pay attention to.

ill
1 *(adj) Are you ill?* sick, unwell, poorly *(informal)*, off colour, ailing, indisposed, under the weather *(informal)*, out of sorts.
OPPOSITES: well, healthy.
2 *(adj) I came off the boat feeling ill.* sick, queasy, groggy *(informal)*, nauseous, green around the gills *(informal)*, peculiar, funny *(informal)*, queer, rough *(informal)*, grotty *(slang)*, weak, faint, delicate, fragile, frail.
OPPOSITES: well, strong.

illegal
1 *(adj) Have you ever done anything illegal?* unlawful, criminal, against the law, illicit, forbidden, outlawed, banned, prohibited, proscribed.
OPPOSITES: legal, above board.
2 *(adj) Dodgy Dave sells illegal whisky.* unlicensed, black market, bootleg, under-the-counter *(informal)*, contraband.
OPPOSITE: legal.

illegible
(adj) Mrs Badger says my handwriting is illegible. impossible to read, hard to make out, indecipherable, unreadable, unclear, unintelligible, scribbled, scrawled, squiggly.
OPPOSITES: legible, clear.

illness
1 *(n) Araminta is absent with a mysterious illness.* ailment, complaint, disorder, sickness, disease, infection, virus, bug *(informal)*, lurgy *(slang)*, malady, indisposition, affliction, attack.
2 *(n) Our family has been plagued by illness.* ill health, poor health, sickness, disease, disability, infirmity.
OPPOSITES: good health, fitness.

illusion
1 *(n) That white lady you saw was just an illusion.* hallucination, apparition, figment of your imagination, phantom, spectre, fantasy, dream, mirage *(illusion of water)*.
OPPOSITE: reality.

2 *(n) One line looks longer than the other, but that's an illusion.* trick, optical illusion, false impression, deception, misperception.

illustrate
(v) Write out your poem and illustrate it. add pictures to, add drawings to, provide artwork for, depict, decorate, adorn, embellish, ornament.

illustration
1 *(n) Look at the illustration on page 14.* picture, drawing, sketch, artwork, graphics *(plural)*, figure, plate, diagram, graph.
2 *(n) Give me an illustration of what you mean.* See **example** 1.

image
1 *(n) Can you see an image on your computer screen?* picture, symbol, figure, icon, photograph, reflection.
2 *(n) You're the image of your dad.* double, living image, spitting image *(informal)*, twin, clone, dead ringer for *(slang)*, chip off the old block *(informal)*.
3 *(n) People have the wrong image of me.* idea, impression, picture, perception.
4 *(n) Flash Frank is worried about his image.* public persona, reputation, public perception, outward appearance, aura.

imaginary
1 *(adj) Dragons aren't real; they're imaginary.* make-believe, fictional, nonexistent, unreal, fantastic, legendary, mythical, mythological, fairy-tale.
OPPOSITE: real.
2 *(adj) Justin has an imaginary illness.* made-up, pretend, invented, imagined, notional, nonexistent.
OPPOSITES: real, actual.

imagination
1 *(n) Designers need imagination.* creativity, inventiveness, originality, inspiration, vision, flair, ingenuity, insight.
2 *(n) The monster only exists in your imagination.* mind, fantasies *(plural)*, dreams *(plural)*, head.

imaginative
(adj) Jabir is full of imaginative ideas. creative, original, inspired, inventive, innovative, ingenious, resourceful.
OPPOSITES: unimaginative, unoriginal.

imagine
1 *(v) Can you imagine a world without flowers?* picture, envisage, visualize, see in your mind's eye, conceive of, think of, conjure up, dream up.
2 *(v) I imagine you'd like some lunch.* See **assume**.

imitate
1 *(v) Felix can imitate Elvis Presley.* do an impression of, impersonate, mimic, do *(informal)*, take off *(informal)*, send up *(informal)*, parody, ape, caricature.
2 *(v) Try to imitate the style of this poem.* copy, match, duplicate, emulate, follow, take as a model, follow the example of.
3 *(v) Do soaps on TV imitate real life?* reflect, mirror, echo, parallel, simulate.

imitation
1 (n) Is this painting real or is it an imitation? See **copy** 2.
2 (n) Bobby does a good imitation of Elvis Presley. See **impression** 4.
3 (adj) My bag is made of imitation leather. synthetic, artificial, mock, fake, man-made, simulated, sham.
OPPOSITES: real, genuine.

immature
(adj) Act your age and don't be so immature! childish, babyish, juvenile, infantile, puerile, adolescent, callow, unsophisticated, inexperienced, green.
OPPOSITES: mature, grown-up.

immediate
(adj) I received an immediate reply. instant, instantaneous, prompt, quick, speedy, swift, direct, punctual.

immediately
(adv) Come here immediately! at once, straightaway, right away, instantly, without delay, promptly, directly, now, right now, this minute, this instant, in the twinkling of an eye.

immense see **huge**.
immerse see **dip** 3.
immoral
1 (adj) How could anyone be so immoral? unprincipled, dishonest, unscrupulous, amoral, unethical, depraved, perverted, corrupt, debauched, degenerate, dissolute, promiscuous, evil, wicked, sinful, bad.
OPPOSITES: moral, upright, virtuous.
2 (adj) It's immoral to show violent films to young children. See **wrong** 2.

immortal
(adj) An immortal being. eternal, undying, everlasting, indestructible, timeless, ageless, deathless, divine.
OPPOSITE: mortal.

impact
1 (n) The car headlights were shattered by the impact. blow, collision, crash, bump, bang, jolt, smash, knock, clash.
2 (n) What sort of impact did the book have? effect, influence, significance, consequences (plural), repercussions (plural), impression, splash (informal).

impartial see **neutral**.
impatient
1 (adj) Waiting makes me feel impatient. restless, fidgety, edgy, on edge, irritable, agitated, fretful, anxious, nervous, tense, wound up (informal), jittery (informal), excited, like a caged lion.
OPPOSITES: patient, calm.
2 (adj) Aunt Bertha was very impatient with me. abrupt, brusque, curt, snappy, short, intolerant, short-tempered, peevish.
OPPOSITES: patient, tolerant.
3 (adj) I was impatient to open my presents. See **eager** 2.

impersonate see **imitate** 1.
impertinent see **cheeky**.

imply see **hint** 4.
importance
(n) Mrs Badger stressed the importance of the situation. significance, seriousness, gravity, momentousness, urgency.

important
1 (adj) This is an important decision. significant, major, serious, momentous, vital, critical, crucial, key, grave, weighty, far-reaching, historic, once-in-a-lifetime, earthshaking (informal).
OPPOSITES: insignificant, trivial.
2 (adj) It's important that you come on time. essential, vital, necessary, crucial.
OPPOSITES: unimportant, unnecessary.
3 (adj) Underline the important points in your notes. See **main**.
4 (adj) I'd like to be an important person. influential, powerful, prominent, high-ranking, leading, eminent, distinguished, outstanding, notable, famous.
OPPOSITES: unimportant, insignificant.

impose on
(v) I don't want to impose on you. be a nuisance to, take advantage of, inconvenience, put you out, make you go out of your way, abuse your hospitality, exploit, burden, saddle (informal).

imposing see **impressive** 1.
impossible
1 (adj) Pigs can't fly - it's impossible! out of the question, beyond the bounds of possibility, unthinkable, inconceivable, unimaginable, not to be thought of.
OPPOSITE: possible.
2 (adj) Don't set yourself impossible goals. unrealistic, unreasonable, unachievable, unattainable, impractical, unworkable, ridiculous, ludicrous, preposterous, crazy.
OPPOSITES: reasonable, realistic.
3 (adj) I'm in an impossible situation. hopeless, intolerable, unbearable, unacceptable, catch-22, no-win (slang).
4 (adj) (informal) Evie is being impossible again! See **awkward** 4.

impractical
1 (adj) An impractical plan. unworkable, impossible, unrealistic, useless, wild, crazy.
OPPOSITES: practical, viable.
2 (adj) Daisy is so impractical. unrealistic, unbusinesslike, up in the clouds, idealistic, romantic, starry-eyed.
OPPOSITES: sensible, down-to-earth.

impress
1 (v) Did the film impress you? make an impression on, affect, inspire, move, touch, excite, stir, leave its mark on, stick in your mind (informal), grab (informal), influence.
2 (v) Justin wore a smart suit in order to impress. make an impact, stand out, cause a stir, be conspicuous, arouse comment, attract attention, make a hit (informal).

impression
1 (n) This book made a big impression on me. impact, effect, influence, mark.

2 (n) What was your impression of the film? opinion, view, memory, recollection.
3 (n) I got the impression something was wrong. See **feeling** 2.
4 (n) Do your impression of Elvis Presley. impersonation, imitation, takeoff (informal), send-up (informal), parody.

impressive
1 (adj) An impressive view of the mountains. striking, imposing, magnificent, splendid, majestic, awe-inspiring, breathtaking, remarkable, grand.
2 (adj) An impressive film. powerful, inspiring, remarkable, memorable, magnificent, great, stunning (informal), stirring, moving, touching, thrilling.

imprison see **jail** 2.
improbable see **unlikely**.
improve
1 (v) Jamal has begun to improve this term. make progress, get better, develop, make strides, make headway, progress, come on, advance, shape up (informal).
OPPOSITES: get worse, fall behind.
2 (v) Mum hopes that business will improve soon. get better, pick up, perk up, look up, recover, rally, take a turn for the better (informal).
OPPOSITES: worsen, fall off.
3 (v) I'm doing my best to improve the situation. make better, put right, rectify, correct, help, mend, ameliorate.
OPPOSITES: make worse, aggravate.
4 (v) The patient is starting to improve. get better, recover, be on the mend, be on the road to recovery, recuperate, rally, convalesce, heal, turn the corner.
OPPOSITES: get worse, deteriorate.

improvement
1 (n) I've seen some improvement in your work. progress, development, advance.
OPPOSITE: deterioration.
2 (n) Our flat needs some improvement. renovation, refurbishment, redecoration, modernization, alterations (plural).

improvise
(v) If you haven't prepared a speech, you'll have to improvise. ad-lib, make it up as you go along, wing it (informal), speak off the cuff (informal), extemporize.

impudent see **cheeky**.
impulsive
1 (adj) Letty is such an impulsive person. impetuous, unpredictable, spontaneous, hot-headed, rash, reckless, capricious.
OPPOSITES: cautious, prudent.
2 (adj) Jen took an impulsive decision to become a vegetarian. See **sudden** 2.

inaccessible see **remote**.
inaccurate
(adj) This account is inaccurate. incorrect, inexact, imprecise, untrue, false, wrong, flawed, unreliable, unsound, misleading, vague, full of errors, wide of the mark.
OPPOSITES: accurate, exact.

inadequate
1 *(adj) Our supplies are inadequate.* insufficient, not enough, meagre, scanty, sparse, in short supply, low.
OPPOSITES: adequate, sufficient.
2 *(adj) Mrs Badger said my essay was inadequate.* unsatisfactory, unacceptable, not good enough, not up to scratch *(informal)*, incomplete, deficient, sketchy.
OPPOSITES: adequate, satisfactory.
3 *(adj) My older sister makes me feel inadequate. See* **inferior** 2.

incessant *see* **constant** 1

in charge *see* **responsible** 3.

incident
1 *(n) That was a memorable incident! See* **event** 1.
2 *(n) I hope there won't be an incident at the match.* disturbance, clash, skirmish, confrontation, scene, commotion, row, fracas, fight, contretemps.

include
1 *(v) This kit should include everything you need.* contain, incorporate, hold, consist of, comprise, involve, take in, encompass, embrace.
OPPOSITES: exclude, leave out.
2 *(v) Try to include this point in your essay.* incorporate, bring in, build in, cover, take into account, deal with, introduce, put in, insert, slip in, add, enter.
OPPOSITES: leave out, omit.

incompetent
(adj) Mum thinks her boss is totally incompetent. incapable, inept, inadequate, ineffectual, inexpert, useless *(informal)*, hopeless *(informal)*, inefficient, unqualified.
OPPOSITES: competent, capable.

inconsiderate *see* **thoughtless**

inconvenient
1 *(adj) You've picked an inconvenient moment to arrive.* awkward, inopportune, ill-timed, untimely, unfortunate, unsuitable, embarrassing, bad.
OPPOSITES: convenient, suitable.
2 *(adj) It's inconvenient when the water is cut off.* awkward, tiresome, annoying, irritating, troublesome, a nuisance, a bore.
OPPOSITES: convenient, handy.
3 *(adj) This parcel is an inconvenient shape. See* **awkward** 3.

increase
1 *(v) Pupil numbers should increase.* rise, grow, multiply, escalate, climb, soar, shoot up, rocket, snowball, spiral, mushroom.
OPPOSITES: decrease, decline.
2 *(v) The noise began to increase when Mrs Badger left the room.* grow, rise, build up, intensify, mount, escalate, heighten.
OPPOSITES: decrease, diminish.
3 *(v) Jet wants to increase her CD collection.* expand, extend, enlarge, build up, widen, broaden, develop, add to, boost, swell, enhance, augment.
OPPOSITES: reduce, decrease.

4 *(n) There has been an increase in crime.* rise, growth, explosion, escalation, upsurge, upturn, leap.
OPPOSITES: decrease, fall.

incredible
1 *(adj) Jojo told an incredible tale about meeting an alien.* unbelievable, far-fetched, unlikely, implausible, improbable, impossible, unconvincing, amazing, extraordinary, absurd, preposterous.
2 *(adj) (informal) I had an incredible time at the party. See* **fantastic** 3.

indecent
1 *(adj) An indecent joke. See* **rude** 2.
2 *(adj) Indecent clothes.* immodest, improper, unseemly, revealing, titillating, outrageous, shocking, tasteless, vulgar.
OPPOSITES: decent, respectable.

indecisive
(adj) Bart is so indecisive, he just can't make up his mind. irresolute, dithery, tentative, hesitant, undecided, uncertain, vacillating, in two minds.
OPPOSITES: decisive, certain.

independent
1 *(adj) Europe is made up of many independent countries.* separate, distinct, unconnected, individual, self-governing, autonomous, sovereign, non-aligned.
2 *(adj) Fenella is too independent to work well in a team.* self-reliant, self-sufficient, self-contained, individualistic, unconventional, free-thinking, liberated.

indicate *see* **show** 2, 5.

indifferent
(adj) How can you be so indifferent when people are suffering? unconcerned, unfeeling, apathetic, unsympathetic, uncaring, unmoved, impassive, heedless, blasé, detached, unemotional, cold.
OPPOSITES: caring, concerned.

indignant *see* **annoyed**.

indirect
(adj) I took an indirect route home. roundabout, circuitous, winding, meandering, rambling, tortuous, long.
OPPOSITES: direct, straight.

individual
1 *(adj) You can buy individual portions of butter.* single, separate, personal.
2 *(adj) Maisie has an individual style.* unique, distinctive, personal, idiosyncratic, particular, characteristic, special, singular.

indulge
1 *(v) Gran loves to indulge us. See* **spoil** 3.
2 **indulge in** *(v) Why don't you indulge in a relaxing bath?* treat yourself to, wallow in, luxuriate in, revel in, bask in.

indulgent
(adj) I wish my parents were as indulgent as yours. lenient, permissive, tolerant, liberal, easy-going, understanding, sympathetic, forbearing, generous, doting, fond, overindulgent, soft.
OPPOSITE: strict.

inevitable
(adj) This disaster was inevitable. unavoidable, unpreventable, inescapable, bound to happen, certain, fated, destined, ordained, decreed, out of your hands.

inexperienced
(adj) An inexperienced team member. new, untried, untrained, untutored, unpractised, unseasoned, unqualified, green, raw.
OPPOSITE: experienced.

infatuated *see* **in love with**.

infect
(v) This virus could infect our water supply. contaminate, poison, pollute, blight, taint.

infectious *see* **catching**.

inferior
1 *(adj) This is inferior work. See* **poor** 2
2 *(adj) My older sister makes me feel inferior.* inadequate, useless *(informal)*, worthless, ineffectual, small, no good

infinite
1 *(adj) Infinite time.* unlimited, endless, never-ending, eternal, everlasting.
2 *(adj) Infinite space.* boundless, limitless, bottomless, immeasurable, fathomless.
3 *(adj) There are an infinite number of stars in the sky.* countless, incalculable, untold, numberless, unimaginable.

inflate *see* **blow up** 3.

influence
1 *(n) Jak has a lot of influence in my life.* control, clout, pull, sway, impact, effect, authority, dominance, mastery.
2 *(v) I don't want to influence your decision.* affect, sway, control, bring pressure to bear on, prejudice, guide, determine, direct, manipulate, alter.

inform
1 *(v) We need to inform everyone of the new arrangements. See* **tell** 1.
2 **inform on** *(v) Burglar Beryl doesn't want to inform on her friends.* betray, denounce, incriminate, accuse, tell on *(informal)*, blow the whistle on *(informal)*, grass on *(slang)*, shop *(slang)*, squeal on *(slang)*, snitch on *(slang)*, rat on *(informal)*.

informal
1 *(adj) The party will be quite informal.* casual, relaxed, simple, unpretentious, cosy, unceremonious, unofficial, easy.
OPPOSITES: formal, official.
2 *(adj) Sanjay has an informal manner. See* **casual** 1.
3 *(adj) Don't use informal language in your essay.* colloquial, slangy, chatty.
OPPOSITE: formal.

information
1 *(n) Computers store information.* data, facts *(plural)*, statistics *(plural)*, details *(plural)*, material, knowledge.
2 *(n) I'd like some information about camping.* details *(plural)*, advice, info *(informal)*, bumf *(informal)*, gen *(informal)*, inside knowledge, lowdown *(informal)*.

infuriating *see* **annoying**.

initiative

(n) You need lots of initiative to set up a theatre company. resourcefulness, enterprise, get-up-and-go *(informal)*, dynamism, drive, ambition, push *(informal)*, leadership, inventiveness, originality, creativity.

injection

(n) My arm was sore after the injection. jab *(informal)*, inoculation, vaccination, shot *(informal)*, booster.

injure

(v) Did the terrorists injure many people? hurt, harm, wound, maim, stab, shoot, beat up *(informal)*, bruise, cripple, disable, mutilate, mangle, damage.

injustice

(n) Todd wants to fight against injustice. unfairness, discrimination, prejudice, inequality, oppression, partisanship, bias.
OPPOSITES: justice, fairness.

in love with

(phrase) Maisie is in love with Famous Fred. attracted to, infatuated with, head over heels in love with, besotted with, passionate about, crazy about *(informal)*, smitten with, devoted to, enamoured of.

innocent

1 *(adj) Burglar Beryl insists that she is innocent.* not guilty, in the clear *(informal)*, free from blame, blameless, guiltless, above suspicion, clean *(slang)*.
OPPOSITE: guilty.
2 *(adj) It was just an innocent remark. See* **harmless** 2.
3 *(adj) When Jet left home she was still very innocent.* naive, inexperienced, childlike, gullible, credulous, trusting, unworldly, wet behind the ears *(informal)*.
OPPOSITES: sophisticated, worldly.

inquire *see* **ask** 1.

inquisitive

1 *(adj) Don't you hate inquisitive neighbours? See* **nosy**.
2 *(adj) Lara has an inquisitive approach to life.* inquiring, questioning, interested, curious, lively, alert, probing, sceptical.

insane *see* **mad** 1, 2, 3.

inscription

(n) Can you read the inscription on this stone? writing, lettering, words *(plural)*, engraving, carving, etching.

insect

(n) creepy-crawly *(informal)*, bug.

insensitive *see* **thoughtless**.

inside

1 *(n) We cleaned the inside of the car.* interior, contents *(plural)*.
OPPOSITES: outside, exterior.
2 *(adv) Stay inside!* indoors, under cover.
OPPOSITE: outside.
3 *(adj) The inside walls are flimsy.* interior, internal, indoor, inner, innermost.
OPPOSITE: outside.

insignificant *see* **unimportant**.

insincere

1 *(adj) I despise insincere politicians.* hypocritical, two-faced, deceitful, devious, evasive, untruthful, dishonest, shifty.
OPPOSITES: sincere, honest.
2 *(adj) Jessie gave me an insincere smile.* false, artificial, feigned, affected, put-on, phoney *(informal)*, flattering.
OPPOSITES: sincere, genuine.

insist

1 *(v) I insist that you tidy your room.* demand, require, command, urge, order.
2 *(v) If anyone objects, you must insist.* stand firm, stand your ground, make a stand, put your foot down, be resolute, be determined, not take no for an answer.
OPPOSITES: back down, give way.
3 *(v) Beryl continues to insist that she is innocent.* claim, assert, maintain, affirm, emphasize, stress, swear, vow.

inspect

(v) Experts came to inspect our school. examine, check, monitor, look over, check out, scrutinize, investigate, study, survey, view, observe, appraise.

inspiration

1 *(n) What was the inspiration for your poem?* stimulus, idea, spur, motivation, starting point, influence, encouragement.
2 *(n) I've had an inspiration! See* **idea** 1.

inspire

(v) This book should inspire you. stimulate, fire your imagination, motivate, spark you off, spur you on, encourage, enthuse, energize, galvanize, stir, hearten.

instant

1 *(n) I'll go in an instant. See* **moment** 1.
2 *(adj) An instant reply. See* **immediate** 1.

instinct

1 *(n) Oscar has an instinct for saying the right thing.* knack, gift, talent, genius, intuition, aptitude, capacity, predisposition.
2 *(n) I had an instinct that someone was following me.* feeling, hunch, sense, gut feeling *(informal)*, presentiment, intuition, sixth sense, gut reaction *(informal)*.

instructions

(plural n) Follow the instructions carefully. directions *(plural)*, rules *(plural)*, guidelines *(plural)*, recommendations *(plural)*, advice.

instrument *see* **musical instrument**.

insult

1 *(v) I hope the boys won't insult you.* be rude to, call you names, slag you off *(slang)*, put you down, sneer at, abuse, offend, snub, slight, hurt your feelings, mortify, humiliate, wound, revile, slander.
2 *(n) Your insult really hurt me.* abuse, taunt, gibe, put-down, snub, slur, slight.

insulting

(adj) Insulting comments. rude, abusive, hurtful, wounding, offensive, snide, disparaging, patronizing, scornful, humiliating, slanderous, scurrilous.

intelligent

1 *(adj) An intelligent pupil. See* **clever** 1.
2 *(adj) An intelligent comment.* astute, perceptive, discerning, sensible, shrewd, apt, well-informed, profound, wise, clever.
OPPOSITES: stupid, ignorant.

intend *see* **mean** 3.

intense

1 *(adj) I felt an intense pain in my leg.* sharp, agonizing, excruciating, severe, acute, violent, extreme, great, fierce.
OPPOSITES: slight, mild.
2 *(adj) Jan was seized by an intense desire to win. See* **strong** 6.

intentional *see* **deliberate**.

interest

1 *(n) The poster has attracted lots of interest.* attention, curiosity, notice, concern, suspicion, scrutiny, awareness, response, reaction, sympathy.
2 *(n) The lecture was of no interest to me.* relevance, concern, importance, significance, consequence, value, note.
3 *(n) Taking up a new interest is a good way to meet people. See* **hobby**.
4 *(v) I think this game should interest you.* appeal to, arouse your curiosity, capture your imagination, hold your attention, amuse, attract, intrigue, turn you on *(slang)*, grab *(informal)*, fascinate, captivate, enthral, absorb, engross, rivet.
OPPOSITE: bore.

interested

1 *(adj) I'm interested to know how the story ends.* curious, fascinated, intrigued, keen, eager, excited, concerned.
2 *(adj) Benji is an interested pupil.* enthusiastic, keen, attentive, responsive.
OPPOSITES: apathetic, bored.
3 interested in *(adj) Yoko is interested in science fiction.* into *(informal)*, keen on, fascinated by, enthusiastic about, fond of.

interesting

1 *(adj) This TV programme is really interesting.* fascinating, intriguing, compelling, enthralling, absorbing, gripping, riveting, engrossing, thought-provoking, stimulating, entertaining, spell-binding, captivating, compulsive.
OPPOSITES: boring, dull.
2 *(adj) Barney has an interesting job.* fascinating, varied, stimulating, exciting, challenging, unpredictable, unusual.
OPPOSITES: boring, tedious.

interfere

1 *(v) It's best not to interfere.* get involved, poke your nose in *(informal)*, stick your oar in *(informal)*, intervene, be a busybody, meddle, tamper, intrude, pry, butt in.
2 interfere with *(v) Bad weather will interfere with our plans. See* **upset** 2.

international

(adj) Pollution is an international problem. global, worldwide, universal.
OPPOSITES: national, regional, local.

interrogate see **question** 5.

interrupt
1 *(v) Don't interrupt when I'm talking.* butt in, barge in *(informal)*, cut in, chip in *(informal)*, chime in *(informal)*, heckle, muscle in *(informal)*, disturb, intrude.
2 *(v) We must interrupt this programme to bring you a newsflash.* break off, break into, suspend, cut short, discontinue.

interview
1 *(v) We will interview six candidates for the job.* talk to, sound out, question, quiz.
2 *(v) The detective was keen to interview Burglar Beryl. See* **question** 5.
3 *(n) I had an interview with the careers teacher. See* **talk** 6.

intimate
1 *(adj) Jade is an intimate friend of mine.* close, dear, bosom, treasured, special.
2 *(adj) My diary contains my most intimate secrets. See* **private** 1.
3 *(adj) This cottage has an intimate feel.* cosy, friendly, warm, welcoming, inviting.

intimidate see **scare** 2.

intolerable see **unbearable**.

intolerant
(adj) Why is Aunt Bertha so intolerant? critical, disapproving, narrow-minded, small-minded, bigoted, prejudiced, illiberal, racist, sexist, ageist, homophobic, chauvinist, xenophobic.
OPPOSITES: tolerant, broad-minded.

intriguing see **fascinating**.

introduce
1 *(v) May I introduce you to Jon?* present, make you known, acquaint you with.
2 *(v) Simon will introduce the magic act. See* **announce** 2.
3 *(v) Mrs Badger wants to introduce a new system of rewards.* bring in, set up, start, establish, initiate, launch, inaugurate, institute, set in motion, pioneer.

introduction
(n) Listen to this introduction. opening, intro *(informal)*, lead in, preamble, opening remarks *(plural)*, foreword *(book)*, preface *(book)*, overture *(music)*, opening bars *(plural)* *(music)*, prologue *(play)*.
OPPOSITE: conclusion.

invade
(v) The soldiers will invade the city. attack, storm, march into, enter, descend on, take over, overrun, occupy, raid, plunder.

invasion see **attack** 4.

invent
(v) Gita loves to invent new recipes. make up, think up, devise, create, concoct, dream up, come up with, improvise, formulate, design.

invention
(n) Professor Peabody has come up with a new invention. creation, discovery, innovation, design, brainchild *(informal)*, gadget, contraption, contrivance, device.

investigate
(v) We need to investigate the causes of the accident. inquire into, look into, go into, make inquiries about, gather evidence about, study, examine, consider, explore, research, probe, scrutinize, analyse, inspect, check out.

investigation
1 *(n) Please work on this investigation for homework.* study, exploration, research, analysis, survey, review, examination.
2 *(n) The police are conducting an investigation.* inquiry, postmortem (examination of a dead body), hearing, inquest, fact-finding exercise, review.

invisible
(adj) The camouflaged soldiers were invisible in the bushes. hidden, concealed, disguised, undetectable, indiscernible, inconspicuous, out of sight.
OPPOSITES: visible, conspicuous.

invite
(v) The king and queen invite you to the ball. ask, request the pleasure of your company at, summon, bid *(old-fashioned)*.

inviting see **tempting**.

involve
1 *(v) The pantomime will involve everyone.* affect, concern, draw in, include, touch.
OPPOSITE: exclude.
2 *(v) I won't involve you in this crazy plan.* include, mix you up, implicate, embroil.
3 *(v) What will the job involve?* entail, require, demand, necessitate, mean, imply.

involved
1 *(adj) I don't like story lines that are too involved.* See **complicated**.
2 *(adj) Do you know who was involved in the robbery?* mixed up, implicated, caught up, in on *(informal)*, included, associated, concerned, taking part, participating.

irrelevant
(adj) Your comments are irrelevant to the subject. unrelated, unconnected, beside the point, neither here nor there, inappropriate, unnecessary, inessential, immaterial, pointless, extraneous.
OPPOSITES: relevant, pertinent.

irresistible
(adj) I felt an irresistible urge to laugh. powerful, overpowering, overwhelming, compelling, uncontrollable, urgent.

irresponsible
(adj) You're too irresponsible to be trusted. unreliable, untrustworthy, reckless, careless, immature, harebrained, wild, scatterbrained, erratic, flighty, feckless.
OPPOSITES: responsible, reliable.

irritable see **bad-tempered**.

irritate
1 *(v) Seb's jokes irritate me. See* **annoy** 1.
2 *(v) Will this cardigan irritate the baby's skin?* chafe, rub, scratch, itch *(informal)*, hurt, tickle, inflame, redden, make itchy.

irritated see **annoyed**.

irritating see **annoying**.

isolated
1 *(adj) The cottage was very isolated.* remote, out-of-the-way, inaccessible, lonely, in the middle of nowhere, secluded, off the beaten track, cut off.
2 *(adj) Imogen felt isolated in her new school. See* **alone** 2.

issue
1 *(n) Gus feels strongly about the issue of whaling. See* **subject**.
2 *(n) Have you read the November issue of "Rap Weekly"?* edition, copy, instalment, publication, number.
3 *(v) The police will issue a description of Burglar Beryl. See* **release** 3.
4 *(v) The prison will issue you with a uniform.* supply, provide, furnish, equip.

itch
1 *(n) I've got an itch on my back.* tickle, prickle, tingling, itchiness, irritation.
2 *(v) Chickenpox makes your skin itch.* tickle, prickle, tingle, crawl, burn.

itchy
(adj) The nettles gave me an itchy rash. prickly, tickly, irritating, maddening, uncomfortable, painful, burning.

item
1 *(n) Jen added another item to her list.* object, article, thing, point, detail, entry.
2 *(n) I saw an interesting item in the newspaper. See* **article** 1.

jab
1 *(v) Jo began to jab at the paper with her brush.* stab, poke, lunge, thrust, punch.
2 *(n) Andy gave me a jab in the ribs.* dig, poke, prod, nudge, stab, punch.
3 *(n) (informal) Did the doctor give you a jab? See* **injection**.

jacket see **clothes**.

jagged
1 *(adj) The knife had a jagged edge.* uneven, serrated, ragged, notched, barbed, toothed, irregular, zigzag, spiky.
2 *(adj) I walked carefully over the jagged rocks.* craggy, sharp, uneven, spiky, pointed, ridged, rough, angular.

jail
1 *(n) Burglar Beryl spent a month in the local jail.* gaol, prison, detention centre, cells *(plural)*, nick *(slang)*, can *(slang)*, slammer *(slang)*, clink *(slang)*.
2 *(v) The judge decided to jail Burglar Beryl.* send to prison, lock up, send down *(informal)*, imprison, put away, put behind bars, detain, incarcerate, confine.
OPPOSITES: free, release.

jam

jam
1 *(n) The accident caused a jam on the bypass.* traffic jam, hold-up, snarl-up *(informal)*, tailback, bottleneck, blockage, obstruction, gridlock, congestion.
2 *(v) I tried to jam all my clothes into the case. See* **cram** 1.
3 *(v) All these cars will jam the town centre.* clog, congest, block, obstruct, overcrowd, bung up.

jangle
(v) I heard the keys jangle in the lock. clink, clank, clang, rattle, clatter, chime *(bell).*

jealous
1 *(adj) I was jealous when I saw Liam's new bike. See* **envious**.
2 *(adj) Clarissa's boyfriend is so jealous.* possessive, suspicious, distrustful, doubting, insecure, clingy, overprotective.

jealousy
1 *(n) I was filled with jealousy when I saw Carl's new bike. See* **envy** 1.
2 *(n) Jon's jealousy drove his girlfriend away.* suspicion, suspiciousness, distrust, possessiveness, insecurity.

jeer
1 *(v) Let's jeer at the villain! See* **boo**.
2 jeer at *(v) I'm scared Bozo will jeer at me. See* **make fun of**.

jerk
1 *(v) Jerk the rope when you're ready.* tug, yank, pull, twitch, tweak, jiggle, wrench.
2 *(v) I felt the train jerk. See* **jolt** 1.

jerky
(adj) The robot moved with jerky steps. jumpy, twitchy, shaky, jolting, lurching, fitful, spasmodic, convulsive.
OPPOSITES: smooth, gliding.

jet
(n) A jet of water gushed from the pipe. spurt, fountain, stream, spout, spray, gush.

jewel
(n) gem, precious stone, gemstone, stone, rock *(slang),* sparkler *(informal).*
TYPES OF JEWEL: amethyst, aquamarine, diamond, emerald, garnet, jade, jasper, jet, lapis lazuli, moonstone, onyx, opal, pearl, ruby, sapphire, topaz, turquoise, zircon.
❖ *Also see* **treasure words**.

jewellery
(n) Shall I wear my jewellery? jewels *(plural),* trinkets *(plural),* finery, gems *(plural),* regalia, costume jewellery.
TYPES OF JEWELLERY: anklet, bangle, beads *(plural),* bracelet, brooch, chain, charm bracelet, choker, crucifix, cuff links *(plural),* earring, engagement ring, eternity ring, locket, medallion, necklace, nose ring, pendant, pin, signet ring, tiara, tiepin, watch, wedding ring.

jingle
1 *(v) Can you hear the sleigh bells jingle?* ring, tinkle, jangle, chime, clink, clank.
2 *(n) I can't get that jingle out of my head.* song, tune, melody, ditty, chorus.

jittery *(informal) see* **nervous**.

job
1 *(n) It's my job to keep the classroom tidy.* responsibility, duty, task, chore, role, function, contribution.
2 *(n) What type of job are you interested in?* work, career, employment, occupation, profession, trade, business, line of work.
3 *(n) Mum is looking for a new job.* post, position, situation, appointment.

jog
1 *(v) I jog every day.* run, go running, go jogging, exercise.
2 *(v) Don't jog me when I'm writing.* nudge, prod, poke, push, knock, tap, elbow, jiggle, jolt, jerk, jar, jostle.
3 *(v) This picture should jog your memory.* refresh, jolt, prompt, stir, stimulate, prod.

join
1 *(v) Join the pieces together.* attach, fasten, fix, fit, link, connect, stick, glue, tie, bind, pin, nail, fuse, weld, solder, cement.
OPPOSITES: detach, separate.
2 *(v) Do you want to join our club?* become a member of, enrol in, sign up for, register with, enlist in, affiliate with.
3 *(v) Where do the two roads join?* meet, come together, converge, cross, intersect.
OPPOSITES: fork, divide.

join in
(v) I want you all to join in. take part, participate, contribute, pitch in, pull your weight, do your bit, lend a hand.

joint
(adj) The garden is our joint responsibility. shared, mutual, common, collective, combined, united, communal, cooperative.
OPPOSITE: individual.

joke
1 *(n) Have you heard the joke about the purple cat?* gag *(informal),* wisecrack *(informal),* one-liner *(informal),* quip, pun.
2 *(n) Let's play a joke on Joel. See* **trick** 2.
3 *(v) It's a serious matter; don't joke.* make jokes, crack jokes, jest, fool around *(informal),* tease, mock, be facetious.

jolly *see* **merry**.

jolt
1 *(v) I felt the train jolt as it moved off.* lurch, jerk, jar, start, bump, shake, jounce.
2 *(v) Don't jolt me! See* **jog** 2.

jostle
(v) Don't let the others jostle you out of the way. push, shove, elbow, crowd, hustle, press, squeeze, force, knock, bump.

journalist *see* **reporter**.

journey
1 *(n) The explorers set out on their journey.* voyage, travels *(plural),* expedition, trek, safari, adventure, odyssey.
2 *(n) Write about your journey to France.* trip, excursion, outing, jaunt, tour, flight, crossing, cruise, drive, voyage.
3 *(v) I must journey home. See* **travel** 1.

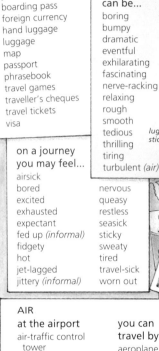

journey words

for your journey you may need...
boarding pass
foreign currency
hand luggage
luggage
map
passport
phrasebook
travel games
traveller's cheques
travel tickets
visa

journeys can be...
boring
bumpy
dramatic
eventful
exhilarating
fascinating
nerve-racking
relaxing
rough
smooth
tedious
thrilling
tiring
turbulent *(air)*

luggage sticker

on a journey you may feel...
airsick
bored
excited
exhausted
expectant
fed up *(informal)*
fidgety
hot
jet-lagged
jittery *(informal)*
nervous
queasy
restless
seasick
sticky
sweaty
tired
travel-sick
worn out

AIR

at the airport
air-traffic control tower
arrivals hall
bureau de change
check-in desk
customs
departure lounge
duty-free shop
flight indicator board
information desk
luggage carousel
luggage trolley
observation terrace
passenger bus
passenger terminal
passport control
restaurant
runway
X-ray machine

you can travel by...
aeroplane
airliner
executive jet
helicopter
jumbo jet *(informal)*
light aircraft

planes...
ascend
bank
circle
climb
cruise
descend
drop
glide
land
mount
nose-dive
rise
soar
take off
taxi

hovering helicopter

RAIL

at the station
arrivals and
  departures board
concourse
  (large central area)
left-luggage office
luggage locker
luggage trolley
platform
railway track
snack bar
station
  announcement
taxi rank
ticket machine
ticket office
waiting room

**you can
travel by...**
commuter train
express train
high-speed train
locomotive
monorail
overnight train
steam train
tube
underground
  train

*luggage
label*

trains...
glide
grind to a halt
hurtle
jerk
jolt
judder
  (informal)
lurch
pull away
pull in
rock
shake
shudder
sway
trundle

train sounds
clank
clatter
click
creak
grind
hum
rattle
squeal
swish
whistle
whoosh

*rail
tickets*

trains can be...
airless
comfortable
cramped
crowded
draughty
jam-packed
shabby
stuffy

rail problems
cancellation
derailment
obstruction on
  the line
points failure
rail strike
signal failure

*network
map*

*high-speed
train*

SEA

**you can
travel by...**
catamaran
cruise ship
ferry
hovercraft
hydrofoil
liner

ships...
berth
cruise
dock
glide
list
pitch
plough through
  the waves
put to sea
roll
sail
set sail
skim
steam
tilt
toss
wallow

on the ship
bridge
cabin
cafeteria
car deck
cinema
control room
deck
duty-free shop
engine room
funnel
lifeboat
lookout tower
passenger lounge
porthole
restaurant
snack bar
sun deck

problems at sea
cancelled crossing
choppy seas
delayed crossing
engine failure
running aground
stormy seas

*cruising
catamaran*

*airliner leaving
the runway*

**plane
sounds**
drone
hum
roar
shriek
throb
vibrate
whine

on the plane
air steward
aisle
captain
emergency exit
flight deck
foldaway table
galley (kitchen)
in-flight
  entertainment
life jacket
overhead
  compartment
safety
  demonstration
seat belt
window seat

*foreign
coins*

**air travel
problems**
air pockets
bad weather
cancelled flight
delayed flight
lost luggage
turbulence

*hire car
key*

ROAD

**you can
travel by...**
bicycle
bus
camper van
car
coach
hire car
minibus
moped
motorcycle
scooter
taxi

vehicles...
accelerate
brake
crawl
cruise
nose forward
overtake
park
pass
reverse
skid
speed
stall
swerve

**traffic
sounds**
beep
chug
cough
growl
honk
hum
purr
rev
roar
screech
splutter
toot
vroom

roads can be...
bumpy
busy
chock-a-block
congested
empty
endless
hazardous
narrow
scenic
single-track
smooth
steep
straight
treacherous
tree-lined
twisting
wide
winding

**problems on
the road**
accident
bad weather
breakdown
hold-up
pile-up *(informal)*
roadworks
tailback
traffic diversion
traffic jam

*camper
van*

*Also see **aircraft**, **boat**.*

joy

joy *see* **happiness**.

joyful *see* **happy** 1.

judge
1 *(v) Who will judge Burglar Beryl's case?* try, hear, examine, give a verdict on, pass sentence on.
2 *(v) Mrs Badger will judge the competition entries.* assess, evaluate, appraise, size up, examine, weigh up, review, criticize.
3 *(v) It was hard to judge if Seb was lying.* gauge, decide, work out, guess, determine, discern, ascertain.
4 *(n) I like this painting, but I'm not much of a judge.* expert, authority, critic, connoisseur.

judgment
1 *(n) What was the court's judgment?* verdict, ruling, decision, conclusion, finding, decree, sentence.
2 *(n) Sam showed a complete lack of judgment.* common sense, good sense, intelligence, discernment, understanding, wisdom, shrewdness, discretion, taste.

jug
(n) A jug of water. pitcher, ewer, carafe, decanter, flagon, crock, urn.

juicy
1 *(adj) Juicy plums.* succulent, luscious, moist, squelchy, soft.
OPPOSITES: dry, shrivelled.
2 *(adj) Juicy gossip.* sensational, spicy (informal), tasty (informal), racy, hot (informal), scandalous, risqué, fascinating, exciting, colourful.

jumble
1 *(v) Don't jumble my papers!* muddle, muddle up, mix up, mess up, make a mess of, shuffle, tangle, disturb, disorganize.
2 *(n) Tidy up this jumble!* mess, chaos, confusion, muddle, clutter, litter, shambles, hotchpotch, hodgepodge, mishmash.

jump
1 *(v) Look at the frog jump!* leap, bound, spring, bounce, hop, skip.
2 *(v) Watch me jump that fence!* clear, vault, hurdle, leap over, sail over.
3 *(v) The noise of the fireworks made me jump.* flinch, start, jerk, recoil, wince, twitch, quiver.
4 *(v) I could jump for joy! See* **dance** 4.
5 *(n) The horse cleared the final jump.* hurdle, fence, gate, rail, hedge, obstacle, barrier, ditch, gap.
6 *(n) I woke with a jump.* jolt, start, jerk, twitch, shudder, shake, quiver.
7 *(n) We predict a jump in prices.* See **rise** 5.

jumper
(n) Put on your jumper. sweater, jersey, pullover, woolly. ❖ *Also see* **clothes**.

jumpy *see* **nervous**.

jungle
(n) rainforest, tropical forest, equatorial forest.

jungle words
clearing (open space)
foliage
forest floor
leaf canopy
quagmire
river
stream
swamp
undergrowth

jungles can be...
airless
claustrophobic
damp
dank
dark
dim
gloomy
humid
misty
muddy
muggy
murky
rainy
shady
slimy
squelchy
steamy
sticky
stifling
swampy
treacherous
unexplored

tree snake

jungle trees and plants
avocado tree
banana tree
cacao tree
ebony tree
fern
liana (creeper)
mahogany tree
mangrove (shrub growing in a swamp)
moss
orchid
palm tree
pineapple tree
rubber tree
teak tree

jungle foliage can be...
bushy
dense
impenetrable
knotted
lush
luxuriant
rotting
tangled

tree frog

chameleon

jungle creatures
alligator
ant
anteater
armadillo
beetle
bird of paradise
butterfly
chameleon
crocodile
gorilla
hummingbird
jaguar
leech (bloodsucker)
leopard
macaw
monkey
mosquito
parrot
piranha (flesh-eating fish)
porcupine
snake
spider
termite
tiger
toucan
tree frog
tree snake

orchid

jungle creatures may...
attack
bite
crawl
creep
dart
flit
flutter
hover
hunt
lie in wait
pad
pounce
prey on other creatures
prowl
scamper
scuttle
slither
spring
stalk
sting
suck blood
swarm
swoop

macaw

jungle sounds
burble
buzz
croak
growl
grunt
gurgle
hiss
rustle
screech
shriek
splash
squawk
squeak
squeal
squelch

toucan

in the jungle you might...
become disorientated
be eaten alive
break into a run
develop a fever
climb
creep
crouch
faint
forage (search for food)
get stuck in a swamp
hack through the undergrowth
hide
itch
lose your way
panic
pant
scrabble
scramble
scratch
slither
slog
splash through streams
squirm
stagger
stumble
sweat
swim
swing from creepers
trek
trip
trudge
wade through mud

hummingbird

liana

armadillo

forest floor

jaguar

junk
(n) Please throw out this junk. rubbish, trash, garbage, litter, scrap, clutter, odds and ends *(plural),* bric-a-brac.

just
1 *(adj) Mrs Badger is strict but she's always just. See* **fair** 2.
2 *(adj) Burglar Beryl received a just sentence.* fitting, appropriate, suitable, proper, apt, rightful, well-deserved.
OPPOSITES: unjust, inappropriate.

justify *see* **excuse** 2.

keen
1 *(adj) Tejal is a keen student.* committed, motivated, enthusiastic, eager, interested, willing, conscientious, diligent, ambitious.
OPPOSITES: unenthusiastic, apathetic.
2 *(adj) Kate is keen to open her birthday presents. See* **eager** 2.
3 **keen on** *(adj) Jenny is keen on football. See* **interested** 3.

keep
1 *(v) Keep the champagne for a special occasion.* hold on to, keep hold of, hang on to, save, put aside, reserve, put away, store, stash away *(informal).*
OPPOSITES: get rid of, use
2 *(v) Oil the wood to help it keep its shine.* retain, maintain, hold, preserve, conserve, keep intact, prolong
OPPOSITE: lose.
3 *(v) Just keep walking. See* **continue** 1.
4 *(v) Keep off the grass!* stay, remain.
5 *(v) It costs a lot to keep a family.* provide for, feed, support, maintain, nourish.
6 *(v) Does your dad keep pigeons?* have, own, care for, look after, tend, mind.

keep on *see* **continue** 1

keep up with
(v) I'm doing my best to keep up with the others. keep pace with, keep abreast of, compete with, rival, match, vie with.

key
1 *(n) This key will open the door.* latchkey, master key, pass key, skeleton key.
2 *(n) Detectives are looking for a key to the mystery. See* **clue**.
3 *(adj) Select the key facts. See* **main**.

kick
1 *(v) Kick the ball.* boot, dribble, pass.
2 *(v) (informal) Mum is trying to kick smoking. See* **stop** 3.

kid
1 *(n) (informal) Stop acting like a kid! See* **child**.
2 *(v) (informal) Who are you trying to kid? See* **deceive** 1.

kidnap
(v) In fairy tales, elves sometimes kidnap babies. snatch, seize, abduct, carry off, steal, hold to ransom, hold hostage.

kill
1 *(v) A hit man was paid to kill the President.* murder, assassinate, take the life of, do away with, bump off *(slang),* do in *(slang),* take out *(slang),* top *(slang).*
2 *(v) The soldiers were ordered to kill the enemy troops.* put to death, slaughter, massacre, butcher, slay, wipe out, destroy, annihilate, obliterate, eradicate, exterminate, liquidate, decimate, waste *(informal),* execute, hang, behead.
3 *(v) (informal) Don't run the marathon - it'll kill you!* tire you out, exhaust, wear you out, overtire, overtax, strain.

killer *see* **murderer**.

killing
1 *(n) Police are investigating the killing.* murder, assassination, homicide, manslaughter, massacre, slaying.
2 *(n) The killing must stop.* bloodshed, slaughter, carnage, butchery, genocide.
3 *(adj) (informal) The runners set off at a killing pace. See* **exhausting**.

kind
1 *(adj) Mr Badger is a kind person.* kind-hearted, kindly, caring, thoughtful, considerate, sympathetic, understanding, unselfish, compassionate, warm-hearted, softhearted, generous, charitable, hospitable, helpful, obliging, neighbourly, friendly, gentle, patient, well-meaning.
OPPOSITES: unkind, cruel.
2 *(n) What kind of food do you like?* sort, type, style, variety, make, brand.
3 *(n) What kind of bird is that?* sort, type, breed, species, family, class, category.

kindness
(n) I appreciate your kindness. helpfulness, thoughtfulness, consideration, generosity, hospitality, sympathy, compassion, understanding, patience, tolerance.

king
(n) monarch, sovereign, ruler.

kingdom *see* **country** 1.

kiss
1 *(v) I don't mind if people kiss in public.* embrace, exchange kisses, blow a kiss, smooch *(informal),* neck *(informal),* snog *(slang),* canoodle *(slang).*
2 *(n) Ned gave me a kiss on the cheek.* peck *(informal),* smacker *(slang).*

kit
1 *(n) The explorers packed their kit into rucksacks.* gear, equipment, tackle, stuff, paraphernalia, apparatus, instruments *(plural),* tools *(plural),* supplies *(plural),* provisions *(plural),* baggage, luggage.
2 *(n) I like your new sports kit.* gear, strip, rigout *(informal),* outfit, colours *(plural),* clothes *(plural),* uniform.

knack
(n) I'd love to be able to juggle, but I don't have the knack. skill, ability, talent, aptitude, expertise, capability, gift, flair.

kneel
(v) Kneel before the king! get down on your knees, fall to your knees, bow down.

knock
1 *(v) Knock the nails into the wood.* tap, hammer, bang, drive, rap, pound, hit.
2 *(v) Don't knock your head on that shelf. See* **hit** 2.
3 *(n) I heard a loud knock on the door.* tap, rap, bang, thud, ratatat-tat.

knock down
1 *(v) The builders were told to knock down this house. See* **demolish**.
2 *(v) If you insult me again, I'll knock you down!* knock you to the floor, throw you to the ground, floor, deck *(slang).*
3 *(v) Be careful that bus doesn't knock you down! See* **run over**.

knock out
(v) A blow on the head could knock you out. make you unconscious, knock you out cold, floor, knock you for six *(informal),* put you out for the count, KO *(slang).*

knot
1 *(n) I can't undo this knot in my shoelace.* loop, twist, bow, tangle.
2 *(v) Knot the two ropes together.* tie, loop, bind, twist, weave, braid, secure.

know
1 *(v) You need to know these facts for the test.* be familiar with, be acquainted with, be conversant with, have a knowledge of, be aware of, have memorized, have learnt by heart, understand
OPPOSITE: be ignorant of.
2 *(v) How can you know that ghosts exist?* know for certain, be sure, be certain, be positive, be confident.
3 *(v) You can't possibly know what I'm going through.* realize, understand, comprehend, tell, be aware of, be conscious of, sense, have experience of.
4 *(v) I used to know Famous Fred.* be acquainted with, have dealings with, socialize with, associate with, be friends with, be on good terms with, be close to.

knowledge
1 *(n) Books are a great source of knowledge.* information, facts *(plural),* data, learning, wisdom, enlightenment.
2 *(n) Penny's knowledge of the subject is good.* understanding, grasp, awareness, comprehension, expertise in.
OPPOSITE: ignorance.

knowledgeable
1 *(adj) The professor is a knowledgeable person.* well-informed, educated, well-read, learned, scholarly, erudite, intelligent.
2 **knowledgeable about** *(adj) Are you knowledgeable about the rules of football? See* **familiar** 2.

Ll

label
1 (n) The price is on the label. tag, tab, sticker, ticket, docket, marker.
2 (v) Label your luggage. attach a label to, put a sticker on, name, mark, tag, stamp.
3 (v) It's unfair to label a child as "difficult". identify, describe, define, brand, class, categorize, classify, call, term, dub.

lack
1 (n) There's a distinct lack of books in our school. See **shortage**.
2 (v) The refugees seem to lack basic medicines. be without, be lacking, be short of, be missing, need, require, want.
OPPOSITES: have, possess.

lacy
(adj) Lacy material. gauzy, cobwebby, wispy, gossamer, delicate, frilly, meshy.

lag behind see drop behind.
laid-back (informal) see relaxed 1, 2.
lair
(n) The creature returned to its lair. den, hole, haunt, cave, tunnel, burrow (rabbit), warren (rabbit), earth (fox), sett (badger).

lake
(n) We paddled in the lake. loch (Scottish), lough (Irish), lagoon, tarn (mountain lake), reservoir, boating lake, pool, pond.

land
1 (n) The sailors were glad to be back on land. dry land, solid ground, terra firma.
2 (n) This land is very fertile. ground, soil, earth, clay, loam, farmland, countryside.
3 (n) Lord Lucre's wealth comes from his land. property, real estate, estate, grounds (plural), acres (plural), farmland.
4 (n) Indiana is visiting a distant land. See **country** 1.
5 (v) When will the plane land? touch down, come in to land, arrive.
OPPOSITE: take off.

landscape
(n) We admired the landscape. countryside, scenery, view, panorama, scene, vista, outlook.

lane
(n) Our garden opens on to a narrow lane. path, pathway, footpath, track, passageway, passage, alley, alleyway.

lank
(adj) Lank hair. limp, straggly, straight, long, dull, lifeless, lustreless, drooping.
OPPOSITES: bouncy, shiny.

lanky
(adj) A lanky youth. tall, long-legged, rangy, gangling, thin, skinny, scrawny, bony, spindly, weedy (informal).
OPPOSITES: dumpy, squat.

lap
1 (n) Pickles settled on my lap. knee.
2 (n) I ran a lap of the track. circuit, circle.
3 (v) Look at Pickles lap his milk. drink, lick up, sip, slurp (informal), sup.
4 (v) Listen to the water lap against the boat. wash, slap, splash, slosh, plash, swish, ripple, gurgle.

large
1 (adj) Mum gave me a large helping of chips. big, huge, enormous, substantial, generous, liberal, sizable, ample, massive, immense, colossal, gigantic, giant, mammoth, mountainous, prodigious, outsize, king-size, whopping (informal).
OPPOSITES: small, modest.
2 (adj) Aunt Bertha is a large woman. big, well-built, big-boned, stout, hefty, thickset, heavy, burly, strapping, fat, corpulent.
OPPOSITES: small, slight.
3 (adj) Lord Lucre lives in a large mansion. great, huge, enormous, spacious, roomy, vast, immense, massive, extensive, sizable, palatial, towering, monumental.
OPPOSITES: small, poky.

last
1 (adj) Read the last chapter of the book. final, concluding, closing, ultimate.
OPPOSITES: first, opening.
2 (adj) Why am I always last? at the end, at the back, at the rear, last in line.
OPPOSITE: first.
3 (adj) What was the last film you saw? most recent, latest.
4 (v) That plant won't last much longer. live, survive, hold out, hold on, live on, linger, endure, continue.
5 (v) The rain could last for hours. See **continue** 2.

lasting see permanent 2.
lastly see finally 2.
late
1 (adj) Why was the train late? behind schedule, not on time, delayed.
OPPOSITES: early, on time.
2 (adj) Minty is always late. unpunctual, behind time, behind, tardy, slow.
OPPOSITES: early, punctual.
3 (adj) I'm sorry about your late birthday present. belated, overdue.
OPPOSITE: early.
4 (adj) The funeral of the late Mr Ray was held yesterday. deceased, departed, dead.

later
(adv) I'll come over later. later on, in a while, afterwards, in a bit, by and by, at a later date, at some point in the future.

lather see foam 1, 3.
laugh
1 (v) This joke will make you laugh. chuckle, giggle, chortle, titter, snigger, roar with laughter, guffaw, split your sides, crack up (informal), fall about (informal), crease up (informal), have hysterics (informal), be in stitches (informal).

2 (n) Bruce is such a laugh! clown, joker, comedian, comic, scream (informal), hoot (informal), card (informal), wit.
3 laugh at (v) Don't laugh at me. See **make fun of**.

laughable see ridiculous.
laughter
1 (n) The sound of laughter filled the air. laughing, giggling, chuckling, chortling, tittering, sniggering, guffawing.
2 (n) Dom's jokes are a great source of laughter. amusement, hilarity, mirth, merriment, entertainment.

lavatory see toilet.
lavish
1 (adj) Lord Lucre is lavish with his money. See **generous**.
2 (adj) Posy spooned on a lavish amount of cream. copious, abundant, plentiful, profuse, generous, liberal, extravagant, excessive, immoderate, wasteful.
OPPOSITES: meagre, frugal.

law
(n) This new law prohibits smoking in public places. rule, regulation, order, directive, command, decree, edict, pronouncement, bill, statute, act.

lawful see legal.
lay
1 (v) Lay the photos on the table. put, place, spread, leave, arrange, set out, set, set down, position, deposit.
2 (v) Hens don't normally lay golden eggs. produce, bring forth, bear, deposit.
3 (v) Please lay the table. See **set** 3.

layer
1 (n) A layer of snow settled on the ground. covering, coating, sheet, film, blanket, mantle, sprinkling, dusting, coat.
2 (n) Each layer of rock was a different colour. stratum, seam, vein, bed, thickness, level, row, tier.

lay into (informal) see attack 2, 3.
layout see design 3.
lay out see set out 2.
laze
(v) I'm going to laze on the beach all day. sit about, lie about, lounge, loll about, loaf about, do nothing, relax, unwind, rest, veg out (slang).

lazy
1 (adj) Mrs Badger says I'm lazy. idle, slothful, workshy, indolent, slack, lax.
OPPOSITES: industrious, hard-working.
2 (adj) I feel really lazy today. sluggish, listless, lethargic, languid, inactive, drowsy.
OPPOSITE: energetic.

lead
1 (v) I can lead you to the treasure. take, show you the way, lead the way, guide, conduct, escort, steer, usher, pilot.
2 (v) Will you lead the team? be in charge of, head, direct, command, manage, supervise, oversee, head up (informal).

3 *(v) Sally managed to lead until the last lap.* be in the lead, head the field, be in front, be out in front, be ahead, come first, blaze a trail.

4 *(v) Rob seems to lead a lonely life.* live, have, spend, pass, experience, undergo.

5 *(v) Your behaviour might lead me to change my mind.* cause, persuade, influence, prompt, induce, incline, move, dispose, sway, make.

6 *(n) Follow Amanda's lead.* example, direction, guidance, leadership, model.

7 *(n) After the first lap, Harry was in the lead.* first place, leading position, front.

8 *(n) Sally has quite a lead over the others.* advantage, edge, margin, start, head start.

9 *(n) I was desperate to play the lead in the school play.* leading role, starring role, title role, principal character, main part, male lead, female lead, hero, heroine.

10 *(n) The police need a lead. See* **clue**.

11 *(n) Connect this lead to the television.* wire, flex, cable.

12 *(n) Fasten the lead to your dog's collar.* leash, strap, chain, rope, cord, tether, rein.

leader

1 *(n) The country needs a strong leader.* ruler, premier, prime minister, president, governor, chancellor, dictator, figurehead.

2 *(n) Take me to your leader!* chief, boss *(informal),* skipper, captain, commander, superior, director, manager, supervisor, number one *(informal),* ringleader.
OPPOSITE: follower.

lead to *see* **cause** 1.

leaflet

(n) Someone pushed a leaflet through the door. hand-out, circular, flyer, pamphlet, booklet, brochure, handbill, mailshot.

leak

1 *(n) There's a leak in this pipe.* hole, crack, chink, break, fissure, puncture, cut, gash, slit, crevice, opening.

2 *(v) Water began to leak from the pipe.* escape, drip, dribble, seep, trickle, ooze, spill, gush, percolate.

3 *(v) Someone is bound to leak this story to the press.* tell, reveal, disclose, divulge, pass on, make known, make public, let slip, let the cat out of the bag, spill the beans *(informal),* blow wide open *(slang)*

leaky

(adj) We must fix this leaky pipe. leaking, dripping, cracked, split, broken, punctured, perforated, holey.

lean

1 *(v) The tower began to lean.* tilt, tip, heel over, slant, slope, incline, list *(ship).*

2 *(v) Lean against the wall if you feel tired.* support yourself, prop yourself up, rest, recline, steady yourself.

3 *(adj) The gymnast had a lean, muscular body. See* **thin** 1.

4 *(adj) I prefer lean meat.* low-fat, unfatty.
OPPOSITE: fatty.

lean on *see* **depend on** 1.

---

leaping frog

leap

1 *(v) Watch that frog leap!* jump, hop, bound, bounce, skip, spring.

2 *(v) Sita began to leap about when she heard the news. See* **dance** 4.

3 *(n) With one giant leap, I cleared the fence.* jump, bound, spring, vault, hop.

4 *(n) We'll see a leap in prices. See* **rise** 5.

learn

1 *(v) Chinese is a hard language to learn.* study, grasp, master, become competent in, take in, absorb, pick up, acquire.

2 *(v) Try to learn the words of the song.* memorize, learn by heart, remember, commit to memory, get off pat, get word-perfect, swot up on *(informal).*

3 *(v) I was sorry to learn that Tom was leaving.* hear, discover, find out, be told, get word, gather, become aware.

learner

(n) beginner, novice, pupil, student, trainee, apprentice, greenhorn, L-driver.

leave

1 *(v) Do you have to leave so soon?* go, set off, set out, depart, make tracks, get going, start, be on your way, be off, disappear, say goodbye, go away, go off.
OPPOSITES: arrive, come.

2 *(v) The demoralized soldiers decided to leave.* run away, abscond, desert, make off, clear off *(informal),* take off *(informal),* slope off, pull out, disappear, split *(informal),* flit *(informal),* scarper *(slang),* do a bunk *(slang),* hook it *(slang).*
OPPOSITE: stay.

3 *(v) If you don't like your job you should leave. See* **resign** 1.

4 *(v) Don't leave me! See* **desert** 1.

5 *(v) Leave your bag in the hall. See* **put** 1.

6 *(v) Did you leave your umbrella on the train?* leave behind, forget, lose, mislay.

7 *(v) The sauce will leave a stain on your skirt.* leave behind, produce, cause, make.

8 *(v) You can leave this job to Mr Badger.* entrust, assign, hand over, consign, refer.

9 *(v) Did your grandma leave you any money?* bequeath, hand down, will.

10 *(n) How much leave do you have?* holiday, vacation, time off, leave of absence, furlough, sabbatical.

leave out

1 *(v) Leave out chapter three. See* **omit**.

2 *(v) Don't leave me out! See* **exclude**.

lecture

1 *(n) I went to an interesting lecture on astronomy.* talk, speech, address.

2 *(n) I got a real lecture when I stayed out late.* scolding, reprimand, telling-off *(informal),* talking-to *(informal),* going-over *(informal),* dressing-down *(informal).*

3 *(v) Please don't lecture me. See* **tell off**.

ledge

(n) The climbers sheltered under a rocky ledge. overhang, shelf, sill, ridge.

---

leftover

(adj) What will we do with the leftover food? remaining, extra, surplus, excess, spare, uneaten, unused, unwanted.

leftovers *see* **scraps**.

legal

(adj) Are Dodgy Dave's activities legal? lawful, legitimate, above board, permissible, allowed, permitted, acceptable, authorized, valid, legit *(slang).*
OPPOSITES: illegal, unlawful.

legalize

(v) Should the government legalize the use of cannabis? make legal, permit, allow, decriminalize, ratify, authorize, sanction.
OPPOSITES: ban, outlaw.

legend

(n) Do you know the legend of the glass mountain? story, tale, myth, folk tale, saga, fairy tale, fable, epic.

leisure

(n) Everyone needs some leisure. free time, spare time, time off, relaxation, recreation, rest, breathing space, holiday, vacation.
OPPOSITE: work.

leisurely

(adj) A leisurely walk. relaxed, unhurried, gentle, easy, laid-back *(informal),* restful, comfortable, slow, lazy, lingering.
OPPOSITES: brisk, hasty, rushed.

lend

(v) I'd be happy to lend you my bike. loan, let you use, give you the loan of, let you have the use of, advance *(money).*
OPPOSITE: borrow.

length

1 *(n) Work out the length of the bridge from end to end.* extent, span, distance, reach, measurement.

2 *(n) Burglar Beryl spent a length of time in jail.* period, stretch, spell, term, space, span, duration.

lengthen

1 *(v) I asked Mum to lengthen my skirt.* let down, make longer.
OPPOSITES: shorten, take up.

2 *(v) This detour will lengthen our journey.* make longer, increase, extend, add to, prolong, stretch out, draw out, protract.
OPPOSITES: shorten, cut down.

lengthy *see* **long** 1, 2.

lenient

(adj) Pandora's parents are really lenient. easy-going, tolerant, indulgent, soft, gentle, kind, forgiving, forbearing, compassionate, merciful.
OPPOSITE: strict.

lesson

1 *(n) When does the next lesson start?* period, class, lecture, tutorial, seminar.

2 *(n) This story contains a lesson for us all.* message, moral, warning, rebuke, deterrent, example, model.

let

let
(v) Will your parents let you go to the disco? allow, give you permission, permit, give you the go-ahead *(informal)*, give you the green light, give you the thumbs up, authorize, agree to, consent to.
OPPOSITE: forbid.

letdown
(n) After all the hype, the concert was a letdown. anticlimax, disappointment, comedown *(informal)*, fiasco, washout *(informal)*.

let down
1 *(v) If you trust me, I won't let you down.* disappoint, fail, leave you in the lurch, leave you stranded, desert, forsake.
2 *(adj) I felt let down when I learnt the truth about Mark. See* **disappointed**.

let go *see* **release** 1, 2.

lethal *see* **deadly** 1, 2.

lethargic
(adj) This heat makes me feel lethargic. listless, sluggish, languid, lazy, weary, slow, drowsy, sleepy, heavy, torpid, slothful, apathetic, passive, unenthusiastic.
OPPOSITES: lively, energetic.

let in
(v) We can't let you in without a ticket. allow you to enter, admit, give you access, take you in, receive, welcome.

let off
1 *(v) It's your turn to wash up, but I'll let you off.* excuse, spare, exempt.
2 *(v) The judge may let Burglar Beryl off. See* **release** 2.
3 *(v) Don't let off the fireworks yet.* set off, detonate, light, ignite, explode.

let on
(v) (informal) Don't let on that you know Justin's secret. let slip, give away, let out, reveal, divulge, disclose, tell, admit, let the cat out of the bag.

letter
1 *(n) What's the last letter in the alphabet?* character, symbol.
2 *(n) Thank you for your letter.* note, message, reply, answer, epistle, communication.

medieval decorated letter

level
1 *(adj) The football pitch should be level.* flat, even, smooth, horizontal.
OPPOSITES: uneven, sloping.
2 *(adj) Is this picture level?* straight, horizontal, flush, square, in line, aligned.
OPPOSITES: crooked, tilted.
3 *(adj) The two teams are level.* equal, evenly balanced, well-matched, all square, on a level, neck and neck, at level pegging *(informal)*, on a par, the same.
OPPOSITE: unequal.
4 *(v) Level the icing on the cake.* level out, even out, smooth out, smooth, flatten.

5 *(n) The river rose to an alarming level.* height, depth, altitude.
6 *(n) Mr Badger has reached a senior level at work.* position, grade, rank, status.

lick
1 *(v) Can I lick your ice cream?* taste, suck.
2 *(v) The flames began to lick around the curtains.* flicker, dart, flick, ripple, play.

lid
(n) Put the lid on the toothpaste. cap, top, stopper, cover, plug, cork *(bottle)*.

lie
1 *(v) I love to lie in front of the fire.* stretch out, recline, sprawl, loll, lounge, relax, rest, be prostrate, be horizontal.
2 *(v) Where is the treasure supposed to lie?* be, be situated, be located, be found.
3 *(v) Don't lie, if you want to be trusted.* tell lies, tell untruths, fib, falsify the facts, make up stories, bluff, perjure yourself, be economical with the truth.
OPPOSITE: tell the truth.
4 *(n) Bo told a lie.* fib, untruth, falsehood, barefaced lie, white lie, whopper *(informal)*, porky *(slang)*, cock-and-bull story *(informal)*, tall tale *(informal)*.
5 **lies** *(plural n) That rumour is pure lies.* fabrication, fiction, invention, deceit.
OPPOSITE: truth.

life
1 *(n) There's no life in a stone statue.* animation, vitality, breath, growth.
2 *(n) You will have many adventures in your life.* lifetime, career, the course of your life, lifespan, time on earth, existence.
3 *(n) Could there be life on Mars?* living things *(plural)*, living creatures *(plural)*, living beings *(plural)*, flora, fauna, wildlife.
4 *(n) What do you know about the life of the Vikings?* way of life, lifestyle, daily life, everyday life, activities *(plural)*, behaviour, habits *(plural)*, customs *(plural)*.
5 *(n) Aisha is so full of life.* energy, vitality, enthusiasm, get-up-and-go *(informal)*, vigour, verve, dynamism, exuberance, high spirits *(plural)*, sparkle, pizzazz *(informal)*, oomph *(informal)*, zip *(informal)*.

lifelike *see* **realistic** 2.

lift
1 *(v) Can you lift this case?* pick up, carry, lift up, raise, hoist.
2 *(v) The balloon began to lift off the ground. See* **rise** 1.
3 *(v) Wait for the fog to lift. See* **clear** 10.
4 *(n) Can I have a lift in your car?* ride, run, drive, trip, spin *(informal)*.

light
1 *(v) We waited for Mum to light the bonfire.* set light to, set fire to, set alight, put a match to, kindle, ignite.
OPPOSITES: put out, extinguish.
2 *(n) I saw a strange light in the sky.* flash, flare, glare, blaze, glow, gleam, glimmer, shimmer, glint, sparkle, twinkle, glitter, ray of light, beam of light, shaft of light, brightness, illumination, radiance.

3 *(n) You need a light to see at night.* lamp, bulb, torch, flashlight, lantern, candle, taper, flare, beacon.
4 *(n) I woke as soon as it was light.* day, daylight, daytime, daybreak, morning, sunrise, dawn, first light.
OPPOSITES: dark, dusk.
5 *(adj) Big windows make a room really light.* bright, full of light, sunny, well-lit.
OPPOSITES: dark, gloomy.
6 *(adj) My shirt is light blue. See* **pale** 3.
7 *(adj) This box is really light.* lightweight, insubstantial, flimsy, easy to carry, portable, underweight *(person)*.
OPPOSITES: heavy, weighty.
8 *(adj) I just had a light lunch.* small, modest, frugal, scanty, snack, digestible.
OPPOSITES: heavy, rich.
9 *(adj) The dancer moved with light steps.* agile, graceful, nimble, lithe, deft, sprightly, light-footed, airy, sylphlike.
OPPOSITES: heavy, clumsy.
10 *(adj) A light breeze. See* **gentle** 2.
11 *(adj) A light workload. See* **easy** 2.

light up
(v) Those lamps light up the street beautifully. illuminate, lighten, brighten, shed light on, flood with light, floodlight.

likable *see* **pleasant** 3.

like
1 *(v) I used to like mushy peas.* love, be partial to, have a taste for, enjoy, be keen on, be fond of, adore *(informal)*, relish.
OPPOSITES: hate, loathe.
2 *(v) I'm sure Robbie will like badminton.* enjoy, be keen on, be interested in, go in for, be into *(informal)*, love, take pleasure in, get a kick out of *(informal)*.
OPPOSITES: dislike, hate.
3 *(v) I used to like Melissa.* be fond of, have a soft spot for, admire, think a lot of, think highly of, respect, have a high regard for, love, be attracted to, fancy *(informal)*.
OPPOSITES: dislike, detest.
4 *(v) Choose whichever cake you like.* want, wish, fancy, please, prefer, desire.
5 *(adj) Our house is like yours.* similar to, much the same as, not unlike, identical to, comparable to, equivalent to, resembling.
OPPOSITES: unlike, different from.

likely
1 *(adj) It's likely that we'll win.* probable, to be expected, anticipated, on the cards, odds-on, possible, plausible, feasible.
OPPOSITE: unlikely.
2 *(adj) Jon is likely to lose his temper if we are late.* liable, apt, inclined, prone.
OPPOSITE: unlikely.

limit
1 *(n) This fence marks the limit of our property.* boundary, border, edge, end, furthest extent, cut-off point, frontier, perimeter, periphery, confines *(plural)*.
2 *(n) There's a limit on how fast you can drive.* limitation, restriction, constraint, check, curb, ceiling, maximum.

3 *(v) Mum is going to limit my TV viewing.* restrict, ration, curb, keep within bounds, hold in check, control, regulate, reduce.

limited
(adj) Our time at the pool is limited. restricted, rationed, fixed, controlled, finite, insufficient, inadequate, minimal.
OPPOSITES: unlimited, unrestricted.

limp
1 *(v) I hurt my leg and had to limp.* hobble, shuffle, shamble, hop.
2 *(adj) Let your arms go limp.* floppy, relaxed, slack, loose, droopy, soft, flexible, flabby, flaccid.
OPPOSITES: stiff, firm, tense.

line
1 *(n) Draw a line on the page.* rule, stroke, underline, slash, dash, hyphen.
2 *(n) My shirt has a red line on the collar.* stripe, band, strip, bar, streak, mark.
3 *(n) The pupils formed a line.* queue, column, row, crocodile *(informal),* file, procession, cordon, chain, string.
4 *(n) Copy this line of figures.* row, column, list, series, sequence.
5 *(n) Don't step over the line.* boundary, borderline, demarcation line, mark, limit, edge, border, frontier.
6 *(n) Mum spotted a new line on her face.* wrinkle, crease, furrow, crow's foot, groove, scar.
7 *(n) Throw me a line. See* **rope**.

linger
1 *(v) The smell of garlic tends to linger.* hang around, stay around, stick around *(informal),* persist, endure, last, remain.
OPPOSITES: go, disappear.
2 *(v) Don't linger on your way to school. See* **dawdle**.

link
1 *(n) Our town has a close link with yours.* connection, association, relationship, tie, attachment, affiliation, liaison, bond.
2 *(v) The police will link Burglar Beryl with the robbery. See* **associate** 2.
3 *(v) Link the two ends of the chain. See* **join** 1.

liquid
1 *(n) Drink this liquid.* fluid, juice, solution.
OPPOSITE: solid.
2 *(adj) Liquid gold.* liquified, fluid, runny, flowing, molten, wet, watery, sloppy.
OPPOSITES: solid, solidified.

list
1 *(n) Is there a list of items for sale?* listing, record, inventory, catalogue, register, directory, file, index, schedule.
2 *(v) List everything that you will need.* write down, note down, jot down, itemize, record, log, enter, set down, catalogue.

listen
1 *(v) The music is about to start, so please listen.* pay attention, prick up your ears, keep your ears open, pin back your ears *(informal),* be all ears, lend an ear, concentrate, attend, be attentive.

2 *(v) Listen when I tell you what to do!* pay attention, take notice, take heed, obey, do as you are told.
3 **listen to** *(v) Did you listen to what I said? See* **hear** 1.

listless *see* **lethargic**.

litter
1 *(n) Don't drop litter. See* **rubbish** 1.
2 *(v) Don't litter the room with your magazines. See* **mess up** 3.

little
1 *(adj) A little speck of dust.* small, tiny, minute, minuscule, microscopic, infinitesimal, wee, titchy *(slang),* teeny.
OPPOSITE: large.
2 *(adj) A little dancer.* petite, diminutive, dainty, small-boned, slight, slender, elfin, short, pint-sized *(informal),* Lilliputian.
OPPOSITE: large.
3 *(adj) Little kittens.* young, baby, infant, immature, undeveloped.
OPPOSITES: adult, mature.
4 *(adj) A little helping of ice cream.* small, modest, meagre, measly *(informal),* inadequate, insufficient, mean, stingy, mingy *(informal),* scant, skimpy.
OPPOSITES: large, generous.
5 *(adj) A little problem.* trivial, minor, unimportant, insignificant, trifling, paltry.
OPPOSITES: major, important.
6 *(n) There's only a little left.* small amount, bit, spot, scrap, trace, dash, smidgen *(informal),* pinch, taste, touch, dab, tad *(informal),* speck, grain.
OPPOSITES: lot, plenty.

live
1 *(v) I will love you for as long as I live.* have life, draw breath, breathe, exist, have being, walk the earth.
OPPOSITE: die.
2 *(v) Where will you live when you grow up?* have your home, reside, dwell *(old-fashioned),* settle, stay, hang out *(informal),* lodge, hang your hat *(informal).*
3 *(v) Can you live on your salary?* survive, support yourself, make a living, make ends meet, get by *(informal),* pay the bills.
4 *(v) The memory of this will live for ever.* last, endure, survive, persist, stay alive, be remembered, abide *(old-fashioned).*
OPPOSITES: die, fade.
5 *(adj) I saw a live snake.* living, alive.
OPPOSITE: dead.

lively
1 *(adj) Mo is so lively.* full of life, vivacious, high-spirited, energetic, bubbly, bouncy, feisty *(informal),* animated, enthusiastic, exuberant, cheerful, chirpy *(informal).*
OPPOSITES: lifeless, listless.
2 *(adj) Our puppies are really lively.* frisky, active, energetic, boisterous, playful, alert.
OPPOSITES: inactive, sluggish.
3 *(adj) The film provoked a lively discussion.* animated, heated, enthusiastic, excited, spirited, interesting, stimulating.
OPPOSITES: dull, apathetic.

4 *(adj) This café looks lively.* buzzing, bustling, jumping *(slang),* busy, crowded, swarming, thronging, hectic, astir.
OPPOSITES: dull, quiet.

livid *see* **angry**.

living *see* **alive** 1, 2.

load
1 *(n) Customs officers inspected the load.* cargo, consignment, shipment, vanload, lorryload, containerload, freight.
2 *(n) You've taken a load off my mind.* weight, burden, worry, millstone, strain.
3 *(v) Load the car with shopping.* fill, fill up, pack, cram, stuff, pile, heap, stack.
OPPOSITE: unload.

loathe *see* **hate** 1.

loathing *see* **disgust** 1.

local
(adj) Let's meet in the local hall. nearby, neighbourhood, community, municipal, district, regional, village, parish, town, city.

lock
1 *(v) Make sure you lock the gate.* bolt, bar, padlock, secure, chain up, fasten.
OPPOSITE: unlock.
2 *(n) I'd love to have a lock of Famous Fred's hair.* strand, tuft, curl, ringlet.

logical
(adj) Try to think in a logical way. rational, systematic, methodical, clear, coherent, consistent, well-organized, reasonable, sensible, intelligent.
OPPOSITES: illogical, unsystematic.

loiter *see* **hang around** 1.

lonely
1 *(adj) A lonely person.* friendless, solitary, lonesome, alone, neglected, abandoned, outcast, rejected, forsaken, forlorn.
2 *(adj) A lonely cottage. See* **isolated** 1.

loner
(n) Don't expect Nicholas to join in; he's a loner. outsider, individualist, lone wolf, recluse, hermit.

long
1 *(adj) Nasim crawled down a long tunnel.* lengthy, extensive, endless, never-ending.
OPPOSITE: short.
2 *(adj) Aunt Bertha is recovering from a long illness.* lengthy, prolonged, long-drawn-out, lingering, protracted, seemingly endless, interminable.
OPPOSITES: short, brief.
3 **long for** *(v) It's pointless to long for something you can't have.* yearn for, wish for, hanker after, eat your heart out over, pine for, dream of, crave, hunger for, thirst for, ache for, hope for, want, desire.

longing *see* **desire** 2.

long-winded
(adj) A long-winded speech. long, lengthy, overlong, rambling, wordy, verbose, long-drawn-out, repetitious, boring, tedious.
OPPOSITES: brief, concise.

loo *(informal) see* **toilet**.

look

look
1 (v) Please don't look! watch, stare, peep, peek, gape, gawp (slang), ogle.
2 (v) Do I look tired? seem, appear, strike you as, give the impression of being.
3 (v) Let's look for clues. See **search** 2.
4 (n) Take a look over here! glance, peek, peep, glimpse, squint (informal), look-see (slang), butcher's (slang), shufti (slang).
5 (n) Famous Fred has the look of a film star. appearance, air, manner, bearing, demeanour, face, expression.
6 (n) What a sad look! See **expression** 1.

look after
(v) Please look after my rat while I'm away. take care of, care for, mind, keep an eye on, watch, guard, protect, attend to.

lookalike
(n) Sidney is a lookalike of Elvis Presley. double, living image, clone, twin, spitting image (informal), dead ringer for (slang).

look at
1 (v) Look at those acrobats! take a look at, watch, see, check out (informal), get a load of (informal), clock (slang).
2 (v) Could you look at my homework? take a look at, glance at, cast your eye over, run your eyes over, skim through, scan, check, read, scrutinize, examine.
3 (v) I love to look at the waves crashing on the shore. watch, gaze at, stare at, contemplate, study, survey, observe, view.

look down on see **scorn** 1.

look forward to
(v) I look forward to your next letter. long for, count the days until, await, anticipate, wait for, hope for.

look like
(v) Don't the girls look like their mum? resemble, take after, remind you of, bear a resemblance to, look similar to, put you in mind of, have a look of, favour (informal).

look out
(v) Look out or you'll get hurt! watch out, pay attention, keep your eyes open, be careful, beware, be alert, keep an eye out.

look up to see **admire** 1.

loop
1 (n) Make a loop in the rope. coil, circle, hoop, ring, spiral, twist, kink, curl, curve.
2 (v) Loop the rope round this post. coil, wind, twist, knot, entwine, circle, spiral, curl, bend.

loose
1 (adj) Wear loose clothing on the plane. loose-fitting, baggy, sloppy, loosened, unbuttoned, slack, flowing.
OPPOSITES: tight, close-fitting.
2 (adj) Don't let the leads become loose. free, unattached, unfastened, untied, detached, disconnected, insecure, wobbly.
OPPOSITES: secure, firm.
3 (adj) Tighten the rope so it isn't loose. slack, floppy, dangling, hanging, free.
OPPOSITES: taut, tight.

4 (adj) My hamster is loose in the kitchen! on the loose, free, at large, at liberty, roaming, unconfined, unrestricted.

loosen
(v) Uncle Walter had to loosen his belt. let out, slacken, undo, release, unfasten, unbutton, unhook, untie.
OPPOSITE: tighten.

loot
1 (n) Burglar Beryl ran home with the loot. booty, spoils (plural), swag (slang), haul, plunder, stolen goods (plural), takings (plural), ill-gotten gains (plural).
2 (v) The rioters began to loot the shops. raid, steal from, ransack, rob, plunder, burgle, pillage.

lopsided
(adj) That clay pot looks lopsided. off-balance, crooked, uneven, cockeyed (informal), skewwhiff (informal), askew, asymmetrical, warped, out of true.
OPPOSITES: symmetrical, straight.

lorry
(n) Tim's dad drives a lorry. truck, HGV (heavy goods vehicle), articulated lorry, artic (informal), van, juggernaut, tanker.

lose
1 (v) I'm scared I might lose my bus fare. mislay, misplace, drop, be unable to find.
OPPOSITE: find.
2 (v) I knew I would lose. be beaten, be defeated, be the loser, be thrashed, lose out (informal), suffer defeat, take a licking (informal), come a cropper (informal).
OPPOSITE: win.
3 (v) Don't lose your chance to go on the outing. See **miss** 3.

lose your temper
(phrase) There's no need to lose your temper! fly into a rage, blow up (informal), blow your top (informal), throw a fit (informal), fly off the handle (informal), go off the deep end (informal), go berserk, blow a fuse (informal), go mad (informal), go crazy (informal), see red (informal), lose your cool (slang), lose it (slang).

loss
1 (n) You may notice a loss of sound. lack, absence, disappearance, failure.
2 (n) Granny never recovered from the loss of her home. ruin, destruction, wrecking, demolition, eradication.
3 (n) I sent my friend a card consoling her on her loss. bereavement, misfortune.
4 (n) The company made a loss last year. deficit, shortfall.
OPPOSITES: profit, gain.

lost
1 (adj) I'm sad because my kitten's lost. missing, disappeared, vanished, gone, strayed, untraceable.
OPPOSITE: found.
2 (adj) We keep lost items in this cupboard. mislaid, misplaced, missing, forgotten, unclaimed, abandoned.
OPPOSITE: found.

3 (adj) The explorers realized they were lost. off-course, off-track, adrift, astray, disoriented, going round in circles, at sea.
4 (adj) You may feel lost when you start at your new school. confused, bewildered, baffled, at a loss, out of your depth, at sea, helpless, mystified, perplexed.
5 (adj) Joel was lost in his own thoughts. absorbed, engrossed, deep, rapt, preoccupied, distracted, spellbound.
6 (adj) Think of those lost opportunities. wasted, missed, squandered, frittered away, misspent, misused.

lots (informal) see **many**.

loud
1 (adj) Loud music came from the disco. noisy, deafening, ear-splitting, booming, blaring, piercing, ear-piercing, thunderous, resounding, clamorous, strident.
OPPOSITES: quiet, soft.
2 (adj) I hate loud shirts. See **gaudy**.
3 (adj) Barry can't help being loud. brash, vulgar, loudmouthed (informal), rowdy, boisterous, raucous, offensive, brazen, coarse, crude, crass, pushy (informal).
OPPOSITES: quiet, retiring.

lovable see **adorable**.

love
1 (v) I will always love you. adore, be devoted to, be in love with, think the world of, dote on, worship, idolize, be infatuated with, care for, have a soft spot for, be fond of, be attached to, treasure, cherish, desire, fancy (informal).
OPPOSITES: hate, loathe.
2 (v) I used to love fudge. See **like** 1.
3 (n) My love for you will never die. affection, passion, fondness, tenderness, desire, devotion to, infatuation with, adoration, yearning, adulation, regard.
OPPOSITES: hatred, loathing.
4 (n) Pirate Peg's love for adventure is well known. fondness, liking, taste, relish, soft spot, weakness, enjoyment of.
5 fall in love with see **fall in love with**.
6 in love with see **in love with**.

lovely
1 (adj) Laura looks lovely. beautiful, gorgeous, stunning (informal), enchanting, ravishing, bewitching, captivating, appealing, adorable, alluring, charming, pretty, elegant, attractive, glamorous.
OPPOSITES: unattractive, hideous.
2 (adj) We had a lovely day at the seaside. delightful, blissful, enjoyable, wonderful, fabulous (informal), fantastic (informal), marvellous, brilliant, glorious, pleasant.
OPPOSITES: awful, terrible.
3 (adj) Mrs Honey is a lovely person. delightful, engaging, warm, charming, sweet, agreeable, pleasant, amiable.
OPPOSITES: obnoxious, disagreeable.

loving
(adj) Loving parents. affectionate, caring, devoted, fond, adoring, doting, kind, warm-hearted, tender, demonstrative.

low

1 *(adj) A low hedge.* small, little, short, stumpy, stubby, squat, stunted, knee-high.
OPPOSITES: high, tall.
2 *(adj) A low salary.* small, meagre, paltry, inadequate, pathetic *(informal)*, poor.
OPPOSITE: high.
3 *(adj) A low rank.* junior, inferior, humble, menial, lowly *(old-fashioned)*.
OPPOSITES: high, senior.
4 *(adj) This work is of a low standard.* inferior, poor, mediocre, second-rate, unacceptable, substandard.
OPPOSITE: high.
5 *(adj) Supplies are low.* meagre, scanty, inadequate, sparse, few, depleted, reduced, diminished, wanting, deficient.
OPPOSITE: ample.
6 *(adj) A low whisper. See* **quiet** 1.
7 *(adj) Low prices.* reasonable, cheap, modest, inexpensive, economical.
OPPOSITES: high, exorbitant.
8 *(adj) Low notes. See* **deep** 3.
9 *(adj) I'm feeling low. See* **miserable** 1.

lower

1 *(adj) We offer lower prices.* reduced, decreased, slashed, pruned, cut, diminished, pared down.
OPPOSITES: higher, increased.
2 *(adj) These soldiers are in the lower ranks.* junior, subordinate, inferior, minor.
OPPOSITES: higher, senior.
3 *(v) Lower your speed. See* **reduce** 3.
4 *(v) Lower your voice.* tone down, soften, quieten, moderate, hush, muffle.
OPPOSITE: raise.
5 *(v) Lower the sail.* take down, let down, pull down, haul down, drop, let fall.
OPPOSITE: raise.

lower yourself

(v) Don't lower yourself by answering back. demean yourself, degrade yourself, humiliate yourself, debase yourself, belittle yourself, humble yourself, discredit yourself, stoop, sink, condescend.

loyal

(adj) A loyal friend. faithful, devoted, firm, true, steadfast, staunch, trustworthy, constant, dependable, unwavering.
OPPOSITES: disloyal, fickle.

lucid *see* **clear** 7.

luck

1 *(n) We found the right path by luck.* chance, accident, coincidence, fluke, good fortune, a stroke of luck, serendipity.
2 *(n) I wish you luck.* good luck, good fortune, success, happiness, prosperity.

lucky

1 *(adj) Who are the lucky winners?* fortunate, favoured, jammy *(slang)*, successful, happy.
2 *(adj) This book was a lucky find.* fortunate, happy, fluky *(informal)*, chance, accidental, fortuitous, providential, opportune, timely.

ludicrous *see* **ridiculous**.

luggage

(n) Don't forget your luggage! baggage, bags *(plural)*, cases *(plural)*, belongings *(plural)*, things *(plural)*, gear.

lukewarm

1 *(adj) This water is lukewarm.* tepid, warm, at room temperature.
2 *(adj) I feel lukewarm about this plan. See* **half-hearted** 1.

lump

1 *(n) A lump of cheese.* piece, wedge, slab, chunk, hunk, block, bit, nugget, wodge *(informal)*, mass.
2 *(n) Robyn has a lump on her knee.* bump, bruise, bulge, swelling, growth, cyst, tumour, hump.

lumpy

1 *(adj) This custard is lumpy.* full of lumps, granular, clotted, curdled.
OPPOSITE: smooth.
2 *(adj) My mattress is lumpy.* bumpy, uneven, knobbly, bulging.
OPPOSITES: flat, even.

lunge

(n) Bozo made a lunge at me. charge, rush, dive, swipe *(informal)*, swing, jab, stab.

lurch

1 *(v) The drunk began to lurch towards us.* stagger, totter, teeter, stumble, sway, reel, weave, lunge, jerk.
2 *(v) The storm made the ship lurch.* wallow, roll, pitch, tilt, list, lean, heel.

lure

(v) The wizard tried to lure the princess into his castle. entice, tempt, ensnare, inveigle, draw, seduce, cajole, attract.

lurid *see* **sensational** 1.

lurk

(v) Wolves lurk in this forest. skulk, lie in wait, lie low, hide, crouch, wait, prowl, slink, steal, take cover.

luscious *see* **delicious**.

lush

(adj) We pushed our way through the lush vegetation. luxuriant, flourishing, overgrown, dense, thick, verdant, green, profuse, abundant, teeming, riotous.
OPPOSITE: sparse.

luxurious

(adj) A luxurious hotel. comfortable, sumptuous, plush *(informal)*, lavish, opulent, ritzy *(slang)*, de luxe, grand, magnificent, posh *(informal)*, swish *(informal)*, swanky *(informal)*, up-market.
OPPOSITES: basic, Spartan.

luxury

1 *(n) Let's have a day of luxury.* comfort, pleasure, indulgence, ease, enjoyment, bliss, self-indulgence, opulence, affluence, high living, splendour, hedonism.
OPPOSITES: discomfort, self-denial.
2 *(n) Caviar is a luxury.* treat, extravagance, indulgence, extra, frill, nonessential.
OPPOSITE: essential.

machine

(n) Is there a machine to do this job? appliance, contraption, device, gadget, instrument, tool, mechanism, apparatus.

machinery

(n) Do you have the machinery for this job? machines *(plural)*, apparatus, equipment, gear, tackle, mechanism, tools *(plural)*.

macho

(adj) Bozo thinks it's good to be macho. virile, manly, butch *(slang)*, hard, tough, masculine, muscular, Ramboesque, strong, strapping, chauvinist, sexist.

mad

1 *(adj) The doctor thought her patient might be mad.* insane, deranged, psychotic, manic, of unsound mind, unbalanced, mentally ill.
OPPOSITES: sane, rational.
2 *(adj) You must be mad to dress up as a gorilla.* crazy, insane, demented, out of your mind, raving mad *(informal)*, unhinged, barmy *(slang)*, bonkers *(slang)*, batty *(slang)*, screwy *(slang)*, loopy *(informal)*, nuts *(slang)*, bananas *(slang)*, off your head *(slang)*, off your trolley *(slang)*, round the twist *(slang)*, nutty as a fruitcake *(slang)*, out to lunch *(slang)*.
3 *(adj) Bathing in baked beans is a mad thing to do.* crazy, absurd, ridiculous, insane, daft *(informal)*, ludicrous, nonsensical, preposterous, wild.
4 *(adj) (informal) Mum was mad that I'd broken her best vase. See* **angry**.
5 *(adj) Kevin is mad about football.* crazy *(informal)*, fanatical, passionate, wild, nuts *(slang)*, bonkers *(slang)*, hooked on, devoted to, keen on, into *(informal)*.

made-up

1 *(adj) Is that a made-up story?* invented, fictional, make-believe, imaginary, fantasy, mythical, fairy-tale.
OPPOSITES: true, real-life.
2 *(adj) I don't want to hear any of your made-up excuses.* fabricated, invented, trumped up, concocted, manufactured, false, untrue, spurious.
OPPOSITES: true, genuine.

magazine

(n) journal, weekly, monthly, quarterly, glossy, fanzine, mag *(informal)*, paper, comic, colour supplement, periodical.

magic

1 *(n) The witch was an expert in magic.* sorcery, enchantment, witchcraft, wizardry, black magic, the black arts *(plural)*, voodoo, spell-making.
2 *(n) Miraculous Marvello produced a rabbit by magic.* conjuring, hocus-pocus, illusion, sleight of hand, trickery, wizardry.

magician
1 *(n) The magician cast a spell.* sorcerer, wizard, enchanter, sorceress, enchantress.
2 *(n) The magician did an amazing trick.* conjurer, illusionist.

magnificent
1 *(adj) What a magnificent palace!* splendid, impressive, imposing, majestic, superb, grand, noble, stately, regal, resplendent, sumptuous, opulent, ornate, lavish, elegant, awe-inspiring, stunning *(informal)*, striking.
2 *(adj) Maggie gave a magnificent performance.* splendid, superb, stunning *(informal)*, masterly, excellent, accomplished, skilful, brilliant, terrific *(informal)*, wonderful, virtuoso.

magnify
(v) The scientist used a microscope to magnify the cells. enlarge, make larger, expand, increase, blow up *(informal)*.

mail *see* **post** 2, 4.

main
(adj) What are the main arguments in your essay? major, central, principal, chief, leading, important, key, basic, essential, fundamental, critical, pivotal, vital, prime, primary, foremost.

mainly *see* **mostly** 1, 2.

maintain
1 *(v) I can't maintain this effort for long.* keep up, sustain, continue, uphold, prolong, keep alive, perpetuate.
2 *(v) Oil the wood to help it maintain its shine. See* **keep** 2.
3 *(v) Do you know how to maintain your bike?* look after, take care of, service, keep in good repair, keep in good condition.
4 *(v) Burglar Beryl continues to maintain that she is innocent. See* **insist** 3.

major
1 *(adj) New York is one of the world's major cities.* largest, biggest, great, most important, main, principal, leading, chief.
OPPOSITE: minor.
2 *(adj) We're making some major changes.* great, significant, wide-ranging, extensive, drastic, radical, serious, important, crucial, large-scale, wholesale.
OPPOSITES: minor, insignificant.
3 *(adj) The play was a major success.* great, outstanding, huge, enormous, phenomenal, notable, mega *(informal)*.

make
1 *(v) Kim loves to make things.* construct, put together, assemble, build, produce, create, fashion, shape, model, mould, devise, form, manufacture, mass-produce.
2 *(v) I don't want to go, so don't make me! See* **force** 1.
3 *(v) Can you make this sheet into a ghost costume? See* **turn** 3.
4 *(v) Let's make some money. See* **earn** 1.
5 *(v) Five and five make ten.* add up to, come to, amount to, total.

6 *(v) We want to make you captain.* appoint, elect, nominate, name, create.
7 *(v) We must make some new rules.* draw up, decide on, agree on, formulate, put together, frame, introduce, bring in.
8 *(v) Joe may make trouble. See* **cause** 1.
9 *(v) Anne will make a good doctor.* be, become, grow into, develop into.
10 *(v) You might make the train if you run.* catch, get, arrive in time for.
OPPOSITE: miss.
11 *(v) I make the total to be 65.* calculate, estimate, reckon, work out, judge, gauge.
12 *(n) Which make of chocolate do you prefer?* brand, type, sort, kind, variety.

make a mess of
(phrase) I hope I don't make a mess of this. muff, botch, mess up, bungle, fudge, make a hash of *(informal)*, screw up *(informal)*, muck up *(slang)*, cock up *(slang)*, make a pig's ear of *(slang)*.

make-believe
1 *(n) Josephine lives in a world of make-believe.* fantasy, imagination, invention, romance, pretence, play-acting, illusion, unreality, dreams *(plural)*.
OPPOSITE: reality.
2 *(adj) A dragon is a make-believe animal. See* **imaginary** 1.

make believe *see* **pretend** 1.

make better
1 *(v) How can we make the situation better? See* **improve** 3.
2 *(v) This ointment will make your rash better. See* **cure**.

make fun of
(phrase) Don't make fun of me because I'm small. laugh at, poke fun at, tease, take the mickey out of *(informal)*, taunt, scoff at, jeer at, sneer at, mock, ridicule.

make love
(phrase) have sex, sleep together, go to bed together, have sexual intercourse, copulate.

make out
1 *(v) I could just make out a figure coming through the fog.* distinguish, recognize, see, perceive, discern, detect, pick out.
2 *(v) Can you make out what this means? See* **understand** 2.
3 *(v) Edwin tried to make out that he was 18.* pretend, bluff, claim, suggest, give the impression, let on *(informal)*, imply.
4 *(v) I wonder how Marco will make out as an actor.* fare, get on, shape up *(informal)*, manage, cope, succeed.

make-up
(n) Put on your make-up and let's go out! cosmetics *(plural)*, war paint *(informal)*, greasepaint *(theatre)*, face paint.

make up
1 *(v) Oz will make up a silly excuse.* invent, fabricate, manufacture, cook up *(informal)*, trump up, concoct, dream up, hatch, come up with, conjure up.

2 *(v) Ruby loves to make up new songs.* compose, invent, write, originate, devise, create, think up, dream up.
3 *(v) How many players make up a team?* form, constitute, comprise, compose.
4 *(v) I'm sick of fighting; let's make up.* be friends, shake hands, call it quits, bury the hatchet, forgive and forget, make peace.

make up for
(v) How can I make up for forgetting your birthday? compensate for, make amends for, atone for, recompense you for.

make up your mind
(phrase) You'll have to make up your mind soon. decide, make a decision, come to a decision, reach a decision, choose.

make worse
(v) Arguing will only make the situation worse. worsen, exacerbate, aggravate.

malicious *see* **spiteful**.

man
1 *(n) Who's that man over there?* guy *(informal)*, bloke *(informal)*, chap *(informal)*, gentleman, fellow.
2 *(n) Sonia joined a dating agency to find herself a man.* boyfriend, partner, husband, lover, spouse, bloke *(informal)*.
3 *(n) Man is descended from the apes.* human beings *(plural)*, people *(plural)*, mankind, the human race, humankind.

manage
1 *(v) I wonder how I'll manage at my new school?* cope, get on, get along, survive, make out, fare.
2 *(v) Mum has always wanted to manage her own business.* run, be in charge of, be in control of, be the manager of, preside over, direct, administer, organize, oversee, supervise, head up *(informal)*.
3 *(v) See what you can manage in an hour. See* **achieve**.
4 *(v) A large family can be hard to manage.* look after, cope with, deal with, handle, organize, control.

man-made *see* **artificial** 1.

manners
1 *(plural n) Haven't you learnt any manners?* etiquette, good manners *(plural)*, social graces *(plural)*, politeness, courtesy, civility, refinement, decorum.
2 *(plural n) Pip's manners are terrible.* behaviour, conduct.

manufacture *see* **make** 1.

many
(adj) Nadya received many presents. lots of *(informal)*, a lot of, masses of *(informal)*, a great many, loads of *(informal)*, scores of *(informal)*, tons of *(informal)*, heaps of *(informal)*, stacks of *(informal)*, piles of *(informal)*, oodles of *(informal)*, countless, innumerable, numerous.

map
(n) We need a map to find the way. plan, guide, street map, town plan, road atlas, route map, atlas, chart *(sea, air)*.

banner

protest
march

march
1 *(v) We watched the soldiers march past.* file, troop, parade, strut.
2 *(v) Dan loves to march across the moors.* stride, pace, stomp *(informal)*, walk, hike, trek, tramp, slog, stalk.
3 *(n) Please join our march against war.* demonstration, demo *(informal)*, protest march, protest, parade, procession.

mark
1 *(n) What's that mark on the wall?* spot, blot, blotch, smear, smudge, streak, splotch, speck, dot, stain, scribble, line, scratch, dent, nick, chip, notch, pit, pock, score, gash, cut, blemish, flaw, impression.
2 *(n) Ed has a mark on his face.* blemish, birthmark, scar, scratch, bruise, tattoo.
3 *(n) Did the thief leave any mark?* trace, sign, trail, tracks *(plural)*, footprints *(plural)*, fingerprints *(plural)*, vestige.
4 *(n) Zanzi got a good mark for her test.* grade, percentage, rating, valuation.
5 *(n) Did the experience leave a mark on you?* lasting impression, scar, impression, effect, impact, influence, imprint.
6 *(v) Don't mark the paintwork!* damage, make a mark on, dirty, stain, smear, smudge, scratch, dent, chip, nick, score, cut, scribble on, spoil, blemish, deface.
7 *(v) Mrs Badger will mark our tests fairly.* correct, assess, grade, evaluate, appraise.
8 *(v) Mark the spot clearly.* identify, label, show, tag, signpost, flag, highlight, name, initial, stamp.

market
(n) You'll find great bargains in the market. open-air market, covered market, flea market, bazaar, fair, marketplace.

marooned see stranded.

marriage
1 *(n) My parents are celebrating 15 years of marriage.* matrimony, wedlock, union.
2 *(n) We've been invited to Simon's marriage.* wedding, wedding ceremony, marriage ceremony, nuptials *(plural)*.

marry
(v) Luke and Lucy are planning to marry. get married, become man and wife, wed, tie the knot *(informal)*, walk down the aisle *(informal)*, get hitched *(slang)*, get spliced *(informal)*, take the plunge *(informal)*.
OPPOSITES: stay single, divorce.

marsh
(n) We squelched through the marsh. bog, swamp, marshland, fen, wetland, morass, quagmire, mire, mud flats *(plural)*.

marshy
(adj) Marshy ground. swampy, boggy, soggy, waterlogged, squelchy, spongy, muddy, wet.

marvel
1 *(n) The pyramids were a marvel of the Ancient World.* See **wonder** 2.
2 *(n) Oz is a marvel at art.* See **genius**.
3 **marvel at** *(v) You'll marvel at the skill of the acrobats.* be amazed by, be astonished by, be filled with amazement at, wonder at, gape at, goggle at, admire, applaud, not believe your eyes.

marvellous see wonderful 1, 2.

mash
(v) Did you mash the vegetables? purée, pulp, crush, pound, pulverize, squash, smash, beat, reduce to a pulp.

mask
1 *(n) Ben wore a gruesome mask to the Hallowe'en party.* false face, disguise.
2 *(n) Wear this mask to protect your face.* protective mask, visor, shield, safety goggles *(plural)*.
3 *(n) Dean's charming manner is just a mask.* See **front** 4.
4 *(v) The soldiers used bushes to mask the tank.* See **disguise** 3.

mass
1 *(n) A mass of papers covered the desk.* load, lot, quantity, heap, mound, pile, stack, bundle, bunch, collection.
2 *(n) A mass of people packed the stadium.* See **crowd** 1.
3 *(n) The statue was carved from a mass of rock.* block, lump, piece, chunk, hunk.
4 *(v) A crowd began to mass in the square.* See **collect** 3.
5 *(adj) There was mass rioting after the match.* widespread, general, large-scale, wholesale, extensive, indiscriminate.
6 **masses** *(plural n) (informal) Gita has masses of CDs.* See **many**.

massive see huge.

master
1 *(v) Greek is hard to master.* See **learn** 1.
2 *(v) Indy will master the situation.* take command of, gain control of, take charge of, get the better of, manage, control, handle, get the upper hand.
3 *(n) Jan is a master at golf.* See **expert** 2.

match
1 *(n) When does the match start?* game, contest, competition, tournament, event, trial, head-to-head, tie, bout *(boxing, wrestling)*, test match *(cricket)*.
2 *(v) This top should match my leggings.* go with, coordinate with, tone in with, be the same colour as, complement, blend with, team with, harmonize with.
3 *(v) The coach will match you with a suitable partner.* link you up, pair, put you together, team you up, join you up.
4 *(v) Nothing can match a steaming hot bath.* See **equal** 5.

matching
(adj) The twins wore matching clothes. identical, similar, the same, coordinating, corresponding, toning, harmonizing.

material
(n) What sort of material is your shirt made of? fabric, cloth, stuff, textile.
TYPES OF MATERIAL: acrylic, calico, canvas, cashmere, chambray, cheesecloth, chiffon, chintz, corduroy, cotton, crêpe de chine, damask, denim, felt, flannel, gauze, gingham, hessian, jersey, lace, lamé, linen, lycra, muslin, net, nylon, oilcloth, polyester, rayon, satin, seersucker, silk, taffeta, tulle, tweed, velours, velvet, viscose, wool.

matter
1 *(v) Will the way I dress matter?* make a difference, be important, carry weight, count, be relevant, signify, be of any consequence, make any odds.
2 *(n) What's the matter, Kirsty?* trouble, problem, difficulty, worry, wrong.
3 *(n) Mrs Badger dealt with the matter quickly.* situation, incident, episode, affair, occurrence, subject, issue, question.

matter-of-fact
(adj) Guy gave a matter-of-fact account of the accident. factual, straightforward, down to earth, sober, unemotional, prosaic, mundane, unimaginative, plain, unvarnished, unsentimental, humdrum.
OPPOSITES: emotional, imaginative.

mature
(adj) Carl is mature for his age. grown-up, advanced, well-developed, adult, sensible, responsible, sophisticated, wise, shrewd.
OPPOSITES: immature, childish.

meadow see field 1.

meal
(n) What a delicious meal! spread *(informal)*, feast, banquet, snack, picnic, barbecue, blowout *(slang)*, nosh-up *(slang)*, tuck-in *(informal)*, beanfeast *(informal)*, repast *(old-fashioned)*. ❖ Also see **food & flavours**.

mean
1 *(v) What do those initials mean?* stand for, indicate, represent, signify, symbolize, denote, convey, communicate, spell, say.
2 *(v) What does Hamlet mean in this speech?* suggest, imply, hint at, drive at, insinuate, indicate, allude to, say, convey.
3 *(v) Did you mean to break the record?* intend, plan, set out, want, resolve, determine, have plans, aim, wish, hope, aspire, have in mind, have the intention.
4 *(v) Being in the team will mean a lot of work.* involve, entail, necessitate, require, lead to, result in, give rise to.
5 *(adj) Scrooge was too mean to share his money.* miserly, stingy, tightfisted, niggardly, tight, mingy *(informal)*, selfish, grasping, penny-pinching *(informal)*.
OPPOSITE: generous.
6 *(adj) That was a mean thing to do.* nasty, horrible, spiteful, malicious, cruel, unkind, shabby, cheap, sneaky, shameful, despicable, contemptible, lousy *(slang)*, rotten *(informal)*, beastly *(informal)*, low-down *(informal)*.

meaning

1 *(n) Use a dictionary to find the meaning of this word.* definition, sense, explanation.

2 *(n) Did you grasp the meaning of my poem?* sense, gist, drift, message, thrust, implication, significance, import.

3 *(n) What's the meaning of your awful behaviour?* reason for, explanation for, point, purpose, aim, objective, intention.

meaningless

1 *(adj) I can't understand Ziggy's meaningless babble.* unintelligible, incomprehensible, incoherent, senseless.

2 *(adj) I wasted the day in meaningless pursuits.* See **empty** 4.

meant

1 *(adj) You're not meant to walk here.* supposed, allowed, permitted, authorized.

2 *(adj) I don't know what we're meant to do.* supposed, expected, required.

3 *(adj) We seem to be meant for each other.* made, destined, intended, fated, suited to, cut out, designed.

measure

(v) Can you measure the amount of sugar in this cup? determine, find out, quantify, calculate, work out, compute, gauge, estimate, assess, judge, evaluate, weigh, calibrate, mark off, pace off, time.

measurement

1 *(n) Your measurement must be accurate.* calculation, estimation, assessment, reckoning, computation, calibration, timing, survey.

2 **measurements** *(plural n) Work out the measurements of this box.* dimensions *(plural)*, size, length, width, height, depth, area, volume, capacity, mass, weight.

meat

(n) flesh, red meat, white meat.

TYPES OF MEAT: bacon, beef, beefburger, chicken, chop, corned beef, cutlet, duck, escalope, game, gammon, goose, ham, hamburger, joint, kebab, kidney, lamb, liver, meatloaf, mince, mutton, offal, pâté, pheasant, pork, poultry, rissole, roast, salami, sausage, smoked ham, sparerib, steak, tripe, turkey, veal, venison.

mechanical

1 *(adj) Ken's dad drives a mechanical digger.* automatic, automated, motor-driven, power-driven, machine-driven. **OPPOSITE:** manual.

2 *(adj) Blinking is a mechanical response.* See **automatic** 2.

meddle *see* **interfere** 1.

medicine

(n) Take your medicine! medication, medicament, drug, remedy, cure.

TYPES OF MEDICINE: antibiotic, antiseptic, capsule, cream, decongestant, drops *(plural)*, herbal remedy, linctus, lotion, lozenge, ointment, over-the-counter drug, painkiller, pill, powder, prescription drug, spray, syrup, tablet, tonic, tranquilliser.

medieval life

jester

some medieval people

baker	dog handler	knight	minstrel	pilgrim
baron	falconer	lady	(musician)	priest
beggar	(falcon handler)	lady-in-waiting	monk	queen
bishop	foot soldier	lord	nun	serf (slave)
blacksmith	friar	man-at-arms	ostler	servant
candlemaker	(travelling priest)	(mounted	(groom)	squire
carpenter	goldsmith	soldier)	page	(trainee
cook	jester	merchant	peasant	knight)
craftsman	king	miller	pedlar	stonemason

medieval clothes and jewellery

chaperon hat
scarf
undertunic
gold necklet
houppeland gown
fur-lined sleeve
hose (tights)
long-toed shoe
lord
embroidered gown
undergown

hennin
veil
jewelled necklace
hose (tights)
lady

hood
shoulder cape with dagged edge
hood
liripipe
short tunic
pouch
peasant

hood
short tunic
apron
overgown
undergown
servant

medieval pastimes

archery
chess
dancing
embroidery
fairs
 (with acrobats, jugglers and dancing bears)
falconry
 (hunting with falcons)
feasting
hunting
jousting
music
singing
storytelling
tournaments

falconry

chess

fair

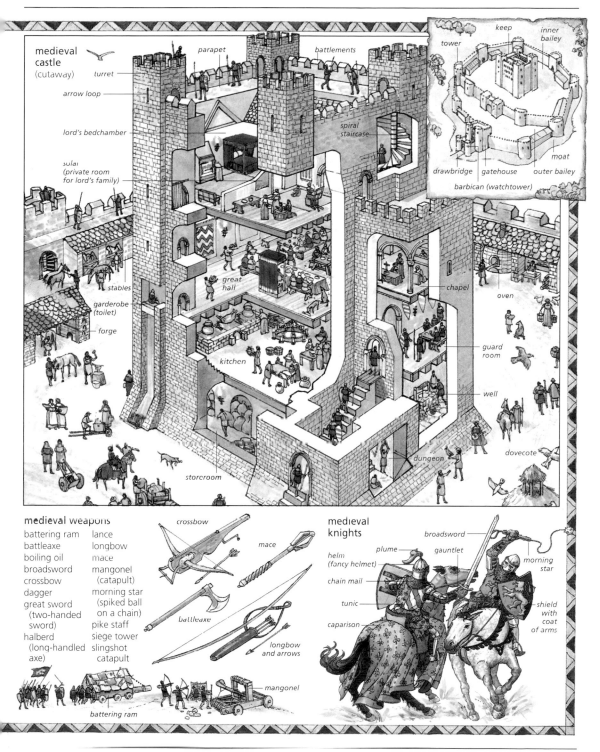

medieval castle
(cutaway)

parapet
turret
arrow loop
lord's bedchamber
solar
(private room
for lord's family)
stables
garderobe
(toilet)
forge
great
hall
kitchen
storeroom

battlements
spiral
staircase
chapel
oven
guard
room
well
dungeon
dovecote

tower
keep
inner
bailey
drawbridge
gatehouse
outer bailey
barbican (watchtower)
moat

medieval weapons

battering ram	lance
battleaxe	longbow
boiling oil	mace
broadsword	mangonel
crossbow	(catapult)
dagger	morning star
great sword	(spiked ball
(two-handed	on a chain)
sword)	pike staff
halberd	siege tower
(long-handled	slingshot
axe)	catapult

crossbow
mace
battleaxe
longbow
and arrows
mangonel
battering ram

**medieval
knights**

broadsword
helm
(fancy helmet)
plume
gauntlet
chain mail
morning
star
tunic
caparison
shield
with
coat
of arms

mediocre

mediocre *see* **average** 2.

medium
(adj) Susie is of medium height. average, moderate, middling, normal, middle.

meek
(adj) A meek tone of voice. timid, humble, mild, submissive, docile, quiet, soft, gentle, unassuming, deferential, resigned.
OPPOSITES: arrogant, assertive.

meet
1 *(v)* I didn't expect to meet you here! bump into *(informal)*, run into, come across, run across, find, see, come upon, encounter, come face to face with.
2 *(v)* Is anyone coming to meet you? fetch, pick you up, greet, welcome.
3 *(v)* On Fridays all the pupils meet in the hall. gather, assemble, congregate, come together, get together, collect, convene.
OPPOSITES: disperse, scatter.
4 *(v)* The two paths meet here. See **join** 3.

meeting
1 *(n)* Al's parents arranged a meeting with his teacher. appointment, get-together *(informal)*, interview, chat, rendezvous.
2 *(n)* We all attended the meeting about animal rights. discussion group, gathering, seminar, rally, conference, convention, forum, assembly, council, congress.
3 *(n)* Tim had an unexpected meeting with a bull. encounter, confrontation, brush.

melancholy
1 *(adj)* Melancholy music makes me feel low. mournful, sombre, sad, depressing, gloomy, dismal, doleful, lugubrious.
OPPOSITES: cheerful, lively.
2 *(adj)* I feel melancholy. See **depressed**.

melt
1 *(v)* The ice will melt soon. thaw, defrost.
OPPOSITE: freeze.
2 *(v)* If you heat the butter it will melt. soften, dissolve, liquefy, run.
OPPOSITES: harden, solidify.

memorize *see* **learn** 2.

menace
(n) That driver is a menace to other motorists. threat, danger, hazard, risk.

menacing
(adj) Bozo gave me a menacing look. threatening, intimidating, ominous, forbidding, grim, sinister, frightening, dark.

mend
1 *(v)* I must mend my bike. See **repair** 1.
2 *(v)* Can you mend my trousers? sew up, stitch, darn, patch, repair.
3 *(v)* Broken bones mend slowly. See **heal** 2.

mention
1 *(v)* Mrs Badger happened to mention that she was leaving. say, remark, observe, let slip, let on *(informal)*, reveal, divulge, disclose, make known, declare, state.
2 *(v)* Don't mention this subject again! bring up, raise, broach, refer to, speak about, allude to, touch upon, hint at.

merciful
(adj) Burglar Beryl hoped the judge would be merciful. compassionate, lenient, forgiving, pitying, forbearing, sympathetic, humane, tenderhearted, generous, kind.
OPPOSITES: merciless, hardhearted.

merciless *see* **ruthless**.

mercy
(n) The judge showed no mercy. pity, compassion, leniency, forgiveness, sympathy, understanding, feeling, kindness, charity, clemency.
OPPOSITES: severity, harshness.

merge
1 *(v)* The two schools are going to merge. amalgamate, join together, unite, link up, combine, integrate, join forces, team up.
OPPOSITES: separate, split up.
2 *(v)* The trees seemed to merge into the background. blend, melt, mingle, fuse, mix, become lost in, be swallowed up by.

merry
(adj) A merry smile. happy, cheerful, cheery, chirpy *(informal)*, carefree, bright, jolly, jovial, joyful, gleeful.
OPPOSITES: sad, serious.

mess
1 *(n)* Clear up this mess! clutter, rubbish, jumble, litter, dirt, muck, gunge *(informal)*, gunk *(informal)*, grot *(slang)*.
2 *(n)* My room is in a total mess. muddle, shambles, jumble, state *(informal)*, chaos, confusion, disarray, disorder, turmoil.
3 *(n)* You got me into this mess! predicament, difficulty, quandary, dilemma, muddle, mix-up, fix *(informal)*, jam *(informal)*, pickle *(informal)*, stew *(informal)*, tight spot, hot water *(informal)*.
4 **make a mess of** *see* **make a mess of**.

mess about
1 *(v)* I like to mess about on the beach. potter about, play about, footle about *(informal)*, muck about *(slang)*, loaf about, lounge about, fiddle about *(informal)*.
2 *(v)* Don't mess about with my computer! interfere, tamper, meddle, tinker, fiddle *(informal)*, play about, muck about *(slang)*.
3 *(v) (informal)* Don't mess about in class. See **fool around**.

message
1 *(n)* I sent you a message. note, memo, communication, letter, fax, e-mail, text message, bulletin, dispatch, communiqué, report, statement, announcement, news.
2 *(n)* The message of this story is clear. meaning, moral, point, theme, thrust, idea.

messenger
(n) A messenger delivered the parcel. courier, carrier, dispatch rider, runner, delivery boy *(old-fashioned)*, go-between.

mess up
1 *(v)* I hope I don't mess up this exam. See **make a mess of**.
2 *(v)* Don't mess up my papers. See **jumble** 1.

3 *(v)* Don't mess up the room with your comics. clutter, litter, strew, make untidy, throw into disorder, dirty.
OPPOSITES: tidy up, clean up.

messy
1 *(adj)* Josie's room always looks messy. untidy, cluttered, chaotic, in a muddle, shambolic *(informal)*, in disarray, littered, dirty, grubby, filthy, mucky.
OPPOSITES: neat, tidy.
2 *(adj)* Why do you always look so messy? untidy, scruffy, unkempt, dishevelled, rumpled, crumpled, slovenly, shambolic *(informal)*, tousled *(hair)*, windswept.
OPPOSITES: neat, tidy.
3 *(adj)* Mrs Badger criticized my messy work. untidy, careless, slapdash, sloppy *(informal)*, slipshod, disorganized.
OPPOSITES: neat, meticulous.

metal
(n) TYPES OF METAL: aluminium, brass, bronze, chrome, copper, gold, iron, lead, mercury, nickel, pewter, platinum, silver, steel, tin, zinc.

method
(n) What method did you use in your experiment? procedure, process, approach, technique, system, practice, scheme, plan.

methodical
(adj) Jo has a methodical approach to her work. orderly, well-organized, systematic, structured, logical, disciplined, businesslike, efficient, careful, painstaking, meticulous.
OPPOSITES: haphazard, chaotic.

middle
1 *(n)* We ate our picnic in the middle of the wood. centre, heart, thick, depths *(plural)*, midst *(old-fashioned)*, core.
2 *(n)* Tie this scarf around your middle. waist, midriff, tummy *(informal)*, waistline.
3 *(adj)* The middle window is smaller than the others. central, inner, inside.
4 *(adj)* Find the middle point of the line. mid, halfway, midway, central, median.

miffed *(informal) see* **annoyed**.

mighty *see* **strong** 1.

mild
1 *(adj)* Mr Badger has a mild manner. gentle, placid, meek, docile, calm, easygoing, peaceable, serene, amiable, affable.
OPPOSITES: aggressive, violent.
2 *(adj)* It was a mild evening. warm, balmy, pleasant, temperate *(climate)*.
OPPOSITES: cool, cold.
3 *(adj)* This soup has a mild flavour. delicate, subtle, faint, bland, insipid.
OPPOSITE: strong.

mime
(v) Can you mime the title of the film? act out, use gestures to indicate, gesture.

mimic
1 *(v)* Dominic can mimic Elvis Presley. See **imitate** 1.
2 *(n)* Tony is an excellent mimic. impressionist, impersonator, imitator.

mind
1 *(n) Use your mind to work out the answer.* brain, head, intelligence, intellect, brains *(plural) (informal)*, brainpower, powers of reasoning *(plural)*, wits *(plural)*, judgment, grey matter *(informal)*.
2 *(n) Don't let your mind wander.* attention, thoughts *(plural)*, concentration.
3 *(n) I must be losing my mind!* sanity, wits *(plural)*, senses *(plural)*, judgment, reason, marbles *(plural) (informal)*.
4 *(v) I won't mind if you go without me.* object, take offence, be upset, care, worry, be bothered, be resentful, disapprove.
5 *(v) Mind the cars!* watch out for, look out for, be careful of, beware of, be wary of, remember, pay attention to.
6 *(v) Please mind my rat while I'm away.* See **look after**.
7 change your mind see **change your mind**.
8 make up your mind see **make up your mind**.

mingle
1 *(v) Irina likes to mingle with people of her own age. See* **mix** 3.
2 *(v) Let the paints mingle together on the page. See* **merge** 2.

minor
(adj) Don't worry about such a minor mistake. small, slight, trivial, insignificant, unimportant, negligible, trifling, petty.
OPPOSITE: major.

minute
1 *(n) I'll be with you in a minute. See* **moment** 1.
2 *(adj) A minute speck of dust. See* **tiny** 2.

miracle
(n) It's a miracle how I passed my exams! wonder, mystery, marvel, phenomenon.

miraculous see **wonderful** 2.

mischievous
1 *(adj) A mischievous child. See* **naughty** 1.
2 *(adj) A mischievous smile.* impish, playful, teasing, roguish, wicked, arch.

miserable
1 *(adj) Carl is feeling miserable.* depressed, unhappy, low, down, blue, glum, gloomy, down in the dumps *(informal)*, down in the mouth *(informal)*, dejected, despondent, melancholy, tearful, mournful, downcast, forlorn, doleful, wretched, heartbroken, grief-stricken, brokenhearted.
OPPOSITES: cheerful, happy.
2 *(adj) It was a miserable day.* dismal, dreary, depressing, gloomy, grey, dull.
OPPOSITES: fine, bright.
3 *(adj) Conditions in the prison were miserable.* grim, hard, harsh, cheerless, filthy, squalid, sordid, desperate, wretched, inhuman, unbearable, distressing, pitiful, disgraceful, shameful, deplorable.
OPPOSITES: comfortable, pleasant.

miserly see **mean** 5.

misery
1 *(n) Gemma couldn't hide her misery when her dog died.* sadness, sorrow, unhappiness, grief, anguish, pain, agony, despair, heartache, distress, suffering, torment, desolation, depression.
OPPOSITES: joy, happiness.
2 *(n) The film showed the misery of the refugees' lives.* hardship, wretchedness, poverty, squalor, deprivation, discomfort, trials *(plural)*, tribulations *(plural)*.
OPPOSITES: ease, comfort.
3 *(n) (informal) Don't be such a misery!* wet blanket *(informal)*, misery guts *(informal)*, moaner, spoilsport *(informal)*, killjoy, grouch *(informal)*, pessimist.

misfortune
(n) I had the misfortune to be ill on my birthday. bad luck, hard luck.
OPPOSITES: good fortune, good luck.

misjudge
1 *(v) It's easy to misjudge how fast traffic is moving.* miscalculate, underestimate, overestimate, make a mistake about, be wrong about, guess wrongly.
2 *(v) People misjudge Ziggy because of how he looks.* get the wrong idea about, jump to the wrong conclusion about, underrate, undervalue, overrate.

mislead see **deceive** 1.

misleading
1 *(adj) A misleading signpost.* confusing, ambiguous, muddling, puzzling, deceptive.
OPPOSITE: clear.
2 *(adj) A misleading answer.* deceitful, deceptive, ambiguous, evasive, tricky, dishonest, false, wrong.
OPPOSITES: straightforward, honest.

miss
1 *(v) That shot will miss the dartboard by a mile.* be wide of, fall short of, fail to hit.
OPPOSITE: hit.
2 *(v) Hurry up or you'll miss the train.* be too late for, fail to catch.
OPPOSITE: catch.
3 *(v) You mustn't miss the chance to go skiing.* miss out on, pass up *(informal)*, forgo, let slip, lose, let go, fail to grasp.
OPPOSITES: take, seize.
4 *(v) I know I'll miss school tomorrow.* be away from, be absent from, play truant from, skip *(informal)*, skive off *(informal)*, bunk off *(slang)*, dodge, avoid.
OPPOSITE: attend.
5 *(v) I know I'll miss my mum when I'm away.* be homesick for, want, need, long to see, long for, pine for, yearn for.

missing see **lost** 1, 2.

miss out
1 *(v) Don't miss out any questions in the exam.* leave out, omit, skip, overlook, pass over, fail to notice, forget, ignore.
2 miss out on *(v) If you go now, you'll miss out on all the fun.* miss, be deprived of, lose out on *(informal)*, be left out of, forgo, pass up *(informal)*.

mist
(n) I couldn't see through the mist. fog, haze, spray, steam, vapour, condensation.

mistake
1 *(n) Rani spotted a mistake in her maths homework.* error, inaccuracy, slip, fault, miscalculation, slip-up *(informal)*, boob *(informal)*, blunder, howler *(informal)*, bloomer *(informal)*, oversight, flaw, lapse.
2 *(n) It was a mistake to invite Stan to the party.* error of judgment, faux pas, gaffe, misjudgment, blunder, clanger *(informal)*.
3 mistake for *(v) I often mistake you for your sister. See* **confuse** 2.

misty
1 *(adj) A misty day.* hazy, foggy, murky.
OPPOSITE: clear.
2 *(adj) Misty glass.* steamy, cloudy, opaque, frosted.
OPPOSITE: clear.

mix
1 *(v) Mix the sugar and butter in a bowl.* combine, blend, stir together, mingle.
OPPOSITE: separate.
2 *(v) Mix the two packs of cards.* shuffle, jumble, combine, join, merge, mingle.
OPPOSITE: separate.
3 *(v) Zoë prefers to mix with people of her own age.* socialize, associate, go around, hang out *(informal)*, mingle, hobnob, rub shoulders *(informal)*, circulate, meet.

mixed
1 *(adj) I'd like a bag of mixed sweets.* assorted, different, various, miscellaneous.
2 *(adj) I have mixed feelings about moving house.* confused, ambivalent, uncertain.
3 *(adj) Do you go to to a mixed school?* coeducational, co-ed.
OPPOSITE: single-sex.

mixed-up
(adj) After her parents' divorce, Lucy was really mixed-up. confused, disturbed, screwed up *(informal)*, bewildered, upset, untogether *(slang)*, maladjusted.

mixture
1 *(n) This box contains a mixture of chocolates.* assortment, selection, variety, range, choice, collection.
2 *(n) The house was a mixture of styles.* blend, combination, fusion, amalgamation, mix, jumble, hotchpotch, mishmash, mixed bag, potpourri, hybrid, conglomeration.
3 *(n) We created a horrible mixture.* concoction, brew, potion, compound.
4 *(n) Drink up your cough mixture.* medicine, syrup, linctus.

mix-up
(n) We need to sort out this mix-up. mistake, misunderstanding, confusion, muddle, mess, snarl-up *(informal)*.

moan
1 *(v) Tom began to moan with pain.* groan, whimper, whine, sob, wail, sigh.
2 *(v) Samantha will moan if we're late. See* **complain**.

mob

1 *(n) The police tried to control the angry mob.* crowd, rabble, throng, horde, swarm, pack, mass, gang.
2 *(v) The fans will mob Famous Fred when he appears.* crowd around, swarm around, surround, besiege, jostle, converge on.

mock *see* **make fun of**.

mocking

(adj) Jacinta gave me a mocking smile. sneering, scornful, disdainful, contemptuous, disparaging, sardonic, ironic, sarcastic, taunting, teasing.

model

1 *(n) This dinosaur is only a model.* copy, imitation, replica, dummy, mock-up.
2 *(n) Our car is the latest model.* version, type, design, style, shape, mark.
3 *(adj) Helen collects model aeroplanes.* miniature, toy, scaled down, imitation.
OPPOSITES: real, full-size.
4 *(adj) Jason is a model pupil.* perfect, ideal, exemplary, dream.
5 *(v) Can you model a hippo out of clay?* mould, shape, form, make, create, fashion *(old-fashioned)*, sculpt, carve, chisel, cast.
6 *(v) Claudia will model the latest style in beachwear.* wear, display, show off, sport *(informal)*.

moderate

1 *(adj) I have a moderate amount of homework.* fair, average, middling, reasonable, normal, ordinary, unexceptional, modest, limited, adequate.
OPPOSITE: excessive.
2 *(adj) My parents have moderate views.* middle-of-the-road, reasonable, restrained, rational, fair, sensible, temperate, mild.
OPPOSITE: extreme.

modern

(adj) Do you like modern music? contemporary, current, present-day, recent, new, up-to-date, up-to-the-minute, the latest, fashionable, trendy *(informal)*.
OPPOSITES: ancient, old-fashioned.

modernize

(v) The editor wants to modernize the magazine. bring up to date, update, revamp, remodel, give a face-lift to, make over, refresh, renovate *(building)*.

modest

1 *(adj) Akin was modest about his success.* humble, self-effacing, self-deprecating, unassuming, unpretentious, reticent, quiet.
OPPOSITES: conceited, boastful.
2 *(adj) Di is too modest to get undressed with the others.* self-conscious, shy, embarrassed, bashful, diffident, demure, coy, reserved, prudish, prim and proper.
3 *(adj) I've saved a modest sum of money.* See **moderate** 1.

moist

1 *(adj) The cave walls felt moist.* damp, dank, dripping, wettish, wet.
OPPOSITE: dry.

2 *(adj) The air feels moist.* humid, clammy, muggy, steamy, sticky, damp, dank, misty.
OPPOSITES: dry, arid.

moisten *see* **wet** 5.

moisture

1 *(n) I could feel the moisture in the air.* humidity, dampness, dankness, wetness, condensation, steam, vapour.
2 *(n) Drops of moisture ran down Garth's face.* perspiration, sweat, water, liquid.

moment

1 *(n) I'll be with you in a moment.* minute, second, bit, tick *(informal)*, instant, jiffy *(informal)*, two shakes of a lamb's tail *(informal)*, flash, trice, the twinkling of an eye, no time.
2 *(n) At that moment, the clock struck midnight.* minute, second, instant, point, point in time, juncture, stage.

money

1 *(n) Lord Lucre may leave his money to the dogs' home.* cash, wealth, riches *(plural)*, funds *(plural)*, capital, hard cash, gold, silver, dosh *(slang)*, lolly *(slang)*, dough *(slang)*, readies *(plural)* *(informal)*.
2 *(n) Take some foreign money with you.* currency, coins *(plural)*, notes *(plural)*.

monotonous

1 *(adj) Harvey has such a monotonous voice.* boring, dull, flat, droning, toneless, colourless, unvarying, samey *(informal)*.
OPPOSITES: animated, lively.
2 *(adj) A monotonous job. See* **boring**.

monster

1 *(n) I dreamt about a big green monster.* creature, beast, dragon, sea monster, giant, ogre, troll, goblin, ghoul, werewolf, zombie, vampire, gremlin, mutant.
2 *(n) Heidi's brother is a little monster.* terror, horror, devil, demon, fiend, brute.
3 *(adj) I had a monster portion of ice cream. See* **enormous**.

monstrous

1 *(adj) I dreamt of a monstrous creature with two heads.* hideous, gruesome, grotesque, repulsive, horrible, frightful, fiendish, hellish, freakish, mutant.
2 *(adj) A monstrous crime. See* **horrible** 1.
3 *(adj) A monstrous amount of chocolate. See* **enormous**.

monument

(n) This monument is dedicated to those who died in battle. memorial, statue, column, pillar, shrine, cenotaph, obelisk, cairn, mausoleum, sepulchre, tombstone.

mood

1 *(n) What sort of mood are you in?* frame of mind, state of mind, humour, temper.
2 *(n) I wish you'd snap out of this mood.* bad mood, bad temper, sulk, huff, grumps *(plural)* *(informal)*, depression, blues *(plural)*, doldrums *(plural)*, melancholy.
3 *(n) How would you describe the mood of the film?* atmosphere, feel, tone, flavour, character, ambience.

moody

1 *(adj) Tricia gets moody if she doesn't have her own way.* cross, grumpy, bad-tempered, irritable, ratty *(informal)*, sulky, in a huff, peevish, touchy, snappy, crotchety *(informal)*, crabby, sullen, miserable, depressed, down in the dumps *(informal)*, down in the mouth *(informal)*, in the doldrums, glum, gloomy.
OPPOSITES: cheerful, contented.
2 *(adj) Jason is so moody, you can't tell how he'll react.* unpredictable, erratic, temperamental, volatile, mercurial, impulsive, capricious, unstable.
OPPOSITES: steady, predictable.

moor

1 *(n) We hiked across the moor.* heath, moorland, fell.
2 *(v) Moor the dinghy or it will drift away.* tie up, secure, make fast, anchor, berth.

mope

1 *(v) Don't mope; it will all come right in the end.* be miserable, be despondent, be dejected, fret, pine, be down in the mouth *(informal)*, eat your heart out, brood, sulk.
2 **mope about** *(v) Barney tends to mope about on his own.* drift about, mooch about *(slang)*, hang around, knock around, wander about, languish, idle.

moral

(n) What is the moral of this story? lesson, teaching, message, meaning, point.

morbid

1 *(adj) Don't be so morbid!* pessimistic, gloomy, glum, melancholy, morose, obsessed with death, preoccupied with death, fixated with death.
OPPOSITE: cheerful.
2 *(adj) Carla has a morbid fascination with graveyards.* unhealthy, unwholesome, grim, ghoulish, macabre, grisly, gruesome, horrible, sick *(informal)*, brooding.
OPPOSITE: healthy.

more

(adj) This extension will give us more space. extra, additional, added, further, supplementary, spare, fresh, new.
OPPOSITE: less.

morning

(n) dawn, daybreak, break of day, sunrise, morn *(old-fashioned)*, forenoon *(old-fashioned)*.

mostly

1 *(adv) Mostly I shop at the supermarket.* usually, normally, generally, as a rule, mainly, in general, on the whole, typically, most often, for the most part, in the main.
2 *(adv) Miranda's bedroom is mostly blue.* mainly, almost entirely, predominantly, largely, primarily, for the most part, chiefly.

mother

1 *(n) Jemima lives with her mother.* mum *(informal)*, mummy *(informal)*, ma *(informal)*, mamma *(informal)*, old woman *(informal)*, old lady *(informal)*.

2 *(v) Alexander likes to mother his little sister.* look after, care for, protect, comfort, nurse, fuss over, baby, pamper, indulge, spoil.

motionless see **still** 1, 2.

motivate
1 *(v) Maybe this news will motivate you to take some action.* See **prompt** 1.
2 *(v) A good teacher should be able to motivate you.* inspire, get you going, spur you on, give you some incentive, stimulate.

motive
(n) There seemed to be no motive for the murder. reason, cause, motivation, rationale, grounds *(plural)*, purpose, stimulus, spur, incentive.

mould
1 *(n) The damp walls were covered in mould.* fungus, mildew.
2 *(n) Pour the jelly into a mould.* cast, form, shape.
3 *(v) Can you mould a hippo out of clay?* See **model** 5.

mouldy
1 *(adj) This plum is mouldy.* bad, rotten, mildewed, spoiled, decaying, putrefying. OPPOSITE: fresh.
2 *(adj) I hate the smell of mouldy clothes.* mildewed, musty, fusty.

mound
1 *(n) A mound of dirty clothes.* See **pile** 1.
2 *(n) A grassy mound.* bank, hill, hillock, hummock, knoll, embankment, dune.

mountain
1 *(n) The mountain was hidden by clouds.* peak, hill, fell, pinnacle, alp.
2 *(n) Please move this mountain of rubbish.* See **pile** 1.

mountainous
(adj) The picture shows a mountainous landscape. alpine, highland, hilly, rugged, craggy, rocky. OPPOSITE: flat.

mourn see **grieve**.

move
1 *(v) Stay there and don't move!* budge, stir, shift, fidget, change position.
2 *(v) Please move your things into the spare room.* shift, take, carry, bring, transfer, switch, transport.
3 *(v) Try to move steadily through the forest.* advance, proceed, walk, make your way, go, march, journey, pass.
4 *(v) I may have to move to Spain.* move house, relocate, move away, emigrate.
5 *(v) It's time to move!* go, set off, get moving, make tracks, get started, get going, make a move, take action, act.
6 *(v) This film will really move you.* touch, affect, upset, make you cry, reduce you to tears, tug at your heartstrings, get to *(informal)*, disturb, have an effect on, make an impression on, stir, inspire.
7 *(v) I hope this news will move you to take some action.* See **prompt** 1.
8 *(n) One move and I'll shoot!* movement, motion, gesture, change of position.
9 *(n) Taking the train was a good move.* step, thing to do, manoeuvre, tack, plan, stratagem, tactic, ploy, trick.
10 *(n) It's your move now.* go, turn.

movement
(n) I saw some movement in the bushes. activity, motion, action, moving, stirring.

moving
1 *(adj) This model car has moving parts.* movable, mobile, working. OPPOSITES: fixed, immovable.
2 *(adj) The film was so moving it made me cry.* touching, emotional, poignant, heart-rending, inspiring, stirring, heart-warming, tear-jerking *(informal)*, sentimental.

muck
(n) Clean that muck off your shoes! dirt, filth, mud, grime, slime, sludge, gunge *(informal)*, gunk *(informal)*, manure, dung.

mucky see **dirty** 1.

mud
(n) My boots are covered in mud. clay, dirt, soil, silt, muck, sludge, slime, slurry, ooze.

muddle
1 *(v) Please don't muddle my papers.* See **jumble** 1.
2 *(v) Complex instructions muddle me.* See **confuse** 1.
3 *(n) Tabitha's room is in a total muddle.* See **mess** 2.

muddled
1 *(adj) All these instructions make me feel muddled.* See **confused**.
2 *(adj) Your essay is very muddled.* disorganized, confused, jumbled, chaotic, incoherent, woolly, unclear, mixed-up, scrambled, higgledy piggledy *(informal)*. OPPOSITES: clear, well-organized.

muddy
1 *(adj) How did your boots get so muddy?* dirty, mucky, filthy, grubby, grimy, caked with mud, mud-spattered. OPPOSITE: clean.
2 *(adj) We squelched across a muddy field.* marshy, mucky, soggy, waterlogged, swampy, boggy, miry, sodden, slimy. OPPOSITES: dry, firm.
3 *(adj) The water in our pond is muddy.* cloudy, murky, dirty, opaque. OPPOSITES: clear, clean.

muffled
(adj) I heard a muffled cry from the cellar. faint, indistinct, dull, smothered, stifled, muted, suppressed, strangled.

mug
1 *(n) Wash up your mug.* cup, beaker, tankard, jug, flagon *(old-fashioned)*.
2 *(v) (informal) Someone tried to mug Dodgy Dave.* attack, rob, set upon, beat up *(informal)*, assault, lay into *(informal)*, rough up *(informal)*, duff up *(slang)*, do over *(slang)*, work over *(slang)*.

---

mountain words

mountains can be...

awe-inspiring	massive
bare	rocky
barren	rugged
breathtaking	shrouded in
craggy	mist
forbidding	snowcapped
jagged	soaring
lofty	spectacular
looming	towering
majestic	treacherous

glacier

in the mountains

alpine flowers	ice field
alpine meadow	ledge
avalanche	log cabin
boulder	mountain
cable car	pass
cave	mountain
chair lift	range
chalet	peak
conifers	precipice
crevasse	ridge
(crack in	scree (loose
glacier)	stones)
crevice (crack	slope
in rock face)	stream
glacier	summit
(river of ice)	tunnel
gorge	waterfall

in the mountains you may feel...

alone
awestruck
breathless
chilled to
the bone
daunted
dazzled
dizzy
dwarfed
exhilarated
insignificant
overawed

mountain activities

abseiling	snowblading
bobsleighing	snowboarding
climbing	tobogganing
hang-gliding	walking
hiking	white-water
mountain	rafting
biking	
mountaineering	
paragliding	
skiing	

snowboarding

muggy

(adj) *This muggy weather makes me sweat.* sticky, sultry, humid, steamy, clammy, oppressive, close, stuffy, airless.

mumble

(v) *Speak up and don't mumble!* mutter, murmur, stutter, stammer, hem and haw.

munch *see* **chew**.

murder

1 *(n)* *The police are investigating the murder.* See **killing** 1.
2 *(v)* *A hit man was paid to murder the President.* See **kill** 1.

murderer

(n) killer, assassin, hit man *(slang)*, cutthroat, butcher, slayer, slaughterer.

murky

1 *(adj)* *It was a murky Autumn day.* dark, dull, foggy, misty, grey, cloudy, overcast, gloomy, dismal, dreary, cheerless.
OPPOSITES: bright, clear.
2 *(adj)* *I won't swim in such murky water.* cloudy, muddy, dirty, opaque.
OPPOSITE: clear.

murmur

1 *(v)* *Did you murmur something?* mutter, mumble, whisper, say under your breath.
2 *(n)* *The hall was filled with the murmur of voices.* hum, buzzing, whispering, muttering, drone, mumble, babble, burble.

muscular *see* **strong** 1.

mushy

1 *(adj)* *Mushy peas.* pulpy, squashy, squelchy, slushy, squidgy, soft.
2 *(adj)* *(informal)* *A mushy love story.* See **sentimental** 2.

music

(n) melody, harmony, rhythm.

musical

(adj) *The bells made a musical sound.* tuneful, melodious, melodic, harmonious, lilting, sweet-sounding, dulcet.
OPPOSITES: discordant, cacophonous.

musical instrument

(n) TYPES OF MUSICAL INSTRUMENT:
BRASS: bugle, cornet, euphonium, French horn, sousaphone, trombone, trumpet, tuba. KEYBOARD: accordion, harpsichord, organ, piano, synthesizer. PERCUSSION: bass drum, bongos, cabasa, castanets, chime bars, claves, cymbals, finger cymbals, glockenspiel, guiro *(West Indies)*, maracas, rattle, side drum, sleigh bells, steel drum *(West Indies)*, tabla *(India)*, tambourine, tam-tam *(gong)*, timpani *(kettle drums)*, triangle, tubular bells, vibraphone, wood block, xylophone. STRINGS: balalaika *(Russia)*, banjo, cello, double bass, guitar, harp, lute, lyre, mandolin, sitar *(India)*, ukulele, viola, violin, zither. WIND: bagpipes, bassoon, clarinet, cor anglais, didgeridoo *(Australia)*, fife, flute, harmonica *(mouth organ)*, oboe, panpipes *(South America)*, penny whistle, piccolo, recorder, saxophone.

musician

(n) performer, player, instrumentalist, minstrel *(old-fashioned)*, singer.
TYPES OF MUSICIAN: accompanist, bandsman, bassoonist, bugler, busker, cellist, clarinettist, composer, conductor, cornetist, drummer, fiddler, flautist, guitarist, harpist, oboist, organist, percussionist, pianist, piper, soloist, timpanist, trombonist, trumpeter, violinist.
Also see **singer**.

must

1 *(v)* *I must go now.* See **have to** 1.
2 *(n)* *Sensible shoes are a must if you want to go hiking.* necessity, essential, requirement, prerequisite.
OPPOSITE: option.

musty

(adj) *The cellar smells musty.* mouldy, mildewy, fusty, damp, dank, stale, stuffy, airless, frowsty.
OPPOSITES: fresh, airy.

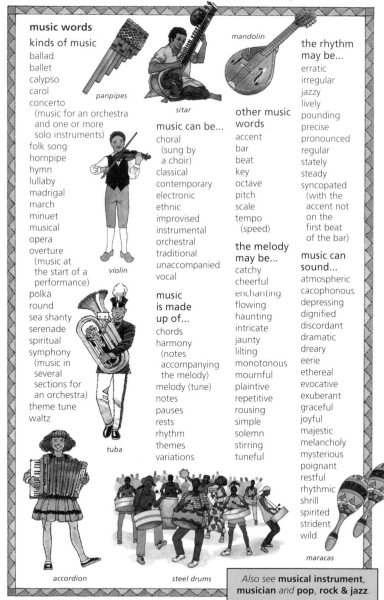

music words

kinds of music
ballad
ballet
calypso
carol
concerto
(music for an orchestra
and one or more
solo instruments)
folk song
hornpipe
hymn
lullaby
madrigal
march
minuet
musical
opera
overture
(music at
the start of a
performance)
polka
round
sea shanty
serenade
spiritual
symphony
(music in
several
sections for
an orchestra)
theme tune
waltz

panpipes

sitar

mandolin

violin

music can be...
choral
(sung by
a choir)
classical
contemporary
electronic
ethnic
improvised
instrumental
orchestral
traditional
unaccompanied
vocal

**music
is made
up of...**
chords
harmony
(notes
accompanying
the melody)
melody (tune)
notes
pauses
rests
rhythm
themes
variations

**other music
words**
accent
bar
beat
key
octave
pitch
scale
tempo
(speed)

**the melody
may be...**
catchy
cheerful
enchanting
flowing
haunting
intricate
jaunty
lilting
monotonous
mournful
plaintive
repetitive
rousing
simple
solemn
stirring
tuneful

**the rhythm
may be...**
erratic
irregular
jazzy
lively
pounding
precise
pronounced
regular
stately
steady
syncopated
(with the
accent not
on the
first beat
of the bar)

**music can
sound...**
atmospheric
cacophonous
depressing
dignified
discordant
dramatic
dreary
eerie
ethereal
evocative
exuberant
graceful
joyful
majestic
melancholy
mysterious
poignant
restful
rhythmic
shrill
spirited
strident
wild

tuba

accordion

steel drums

maracas

Also see **musical instrument**, **musician** *and* **pop, rock & jazz**.

mutter
(v) *Did I hear you mutter that you weren't satisfied?* mumble, murmur, say under your breath, grumble, complain, grouse.

mysterious
(adj) *A mysterious crime.* baffling, puzzling, perplexing, mystifying, unexplained, inexplicable, insoluble, cryptic, enigmatic, strange, curious, bizarre, weird, uncanny.

mystery
1 (n) *Can you solve the mystery of the green cat?* enigma, puzzle, riddle, conundrum, problem, secret.
2 (n) *Nadia reads one mystery after another.* detective story, crime story, whodunit (informal), thriller.

nag
(v) *Don't nag me!* scold, keep on at, go on at (informal), harp on at, find fault with, badger, pester, hassle (informal), henpeck.

naive
(adj) *Emily is so naive, she trusts everybody.* gullible, unsuspecting, trusting, credulous, innocent, green, inexperienced, unworldly, unsophisticated, childlike.
OPPOSITES: experienced, cynical.

naked
(adj) *It's normal to be naked in the bath.* nude, bare, in the nude, undressed, stark naked, starkers (informal), in your birthday suit (informal), in the altogether (informal), without a stitch on.
OPPOSITES: dressed, fully clothed.

name
1 (v) *What shall we name our gang?* call, entitle, label, term, style, tag, dub.
2 (v) *Can you name all the European capitals?* identify, list, cite, reel off, recite.
3 (n) *What is your name?* first name, given name, Christian name, surname, family name, middle name, maiden name, married name, nickname, alias, pseudonym (pen name), handle (informal).

nap see **sleep** 3.

narrow
1 (adj) *What a narrow space!* tight, confined, cramped, restricted, limited.
OPPOSITES: wide, ample.
2 (adj) *This chair has narrow legs.* thin, slim, slender, tapering, fine.
OPPOSITES: wide, broad.

nasty
1 (adj) *What a nasty smell!* disgusting, revolting, horrible, unpleasant, foul, repulsive, nauseating, sickening, vile, loathsome, odious, obnoxious, offensive, repugnant, repellent, yucky (slang).
OPPOSITES: pleasant, nice.

2 (adj) *Don't be nasty! See* **horrible** 3.
3 (adj) *Ria has a nasty illness.* unpleasant, serious, bad, severe, major, critical, painful.
4 (adj) *Should nasty videos be banned?* pornographic, obscene, blue, dirty, smutty, indecent, off colour, violent, offensive.

national
(adj) *Tomorrow will be a national holiday.* public, state, nationwide, countrywide, general, widespread, coast-to-coast.

natter see **talk** 1, 5.

natural
1 (adj) *It's natural to grieve when someone dies.* normal, healthy, understandable, usual, common, typical.
OPPOSITES: abnormal, unnatural.
2 (adj) *Dom has a natural musical ability.* innate, inborn, instinctive, intuitive, intrinsic, inherent, inherited.
3 (adj) *I prefer to eat natural foods.* unprocessed, pure, organic, additive-free, chemical-free, unrefined, uncoloured, unbleached, whole, plain, wholesome.
OPPOSITES: processed, synthetic.
4 (adj) *Jenny has a natural manner.* unaffected, artless, genuine, open, frank, spontaneous, easy, unselfconscious, unsophisticated, unpretentious, unstudied.
OPPOSITES: affected, artificial.

nature
(n) *I enjoy learning about nature.* the environment, the countryside, natural history, wildlife, the living world, the natural world, the earth.

naughty
1 (adj) *A naughty child.* disobedient, badly behaved, mischievous, unruly, defiant, unmanageable, wild, wilful, wayward, undisciplined, cheeky, exasperating.
OPPOSITES: well-behaved, obedient.
2 (adj) *A naughty joke. See* **rude** 2.

near
1 (prep) *I live near the shops.* close to, not far from, next to, adjacent to, handy for, within sniffing distance of (informal).
OPPOSITE: far from.
2 (adj) *Winter is near.* coming, approaching, looming, just around the corner, close at hand, imminent.
OPPOSITES: far off, distant.

nearly
(adv) *I've nearly finished.* almost, just about, practically, virtually, as good as, to all intents and purposes, not quite.

neat
1 (adj) *Ned's room looks neat. See* **tidy** 2.
2 (adj) *The carpenter did a neat job.* careful, precise, meticulous, skilful, deft, expert, competent, accurate, efficient.
OPPOSITES: clumsy, messy.

necessary
(adj) *A hard hat is necessary for riding.* essential, vital, compulsory, obligatory, needed, indispensable, mandatory.
OPPOSITES: unnecessary, optional.

need
1 (v) *This project will need a lot of work.* require, demand, call for, necessitate, entail, want.
2 (v) *Come back - I need you!* want, miss, rely on, depend on, yearn for, pine for.
3 (n) *There's a need for qualified teachers.* demand, call, lack of, shortage of, want of.
4 **needs** (plural n) *Will this money satisfy your needs?* requirements (plural), demands (plural), wants (plural), wishes (plural), desires (plural).
5 **need to** (v) *I need to revise for the test. See* **have to** 1.

neglect
1 (v) *Don't neglect your dog.* fail to look after, fail to care for, abandon, leave alone, forsake.
OPPOSITES: look after, care for.
2 (v) *If you neglect your studies, you'll fail the exam.* let slide, pay no attention to, skimp on, leave undone, shirk, avoid.
OPPOSITES: pay attention to, attend to.

neglected
1 (adj) *A neglected animal.* abandoned, uncared for, unfed, mistreated, unloved.
2 (adj) *A neglected flowerbed.* untended, overgrown, unweeded, uncared-for, derelict (building), run-down (building).

neighbourhood see **area** 1.

nervous
(adj) *I'm always nervous before a concert.* anxious, apprehensive, worried, scared, frightened, on edge, uneasy, edgy, tense, jittery (informal), uptight (informal), twitchy, jumpy, fidgety, nervy (informal), hyper (informal), agitated, overwrought, flustered, highly strung, excitable.
OPPOSITES: calm, confident.

neutral
(adj) *A referee must remain neutral.* impartial, objective, detached, unbiased, nonpartisan, unprejudiced, dispassionate, uninvolved, sitting on the fence.
OPPOSITE: biased.

never
(adv) *Do you tell lies? No, never!* certainly not, no way, not at all, under no circumstances, on no account, not ever, at no time, not on your life (informal).
OPPOSITES: sometimes, always.

new
1 (adj) *We have some new information.* fresh, recent, up-to-date, current, up-to-the-minute, extra, additional, more.
OPPOSITES: old, outdated.
2 (adj) *Have you tried this new product?* brand-new, state-of-the-art, revolutionary, innovative, ground-breaking, advanced, modern, ultramodern, novel, original.
OPPOSITES: obsolete, out of date.
3 (adj) *Start on a new page. See* **fresh** 4.
4 (adj) *Let's explore a new path.* different, unfamiliar, unknown, untried, unexplored, uncharted, untouched, untrodden, fresh.
OPPOSITE: familiar.

news

1 (n) *The news from the war zone shocked the nation.* report, bulletin, news item, newsflash, story, press release, announcement, communiqué, dispatch, message, account, statement, information, facts (plural), intelligence, info (informal), update, leak, disclosure, revelation.
2 (n) *Have you heard the news about Jason?* latest (informal), rumours (plural), gossip, lowdown (informal), word, talk, stories (plural), tittle-tattle, gen (informal), scandal, dirt (slang).
3 **the news** (n) *I like to keep up with the news.* current affairs (plural), world events (plural).

newspaper

(n) paper, daily, weekly, Sunday paper, national paper, local paper, tabloid, broadsheet, rag (informal).

next

1 (adj) *We planned our work for the next four weeks.* following, succeeding, ensuing, subsequent, coming.
OPPOSITES: previous, past.
2 (adj) *Can you hear voices in the next room?* adjacent, adjoining, neighbouring, nearest, closest.
3 (adv) *Next add the sugar.* then, after that, afterwards, later, subsequently.

nibble

1 (v) *The mouse began to nibble the cheese.* bite, gnaw, peck at, chew on, munch, pick at, eat, taste.
2 (n) *I've only had a nibble of my sandwich.* See **bite** 3.

night

(n) dark, darkness, night-time, small hours (plural), hours of darkness (plural).

night...	the night is...	the moon is...	in the sky you see...	night-time creatures
closes in	moonless	bright	clouds	badger
descends	moonlit	ghostly	constellations	bat
falls	pitch-black	gleaming	crescent	firefly
settles	shadowy	hazy	moon	frog
	silent	hidden	full moon	glow-worm
darkness...	starless	luminous	Milky Way	hedgehog
blots out	starlit	pale	planets	mosquito
cloaks	still	remote	shooting stars	moth
conceals		shining		nightingale
engulfs	**the sky is...**	silvery	**night-time sights**	owl
envelops	clear	veiled	Catseyes	
hides	cloudy		(reflectors	**night-time sounds**
masks	illuminated	**the stars...**	on roads)	
obscures	inky	flicker	city lights	bats squeaking
swallows up	jet-black	glimmer	floodlit	cats yowling
veils	lit up	glitter	buildings	clocks chiming
	starry	shimmer	headlights	frogs croaking
	star-studded	sparkle	illuminations	mosquitoes
	vast	twinkle	neon signs	whining
	velvety	wink	streetlights	owls hooting
				sirens wailing

nice

a nice person	a nice meal	a nice view	I had a nice time.	You look nice.
agreeable	appetizing	beautiful	agreeable	attractive
amiable	delectable	breathtaking	amusing	beautiful
caring	delicious	glorious	brilliant	divine
charming	lovely	gorgeous	enjoyable	(informal)
considerate	luscious	impressive	entertaining	gorgeous
delightful	mouthwatering	lovely	excellent	handsome
friendly	scrumptious	magnificent	fabulous	lovely
generous	(informal)	picturesque	(informal)	pretty
gentle	tasty	spectacular	fantastic	ravishing
good-natured	yummy (slang)	splendid	(informal)	stunning
helpful	**nice weather**	superb	fun	(informal)
kind	beautiful	wonderful	good	wonderful
likable	bright	**a nice piece of work**	great	
lovely	dry		(informal)	**Nice people don't swear.**
obliging	fair	accurate	interesting	courteous
pleasant	fine	careful	lovely	genteel
sweet	glorious	methodical	marvellous	gentlemanly
sympathetic	gorgeous	meticulous	pleasant	ladylike
thoughtful	lovely	neat	super	polite
understanding	mild	painstaking	(informal)	refined
unselfish	pleasant	pleasing	terrific	respectable
warm-hearted	sunny	well-presented	(informal)	well-bred
	warm	well-written	wonderful	

nightmare

1 (n) *You've had a nightmare.* bad dream.
2 (n) *The test was a nightmare.* ordeal, torment, torture, agony, horror, trial.

nimble

(adj) *You must be nimble to be a good footballer.* light on your feet, agile, lithe, nippy (informal), speedy, quick, swift, supple, acrobatic, deft, skilful, proficient.

noble

(adj) *Many noble lords attended the banquet.* aristocratic, titled, highborn, blue-blooded, distinguished.

nod

(v) *Nod your head if you agree.* incline, bow, bob, dip, duck, shake up and down.

noise

1 (n) *I heard a faint noise.* sound.
2 (n) *The noise in the classroom was unbelievable.* din, racket, row, clamour, uproar, hullabaloo, tumult, rumpus, hubbub, commotion, pandemonium.

noisy

1 (adj) *A noisy aeroplane.* See **loud** 1.
2 (adj) *A noisy gang of kids.* boisterous, riotous, rowdy, uproarious, raucous, clamorous, rackety, talkative, vociferous.
OPPOSITES: quiet, subdued.

nonsense
1 *(n) Don't talk nonsense.* rubbish, drivel, garbage, rot, guff *(informal)*, baloney *(informal)*, twaddle, balderdash, piffle, claptrap *(informal)*, codswallop *(slang)*, poppycock *(informal)*, gibberish, double Dutch *(informal)*, gobbledegook *(informal)*. OPPOSITE: sense.
2 *(n) Mum won't stand for any nonsense.* silliness, foolishness, stupidity, tomfoolery, monkey business *(informal)*, misbehaviour, mischief, antics *(plural)*, high jinks *(plural)*.

normal
1 *(adj) It's normal for babies to cry.* common, usual, commonplace, natural, typical, standard, accepted, expected. OPPOSITES: unusual, unnatural.
2 *(adj) Our normal routine was disrupted.* See **usual**.
3 *(adj) A normal person wouldn't behave like that.* sane, well-adjusted, rational, well-balanced, reasonable. OPPOSITES: abnormal, insane.

nosy
(adj) (informal) Nosy neighbours. inquisitive, prying, snooping *(informal)*, eavesdropping, curious, overcurious, interfering, meddlesome, intrusive.

note
1 *(n) I must send Henry a note.* message, letter, reminder, memo, memorandum, line *(informal)*, communication.
2 *(v) Note down this date.* See **write** 1.

nothing
1 *(pronoun) There's nothing in the box.* not a thing, nothing at all, zilch *(slang)*, not a sausage *(informal)*.
2 *(pronoun) We scored nothing.* nought, zero, nil, love *(tennis)*, a duck *(cricket)*.

notice
1 *(v) Did you notice Burglar Beryl's new brooch?* see, spot, observe, catch sight of, note, take in, take note of, spy, detect, discern, perceive, get a load of *(informal)*.
2 *(n) Have you seen the notice about the sale?* announcement, poster, sign, advertisement, circular, leaflet, pamphlet, brochure, bulletin, communication.

noticeable
(adj) There has been a noticeable change in Toni's behaviour. distinct, perceptible, discernible, unmistakable, obvious, clear, marked, visible, pronounced, striking, conspicuous, definite, significant, evident. OPPOSITE: imperceptible.

now
1 *(adv) I must go now.* See **immediately**.
2 *(adv) Most families now have a TV.* nowadays, these days, today, in this day and age, at the moment, at present.

nude *see* **naked**.

nudge
(v) Don't nudge me when I'm writing. poke, prod, jog, jolt, bump, knock, jab, push, shove, touch, elbow.

nuisance
1 *(n) It's a nuisance when you miss the bus.* inconvenience, problem, pain *(informal)*, pain in the neck *(informal)*, hassle *(informal)*, drag *(informal)*, headache *(informal)*, bore, disadvantage.
2 *(n) Jemima is such a nuisance.* pest, pain *(informal)*, pain in the neck *(informal)*, problem, bother, plague, bore.

numb
(adj) My fingers feel numb. dead, paralysed, frozen, chilled, anaesthetized, without feeling, asleep, desensitized.

number
1 *(n) Think of a number between one and ten.* figure, digit, numeral, integer, unit.
2 *(n) Count the number of sweets in the bag.* amount, quantity, total, sum, tally.
3 *(n) A large number of people gathered in the hall.* group, crowd, throng, horde, mass, collection, company, multitude.

obedient
(adj) An obedient child. well-behaved, dutiful, respectful, biddable, submissive, compliant, manageable, amenable, docile, meek, well-trained *(animal)*. OPPOSITES: disobedient, rebellious.

obey
1 *(v) You must obey the school rules.* observe, follow, keep to, stick to, abide by, comply with, adhere to, respect, submit to, conform to, be ruled by, heed. OPPOSITES: disobey, defy.
2 *(v) You'll get into trouble if you don't obey.* do as you are told, follow orders, toe the line, knuckle under *(informal)*. OPPOSITES: rebel, revolt.

object
1 *(n) What's that red object?* See **thing** 1.
2 *(v) My parents object when I play loud music.* See **disapprove** 1.

obscene
(adj) An obscene film. indecent, pornographic, blue, immoral, corrupting, offensive, shocking, sickening, vile, lewd, vulgar, smutty, suggestive, raunchy *(slang)*, dirty, filthy, kinky *(slang)*, sick *(informal)*. OPPOSITE: decent.

observant
(adj) Spies need to be observant. watchful, alert, eagle-eyed, sharp-eyed, perceptive, attentive, vigilant, wide-awake, aware. OPPOSITES: unobservant, oblivious.

observe
1 *(v) The police will observe Beryl's actions.* watch, keep an eye on, monitor, keep under observation, keep tabs on *(informal)*, keep under surveillance, spy on.
2 *(v) Did you observe that the clock was five minutes fast?* See **notice** 1.

obsessed
(adj) Leo is obsessed by the fear of failing. consumed, gripped, possessed, haunted, tormented, plagued, preoccupied with.

obstacle
(n) Mum's disapproval could be a major obstacle. difficulty, problem, stumbling block, hurdle, impediment, drawback, disadvantage, snag, deterrent, barrier.

obstinate *see* **stubborn**.

obstruct *see* **block** 2, 3.

obtain *see* **get** 1, 4.

obvious
(adj) Ziggy's boredom is obvious. plain, clear, evident, self-evident, easy to see, crystal clear, visible, apparent, noticeable, conspicuous, striking, unmistakable, undisguised, unconcealed, undeniable, transparent, blatant, glaring, flagrant. OPPOSITES: imperceptible, hidden.

occasion *see* **event** 1, 2.

occasional
(adj) I heard an occasional rumble of thunder. intermittent, periodic, infrequent, sporadic, irregular, odd, rare. OPPOSITES: frequent, continuous.

occupation *see* **job** 2.

occupy
1 *(v) This puzzle will occupy you for hours.* See **amuse** 2.
2 *(v) Does sport occupy a lot of your time?* take up, fill, use up, eat up, consume.
3 *(v) The Smiths occupy a small house.* live in, inhabit, dwell in, reside in, rent, own.

occur
1 *(v) When did this occur?* See **happen** 1.
2 occur to *(v) When did the idea occur to you?* come to, dawn on, enter your head, cross your mind, spring to mind, strike.

ocean *see* **sea** 1.

odd
1 *(adj) Odd behaviour.* See **strange** 1.
2 *(adj) An odd noise.* See **strange** 2.
3 *(adj) Why is there always one odd sock in the wash?* spare, unmatched, leftover, remaining, single, solitary, lone.

off
1 *(adj) Mrs Badger says the trip is off.* cancelled, called off, postponed, shelved.
2 *(adj) Tom is off today.* See **away** 1.
3 *(adj) This yoghurt is off.* bad, mouldy, sour, rancid, turned, curdled, rotten.
4 *(adj) (informal) That comment was really off.* out of order, uncalled-for, unjustified, unwarranted, unacceptable, in bad taste, objectionable, non-pc *(informal)*.

offend
(v) I didn't mean to offend you. upset, hurt your feelings, put your back up, give offence, insult, slight, snub, tread on your toes *(informal)*, put your nose out of joint *(informal)*, annoy, anger, provoke, rile.

offended
(adj) Dad looked offended when I criticized his cooking. hurt, upset, wounded, put out, piqued, affronted, miffed (informal), insulted, resentful, disgruntled, in a huff, annoyed, incensed, outraged.

offensive
1 (adj) An offensive smell. See **nasty** 1.
2 (adj) Offensive remarks. See **rude** 1, 2.

offer
1 (v) Most schools offer a good education. provide, supply, give, give the opportunity of, place at your disposal, make available.
2 (v) Did Jo offer to help? See **volunteer**.
3 (v) Did you offer Grandma some cake? give, hand, proffer, pass, present with.

official
1 (adj) Is that an official certificate? authorized, approved, recognized, valid, bona fide, authentic, legitimate, legal.
2 (adj) The mayor attends many official functions. formal, ceremonial, solemn.

often
(adv) Fifi is often late. frequently, regularly, usually, generally, repeatedly, constantly, habitually, again and again, time after time, over and over again, time and again.
OPPOSITES: rarely, seldom.

O.K. (informal) see **all right** 1, 2, 3.

old
1 (adj) I'll look after you when you're old. older, elderly, getting on, advanced in years, grey-haired, aged, past your prime, over the hill (informal), past it (informal), doddery (informal), decrepit.
OPPOSITE: young.
2 (adj) Our school buildings are old. ancient, historic, antiquated, dilapidated, crumbling, decaying, run-down.
OPPOSITES: new, modern.
3 (adj) Do you have to wear those old clothes? ancient, worn-out, shabby, scruffy, moth-eaten, ragged, tattered, cast-off, second-hand.
OPPOSITE: new.
4 (adj) Flash Frank collects old cars. vintage, veteran, antique.
OPPOSITES: new, modern.
5 (adj) Life was harder in the old days. bygone, former, olden (old-fashioned), early, past, forgotten, of old, of yore.
OPPOSITES: recent, modern.
6 (adj) Kissing under the mistletoe is an old custom. ancient, age-old, long-established, long-standing, time-honoured, traditional, enduring, antiquated.
OPPOSITES: modern, recent.

old-fashioned
(adj) Aunt Bertha's ideas are really old-fashioned. out of date, behind the times, dated, outdated, outmoded, out of fashion, unfashionable, backward-looking, reactionary, old-fogyish, square (informal), ancient, archaic, antiquated, quaint, medieval, out of the ark (informal).
OPPOSITES: up-to-date, modern.

ominous
(adj) An ominous silence. forbidding, menacing, threatening, grim, sinister, dark, unpromising, inauspicious, baleful, fateful.
OPPOSITES: encouraging, promising.

omit
(v) We'll sing the song, but omit verse three. leave out, miss out, skip, pass over, exclude, drop, forget about, cut.

on purpose
(phrase) You did that on purpose! deliberately, intentionally, purposely, wilfully, knowingly, consciously, wittingly.
OPPOSITES: accidentally, by accident.

ooze
(v) Fat began to ooze from the sausage. seep, dribble, trickle, drip, escape, leak.

open
1 (v) Could you open this for me? undo, unfasten, untie, unwrap, unlock, unbolt, unbar, unseal, uncork, unroll, unfold.
OPPOSITES: close, shut.
2 (v) Will you open the discussion? See **start** 4.
3 (adj) The door was left open. ajar, wide-open, unlocked, unfastened, unbolted, unbarred, unlatched, gaping, yawning.
OPPOSITES: closed, locked.
4 (adj) When are the tennis courts open? available, free, accessible, usable, public.
OPPOSITES: unavailable.
5 (adj) We reached some open country. wide-open, empty, clear, undeveloped, unbuilt-up, uncrowded, spacious, unenclosed, unfenced, exposed, wild.
OPPOSITES: enclosed, built-up.
6 (adj) Please be open with me. See **honest** 1.

opinion see **view** 2.

opportunity
1 (n) Take every opportunity that you're offered. chance, opening, break (informal).
2 (n) Is this a good opportunity to talk? moment, time, occasion.

oppose
(v) No one dares to oppose Aunt Bertha. defy, challenge, resist, stand up to, take a stand against, cross, contradict, disagree with, take issue with, confront, quarrel with, argue with, gainsay, thwart.

opposite
1 (adj) I sat opposite Sandy. facing, face-to-face with, across from.
2 (adj) We have opposite views. opposing, conflicting, contradictory, incompatible, differing, different, diametrically opposed.
OPPOSITES: identical, similar.

optimistic
(adj) Ryan is optimistic·about the future. positive, confident, hopeful, cheerful, sanguine, buoyant, upbeat (informal).
OPPOSITES: pessimistic, cynical.

orange
(n) SHADES OF ORANGE: amber, apricot, ginger, ochre, peach, tangerine.

ordeal
(n) I never want to go through this ordeal again. torture, torment, agony, nightmare, distress, anguish, suffering, hardship, trial, tribulation, struggle, difficulty, trouble.

order
1 (v) Didn't I order you to go home? tell, command, instruct, direct, bid, charge.
2 (v) Did you order tickets for the concert? apply for, send away for, book, reserve, request, ring for, place an order for.
3 (n) The general gave the order to advance. command, instruction, direction.
4 (n) Can you see any order in this group of numbers? pattern, structure, sequence, progression, system, plan, organization, regularity, grouping, arrangement.
OPPOSITES: chaos, muddle.
5 (n) Mrs Badger quickly restored order. discipline, control, peace and quiet, calm, tranquillity, harmony, neatness, tidiness, obedience, law and order.
OPPOSITES: disorder, pandemonium.
6 (n) Try to keep your bicycle in good order. condition, shape, nick (informal).

ordinary
1 (adj) Guitar practice is part of my ordinary routine. See **usual**.
2 (adj) I live in an ordinary terraced house. typical, standard, conventional, run-of-the-mill, common or garden (informal), commonplace, simple, modest, humble.
OPPOSITES: unusual, extraordinary.
3 (adj) This is a rather ordinary piece of work. average, mediocre, indifferent, nondescript, unexceptional, unremarkable, unimpressive, unimaginative, uninspired, dull, run-of-the-mill, banal, pedestrian.
OPPOSITES: exceptional, outstanding.

organize
1 (v) Let's organize a trip. See **arrange** 3.
2 (v) Mrs Badger asked me to organize the cake stall. take charge of, be responsible for, set up, run, manage, coordinate, look after, see to, take care of.
3 (v) Try to organize your essay more clearly. structure, plan, construct, put together, shape.
4 (v) I must organize my CDs. See **sort** 3.

original
1 (adj) Who were the original inhabitants of Australia? first, earliest, initial, native, indigenous, aboriginal, primitive, primeval.
2 (adj) Your essay contains lots of original ideas. new, fresh, unique, individual, innovative, novel, ground-breaking, imaginative, ingenious, inspired, inventive, creative, unusual, unconventional.
OPPOSITES: old, familiar.
3 (adj) Is this an original painting? genuine, authentic, real, unique.
OPPOSITES: copied, fake.

ornament
(n) Hang the ornament on the tree. trinket, knick-knack, bauble, decoration, trimming.

outgoing see **extrovert**.

outing see **trip** 1.

outline
1 (n) Show me an outline of your design. rough draft, sketch, drawing, tracing, plan, diagram, layout.
2 (n) Give me an outline of the story. rough idea, quick rundown, summary, shortened version, résumé, synopsis, main points (plural), bare bones (plural).
3 (n) I saw the outline of a man through the mist. shape, silhouette, figure, profile.

outrageous
1 (adj) Conditions in the prison were outrageous. shocking, scandalous, atrocious, barbaric, monstrous, disgraceful, intolerable, unbearable, abominable, vile.
2 (adj) Dodgy Dave sells his cars at outrageous prices. exorbitant, excessive, preposterous, scandalous, unreasonable, over the top, extravagant, OTT (slang).
OPPOSITES: reasonable, fair.

outside
1 (n) We need to paint the outside of our house. exterior, façade, front, surface.
OPPOSITE: inside.
2 (adv) Let's play outside. outdoors, out-of-doors, in the open air, in the fresh air.
OPPOSITE: inside.
3 (adj) The outside walls look damp. external, exterior, outer, outermost.
OPPOSITE: inside.

outspoken see **blunt** 2.

outstanding
(adj) An outstanding writer. exceptional, great, first class, superlative, excellent, remarkable, impressive, distinguished, notable, important, celebrated, eminent.
OPPOSITES: unremarkable, insignificant.

over
1 (adj) I'm glad that unpleasant affair is over. over and done with, at an end, finished, ended, past, closed, concluded, settled, ancient history (informal).
2 (prep) We've invited over 20 people. more than, in excess of, above.

overcome see **conquer** 1, 2.

overhear
(v) Did you overhear our conversation? listen in on, eavesdrop on, pick up, catch.

overpowering
1 (adj) I felt an overpowering urge to laugh. See **irresistible**.
2 (adj) The smell of Wayne's aftershave is overpowering. suffocating, sickening, nauseating, stifling, unbearable.

overtake
(v) Let's try to overtake that car. pass, get past, get by, go past, outdistance, outstrip, outdo, go faster than, leave behind.

overweight
(adj) Dad is getting overweight. heavy, chubby, tubby, plump, podgy, stout, portly, paunchy, fleshy, hefty, corpulent, fat, obese, huge, massive, outsize, gross.
OPPOSITE: underweight.

own
1 (v) I hope to own a pony one day. have, be the owner of, possess, keep, be in possession of, be responsible for.
2 (adj) Everyone needs their own space. personal, individual, private, particular.

own up see **confess** 1, 2.

Pp

pace
1 (n) Take one pace forwards. See **step** 2.
2 (v) Don't pace about; it makes me nervous. march, walk, stride, tramp, pad.

pack
(v) Can you pack all your books in this box? put, place, load, stow, fit, stuff, cram, bundle, squeeze, jam, wedge, ram.

paddle
(v) Let's paddle in the sea. wade, splash about, slosh about, dabble.

page
(n) Take a new page for each question. side, sheet, piece of paper, leaf, folio.

pain
1 (n) You may feel a little pain. soreness, discomfort, tenderness, irritation, twinge, pang, spasm, throbbing, ache, cramp.
2 (n) This behaviour will cause your parents great pain. See **distress** 1.

painful
1 (adj) Is your arm painful? See **sore**.
2 (adj) Splitting up with your boyfriend can be painful. upsetting, distressing, unpleasant, hard, tough, heartbreaking, traumatic, agonizing, harrowing.

paint
1 (n) This paint will hide the dirt. colour, pigment, dye, tint, stain, emulsion, gloss, whitewash, undercoat, primer.
2 (v) Can you paint the sunset? depict, portray, represent.
3 (v) Dad plans to paint the house himself. decorate, redecorate, do up (informal).

painting
(n) TYPES OF PAINTING: abstract painting, altarpiece, fresco, landscape, miniature, mural, oil painting, portrait, seascape, self-portrait, still life, watercolour.

pair
(n) Sam and Seb are a good pair. couple, match, combination, partnership, double act, twosome, duo, team.

palace
(n) chateau, stately home, mansion, castle, official residence. ❖ Also see **building**.

pale
1 (adj) Megan has a pale complexion. fair, light, creamy, ivory, pallid, waxen, pasty.
OPPOSITES: rosy, ruddy.

2 (adj) You look pale. peaky (informal), washed out (informal), drained, white, ashen, anaemic, sickly, grey, green, like death warmed up (informal).
OPPOSITES: flushed, blooming.
3 (adj) Claire's room is decorated in pale shades of blue. light, soft, subtle, pastel, muted, subdued, faint, faded, bleached.
OPPOSITES: dark, bright, strong.

pamper see **spoil** 3.

panic
1 (n) The sight of the fire filled us with panic. alarm, horror, fear, terror, dread, consternation, hysteria, confusion, dismay.
2 (v) Don't panic! be alarmed, be scared, become hysterical, overreact, go to pieces, lose your head, lose your nerve, freak out, get into a tizzy (informal), lose your cool (slang), throw a wobbly (slang).

pant
(v) Exercise makes me pant. gasp, wheeze, breathe heavily, puff, huff and puff.

paper
1 (n) I need some more paper. writing paper, notepaper, stationery, file paper, rough paper, scrap paper, cartridge paper, graph paper, tracing paper.
2 (n) Which paper do your parents read? See **newspaper**.
3 papers (plural n) These papers prove that Dodgy Dave is guilty. documents (plural), records (plural), files (plural), certificates (plural), forms (plural), deeds (plural), diaries (plural), archives (plural).

parade
(n) Crowds lined the street to watch the parade. procession, cavalcade, march past (troops), motorcade, cortege (funeral procession), display, spectacle, pageant.

paradise see **heaven** 1, 2.

parcel
(n) Is this parcel for me? package, packet, box, carton, pack, bundle.

pardon see **forgive**.

park
(n) Let's walk around the park. public park, recreation ground, gardens (plural), botanical gardens (plural), green, common, woodland, parkland, grounds (plural).

part
1 (n) Have a part of my orange. See **bit** 2.
2 (n) Which part of the course do you prefer? bit, section, element, unit, module, component, constituent.
3 (n) Which part of the company interests you? bit, area, branch, division, section, department, sector, segment.
4 (n) Which part of the country are you from? bit, area, region, district, neck of the woods (informal), neighbourhood.
5 (n) I'd love to play a part in the pantomime. role, character, starring role, lead, supporting role, speaking part, bit part, walk-on part, extra, cameo role.
6 take part see **take part**.

participate

participate *see* **take part**.

particular
1 *(adj) This sauce has a particular flavour.* distinct, unique, special, unmistakable, specific, definite, individual, certain. OPPOSITES: vague, general.
2 *(adj) Aunt Bertha is particular about her food. See* **fussy**.

partner
1 *(n) Bring your partner to the dance.* boyfriend, girlfriend, wife, husband, spouse, other half *(informal)*, mate.
2 *(n) Dad had a business lunch with his partner.* associate, colleague, collaborator, ally, sidekick *(informal)*, accomplice.

party
1 *(n) Let's have a party!* celebration, gathering, get-together *(informal)*, bash *(informal)*, thrash *(informal)*, do *(informal)*, rave-up *(slang)*, shindig *(informal)*, knees-up *(informal)*, function, reception.
2 *(n) Which party do you belong to?* group, faction, alliance, association, camp, side, team, gang, crew *(informal)*, band.

pass
1 *(v) The guard let us pass.* go by, go past, pass by, move past, move on, proceed, go on, go ahead, go through, enter.
2 *(v) The time seemed to pass so quickly.* go, go by, go past, pass by, elapse, slip by, tick away, fly by, glide by, flow by, roll by.
3 *(v) Can we pass that car? See* **overtake**.
4 *(v) Your anger will pass.* blow over, run its course, come to an end, die away, fade away, disappear, evaporate, peter out.
5 *(v) How do you pass the time?* occupy, fill, spend, while away, fritter away, kill.
6 *(v) Pass me your plate. See* **hand** 4.
7 *(v) This exam is so hard; I hope I'll pass.* succeed, get through, come up to scratch *(informal)*, pass muster, qualify, graduate. OPPOSITE: fail.

passage
1 *(n) The thieves escaped down a narrow passage.* passageway, alley, alleyway, lane, path, track, corridor, tunnel.
2 *(n) Listen to this passage from "Oliver Twist".* excerpt, extract, quotation, piece, section, episode, scene, paragraph, verse.

passion
1 *(n) The actor played his part with passion.* feeling, emotion, intensity, fervour, zeal, warmth, fire, zest, gusto, enthusiasm, energy, animation.
2 *(n) Jason is consumed with passion for Jodie.* love, adoration, desire, lust, longing, yearning, hunger, the hots *(plural) (slang)*.

passionate
1 *(adj) A passionate argument.* heated, emotional, impassioned, intense, fierce, vehement, furious, violent, fiery, stormy. OPPOSITES: cool, dispassionate.
2 *(adj) A passionate embrace.* loving, ardent, amorous, steamy *(informal)*, sensual, lustful, urgent, burning, frenzied. OPPOSITE: cool.

past
1 *(adj) Those times are past. See* **over** 1.
2 *(adj) You can learn a lot from past events.* former, bygone, earlier, previous, prior, recent, historical, ancient. OPPOSITE: future.
3 **the past** *(n) I like learning about the past.* history, past times, former times, days gone by, the olden days, the good old days, yesteryear *(old-fashioned)*, recent history, ancient history, prehistory. OPPOSITE: the future.

pastel *see* **pale** 3.

pastime *see* **hobby**.

pat
1 *(v) Come and pat Fido.* stroke, pet.
2 *(v) Pat Joe on the back; he's coughing!* slap, thump, hit, smack, bang, clap, tap.

patch
1 *(v) I must patch my jeans.* mend, sew up, stitch up, reinforce, darn, repair, fix.
2 *(n) We grow turnips on this patch.* plot, piece of land, spot, bed, lot, allotment, ground, area, stretch, tract, clearing.

path
(n) footpath, pathway, pavement, towpath, bridle path, track, trail, lane.

pathetic
1 *(adj) Fido gave a pathetic whimper.* pitiful, plaintive, forlorn, doleful, mournful, woeful, touching, moving, poignant, heart-rending, heartbreaking, distressing.
2 *(adj) Dad made a pathetic attempt to be trendy.* feeble, unsuccessful, unconvincing, pitiful, dismal, woeful, sorry, sad *(slang)*.
3 *(adj) (informal) I'm pathetic at maths. See* **hopeless** 4.

patient
1 *(adj) Mrs Badger is always patient with us.* tolerant, long-suffering, forbearing, understanding, sympathetic, calm, even-tempered, accommodating, indulgent. OPPOSITES: impatient, short-tempered.
2 *(adj) Try to be patient; you'll get there in the end.* persistent, persevering, steady, unhurried, resolute, determined, dogged, resigned, philosophical, stoical. OPPOSITES: impatient, restless.

patronizing *see* **condescending**.

pattern
1 *(n) Use this as a pattern for your sketch.* guide, model, example, master, blueprint, template, stencil, standard.
2 *(n) A floral pattern. See* **design** 2.

pause
1 *(v) Don't pause at the end of every sentence.* stop, break off, hesitate, wait, delay, rest, take a break, have a rest, halt.
2 *(n) There will be a pause between each act. See* **gap** 2.

pay
1 *(v) Who will pay for the party?* foot the bill, pay up, settle the bill, meet the cost, shell out *(informal)*, cough up *(informal)*, stump up *(informal)*, fork out *(slang)*.
2 *(v) I didn't pay much. See* **spend** 1.
3 *(v) Mum said she'd pay me if I washed the car.* reward, reimburse, compensate.
4 *(v) You'll pay for this!* suffer, be punished, answer, pay the price, make amends, get your comeuppance *(informal)*.
5 *(n) At your interview, ask about the pay.* salary, wages *(plural)*, earnings *(plural)*, fee, payment, remuneration.

pay attention
(v) Pay attention or you won't know what to do. listen, watch, concentrate, take notice, listen up *(slang)*.

pay back
1 *(v) You must pay back the money.* repay, return, refund, reimburse.
2 *(v) I'll pay you back for taking my pen!* repay, get revenge on, get even with *(informal)*, get *(informal)*, settle the score with, retaliate against, hit back at.

peace
1 *(n) I wish there could be peace all over the world.* harmony, goodwill, agreement, accord, friendship, reconciliation.
2 *(n) The two armies agreed to a permanent peace.* truce, ceasefire, armistice, cessation of hostilities, reconciliation, alliance, treaty, pact.
3 *(n) I love the peace of the countryside.* peace and quiet, tranquillity, peacefulness, calm, stillness, quietness, silence, hush.

peaceful
1 *(adj) It's so peaceful here.* tranquil, restful, quiet, still, calm, relaxing, soothing. OPPOSITES: noisy, bustling.
2 *(adj) Alice looks so peaceful.* tranquil, serene, at peace, relaxed, untroubled, unruffled, unworried, calm, placid.

peak
1 *(n) A snowy mountain peak. See* **top** 1.
2 *(n) Famous Fred is at the peak of his career.* height, high point, climax, zenith.

peculiar
1 *(adj) Peculiar behaviour. See* **strange** 1.
2 *(adj) A peculiar noise. See* **strange** 2.
3 *(adj) I feel peculiar. See* **ill** 2.

peep
(v) Did you peep at your presents? peek, steal a look, sneak a look, take a sly look.

peer
(v) I saw you peer through the window. spy, peek, peep, squint, snoop, try to see, look closely, screw up your eyes.

people
1 *(plural n) What makes people different from animals?* humans *(plural)*, human beings *(plural)*, the human race, mankind.
2 *(plural n) How many people were hurt?* men and women *(plural)*, children *(plural)*, individuals *(plural)*, persons *(plural)*.
3 *(plural n) The king addressed the people.* nation, citizens *(plural)*, populace, general public, community, population, crowd, masses *(plural)*, multitude, mob, rabble, rank and file, hoi polloi.

perceptive
(adj) Perceptive comments. shrewd, discerning, astute, penetrating, incisive, observant, sensitive, understanding.

perfect
1 (adj) If you buy something new, you expect it to be perfect. flawless, in mint condition, undamaged, unblemished, unscratched, unbroken, clean, spotless, immaculate, intact, complete, whole.
OPPOSITES: imperfect, faulty.
2 (adj) Ali gave a perfect performance. flawless, faultless, exemplary, unerring, impeccable, consummate, unrivalled, matchless, unequalled, ideal, definitive.
OPPOSITES: flawed, poor.
3 (adj) A perfect copy. See **exact** 3.
4 (adj) A perfect choice. See **ideal** 2.

perform
1 (v) Will you perform in the concert? take part, appear, play, act, dance, sing, star:
2 (v) Let's perform a play. See **stage** 3.

performance
(n) I'm sure you'll enjoy the performance. show, production, play, concert, recital, gig (informal), act, presentation, display, spectacle, entertainment, matinée, debut, premiere, preview, dress rehearsal.

perfume see **scent** 1, 2.

period
1 (n) I spent a period in Spain. See **time** 1.
2 (n) We're studying the medieval period See **age** 1.

permanent
1 (adj) Billy has a permanent cough. constant, continual, perpetual, persistent.
2 (adj) Is this a permanent arrangement? fixed, firm, definite, unalterable, unchangeable, irreversible, immutable, binding, lasting, enduring, stable.
OPPOSITES: short-lived, temporary.

permission
(n) We need police permission to hold a street party. authorization, approval, authority, consent, leave, go-ahead (informal), rubber stamp, green light.

permit see **allow** 1, 2.

perplexing see **puzzling**.

persecute
(v) The refugees feared the officials would persecute them. hound, plague, pursue, harass, harry, bully, terrorize, victimize, oppress, ill-treat, torment, molest, torture.

persevere
(v) Try to persevere when life gets hard. keep going, carry on, soldier on, stick at it, keep at it, hang in there (informal), be resolute, persist, plug away (informal)

person
(n) Each person is different. human being, individual, character, living being, soul.

personal
1 (adj) Cynthia has her own personal style. See **individual** 2.

2 (adj) Don't open that letter; it's personal! See **private** 2.
3 (adj) Don't make personal comments. insulting, offensive, rude, nasty, critical, negative, hurtful, disparaging, derogatory.

personality see **character** 1.

perspire see **sweat** 2.

persuade
(v) Can I persuade you to try some squid? coax, tempt, entice, induce, cajole, urge, prompt, prevail on, convince, talk you into, wheedle you into, sweet-talk you into (informal), win you over, bring you round.
OPPOSITES: dissuade, deter.

persuasive
(adj) The salesman was very persuasive. convincing, compelling, forceful, plausible, credible, believable, eloquent, silver-tongued, seductive, coaxing, winning.
OPPOSITES: unconvincing, implausible.

pessimistic
(adj) I feel pessimistic about the future. gloomy, hopeless, negative, despondent, despairing, depressed, glum, melancholy, fatalistic, defeatist, resigned, cynical.
OPPOSITES: optimistic, positive.

pester
(v) Answer my question and I won't pester you anymore. badger, bother, plague, torment, hound, harass, harry, hassle (informal), disturb, annoy, nag, be on your back (slang), get in your hair (informal).

petrified see **scared** 1.

phase see **stage** 2.

phone
1 (v) Did Sid phone you? call, telephone, ring you up, ring, give you a call, give you a bell (slang), give you a tinkle (informal), give you a buzz (informal), get on the blower to you (informal).
2 (n) We've bought a new phone. telephone, mobile phone, cordless phone, car phone, cellphone, answerphone, videophone, handset, blower (informal).

photograph
1 (n) Look at this photograph of Granddad. photo (informal), picture, print, snap (informal), snapshot, shot, slide, transparency, enlargement, likeness.
2 (v) I want to photograph you in your clown suit. take a photograph of, take a picture of, capture you on film, get a shot of, shoot, film, snap (informal), record.

phrase see **expression** 2.

pick
1 (v) Pick a number. See **choose** 1.
2 (v) Shall I pick some flowers? gather, cut, collect, pluck, harvest (fruit).

pick on
(v) Pick on someone else for a change! criticize, find fault with, blame, nag, get at, tease, torment, badger, bully.

pick up
1 (v) Pick up that box. See **lift** 1.

2 (v) I'll pick you up at two o'clock. call for, come for, collect, give you a lift, fetch.
3 (v) Did you pick up any French on holiday? acquire, learn, get the hang of (informal), grasp, master.

picture
1 (n) That's a good picture of your dad. likeness, portrayal, depiction, representation, study, portrait, photograph, drawing, sketch, painting, caricature, cartoon, silhouette, etching, engraving, print, poster.
2 (v) I can't picture Aunt Bertha as a teenager. See **imagine** 1.

picturesque see **pretty** 2.

piece
1 (n) I'd like a piece of cheese. See **bit** 1.
2 (n) I dropped a piece of food on the floor. bit, scrap, morsel, mouthful, fragment, crumb, speck, particle.
3 (n) I cut my foot on a piece of glass. bit, fragment, sliver, splinter, shard, chip.
4 (n) Do you need that piece of material? bit, scrap, snippet, shred, remnant, length.
5 (n) Have a piece of my apple. See **bit** 2.
6 (n) This kit has a piece missing. bit, part, section, element, component.
7 (n) I'm learning a new piece for the concert. work, composition, item.
8 (v) Piece the parts together. See **fit** 2.

pierce
(v) Did the spear pierce the dragon's skin? puncture, penetrate, make a hole in, enter, go through, pass through, perforate, prick, wound, stab, spike, skewer.

pile
1 (n) Matt has a huge pile of magazines in his room. stack, heap, mound, mountain, mass, bundle, load, hoard, store, stockpile.
2 (v) Pile the papers here. stack, heap, gather, collect, amass, assemble, store

pill
(n) tablet, capsule, lozenge.

pillar
(n) That pillar holds up the roof. column, post, pole, support, upright, prop, shaft.

pinch
1 (v) Don't pinch my leg. nip, squeeze.
2 (v) These shoes pinch my feet. hurt, cramp, squeeze, crush, confine, chafe.
3 (n) Add a pinch of salt. bit, taste, touch, dash, smidgen (informal), soupçon, small amount, trace, tad (informal), speck.

pink
(adj) Pink cheeks. rosy, flushed.
SHADES OF PINK: cerise, coral, flesh-colour, rose, salmon, shell pink, shocking pink.

pipe
(n) Water flowed through the pipe. tube, hose, duct, water main, pipeline, drainpipe, channel, conduit.

pirate
(n) buccaneer, raider, marauder, freebooter, cutthroat. ❖ Also see **pirates & shipwrecks**.

pirates

pirates and shipwrecks

pirates may be...

barbaric
black-hearted
bloodthirsty
bold
brutal
daring
dastardly
drunken
grasping
greedy

heartless
infamous
lawless
murderous
notorious
remorseless
ruthless
swashbuckling
vengeful
villainous

cutlass

pirates may...

board ships
bury treasure
drop anchor
keelhaul
  mutineers (drag
  rebels by a rope
  under the ship)
lie in wait
loot
make prisoners
  walk the plank
mutiny (rebel)
pillage

plunder
pursue
raid
ransack
rob
sail the high seas
seek revenge
sink ships
slit throats
take prisoners
weigh anchor
  (raise the
  anchor)

whale

pirates may have...

booty
bottle of rum
breeches
cockatoo
cocked hat
cutlass
doubloons
  (gold coins)
ducats (gold or
  silver coins)
eye patch
gold earrings
grog
  (diluted rum)
hook

kerchief
  (headscarf)
logbook
parrot
peg leg
  (wooden leg)
pieces of eight
  (coins)
pigtail
pistol
scar
sea chart
tattoo
telescope
treasure map

on board a pirate ship

bow (front)
cabin
cannon
crow's nest
deck
fo'c'sle
  or forecastle
hammock
hull (main
  body of ship)
Jolly Roger
  (flag with
  skull and
  crossbones)

keel
  (ship's bottom)
mast
poop deck
port
  (left side)
rigging
rudder
sail
ship's lantern
starboard
  (right side)
stern (back)
wheel

Jolly Roger
mast
crow's nest
rigging
bow
hull
fo'c'sle
poop deck
stern
rudder

in a storm, a ship may...

break up on the rocks
capsize
creak
disintegrate
founder (sink)
groan
list
lurch
pitch
run aground
shatter
shudder
sink beneath the waves
splinter
split apart

jagged rocks
message in a bottle
sea battle
shipwreck

on a desert island you might find...

buried treasure
coral reef
dense jungle
driftwood
footprints
lagoon
palm trees
pirates' hide-out
silver sand
volcano

footprints
quicksand
volcano
jellyfish

on the island you might...

build a shelter
climb trees
collect berries
dive down to the wreck
drink coconut milk
explore the island
fish
forage for food
hunt
light a fire
make a raft
search through the wreckage
send a message in a bottle
send smoke signals

desert island dangers

contaminated water
jellyfish
poisonous berries
quicksand (sinking sand)
shark-infested waters
swamps
treacherous currents
venomous snakes
wild beasts

treasure island
survivors
shark
raft

after a shipwreck you might...

be marooned
be the sole survivor
be washed ashore
cling to the wreckage
encounter sharks
go down with the ship
go to a watery grave
swim for the shore

pieces of eight
telescope

cocked hat
eye patch
pistol
pigtail

WANTED
Dead or Alive

Also see **sea & seashore**, **storm words**, **treasure words**.

planets in the solar system · Jupiter — Jupiter's rings — Saturn — Saturn's rings — Uranus — Pluto — Mercury — Earth — Venus — Mars — Neptune

pity

1 (n) *The judge showed no pity.* sympathy, compassion, understanding, fellow feeling, mercy, charity, kindness, emotion, feeling.
2 (n) *It's a pity you can't come.* shame, crying shame, stroke of bad luck, bummer (slang), misfortune, tragedy, sin.
3 (v) *I pity anyone out in this blizzard.* feel sorry for, sympathize with, feel for, commiserate with, feel pity for, have compassion for, weep for, grieve for.

place

1 (n) *What a good place for a picnic!* spot, position, site, location, situation, setting
2 (n) *Riverdale is an interesting place to visit.* village, town, city, neighbourhood, district, area, region, spot, locality.
3 (n) *Save me a place!* seat, chair, space.
4 (v) *Place the fruit in the bowl.* See **put** 1.

placid

(adj) *Anna is a placid child.* calm, even-tempered, docile, easy-going, peaceable, serene, self-possessed, composed, level-headed, unexcitable, steady.
OPPOSITES: excitable, temperamental.

plain

1 (adj) *The room was decorated in a plain style.* simple, basic, restrained, subdued, unpretentious, austere, stark, severe, Spartan, unadorned, unembellished, undecorated, unpatterned.
OPPOSITES: fancy, elaborate.
2 (adj) *Aunt Bertha likes plain food.* simple, basic, ordinary, homely, everyday, unsophisticated, unexciting, frugal.
OPPOSITES: fancy, elaborate.
3 (adj) *Martha is a plain child.* ordinary-looking, unattractive, unprepossessing.
OPPOSITES: attractive, good-looking.
4 (adj) *Mrs Badger's feelings were plain.* See **obvious**.

plan

1 (n) *That sounds like a sensible plan.* idea, scheme, plan of action, suggestion, proposal, proposition, strategy, procedure, system, method, tactic.
2 (n) *Look at this plan of our new house.* drawing, scale drawing, blueprint, layout, diagram, sketch, outline, representation, illustration, map, chart, bird's-eye view.
3 (v) *I didn't plan to cheat.* See **mean** 3.
4 (v) *Plan your project before you start.* think out, sketch out, map out, outline, organize, prepare, draft, design, formulate, devise, shape, frame.

plane see **aircraft**.

planet

(n) *The planet floated in space.* sphere, orb, globe, satellite, heavenly body.
PLANETS IN THE SOLAR SYSTEM: Earth, Jupiter, Mars, Mercury, Neptune, Pluto, Saturn, Uranus, Venus. ❖ Also see **space adventure**.

plant

(n) *What's that unusual plant?* flower, bloom, seedling, weed, shrub, bush, climber, creeper, herb, vegetable, grass, fern, cactus, moss, lichen.

plaster see **smear** 1.

play

1 (v) *You have all day to play.* amuse yourself, entertain yourself, enjoy yourself, have fun, play games, mess about.
2 (v) *The others won't let me play.* join in, take part, participate, be in the game.
3 (v) *Rangers will play United.* play against, take on, challenge, compete against, rival, vie with, contend with.
4 (v) *Gill will play Cinderella.* act, be, take the part of, take the role of, portray.
5 (n) *Did you enjoy the play?* show, production, performance, drama.
TYPES OF PLAY: comedy, farce, historical play, melodrama, mime, musical, nativity play, pageant, pantomime, puppet show, radio play, satire, tragedy, TV play.

play about see **mess about** 1, 2

playful

1 (adj) *Playful puppies.* See **lively** 2.
2 (adj) *A playful grin.* See **mischievous** 2.

plead with see **beg** 2.

pleasant

1 (adj) *A pleasant day out.* See **enjoyable**.
2 (adj) *What pleasant weather!* lovely, beautiful, glorious, delightful, fine, mild, warm, sunny, balmy.
OPPOSITES: unpleasant, nasty.
3 (adj) *Mrs Honey is a pleasant person.* likable, lovely, good-natured, amiable, delightful, charming, agreeable, friendly.
OPPOSITES: unpleasant, obnoxious.
4 (adj) *This makes a pleasant change.* agreeable, welcome, refreshing, pleasing, satisfying, appreciated.
OPPOSITES: unwelcome, unpleasant.

please

1 (v) *I'm doing my best to please you.* make you happy, give you pleasure, satisfy, cheer you up, delight, charm, entertain, amuse, indulge, gratify, humour, suit.
2 (v) *Do as you please.* See **like** 4.

pleased

(adj) *Kim was pleased when she passed her exams.* happy, delighted, glad, contented, satisfied, thrilled, overjoyed, jubilant, elated, euphoric, over the moon (informal), thrilled to bits (informal), chuffed (slang).

pleasure

(n) *Lord Lucre leads a life of pleasure.* enjoyment, contentment, satisfaction, comfort, ease, gratification, entertainment, amusement, bliss, delight.
OPPOSITES: misery, suffering.

plenty

(n) *Lord Lucre has plenty of money.* a great deal, a lot, lots (plural) (informal), a large amount, more than enough, enough, sufficient, a fund, heaps (plural) (informal), loads (plural) (informal), masses (plural) (informal), oodles (plural) (informal), piles (plural) (informal), stacks (plural) (informal).

plot

1 (n) *The pirates hatched a plot.* scheme, conspiracy, plan, stratagem, intrigue.
2 (n) *Can you follow the plot of this play?* storyline, story, narrative, thread, structure.
3 (v) *Let's plot to get our revenge.* plan, scheme, conspire, intrigue, manoeuvre.

plough

1 (v) *Farmer Phyllis plans to plough this field.* cultivate, till, turn over, dig up.
2 (v) *We tried to plough through the mud.* plunge, push, wallow, wade, cut, drive.

plump

(adj) *Mrs Honey is rather plump.* chubby, tubby, podgy, dumpy, pudgy, roly-poly, well-rounded, stout, portly, corpulent, fat, well-padded, fleshy, buxom, matronly.
OPPOSITES: slim, slender.

plunge see **dive** 1, 2.

plush (informal) see **luxurious**.

poem

(n) rhyme, verse, ditty, ballad, ode, sonnet, limerick, haiku, elegy, epic, jingle.

poetic

(adj) *This story is written in a poetic style.* lyrical, imaginative, creative, artistic, flowing, lilting, graceful, songlike, flowery.

poignant see **sad** 2.

point

1 (n) *This is the point where we started.* spot, place, position, site, location.
2 (n) *At that point, Zak left.* moment, very moment, instant, second, stage, juncture.
3 (n) *This spear has a sharp point.* tip, end, spike, prong, sharp end.
4 (n) *What is the point of this game?* purpose, aim, objective, object, use.
5 (n) *I don't understand the point of this story.* meaning, significance, relevance, thrust, drift, theme, main idea, substance.
6 (n) *I covered that point in my talk.* detail, aspect, item, feature, particular, facet.
7 (v) *Point me to the station.* See **direct** 6.
8 (v) *Point your arrow at the bull's-eye.* See **aim** 3.

pointless *see* **useless** 1.

point out
(v) *Why didn't you point out this problem earlier?* draw attention to, mention, bring up, allude to, refer to, indicate, identify.

poisonous
(adj) *Bleach is a poisonous substance.* toxic, noxious, lethal, deadly, harmful, venomous *(snakes, spiders)*.
OPPOSITES: harmless, nontoxic.

poke
1 (v) *Don't poke your finger in the trifle!* See **stick** 6.
2 (v) *Poke me if I start to snore.* prod, jab, nudge, elbow, butt, hit.

poky
(adj) *This room is so poky.* cramped, small, tiny, narrow, confined, cell-like.
OPPOSITES: spacious, large.

pole
(n) rod, bar, post, stake, stick, staff, spar.

polish
1 (n) *Look at the polish on that table!* See **shine** 4.
2 (v) *Polish your shoes.* shine, buff up, rub, wax, brush, clean, burnish *(metal)*.

polite
1 (adj) *Cyril is always polite.* courteous, well-behaved, well-mannered, civil, tactful, diplomatic, respectful, deferential, obliging, considerate, thoughtful.
OPPOSITES: rude, discourteous.
2 (adj) *It's not polite to gobble your food.* acceptable, done, proper, seemly, nice, genteel, civilized, ladylike, gentlemanly.
OPPOSITES: rude, ignorant.

pollute
(v) *Cars pollute the air.* contaminate, poison, dirty, foul up, taint, blight, infect.

pool
(n) puddle, pond, fish pond, duck pond, millpond, oasis, water hole, lake, tarn, swimming pool, paddling pool.

poor
1 (adj) *I hate being poor.* short of money, badly off, hard up *(informal)*, penniless, poverty-stricken, destitute, down-and-out, on the rocks, impoverished, broke *(informal)*, flat broke *(informal)*, stony-broke *(slang)*, skint *(slang)*.
OPPOSITES: rich, wealthy.
2 (adj) *This is a poor piece of work.* inadequate, unsatisfactory, second-rate, mediocre, inferior, substandard, below average, disappointing, feeble, worthless, dismal, rubbishy, shoddy, rotten *(informal)*.
OPPOSITES: good, excellent.
3 (adj) *The poor kitten was soaked!* unfortunate, unlucky, wretched, luckless, hapless, miserable, pathetic, pitiable.
4 (adj) *Eva earns a poor salary.* See **low** 2.

pop
(v) *Can you hear the firecrackers pop?* bang, crack, snap, go bang, explode, go off, go off with a bang, detonate, burst.

---

pop, rock and jazz

musical styles

acid jazz	dub	hip-hop	rave
beat	easy listening	house	reggae
bebop	folk	indie	rhythm
big band	funk	jazz	and blues
blues	garage	jungle	rock 'n' roll
country and	glam rock	pop	salsa
western	gospel	psychedelia	ska
dance	hardcore	punk	soul
disco	hard rock	ragga	swing
doo-wop	heavy metal	rap	techno

jazz musician

drummer

volume control — tempo control (changes speed) — display screen — sound editing buttons

vibrato — synthesizer — keyboard

pitch blend (changes pitch)

you might listen to...

acoustic version	live recording
album	new release
chart music	remix
compilation album	single
concept album	soundtrack
cover version	track
hit single	unplugged
live performance	version

a band may use...

acoustic guitar	PA system
amplifier	record deck
bass guitar	sampler
drum kit	(equipment to
drum machine	mix in sounds)
electric guitar	sequencer
headphones	(equipment to
keyboard	memorize a
microphone	sequence of
mixing desk	notes)
multitrack tape	speakers
machine	synthesizer

crash cymbal — ride cymbal — tom-toms — hi-hat cymbal — snare drum — floor tom — pedal — bass drum — pedal

drum kit

vocalist

punk

on a track you might hear...

backing vocals	key change
bass line	lyrics
beat	melody
bridge (link)	refrain (chorus)
chords	rhythm
drum break	riff (repeated
(drum solo)	chord
echo effects	sequence)
fade	sample
harmony	(mixed-in
hook	extract from
(catchy phrase)	another record)
improvisation	scratching
instrumental	sound effects
section	theme
intro *(informal)*	vocals (singing)

a track may sound...

bland	original
catchy	polished
dreamy	raucous
fresh	repetitive
funky	rhythmic
(informal)	sexy *(informal)*
futuristic	slick
haunting	smooth
laid-back	soulful
(informal)	tinny
manic	tribal
melancholy	tuneless
mellow	unoriginal
melodic	upbeat
(tuneful)	*(informal)*
monotonous	weird

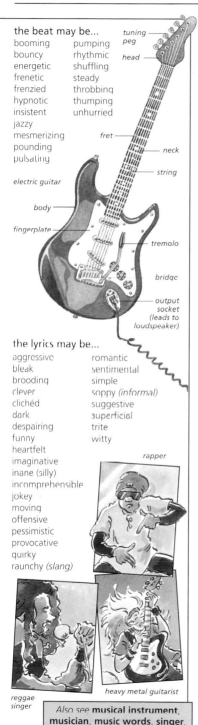

the beat may be...

booming	pumping
bouncy	rhythmic
energetic	shuffling
frenetic	steady
frenzied	throbbing
hypnotic	thumping
insistent	unhurried
jazzy	
mesmerizing	
pounding	
pulsating	

electric guitar

Labels: tuning peg, head, fret, neck, string, body, fingerplate, tremolo, bridge, output socket (leads to loudspeaker)

the lyrics may be...

aggressive	romantic
bleak	sentimental
brooding	simple
clever	soppy *(informal)*
clichéd	suggestive
dark	superficial
despairing	trite
funny	witty
heartfelt	
imaginative	*rapper*
inane (silly)	
incomprehensible	
jokey	
moving	
offensive	
pessimistic	
provocative	
quirky	
raunchy *(slang)*	

reggae singer

heavy metal guitarist

Also see **musical instrument, musician, music words, singer**.

popular
1 *(adj)* Josie has always been popular. well-liked, admired, in demand, in favour, sought-after, accepted, loved, idolized. OPPOSITE: unpopular.
2 *(adj)* Short hair is popular at the moment. fashionable, in fashion, in, in favour, trendy *(informal)*, hip *(slang)*. OPPOSITES: unfashionable, out.
3 *(adj)* There's a popular theory that chocolate gives you spots. common, widespread, general, well-known, current, prevailing, prevalent.

port
(n) The ship approached the port. harbour, dock, seaport, marina, anchorage, wharf, quay, landing stage, dockyard, dry dock.

portion see **helping**.

portrait
(n) Do you like this portrait of Fergus? picture, self-portrait, painting, drawing, sketch, photograph, study, likeness, portrayal, image, depiction, impression.

posh
1 *(adj) (informal)* We stayed in a posh hotel. grand, luxurious, plush *(informal)*, up-market, classy *(slang)*, swish *(informal)*, swanky *(informal)*, ritzy *(slang)*, high-class. OPPOSITES: modest, humble.
2 *(adj) (informal)* Araminta is much too posh to talk to us. grand, superior, swanky *(informal)*, upper class, refined, genteel, snooty *(informal)*, toffee-nosed *(slang)*, stuck-up *(informal)*, la-di-da *(informal)*.

position
1 *(n)* What a perfect position for a house! See **place** 1.
2 *(n)* Ben's request put me in a difficult position. situation, predicament, spot, plight, dilemma, state.
3 *(n)* What's your mum's position in the company? See **rank**.
4 *(n)* Mrs Badger applied for the position of deputy head. See **job** 3.
5 *(n)* I can't hold this position for much longer. pose, stance, posture, attitude.

positive
1 *(adj)* Are you positive that you saw a ghost? See **certain** 1.
2 *(adj)* Do you have any positive proof? real, actual, definite, clear-cut, firm, concrete, categorical, absolute, conclusive, indisputable, undeniable, irrefutable.
3 *(adj)* Mrs Badger made some positive suggestions. helpful, constructive, encouraging, useful, practical, beneficial. OPPOSITES: negative, unhelpful.

possible
1 *(adj)* Anything is possible if you try. achievable, attainable, feasible, within reach, practicable, workable, doable. OPPOSITES: impossible, unattainable.
2 *(adj)* This story has only one possible ending. conceivable, imaginable, plausible, credible, likely, probable, potential. OPPOSITES: inconceivable, unthinkable.

post
1 *(n)* Stick the post in the ground. stake, pole, upright, support, pillar, gatepost.
2 *(n)* Don't open my post. mail, letters *(plural)*, correspondence.
3 *(n)* May I apply for this post? See **job** 3.
4 *(v)* I must post this parcel. mail, send, send off, dispatch.

postpone
(v) We'll have to postpone the match. put off, put back, defer, hold over, delay, shelve, suspend, adjourn, put on the back burner *(informal)*, take a rain check on *(informal)*, put on ice *(informal)*.

potion
(n) A magic potion. brew, concoction, mixture, drink, draught, elixir, drug.

potter about see **mess about** 1.

pounce
1 *(v)* The eagle will pounce when it sees its prey. strike, attack, swoop down, drop down, descend.
2 **pounce on** *(v)* Ed is waiting to pounce on you. jump on, leap out at, spring on, swoop on, lunge at, make a grab for, ambush, attack, take you by surprise.

pour
1 *(v)* Water began to pour from the pipe. See **flow** 1
2 *(v)* Please pour the tea. pour out, serve.
3 *(v)* It's going to pour. See **rain** 1.

powdery
(adj) Powdery earth. crumbly, fine, dry, loose, dusty, sandy, chalky, grainy.

power
1 *(n)* You'll need all your power to lift that sack. See **strength** 1.
2 *(n)* I wish I had the power to fly. ability, capacity, capability, potential.
3 *(n)* The king has power over his people. control, authority, command, mastery, supremacy, dominance, sovereignty, influence, sway, clout.
4 *(n)* Nuclear power. energy, fuel

powerful
1 *(adj)* A powerful leader. strong, forceful, influential, dominant, commanding, high-powered, authoritative, mighty, supreme, invincible, all-powerful, omnipotent. OPPOSITES: weak, powerless.
2 *(adj)* A powerful wrestler. See **strong** 1.
3 *(adj)* A powerful film. compelling, effective, impressive, convincing, forceful, inspiring, stirring, moving, disturbing.

powerless see **helpless** 2.

practical
1 *(adj)* Mandy is a practical person. sensible, down-to-earth, matter-of-fact, no-nonsense, hard-headed, businesslike, efficient, realistic, pragmatic. OPPOSITES: impractical, idealistic.
2 *(adj)* Your idea isn't really practical. practicable, workable, feasible, viable, doable, possible, realistic, sensible, sound. OPPOSITES: impractical, unworkable.

practice

practice
1 (n) To be a good pianist you must do lots of practice. training, exercises (plural), drill, repetition, preparation.
2 (n) This is the last practice before the concert. See **rehearsal**.

practise
1 (v) Let's practise our performance. rehearse, work at, go over, run through, go through, prepare, polish, fine-tune.
2 (v) Dancers practise daily. See **train** 3.

praise
1 (n) Neesha would flourish if you gave her more praise. compliments (plural), approval, appreciation, congratulations (plural), acclaim, applause, admiration.
OPPOSITES: criticism, censure.
2 (v) I'm sure the critics will praise your performance. compliment you on, congratulate you on, commend, acclaim, rave about (informal), sing the praises of, eulogize about, admire, applaud, cheer.
OPPOSITES: criticize, revile.

prance
(v) Look how the ponies prance about! leap, jump, skip, caper, cavort, romp, frisk, dance, gambol.

prank see **trick** 2.

prattle
(v) Sophie can prattle for hours. chatter, natter, gossip, gabble, jabber, twitter, babble, rattle on, rabbit on (informal), waffle, witter on (informal), go on (informal), yak (slang), jaw (slang).

precarious
(adj) Indy is in a precarious position. dangerous, risky, hazardous, perilous, tricky, dicey (informal), dodgy (informal), hairy (slang), vulnerable, insecure, unstable, uncertain, touch and go.
OPPOSITES: safe, secure.

precious
1 (adj) Precious jewels. See **valuable** 1.
2 (adj) Don't hurt my precious child. beloved, adored, cherished, treasured, darling, dearest, idolized, valued, prized.

precise
1 (adj) Please take precise measurements. See **accurate** 1.
2 (adj) At that precise moment, Eve burst in. very, exact, specific, particular, actual.
3 (adj) Jo is so precise; she even keeps her CDs in alphabetical order. particular, methodical, meticulous, careful, exact, finicky, fastidious, fussy, prim.
OPPOSITES: sloppy (informal), careless.

predicament see **mess** 3.

predict
(v) It's hard to predict what problems may arise. foresee, foretell, anticipate, forecast, prophesy, guess, second-guess (informal).

prefer
(v) Which team do you prefer? like better, favour, fancy, incline towards, support, back, go for, opt for, recommend.

pregnant
(adj) Auntie Penny is pregnant. expecting (informal), having a baby, in the family way (informal), in the club (slang), in the pudding club (slang), preggers (informal).

prejudiced
(adj) Don't be so prejudiced; try to keep an open mind. bigoted, biased, intolerant, narrow-minded, opinionated, partisan, one-sided, unfair, racist, sexist, chauvinist, ageist, homophobic, xenophobic.
OPPOSITES: open-minded, tolerant.

prepare
1 (v) We must prepare for the play. get ready, plan, make arrangements, gear up, practise, rehearse, train, get into shape.
2 (v) Let's prepare this room for our visitors. get ready, make ready, arrange, sort out, organize, fix up, set up.
3 **prepare yourself** (v) Prepare yourself for a shock. get ready, be prepared, brace yourself, steel yourself, gear yourself up, psych yourself up (informal).

present
1 (n) Thank you for the present. gift, pressie (informal), offering, contribution, donation, hand-out, freebie (informal).
2 (n) Try to live for the present. here and now, present day, today, this day and age.
OPPOSITES: past, future.
3 (adj) Let's consider the present situation. current, existing, immediate.
OPPOSITES: past, future.
4 (adj) Is everyone present? here, there, on the spot, at hand, ready, in attendance, available, accounted for.
OPPOSITES: absent, away.
5 (v) Lord Lucre will present the prizes. give, hand out, distribute, give out, hand over, award, bestow, donate, grant.

press
1 (v) Press the mixture into the tin. push down, squeeze, compress, force down, cram, jam, crush, flatten, smooth out.
2 (v) Look how the fans press round their team. push, crowd, surge, swarm, cluster, throng, flock, mill, huddle, squeeze.
3 **the press** (n) What does the press say? papers (plural), newspapers (plural), media, journalists (plural), reporters (plural).

pressure
1 (n) The ice will break under the pressure. weight, force, load, burden, stress, strain.
2 (n) I can't stand all this pressure! stress, strain, tension, anxiety, worry, hassle (informal), demands (plural).
3 (n) I only came here under pressure. duress, obligation, constraint, compulsion, coercion, force.

pressurize
(v) I don't want to go, so don't pressurize me. push, pressure, put pressure on, press, browbeat, bully, force, drive, compel, coerce, bulldoze (informal), dragoon, try to persuade, lean on (informal).

presume see **assume**.

pretence see **front** 4.

pretend
1 (v) Let's pretend we're space aliens. imagine, make believe, suppose, fantasize.
2 (v) I don't know how to speak Chinese, but I could pretend. bluff, fake it, put on an act, play-act, put it on, sham, feign.

pretentious
(adj) Araminta is so pretentious; she's always putting on airs. affected, phoney (informal), false, unnatural, pseudo (informal), showy, ostentatious, stagy.
OPPOSITES: unpretentious, unassuming.

pretty
1 (adj) Yasmin is really pretty. attractive, good-looking, cute, beautiful, lovely, fetching (informal), striking, appealing.
OPPOSITES: plain, ugly.
2 (adj) What a pretty village! picturesque, quaint, charming, beautiful, old-world, scenic, chocolate-box (informal).
OPPOSITES: ugly, unattractive.
3 (adv) (informal) I did pretty well. See **quite** 1.

prevent
1 (v) Try to prevent any accidents. avoid, avert, ward off, head off, stave off, pre-empt, forestall, nip in the bud (informal).
OPPOSITE: cause.
2 (v) We must prevent Joel from leaving. stop, deter, hinder, hamper, impede, obstruct, thwart, deflect, foil, hold back.

price
1 (n) I can't afford such a high price. cost, charge, amount, figure, sum, rate, payment, fee, outlay, expenditure.
2 (n) Fred has discovered the price of being famous. cost, consequence, result, outcome, penalty, sacrifice, punishment.

priceless
(adj) Don't break that vase; it's priceless. beyond price, irreplaceable, precious, valuable, expensive, costly, worth a king's ransom, worth its weight in gold, rare, treasured, cherished, prized.
OPPOSITE: worthless.

prick
(v) Prick the balloon with a pin. jab, stab, puncture, pierce, put a hole in, perforate, spike, nick, jag (informal).

prickly
1 (adj) Ned scratched himself on a prickly branch. thorny, spiky, spiny, brambly, barbed, bristly, briery.
2 (adj) This rash gives me a prickly feeling. itchy, scratchy, tingly, stinging, crawling.

pride
1 (n) It hurts my pride when people laugh at me. self-esteem, self-respect, self-worth, dignity, self-image, ego, feelings (plural).
2 (n) Pride is one of the seven deadly sins. conceit, vanity, arrogance, haughtiness, self-importance, bigheadedness (informal), self-love, egotism.
OPPOSITE: humility.

3 *(n) You can take pride in a job well done.* pleasure, satisfaction, delight, joy.
OPPOSITES: shame, dissatisfaction.

prim
(adj) Aunt Bertha is too prim to join in the fun. strait-laced, starchy, stuffy, proper, prissy, priggish, prudish, stiff, formal.

prison *see* **jail** 1.

prisoner
1 *(n) Burglar Beryl shared a cell with another prisoner.* convict, jailbird, con *(slang)*, lifer *(informal)*.
2 *(n) Granddad was a prisoner during the war.* captive, hostage, POW (prisoner of war), detainee.

private
1 *(adj) Flash Frank has his own private jet.* personal, individual, special, exclusive, particular, privately owned.
OPPOSITE: public.
2 *(adj) This letter contains private information.* confidential, personal, intimate, secret, restricted, classified, unofficial, off the record, hush-hush *(informal)*, inside.
OPPOSITE: public.
3 *(adj) This beach seems very private.* secluded, solitary, remote, isolated, secret, quiet, sequestered, unknown, hidden.

prize
1 *(n) Kirsty won a prize on Sports Day.* award, trophy, cup, medal, shield, badge, rosette, certificate, reward, accolade.
2 *(n) How did you spend your prize from the lottery?* winnings *(plural)*, jackpot, windfall, haul.

probable *see* **likely** 1.

problem
1 *(n) I can't cope with this problem alone.* difficulty, dilemma, predicament, mess, setback, snag, complication, worry, burden, trouble, quandary.
2 *(n) Mrs Badger gave us a problem to solve.* question, puzzle, riddle, brain-teaser *(informal)*, conundrum, poser, mystery.

procession *see* **parade**.

prod *see* **poke** 2.

produce
1 *(v) How many cars can the factory produce in a week?* turn out, manufacture, make, put together, build, assemble, construct, supply, churn out *(informal)*.
2 *(v) We produce all our own vegetables.* grow, cultivate, supply.
3 *(v) The police can't produce any evidence.* supply, provide, furnish, offer, put forward, reveal, show, present, display
4 *(v) This decision will produce a lot of ill feeling.* cause, give rise to, result in, lead to, provoke, generate, bring about, make for, engender, spark off, trigger.

programme
1 *(n) What's the programme for today?* plan, schedule, timetable, order of events, agenda, line-up, order of the day.

2 *(n) Would you like to buy a programme?* brochure, leaflet, guide, list of events, list of performers, list of players.
3 *(n) What's your favourite TV programme?* show, broadcast, production.
❖ *Also see* **television & film**.

progress
1 *(n) Have you made any progress on your project?* headway, advance, improvement, steps forward *(plural)*, progression, development, breakthrough.
2 *(v) You've really begun to progress this term. See* **improve** 1.

prohibit *see* **forbid**.

project
1 *(n) Have you finished your science project?* assignment, topic, task, activity, investigation, research, piece of work.
2 *(n) I'm involved in a project to clean up the pond.* scheme, campaign, venture, operation, programme, plan, undertaking.

promise
1 *(v) Promise you'll love me always!* vow, swear, give your word, pledge, guarantee, take an oath, undertake, cross your heart.
2 *(n) I give you my promise.* word, word of honour, assurance, guarantee, pledge, vow, oath, commitment, undertaking.
3 *(n) Your work shows promise.* potential, ability, aptitude, talent, flair.

promising
1 *(adj) The future looks promising. See* **hopeful** 2.
2 *(adj) Benji is a promising young actor.* talented, gifted, up-and-coming, budding.

promote
1 *(v) If you work hard the company may promote you.* give you promotion, upgrade, advance, move you up, move you up the ladder, give you a rise.
OPPOSITES: demote, downgrade.
2 *(v) Famous Fred is keen to promote his new album.* publicize, advertise, push, plug *(informal)*, hype, market, sell.

prompt
1 *(v) This news may prompt Judd to take some action.* motivate, induce, lead, cause, move, persuade, influence, encourage, inspire, rouse, stir, stimulate, provoke.
2 *(v) I'll prompt you if you forget your lines. See* **remind** 1.
3 *(adj) I need a prompt reply. See* **quick** 2.

proof
(n) Is there any proof that Burglar Beryl is guilty? evidence, confirmation, verification, corroboration, testimony.

proper
1 *(adj) I need the proper equipment for diving.* right, correct, appropriate, suitable.
OPPOSITES: inappropriate, unsuitable.
2 *(adj) This is the proper way to use chopsticks.* right, correct, usual, normal, conventional, accepted, established, acceptable, orthodox.
OPPOSITES: wrong, unconventional.

3 *(adj) Aunt Bertha expects proper behaviour.* decent, seemly, respectable, polite, fitting, genteel, refined, ladylike, gentlemanly, sedate, decorous, dignified.
OPPOSITES: improper, unseemly.

property
(n) Keep your hands off my property! possessions *(plural)*, belongings *(plural)*, things *(plural)*, personal effects *(plural)*, land, ground, estate, house, money, wealth, riches *(plural)*, assets *(plural)*.

protect
1 *(v) Don't worry; I'll protect you.* look after, watch over, keep you safe, take care of, shield, shelter, guard, defend, save, stick up for *(informal)*, cover up for.
OPPOSITES: expose to danger, betray.
2 *(v) The soldiers did their best to protect the city. See* **defend** 1.
3 *(v) These goggles will protect your eyes.* shield, cover, safeguard, save, preserve, screen, mask, conceal.
OPPOSITES: expose, endanger.

protest
1 *(n) If there's any protest we'll go home.* objection, opposition, complaint, dissent, disagreement, disapproval, outcry, fuss.
2 *(n) Mel took part in a protest against fox-hunting. See* **demonstration** 2.
3 **protest against** *(v) We will protest against the education cuts.* oppose, fight, take a stand against, object to, say no to, speak out against, raise objections to, put up a fight against, kick up a fuss about *(informal)*, complain about, grumble about, demonstrate against.
OPPOSITES: accept, go along with.

proud
1 *(adj) I felt proud to be chosen.* pleased, gratified, full of pride, honoured, chuffed *(slang)*, satisfied, contented, happy.
OPPOSITE: ashamed.
2 *(adj) Araminta is so proud; she looks down on everyone.* arrogant, haughty, high and mighty *(informal)*, supercilious, disdainful, conceited, vain, self-satisfied, self important, overbearing, snobbish, stuck-up *(informal)*, snooty *(informal)*, toffee-nosed *(slang)*, uppity *(informal)*.
OPPOSITES: humble, unassuming.

prove
(v) This letter will prove that I am right. demonstrate, show, establish, confirm, provide evidence, give proof, bear out.
OPPOSITES: disprove, refute.

provide
1 *(v) Can you provide enough food for everyone?* supply, lay on, offer, produce, contribute, deliver, donate, grant.
2 **provide for** *(v) Uncle Pete works hard to provide for his family. See* **support** 2.

provoke
1 *(v) Don't provoke me! See* **annoy** 1.
2 *(v) This news may provoke a riot.* cause, start, spark off, trigger, incite, give rise to, lead to, produce, prompt, precipitate.

public

1 *(adj) I think education should be a public service.* state, national, social, civic, nationwide, countrywide, universal.
OPPOSITE: private.
2 *(adj) Is this road public?* open to the public, free to all, accessible to all, unrestricted, communal.
OPPOSITES: private, restricted.
3 *(adj) Charles's secret soon became public.* widely known, well-known, publicized, famous, notorious, obvious, apparent, evident, plain, exposed, visible.
OPPOSITES: secret, unknown.
4 *(n) What will the public say about this?* people *(plural)*, country, nation, society, community, citizens *(plural)*, populace, voters *(plural)*, electorate, masses *(plural)*, hoi polloi, rank and file, Joe Public *(slang)*.

pudding *see* **dessert**.

puff

1 *(n) Did you feel that puff of wind?* gust, breath, blast, whiff, flurry, draught.
2 *(v) Running makes me puff. See* **pant**.

puffy *see* **swollen**.

puke *(slang) see* **vomit**.

pull

(v) Pull the sledge up the hill. drag, haul, tug, heave, lug, tow, trail, draw, yank, jerk.
OPPOSITE: push.

pull through *see* **recover** 1.

pull yourself together

(phrase) get a grip on yourself, control yourself, snap out of it *(informal)*.

pump

1 *(v) Pump the water through the pipe.* siphon, force, push, drive, send, drain.
2 pump up *(v) You need to pump up your tyres.* inflate, blow up.

punch

(v) Let me past or I'll punch you! hit, thump, sock *(slang)*, bash *(informal)*, belt *(slang)*, biff *(slang)*, whack, thwack, slug, clout *(informal)*, strike, clobber *(slang)*, wallop *(informal)*, hammer, pummel.

punctual

(adj) Carly is always punctual. on time, prompt, early, in good time, on the dot.
OPPOSITES: unpunctual, late.

punish

(v) The head will punish you if you cheat in exams. penalize, discipline, teach you a lesson, correct, scold, chastise, slap your wrists, rap your knuckles, sentence.

pure

1 *(adj) Is this water pure?* clean, fresh, uncontaminated, unpolluted, clear, untainted, natural, germ-free, uninfected, sterilized, pasteurized *(milk)*, undiluted.
OPPOSITES: contaminated, polluted.
2 *(adj) Despite temptations, Eve remained pure.* chaste, virtuous, uncorrupted, undefiled, unstained, blameless, innocent, true, upright, squeaky-clean *(informal)*.
OPPOSITES: impure, corrupt.

3 *(adj) That goal was pure magic! See* **absolute**.

purple

(n) SHADES OF PURPLE: aubergine, burgundy, grape, lavender, lilac, maroon, mauve, mulberry, plum, puce, violet.

purpose

1 *(n) What was your purpose in cycling to Rome?* aim, object, goal, objective, target, motive, intention, plan, reason, rationale.
2 *(n) What is the purpose of this machine?* use, function, point, value, advantage.
3 on purpose *see* **on purpose**.

pursue *see* **follow** 1.

push

1 *(n) Give the door a push.* shove, nudge, prod, jolt, thrust.
OPPOSITE: pull.
2 *(v) Push this button.* press, press down, push down, depress, put pressure on.
3 *(v) Bozo tried to push me into the pool.* shove, propel, force, drive, thrust, ram.
4 *(v) Can you push through the crowd?* force your way, squeeze, press, shove, barge *(informal)*, elbow, shoulder, jostle.
5 *(v) Mum has to push me to do my piano practice. See* **pressurize**.
6 *(v) Famous Fred is keen to push his new album. See* **promote** 2.

pushy

(adj) (informal) Jemima is so pushy; she's invited herself to the party! assertive, forceful, forward, aggressive, bumptious, brash, loud, bold, cocksure, ambitious.
OPPOSITES: timid, retiring.

put

1 *(v) Put the files on the desk.* place, lay, leave, set, stand, rest, plonk, dump, park *(informal)*, set down, dump.
2 *(v) Don't put your finger in the trifle! See* **stick** 6.
3 *(v) I bet Mrs Badger will put you in the top stream.* place, assign you to, consign you to, allocate you to, rank, grade.

put away

(v) Put away your clothes. tidy away, clear away, tidy up, put back, replace.

put down

1 *(v) The vet had to put down the sick animal.* put to sleep, put out of its misery, destroy, do away with, put away.
2 *(v) My friends never put me down.* belittle, humiliate, disparage, denigrate, sneer at, deflate, crush.

put off

1 *(v) We'll have to put off the match until next week. See* **postpone**.
2 *(v) Don't let the spectators put you off. See* **distract**.
3 *(v) Don't let this one setback put you off.* discourage, dissuade, deter, dishearten, dismay, daunt, perturb, faze, throw *(informal)*, rattle *(informal)*.
4 *(v) Doesn't lumpy custard really put you off? See* **disgust** 2.

put on

1 *(v) Why don't you put on your jeans?* slip into, change into, don, get dressed in.
OPPOSITE: take off.
2 *(v) It doesn't matter if you put on a bit of weight.* gain, add.
OPPOSITES: take off, lose.
3 *(v) Araminta likes to put on a posh accent.* affect, fake, feign, assume.
4 *(v) We're hoping to put on a pantomime. See* **stage** 3.

put out

1 *(v) Put out the flames!* extinguish, quench, douse, smother, stifle, stamp out, blow out, snuff out *(candle)*.
2 *(adj) Kim felt put out that she hadn't been invited. See* **offended**.

put up

1 *(v) Dad plans to put up a new garage. See* **build** 1.
2 *(v) We can easily put you up for the night.* take you in, give you a bed, give you a room, accommodate, give you lodging.

put up with *(informal) see* **stand** 4.

puzzle

1 *(n) I can't get my head round this puzzle.* problem, question, brain-teaser *(informal)*, poser, riddle, conundrum, mystery, enigma, paradox, crossword.
2 *(v) The crime seemed to puzzle the police.* baffle, mystify, perplex, flummox, floor *(informal)*, stump, bewilder, confuse, confound, defeat, nonplus.

puzzling

(adj) A puzzling code. baffling, perplexing, mystifying, cryptic, bewildering, confusing, mindboggling *(informal)*, insoluble, incomprehensible, mysterious, strange.
OPPOSITES: simple, straightforward.

quaint

(adj) Tourists think our village is quaint. old-fashioned, picturesque, charming, old-world, antiquated, twee *(informal)*.

quality

1 *(n) This work is of a poor quality.* standard, level, grade, class.
2 *(n) Aren't you impressed by the quality of the acting?* high standard, calibre, excellence, superiority, distinction, merit.
3 *(n) Honesty is a quality I value in a friend. See* **characteristic**.

quantity *see* **amount** 1, 2.

quarrel

1 *(v) My sisters quarrel all the time. See* **argue** 1.
2 *(n) We had a quarrel about who should pay. See* **argument** 1.

3 *(n) The quarrel between the two families lasted for years.* feud, dispute, disagreement, misunderstanding, argument, hostility, enmity, conflict, vendetta, bad blood, rivalry.

quarrelsome
(adj) Andy is so quarrelsome; he's always fighting with someone. argumentative, belligerent, aggressive, pugnacious, cantankerous, irritable, irascible.
OPPOSITES: easy-going, even-tempered.

quay
(n) We tied up our boat at the quay. jetty, wharf, landing stage, dock, harbour.

queasy see **sick** 2.

queen
(n) monarch, sovereign, ruler.

quest
(n) The white knight set out on a perilous quest. mission, search, hunt, expedition, adventure, voyage, journey, crusade.

question
1 *(n) Do you have a question?* query, inquiry.
OPPOSITES: answer, reply.
2 *(n) Mrs Badger set us a difficult question. See* **problem** 2.
3 *(n) There's some question about who won the race.* doubt, uncertainty, dispute, debate, argument, controversy, confusion.
4 *(n) That's an interesting question for a debate. See* **subject**.
5 *(v) Detectives want to question Burglar Beryl.* interview, interrogate, cross-examine, cross-question, quiz, grill *(informal)*, pump, give the third degree to.
6 *(v) Why do you question everything I say?* query, call into question, challenge, dispute, raise objections to, oppose, throw doubt on, suspect.
OPPOSITES: accept, believe.

queue
1 *(n) There was a long queue of traffic at the lights.* line, string, column, row, tailback, chain, file.
2 *(v) You must queue for tickets.* line up, wait in line, stand in line, form a queue.

quick
1 *(adj) The sprinter ran at a quick pace.* fast, swift, rapid, brisk, speedy, spanking *(informal)*, breakneck, headlong.
OPPOSITES: slow, sluggish.
2 *(adj) I need a quick response.* instant, immediate, instantaneous, prompt, early, swift, rapid, speedy.
OPPOSITES: slow, delayed.
3 *(adj) We paid a quick visit to Aunt Bertha. See* **short** 3.
4 *(adj) Let's go home the quick way. See* **short** 4.
5 *(adj) Ed will see the problem right away; he's very quick.* bright, sharp, astute, quick on the uptake *(informal)*, quick-witted, shrewd, clever, perceptive, discerning, intelligent, able, all there *(informal)*.
OPPOSITES: slow, stupid.

6 *(adj) Sharmeen is always quick to help. See* **willing**.

quiet
1 *(adj) Ellen spoke in a quiet voice.* soft, low, hushed, scarcely audible, muted.
OPPOSITE: loud.
2 *(adj) Toni crept past with quiet steps.* silent, soundless, noiseless, inaudible.
OPPOSITES: noisy, loud.
3 *(adj) Frances is a quiet member of the class.* reserved, uncommunicative, unforthcoming, taciturn, silent, shy, retiring, diffident, unassertive, introverted, unobtrusive, subdued, restrained.
OPPOSITES: noisy, talkative.
4 *(adj) Everything was quiet before the storm.* still, calm, peaceful, tranquil.
OPPOSITES: restless, agitated.
5 *(adj) The cottage stood in a quiet valley.* peaceful, sleepy, secluded, isolated, lonely, remote, out-of-the-way, private.
OPPOSITES: bustling, crowded.
6 **be quiet** *(phrase) Be quiet and listen!* stop talking, shut up *(informal)*, shush, quieten down, don't say a word, don't make a sound, hush, hold your tongue, put a sock in it *(slang)*, belt up *(slang)*, shut your trap *(slang)*, pipe down *(slang)*.

quite
1 *(adv) It's quite windy today.* rather, fairly, pretty *(informal)*, moderately, reasonably, relatively, a bit, somewhat.
OPPOSITE: very.
2 *(adv) Your answer is quite correct.* absolutely, completely, totally, perfectly, entirely, wholly, utterly.
OPPOSITES: partly, more or less.

quiver see **shiver**.

quote
1 *(v) Try to quote plenty of examples in your essay.* give, mention, cite, refer to, allude to, name.
2 *(v) Can you quote any lines from Shakespeare?* recite, repeat, recall, recollect, reel off.

race
1 *(n) Lateefah took part in the race.* competition, contest, heat, final, relay race, sprint, marathon, cross-country, steeplechase, hurdles.
2 *(n) The Ancient Greeks were a civilized race.* people, nation, tribe, ethnic group.
3 *(v) I must race for my bus. See* **run** 1.
4 *(v) I'll race you to the corner.* have a race with, try to beat, compete with, take you on, run faster than.

racket see **noise** 2.

rage see **anger** 1.

ragged
1 *(adj) The little boy's trousers were ragged.* tattered, torn, frayed, worn-out, in tatters, in holes, in shreds, in ribbons, threadbare, patched, shabby, tatty.
2 *(adj) The torn page had a ragged edge.* uneven, rough, jagged, irregular, serrated.
OPPOSITES: smooth, even.

raid
1 *(n) There's been a raid at the bank.* robbery, hold-up, heist *(slang)*, smash-and-grab *(informal)*, stick-up *(slang)*, break-in, ram raid *(informal)*.
2 *(n) We hid underground during the raid. See* **attack** 4.
3 *(v) Pirate Peg planned to raid the enemy's hide-out.* attack, invade, break into, storm, charge, rush, swoop on, rob, loot, plunder, pillage, ransack, rifle.

rain
1 *(v) Suddenly it began to rain.* pour, pelt down, bucket down, lash down, teem, rain cats and dogs *(informal)*, come down in torrents, spit, drizzle, sleet, hail.
2 *(n) I wish this rain would stop.* shower, drizzle, downpour, deluge, thunderstorm, cloudburst, torrential rain, driving rain, rainfall, raindrops *(plural)*, sleet, hail.

rainforest see **jungle**

rainy
(adj) I like to stay inside on rainy days. wet, drizzly, showery, damp.
OPPOSITES: dry, fine, sunny.

raise
1 *(v) We'll need a crane to raise those girders.* lift, hoist, pick up, heave up, jack up, put up, elevate, set upright.
OPPOSITE: lower.
2 *(v) Supermarkets may raise their prices.* put up, increase, hike *(informal)*, inflate.
OPPOSITES: lower, reduce, cut.
3 *(v) We need to raise a lot of money for our new computer.* make, collect, get together, gather together, scrape together, pull in, drum up, obtain.
4 *(v) This campaign will raise awareness about drugs.* heighten, increase, promote, boost, strengthen, improve, enhance.
5 *(v) How can we raise some enthusiasm for the campaign?* arouse, awaken, stimulate, stir up, whip up, drum up, summon up, excite, kindle, foster.
6 *(v) It's hard to raise a family on your own. See* **bring up** 1.
7 *(v) Please don't raise that subject again. See* **mention** 2.

ram
1 *(v) Saul tried to ram my Dodgem car.* crash into, slam into, smash into, bump into, drive into, run into, collide with, hit.
2 *(v) Ram your stuff in here. See* **cram** 1.

ramshackle
(adj) A ramshackle cottage. tumbledown, dilapidated, run-down, derelict, neglected, decrepit, crumbling, rickety, unsafe, falling to pieces, gone to rack and ruin.

random

(adj) I jotted down my ideas in a random way. haphazard, arbitrary, indiscriminate, casual, unplanned, unsystematic, unmethodical, aimless, desultory.
OPPOSITES: deliberate, orderly.

range

1 *(n) This shop stocks a wide range of CDs.* variety, assortment, selection, choice, collection, array.
2 *(n) The ship is outside the range of our radar.* reach, scope, field, span, sweep, radius, limits *(plural)*, bounds *(plural)*.
3 *(v) Your marks range from good to excellent.* vary, fluctuate, stretch, extend.

rank

(n) Mum has a high rank in the company. grade, status, position, level, standing.

rapid *see* **fast** 1.

rare

(adj) Vases like this one are rare. unusual, out of the ordinary, scarce, few and far between, uncommon, exceptional, remarkable, thin on the ground, sparse, irreplaceable, unique, valuable, precious.
OPPOSITES: common, plentiful.

rarely

(adv) We rarely see Lucy. hardly ever, seldom, scarcely ever, almost never, once in a while, once in a blue moon *(informal)*, on rare occasions, infrequently.
OPPOSITES: often, frequently.

rash

1 *(n) Your rash should soon clear up.* spots *(plural)*, allergy, itch, hives *(plural)*.
2 *(adj) Don't make any rash decisions.* reckless, impetuous, impulsive, hasty, sudden, hurried, foolhardy, harebrained, madcap, imprudent, ill-considered, ill-advised, risky, careless, thoughtless.
OPPOSITES: careful, considered.

rate

1 *(n) Gus raced off at a tremendous rate.* speed, pace, velocity.
2 *(n) What's the rate for a single room?* charge, cost, price, fee, tariff, payment, damage *(informal)*, figure.
3 *(v) Would you rate my performance as good?* regard, consider, judge, count, evaluate, assess, appraise, classify, rank.
4 *(v) (slang) I don't rate our new teacher at all. See* **admire** 1.

rather *see* **quite** 1.

rattle

(v) The wind made the shutters rattle. clatter, bang, clank, clink, clunk, clack, shake, vibrate, jiggle.

rave

1 *(adj) (informal) Our play got rave reviews.* rapturous, enthusiastic, ecstatic, excellent, favourable.
OPPOSITES: lukewarm, critical.
2 *(n) (slang) I hear there was a rave last night.* party, warehouse party, disco, rave-up *(slang)*, bash *(informal)*.

ravenous *see* **hungry** 1.

raw

1 *(adj) Raw meat.* uncooked, unprepared, bloody, underdone, rare, fresh *(vegetables, fruit)*.
OPPOSITES: cooked, well-done.
2 *(adj) Raw materials.* unprocessed, unrefined, untreated, natural, basic, crude, unfinished, coarse, rough.
OPPOSITES: refined, processed.
3 *(adj) Raw skin.* chafed, grazed, scraped, scratched, red, inflamed, sensitive, sore.
4 *(adj) A raw winter's day. See* **cold** 1.

ray

(n) A ray of sunlight. beam, shaft, stream, gleam, streak, flash, glimmer, glint, flicker.

reach

1 *(v) Can you reach that book on the top shelf?* get at, get hold of, touch, grab, grasp, catch at, clutch at, seize.
2 *(v) Did the explorers reach the North Pole?* get to, make, make it to *(informal)*, get as far as, arrive at, set foot on, land at.
3 *(v) The mountains seemed to reach the sky.* touch, stretch to, extend to.
4 *(v) (informal) Please reach me that book.* pass, hand, give, hand over.
5 *(v) I tried to reach you yesterday, but you were out. See* **contact**.

reach out

(v) Reach out and grab the railing. stretch out, hold out your hand, stick out your hand, lean out, lean over.

react

(v) How did Zak react when he heard the news? respond, behave, act, cope, reply.

reaction

(n) Did you get any reaction to your suggestion? response, reply, answer, feedback, comeback *(informal)*, backlash.

read

1 *(v) Did you read the paper yesterday?* look at, study, browse through, scan, skim through, glance at, run your eye over, dip into, pore over, wade through, peruse.
2 *(v) I have to read a poem in assembly.* read out, read aloud, recite, say, deliver.
3 *(v) Your writing is hard to read.* make out, decipher, understand, interpret, comprehend, decode.

ready

1 *(adj) Is everything ready?* prepared, arranged, organized, set up, finished, completed, finalized, ready and waiting, in readiness, primed, all set, fitted out.
OPPOSITES: unprepared, unfinished.
2 *(adj) Grandma is always ready to babysit. See* **willing**.
3 *(adj) Have you got your bus fare ready? See* **handy** 2.
4 *(adj) Louise looked ready to cry.* about, likely, liable, close, in danger of, on the brink of, on the point of, on the verge of.

real

1 *(adj) Is that real gold? See* **genuine** 1.

2 *(adj) These are the real facts.* true, actual, veritable, unquestionable, correct, certain, positive, tangible, truthful, factual.
OPPOSITES: false, imaginary.
3 *(adj) I can't hide my real feelings.* true, genuine, sincere, honest, heartfelt.
OPPOSITES: feigned, insincere.

realistic

1 *(adj) You must be realistic about your job prospects.* practical, sensible, level-headed, clear-sighted, rational, objective, pragmatic, down-to-earth, businesslike, hard-headed, unromantic, unsentimental.
OPPOSITES: unrealistic, idealistic.
2 *(adj) What a realistic model!* lifelike, convincing, true-to-life, naturalistic, authentic, faithful, accurate, precise.
OPPOSITES: unrealistic, unconvincing.

realize

(v) I didn't realize what had happened. understand, appreciate, grasp, comprehend, take in, absorb, twig *(informal)*, catch on to *(informal)*, cotton on to *(informal)*, notice, recognize.

really

1 *(adv) This film is really gruesome.* totally, utterly, absolutely, truly, extremely, thoroughly, completely, positively, very.
2 *(adv) Archie says that he's nine, but he's really only seven.* actually, in fact, in reality, in truth, as a matter of fact.

reason

1 *(n) Do you have any reason for being late?* grounds *(plural)*, cause, explanation, excuse, justification, pretext, rationale.
2 *(n) What is the reason behind your visit? See* **purpose** 1.
3 **reason with** *(v) It's a waste of time trying to reason with you.* argue with, persuade, dissuade, talk you round, win you over, bring you round, plead with, show you the error of your ways.

reasonable

1 *(adj) That sounds like a reasonable explanation.* sensible, logical, rational, credible, plausible, believable, intelligent, well-thought-out, reasoned, sound.
OPPOSITES: irrational, incredible.
2 *(adj) Mr Badger is a reasonable man.* moderate, fair, just, sensible, rational, wise, open to reason.
OPPOSITE: unreasonable.
3 *(adj) Your exam results are reasonable. See* **all right** 3.
4 *(adj) Reasonable prices. See* **low** 7.

reassure

(v) Did Mrs Badger's comments reassure you? put your mind at rest, comfort, calm, soothe your fears, encourage, give you confidence, cheer you up, hearten, bolster.
OPPOSITES: discourage, worry.

reassuring

(adj) Dad gave me a reassuring smile. encouraging, supportive, comforting, heartening, sympathetic, soothing.
OPPOSITES: discouraging, disturbing.

relax

rebel
1 (v) *The citizens threatened to rebel.* revolt, riot, rise up, mutiny, take to the streets, take up arms, man the barricades, take a stand, resist.
2 **rebel against** (v) *Teenagers sometimes rebel against their parents.* See **disobey** 1.

rebellion *see* **revolution** 1.

rebellious
1 (adj) *A rebellious teenager.* defiant, disobedient, unruly, difficult, stroppy (informal), obstinate, uncontrollable, wild. OPPOSITES: obedient, compliant.
2 (adj) *Rebellious soldiers.* mutinous, insubordinate, rioting, disloyal, disaffected, rebel, revolutionary, insurgent. OPPOSITES: loyal, obedient.

receive
1 (v) *I was thrilled to receive a prize.* be given, be awarded, get, accept, collect, pick up, obtain, gain, come by. OPPOSITE: give.
2 (v) *I hope to receive some good news.* hear, be given, be told, be informed of.

recent
(adj) *A recent invention.* new, modern, present-day, contemporary, fresh, novel, up-to-the-minute, current, up-to-date. OPPOSITES: old, early.

recite
(v) *Can you recite the alphabet backwards?* say, repeat, reel off, read aloud, run through, go through, perform, deliver.

reckless *see* **rash** 2.

reckon *see* **think** 1, 2.

recognize
1 (v) *I didn't recognize you with short hair.* know, spot, identify, notice, pick you out, remember, recall, place.
2 (v) *Do you recognize what you've done wrong?* realize, see, understand, know, accept, acknowledge, appreciate, admit to.

recommend
1 (v) *What did the doctor recommend?* advise, suggest, propose, advocate, urge.
2 (v) *All my friends recommend this film.* speak highly of, praise, rave about (informal), approve of, commend, vouch for, put in a good word for, applaud.

record
1 (n) *Is there a record of this trip?* account, report, chronicle, diary, log, journal, note, memo, file, dossier, document, archives (plural).
2 (n) *Have you heard Famous Fred's new record?* See **release** 4.
3 (n) *Leo has a good record of punctuality.* track record (informal), history, background, past performance, reputation.
4 (v) *Record your progress every day.* document, log, note, write down, set down, enter, chronicle, put on record, put in writing, jot down, tape, video.
5 (v) *The band hope to record a single.* cut, make a recording of, lay down (slang).

recover
1 (v) *I'm sure you'll soon recover.* get better, get well, improve, get back on your feet, bounce back, rally, pull through, recuperate, convalesce, heal, mend. OPPOSITES: deteriorate, get worse.
2 (v) *I tried to recover my lost suitcase.* See **retrieve**.

red
1 (n) SHADES OF RED: beetroot red, blood red, brick red, burgundy, cardinal red, cherry red, crimson, flame red, magenta, maroon, pillar-box red, poppy red, puce, ruby, scarlet, tomato, vermilion.
2 (adj) *Red hair.* ginger, auburn, carroty, chestnut, coppery, sandy, reddish, flame-coloured, rust-coloured, russet, Titian.
3 (adj) *A red face.* flushed, flaming, burning, rosy, glowing, ruddy, florid, sunburnt, rosy-cheeked, apple-cheeked.
4 (adj) *Red eyes.* bloodshot, red-rimmed.

reduce
1 (v) *We will reduce our prices.* lower, bring down, cut, slash, discount, trim, halve, mark down, knock down (informal). OPPOSITES: raise, increase.
2 (v) *Earplugs will reduce the sound.* cut down, decrease, lessen, lower, diminish, minimize, tone down, muffle, dull. OPPOSITES: increase, amplify
3 (v) *Please reduce your speed.* lower, decrease, cut down, cut, lessen, ease off. OPPOSITE: increase.

refer to
1 (v) *Who could this rude note refer to?* apply to, relate to, concern, be aimed at, be directed at, be relevant to, pertain to
2 (v) *Did the letter refer to our visit?* mention, make reference to, speak about, touch on, allude to, comment on, hint at.
3 (v) *Refer to your textbooks.* consult, look at, turn to, look up.

reflect
1 (v) *The lakes reflect the trees.* mirror.
2 (v) *Do soaps on TV reflect real life?* See **imitate** 3.
3 (v) *Your marks reflect your ability.* do justice to, demonstrate, display, reveal, indicate, bear out, speak volumes about.

refreshing
1 (adj) *This drink is very refreshing.* thirst-quenching, cooling, reviving, revitalizing, rejuvenating, fortifying, restorative.
2 (adj) *I've just had a refreshing swim.* bracing, invigorating, cooling, freshening, exhilarating, revitalizing.

refuse
1 (v) *Here's an offer you can't refuse.* turn down, say no to, decline, reject, pass up (informal), resist, spurn, rebuff, dismiss. OPPOSITE: accept.
2 (v) *Damian's parents refuse him nothing.* See **deny** 2.

region
(n) *A mountainous region.* area, place, district, land, country, province, territory.

regret
1 (v) *Don't you regret that you lied to me?* feel sorry, feel ashamed, feel remorse, reproach yourself, have qualms, repent.
2 (v) *When you're older you'll regret this lost opportunity.* feel sorry about, pine over, fret over, bemoan, weep over.
3 (n) *Amir was filled with regret.* remorse, shame, guilt, self-reproach, contrition, repentance, sadness, sorrow, grief. OPPOSITES: satisfaction, pleasure.

regular
1 (adj) *Guitar practice is part of my regular routine.* See **usual**.
2 (adj) *You'll receive a regular progress report.* periodic, frequent, yearly, quarterly, termly, monthly, weekly, daily, hourly. OPPOSITES: occasional, infrequent.
3 (adj) *The trees were planted at regular intervals.* constant, fixed, set, equal, even, uniform, unvarying, consistent, measured. OPPOSITES: irregular, erratic.

rehearsal
(n) *We need another rehearsal before the performance.* practice, practice session, run-through, trial run, dress rehearsal, dummy run, dry run (informal).

reign
(v) *Who will reign when the king dies?* be king, be queen, sit on the throne, wear the crown, rule, govern, hold power

reinforce *see* **strengthen** 2, 3.

reject
1 (v) *I bet the head will reject our plans.* say no to, veto, disallow, give the thumbs down to, throw out, scrap, discard, bin OPPOSITES: accept, approve.
2 (v) *How could you reject your best friend?* disown, turn your back on, spurn, abandon, cast aside, forsake, drop (informal), dump (informal), ditch (slang).
3 (v) *Don't reject my offer.* See **refuse** 1.

rejoice
(v) *The whole school will rejoice if we win.* be happy, be pleased, be glad, be delighted, be jubilant, be overjoyed, jump for joy, celebrate, triumph, exult. OPPOSITES: mourn, grieve.

related
(adj) *The two crimes seem to be related.* connected, linked, interconnected, associated, similar, comparable, parallel.

relation
(n) *Aunt Bertha is a close relation.* relative, member of the family, family member, blood relative, relative by marriage.

relax
1 (v) *Relax your grip.* loosen, slacken, ease, weaken, unclench, lessen, reduce, release. OPPOSITE: tighten.
2 (v) *You can relax after the exams.* unwind, take it easy, rest, ease up, put your feet up, laze about, chill out (slang), hang loose (informal), let your hair down, lighten up (slang).

relaxed

1 *(adj) Bianca has a relaxed attitude to her work.* easy-going, laid-back *(informal),* casual, free and easy, leisurely, nonchalant, blasé, unconcerned, slack.
OPPOSITES: uptight *(informal),* serious.
2 *(adj) We had a relaxed lunch.* leisurely, unhurried, restful, informal, laid-back *(informal),* cosy, comfortable.
OPPOSITES: formal, tense.

relaxing

(adj) We spent a relaxing day on the beach. restful, peaceful, quiet, leisurely, unhurried, lazy, languid, soothing.
OPPOSITE: stressful.

release

1 *(v) Let's campaign to release the hostages.* free, set free, liberate, deliver, emancipate, let go, let out, turn loose.
OPPOSITE: imprison.
2 *(v) The judge decided to release Burglar Beryl.* free, let go, let off, spare, excuse, acquit, discharge, pardon, absolve.
OPPOSITE: detain.
3 *(v) The police will release a description of the criminal.* issue, put out, publish, broadcast, circulate, distribute, make public, make known, reveal, disclose.
OPPOSITES: withhold, suppress.
4 *(n) Listen to this new release.* recording, record, disc, tape, CD, single, album, EP (extended play), 12-inch, remix, rerelease.

relevant

(adj) Is that remark relevant to the discussion? related, pertinent, connected, linked, applicable, essential, significant.
OPPOSITES: irrelevant, beside the point.

reliable

1 *(adj) Lateefah is a reliable friend.* dependable, trustworthy, trusty, staunch, faithful, loyal, devoted, unfailing, constant, steady, true, responsible, honest.
OPPOSITES: unreliable, fickle.
2 *(adj) Is your information reliable?* dependable, well-founded, sound, tried and tested, trustworthy, credible, true.
OPPOSITES: unreliable, dodgy *(informal).*

relieve

1 *(v) This ointment will relieve the pain.* ease, alleviate, soothe, lessen, reduce, deaden, dull, numb, blunt.
OPPOSITES: increase, intensify.
2 *(v) A substitute will relieve you at half-time.* take over from, replace, stand in for, take your place, give you a break.

religion

(n) What is your religion? faith, belief, creed, denomination, sect.

religious

1 *(adj) Religious books.* theological, devotional, spiritual, sacred, holy, divine.
OPPOSITE: secular.
2 *(adj) A religious woman.* pious, devout, God-fearing, godly, churchgoing.

reluctant *see* unwilling.

rely on *see* **depend on** 1, 2.
remain *see* **stay** 1, 4.

remains

1 *(plural n) What shall we do with the remains of this meal?* leftovers *(plural),* scraps *(plural),* remnants *(plural),* crumbs *(plural),* dregs *(plural) (drink),* rest, residue.
2 *(plural n) Experts sifted through the remains.* rubble, debris, wreckage, ruins *(plural),* ashes *(plural),* bones *(plural).*

remark *see* **comment** 1, 2.

remarkable

(adj) What a remarkable painting! amazing, astonishing, incredible, extraordinary, astounding, surprising, startling, striking, distinctive, unusual, strange, outstanding, exceptional.
OPPOSITES: ordinary, unremarkable.

remember

1 *(v) Can you remember my name?* think of, recall, recollect, call to mind, place.
OPPOSITE: forget.
2 *(v) It took me ages to remember my lines. See* **learn** 2.
3 *(v) Granny likes to remember her youth.* reminisce about, think about, think back on, look back on, hark back to, recall, recollect, talk about, be nostalgic about.
OPPOSITE: forget about.

remind

1 *(v) I'll remind you when it's time to go.* prompt, jog your memory, refresh your memory, give you a reminder, prod.
2 **remind you of** *(v) This song will remind you of our holiday.* make you think of, bring back memories of, take you back to, awaken memories of, put you in mind of.

remote

(adj) Pirate Peg landed on a remote island. faraway, far-off, distant, far-flung, outlying, out-of-the-way, isolated, lonely, inaccessible, secluded, godforsaken.
OPPOSITES: accessible, nearby.

remove

1 *(v) Please do not remove these books.* take, take away, take out, carry away, move, shift, dislodge, withdraw, borrow, throw out, steal.
2 *(v) This liquid will remove stains.* get rid of, eradicate, eliminate, dislodge, shift, move, budge, erase, wipe out, root out.
3 *(v) Remove your hat. See* **take off** 1.

repair

1 *(v) Can you repair my radio?* fix, mend, put right, restore to working order, patch up, sort out, overhaul, rebuild, recondition.
2 *(v) I must repair my jeans. See* **mend** 2.

repay *see* **pay back** 1, 2.

repeat

1 *(v) Don't repeat this story to anyone!* tell, pass on, quote, relate, recount, reiterate, retell, restate, recite.
2 *(v) Listen to the violins repeat the tune.* echo, reiterate, re-echo, restate, replay, play back, copy, duplicate, reproduce.

replace

1 *(v) Please replace the knives and forks.* put back, put away, return.
2 *(v) You must replace those worn tyres.* change, renew, exchange, swap, switch.
3 *(v) Who will replace Jodie on the team?* take the place of, stand in for, substitute for, deputize for, cover for, take over from, succeed, follow, supplant, supersede.

reply *see* **answer** 1, 2, 3.

report

1 *(n) Have you read this report?* account, description, statement, write-up, article, news story, piece, message, communiqué, communication, note, summary, narrative.
2 *(v) The committee will report their findings.* present, state, announce, declare, publish, make public, communicate, outline, document, detail, give an account of, put in writing, broadcast, circulate.
3 *(v) I'm going to report you to the head.* complain about, denounce, tell on *(informal),* inform on, blow the whistle on *(informal),* shop *(slang),* snitch on *(slang).*

reporter

(n) journalist, correspondent, hack, newshound *(informal),* writer, investigator, commentator, broadcaster, feature writer, columnist, member of the press.

represent

1 *(v) What do the letters "PC" represent? See* **stand for**.
2 *(v) Rose will represent our class on the school council.* speak for, act on behalf of, be the voice of, be the spokesperson for.

repulsive *see* **disgusting** 1.

reputation

(n) This rumour could damage Famous Fred's reputation. name, good name, character, honour, respectability, standing, status, position, prestige, fame, renown.

request

1 *(n) The police issued a request for information.* appeal, call, plea, demand.
2 *(v) The genie will do anything you request. See* **ask** 4.

require

1 *(v) This project will require a lot of work. See* **need** 1.
2 *(v) I expect Dad will require an apology. See* **demand** 1.

rescue

1 *(v) Don't panic; I'll rescue you!* save, save your life, help, come to your rescue, free, release, set you free, get you out, deliver you from danger, liberate.
2 *(v) Pirate Peg managed to rescue her map from the wreck.* recover, retrieve, salvage, save, extricate, fish out.
3 *(n) We watched the rescue on television.* rescue operation, rescue attempt, air-sea rescue, recovery, salvage operation, relief operation.
4 *(n) Please come to my rescue.* aid, help, assistance.

rescue words

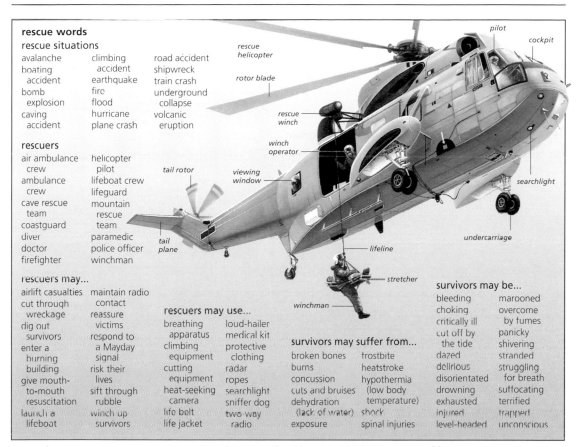

rescue situations

avalanche	climbing	road accident
boating	accident	shipwreck
accident	earthquake	train crash
bomb	fire	underground
explosion	flood	collapse
caving	hurricane	volcanic
accident	plane crash	eruption

rescuers

air ambulance	helicopter
crew	pilot
ambulance	lifeboat crew
crew	lifeguard
cave rescue	mountain
team	rescue
coastguard	team
diver	paramedic
doctor	police officer
firefighter	winchman

rescuers may...

airlift casualties	maintain radio
cut through	contact
wreckage	reassure
dig out	victims
survivors	respond to
enter a	a Mayday
burning	signal
building	risk their
give mouth-	lives
to-mouth	sift through
resuscitation	rubble
launch a	winch up
lifeboat	survivors

rescuers may use...

breathing	loud-hailer
apparatus	medical kit
climbing	protective
equipment	clothing
cutting	radar
equipment	ropes
heat-seeking	searchlight
camera	sniffer dog
life belt	two-way
life jacket	radio

survivors may suffer from...

broken bones	frostbite
burns	heatstroke
concussion	hypothermia
cuts and bruises	(low body
dehydration	temperature)
(lack of water)	shock
exposure	spinal injuries

survivors may be...

bleeding	marooned
choking	overcome
critically ill	by fumes
cut off by	panicky
the tide	shivering
dazed	stranded
delirious	struggling
disorientated	for breath
drowning	suffocating
exhausted	terrified
injured	trapped
level-headed	unconscious

Image labels: pilot, cockpit, rescue helicopter, rotor blade, rescue winch, winch operator, tail rotor, viewing window, searchlight, tail plane, undercarriage, lifeline, stretcher, winchman

---

research

1 (n) I need to do some research for my project. reading, background reading, groundwork, fact-finding, investigation, study, experiments (plural), tests (plural).
2 (v) I've decided to research my family history. See **investigate**.

resent

1 (v) Aunt Bertha will resent not being invited. feel bitter about, feel aggrieved at, be offended at, take offence at, take umbrage at, bear a grudge about, have hard feelings about, take exception to.
2 (v) Try not to resent your sister's success. begrudge, feel bitter about, envy, be jealous of, feel aggrieved at.

resentful see **bitter** 2.

reserve

1 (v) Please reserve a room. See **book** 3.
2 (n) Who will be the reserve? substitute, replacement, stand-in (informal), deputy.

resign

1 (v) If you don't like your job, why don't you resign? leave, hand in your notice, give notice, quit, stand down, step down (informal), give up, pack it in (informal).

2 **resign yourself to** (phrase) Revising is dull, but you'll have to resign yourself to it. reconcile yourself to, accept, come to terms with, put up with (informal), grin and bear (informal), make the best of.

resigned

(adj) How can Dad be so resigned about losing his job? accepting, philosophical, stoical, patient, long-suffering, calm, reasonable, unresisting, passive, defeatist.

resist

1 (v) How can you resist eating that cake? prevent yourself from, keep from, avoid, refrain from, abstain from, stop.
2 (v) I can't resist your offer. See **refuse** 1.
3 (v) We will resist any attempt to close our school. See **fight** 4.

respect

1 (n) You should have more respect for people's feelings. consideration, concern, regard, deference, appreciation, reverence. OPPOSITES: contempt, disdain.
2 (v) People respect Mr Badger. think highly of, think well of, have a high opinion of, admire, look up to, revere. OPPOSITES: look down on, scorn.

respectable

1 (adj) Mr Badger is a respectable citizen. respected, upstanding, decent, law abiding, upright, honest, well-regarded. OPPOSITE: disreputable.
2 (adj) Put on your dressing gown; you're not respectable! See **decent** 1.

respond

1 (v) Didn't Ed respond when you tickled him? react, retaliate, hit back, reciprocate.
2 (v) I heard Kate respond. See **answer** 2.
3 **respond to** (v) I must respond to this letter. See **answer** 1.

response see **answer** 3.

responsible

1 (adj) We need a responsible babysitter. reliable, dependable, trustworthy, sensible, level-headed, conscientious, mature. OPPOSITES: irresponsible, unreliable.
2 (adj) What a mess! Who is responsible? guilty, to blame, at fault, culpable.
3 **be responsible for** (phrase) Who will be responsible for the team's actions? take responsibility for, be in charge of, take control of, be accountable for, be answerable for, take the blame for.

rest

1 (n) *Granny is having a rest. See* **sleep** 3.
2 (n) *You deserve a rest after your hard work.* break, breather (informal), holiday, vacation, time off, leave, breathing space.
3 (n) *What shall I do with the rest?* remainder, surplus, excess, balance, residue, remains (plural), remnants (plural), leftovers (plural) (food), others (plural).
4 (v) *You should rest for a while.* take a break, have a rest, take a breather (informal), relax, take it easy, sit down, lie down, put your feet up, take a nap, have forty winks (informal).
5 (v) *Rest your bike against the wall.* lean, prop, support, stand, balance, steady.

restaurant

(n) TYPES OF RESTAURANT: bistro, brasserie, burger bar, café, cafeteria, canteen, carvery, diner, grill, pizzeria, snack bar, steakhouse, takeaway.

restful *see* relaxing.

restless

1 (adj) *Before the show, all the cast were restless.* unsettled, agitated, fidgety, jittery (informal), excitable, impatient, edgy, nervous, on edge, jumpy, anxious, fretful.
OPPOSITES: calm, composed.
2 (adj) *I had a restless night.* sleepless, wakeful, disturbed, unsettled, troubled.
OPPOSITES: peaceful, undisturbed.

restrict *see* limit 3.

result

1 (n) *The meeting had an unexpected result.* outcome, consequence, effect, upshot, aftermath, sequel, legacy, end product, repercussion, side effect, spin-off.
2 (v) *If the two countries can't agree, war may result.* follow, ensue, develop, come about, take place, happen, occur, arise.
3 result in (v) *These talks could result in a solution.* lead to, bring about, give rise to, produce, create, culminate in, end in, finish in, conclude in, terminate in.

retreat

(v) *The soldiers were forced to retreat.* withdraw, draw back, back off, back away, pull back, pull out, give ground, flee, take flight, turn tail, bolt, retire, depart.
OPPOSITE: advance.

retrieve

(v) *I tried to retrieve my lost suitcase.* get back, reclaim, recover, track down, find, salvage, rescue, regain, recapture.

return

1 (v) *Dad said he would return after tea.* come back, be back, get back, go back, reappear, come home.
2 (v) *If you return the same way you may find your keys.* go back, walk back, retrace your steps, double back, backtrack, retreat.
3 (v) *I asked Shelley to return my pen.* give back, put back, replace, send back.
4 (n) *I couldn't wait for Dad's return.* homecoming, reappearance, arrival.

reveal

1 (v) *Does this skirt reveal too much leg?* expose, show, display, bare, uncover.
OPPOSITES: cover up, conceal.
2 (v) *Will Melissa reveal her true feelings?* give away, betray, let out, let slip, disclose, divulge, declare, make known, make public, broadcast, display, lay bare, unveil.
OPPOSITES: hide, conceal.

revenge

1 (n) *We think the attack was an act of revenge.* vengeance, retaliation, reprisal, retribution, vindictiveness, tit for tat.
2 take revenge for (phrase) *You must take revenge for this injustice.* avenge, wreak your revenge for, get your own back for (informal), even the score for, repay, retaliate against, hit back at.

reverse

1 (v) *You'll have to reverse up the drive.* back, go backwards, drive backwards, go into reverse, back away, retreat, backtrack.
2 (v) *The head won't reverse her decision.* overturn, go back on, revoke, change, alter, undo, overrule, retract, repeal.
3 (n) *The instructions are on the reverse.* other side, back, rear, opposite side, flip side, underside, underneath.

review

1 (n) *Write a review of this book.* criticism, critique, appreciation, evaluation, assessment, appraisal, report, write-up.
2 (v) *Will you review the school play for our magazine?* give your opinion of, comment on, discuss, write a critique of, evaluate, assess, appraise, criticize.

revise

(v) *I must revise these facts before the test.* go over, run through, memorize, learn, swot up on (informal), mug up on (slang), reread, study.

revive

1 (v) *Doctors tried to revive the patient.* resuscitate, bring back to life, breathe life into, save, bring round, rouse, awaken.
2 (v) *The patient began to revive.* come round, regain consciousness, rally, recover.

revolt

1 (n) *An armed revolt. See* **revolution** 1.
2 (v) *The citizens will revolt. See* **rebel** 1.

revolting *see* disgusting 1.

revolution

1 (n) *Troops were brought in to crush the revolution.* uprising, rebellion, revolt, coup, coup d'état, mutiny, riot, insurrection, insurgency, armed struggle, civil war.
2 (n) *Computers have caused a revolution in the way we work.* complete change, radical change, transformation, sea change, turnaround, shift, upheaval.

revolve

1 (v) *Watch the cogs revolve. See* **turn** 1.
2 revolve around (v) *Satellites revolve around the earth.* circle, orbit, travel round, spin round, rotate around.

reward

1 (n) *Do we get a reward for effort?* prize, payment, remuneration, recompense, bonus, tip, compensation, award.
OPPOSITES: penalty, punishment.
2 (v) *The leader will reward you if you succeed.* repay, pay, compensate, make it worth your while, recompense, honour.
OPPOSITES: penalize, punish.

rhythm

(n) *Listen to the rhythm of the music.* beat, pulse, throbbing, pounding, tempo, phrasing, pattern, lilt, swing, syncopation.

rich

1 (adj) *Lord Lucre is rich.* wealthy, well-off, affluent, prosperous, well-to-do, well-heeled (informal), made of money (informal), stinking rich (informal), loaded (slang), rolling in it (slang).
OPPOSITE: poor.
2 (adj) *The walls were hung with rich tapestries.* costly, expensive, valuable, priceless, sumptuous, luxurious, opulent, lavish, ornate, elaborate, fine, exquisite, magnificent, splendid, gorgeous.
OPPOSITES: worthless, shabby.
3 (adj) *Red is a rich colour.* strong, deep, warm, vibrant, vivid, bright, intense.
OPPOSITES: pale, insipid.
4 (adj) *This sauce is too rich for me.* heavy, fatty, creamy, spicy, highly flavoured, indigestible, full-bodied (wine).
OPPOSITES: light, bland.

rickety

(adj) *A rickety bridge.* broken-down, wobbly, tumbledown, ramshackle, flimsy, unstable, unsafe, weak, decrepit.
OPPOSITES: strong, stable.

riddle *see* puzzle 1.

ride

1 (v) *Rod's moped is hard to ride.* control, handle, manage, steer, pedal, drive.
2 (v) *I love to ride on the bus.* travel, go, take a trip on, journey, sit, stand.
3 (n) *Come for a ride in our new car! See* **drive** 4.

ridiculous

(adj) *The idea of a flying pig is ridiculous.* absurd, ludicrous, crazy, mad, incredible, preposterous, outrageous, unbelievable, laughable, farcical, comical, hilarious, daft (informal), foolish, silly, nonsensical, zany.
OPPOSITE: sensible.

right

1 (adj) *Is this the right answer?* correct, proper, true, exact, precise, perfect, most accurate, valid, spot-on (informal).
OPPOSITES: wrong, incorrect.
2 (adj) *I try to do what's right.* just, fair, honourable, good, honest, decent, ethical, moral, proper, legal, above board.
OPPOSITES: wrong, immoral.
3 (adj) *Is this outfit right for a funeral?* suitable, appropriate, fitting, fit, proper, seemly, sensible.
OPPOSITES: inappropriate, unsuitable.

4 (n) *Do you have the right to do that?* authority, power, entitlement, prerogative, privilege, permission, authorization, justification, licence, freedom, liberty.

rigid

1 (adj) *Rigid plastic. See* **stiff** 1.

2 (adj) *Rigid rules. See* **strict** 2.

ring

1 (n) *Make a paper ring.* circle, disc, hoop, loop, band, cordon.

2 (n) *The police are investigating a drugs ring.* circle, gang, group, organization, band, syndicate, cartel, cell, mob.

3 (v) *Listen to the bells ring.* chime, peal, toll, tinkle, jingle, jangle, clang, ding, ping, sound, resound, reverberate, fill the air.

4 (v) *Please ring me tonight. See* **phone** 1.

riot

1 (n) *This news may cause a riot.* uprising, revolt, breach of the peace, insurrection, rebellion, upheaval, disturbance, street fight, brawl, scuffle, free-for-all (informal), violence, unrest, fighting, uproar, anarchy.

2 (v) *The people will riot when they hear the news.* run riot, rise up, take to the streets, revolt, rebel, take the law into their own hands, run amok, go on the rampage.

rip *see* **tear** 1, 2, 4.

ripe

(adj) *Wait until the fruit is ripe.* matured, mellow, ready to eat, fully developed, seasoned, perfect, fully grown.

rise

1 (v) *Watch the plane rise into the air.* lift, climb, ascend, soar, go up, fly up, shoot up, rocket, mount, spiral, take off
OPPOSITES: fall, descend.

2 (v) *House prices may rise.* increase, go up, climb, escalate, spiral, soar, shoot up, rocket, surge, jump, leap, grow.
OPPOSITES: fall, drop.

3 (v) *Can you see the mountain rise above us?* tower, loom, soar, rear up, stand out.

4 (v) *The path began to rise.* get steeper, climb, incline, go uphill, slope upwards.
OPPOSITE: fall.

5 (n) *I predict a rise in prices.* jump, increase, leap, surge, escalation, upturn.
OPPOSITES: drop, fall.

risk

1 (n) *There's a risk of snow. See* **chance** 2.

2 (n) *Dodgy Dave took a risk.* gamble, chance, leap in the dark, speculation.

3 (n) *There's some risk involved in motor racing.* danger, hazard, peril, uncertainty.

4 (v) *Don't risk all your money on a bet.* gamble, hazard, chance, speculate with.

5 (v) *Would you risk your life to save me?* endanger, put at risk, put in jeopardy, imperil, jeopardize, gamble with.

risky

(adj) *Skating on thin ice is risky.* dangerous, hazardous, fraught with danger, perilous, unsafe, precarious, dicey (informal), chancy (informal), dodgy (informal), iffy (informal).
OPPOSITE: safe.

river

(n) stream, brook, creek, rivulet, tributary, waterway, torrent.

along a river you might see...
estuary (river mouth)
ford (crossing)
gorge (deep river valley)
island
lock
meander (loop)
pool
rapids (fast-moving water)
reeds
river bank
river bed
rushes
stepping stones
towpath
waterfall
weeds
weir

rivers may be...
choked up
clean
contaminated
crystal clear
dark
deep
fast-flowing
foaming
frothing
glassy
glittering
icy
muddy
polluted
shallow
shimmering
silted up
silvery
slow-moving
sluggish
sparkling
turbulent
wide

rivers may...
babble
bubble
burble
cascade
eddy
flood
flow
glide
gurgle
gush
meander
murmur
plunge
race
ripple
roar
rush
snake
splash
stream
surge
sweep
swirl
thunder
trickle
tumble
twist
wind

river activities
angling
canoeing
cruising
fishing
paddling
punting
rowing
sailing
swimming
wading
white-water rafting

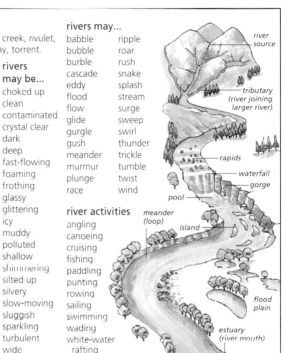

river source
tributary (river joining larger river)
rapids
waterfall
gorge
pool
meander (loop)
island
flood plain
estuary (river mouth)

road

(n) *Which road do we take?* route, way, direction, course.
TYPES OF ROAD: alley, avenue, backstreet, boulevard, bypass, close, crescent, cul-de-sac, drive, dual carriageway, high street, highway, lane, main road, minor road, motorway, one-way street, ring road, side street, single-track road, street, track.

roar

1 (v) *The giant began to roar.* bellow, thunder, shout, yell, bawl, howl, shriek.

2 (v) *Listen to the thunder roar.* boom, rumble, roll, growl, crash, thunder.

rob

1 (v) *Someone tried to rob the post office.* burgle, break into, hold up, raid, loot, steal from, ransack, ram raid (informal).

2 (v) *Don't let anyone rob you.* steal from, pick your pocket, mug (informal), swindle, con (informal), defraud, cheat, diddle (informal), rip you off (slang).

robber

(n) thief, burglar, pickpocket, shoplifter, housebreaker, looter, mugger (informal), bandit, brigand, highwayman, pirate.

robbery

1 (n) *Beryl was found guilty of robbery.* burglary, theft, stealing, housebreaking, ram raiding (informal), shoplifting, pilfering, swindling, fraud, embezzlement.

2 (n) *There's been a robbery in town.* burglary, break in, smash-and-grab (informal), hold up, raid, heist (slang), stick-up (slang), ram raid (informal).

robot

(n) android, automaton, machine.

rock

1 (n) *Crispin sat on a rock.* boulder, stone, crag, rocky outcrop.

2 (v) *The waves made the boat rock.* sway, roll, toss, pitch, lurch, wobble, swing.

rocky

(adj) *We scrambled over the rocky ground.* stony, boulder-strewn, pebbly, rough, hard, rugged, craggy, jagged, barren.

rod

(n) *A wooden rod.* stick, pole, switch, cane, birch, wand, baton, staff, crook, bar.

roll

1 (v) *Look at the coin roll across the floor.* trundle, travel, spin, wheel, twirl, whirl.

2 (v) *Let's roll in the snow!* tumble, somersault, go head over heels.

3 (v) *The wheels roll smoothly. See* **turn** 1.

4 (v) *Roll your hair around your fingers.* curl, coil, wind, wrap, twist, entwine, bind.

5 (v) *Use a rolling pin to roll the dough.* roll out, flatten, smooth, even out, level, spread out, press down.

6 (n) *I need another roll of paper.* spool, reel, cylinder, drum, scroll, tube, bobbin.

Roman life

Roman life

Roman gods and goddesses

Apollo (god of the sun, music and healing)
Diana (goddess of hunting and the moon)
Juno (goddess of women and childbirth)
Jupiter (king of the gods)
Mars (god of war)
Mercury (messenger of the gods)
Minerva (goddess of wisdom and war)
Neptune (god of the sea)
Venus (goddess of love and beauty)

Neptune

Mercury

Venus

some Roman people

architect
astrologer
centurion (army officer)
citizen (man with the right to vote)
consul (senior government official)
emperor
engineer
farmer
freed man (former slave)
gladiator
lawyer
legionary (foot soldier)
merchant
paedagogus (slave who supervised a child's education)
patrician (nobleman or noblewoman)
plebeian (commoner)
poet
politician
priest
scribe
senator (statesman)
slave
teacher

Roman emperor Nero

Roman town house

(cutaway)

tiled roof
mosaic
atrium (central room)
mosaic floor
impluvium (pool for catching rainwater)
kitchen
triclinium (dining room)
tablinum (study)
shrine of the household gods
peristylium (walled garden)

Roman clothes and jewellery

fibula (cloak pin)
tunic
belt
cloak
tunic
belt
tunic
slave
farmer
sandal
hairpin
gold chain
toga (robe made from one length of cloth)
gold earring
garnet ring
senator
palla (wrap)
cameo
stola (robe)
ivory hairpins
snake bracelets
sandal
patrician

Roman town

amphitheatre (sports arena)
apartment block
aqueduct (bridge for carrying water)
arch
basilica (public building used as law court)
circus (racetrack)
curia (town hall)
domus (town house)
forum (main square)
fountain
gate
inn
library
market stall
monument
public baths
shops
temple
theatre
town wall
viaduct (bridge)
villa (country house)

gate
temple
public baths
apartment block
town wall
amphitheatre

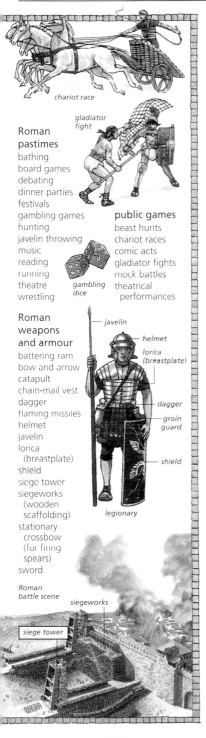

chariot race

gladiator fight

Roman pastimes
bathing
board games
debating
dinner parties
festivals
gambling games
hunting
javelin throwing
music
reading
running
theatre
wrestling

gambling dice

public games
beast hunts
chariot races
comic acts
gladiator fights
mock battles
theatrical performances

Roman weapons and armour
battering ram
bow and arrow
catapult
chain-mail vest
dagger
flaming missiles
helmet
javelin
lorica (breastplate)
shield
siege tower
siegeworks (wooden scaffolding)
stationary crossbow (for firing spears)
sword

— *javelin*
— *helmet*
— *lorica (breastplate)*
— *dagger*
— *groin guard*
— *shield*

legionary

Roman battle scene

siegeworks

siege tower

romantic
1 *(adj) Romantic films make me cry.* sentimental, lovey-dovey, emotional, heart-warming, soppy *(informal)*, slushy *(informal)*, schmaltzy, mushy *(informal)*.
2 *(adj) Ed held Eve in a romantic embrace.* loving, tender, fond, amorous, passionate.
3 *(adj) Daisy is hopelessly romantic.* dreamy, starry-eyed, unrealistic, idealistic, optimistic, impractical.
OPPOSITES: down-to-earth, realistic.
4 *(adj) Paris is a romantic city.* colourful, fascinating, glamorous, exciting, exotic, charming, picturesque, idyllic, inspiring.
OPPOSITES: unromantic, banal.

room
1 *(n) I need more room. See* **space** 2.
2 *(n) A secret room.* chamber.
TYPES OF ROOM: attic, ballroom, basement, bathroom, bedroom, boudoir *(old-fashioned)*, breakfast room, cellar, cloakroom, conservatory, den, dining room, drawing room, dressing room, gallery, games room, guest room, hall, kitchen, landing, larder, lavatory, library, living room, loft, loo *(informal)*, lounge, music room, nursery, office, pantry, parlour, playroom, scullery *(old-fashioned)*, sitting room, spare room, store room, studio, study, toilet, utility room, WC *(water closet)*. ❖ *Also see* **building**.

rope
(n) Pull the rope tight. cord, cable, line, string, twine, guy rope, lasso.

rot
1 *(v) These tomatoes will rot if we don't eat them soon.* go bad, go mouldy, spoil, deteriorate, go off *(informal)*, decay, perish, decompose, fester, putrefy.
2 *(v) The wallpaper had started to rot.* fall apart, disintegrate, crumble, perish, decay.
3 *(v) Sweets can rot your teeth.* eat away, eat into, decay, erode, corrode *(metal)*.

rotten
1 *(adj) These tomatoes are rotten.* bad, mouldy, spoiled, off, sour *(milk)*, putrid, festering, foul, fetid, decomposing.
OPPOSITE: fresh.
2 *(adj) Be careful! The floorboards are rotten.* decayed, decaying, crumbling, disintegrating, unsound, corroded *(metal)*.
OPPOSITE: sound.
3 *(adj) (informal) I feel rotten.* ill, unwell, sick, off colour, ghastly, rough *(informal)*, under the weather *(informal)*, poorly *(informal)*, grotty *(slang)*, lousy *(slang)*.
OPPOSITE: well.
4 *(adj) (informal) That was a rotten trick! See* **mean** 6.
5 *(adj) (informal) This is a rotten piece of homework. See* **poor** 2.

rough
1 *(adj) The cave walls felt rough.* uneven, bumpy, irregular, jagged, craggy, pitted, ridged, lumpy, rugged, rocky, stony.
OPPOSITE: smooth.

2 *(adj) The sea is rough today.* choppy, stormy, turbulent, tempestuous, wild.
OPPOSITES: calm, smooth.
3 *(adj) Granddad's skin feels rough.* scratchy, bristly, unshaven, leathery, callused, chapped, wrinkled.
OPPOSITES: smooth, soft.
4 *(adj) My dog has a rough coat.* coarse, bristly, wiry, fuzzy, shaggy, tangled.
OPPOSITES: smooth, silky.
5 *(adj) Peg has a rough voice. See* **gruff** 1.
6 *(adj) Cynthia hates rough games.* rowdy, boisterous, violent, tough, unruly, wild.
OPPOSITES: gentle, quiet.
7 *(adj) Nat made a rough drawing.* basic, quick, sketchy, crude, clumsy, rough-and-ready, hasty, incomplete, unfinished.
OPPOSITES: detailed, precise.
8 *(adj) I only have a rough idea of what to do. See* **vague** 2.

round
1 *(adj) I saw a round object in the sky.* circular, spherical, ball-shaped, balloon-like, curved, globular, bulbous, cylindrical.
2 *(adj) Augustus has a round face.* rounded, full, chubby, plump, podgy, fat, fleshy, moon-shaped, babyish.
3 *(n) I got to the last round of the contest.* stage, phase, level, heat, game, lap.

routine
1 *(n) My normal routine was disrupted.* procedure, schedule, pattern, programme, system, practice, custom, habit.
2 *(adj) This is just a routine checkup.* normal, ordinary, standard, typical, regular, everyday, usual, customary, conventional.
OPPOSITES: unusual, special.

row
1 *(v) I hate it when we row. See* **argue** 1.
2 *(n) Anita and Alice are having a row. See* **argument** 1.
3 *(n) What's that awful row? See* **noise** 2.
4 *(n) Look at that long row of cars.* line, queue, string, column, file, chain.
5 *(v) Let's row down the river.* paddle, scull, canoe, punt, boat.

rowdy
(adj) A rowdy class. unruly, noisy, boisterous, loud, riotous, obstreperous, disorderly, rough, loutish, wild.
OPPOSITES: quiet, subdued.

rub
1 *(v) Rub the lamp until it gleams.* polish, buff up, scrub, clean, shine, burnish, scour.
2 *(v) I knew the label would rub my neck.* chafe, irritate, scratch, scrape, graze.
3 *(v) Shall I rub suntan lotion on to your back?* smear, smooth, massage, spread, stroke, apply, work in.

rubbish
1 *(n) Put the rubbish in the bin.* litter, waste, refuse, garbage, trash, junk *(informal)*, scraps *(plural)*, leftovers *(plural)*, dregs *(plural)*, debris.
2 *(n) Don't talk rubbish! See* **nonsense** 1.
rub out *see* **erase**.

rude

rude
1 *(adj) That was a rude remark.* insolent, impertinent, cheeky, impudent, impolite, insulting, offensive, abusive, discourteous, disrespectful, inconsiderate, tactless.
OPPOSITES: polite, civil.
2 *(adj) Bozo told a rude joke.* dirty, smutty, crude, coarse, vulgar, filthy, indecent, obscene, blue, lewd, suggestive, risqué, naughty, saucy, tasteless, offensive.
OPPOSITES: clean, decent.

rugged
(adj) A rugged coastline. rocky, craggy, jagged, rough, stony, irregular, uneven.

ruin
1 *(v) This haircut could ruin my image.* wreck, destroy, shatter, spoil, damage, play havoc with, harm, mar, undermine, screw up *(informal)*, blow *(slang)*.
2 *(v) Earthquakes can ruin whole cities.* See **destroy** 1.
3 *(v) If your business fails, it could ruin you.* bankrupt, break, destroy, crush, make you a pauper, impoverish, bring you down.
4 *(n) This mistake could lead to ruin.* disaster, defeat, failure, collapse, breakdown, destruction, devastation, bankruptcy, insolvency, destitution.

ruined
(adj) The ruined castle looked ghostly in the moonlight. crumbling, derelict, dilapidated, ramshackle, tumbledown.

ruins
(plural n) Rescuers searched the ruins. rubble, wreckage, debris, remains *(plural)*.

rule
1 *(n) You must obey this rule.* regulation, ruling, guideline, directive, order, commandment, law, decree, statute.
2 *(v) Who will rule the country? See* **govern**.

rumble
1 *(v) I felt the ground rumble under my feet.* thunder, reverberate, boom, roar, murmur, groan, shake.
2 *(v) My tummy began to rumble.* gurgle, grumble, growl, murmur.

rumour
(n) Have you heard the rumour about Famous Fred? gossip, talk, word, news, story, buzz, hearsay, scandal, dirt *(slang)*.

run
1 *(v) You'll have to run to catch the bus.* race, sprint, jog, dash, hurry, rush, hotfoot it, leg it *(informal)*, get a move on *(informal)*, tear along, speed along, charge along, hare along *(informal)*, career along, scoot, scurry, scamper, gallop.
2 *(v) Does this car run on unleaded petrol?* go, work, function, operate, perform.
3 *(v) Water began to run down the walls.* trickle, dribble, drip, pour, flow, stream, cascade, course, spill, gush, spout.
4 *(v) These skis run smoothly over the snow.* glide, skim, slide, move, go.

5 *(v) I hope to run a music shop one day.* See **manage** 2.
6 *(v) I hope the colours don't run.* bleed, mix, spread, wash out.
7 *(n) Let's go for a run around the park.* jog, sprint, race, trot, gallop, marathon.

run after *see* **chase**.

run away
(v) Run away or you'll get caught! run off, take off *(informal)*, make a run for it, take to your heels, bolt, escape, flee, scram *(informal)*, scarper *(slang)*, beat it *(slang)*, do a runner *(slang)*, do a bunk *(slang)*.

runny
1 *(adj) This paint is too runny.* thin, watery, liquid, fluid, diluted, flowing.
OPPOSITES: thick, solid.
2 *(adj) I've got a runny nose.* streaming.

run out
1 *(v) When does your season ticket run out?* expire, lapse, finish, end, terminate.
2 *(v) Our supplies will soon run out.* be finished, be used up, dry up, be exhausted, give out, peter out.

run over
(v) Watch out or that bus will run you over. knock you down, run you down, knock you over, hit, bump into.

rush
1 *(v) We must rush or we'll be late. See* **hurry** 1.
2 *(v) You can't rush such an important decision. See* **hurry** 2.
3 *(n) It was a rush to get there on time.* race, scramble, struggle, mad dash.
4 *(n) Take your time; there's no rush.* hurry, urgency, pressure.

rustle
(v) The wind made the leaves rustle. swish, whisper, crackle, crinkle.

ruthless
(adj) The king was ruthless in his revenge. merciless, pitiless, heartless, remorseless, relentless, without pity, cruel, hardhearted, callous, unfeeling, unrelenting, implacable, inhuman, ferocious.
OPPOSITES: merciful, compassionate.

Ss

sack *(informal) see* **dismiss** 1.

sad
1 *(adj) Leah felt sad.* unhappy, miserable, depressed, down, blue, low, glum, gloomy, down in the dumps *(informal)*, dejected, melancholy, mournful, sorrowful, forlorn, wistful, despondent, upset, tearful, heartbroken, brokenhearted, grief-stricken, sick at heart, wretched, despairing.
OPPOSITES: happy, cheerful.

2 *(adj) This film has a sad ending.* unhappy, poignant, tear-jerking *(informal)*, heartbreaking, heart-rending, touching, moving, tragic, depressing, sombre, dark.
OPPOSITE: happy.
3 *(adj) I have some sad news for you.* bad, serious, grave, unfortunate, upsetting, painful, regrettable, distressing, tragic, heartbreaking, grim, harrowing.
OPPOSITES: happy, good.
4 *(adj) (slang) Dad made a sad attempt to be trendy. See* **pathetic** 2.

sadden
(v) It will sadden you to hear this tragic news. upset, grieve, distress, break your heart, pain, dismay, make you cry, bring tears to your eyes, make your heart bleed.
OPPOSITES: cheer, comfort.

sadness *see* **sorrow**.

safe
1 *(adj) All the explorers are safe.* unharmed, unhurt, uninjured, unscathed, safe and sound, alive and well, in one piece *(informal)*, out of danger, all right.
OPPOSITES: hurt, injured.
2 *(adj) The villagers were safe inside the castle.* secure, protected, out of harm's way, sheltered, defended, shielded, guarded, invulnerable, unassailable, out of danger, free from harm.
OPPOSITES: in danger, at risk.
3 *(adj) Mum is a safe driver.* careful, prudent, sensible, responsible, reliable, dependable, cautious, unadventurous.
OPPOSITES: dangerous, reckless.
4 *(adj) This snake is quite safe.* harmless, docile, tame, nonpoisonous, innocuous.
OPPOSITE: dangerous.
5 *(adj) Is the tap water safe?* pure, uncontaminated, unpolluted, drinkable, nontoxic, wholesome, edible *(food)*.
OPPOSITES: unsafe, harmful.
6 *(n) Put your valuables in the safe.* safe-deposit box, cash box, deposit box, strongbox, coffer, strongroom, vault.

sag
(v) My bed is starting to sag in the middle. sink, slump, droop, dip, cave in, give way, subside, hang down, drop, fall.

sail
1 *(v) Pirate Peg is ready to sail.* set sail, put to sea, leave port, weigh anchor, hoist sail, get under way, embark.
2 *(v) Did you sail to France?* go by boat, cruise, go by sea, steam, ride the waves, voyage.
3 *(v) Watch the balloon sail through the air. See* **glide** 1.

same
1 *(adj) That's the same tune I heard before.* selfsame, very same, very, identical.
OPPOSITE: different.
2 **the same** *(adj) Our hats are the same.* identical, alike, matching, like peas in a pod *(informal)*, indistinguishable.
OPPOSITES: different, dissimilar.

3 the same *(adj) These two experiments should give the same results.* identical, matching, corresponding, equivalent, parallel, comparable, similar.
OPPOSITES: different, dissimilar.
4 the same *(adj) At the North Pole, the weather is always the same.* unchanging, unvarying, consistent, constant, uniform.
OPPOSITES: variable, changeable.

sarcastic
(adj) Sarcastic comments. cutting, scathing, caustic, biting, withering, acerbic, sharp-tongued, disparaging, contemptuous, scornful, mocking, sneering, taunting, jeering, sarky *(informal)*, ironic, sardonic.

satisfactory see **all right** 3.

satisfied
1 *(adj) After his enormous tea, Augustus felt satisfied.* See **full** 3.
2 *(adj) Once she's won the prize, Lucy will feel satisfied.* content, contented, pleased, gratified, happy, glad, at ease, self-satisfied, complacent, smug, like the cat that swallowed the cream *(informal)*.
OPPOSITES: dissatisfied, discontented.

savage
1 *(adj) Savage animals.* wild, ferocious, fierce, vicious, untamed, undomesticated.
OPPOSITES: tame, gentle.
2 *(adj) A savage attack.* brutal, vicious, ferocious, violent, bloody, bloodthirsty, barbaric, murderous, sadistic, cruel, callous, cold-blooded, merciless, pitiless, ruthless, inhuman, diabolical, bestial.

save
1 *(v) Don't panic; I'm coming to save you!* See **rescue** 1.
2 *(v) Try to save your money.* hold on to, hang on to, be sparing with, be thrifty with, be frugal with, economize, set aside, put aside, put away, stash away *(informal)*, keep for a rainy day, hoard, accumulate, amass, bank, deposit, invest.
OPPOSITES: squander, waste.
3 *(v) Let's campaign to save the whales.* protect, preserve, conserve, safeguard, defend, guard, keep safe, look after.
OPPOSITES: endanger, imperil.

say
1 *(v) Sam couldn't say what was bothering her.* put into words, articulate, express, communicate, give voice to, convey, put across, mention, tell, relate, reveal, disclose, divulge, come out with.
2 *(v) Say your lines out loud.* recite, repeat, speak, deliver, perform, rehearse, declaim, read.
3 *(v) What does the recipe say?* specify, state, suggest, indicate.
4 *(v) I would say it's about four o'clock.* See **think** 2.
5 *(v) People say Dodgy Dave is a crook.* claim, allege, suggest, put about, report.
6 *(n) Do I have any say in this decision?* input, voice, share, part, vote, influence, clout, sway, weight.

say words

Please may I go to the party?

"I'm leaving home," Ziggy...
announced
declared
exclaimed
proclaimed
pronounced
stated

I'm leaving home.
Ziggy declared

"It's a lovely day," Kamal...
commented
mentioned
noted
observed
pointed out
reflected
remarked

"I broke the window," Sam...
acknowledged
admitted
blurted out
confessed
confirmed
disclosed
divulged
revealed

"What are you doing?" Poppy...
asked
demanded
inquired
queried
questioned

"It's none of your business," Ben...
answered
rejoined
replied
responded
retorted

What are you doing?
Poppy inquired

"I'm innocent," Melissa...
affirmed
asserted
claimed
emphasized
insisted
maintained
professed
protested
stressed

It's none of your business!
Ben retorted

"I'm bored," Josh...
complained
drawled
groaned
grumbled
moaned
sighed
wailed
whined
whinged

"I can't find my kitten," Shama...
babbled
cried
gabbled
gasped
gulped
sobbed
spluttered
stammered
stuttered
whimpered

"I'm sorry," Matt...
mumbled
murmured
muttered
whispered

I'm bored.
Lopa pleaded
whined

"Please may I go to the party?" Lopa...
begged
beseeched
entreated
implored
pleaded
wheedled

"Keep out of my room!" Edwin...
barked
bawled
bellowed
commanded
growled
ordered
roared
screamed
shouted
shrieked
snapped
snarled
yelled

Keep out of my room!
KEEP OUT
snarled

You look funny in that hat
chuckled

"You look funny in that hat," Jemima...
chortled
chuckled
giggled
laughed
sneered
sniggered
tittered

scalding see **hot** 2.

scamper
1 *(v) Watch the mouse scamper across the floor.* scurry, scuttle, scoot, scramble, dart, dash, run, sprint, race, beetle *(informal)*.
2 **scamper about** *(v) My rabbit loves to scamper about in the grass.* run about, romp, frisk, frolic, gambol, cavort.

scan
1 *(v) Scan the front page.* See **look at** 2.
2 *(v) Beryl stopped to scan the street for police.* survey, search, scrutinize, scour, inspect, take stock of, check out *(informal)*, recce *(informal)*, look up and down.

scandal
1 *(n) Don't believe the scandal you read in the papers.* gossip, rumours *(plural)*, dirt *(slang)*, tittle-tattle, libel *(written)*, slander *(spoken)*, muckraking, smear campaign.
2 *(n) It's a scandal that so many people are homeless.* disgrace, outrage, crime, sin, shame, crying shame.

scandalous
1 *(adj) Dodgy Dave's behaviour is scandalous.* See **disgraceful** 1.
2 *(adj) Who started that scandalous rumour?* slanderous *(spoken)*, libellous *(written)*, scurrilous, malicious, untrue.

scarce

scarce
(adj) Bananas were scarce during the war.
in short supply, few and far between,
seldom seen, hard to find, thin on the
ground, rare, uncommon.
OPPOSITES: plentiful, common.

scarcely *see* **hardly**.

scare
1 *(v) This film will scare you.* frighten,
scare you out of your wits, scare you stiff,
terrify, horrify, petrify, make your hair
stand on end, send shivers down your
spine, make your blood run cold, make
your flesh creep, unnerve, alarm, startle.
2 *(v) Don't let Bozo scare you.* intimidate,
frighten, terrorize, bully, threaten, menace,
put the wind up *(informal)*, cow, daunt.
3 *(n) The news gave me a real scare.*
fright, shock, panic, start, jolt.
4 *(n) The shops are closed because of a
bomb scare.* alert, alarm, hoax.

scared
1 *(adj) Weren't you scared when the lights
went out?* afraid, frightened, terrified,
petrified, scared stiff, scared out of your
wits, panic-stricken, terror-stricken,
panicky, apprehensive, alarmed, anxious,
fearful, startled, horrified, horrorstruck.
2 **be scared of** *(phrase) There's no need
to be scared of spiders.* be afraid of, be
frightened of, fear, have a phobia about,
have a horror of, dread, shudder at,
tremble at, live in fear of, shake in your
shoes, be in a blue funk *(informal)*.

scarred
(adj) A scarred face. disfigured, blemished,
marked, pockmarked, pitted.

scary *(informal) see* **frightening**.

scatter
1 *(v) Don't scatter your magazines over
the floor.* strew, spread, throw, fling, toss,
drop, shower, sprinkle, distribute.
2 *(v) The crowd began to scatter.* break
up, disperse, disband, separate, dissolve.

scatterbrained
*(adj) Don't rely on Kylie; she's much too
scatterbrained!* absent-minded, forgetful,
muddleheaded, disorganized, vague, scatty
(informal), featherbrained, bird-brained
(informal), empty-headed, giddy, dizzy,
flighty, unreliable, not with it *(informal)*.

scene
1 *(n) We admired the scene. See* **view** 1.
2 *(n) Let's investigate the scene of the
crime.* site, location, setting, place, area,
spot, position, whereabouts, locality,
locale, neighbourhood, region.
3 *(n) In this scene the hero dies.* act,
episode, sequence, shot, clip, take.
4 *(n) The curtain rose on a stunning scene.*
set, stage, setting, tableau, backdrop.

scenery
1 *(n) Isn't the scenery beautiful!*
landscape, countryside, surroundings
(plural), terrain, view, vista, panorama.

2 *(n) Natalie designed the scenery for our
school play.* set, stage set, staging, setting,
backdrop, backcloth, décor.

scent
1 *(n) Don't these roses have a wonderful
scent!* perfume, fragrance, smell, bouquet,
aroma *(food, drink)*.
2 *(n) Do you like my new scent?* perfume,
fragrance, eau de Cologne, cologne, body
spray, toilet water, aftershave.

schedule
(n) Try to keep to the schedule. plan,
programme, timetable, agenda, itinerary.

scheme
1 *(n) The government announced a
scheme to cut crime. See* **plan** 1.
2 *(n) Dodgy Dave has a new scheme to
make money.* plan, idea, stratagem, ploy,
plot, ruse, intrigue, dodge, manoeuvre,
subterfuge, conspiracy, racket *(informal)*.
3 *(v) Let's scheme to get our revenge. See*
plot 3.

school
(n) college, academy.
TYPES OF SCHOOL: boarding school,
co-ed (coeducational school),
comprehensive school, day school,
grammar school, grant-maintained school,
high school, independent school, infant
school, junior school, kindergarten, middle
school, mixed school, nursery school, prep
school (preparatory school), primary
school, private school, public school,
secondary school, selective school, single-
sex school, sixth-form college, state school,
technology college.

scold *see* **tell off**.

scorch
(v) Don't scorch the paintwork! burn,
singe, char, blacken, blister, sear, roast.

scorching *see* **hot** 1.

score
1 *(n) What was the score at half-time?*
tally, result, number of points, total, mark.
2 *(v) We need to score ten points.* win,
earn, gain, achieve, make, total, chalk up
(informal), notch up *(informal)*, amass.
3 *(v) Don't score your name in the desk!
See* **cut** 5.

scorn
1 *(v) Don't scorn my efforts at sewing.*
sneer at, scoff at, jeer at, look down on,
despise, be contemptuous of, turn up your
nose at *(informal)*, mock, deride.
OPPOSITES: admire, respect.
2 *(n) Hilda viewed my painting with scorn.*
contempt, derision, disdain, disgust,
mockery, ridicule, sarcasm.
OPPOSITES: admiration, respect.

scornful
*(adj) Maddy gave her brother a scornful
look.* disdainful, contemptuous, scathing,
withering, condescending, supercilious,
sneering, derisive, sarcastic, mocking.
OPPOSITES: admiring, respectful.

scowl
(v) Mum will scowl at you if you snigger.
frown, grimace, glower, glare, look
daggers, give you a dirty look.

scramble
1 *(v) Can you scramble up this cliff?*
clamber, scrabble, climb, crawl, struggle,
swarm, scale, scurry.
2 *(v) Watch the fans scramble for a seat.*
jostle, scrabble, fight, scuffle, struggle,
jockey, battle, vie, rush, dash, scurry.

scrap
1 *(n) Pick up that last scrap.* piece, bit,
fragment, crumb, morsel, speck, grain,
snippet, sliver, remnant, mouthful, drop.
2 *(n) (informal) The boys had a scrap in
the playground. See* **fight** 6.
3 *(v) Don't scrap that paper! See* **throw
away** 1.
4 *(v) Let's scrap the match. See* **cancel**.

scrape
1 *(v) How did you scrape your knee?*
graze, scratch, skin, scuff.
2 *(v) Scrape the food off the floor.* scoop,
shovel, scrub, scour, clean.
3 *(v) Can you hear my fingernails scrape
against the blackboard?* grate, scratch,
rasp, squeak, grind, screech.

scraps
(plural n) Leave the scraps for the birds.
leftovers *(plural)*, remains *(plural)*, leavings
(plural), pickings *(plural)*, scrapings *(plural)*,
crumbs *(plural)*, remnants *(plural)*.

scratch
1 *(v) Don't scratch the table.* score, mark,
scrape, cut, gouge, claw at, damage.
2 *(n) I have a scratch on my leg.* cut,
graze, scrape, gash, nick, abrasion, mark.

scrawl *see* **scribble** 1, 2.

scrawny *see* **thin** 1.

scream
*(v) I'll scream if you put that spider down
my neck.* shriek, screech, squeal, squawk,
cry out, yell, howl, yelp, yowl, wail, holler
(informal), bawl, bellow, shout.

scribble
1 *(v) I just had time to scribble a message.*
scrawl, dash off, jot down, write, pen.
2 *(v) Don't scribble on the walls!* doodle,
scrawl, write, draw, write graffiti.

scrounge
*(v) (informal) Let's scrounge some money
off Dad.* cadge, sponge, beg for, wheedle.

scrub
*(v) We'll have to scrub the floor to get the
dirt off.* scour, wash, clean, rub, swab.

scruffy
1 *(adj) Barney always looks scruffy.*
dishevelled, unkempt, untidy, messy,
down-at-heel, bedraggled, shabby.
OPPOSITES: smart, neat.
2 *(adj) I like wearing scruffy jeans.* tatty,
shabby, worn, tattered, ragged, holey,
sloppy, grungy *(slang)*.
OPPOSITE: smart.

3 (adj) Ziggy lives in a scruffy part of town. shabby, tatty, run-down, dilapidated, seedy, disreputable, squalid, dirty, dingy, grotty *(slang)*, rough.
OPPOSITE: smart.
scrumptious *(informal) see* **delicious**.
scuffle *see* **fight** 2, 6.
sea
1 *(n) Pirate Peg sailed across the sea.* ocean, waves *(plural)*, high seas *(plural)*, briny *(informal)*, deep, drink *(informal)*.
2 *(adj) An octopus is a sea creature.* saltwater, aquatic, marine.

seal
1 *(v) Seal the bottle.* stop up, plug, cork, make airtight, make waterproof, bung.
2 *(v) The police decided to seal the room.* close up, shut up, lock, secure, seal off, close off, board up, wall up, cordon off.
search
1 *(v) Rescuers had to search the wreckage.* hunt through, look through, comb, scour, sift through, rummage through, rifle through, examine, scrutinize, investigate, go over with a fine-tooth comb, turn upside down, turn inside out, ransack.

2 *(v) The police began to search for clues.* look, hunt, poke about, nose about, ferret around, scout around, cast around, look high and low, seek, probe, pry, leave no stone unturned.
3 *(n) Hundreds of people joined in the search.* hunt, pursuit, quest, investigation, inquiry, exploration, chase.
seaside
(n) We spent our holiday at the seaside. beach, coast, shore, seashore, sands *(plural)*, seaside resort, coastal resort.
❖ *Also see* **seaside words**.

sea and seashore

sea words
breaker, crest (top of wave), current, high tide, low tide, spray, spume (foam), surf, swell, tidal wave, white horses (waves with white crests)

the sea may be...
aquamarine, billowing, calm, choppy, crystal clear, emerald green, glassy, grey, heaving, raging, rough, sapphire blue, shimmering, silvery, sparkling, stormy, tempestuous, tranquil, turbulent, turquoise, wild

the waves may...
billow, break, churn, crash, curl, foam, froth, lap, plash, plunge, pound, race, ripple, roar, roll, rush, spill, splash, surge, swirl, swish, thunder, tumble, wash

shore words
bay, beach, boulder, cave, cliff, coast, cove (small bay), driftwood, estuary (place where river meets sea), headland, inlet, mud flat, pebble, rock arch, rock pool, sand dune, seaweed, shell, shingle, spit (ridge of sand jutting into sea), stack (rock pillar)

the cliffs may be...
bare, chalky, craggy, crumbling, dramatic, jagged, jutting, overhanging, precipitous, rocky, rugged, sheer, spectacular, towering, treacherous, vertical

the beach may be...
crowded, deserted, exposed, golden, idyllic, inaccessible, isolated, jam-packed, lonely, muddy, pebbly, polluted, remote, sandy, secluded, sheltered, shelving (sloping), shingly, stony, sun-drenched, unspoilt, windswept

sea birds
albatross, auk, booby, cormorant, fulmar, gannet, guillemot, gull, kittiwake, pelican, penguin, petrel, puffin, razorbill, shag, skua, tern

sea creatures
dolphin, eel, octopus, porpoise, sea horse, seal, sea lion, sea otter, sea snake, shark, squid, stingray, turtle, whale

seashore wildlife
barnacle, clam, coral, crab, cuttlefish, jellyfish, limpet, lobster, mussel, oyster, prawn, sandhopper (sand flea), sea anemone, sea snail, sea urchin, shrimp, sponge, starfish, whelk, worm

stack *rock arch* *booby* *puffin* *octopus* *squid* *shark* *whale* *raging sea* *jellyfish* *sea urchin* *coral reef*

Also see **seaside words**.

seaside

seaside words

at a seaside resort
amusement arcade
aquarium
boating lake
campsite
caravan park
disco
fairy lights
funfair
guesthouse
harbour
hotel
ice-cream kiosk
jetty
marina
nightclub
pier
promenade
souvenir shop

on the beach
beach ball
beach café
beach hut
breakwater
bucket and spade
deckchair
parasol
Punch and Judy show
sandcastle
sun-lounger
volleyball net
windbreak

seaside food
candyfloss
fish and chips
ice cream
ice lolly *(informal)*
seafood
seaside rock
shellfish

a resort may be...
bustling
busy
buzzing
crowded
elegant
fashionable
jumping *(slang)*
lively
noisy
packed
peaceful
picturesque
quiet
shabby
sleepy
smart
tacky *(informal)*
tatty
touristy *(informal)*
up-market

mask
snorkel

seaside activities
beachcombing
boat trips
collecting shells
donkey rides
exploring caves
fishing trips
jet skiing
paddling
parasailing
sailing
sandsailing
scuba diving
shrimping
snorkelling
sunbathing
surfing
swimming
volleyball
water-skiing
windsurfing

candy floss

Also see **sea & seashore**.

seat
(n) Find yourself a seat. chair, stool, bench, place. *Also see* **chair, sofa.**

second
1 *(adj) I asked for a second helping of pudding.* extra, additional, further, other.
2 *(n) The butterfly was gone in a second.* See **moment** 1.

secret
1 *(adj) This information must remain secret.* hidden, concealed, under wraps, unpublished, undisclosed, private, confidential, restricted, classified, off the record, hush-hush *(informal).*
OPPOSITES: public, well-known.
2 *(adj) Agent Arthur was sent on a secret mission.* undercover, covert, cloak-and-dagger, underground, clandestine, hush-hush *(informal),* furtive, surreptitious.
OPPOSITES: open, well-known.
3 *(adj) The treasure chamber had a secret entrance.* concealed, hidden, camouflaged, disguised, invisible.
OPPOSITES: obvious, visible.
4 *(adj) Can you read this secret message?* cryptic, encoded, mysterious, hidden.
OPPOSITE: straightforward.
5 *(n) Don't tell Mum - it's a secret!* private matter, confidential matter, confidence.
6 *(n) What is the secret of eternal youth?* formula, recipe, key, solution, answer.

section
1 *(n) Have a section of my pear.* See **bit** 2.
2 *(n) What section of the company do you work in?* See **part** 3.
3 *(n) Read the next section for homework.* bit, part, passage, paragraph, chapter, unit, module, page, instalment.

secure
1 *(adj) I feel secure at my new school.* safe, confident, at ease, unworried, relaxed, comfortable, reassured.
OPPOSITES: insecure, uneasy.
2 *(adj) Is that ladder secure?* firm, steady, stable, fixed, immovable, safe, strong.
OPPOSITES: unsafe, precarious.
3 *(adj) Make sure the windows are secure.* fastened, locked, shut, closed, barred.
4 *(adj) The villagers were secure inside the castle.* See **safe** 2.
5 *(v) Secure your bike to the railings.* See **fasten** 1.

see
1 *(v) Did you see the comet?* catch sight of, catch a glimpse of, spot, notice, glimpse, make out, identify, observe, sight, note, spy, witness, clap eyes on *(informal).*
2 *(v) It was hard to see what Alice meant.* understand, grasp, follow, take in, make out, know, make sense of, comprehend, get the drift of, get the hang of *(informal),* catch on to *(informal),* get, twig *(informal).*
3 *(v) Mrs Badger wants to see my parents.* talk to, speak to, meet, consult, confer with, interview, visit.
4 *(v) Can you see when the film starts?* find out, have a look, ask, discover, ascertain, determine, investigate.
5 *(v) See that Tommy doesn't hurt himself.* make sure, mind, see to it, take care, make certain, ensure.
6 *(v) "Can I go to the disco?" "I'll see."* think about it, give it some thought, think it over, consider it, mull it over.
7 *(v) I'll see you to your car.* show, walk, accompany, escort, lead, usher.
8 *(v) I can't quite see you as a film star.* picture, imagine, visualize, envisage.
9 *(v) I see problems ahead.* foresee, envisage, anticipate, predict, foretell.

seem
(v) Do I seem sad? appear, look, strike you as, give the impression of being, sound.

see-through *see* **transparent**.

see to
(v) Can you see to the baby? attend to, check up on, look after, take care of, be responsible for, manage, take charge of.

seize
1 *(v) I felt someone seize me by the arm.* See **grab** 1.
2 *(v) Customs officials were quick to seize the drugs.* See **confiscate**.

seldom *see* **rarely**.

select *see* **choose** 1.

selection
1 *(n) This shop stocks a wide selection of CDs.* See **choice** 2.
2 *(n) This book contains a selection of poems.* collection, anthology, miscellany, choice, variety, range, medley, potpourri.

self-centred *see* **selfish**.

self-confident *see* **confident** 1.

self-conscious
(adj) Zoë feels self-conscious when she has to sing in public. awkward, embarrassed, uncomfortable, ill at ease, shy, diffident, nervous, insecure, bashful, mortified.

self-control
(n) It took great self-control not to shout at my brother. self-discipline, self-restraint, restraint, willpower, strength of mind, patience, composure, coolness, calmness.

selfish
(adj) Nev is so selfish; he never thinks of others. self-centred, egocentric, egotistical, self-absorbed, demanding, greedy, mean.
OPPOSITES: unselfish, generous.

self-satisfied *see* **smug**.

sell
1 *(v) We're planning to sell our house.* put up for sale, put on the market, auction off.
OPPOSITE: buy.
2 *(v) Dodgy Dave is trying to sell stolen goods.* sell off, dispose of, peddle, hawk, tout, exchange, deal in, traffic in, handle.

3 *(v) Does this shop sell balloons?* stock, keep *(informal)*, supply, carry, trade in, deal in, offer for sale, retail.
4 *(v) Famous Fred is keen to sell his new single. See* **promote** 2.

send
1 *(v) Don't forget to send your card to Granny. See* **post** 4.
2 *(v) Can you send this message for me?* convey, relay, forward, transmit, dispatch, radio, fax, e-mail, broadcast.
3 *(v) Will your parents send you to boarding school?* pack you off, ship you off, farm you out, dispatch, consign.

send for *see* **summon**.

sensational
1 *(adj) A sensational newspaper article.* dramatic, melodramatic, lurid, shocking, scandalous, electrifying, startling, staggering, spectacular, astounding, horrifying, alarmist, shock-horror.
2 *(adj) (informal) A sensational party. See* **fantastic** 3.

sense
1 *(n) I had a sense that something was wrong.* feeling, impression, hunch, sensation, awareness, instinct, intuition, premonition, presentiment.
2 *(n) I can't work out the sense of this poem. See* **meaning** 2.
3 *(n) Adrian has no sense.* common sense, brains *(plural) (informal)*, wit, judgment, understanding, intelligence, nous *(slang)*.
4 *(v) Didn't you sense that Mrs Badger was annoyed?* feel, get the impression, get the feeling, have a hunch, suspect, notice, pick up, perceive, observe, realize.

sensible
1 *(adj) A sensible girl.* level-headed, down-to-earth, practical, matter-of-fact, serious-minded, thoughtful, mature, steady.
OPPOSITES: silly, foolish.
2 *(adj) A sensible choice.* wise, prudent, intelligent, logical, rational, reasonable, sound, realistic, shrewd, well-thought-out.
OPPOSITES: foolish, stupid.
3 *(adj) Sensible shoes.* practical, comfortable, functional, suitable, hard-wearing, serviceable.
OPPOSITES: impractical, unsuitable.

sensitive
1 *(adj) Don't tease Mary; she's very sensitive.* thin-skinned, touchy, easily upset, oversensitive, hypersensitive.
OPPOSITES: thick-skinned, tough.
2 *(adj) My skin is sensitive.* easily irritated, delicate, soft, tender, painful, sore, raw.
OPPOSITE: tough.
3 *(adj) Karen will notice if you're unhappy; she's very sensitive.* perceptive, discerning, receptive, responsive, impressionable.
OPPOSITES: obtuse, insensitive.
4 *(adj) Try to deal with this situation in a sensitive way.* discreet, diplomatic, tactful, sympathetic, thoughtful, understanding.
OPPOSITES: insensitive, heavy-handed.

5 *(adj) This is a sensitive issue.* delicate, difficult, awkward, controversial, contentious, problematic, thorny, ticklish.

sentimental
1 *(adj) Old love songs make Granny feel sentimental.* emotional, nostalgic, tearful, weepy *(informal)*, dewy-eyed, maudlin, softhearted, tenderhearted, warm.
2 *(adj) I hate sentimental poetry.* romantic, lovey-dovey, mawkish, soppy *(informal)*, slushy *(informal)*, corny *(slang)*, mushy *(informal)*, schmaltzy, sugary, syrupy, weepy *(informal)*, tear-jerking *(informal)*.

separate
1 *(v) The police tried to separate the fighting fans.* split up, break up, part, disentangle, divide, come between, keep apart, segregate, isolate, scatter, disperse.
2 *(v) Be careful! The pieces could separate in your hands.* come apart, fall apart, break apart, come away, detach, split, divide, disconnect, disintegrate, scatter.
3 *(v) I'm sorry that you and Jason have decided to separate.* split up, break up, part, part company, go your separate ways, live apart, divorce.
4 *(v) At the big tree, the two paths separate. See* **divide** 1.
5 *(adj) The two schools are quite separate.* unconnected, unrelated, distinct, different, independent, autonomous, detached.

series
(n) A series of disasters. sequence, string, chain, run, row, succession, train, procession, progression, set, cycle.

serious
1 *(adj) Edwin is a serious boy.* solemn, earnest, sober, grave, pensive, thoughtful, sedate, staid, humourless, sombre.
OPPOSITES: frivolous, cheerful.
2 *(adj) We had a serious discussion.* earnest, grave, weighty, heavy, deep, profound, sincere, important, significant.
OPPOSITES: frivolous, trivial.
3 *(adj) Pollution is a serious problem.* grave, major, urgent, pressing, acute, critical, far-reaching, worrying, alarming.
OPPOSITES: minor, insignificant.
4 *(adj) Aunt Bertha has a serious illness.* major, severe, grave, critical, dangerous, acute, incapacitating, crippling, incurable, inoperable, fatal, terminal, malignant.
OPPOSITES: mild, minor.
5 *(adj) A serious accident occurred.* major, catastrophic, calamitous, tragic, fatal.
OPPOSITE: minor.
6 *(adj) You must be serious if you want to learn ballet.* committed, determined, in earnest, sincere, resolved, resolute, dedicated, single-minded, unwavering, conscientious, hard-working, diligent.
OPPOSITES: half-hearted, casual.

servant
(n) attendant, helper, assistant, help, hired help, retainer, hireling, domestic, dogsbody *(informal)*, skivvy, drudge, slave.

serve
1 *(v) The genie will serve the owner of the lamp.* work for, obey, assist, help, be of use to, wait on, attend to, minister to.
2 *(v) Shall I serve tea?* put out, set out, dish up, give out, hand round, pass round.
3 *(v) Do you serve refreshments?* supply, provide, offer, sell, lay on.

service
(n) We all joined in the service. ceremony, act of worship, worship, prayers *(plural)*, celebration, assembly, meeting.

serving *see* **helping**.

set
1 *(v) Set the dish on the table. See* **put** 1.
2 *(v) Let's set a date. See* **fix** 2.
3 *(v) Please set the table for tea.* lay, spread, prepare, arrange, make ready.
OPPOSITE: clear.
4 *(v) Wait for the jelly to set.* jell, harden, solidify, thicken, stiffen, take shape, congeal, crystallize, cake, coagulate.
5 *(v) The sun began to set.* go down, sink, drop below the horizon, disappear, vanish.
OPPOSITE: rise.
6 *(v) Can you set the video timer?* adjust, regulate, fix, programme, synchronize.
7 *(adj) We have our meals at set times.* fixed, established, agreed, definite, appointed, arranged, scheduled, regular.
OPPOSITES: flexible, varying.
8 *(adj) Aunt Bertha has set views.* fixed, definite, hard and fast, inflexible, unbending, firm, strict, entrenched, deep-seated, hidebound, narrow-minded.
OPPOSITES: flexible, open-minded.
9 *(adj) The story is set in India.* located, supposed to take place, situated, placed.
10 *(n) I'm collecting the whole set.* series, range, collection, group, batch, class, kit.
11 *(n) Tanya designed the set for our play. See* **scenery** 2.
12 *(n) Which set are you in for English? See* **class**.

setback
(n) Don't let this setback discourage you. hitch, difficulty, problem, snag, hiccup *(informal)*, complication, obstacle, disappointment, misfortune, blow, relapse.

set fire to *see* **light** 1.

set free *see* **release** 1.

set off
1 *(v) It's time to set off. See* **leave** 1.
2 *(v) Don't set off the fireworks.* let off, detonate, light, ignite, trigger off, explode.

set out
1 *(v) It's time to set out. See* **leave** 1.
2 *(v) Set out your work neatly.* lay out, present, arrange, organize, display, exhibit.
3 *(v) I didn't set out to cheat. See* **mean** 3.

setting
(n) Paris is the ideal setting for a romantic weekend. place, location, situation, venue, backdrop, scene, background, environment, surroundings *(plural)*.

settle
1 *(v) Do you plan to settle in Australia?* stay, set up home, make your home, put down roots, take up residence, become established, move to, emigrate to, live.
2 *(v) The moth may settle on your hand.* come to rest, stop, rest, stay, land, alight.
3 *(v) We need to settle this dispute.* sort out, resolve, clear up, put an end to, end, patch up, decide, deal with.
4 *(v) Wait for the dust to settle.* die down, subside, sink, clear.
5 **settle on** *(v) Let's settle on a date. See* **agree** 2.

settle down
1 *(v) Settle down and get on with your work.* calm down, quieten down, be quiet.
2 *(v) Settle down and enjoy the film.* sit down, relax, make yourself comfortable, snuggle down, curl up.

set up *see* **start** 5.

severe
1 *(adj) Aunt Bertha always looks so severe. See* **stern** 1.
2 *(adj) Jamie is recovering from a severe illness. See* **serious** 4.
3 *(adj) We should expect severe weather conditions.* bad, extreme, harsh, rough, violent, fierce, drastic, dangerous, freezing. OPPOSITES: mild, moderate.

sew
1 *(v) Can you teach me how to sew?* stitch, tack, embroider, do needlework, make clothes, do dressmaking.
2 **sew up** *(v) I need to sew up this hole in my shirt. See* **mend** 2.

sex
1 *(n) What sex is your kitten?* gender.
2 *(n) Should children be taught about sex at school?* the facts of life *(plural)*, sexual intercourse, sexuality, reproduction.
3 **have sex** *see* **make love**.

sexy
1 *(adj) (informal) Sam is really sexy.* desirable, sexually attractive, seductive, sultry, sensuous, voluptuous *(female)*, shapely, kissable, fit *(slang)*.
2 *(adj) (informal) Mum thinks my dress is too sexy.* slinky, seductive, titillating, provocative, revealing.
3 *(adj) (informal) This song has very sexy lyrics.* suggestive, raunchy *(slang)*, erotic, risqué, pornographic, obscene.

shabby
1 *(adj) Your jeans are looking shabby.* worn, faded, threadbare, tatty, scruffy, worn-out, frayed, ragged, tattered. OPPOSITES: smart, new.
2 *(adj) Ziggy lives in a shabby part of town. See* **scruffy** 3.

shade
1 *(n) Those trees will provide some shade.* shadow, shelter, protection, coolness.
2 *(n) That shade of green suits you.* colour, tone, hue, tint, tinge.

shadow
1 *(n) Emma sat in the shadow of a tree. See* **shade** 1.
2 *(n) I saw a shadow on the wall.* shape, silhouette, outline, figure, image.
3 **shadows** *(plural n) I saw a figure lurking in the shadows.* dark, darkness, gloom, dimness, blackness, dusk, semi-darkness.
4 *(v) The detectives decided to shadow Burglar Beryl. See* **follow** 1.

shadowy *see* **dim** 2.

shady
1 *(adj) We walked through a shady wood.* shadowy, shaded, dim, dark, cool, leafy, sunless, gloomy, sun-dappled. OPPOSITES: sunny, sunlit.
2 *(adj) (informal) Dodgy Dave is a shady character. See* **suspicious** 2.

shaggy
(adj) Shaggy hair. bushy, thick, tousled, tangled, unkempt, untidy, rough, woolly.

shake
1 *(v) The earthquake made the buildings shake.* vibrate, quake, shudder, judder *(informal)*, tremble, totter, sway, wobble, quiver, shiver, jiggle, joggle, convulse.
2 *(v) Shake the mixture.* shake up, stir up, churn up, agitate, swirl, jiggle, joggle.
3 *(v) Don't shake that stick at me.* brandish, flourish, wave, waggle, jiggle.

shaky
1 *(adj) Don't stand on that shaky chair.* wobbly, rickety, unsteady, rocky, flimsy, unsafe, unstable, tottery, teetering, weak. OPPOSITES: steady, firm.
2 *(adj) I answered the questions in a shaky voice.* faltering, tremulous, trembling, quavering, quivery, quivering, unsteady, wavering, wobbly, weak, nervous. OPPOSITES: steady, firm.
3 *(adj) I felt shaky when I got up this morning. See* **dizzy**.

shallow
(adj) Mrs Badger said my essay was too shallow. superficial, trivial, empty, flimsy, slight, lightweight, insubstantial, glib, frivolous, facile, unconvincing, skin-deep. OPPOSITES: thoughtful, thorough.

shame
1 *(n) Casper was filled with shame for what he had done.* remorse, self-reproach, guilt, guilty conscience, disgust, self-loathing, mortification, chagrin. OPPOSITE: pride.
2 *(n) I can't bear the shame of losing.* humiliation, disgrace, ignominy, degradation, indignity, embarrassment, dishonour, scandal, stigma, stain, infamy. OPPOSITES: honour, glory.
3 *(n) It's a shame that Dad is so strict.* pity, crying shame, hard luck, disgrace, outrage, scandal, tragedy, sin.
4 *(v) Your mum would never shame you in public. See* **humiliate**.

shameful *see* **humiliating**.

shape
1 *(n)* TYPES OF SHAPE: circle, cone, cube, cylinder, diamond, hexagon, oblong, octagon, oval, parallelogram, pentagon, prism, pyramid, rectangle, rhombus, sphere, square, trapezium, triangle.
2 *(n) Can you recognize the shape of France on a map?* outline, form, contours *(plural)*, profile, silhouette, lines *(plural)*.
3 *(n) The enchanter took on the shape of a serpent.* form, guise, likeness, look, semblance, aspect.
4 *(n) I try to keep in good shape. See* **condition** 1.
5 *(v) Can you shape a hippo out of clay? See* **model** 5.

shapeless
1 *(adj) A shapeless cloud.* nebulous, formless, vague, undefined, unformed, ill-defined, amorphous, indeterminate.
2 *(adj) A shapeless dress.* loose, baggy, sack-like, sloppy, unfitted, ill-fitting.

share
1 *(n) We all had a share of the profits.* portion, part, fraction, proportion, percentage, quota, ration, cut *(informal)*, helping, whack *(informal)*, piece, slice.
2 *(v) Share the sweets between you.* share out, divide, split, distribute, deal out, dole out, allocate, apportion, measure out, go halves, go fifty-fifty *(informal)*.

sharp
1 *(adj) Don't cut yourself on that sharp knife.* razor-sharp, pointed, keen-edged, serrated, sharpened, jagged, barbed. OPPOSITE: blunt.
2 *(adj) The rocks are sharp. See* **jagged** 2.
3 *(adj) I felt a sharp pain.* piercing, stabbing, shooting, violent, excruciating, agonizing, intense, severe, acute. OPPOSITE: dull.
4 *(adj) Aunt Bertha gave a sharp reply.* cutting, stinging, caustic, scathing, sarcastic, barbed, curt, tart, acid, acerbic. OPPOSITE: gentle.
5 *(adj) Lemons taste sharp. See* **sour** 1.
6 *(adj) We came to a sharp bend.* tight, sudden, abrupt, unexpected, hairpin. OPPOSITES: gentle, gradual.
7 *(adj) In front of us was a sharp drop. See* **steep** 1.
8 *(adj) Try to get a sharp picture on the TV. See* **clear** 5.

shatter *see* **smash** 2.

shattered
1 *(adj) Kim was shattered by the news.* devastated, stunned, dazed, crushed, heartbroken, destroyed, upset, shocked.
2 *(adj) (informal) I was shattered after the race. See* **exhausted**.

shed
(n) garden shed, tool shed, potting shed, woodshed, hut, shack, shelter, outhouse.

sheer
1 *(adj) That goal was sheer magic! See* **absolute**.

2 *(adj) In front of us was a sheer drop.* See **steep** 1.
3 *(adj) The bride wore a veil of sheer silk.* See **fine** 5.

sheet
1 *(n) Start each question on a new sheet.* piece of paper, page, side, leaf, folio.
2 *(n) A metal sheet covered the window.* panel, plate, piece, slab, pane *(glass)*.
3 *(n) A sheet of snow covered the ground.* See **layer** 1.

shelf
(n) Put the clock on that shelf. ledge, mantelpiece, windowsill, bracket.

shell
(n) Some seeds are protected by a hard shell. casing, covering, case, pod, husk, exterior, outside, outer layer.

shelter
1 *(v) The trees will shelter us from the rain.* protect, shield, screen, provide cover for, provide protection for, provide refuge for, safeguard.
2 *(v) Where can we shelter from the storm?* take cover, take shelter, take refuge, seek refuge, seek protection.
3 *(n) The refugees looked for shelter.* cover, protection, refuge, safety, asylum, sanctuary, safe haven.

sheltered
1 *(adj) Our garden is sheltered because of the trees.* protected, shielded, shaded, screened, secluded, snug, windless.
OPPOSITES: exposed, open.
2 *(adj) Mary had a sheltered childhood.* quiet, protected, cloistered, unadventurous, unexciting, secluded, isolated, reclusive.

shield see **protect** 1, 3.

shift
1 *(v) Shift your things into the spare room.* See **move** 2.
2 *(v) You'll need hot water to shift that stain.* See **remove** 2.

shimmer see **shine** 2.

shine
1 *(v) Light bulbs are supposed to shine.* give out light, shed light, emit light, be bright, be luminous.
2 *(v) I saw something shine in the sky.* gleam, glow, shimmer, glimmer, twinkle, sparkle, glint, glitter, glisten, blaze, flash, flicker, beam, glare.
3 *(v) Jo manages to shine at everything she does.* excel, do well, stand out, be brilliant, be expert, show talent, star.
4 *(n) Look at the shine on that table!* polish, sheen, gloss, gleam, sparkle, lustre, finish, patina.

shining
(adj) I saw a shining light in the sky. bright, brilliant, dazzling, blazing, radiant, luminous, glowing, beaming, gleaming, shimmering, sparkling, glittering, glistening, glaring, fluorescent.

shiny
1 *(adj) A shiny golden goblet.* gleaming, shining, sparkling, glistening, glittering, dazzling, bright, polished, burnished.
OPPOSITES: dull, matt.
2 *(adj) Shiny hair.* glossy, shining, gleaming, sleek, lustrous, silky, satiny.
OPPOSITE: dull.

ship see **boat**.

shiver
(v) Ghost stories make me shiver. shudder, shake, tremble, quiver, quake.

shock
1 *(v) This news may shock you.* stun, stagger, startle, take your breath away, amaze, astonish, astound, surprise, alarm, dismay, shake, shake you up *(informal)*, shatter, devastate, disturb, distress, traumatize, perturb, daze, numb, stupefy.
2 *(v) Rude jokes shock Aunt Bertha.* horrify, disgust, offend, scandalize, appal, outrage, revolt, sicken, nauseate.
3 *(n) You gave me a shock!* See **scare** 3.
4 *(n) The news came as a shock.* surprise, blow, bombshell, bolt from the blue, revelation, eye-opener *(informal)*.

shocking
1 *(adj) Have you heard the shocking news about Mrs Badger?* astonishing, surprising, startling, staggering, stunning, stupefying, unexpected, disturbing, perturbing, upsetting, disquieting, unsettling.
2 *(adj) Bozo's behaviour is shocking.* outrageous, disgusting, scandalous, appalling, disgraceful, offensive, revolting, repugnant, sickening, nauseating, atrocious, monstrous, indecent.
3 *(adj) There has been a shocking accident.* horrific, horrendous, horrifying, appalling, ghastly, harrowing, grisly, gruesome, terrible, dreadful, frightening.

shoddy
(adj) Mrs Badger criticized my shoddy work. second-rate, poor-quality, inferior, careless, messy, slapdash, sloppy *(informal)*, slovenly, slipshod, untidy, tatty.
OPPOSITES: careful, meticulous.

shoe
(n) footwear.
TYPES OF SHOE: ballet shoe, boot, bootee, brogue, clog, court shoe, deck shoe, dolly shoe, espadrille, flip-flop, gym shoe, high-heeled shoe, lace-up, loafer, moccasin, mule, patent shoe, peep-toe, platform shoe, plimsoll, pump, running shoe, sandal, slingback, slip-on, slipper, sneaker, stiletto, suede shoe, tennis shoe, trainer, winklepicker.

shoot
1 *(v) "Don't move or I'll shoot you!" Arnie said.* fire at, open fire on, gun you down, snipe at, blow your brains out, take a pot shot at, pump you full of lead *(slang)*, riddle you with bullets, zap *(slang)*, shell.
2 *(v) Shoot the arrows at the target.* fire, aim, launch, propel, let fly.
3 *(v) Watch the comet shoot through the sky.* fly, hurtle, streak, flash, speed, whiz *(informal)*, zoom, zip, tear, race, dash.
4 *(n) A shoot will grow.* bud, offshoot, tendril, sprout, new growth, stem, twig.

shop
(n) corner shop, supermarket, store, department store, superstore, megastore, hypermarket, boutique, market, cash-and-carry, emporium *(old-fashioned)*.

shore
(n) We walked along the shore. seashore, beach, coast, sand, sands *(plural)*, water's edge, waterside, waterfront, lakeside, seafront, foreshore, shingle, strand. ❖ Also see **sea & seashore**, **seaside words**.

short
1 *(adj) Dil is rather short.* small, squat, little, tiny, petite, diminutive, dumpy, stubby, stumpy, pint-sized *(informal)*.
OPPOSITE: tall.
2 *(adj) Write a short account of your trip.* brief, concise, succinct, pithy, compressed, to the point, abridged, abbreviated.
OPPOSITES: long, long-winded.
3 *(adj) We paid a short visit to Aunt Bertha.* brief, quick, fleeting, hurried, hasty, short-lived, cursory.
OPPOSITES: long, leisurely.
4 *(adj) Shall we go home the short way?* quick, direct, straight, obvious.
OPPOSITES: long, indirect.

shortage
(n) There's a noticeable shortage of books in our school. lack, scarcity, shortfall, absence, dearth, deficiency.
OPPOSITES: abundance, surplus.

shorts see **clothes**.

shot
1 *(n) Did you hear that shot?* gunshot, crack, bang, pop, report, explosion, blast.
2 *(n) That was a great shot!* hit, stroke, volley, lob, smash, throw, pass, kick, header, drive, putt, pot, pot shot.
3 *(n) (informal) Have a shot!* See **try** 1.

shout
(v) Please don't shout. yell, raise your voice, bawl, bellow, holler *(informal)*, scream, shriek, screech, roar, call out, cry out.

brogue   deck shoe   loafer   slingback   winklepicker
espadrille   mule   stiletto

shove

shove see **push** 1, 3, 4.

show
1 (v) Will this mark show? show up, be visible, be seen, stand out, be noticeable, catch the eye, attract attention.
2 (v) Todd tried not to show his true feelings. display, make obvious, make plain, make known, indicate, express, betray, reveal, expose, disclose, divulge.
3 (v) I want to show an alien in my painting. depict, portray, illustrate, represent, feature.
4 (v) Delia will show you how to make an omelette. See **demonstrate** 1.
5 (v) This letter will show that I am telling the truth. indicate, demonstrate, make clear, prove, establish, confirm, clarify.
6 (n) Enjoy the show! See **performance**.
7 (n) You'll see all kinds of cars at the show. exhibition, fair, expo (informal), display, demonstration, presentation.
8 (n) Nina put on a show of affection for Aunt Bertha. display, appearance, pretence, pose, affectation, illusion.

shower
1 (n) The sudden shower surprised us. downpour, cloudburst, deluge, rainfall.
2 (v) Be careful the elephants don't shower you with water! See **spray** 1.

show-off
(n) (informal) Jeremy is such a show-off. bighead (informal), boaster, poser (informal), exhibitionist, braggart.

show off
1 (v) Al is keen to show off his computer. flaunt, parade, display, demonstrate.
2 (v) (informal) Don't show off about all your prizes. See **boast**.

show up
1 (v) This orange shirt will certainly show up. be visible, stand out, be conspicuous, catch the eye, leap out at you.
2 (v) Bright light will show up my spots. accentuate, draw attention to, highlight, expose, reveal.
3 (v) (informal) Don't you hate it when your parents show you up! let you down, embarrass, humiliate, disgrace, shame, mortify, show you in a bad light.

shred
1 (n) The detectives found a shred of cloth. scrap, snippet, strip, bit, piece, fragment, ribbon, rag, tatter, wisp.
2 (n) There isn't a shred of evidence against Burglar Beryl. scrap, bit, jot, iota, trace, grain, speck, crumb, atom, particle.

shriek see **scream**.

shrill
(adj) A shrill sound. high-pitched, piercing, ear-piercing, ear-splitting, penetrating, strident, screeching, piping, sharp.

shrink
1 (v) This balloon is starting to shrink. grow smaller, deflate, contract, shrivel up.
OPPOSITES: expand, swell.

2 (v) Famous Fred's record sales may shrink. decrease, decline, dwindle, drop off, fall off, diminish, contract, reduce.
OPPOSITES: expand, increase.
3 (v) Don't shrink away from me. See **cower**.

shrivel
(v) The flowers will shrivel in the sun. wither, dry up, wilt, droop, dry out, dehydrate, shrink, wrinkle up, pucker up.

shudder see **shiver**.

shuffle
1 (v) Shuffle the cards. mix, mix up, jumble up, rearrange, reorganize.
2 (v) I hate the way you shuffle around in those shoes. shamble, drag your feet, paddle, pad, hobble, stumble, limp.

shut
1 (v) Shut the door. close, slam, lock, bolt, bar, secure, fasten, latch, pull to, push to.
OPPOSITE: open.
2 (v) Shut the curtains. close, draw, pull.
OPPOSITE: open.
3 (v) Why did the king shut the princes in the tower? lock, imprison, incarcerate, shut up, keep, confine, detain, enclose, coop up, wall up, cage, box.
4 (adj) Is the shop shut? closed, locked up, shut up, bolted and barred, closed down.
OPPOSITE: open.

shut down
(v) The car factory may have to shut down. close down, cease operating, cease production, cease trading (shop, business).

shut out see **exclude**.

shut up
(v) (informal) Shut up and listen! be quiet, stop talking, keep quiet, shush, hush, hold your tongue, put a sock in it (slang), belt up (slang), shut your trap (slang).

shy
(adj) Amy is too shy to come to the party. timid, diffident, reserved, retiring, mousy, bashful, self-conscious, inhibited, reticent, introverted, wary, coy.
OPPOSITES: self-assured, assertive.

sick
1 (adj) Kamilah can't come to school because she's sick. See **ill** 1.
2 (adj) I feel sick. nauseous, queasy, bilious, green around the gills (informal).
3 (adj) Bozo's behaviour makes me sick. disgusted, sickened, appalled, revolted, nauseated, upset, distressed, outraged, repelled, offended, horrified.
4 (adj) (informal) Harriet has a sick sense of humour. twisted, black, perverted, morbid, macabre, ghoulish, sadistic.
5 sick of (adj) (informal) I'm sick of staying at home. See **fed up with**.
6 be sick (v) I'm going to be sick! See **vomit**.

sickening
1 (adj) The smell from the drains was sickening. See **disgusting** 1.

2 (adj) The way Araminta sucks up to Mrs Badger is sickening. loathsome, disgusting, nauseating, distasteful, cringe-making (informal), repellent, repulsive, obnoxious, odious, objectionable, stomach-turning.

sickly
1 (adj) A sickly baby. See **delicate** 2.
2 (adj) A sickly dessert. sugary, syrupy, treacly, cloying, nauseating, saccharine.

side
1 (n) Paint one side of the box. face, surface, facet, flank, elevation (building).
2 (n) Stand at the side of the pool. edge, rim, brink, perimeter, periphery, boundary, verge (road), kerb (pavement).
3 (n) The side of the page was covered with notes. edge, margin, border.
4 (n) Start each question on a new side. See **page**.
5 (n) Which side won? team, group, faction, camp, party, army, sect, cause.
6 (n) Try to look at the problem from every side. angle, aspect, perspective, point of view, viewpoint, standpoint, position.
7 side with (v) Did you side with Dalal in the argument? agree with, support, back, take the part of, go along with, team up with, ally with, champion, second.

sieve
1 (v) Sieve the mixture. strain, sift, filter, separate, pan (gold).
2 (n) Pass me the sieve. strainer, colander.

sigh
1 (v) Did I hear you sigh? exhale, let out your breath, moan, groan.
2 (v) The wind began to sigh through the branches. whisper, rustle, moan.

sight
1 (n) I'm worried about Matty's sight. eyesight, vision, eyes (plural), short-sightedness, long-sightedness.
2 (n) We watched the balloon until it was out of sight. view, range, eyeshot, range of vision, field of vision.
3 (n) What a beautiful sight! scene, vision, spectacle, picture, image, view, vista, panorama, display, prospect, outlook.
4 (n) (informal) You look a sight! fright (informal), mess (informal), wreck, eyesore.

sign
1 (n) Is there any sign that Burglar Beryl has been here? indication, hint, suggestion, clue, evidence, proof, pointer, trace, vestige, giveaway, telltale sign.
2 (n) Did you read the sign? notice, poster, placard, board, signpost.
3 (n) Let's design a secret sign for our gang. symbol, badge, emblem, identification mark, logo, insignia.
4 (n) Give me a sign when it's time to begin. signal, indication, tip-off, cue, message, hint, reminder, warning, wave, nod, wink, gesture, go-ahead (informal).
5 (n) Arthur knew the pile of bones was a sign. warning, omen, portent, forewarning, message, token, pointer.

6 (v) Please sign this postcard. write your name on, autograph, initial, inscribe, put your name to, put your mark on.

signal
1 (n) Give me a signal when it's time to begin. See **sign** 4.
2 (v) I'll signal to you when it's safe. indicate, make a sign, gesture, sign, motion, wave, nod, beckon, gesticulate.

significant see **important** 1.

silence
1 (n) I love the silence of evening. quietness, stillness, calm, tranquillity, peacefulness, peace, quiet, hush.
OPPOSITE: noise.
2 (n) Sarah's silence puzzled us. lack of speech, dumbness, muteness, reticence, uncommunicativeness.
3 (v) How can we silence the sound of Paula's trumpet? quieten, muffle, stifle, smother, deaden, suppress, subdue.

silent
1 (adj) Ravi approached with silent steps. soundless, noiseless, inaudible, muffled.
OPPOSITES: noisy, loud.
2 (adj) The shock made me silent for a while. speechless, tongue-tied, dumbstruck, unable to get a word out, mute, dumb, mum
3 (adj) Edward is a rather silent member of the class. See **quiet** 3.
4 (adj) Everything was silent before the storm. See **still** 3.
5 (adj) We watched with silent approval. unspoken, unvoiced, unexpressed, wordless, tacit, implied, implicit.

silhouette see **outline** 3.

silky
(adj) I stroked the horse's silky coat. sleek, smooth, velvety, satiny, shiny, glossy, soft.
OPPOSITES: rough, matted.

silly
1 (adj) What a silly idea! stupid, foolish, daft (informal), idiotic, crazy, absurd, ridiculous, preposterous, ludicrous, senseless, nonsensical, brainless, irrational, illogical, misguided, half-baked (informal), inane, harebrained, foolhardy, reckless.
OPPOSITES: sensible, clever.
2 (adj) Daisy can be so silly. idiotic, brainless, daft (informal), foolish, stupid, senseless, dotty (slang), dippy (slang), dopey (slang), goofy (informal), immature, childish, infantile, puerile, irresponsible, featherbrained, giddy, flighty, frivolous.
OPPOSITES: sensible, mature.

silver
(adj) A silver moon. silvery, pearly, ivory.

similar
(adj) Our answers are similar. alike, comparable, much the same, close, in agreement, corresponding, matching.
OPPOSITES: different, dissimilar.

simple
1 (adj) The test was simple! See **easy** 1.

2 (adj) The instructions are written in simple language. clear, straightforward, uncomplicated, plain, intelligible, understandable, comprehensible, easy to follow, foolproof, uninvolved
OPPOSITES: complicated, complex.
3 (adj) The peasants lived in a simple cottage. modest, ordinary, humble, plain, basic, unpretentious, undecorated, austere, stark, Spartan, poor, lowly, rustic.
OPPOSITES: grand, fancy.
4 (adj) I like simple meals. See **plain** 2.
5 (adj) Give me the simple truth. plain, honest, naked, stark, bald, basic, unvarnished, unembellished, unadorned.

sincere
1 (adj) Peter's sympathy seems to be sincere. genuine, real, wholehearted, heartfelt, in earnest, unfeigned, bona fide.
OPPOSITES: insincere, feigned.
2 (adj) Mr Badger is a sincere person. truthful, honest, frank, candid, open, straightforward, genuine, artless, guileless, upfront (informal), plain-dealing.
OPPOSITES: insincere, deceitful.

sing
1 (v) Dad likes to sing in the shower. warble, croon, carol, yodel, chant, serenade, hum, whistle.
2 (v) The nightingale began to sing. trill, warble, twitter, chirrup, cheep, chirp, whistle, pipe, peep, squawk.

singer
(n) vocalist, songster, songstress.
TYPES OF SINGER: alto, backing singer, baritone, bass, choirboy, choirgirl, chorister, contralto, countertenor, crooner, folk singer, jazz singer, lead singer, mezzo-soprano, opera singer, pop singer, prima donna (leading female opera singer), rapper, rock singer, soloist, soprano, tenor, treble, troubadour (old-fashioned).

single
1 (adj) Do you have single rooms? individual, separate, personal, unshared.
OPPOSITES: shared, double.
2 (adj) A single tree stood on the hill. lone, solitary, isolated, unique, individual, unaccompanied, on its own, solo.
3 (adj) Do you think you'll stay single? unattached, unmarried, celibate, on your own, unwed, partnerless, not tied down, free, fancy-free, footloose.
OPPOSITES: attached, married.

sinister
(adj) The shadows looked sinister. threatening, menacing, ominous, forbidding, frightening, disturbing, spooky (informal), malevolent, evil, malign.

sink
1 (v) The ship is going to sink! go down, go under, founder, submerge, go to the bottom, go to Davy Jones's locker, drown.
OPPOSITE: float.
2 (v) The plane began to sink. See **drop** 2.
3 (v) We watched the sun sink. See **set** 5.

4 (v) Oliver tried to sink his toy boat. submerge, scupper, scuttle, capsize, drown, swamp, flood, immerse, engulf, dunk, duck, torpedo.
5 (v) How could you sink to that level of meanness? lower yourself, stoop, be reduced, debase yourself, succumb, yield.
OPPOSITES: aspire, rise.
6 (n) Fill the sink. washbasin, basin.

sit
(v) You can sit here. sit down, be seated, seat yourself, take a seat, settle down, perch, squat, rest, take the weight off your feet, loll, sprawl, flop, collapse.

situation see **position** 2.

sketch
1 (v) Why don't you sketch your cat? See **draw** 1.
2 (n) We admired Meg's sketch. drawing, picture, study, design, outline, diagram, plan, representation, rough drawing.

skid
(v) The car began to skid. slide, slip, spin, go into a skid, go into a spin, go out of control, sideslip, veer, glide, aquaplane.

skilful
(adj) Ryan is a skilful footballer. skilled, accomplished, talented, expert, capable, proficient, deft, versatile, ace (informal).
OPPOSITES: inept, incompetent.

skill
(n) We admired the potter's skill. expertise, technique, prowess, talent, ability, artistry, craftsmanship, workmanship, art, craft, deftness, dexterity, versatility, finesse.

skim
1 (v) Watch me skim over the ice! glide, slide, skate, sail, fly, float, coast.
2 (v) See how the dragonflies skim the surface of the pond. brush, graze, touch.
3 skim through (v) Skim through this booklet. glance through, look through, run your eye over, leaf through, scan, flip through, skip through, thumb through.

skin
1 (n) With your fair skin you should avoid the sun. complexion, colouring, skin tone.
2 (n) This fruit has a tough skin. rind, peel, outer layer, exterior, surface, casing, covering, shell, husk, pod.
3 (n) Is this jacket made from an animal's skin? hide, pelt, coat, fleece, fur.
4 (n) I hate custard with a skin on top. film, coating, layer, crust, scum.

skinny see **thin** 1

skip
1 (v) I love to see the children skip around the garden! prance, dance, bounce, frolic, gambol, cavort, bound, jump, leap, hop.
2 (v) Let's skip this page. See **miss out** 1.
3 (v) (informal) You mustn't skip school. miss, play truant from, dodge, skive off (informal), bunk off (slang), cut (informal), play hooky from (informal).

skirt see **clothes**.

skulk

skulk *see* **lurk**.

sky
(n) My balloon floated up into the sky. air, atmosphere, skies *(plural)*, space, heavens *(plural)*, stratosphere, blue, firmament.

slab *see* **block** 1.

slag off *(slang) see* **criticize** 1.

slant
1 *(v) That chimney seems to slant to one side. See* **lean** 1.
2 *(n) Look at the slant of that table top! See* **slope** 1.
3 *(n) Veena gave the story a new slant.* angle, emphasis, twist, perspective, bias.

slap
1 *(v) Don't slap Caroline! See* **smack**.
2 *(v) Sam started to slap paint on the walls.* slop, splash, slosh *(informal)*, daub, dollop *(informal)*, plaster, spread.

slapdash *see* **careless** 1.

slash
1 *(v) The vandals began to slash the furniture.* cut, slit, gash, rip, tear, lacerate, score, knife, hack at.
2 *(v) Supermarkets may slash their prices. See* **reduce** 1.

slaughter
1 *(n) The slaughter must be stopped. See* **killing** 2.
2 *(v) The farmers had to slaughter their sick cattle. See* **kill** 2.
3 *(v) (informal) We'll slaughter the other team. See* **beat** 2.

sleazy
(adj) The street was full of sleazy bars. sordid, seedy, disreputable, squalid, run-down, tacky *(informal)*, crummy *(slang)*.
OPPOSITES: respectable, up-market.

sleek *see* **silky**.

sleep
1 *(v) You can sleep at my house.* spend the night, stay, sleep over, kip *(slang)*, doss down *(slang)*, crash out *(slang)*.
2 *(v) Aunt Bertha likes to sleep after lunch.* doze, take a nap, snooze *(informal)*, catnap, drowse, have forty winks *(informal)*, get some shuteye *(informal)*, drop off *(informal)*, nod off *(informal)*, rest.
3 *(n) Granny is having a sleep.* nap, rest, siesta, snooze *(informal)*, doze, catnap, lie-down, forty winks *(plural) (informal)*, kip *(slang)*, shuteye *(informal)*, zizz *(informal)*.

sleeping *see* **asleep**.

sleepy
1 *(adj) Do you feel sleepy?* tired, drowsy, half-asleep, weary, exhausted, unable to keep your eyes open, lethargic, sluggish, dozy, dopey *(informal)*, ready for bed.
OPPOSITES: wide-awake, alert.
2 *(adj) Nothing ever happens in this sleepy town.* quiet, peaceful, dozy, unexciting, boring, dull, dreary, dead.
OPPOSITES: lively, bustling.

slender *see* **slim** 1, 2.

slice
1 *(n) Have a slice of cake.* piece, segment, slab, wedge, sliver, doorstep *(informal)*, chunk, portion, helping, wodge *(informal)*.
2 *(v) Will you slice the pineapple?* cut up, divide, carve, segment, dissect.

slide
(v) Felix began to slide across the ice. slip, slither, skid, glide, skate, skim, sideslip, veer, toboggan, ski.

slight
(adj) There's been a slight improvement in your work. small, minor, modest, negligible, imperceptible, insignificant, trivial, tiny, trifling, measly *(informal)*.
OPPOSITES: great, considerable.

slim
1 *(adj) Natasha has a slim figure.* slender, trim, slight, lean, thin, willowy, sylphlike, svelte, graceful.
OPPOSITES: chubby, fat.
2 *(adj) There's a slim chance that we might survive.* slight, small, slender, faint, remote, outside.

slimy
1 *(adj) We squelched through a slimy swamp.* slippery, sludgy, oozy, gooey *(informal)*, sticky, muddy, mucky.
2 *(adj) Flash Frank is a slimy character.* smooth, smarmy *(informal)*, oily, greasy, obsequious, ingratiating, grovelling, fawning, toadying, sycophantic, unctuous.

sling *see* **throw** 1.

slink
(v) The thieves tried to slink through the bushes. creep, sneak, steal, slip, sidle, prowl, skulk, tiptoe, pussyfoot *(informal)*.

slinky
(adj) Naomi wore a slinky black dress. clinging, figure-hugging, skintight, close-fitting, sleek, sexy *(informal)*.

slip
1 *(v) It's easy to slip if the pavement is icy.* skid, lose your balance, lose your footing, fall, trip, slide, slither, glide, skate.
2 *(v) Try to slip out of the house unnoticed. See* **creep** 2.
3 *(n) I made a slip in my calculations. See* **mistake** 1.
4 *(n) Write your phone number on this slip of paper.* scrap, piece, bit, strip, snippet.
5 *(n) Your slip is showing.* petticoat, underskirt.

slippery
1 *(adj) The path is slippery.* icy, greasy, oily, slimy, slithery, slippy *(informal)*, skiddy *(informal)*, glassy, treacherous.
2 *(adj) Dodgy Dave is a slippery character. See* **deceitful**.

slip up *(informal) see* **go wrong** 1.

slit
1 *(n) Jamie has a slit in his trousers.* cut, split, slash, tear, rip, gash.
2 *(n) I peeped through a slit in the rock. See* **crack** 2.

slither
(v) Watch the snake slither over the sand! slide, glide, slip, wriggle, squirm, skitter, slink, writhe, twist, snake, worm, creep.

slobber
(v) Look at Fido slobber over his bone. drool, slaver, dribble, salivate.

slope
1 *(n) Look at the slope of that roof!* slant, angle, tilt, rake, pitch, skew, incline, gradient, camber *(road)*.
2 *(n) Our house is built on a slope.* hill, hillside, bank, rise, incline, ramp.
3 *(v) The path began to slope steeply.* rise, fall, drop, descend, ascend, incline, shelve.
4 *(v) That chimney seems to slope to one side. See* **lean** 1.

sloppy
1 *(adj) A sloppy trifle.* runny, slushy, watery, soggy, squidgy, oozy, liquid.
OPPOSITES: firm, solid.
2 *(adj) (informal) Sloppy work. See* **careless** 1.
3 *(adj) A sloppy jumper. See* **loose** 1.

slot
(n) Insert a knife in the slot. slit, crack, opening, hole, groove, notch, channel.

slouch
(v) Sit up and don't slouch! slump, stoop, droop, hunch, loll, lounge, sprawl, sag.

slow
1 *(adj) Tortoises move at a slow pace.* unhurried, steady, plodding, sluggish, ponderous, snail-like, dawdling, crawling, leisurely, easy, lazy, measured, deliberate.
OPPOSITES: fast, quick.
2 *(adj) Aunt Bertha's recovery was slow.* gradual, long drawn out, protracted, prolonged, lingering, interminable.
OPPOSITES: fast, rapid.
3 *(adj) Rory was slow in handing in his project.* late, delayed, unpunctual, tardy, behind, dilatory.
OPPOSITE: prompt.
4 *(adj) This film is so slow!* slow-moving, uneventful, tedious, monotonous, dull, boring, tiresome, wearisome.
OPPOSITES: fast-moving, action-packed.

slow down
1 *(v) Slow down; you're going too fast!* reduce your speed, slacken your speed, decelerate, put the brakes on, brake.
OPPOSITES: speed up, accelerate.
2 *(v) Don't slow me down. See* **delay** 2.

sly
(adj) That was a sly trick you played. crafty, sneaky, cunning, wily, artful, devious, deceitful, underhand, stealthy, furtive, insidious, scheming, clever, smart, shrewd.
OPPOSITES: straightforward, honest.

smack
(v) Should parents smack their children? slap, hit, strike, whack, spank, wallop *(informal)*, belt *(slang)*, thump, cuff, clout *(informal)*, biff *(slang)*, beat.

small				
a small person	**a small child**	**a small helping of pudding**	**a small space**	**a small mistake**
dainty	little	inadequate	confined	insignificant
diminutive	teeny	insubstantial	cramped	minor
elfin	tiny	meagre	limited	negligible
Lilliputian	wee	mean	narrow	slight
little	young	measly	poky	trifling
petite		measly *(informal)*	restricted	trivial
pint-sized *(informal)*	**a small radio**	mingy *(informal)*		unimportant
puny	compact	moderate	**a small speck**	**Don't make me feel small!**
short	dinky *(informal)*	modest	infinitesimal	foolish
slender	mini	scanty	microscopic	humiliated
slight	miniature	skimpy	minuscule	ridiculous
squat	pocket-sized	stingy	minute	sheepish
tiny	tiny	tiny	teeny	silly
titchy *(slang)*	toy	titchy *(slang)*	teeny-weeny	stupid
undersized			tiny	

smart
1 *(adj)* Ellie always looks smart. elegant, stylish, chic, well-dressed, well-groomed, presentable, spruce, neat, tidy, dashing, dapper, natty *(informal)*, snazzy *(informal)*.
OPPOSITES: scruffy, dowdy.
2 *(adj)* That was a smart move. clever, intelligent, shrewd, crafty, astute, quick witted, bright, ingenious, wise, sensible.
OPPOSITES: stupid, idiotic.
3 *(adj)* Oliver loves to make smart remarks. clever, witty, facetious, impertinent, cheeky, saucy, smart alecky *(informal)*, clever-clever *(informal)*, clever-Dick *(informal)*, droll, waggish.
4 *(v)* If you get soap in your eyes it will smart. See **sting**.

smash
1 *(n)* Was anyone injured in the smash? See **crash** 2.
2 *(v)* If you drop that bowl it will smash. shatter, splinter, smash to smithereens, break, break into pieces, crack, split, fracture, disintegrate.
3 smash into *(v)* Try not to smash into that tree. See **hit** 4.

smear
1 *(v)* Don't smear paint on the walls! spread, daub, plaster, smudge, wipe, rub.
2 *(n)* You've got a smear of paint on your nose. streak, smudge, splodge, blotch, splotch, daub, spot, mark.

smell
1 *(n)* What a wonderful smell! fragrance, scent, perfume, aroma, bouquet, odour.
2 *(n)* What a horrible smell! stink, stench, pong *(informal)*, odour, whiff, reek.
3 *(v)* Your feet smell! See **stink** 1.
4 *(v)* A fox can smell chickens from miles away. scent, sniff out, nose out, sense, detect, track down, get wind of *(informal)*.
5 *(v)* Smell that lovely aroma! inhale, breathe in, take in, sniff, get a whiff of.

smelly
(adj) Throw away that smelly cheese. stinking, reeking, pongy *(informal)*, whiffy *(slang)*, stinky *(informal)*, pungent, strong-smelling, foul-smelling, evil-smelling, malodorous, high, putrid, fetid.
OPPOSITES: sweet smelling, fragrant.

smile
1 *(v)* Smile for the camera! grin, beam, look happy, smirk, simper, say cheese.
2 *(n)* The witch gave a horrible smile. grin, smirk, leer, grimace, sneer.

smoke
1 *(v)* Please don't smoke. light up, chain-smoke, puff away, have a drag *(informal)*, have a fag *(slang)*, inhale.
2 *(v)* The fire started to smoke. smoulder, give off smoke, emit smoke, billow.
3 *(n)* The air was filled with smoke. clouds of smoke *(plural)*, exhaust fumes *(plural)*, pollution, smog, haze.

smooth
1 *(adj)* You need a smooth lawn for bowls. level, flat, even, horizontal, flush.
OPPOSITES: bumpy, uneven.
2 *(adj)* Clare has smooth skin. soft, velvety, silky, downy, flawless, unlined, unwrinkled.
OPPOSITES: rough, coarse.
3 *(adj)* This table has a smooth surface. polished, shiny, glossy, satiny, sleek, even.
OPPOSITES: rough, bumpy.
4 *(adj)* Nothing disturbed the smooth surface of the lake. calm, still, unruffled, glassy, mirror-like, tranquil, placid, flat.
OPPOSITES: choppy, rough.
5 *(adj)* You'll love the smooth taste of this sauce. mild, mellow, creamy, velvety, pleasant, agreeable, bland.
6 *(adj)* I hope you have a smooth journey. easy, comfortable, straightforward, effortless, peaceful, uneventful, uninterrupted, trouble-free, stress-free.
OPPOSITES: difficult, stressful.

7 *(adj)* Ballet dancers should have smooth movements. easy, effortless, flowing, fluid, graceful, steady, rhythmic, regular.
OPPOSITES: jerky, erratic.
8 *(adj)* Flash Frank has a smooth manner. suave, polished, glib, charming, persuasive, flattering, ingratiating, sophisticated, urbane, slick, smarmy *(informal)*, slimy.
OPPOSITES: rough, abrasive.
9 *(v)* Smooth the sheets before you fold them. smooth out, flatten, iron, press.
OPPOSITES: crumple, crease.
10 *(v)* I must smooth the edges of this box. file, sand, plane, even, level off.

smother
1 *(v)* Don't smother me with that pillow! suffocate, stifle, asphyxiate, choke.
2 *(v)* Try to smother your giggles. stifle, suppress, hold back, keep in, muffle, hide.
3 *(v)* Let's smother the cake with cream. cover, plaster, heap, pile, envelop, drown, swamp, engulf, surround, blanket.

smudge
1 *(n)* There's a smudge on the front of this book. smear, streak, dirty mark, blotch, splotch, blot, spot, stain, smut.
2 *(v)* Try not to smudge the glass. smear, streak, blur, dirty, mark, blotch, stain

smug
(adj) Don't look so smug when you get the answer right. self-satisfied, pleased with yourself, complacent, superior, conceited, self-righteous, holier-than-thou, priggish.

snake
1 *(n)* I saw a snake in the grass. serpent.
TYPES OF SNAKE: adder, boa constrictor, cobra, grass snake, python, rattlesnake, sea snake, sidewinder, tree snake, viper.
2 *(v)* The path began to snake up the mountain. See **wind** 2.

snap
1 *(v)* I hope this rope doesn't snap! break, break in two, give way, split, come apart.
2 *(v)* Can you hear the twigs snap under your feet? crack, crackle, pop, crunch.
3 snap at *(v)* Did the dog snap at you? bite, nip, go for, have a go at *(informal)*, snarl at, yap at, bark at, growl at.

snarl
1 *(v)* Don't snarl, Fido! growl, show your teeth, bare your teeth.
2 *(n)* "Clear off!" the man said with a snarl. growl, scowl, sneer, grimace.

snatch
(v) A thief tried to snatch my bag. grab, seize, take, wrench away, make off with, run off with, steal, nick *(slang)*, nab *(informal)*, swipe *(slang)*.

sneak
1 *(v)* Try to sneak past the guard. See **creep** 2.
2 *(v)* I tried to sneak the kitten into my bedroom. smuggle, slip, spirit.
3 sneak on *(v)* *(informal)* Will your sister sneak on us? See **tell on**.

sneaky see **sly**.

sneer
1 (n) "It's your own fault," said Edwin with a sneer. smirk, snigger, curl of the lip.
2 **sneer at** (v) Don't sneer at my efforts. See **scorn** 1.

sniff
(v) Don't sniff! sniffle, snuffle, snort, snivel.

snigger see **giggle**.

snobbish
(adj) Araminta is so snobbish; she looks down on everyone. condescending, snooty (informal), stuck-up (informal), superior, haughty, arrogant, disdainful, patronizing, hoity-toity (informal), toffee-nosed (slang).

snooze (informal) see **sleep** 2, 3.

snub
(v) Did Araminta snub you at the party? ignore, cut, cut you dead (informal), give you the cold shoulder, give you the brush-off (slang), put you down, humiliate, slight.

snug see **cosy**.

snuggle
(v) Watch the piglets snuggle against their mother. cuddle, nestle, nuzzle, curl up.

soak
1 (v) Soak the fruit in the liquid. immerse, steep, saturate, marinate, submerge, wet.
2 (v) This rain will soak my shoes. saturate, drench, seep through, penetrate.
3 **soak up** (v) This cloth will soak up the water. absorb, mop up, take in, take up.

soaking
(adj) My shoes are soaking. wet through, sopping wet, dripping wet, wringing wet, sodden, saturated, drenched, dripping, soggy, waterlogged (ground).
OPPOSITES: dry, bone-dry (informal).

soar see **rise** 1, 2, 3.

sob see **cry** 1.

sofa
(n) settee, couch, sofa bed, divan, chaise longue, futon, ottoman.

soft
1 (adj) Clare's skin is so soft. smooth, delicate, tender, silky, velvety, downy.
OPPOSITES: rough, tough.
2 (adj) The baby animals felt soft. fluffy, furry, fleecy, silky, downy, feathery, velvety, satiny, sleek, smooth.
OPPOSITES: rough, coarse.
3 (adj) This sofa is really soft. comfortable, well-padded, well-cushioned, squashy, bouncy, springy, yielding.
OPPOSITES: hard, uncomfortable.
4 (adj) Uri rubbed the spoon until it was soft. bendy, pliable, flexible, supple, malleable, bendable, limp, floppy.
OPPOSITES: hard, rigid.
5 (adj) This biscuit is soft. See **soggy** 2.
6 (adj) Be careful! The ground is soft. spongy, soggy, boggy, swampy, marshy, waterlogged, muddy, crumbly, yielding.
OPPOSITES: hard, firm.

7 (adj) Mum spoke in a soft voice. quiet, low, gentle, soothing, hushed, faint, scarcely audible, whispered, murmured.
OPPOSITES: loud, harsh.
8 (adj) The room was bathed in a soft light. gentle, dim, subdued, faint, low, pale, subtle, muted, restful, diffuse.
OPPOSITES: harsh, glaring.

soggy
1 (adj) The rain has made my shoes soggy. See **soaking**.
2 (adj) These biscuits are soggy. soft, mushy, spongy, squashy, pulpy, doughy.
OPPOSITES: crisp, crunchy.

soil see **earth** 2.

soldier
(n) fighter, trooper, serviceman, warrior (old-fashioned), marine, paratrooper, commando, guardsman, sentry, gunner, rifleman, cavalryman, infantryman, mercenary, conscript.

solemn
1 (adj) Sara looks solemn. See **serious** 1.
2 (adj) The coronation was a solemn occasion. stately, ceremonial, formal, grand, dignified, majestic, imposing, awe-inspiring, momentous, impressive.
OPPOSITES: frivolous, informal.

solid
1 (adj) Cement becomes solid when it sets. hard, firm, rigid, set, unyielding, thick, dense, compact.
OPPOSITES: liquid, powdery.
2 (adj) The castle walls are solid. thick, strong, sturdy, firm, substantial, stout, sound, unshakable, well-built, well-made.
OPPOSITES: flimsy, shaky.
3 (adj) My ring is solid silver. pure, real, genuine, unalloyed, unadulterated.
4 (adj) The traffic formed a solid line. continuous, unbroken, uninterrupted.

solve
(v) Can you solve this mystery? work out, figure out (informal), unravel, clear up, decipher, get to the bottom of, find the answer to, resolve, crack, find the key to, find the solution to, suss out (slang).

song
(n) Listen to this song. tune, ditty, air, melody, number, chorus.
TYPES OF SONG: anthem, aria, ballad, calypso, canon, carol, chant, folk song, hymn, jingle, love song, lullaby, madrigal, nursery rhyme, pop song, psalm, round, sea shanty, serenade, spiritual. ❖ Also see **music words** and **pop**, **rock & jazz**.

soothing
(adj) Let's listen to some soothing music. restful, relaxing, peaceful, calming, gentle.

sophisticated
(adj) Eva has become quite sophisticated since she went to Paris. stylish, poised, cultured, cultivated, urbane, refined, cosmopolitan, worldly, worldly-wise, blasé.
OPPOSITES: unsophisticated, naive.

soppy (informal) see **sentimental** 2.

sore
(adj) My knee is sore where I scraped it. painful, tender, raw, hurting, smarting, stinging, throbbing, aching, bruised, burning, inflamed, chafed, irritated.

sorrow
(n) Demi's sorrow was unbearable. sadness, grief, misery, anguish, despair, distress, unhappiness, heartache, heartbreak, wretchedness, woe, melancholy, gloom, despondency.
OPPOSITES: happiness, joy.

sorry
1 (adj) I hope you're sorry about breaking that window! repentant, remorseful, regretful, conscience-stricken, penitent, contrite, apologetic, ashamed, guilt-ridden.
OPPOSITES: unrepentant, unapologetic.
2 (adj) I was sorry when I heard that your cat had died. sad, upset, distressed, unhappy, miserable, sorrowful, grieved, concerned, disconsolate, crestfallen.
OPPOSITES: unconcerned, unmoved.
3 **feel sorry for** (phrase) You should feel sorry for the losing team. feel for, feel pity for, feel compassion for, sympathize with, commiserate with, condole with.

sort
1 (n) What sort of bread shall I buy? See **kind** 2.
2 (n) What sort of dog is that? See **kind** 3.
3 (v) Sort your books according to subject. organize, group, put in order, order, arrange, file, separate, divide, subdivide, classify, categorize, grade, rank, catalogue.

sound
1 (n) Can you hear a sound? noise.
2 (adj) Are these old floorboards sound? solid, sturdy, strong, substantial, intact, whole, undamaged, in good condition.
OPPOSITES: flimsy, weak.
3 (adj) Nadia gave me some sound advice. See **sensible** 2.

sour
1 (adj) Lemons taste sour. sharp, tangy, acid, tart, bitter, vinegary, piquant, unripe.
OPPOSITE: sweet.
2 (adj) This milk is sour. curdled, rancid, off, turned, bad, spoiled, fermented.
OPPOSITE: fresh.

space
1 (n) How can we fill this space? gap, hole, opening, blank, blank space, interval, area, expanse, stretch, vacuum.
2 (n) We need more space for our activities. room, scope, capacity, freedom, elbow room, room to manoeuvre, leeway.
3 (n) Vijay stared into space. infinity, emptiness, nothingness, the distance, thin air, the void, the blue.
4 (n) I'm reading a book about space. the universe, outer space, interplanetary space, interstellar space, intergalactic space, the galaxy, the solar system, the stars (plural), the planets (plural), astronomy.

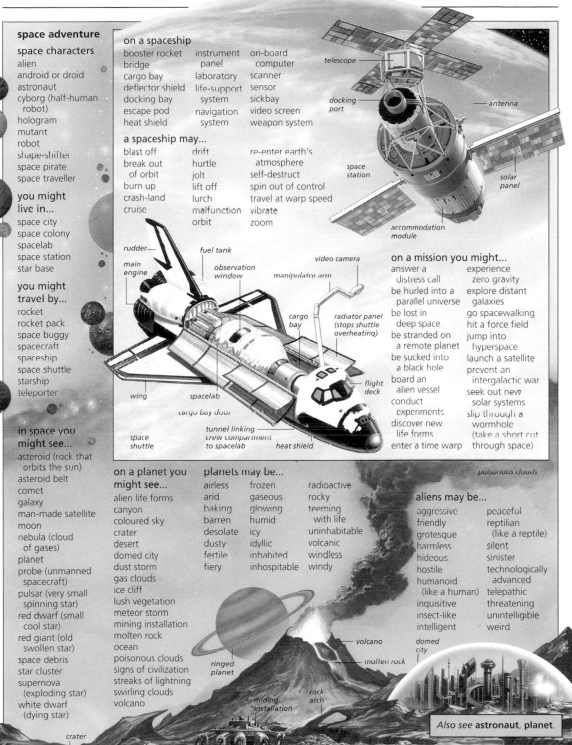

space adventure

space characters
alien
android or droid
astronaut
cyborg (half-human
  robot)
hologram
mutant
robot
shape-shifter
space pirate
space traveller

you might
live in...
space city
space colony
spacelab
space station
star base

you might
travel by...
rocket
rocket pack
space buggy
spacecraft
spaceship
space shuttle
starship
teleporter

in space you
might see...
asteroid (rock that
  orbits the sun)
asteroid belt
comet
galaxy
man-made satellite
moon
nebula (cloud
  of gases)
planet
probe (unmanned
  spacecraft)
pulsar (very small
  spinning star)
red dwarf (small
  cool star)
red giant (old
  swollen star)
space debris
star cluster
supernova
  (exploding star)
white dwarf
  (dying star)

on a spaceship
booster rocket
bridge
cargo bay
deflector shield
docking bay
escape pod
heat shield
instrument
  panel
laboratory
life-support
  system
navigation
  system
on-board
  computer
scanner
sensor
sickbay
video screen
weapon system

a spaceship may...
blast off
break out
  of orbit
burn up
crash-land
cruise
drift
hurtle
jolt
lift off
lurch
malfunction
orbit
re-enter earth's
  atmosphere
self-destruct
spin out of control
travel at warp speed
vibrate
zoom

telescope

docking
port

antenna

space
station

solar
panel

accommodation
module

rudder
fuel tank
main
engine
observation
window
video camera
manipulator arm
cargo
bay
radiator panel
(stops shuttle
overheating)
wing
spacelab
flight
deck
cargo bay door
tunnel linking
crew compartment
to spacelab
space
shuttle
heat shield

on a mission you might...
answer a
  distress call
be hurled into a
  parallel universe
be lost in
  deep space
be stranded on
  a remote planet
be sucked into
  a black hole
board an
  alien vessel
conduct
  experiments
discover new
  life forms
enter a time warp
experience
  zero gravity
explore distant
  galaxies
go spacewalking
hit a force field
jump into
  hyperspace
launch a satellite
prevent an
  intergalactic war
seek out new
  solar systems
slip through a
  wormhole
(take a short cut
  through space)

on a planet you
might see...
alien life forms
canyon
coloured sky
crater
desert
domed city
dust storm
gas clouds
ice cliff
lush vegetation
meteor storm
mining installation
molten rock
ocean
poisonous clouds
signs of civilization
streaks of lightning
swirling clouds
volcano

planets may be...
airless
arid
baking
barren
desolate
dusty
fertile
fiery
frozen
gaseous
glowing
humid
icy
idyllic
inhabited
inhospitable
radioactive
rocky
teeming
  with life
uninhabitable
volcanic
windless
windy

poisonous clouds

aliens may be...
aggressive
friendly
grotesque
harmless
hideous
hostile
humanoid
  (like a human)
inquisitive
insect-like
intelligent
peaceful
reptilian
  (like a reptile)
silent
sinister
technologically
  advanced
telepathic
threatening
unintelligible
weird

volcano
domed
city
molten rock
ringed
planet
mining
installation
rock
arch
crater

Also see **astronaut, planet.**

spank

spank see **smack**.

spare
1 *(adj) Take some spare socks.* extra, additional, supplementary, reserve.
2 *(adj) Is that sandwich spare?* left over, going begging, unwanted, unneeded, superfluous, surplus to requirements.
3 *(adj) In my spare time I play tennis.* free, leisure, unoccupied, remaining, available.
4 *(v) I can spare a few pounds for a good cause.* afford, part with, donate, give up, sacrifice, let you have, give, provide.
5 *(v) I can spare this piece of cake.* let you have, do without, manage without, get along without, dispense with.
6 *(v) The judge decided to spare Burglar Beryl.* have mercy on, be lenient towards, go easy on *(informal)*, pardon, let off, reprieve, release, free, let go.
OPPOSITES: punish, condemn.

spark
(n) The firework sent out a spark of light. flash, flicker, flare, glint, gleam, glimmer.

sparkle
(v) Look how the stars sparkle in the sky. twinkle, flicker, shimmer, flash, glitter, glisten, glint, glimmer, gleam, shine, glow.

speak
1 *(v) Why didn't you speak earlier?* say something, speak out, speak up, make yourself heard, open your mouth, have your say, express yourself, pipe up.
2 *(v) Can you speak Chinese?* talk, communicate in, express yourself in, hold a conversation in, get by in *(informal)*.
3 *(v) Please speak your words more clearly.* pronounce, enunciate, articulate.
4 *(v) Dad can speak for hours on any subject.* talk, hold forth, lecture, spout *(informal)*, sermonize, spiel, speechify, give a talk, give a speech, deliver an address.

speak to
(v) Mrs Badger would like to speak to you. talk to, have a word with, chat to, have words with, have a discussion with, converse with, bend your ear *(informal)*.

special
1 *(adj) Eliza has a special talent for drawing.* extraordinary, exceptional, remarkable, unusual, rare, outstanding, notable, unique, singular.
OPPOSITES: unexceptional, commonplace.
2 *(adj) This is a special day for our school.* important, momentous, significant, noteworthy, memorable, red-letter, gala.
OPPOSITES: normal, ordinary.
3 *(adj) Soy sauce has a special flavour.* distinctive, unique, unmistakable, characteristic, distinct, definite, specific, particular, individual, peculiar.
OPPOSITES: unremarkable, undistinctive.

speck
1 *(n) I've got a speck of paint on my shirt.* spot, fleck, speckle, dot, smudge, mark.
2 *(n) There isn't a speck of food left.* bit, crumb, grain, shred, trace, jot, iota, atom.

speckled
(adj) A speckled egg. flecked, freckled, spotted, spotty, stippled, mottled, dappled.

spectacular
(adj) The acrobats gave a spectacular display. breathtaking, dazzling, eye-catching, dramatic, daring, extraordinary, remarkable, staggering, striking, stunning *(informal)*, sensational, magnificent, impressive, astonishing, amazing.

spectator
(n) onlooker, viewer, observer, looker-on, bystander, passer-by, witness, eyewitness.

speech
1 *(n) The speech lasted for hours.* talk, address, lecture, sermon, oration, spiel.
2 *(n) Mum says my speech isn't clear.* pronunciation, diction, enunciation, articulation, accent, voice, dialect.

speechless
(adj) Your news left me speechless. dumbstruck, dumbfounded, thunderstruck, stunned, at a loss for words, tongue-tied, silent, mute.

speed
1 *(n) The speed of the car amazed us.* pace, swiftness, rapidity, quickness, velocity, acceleration, momentum.
OPPOSITES: sluggishness, slowness.
2 *(n) Jo walks at a great speed.* rate, pace.
3 *(v) You may be fined if you speed.* break the speed limit, exceed the speed limit, go over the speed limit, drive too fast.
4 *(v) I saw you speed past on your bike.* race, zoom, flash, fly, whiz *(informal)*, whoosh *(informal)*, zip, hurtle, tear, bomb, belt *(slang)*, streak, career, dash, go like the wind, go like a bat out of hell *(slang)*.
OPPOSITES: dawdle, crawl.

speed up
1 *(v) The train began to speed up.* accelerate, pick up speed, gather speed, go faster, quicken, gain momentum, put on a spurt, get a move on *(informal)*.
OPPOSITES: slow down, decelerate.
2 *(v) We need to speed up the wedding preparations.* See **hurry** 2.

speedy see **fast** 1, 2.

spell
(n) The witch used a spell to turn the prince into a frog. charm, incantation, magic formula, magic words *(plural)*, curse.

spend
1 *(v) How much money did you spend?* pay, pay out, get through, part with, lay out *(informal)*, shell out *(informal)*, fork out *(slang)*, cough up *(informal)*, lash out *(informal)*, splurge, blow *(slang)*, squander, waste, fritter away.
OPPOSITE: save.
2 *(v) How shall we spend the day?* occupy, fill, pass, while away, use up.
3 *(v) You should spend more time on your homework.* put in, concentrate, invest, lavish, devote.

spice
(n) This curry needs more spice. flavouring, seasoning, taste, flavour, bite, piquancy.
TYPES OF SPICE: allspice, caraway seed, cardamom, cayenne, chilli, cinnamon, clove, coriander, cumin, curry powder, ginger, mace, nutmeg, paprika, pepper, pimento, saffron, star anise, turmeric.

spicy
1 *(adj) A spicy curry.* hot, peppery, fiery, piquant, aromatic, highly seasoned.
OPPOSITES: bland, mild.
2 *(adj) (informal) Spicy gossip.* See **juicy** 2.

spike
(n) Be careful of that spike! point, prong, barb, stake, nail, thorn, prickle, needle.

spiky see **prickly** 1.

spill
1 *(v) Try not to spill your drink.* knock over, overturn, tip over, upset.
2 *(v) Lift the bucket slowly so the water doesn't spill.* spill out, slop over, run over, brim over, overflow, pour out, flow out.

spin
(v) Open the music box and watch the ballerina spin. go round, turn, twirl, whirl, pirouette, revolve, rotate, gyrate, wheel.

spine see **back** 1.

spine-chilling see **frightening**

spirit
1 *(n) Do you think your spirit will live on after you die?* soul, inner self, psyche.
2 *(n) The castle was haunted by a spirit.* See **ghost**.
3 *(n) The explorers showed great spirit in the face of danger.* See **courage**.
4 *(n) It's hard to suppress Lydia; she's got so much spirit.* energy, life, enthusiasm, sparkle, fire, vigour, zest, verve, zip *(informal)*, willpower, determination.

spit
1 *(v) Don't spit on the floor!* gob *(informal)*, spew, expectorate, hawk.
2 *(v) Graham tends to spit when he talks.* splutter, sputter, spray, hiss.

spiteful
(adj) Tania's spiteful comments upset me. malicious, snide, hurtful, cruel, nasty, unkind, catty *(informal)*, bitchy *(informal)*, vicious, vindictive, poisonous, venomous.

splash
1 *(v) Marcus began to splash paint on the walls.* slap, slop, slosh *(informal)*, spatter, splatter, sprinkle, squirt, spray, shower, spill, daub, splodge.
2 *(v) Can you hear the waves splash against the rocks?* break, dash, wash, surge, smack, swish, swash, plash, plop.
3 *(v) I love to splash in the river.* paddle, wallow, wade, dabble, bathe, plunge.

splendid
1 *(adj) Splendid tapestries.* magnificent, gorgeous, impressive, rich, costly, sumptuous, opulent, ornate, dazzling, glittering, resplendent, lavish, luxurious.

2 *(adj) A splendid essay. See* **excellent**.

splinter
1 *(n) A small splinter broke off the table.*
See **chip** 2.
2 *(v) The explosion made the glass*
splinter. See **smash** 2.

split
1 *(v) I hope this bag doesn't split.* burst,
tear, rip, come apart, break, give way.
2 *(v) The ground seemed to split beneath*
my feet. open, crack, gape, yawn, part.
3 *(v) Where does the path split in two?*
See **divide** 1.
4 *(v) Let's split the money between us.*
See **divide** 3.
5 *(n) I have a split in my jeans. See* **tear** 4.

split up *see* **separate** 1, 3.

spoil
1 *(v) One mistake could spoil your chances*
of winning. See **ruin** 1.
2 *(v) I didn't mean to spoil your painting.*
damage, ruin, wreck, deface, mess up,
smudge, blemish, mark, stain, botch.
3 *(v) I wish Granny wouldn't spoil you.*
indulge, overindulge, pamper,
mollycoddle, wait on you hand and foot,
cosset, spoon-feed, baby, pander to.

spoilsport
(n) Don't be such a spoilsport! killjoy, wet
blanket *(informal)*, party pooper *(informal)*,
misery *(informal)*, dog in the manger

spoof
(n) (informal) This film is a spoof of a
disaster movie. takeoff *(informal)*, send-up
(informal), parody, pastiche, satire.

spooky
(adj) (informal) The castle looks spooky in
the moonlight. eerie, creepy *(informal)*,
mysterious, ghostly, uncanny, unearthly,
weird, frightening, spine-chilling, haunted.
❖ *Also see* **ghosts & hauntings**.

sport
(n) Sport is good for you. exercise, games
(plural), physical activity, PE (physical
education), physical recreation.
TYPES OF SPORT: aikido, American
football, angling, archery, athletics,
badminton, baseball, basketball, beach
volleyball, billiards, bobsleighing, bowls,
boxing, canoeing, cricket, croquet, curling,
cycling, darts, diving, dressage, eventing,
fencing, Gaelic football, golf, greyhound
racing, gymnastics, handball, hockey,
horse racing, hurling, ice hockey, judo,
jujitsu, karate, lacrosse, luge, motorcycle
racing, motor racing, mountaineering,
netball, orienteering, polo, pool, rallycross,
rock climbing, rounders, rowing, rugby
league, rugby union, sailing, shooting,
show jumping, skating, skiing, snooker,
soccer, softball, squash, surfing,
swimming, synchronized swimming, table
tennis, tae kwon do, tennis, trampolining,
volleyball, water polo, water-skiing,
weightlifting, windsurfing, wrestling,
yachting. *Also see* **athletics**.

---

sport words

types of sporting event
challenge	play-off
championship	preliminary
competition	round
contest	qualifying
final	round
fixture	quarterfinal
friendly match	race
game	regatta
head-to-head	replay
heat	semifinal
match	test match
Olympic Games	time trial
Paralympics	tournament

gymnasts tumble

fencers lunge

mask

foil

sport moves
attack	evade	pass	speed
block	field	pitch	spin
bowl	glide	punch	sprint
catch	hurtle	race	stretch
chase	intercept	reach	strike
corner	jump	retrieve	swerve
dart	kick	save	swing
defend	leap	score	tackle
deflect	lob	shoot	throw
dive	lunge	skim	tumble
dodge	mark	slam	twist
dribble	overtake	slide	vault
duck	parry	smash	volley

motorcyclists corner

competitors may...
be disqualified	go flat out	storm ahead
be stretchered off	miss a shot	take a penalty
break a record	play safe	take evasive
cheat	put on a spurt	action
clinch the match	reach a new	take the lead
commit a foul	personal best	use tactics
draw level	run out of steam	work as a
equalize	score a hat-trick	team
fend off a tackle	set the pace	
follow a game plan		

sporting events can be...
dangerous	hotly
demanding	contested
draining	nail-biting
dramatic	nerve racking
dull	punishing
electrifying	strenuous
emotional	tedious
exhausting	tense
exhilarating	testing
frustrating	thrilling
gruelling	uneventful

skaters spin

goalkeepers leap

ski pole

skiers swerve

mast

baseball players swing at the ball

sail

batten

boom

window

board

judo players throw their opponents

windsurfers skim the waves

basketball players dribble

sporting events can end in...
celebration	humiliation
controversy	injury time
dead heat	photo finish
defeat	riot
disaster	success
draw	tie
extra time	triumph
failure	victory

stadium

tiered seating

track

tennis court

sports complex

field

sports hall

swimming pool

sporty
(adj) Tabby is very sporty. athletic, active, energetic, fit, hearty, outdoorsy *(informal).*

spot
1 *(v) Did you spot the difference between the pictures?* notice, detect, identify, pinpoint, discover, pick out, single out, observe, put your finger on *(informal).*
2 *(v) Did you spot my note? See* **notice** 1.
3 *(v) Try to rub that spot off the wall.* mark, stain, speck, fleck, smudge, blotch, blob, blot, splotch, patch, blemish.
4 *(n) Jilly has a spot on her chin.* pimple, zit *(slang),* blackhead, boil, pustule, mole.
5 *(n) We found a perfect spot to camp. See* **place** 1.
6 **spots** *(plural) Our curtains are blue with yellow spots.* dots *(plural),* polka dots *(plural),* circles *(plural),* blobs *(plural).*

spotless *see* **clean** 2.

spotty
(adj) Spike has a spotty face. pimply, acne-covered, blotchy, blemished, freckled.

sprawl
(v) I love to sprawl in front of the telly. stretch out, lie around, lounge, loll, flop, slouch, slump, spread-eagle.

spray
1 *(v) Don't spray water over me!* sprinkle, shower, spatter, splash, scatter, squirt.
2 *(n) The fountain sent out a spray of water.* jet, shower, sprinkling, mist, drizzle, squirt, droplets *(plural),* vapour.

spread
1 *(v) Spread the rug on the ground.* spread out, stretch out, open out, lay out, unroll, unfold, arrange, display.
2 *(v) Spread the glue thickly.* apply, smear on, plaster on, lay on, daub, coat.
3 *(v) See the puddle spread! See* **grow** 2.
4 *(v) The violence may spread.* increase, escalate, mushroom, grow, proliferate.
5 *(v) Spread the news!* pass on, circulate, broadcast, publicize, make known, make public, proclaim, disseminate, transmit.

spring *see* **jump** 1.

springy *see* **bouncy** 1.

sprinkle
1 *(v) Sprinkle sugar over the cake.* scatter, strew, shower, spread, dust, pepper.
2 *(v) Don't sprinkle water everywhere! See* **spray** 1.

sprint *see* **run** 1.

spurt
1 *(v) Water began to spurt from the pipe. See* **squirt**.
2 *(n) I felt a spurt of speed as the car accelerated.* burst, surge, rush, explosion.

spy
1 *(n) Could Stanley be a spy?* secret agent, undercover agent, enemy agent, mole *(informal),* double agent, infiltrator.
2 **spy on** *(v) Let's spy on Leo!* keep watch on, keep an eye on, follow, shadow, tail, trail, snoop on, eavesdrop on.

squabble *see* **argue** 1.

squash
1 *(v) Don't squash the strawberries!* crush, squeeze, squish, flatten, pulp, pulverize, smash, mash, mangle, compress, pound, stamp on, tread on, trample on, crumple.
2 *(v) I can't squash any more food into the fridge. See* **squeeze** 1.

squashy
(adj) I hate squashy bananas. soft, squishy, squidgy, mushy, pulpy, spongy, soggy.

squat
1 *(v) Squat behind this bush! See* **crouch**.
2 *(adj) Angus has a squat figure.* dumpy, stocky, chunky, stubby, thickset, short.
OPPOSITE: lanky.

squawk
(v) The parrot began to squawk. screech, shriek, squeal, cackle, crow, cheep, hoot.

squeak
(v) Can you hear my brakes squeak? squeal, screech, creak, scrape, grate, peep.

squeal *see* **scream**.

squeeze
1 *(v) I can't squeeze any more food into the fridge.* squash, cram, stuff, pack, crowd, jam, ram, force, wedge.
2 *(v) Try to squeeze the water out of the cloth.* wring, force, twist, screw, extract.
3 *(v) Don't squeeze my hand like that!* grip, clasp, clutch, pinch, nip, press, crush, squash, compress.
4 *(v) Try to squeeze your way through the crowd.* edge, shoulder, worm, wriggle, squirm, wiggle, elbow, jostle, push, shove.
5 *(n) I gave Anna a friendly squeeze.* hug, embrace, cuddle, clasp, grasp, bear hug.

squirm
1 *(v) Don't squirm about! See* **wriggle** 1.
2 *(v) Dad's jokes make me squirm.* cringe, wince, die of shame *(informal),* curl up and die *(informal),* flinch, blench, writhe.

squirt
(v) Watch the water squirt out of the hose. spurt, shoot, gush, spout, jet, spray, splash, spatter, pour, spit, spew, shower.

stab
(v) Stab the dragon through the heart! pierce, spear, knife, spike, lance, skewer, impale, run through, gore, transfix.

stack *see* **pile** 1, 2.

stage
1 *(n) Stand on the stage to recite your poem.* platform, dais, rostrum, podium.
2 *(n) We completed the final stage of our journey.* phase, leg, section, step, lap.
3 *(v) Let's stage a play next term.* perform, put on, produce, present, mount.

stagger
1 *(v) The weight of the parcel made me stagger.* totter, teeter, reel, lurch, stumble, wobble, sway, falter.
2 *(v) The height of the skyscrapers will stagger you. See* **astonish**.

stagnant
(adj) A pool of stagnant water. motionless, still, stale, foul, dirty, filthy, polluted.
OPPOSITES: flowing, fresh.

stain
1 *(n) I must get this stain off my shirt.* mark, spot, blotch, smudge, smear, blot.
2 *(n) The rumour left a stain on my reputation.* smear, slur, blot, blemish, taint.
3 *(v) Those sweets will stain your tongue blue.* dye, colour, tinge, tint, discolour.

stairs
(plural n) steps (plural), flight of stairs, staircase, stairway.

stale
1 *(adj) This bread is stale.* old, dry, dried up, dried out, hard, mouldy.
OPPOSITE: fresh.
2 *(adj) The air in the cellar smelt stale.* musty, fusty, frowsty, stuffy, foul, damp.
OPPOSITE: fresh.

stammer
(v) I always stammer when I'm nervous. stutter, splutter, falter, hesitate, stumble.

stamp
1 *(n) Look for the maker's stamp on the vase.* mark, imprint, hallmark, seal, label, logo, signature, impression, brand.
2 *(v) Please don't stamp around the house.* stomp *(informal),* clump, clomp, tramp, pound, thump, thud.
3 **stamp on** *(v) Don't stamp on the flowers! See* **trample on**.

stand
1 *(v) Stand when the judge comes in.* stand up, rise, get to your feet, get up.
OPPOSITES: sit, sit down.
2 *(v) Don't stand on my toes! See* **step** 5.
3 *(v) Stand the photograph on the shelf.* put, place, set, position, set upright, prop.
4 *(v) I can't stand the sight of blood!* bear, stick *(slang),* endure, abide, tolerate, stomach, take, handle, cope with, put up with *(informal).*

standard
1 *(n) Are you pleased with the standard of my work? See* **quality** 1, 2.
2 *(n) Steve's tennis is below standard.* average, the norm, par.
3 *(adj) It's standard practice to brush your teeth in the morning. See* **normal** 1.

stand by
1 *(v) I'll stand by you whatever happens.* support, be loyal to, stay with, stick with *(informal),* back, take your side, defend.
2 *(v) Stand by for takeoff!* be prepared, be ready, wait, wait in the wings.

stand for
(v) What does "PC" stand for? represent, mean, indicate, denote, signify, symbolize.

stand in for
(v) I'll stand in for you if you're ill. take your place, fill in for, cover for, deputize for, take over from, substitute for, replace, represent, understudy *(theatre).*

stand out
(v) *You'll certainly stand out in that orange shirt!* stick out, be noticed, attract attention, be conspicuous, be eye-catching, stand out from the crowd.

stand up for
(v) *I'll stand up for you.* stick up for (informal), defend, come to your defence, back, support, take your side, stand by.

star
1 (n) *Astronomers have sighted a new star.* ❖ See **space adventure**.
2 (n) *Jodie longs to be a star.* celebrity, superstar, megastar, big name, top draw, idol, screen goddess, starlet, celeb (informal), VIP (very important person).
3 (v) *Who will star in this film?* take the lead, play the starring role, head the cast, top the bill, co-star, feature.

stare
1 (v) *When I met Famous Fred, all I could do was stare.* gape, gaze, look, gawp (slang), gawk, goggle, be open-mouthed, ogle, rubberneck (slang).
2 (n) *A hard stare.* glare, look, dirty look.

start
1 (v) *You've got lots to do, so you'd better start soon.* get started, make a start, make a beginning, begin, get going, get moving, get weaving (informal), take the plunge (informal), get the show on the road (informal), pull your finger out (informal). OPPOSITE: stop.
2 (v) *When did life on earth first start?* See **begin** 4.
3 (v) *Are you packed and ready to start?* See **leave** 1.
4 (v) *Who will start the discussion?* begin, commence, open, initiate, kick off (informal), set in motion, kick-start, get going, get under way, start the ball rolling. OPPOSITES: end, finish.
5 (v) *Mum wants to start her own business.* set up, establish, launch, create, found, form, pioneer, get off the ground (informal), get going, set in motion. OPPOSITES: wind up, close down.
6 (n) *Danni missed the start of the show.* beginning, opening, commencement, kickoff (informal), introduction. OPPOSITE: end.
7 (n) *Greg got a start on the others at the beginning of the race.* head start, lead, advantage, edge, margin.
8 (n) *Bo woke with a start.* See **jump** 6.

startle
(v) *Did the firecracker startle you?* alarm, scare, frighten, make you jump, give you a start, catch you unawares, shock, surprise, unnerve, unsettle, disturb, disconcert.

starving
1 (adj) *The refugees were starving.* hungry, starved, famished, underfed, malnourished, dying of starvation.
2 (adj) (informal) *I'm starving!* ravenous, famished, hungry.

state
1 (v) *Did Beryl state that she was innocent?* declare, say, assert, affirm, announce, proclaim, profess, reveal.
2 (v) *You'll have a chance to state your opinion.* put, express, voice, present, put across, explain, communicate, submit.
3 (n) *The castle is owned by the state.* nation, country, government, people (plural), citizens (plural), republic, kingdom, realm (old-fashioned), commonwealth.
4 (n) *What sort of state are the survivors in?* condition, shape, frame of mind, mood, spirits (plural), form, health.

stay
1 (v) *Don't stay in town too long.* remain, hang around, linger, loiter, delay, stop, wait around, dally.
2 (v) *We're hoping to stay in a luxury hotel.* spend the night, stop over, take a room, put up, lodge, board.
3 (v) *If we like Australia we might stay there.* See **settle** 1.
4 (v) *Please stay standing.* remain, keep, continue, carry on, go on.
5 (n) *Enjoy your stay in London!* holiday, break, stopover, visit, vacation.

steady
1 (adj) *This chair isn't very steady.* firm, stable, safe, secure, solid. OPPOSITES: unsteady, wobbly.
2 (adj) *The steady rain kept us indoors.* continuous, constant, incessant, nonstop, endless, persistent, ceaseless, unremitting. OPPOSITES: intermittent, sporadic.
3 (adj) *The drummer kept up a steady beat.* regular, rhythmic, even, constant, repeated, unvarying, uniform, unhurried. OPPOSITES: irregular, uneven.

steal
1 (v) *It's wrong to steal.* thieve, pilfer, shoplift, pick pockets, commit a theft.
2 (v) *Someone tried to steal my purse.* take, make off with, walk off with, pocket, filch, misappropriate, pinch (informal), nick (slang), lift (informal), swipe (slang).

steep
1 (adj) *There's a steep drop down to the beach.* sheer, precipitous, sharp, sudden, abrupt, vertical, perpendicular. OPPOSITES: gentle, gradual.
2 (v) *Steep your shirt in water.* See **soak** 1.

steer
(v) *The car was hard to steer.* control, handle, drive, direct, navigate, pilot.

step
1 (n) *My foot slipped off the step.* stair, rung (ladder), doorstep, tread (staircase).
2 (n) *Take one step forwards.* pace, stride.
3 (n) *We must plan our next step carefully.* move, manoeuvre, course of action, act.
4 (n) *Learning to read is an important step for a child.* step forward, advance, development, progression, stage, phase.
5 (v) *Don't step on my toes!* tread, stand, tramp, trample, walk, stamp.

stern
1 (adj) *A stern look.* severe, grim, forbidding, serious, disapproving, tight-lipped, steely-eyed, frowning, unsmiling, unsympathetic, sombre, sober, austere.
2 (adj) *A stern teacher.* See **strict** 1.

stick
1 (n) *Throw another stick on the bonfire.* branch, twig, switch, piece of wood.
2 (n) *Grandpa uses a stick when he walks.* walking stick, cane, crutch, staff, crook.
3 (n) *Don't hit me with that stick!* rod, cane, switch, birch, truncheon, baton, club, cudgel, cosh.
4 (n) *Tie the ivy to a stick so it won't droop.* cane, pole, stake, post.
5 (v) *Stick the pieces together.* glue, tape, paste, gum, fix, fasten, attach, join, bond.
6 (v) *Don't stick your finger in the trifle!* put, poke, jab, stab, dig, thrust, insert.
7 (v) *Let's hope the car doesn't stick in the mud.* get stuck, get bogged down, get embedded, get lodged, get clogged up.
8 (v) *I felt a bone stick in my throat.* catch, lodge, wedge, jam, get trapped, snag.
9 (v) (informal) *Stick your trainers in the wardrobe.* See **bung**.
10 (v) (slang) *I can't stick this noise any longer!* See **stand** 4.

stick at see **persevere**.

stick out
1 (v) *How far does the ledge stick out?* jut out, extend, project, protrude, overhang.
2 (v) *You'll certainly stick out in that orange shirt!* See **stand out**.

sticky
1 (adj) *A sticky label.* gummed, adhesive.
2 (adj) *A sticky mixture.* gluey, gooey (informal), tacky, glutinous, viscous.
3 (adj) *A sticky bun.* gooey (informal), syrupy, treacly, sugary, creamy, jammy.
4 (adj) *Sticky weather.* See **muggy**.

stiff
1 (adj) *I can't bend this plastic; it's too stiff.* rigid, hard, firm, inflexible, unbending, unyielding, inelastic, brittle. OPPOSITES: flexible, pliable.
2 (adj) *After the climb my muscles felt stiff.* tight, tense, taut, unsupple, painful, aching, sore, creaky (informal), arthritic. OPPOSITE: supple.
3 (adj) *The robot's movements looked stiff.* See **awkward** 2.

stifle see **smother** 1, 2.

still
1 (adj) *Andy stood still and stared.* motionless, stock-still, rooted to the spot, without moving, immobile, stationary, paralysed, transfixed, spellbound, frozen.
2 (adj) *The clouds were reflected in the still water.* calm, motionless, smooth, unruffled, undisturbed, stagnant. OPPOSITE: turbulent.
3 (adj) *What a still evening!* quiet, silent, calm, tranquil, peaceful, windless, airless. OPPOSITES: stormy, noisy.

sting

sting
(v) *If you get soap in your eyes it will sting.* smart, burn, prick, hurt, tingle, irritate.

stingy see **mean** 5.

stink
1 (v) *Those rotten eggs really stink.* smell, reek, pong (informal), stink to high heaven (informal), hum (slang), whiff (slang).
2 (n) *What's making that stink?* stench, bad smell, foul odour, pong (informal).

stir
1 (v) *Stir the ingredients together.* mix, blend, whisk, beat, whip.
2 (v) *The leaves began to stir in the breeze.* move, quiver, tremble, flutter, rustle, shake, twitch.
3 **stir up** (v) *Oscar loves to stir up trouble.* make, cause, start, provoke, spark off, trigger off, incite, instigate, inflame.

stomach
1 (n) *Tabitha has a pain in her stomach.* tummy (informal), belly, abdomen, insides (plural) (informal), guts (plural).
2 (n) *Trevor has a huge stomach.* tummy (informal), paunch, gut (slang), beer belly (slang), spare tyre (informal), potbelly.

stone
1 (n) *I found a smooth stone on the beach.* pebble, rock, boulder.
2 (n) *Flash Frank wears a ring with a huge stone in it.* See **jewel**.
3 (n) *Don't eat the stone in the middle of the fruit.* pip, seed, kernel, nut.
4 (n) *The grave was marked by a stone.* gravestone, headstone, tombstone, monument, memorial stone, tablet.
5 **stones** (plural n) *Don't slip on the stones!* gravel, scree, shingle, pebbles (plural), cobbles (plural).

stony
(adj) *We struggled over the stony ground.* rocky, rough, pebbly, gravelly, shingly (beach), boulder-strewn, hard, flinty.

stoop
1 (v) *You'll have to stoop to get into the cave.* duck, crouch, bend down, lean down, bow down, bend your head, lower your head, hunch your shoulders, squat.
2 (v) *How could you stoop to playing such a mean trick?* See **lower yourself**.

stop
1 (v) *Wait for the bus to stop before you get off.* come to a stop, come to a halt, come to a standstill, pull up, draw up, halt, come to rest, grind to a halt.
OPPOSITES: go, start.
2 (v) *Let's stop now; I'm tired.* pause, have a break, rest, finish, call it a day (informal), knock off (informal), down tools.
OPPOSITES: keep going, carry on.
3 (v) *Dad has decided to stop smoking.* finish, cease, quit, give up, desist from, refrain from, leave off, cut out (informal), pack in (informal), kick (informal).
OPPOSITES: start, take up.

4 (v) *The college may stop our pottery classes.* put an end to, call a halt to, end, finish, wind up, shut down, discontinue, cut short, break off, axe (informal), drop.
OPPOSITES: start, set up.
5 (v) *You can't stop me from going to the disco.* See **prevent** 2.
6 (v) *Stop that man!* catch, seize, restrain, hold, capture, intercept, arrest, detain.
7 (v) *We must stop the bleeding.* stem, staunch, check, hold back, control.
8 (v) *Will you stop anywhere on your way to Paris?* break your journey, spend time, stay, spend a night, stay over, put up, visit.
9 (n) *Is this your stop?* bus stop, station, halt, terminus, destination, depot.

store
1 (v) *Farmers have to store hay for the winter.* stock up on, set aside, put by, lay in, save, reserve, stash away (informal), salt away, accumulate, amass, hoard, stockpile.
2 (n) *Pirate Peg has a huge store of gold.* hoard, stock, stockpile, quantity, supply, fund, reserve, cache, accumulation.

storm
1 (n) *The storm wrecked our garden.* gale, squall, tempest, thunderstorm, blizzard, hurricane, typhoon, cyclone, tornado, whirlwind, twister (informal), monsoon.
2 (v) *Why did Josie storm out of the room like that?* flounce, stamp, stomp (informal), rush, charge, fly, stalk, march, stride.

stormy
1 (adj) *Stormy weather.* rough, windy, squally, blustery, gusty, thundery, rainy, foul, dirty, wild, violent.
OPPOSITES: calm, fine.
2 (adj) *Stormy seas.* See **rough** 2.

story
1 (n) *Tell me the story of the giant octopus!* tale, yarn (informal), anecdote, account, history, narrative.
TYPES OF STORY: adventure story, allegory, crime story, detective story, fable, fairy tale, fantasy story, folk tale, ghost story, historical romance, horror story, legend, love story, mystery, myth, novel, parable, romance, saga, science fiction story, spy story, thriller, whodunit (informal).
2 (n) *Clark wrote a good story for "Rap Weekly".* See **article** 1.

stout see **plump**.

straight
1 (adj) *This wall isn't straight.* level, even, horizontal, perpendicular, vertical, upright, true, flush, plumb, square, aligned, in line.
OPPOSITES: crooked, bent.
2 (adj) *We took the straight route to the coast.* direct, short, undeviating, quick.
OPPOSITES: indirect, circuitous.
3 (adj) *Our team has had five straight wins.* consecutive, successive, unbroken, uninterrupted, continuous, in a row.
4 (adj) *A straight answer.* See **honest** 1.

storm words

in a storm	thunder may...	the rain may...	storms can...	storms can be...
billowing clouds	boom	beat down	block roads	awe-inspiring
cloudburst	crack	bucket down	bring down power lines	cataclysmic
deluge	crash	lash down	cut off villages	catastrophic
downpour	echo	pelt down	damage crops	deafening
driving rain	growl	pour down	destroy buildings	destructive
forked lightning	resound	teem down	flatten fences	devastating
gale	reverberate		flood homes	dramatic
gust of wind	roar	the wind may...	mangle cars	ear-splitting
hailstones	roll	batter	maroon motorists	fierce
inky sky	rumble	blast	rip off roof tiles	frightening
lashing rain		blow	smash windows	furious
leaden sky	lightning may...	buffet	start fires	powerful
peal of thunder	flare	gust	swell rivers	raging
sheet of lightning	flash	howl	topple chimneys	savage
streak of lightning	flicker	moan	uproot trees	short-lived
	light up the sky	rage	wreck ships	spectacular
thunderbolt	streak across the sky	roar		squally
thunderclap	strike	shriek		tempestuous
torrential rain	zigzag	swirl		turbulent
		wail		unrelenting
		whirl		violent
				wild

5 (adv) Go straight to school. directly, immediately, at once, instantly, without delay, by the shortest route.

straightaway see **immediately**.

strain
1 (n) I can't take the strain any longer! See **pressure** 2.
2 (v) Did you strain a muscle? pull, sprain, injure, damage, hurt, twist, tear, wrench.
3 (v) Reading in the dark can strain your eyes. tire, weaken, tax, fatigue, damage.
4 (v) Strain the mixture. sieve, sift, filter, separate, percolate (coffee).

stranded
(adj) Pirate Peg was stranded on a desert island. marooned, shipwrecked, cast away, left high and dry, stuck, abandoned.

strange
1 (adj) Ziggy wears some really strange clothes. unusual, extraordinary, remarkable, funny, odd, peculiar, curious, queer, weird, bizarre, outlandish, eccentric, way-out (informal), wacky (slang), off-the-wall (slang), uncommon, abnormal.
OPPOSITES: normal, standard.
2 (adj) I heard a strange noise outside the window. odd, peculiar, funny, weird, mysterious, eerie, spooky (informal), uncanny, unnatural, unearthly, puzzling, perplexing, mystifying, inexplicable.
OPPOSITES: ordinary, unremarkable.
3 (adj) The new school seemed strange to me. unfamiliar, alien, foreign, different, new, novel, unknown.
OPPOSITES: familiar, well-known.
4 (adj) Indiana was alone in a strange land. unfamiliar, foreign, alien, exotic, remote, little-known, unexplored.
OPPOSITES: familiar, well-known.
5 (adj) I felt strange being the only girl in the class. odd, awkward, ill at ease, uncomfortable, out of place, lost.
OPPOSITES: at ease, comfortable.

strangle
(v) Don't strangle yourself with that scarf! choke, throttle, strangulate, garrotte.

strap
(v) Strap the parcel to your bicycle rack. buckle, lash, fasten, attach, secure, tie.

stray
1 (adj) We're looking after a stray dog. abandoned, lost, homeless, unclaimed.
2 (v) Don't stray too far from the path. wander, roam, ramble, drift, straggle, rove, range, deviate, go off course, go astray.

streak
1 (n) Our car has a black streak down the side. stripe, strip, line, band, slash, zigzag, smear, smudge, mark.
2 (n) Look at that streak of lightning! flash, bolt, fork, stroke, sheet.

stream
1 (n) Gregory paddled in the stream. brook, river, spring, beck, burn, creek, rivulet, tributary. ❖ Also see **river**.

2 (n) A stream of water poured from the washing machine. flood, torrent, cascade, jet, gush, rush, surge, flow, outpouring.
3 (v) Tears began to stream down Anji's face. See **run** 3.

street see **road**.

strength
1 (n) Wilf hasn't the strength to lift a paper bag! power, might, muscle, brawn, force, energy, stamina, vigour.
OPPOSITES: weakness, frailty.
2 (n) Jade showed great strength under pressure. courage, bravery, fortitude, strength of character, spirit, grit, determination, firmness, backbone.
OPPOSITE: weakness.
3 (n) Don't underestimate the strength of my feelings. intensity, depth, force, vehemence, ardour.

strengthen
1 (v) Fluoride can strengthen your teeth. harden, toughen, make stronger, build up.
OPPOSITE: weaken.
2 (v) The soldiers tried to strengthen the castle walls. reinforce, fortify, make stronger, support, brace up, buttress.
OPPOSITE: weaken.
3 (v) This success should strengthen your desire to do well. reinforce, increase, heighten, deepen, intensify, confirm.
OPPOSITES: weaken, undermine.

strenuous see **exhausting**.

stress
1 (n) Too much stress can make you ill. pressure, strain, tension, anxiety, worry, hassle (informal), nervous tension.
2 (n) Put the stress on the first word. emphasis, accent, weight, beat.
3 (v) I must stress the importance of safety. See **emphasize**.

stressed
(adj) I always feel stressed at exam time. under pressure, pressurized, hassled (informal), tense, anxious, overworked, overstretched, pushed to the limit.
OPPOSITE: relaxed.

stressful
1 (adj) The exam period can be a stressful time. tense, worrying, anxious, nerve-racking, nail-biting, agonizing, traumatic.
2 (adj) Teaching is a stressful job. pressurized, high-pressure, demanding, tough, taxing, challenging, difficult, trying.

stretch
1 (v) Stretch the elastic. pull, extend, draw out, tighten, tauten, lengthen, elongate.
2 (v) Balloons stretch when you blow them up. expand, inflate, swell, distend.
3 (v) I hope this jumper doesn't stretch. pull out of shape, get larger, get bigger, widen, lengthen.
OPPOSITE: shrink.
4 (v) How far does the desert stretch? extend, spread, reach, continue, range.
5 (v) This test will stretch you. challenge, push you to the limit, tax, extend.

stretchy
(adj) Rubber bands are stretchy. elastic, stretchable, rubbery, springy.

strict
1 (adj) Jason's dad is really strict. stern, firm, severe, harsh, hard, tough, inflexible, uncompromising, authoritarian, autocratic, iron-handed, iron-fisted, tyrannical.
OPPOSITES: lenient, lax.
2 (adj) Our school has strict rules about uniform. stringent, rigid, hard and fast, rigorous, exacting, inflexible, tight, set.
OPPOSITES: flexible, lax.

stride
1 (v) We watched the sentry stride up and down. pace, march, pound, parade, strut.
2 (n) With one stride the giant crossed the river. step, pace, bound, leap.

strike
1 (v) Should parents ever strike their children? See **hit** 1.
2 (v) Strike the ball hard. See **hit** 3.
3 (v) I saw the car strike a tree. See **hit** 4.
4 (v) When did it strike you that you'd forgotten your key? See **occur** 2.
5 (v) The workers decided to strike. go on strike, walk out, take industrial action, stop work, down tools, come out.
6 (n) Do you support the teachers' strike? industrial action, walkout, stoppage, sit-in.

striking
1 (adj) The similarity between the sisters is striking. obvious, unmistakable, evident, noticeable, conspicuous, visible, remarkable, extraordinary, incredible.
2 (adj) That's a striking painting. eye-catching, distinctive, unusual, arresting, dazzling, stunning (informal), memorable.

string
1 (n) Tie the parcel up with string. cord, twine, yarn, rope.
2 (n) Sasha is wearing a string of pearls. row, strand, rope, necklace.
3 (n) I had a string of disasters. See **series**.

strip
1 (v) You have to strip before you shower. take your clothes off, get undressed, undress, strip off (slang), peel off (slang), remove your clothes, strip naked.
OPPOSITES: get dressed, dress.
2 (v) Strip the paper off the walls. peel, scrape, tear, rip, flake, remove, clear.
3 (n) My sweatshirt has a red strip round the bottom. stripe, band, line, bar.
4 (n) Cut off a strip of material. band, piece, bit, ribbon, swathe, slip, shred.

stripe see **strip** 3.

stroke
1 (v) Fido loves it when you stroke his ears. rub, pat, fondle, caress, pet.
2 (n) What a brilliant stroke! See **shot** 2.

stroll
(v) Why don't you stroll into town? amble, wander, saunter, walk, make your way, mooch (slang), mosey (informal), ramble.

strong
1 *(adj) A strong giant has uprooted the trees!* powerful, mighty, muscular, brawny, hefty, strapping, athletic, sinewy, wiry, sturdy, burly, Ramboesque.
OPPOSITES: weak, puny.
2 *(adj) Clint is a strong character who always gets his way.* forceful, strong-willed, assertive, aggressive, tough, determined, tenacious, unyielding.
OPPOSITES: weak, spineless.
3 *(adj) Ellie has been very strong since her mum fell ill.* brave, courageous, plucky, resilient, gutsy *(informal)*, resourceful.
OPPOSITES: feeble, pathetic.
4 *(adj) The walls are strong. See* **solid** 2.
5 *(adj) Farmer Phyllis wears strong boots.* stout, sturdy, hard-wearing, heavy, heavy-duty, durable, indestructible, robust.
OPPOSITES: lightweight, flimsy.
6 *(adj) Karen has a strong desire to win.* deep, deep-seated, passionate, fervent, intense, keen, fierce, heartfelt, ardent.
OPPOSITES: superficial, half-hearted.
7 *(adj) There are strong arguments against smoking.* compelling, convincing, persuasive, forceful, cogent, potent.
OPPOSITES: unconvincing, weak.
8 *(adj) Ziggy's room is painted in strong colours.* bright, bold, vivid, loud, glaring, dazzling, brilliant, stark, clear, intense.
OPPOSITES: pale, muted.
9 *(adj) This soup has a strong flavour.* intense, concentrated, overpowering, spicy, tangy, piquant, pungent, sharp, biting, fiery, highly flavoured.
OPPOSITES: bland, delicate.
10 *(adj) This drink is too strong for me.* concentrated, overpowering, alcoholic, intoxicating, potent, heady.
OPPOSITES: weak, nonalcoholic.
11 *(adj) A strong wind blew in off the sea.* stiff, high, brisk, fresh, gusting, gale-force.
OPPOSITES: light, gentle.

stroppy *(informal) see* **awkward** 4.

struggle
1 *(v) You will have to struggle to stay in the race.* work hard, strain every muscle, exert yourself, do your utmost, make a huge effort, go all out *(informal)*, bust a gut *(informal)*, break your neck *(informal)*.
2 *(v) Indiana had to struggle with the monster.* grapple, wrestle, tussle, fight, scuffle, skirmish, brawl, scrap *(informal)*, clash, do battle, slog it out, spar, vie.
3 *(v) The puppy will struggle when you put him on the lead.* strain, wriggle, squirm, writhe, flail about.
4 *(n) It was a struggle to complete the assault course.* effort, grind *(informal)*, battle, challenge, slog, long haul.

strut *see* **swagger**.

stubborn
(adj) Don't be so stubborn! obstinate, pig-headed, headstrong, wilful, self-willed, inflexible, defiant, determined.

stuck
1 *(adj) Should the pieces be stuck together?* fixed, fastened, joined, attached, glued, taped, pasted, gummed, cemented.
2 *(adj) I'm stuck in a hole!* stuck fast, stuck tight, wedged, jammed, stranded.
3 *(adj) (informal) Ask Mrs Badger to help you if you're stuck.* stumped, baffled, at a loss, at a standstill, bogged down, beaten, up against a brick wall, at your wits' end.

stuck-up *(informal) see* **snobbish**.

study
1 *(v) Study this chapter for the test.* work on, look at, revise, read up on, swot up on *(informal)*, mug up on *(slang)*, cram *(informal)*, burn the midnight oil.
2 *(v) Dustin wants to study Spanish at college.* learn, take, read, master.
3 *(v) The detectives will study the evidence. See* **examine**.
4 *(n) We're doing a study of local traffic problems. See* **survey**.

stuff
1 *(n) Pick up all your stuff! See* **things**.
2 *(n) The alien's clothes were made of some odd green stuff.* substance, material, fabric, cloth, textile, fibres *(plural)*.
3 *(v) I can't stuff anything more into this case. See* **squeeze** 1.

stuffy
(adj) It was stuffy in the attic. airless, fusty, musty, stale-smelling, frowsty, fuggy, stifling, suffocating, oppressive, poorly ventilated, close, muggy.
OPPOSITES: airy, well-ventilated.

stumble *see* **trip** 2.

stunned
1 *(adj) The blow from the cricket ball left Ian stunned.* dazed, semiconscious, reeling, seeing stars, dizzy, groggy *(informal)*, senseless, in a stupor, unconscious, knocked out, out for the count *(informal)*.
2 *(adj) The news left us stunned.* amazed, astonished, staggered, dazed, shocked, numb, dumbstruck, flabbergasted *(informal)*, dumbfounded, thunderstruck, stupefied, gobsmacked *(slang)*, devastated.

stupid
1 *(adj) Andy isn't usually so stupid!* dim, dense, idiotic, brainless, thick, slow, clueless *(slang)*, gormless *(informal)*, dopey *(slang)*, dumb *(informal)*, dull, obtuse.
OPPOSITES: clever, intelligent.
2 *(adj) What a stupid idea!* idiotic, foolish, daft *(informal)*, crackbrained, ludicrous, silly, senseless, pointless, irresponsible, foolhardy, rash, half-baked *(informal)*.
OPPOSITES: sensible, clever.

sturdy *see* **strong** 1, 5.

stutter *see* **stammer**.

style
1 *(n) I love the style of this skirt.* cut, design, shape, lines *(plural)*.
2 *(n) These jeans are the latest style. See* **fashion** 1.

subject
(n) Choose a subject to debate. topic, issue, question, theme, point, motion.

subtle
1 *(adj) A subtle shade of green.* delicate, understated, gentle, pale, muted, unobtrusive, low-key, tasteful.
2 *(adj) A subtle hint.* gentle, indirect, veiled, implied, tactful, insinuated, crafty.

succeed
1 *(v) I'm sure you'll succeed.* do well, be successful, prosper, thrive, flourish, get on, get to the top, make it *(informal)*, make good, arrive *(informal)*, triumph.
OPPOSITES: fail, be unsuccessful.
2 *(v) My scheme didn't succeed.* work, work out, turn out well, produce results, come off *(informal)*, bear fruit.
OPPOSITES: fail, fall flat.

success
1 *(n) I hope our play will be a success.* hit *(informal)*, smash hit *(informal)*, sensation, triumph, winner, crowd puller *(informal)*, sellout *(informal)*, blockbuster *(informal)*.
OPPOSITES: failure, flop *(informal)*.
2 *(n) Success hasn't spoiled Famous Fred.* stardom, fame, good fortune, glory, honour, acclaim, recognition, prosperity.
OPPOSITE: failure.

successful
1 *(adj) Mum runs a successful business.* profitable, thriving, flourishing, booming, lucrative, fruitful, productive, profit-making, moneymaking, rewarding.
OPPOSITES: failing, unsuccessful.
2 *(adj) Mr Mustafa is a successful businessman.* wealthy, prosperous, well-off, high-earning, high-flying, high-powered, top, best-selling *(writer)*.
OPPOSITES: unsuccessful, failed.
3 *(adj) Our team has been successful all year.* victorious, unbeaten, on a winning streak, out in front *(informal)*, triumphant.
OPPOSITES: unsuccessful, defeated.

suck
(v) Suck your drink through a straw. drink, suck up, slurp *(informal)*, draw up, take in.

suck up *(informal) see* **crawl** 3.

sudden
1 *(adj) A sudden noise.* unexpected, startling, surprising, unforeseen.
OPPOSITES: expected, anticipated.
2 *(adj) A sudden decision.* instant, quick, speedy, hasty, snap, spur-of-the-moment, immediate, hurried, impetuous, impulsive, spontaneous, rash, unconsidered.
OPPOSITES: considered, careful.
3 *(adj) Sudden movements.* abrupt, jerky, rapid, quick, unpredictable, unexpected.
OPPOSITES: slow, gradual.

suddenly
(adv) Suddenly the car swerved. all of a sudden, all at once, without warning, unexpectedly, out of the blue *(informal)*, on the spur of the moment, abruptly.

suffer

1 *(v) The vet made sure that Fido wouldn't suffer.* be in pain, feel any pain, be hurt, be in agony, be racked with pain, be sore.
2 *(v) If parents fight, their children will suffer.* be distressed, be upset, be hurt, feel miserable, feel wretched, have a bad time, go through hell *(informal)*, grieve.
3 *(v) I can't suffer another day of this misery.* go through, endure, tolerate, put up with *(informal)*, bear, stand, take, stick *(slang)*, cope with, handle.

suffocate *see* **smother** 1.

suggest

1 *(v) What did Dr Honey suggest?* propose, advise, recommend, advocate, put forward, counsel, urge, prescribe.
2 *(v) The pictures suggest that the hotel has a pool.* give the impression, give the idea, lead you to believe, make you think, indicate, show, imply, hint, insinuate.

suit

1 *(n) That's a very smart suit.* outfit, ensemble. ❖ *Also see* **clothes**.
2 *(v) Those jeans suit you.* look good on, look right on, do something for, flatter, suit your image, become *(old-fashioned)*.
3 *(v) Would three o'clock tomorrow suit you?* be convenient for, be good for, be acceptable to, do for, meet your requirements, please, satisfy.

suitable

1 *(adj) This video isn't suitable for children.* appropriate, fit, acceptable, meant, cut out, right, fitting, relevant to.
OPPOSITES: unsuitable, inappropriate.
2 *(adj) Is this a suitable moment to talk?* convenient, appropriate, opportune, good.
OPPOSITES: inappropriate, awkward.

sulky

(adj) There's no need to be sulky just because you lost. in a sulk, in a huff, resentful, disgruntled, put out, piqued, grumpy, cross, petulant, peevish, grouchy *(informal)*, sullen, moody, bad-tempered, in a strop *(slang)*, morose, surly, sour.

summary

(n) Write a summary of what happened in the first chapter. outline, résumé, précis, synopsis, overview, rundown, survey, analysis, review, summing-up.

summon

(v) Summon the king's musicians! send for, call for, call, fetch, call together, assemble, gather, muster, demand the presence of.

sum up

(v) Can you sum up what happened in the last chapter? summarize, give a summary of, outline, give a rundown of, give the main points of, put in a nutshell, encapsulate, précis, review.

sunburnt

(adj) Dad looks sunburnt. red, scarlet, like a lobster, burnt, blistered, peeling, tanned, suntanned, brown as a berry, bronzed.

sunny

(adj) Sunny weather. sunshiny, fine, summery, bright, clear, cloudless, brilliant.
OPPOSITES: cloudy, dull.

sunrise *see* **dawn** 1.

sunset *see* **dusk**.

sunshine

(n) Open the curtains and let in the sunshine. sun, sunlight, sunbeams *(plural)*, sun's rays *(plural)*, daylight, light.

supple

(adj) A supple gymnast. lithe, agile, loose-limbed, nimble, flexible, lissom, limber.
OPPOSITES: stiff, awkward.

supply

1 *(v) Can you supply some backing for our project?* provide, contribute, produce, give, offer, donate, come up with, fork out *(slang)*, grant, pass on.
2 *(v) The school will supply you with books.* provide, equip, furnish, kit you out.
3 *(n) Anjali keeps a supply of chocolate in her bedroom.* hoard, store, stock, stockpile, quantity, fund, reserve, cache.
4 **supplies** *(plural n) Do we have enough supplies for the trip?* food, rations *(plural)*, provisions *(plural)*, stores *(plural)*, equipment, materials *(plural)*.

support

1 *(v) These pillars support the ceiling.* hold up, keep up, prop up, carry, bear, underpin, shore up, strengthen, reinforce.
2 *(v) Uncle Pete works hard to support his family.* provide for, keep, take care of, look after, finance, maintain, sustain, nourish.
3 *(v) Do you support animal rights?* agree with, go along with, back, defend, uphold, stand up for, stick up for *(informal)*, speak out for, argue for, promote, champion.
OPPOSITE: oppose.
4 *(n) I'm grateful for the support of my parents.* encouragement, moral support, backing, backup, help, assistance, approval, reassurance, loyalty, friendship.

suppose

1 *(v) I suppose Tom is ill. See* **assume**.
2 *(v) Let's suppose that pigs could fly!* imagine, pretend, make believe, fantasize.

sure *see* **certain** 1, 3.

surface

1 *(n) This fruit has a knobbly surface.* exterior, covering, outside, skin, outer face, wall, crust, coat.
2 *(n) The table has a shiny surface.* top, coating, finish, veneer, sheen, polish, patina, appearance, texture.
3 *(n) Paint each surface of the box a different colour. See* **side** 1.

surge

1 *(v) We watched the waves surge around the rocks.* gush, rush, swirl, eddy, billow, seethe, stream, well up, heave, roll.
2 *(v) Did you see the fans surge on to the pitch?* rush, charge, stampede, swarm, stream, throng, flood, sweep, push.

surprise

1 *(v) This news will surprise you.* amaze, astonish, astound, stun, stagger, shock, take your breath away, bowl you over *(informal)*, leave you open-mouthed, throw *(informal)*, wow *(slang)*.
2 *(v) Did Mum surprise you as you were raiding the fridge?* burst in on, catch you out, catch you unawares, take you by surprise, catch you in the act, catch you red-handed, startle, ambush.
3 *(n) Kate's eyes opened wide with surprise.* amazement, astonishment, incredulity, wonder, shock, bewilderment.
4 *(n) What a surprise! See* **shock** 4.

surprised

(adj) I bet you're surprised to see me! amazed, astonished, astounded, startled, taken aback, taken by surprise, shocked, stunned, staggered, thunderstruck, flabbergasted *(informal)*, gobsmacked *(slang)*, bowled over *(informal)*.

surprising

(adj) A surprising result. amazing, astonishing, astounding, incredible, staggering, startling, extraordinary, unexpected, unforeseen, unpredicted, unusual, remarkable, shocking.
OPPOSITES: predictable, unsurprising.

surrender

(v) Will you surrender? give in, admit defeat, give yourself up, submit, yield, cave in *(informal)*, lay down your arms, show the white flag, throw in the towel, quit.

surround

(v) The soldiers planned to surround the castle. circle, ring, close in on, encircle, hem in, fence in, hedge in, encompass, enclose, envelop, besiege, lay siege to.

surroundings

(plural n) The hotel is situated in pleasant surroundings. environment, location, neighbourhood, setting, vicinity, locality.

survey

(n) Show the results of your survey in a graph. study, investigation, inquiry, examination, analysis, research, review, poll, questionnaire, ballot, count, census.

survive

1 *(v) The explorers managed to survive.* stay alive, hold out, get by *(informal)*, cling to life, keep body and soul together *(informal)*, pull through, live, exist.
2 *(v) Did the daffodils survive the storm?* come through, withstand, weather, live through, outlast, outlive.

suspect

1 *(v) Why should Oz suspect you?* distrust, doubt, have suspicions about, have doubts about, have misgivings about, have qualms about, be sceptical about, disbelieve, mistrust, think you are guilty, smell a rat.
2 *(v) I suspect we'll lose.* have a feeling, have a hunch, have a sneaking suspicion, think, guess *(informal)*, imagine, suppose.

suspense
(n) The suspense is killing me! tension, uncertainty, anticipation, expectation, excitement, anxiety.

suspicious
1 (adj) Don't be so suspicious; you can trust me. distrustful, wary, doubtful, uneasy, apprehensive, sceptical, jealous.
OPPOSITES: trusting, unsuspecting.
2 (adj) That man in the dark glasses looks suspicious. questionable, suspect, dubious, shifty, dodgy (informal), shady (informal), fishy (informal), disreputable, slippery.
OPPOSITES: above board, respectable.

swagger
(v) Look at Bozo swagger about in his leather jacket! strut, parade, prance, swank (informal), show off (informal).

swallow
1 (v) Swallow your bun. See **eat** 2.
2 (v) Swallow your juice. See **drink** 1.

swamp
(n) bog, marsh, marshland, morass, mire, quagmire, fen, quicksand.

swap see **exchange**.

swarm see **crowd** 1, 2.

sway
(v) The wind made the trees sway. bend, lean, wave, move to and fro, rock, swing.

swear
1 (v) Don't swear! use bad language, curse, be foul-mouthed, blaspheme, turn the air blue (informal), cuss (informal).
2 (v) Swear you'll always love me! See **promise** 1.

sweat
1 (n) I'm covered in sweat. perspiration.
2 (v) The runners began to sweat. perspire, break out in a sweat, drip with perspiration, swelter, glow, steam.

sweaty
(adj) I was sweaty after the match. sweating, perspiring, dripping with perspiration, drenched in sweat, sticky, clammy, glowing.

sweep
1 (v) Sweep the crumbs off the table. brush, clear, clean, dust, remove, push.
2 (v) Fire began to sweep through the building. spread, race, tear, rip, whip, whoosh (informal), fly, streak, course.

sweet
1 (adj) This pudding tastes really sweet. sugary, syrupy, sickly, cloying, treacly, sweetened, saccharine.
OPPOSITES: bitter, sour, savoury.
2 (adj) The sweet smell of roses filled the air. fragrant, sweet-smelling, aromatic, balmy, fresh, cloying, sickly.
OPPOSITES: foul, acrid.
3 (adj) What a sweet child! cute, appealing, lovable, charming, endearing, winsome, engaging, delightful, sweet-tempered, pretty, lovely, attractive.
OPPOSITES: nasty, obnoxious.

4 (adj) I love the sweet sound of the lark's song. tuneful, melodious, musical, dulcet, harmonious, mellow, soft, soothing.
OPPOSITES: harsh, discordant.
5 (n) What's for sweet? See **dessert**.
6 **sweets** (plural n) Inga spends all her money on sweets. confectionery, sweeties (plural) (informal), candy, bonbons (plural).

swell
1 (v) My ankle started to swell. puff up, balloon, bulge, blow up, become bloated.
2 (v) The sails began to swell. fill out, billow, inflate, expand, balloon, bulge.

swerve
(v) The car had to swerve. veer, turn aside, change direction, take evasive action, go off course, dodge, weave, swing, wheel.

swift see **fast** 1.

swim
1 (v) I can't swim. float, doggy-paddle, do breaststroke, do the crawl, do backstroke, do butterfly, tread water.
OPPOSITE: sink.
2 (v) Let's swim in the lake. go for a swim, go swimming, take a dip, bathe, splash about, go skinny-dipping, dive, plunge.

swing
1 (v) Monkeys like to swing by their tails. hang, dangle, move back and forth, rock, sway, be suspended.
2 (v) Nola's mood can swing from one extreme to the other. shift, fluctuate, veer, waver, seesaw, change, vary, alter.

swirl see **whirl**.

switch see **change** 4, 5, 6.

swivel
(v) Press the button to make the robot's head swivel. pivot, rotate, revolve, spin, turn, swing round, gyrate, twirl, wheel.

swollen
(adj) After the fight, Rocky had a swollen nose. puffy, inflamed, bulbous, enlarged, bulging, distended, bloated, puffed up.

swoop
(v) Watch the eagles swoop. dive, plunge, sweep down, drop, plummet, descend, fly down, nose-dive, pounce, lunge.

sword
(n) blade, steel.
TYPES OF SWORD: broadsword, cutlass, dagger, dirk, foil, machete, rapier, sabre, samurai sword, scimitar.

symbol
1 (n) A horseshoe is a symbol of good luck. sign, token, emblem, mark, image.
2 (n) The school symbol is a swan. badge, emblem, insignia, logo, sign, motif.

sympathetic
(adj) Mum was sympathetic when I had to change schools. understanding, supportive, caring, concerned, kind, comforting, considerate, consoling, sorry, compassionate, encouraging, approving.
OPPOSITES: unsympathetic, callous.

Tt

tackle
1 (v) Try to tackle Simon before he scores. challenge, intercept, block, take on, bring down, grab, seize, stop.
2 (v) I'm ready to tackle the next question. get to work on, embark on, set about, get stuck into (informal), wade into, attempt, try, have a go at (informal), have a stab at (informal), deal with, get to grips with, grapple with.
3 (v) Who will tackle Dad about bedtimes? confront, challenge, talk to, speak to, take on, have a go at (informal), face up to.

tactful
(adj) It's not tactful of you to laugh at my hair. diplomatic, discreet, polite, subtle, sensitive, considerate, thoughtful.
OPPOSITES: tactless, insensitive.

tactless
(adj) Dom made a tactless remark about Dad's bald patch. indiscreet, undiplomatic, unsubtle, indelicate, blundering, clumsy, heavy-handed, insensitive, thoughtless, inconsiderate, impolite, rude, hurtful.
OPPOSITES: tactful, diplomatic.

take
1 (v) Take your suitcase upstairs. carry, bring, move, cart, lift, haul.
2 (v) Take my hand! take hold of, hold on to, grab, grasp, grip, clutch, hang on to.
3 (v) Dad will take you to school. bring, drive, run, give you a lift, accompany, walk, escort, ferry, transport, convey.
4 (v) Please take a piece of cake. have, help yourself to, pick out, choose, select.
5 (v) Did the burglars take anything valuable? See **steal** 2.
6 (v) Did the terrorists take any hostages? capture, seize, abduct, kidnap, snatch, carry off, detain, arrest.
7 (v) Take your medicine. swallow, gulp down, get down, drink, consume, inhale.
8 (v) Do you take the bus? catch, travel by, go by, come by, use.
9 (v) Card tricks take a lot of practice. need, require, call for, demand.
10 (v) I can't take this noise. See **stand** 4.

take advantage of
(phrase) Don't take advantage of your friends. exploit, use, walk all over (informal), impose on, manipulate, milk, squeeze dry, rip off (slang).

take away
(v) Take away three from eight. subtract, take, deduct, minus, remove.
OPPOSITE: add.

take in
(v) I can't take in all this information at once. absorb, digest, assimilate, make sense of, grasp, understand, comprehend.

take off
1 (v) Take off your clothes. remove, strip off, peel off, throw off, drop, discard.
OPPOSITE: put on.
2 (v) We watched the plane take off. leave the ground, take to the air, rise into the air, become airborne, lift off, climb.
OPPOSITE: land.

take part
(phrase) Do you want to take part? join in, participate, be involved, contribute, play a part, be included, enter (competition).

talented
1 (adj) I really envy Jemima; she's so talented. gifted, accomplished, versatile, clever, able, brilliant, artistic, musical.
2 (adj) Gary is a talented footballer. accomplished, skilful, brilliant, gifted, skilled, expert, proficient, capable, deft.

talk
1 (v) Mum can talk for hours. speak, chat, chatter, converse, hold forth, spout (informal), natter, gossip, rattle on, prattle on, rabbit on (informal), witter on (informal), jabber on, go on (informal), yak (slang), jaw (slang), spiel, gabble, babble.
2 (v) Can you talk Italian? See speak 2.
3 (v) If you're upset it helps to talk. express your feelings, discuss things, share your thoughts, get things off your chest (informal), put things into words.
4 (v) The police quizzed Burglar Beryl but she wouldn't talk. blab, let the cat out of the bag, give the game away, speak out, confess, tell, tell tales, spill the beans (informal), squeal (slang), grass (slang).
5 (n) Sophie and I had a talk on the phone. chat, conversation, word, gossip, natter, chinwag (informal), confab (informal), heart to heart, tête à tête.
6 (n) I had a long talk with the careers teacher. chat, conversation, discussion, meeting, interview, consultation.
7 (n) Dad gave a talk. See speech 1.

talkative
(adj) Zoë is so talkative, it's hard to shut her up. chatty, gossipy, garrulous, loquacious, voluble, gushing, effusive.

tall
1 (adj) Fran is quite tall. big, lanky, rangy, long-legged, leggy, gangling, statuesque.
OPPOSITES: short, small.
2 (adj) Tall towers loomed over us. high, lofty, giant, towering, soaring, sky-high.
OPPOSITES: small, low.

tame
(adj) Is your pet tame? domesticated, used to humans, safe, docile, gentle, manageable, obedient, trained, house-trained, broken in (horse).
OPPOSITES: wild, untamed.

tamper
(v) Don't tamper with my computer! interfere, meddle, tinker, fiddle (informal), mess about, muck about (slang), monkey around, fool around (informal), damage.

tangle
1 (n) Can you sort out this tangle of threads? jumble, muddle, mass, mess, knot, snarl, coil, mesh, web, confusion.
2 (v) Don't tangle yourself in that wire. entangle, ensnare, enmesh, get tangled up, get snarled up, get muddled up, trap.
OPPOSITES: untangle, extricate, free.

tangled
(adj) I can't straighten out these tangled threads. snarled, twisted, knotted, jumbled, scrambled, messy, matted, tousled (hair), dishevelled (hair).

tanned
(adj) Kit looks tanned. suntanned, brown, bronzed, sunburnt, weather-beaten.

tantrum see temper 1.

tap
1 (n) Water gushed out of the tap. spout, valve, stopcock, mixer tap.
2 (n) I heard a tap. See knock 3.
3 (v) Did you hear something tap against the window? knock, rap, thud, bang, beat, drum, hammer, strike, hit.
4 (v) Tap Ed on the back. touch, pat, slap.

tape
1 (n) Wrap some tape round the parcel. sticky tape, adhesive tape, ribbon, string.
2 (n) What's on this tape? cassette, video, video tape, video cassette, audiocassette.
3 (v) Tape the pieces together. stick, fasten, fix, attach, tie, bind, secure.
4 (v) Did you tape the concert? record, video, tape-record.

target
1 (n) Aim at the target. bull's-eye, mark.
2 (n) My target is to run a mile. See aim 1.

task
(n) I have a task to complete. job, chore, duty, assignment, activity, undertaking, piece of work, exercise, challenge, mission.

taste
1 (n) This dish doesn't have much taste. flavour, tang, flavouring, savour, relish, character, zest, aftertaste. ❖ Also see food & flavours.
2 (n) Give me a taste of your supper. mouthful, spoonful, bite, nibble, sip, drop, morsel, titbit, try, swallow.
3 (n) Kylie has no taste! style, flair, class, fashion sense, judgment, discernment, colour sense, design sense.
4 (n) Flash Frank has a taste for fast cars. liking, penchant, fondness, preference, appetite, desire, fancy, relish, weakness.
5 (v) Taste this snack. try, sample, try out, test, nibble, sip, relish, savour.
6 (v) The sauce should taste of orange. have a flavour, smack, savour, have a tang.
7 (v) Can you taste the garlic in this dish? make out, distinguish, identify, recognize.

tasteless
1 (adj) Tasteless soup. flavourless, bland, insipid, unexciting, uninteresting, boring, weak, watery, mild, dull, watered down.

2 (adj) A tasteless comment. crude, vulgar, crass, uncouth, coarse, cheap, offensive, distasteful, insensitive, tactless.
3 (adj) Tasteless clothes. See vulgar 2.

tasty see delicious.

taunt see make fun of.

taut see tight 1.

teach
1 (v) Dan wants to teach photography. be a teacher of, give lessons in, give classes in, give instruction in, lecture in, demonstrate.
2 (v) Mrs Badger aims to teach her students thoroughly. educate, instruct, tutor, coach, train, drill, inform, enlighten.
3 (v) Can you teach Daisy how to tie her shoelaces? show, explain to, demonstrate to, train, instruct.

teacher
(n) TYPES OF TEACHER: coach, don, governess, guide, guru, headteacher, instructor, lecturer, mentor, professor, schoolteacher, trainer, tutor.

team
(n) Please join our team. side, crew, squad, troupe, line-up, club, gang, band, group, company, unit, staff, alliance, party.

tear
1 (v) The brambles will tear your dress. rip, cut, rip to shreds, slit, slash, split, pull to pieces, snag, pierce, mangle, claw at.
2 (v) Louis started to tear the paper off his present. rip, pull, yank, wrench, peel.
3 (v) I saw Jim tear past. See speed 4.
4 (n) There's a tear in my shorts. rip, split, slit, slash, cut, hole, gash, snag, run.

tease
(v) Does your brother tease you? pull your leg (informal), wind you up (informal), have you on (informal), kid (informal), make fun of, laugh at, taunt, mock, goad, torment, pester, annoy, provoke.

teenager
(n) adolescent, young person, youngster, youth, juvenile.

telephone see phone 1, 2.

television
(n) What's on the television tonight? TV, telly (informal), box (informal), gogglebox (slang), small screen (informal).
TYPES OF TELEVISION PROGRAMME: arts programme, cartoon, chat show, children's programme, classic drama, comedy, costume drama, courtroom drama, current affairs programme, debate, detective series, discussion programme, docudrama, documentary, drama, film, game show, hospital drama, live show, magazine programme, miniseries, murder mystery, natural history programme, news broadcast, newsflash, play, police drama, quiz, real-life drama, serial, series, sitcom (situation comedy), soap (soap opera), sports programme, talk show, variety show, whodunit (informal). ❖ Also see television & film.

television and film

television and film

TV and film people

broadcaster	interviewer
camera	narrator
operator	newsreader
cast (actors	presenter
and actresses)	producer
commentator	reporter
director	researcher
film crew	scriptwriter
floor manager	sound engineer
game show	stuntman
host	stuntwoman

costume

TV programmes and films can be...

banned
censored
cut
dubbed
edited for language
subtitled

hair-raising stunt

TV and film people use...

autocue	microphone
camera	props
costume	scenery
lighting	script
locations	sets
make-up	studio

films and TV dramas may contain...

action	happy ending	sound effects
car chase	humour	soundtrack
climax	incidental music	special effects
close-up shots	intrigue	stunts
computer animation	love scene	suspense
dialogue	murder hunt	sword fight
flashback	plot (storyline)	theme music
gratuitous violence	shoot-out	trick photography

swashbuckling sword fight

romantic love scene

TV programmes may contain...

action replay	exclusive
audience	footage
participation	highlights
background	in-depth
music	investigation
canned	interview
laughter	library pictures
commentary	live coverage
commercial	news report
break	outside
computer	broadcast
graphics	phone-in
crime	satellite link-up
reconstruction	title music
debate	video clip
discussion	voice-over

news report

audience participation

films and TV dramas can be...

action-packed	harrowing	slow-moving
atmospheric	heart-	spectacular
chilling	warming	spooky *(informal)*
cliffhanging	inspiring	stirring
compelling	intriguing	swashbuckling
depressing	melodramatic	tear-jerking
disturbing	moving	*(informal)*
dramatic	nail-biting	tense
enthralling	poignant	terrifying
gory	predictable	thrilling
gripping	realistic	touching
grisly	romantic	violent
gruesome	sentimental	visually stunning
hair-raising	shocking	

TV studio

lighting
monitor
period costume
microphone
boom
prop
sound engineer
TV camera
camera operator
floor manager
dolly (camera stand on wheels)

nail-biting car chase
microphone
movie camera
arc lamp

comedies can be...

amusing	riotous
anarchic	satirical
entertaining	side-splitting
farcical	slapstick
frenetic	wacky
hilarious	*(slang)*
idiotic	way-out
inane (silly)	*(informal)*
offbeat	witty
quirky	zany

current affairs programmes and documentaries can be...

alarmist	hard-hitting
controversial	informative
distressing	provocative
disturbing	revealing
educational	shocking
enlightening	superficial
factual	thought-
fascinating	provoking

Also see **comedy, film, television.**

tell
1 (v) I'll tell you where the treasure is buried. let you know, inform, notify, reveal to, disclose to, divulge to, describe to, recount to, relate to, mention to, report to, confess to, own up to, tip you off about.
2 (v) The signs tell you that it isn't safe to swim. show, inform, advise, indicate to, warn, notify, tip you off, proclaim to.
3 (v) Didn't I tell you to be home by ten o'clock? See **order** 1.
4 (v) I'll tell the story while you act it out. relate, narrate, recount, recite, describe.
5 I couldn't tell which twin it was. make out, work out, identify, recognize, distinguish, discern, discover, differentiate.

tell off
(v) (informal) Dad will tell you off if you're late. scold, reprimand, lecture, tick you off (informal), bawl you out (informal), tear you off a strip (informal), read you the riot act, give you a rocket (informal), give you a dressing-down (informal), haul you over the coals (informal), rebuke, castigate.

tell on
(v) (informal) Your secret is safe; I won't tell on you! betray, give you away, tell tales about, sneak on (informal), snitch on (slang), rat on (informal), grass on (slang), report, shop (slang), breathe a word.

temper
1 (n) Dad's in a temper. rage, fury, bad temper, foul temper, tantrum, bad mood.
2 (n) People avoid Danielle because of her temper. quick temper, hot temper, irritability, peevishness, irascibility, hot-headedness, unpredictability, volatility.
3 lose your temper see **lose your temper**.

temporary
1 (adj) Jo's bad moods are only temporary. short-lived, brief, passing, fleeting, momentary, a flash in the pan, transient, impermanent, ephemeral.
OPPOSITES: permanent, long-lasting.
2 (adj) This is a temporary arrangement. provisional, interim, stopgap, short-term.
OPPOSITES: permanent, long-term.

tempt
(v) The witch tried to tempt the princess off the path. lure, entice, draw, lead, coax, persuade, woo, inveigle, seduce, bribe.

tempting
(adj) The thought of a tropical holiday is so tempting! inviting, irresistible, enticing, attractive, alluring, tantalizing, seductive, appetizing (food), mouthwatering (food).

tender
1 (adj) Cook the meat until it's tender. soft, succulent, juicy, coming off the bone.
OPPOSITES: tough, chewy.
2 (adj) Is your finger still tender? See **sore**.
3 (adj) Max gave me a tender look. affectionate, loving, gentle, sympathetic, caring, tenderhearted, warm, kind, doting.
OPPOSITES: cold, unsympathetic.

tense
1 (adj) I feel tense. wound up (informal), worked up, keyed up, uptight (informal), stressed, under pressure, nervous, edgy, on edge, jumpy, jittery (informal), anxious.
OPPOSITE: relaxed.
2 (adj) We had some tense moments waiting for the result. See **stressful** 1.
3 (adj) My muscles were tense as I waited for the race to start. taut, tight, strained, stretched, rigid, flexed, braced, stiff.
OPPOSITE: relaxed.

tension
(n) I can't bear the tension of waiting. suspense, stress, strain, anxiety, worry, uncertainty, anticipation, excitement.

terrible
1 (adj) A terrible crime. See **dreadful** 1.
2 (adj) A terrible essay. See **dreadful** 2.
3 (adj) A terrible smell. See **horrible** 2.
4 (adj) A terrible predicament. See **desperate** 3.

terrific
1 (adj) A terrific storm. tremendous, enormous, gigantic, huge, great, mighty, fierce, violent, intense, severe, dreadful, awful, terrible, horrific, awesome.
2 (adj) (informal) A terrific party. See **great** 9.

terrified see **scared** 1.

terrifying see **frightening**.

terror see **fear** 1, 2.

test
1 (n) Did you pass the test? exam, examination, assessment, oral test, written test, practical, audition, medical (informal).
2 (v) This quiz will test your general knowledge. put to the test, assess, evaluate, check, examine, probe, appraise.
3 (v) Scientists test medicines to make sure they are safe. run tests on, investigate, analyse, experiment on, check, check out, research, inspect, scrutinize.

thank
(v) Remember to thank Granny for the present. say thank you to, show your appreciation to, express gratitude to.

thankful see **grateful**.

thaw
(v) Don't let the ice cream thaw. defrost, melt, soften, liquefy, warm up, unfreeze.
OPPOSITE: freeze.

then see **next** 3.

theory
(n) The detective's theory was proved right. idea, hypothesis, supposition, conjecture, speculation, notion, belief, assumption.

thick
1 (adj) Thick walls. broad, wide, deep, solid, substantial, sturdy, stout, chunky.
OPPOSITES: thin, flimsy.
2 (adj) A thick book. fat, chunky, bulky, heavy, weighty, big, large.
OPPOSITES: thin, slim.

3 (adj) Thick hair. abundant, luxuriant, bushy, shaggy, coarse, wiry, frizzy, woolly.
OPPOSITES: thin, sparse.
4 (adj) Thick jungle. dense, impenetrable, impassable, heavy, lush, closely packed.
OPPOSITES: sparse, thin.
5 (adj) Thick fog. dense, heavy, soupy, impenetrable, murky, smoggy, opaque.
OPPOSITES: thin, light.
6 (adj) Thick custard. condensed, concentrated, solid, viscous, gelatinous, congealed, coagulated, firm, stiff.
OPPOSITES: thin, runny.

thicken
(v) Wait for the mixture to thicken. set, jell, solidify, coagulate, congeal, cake, condense, reduce, clot (blood).

thief
(n) pickpocket, shoplifter, pilferer, poacher, burglar, housebreaker, robber, mugger (informal), swindler, embezzler, fraudster.

thin
1 (adj) A thin girl. slim, slender, slight, lean, lanky, skinny, underweight, spindly, scrawny, bony, gaunt, scraggy, flat-chested, waiflike, skeletal, emaciated, undernourished, anorexic.
OPPOSITES: plump, fat, obese.
2 (adj) A thin crack. See **fine** 4.
3 (adj) Thin curtains. light, lightweight, flimsy, fine, delicate, floaty, gauzy, filmy, gossamer, diaphanous, sheer, translucent, transparent, see-through, threadbare.
OPPOSITES: thick, heavy.
4 (adj) Thin hair. sparse, wispy, fine, straggly, thinning, scanty, scarce.
OPPOSITES: thick, luxuriant.
5 (adj) Thin gravy. runny, watery, diluted, wishy-washy (informal), weak.
OPPOSITES: thick, concentrated.

thing
1 (n) What's that thing on the table? object, article, item.
2 (n) There's a thing crawling out of the swamp! creature, being, entity.
3 (n) We have a thing for crushing cans. gadget, device, machine, contraption, appliance, tool, instrument, implement.
4 (n) A funny thing happened. incident, occurrence, happening, phenomenon.
5 (n) There's one more thing I have to do. job, task, chore.
6 (n) What made you do such a crazy thing? act, deed, exploit, feat.
7 (n) A worrying thing occurred to me. thought, idea, notion, theory.
8 (n) What's the thing you like best about this book? aspect, feature, quality, characteristic, attribute, detail, point.

things
(plural n) Put your things away. belongings (plural), stuff, paraphernalia, bits and pieces (plural), odds and ends (plural), possessions (plural), clothes (plural), gear, kit, equipment, tools (plural), tackle, junk (informal), clobber (slang), baggage.

think

think

1 *(v) I used to think that girls were silly.* believe, consider, reckon, be convinced, be of the opinion, maintain, feel.
2 *(v) I think it's about four o'clock.* reckon, imagine, suppose, guess *(informal),* would say, estimate, assume, presume, believe.
3 *(v) I didn't think that you'd come.* expect, foresee, anticipate, envisage, suppose, imagine, dream.
4 *(v) Lauren likes to sit in her room and think.* meditate, contemplate, cogitate, deliberate, reflect, ponder, muse, brood.
5 **think about** *(v) You should think about your future.* consider, give thought to, put your mind to, concentrate on, reflect on, mull over, chew over, weigh up, work out.

think up

(v) We must think up a cunning plan. dream up, come up with, make up, concoct, devise, invent, create, contrive.

thirsty

(adj) The explorers were thirsty. parched, dry *(informal),* dehydrated, gasping, panting, dying of thirst *(informal).*

thorough

(adj) A thorough investigation. detailed, in-depth, extensive, comprehensive, exhaustive, full, complete, wide-ranging, meticulous, painstaking, methodical.

thought

1 *(n) This plan will need a lot of thought.* consideration, reflection, deliberation, thinking, brainwork, concentration, reasoning, contemplation, meditation.
2 *(n) An interesting thought. See* **idea 1.**

thoughtful

1 *(adj) It was thoughtful of you to visit Granny.* considerate, kind, caring, unselfish, friendly, helpful, compassionate.
OPPOSITES: thoughtless, selfish.
2 *(adj) Tessa wrote a thoughtful essay.* well-thought-out, perceptive, insightful, profound, penetrating, discerning.
OPPOSITES: superficial, shallow.
3 *(adj) Hanif is in a thoughtful mood.* pensive, reflective, contemplative, philosphical, meditative, introspective, brooding, wistful, dreamy.

thoughtless

(adj) A thoughtless remark. insensitive, tactless, inconsiderate, unkind, uncaring, unsympathetic, cruel, rude, indiscreet.
OPPOSITES: thoughtful, tactful.

thrash *see* **beat 1, 2.**

thread

(n) Pull the thread tight. strand, cotton, string, yarn, twine, wool, silk.

threaten

1 *(v) Did Bozo threaten you?* intimidate, bully, terrorize, make threats to, menace, browbeat, pressurize, lean on *(informal).*
2 *(v) Reckless drivers threaten lives.* put at risk, endanger, imperil, put in jeopardy.

threatening *see* **menacing.**

thrill

(n) Luke gets a thrill out of surfing. sense of excitement, feeling of exhilaration, kick *(informal),* buzz *(slang),* charge *(slang).*

thrilling *see* **exciting.**

throb

(v) Loud music began to throb through the house. pulsate, pound, thump, thud, beat, vibrate, reverberate, pulse.

throw

1 *(v) Throw the ball.* hurl, fling, chuck *(informal),* lob *(informal),* sling, toss, pitch, shy, heave, send, launch, propel, let fly.
2 *(v) (informal) Did Aunt Bertha's arrival throw you?* faze, disconcert, put you off, throw you off your stride, worry, unsettle, unnerve, upset, rattle *(informal).*

throw away

1 *(v) Throw away your rubbish.* get rid of, throw out, dispose of, chuck out *(informal),* bin, dump *(informal),* scrap, ditch *(slang),* discard, jettison.
2 *(v) Don't throw away this opportunity. See* **waste.**

throw out

(v) Why did the football club throw you out? expel, eject, kick you out *(informal),* turf you out *(informal),* oust, banish, evict.

throw up *(informal) see* **vomit.**

thump

1 *(v) Don't thump your brother! See* **hit 1.**
2 *(v) My heart began to thump loudly. See* **beat 3.**
3 *(n) Jack fell out of the tree with a thump.* thud, crash, bang, clunk, clonk, clump, clomp, thwack, smack, wham.

tidy

1 *(adj) Jo always looks tidy.* neat, smart, well-turned-out, well-groomed, trim, spruce, spick-and-span, presentable.
OPPOSITES: untidy, messy.
2 *(adj) Adam keeps his room tidy.* neat, uncluttered, clean, well-organized, in good order, shipshape, spick-and-span, immaculate, in apple-pie order *(informal).*
OPPOSITES: untidy, messy.
3 *(v) Please tidy your room.* sort out, tidy up, clear up, neaten up, put straight.

tie

1 *(v) Tie the boat to the post.* tie up, secure, fasten, attach, make fast, tether, lash, knot, moor, hitch, bind, rope, chain.
2 *(v) Please tie your shoelaces.* tie up, do up, knot, make a bow in, make a knot in.
3 *(n) The result was a tie. See* **draw 6.**
4 *(n) Dad wore a spotty tie.* necktie, bow tie, dicky bow, cravat, neckerchief.

tight

1 *(adj) Pull the rope until it's tight.* taut, rigid, stretched, strained, tense.
OPPOSITES: slack, loose.
2 *(adj) Mo wore a tight skirt.* tight-fitting, close-fitting, skintight, figure-hugging, snug, clinging, straining at the seams.
OPPOSITES: baggy, roomy.
3 *(adj) Screw the lid on until it's tight.* sealed, secure, airtight, watertight.
OPPOSITE: loose.
4 *(adv) Hold on tight!* tightly, firmly, fast.

tilt *see* **lean 1.**

time

1 *(n) Burglar Beryl spent a short time in prison.* period, while, spell, interval, stretch, term, season, session, duration.
2 *(n) What did people wear in the time of Queen Victoria? See* **age 1.**
3 *(n) The bomb could blow up at any time.* moment, minute, second, instant, point, point in time, stage, juncture.
4 *(n) What time would suit you?* day, date, time of day, hour, week, month, season, year, decade, century, millennium.
5 *(v) Time how long the journey takes.* measure, count, clock, record, calculate.

timid *see* **shy.**

tingle

(v) Can you feel your skin tingle? prickle, prick, tickle, itch, sting, come up in goose pimples, have pins and needles *(informal).*

tinkle *see* **jingle 1.**

tiny

1 *(adj) A tiny girl.* small, slight, petite, titchy *(slang),* undersized, pint-sized *(informal),* diminutive, Lilliputian.
OPPOSITES: big, tall, enormous.
2 *(adj) A tiny speck.* minute, minuscule, microscopic, infinitesimal, teeny, weeny, teeny-weeny, itsy-bitsy *(informal).*
OPPOSITES: huge, enormous.

tip

1 *(n) The tip of an iceberg.* top, peak, pinnacle, summit, point, cap, crown, apex.
2 *(n) A pencil tip.* end, point, sharp end.
3 *(n) A useful tip.* piece of advice, hint, suggestion, pointer, tip-off, clue.
4 *(v) Tip the scraps into the bin.* pour, empty, dump, unload, slide.
5 **tip over** *(v) Don't let the desk tip over!* fall over, topple over, keel over, overturn, upend, capsize *(boat).*

tired

1 *(adj) You must be tired after your hard work.* worn out, exhausted, weary, sleepy, drowsy, ready to drop, dead tired, drained, shattered *(informal),* done in *(informal),* dead on your feet *(informal),* whacked *(informal),* bushed *(slang),* zonked *(slang).*
OPPOSITES: wide-awake, rested.
2 **tired of** *(adj) I'm tired of your moaning. See* **fed up with.**

tiring

(adj) Teaching is a tiring job. exhausting, draining, wearing, wearying, taxing, demanding, tough, arduous, strenuous.

toilet

(n) lavatory, loo *(informal),* WC (water closet), public convenience, urinal, bog *(slang),* john *(slang),* khazi *(slang),* ladies *(informal),* gents *(informal),* cloakroom, bathroom, powder room, washroom.

tolerant
1 *(adj) I try to be tolerant about other people's views.* open-minded, broad-minded, unprejudiced, unbigoted, fair, liberal, understanding, sympathetic.
OPPOSITES: intolerant, narrow-minded.
2 *(adj) Amy's dad is so tolerant; he lets her do anything.* easy-going, permissive, free and easy, indulgent, lenient, soft, patient, long-suffering, unshockable, forgiving.
OPPOSITES: strict, authoritarian.

tolerate *see* **endure** 1.

tomb
(n) grave, burial place, sarcophagus, burial chamber, vault, crypt, sepulchre, mausoleum, catacomb, final resting place.

tool
(n) implement, instrument, device, utensil, gadget, appliance, machine, contraption.

tooth
(n) An animal's tooth. fang, tusk.

top
1 *(n) I climbed to the top of the mountain.* peak, summit, pinnacle, crest, tip, crown *(hill)*, brow *(hill)*, highest point, apex.
2 *(n) Put the top back on.* lid, cap, cover, stopper, cork, covering.
3 *(n) Paula has a new top.* ❖ *See* **clothes**.
4 *(adj) The jug is on the top shelf.* highest, topmost, upper, uppermost.
OPPOSITES: bottom, lowest.
5 *(adj) Who got the top marks in the test?* highest, best, most, maximum, winning.
OPPOSITES: lowest, bottom.
6 *(adj) Professor Peabody is a top scientist.* leading, eminent, outstanding, great, important, famous, celebrated, renowned, noted, high-ranking, crack *(slang)*.
OPPOSITES: second-rate, obscure.

topic *see* **subject**.

torment *see* **torture** 1, 2.

torture
1 *(v) Will the kidnappers torture their prisoners?* inflict pain on, hurt, abuse, maltreat, ill-treat, be cruel to, torment, use force on, intimidate, persecute, bully.
2 *(n) You can't imagine the torture I went through.* agony, torment, anguish, pain, suffering, misery, distress, hell *(informal)*.

toss
1 *(v) Toss the ball to me. See* **throw** 1.
2 *(v) Bad dreams made me toss around all night.* thrash, toss and turn, roll, twist and turn, writhe, wriggle, wallow, tumble.
3 *(v) Look at the boats toss on the waves.* bob, wallow, lurch, pitch, tumble, heave.

total
1 *(n) Add up the figures and tell me the total.* tally, full amount, sum total, grand total, answer, sum, aggregate, gross.
2 *(n) What's the total population of the two towns?* overall, complete, sum, full, gross, entire, whole, combined.
3 *(adj) A total disaster. See* **complete** 2.

totter *see* **stagger** 1.

touch
1 *(v) Don't let the wires touch!* come into contact, connect, meet, come together.
2 *(v) I felt the cobweb touch my face.* brush, graze, tickle, rub against.
3 *(v) Don't touch the animals!* lay a finger on, handle, feel, stroke, pat, rub, fondle, caress, nuzzle, tickle, pick up.
4 *(v) Don't touch my radio!* lay a finger on, move, pick up, interfere with, fiddle with *(informal)*, tamper with, finger.
5 *(v) I only managed to touch the ball once in the match.* hit, strike, kick, head, tap, knock, come into contact with.
6 *(v) Never touch drugs!* get involved with, have anything to do with, concern yourself with, handle, consume, use.

touchy
(adj) Treat Amy carefully; she's very touchy. sensitive, easily offended, thin-skinned, oversensitive, irritable, ratty *(informal)*, tetchy, grouchy *(informal)*, bad-tempered.
OPPOSITES: easy-going, thick-skinned.

tough
1 *(adj) Bulletproof glass needs to be tough.* strong, hard, thick, solid, durable, resilient, hard-wearing, unbreakable, indestructible, sturdy, inflexible, firm, rigid.
OPPOSITES: flimsy, fragile.
2 *(adj) You must be tough to go on this expedition.* fit, strong, sturdy, hardy, robust, resilient, brawny, muscular.
OPPOSITES: feeble, delicate.
3 *(adj) Gangsters are pretty tough characters.* rough, hard, hardened, hard-bitten, ruffianly, wild, vicious, violent, lawless, rowdy, hard as nails.
OPPOSITES: gentle, civilized.
4 *(adj) This steak is tough.* chewy, leathery, rubbery, stringy, gristly, sinewy.
OPPOSITES: tender, succulent.
5 *(adj) A tough puzzle. See* **difficult** 1.
6 *(adj) A tough job. See* **difficult** 2.

tower
(n) Let's climb up this tower. turret, keep, clock tower, bell tower, steeple, spire, belfry, minaret, column, pillar, obelisk.

trace
1 *(n) There's just a trace of sherry in this trifle.* dash, touch, spot, bit, drop, splash, smattering, hint, whiff, tinge, soupçon.
2 *(n) Indy found no trace of the temple.* sign, evidence, indication, record, remains *(plural)*, remnants *(plural)*, vestiges *(plural)*.
3 *(v) Police are trying to trace Dodgy Dave.* find, locate, track down, hunt down, seek out, uncover, unearth, get in touch with.

track
1 *(n) The fox left a track.* trail, scent, spoor, footprints *(plural)*, prints *(plural)*, marks *(plural)*, traces *(plural)*.
2 *(n) We cycled along a narrow track.* path, pathway, bridle path, footpath, trail.
3 *(n) The competitors sped round the track.* racetrack, circuit, running track, racecourse, speedway.

tradition *see* **custom**.

tragic
1 *(adj) A tragic ending. See* **sad** 2.
2 *(adj) A tragic accident.* catastrophic, disastrous, calamitous, terrible, appalling, dreadful, awful, shocking, fatal, deadly.

trail
1 *(n) Angus left a trail of rubbish.* line, train, stream, track, path, wake, wash.
2 *(n) Follow the fox's trail. See* **track** 1.
3 *(v) Let the streamers trail from the ceiling. See* **hang** 1.
4 *(v) Watch the queen's robes trail behind her.* drag, sweep, fall, stream out, flow.
5 *(v) Don't trail behind. See* **drop behind**.

train
1 *(n) The train pulled into the station.* locomotive, engine.
TYPES OF TRAIN: boat train, bullet train *(Japan)*, diesel train, electric train, express train, freight train, goods train, high-speed train, intercity train, maglev, monorail, steam train, tube train, underground train.
❖ *Also see* **journey words**
2 *(v) Matt wants to train to be a nurse.* study, learn, qualify, prepare.
3 *(v) Athletes train regularly.* practise, exercise, work out, prepare, get fit.
4 *(v) Who will train the team?* coach, prepare, drill, instruct, guide, teach.

tramp *see* **trudge**.

trample on
(v) Don't trample on the tulips! tread on, tramp all over, step on, stamp on, walk on, squash, crush, flatten, grind under foot.

transform *see* **change** 2.

transparent
(adj) Transparent material. see-through, clear, glassy, crystal clear, translucent, sheer, filmy, gauzy, diaphanous.
OPPOSITE: opaque.

trap
1 *(n) The creature was caught in a trap.* snare, noose, net, pit, mousetrap, mantrap, booby trap, web.
2 *(v) The police managed to trap Burglar Beryl.* catch, capture, snare, ensnare, corner, cut off, ambush, smoke out.

travel
1 *(v) Which way will you travel?* go, journey, voyage, head, proceed, drive, walk, cycle, ride, fly, sail, cruise, motor, ramble, roam, wander, trek, commute.
❖ *Also see* **journey words**.
2 *(v) Uncle Walter loves to travel.* see the world, go abroad, go on trips, go on journeys, tour, go globetrotting, sightsee.

treasure
1 *(n) Pirate Peg buried her treasure.* riches *(plural)*, valuables *(plural)*, fortune, hoard, jewels *(plural)*, coins *(plural)*, gold, silver, money. ❖ *Also see* **treasure words**.
2 *(v) Clare will treasure this gift.* cherish, value, prize, appreciate, love, adore, dote on, be careful with, keep safe, look after.

treasure words

treasure words

types of treasure

anklet	earring	medallion
bangle	flagon (jug)	necklace
bracelet	goblet	pendant
brooch	gold bars	platter
chain	gold bullion	(plate)
chalice	(bars or	ring
(drinking	nuggets)	shield
cup)	gold coins	silver coins
coronet	gold nuggets	statue
crown	helmet	sword
dagger	locket	tiara

treasure can be made of...

agate	emerald	onyx
amber	garnet	opal
amethyst	gold	pearl
aquamarine	ivory	ruby
bronze	jade	sapphire
copper	jasper	silver
coral	jet	topaz
crystal	lapis lazuli	turquoise
diamond	moonstone	

treasure can be...

breathtaking	glittering
burnished	grimy
(polished)	inlaid with
dazzling	precious
dusty	stones
encrusted	priceless
with jewels	shimmering
fabulous	shiny
gleaming	sparkling
glinting	tarnished

treasure can be kept in...

casket	treasure
(small chest)	chamber
coffer (chest)	treasure chest
pouch	trunk
strongbox	vault

locket

medallion

casket

gold nuggets

amethyst brooch

garnet

topaz

aquamarine

lapis lazuli necklace

turquoise ring

sword *ruby*

anklet

jewel-encrusted chalice

flagon *golden coronet* *silver platter*

treat

1 (n) *I enjoyed my birthday treat.* present, gift, entertainment, party, outing, surprise, celebration, fun.
2 (v) *How did your penfriend's family treat you?* behave towards, act towards, relate to, look upon, talk to, deal with, handle.
3 (v) *Does the doctor treat outpatients?* look after, take care of, give treatment to, care for, see to, attend to, patch up.

tree

(n) *Look at that tree!* conifer, evergreen, deciduous tree, fruit tree, sapling, bonsai.
TYPES OF TREE: alder, apple, apricot, ash, aspen, beech, birch, cedar, cherry, cypress, ebony, elder, elm, eucalyptus, fig, fir, hawthorn, hazel, holly, horse chestnut, juniper, laburnum, larch, lemon, lime, magnolia, mahogany, mango, maple, mimosa, monkey puzzle, oak, olive, orange, palm, peach, pear, pine, plane, plum, poplar, redwood, rowan, rubber, sequoia, spruce, sweet chestnut, sycamore, walnut, weeping willow, willow, yew.

tremble *see* shiver.

tremendous

1 (adj) *A tremendous bang.* terrific, enormous, colossal, mighty, stupendous, almighty (informal), dreadful, awful, terrible, frightful, deafening, ear-splitting.
2 (adj) (informal) *A tremendous experience. See* fantastic 3.

trick

1 (n) *We were amazed by the magician's trick.* conjuring trick, illusion, magic trick, stunt, sleight of hand.
2 (n) *Mum wasn't amused by our trick.* joke, practical joke, prank, leg-pull (informal), wind-up (slang), hoax, gag (informal), stunt, jape, April fool.
3 (v) *Don't let Ed trick you. See* deceive 1.

trickle *see* dribble 2.

tricky *see* awkward 5, 6.

trip

1 (n) *We're going on a trip to France.* outing, visit, excursion, jaunt, expedition, coach trip, day trip, field trip, tour, journey.
2 (v) *Be careful not to trip!* trip up, fall, fall over, lose your footing, lose your balance, go head over heels, stumble, take a tumble, slip, stagger, catch your foot.

trivial

(adj) *Don't waste my time with trivial details.* unimportant, insignificant, inconsequential, petty, minor, negligible, trifling, piffling, worthless, frivolous.
OPPOSITES: important, significant.

trouble

1 (n) *Our new car has caused us a lot of trouble.* bother, problems (plural), hassle (informal), inconvenience, difficulty, irritation, annoyance, worry, anxiety.
OPPOSITES: pleasure, convenience.

2 (n) *Granny has had a lot of trouble in her life.* difficulty, hardship, adversity, problems (plural), trials (plural), tribulations (plural), misfortune, bad luck, sadness, unhappiness, heartache, pain, suffering.
OPPOSITES: happiness, good fortune.
3 (v) *I didn't mean to trouble you. See* bother 1, 2.
4 in trouble (phrase) *Call me if you're in trouble.* in difficulty, having problems, in a predicament, in a mess, in hot water (informal), in dire straits, in danger.

trousers *see* clothes.

truck *see* lorry.

trudge

(v) *I watched you trudge through the snow.* plod, tramp, slog, stomp (informal), traipse (informal), trek, hike, clomp, yomp, lumber, drag your feet, shuffle.

true

1 (adj) *This is a true story.* real, real-life, factual, actual, based on real life.
OPPOSITES: fictional, made-up.
2 (adj) *Is your account true?* correct, accurate, right, truthful, faithful, exact, precise, reliable, genuine, confirmed.
OPPOSITES: false, fabricated.
3 (adj) *Tell me your true feelings. See* real 3.

trust

(v) *You can trust me; I won't let you down.* put your trust in, have confidence in, have faith in, be sure of, rely on, depend on, count on, pin your hopes on, confide in.

truthful *see* honest 1, 2.

try

1 (n) *Have a try!* attempt, go (informal), bash (informal), stab (informal), shot (informal), crack (informal), effort.
2 (v) *You should try to break the record.* attempt, make an attempt, endeavour, aim, seek, strive, make an effort, do your best, exert yourself, go all out (informal), bend over backwards (informal).
3 (v) *Let's try that new restaurant.* try out, check out (informal), sample, investigate, experience, test, give it a whirl (informal).

tug *see* pull.

tumble *see* fall 1, 3, 6.

tummy (informal) *see* stomach 1, 2.

tune

(n) *A catchy tune.* melody, song, theme, air, refrain. ❖ *Also see* music words.

tunnel

(n) passageway, passage, shaft, mine, burrow, hole, subway, underpass.

turn

1 (v) *Watch the wheels turn.* go round, spin, revolve, rotate, gyrate, roll, circle, wheel, pivot, swivel, twirl, whirl.
2 (v) *It's unlikely that this frog will turn into a prince. See* change 3.
3 (v) *Let's turn the garage into a games room.* convert, adapt, transform, change, make, remodel, alter, make over.

4 *(n) We came to a turn in the road.* bend, curve, twist, hairpin bend, U-turn, corner, turning, turn-off, angle, loop, zigzag.
5 *(n) Everyone will have a turn on the computer.* go *(informal)*, try, chance, shot *(informal)*, opportunity, attempt, bash *(informal)*, stab *(informal)*, spell, stint.

turn out
(v) How did things turn out? work out, end up, develop, pan out *(informal)*, evolve, come about, happen, transpire *(informal)*.

TV *see* **television**.

twinkle *see* **sparkle**.

twist
1 *(v) Twist the threads together.* weave, wind, entwine, intertwine, tangle, plait, braid, knot, loop, wreathe, coil, wrap.
2 *(v) The noise made Posy twist round in her seat.* turn, spin, swivel, swing, pivot.
3 *(v) The path began to twist. See* **wind** 2.
4 *(v) Try not to twist your ankle.* sprain, turn, wrench, strain, rick *(neck)*.
5 *(v) Reporters can twist what you say.* distort, slant, warp, garble, misquote, misrepresent, falsify, change, alter.

twisted
1 *(adj) A twisted tree trunk.* distorted, contorted, crooked, bent, deformed, misshapen, gnarled, knotted.
2 *(adj) Twisted threads. See* **tangled**.

twitch
(v) Do you twitch in your sleep? jerk, fidget, wriggle, squirm, writhe, quiver, shiver, tremble, start, jump.

type *see* **kind** 2, 3.

typical
1 *(adj) It was a typical weekend at home.* normal, average, standard, ordinary, usual, commonplace, everyday, run-of-the-mill.
OPPOSITES: extraordinary, remarkable.
2 *(adj) Woodchester is a typical English village.* archetypal, quintessential, classic, characteristic, representative, stereotypical.
OPPOSITES: atypical, unique.
3 *(adj) It's typical of Dan to be late.* characteristic, in character, true to type, true to form, in keeping, unsurprising.
OPPOSITE: unusual.

ugly
1 *(adj) You look ugly in that mask.* hideous, grotesque, horrible, repulsive, disgusting, revolting, ghastly, monstrous, deformed, disfigured, misshapen.
OPPOSITES: beautiful, lovely.
2 *(adj) What an ugly building!* unsightly, unattractive, hideous, horrible, ghastly, vile, grim, inelegant, tasteless, monstrous.
OPPOSITES: beautiful, lovely.

unavoidable *see* **inevitable**.
unaware *see* **ignorant** 1, 3.
unbearable
(adj) The noise is unbearable. intolerable, unendurable, insupportable, insufferable, unacceptable, too much *(informal)*.

unbelievable *see* **incredible** 1.
uncertain
1 *(adj) I'm uncertain about what to do.* unsure, doubtful, dubious, undecided, hesitant, in two minds, unclear, vague.
2 *(adj) It's uncertain who won the race.* unclear, undecided, unresolved, unconfirmed, inconclusive, arguable, open to question, ambiguous, up in the air.

unclear
(adj) This message is unclear. hard to read, illegible, hard to understand, unintelligible, indecipherable, cryptic, ambiguous, vague, confused, garbled, mystifying, puzzling.

uncomfortable
1 *(adj) My new shoes are uncomfortable.* tight, cramped, hard, stiff, painful.
OPPOSITE: comfortable.
2 *(adj) I feel uncomfortable in this situation.* awkward, ill at ease, self-conscious, embarrassed, out of place, uneasy, tense, on edge, nervous, edgy.
OPPOSITES: comfortable, at ease.

unconscious
(adj) The patient lay unconscious. senseless, comatose, out cold, knocked out, concussed, stunned, sleeping.

underground
(adj) An underground chamber. subterranean, sunken, buried, covered.

understand
1 *(v) I didn't understand what you meant.* realize, see, grasp, know, recognize, take in, comprehend, follow, get, catch on to *(informal)*, cotton on to *(informal)*, twig *(informal)*, get the drift of.
2 *(v) I can't understand this code.* make sense of, make head or tail of *(informal)*, make out, work out, figure out *(informal)*, suss out *(slang)*, decipher, decode.
3 *(v) I understand that you're leaving.* believe, hear, gather, learn.

understanding
1 *(n) Samirah has a good understanding of history. See* **grasp** 4.
2 *(adj) My dad is very understanding.* sympathetic, compassionate, tolerant, forgiving, forbearing, patient, kind, considerate, thoughtful, sensitive.

undo
(v) Can you undo this? unfasten, open, loosen, untie, unwrap, unbutton, unzip, unlace, unhook, unclip, unclasp, unscrew, unpin, unlock, unchain, disentangle, untangle, unravel, release.

undress
(v) Undress before you shower. get undressed, take your clothes off, strip, strip off *(slang)*, peel off *(slang)*, disrobe.

unemployed
(adj) Justin's dad is unemployed. out of work, out of a job, on the dole *(informal)*, jobless, laid off, redundant.

uneven *see* **bumpy** 1.

unexpected *see* **surprising**.

unfair
(adj) An unfair decision. unjust, biased, prejudiced, one-sided, partisan, arbitrary, unreasonable, unjustified, uncalled-for.
OPPOSITES: fair, just.

unfamiliar *see* **strange** 3, 4.

unfortunate
(adj) An unfortunate accident. unlucky, regrettable, dreadful, disastrous, calamitous, tragic, lamentable.

unfriendly
(adj) Unfriendly neighbours. unsociable, aloof, distant, standoffish, cold, cool, chilly, disagreeable, unpleasant, uncivil, hostile, aggressive, antisocial.

unhappy *see* **sad** 1, 2.

unhealthy
1 *(adj) The stray dog looked unhealthy.* ill, sick, in poor health, unwell, sickly, poorly *(informal)*, ailing, infirm, weak, feeble, frail, undernourished, unfit, out of condition.
OPPOSITES: healthy, well.
2 *(adj) The refugees lived in unhealthy conditions.* insanitary, unhygienic, squalid, dirty, disease-ridden, polluted, harmful.
OPPOSITES: clean, healthy.
3 *(adj) A diet of chips and fizzy drinks is unhealthy.* bad for you, unwholesome, unnourishing, harmful, damaging.

unimportant
(adj) Leave out anything that is unimportant. of no importance, trivial, insignificant, inessential, inconsequential, of no consequence, irrelevant, immaterial.
OPPOSITES: important, significant.

uninhabited
1 *(adj) An uninhabited flat. See* **empty** 3.
2 *(adj) An uninhabited planet.* unpopulated, unpeopled, uncolonized, unsettled, deserted, desolate, barren.

unique
(adj) Ziggy's hairstyle is unique. distinctive, in a class of its own, one-off *(informal)*, without equal, unparalleled, unrivalled.

united
1 *(adj) Let's make a united effort to win.* combined, joint, concerted, cooperative, collaborative, collective, common, unified.
2 *(adj) We are united in our opposition to the plan.* agreed, in agreement, undivided, at one, of one mind, unanimous.
OPPOSITES: divided, at odds.

unkind
(adj) It was unkind of you to laugh at me. cruel, nasty, mean, heartless, uncaring, callous, unfriendly, inconsiderate, insensitive, thoughtless, hurtful, spiteful.
OPPOSITES: kind, considerate.

unknown

unknown
1 *(adj) The causes of the disease are unknown.* unidentified, undiscovered, undecided, unrecognized, mysterious, undisclosed, hidden, concealed, secret.
2 *(adj) This song is by an unknown band called Purple Pig.* little-known, obscure, unheard-of, unfamiliar, insignificant.
3 *(adj) Pirate Peg sailed into unknown waters.* unfamiliar, unexplored, uncharted, unmapped, undiscovered, new, strange.

unlikely
(adj) It's unlikely that there's life on Venus. improbable, not likely, doubtful, questionable, inconceivable, unimaginable.

unlucky
1 *(adj) You really are unlucky, aren't you?* unfortunate, accident-prone, jinxed, cursed, ill-fated, ill-starred, star-crossed, out of luck, down on your luck, luckless.
OPPOSITES: lucky, fortunate.
2 *(adj) Seeing a magpie is supposed to be unlucky.* bad luck, a bad sign, a bad omen, inauspicious, ominous, ill-omened.
OPPOSITES: lucky, auspicious.

unnecessary
(adj) Smart clothes are unnecessary on a cycling holiday. inessential, nonessential, uncalled-for, superfluous, surplus to requirements, redundant, dispensable.
OPPOSITES: necessary, essential.

unpleasant
1 *(adj) An unpleasant child.* disagreeable, objectionable, bad-tempered, unfriendly, unkind, nasty, spiteful, hateful, unlovable.
2 *(adj) An unpleasant smell. See* **nasty** 1.

unpopular
(adj) You'll be unpopular if you start telling tales. disliked, friendless, unwanted, unwelcome, out of favour, detested, hated, despised, avoided, ignored, rejected, shunned.
OPPOSITES: popular, well-liked.

unrealistic *see* **impractical** 1, 2.

unreasonable
(adj) Don't be so unreasonable! irrational, illogical, inconsistent, opinionated, obstinate, headstrong, biased, prejudiced.

unreliable
(adj) Don't trust Oz; he's too unreliable. undependable, irresponsible, erratic, inconsistent, unpredictable, untrustworthy.
OPPOSITES: reliable, dependable.

unselfish
(adj) It was unselfish of you to give me your last chocolate. self-sacrificing, selfless, noble, generous, magnanimous, kind, big-hearted, big, altruistic, charitable.

unsuccessful
(adj) My attempts to talk Dad round were unsuccessful. fruitless, futile, in vain, to no avail, useless, abortive, unproductive, ineffective, foiled, thwarted, frustrated.
OPPOSITES: successful, fruitful.

unsure *see* **uncertain** 1.

untidy
1 *(adj) My desk is untidy.* messy, chaotic, cluttered, disorganized, muddled, jumbled, littered, topsy-turvy, shambolic *(informal)*.
OPPOSITES: tidy, neat.
2 *(adj) You look untidy. See* **messy** 2.
3 *(adj) What untidy work! See* **messy** 3.

unusual
1 *(adj) Pat has an unusual ability to learn languages.* extraordinary, exceptional, rare, remarkable, phenomenal, singular, uncommon, abnormal, freak, atypical.
2 *(adj) Ziggy dresses in an unusual way.* strange, peculiar, odd, weird, bizarre, eccentric, unconventional, outlandish, curious, offbeat, original, different, exotic.

unwilling
(adj) Andy was unwilling to volunteer. reluctant, loath, slow, disinclined, not in the mood, ill-disposed, unenthusiastic.
OPPOSITES: willing, eager.

upset
1 *(v) I didn't mean to upset you.* hurt, distress, offend, rub you up the wrong way, annoy, irritate, worry, alarm, disturb, ruffle, fluster, faze, dismay, unsettle.
2 *(v) Don't upset our plans.* disrupt, interfere with, spoil, ruin, wreck, mess up, throw into confusion, turn upside down.
3 *(adj) I can see that you're upset.* hurt, distressed, worried, troubled, disturbed, bothered, agitated, in a state *(informal)*, put out, offended, angry.

urge
(n) I felt a sudden urge to scream. impulse, desire, compulsion, need, drive, longing, yearning, inclination, wish, whim.

urgent
(adj) I must see the doctor; it's urgent. imperative, vital, essential, critical, crucial, important, high-priority, serious, pressing.

use
1 *(v) Can you use these empty boxes?* find a use for, make use of, put to good use, utilize, do something with.
2 *(v) This whisk is easy to use.* operate, control, work, manage, handle.
3 *(v) Fenella will use you to get what she wants. See* **take advantage of**.
4 *(n) What's the use of complaining?* point, purpose, good, advantage, benefit, value, usefulness, worth.

used to
(adj) I'm used to coming last. accustomed to, resigned to, hardened to, familiar with, at home with, in the habit of, given to.

useful
1 *(adj) A useful gadget.* practical, handy, convenient, effective, helpful, valuable, functional, multipurpose, all-purpose.
OPPOSITES: useless, ineffective.
2 *(adj) Useful suggestions.* helpful, practical, worthwhile, valuable, invaluable, constructive, positive, beneficial.
OPPOSITES: useless, unhelpful.

useless
1 *(adj) The search was useless.* futile, pointless, a waste of time, in vain, fruitless, unsuccessful, hopeless, unproductive.
OPPOSITES: worthwhile, fruitful.
2 *(adj) This knife is useless.* no use, unusable, ineffective, impractical, hopeless *(informal)*, faulty, defective, broken.
OPPOSITES: useful, effective.

usual
(adj) Jogging is part of my usual routine. normal, regular, customary, accustomed, everyday, daily, ordinary, typical, standard, general, familiar, set, fixed, established.

Vv

vacant
1 *(adj) A vacant flat. See* **empty** 3.
2 *(adj) A vacant seat.* empty, available, free, unoccupied, not in use, not taken.
OPPOSITES: occupied, in use.
3 *(adj) A vacant stare.* blank, glazed, expressionless, faraway, dreamy, absent-minded, abstracted, vague, inattentive.

vague
1 *(adj) I could see a vague shape through the fog.* indistinct, hazy, shadowy, ill-defined, blurred, fuzzy, dim, faint.
OPPOSITES: clear, distinct.
2 *(adj) Justin has a vague idea of history.* hazy, woolly, foggy, inexact, imprecise, rough, broad, generalized.
OPPOSITES: clear, well-defined.
3 *(adj) Professor Peabody is terribly vague. See* **absent-minded**.

vain
(adj) Too much praise can make you vain. conceited, bigheaded *(informal)*, swollen-headed *(informal)*, self-satisfied, proud, arrogant, narcissistic, cocky, puffed up.
OPPOSITES: modest, humble.

valuable
1 *(adj) A valuable painting.* expensive, precious, costly, priceless, invaluable, dear, treasured, highly prized.
OPPOSITES: worthless, inexpensive.
2 *(adj) A valuable clue. See* **useful** 2.

vanish
(v) The figure seemed to vanish. disappear, become invisible, vanish into thin air, dematerialize, vanish off the face of the earth, fade away, melt away.
OPPOSITES: appear, materialize.

vast
1 *(adj) The universe is vast.* immense, huge, boundless, infinite, immeasurable, never-ending, limitless, unending, unbounded, sweeping, extensive.
OPPOSITES: tiny, limited.
2 *(adj) A vast appetite. See* **enormous**.

vegetable
(n) greens (plural), garden produce.
TYPES OF VEGETABLE: artichoke, asparagus, aubergine, beetroot, broad bean, broccoli, Brussels sprout, cabbage, carrot, cauliflower, celery, chicory, courgette, cucumber, fennel, garlic, haricot bean, kale, leek, lettuce, mangetout, marrow, mushroom, okra, onion, parsnip, pea, potato, pumpkin, radish, rocket, runner bean, shallot, spinach, spring greens (plural), spring onion, squash, string bean, swede, sweet corn, sweet pepper, sweet potato, turnip, watercress.

very
1 (adv) I was very sad to hear your news. extremely, really, terribly, dreadfully, deeply, truly, profoundly, intensely, acutely, awfully (informal).
2 (adv) Mrs Badger was very impressed with Oscar's work. extremely, really, tremendously, highly, greatly, most, exceedingly, enormously, hugely, mightily.

vibrate see **shake** 1.

vicious see **fierce** 1.

victory
(n) The team were excited by their victory. win, success, triumph, conquest.
OPPOSITE: defeat.

view
1 (n) What a beautiful view! vista, scene, sight, outlook, prospect, panorama, landscape, seascape, spectacle, picture.
2 (n) Kali shared my view that the film was awful. opinion, point of view, judgment, belief, conviction, assessment, way of thinking, idea, feeling, impression.

viewpoint
(n) Try to see the problem from a different viewpoint. angle, perspective, point of view, standpoint, position, side, slant.

vile see **horrible** 1, 2.

violent
1 (adj) A violent attack. savage, vicious, brutal, bloody, bloodthirsty, ferocious, fierce, barbaric, murderous, frenzied.
2 (adj) Violent emotions. powerful, uncontrollable, passionate, burning, intense, vehement, tempestuous, overwhelming, ungovernable, extreme.
3 (adj) A violent storm. raging, tempestuous, tumultuous, turbulent, wild, blustery, fierce, severe, devastating.
4 (adj) A violent stab of pain. See **sharp** 3.

visible see **noticeable**.

visit
1 (v) May I visit you next summer? come to see, go to see, call in on, drop in on (informal), look you up, pay you a visit, stay with, be your guest, descend on.
2 (n) Enjoy your visit to Paris! See **trip** 1.

vital
(adj) The doctor made a vital decision. critical, crucial, life-or-death, urgent, serious, significant, important, key, major.

vivid
1 (adj) I love vivid colours. brilliant, vibrant, glowing, bright, bold, strong, rich, deep, clear, luminous, fluorescent, dazzling.
OPPOSITES: dull, pale.
2 (adj) Gita gave a vivid account of her travels. graphic, dramatic, colourful, lively, exciting, striking, powerful, expressive, imaginative, true-to-life, realistic, lifelike.
OPPOSITES: dull, lifeless.

volcano
volcanoes...

belch	growl	smoulder
blow up	grumble	spew
erupt	roar	spurt
explode	rumble	steam
flare up	smoke	thunder

volcanoes send out...

burning rock	smoke
cinders	steam
lava (molten rock)	suffocating
lava flow	clouds
poisonous gas	volcanic ash

lava may...

burn	flow	solidify
bury	gush	spread
destroy	harden	stream
devastate	pour	surge
engulf	slide	sweep

lava can be..

bubbling	glimmering	runny
fiery	glowing	sticky
flaming	lumpy	viscous
fluid	red-hot	(thick)

volcanoes can be...

active
dormant
extinct
underwater

volcanic bomb
(lump of solidified lava)

smoke

cone

lava fountain

crater

river of lava

volunteer
(v) Did you volunteer to help? offer, put yourself forward, come forward, step forward, offer your services.

vomit
(v) I think I'm going to vomit! be sick, throw up (informal), puke (slang), spew up, retch, heave, gag, bring up, do a technicolour yawn (slang).

vote
1 (n) What was the result of the vote? poll, ballot, show of hands, election.
2 **vote for** (v) I didn't know who to vote for. cast a vote for, choose, elect, return, nominate, opt for, select, pick, support.

voyage see **journey** 1, 2.

vulgar
1 (adj) Vulgar jokes. See **crude**.
2 (adj) Vulgar jewellery. tasteless, flashy, showy, gaudy, garish, ostentatious, tawdry, tacky (informal), cheap and nasty.
OPPOSITE: tasteful.

Ww

waffle
(v) Don't waffle! Stick to the point! ramble, witter (informal), rabbit on (informal), blather, beat about the bush.

wail
(v) Babies wail when they're hungry. cry, howl, yowl, sob, weep, bawl, shriek, caterwaul, moan, whine, complain.

wait
1 (v) Wait until it's your turn. be patient, hold on (informal), hang on (informal), sit tight, stand by, hold back, hold your horses, cool your heels, hang fire.
2 (v) Wait here until I get back. stay, stop, remain, stay put, hang around.

wake up
(v) I didn't wake up until midday. wake, stir, surface (informal), get up, rise, come to life, awaken (old-fashioned).

walk
1 (v) I usually walk to school. go on foot, travel on foot, foot it, hoof it (slang).
WAYS TO WALK: amble, crawl, creep, dodder, hike, hobble, limp, lope, march, mince, mooch (slang), pace, pad, parade, plod, prowl, ramble, saunter, scuttle, shamble, shuffle, slink, stagger, stalk, stomp (informal), stride, stroll, strut, stumble, swagger, teeter, tiptoe, toddle, totter, traipse (informal), tramp, trek, trot, trudge, waddle, wander.
2 (v) Don't walk on the tulips! tread, trample, tramp, step, stamp, walk all over.
3 (n) Let's go for a walk. stroll, saunter, wander, ramble, hike, tramp, trek, march.

wander

wander
1 *(v) I'll just wander round town.* drift, saunter, stroll, amble, mooch *(slang),* traipse *(informal),* roam, ramble, cruise.
2 *(v) Don't wander off! See* **stray** 2.

want
(v) The genie will give you whatever you want. desire, wish for, fancy, like, dream of, crave, long for, yearn for, hanker after, set your heart on, covet, pine for, need.

war
(n) Many soldiers were killed in the war. conflict, fighting, hostilities *(plural),* armed conflict, struggle, confrontation, combat.

warm
1 *(adj) A warm evening.* mild, balmy, hot, sultry, sunny, summery, fine, pleasant. OPPOSITES: cool, cold.
2 *(adj) Warm water.* lukewarm, tepid. OPPOSITES: cool, cold.
3 *(adj) A warm coat.* thick, heavy, woolly, fleecy, cosy, snug, thermal, padded. OPPOSITES: thin, lightweight.
4 *(adj) A warm welcome.* hearty, cordial, friendly, heartfelt, fervent, enthusiastic, emotional, effusive, ecstatic, rapturous. OPPOSITES: cool, hostile.

warn
1 *(v) I'll warn you if anyone comes.* alert, tip you off, let you know, inform, notify, give you fair warning, raise the alarm.
2 *(v) Didn't I warn you not to hitchhike?* caution, tell, advise, counsel, urge, remind.

warning
(n) Did you have any warning of what would happen? advance notice, forewarning, tip-off, notification, word, sign, hint, indication, premonition, omen.

wash
1 *(v) Did you wash before you went to bed?* have a wash, wash yourself, have a bath, have a shower, bath, shower.
2 *(v) We must wash our car.* clean, shampoo, sponge down, scrub, soap, swab down, wipe, mop, launder *(clothes).*

waste
(v) Don't waste all your money at the fair. squander, fritter away, throw away, blow *(slang),* use up, run through, exhaust.

watch
1 *(v) I like to watch the people.* look at, observe, see, gaze at, stare at, survey, view, contemplate, check out *(informal),* scrutinize, inspect, peer at, peep at, gape at, gawp at *(slang),* ogle, clock *(slang).*
2 *(v) Watch what I do first.* observe, look at, notice, pay attention to, mark, note.
3 *(v) I'll watch your bike for you.* keep watch over, keep an eye on, guard, mind, take care of, look after, protect.

watch out
(v) Watch out for signs of trouble. look out, be on the lookout, keep a lookout, keep your eyes open, be on the alert, be on your guard, be vigilant, be watchful.

wave
1 *(v) Wave when the coast is clear.* signal, indicate, gesture, motion, sign, beckon.
2 *(v) Don't wave that stick at me!* shake, waggle, brandish, flourish, swing, twirl.
3 *(v) Watch the grass wave in the breeze.* sway, stir, ripple, quiver, shake, flutter.
4 *(n) The surfer was carried along on the wave.* breaker, roller, billow, surf, swell, white horses *(plural),* tidal wave.

way
1 *(n) Is this the right way home?* route, direction, road, path, street, lane, track.
2 *(n) Think of a way to solve the puzzle.* method, technique, procedure, system, means *(plural),* plan, approach, scheme.

weak
1 *(adj) Mia felt weak after her illness.* frail, feeble, delicate, fragile, faint, shaky, unsteady, debilitated, infirm, incapacitated, sickly, tired, exhausted, wasted, puny. OPPOSITES: strong, energetic.
2 *(adj) The bridge is too weak to support us.* flimsy, insubstantial, rickety, unsafe, shaky, unsteady, thin, fragile, delicate. OPPOSITES: strong, sturdy.
3 *(adj) Don't be weak!* feeble, spineless, timid, cowardly, pathetic, wet *(informal),* soft, wimpish *(informal),* weedy *(informal).* OPPOSITES: assertive, brave.
4 *(adj) This drink is too weak.* watery, diluted, watered down, wishy-washy *(informal),* tasteless, insipid, thin. OPPOSITES: strong, concentrated.
5 *(adj) A weak excuse. See* **feeble** 3.
6 *(adj) A weak cry. See* **faint** 4.

weakness
1 *(n) Nat's weakness is laziness.* failing, shortcoming, fault, flaw, defect, problem. OPPOSITES: strength, asset.
2 *(n) Jo has a weakness for sweets.* liking, fondness, taste, passion, love, soft spot.

wealthy *see* **rich** 1.

weapons
(plural n) arms *(plural),* munitions *(plural),* armaments *(plural),* weaponry, offensive weapons *(plural).*
TYPES OF WEAPON: battering ram, battleaxe, bayonet, bazooka, biological weapons *(plural),* blowpipe, bomb, boomerang, bow and arrow, cannon, catapult, cosh, crossbow, cudgel, dagger, flame-thrower, grenade, guided missile, gun, harpoon, lance, longbow, missile, mortar, mustard gas, nerve gas, pike, rocket, shell, spear, sword, tear gas, tomahawk, torpedo, truncheon, warhead. *Also see* **bomb**, **gun**, **sword**.

wear
(v) What will you wear? put on, dress in, be dressed in, have on, sport *(informal).*

wear away
(v) The sea will slowly wear away the rocks. erode, eat away, wear down, grind down, wash away, crumble, dissolve, corrode *(metal),* eat into, rot, decay.

wear out
(v) My shirt is starting to wear out. become worn, show signs of wear, wear thin, fray, go into holes, become threadbare.

weather
(n) climate, weather conditions *(plural).*

it is hot
baking
blistering
boiling
roasting
scorching
searing
sizzling
sweltering
torrid

a stormy day

it is cloudy
dark
dismal
dreary
dull
gloomy
grey
overcast
sunless

it is windy
blowy
blustery
breezy
gusty
squally
stormy

it is cold
bitter
bracing
chilly
cool
crisp
freezing
fresh
frosty
icy
nippy
numbing
parky *(informal)*
perishing *(informal)*
raw
snowy
wintry

a scorching day

it is humid
clammy
close
muggy
oppressive
steamy
sticky
stifling
stuffy
suffocating
sultry

it is fine
balmy
bright
calm
clear
cloudless
dry
fair
mild
pleasant
still
summery
sunny
sunshiny
warm

it is wet
bucketing *(informal)*
coming down in torrents
damp
drizzly
lashing down
pelting down
pouring
rainy
showery
spitting
teeming
tipping down *(informal)*

it is foggy
hazy
misty
murky
smoggy

a murky evening

a frosty morning

Also see **ice, frost & snow, storm words.**

wedding *see* **marriage** 2.

weird *see* **strange** 1, 2.

welcome
*(adj) Emily's parents made me feel
welcome.* at home, one of the family,
accepted, appreciated, wanted, included.
OPPOSITES: unwelcome, excluded.

well
1 *(adj) You look well.* healthy, fit, in good
health, blooming, strong, robust, thriving.
OPPOSITES: unwell, ill.
2 *(n) The well provided water for the
village.* water hole, borehole, spring, water
source, oasis, artesian well, wishing well.

well-behaved
(adj) A well-behaved child. good, obedient,
cooperative, amenable, compliant, docile,
polite, well-mannered, dutiful.
OPPOSITES: badly behaved, naughty.

well-known *see* **famous**.

wet
1 *(adj) My clothes are wet.* damp, soaking,
dripping, sopping wet, sodden, drenched,
wringing wet, saturated, wet through.
OPPOSITES: dry, bone-dry *(informal)*.
2 *(adj) After the rain, the ground was wet.*
damp, moist, sodden, waterlogged,
saturated, soggy, spongy, muddy, dewy.
OPPOSITES: dry, parched.
3 *(adj) If it's wet we won't go out.* rainy,
raining, pouring, drizzly, showery, damp,
misty, dank, clammy, humid.
OPPOSITES: dry, fine.
4 *(adj) (informal) Stand up for yourself and
don't be so wet! See* **weak** 3.
5 *(v) Wet the cloth.* dampen, moisten,
soak, drench, saturate, steep, douse,
splash, sprinkle, spray, irrigate *(ground)*.

whine
1 *(v) The toddler began to whine.*
whimper, wail, cry, grizzle *(informal)*.
2 *(v) Cecil always finds something to
whine about. See* **complain**.

whip *see* **beat** 1, 4.

whirl
*(v) Watch the dancers whirl round the
room.* spin, twirl, swirl, circle, wheel, reel,
pirouette, gyrate, revolve, rotate, swivel.

whisper
1 *(v) I can't hear you when you whisper.*
speak under your breath, speak in hushed
tones, talk quietly, speak softly, keep your
voice down, murmur, mutter.
2 *(n) Sandy spoke in a whisper.* low voice,
quiet voice, soft voice, murmur, stage
whisper, undertone, hushed tones *(plural)*.

white
1 *(adj) The statue looked white in the
moonlight.* milky, chalky, pearly, silvery,
snow-white, alabaster, ivory, ghostly.
2 *(adj) Granny has white hair.* snowy,
snow-white, silver, silvery, hoary.
3 *(adj) Edmund's face was white with
fear.* ashen, pale, pallid, bloodless, wan,
pasty, waxen, chalky, drained.

whole
*(adj) Will the whole film be shown on
television?* entire, complete, full, total,
uncut, unedited, unabridged *(book)*.

wicked
1 *(adj) A wicked criminal.* evil, bad, sinful,
immoral, corrupt, depraved, villainous,
vicious, vile, fiendish, diabolical, devilish,
black-hearted, lawless.
OPPOSITES: good, virtuous.
2 *(adj) A wicked grin. See* **mischievous** 2.

wide *see* **broad** 1, 2.

wild
1 *(adj) That dog is quite wild.* untamed,
undomesticated, savage, fierce, ferocious.
OPPOSITES: tame, domesticated.
2 *(adj) We crossed some wild country.*
uncultivated, unspoilt, untamed, natural,
deserted, empty, waste, barren, desolate,
bleak, rough, rugged, overgrown.
OPPOSITES: cultivated, inhabited.
3 *(adj) What wild weather! See* **stormy** 1.
4 *(adj) The boys are very wild.* rowdy,
boisterous, unruly, uncontrollable,
undisciplined, wayward, out of control,
rough, noisy, violent, rude, riotous.
5 *(adj) Ziggy had a wild idea. See* **mad** 3.
6 *(adj) Al is wild about soccer. See* **mad** 5.

willing
(adj) Helen is always willing to help. glad,
happy, pleased, ready, quick, prepared,
eager, keen, game *(informal)*.
OPPOSITES: unwilling, reluctant.

wilt *see* **wither**.

win
1 *(v) I hope that I will win.* come first, be
the winner, get first place, take first prize,
finish first, be victorious, triumph, succeed.
OPPOSITES: lose, come last.
2 *(v) Mo wants to win a medal.* gain, earn,
secure, obtain, receive, collect, pick up.

wince *see* **flinch**.

wind
1 *(n) A strong wind can cause a lot of
damage.* breeze, gust, blast, squall,
headwind, crosswind, tailwind, gale,
tornado, cyclone, whirlwind, twister
(informal). ❖ *Also see* **storm words**.
2 *(v) The path began to wind up the
mountain.* meander, snake, twist and turn,
twist, zigzag, weave, spiral, corkscrew.
3 *(v) Wind the tinsel round the tree.* loop,
twist, coil, entwine, wrap, curl, thread.

window
(n) TYPES OF WINDOW: bay window,
bow window, casement window, dormer
window, fanlight, French window, leaded
window, louvred window, oriel window,
picture window, plate-glass window,
porthole, rose window, sash window,
skylight, stained-glass window.

windy
1 *(adj) A windy day.* breezy, blustery,
blowy, gusty, squally, stormy, wild.
OPPOSITES: calm, still.

2 *(adj) A windy spot.* exposed, open,
unprotected, windswept, bleak, desolate.
OPPOSITE: sheltered.

winner
(n) Who is the winner? victor, champion,
prizewinner, medallist, champ *(informal)*.
OPPOSITE: loser.

wipe
(v) Wipe the surface. clean, sponge, mop,
swab, wash, dust, polish, rub, brush.

wise
1 *(adj) A wise ruler.* learned, clever,
knowledgeable, intelligent, astute, shrewd,
perceptive, discerning, understanding,
enlightened, experienced, deep-thinking.
OPPOSITE: foolish.
2 *(adj) A wise choice. See* **sensible** 2.

wish
1 *(n) Josie has a secret wish to be famous.*
desire, longing, hankering, yearning,
craving, hunger, ambition, aspiration,
hope, dream, fancy, whim.
2 *(n) The genie will carry out your every
wish.* request, desire, demand, command,
order, instruction, bidding.
3 **wish for** *(v) The genie will give you
whatever you wish for. See* **want**.

wistful
*(adj) You look wistful; what are you
thinking about?* sad, forlorn, melancholy,
disconsolate, thoughtful, pensive, dreamy.

witch
(n) sorceress, enchantress, crone.

wither
*(v) The daffodils will wither if you don't
water them.* wilt, dry up, shrivel up, fade,
droop, go limp, flop, sag, flag, die.
OPPOSITES: flourish, bloom.

witty
(adj) Tim's witty remarks made me laugh.
funny, humorous, amusing, clever, quick-
witted, sparkling, lively, droll, facetious.

wizard *see* **magician** 1.

wobble
1 *(v) Can you make the bottle wobble
without knocking it over?* teeter, totter,
rock, sway, waver, seesaw, oscillate.
2 *(v) Look at the jelly wobble!* quiver,
tremble, shake, vibrate, quake.

woman
(n) Who's that woman? lady, girl, female,
dame *(slang)*, lass, maiden *(old-fashioned)*.

wonder
1 *(n) We gazed at the magician in
wonder.* amazement, astonishment, awe,
wonderment, admiration, curiosity,
bewilderment, surprise, disbelief.
2 *(n) The pyramids were a wonder of the
Ancient World.* marvel, phenomenon,
miracle, spectacle, curiosity, attraction.
3 *(v) It's pointless to wonder what might
have happened.* think about, ponder,
speculate about, ask yourself, puzzle over,
reflect on, meditate on, query, question,
be curious about, be inquisitive about.

wonderful
1 (adj) *What a wonderful party!* fantastic (informal), marvellous, great (informal), terrific (informal), superb, excellent, fabulous (informal), tremendous (informal), amazing (informal), sensational (informal), magnificent, wicked (slang), decent (informal), cool (informal).
OPPOSITES: terrible, dreadful.
2 (adj) *Modern medicine can do wonderful things.* amazing, astonishing, incredible, astounding, extraordinary, remarkable, staggering, marvellous, miraculous, phenomenal, awe-inspiring.
OPPOSITES: commonplace, unremarkable.

wood
1 (n) *Don't get lost in the wood.* woods (plural), woodland, copse, spinney, thicket, coppice, forest, trees (plural).
2 (n) *The shed was made of wood.* timber, logs (plural), planks (plural), boards (plural).

word
1 (n) *What's the proper word for this thing?* name, term, expression.
2 (n) *Give me your word you'll be there.* See **promise** 2.

work
1 (v) *You'll have to work if you want to pass your exams.* slog away, slave, graft (informal), sweat (informal), labour, toil, exert yourself, beaver away (informal), peg away, keep your nose to the grindstone.
2 (v) *Lord Lucre doesn't need to work.* have a job, go to work, earn a living.
3 (v) *This whisk is easy to work.* See **use** 2.
4 (v) *Our CD player doesn't work properly.* function, go, perform, run, operate, play.
5 (v) *My plan might work.* See **succeed** 2.
6 (n) *I need a rest after all that work.* hard work, effort, toil, labour, exertion, drudgery, graft (informal), hard grind (informal), donkey-work, slavery.
7 (n) *What work do you do?* See **job** 2.

work out
1 (v) *Can you work out the answer to this question?* figure out (informal), calculate, deduce, puzzle out, suss out (slang), find out, discover, solve, find the solution to.
2 (v) *We must work out a plan.* think up, come up with, concoct, devise, construct, put together, decide on, formulate.
3 (v) *Pamela likes to work out on the beach.* exercise, do exercises, train, keep fit, tone up, lift weights, pump iron (slang).

world
1 (n) *Captain Stardust travelled round the world.* earth, globe, planet.
2 (n) *How did the world begin?* earth, universe, cosmos, life, existence, human life, nature, creation, everything.

worn out see **exhausted**.
worried see **anxious** 1.

worry
1 (v) *Don't worry about the exams.* fret, be anxious, be apprehensive, get in a state (informal), get worked up, get in a stew (informal), agonize, torment yourself.
2 (v) *Don't let this small problem worry you.* trouble, concern, bother, distress, upset, disturb, unsettle, make you anxious.
3 (n) *Ziggy has caused his parents a lot of worry.* anxiety, concern, unease, distress, bother, hassle (informal), problems (plural).

worthwhile
(adj) *I want to do a job that's really worthwhile.* useful, valuable, helpful, worth the effort, constructive, beneficial, important, rewarding, profitable.
OPPOSITES: worthless, pointless.

wound
1 (n) *The doctor examined the wound.* cut, gash, laceration, knife wound, stab wound, bullet wound, incision, injury.
2 (v) *Did the terrorists wound anyone? See* **injure**.

wrap
1 (v) *Wrap the ornament in cotton wool.* pack, cover, bundle up, surround, swathe, drape, enfold, enclose, envelop, cocoon.
2 (v) *Wrap the tape round the pole.* wind, loop, twist, roll, coil, twine, bind.

wreck
1 (v) *Don't wreck the furniture!* destroy, demolish, break, smash, trash (slang), total (slang), write off (car) (informal).
2 (v) *One mistake could wreck our chances of winning.* See **ruin** 1.
3 (n) *Divers explored the wreck.* shipwreck, sunken ship, wreckage, hulk.

wreckage
(n) *Rescuers sifted through the wreckage.* debris, remains (plural), rubble, ruins (plural), fragments (plural).

wriggle
1 (v) *Sit still and don't wriggle!* fidget, squirm, jiggle about, twist around, writhe around, shift around, jerk about.
2 (v) *Watch the snake wriggle across the grass.* wiggle, zigzag, twist and turn, writhe, snake, worm, slither, crawl, slink.

wrinkled
1 (adj) *A wrinkled face.* lined, wrinkly, furrowed, wizened, crinkly, creased.
2 (adj) *A wrinkled shirt.* creased, crumpled, rumpled, crinkled, unironed.

write
1 (v) *I'll write your number on this pad.* write down, note down, jot down, take down, make a note of, record, scribble, scrawl, print, put in writing, copy, inscribe.

2 (v) *I have to write a story for homework.* make up, invent, create, compose, draft, pen, dash off, put together, concoct.

writer
(n) author, novelist, scriptwriter, dramatist, playwright, poet, biographer, journalist.

writing
(n) *I can't read this writing.* handwriting, scrawl, scribble, script, print, letters (plural), characters (plural), calligraphy.

wrong
1 (adj) *My theory turned out to be wrong.* incorrect, inaccurate, mistaken, off target, wide of the mark, erroneous, false, untrue, off beam (informal), way out (informal).
OPPOSITES: right, correct.
2 (adj) *It's wrong to sell stolen goods.* illegal, unlawful, criminal, immoral, unethical, dishonest, corrupt, deceitful, crooked (informal), wicked, sinful, evil.
OPPOSITES: right, legal.
3 (adj) *It would be wrong to wear a bikini to school.* inappropriate, unsuitable, unfitting, unseemly, improper, unacceptable, not done, unconventional, funny, incongruous, incorrect.
OPPOSITES: right, proper.
4 go wrong see **go wrong** 1, 2.

xylophone
(n) glockenspiel, chime bars (plural).
yearn see **long** 3.
yell see **shout**.
yellow
(n) SHADES OF YELLOW: amber, buttercup yellow, canary yellow, gold, lemon, mustard, ochre, primrose, saffron.

young
1 (adj) *Young children can't look after themselves.* small, little, infant, newborn.
OPPOSITES: old, grown-up.
2 (adj) *Zak is so young for his age.* childish, babyish, immature, juvenile, infantile, puerile, adolescent.
OPPOSITES: mature, grown-up.
3 (adj) *My parents still seem young.* youthful, boyish, girlish, fresh-faced, sprightly, spry, well-preserved, active.
OPPOSITES: old, elderly.
4 (plural n) *Animals try to protect their young.* babies (plural), offspring (plural), little ones (plural), litter, brood, family.
zero see **nothing** 2.
zoom see **speed** 4.